Warman's®

Civil War COLLECTIBLES

John F. Graf

Published by

kp krause publications
An F&W Publications Company

700 East State Street • Iola, WI 54990-0001
715-445-2214 • 888-457-2873
www.krause.com

Our toll-free number to place an order or obtain a free catalog is 800-258-0929

Edited by Tracy Schmidt
Designed by Kay Sanders

Library of Congress Catalog Number: 2002105777
ISBN: 0-87349-437-7

Printed in the United States of America

Back cover images courtesy of: Battleground Antiques, Inc. & J.C. Devine Inc.
Spine image courtesy of: J.C. Devine Inc.

Dedication

I humbly dedicate this book
to the finest historian I have ever known,

my father,
John Milton Graf.

Contents

Acknowledgments

A work of this nature does not evolve over a short period of time. Rather, it has taken 35 years to develop the familiarity with the material culture of the mid-nineteenth centure to even feel comfortable considering such a project. I would not have the foundation on which to build an appreciation for Civil War history and the artifacts associated with it were it not for my grandmother, Celine Robertson. When I was a boy of three or four years old, she never denied my request to have her read the *How and Why Book of the Civil War* to me, no matter how many times before she had already led me through the pages. it may seem silly to some to acknowledge such a long-gone activity, but I want to acknowledge that it was my grandmother's patience with me as she reread that same book to me or waited while I studied its drawings of uniforms and weapons, that provided the foundation for my life-long passion for the Civil War and nineteenth century material culture.

More recently, I wish to extend my gratitude to Gregory Smith and Bill Krause of Krause Publications, an F & W Company, for their patience and understanding. As with many students of history, I am susceptible to not knowing, "when to say when." Without their occasional pep talks that brought me in from the ledge, I would have spun on and on, forever collecting data and would not have been able to have seen this project through to completion.

Several fine dealers in Civil War Memorabilia came forward and contributed past catalogs, auction and sale results, photographs, and their specialized knowledge. This group of individuals includes: Jefferson Shrader of Advance Guard Militaria; Dale C. Anderson of Dale C. Anderson Co. Militaria and Americana; Ted and Sallie Caldwell of Caldwell and Company Civil War Antiques; Dan and Teresa Patterson of The Civil War Connection; Harry Ridgeway, The Civil War Relicman; Eric P. Kane of Drumbeat Civil War Memorabilia; Norm Flayderman of N. Flayderman & Co., Inc.; P. and J. Frohne, owners of Frohne's Historic Military; Will and Lynn Gorges and Scott Ford of Battleground Antiques; Brian and Maria Green of Brian & Maria Green, Inc.; Dan and Teresa Patterson at the Civil War Connection; Dave Taylor of Dave Taylor's Civil War Antiques; Dr. Michael Echols; Gary Hendershott of Hendershott Museum Consultants; Chet, Pat, Sam, and Wes Small of The Horse Soldier; Jacques Noel Jacobsen, Jr., proprietor of Collector's Antiquities, Inc.; Kim Ralph of J.C. Devine, Inc.; Phillip B. Lamb, owner of Phillip B. Lamb, Ltd., and Colonel Lamb's Antiques; Larry and Deb Hicklin, owners of Middle Tennessee Relics; Shannon and Lesia Pritchard, proprietors of Old South Military Antiques; Bob Daly and Cliff Sophia of The Powder Horn Gunshop, Inc.; Donald E. Stoops owner of the Sharpsburg Arsenal; and William Leigh III, owner of www.civilwarbuttons.com. If I have left anyone from this list, it is not out of malice, but rather, the result of a messy filing system! Thank you all, for making this book available to the thousands of Civil War collectors and enthusiasts.

Finally, I wish to acknowledge the long hours that friends and fellow collectors have spent sharing their knowledge with me or simply listening to me formulate ideas about this book. At the very top of this list is the late Perk Steffen. As an editor of a Minnesota newspaper during the first half of the twentieth century, Perk met many veterans of the Civil War and, in addition to collecting their stories, collected much of the memorabilia of their service. As a young boy, I visited Perk every Saturday and he would go over a Civil War book that both of us studied the previous week. Each visit culminated with his pulling out a sword, musket, or some other relic that he had collected from a local veteran many years prior. My young eyes devoured the weekly "Civil War treat" and I came to treasure those afternoons sitting with Perk.

I would be remiss if I did not thank Diane Adams-Graf of the Minnesota Historical Society. She is the finest museum professional I have ever known. She unselfishly spent countless hours teaching the details of proper labeling, care, and storage of historic artifacts to me. Thomas Shaw of Historic Fort Snelling was never short in sharing his vast knowledge of pre-1865 uniforms and men's clothing. Similarly, Joseph S. Covais, founder of New Columbia, coached me through the examination of many uniforms and headgear, pointing out the details that only an accomplished tailor as himself would notice. Bill Brewster of the Wisconsin Veteran's Museum was very kind to meet with me and allow me to study the Museum's extensive collection of Civil War artifacts. Thomas Kailbourn was forthcoming with so much of the details that he has uncovered in his own study of pre-1865 photography that I am truly indebted to him. My daughter, Trisha Graf deserves a note of thanks as well. She was very patient with her father as we missed countless nights together as I wrapped up the final pages of the book. To all of these people, I am grateful.

And finally, I must thank my parents, Milton and Helen Graf. Without their accepting my fascination with the Civil War as a young boy and then helping me to discover the possibilities that scholarship, study, and perseverance provide, this book, or my enjoyment of exploring the history of the Civil War, would never have been realized.

Photos courtesy of: Middle Tennesee Relics, J.C. Devine Inc., Dale C. Anderson, and Hendershott Museum Consultants

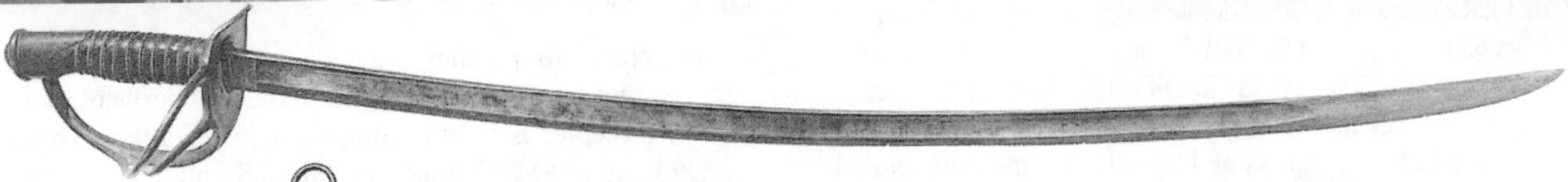
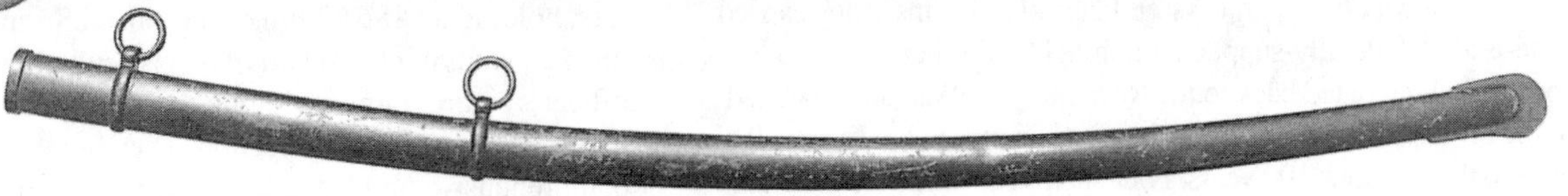

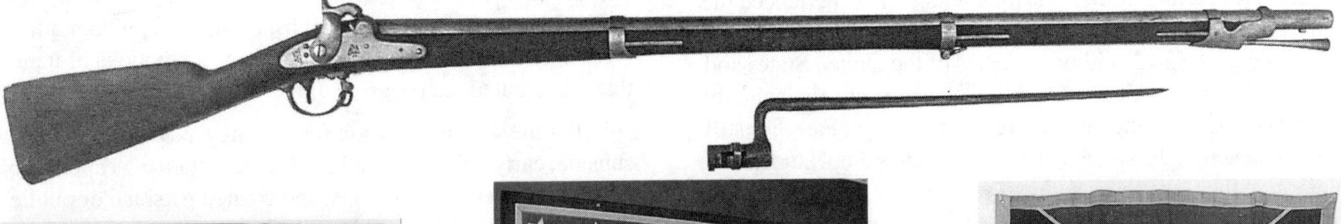

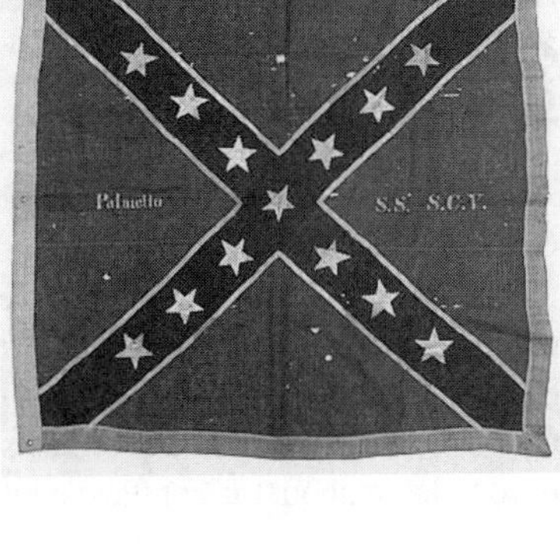

Introduction

What is it that causes a deep stir within the spirit of some at the sight of a tattered Confederate flag under glass or the bright steel of a cavalry saber? Perhaps such items evoke a long-forgotten school lesson about how nearly four million men answered the call to serve either the Union or the Confederacy between 1861 to 1865. Or, maybe these relics clarify a moment in time when the romantic image of a pioneering America ended and the modern age began. Whatever the reason, more than 300,000 Americans currently categorize themselves as Civil War buffs.

The Civil War's Longevity

Between the bombardment of Fort Sumter on April 12, 1861, and the final surrender of Confederate troops on May 26, 1865, the way wars were fought and the tools soldiers used, changed irrevocably. When troops first formed lines of battle to face each other near Bull Run Creek in Virginia on June 21, 1861, they were dressed in a widely disparate assemblage of uniforms. They carried state-issued, federally-supplied, or brought-from-home weapons, some of which dated back to the Revolutionary War, and marched to the orders and rhythms of tactics that had served land forces for at least the previous 100 years. Four short years later, the generals and soldiers had perfected the art of warfare on the North American continent, having developed such leaps as the use of the repeating rifle combat, moving siege artillery by rail, extensive employment of trenches and field fortifications, ironclad ships to engage in combat, the widespread use of portable telegraph units on the battlefield, the draft, organized use of African American troops in combat, and even an income tax levied to finance the war.

This change levied a toll on the nation, however, in the form of more than one million casualties (over 620,000 war-related deaths). At that rate, nearly one in four soldiers experienced the pains of war firsthand. It was impossible that this did not impact every one of the 34.3 million residents of the United States and former Confederate States. Over the ensuing years, the pain, for most, subsided, but the memory remained strong. Families still pay homage to their veteran ancestors, grade school students memorize the Gettysburg address, we bow our heads on Memorial Day and hardly a NASCAR event occurs where a Confederate battle flag isn't prominently and defiantly waved.

The Civil War Experience

Many Americans satisfy their desire to feel connected with the Civil War by exploring battlefields or cemeteries or researching their own family ancestors who served. Some people even read countless biographies, regimental histories, or battle accounts, even joining Civil War study groups or "Round Tables." For many, these very private explorations are enough to satiate their need to learn about the conflict and the lives of its participants.

For some though, simply memorializing the war isn't sufficient to satisfy that need to remain connected to the events of 1861-1865. Some will painstakingly recreate uniforms and equipment to don on weekend campaigns and refight battles, this time firing at their fellow countrymen with muskets and cannons charged with powder and paper instead of canisters of grape shot or loads of buckshot. For these reenactors, such events help them come close to experiencing the daily work, inconveniences, and feelings of Civil War soldiers. Of course, at the end of the weekend, these modern "Sessesh" and "Billy Yanks," return to their twenty-first-century lives, leaving the recreated image of maimed fellow soldiers, dysentery, and lice-infested clothing behind.

And finally, for another group of Civil War enthusiasts, the best medium for understanding the heritage and role of thousands who served is by collecting war relics. For these collectors, holding an 1861 Taunton-produced Springfield rifled musket, studying the detail of a Nashville Plow Works' foot officer's sword, or admiring the style of a Confederate artilleryman's kepi are a fast connection. They represent direct links to a comprehensive understanding of the depth of commitment, sacrifice, and engagement that the soldiers felt.

Collectors and Accumulators

Collecting mementos and artifacts from the Civil War is not a new hobby. Even before the war ended, people were already gathering remembrances. The first collectors, as with any period of warfare, were the participants themselves. Soldiers sent home scraps of flags collected minie-ball shattered logs, purchased privately marketed unit insignias, or obtained a musket or carbine for their own use after the war. Civilians wrote to prominent officers asking for autographs, exchanged photographs ("carte de visites") with soldiers, or kept scrapbooks of items that represented the progress of the conflict.

After the war, the passion for owning a piece of it did not subside, early collectors gathered representative weapons, collected battlefield-found relics, and created personal or public memorials to the veterans. For nearly eighty years following the end of hostilities, veterans would gather for annual reunions to swap stories and pay homage to their fallen comrades. When these old soldiers gathered, collectors were right there to acquire any tidbits or mementos that the veterans would release.

Simultaneously, and not unlike the time following any major conflict, a grand scale of surplus sales emerged. This was the heyday of Civil War collecting. Dealers such as Francis Bannerman made hundreds of Civil War relics available to the general public. For as little as $3.50, a person could buy a Springfield Musket. Ten dollars would secure a Confederate Richmond-made version. Unissued Union cavalry shell jackets could be had for $3.85 each (or $1.50 if you ordered a dozen!), and an actual 3" rifled cannon for $350. Though a lot of sales were made to early collectors, much of the surplus was sold in bulk to other governments, outdoors enthusiasts, and a lot was sold simply for its scrap value.

Following World War II, a new wave of collecting emerged. Reveling in the victories in Japan and in Europe, Americans were charged with a renewed sense of patriotism and heritage. At the same time, the newspapers started to track the passing of the last few veterans of Civil War. As the nation paid tribute to the few survivors of the Rebellion, it also acknowledged that the 100-year anniversary of the war was fast upon them. In an effort to capture a sense of the heritage, Civil War buffs began to collect in earnest.

With the high profile of the Civil War Centennial, in the 1960s, thousands of outstanding relics seemingly emerged from closets, attics, and long-forgotten chests. Collectors eagerly bought and sold firearms, swords, and uniforms. It was during this time when metal detectors first played a large role in Civil War collecting, as hundreds donned headphones and swept battlefields and campsites, uncovering thousands of spent bullets, buttons, belt plates, and artillery projectiles.

By the 1970s, as this first wave of prominent and easily recognized collectibles disappeared into collections, Civil War buffs discovered carte de visites, tintypes, and ambrotypes. All of the early photographs of the period were fantastic, visual documents of personalities, uniforms, and weapons. With a fervor matched only by collectors of baseball cards, these wonderful items were bought and sold. Simultaneously, more interest turned to the common soldiers. Accoutrements started to reach prices that far outstretched what surplus dealers could have only hoped for, just a few years prior. The demand for letters and diaries written by the soldiers forced people to open boxes and drawers to rediscover long-forgotten manuscript records of battles and campaigns.

By the end of the twentieth century, Civil War collecting had peaked. Some thought all the good stuff was gone. Little did these skeptics realize, collectors are not the end user. Rather, a collector is merely the caretaker who provides a good home for an object until that time when they choose, or no longer are able, to care for the item. Then, these relics, thought to be gone, suddenly reemerge on the market. And it is this era of Civil War relic reemergence in which we currently live.

The fabulous collections of early relics that were assembled in the late 1940s and early 1950s are reappearing. Granted, the prices have increased considerably, but nevertheless, relics like no one has seen available for fifty years are suddenly appearing at auctions, shows, and in private dealer's lists.

Today, we benefit from the many years of research that has resulted from the earlier collecting frenzies. Books that the first generation of collectors could only have dreamed of are now available on specialized topics such as Confederate saddles, Gwyn & Campbell carbines, or Federal shelter tents. At no time since the Civil War, has so much information and material been available at one time.

As we enter this "glory period" of Civil War collecting, though, many lessons need to be relearned. Whereas an old-time collector could look at a saber and recognize offhand that it was the product of the Griswold factory or quantify the variations of percussion conversion done to flintlock muskets at Federal arsenals, many of these outstanding artifacts have not been available for study for many years. Collectors are learning many of the nuances that affect desirability and value for the first time (often at the expense of the old-timer's patience!).

Using the Book

This book is organized into eighteen chapters representing eighteen different areas of Civil War relic collecting that are popularly pursued today. Great care has been made to not give a false impression of the current marketplace by misrepresentative balance within these pages. For example, the number of flag-related items account for only a handful of listings in this book. That is because, even though widely sought after, very few actual flags carried by soldiers hit the market. When they do, as the reader will discover, the prices are well beyond the reach of the average collector.

This book deals only with items made before the summer of 1865 when the last troops of the Confederacy laid down their weapons. The items listed are typical of what a soldier would have carried or encountered on a daily basis. It does not address items primarily used by civilians from this period (such as furniture, glassware, toys, or other decorative arts) or produced after the cessation of hostilities. Therefore, there are no veteran group items (for example, items issued by the Grand Army of the Republic (G.A.R.) or the United Confederate Veterans (U.C.V.) listed in this book. Similarly, commemorative items or publications produced after 1865 are not covered.

Frohne's Historic Military

Rarity, Availability, and Reproduction Alert

At the beginning of each chapter, there is a rating chart. Three ratings are represented: Availability, Price, and Reproduction Alert. An attempt has been to make a general rating for each category. Each ratings is represented by one to five stars with the meaning as follows:

Availability:

***** = Very rare, available through advanced dealers.
**** = May find the items through private sales lists.
*** = Encountered with frequency at Civil War relic shows.
** = Commonly found through online auctions or through most dealers.
* = You should be able to find these items at a general antique show.

Price:

*****.................................Less than $50
****.................................. $51-$250
***..................................$251-$1,000
**................................. $1,001-$5,000
*.................................. $5,001-and up

Reproduction Alert

***** Items in this category rarely, if ever reproduced.
**** Reproductions might exist, but most often, misidentification is of more concern.
*** Be careful. Reproductions are known to exist and misrepresented.
** Be extremely careful. Reproductions are misrepresented as original on a regular basis.
* Extreme care needed. It is safe to assume that the item you have encountered is a reproduction. Get proof that it isn't before making a purchase.

In each category, you will find items listed using the language from the seller's descriptions. Claims of rarity, condition, or value are that of the original seller. Often, you will find several listings for very similar items. This has been done to show how prices are often not fixed for particular type of item. Rather, price may depend on how willing a dealer is to part with his item. Since the market is not fixed, these multiple listings should provide the opportunity to compare similar items that were sold for different prices. In so doing, the reader will gain a much stronger feeling for the marketplace.

Several pros and cons for collecting the items represented in a particular chapter are also listed. These are not provided as a definitive list of reasons to collect or not collect that group of objects, but rather, to cause the reader to learn to consider things such as liability, storage, and fraudulent representation before making a purchase.

Why Multiple Listings?

Throughout the different chapters and categories, the reader will find listings for several similar items that have sold during the past two years. For example, under the heading of "Revolvers," the reader will notice several separate listings for Colt Model 1860 New Army revolvers. This sort of duplication should not go by unstudied, as the many nuances that affect price are listed in the descriptions. A revolver engraved and cased will command a higher price than an attic relic with parts missing. Similarly, if the original owner of the revolver is identified, the price will reflect that additional history. By studying such comparative listings, you will be able to develop a sense for what contributes to the value of a Civil War artifact.

As an example of this idea, consider three entries for three Model 1842, .69-caliber muskets. Normally, one can expect to pick up a decent, complete Model 1842 for between $900 and $1800. Here, however, the range swung to either side of that spectrum:

Musket, U.S., Model 1842

Harpers Ferry, percussion .69-caliber musket with a 34" barrel that has been bored out to smoothbore. Lock dated 1850. Stock shortened to 9" in front of lock. Condition is poor. Barrel with later browned finish and areas of pitting. Lock with dark patina. Stock cleaned and modified. **$127.00**

.69-caliber smoothbore with a barrel cleaned back to the original armory bright color. Very fine salt and peppering around the breech. Crisp "V/P"/eagle at left breech. Dated 1853 on tang. Very good lock and hammer also cleaned to bright with very crisp eagle/"U.S." in the center and, "Spring/Field/1852," to the rear of the hammer. Original iron furniture has been brightened but other than the rear sling swivel is original. Fine oil-finished stock with shadow of cartouche at the left flat. Smooth bore, fine mechanics. **$1,775.00**

.69 cal., 42" round barrel, marked on the side of the breech, "W.G. & Co.," and on top of the breech is, "V/P/(palmetto tree)." The lockplate is marked vertically behind the hammer with, "Columbia/S.C. 1852," and in front of the hammer is the palmetto tree encircled by, "Palmetto Armory S*C." The heel of the buttplate is marked, "SC." All the iron has a gray patina with pitting on the breech and bolster and only minor pitting elsewhere. The brass bands have a light ochre patina. All of the metal markings are clear. The stock is in fine condition with sharp edges and some raised grain evident, relatively few light handling marks, but has probably had a little extra oil wiped on through the years. The original ramrod is about 1" short. **$4,750.00**

At first glance, it's obvious that there has to be some good reasons why three weapons of similar nature have such a varying spread of prices. Examining the description of the first musket, it becomes obvious that the musket has been shortened, and its condition overall is poor. Most likely, only the lock and some of the hardware were salvageable. No wonder this weapon sold for only $127!

The second weapon, however, sold for a bit more, but was directly in line with the current market trends. It was cleaned to an armory bright finish, thereby cutting into its collector value, but certainly increasing its "eye-appeal." It retained all of its original furniture and was embossed with the desirable Springfield logo and eagle. Dated 1853, it sold right at the top end of the wall-hanger price range. Again, after studying the description, no surprises.

And finally, the third weapon sold for a price well beyond the normal range—$4,750! Why? Its stock was full-length in decent, but not extraordinary condition (possibly even a bit over-oiled). The metal was dull and unclean. So why the almost $3,000 paid over value for a Model 1842? Study the description again. What should become clear is that this is not an ordinary '42. For starters, it has brass and not steel barrel bands. Furthermore, its lock signifies that it was made at the Palmetto Armory in South Carolina in 1853. U.S. Martial arms made in southern armories before the war are regarded as prime examples of Southern-carried weapons. But generally, that supposition alone is not enough to double or triple the price of a particular firearm. The final factor that affected the price of this weapon was the "SC" surcharge on the buttplate, confirming that this weapon was, indeed, a southern armory piece.

Provenance—"Whose was it?"

Comparing prices of similar items, the reader will discover that known provenance will almost always dramatically affect the price of a Civil War relic. Both dealers and collectors like to refer to such items as "identified," meaning that the name of the original Civil War soldier who owned the object is still known. Although it has always been important to collectors to know who carried or used what items during the war, now, more than ever, premium prices are being paid for an item with history. Not only are items being touted as, to who originally used an item during the war, now the items subsequent owners are affecting prices as well. Pieces that once sat in a prominent collection have gained a degree of legitimacy (and value) greater than an identical object with no known history.

Provenance has probably affected price more than any other factor in recent years, so it stands to reason that many items have acquired a provenance. When you are paying for an item and its history, be careful. It is easy for a seller to tell a story when handing over an object, but it is a lot more difficult to verify or prove it. The best provenance will be in the form of period inscriptions or written notes attributing an object to a particular soldier.

A boon to the provenance-oriented collector has been the thousands of excavated items that have flooded the market in the last fifty years. A collector who would generally be afraid to purchase an oval "C.S." belt plate will gladly consider a dug example. The patina acquired by years of being underground is more reassuring than any number of stories from a fast-talking dealer. Some very important collections have been assembled consisting of only dug items. But like any deal that is 100% fool-proof, collecting excavated relics is no longer devoid of danger. Unscrupulous dealers have found ways to age good reproductions into looking like excavated originals. Also, it is not out of the question for a dealer to strengthen an item's history. Who is to say the sword blade represented as having been dug near the Sunken Road at Antietam didn't really come from a trash pit of an Oregon Territory outpost? Collecting excavated relics with provenance requires that the buyer trusts his dealer.

Though many dealers and collectors like to segregate dug from non-dug items, this book does not differentiate these items other than stating their current condition and price at time of the sale. Therefore, a reader should quickly determine the effect on the price of similar items (such as an excavated cartridge for a Burnside Carbine versus a non-dug example).

The Artifact's Context

Finally, it is the goal of this book to help the collector understand the context of the artifact. Depending on how it is viewed, the context can be varied. For example, a 10 lb Parrot shell dug at Stone's River is, in the most base of contexts, an item worth about $250. Stepping up the ladder, it represents the strides in rifled artillery development made in a few short years of the Civil War. Even higher up the ladder of consciousness, it might represent the need of a modern society to feel connected with its past. Context is, obviously, a very personal consideration. Feelings and emotions aside, however, it is factually correct that these items represent a time in the United States' history when a pervasive feeling of states rights and isolation from its government caused a people to sever themselves from the nation. What ensued was the overwhelming willingness of the masses to die to protect that right or to protect the integrity of the Union. This is the context that we, as collectors of relics of this great struggle, can never forget.

The Civil War Relicman

Chapter 1
Accoutrements

Accoutrements provide collectors with a feeling of direct connection to the Civil War soldier. These were, after all, the tools of his trade—the very trappings that he wore on campaign, in battle, on the drill field, and the souvenirs of his service he decided to take home.

All accoutrements did not survive at the same rate. Nearly every Union foot soldier was issued a haversack, canteen, cartridge box, cap pouch, belt, knapsack, blanket, shelter half, and rubber blanket. However, one doesn't find the same proportion of these items today. Cap pouches, cartridge boxes, canteens, belts, and even knapsacks have passed down through the ages by the thousands. Original blankets, haversacks, shelter halves, and gum blankets, though, are exceedingly rare.

Any Confederate accoutrement with provenance is seldom encountered. Because much of the South's hardware was confiscated from Federal arsenals, it is often difficult to assign a Southern provenance to an accoutrement. Once the war commenced, however, some Southern manufacturers did produce equipment for the Confederate army and navy. When a legitimate, Southern-made, or Confederate-attributed piece is located, adding it to your collection requires a thick pocketbook of cash.

The abundance of some items (like cap pouches or cartridge boxes) enables a collector to specialize in one particular accoutrement by seeking out variations and various makers' marks. Others find it satisfying to amass all of the trappings worn by a typical officer or enlisted man.

It is a common practice with dealers to assign the term "Confederate" to accoutrements that are not regulation U.S. issue. Approach such items with caution. If a specific item does not have solid Confederate association, you may not want to pay the higher price by including "C.S." in the title. Just because a canteen may be a "tin, drum-style," does not mean that it was carried by a Confederate solider. Many states (both northern and southern) purchased tin drum-style canteens and issued them to their volunteers.

The color of leather goods is one point to consider when determining an item's origin and authenticity. However, it should not be the sole determinate. For example, a brown-dyed leather belt is not automatically a Confederate-issued piece. Similarly, an oval "C.S." buckle attached to a black, buff leather belt should not immediately be dismissed as a married item. Color should be considered as only one of several clues when examining original leather items.

Collecting Hints

Pros:

- Fakes are not as prevalent, because it is extremely difficult to fake the age and patina that most leather or tarred goods acquire naturally.
- Due to the volume of equipment produced during the Civil War, there are a wide variety of variations and manufacturers for most accoutrements. Therefore, assembling wide study collection is fun.
- Accoutrements, by their very nature, have a "personal" feel to them. By collecting the complete trappings of a soldier, a collector can develop a keen sense of a typical Civil War soldier's burden.

Cons:

- Leather and metal accoutrements can be hard to properly store. Leather requires special treatment and is prone to flaking and dryness. Ideally, it is stored in a slightly humid environment. Metal items, are especially tin-dipped iron such as canteens, are prone to rust, and must be kept dry.
- Different types of accoutrements survived at disproportionate rates. As an example, cartridge boxes have survived by the thousands, but very few haversacks have passed down through the ages. Therefore, assembling a complete soldier's kit is costly.
- Many interesting accoutrement variations are often erroneously labeled Confederate. The result is artificially high prices.
- Union accoutrements are relatively inexpensive, but anything concretely identified as Southern manufacture bears an astronomical price. Assembling typical kits of *both* Union and Confederate soldiers is difficult.

Availability ★★
Price ★★★
Reproduction Alert ★★★★★

Belts

U.S.

Some basic Civil War enlisted man's accoutrements (clockwise from center): Model 1855 Knapsack, buff leather belt with keeper and plate, cap pouch (square front), cap pouch (standard front), bayonet with scabbard, carbine cartridge box, and revolver cartridge box.

Powder Horn Militaria LLC

Buff Leather

Artillery belt, no buckle. From a small lot that surfaced years ago from a G.A.R. post. **$395.00**

Regulation Civil War U.S. infantry belt, fine condition, brown buff leather with brass adjuster or keeper. **245.00**

Regulation NCO waist belt (designed to accept the rectangular eagle buckle with silver wreath), mint condition with sliding loop adjuster and brass hook. Early war example with brass keeper secured by stitching only (no rivets). **295.00**

U.S. issued, no buckle; just the belt with brass adjuster. **195.00**

Cavalry, absolutely top-notch with all straps present, including the "over-the-shoulder" strap, beautiful silver wreath buckle with serial number matched to keeper. **1,975.00**

Harness Leather

Just the belt (no buckle), excellent condition with 98% of original black finish, complete with brass adjuster. Nicely marked with an oval inspector's cartouche. **275.00**

Buff examples of these are getting hard to find, samples in black harness leather are virtually impossible to purchase. Complete with brass adjuster and crisp maker's and inspector's stamps, slightest handling age on belt edges. **675.00**

Canteens

Confederate

Tin Drum

4-1/4" d, 1-1/4" w, japanned tin (sheet iron), convex front and flat back with large belt loop, complete with cork, japanned finish 80%, excellent condition. **200.00**

The smooth-sided, tin drum canteen is often referred to as the "Virginia" style and usually attributed to Confederate usage.

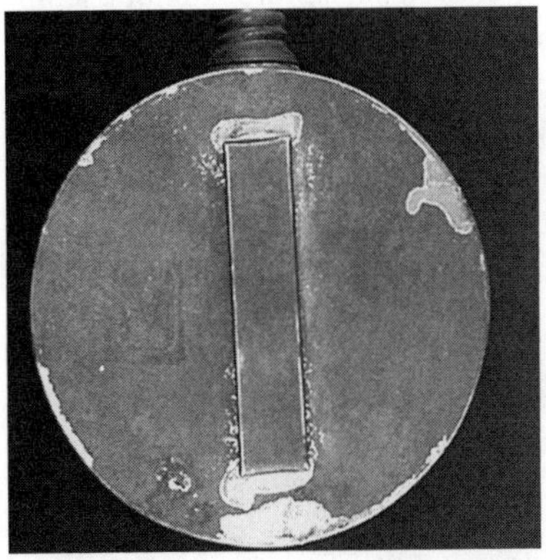

Though long-considered postwar manufacture, recent research has demonstrated that screw-top canteens existed as early as 1858.

Dale C. Anderson Co.

5-1/3" x 1-1/2", standard Virginia style with smooth convex face and flat reverse. Small canteen, three strap loops for the cotton cord strap, cord is unbroken. Condition is complete and outstanding, retaining about 40% plus of original black paint, body has no holes or broken seams. There are a few small handling dents. Stopper assembly is retained by a small cord and is complete, small chip in cork's bottom. An example of this canteen style can be found in Sylvia and O'Donnell's book, *Civil War Canteens*. **494.00**

Tin Drum, cont.

Drum style, a bit over 4-1/4" d, flat backside with tall belt loop soldered on, front has convex face, screw cap spout, fine condition, no dents. **165.00**

This style of screw-top canteen (missing its original cap) has been attributed to Confederate use.

Dale C. Anderson Co.

Rarer than standard tin drum, has its original screw spout. Very fine example, uncommon variation, particularly valuable for reference collection. Body very fine, 6-7/8" d, 1-7/8" on the side, three sling guides. Both sides convex around the edge with ring design about 1-1/4" from edge. One side is smooth, lustrous gray tin with no dents. Edges have considerable bright tin. Reverse is mottled brown bright to dark gray with deposit of finish off oilcloth haversack with which it had been stored, missing cap................**750.00**

Roughly 6" d, slightly convex sides, three tin loop strap brackets, and short tin spout, uniform undisturbed aged-tin patina, possibly pre-war militia manufacture, or Confederate made. Strap brackets are simple cut tin (not folded for strength) attached in "loop" form, so that the strap or perhaps a piece of rope could pass through them. **295.00**

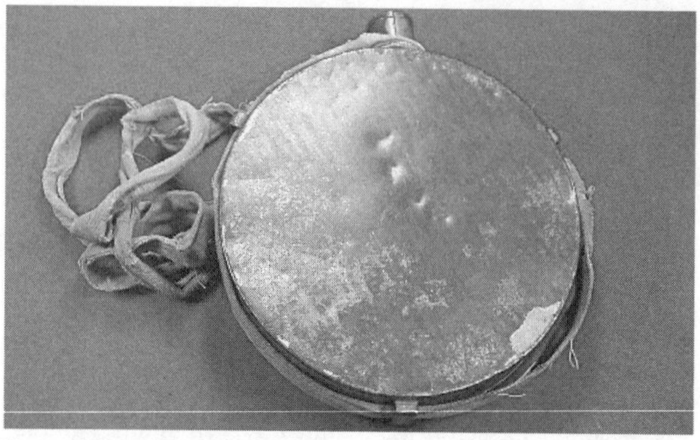

The original linen strap along with faint writing and the soldier's initials on this tin drum made it very appealing.

Middle Tennessee Relics

Nice condition, original linen sling, flat on one side and slightly convex on the other, soldier's initials and lots of faint writing on both sides. This style of canteen is often attributed to Confederate usage. **1,150.00**

The lack of side brackets on this tin drum canteen might indicate that it was originally fabric covered.

Dale C. Anderson Co.

This one is 6" d and 2" on the side with a thin, sheet tin spout. Lacks sling and cork, both simply reproduced for display. Excellent condition, thin, gray-brown patina about 50% bright tin showing, no visible rust on outside, one sling guide at bottom center. Never had guides on the side, which means it was probably fabric covered. **545.00**

The carving assisted in attributing this cedar canteen to the 4th Texas Volunteer Infantry.

Old South Military Antiques

Wood Drum

Attributed to member of 4th Texas Infantry. . . **9,000.00**

Cedar, completely untouched with original, coarse cotton sling, pencil identification of "Lt. Col. Benjamin Thompson," a New York officer who ultimately served in the U.S. Colored Troops. Probably a battlefield pickup as there are numerous other names on the reverse. **3,200.00**

Excellent Confederate Gardner-pattern cedar canteen, fine overall with only minor shrinkage, partial old initials carved in one side, complete with tin spout and original, coarse cotton sling, beautiful patina overall. **2,650.00**

Rare and extremely fine, carved Kentucky-identified cedar canteen, inscribed with the initials "W.B.K. Cap't," and "W.H.C. Late Cap't," with the year "1862" penciled above the initials. Research identifies Captain William B. Kelly and Captain William H. Cundiff both of the Union 19th Kentucky, Infantry, Company A. The 19th Kentucky Infantry was organized at Harrodsburg, Kentucky, in January 1862. The regiment fought at the battles of Port Gibson, Champion's Hill, Big Black River Bridge, Vicksburg, Red River Campaign, Sabine Crossroads, and Pleasant Hill, mustering out in January 1865. Captain Cundiff enlisted in January 1862, was wounded at Port Hudson, wounded and captured at Sabine Crossroads, reported back to duty October 1864, and remained on duty until he resigned January 1865. Captain Kelly served for nearly three years until he also resigned in January 1865. Both men's records are included. This canteen was found in Harrodsburg, Kentucky. **4,850.00**

Excellent condition, 7-1/2" d, one side in crude carving says, "Look Out Mt. Nov. 28, 1863 Tenn.," other side says "C A 4th C.S.A.," intact leather strap . . . **520.00**

Rarer style with raised central teat on both faces, original course woven cotton strap is flawless, unique original mouthpiece which utilizes an artillery shell fuse and retains its original lathe-turned, soft-wood stopper. Initials "R.A.L." carved on one side. **6,800.00**

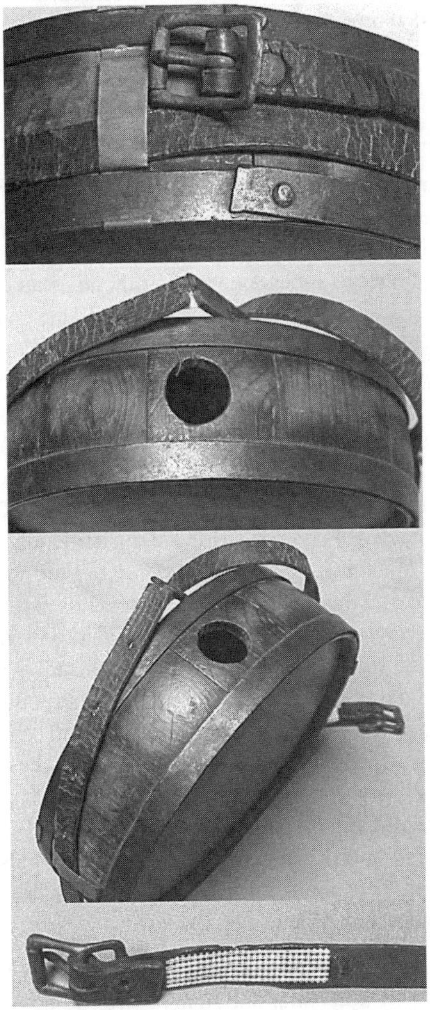

Private Tobias J. Hyatt, Company C, 60th North Carolina Regiment Volunteer Infantry carried this drum canteen.

Sharpsburg Arsenal

Wood Drum, cont.

Cedar with strap, carried during the Civil War by Private Tobias J. Hyatt, who enlisted in Co. C of the 60th North Carolina Regiment Volunteer Infantry on July 8, 1862. He participated in the battles of Chattanooga and Missionary Ridge, Tennessee. Original leather strap, web tape reinforcement on the underside. From the collection of Steve Mullinax. **4,250.00**

Private N.P. Reid of Company A, 2nd Alabama Cavalry, carried this iron-banded cedar canteen.

Old South Military Antiques

Excellent condition, tight with pleasing patina, carried during the war by Private N.P. Reid of the 2nd Alabama Cavalry, Company A. Reid's official records indicate that the 2nd organized in March 1862. Reid continues to appear on various official documents until March of 1864. It is likely he survived the war, though never surrendered. Private Reid's service would have, out of necessity, paralleled that of the 2nd, whose companies were formed from the counties of Calhoun, Shelby, Greene, Montgomery, Tuscaloosa, Butler, Coosa, Monroe, and Dallas. The regiment operated in Florida and Mississippi before being assigned to Samuel W. Ferguson's Brigade. It saw action during the Atlanta Campaign, the defense of Savannah and went into the Carolinas with General Joseph Johnston. It received its fame as part of President Jefferson Davis' escort during his escape southward at the close of the war. The 2nd Alabama Cavalry surrendered at Forsyth, Georgia, in May 1865, with 450 officers and men. "N. P. Reid" is deeply carved into the canteen's face along with his initials, indicating that he carried it for some time. The initials "J E R" and "E R" are also carved into the canteen. It has both iron bands and loops. The mouth has been only slightly elongated by a mouse sometime during the last 140 years. . . **5,600.00**

Cedar, very good condition, wood is very tightly held in place by iron bands and strap holders, attractive color, missing spout. When this type of canteen was without water for a long period of time, the wood shrank and the spout would be lost. There is nice wear on one side of the canteen, mouse damage at spout hole. **2,650.00**

Absolutely beautiful with original stopper and sling, this wood canteen is engraved with the owner's initials, "R.A.L."

Old South Military Antiques

Unique C.S.-style wooden canteen. **6,800.00**

Traditional Confederate style with iron hoops and three copper sling loops. Canteen still retains mouthpiece, often missing, patina mostly removed by partial cleaning, rudimentary carvings of sailing ship on both faces. **1,500.00**

Confederate-style, wood drum canteen decorated with a couple of floral patterns.

Middle Tennessee Relics

Beautiful condition red cedar, out of a central Georgia estate, rich red, uncleaned patina with all three sling loops intact, has two flowers that were formed using a woodworking tool. **2,250.00**

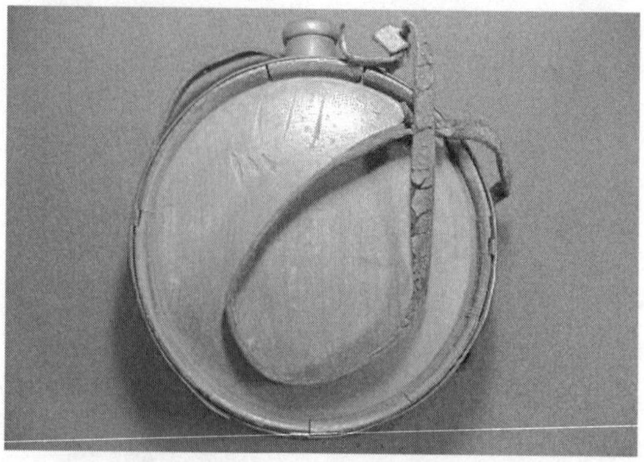

Cedar canteen complete with spout, three strap holders, and leather strap.

Middle Tennessee Relics

Though a leather-covered glass canteen would seem impractical as an accoutrement for a field soldier, these have been positively attributed to having been used during the Civil War.

Middle Tennessee Relics

Nice condition Confederate cedar complete with spout, original leather sling, and all three sling loops, very pleasing "out-of-the-attic" look. This canteen is out of the "Rattle and Snap" Polk Historic Home near Mt. Pleasant, Tennessee, where it was on display for several years. **2,450.00**

Leather-Covered Glass, carried by both Union and Confederate soldiers, excellent condition, name "RING" faintly carved into one side. **795.00**

U.S.

Model 1858

Nice example of concentric ring Civil War issue canteen, brown wool cover shows only light age, original stopper (no shoulder strap). **350.00**

Regulation M1858 U.S. army smooth-side canteen complete with all three brackets, pewter spout, brown wool original cover, repeated rectangular pattern designs in the cloth. Much more interesting than the common brown wool specimens. This one was covered by the soldier in the field just as prescribed by directive when canteens were issued without covers, great example (no stopper). **295.00**

About perfect condition standard smooth-side canteen. **149.00**

About perfect condition standard smooth-side canteen, original stopper still attached to top bracket with chain, tin spout pattern (as opposed to pewter) attributed to manufacture in St. Louis or Cincinnati. **169.00**

Excellent example (no stopper) of regulation Model 1858 smooth-side army canteen complete with the full brownish-gray wool cover and the full length (unbroken) "folded and sewn" cotton shoulder strap. Interestingly, this one was actually issued and is not a surplus example. Faintly visible on one side of the canteen in worn black stenciled letter "E" and what appears to be a worn "6." **455.00**

Excellent example, stopper and chain, regulation Model 1858 smooth-side army canteen complete with the full brownish-gray wool cover and the full length (unbroken) "folded and sewn" cotton shoulder strap. Truly excellent condition with light dirt and expected age, unit markings on the front cover of "M 35" which tend to indicate issuance to cavalry or heavy artillery. **475.00**

Excellent example, regulation Model 1858 smooth-side Army canteen, complete with the full brownish-gray wool cover and the full length (unbroken) "folded & sewn" cotton shoulder strap. The condition is truly excellent with only a couple very tiny moth holes. Interestingly, this one was actually issued and is not a surplus example. Faintly visible on one side of the canteen in worn black stenciled letters is "E."? A very fine example with great appeal. **435.00**

Brown wool cover and shoulder strap, virtually defect-free except for expected age stains and light surface dirt. The spout is stamped with the maker's mark. **650.00**

Bull's-eye pattern with all three strap brackets and pewter spout. Overall, very good and solid with no bad dents, clear marker stamp on spout, "R. H. Gratz Phila." **159.00**

Model 1858, cont.

Classic example of a smooth-sided Model 1858 canteen with cover.

Bull's-eye-style canteen with strap and cover. Cover appears gray-brown, but is probably a faded blue, surface rust on body, pewter spout. **330.00**

Complete brown cover shows some wear, retains original cotton strap, maker's mark on spout: "A. Jewett." Stopper and chain missing. **485.00**

Complete with cover, strap, and stopper. Almost mint except for very small wear spot in the cover.. **495.00**

Spherical tinned-iron canteen with smooth-sides, three strap loops, and tin spout. Painted white with owner's initials, "MHH," in a floral design worked in red and green, worn finish, body holes rusted through the base on both sides, retains remnant of a crimson tassel and old address label, which may aid in identification. **125.00**

Nice solid bull's-eye example with all three strap brackets, pewter spout, very good and solid, nice age patina. **189.00**

Nice solid bull's-eye with complete brown wool cover in very good condition, just having a couple small holes from age and wear. Very nice look to it, very solid condition, priced fairly.................. **285.00**

Nice solid bull's-eye with very scarce dark blue wool cover in very good condition, a couple small age/wear holes, but very appealing, 80% of the original cloth shoulder strap which is broken and frayed, Philadelphia maker's mark stamped into spout. **550.00**

Solid specimen, all three strap brackets, pewter spout, very nice age patina, solid. These concentric ring canteens were manufactured only during the war years. The rings were thought to impart added strength, but this was not the case, so they were discontinued after the Civil War. **189.00**

Really sharp with excellent cover, no moth damage, nice Philadelphia maker's stamp in the spout. The top left strap bracket is missing, and was obviously missing since the Civil War, as there is an area of reinforcement in that spot where the shoulder strap (no longer present) was actually sewn in place. Top-notch shape and very rare with the dark blue cover. **345.00**

Regulation army canteen, 100% complete with cover, strap, and stopper, excellent condition with tiny wear spots on cover. **465.00**

Regulation canteen in very good condition, shows honest age and wear with a few small dents from wartime use. **139.00**

Regulation smooth-side canteen with portions of tweed/brown cover around the outer edges. Nice and appealing with some war-use dents. **139.00**

Regulation smooth-side canteen in overall very good condition, complete w/all strap brackets, rolled tin spout like the St. Louis arsenal examples, nice deep age patina. **149.00**

Retains original covering and canvas strap, stopper, chain, and cork. There are no repairs, additions, or subtractions. There is a date stamped on the spout that reads, "Feb. 15/65," and above that a stamp of what appears be the manufacturer's name. ... **360.00**

Smooth-sides, covered in butternut-colored wool. Complete with cork stopper and linen cloth sling, fine condition. Sling has inspector's stamp. .. **325.00**

Original covers are a factor that will elevate the price of a Model 1858 canteen. This example has only about 70% of its original butternut wool cover.

Middle Tennessee Relics

Smooth-type Union canteen that has portions (approximately 70%) of the original butternut cover. **250.00**

Well-used St. Louis Arsenal-style canteen complete with butternut cover and the remnants of the linen sling. St. Louis canteens are distinctive because of their tin spouts. They were used by both Union and Confederate soldiers during the war. **395.00**

Dark blue wool cover, shows only light age and moderate fading, lacks bottom strap bracket, but otherwise is very fine (no shoulder strap). . . . **350.00**

This came from an ages-old Ohio collection put together in the 1940s. Excellent condition, fine deep-brown wool cover that is perfect on one side, and has a small "L"-shaped tear in the other. Painted on the perfect side are the original unit markings, which have partially flaked. What appears to be the soldier's initials are over the letters "Co" above the letter "M." With this, is an old (but not Civil War period) leather shoulder strap that adds greatly to its display value. **345.00**

Classic army canteen with smooth-side body, pewter spout, and all three strap brackets. Overall excellent condition, several honest minor dents from wartime use. **149.00**

Classic army canteen with smooth-side body, pewter spout and all three strap brackets. Overall good condition, several honest minor dents and a deep, brown rust age patina. **139.00**

Classic army canteen with smooth-side body, pewter spout, all three strap brackets and stopper. Overall excellent condition, very attractive green, aged tin patina, just the right amount of light dings to let you know it was there. **179.00**

Boldly painted in neat-stenciled characters, "G 12 V.R.C.," designating Company "G" 12th Regiment, Veteran Reserve Corps, condition very worn and tattered. The brown wool cover is badly worn with much back shredding and some face shredding with the paint. The shoulder strap is present, but is shredded and torn. The cloth shows great wear, but the unit identification is really fine and very visual. . . . **495.00**

Entirely complete with original heavy fabric sling, stopper, and gray cover with absolutely no holes, and only a bit of rust stain coming through the center on one side. Canteen is smooth-sided and without dents, cover is clean. Linen strap has dulled to off-white, beige from age. An exceptionally nice canteen that is complete and original. **575.00**

Possible Confederate copy of the Model 1858 canteen or perhaps one of the tin spout specimens made in Cincinnati, Ohio. Body has a deep, rust-brown patina and remnants of the original woven shoulder strap (40%) are still present in a greatly deteriorated state, rare pattern. **195.00**

Regulation smooth-side canteen surfaced at a home sale in eastern Ohio, excellent condition with all three strap brackets and a full complement of light-brown wool cover (excellent with one modest wear spot on each side just below the spout). Also attached is an old leather shoulder strap. **250.00**

Model 1858 canteens were reinforced by stamping with concentric rings. Collectors refer to these as "bull's-eye" canteens to differentiate them from the smooth-sided canteens they replaced. Often, a bull's-eye-styled canteen was covered with wool fabric, but photographic evidence shows that soldiers carried them uncovered as well.

Solid Union bull's-eye canteen, two small dings, traces of original paint coating remain between the bull's-eye rings, some surface rust on one side, giving it character. The pewter spout is maker-marked, "Hadden, Porter & Booth, Phila." Stopper is original, however, the chain that connects the stopper to the canteen may (or may not) be an old replacement. If the chain is a replacement, it is a good one, being exactly like the original chain. Purchased locally in Richmond, Virginia. **185.00**

Very good condition with cotton strap, original plug, and guides for the carrying strap. Believed to be from the New Jersey National Guard, circa 1860, nice brown wool jean covering. **312.00**

Wool covering, tin spout with ring and cork plug, 8" deep (some hole in cloth), later carrying strap. **275.00**

Very representative example unquestionably actually issued, has great appeal. The cover is nice very solid tan wool. One side of the cover is perfect; the other has a wear spot near the center (about the size of a silver dollar). Original woven sling strap, which is broken in two spots, but could be easily repaired. Original stopper and original string twine ties the stopper to the spout, which bears a Philadelphia maker's stamp. Uniformly dirty from 135 years of storage in a New York attic. **345.00**

Cap Pouches

Confederate

The long tongue is one of the distinguishing factors of an Augusta Arsenal-produced cap box for the Confederate Army.

Old South Military Antiques

Augusta Arsenal. **7,200.00**

The single belt loop and tarred leather finish distinguish this as a Confederate cap pouch.

Middle Tennessee Relics

Percussion, excellent condition, single-loop tarred leather Confederate percussion, crudely molded teardrop-shaped pattern, brass finial, intact including leather closure tab. **1,250.00**

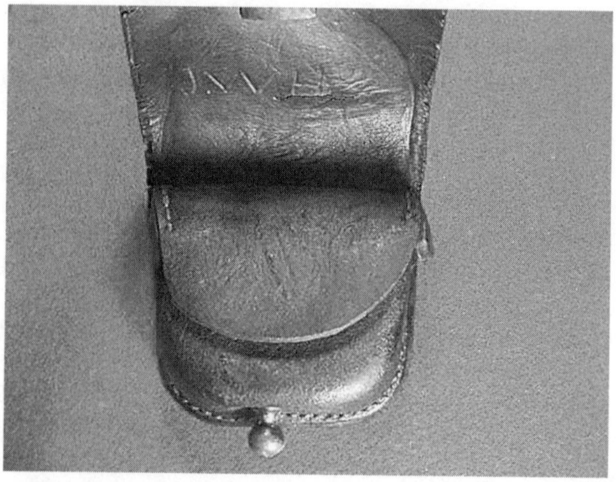

The lead finial on this cap box is what gives credibility to a Confederate attribution.

Middle Tennessee Relics

Extremely rare, lead-finial Confederate cap pouch, nice condition with crude, hand-sewn construction, Confederate soldier's initials, "J.W.H." cut into the underside of outside flap. Except for the tip of the leather closure tab, this is a nice lead-finial C.S. pouch. **1,250.00**

Percussion with "Texas" and five-pointed star carved on front. **2,500.00**

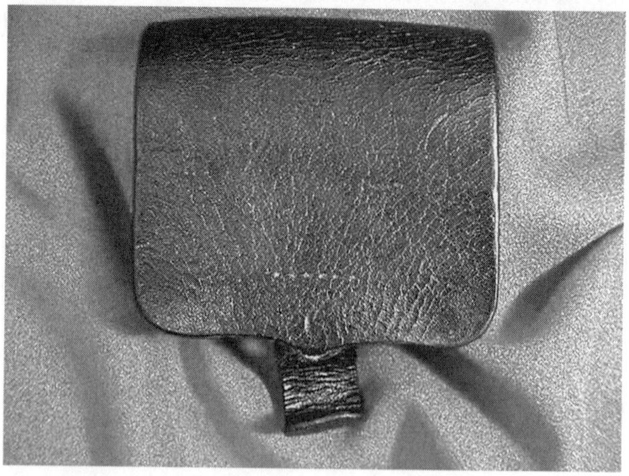

The square-front cap pouch is very typical of Confederate design.

Old South Military Antiques

Perfect percussion pouch. **1,420.00**

Lead-finial-equipped cap pouch with the closure flap torn off.

Middle Tennessee Relics

Rare, single-loop, lead finial Confederate cap pouch that is made of hand-stitched, dark-brown leather. The closure tab's tip is missing, as are the two small sidepieces that are attached to the inner flap. Otherwise, this is a solid, pliable C.S. pouch. **1,150.00**

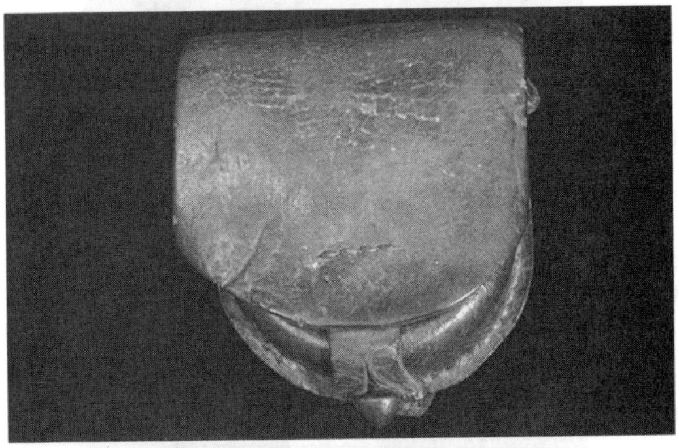

Stunning Selma Arsenal Confederate cap pouch.

Old South Military Antiques

Selma Arsenal-marked. **8,500.00**

Box brought home by Michael Moyer, 46th Regiment Illinois Volunteers. Separately applied latch tab, strong hand-stitched seams on all edges, single, wide belt loop on the reverse, cast-lead finial, constructed of excellent-condition, brown-russet leather with excellent finish. The latch tab is connected to the front flap by being sewn to the outside with two rows of vertical blonde stitching, then the tab passes through a bottom slot on the front flap to engage the lead finial. In addition, the side ears of the cap pouch are sewn directly to the front flap with blonde thread. The latch tab is missing, the very end having broken off at the hole that accepts the finial. **1,495.00**

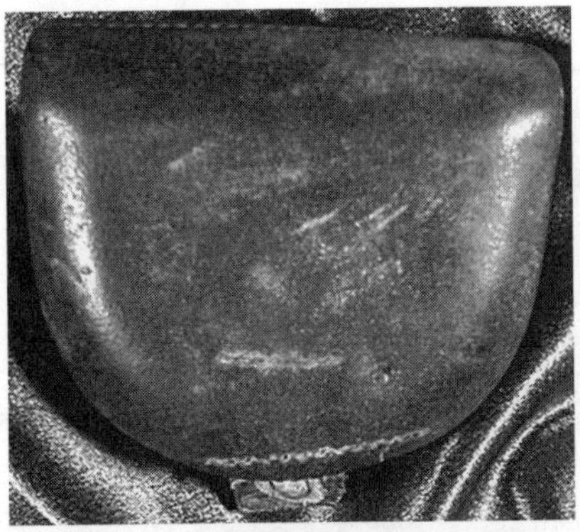

Constructed from reclaimed leather from a Campbell & Company, London, accoutrement, this cap pouch is a fine example of Confederate frugality.

Old South Military Antiques

Percussion pouch manufactured using leather reclaimed from an S. Isaac, Campbell & Co., London, marked accoutrement. Isaac, Campbell & Co. supplied numerous articles of war to the fledgling Confederacy. Occasionally, knapsacks, cartridge boxes, belts, cap pouches, swords, buttons, and firearms of English manufacture are encountered bearing Isaac & Campbell's mark. This is the only truly Confederate-manufactured accoutrement bearing the Isaac & Campbell mark. This is a case of their having reclaimed their own damaged material. Confederate armory workers reused the leather from damaged accoutrements to make new ones. This remanufactured cap pouch includes the classic Confederate lead finial and the wide, single belt loop. Box in excellent condition throughout, even retains its vent pick. **3,600.00**

Wide, single belt loop and brass finial, typical crude manufacture, leather condition very good. . . . **1,250.00**

U.S.

1863 dated, brown, with Maine maker's stamp, near-mint condition (no wool or pick inside). The leather is a pretty brown color with much life, stamped on the inner flap, "Carcelon & Covell 1863 Lewiston Me." . . **235.00**

Regulation mid-war with a Model 1839 small "US" cartridge box plate attached to the front flap by means of the plate loops being bent over inside the flap. . . **245.00**

Excellent regulation Union specimen, maker unknown, super finish on leather, embossed decorative edge line impressed around the perimeter of outer flap—an added feature not seen on government contract boxes. . **169.00**

Excellent, russet-brown Union army cap pouch with remnants of lamb's wool still inside. Leather is somewhat dry, and the overall condition rates very good. Inside the inner flap is a name written in pencil (perhaps "Williams"). **150.00**

Black leather, marked, "E. Gaylord Chicopee, Mass.," in three lines on inner flap, excellent condition but shows use. Both belt loops and the tie-down strap are intact. **195.00**

Cartridge Box, cont.

in ink. Presumably a Civil War cadet box that wasn't fitted with the box plate. For an identical specimen with an original VMI box plate, reference the Steuart Collection at the Virginia Historical Society, Richmond, Virginia. **1,200.00**

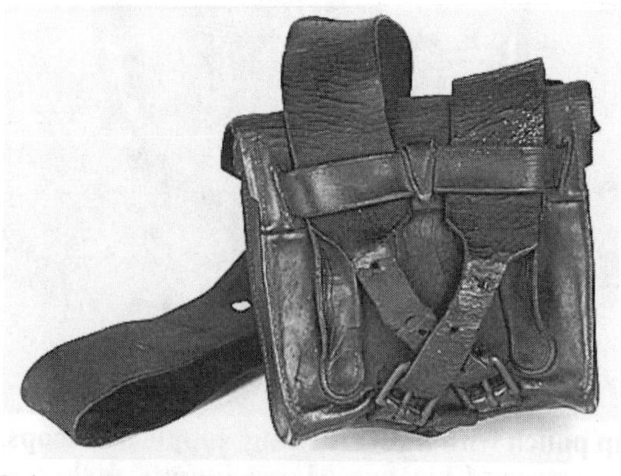

Private Daniel W. Kline of Company F, 25th Virginia Infantry was wearing this cartridge box when he was captured on July 13, 1861.

Hendershott Museum Consultants

This Confederate-made cartridge box was carried by Private Daniel W. Kline of Company F, 25th Virginia Infantry. Pvt. Kline carved his name into the flap, "D.W. Kline." Very-fine condition, with the leather in good shape and the original leather strap still intact. Pvt. Kline served with the 25th Virginia and was captured in the very early days of the war in the Battle of Rich Mountain, Virginia, in July 1861. He was under the command of Confederate Colonel John Pegram who led his men against 2,000 of General McClellan's federal troops. Pegram was forced to surrender 555 Confederates on July 13 due to the fact that he was outflanked by McClellan's men. Private Kline was one of these 555 men. He was paroled and exchanged in August 1862. This identified Confederate cartridge box is beautifully homemade with crossed "X-"style harness straps. **4,500.00**

R. J. Higgins scratched his name into the outer flap's center of this Confederate-manufactured cartridge box. Pvt. Higgins enlisted in the 3rd South Carolina Volunteers during the patriotic rush following the firing upon Fort Sumter. This would, a year later, cost him his life. The 3rd was one of the first South Carolina regiments which arrived in time to fight under General Bonham at Bull Run. The following spring, the 3rd was serving under General Kershaw in the bloody Seven Days around Richmond. Kershaw's Brigade, on June 29th, led the assault at Savage Station. Pvt. Higgins was slain when this single brigade attacked Sumner's entire corps. The other name on the box is L. L. White. He was a private in the 2nd South Carolina Volunteers that subsequently became the 9th South Carolina Volunteers. White was discharged due to illness during February 1862. He appears on Confederate records again in August 1863, serving in the 3rd Palmetto Battalion Light Artillery. He served with them for the remainder of the war or at least until February 1865, after which no further record can be found. The cartridge box is in flawless condition. **9,500.00**

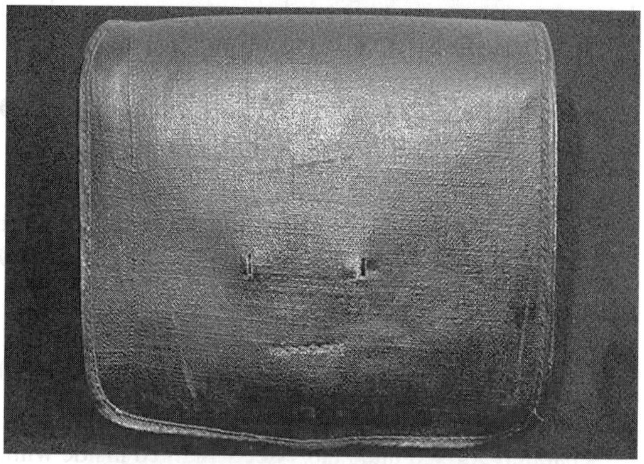

N. Crown & Co. Confederate box sporting a tarred linen flap.

Old South Military Antiques

.58 Rifle, N. Crown & Company cartridge box. . . **24,000.00**

U.S.

.58 Rifle Enfield

Classic example of what many U.S. and C.S. soldiers carried with their Enfield rifle muskets. Rig is in superb condition, box is near mint and marked inside outer flap with maker's name and 1861 date, original tin liner, buff leather latch tab, and all the straps and buckles are firmly in place. Standard U.S. example shoulder strap, oval U.S. inspector's cartouche visible near where strap meets box, shows slight handling age, never cut for the eagle "breastplate." . . **1,395.00**

Excellent condition, complete with all straps, tab, and buckles firmly in place, large tin liner inside the box. Outstanding leather with great finish and life, front flap's underside has oval maker's cartouche with "1861" date, "WD, as well as a number "4219" as is seen on the butt plates of Confederate Enfield rifles. **1,250.00**

.58 Rifle Mann's Patent

Near-mint example of this scarce and desirable box boldly marked in a huge cartouche on the front flap, "Col Mann's Patent Re-Issued June 7th 1864 E. Gaylord Maker Chicopee, Mass." All of this wording surrounds a large embossed, "US." Patented tin liner inside, shoulder strap removed, inspected by T.J. Shepherd. **395.00**

Cartridge box stamped "E.Gaylord, Inspector." 1864 dated, very fine.. . . . . **450.00**

Large 7" x 8" box for rifled musket, clear "US" oval embossed on flap, "Mann Patents" around the edge, retains pull-up tin liner with finger loop, torn closing strap. Complete sling strap arrangement, several pieces need restoration. **475.00**

Maker mark, "E. Gaylord, Maker, Chicopee, Mass." present on this pouch. Leather is strong and supple, box has metal interior, and brass stud latch on base. **250.00**

M1864 Mann's infantry box, short body (as opposed to the same year's long body pattern), fine to excellent condition good finish, all straps and hooks firmly in place, Mann's patent tin liner inside, well marked, complete & unbroken pair of shoulder straps. Mann's patent data, Gaylord maker's data, large "US," and Laidley inspector's cartouche nicely marked on front cover. Most of these boxes had the straps removed after the war. Finding an as-issued example like this one is quite difficult. **975.00**

Model 1855

Dark leather box has no maker's mark, leather is dry with surface crazing; seams and tabs are intact, sling has lots of crazing and a repaired break, box has oval brass U.S. plate, and sling has circular brass eagle plate. **175.00**

With the U.S. plate still attached to its flap, this Model 1855 cartridge box also had the owner's initial scratched into it.

Middle Tennessee Relics

Good, solid, middle-grade example of a .58 model 1855 Union cartridge box, reasonably pliable, all buckles and tabs intact, original lead-filled, large, oval "US" box plate on outside flap and one of the original cartridge tins inside. The soldier's initials, "W.A.M.," are carved into the back of the box. **425.00**

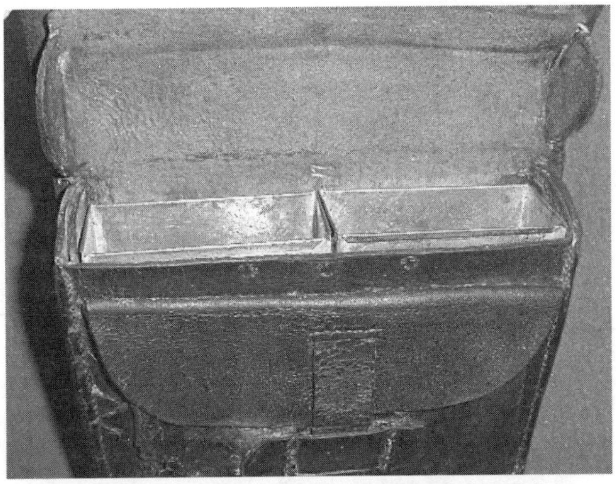

Each cartridge box had some method of keeping cartridges organized. In the cases of the Models 1855, 1861, and 1864 cartridge boxes, two tin containers served this function. On this particular box, the owner's name "D. Day" was lightly scratched into this Model 1855 cartridge box.

Middle Tennessee Relics

Very attractive 58-caliber Union cartridge box complete with lead-filled, "US" oval cartridge box plate and both cartridge tins, box also retains the leather closure tab, both iron roller buckles, and both leather belt loops. Faint, "C.S. Storm," maker mark on side of box, and the name, "D.A. DAY," is cut with a pin knife into the outer flap's underside, a good solid cartridge box with typical leather flaking.. . . . **475.00**

Model 1861

The latch tab is secured by a single row of stitching only (no rivet), the belt loops are sewn and riveted, and the bottom buckles are held in place by stitching only. Box finish very good with some light surface scuffs and a little crazing, shoulder strap in identical condition with light surface wear and one small snag where the strap hung on a peg for years. It has the circular eagle breastplate still present, as well as the "US" oval cartridge box plate. Not marked in any fashion, the front flap of the box is cut for the box plate, but it is not present. **1,175.00**

.58-caliber, black harness-leather cartridge box, shield-front flap with removed box plate, sewn closure billet intact and pliable, interior has, "H.A.DINGEE/ N.YORK," contractor stamp, implement pouch complete with flap and closure tab, and one ammunition tin (the other lacking) which contains the loose side ear from the interior flap. Black leather sling has been affixed by sewing where the sling buckle tabs should be at the base, fitted with reproduction eagle breastplate. Reverse of sling has museum accession number indicating that it was processed into a collection in 1966, leather remains good and pliable. **225.00**

Model 1861, cont.

7" x 8" black saddle-leather cartridge box, complete with original shoulder sling, both breast and box plate, tool pouch, and tin liners. Leather is in very-good supple condition, box has wrinkles, but no real crazing, sling is slightly crazed at pressure points, no markings. **1,300.00**

Superb example of early-war pattern, .58-caliber cartridge box. Latch tab secured by a single row of stitching only (no rivets), belt loops are sewn and riveted, and bottom buckles are held in place by stitching. Outstanding box finish without any flakes or flaking, only a little surface scuffing on the outer flap, unmarked, complete with tin liners, and was never cut for the cartridge box front flap plate. **465.00**

Excellent condition, early war, Union army infantry cartridge box. Strong and solid leather with a couple small areas of finish wear on outer flap. Unusual manufacture with two copper rivets on the bottom corners of the inside implement pouch. The inner flap is deeply marked, "Watertown Arsenal 1864." Both tin liners are still inside. All straps and buckles are firmly in place, latch tab is secured by a line of stitching and one rivet. The bottom buckles are sewn and riveted, oval, brass "US" cartridge box plate on the front flap in very-fine condition. A scarce variant. **550.00**

A very-fine 1861 box with a pretty plate, one tin liner, great finish, and very solid. Crisp, "Hoover Calhoun," maker stamp, perfect, except one roller buckle has been reattached, ancient small museum tag on front with, "#4," and, "XA2105." **350.00**

Complete with very pretty "US" box plate and bold maker's stamp, "A. W Decrow Bangor Me." Very solid with good life and finish to the leather, light handling wear. **395.00**

Fine example, early-war-pattern .58-caliber cartridge box. Latch tab secured by single row of stitching only (no rivet), the belt loops are sewn and riveted, and the bottom buckles are stitched in place. Box's finish is very good with just some light surface scuffs and a little crazing, unmarked in any fashion, the front flap is cut for the box plate (not present). **435.00**

Freshly found "really issued" example in nice, solid condition, 1861 pattern box with a provision for box plate (not present) on flap. Marked, "Watertown Arsenal 1863," on inner flap, and both tin liners are still inside, all straps and buckles are firmly in place, still has the original shoulder strap with it w/provision for eagle plate (not present). Solid condition with good finish on the leather. **495.00**

Good, solid specimen. Complete with all straps and buckles, maker's stamp, "E.A. Corben/St. Louis," has U.S. plate, and shows light age and handling, but very solid (no tins)......................... **325.00**

This desirable Model 1861 box is enhanced by a strong ink identification to John H. Miller, 184th Pennsylvania Infantry.

Sharpsburg Arsenal

Identified to John H. Miller, 184th Pennsylvania Infantry, black leather, .58-caliber box with lead-filled "US" box plate with records included. Name paper attached under lid shows box was property of "John H. Miller, Co. G, 184th PA Inf." Miller was wounded on October 27, 1864, in the fighting before Richmond. He was later taken prisoner and confined in a rebel prison in Richmond, Virginia, and paroled on February 25, 1865. His regiment was also present at Lee's surrender at Appomattox Court House. **895.00**

Near perfect, unoiled 8" x 7" black saddle-leather cartridge box, very smooth overall. Perfect tool pouch, sling buckles, tins, and belt loops. Crisp "J.B. Sickles & Co./St. Louis, Mo." stamp on inner flap. Super "SNY" box plate is a deep, untouched mustard color with black tarnish spots............ **1,250.00**

Standard 1861 pattern box constructed with sewn latch tab, sewn and riveted bottom buckles, and sewn and riveted belt loops on the back, both tin liners inside, nicely marked, "E Gaylord," on inner flap. Unusual feature is that the front flap sports a circular eagle shoulder belt plate (breastplate) instead of the U.S. plate. You can see that there was a standard U.S. plate on this at one time, but that the breastplate was then added. Normal scuffs and scrapes on the front cover. **395.00**

Worn, but solid, example of the 1861 pattern, .58 cartridge box with maker's stamp, "Baker-McKenney NY." Complete and solid with all buckles and straps intact. **375.00**

1861 pattern somewhat taller than a Model 1855 box, overall fine condition with good life and finish, complete with tin liners, lacking the latch tab. Excining element is front cover with a large cast-brass British crest attached with the unicorn and lion and crest, above crest is his cap insignia which consists of a letter "G" and numerals "87.". . . **375.00**

Model 1863, manufactured by, "Edwin A. Crossman & Co., Newark, NJ." 1864 contract for 15,000 sets of "Infantry Accoutrements." This is complete with U.S. sub-inspector stamp, leather is in absolutely excellent condition. **1,250.00**

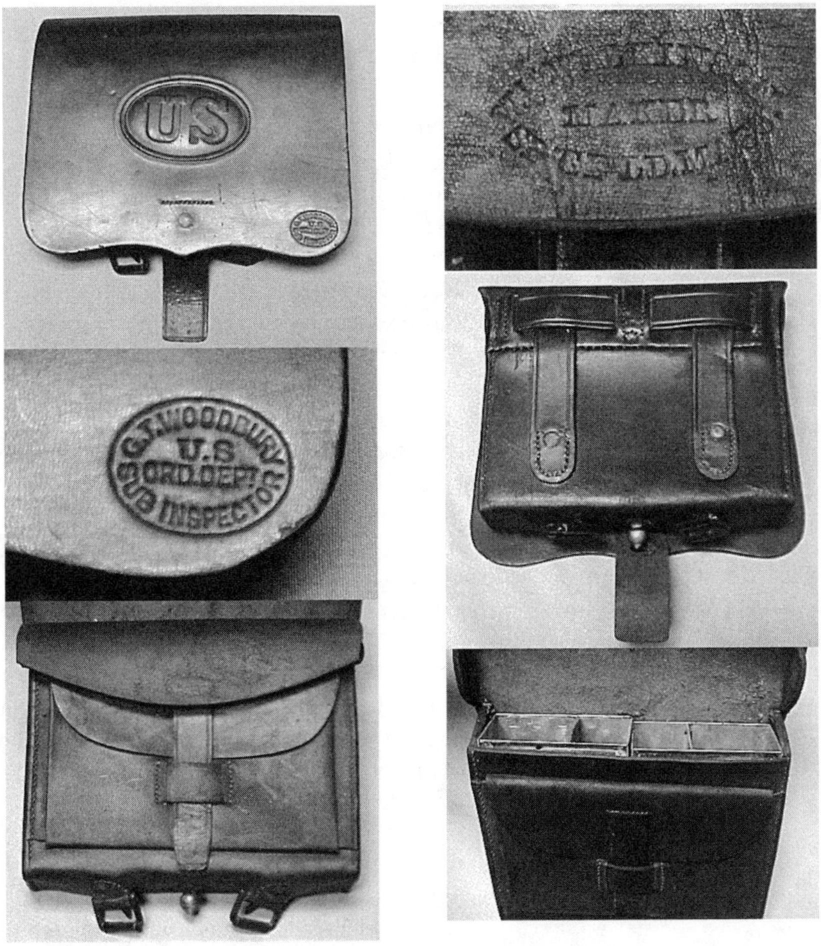

Model 1864

Manufactured by W.H. Wilkinson, Springfield with Ordinance Dept. sub-inspector stamp, superb condition. **1,200.00**

The Model 1864 box is distinguished by having the oval U.S. plate embossed directly onto the flap, rather than an attached brass plate.

Sharpsburg Arsenal

Model 1864, cont.

6" x 8" black saddle-leather cartridge box, original M1864 leather sling with no eagle plate (no piercing for one either). Excellent box with handsome mustard-colored, lead-filled, brass "US" box plate. Closing tab reinforced with copper rivet (M1864), inner flap crisply stamped, "Arsenal/1864/US." Box retains the original tool pouch, tins, and acorn-shaped finial, smooth surface on leather, very-fine box. **1,250.00**

A good, solid example with minor finish wear, all straps and buckles firmly in place, nice inspector's stamp on outer flap, Wilkinson maker's stamp inside, no tins, embossed "US" on flap. **235.00**

Solid example with all straps and buckles firmly in place, marked, "Watertown Arsenal 1864," on the inner flap. Some crazing to the finish, but a solid strong box with good finish and appeal, replaced tins. **265.00**

Standard 1864 box with the latch tab, buckles, and belt loops all secured by rivets and stitching, front flap nicely embossed with the "US" in an oval panel, overall condition very-good to fine with nice leather finish, tin liners inside, embellished with the soldier's name, "Hilliard," scratched into inner flap. Also remnants of two old paper tags inside the outer flap, neither legible except for one which has, "17 W?M?" The outer flap shows evidence of once having a box plate (no longer present) over the embossed "US" mark. **365.00**

Very good, solid example showing honest use and age, complete with all the buckles and straps firmly in place (no tin liners), boldly marked with a "Nece" maker's stamp and "Laidley" inspector's stamp on inner flap. The leather shows scuffs and handling, but no abuse or rot whatsoever. This is the last pattern cartridge box issued during the Civil War, and this example is a fine solid specimen. **245.00**

Complete with tins, all straps, and buckles (tie down strap is an old replacement). Minor crazing to the black leather, has sub-inspector's stamp and Philadelphia maker's stamp on inner flap, embossed U.S. in an oval on the outer flap. **375.00**

"US" embossed in the oval on the front flap. Inspector's mark also on the front flap. This piece is in good condition with both tins, all buckles, and straps. Soft and supple leather with only one side of the fastening strap hole torn. There are also inspector's initials and other words on the inside tool pouch. **395.00**

Condition is everything when buying leather goods. Though flaking on the underside of this Model 1864 box is a bit much, the maker's mark is still visible on the front.

Middle Tennessee Relics

Model 1864 Union leather cartridge box with the closure tab, both roller buckles, both belt loops, and both original cartridge tins perfectly intact. Pliable leather with only a small amount of normal flaking. A nice inspector's mark is visible on the outside flap. **350.00**

This 1864 box is complete with all the straps intact, as well as the bottom buckles and original shoulder belt. This rig was never cut for plates. Leather is very solid and the finish is intact with expected age and dirt wear. Complete as issued except for no tin liners. One small break in the strap leather where the strap passes through the bottom buckle. **475.00**

Rare trial box prepared during the closing hours of the Civil War and the early days of the Custer era. Regulation 1864 pattern cartridge box with maker's stamp by "Metzger" and a bold inspector's cartouche. It is complete with all the straps and buckles firmly in place and the original tin liners. The only aspect of this cartridge box that is different is the addition of a solid cast-brass hook attached to the outer flap's top by a riveted leather loop. **295.00**

Truly a top-shelf example of the 1864 box with embossed, "US," on the front flap and crisp inspector's cartouche, "R White US ORD DEPT Sub Inspector," on the lower-left corner of the front flap. Complete with tin liners. Slight crackling on parts of the finish, otherwise excellent. **450.00**

Truly excellent condition, crisp oval "US" embossed on front cover, both tin liners inside, all straps and buckles firmly in place, tight, sound, good finish, and, "Haedrich/Phila," maker's stamp on inner flap. There is some storage dirt inside. **365.00**

U.S.

Carbine, Burnside

Black leather carbine box for the .54 cartridge. Complete with wood block for 20 cartridges and both inner flaps and one horizontal belt loop on back. The two buckles with button have been removed so it could be worn on waist belt, has maker, "JE Condice 57 White St. New York," on inner flap....... **325.00**

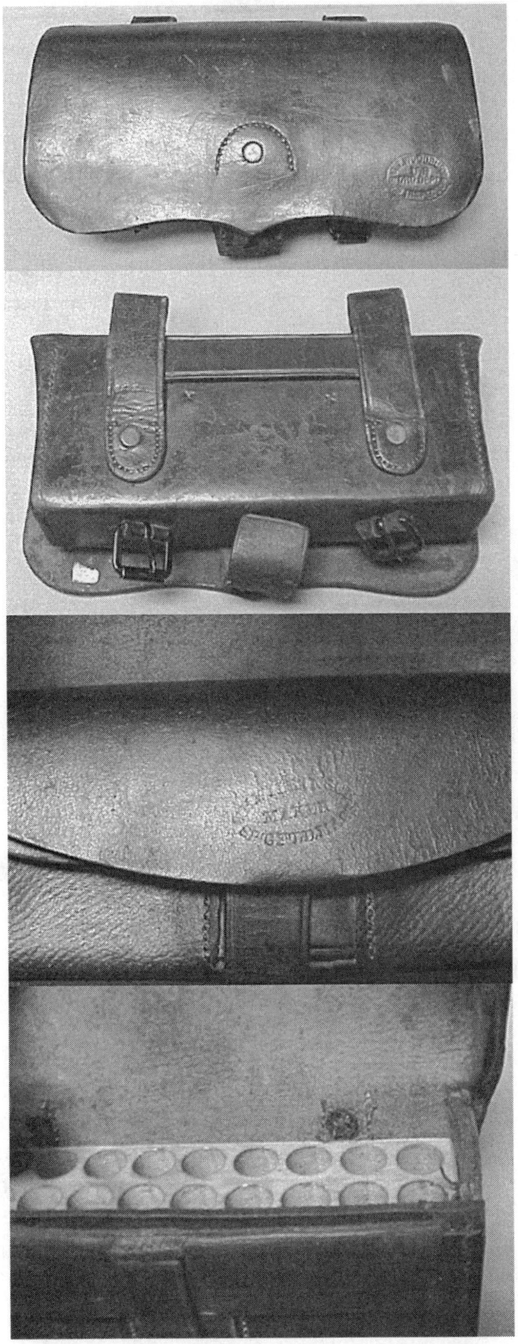

Nearly pristine, it is doubtful whether or not this carbine cartridge box was ever actually issued. Originally intended for use with the versatile Burnside carbine.

Sharpsburg Arsenal

Manufactured by W.H. Wilkinson, Springfield, Massachusetts. Box is in excellent condition with no flaking of leather, closing tab complete, and original wood interior complete. Strong, "US Ordnance Dept.," mark on front flap............... **1,295.00**

Regulation box with wooden block liner drilled to hold 20 cartridges. All straps and buckles firmly in place, good finish with just the lightest flakes from the finish, nice Davy maker's stamp, and very solid. **345.00**

Regulation carbine box boldly stamped on the inner flap, "Sickles & Co./St. Louis/Mo.," in an oval cartouche. Excellent condition in black harness leather and complete with the wooden block liner drilled to accept 20 cartridges. All buckles and straps are firmly in place.............................. **450.00**

Carbine, Maynard, maker-marked "Hoover Calhoun & Co. New York." The wooden block liner holds 20 rounds of Maynard carbine ammunition. Some crackling to the surface finish on the leather, but solid and 100% complete. **395.00**

Carbine, Model 1855 Pistol

Super condition, excellent finish and strength, both perfect tin liners still inside, once had a "US" plate on the front flap, but is no longer present..... **750.00**

This box, which is roughly half the size of a musket cartridge box and is constructed virtually the same (implement pouch, inner flap etc.), was intended for use with the M1855 Springfield single-shot pistol with detachable shoulder stock. Complete with damaged tin liner inside, all straps and buckles firmly in place. Soldier's name scratched into the outer flap, "W.V. Bi?" Very-good condition with some finish crackling and evidence of actual use. There is a professional repair to the latch tab that is unnoticeable unless you look very closely. **425.00**

Carbine, Spencer, "as found" box with some finish scuffing and wear. Both belt loops firmly in place on the back, while the bottom buckles were removed long ago. Wooden block is still inside, but the latch tab is broken, boldly marked inside the inner flap, "Hoover Calhoun & Co. Makers NY." **145.00**

Carbine

A rare, variant carbine box that has roller buckles riveted to the upright belt loops on the back! Manufactured without bottom roller buckles. Bears maker's stamp, "J Cummings/Springfield Mass.," on inner flap, solid condition, broken latch tab... **175.00**

Unusual cartridge box made in the style of a regulation pistol carbine cartridge box or rifle cartridge box. Inside tin has a separator, dividing it into 2-3/4" and 3-1/4" compartments. The tin retains 100% original finish. The box measures 4-7/8" x 7", while the inner box is about 3-1/2" deep. There is a leather inner flap. The cover leather is crazed, but all leather is solid with an excellent closing tab. The finial is black japanned iron. The loops on the back take a standard 2" wide belt. **228.50**

Carbine, cont.

Cavalry soldier's cartridge box nicely marked, "J Davy & Co/Newark NJ," on the front flap. Very worn, but a really good display item. Damaged latch tab, no bottom buckles and no wooden block inside. Both belt loops intact with damage on one. **65.00**

Extremely rare style of carbine cartridge box, known as the "Kittredge Box" (named for its inventor), is thought to have been intended for use with Henry rifles and Frank Wesson carbines.

Sharpsburg Arsenal

Kittredge & Co. cartridge box complete with lid spring and belt attachments on back. Said to have been issued with Henry rifles and Frank Wesson carbines. This box has no dents and has a wonderful mellow patina. **1,295.00**

Mann's Patent cavalry carbine box, has patent date, "1864," but was later converted into an Indian War Cavalry box with a wood block that accommodated 32 .45/50 cartridges. The box is in good condition with only one small end panel that fastens to the front flap missing. **350.00**

Regulation box for holding 20 rounds of Joslyn or Spencer ammunition. Crisp, "J. Davy," maker's stamp on outer flap, wooden block liner inside, both buckles firmly in place as are all the straps. Excellent condition with only the lightest wear........ **365.00**

Standard pattern U.S. carbine cartridge box in good, pliable condition.

Standard government issue. Leather and seams are in excellent condition with some wear on black finish. **250.00**

This is a really fine condition regulation Civil War cavalry carbine cartridge box. It is all complete with undamaged belt loops, buckles (with about all the japanned black finish), and latch tab. It has its original wooden cartridge block. Inside it is maker-marked, "DINGEE & LORIGAN MAKERS NEW YORK." Implement pouch is fine as is inside flap. Just minimal crazing on the front flap. **256.00**

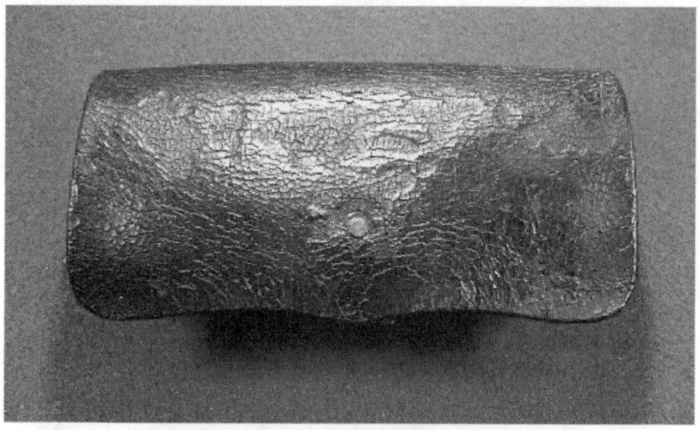

The wood cartridge block still exists in this cavalry carbine cartridge box. Made by E.A. Crossman & Company.

Middle Tennessee Relics

Union cavalry carbine leather cartridge box in solid middle grade condition. The outside flap is pliable and complete, but has surface flaking. Both iron roller buckles are intact, but the end of the leather closure tab is missing. The wood cartridge block remains intact inside. The box is crisply marked, "E.A. Crossman & Co. Newark, N.J.," on the inside flap. **295.00**

Carbine cartridge box in outstanding condition. Measures about 9" x 2" x 5", leather in near-perfect condition. **475.00**

Cartridge Boxes, Pistols, and Revolvers

U.S.

Pistol, Navy, externally, looks like tall version of USN fuse box. Single, wide belt loop on the back, the box's inside has an envelope or implement pouch and inner flap. The front cover is embossed "USN," the inner flap is marked, "Navy Yard Phila 1861." Box's finish is excellent as is overall condition, missing tin liner, small tear in latch tab. **495.00**

Day's Patent, this box is quite ingenious. It consists of a wooden revolving cylinder drilled with holes that rests inside a tin carrier that, in turn, rests inside the leather box. The revolving wooden cylinder is designed to accept cartridges in the drilled holes. The user rotated the cylinder to remove each cartridge. Appears designed for revolver ammo or possibly Henry rifle ammo (holes appear to be roughly .45 caliber). The leather box itself is 4-1/2" by 4-1/2" by 1-7/10" in size, and is shaped with a rounded bottom, leather cover flap accepts brass finial centered on box's front, back has two leather upright belt loops with small extensions of leather strapping at top with small buttonholes in extension ends. Condition is good to very good with some finish wear and flaking. The patent for this device was issued during the Civil War. **975.00**

Revolver, Navy, 5" x 7" black saddle-leather waist carried cartridge box. "USN" stamped in crisp oval on the outer flap. Outside of box is dry, but fairly smooth, crazing on extended belt loop, but still solid, retains inner flap, closing tab, and the oft-times missing oval accoutrement pouch with cover. Box is lined with a six-compartment tin liner for the Colt .36-caliber cartridge blocks. This box could use a coat of leather preservative, but it is quite presentable and very rare, because most of these had the accoutrement pouch cut out and wooden block tacked in for cartridge weapons. **650.00**

Revolver, Plant's, rare box designed to be used with Plant's cartridge revolver, looks just like a miniature carbine-style cartridge box with a delicately scalloped front flap outline. It is roughly half as wide as a carbine box and 80% as tall. It has two belt loops on the reverse and a brass finial. It was made with no inner flap nor an inner implement pouch. The condition is excellent with good finish (just some light surface crazing). The front flap's bottom portion is shaped in a semi-shield shape (coming to a point). The left and right sides of the box are rounded at the top to meet the front flap's contour when closed. **345.00**

Revolver

.36-caliber pistol box for use with cavalry belt, very good solid condition, normal age and wear, a bit dry with outer finish crackling. **145.00**

4" x 6" black saddle-leather cartridge box for two wooden block packets of .36 percussion cartridges. Smooth black leather, only the slightest crazing, crisp, "T.J. Shepard," cartouche over script "US" on the front flap, two or three large areas of crazing on the box's inside face, this does not show nor detract, excellent closing tab with brass acorn finial and belt loops at back.......................... **350.00**

5" x 7" black saddle-leather cartridge box for the wooden .44 cartridge blocks. Nice smooth face, slight crazing, crisp, "J. Davy & Co/Newark, NJ," maker's address on front, fine closing tab, finial, and belt loops. **350.00**

Black saddle-leather cartridge box, front heavily crazed, inspector's cartouche in center, good tab and belt loops................................ **165.00**

Front flap 6-1/4" x 4-1/4". Retains essentially all finish—front and rear of box are smooth, no front cracks, back has a few microscopic cracks. Front flap has light surface wear and some fine finish cracking. Few flakes out of upper bend and along bottom, marked "J. DAVY & CO./NEWARK, N.J." Also has small script, "US," on left corner, rectangular inspector's stamp leaves barely a trace on opposite corner. **250.00**

Nice (fine condition), brown-finished box measuring (box portion measurements) 5" x 1-1/2" x 2-1/2". The bottom portion of the front flap is a semi-shield shape (coming to a point). The latch tab is attached with stitching and a rivet, two belt loops on back attached with stitching and rivets, constructed without an inner flap nor implement pouch, the left and right sides of the inside box portion are rounded at the tops to exactly meet the front flap's contour when closed, unmarked. A rather scarce accoutrement for either cavalry or artillery. **295.00**

Made for the .44 revolver, this is the scarcer of the two patterns being about 15% larger than those made for .36-caliber revolvers, overall excellent condition. **195.00**

Many states equipped their own troops with uniforms, arms, and accoutrements. This is a fine set provided to a cavalryman by a state. It consists of two boxes, one for carbine, and one possibly for pistol cartridges and pistol caps. Both are excellent quality and condition, which if oiled and polished, can look almost as fine as when used. Carbine box is 7-1/2" wide at the front flap and 4-1/4" high. Lustrous thin black finish a bit dusty, lots of fine flex-cracking, two back belt loops, heavy, inside tins divided into three compartments, closing strap missing a bit of top. Other box is smaller, but much larger than a cap pouch: 4-7/8" x 4". Finish is the same as on the other box, tin inside with a small tray on tip, at one end, probably for caps, once had fleece edging. **575.00**

Revolver, cont.

Produced by "Davey & Co." this revolver cartridge box was designed for use with a .44 caliber revolver.

Nice .44 cartridge pouch in outstanding condition, "DAVY & CO.," stamped below tab rivet, "SHEPARD," inspected and stamped as such. "U.S." stamped. No rotten threads, broken rivets, or tears, closing tab intact, leather pliable, measures 6" x 4". Leather has flaking on the closing tab and belt loops, the flap has a few dings, but flawless body. Stamps are clear and crisp, the leather's flesh side is lightly stained, but not greasy from leather conditioner, the threads are strong. Original closing tab, and the leather straps are intact. **160.00**

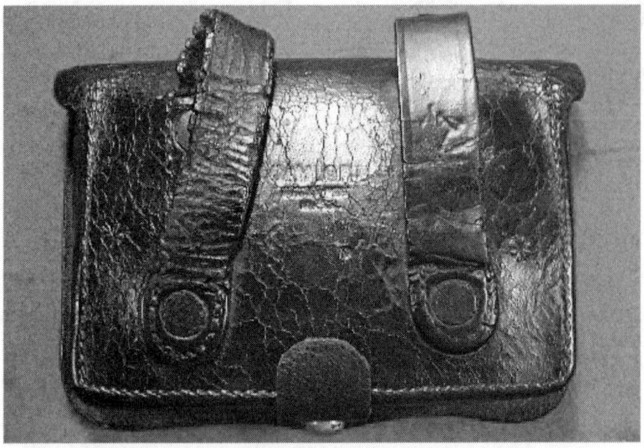

Made by, "Gaylord, Chicopee, Mass.," this revolver cartridge box still has pliable leather and both loops intact.

Middle Tennessee Relics

Nice condition, Union revolver cartridge box with pliable leather, closure tab, and both belt loops, "Gaylord-Chicopee, Mass.," maker's mark on reverse. **275.00**

Perfect, unissued Civil War .36-cartridge box for issue with the Colt Navy and similar revolvers. ...**189.00**

Perfect unissued.36-caliber cartridge box for issue with the Colt Navy and similar revolvers, well-marked cover with Davy maker's stamp, U.S. stamp, and, "TJ Shepard," inspector's stamp. **159.00**

Black saddle leather cartridge box for the .36 Colt Navy revolver, fine smooth finish, maker-stamped on inside, "Felix Chilling-worth/Maker/Greenfield, Mass." **.295.00**

Tarred leather pistol cart box, with large silver letter *"P"* on the flap, solid, but missing latch tab. Single, wide belt loop on back, and brass finial, jammed into the back belt loop is the top section of an 1816 bayonet scabbard and the frog. **59.00**

Fine condition, inspector's mark and stamp on front cover, shows careful handling. **169.00**

Footwear

Confederate

Essentially a pair of squared-toed civilian boots.

Dale C. Anderson Co.

Boots

Black leather, square toed, wood-pegged soles, tiny square nails at toe and larger square nails in heels. Well-used, but flexible and excellent for display. Face of the boot top on one has an extra panel pieced in (totally original), because the lower piece was too short to use otherwise, 11-1/2" heel to toe; 13-1/4" h, top front of boot higher than rear, striped web loop pulls inside top of boots. Few wear-thru spots on soles, heels worn down to 3/4", couple cracks at edges where tops joins soles, one showing period repair.... **.525.00**

False, all-leather boot uppers or Greaves used by Civil War officers. Designed to be worn with low boots or brogans, to simulate high boots and provide the protection of boots when riding. These have a nice fancy stitch design and are spring loaded to allow for firm grip on legs—a very practical and comfortable item to wear that allowed quick removal. ... **550.00**

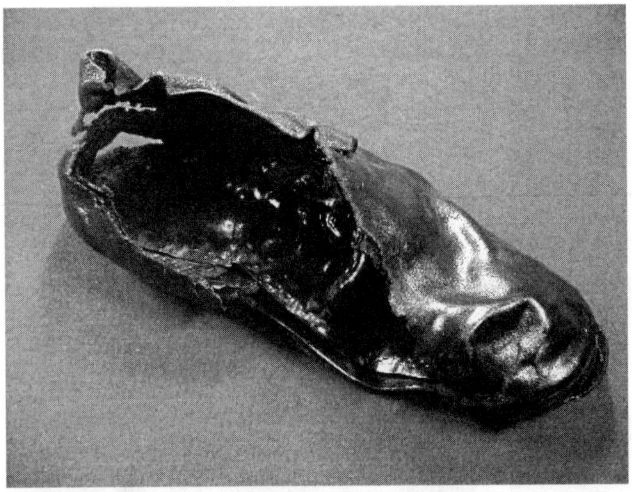

Extremely rare to find as an excavated relic, this Civil War-period brogan emerged from a Nashville, Tennessee trash pit.

Middle Tennessee Relics

Brogan, dug, original, excavated from a huge trash pit at Nashville that produced shoes, sections of uniforms, glassware, and hundreds of other items. Brogan has been treated, coated, and is totally stable and ready for display. **125.00**

This shoe is one of a stylish pair that bears a period tag directing that they be delivered to "Capt. John Woodcock, Penn. Vols." Any footwear identified to a Civil War soldier is exceedingly rare.

Dale C. Anderson Co.

U.S.

Brogans, U.S., Officer, ankle-high black leather brogans of a distinctly different style found only in central Pennsylvania and wherever Dutch/German people settled...which is where this officer came from. Wooden soles, very pointed toes, iron "horseshoes" nailed to sole and heel, and the toe areas have some incised geometric line designs. On one sole, there in an original ink inscription that reads, "SEND TO CAPT. JOHN WOODCOCK, PENN. VOLS. See Bety (sic) for Adress (sic)." Sounds like he needed another pair of shoes at the front and his shoemaker sent them. Capt. Woodcock was in the 124th PA Vol. Infantry nine months (Aug 62- May 63). Shoes are nearly good as new, exceptional display item showing diversity of equipment used. ... **1,495.00**

Fuse Pouches

Confederate

About the size of a regular cartridge box, scalloped front flap, finial is brass, but more of a fat button, inner flap with ears, softer and thinner than the outer flap, box sides are rounded at the top and the sides taper in toward the bottom, just two narrow belt loops sewn on the back, some surface cracking and flexing on the flap top. Inside were two Civil War envelopes that were addressed to a woman in Vicksburg, Mississippi, both of the stamps, no letters. Box is in great condition and has no maker's marks. Belt has been married to the box. The buckle is an old roller-type buckle that is indicative of C.S. use. **950.00**

U.S.

Very fine example of artilleryman's fuse box worn on waist belt, standard-size leather box measures 5-1/2" x 7" and is marked, "US Watervliet Arsenal," on outer flap. Inner flap, closing tab, and belt loops are intact, box was designed to hold artillery fuses and implements, box is dyed black.............................. **475.00**

Navy

Black saddle-leather belt pouch, 3" x 3-1/2" x 2". Shield-shaped front flap, inside crisply stamped, "U.S.N.Y./Boston," within a cartouche, fine condition with closing strap, brass finial, and single belt loop. **375.00**

.36 Caliber, overall fine condition, hand-sewn, full-flap holster, made entirely of brown-finished pigskin. Constructed with the flap cut so that it ends in a strap passed through a sewn loop on the holster's body (not made with a finial). Superb condition with no flaking, just showing light honest age, missing back belt loop. **650.00**

Griswold, authentic Confederate revolver holster from famed Ted Meredith Confederate collection, "found in an old Gettysburg Museum collection with a Griswold and Gunnison revolver." This tooled-leather holster with full flap and closing tab has a rear belt loop riveted in place. There is a brass closing stud, the leather is soft and pliable, one visible area of repair is held with age-old wire reinforcement. A very rare and interesting piece of Confederate leather with solid provenance. **800.00**

U.S.

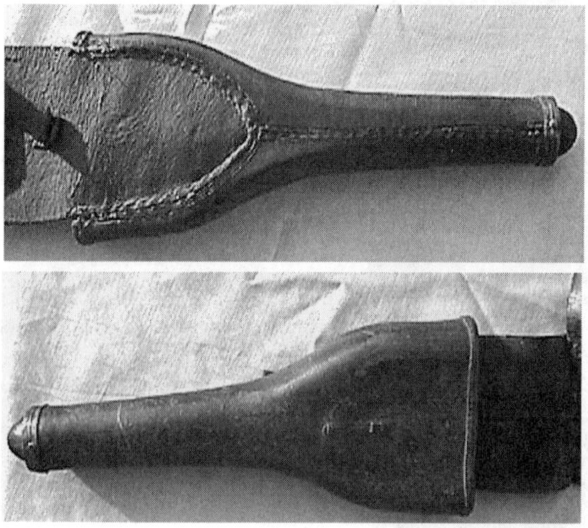

"Saddle Holsters" were nearly outdated by the time of the Civil War. Nevertheless, officers and even some cavalry troopers still kept them with their equipment to hold a pair of single-shot pistols at the ready.

Saddle, pair of pommel holsters 12-3/8" and 5-1/4" x 1-3/4" at the top. There is a copper 7/16" band around the bottom. The 4-3/8" connecting strap has been re-stitched by a previous owner. Other than that, the holsters are very good. **325.00**

Model 1849 Colt

Made for Colt's pocket revolver, large flap and brass stud closure, complete with belt loop and barrel plug. **195.00**

This was for a revolver with a 5" barrel, excellent condition, good solid body contour. Not limp or flat. Has 90-95% original surface finish with a very shallow network of drying cracks on the face. Rear of holster, flap, and belt loop have no cracks, flap has deep finish cracking along the top bend, 1-1/2" break in the flap at bend's rear, full-length closing strap with flexed finish. **395.00**

.36 Caliber, overall fine condition, hand-sewn, full-flap holster, made entirely of brown-finished pigskin. Constructed with flap being cut, so that it terminates in a strap, which passes through a sewn loop on the holster's body (not made with a finial). Superb condition, no flaking, light honest age. The only defect is the missing back belt loop. **395.00**

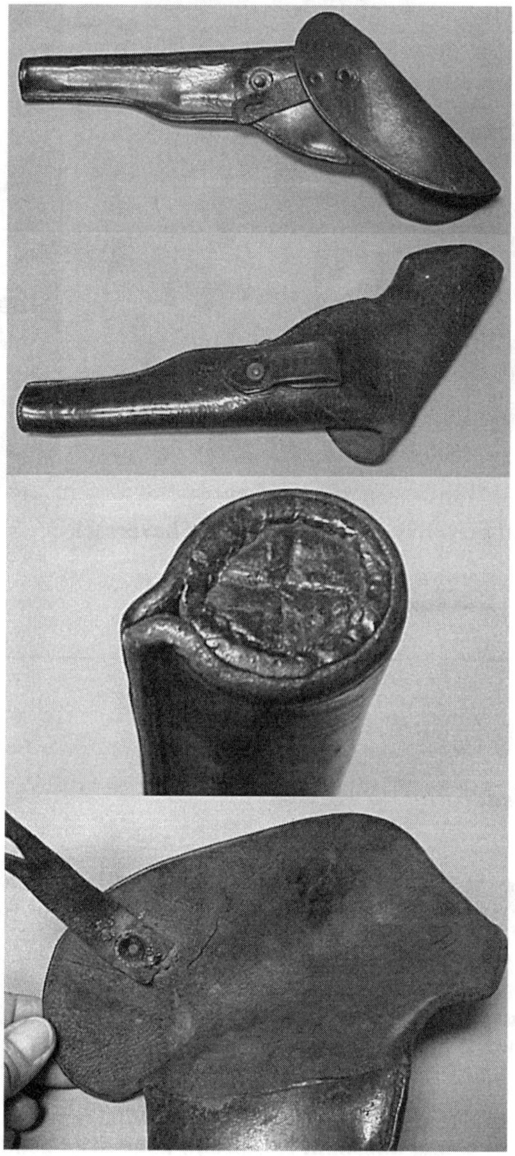

Made from brown-russet harness leather, this holster fits a Colt Model 1851 revolver. It is likely that it was intended for Confederate service.

Model 1851 Colt Navy

Complete with very nice russet-brown saddle leather, small single belt loop on rear, closing tab appears to have been re-riveted a long time ago and is complete, holster has plugged bottom. **725.00**

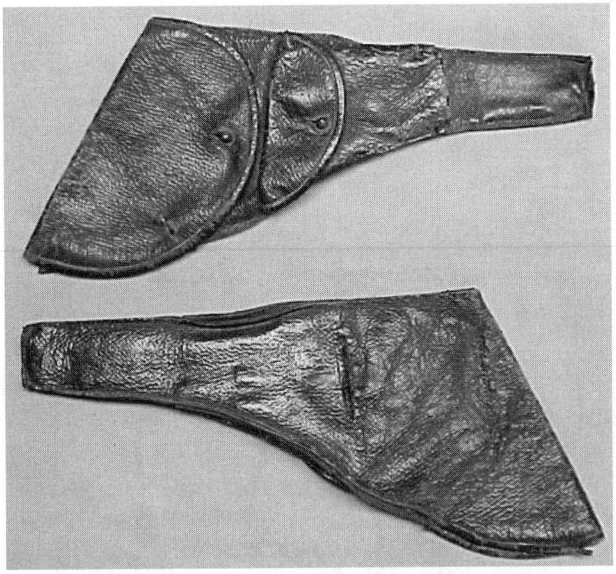

This pigskin holster was made for a Colt Model 1851 revolver.

Sharpsburg Arsenal

Appears to be made of pigskin, Army-style flap and front pouch for percussion caps. Appears to fit a Colt Navy revolver, stitching is weak and in some places, gone, belt loop is missing on rear. **295.00**

Original revolver holster that fits the Colt M1851 Navy perfectly, holster in great condition and comes with an original U.S. belt and belt plate with arrow hooks, rear belt loop is intact, but slightly curled from hanging. **600.00**

Regulation cavalry holster with clear "Condict" maker's stamp on flap, overall very good with tear in belt loop and missing plug, otherwise quite nice with good leather finish. **275.00**

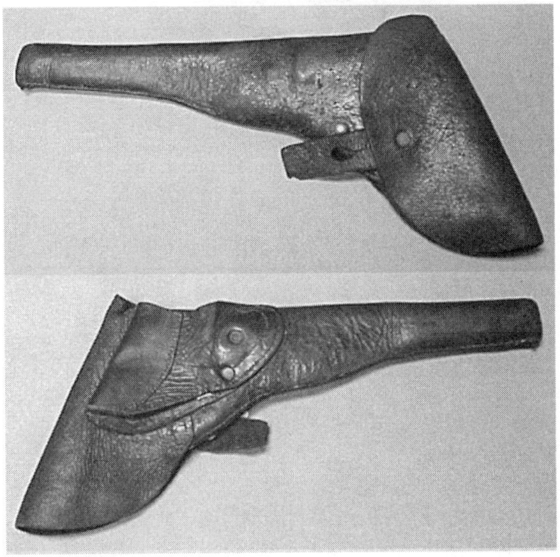

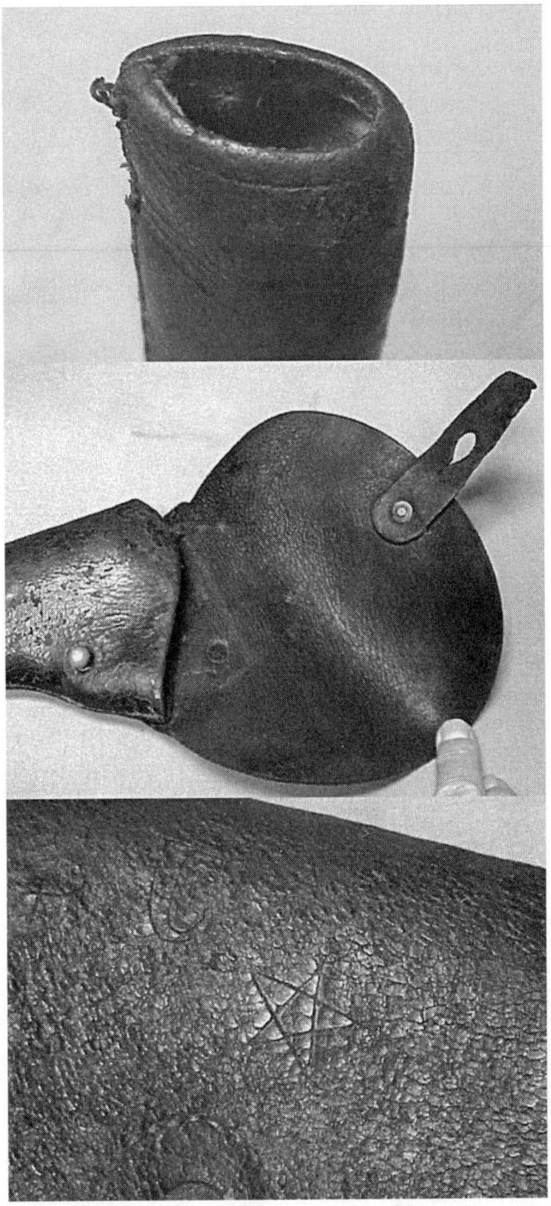

Initials, "S.J.," and a star are carved into the flap of this holster. It was left up to the buyer to decided whether it was a Union or Confederate piece. Made to fit a Colt Model 1860.

Sharpsburg Arsenal

Model 1860 Colt Army

Very-good condition with minor flaking, but pliable leather, closing tab is complete. All seam stitching is strong, missing bottom plug, "S J" and five-pointed star carved into flap. **595.00**

Model 1860 Colt Army, cont.

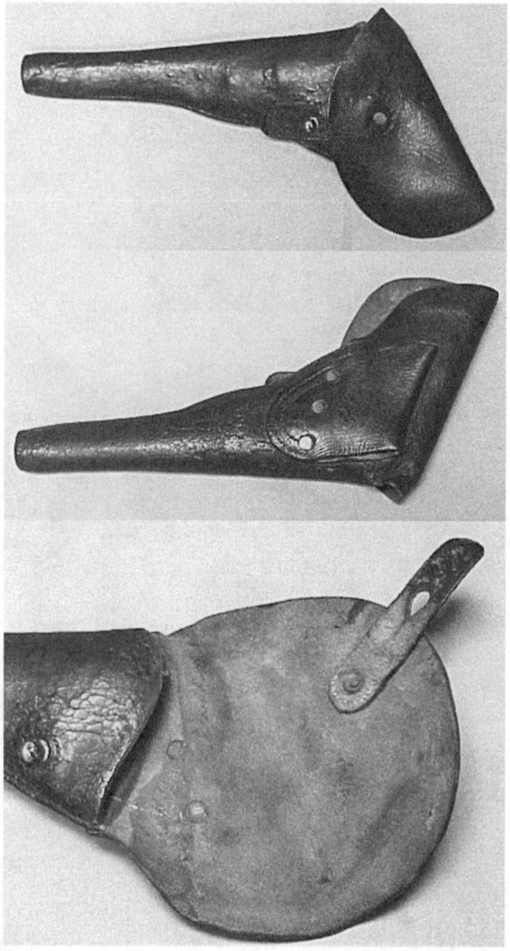

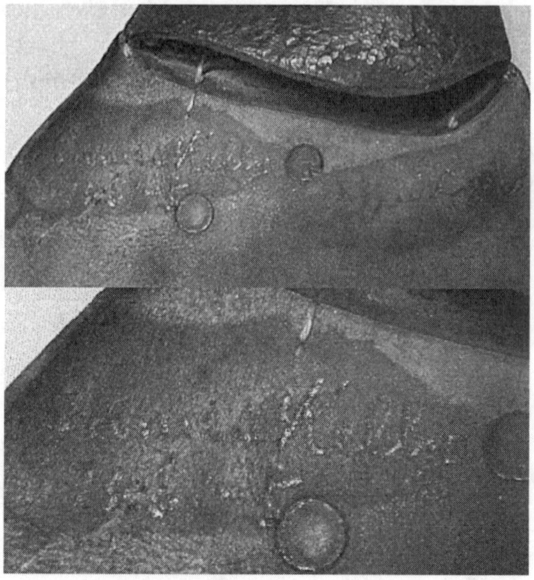

A pencil identification inside the flap added to the appeal of this Wm. Kinsey & Co. holster.

Sharpsburg Arsenal

Maker-marked, "Wm Kinsey & Co. Newark–NJ." Holster has bottom plug and original closing tab, very-good condition leather, could easily still be used. Pencil identification on inside of flap, "James Kelly 1861-5." **695.00**

Holster and waist belt with brass hardware, no belt plate. **432.00**

Knapsacks

U.S.

Box style, measures 15" x 13.25" x 4", made of fruitwood and square pin nailed and glued together. Canvas covered and painted with black pitch. The side panel marked with, "No174." The back lift-up flap is marked with the painted number, "22." Surface with cracking, minor tears and dirty. **350.00**

Model 1855

The style of knapsack issued to most troops, even though several models were used. Thin fabric tarred overall, complete with straps and buckles, displayed by filling the big double bags with some type of soft material, one bag has a number of fractures along the edge, which should be backed by some thin material. One main shoulder strap and a few others have all the finish flaked off. **350.00**

Black tarred canvas knapsack, complete straps, ties, buckles, no envelope tears. "Valentin" maker's stamp on right shoulder strap.................. **275.00**

Fabulous knapsack in great condition, made by, "E. Robinson, New York," who was a contractor to the U.S. **495.00**

Known as the "double-bag" or "soft pack," regulation Model 1855 Knapsacks survived the war inspite of never currying favor with soldiers.

Dale C. Anderson Co.

Optics

Confederate, Field Glasses

All brass with a gold wash, these glasses are 5" extended and 3-7/8" closed. There is a 2-1/16" x 1-1/8" engraved ring for holding, front end is 2-1/4" d. Each eye piece is made of hard rubber and is marked, "*Hyde & Goodrich* New Orleans." **1,895.00**

French, U.S., and Confederate

Black glove leather covered 5" binoculars of about 4X power, excellent optics, eyecups engraved, "A. Lefevre/ Paris," both binoculars and leather covering are near perfect................................. **265.00**

French-imported field glasses, used by both sides, maker-marked, "Chevalier Opticien, Paris," in the ocular lens cups, 6" h, strong, complete leather on brass body of glasses, replacement objective lens, almost indiscernible, field glasses are complete with original case, case missing shoulder strap............ **315.00**

Marked, "U.S.Signal/Army&Navy/Day&Night/Glass," on the tubes. Made by famous Paris maker Chevalier, leather covers on main body, for holding comfort, fine set of field glasses in excellent condition....... **245.00**

Solid brass, finished gloss black, with dark-brown, scotch-grained leather veneer around the main barrels, 3-7/8" long, fully extended, 4-1/4" wide, shows barely any wear, excellent optics. While French-made (as one would expect), they are marked by a New York dealer, both on the eyepieces and in case's lid. There is a tiny bee logo on one of the cross braces showing the French manufacturer, fitted leather case is quite worn, several open seams on the ends. The little push-button opener lacks the tip and part of the latch. Coppery-colored lining a bit loose, gold logo of dealer, "J. PRENTICE/ N.Y.," in lid. **125.00**

The barrels are longer and more narrow than most, and the glasses open to 9-1/2". The rear barrels are nearly as long as the front, solid brass finished gloss black, main barrels covered in thin dark-brown, scotch-grain leather, barely any wear to finish. Leather complete with surface wear and minor shrinkage, fine, adjustable optics, hand-engraved eyepiece, "AUDEMAIR/ PARIS," tiny deer-head logo, on cross piece, "16 Glasses." **175.00**

U.S., Telescope

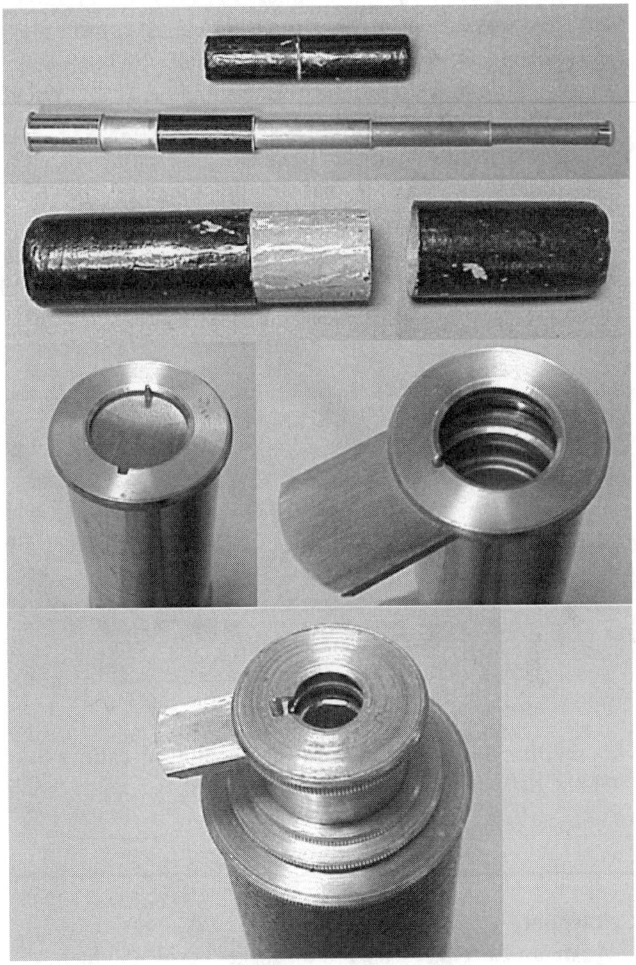

It is difficult to attribute a telescope as specifically having been used during the Civil War. Nevertheless, many were, so it is possible to find representative examples.

Sharpsburg Arsenal

Telescope fully extended measures 23-3/4" long. Constructed of brass with sliding lens protectors on both ends, original leather covering on body and original painted paper case, perfect optics. **495.00**

Civil War era, brass drawtube telescope made about 1850 and engraved by the maker, "L. BACH OPTIKER/ MUNCHEN." Black leather-covered, four-section tube with sunshade, 12 to 15 power, 26-3/4" extended, optics are fine although a little dusty. Covering is in fine condition and includes both original lens covers. Includes letter indicating that this was the property of George Fenwick Jones (1840-1873). **375.00**

U.S., Telescope, cont.

Fine, medium-size, four-draw telescope (body and 3 brass tubes). Body is covered in Mahogany (damaged area on one side of wood), scope measures about 2' when open and 8" when closed, fine optics. **125.00**

Five big sections which open to 36" l. Almost completely opened leather seam, fine optics, and a solid brass lens cap, little internal "eyelid" is missing. **395.00**

U.S., Navy, marked, "Bardou & Son, Paris/US Navy Quartermaster." Wooden barrel covered with black saddle leather. All original with brass sliding tube and end piece. Dust cover over eyehole, barrel length is 25-1/4"; extends to 31-1/2". Perfect optics, replacement leather lens cover. **795.00**

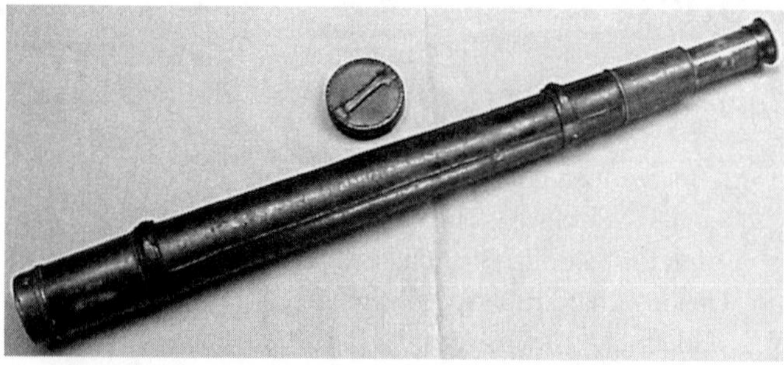

This Paris-made telescope is clearly engraved, "U.S. Navy Quartermaster."

Sharpsburg Arsenal

Scabbards

Confederate

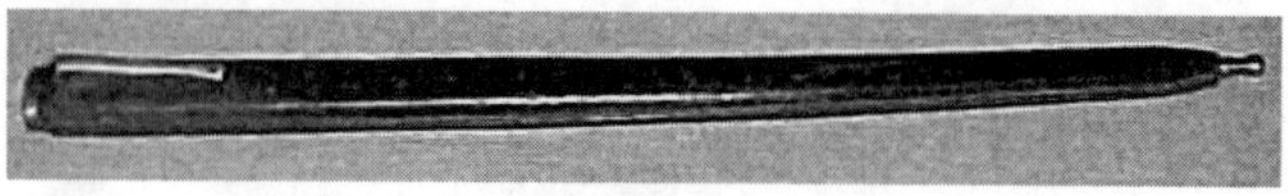

This scabbard is designed to fit the unique .54-caliber Lorenze Rifle.

Battleground Antiques

Bayonet

Austrian Lorenze, scabbard for socket bayonet in fine condition, original iron frog loop, iron tip, leather-covered wooded sheath—fits the unique cruciform "X" pattern blade of the .54 and .58-caliber weapons. **90.00**

U.S.

.58 Remington, a superb, unissued example of the leather scabbard with brass mounts for the M1863 Remington "Zouave" saber bayonet, near-perfect condition, back stitching has separated. **195.00**

.58 Rifle

A very nice example of the standard pattern scabbard in overall fine to excellent condition, harness leather frog secured by seven copper rivets. **189.00**

Regulation seven-rivet-style bayonet scabbard. Solid just showing light wear, not shrunken or stiff, very-good condition. **115.00**

.69 Musket

Frog displays some wear, tight and solid. **85.00**

Early pattern, frog secured by two rivets and a triangular stitching pattern, very-good to fine condition. **.165.00**

Slings and Boots, Carbines, Muskets, and Rifles

U.S. and Confederate

Carbine Boot, U.S.

Black saddle leather "doughnut" with strap and buckle, fine condition, held the muzzle to the saddle of a variety of Civil War carbines. The firearm was attached to the carbine sling over the cavalryman's shoulder. **85.00**

Cavalry carbine "boot" with maker mark, " P. Carter." This attached to saddle strap to hold carbine barrel, mint condition. **65.00**

The carbine "boot" was designed to keep a carbine from bouncing about while a trooper was mounted on his horse.

Sharpsburg Arsenal

Excellent condition, manufactured "E. Metzger Phila." **165.00**

Hard leather "cup" open at both ends and having a strap for attaching to the saddle. This is the regulation cavalryman's socket or thimble that he strapped to his saddle to keep his carbine from banging around. The trooper slid the barrel of his carbine into this socket that held it in place while riding on horseback, solid and dirty. **59.00**

This is the regulation socket or "thimble" that was strapped to the saddle to keep the cavalryman's carbine from banging around, solid & dirty. .. **55.00**

Slides, Saber Strap, U.S., pair of excellent buff leather loop adjusters that went on the saber hanger straps on a buff cavalry belt. **59.00**

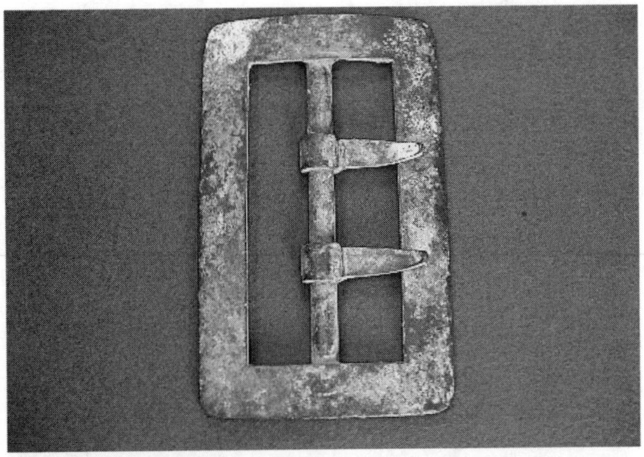

This carbine sling buckle was excavated from the lines around Nashville, Tennessee.

Middle Tennessee Relics

Sling Buckle, U.S., Carbine

Excellent condition, dug, Union cavalry carbine sling buckle. This buckle was excavated from Wilson's cavalry position at the Battle of Nashville, Tennessee. It has perfect form and both hooks intact, buckle is uncleaned as dug. **145.00**

Fine condition, tip and one hook intact, dug near Atlanta, Georgia. **85.00**

Steel swivel used on the cavalry carbine slings to support the carbine. **69.00**

Carbine sling swivel and snap hook, maker-marked, "Gaylord," and, "US," inspector-marked "J Shepard." In near-mint condition, lightest age wear..... **125.00**

Iron swiveling snap hook that goes on the carbine sling, fine condition. **85.00**

Steel swivel used on the cavalry carbine slings to support the carbine. **59.00**

Sling, Carbine, U.S.

Nice example of classic carbine sling, a Bannerman surplus example that has had the leather shortened by four inches. **495.00**

Iron swivel snap, wide black leather, over-the-shoulder sling with brass buckle and batwing finial. Leather bright and supple, stitching has come loose around the buckle, could be easily fixed. Perfect snap hook with crisp, "O.B. North," contractor's stamping. .. **1,050.00**

This example has never been altered and is in overall fine condition with strong, flexible leather and a beautiful untouched patina on the brass buckle and tip. There is a faint arsenal stamp near the brass tip, and the steel swivel is still present and fully functional. The only defect is that two of the four rivets that hold the brass tip in place are damaged (the bases are present, but the heads are gone). **1,195.00**

Sling issued to cavalrymen for carbine support purposes while they're on horseback. It prevents the gun from being lost if dropped from the saddle. The sling was worn across the trooper's chest with the carbine firmly held in place by a steel swivel ring. Rarest

Civil War pattern sling, constructed of dark-brown buff leather (not the common black harness leather). It is in near-mint condition, shows light handling and storage age. Complete with brass buckle, brass tip, and steel sling swivel, and also has the original maker's stamp inked on the cream-colored inside, "J. Davy & Co." Also is marked "3" on the inside. A tiny defect hole is punched into a remote area of the leather where it had been hung on a hook. . . **2,600.00**

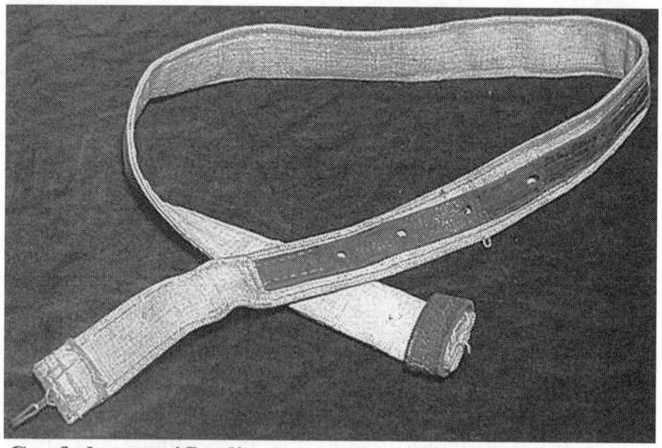

Confederate rifle sling was made of cotton due to leather shortages.

Old South Military Antiques

Sling, Rifle, Confederate, made from cotton during the South's leather shortage. Making the most of what was at hand, two-inch cotton was folded double and hand stitched down each edge. Small amounts of leather were then sewn on to form the end loop and adjustment strip. A doubled iron wire keeper was then sewn onto the end to serve as adjuster. The completed product was totally Confederate-made, excellent condition. **1,050.00**

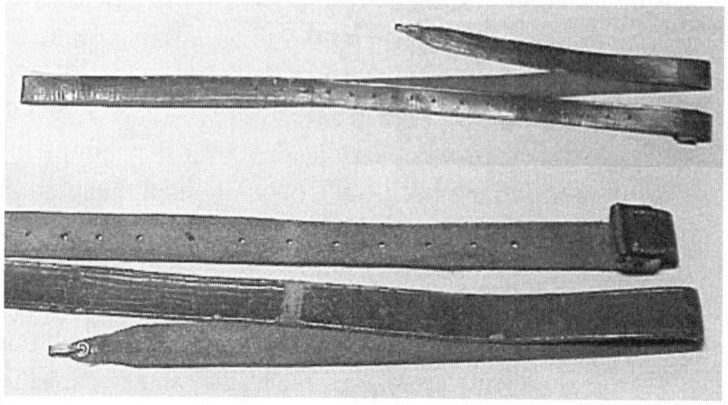

Sling made for the three-band Enfield rifle.

Sharpsburg Arsenal

Sling, Rifle, Enfield

78", leather in good condition with some flaking and cracking, sling is a little weak at brass hook, pliable leather. **350.00**

White buff leather sling for the Enfield Rifle Musket, both keepers, fine supple condition. **100.00**

Sling marked, "N.W. Oliver," Pittsburgh, Pennsylvania.

Sharpsburg Arsenal

Sling, Rifle, Springfield

Stamped, "N.W. Oliver Pittsburgh, PA.," manufactured using two pieces of leather—not a period repair, 64" overall, sling is in very-good, usable condition. . **395.00**

This is an original russet-brown leather sling as used with the Springfield muskets, it is about 42" long and 1-1/8" wide, pliable leather, complete with the loop at one end, brass hook at the other, and the leather keeper. There is an illegible maker's name—the bottom line reads, "NEW YORK." **270.00**

Spurs

Confederate

Clearly a southern spur of undetermined origin, it's a variation of the so-called "Mississippi" spur. More are found on Virginia sites than Mississippi sites, neck missing off this excavated example, recovered in the Shenandoah Valley. **75.00**

Richmond-style spur probably excavvated years ago.

Battleground Antiques

C.S. Richmond Arsenal spur that may have been excavated, and then cleaned many years ago. Very dark reddish-brown patina left in places, signs of heavy usage. **.345.00**

Early pick-up from Tennessee, complete with rowel, several file marks and irregular-cut strap slots. **325.00**

Enlisted Man

Nice, non-excavated, cleaned specimen complete with rowel, many file marks on strap plates. Many have been dug in Virginia. **345.00**

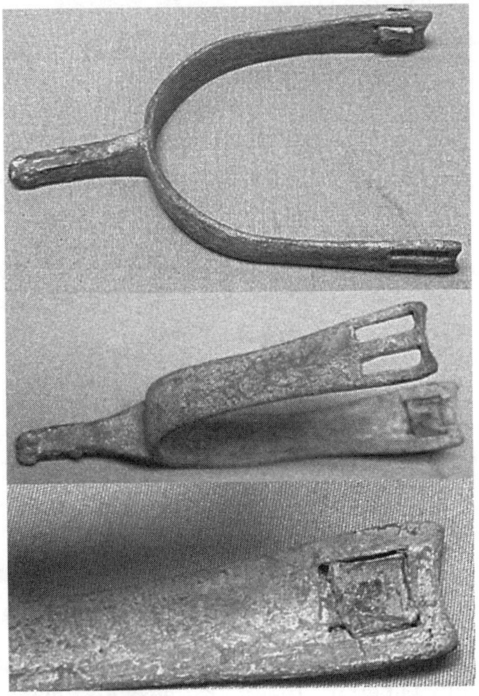

Confederate "Richmond"-style spur was dug near the Antietam battlefield.

Sharpsburg Arsenal

Richmond spur dug in the Antietam Campaign area, super nice with attached leather remnant **395.00**

U.S.

Enlisted Man

Beautiful condition, Tennessee dug, regulation issue Union enlisted man's cavalry spur, slick brown patina with practically no ground action.. . . . . **75.00**

Brass with steel starred rowel, standard issue spur worn by cavalry and horse artillery. A single in excellent condition. **75.00**

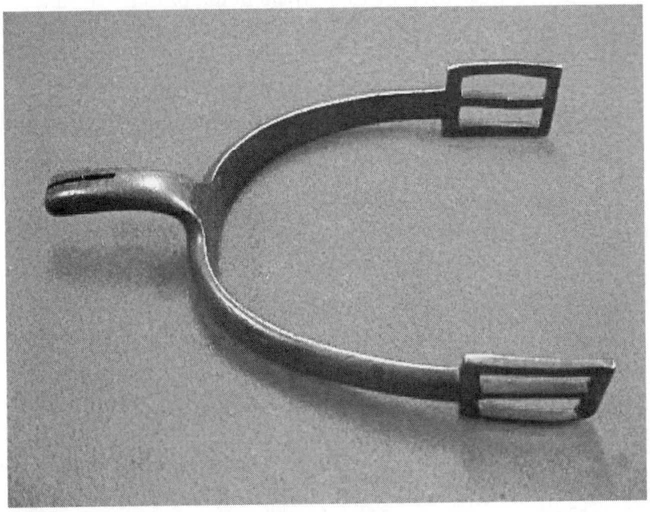

Regulation U.S. spur dug in Tenessee.

Sharpsburg Arsenal

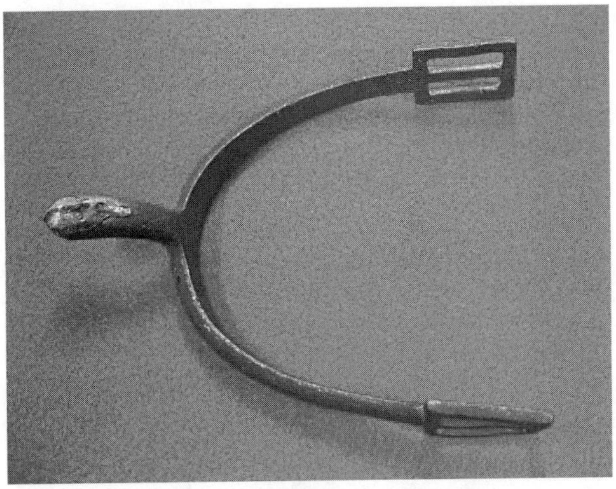

Called a "rooster" style, this U.S. regulation spur came from the Stones River battlefield.

Middle Tennessee Relics

"Rooster neck" Union cavalry spur dug from the Union cavalry camps at Murfreesboro occupied by General David Stanley's troops after the Battle of Stone's River. **75.00**

Nice matched pair of dug, regulation spurs with rowels rusted. **135.00**

Pair of regulation cavalry enlisted spurs with rowels intact and nice brass color. **259.00**

Spurs, U.S., Enlisted Man, cont.

A nice pair of regulation cavalry enlisted spurs with beautiful aged-brass color, still have the rare leather straps and buckles present for attaching to a pair of boots, very-fine condition, one spur lacks rowel. 285.00

Cast, rounded brass spurs with iron rowels, bright, excellent condition. 285.00

Nice, matched pair dug in a Virginia cavalry camp by a 1960s relic hunter, regulation spurs with rowels rusted and a rich ground patina. 135.00

These were found with a metal detector in a Virginia cavalry camp by a 1970s relic hunter and are maker-marked. One spur is stamped, "Allegheny Arsenal," with size number, "1." The other is stamped, "Allegheny Arsenal," with a size number, "2." Rowels rusted away, and a rich ground patina. 250.00

Matching pair of brass Model 1858 enlisted man's spurs.

Battleground Antiques

Model 1858, very fine pair of cast-brass enlisted man's spurs, bright golden color, iron "star"-shaped rowels, very handsome matched pair. 295.00

Model 1859, pair of spurs, brass construction, rowel missing, no bends or breaks. Excavated at Brandy Station Virginia. 110.00

Officer

Style of spur advertised in the 1864 *Schuyler Hartley & Graham* catalog. It employed the "box" locking device popular in European period designs. A box fit in the shoe, the spike fit into the box. Note the screw heads on the side were purely ornamental. The rowel is also pure ornament, as the rotating hole is intentionally way too big, so that whatever angle is used it never protrudes to jab the horse. This great looking pair is a true "gentleman's" spur. Non-excavated pair, everything intact. 250.00

Cast brass with sharp, faceted iron rowels, beautiful matched pair. 350.00

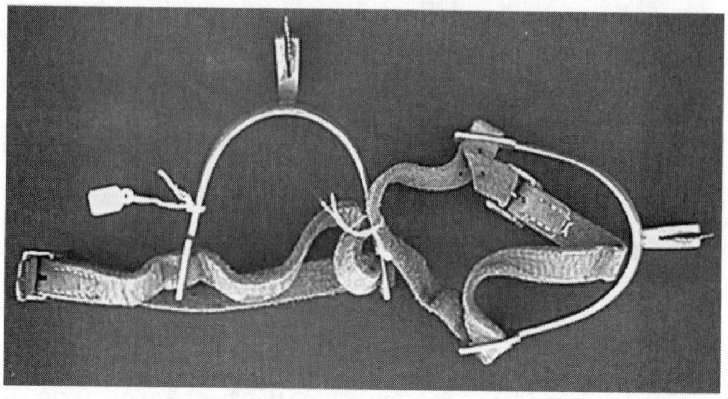

Spurs are seldom found complete with their straps. This pair of officer-quality spurs have all their fittings.

Dale C. Anderson Co.

Nice set complete with original belts/buckles, nickeled brass, essentially the same as enlisted spurs except for the bright silver finish, some minor spotty age to finish, most probably cleanable, leather flexible, lacking finish, pair. 295.00

Steel with steel starred rowels, typical pair of officer's spurs, excellent condition................. 195.00

Pair of spurs in cast brass, lighter weight and better finished than the standard cast-brass enlisted examples. They are gilt finished and retain about 90% of this original gilt. Perfect condition with starburst-style rowels. 225.00

Model 1859, sturdy brass construction, officer's pattern with flourish, rowell missing, minor bends, no breaks, excavated at Monocacy, Maryland. 45.00

Miscellaneous Accoutrements

Confederate and U.S.

Blanket, U.S., 67" x 74" fragment; light-brown, woven wool army blanket with 4" dark-brown stripe woven on the opposite ends of the longer measurement, double line "US" stenciled about 8" above the lower strip, ends not bound so they appear frayed, but are not. Couple of minor moth nips, but nothing major. 1,750.00

Buckle Covers, Confederate, sometimes used as blanket-roll buckle covers. Also used for covering a horse's headstall buckles from snagging in brush and timber. Pictured in Lord's, *Civil War Collector's Encyclopedia,* Vol. 4, matched pair, stamped brass with raised "heart" motif. 125.00

Frog, U.S., NCO Sword, non-regulation belt frog used to support the NCO sword from the waist belt, very similar to the frogs used to support the navy cutlasses, excellent condition, light use and age. 69.00

Hanger, Sword, U.S., spring-loaded brass belt clip crisply stamped on the back, "E. Gaylord Chicopee," wonderful umber patina. Two near-mint black leather sword straps, the longer with a crisp, "A.D. Laidley/US/Ord. Dept/Sub Inspector," stamp. Complete with both buttons and spring-loaded saber hooks. **550.00**

Hangers, Saber, U.S., an excellent example of the Civil War-period saber hangers as used on some Mann's cavalry sets, and also used on plain waist belts. This rig consists of a spring-loaded brass hook designed to attach to a belt, and two saber hanger straps with leather adjusters. Nicely marked, "Frankford Arsenal/US," on brass clip, clear inspector's cartouche on one leather strap. Very good to fine condition, some finish flexing and crazing. **295.00**

Lanyard, NCO's Whistle, U.S., braided white cords with large neck loop at small whistle-attaching loop at opposite end, unused condition. **65.00**

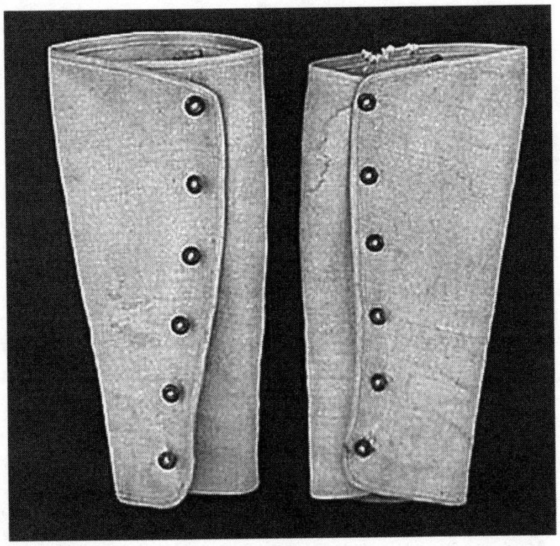

Leggings or "gaiters" were worn to protect the lower portion of a soldier's pants. They figured prominently into the uniform of Zouaves and Chasseurs.

Dale C. Anderson Co.

Leggings, worn by numerous Union Infantry wearing the Regulation Infantry uniform, and by militia who, at times, wore elaborate Zouave styles. Meant to keep dust from getting in the shoes and protected the ankles and pant cuff area in the field. Prime set, very heavy natural-linen canvas (light beige), 12" hight, six brown horn buttons down side, lined on bottom and edges, shows some use, but clean and very excellent. **695.00**

Rattle, U.S. Navy, larger than average, 10" long, double ratchet alarm, marked, "U.S.N.," and, "E. Gaylord Chicopee, Mass." **245.00**

Sling, NCO Sword, superb, near-mint, unissued condition, some light storage/handling scuffs. Made of fine, brown-finished harness leather with much shine on it. Used to support the Model 1840 NCO sword worn by sergeant's of infantry. Cut for the three-prong eagle shoulder belt plate (breastplate) that is not present. **495.00**

Strap, Shoulder, U.S., "over-the-shoulder" support straps for the Model 1851 cavalry saber belts. Very-fine condition, with some dryness and storage age. **125.00**

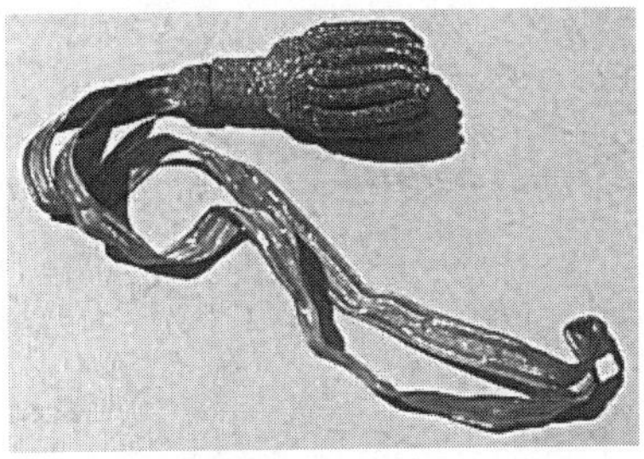

Sword knots were designed to provide the user with a sort of safety in case he lost grip of his blade. Officer knots were often elaborately made utilizing bullion threads, as was this one.

Sword Knot, U.S., Officer, Civil War or perhaps later era officer's sword knot. Ribbon is excellent with no breaks or tears, tassel is excellent as well possessing a nice gold color, one minor isolated spot of fraying on one coil only, no loss of wire. **205.00**

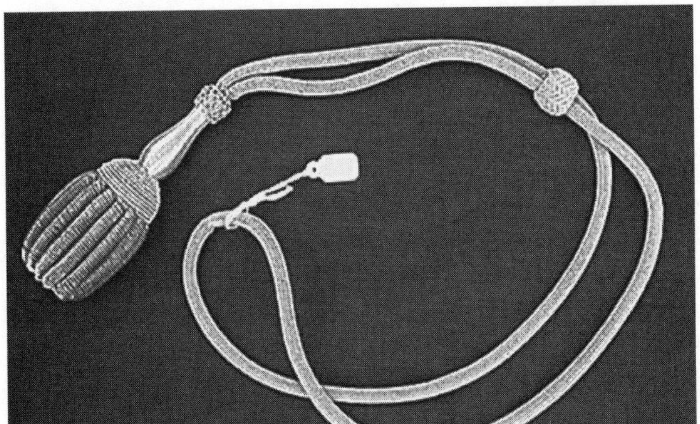

Near pristine condition officer's sword knot.

Sword Knot, U.S., Officer, remarkable for its practically new condition, lush quality, and uniquely long cord, 23" long overall. The bullion "rope" loop is 1/4", with sliding keeper. The conventional knot end is simply more lush than usual, this termination is over 4" long. **475.00**

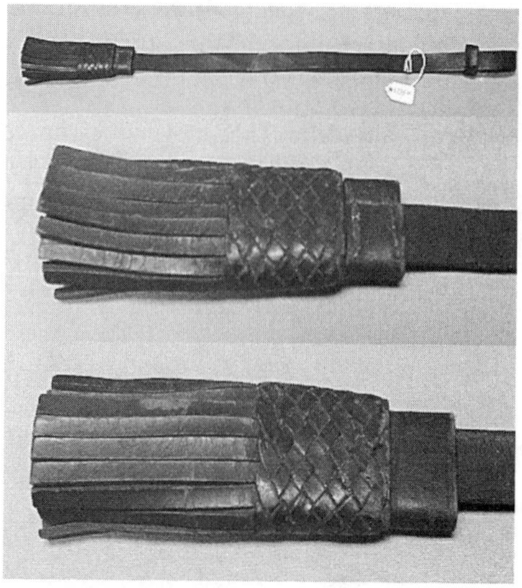

The enlisted man's sword was made of leather.

Sharpsburg Arsenal

Sword Knot, very-good condition, all tassels intact and pliable. **295.00**

Whistle, NCO, U.S. 2-1/2" long, used by sergeants to give field orders and drill just as they do today, a fine specimen. **75.00**

Accoutrement Terminology

Brogan: An early nineteenth-century term meaning shoe. Somewhat erroneously, collectors and reenactors often refer to federally-issued Jefferson Pattern shoes as brogans. The error, though, is very slight as many soldiers also referred to their government-issued footwear as brogans."

Cap pouch: Small leather box carried on the waist belt for the storage and easy retrieval of percussion caps.

Cartridge box: Leather box carried on the waist belt or suspended from a shoulder strap for the storage and easily retrieval of cartridges.

Frog: Generally, a frog is a leather item that slips onto a belt and provides a means for carrying a bayonet scabbard or straight sword scabbard on the belt.

Haversack: A bag used primarily for an individual's eating tools and foodstuffs. Generally carried by means of a shoulder sling.

Kit: Term used to describe the entire trappings of accoutrements assigned to one soldier.

Tarred: Nineteenth-century term used to refer to painted cloth.

Trappings: Nineteenth-century term used to describe the sum of belt, cartridge box, cap pouch, bayonet scabbard, canteen, and haversack.

See also: Groupings, Belts and Buckles, Artillery and Accessories, and Bayonets, Knives, and Pikes.

Chapter 2

Artillery and Accessories

Artillery collectors most often enjoy firing artillery. This brings a host of different people into the mix. Reenactors, skirmishers, and living history buffs will be competing with traditional relic collectors for artillery pieces and accessories.

Whether or not you ever purchase a field piece, there can be a lot of satisfaction in collecting artillery accessories. Because firing artillery has blossomed as a hobby since the 1960s, there are many fine reproductions of artillery implements and tools available. These implements have actually been put to use over the past 40 or 50 years, they have acquired an extremely realistic patina. Be sure to study pieces carefully before you make the acquisition.

If firing an old cannon is your goal, you may be best served by any number of fine American-made reproduction tubes currently available. You must bear in mind—there are no implied warranties with artillery pieces that are a century and a half old! Metal fatigues with age. Just because a tube may have fired non-stop for several hours before Picket launched his attack on July 3, 1863, does not mean that it is up for a 20-minute reenactment firing blank charges. If you happen to purchase a field piece and wish to actually pull the occasional lanyard on a charge, have the piece inspected first.

See also: Groupings; Belts and Buckles; Artillery and Accessories; and Bayonets, Knives and Pikes.

Hendershott Museum Consultants

Collecting Hints

Pros:

- A collection that revolves around a field piece is most certainly impressive!
- Reproduction artillery pieces are obvious and generally are appropriately marked. Accessories, on the other hand, can be more difficult to recognize.

Cons:

- Artillery requires a lot of space once it is in your collection.
- Actual ownership on original artillery pieces can be sketchy and hard to prove. Though you may find an artillery piece in the hands of a reputable dealer, it may have disappeared from a cemetery, town square, or battlefield park many years and dealers before.

Availability ★★
Price ★★★
Reproduction Alert ★★

Described as being made of hard rubber and copper rivets, this "bumper" was purportedly used to cover the muzzle of an artillery piece when not in use. Actually, it appears to be made of leather and is a limber pole cover.

Bumper, Cannon, original 1864 Civil War, fit into the muzzle of the cannon barrel, made of hard rubber with bronze rivets. It has an iron pin, which is removable at the base, top is inscribed, "Allegheny Arsenal 1864," measures 4-1/2" high and 5" across top. The cannon bumper is in very-good condition. **366.00**

Caliper, Gunner's, all brass gunner's caliper used to measuring shells and cannon bores, fully calibrated. Very rare artillery implement to find in any condition, this example is near mint with the usual handling scratches. **3,250.00**

10 lb Parrot on a Confederate carriage.

Hendershott Museum Consultants

Cannon, 10 lb Parrott, America's first rifled cannon made by R.P. Parrott at the West Point Foundry marked, "U.S.," on the barrel as well as marked, "1862," in 4" letters on the side trunnion with early war-date serial number 219. Discovered in a privately-owned soldier's cemetery near the Gettysburg battlefield. Rifled cannons were retired after firing 2,000 rounds because the rifling blew out, which most likely occurred to this 1862 cannon during the famous battle. This cannon fired specially designed 10 lb, 12" long projectiles which were made as solid shot, case shot, canister shot, and shrapnel shells. The carriage that this cannon sits on is a Confederate carriage made in 1862 by Tredegar Iron Works, Richmond, Virginia, which was the largest cannon foundry in the Confederacy. All of the metal parts are completely original and Confederate, including the axle as well as the wheel rims. The wooden part of the carriage has been rebuilt using all of the original parts. A superb showpiece (total weight 2300 pounds) accompanied by notarized bills of sale and title, also accompanied by R.P. Parrott's original military appointment to West Point, signed by John C. Calhoun. **125,000.00**

Cannon, 8 inch, 114" long, mounted on old wood carriage. Gun inspected by U.S. Navy Inspector Timothy Atwater Hunt, 1856-1859 and 1862-1867. The gun served aboard the U.S.S. Jamestown when it blocked the Confederate coastline during 1861-1864 (during which it captured several ships). In 1864, the Jamestown was sent to Japan. **28,000.00**

Cutter, Fuse, Borman-style iron punch blade with half circle brass top. Excellent condition. **135.00**

Friction Primer, Confederate, recovered from the Savannah River site of the Augusta Arsenal, originally used with lanyard to fire cannon. Comes with certificate of authenticity. **45.00**

Friction Primer, U.S., brass, wire ring that attached to hook at the lanyard cord's end. When pulled, it ignited the main charge, firing the gun. **45.00**

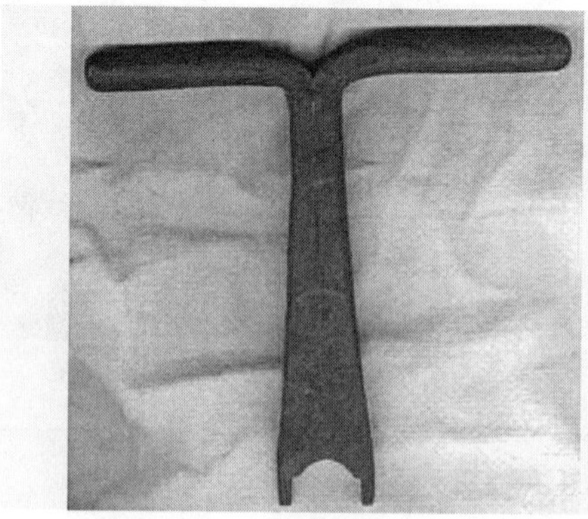

Fuse wrenches were used to pull and place fuses in artillery projectiles.

Fuse Wrench, Gunner's, very nice condition "T"-shape wrench used for removing assorted fuses, approximately 5" long. **228.00**

Gimlet, Gunner's. 9" pointed iron rod with big 2" diameter ring at top. Used for punching down through the vent and breaking a hole in the projectile's powder bag, excellent condition. **65.00**

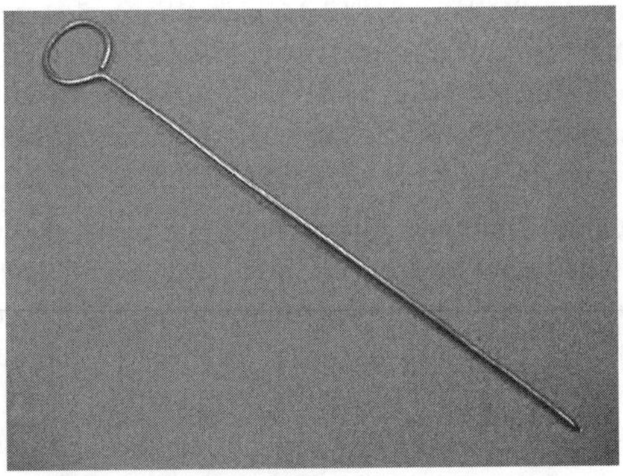

Gunner's gimlet used to tear open the powder bag once it was seated in the breech of the gun.

Dave Taylor Civil War Antiques

Gimlet, Gunner's, this one is 14" l and has a nice, smooth, brown aged patina. **89.00**

Gimlet, Gunner's, somewhat crudely made long vent punch for large artillery piece, possibly Confederate, no markings, used to clear cannon vent hole and perforate powder bag after loading. **95.00**

Grease Bucket

Very nice, complete, for Civil War artillery piece. Condition is excellent with original cover and chain. No rust holes. **450.00**

Painted black, the iron rings and lid on this grease bucket have survived virtually rust-free.

J.C. Devine Inc.

A 7-1/4" riveted metal bucket with pivoting metal lid. The height is 9-1/4" not including the chain and ring suspension handle. The weight is 8-3/4 lbs, painted black, and in fine condition. **125.00**

This and another bucket for water hung below the carriage of each cannon. Very heavy sheet iron construction, riveted base, and hangers. Chain loop over top for hanging. Lacks disc lid, which pivoted on a pin to open and close, very old coat of gray paint which may have been from period of use or later display, in any case, it kept the iron from rusting. 7" d, 8" h. **345.00**

Hammer, Tow, blacksmith shop wrought iron hammer with 14" hooked tail. Civil War artillery shells were packed in cases of linen and cotton waste called "tow." The hammer end was used to tap fuse plugs into shells and the hook end was used to pull the tightly packed tow out from around the shells. Faces of the hammer are chipped, otherwise fine. **175.00**

Level, Gunner's, one of the rarest artillery implements, and almost impossible to find today, this U.S. Waterlivet 1862 marked gunner's level is essential for any complete artillery collection. Mint-condition piece has the original liquid-filled level. **3,500.00**

Limber Pole Pad, interesting, heavily-padded leather, used to protect horses from the pole between the horses attached to the artillery limber, well-marked "Washington Arsenal" and inspected by, "J. P. Hall." It includes the rare pin and leather thong for holding the pad in place, nice condition with some age wear to leather, but a fine displayable example. **325.00**

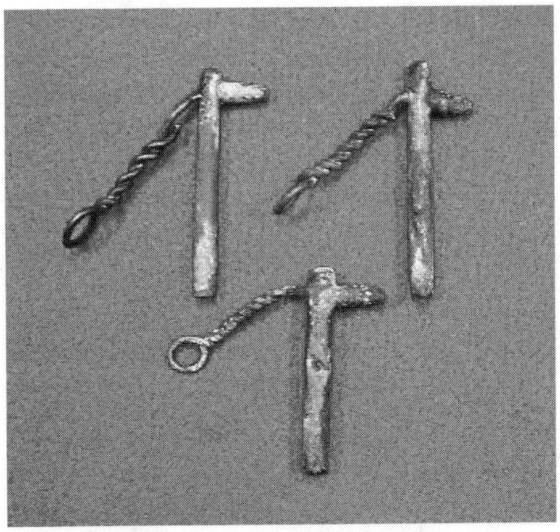

Friction primers were inserted into the vent of a loaded artillery piece. Then, a lanyard was attached to the primer. Pulling the lanyard ignited the primer that, in turn, ignited the charge. Pictured are unfired Confederate primers.

Middle Tennessee Relics

Primer, Confederate, dug, unfired Confederate-made cannon friction primer, excavated from a gun pit location from the Battle of Nashville. **25.00**

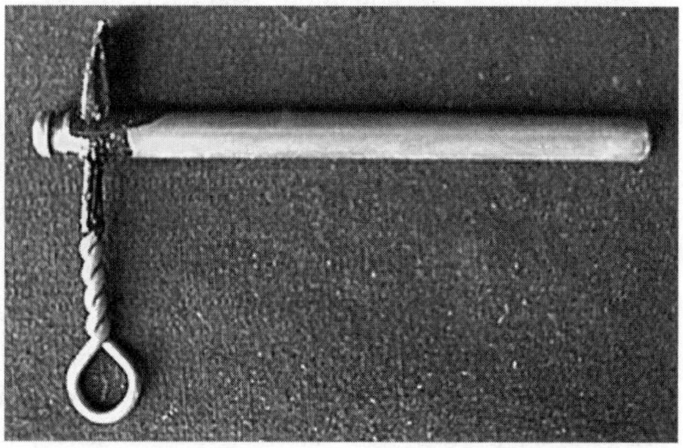

Non-dug, Frankford Arsenal copper primer.

Dale C. Anderson Co.

Primer, Copper, Civil War period, small "T"-shaped items which fit into a cannon's vent hole, and to which the lanyard was attached. Upper crosspiece consists mainly of a twisted wire with loop at end to which the lanyard hooks. Main tube has quick burning powder that is fired by the yanked wire. This ignites the main cannon charge, 2-3/8" l. Mint—right out of the original Frankford Arsenal tin. **35.00**

Primer, Quill, War of 1812-Mexican War U.S. Artillery igniter and surplus used by Confederate troops in the Civil War. Made of a goose quill with tarred slow match. These served until the friction primer came in before the Civil War. **35.00**

Quadrant, Gunner's, all brass artillery quadrant with original wood handcrafted fitted case, overall length 18" with original liquid filled level. This would be used for aiming a large artillery piece such as a fortress cannon. Extremely rare, and in perfect condition, with no maker's markings. **1,895.00**

Sight, Mountain Howitzer, small front sight from 12 lb Mountain Howitzer, marked "12 H," original Civil War issue. **250.00**

Tube, Cannon, bronze, cast with serpents and geometric design on yoke and swivel, approximately 30". .. **1,250.00**

Vent Plug, leather, small, rare, used to keep dirt and rain out of vent hole. **250.00**

Wiper/Worm, 12lb Cannon, original full-length wiper or worm for 12 lb. Civil War cannon. Heavy iron spiral corkscrew-like device on the end of this seven-foot shaft for cleaning cannon barrel and removing unfired charges. Wood is in excellent condition with some original paint. **1,195.00**

Artillery Terminology

Tube: This refers to the "barrel" of the gun, generally of bronze or cast iron.

Limber: A two-wheeled vehicle to which a gun or caisson is attached.

Caisson: A two-wheeled vehicle designed to carry artillery ammunition, pulled by a limber and team.

Fuse: Device used to detonate a shell or case shot.

Primer: Device that when placed in the vent hole of a field piece and attached to a lanyard, is used to fire the gun. It replaces the process of priming the vent hole with fuse and powder and igniting with a slow match.

See also: Uniforms; Accouterments; and Swords

Chapter 3

Bayonets, Knives, and Pikes

Blades of one variety or another hold the fascination of many Civil War collectors. The idea of soldiers marching into battle with bayonets affixed or brandishing large D-Guard Bowies and pikes in bloody hand-to-hand combat are hard notions to dislodge from the spirited collector's mind. Even though blade-related wounds of any variety (including sword or saber-inflicted) were minimal during the war, the weapons that could have delivered such a wound are at the top of many collectors' "premium pieces" list.

Bayonets are a rather straightforward item to collect. Rarely reproduced, plentiful, and with an endless variety, a collector can step into the bayonet arena with a minimum amount of cash and proceed to assemble a very engaging collection.

Knives and pikes, on the other hand, get a bit cloudy. It seems that most dealers have forgotten that the Bowie-style blade was available to folks both south and north of the Mason-Dixon line. In fact, a great many actually were manufactured in England. Nevertheless, most Bowies are sold as Confederate and if not, very few are quick to deny that these were favorites of Rebel troops. Furthermore, since knives were not an issue item, it is extremely difficult to ascertain whether or not a blade actually campaigned with a soldier or sat on a shelf back in some upstate farm.

Pikes are even more difficult to directly associate with Civil War service. Apart from the documented specimens manufactured in Confederate arsenals, many pikes spent the war propped in armory racks. Regardless, there exists a powerful romantic image of the citizen soldier picking up a pike (in the absence of a more potent weapon) to defend his nation and his rights. Therefore, even though there are very few documented incidents of pikes being used in combat during the Civil War, they are one of the most sought-after edged relics.

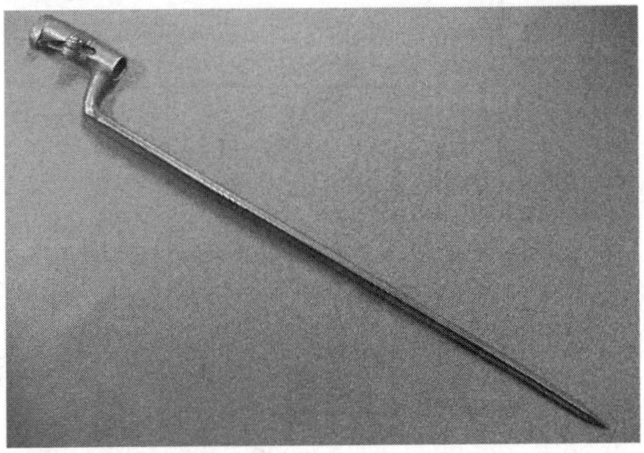

Middle Tennessee Relics

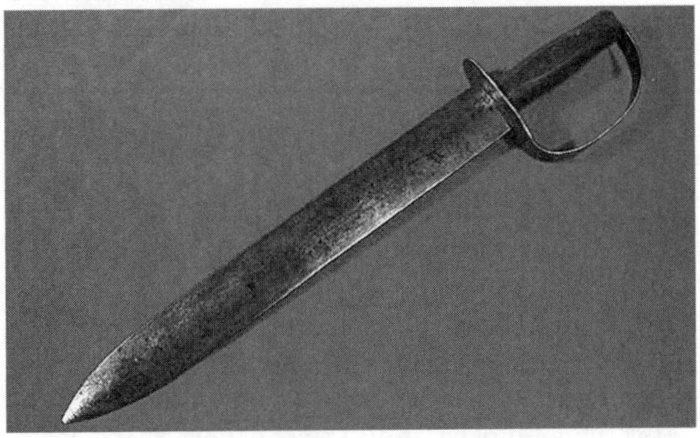

Old South Military Antiques

Collecting Hints

Pros:

- Due to the materials involved, bayonets, knives, and pikes are plentiful.
- There is a wide variety of items.
- A lot of primary research has been done to identify various knife and pike makers, making authentication easier.

Cons:

- Hand-forged items such as pike heads or D-Guard Bowie knives are easily reproduced and aged to appear like authentic, period items.
- Because iron is the primary material, these items are prone to rust if not stored in a very dry environment.
- A lot of nostalgia is attached to the notion of the Bowie knife-wielding Confederate. Therefore, dealers are quick to assign a Rebel attribution to any blade that vaguely resembles a Bowie. A collector may have to pay premium prices simply to acquire a representative knife carried by either a Confederate *or* Yankee.

Availability ★★
Price ★★★
Reproduction Alert ★★★★

Bayonets

Confederate

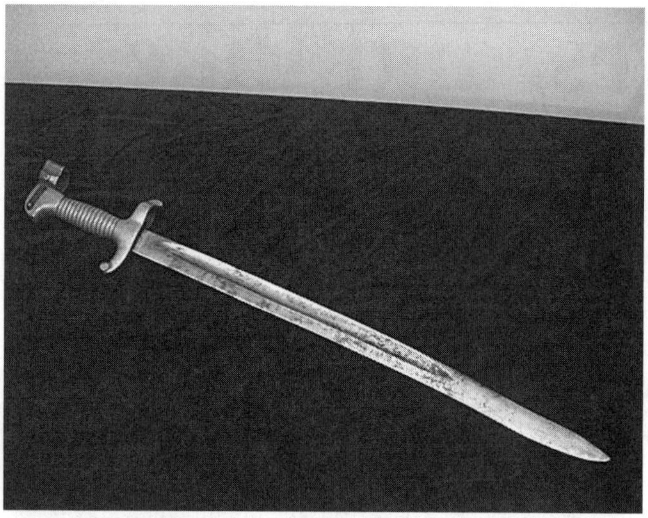

Saber bayonet fitted with an adaptor to use on the Model 1841 rifle. It was made by the Confederate sword maker, Boyle and Gamble.

Old South Military Antiques

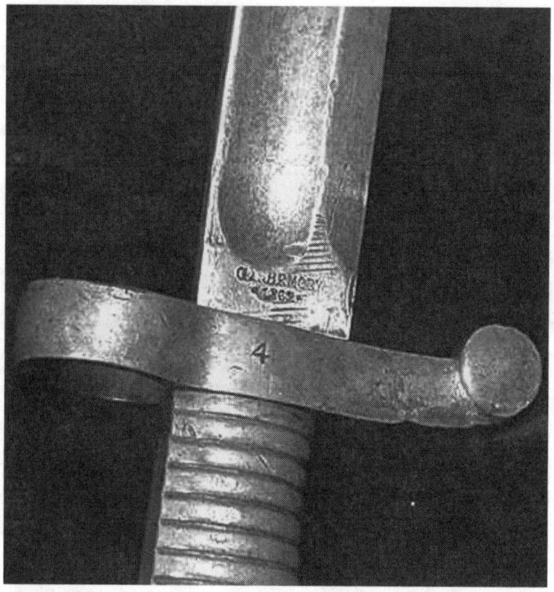

Made by the Georgia State Armory for use with the Model 1855 rifle, is this saber bayonet.

Old South Military Antiques

Boyle and Gamble saber bayonet with adapter for use on the Model 1841 rifle. **2,850.00**

Saber bayonet made by Cook & Brother, New Orleans in 1861 or 1862, marked "1472." Research suggests that this piece was issued to one of the Alabama regiments: 20th Infantry to 30th Infantry or thereabouts. Condition is superb, bayonet lightly cleaned, pleasing appearance, side spring intact, fastening button missing. **2,150.00**

Made into body hook. Dug from the battlefield area of Richmond, Virginia. Rare Confederate-manufactured by Tredegar Iron Works of Richmond. **395.00**

.58 Rifle, uncleaned, original condition, 19-5/16" x 1-1/8" V-ground blade with very heavy patina with medium rust overall, short blade tip, perhaps 3/16" (worn, not broken). Solid brass handle, 4-1/2" long, number "39" stamped near the guard is the only marking present, which is typical of this bayonet pattern. **850.00**

.58 Rifle, Fayetteville Armory, Confederate Fayetteville Arsenal bayonet recovered in Fredericksburg, Virginia in the late 1960s, good condition, blade intact with small pits and rust (dug condition), stamp on handle, "M," as several of them were. **2,250.00**

.58 Rifle, Georgia Armory, made by the Georgia State Armory in Milledgeville, Georgia, in 1862, this saber bayonet has a heavy 22-3/4" blade and measures 26-1/2" overall. The single fuller blade is smooth and semi bright from hilt to point, near-mint brass hilt with beautiful untouched patina, working lock spring and release. It was manufactured in the old state penitentiary at Milledgeville. The armory converted sporting rifles, altered flintlocks, and manufactured the rare Georgia Armory Rifle based on the Model 1855 Harpers Ferry. The armory also manufactured saber bayonets for its rifles. Lower serial numbers 16, 17, and 32 are brass hilted. Higher numbers, 127 and 135 are wooden hilted. The armory never returned to the brass hilted model, so at most, only one out of four were brass hilted. The armory continued using wood slabbed hilts for the remainder of its full production of less than four hundred rifles and bayonets. It is reasonably estimated that less than ten survive of all models combined. The armory manufactured weapons as opposed to altering for only four months, from December 1862 until March 1863, most likely due to a lack of raw materials. The changeover from brass to wooden hilts would tend to support that theory. **5,800.00**

> **"The day of the bayonet is passed except for use in hollow squares, or in resisting cavalry charges, or as an implement in constructing light and temporary fortifications."**
>
> ***— General John B. Gordon***
> ***Confederate States Army***

U.S.

Dated 1861, this saber bayonet for a Sharps rifle was sold at the same auction that the matching number rifle was sold.

J.C. Devine Inc.

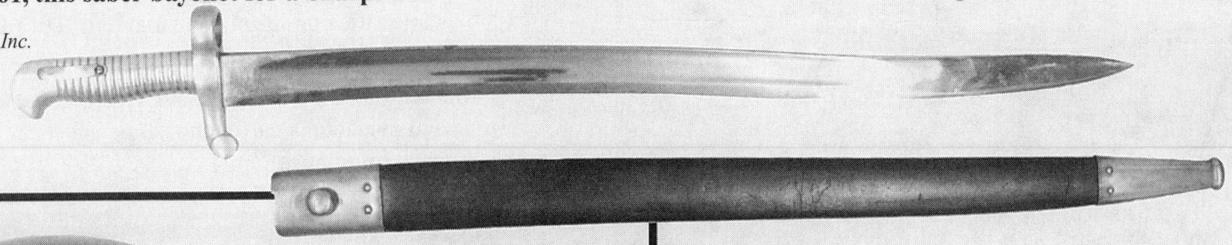

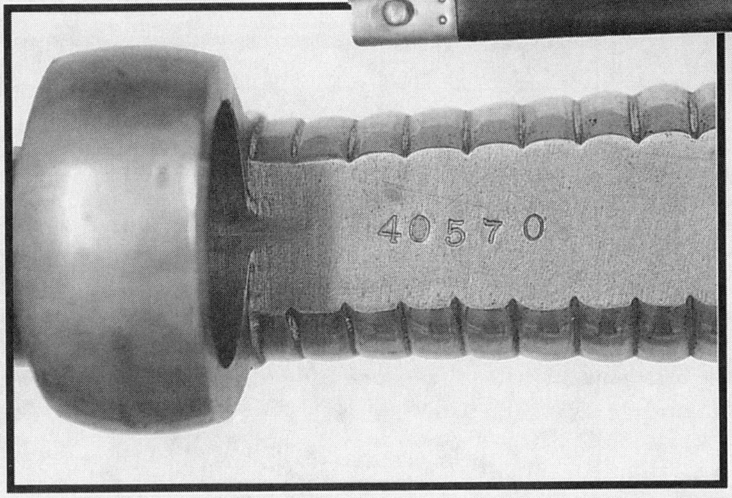

.52 Rifle, Sharps, brass-handled, saber bayonet for the Sharps Rifle that is 22" long and dated on the obverse ricasso, "1861," and marked on the reverse, "Made by/AMES MFG. CO./ CHICOPEE/MASS." Bayonet numbered 40570 on handle, blade bright with much original luster, some light tarnish, and a 1/4" patch of pinprick pitting, original scabbard in very-fine condition with entire original leather surface remaining, very little crazing. **2,800.00**

.54 Rifle, Model 1841, Ames brass-hilted saber bayonet for a New Hampshire state contract alteration of the Model 1841 rifle measuring 26-1/2" overall, with a 22" semi-yataghan iron blade. Crisp Ames address at left ricasso, blade tarnished but fine, mustard-colored brass hilt with spring release, no scabbard. **450.00**

.56 Rifle, Model 1855, Colt, imported S&K brass-handled saber bayonet for the Colt Revolving Rifle measuring 29" overall with a straight 24" blade. Blade is a gray dove patina with very light salt and peppering overall. "S&K" stamp on left ricasso, iron guard, and muzzle ring, cast-brass grips, serial number "721" on pommel. **250.00**

.58 Rifle Musket, Model 1855

Bright steel triangular bayonet with crisp, "US," at the ricasso. Black saddle leather with sheet brass drag has slight crazing on bottom third, otherwise excellent. Buff leather frog with the 1864 eight-rivet reinforcing arrangement. **325.00**

Overall length of the bayonet is 21" with 3" socket and 18" blade and 16-5/8" face flute. Original bright finish in very good condition, three very small spots of surface rust, marked, "U.S.," on the shank, locking ring missing, leather and brass scabbard in very-good condition with only a 1/4" tear at top of leather sling where it hung from the belt. The leather has good body and is not dried out. The brass ferrule has only a few small dents. **138.00**

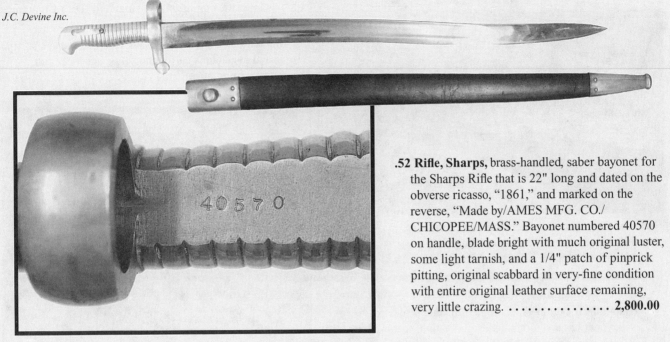

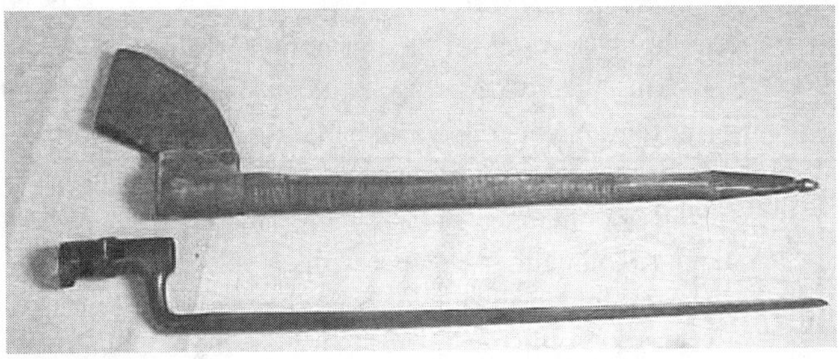

The same bayonet will fit the Model 1855, 1861, 1863, or 1864 rifle musket.

.58 Rifle Musket, Model 1861

Nice example, full scabbard, brass tip, good belt loop, ready to go on a Springfield or contract musket Model 1855, 1861, 1863, or 1864. . . . . **163.00**

A good, cleanable, old, brown 1861 pattern socket, end of socket has small crimp prohibiting it from passing over the gun's muzzle. Scabbard present, but lacks frog and tip. **69.00**

A super example for the Models 1855, 1861, 1863, 1864, and Special Model 1861 rifle muskets, shows just light age. **155.00**

Cleaned, bright and shiny condition, "US" stamped on ricasso. **89.00**

Clear "US" stamp on the ricasso. **155.00**

Light age patina. **169.00**

Light-brown patina overall and some light pitting evident. **105.00**

58 Rifle Musket, Model 1861, cont.

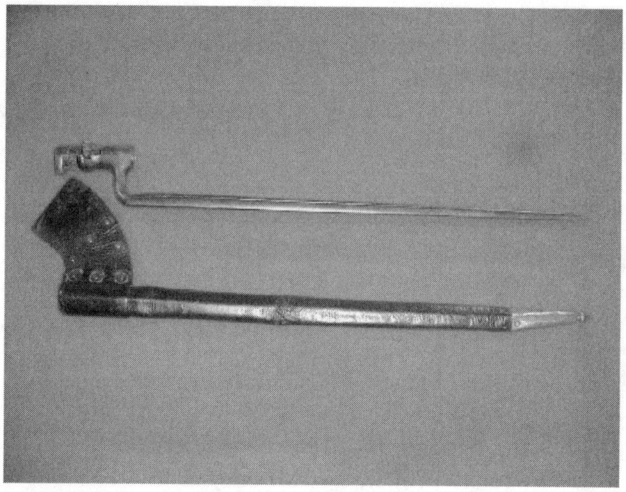

Because so many bayonets are on the market, condition can greatly influence the price.

Middle Tennessee Relics

Triangular socket bayonet, original leather scabbard, bayonet has a smooth, dark, aged patina, scabbard in nice, complete condition with only one weak spot. 295.00

Really shiny bayonet in a top-notch, black harness leather scabbard of seven-rivet design. 425.00

Regulation bayonet for the Springfield, really pitted, lacking the locking ring. 35.00

Springfield bayonet and scabbard (seven-rivet) with faint inspector's cartouche on frog, nice brown leather. 375.00

Standard .58 caliber bayonet with clear "US" stamp on ricasso, clean steel color overall, some light pitting on socket (still clean steel color), and great blade. 135.00

Standard .58 caliber bayonet with faint "US" stamp on the ricasso and a small "J" below the "US." Clean steel color overall, with light age patina. 135.00

Standard socket bayonet in very-good condition with crisp "US" stamp at ricasso, bright steel, and only a couple patches of light pitting............ 125.00

Standard socket bayonet in very-fine condition, nice steel color with just a hint of age patina, crisp "US" stamp.............................. 139.00

Standard socket bayonet in very-fine condition, nice steel color with just a hint of age patina, crisp "US" stamp, would match a gun in the $1,200 to $1,500 price range. 149.00

Standard socket bayonet in very-fine condition, nice steel color with just a hint of age patina, crisp "US" stamp in fine condition. 169.00

Standard socket bayonet in very-fine condition, nice steel color with delicate patina, crisp "US" stamp, excellent condition..................... 189.00

Standard Springfield bayonet, cleaned to very shiny and showing much wear on the edges, very pretty. ..89.00

Excellent, resides in original scabbard in exactly the same attic condition, frog marked, "US J Cummings Springfield, Mass." 295.00

Marked on scabbard frog with Metzger maker's stamp and inspector's cartouche, some age wear and crackling on leather. 450.00

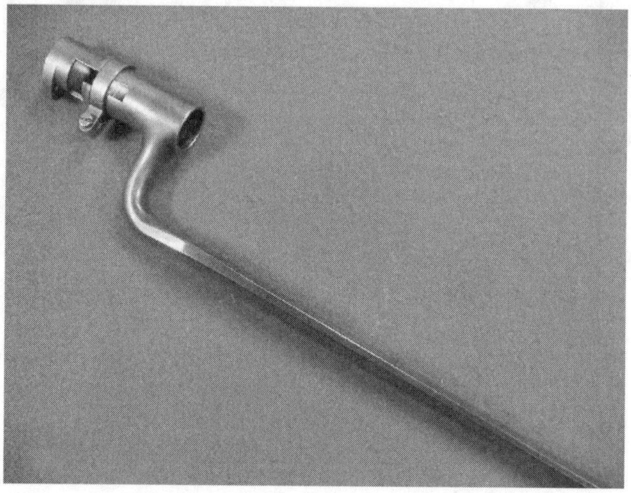

Though bright and clearly stamped, this bayonet did not include a scabbard.

Middle Tennessee Relics

Triangular socket bayonet, bright and clean—just beginning to lightly gray with age, nice, clear "U.S." marking............................. 175.00

Very-good to fine condition, "US" mark, but also has "C & Co" stamp on the socket indicating manufacture by Collins & Company of Hartford, Connecticut, light cleaning done on socket............. 149.00

Nice, patches of light-brown surface rust in areas, overall steel color and solid. 125.00

.58 Rifle, Model 1841

Dated 1861, fits the Colt conversion of the Model 1841 rifle, overall very good to fine condition, clean steel blade mixed with gray, and the brass is clean yellow color with just honest dings. 275.00

Saber bayonet for the Colt conversion of the Model 1841 rifle, a very-good to fine condition example with great steel blade marked with crisp "1861" date on the ricasso, the brass handle is a nice mellow brass color and it has a serial number of 6,854 stamped into it. Complete with spring catch and button.... 289.00

.58 Rifle, Model 1855, saber bayonet, brass-handled for Model 1855 rifle. The 21-7/18" blade is slightly rounded at the tip, missing lock and spring, sharpened blade has a smooth dark patina, no scabbard, very-good condition. 165.00

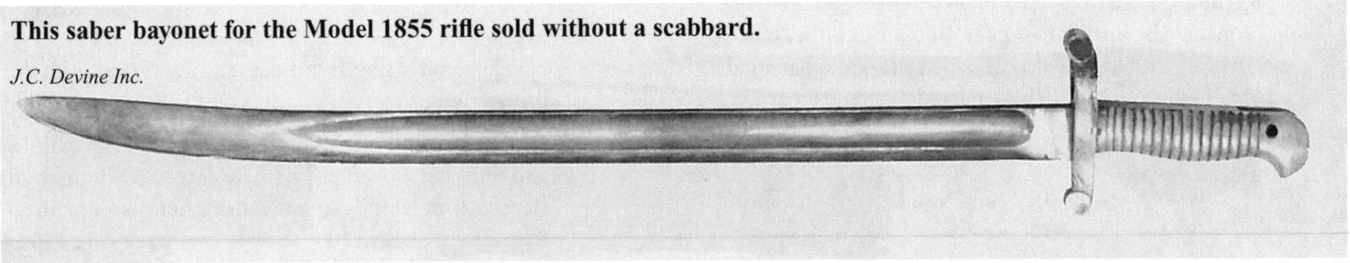

This saber bayonet for the Model 1855 rifle sold without a scabbard.

J.C. Devine Inc.

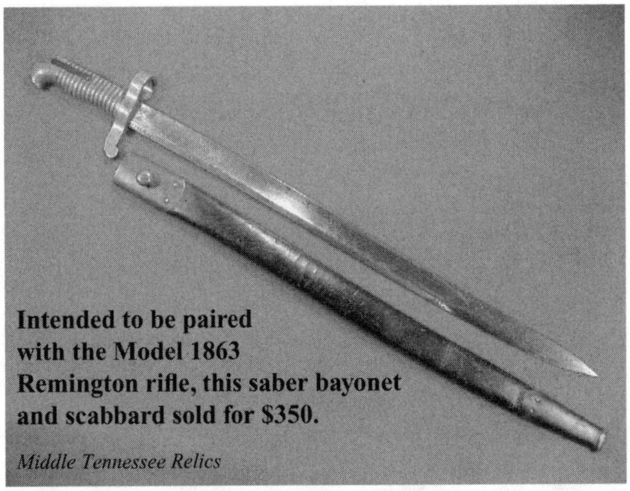

Intended to be paired with the Model 1863 Remington rifle, this saber bayonet and scabbard sold for $350.

Middle Tennessee Relics

.58 Rifle, Model 1863 Remington

"Zouave" rifle bayonet and scabbard, 90+ percent condition, mellow brown patina to match a rifle. **595.00**

Brass-handled saber bayonet for the Model 1863 Remington "Zouave" in original leather scabbard, blade is bright with some areas beginning to darken with age, brass handle is nice with pleasing, uncleaned aged patina, leather scabbard is complete and strong, but does have a few small surface cracks from age. **350.00**

Brass-handled saber bayonet and scabbard for the Model 1863 Remington "Zouave" rifle measuring 26" overall with a brilliant 20" semi-yataghan blade. Bayonet about mint. Scabbard very good with old repaired crack in leather about 6" from the drag........**375.00**

The 20" blade has not been sharpened and has scattered light corrosion, mostly near the tip. The brass-mounted black leather scabbard has a couple of weak spots, very good. **265.00**

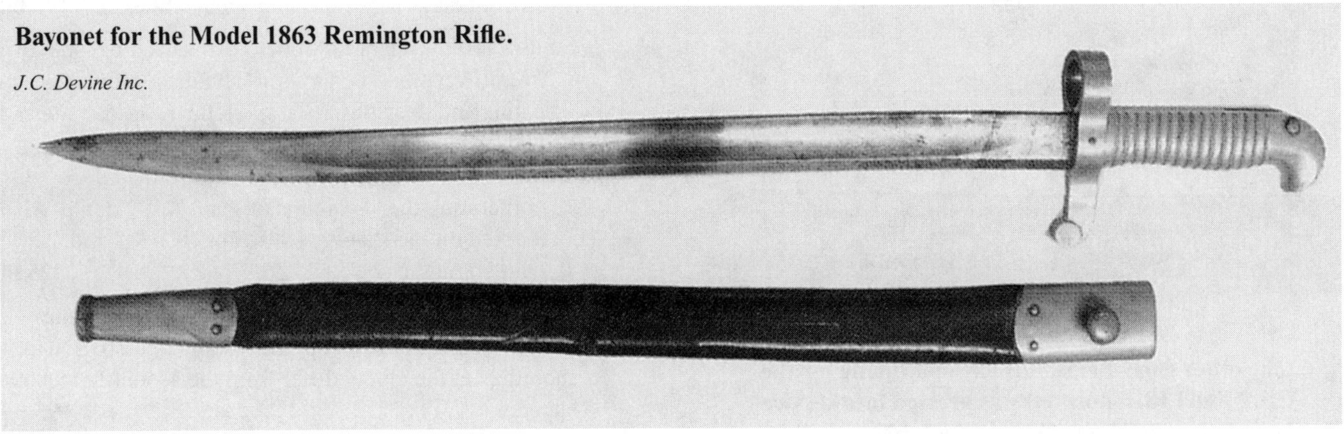

Bayonet for the Model 1863 Remington Rifle.

J.C. Devine Inc.

.58 Rifle, P.S. Justice, rare, brass-handled saber bayonet for the P.S. Justice two-band rifle measuring 26" overall with a tarnished 21-1/2" semi-yataghan blade, mellow brass hilt with spring catch, no scabbard. 435.00

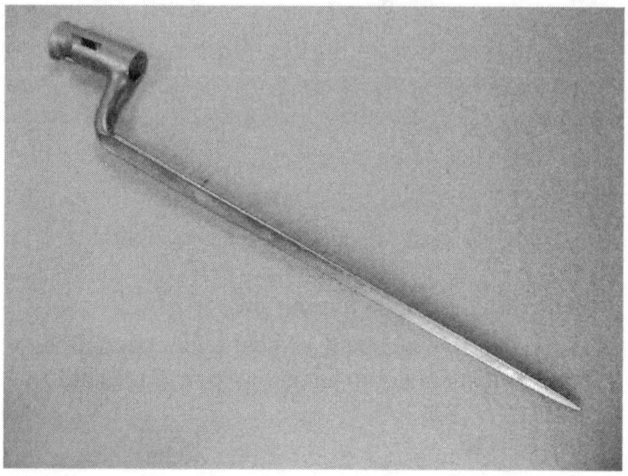

Bayonets made for the U.S. Model 1795 musket were sitting in arsenals at the beginning of the Civil War. When hostilities broke out, the bayonets, however out-of-date, were soon put to service.

Middle Tennessee Relics

.69 Musket, Model 1795, quite rare 1795-1812 pattern .69 friction-fit triangular socket bayonet, smooth, brown, never-cleaned patina. 125.00

.69 Musket, Model 1816

19-1/4" overall with a triangular 16-3/4" blade, "US" stamped on ricasso, bayonet is a smooth mixture of plum and steel patina. 185.00

Early .69 Model 1816 triangular socket bayonet picked up at Stones River in the early 1900s, very solid with the "U.S." marking still visible. 125.00

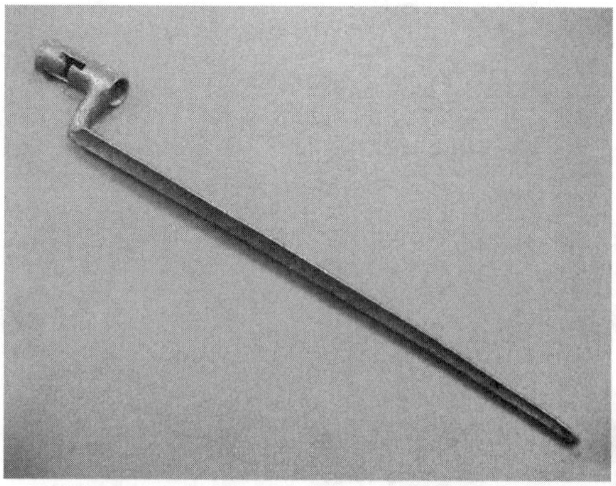

Like other early items, this bayonet (made for the U.S. Model 1816 musket) was pressed into service during the Civil War. This particular blade was found on the Stones River battlefield.

Middle Tennessee Relics

Marking of "U" above the "US" stamp on the ricasso and has an "E 43" mark on the socket. Does not appear to have any significant pitting mixed with the brown patina..........................135.00

Overall very-good condition with a medium age patina and light patches of pitting. Has large "US" stamp on ricasso which tends to indicate earlier manufacture date.................................120.00

Smooth plum patina and crisp, "US/JB," stamped at the ricasso, would clean to fine. 185.00

Socket bayonet for the Hewes & Phillips conversion musket, bright and shiny with "US" stamp at the ricasso, 1816-style socket (but longer) and long-length blade. 145.00

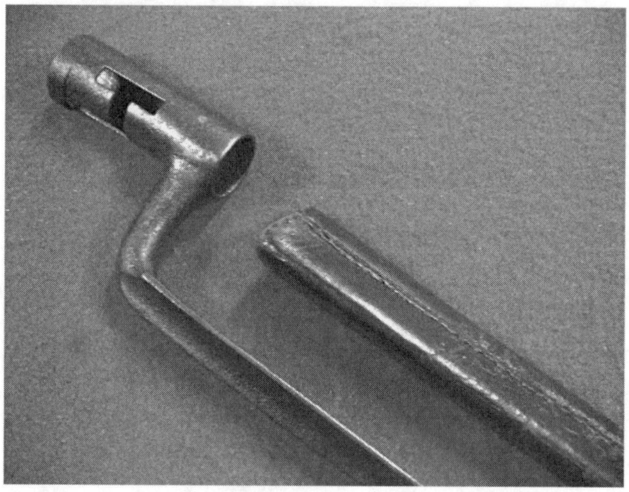

Model 1816 .69 musket bayonet and scabbard.

Middle Tennessee Relics

Friction fit triangular socket bayonet in leather shaft portion of original scabbard. The bayonet has a smooth dark, never-cleaned aged patina. ... 195.00

South Carolina-marked Model 1816 socket bayonet in overall very-good condition with deep-brown age patina and deep "SC" stamp on the ricasso, pattern with the "S" above the "C" on the ricasso (the markings were put on by South Carolina by obliterating the "U" in the original "US" stamp. Also marked on the shank, "LWK," or, "LAK," and marked on the socket." "Z59."..............325.00

.69 Musket, Model 1835, 21" overall with a triangular 18-1/2" bright blade, crisp "US" at the ricasso. Square shoulders at the elbow differ from the Model 1855, .69 bayonet. 195.00

.69 Musket, Model 1842, overall fine condition with clean steel color and good US stamp on the ricasso. 195.00

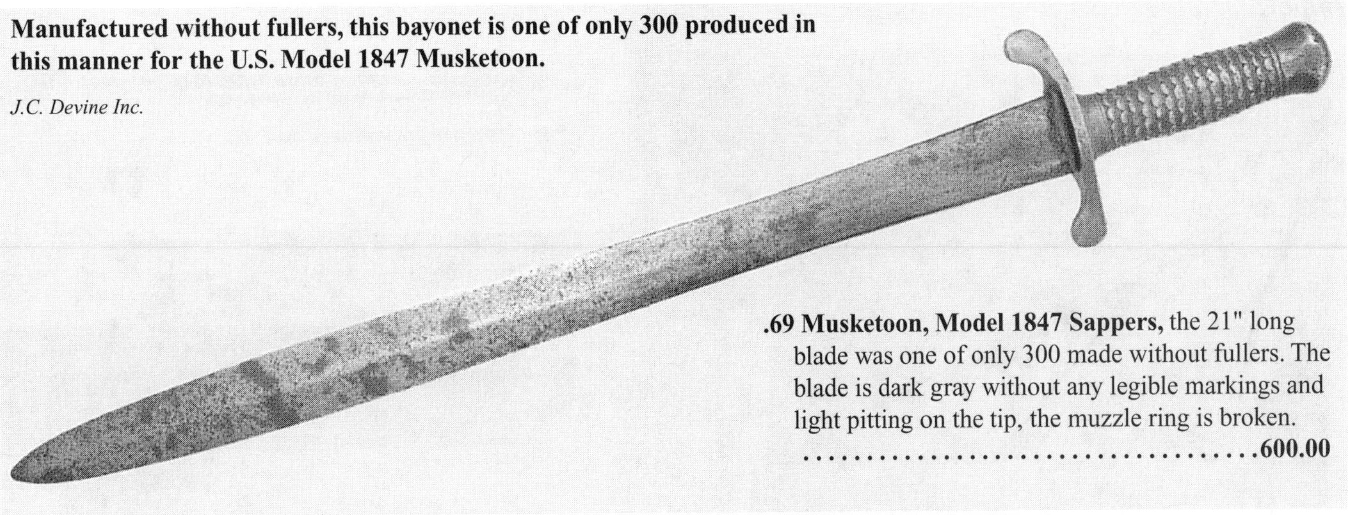

Manufactured without fullers, this bayonet is one of only 300 produced in this manner for the U.S. Model 1847 Musketoon.

J.C. Devine Inc.

.69 Musketoon, Model 1847 Sappers, the 21" long blade was one of only 300 made without fullers. The blade is dark gray without any legible markings and light pitting on the tip, the muzzle ring is broken. **600.00**

.69 Rifle Musket, Model 1835/42, 18" socket bayonet has scalloped comers, face flute, back flutes carried through the elbow, socket complete with locking ring, ricasso has heavy, "A," stamped over and obscuring any U.S. surcharge that may have originally been there. The stamping is in the style of those attributed to 1835/42 bayonets refurbished for issue with the U.S. Model 1847 Musketoon. This bayonet maintains its original 18" length, however, with the 1847 Musketoon bayonets being shortened to 15". Bright finish in good polish has only a few age spots. **125.00**

.69 Rifle Musket, Model 1842, really a fine example with clean steel color overall, clear "US" stamp, and nice pointy tip. **145.00**

.69 Rifle Musket, Model 1855

21" overall with 17" triangular blade, good to fine condition. **135.00**

For the Model 1842 Rifled Musket and used on the conversions, smooth plum-brown patina, would clean to fine, crisp "US" stamped on the ricasso. .. **155.00**

Scabbard .58 Rifle, Musket, Model 1861, attic brown, seven-rivet pattern, very solid with a good "just-found" look to it. **185.00**

Scabbard, .58 Rifle, Model 1863 Remington, near-mint example of the leather scabbard with brass mounts for use with the Remington "Zouave" rifle, brass-handled saber bayonet. Outstanding leather finish, great bright brass mounts, only defect is lightly separated back stitching, which does not affect the soundness of the scabbard. **195.00**

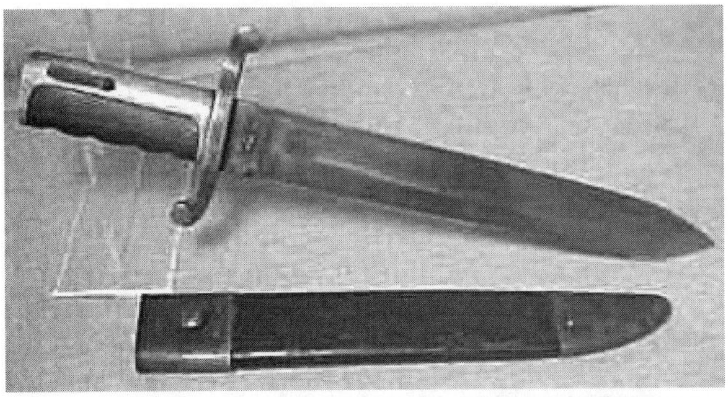

Made to fit the Plymouth/Whitney .69 rifle, this Dahlgren Bowie-style bayonet is quite rare. Be careful, though, there are many reproductions of this bayonet on the market.

Battleground Antiques, Inc.

.69 Rifle, Plymouth/Whitney

Extremely rare, Navy 1862 Ames Dahlgreen bayonet from the ironclad gunboat U.S.S. Cincinnati. These bayonets are Bowie-style, made by Ames Swords for the Plymouth/Whitney Rifle. This was fashioned from a single brass casting. This bayonet has the original scabbard, blade is marked, "U.S.S. Cincinnati Cairo," "U.S.N. D.R. 1862," on the other side, "AMES MFG. CO. CHICOPEE MASS." Brass end on handle is marked "D.R." Scabbard is intact with plaque of Landsmans Mame who owned this bayonet. The piece is in original condition and has not been cleaned. Bayonet measures 17-1/8" from tip to back of handle. **1,750.00**

Fine condition, Ames Dahlgren, crisp example dated and inspected 1864, excellent blade, fine grip, and sheath. Never polished or altered—missing only a couple of tiny brass pins on the drag. **2,050.00**

Import

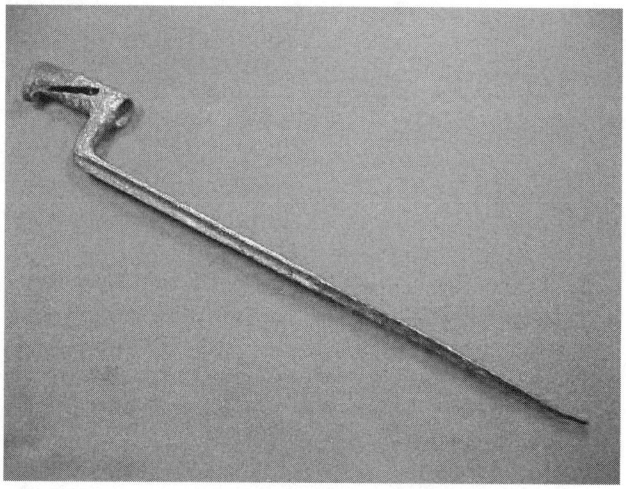

Austrian Lorenz .54 rifle bayonet dug from the Confederate battle lines on the Stones River battlefield.

Middle Tennessee Relics

Bayonet, .54 Rifle, Austrian Lorenz

Four-sided Austrian bayonet recently excavated from the Confederate battle line at Stones River. **85.00**

Complete with locking ring, unique four-sided bayonet with the spiral mortise, goes on the .54 caliber Lorenz. **125.00**

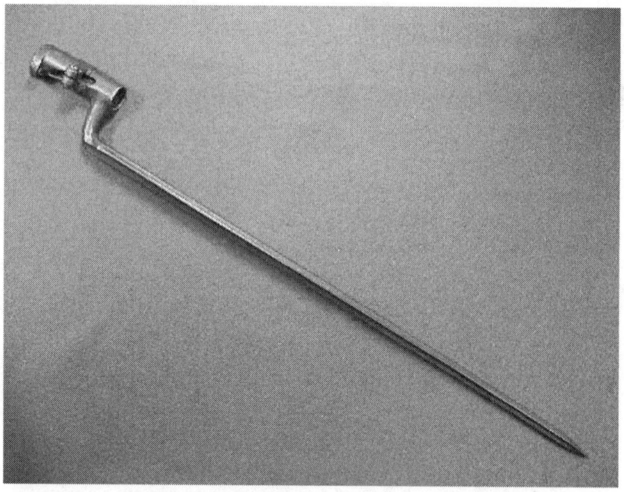

The .54 Austrian Lorenz rifle was one of the more popular import weapons used by both Union and Confederate troops.

Middle Tennessee Relics

Four-sided Austrian socket bayonet with a smooth, never-cleaned, attic-brown patina. **150.00**

The quadrangular socket bayonet for the Lorenz rifle with overall gray and brown patina some surface pitting in the socket. **89.00**

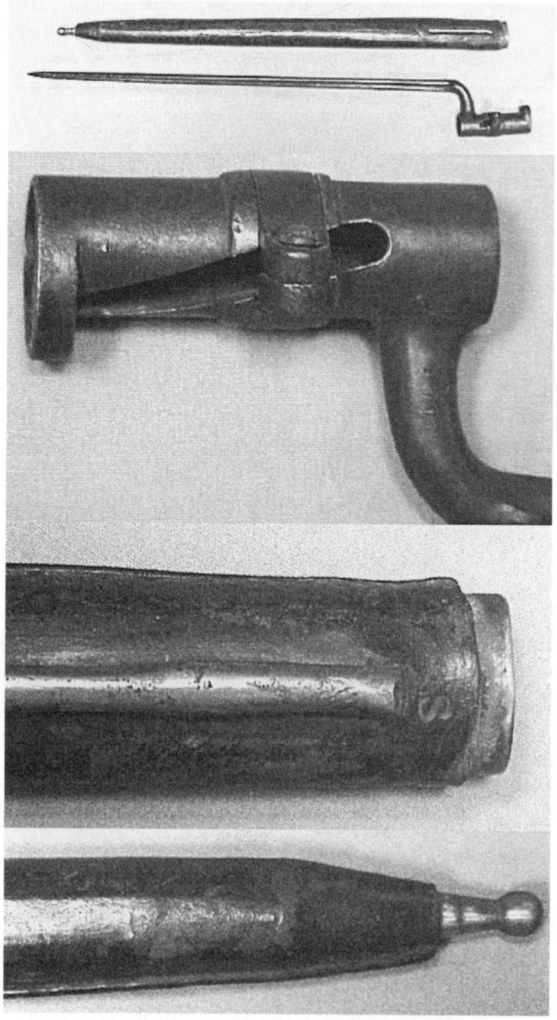

Complete with its original scabbard, this .54 Austrian Lorenz bayonet sold for $425.00.

Old South Military Antiques

Lorenz Bayonet in very-good condition with an excellent scabbard. **475.00**

.577 Rifle Musket, Model 1853 Enfield

A nice brown metal triangular socket bayonet for the Enfield rifle with nice patina and areas of surface scale. **85.00**

Solid example of the Enfield socket bayonet for the Tower Enfield rifle muskets. Good steel color with no rust or pitting. **125.00**

A very representative example, but moderately pitted. **55.00**

Overall about-fine condition socket bayonet for the Tower Enfield rifle musket, nice steel color and patina, good edges, no pitting. **110.00**

Overall about-fine condition socket bayonet for the Tower Enfield rifle musket. Nice steel color, good edges, nice patina, no pitting. Better than average by a good margin. **125.00**

This one is brown and has some age crud on the socket, very solid, and should clean. 79.00

Triangular-sided socket bayonet. Complete with slight split at muzzle. 65.00

Very-fine example of the standard Enfield socket bayonet and scabbard. 145.00

Nice socket bayonet with even, light-brown patina residing in its original U.S. seven-rivet harness leather scabbard. 265.00

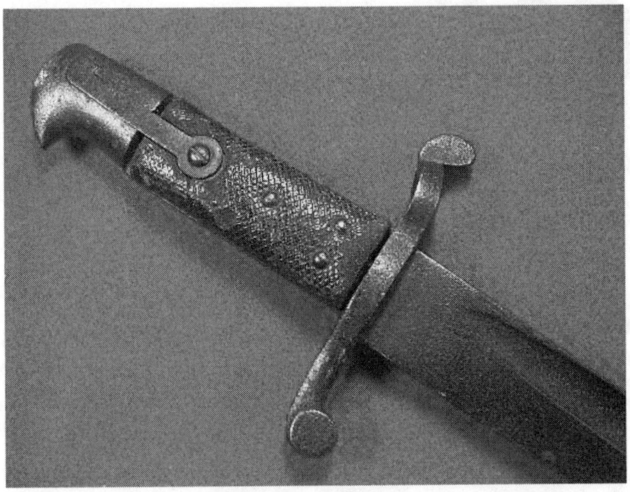

The two-band Model 1858 Enfield rifle was equipped to use a saber bayonet.

Middle Tennessee Relics

.577 Rifle, Model 1858 Enfield

Bayonet for the two-band Enfield rifled musket with both pressed leather grips intact and a smooth, dark, never-cleaned patina. 195.00

Enfield-pattern saber bayonet and scabbard measuring 28" overall with a bright 23" semi-yataghan blade. British proofs at the ricasso, hilt and po mmel are iron, hard black leather, two-piece grips have diamond checkering. Good, solid black-leather scabbard with iron mounts. This bayonet was made for the P1856 Short Rifle. 225.00

Very nice example of the saber bayonet for the two-band Enfield rifle. Steel-mounted with checkered black composition handle (very nice), clean steel blade signed with a maker's "knight's head" cartouche. Nice, bright shiny blade (original luster), a very solid example. 125.00

.58 Rifle, French Import, brown patina with age crud and light pits, this bayonet fits an import French rifle. It looks like a Fayetteville, but the socket is a little smaller in diameter. 85.00

.70 Rifle, Brunswick, saber bayonet with brass handle and 22-inch-long blade. The British Pattern 1845 Brunswick Rifle was purchased during the Civil War only by Confederate purchasing agent Caleb Huse. There are no known U.S. purchases of this musket and bayonet. Nice example with "G 640" stamped on the grip and light sharpening marks on the blade, no blade markings. 175.00

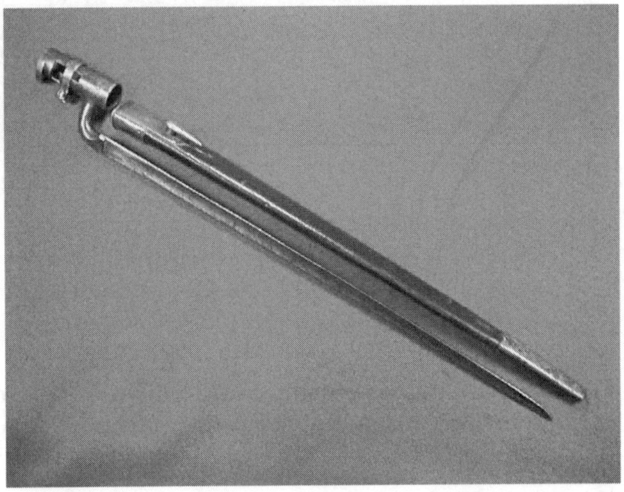

This Enfield bayonet and scabbard were made for a .69 musket.

Middle Tennessee Relics

.69 Musket, Enfield, Enfield triangular-socket bayonet in original leather scabbard. The metal is smooth with an aged gray patina. The leather scabbard is very nice with no breaks or weak spots. 295.00

.69 Musket, French Import, very-good condition triangular socket bayonet with locking ring for the 1842 pattern French import musket. Nice steel color with light age patina, fits a U.S. Model 1835 Musket perfectly. A couple nicks and dings on the socket. 99.00

.69 Musket, Potsdam, very-good steel color socket bayonet for the large-bore German Potsdam musket (with the spring hook mounted under the muzzle). 79.00

.72 Musket, Austrian, this socket bayonet has a quadrangular blade just like a Lorenz, but the socket is larger diameter and has a circular locking ring near the base of the socket (like on a Greene bayonet). Fits a .72-caliber Austrian musket, probably the model 1809, very-good to fine condition. 95.00

.54 Rifle, Austrian Lorenz, two rivets and triangular stitching pattern secure the frog to the body. This one was made in the U.S. to accept the quadrangular Lorenz bayonet. 200.00

Knives

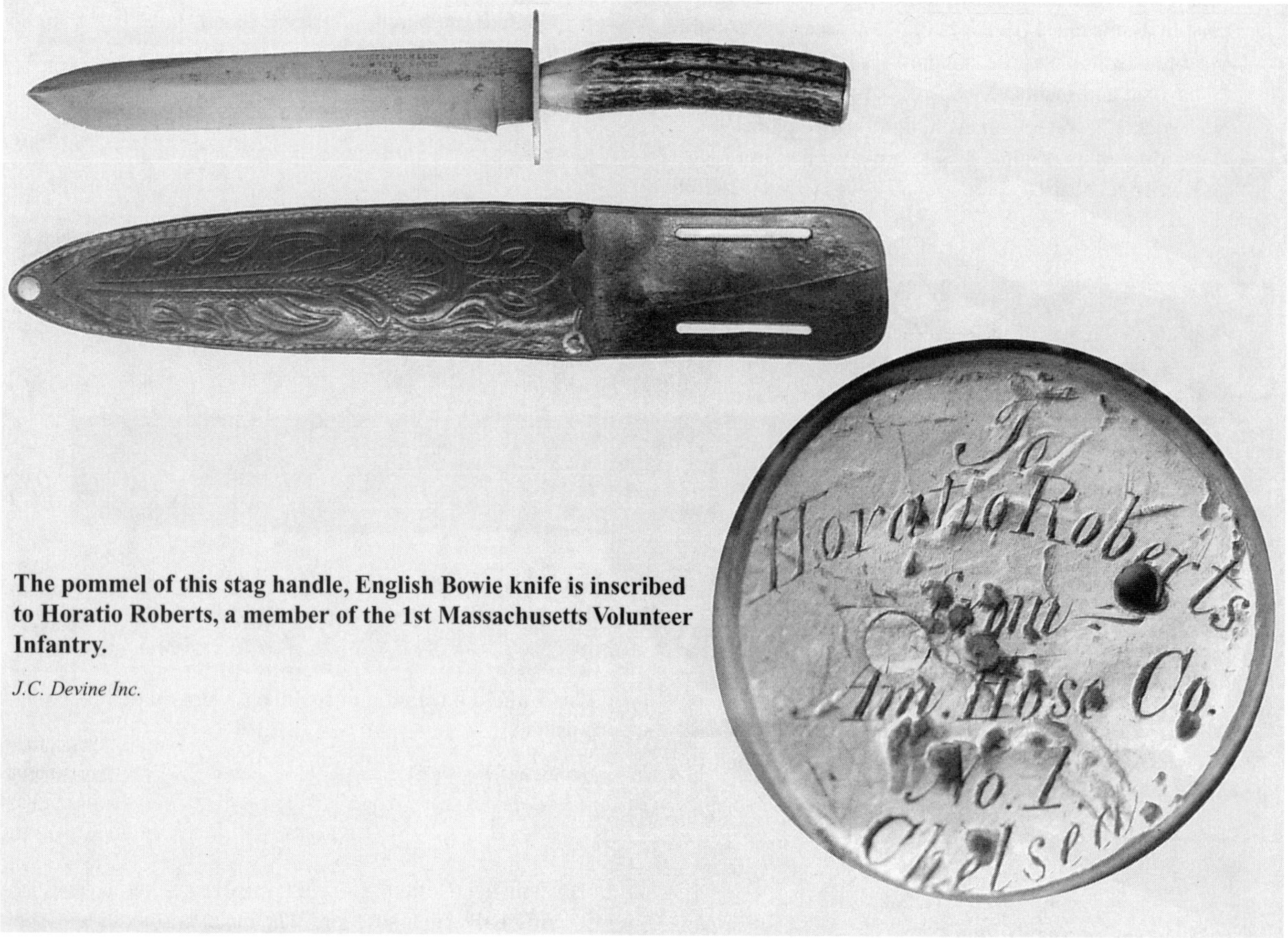

The pommel of this stag handle, English Bowie knife is inscribed to Horatio Roberts, a member of the 1st Massachusetts Volunteer Infantry.

J.C. Devine Inc.

Bowie

English Bowie knife with Civil War presentation to First Lieutenant Horatio Roberts, 1st Regiment Massachusetts Volunteers. The Bowie has a 7-5/8" spear-point blade, an oval German silver guard, and flat pommel with a one-piece stag handle. The ricasso is marked, "IXL," and the blade itself is marked, "G. WOSTENHOLM + SON/WASHINGTON WORKS/ SHEFFIELD." The pommel is neatly engraved, "To/ Horatio Roberts/from/Am. Hose Co./No. 1/Chelsea." The blade has been sharpened and has clean, gray steel with some scattered fine to light pitting, the stag handle has three age cracks at the guard with the pommel missing one retaining pin. The tooled leather scabbard is a later replacement. Included are several dozen photocopies of documents from the National Archives relating to Roberts. He enlisted on May 22, 1861, as a 1st Sergeant in Company H of the First Regiment of Massachusetts Volunteer Infantry. On October 12, 1861, he was promoted to 2nd Lieutenant and on June 24, 1862, he was promoted to First Lieutenant. He was shot at the Second Battle of Bull Run on August 19, 1862, in the left leg, which resulted in the loss of the leg and many months spent in the hospital. He was commissioned into the 143rd Company of the 2nd Battalion of the Veteran Reserve Corps on January 29, 1864. He was transferred to the 20th Regiment of the Veteran Reserve Corps on October 20, 1865 and mustered out of the service on June 30, 1866. . . . . **950.00**

A hefty and substantial Civil War Sheffield bowie that measures roughly 1-1/4" long and has a 7" spear-point blade. The ricasso is deeply marked, "IXL," in large characters. The grips are a lovely aged stag horn and the left slab has a wonderful silver escutcheon plate (oval, narrow and 1-1/4" wide) which is beautifully engraved, "M.A. O'Brien Co "B" 13th Regiment N.Y.S.M." This knife dates to 1861 when the 13th was organized under Colonel Abel Smith and left the state on April 13, 1861, under Lincoln's first call for troops. It served as infantry at Annapolis and Baltimore and was mustered out of service on August 6, 1861. The cross guard on this knife was intentionally removed during its period of use. **1,150.00**

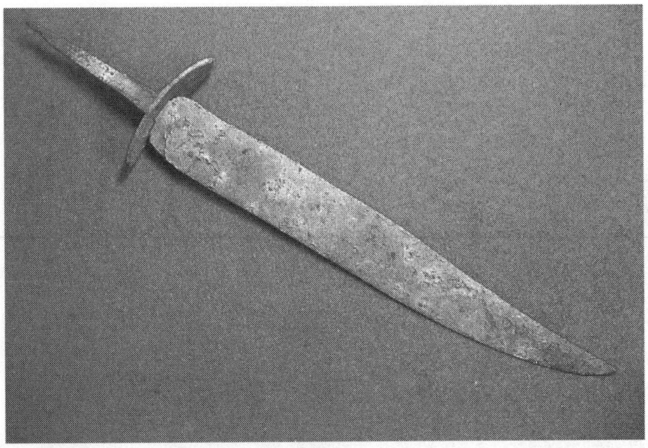

Dug from General Polk's 1863 winter campsite near Shelbyville, Tennessee, this is a relic-condition Bowie knife.

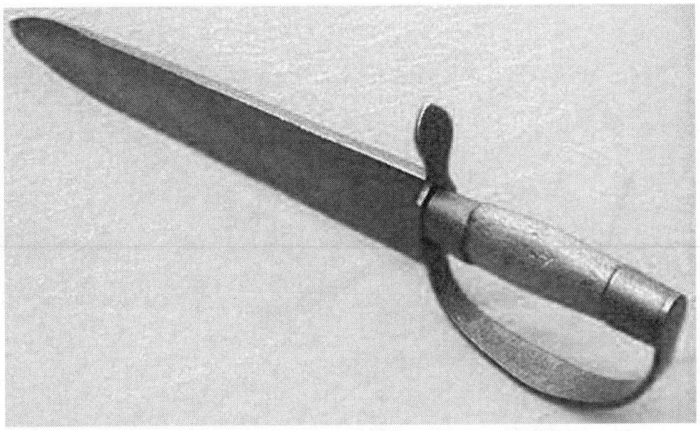

This knife is one of 39 D-Guard Bowies made by T.L. Pruett for the Autauga Guard in 1861.

Old South Military Antiques

Excellent condition, dug, 13" bowie knife. This knife was excavated from General Polk's 1863 winter camps along Duck River near Shelbyville, Tennessee. This knife is 100% complete lacking only the wooden grip. The blade was forged from a file, and numerous file teeth are still visible. **650.00**

Very nice condition 13" stag handle Bowie. This Bowie was purchased out of a Tennessee estate and has a nice clean blade and an excellent stag handle without a single crack. **795.00**

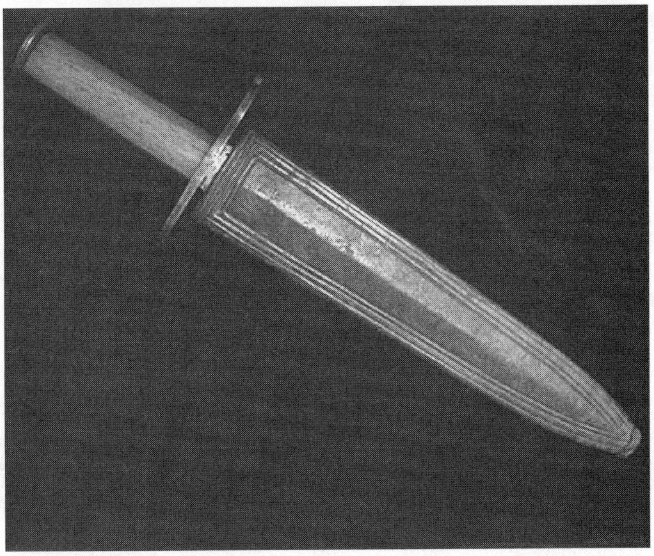

Virginia-made Bowie.

Old South Military Antiques

Virginia-made Bowie. **9,500.00**

D-Guard Bowie

When the secession crisis reached a fever pitch in 1860, forty-year-old T. L. Pruett, a native Kentuckian, was plying his trade just east of Montgomery, Alabama, in Prattville. Pruett was a blacksmith by trade, and evidently a very skilled artisan judging by the workmanship exhibited in his D-guard knives. The huge weapon he produced was of the very highest quality. It is not known how many D-guard Bowies he manufactured, but the production must have been very small, as only three of his Bowies are known to survive. It is known that Pruett made a D-guard knife for each member of the Autauga (Alabama) Guard (that later became Company G, 44th Mississippi Infantry). Pruett supplied all 39 enlisted men in Captain Faulkner's Autauga Guard with a huge iron-mounted D-Guard knife with a 19" blade. Maker-marked, Confederate D-guards are virtually unheard of, but Pruett boldly stamped his name and address into the D-guard: "T. L. PRUETT. MAKER. PRATTVILLE. ALA." The D-guard Pruett created is a whopping 22-1/2" l, over 2" w and over a 1/4" d! The flat spear-point blade has a 3" reverse edge. The handgrip is made of walnut set into two heavy iron ferrules. The guard is made as heftily as the rest of the knife, measuring over 1/8" d and 1" w. This exact knife was displayed at the Ohio Historical Society in the early 1960s. It was photographed, catalogued, and published by the Historical Society in April 1962 and comes with facsimile copies from that publication. Pruett's Confederate record and history are also included. **18,500.00**

D-Guard Bowie, cont.

Measuring 21" overall, this walnut-handled, D-Guard Bowie knife originated in Texas.

J.C. Devine Inc.

From Texas, 21" overall length with a 16-1/2" l double-edged blade, oval iron guard 3-3/4" l, tapered tang with copper or brass riveted walnut scales, copper or brass buttplate secured by two non-ferrous screws. Dark patina on all the metal, negligible pitting, handles are fine. **500.00**

Authentic, non-excavated, blacksmith-made D-guard Bowie knife. Blacksmith-forged from old file blade. Teeth of the file are very prominent, somewhat crude, but very solid. A large and heavily constructed knife, overall length is 17-1/2" with a 12" dark blade. Multiple heavy hammer marks over entire blade. Semi-taper clip point blade. Grip looks to be made of pecan or walnut. The "D" itself is a thick, heavy hand-hammered forged iron guard. All in all, very typical of many of the D-guards that Confederate troops had made by local blacksmiths before they marched off to war. There is no doubt about this knife. This specimen is definitely *not* a Philipino- or Mexican-import such as are often encountered in the market, as well as being sold as original. Nor is this knife a postwar cane or field knife. This is an authentic specimen, and was manufactured to be carried off into the Civil War by Southern soldiers. **2,275.00**

Confederate States Armory Bowie knife that is a rare product of the Confederate States Armory, Kenansville, North Carolina. This massive 16" spear-point bowie is 100% authentic and original. This weapon is a piece of 1862-1864 Southern-made steel and walnut, with a unique tarred-leather grip covering, perhaps indicating its use as a Naval Cutlass. **3,500.00**

Exceptional Confederate D-Guard Bowie that is a superb purebred D-Guard Bowie knife, likely a product of the Augusta Arsenal in Georgia circa 1861-1862, massive 16.5" clip point blade, 100% original.. .... **3,000.00**

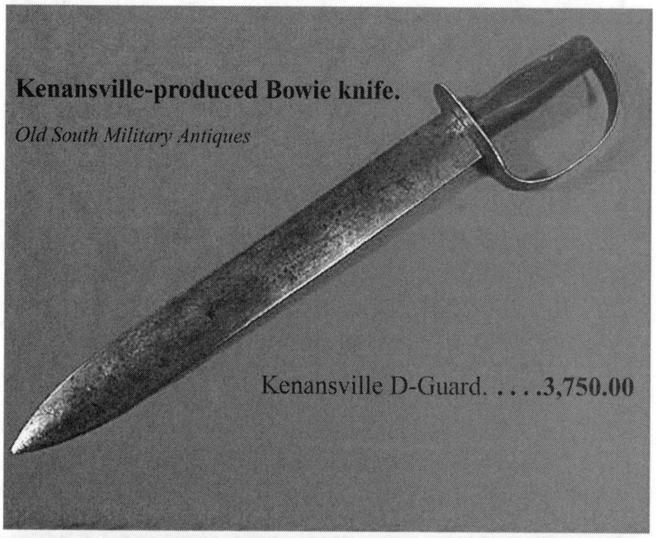

Kenansville-produced Bowie knife.

Old South Military Antiques

Kenansville D-Guard. **3,750.00**

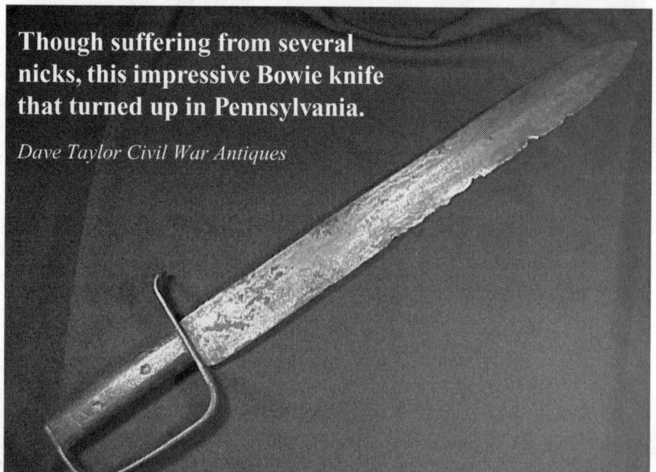

Though suffering from several nicks, this impressive Bowie knife that turned up in Pennsylvania.

Dave Taylor Civil War Antiques

This is a 100% guaranteed original and genuine Confederate soldier's D-Guard Bowie knife, measures over 2" long and was found by a woman in eastern Pennsylvania. The blade has some severe edge nicks from being beaten against something. The wood that forms the grip is likely ash. It is very solid and has great eye appeal. **1,850.00**

D-Guard Bowie knife belonged to Lieutenant Robert Neely Provine of the 29th Mississippi Infantry.

Old South Military Antiques

From a collection of several hundred guns from Arkansas, 23-3/8" long overall with an 18-7/8" single-edged blade, sheet iron guard, dark wood scales fastened by two iron rivets through rectangular strap iron reinforcement plates. All of the iron has a dark patina, the guard is slightly bent and the reverse handle is missing a 1/8" wide splinter. **900.00**

This massive 20-1/2" D-guard has all of the hallmarks of the classic Confederate fighting knife. The elegantly shaped blade is sharp on both edges from ricasso to point. The stag horn grip is ensconced in a forged-iron D-guard having an extended counter stroke guard. The tin scabbard's belt loop is mounted at 45 degrees allowing for a swift cross draw. The knife and scabbard are in excellent, untouched condition. It belonged to Robert Neely Provine who entered service as a Second Lieutenant in the 29th Mississippi Volunteer Infantry on March 6, 1862, at his home in Big Creek, Mississippi. Promoted to First Lieutenant late that same year, he served with the 29th until he was captured at Lookout Mountain on November 24, 1863. He was sent to Johnson's Island prison. He did not take the oath until June 13, 1865. Being an unreconstructed Rebel, he was commander of the J. Gordon #553 Confederate Veterans for many years. He is mentioned many times in the original *Confederate Veteran* magazine including his obituary. He was still at Big Creek, Mississippi at the time of his death. **9,250.00**

Emerging from a gun collection in Arkansas, this D-Guard Bowie measures a whopping 23-3/8" overall.

J.C. Devine Inc.

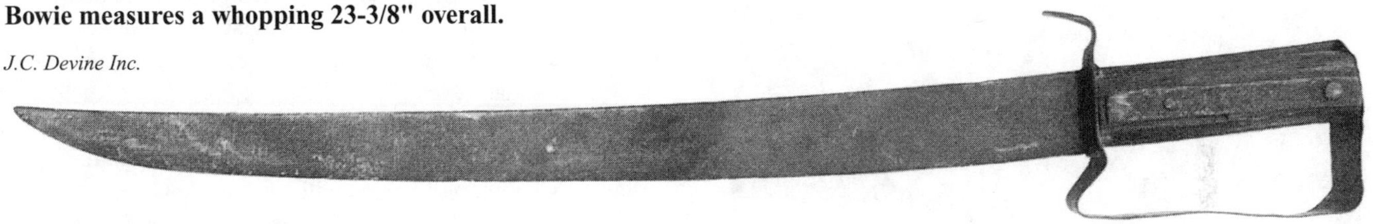

Knife, Confederate

11" overall with a double-edged, spear-pointed, 7" blade made from a file. Still has the turned file handle with brass tang ferrule, fine condition, from the Bray Family, Fincastle, Virginia. **1,250.00**

12-1/2" long with a hand forged, heavily used 7-3/4" single-edged blade and oval iron guard. Two-piece wooden grips held by three rivets. Knife came from the Howard Family of Rockingham County, Virginia. **650.00**

Pikes

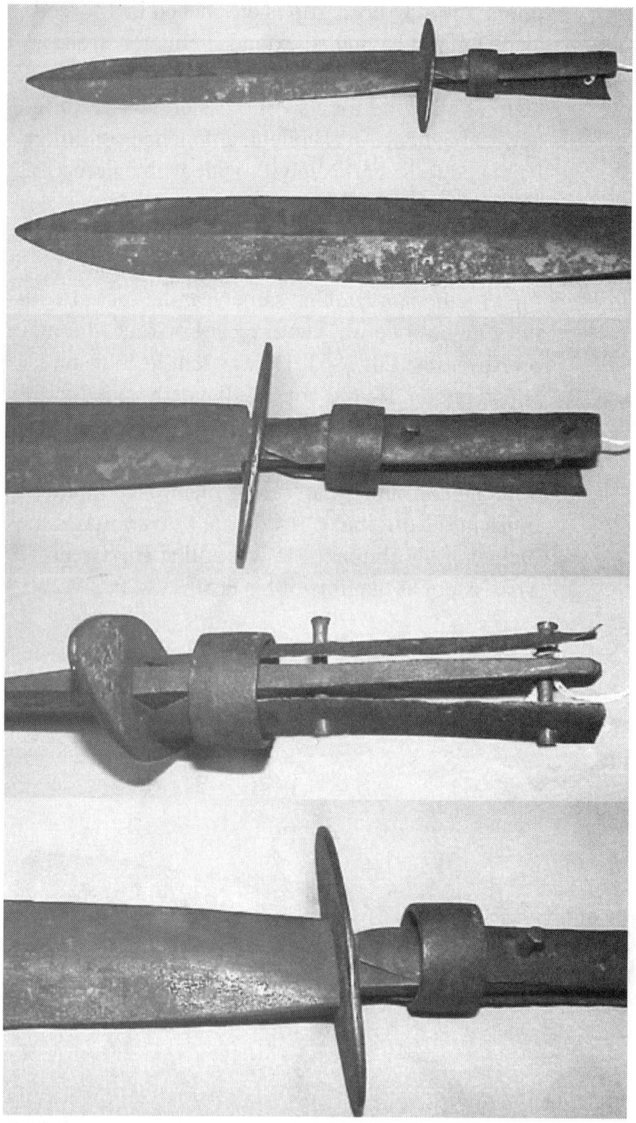

Either the wood handle rotted or was burned away from this Augusta Arsenal-made pike head.

Sharpsburg Arsenal

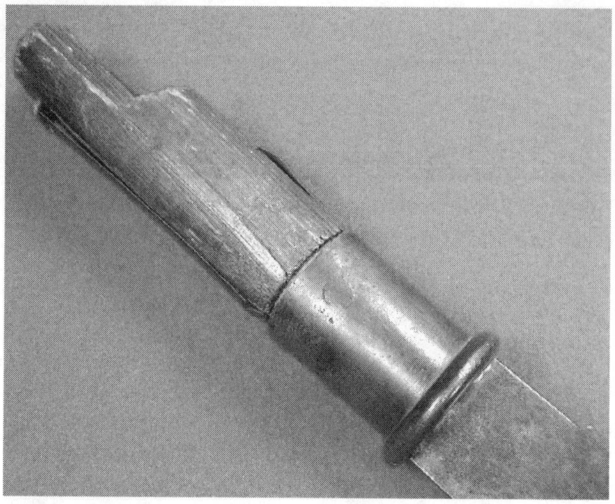

Georgia pike head with a portion of the pole intact.

Middle Tennessee Relics

Confederate

Augusta Arsenal pike head that is complete with retainer bands and rivets in place. Wooden pike handle was either burnt out or rotted away. Metal pieces are all in attached position. **1,195.00**

Beautiful condition Georgia pike head, original brass cuff, several inches of original pole intact. Blade has a smooth, aged, gray-brown patina without even a single nick, brass cuff is perfect with a rich uncleaned patina. **975.00**

Georgia-style pike with full haft is 8' long overall with a spear-pointed, double-edged 12" blade. Blade is a smooth, dark patina with obvious flaws in the iron; oval-shaped iron guard; brass socket or ferrule behind the guard. Iron reinforcing straps extend 18" down the 1-1/2" diameter ash haft. Brass ferrule grounding iron at the bottom tip. Shaft is painted a very handsome milk-based thin red (the original color). Governor Joe Brown of Georgia ordered thousands of these pikes to arm the State Militia early in the War, completely original and in fine condition. **2,250.00**

"Governor Joseph E. Brown, of Georgia, put shops in the State to work, making what were called "Joe Brown's pikes." They were a sort of rude bayonet, or steel lance, fastened, not to guns, but to long poles or handles, and were given to men who had no other arms. Of course, few if any of these pikemen ever had occasion to use these warlike implements..."

—General John B. Gordon
Confederate States Army

Confederate pike head bearing a clear "H. Stevens" mark.

Old South Military Antiques

H. Stevens-marked pike. **12,500.00**

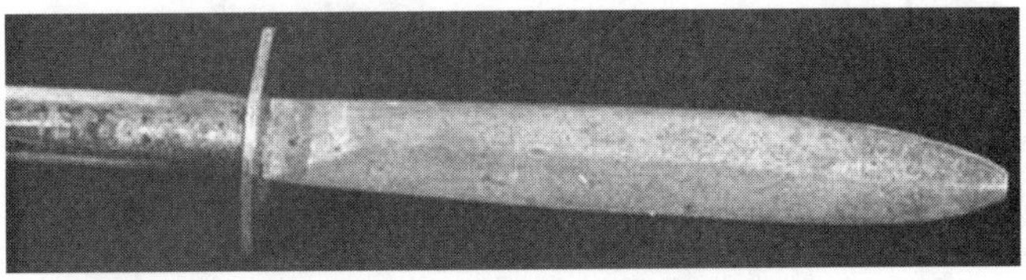

"Joe Brown" pike named for the Georgia governor who placed his reliance on the medieval weapon.

Old South Military Antiques

"Joe Brown" Pike

In early 1862, the South was woefully under armed, causing Joe Brown, the governor of Georgia to lament, "What shall be done in the emergency?" Brown then replied to his own rhetorical question, "Let every army have a large reserve, armed with a good pike and a large, heavy side knife to be brought upon the field with a shout for victory. When the time comes for the charge, let them move in double quick time and rush with terrible impetuosity into the lines of the enemy. When the retreat commences, let the pursuit be rapid, and if the enemy throw down their guns and are likely to outrun us, if need be, throw down the pike and keep close at their heels with the knife until each has hewed down at least one of his adversaries." While Joe Brown is the most recognized proponent of the pike that bears his name, he was by no means alone. Pikes were made at various state arsenals including, but not limited to Alabama, Georgia, Tennessee, and Virginia. The use of the pike was, of course, limited to non-combat roles such as guarding prisoners, home guard, and drilling. This Joe Brown pike is in excellent condition, with the exception that the tip is broken. It still retains much of its original black paint on the reinforcing straps and counter guard. **1,800.00**

Original Confederate "Richmond-style" pike on the original haft measuring 8'7" from tip to bottom of grounding iron. 13-1/4", double-edged, spear-pointed blade that enters into a brass 2" ferrule, which has a rolled edge for strength. Iron rivet through the ferrule holds the blade, 17-1/2" blackened iron reinforcing straps on either side to strengthen the ash haft. Haft has turned almost black with age, but is still in excellent condition. Grounding iron is of heavy folded and hammer welded iron riveted through the haft. Overall the entire pike is in excellent condition. Collectors and historians consider this style pike to be a product of Confederate shops in and around Richmond, Virginia, from the early days of the war. **3,295.00**

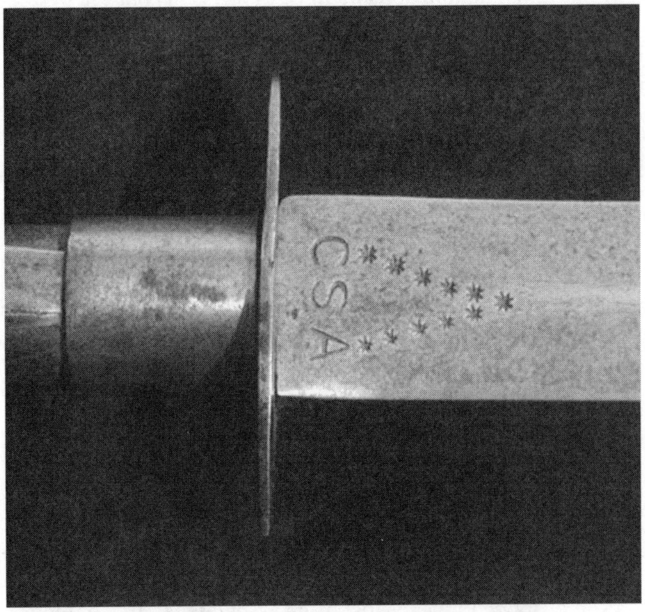

Finding any item clearly marked as being made in the South during the existence of the Confederacy is quite a windfall.

Old South Military Antiques

Rare C.S.A.-marked pike. **14,000.00**

Pike, Confederate, cont.

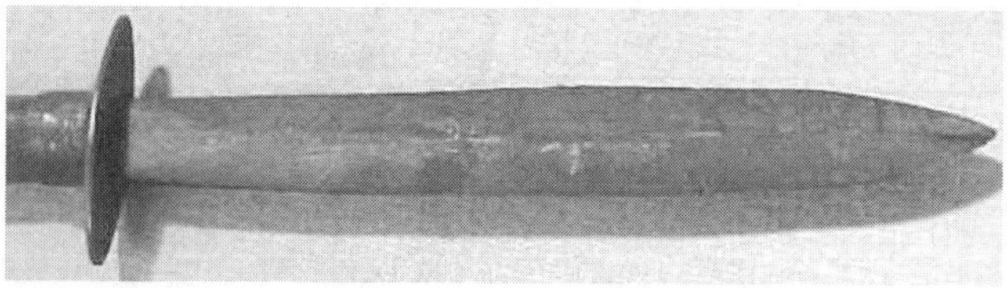

Initialed Richmond Arsenal Confederate pike was probably a souvenir picked up by Captain H.A. Coursen who served in the 7th and 23rd New Jersey Volunteer Infantry.

Battleground Antiques

Superb, identified Confederate, Richmond Armory pike, full-length pole, missing bottom cap, excellent blade. Name clearly inked in wood, "Cap. H.A. Coursen." Coursen served with distinction with both the 7th and 23rd New Jersey Infantry, seeing action at Williamsburg, Seven Pines, Malvern hill, 2nd Bull Run and Fredericksburg! Excellent overall condition, 96-1/2" tip-to-tip. **3,500.00**

U.S.

Navy, 8' long overall with a 12-1/2", four-sided, spike-style blade, 3" langets run down the sides of the haft for reinforcement, one langet marked with an "L," fine, original handle appears to be of ash. This pattern of pikes was used as early 1797, but continued in service through the Civil War, fine condition. **1,650.00**

Miscellaneous

Bayonet, Child's, hand-forged socket bayonet (looks like Revolutionary War style) measuring roughly 10" overall with a socket diameter of 3/5". Made for a small boy's musket and really appealing, overall deep-brown patina with pitting. **65.00**

Utilitarian items are often not passed down through the generations, because the nostalgia value is not immediately recognizable. This Confederate spade, however, did survive.

Sharpsburg Arsenal

Shovel, Confederate, with wood T-handle and strap stamped, "T. Carr CASTSTEEL," 10-1/4" x 7" blade with 18" wood handle. Thomas A. Carr, Mobile, Alabama, advertised in 1838 as maker of military equipments, good condition. All iron has rust and shows age as does wood handle. **695.00**

Bayonet, Knife, and Pike Terminology

D-Guard: This is the term applied to the over-the-fist guard on some Bowie knives. Most often associated with Confederate knives, there are many photographs of Union soldiers posing with D-Guard knives as well.

Ricasso: The flattened portion of the blade that assists in weapon manipulation. Often, one will find the maker's mark stamped here.

Fuller: The "groove" that often runs the blade length of a knife or sword.

Saber bayonet: This is a wide-bladed (most often with a fuller) bayonet that has a handle that attaches to a lug on the rifle barrel's side.

See also: Accoutrements and Groupings.

Chapter 4

Belt Plates and Buckles

Collecting Civil War belt plates can be very satisfying: The pieces look really nice on display, are readily available, and offer many levels for collection growth. Both Union and Confederate troops wore a variety of belt buckles and plates, so it is advisable for beginners to first assemble a representative collection (perhaps consisting of a U.S. oval plate, C.S. oval plate, pattern of 1851 plate, and a frame buckle), and then focusing on a particular variety or style.

Reproductions abound, however, so great care should be exercised when purchasing buckles and plates. Because of the demand by reenactors, even low-grade, common plates have been reproduced in abundance. One would assume that dug buckles would guarantee authenticity, but this is not the case. Because some Confederate buckles can sell for tens of thousands of dollars, a forger has a lot of incentive to make their handiwork look as convincing as possible. On the other hand, a dug U.S. buckle, pattern of 1841, isn't probably going to pose too many authenticity concerns to a buyer—it simply isn't worth a forger's time to artificially age the common plate.

Middle Tennessee Relics

Middle Tennessee Relics

Collecting Hints

Pros:
- Belt plates and buckles are still widely available.
- It is easy to assemble a large collection that does not require a lot of space.
- Belt plates and buckles display well, as they are not adversely affected by light.
- Many belt plates can be purchased for under $150 each.
- Belt plates are very impressive when on display.

Cons:
- Many belt plates have been restruck, reproduced, and faked.
- Variety is virtually unlimited and overwhelming.
- Advanced items require tens of thousands of dollars.

Availability ★★★
Price ★★
Reproduction Alert ★★

Buckles and Plates

Confederate, General Issue

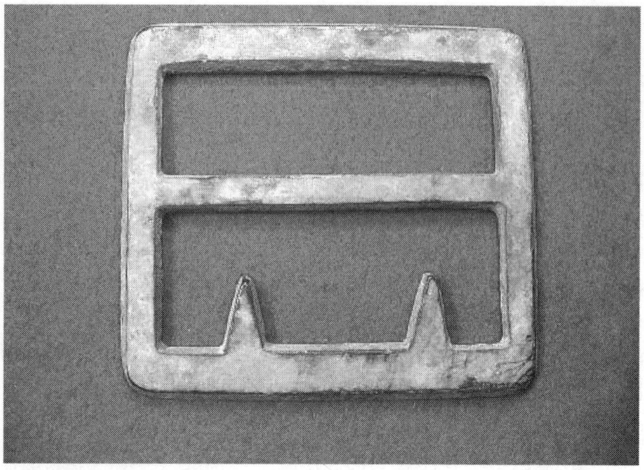

Frame buckles came in a variety of sizes. This is a Georgia "Baby Cavalry" buckle.

Middle Tennessee Relics

Belt Buckle, Frame

"Baby cavalry" Georgia frame that was recently dug from Bragg's C.S. camp near Shelbyville, Tennessee, perfect and not cleaned. **625.00**

Beautiful condition, dug, Confederate cavalry Georgia frame buckle from the camp of the 51st Alabama Cavalry. Pattern manufactured by McElroy & Hunt of Macon, Georgia but is unmarked. Buckle has a pretty, slick, green uncleaned patina. **550.00**

Georgia frame buckle dug in Tennessee.

Middle Tennessee Relics

Beautiful, dug, smooth-type, large-size Confederate Georgia frame buckle, slick brown wood patina dug from C.S. camps along Duck River near Shelbyville, Tennessee. **550.00**

C.S. Georgia frame that is the guttered back style, recently dug from Bragg's C.S. camps near Shelbyville, Tennessee. It is a perfect buckle with an uncleaned brown-green patina. **575.00**

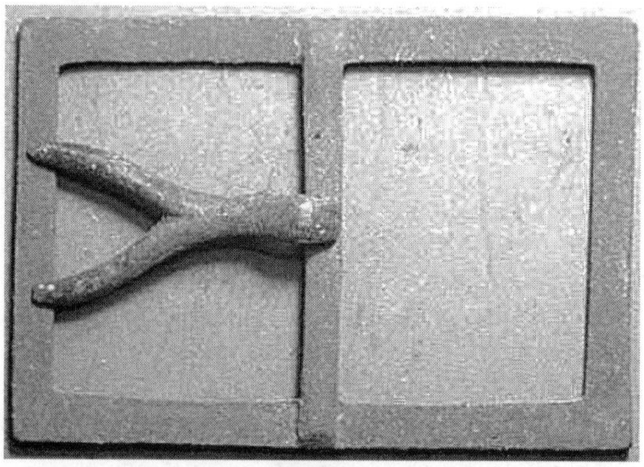

Large Georgia frame buckle was dug in one of General Braxton Bragg's camps.

Middle Tennessee Relics

Excellent, dug, large-size C.S. Georgia frame waist belt buckle that is uncleaned and retains a brown-green patina. Dug from Bragg's camps following the Battle of Stones River. **550.00**

Large-size Confederate "wishbone" or "fork tongue" frame buckle that was dug along the Confederate retreat route out of Shiloh towards Corinth, Mississippi. It is very attractive with a thick pea green patina. **650.00**

Cast brass. Fine, excavated condition, brownish patina. **785.00**

Scarce medium-size Confederate fork tongue frame waist belt buckle. It has a nice wood brown-green patina, and has not even been washed off. . . . **695.00**

Frame buckle with the hooks raised was a popular pattern that could be produced inexpensively. **500.00**

"Wishbone" or "fork tongue" frame buckle.

Middle Tennessee Relics

Belt Buckle, Fork-Tongue Frame

Large-size Confederate "wishbone" or "fork tongue" frame buckle dug along the Confederate retreat route out of Shiloh towards Corinth, Mississippi, very attractive with a thick pea-green patina. **650.00**

Frame buckle sold with a letter of authenticity and guarantee.

Drumbeat Civil War Memorabilia

Classic Confederate forked tongue brass belt buckle, non-dug example in perfect condition, and guaranteed original with letter of authenticity. **1,250.00**

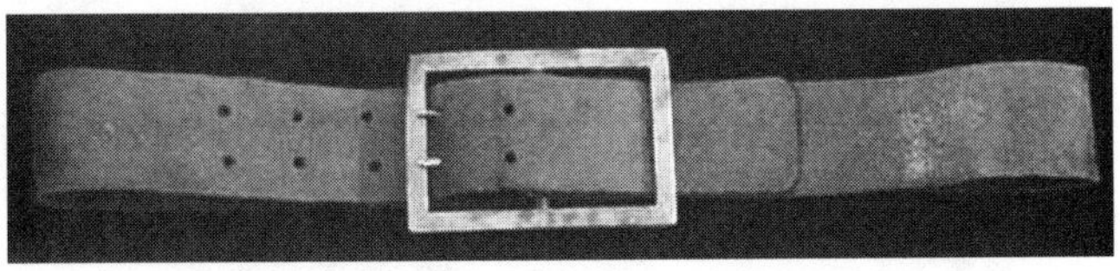

Belts with frame buckles are quite rare.

Old South Military Relics

Belt and buckle known as a "forked tongue frame" waist belt. This style accoutrement belt was widely manufactured and issued throughout the Confederacy. Despite their widespread use, very few of the belts survive. Example is strong and supple, stitching is intact, original, and tight. **8,500.00**

Belt Buckle, Snake, complete, large-size, three-piece Confederate snake buckle. All three pieces are perfect with matching smooth, brown patina. **475.00**

Plate, Belt, Clipped Corner

All three hooks intact. **3,600.00**

Army of Tennessee style, with all three hooks in nice condition. **3,600.00**

Beautiful condition, thick, cast brass, clip corner, plain face, rectangular waist belt plate excavated from General Leonidus Polk's C.S. winter camp along Duck River near Shelbyville, Tennessee. It has a perfect front and back with all three hooks intact. **375.00**

Plate, Belt, Frame, construction is solid brass casting. Missing tongue, buckle probably discarded because of the missing tongue. Another tongue has been found and is included with this piece, but it is not the tongue originally with this piece. **400.00**

Plate, Belt, Sheet Brass, dug rectangular sheet brass, Confederate waist belt plate. Rare pattern with folded edge, beautiful brown-green wood patina with main hook intact on the reverse. **475.00**

Collectors refer to this variation of the C.S. plate as a "Breckinridge-style" plate. Affixed to a remnant of an original Confederate belt.

Middle Tennessee Relics

Plate, Belt, Oval and Belt, this is a non-dug, solid, cast Breckinridge-style C.S. oval waist belt plate on what is left of the original Confederate leather belt. Belt rig is out of a Henry County, Tennessee, family and had been on display at the Lotz House Civil War Museum in Franklin, Tennessee, for the past several years. The plate is absolutely perfect with all three hooks intact. Approximately 70% of the original Confederate leather belt remains with the buckle. **9,500.00**

The stylized edging on this plate lends itself to the nickname "Rope-Border."

The Civil War Relicman

Plate, Belt, Oval

Called the "rope-border" style because there is the faint outline of a rope just inside the rim, these plates were stamped, never lead-filled, and the attachment hooks were individually fashioned from sheet brass. All three hooks are original and intact. Plate shows good bit of wear from actual use. There was a bend in the middle, now straightened, but it was not broken or cracked and has not been repaired in any way. The red color is from having been cleaned with lemon juice at one time, a technique used by some to remove oxidation and other crud.......... **2,500.00**

Dug, rope-border, C.S. oval waist belt plate. This plate was dug near Shiloh and has a smooth, brown-green patina, perfect body curve and all three hooks intact, small amount of professionally-restored chipping along the rim to the lower right of the S. ... **2,850.00**

Dug, rope-border plate.

Middle Tennessee Relics

Dug, rope-border-style stamped-brass oval waist belt plate. Buckle has nice brown patina and all three hooks intact. Plate has a couple tiny hairline freeze cracks, as is typically the case with thin die-struck southern plates. It is, otherwise, a complete, quite solid, very pretty example. **3,250.00**

Egg-shaped, C.S., oval, waist belt plate excavated from N.B. Forrest's Confederate cavalry camp near Spence Springs located at Murfreesboro, Tennessee. Plate is very solid and has been professionally straightened where it was bent downward on each end. This is the stamped-brass, non-lead-filled, western theater variety............................ **1,250.00**

Exceedingly rare, the 11-star border Leech and Rigdon plate.

Middle Tennessee Relics

Leech and Rigdon 11-star C.S. oval is untouched with nice patina, perfect body curve, and all three hooks intact. **22,500.00**

Breckinridge-style C.S. plate emerged from a museum collection.

Middle Tennessee Relics

Rare, stamped brass "Breckinridge style," C.S., oval waist belt plate. This buckle was dug at the Battle of Franklin, Tennessee, and was on display in the Lotz House Civil War Museum in Franklin, Tennessee, for a number of years. The buckle still has the museum's accession number on the back. The plate is very solid with all three hooks intact on the reverse and a green-brown patina........................ **3,850.00**

Cast oval border, C.S. plates are often referred to as the "Army of Tennessee" style.

Battleground Antiques, Inc.

Scarce Army of Tennessee, Confederate, solid, cast oval border "CS" plate, belt, all hooks intact, but tip broken from one. Recovered in a field near a hospital site in Kinston, North Carolina, where the military battle of Wyse Forks took place, fine deep-green patina. **3,000.00**

Dug plate possessing strong character.

Western theater-style Confederate (egg) belt buckle. Dug directly behind the Confederate trench line at the Siege of Port Hudson, Louisiana. The plate is very strong and has a lot of character to it. **620.00**

Very nice, dug, solid cast-brass, Army of Tennessee round-corner C.S. waist belt plate dug from a C.S. camp near Mobile, Alabama. Very attractive, uncleaned, brown-green patina, approximately 80% black enamel still visible in the background, all three hooks intact on reverse with nice deep spun downs around each. **3,250.00**

Pretty, "rope border," C.S., oval waist belt plate. Solid buckle, no cracks, dug at Shiloh, has a beautiful red-brown patina. Portions of the strip brass hooks remain intact on the reverse.............. **3,150.00**

Plate, Belt, Rectangular, and Belt

Beautiful condition, cast-brass, Atlanta-style rectangle "C.S.A." on original Confederate brown leather belt. Plate has prominent file marks and a rich, never-cleaned patina....................... **5,500.00**

Rectangular C.S.A. plate on its original belt.

Old South Military Antiques

The letters "C S A" are well shaped and well defined. Sand casting, using a brass with a high copper content, has resulted in its having a patina with a pleasing reddish hue. It appears to be on its original waist belt, which remains strong, soft, and supple. There is an illegible name inked into the russet side of the belt. **18,500.00**

Collectors refer to this style of rectangular C.S.A. plate as being the "Army of Northern Virginia pattern."

Battleground Antiques, Inc.

Plate, Belt, Rectangular

"CSA" Army of Northern Virginia pattern rectangular, excavated just south of Richmond. Fine overall condition with solid hooks and a smooth face; a pleasing light-brown patina. **2,500.00**

Plate, Belt, Rectangular, cont.

Absolutely beautiful freshly dug cast brass rectangular "C.S.A." waist belt plate, dug near Vicksburg, Mississippi, and has an uncleaned wood brown-green patina. Plate has nice body curve, all three hooks intact, and a good-size piece of original leather belt remaining under the hooks. This is the thinner early-war, Tennessee style with the rim notched for the period after the "A." This is a relatively uncommon pattern in the best of the best condition.. . . . **2,850.00**

The thick, cast-brass, C.S.A. rectangular plates are referred to as being in the "Atlanta style."

Middle Tennessee Relics

Absolutely beautiful non-excavated, cast-brass, rectangular C.S.A. waist belt plate. This is a thick Atlanta style with a rich age patina and all three hooks intact, the plate is out of a North Mississippi estate. **3,250.00**

Atlanta Arsenal plate.

Battleground Antiques, Inc.

Authentic Atlanta Arsenal belt plate, one hook has tip gone and has been filed smooth. All three hooks show a lot of file marks on their sides and also on the edges and back corner of the buckle itself. The edges are very irregular in shape. It is very unevenly made. The thickness of the bronze or brass is thinner at the two-hook end than at the main hook end. It has all original patina and green tarnish from age. It is non-dug and has always been protected from abuse. **3,251.00**

Box-shaped letters are one of the defining characteristics of Atlanta-style plates.

The Civil War Relicman

Atlanta-style plates are noted for the "box-shaped" letters. This is a beautiful, non-dug example with definite copper content. **3,500.00**

This dug, Atlanta-style plate emerged from a museum collection.

Middle Tennessee Relics

Beautiful, thick, cast-brass, Atlanta Arsenal-style rectangular "C.S.A." This buckle was excavated many years ago on the Confederate battle line at Franklin, Tennessee. This plate has a beautiful, uncleaned brown-green patina, and all three hooks are intact. This plate is out of the Lotz House Civil War Museum in Franklin, Tennessee, where it had been on display for several years. The buckle still has the Lotz House accession number on the reverse. **2,850.00**

Dug rectangular sheet brass Confederate belt plate. This is the rare pattern with folded edge. Beautiful, wood brown-green patina with main hook intact on the reverse. **475.00**

Extremely rare, rectangular, pewter C.S.A. waist belt plate manufactured by Noble Bros. of Rome, Georgia. Its brittle nature causes 95% of all excavated examples to be broken in half or into multiple pieces when found. This fine example was totally intact with the exception of one corner that was chipped off and has been expertly replaced. The C.S.A. letters are sharp and crisp and all three iron hooks remain intact. **5,500.00**

Identified to a member of the 7th Tennessee Cavalry.

Middle Tennessee Relics

Rectangular buckle with "C.S.A." on the face. Comes with old original note stating it was worn by Private and later Lt. James Fentress, 7th Tennessee Cavalry, under Gen. Nathan Bedford Forrest. Plate shows wear and use; numerous small nicks to face; one belt prong broken off, another half broken, and one complete. **3,550.00**

The thinner C.S.A. rectangular plates are called "Tennessee-style."

Middle Tennessee Relics

Thinner, Tennessee-style, cast-brass rectangular "C.S.A." waist belt plate recently excavated from General Hood's camp on the Tennessee River near Florence, Alabama. The buckle is perfect with a nice face, body curve, and all three hooks intact. The plate is dug and uncleaned. **2,450.00**

This is a non-excavated example of the Atlanta Arsenal-style. It has a soft-aged patina. **3,850.00**

Very attractive, non-excavated, cast-brass, Atlanta-style, rectangular C.S.A. plate with a rich aged-bronze patina and all three hooks intact. One hook is a little shorter than the others due to an air bubble casting flaw in the end of the hook. The letters are nice and tall, making the "C.S.A." really stand out. **3,250.00**

Stunningly beautiful, cast-brass, early war Tennessee-style, rectangular C.S.A. buckle was dug at General Lydell's Arkansas camps near Bell Buckle, Tennessee. Untouched brown-green wood patina, perfect body curve, and all three hooks intact and straight. **2,850.00**

Highly attractive, non-excavated, cast-brass, Atlanta-style, rectangular C.S.A. The plate has a rich aged-bronze patina and all three hooks intact. One hook is a little shorter than the others due to an air bubble casting flaw in the end of the hook. The letters are nice and tall, making the "C.S.A." really stand out. **2,950.00**

Obvious from the shape, these C.S. plates with round corners are often called "Sardine Can style."

Middle Tennessee Relics

Plate, Belt, Round Corner

Extremely rare, stamped-brass, round-corner, sardine-style C.S. waist belt plate. This plate is very solid with an uncleaned brown-green patina. The plate has several small marks from Civil War-era use. Solder marks are visible on the reverse where the hooks were, but as usual, they were not present when dug. **4,850.00**

Plate, Belt, Round Corner, cont.

Dug, round corner plate.

Middle Tennessee Relics

Very nice, solid cast-brass, Army of Tennessee, round-corner C.S. waist belt plate dug at a C.S. camp near Mobile, Alabama. Very attractive uncleaned brown-green patina and approximately 80% black enamel still visible in the background. All three hooks are intact on the reverse with nice, deep spun downs around each. **3,250.00**

"Bullet-stitch" patterned plates were produced at the Richmond Arsenal.

Middle Tennessee Relics

Plate, Belt, Two Piece, and Belt, extremely rare Richmond Arsenal C.S. tongue-and-wreath on original Confederate waist belt of the very desirable "bullet stitch" pattern. The buckle is an absolute beauty with a rich, deep never-cleaned patina. The belt is sound and reasonably pliable, but does have a couple of very old repairs using brass rivets. **7,500.00**

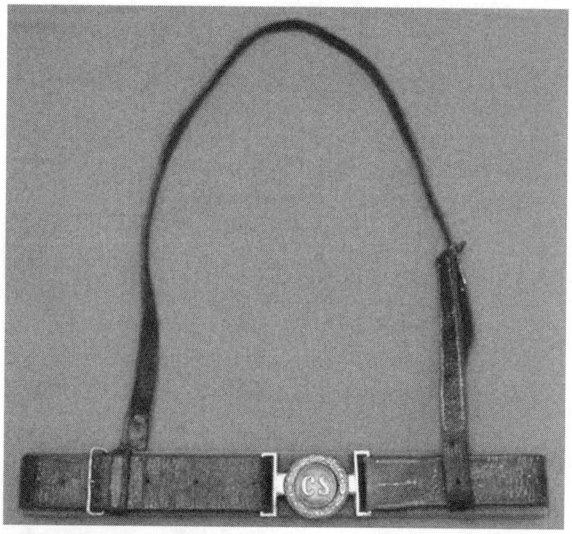

"Richmond-style," two-piece buckle. Sold on its original belt.

Old South Military Relics

Plate, Belt, Two Piece

Because this style of buckle has a strong association with many of Richmond, Virginia's personages and sword manufacturers, it is surmised (and quite reasonably so) by collectors and historians to have been produced in the Capitol of the Confederacy. One will readily see the similarities between this style two-piece buckle and the script "CS." For example, the very finely detailed letters, the beveled bars connecting the buckle to the belt loops, the thin border around the tongue disc and the stepped tongue bar are typical of pieces made with finer detail than common C.S. two-piece buckles. The belt is original to the buckle; all of the stitching on both the tongue and wreath side is tight and original. The belt is strong and supple. It has no repairs or alterations. It still retains its original, slide-on over-the-shoulder belt support. The belt was manufactured for use as a pistol belt, as there is no provision for sword hangers. **14,500.00**

A beautiful, two-piece Confederate belt buckle considered to be made in Richmond, Virginia. This buckle is has a soft, mellow brass patina that has never been cleaned or polished. It is a non-dug example and is in perfect condition. Plate 003 in Mullinex. **3,600.00**

Absolutely beautiful and perfect Richmond Arsenal-style C.S. two-piece officer's sword belt plate. This plate was dug near Brandy Station in the early 1970s. Both pieces were dug together and fit perfectly. The plate has a nice deep chocolate-brown patina and literally could not be prettier. **2,450.00**

This C.S. tongue-and-wreath plate was found in a Richmond, Virginia camp.

Battleground Antiques, Inc.

Excavated two-piece "C.S." tongue and wreath buckle, matching, excellent, mild brown-green patina, fresh from a camp near Richmond, Virginia. **2,250.00**

Wreath of a coin-style C.S. plate.

Middle Tennessee Relics

Flawless condition, wreath portion of a heavy pattern coin-type C.S. two-piece buckle. This wreath was dug from Forrest's and Van Dorn's camps near Spring Hill, Tennessee. It has a smooth, dark brown-green patina. **950.00**

"Richmond-style," two-piece plate.

Old South Military Antiques

Non-dug "Richmond Style" C.S. script two-piece belt buckle. **3,200.00**

Plain face excavated tongue portion of a two-piece tongue and wreath sword belt plate. This buckle was excavated from an 1863 Confederate camp along Duck River near Shelbyville, Tennessee. It is perfect with a smooth, chocolate-brown patina. **175.00**

Extremely unusual and not frequently encountered, rectangular two-piece buckle.

Old South Military Antiques

Rectangular two-piece C.S. sword belt plate. **29,000.00**

This is the exact two-piece C.S. script belt plate photographed and published in *Plates And Buckles of the American Military 1795-1874* by Sydney C. Kerksis. **15,000.00**

Dug near Brandy Station, Virginia, this two-piece buckle emerged intact.

Middle Tennessee Relics

Richmond-style C.S. tongue and wreath, dug in the early years near Brandy Station, Virginia. It was dug together, and was still interlocked. **2,450.00**

Plate, Belt, Two Piece, cont.

Both halves of this two-piece Virginia-style plate were dug near each other.

Middle Tennessee Relics

Two-part Virginia style is noted for the convex curve and straight serif. Beautiful dug example, both halves dug together. 2,700.00

Non-dug, Virginia-style two-piece plate.

Battleground Antiques

Two-piece "C.S." buckle, Army of Northern Virginia pattern. Perfectly matching with excellent patina and original luster......................... 3,250.00

Two-piece buckle, dug near each other, but not interlocked.

Middle Tennessee Relics

Very pretty, dug, two-piece C.S. Richmond Arsenal tongue and wreath sword belt plate. The fit is excellent, and the two pieces were dug in the same area, but were not interlocked. Both halves have a nice uncleaned woods brown-green patina. 2,450.00

When the individual pieces of a two-piece plate are "married" together, the price will be affected.

The Civil War Relicman

Two-part Virginia style is noted for the stepped up back and straight serif. Beautiful dug example, the two halves were found at different sites, but patina and fit is right. This is a much better "marriage" buckle than is typically seen. 1,600.00

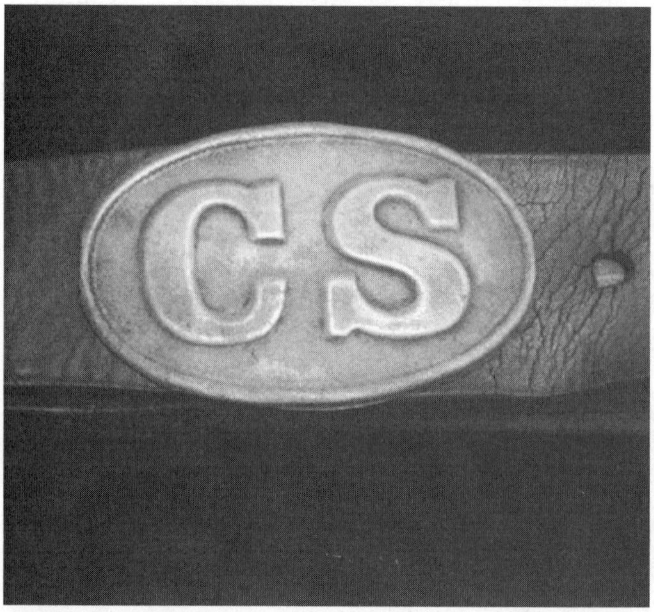

Rope-border plate.

Old South Military Antiques

Belt Plate

"Rope border" C.S. waist belt plate. **7,500.00**

Attributed as a Confederate plate, this plate could just as easily been used by a local militia or civic organization.

Old South Military Antiques

"S S" belt plate. **5,500.00**

Brass or bronze, excellent condition. No damage or repairs. 3-1/4" x 2" when buckled. No maker's mark. **1,875.00**

This Atlanta-style plate was recovered near Marietta, Georgia.

Sharpsburg Arsenal

C.S. belt plate in the "Atlanta Style." Very fine example with one hook half missing, recovered at Marietta, Georgia. **3,300.00**

Die-stamped, 1850-era "star" militia plate. This is a very beautiful and ornate plate that was carried over into the Civil War. Due to its star motif and prewar availability, this plate often is excavated from C.S. campsites, especially Texas and Mississippi. The plate has a perfect face, and the main hook is intact on the reverse. It is, however, missing the belt loop bar. This is a beautiful plate that would look nice in any collection. **450.00**

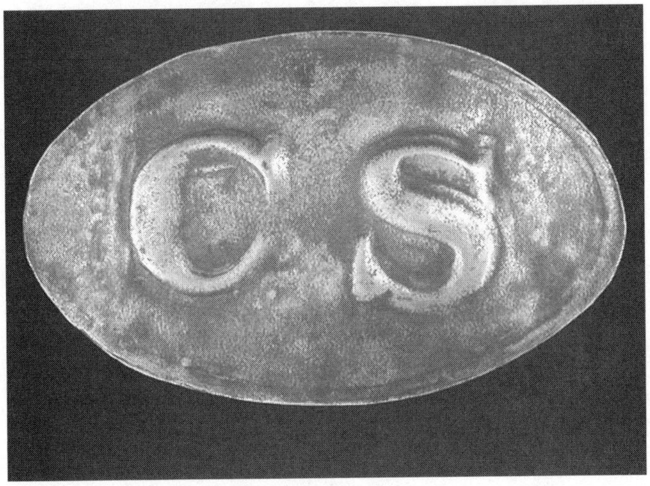

Referred to as an "egg-style" plate.

Old South Military Antiques

Non-dug, C.S. "egg" waist belt plate. **3,800.00**

Confederate, State Issue

This Alabama-issued "AVC" plate is a fine representative of state-issued Confederate plates.

Old South Military Antiques

Plate, Belt, Alabama. Alabama Volunteer Corps waist belt plate. **7,900.00**

Georgia plates are some of the most attractive belt plates worn by Confederate troops. Non-dug examples will command premium prices.

Middle Tennessee Relics

Plate, Belt, Georgia, and Belt

Extremely rare, non-dug, lead-filled Georgia oval state seal waist belt plate on the unquestionably original leather waist belt. The leather belt is 1-1/2" w. The Confederate soldier customized the Georgia oval to the inner circle to make it smaller to better fit the belt. The leather belt is complete, but quite stiff. This belt rig was purchased directly out of a central Georgia estate and has since been on display in a Tennessee museum. **4,850.00**

Some collectors regard the Georgia two-piece officer's plate as being of the finest examples to add to their collections.

Old South Military Antiques

This Georgia officer's sword belt is a southern masterpiece. The heavily gilted belt plate has a die-stamped Georgia state seal affixed onto a stippled background. The belt is also of exceedingly fine quality. It is made of a soft, supple leather, much softer than cowhide. It is given strength by an attractive buff cowhide outer band. The workmanship is the very finest. Large heart-shaped leather panel keeps the Officer's Sword hilt from rubbing against his uniform. This belt and buckle were obviously custom made for a very high-ranking Georgia officer, no weak spots or loose stitching. **19,500.00**

Emerson Gaylord, a northern manufacturer, produced this plate under contract for the State of Georgia in 1860.

Old South Military Antiques

This accoutrement belt buckle was manufactured by Emerson Gaylord under contract to the great state of Georgia. Georgia bought one-thousand of this type belt for issuance to her native soldiers. These were acquired in the fall of 1860, assuring that virtually all saw subsequent Confederate service with the first wave of Georgia patriots who rushed to defend the South. **6,800.00**

Dug Georgia plate.

Sharpsburg Arsenal

Plate, Cartridge Box, Georgia, excavated on the south end of the Antietam Battlefield, near the Potomac River where Lee crossed. **3,100.00**

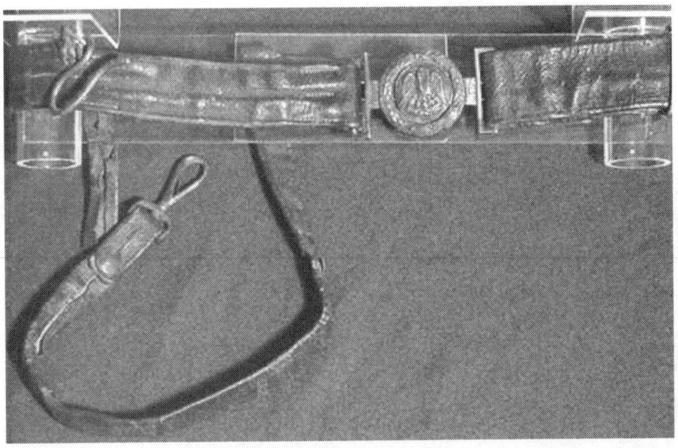

Louisiana two-piece plate still affixed to its original patent leather belt.

Old South Military Antiques

Plate, Belt, Louisiana, and Belt, sword belt consists of a two-piece belt plate and a belt of patent leather over cotton webbing. This alone makes this a very rare and desirable belt. The die-struck disc is mounted upside down and the belt is notched in order to allow the sword hanger to be reversed. The belt is in excellent condition, being strong and supple throughout. The long sword hanger is in excellent condition, but only about four inches of the short hanger remains. **12,500.00**

Non-dug, Maryland plate.

Sharpsburg Arsenal

Plate, Belt, Louisiana, dug, Louisiana state seal buckle that was excavated in Baldwyn, Mississippi. Expertly repaired, the buckle was in three pieces when found. The face has a nice smooth light chocolate patina all over. The hooks are of a scrap brass. **1,990.00**

Plate, Cartridge Box, Louisiana, this incredible, non-excavated Louisiana state cartridge box plate has lead filling in the back. Also, both original iron loops remain. Possibly worn by members of the 5th Louisiana regiment. **1,650.00**

Plate, Belt, Maryland, circa 1860-1865. A beautiful non-dug specimen, over 50% of original gold gilt, belt edge of buckle has a slight bend that does not take away from the buckle at all......................... **4,195.00**

Confederate state-issued cartridge box plates are exceedingly rare. This Maryland plate was manufactured by Emerson Gaylord as part of an 1860 contract.

Battleground Antiques, Inc.

Plate, Cartridge Box, Maryland

Maryland cartridge box plate, non-dug, untouched patina, both hooks! One of the rarest of accoutrement plates, this well-made plate is clearly stamped by the maker, Emerson Gaylord, Chicopee, Massachusetts. Gaylord just about got himself in trouble for selling items to the southern states in 1861 (right up to the time when Lincoln stopped shipments). This plate is circa late 1860-early 1861, and was either shipped south or got intercepted before the final load! Plate came from the noted collection of Richard Steuart (co-author of *Firearms of the Confederacy* with Claude Fuller), who donated a good portion of his extremely advanced Confederate items to Battle Abbey (Virginia Historical Society), in Richmond, Virginia. Plate is also noted with the Gavin reference plate number on reverse................ **5,500.00**

Recovered between Brunswick and Burkittsville, Maryland by local relic hunter. **3,695.00**

Mississippi plate excavated from Fraser's Farm Battlefield.

Sharpsburg Arsenal

Plate, Belt, Mississippi, Oval Mississippi Belt Buckle. This plate was dug in the summer of 1976 at the Fraser's Farm Battlefield. Plate in very-good condition, minor rim repair. **6,500.00**

The 6th North Carolina Troops were the only regiment in the Confederate army known to have belt plates that bore regimental designation.

Sharpsburg Arsenal

Plate, Belt, North Carolina

6th North Carolina Troops, cast-brass buckle with black-enamel background and three brass-soldered belt hooks. Only marked regimental plate worn by Confederates. These were made at a small railway shop in Greensboro, North Carolina, as the 6th Troops prepared to embark for the front. . **4,500.00**

6th North Carolina State Troops waist belt buckle excavated from General Whiting's position on the Gaines Mill Battlefield in the summer of 1977. .... **7,500.00**

Because of the rarity (probably less than 1,000 made), a dug 6th North Carolina plate will sell for nearly as much as a non-excavated example.

Old South Military Antiques

Excavated 6th North Carolina plate. **4,300.00**

Plate, Belt, South Carolina, these plates were originally made for the prewar militia as breastplates. The accoutrement-starved Confederacy needed buckles to support the equipment carried on the belt. A quantity of these plates were taken to a local shop and brass hooks were fashioned from available supplies. The iron wire hooks were clipped and the brass hooks soldered on. Note the distinctive sharp detail of the "Type I" design; plate is missing the long hook. This superb non-dug plate was recovered from a house in Ridgeway, South Carolina that was being demolished. **5,795.00**

Plate, Cartridge Box, South Carolina, this accoutrement plate was worn by South Carolina militia troops prior to the Civil War. However, many were worn by state troops at the war's start. Some of the brass cartridge box shoulder belt plates were converted to waist belt plates due to a shortage of equipment. This lead-filled brass palmetto plate was originally manufactured as a shoulder belt plate and the iron attachment loops were clipped off and the plate was modified with crude-cut brass hooks to convert it to a waist belt plate. This plate shows identical brass conversion hooks on the reverse. The plate's face shows minor surface scratches, but shows no surface wear! The die strike is extremely sharp, and all of the high points remain very sharp and clear. The wartime conversion plate is considered very scarce. **4,250.00**

Produced prior to 1861, Texas troops bound for Confederate service are known to have used this style of belt plate.

Old South Military Antiques

Plate, Belt, Texas, with Belt

This rare Ames-manufactured, two-piece Texas waist belt buckle is on its original belt. The plate is the early die-struck version purchased by Texas prior to 1861. The inside face of the wreath is lathe turned and bears the remnant of inventory number 62. Traces of the original gilt survive in the less exposed areas. Complete and original belt is strong and supple though lots of wear beside the wreath where a holster or accoutrement rode. **6,050.00**

Reportedly, a group of Texas officers purchased these buckles at the time of the Mexican War and then used them later as officers in the Confederacy.

Old South Military Antiques

According to Steve Mullinax, author of *Confederate Belt Buckles and Plates*, these rare rectangular two-piece "Lonestar" waist belts were purchased by a group of Texas officers in the mid-1840s. It was originally intended for use as a dress belt, but has had a contemporary addition of an over the shoulder belt support ring. It was added by means of a course cotton cloth, doubled through a brass ring and sewn back into the belt. The unique inner-adjustment ranger was also extended at this same time in order that its owner could wear it over a coat. These additions, along with the fact that the famed Leech and Rigdon rectangular C.S. two-piece was patterned after it, suggest that this belt was used by the Confederacy. The die-stamped buckle is in mint, new condition, still retaining nearly all of its original lacquer. The patent leather belt is in mint condition as well. **13,800.00**

The oval star plate is often attributed to Texas troops, but was also used by Mississippians as well as several prewar militia units.

Old South Military Antiques

Plate, Belt, Texas, oval star belt buckle. **2,800.00**

James Smith of New York produced these Virginia plates around 1860 for volunteer militia units. Undoubtedly, these early plates found there way into Confederate service.

Old South Military Antiques

Plate, Belt, Virginia, with Belt, manufactured by James Smith & Sons of New York, circa 1860. It was used in conjunction with two web belts that supported a cartridge box and a bayonet. The cross belts were pinned together at the breast and locked into position at the waist with this belt. The plate bears the Virginia coat of arms, a Victorious Virtus wearing the Liberty cap, standing over an uncrowned and defeated Tyranny. The Latin motto, "Sic Semper Tyrannis" or "Thus Ever to Tyrants" arches around "Virtus" or Virtue. . . . **5,900.00**

Plate, Belt, Virginia

Absolutely beautiful, dug, die-struck Virginia State Seal waist belt plate with a smooth brown patina with crisp, sharp detail. Solder marks remain on the reverse where the bar and hook once were. **2,850.00**

The Commonwealth of Virginia purchased these plates from Emerson Gaylord during the late 1850s. Like so many pieces of military goods, these plates were fast pressed into service by Virginians after seceding from the Union.

Old South Military Antiques

From the late 1850s until the fall of Fort Sumter, the Commonwealth of Virginia purchased sword belts from Emerson Gaylord of Chicopee, Massachusetts. Gaylord produced a very high quality plate by first casting and then die stamping to bring out the detail in the Virginia state seal. After casting and die stamping the face, the tongue was brazed on and a keeper was fitted. Both the keeper and the plate were then struck with a matching number. In this case, the number 73. The initials "J W" are carved into the back of the plate, unfortunately this is not enough information to identify its original owner. This particular example shows a lot of wear around the tongue where the keeper rode, indicating long hard service.... **3,850.00**

Has 76 stamped in corner on back, dings on top and bottom edges, light-brown patina, non-dug plate with nice body bend. **3,950.00**

Non-dug Virginia plate.

Old South Military Antiques

Non-excavated Virginia sword belt plate. **3,900.00**

Stamped-brass, rectangular, Virginia waist belt plate with bar and tongue back. This particular plate came from the collection of Norm Flayderman and it still retains his number and identifying card: "Orig Confed Va Buckle, bought from estate of Capt. T. Halan 5th US Vols. In CW from New Bedford Mass. & 3rd Mass Cav'ly & 82nc Col. Inf." **5,700.00**

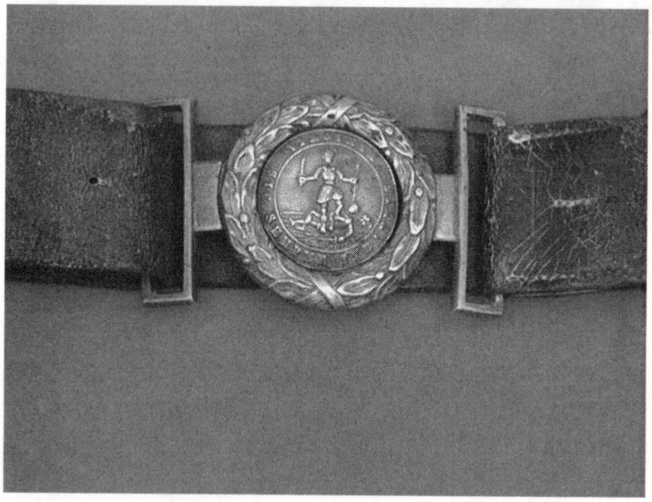

Two-piece Virginia plate.

Old South Military Antiques

Virginia two-piece sword belt plate. **7,500.00**

Stamped brass Virginia belt plate with the familiar seal of Virtue triumphing over Tyranny. The state motto, "Sic Semper Tyrannis" is around the scene. Both belt attachments are off the back. **2,800.00**

Plate, Cartridge Box Sling, Virginia, few southern belt plates can be attributed to a specific maker, and fewer still to a specific unit. This exceedingly rare, die-struck Virginia State Seal Cross belt plate is an exception. By comparing the die-strike with waist belt plates marked James Smith & Sons, New York, it can be identified as a circa 1860 Smith product. There are several images of "Southern Guards" wearing this distinctive cross and waist belt configuration. These cross belt plates are exceedingly rare, and there are no known links to any other unit. Other Virginia units did, however, use the James Smith & Sons' waist belt. **14,500.00**

U.S., General Issue

Buckle, Belt, M1855 Rifleman, an attractive, non-dug example of the interlocking solid brass Rifleman's buckle complete with the two cast-brass keepers that flank the buckle on the belt for use with the knapsack hooks.................................**395.00**

Buckle, Belt, Navy, not much to look at, but quite a scarce plate from the Civil War. A japanned iron-friction buckle (2.5" x 2") with 2" of belt still attached including the floating tin friction plate, a little surface rust. This is the enlisted buckle worn on the buff leather USN belts. **65.00**

Plate, Belt, Navy, and Belt, beautiful, two-piece, cast-brass U.S. Navy belt buckle and original brown leather belt. Buckle measures 1-15/16" by 3-1/4" and retains traces of gilting. The leather belt measures 15/8" by 35". The leather is soft and pliable, but does have a tear and the finish is chaffing some. **405.00**

Plate, Belt, Pattern of 1832, and Belt

Rare belt of the period in very near-mint condition. The leather is very supple and very clean, maker cartouche, "R. Dingee/New York," although very light. In 1832, Dingee contracted with the U.S. government for 3,000 belt plates and artillery belts. These were used through the Civil War. The frog fits the artillery short sword. **1,795.00**

White buff leather accoutrement belt with brass supporting rings inserted to hold the buff leather scabbard frog for a M1832 Ames Foot Artillery Sword. Beautiful cast "US" spoon and wreath-style buckle. Belt is complete with both buff keepers and brass hook adjuster, top-notch condition with only some very slight frog staining. **1,500.00**

Because the original buff belt is still white, this set probably saw service prior to the Civil War and would be appropriate in a Mexican War display.

Drumbeat Civil War Memorabilia

Plate, Belt, Pattern of 1839, and Belt

Beautiful, white buff early belt with leather standing loop, small U.S. brass buckle with single arrow hook on back. Belt and buckle unmarked but definitely original. **800.00**

Fine example of the earliest plate made, oval studs on back instead of arrowhead hooks, and a wide, tapered, and serpentine silvered tongue, instead of a flat sheet brass one. Face has even light patina, shows use, but not dented and very sharp. It is on an original well-used Civil War leather belt. All finish flaked and torn a bit at the keeper end. The reverse has original, faded stenciled unit information: "Co. G. (s?) REGT. G.R. 39," a rare plate these days. **395.00**

Excellent example with this small US buckle having a fantastic undisturbed light age patina, and very, very appealing die design to the US letters, single prong and single arrow hook on the back. It is still on its original black harness belt (1.5" wide) in overall very good condition showing just honest age and use. This had once had the standing leather loop adjuster at the end which is now gone leaving just the stitching outline. Stamped into the body of the belt is, "?? MASS," like the markings seen on Mass. muskets. Written in ancient brown ink inside the belt is, "R.J. Maconkey Harvard Drill Club." **525.00**

Plate, Belt, Pattern of 1839

An excellent non-dug specimen belt buckle, face has crisp U.S. strike and back has full solder fill with the single arrow and prong, fine, light age patina. **325.00**

An excellent, non-dug specimen of this highly desirable belt buckle. The face has a crisp U.S. strike and the back has full solder fill with the single arrow and prong, fine, light age patina. A really fine buckle correct for display with Mexican War or Civil War plates. **325.00**

Beautiful condition excavated 1839 small, oval U.S. waist belt plate. Rare pattern with hooks made of iron and barely enough lead to hold them in place. An early find, and the face couldn't be nicer. There are rusty remnants of what once were the iron hooks on the reverse.. . . . . **275.00**

Nice condition non-dug small U.S. oval waist belt plate with full lead and both hooks intact. **295.00**

This excellent, non-dug specimen has a crisp U.S. strike and the back is lead filled with the single arrow and prong, fine light age patina. **345.00**

Plate, Cartridge Box, Pattern of 1839

Excellent condition, non-excavated, small-size, oval U.S. cartridge box plate with an attractive aged patina. The reverse has full lead and both loops perfectly intact. **295.00**

Mint and original, small size, oval lead-filled box plate with, "WH Smith Brooklyn," stamped in lead on reverse.. . . . . **300.00**

In addition to the belt plates, there were Pattern of 1839 small oval plates for attaching to the flaps of cartridge boxes. The two iron loops in the lead-filled back indicate that this plate is a box plate, rather than a belt plate.

Drumbeat Civil War Memorabilia

Plate, Cartridge Box, Pattern of 1839, cont.

Non-excavated, lead-filled, small oval U.S. cartridge box plate. Plate is beautifully marked, "Boyd & Sons, Boston." Wire loops were clipped off years ago for display on a relic board. **295.00**

Dug, circular, lead-filled Union eagle breastplate excavated at Stones River. Very nice complete face, chocolate-brown patina, full, smooth lead with rust stubs of the two iron loops. **95.00**

Dug, small-size circular "Burnside" breastplate with excellent face, crisp detail, and a smooth chocolate patina, full lead in the reverse, but the two iron loops are rusted away. **195.00**

Excellent condition, non-excavated, circular Union eagle breastplate with a very attractive aged patina, reverse has full lead and both wire loops intact. **195.00**

Nice condition, circular Union eagle breastplate dug April 4, 2001, at Cold Harbor. The reverse has full lead and is marked, "Boyd and Sons-Boston." One and one-half of the two loops remain intact on the reverse. . . **195.00**

Non-dug eagle plate for use on the cartridge box shoulder strap. **195.00**

Rare triple-marked excavated circular eagle breastplate that has a beautiful smooth, chocolate-brown face, smooth lead, and is marked, "T.J. Shepard-U.S.-W.H. Wilkinson Springfield, Mass." This beautiful plate was dug 34 years ago. **275.00**

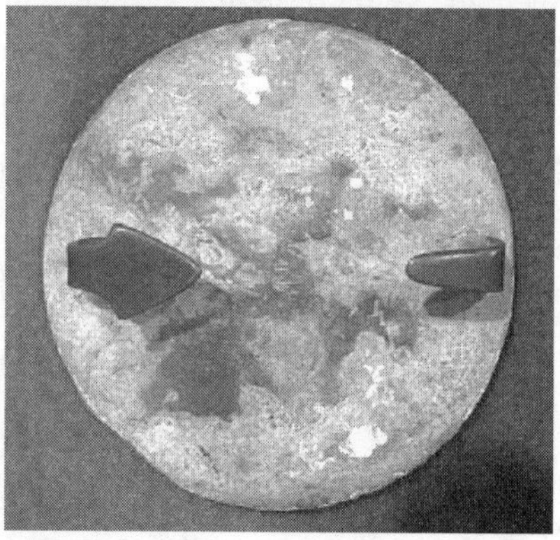

Almost identical to the Pattern of 1839 sling plates, a smaller diameter plate is referred to as the "Burnside-style" sling plate. These smaller plates will generally sell for a bit more than a normal-sized sling plate.

Drumbeat Civil War Memorabilia

Three-prong eagle plate with lead filled back for use with the N.C.O. and musician's sword belts, fine detail and great, light-age patina. **345.00**

Very nice condition, dug, back marked Union eagle breastplate. Plate has an excellent face, full lead, and is marked "H. Dingee." Portions of the back mark are clear, and other portions are somewhat faint. One and one half of the original wire loops remain intact on the reverse.. . . . . **195.00**

Early battlefield pick-up circular Union eagle breastplate, face has a deep, rich, aged patina, and the reverse has full smooth lead and both wire loops intact. This one is nice enough to put back on a sling. **175.00**

Burnside-style eagle belt buckle for circular cartridge box shoulder strap. Plate has field conversion making it into a belt buckle with standard attachment hooks. This dug plate has a wonderful chocolate patina, undamaged face with excellent detail. **400.00**

Exactly the same stamping as the cartridge box sling, this plate has arrow hooks on the back for adjusting on a belt. This style of plate was used in conjunction with the N.C.O. sword sling.

Drumbeat Civil War Memorabilia

Plate, N.C.O. Sling, Pattern of 1839

The rare Eagle plate with arrow hooks on the back, like a belt buckle, lead filled, for the over shoulder N.C.O. sword sling. Mint example has a nice, light age patina, rare version with the arrow hooks on the back. **395.00**

Exceptionally nice condition, dug, three-wire hook, circular Union N.C.O. eagle plate. This plate has sharp detail and a smooth chocolate patina, lead is full and smooth, and all three hooks are intact on the reverse. **295.00**

Scarce and desirable plate, lead-filled back with three prongs for use with the N.C.O. and musician's shoulder support belt for their swords, fine detail and great, light age patina. **345.00**

Plate, Belt, Pattern of 1841, and Belt

Regulation U.S. oval buckle w/arrow hooks (very pretty) on original waist belt with original brass adjuster, very solid and supple, with much finish loss, a very solid example. **295.00**

Issued U.S. buckle on the original harness leather waist belt, complete with the original brass adjuster, slightly shrunken leather near the keeper. . . . **295.00**

A scarce piece of Civil War equipment, very early black harness leather waist belt with the standing leather loop adjuster (keeper). A large U.S. oval buckle with the round "puppy paw" studs (not the later oval studs), attaches in a left to right fashion from the wearer's perspective. This buckle is likely an early product of Boyd & Sons of Boston as the die style of the "U.S." is identical to theirs though this plate is not marked. Condition is very good with a small expert repair on the belt where the buckle attaches. **395.00**

The 1841 regulations called for an oval plate slightly larger than prescribed in the 1839 regulations. These larger U.S. oval plates are referred to as "Pattern of 1841" plates. This example with a bit of its original belt was recovered from the Antietam battlefield.

Drumbeat Civil War Memorabilia

A wonderful U.S. buckle on its original leather belt recovered from the area of Burnside's 9th Corps at Antietam. The buckle has a dark chocolate patina. The belt is soft and pliable but delicate, measuring about 22" l. **495.00**

Absolutely mint new condition, shows just the slightest storage age only. **495.00**

An issued U.S. buckle on the original waist belt. The belt is solid with good finish, just showing honest age and lacking brass adjuster. A good honest example that was really in the Civil War. **325.00**

Complete with the brass adjuster and shows just the right amount of age and wear, very solid and appealing. **395.00**

Mint, unissued surplus U.S. buckles on surplus buff leather waist belt, perfect condition except for the missing brass adjuster. **325.00**

Near-perfect, black buff leather belt with handsome, golden brass "US" belt plate, 1863-style arrow hooks on plate, belt retains brass keeper for excess, unissued. **595.00**

Regulation Union issue oval buckle with arrow hooks and buff leather belt with brass adjuster. Absolutely mint condition never having been put together. Just the way shipped from factory, with the belt holes (for arrow hooks) never touched. **595.00**

The belt is solid with good finish, just showing honest age and lacking brass adjuster. **325.00**

This is a very fine, unissued example of this belt. The black leather has faded to brown (as is often the case with these buff leather belts). The buckle is mint with 100% of the gold gilt, belt has some minor age scuffs. Overall condition is very fine. **600.00**

Attached to a saber belt, this oval Pattern of 1841 plate is right at home with a pistol cartridge pouch and cap box.

Sharpsburg Arsenal

Plate, Belt, Pattern of 1841, and Saber Belt, 1851 dragoon saber belt with black buff leather complete with 1851 pattern buckle, applied nickel-silver wreath. Pistol cartridge pouch and percussion cap pouch included. Leather is very pliable, but has flaking on finish, which is normal for a used cavalry belt rig. **1,195.00**

Plate, Belt, Pattern of 1841

All three puppy paw hooks intact, non-dug. **295.00**

The two studs on the back of a belt plate are referred to as being "puppy paw styled." This style of back is thought to be of earlier production than the arrow back plates.

Beautiful, dug, Smith Contract, oval U.S. belt plate with puppy paw studs. Great patina on this plate with no bends or dents and most all of the lead back is intact, "W.H. Smith, B." Smith was a contractor for the U.S. Government during the Civil War. This belt plate was dug in Tennessee around the Fort Donelson area about 15 years ago. **285.00**

Early-war-style U.S. oval plate with lead-filled back and two oval "puppy paw" studs and prong, very fine. **285.00**

Early-war-style U.S. oval with lead-filled back and two oval "puppy paw " studs and prong as used early in the war. Very fine, showing just honest age. . . **255.00**

Large-size, arrow-hook, U.S. oval waist belt plate excavated from the Union battle lines at Stones River. The buckle has a dark-green patina with full lead and all three hooks intact on reverse. **185.00**

Mint, original U.S. oval Civil War buckle with rich gilt and still with its original tissue paper wrapper. **275.00**

Regulation oval buckle with some letters die stamped into it (owners initials?), nice and solid showing use and age. **135.00**

Regulation oval U.S. buckle with arrow hooks in excellent condition. This one bears maker's stamp of *"S Peters"* in the lead back. **245.00**

Stamped brass with U.S. on the front, lead-filled back with arrow-shaped hooks, the prong broken. Dark patina on brass with many small dings, good condition. **200.00**

Standard Union issue U.S. oval buckle with arrow hook back, excellent condition. **225.00**

Standard U.S. belt plate with lead-filled back. Very nice used condition with dings on the front brass and also on the back. This piece is complete with the tongue and arrowhead hooks. No maker's name present. **145.00**

The standard Union-issue U.S. oval buckle with arrow hook back, excellent condition just showing honest age and patina. **225.00**

U.S., oval, arrow-hook, dug out of an old roadbed used by Rosecran's Army of the Cumberland on their way to Chickamauga. Plate is complete with full lead and all three hooks. It must have been run over by every wagon and every cannon in Rosecran's army to get mashed this flat. **125.00**

Plate, Cartridge Box, Pattern of 1841

Identical to the U.S. oval belt buckles but having two iron wire loops on the back for securing to the flap of the cartridge box, fine, non-dug condition. . . **225.00**

Regulation-size, U.S., oval plate with high-quality plate, gilt finish, a few minor scratches. Under "US" is stamped small "MS." Back in excellent condition. **695.00**

Absolutely beautiful, large-size lead-filled U.S. oval cartridge box plate dug in the 1960s, smooth face, full lead, and both loops intact. **175.00**

Beautiful excavated, backmarked, large, oval U.S. cartridge box plate. This plate was dug at Resaca, Georgia, January 27, 1960, perfect smooth brown face, full lead, both loops, and a super crisp, "W. H. Smith Brooklyn," backmark. **195.00**

Beautiful, non-excavated, large-size, U.S. oval cartridge box plate, face is perfect, reverse has full lead and both wire loops intact. **195.00**

Choice, dug, large, oval, U.S. cartridge box plate. This is an early find from Stones River, perfect face, full, smooth lead, and both loops intact. **175.00**

Excavated from the area of the Battle Of the Wilderness, Virginia. Dark-brown face, complete with both hooks and full lead with only a couple of flakes missing, carved letter "K" on back. **265.00**

Fine, non-dug, U.S. plate for front of cartridge box with two iron-wire loops on the reverse. **175.00**

Freshly dug, large-size, U.S. oval lead-filled cartridge box plate with a pleasing green patina, full lead and both loops intact on reverse. **150.00**

Near-perfect, excavated, U.S. oval cartridge box plate with rich-brown patina, full lead, and both wire loops intact, very slight bend. **129.00**

Nice dug, large-size, lead-filled, U.S. oval cartridge box plate that has an attractive face, full lead, one iron loop intact, and is backmarked, "Boyd & Sons-Boston." **150.00**

Plate was found in a fire pit, but the location is lost now. The face exhibits a very nice dark patina with dings and dents. The lead in the back is mostly all there having melted to one side. Both hooks are present and in very good, strong condition. **110.00**

Non-excavated, large-size, lead-filled, U.S. oval cartridge box plate that has a rich, aged patina. The reverse has full lead, both loops, and is backmarked, "Boyd & Sons-Boston." The loops are 2-1/2" apart. **250.00**

Plate, Pattern of 1851, and Belt

A perfect Civil War eagle buckle with silver wreath. This one shows how the plates continue in service for years after the war, as it resides on a white patent leather waist belt that was probably worn by a New York militia soldier just after the war. **395.00**

Superb Civil War eagle buckle with silver wreath, black harness leather belt that is probably a little later than Civil War. **395.00**

A perfect Civil War eagle buckle with silver wreath. Shows how the plates continued in service for years after the war as it resides on a white patent leather waist belt that was probably worn by a New York militia soldier just after the war. **395.00**

Superb Civil War eagle buckle with silver wreath, black harness leather belt that is probably a little later than Civil War. **395.00**

This piece is most intriguing, possessing a most ingenious repair. The buckle is an officer's pattern M1851 rectangular eagle sword belt plate with cast-brass wreath surrounding the eagle. During its period of service the loop at the buckle's end was damaged and removed. In its place was carefully fitted (and soldered) a replacement loop that was carefully manufactured in copper or bronze. It was fitted so that the buckle appears to not have a repair when viewed from the front. This ingenious plate is attached to a much earlier waist belt (possibly 1830s or 1840s period) by means of two large, crude, copper rivets. It also has the proper brass keeper also riveted to the female belt end. The leather belt itself is made of very soft (almost doe skin) brown leather with a hand-stitched leather edge border that runs the belt's full length. **295.00**

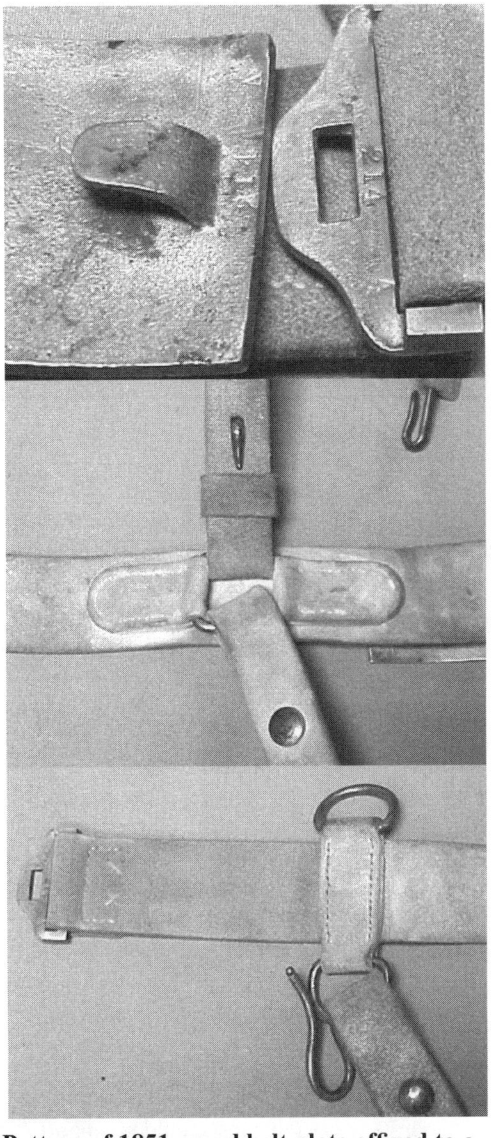

Pattern of 1851 sword belt plate affixed to a white buff belt.

Sharpsburg Arsenal

Plate, Pattern of 1851, and Belt

Beautiful, cast-brass Union eagle sword belt plate with a portion of antique leather waist belt. The plate has a rich uncleaned patina with applied silver wreaths. This is the officer's grade plate where the rays go all the way around the plate, mark of "32" on reverse. **425.00**

Classic Civil War N.C.O. or cavalry rectangular eagle buckle with applied German silver wreath in excellent condition and with great appeal. Resides on a slightly postwar (1872 era) leather waist belt. **375.00**

Officer's applied silver, wreath-style eagle belt plate that is 3-1/2" x 2-1/4" with a small 1/2" tongue on the back stamped with the number "463." The 32" long, folded-over-type belt (actually 7" of belt on the back side so the belt could be at least 4" longer if desired) has an attached sword hook and strap with brass snap hook (originally there was probably also a sliding additional sword strap).The applied silver wreath is perfect (no lifted up or chipped parts like many have) and the belt plate has a wonderful rich patina. The leather belt is good, strong, and supple with just very minor crazing. **349.00**

Perfect, non-dug, specimen possessing good color, great die detail, proper narrow tongue, and perfect one-piece silver wreath on the face. This one was found in New York and comes with 25" of original belt including the brass keeper, which matches and fits the buckle perfectly. **345.00**

Officer's pattern buckle, rectangular, eagle sword belt plate with an integrally cast-brass wreath surrounding the eagle. During its period of service, the "loop" at the buckle's end was damaged and removed. In its place was carefully fitted (soldered) a replacement loop that is manufactured in copper or bronze but fitted so that the buckle appears to not have a repair when viewed from the front. This ingenious plate is attached to a much earlier waist belt (possibly 1830s or 1840s period) by means of two large crude copper rivets. It also has the proper brass keeper also riveted to the female end of the belt. The leather belt itself is made of very soft (almost doe skin) brown leather with a hand-stitched, leather-edge border, which runs the full belt length. . **350.00**

White buff leather belt in excellent condition with over the shoulder strap and sword hangers. Buckle retains 70% original gold gilt. Buckle and keeper have matching benchmark numbers. **2,500.00**

Plate, Pattern of 1851, and Saber Belt

Classic Civil War-issue, buff-leather cavalry belt with silver-wreath eagle buckle and matching keeper, both saber hanger straps, the shoulder support strap, all leather adjusters (keepers) and overall in near mint condition. There is a professional (undetectable) repair 4" in from the keeper. **1,100.00**

Near-mint, black, buff-leather Model 1851 saber belt complete in all respects including the scarce over-the-shoulder support strap. Fine pliable buff leather, rectangular, brass-eagle buckle with applied silver wreath (number on buckle matches on keeper), both saber straps and all the leather adjusters. Marked, *"J. DAVY & CO.,"* on the inside of the leather near the triangular brass hook that secures the belt around the buckle loop. Made in 1864 with two copper rivets in addition to the three rows of stitching holding the brass keeper in place. **1,595.00**

Early war buff leather artillery saber belt (made without provision for shoulder support strap) in very good condition, has three-piece silver-wreath eagle buckle with matched number to the keeper (very pretty). Has both saber straps with all four loop adjusters, just lacks the loop adjuster on the belt portion. Early pattern, the brass keeper is secured to the belt with stitching only (no rivets). **795.00**

Sword belt rig with matching numbered (#280) eagle belt and keeper. Both straps present, though one is broken near the bottom edge, very little original finish to leather, but solid. **1,250.00**

A complete sword belt with hangers and plate can be a standout piece in a Civil War belt plate or cavalry display.

Drumbeat Civil War Memorabilia

Buff belt complete with matching mint buckle and keeper, perfect sword hangers, and the over-the-shoulder strap, maker marked. **2,150.00**

Very nice, rectangular eagle officer's-quality buckle residing on remnants of a buff leather enlisted saber belt (no straps). Buckle is really nice. **325.00**

Plate, Belt, Pattern of 1851, and Sword Belt

Black "folded & sewn" construction, has both saber hanger straps intact (small repair on one) that are affixed to sliding loop keepers. Buckle is pretty eagle with mid-war, medium-wide tongue. **795.00**

Fine horsehide belt with flat brass hook and leather keeper, applied sword hangers with the "S"- shaped rising hook. Superb, rectangular eagle plate, beautifully cast and chiseled with applied silver wreath around the eagle. **850.00**

This high-grade officer's sword belt sold with its hangers and Pattern of 1851 plate.

This high-grade, Civil War officer belt with buckle and original hardware. Complete rig has leather belt with high-grade stitching and M1851-style officer buckle with female hook, original sword hanger hooks and straps. Complete with the heart-shaped leather hip protector. Leather belt a little stiff and has separated in one spot. Leather sword hanger strap starting to separate, but is still completely intact. **405.00**

Model 1851 black, leather, private-purchase sword belt made in the folded construction style. Solid case, eagle belt plate retains shield-shaped, leather coat guard and brass hardware, including both scabbard ring snap hooks. Leather is dry with some crazing to finish, but still supple enough for display. Shoulder sling is broken with some leather lost, saber straps intact, but with one partial tear. **435.00**

Original U.S. sword belt plate on original belt with one hanger. The overall condition is excellent, great patina. The plate is numbered "958" and the keeper is numbered "911." **650.00**

This sword belt still retained its hangers in addition to the Pattern of 1851 plate.

Sharpsburg Arsenal

The buckle measures 3-1/4" x 2". The belt is approximately 33", leather belt has usual wear for this time period, has the sword hangers intact, very good condition. **283.00**

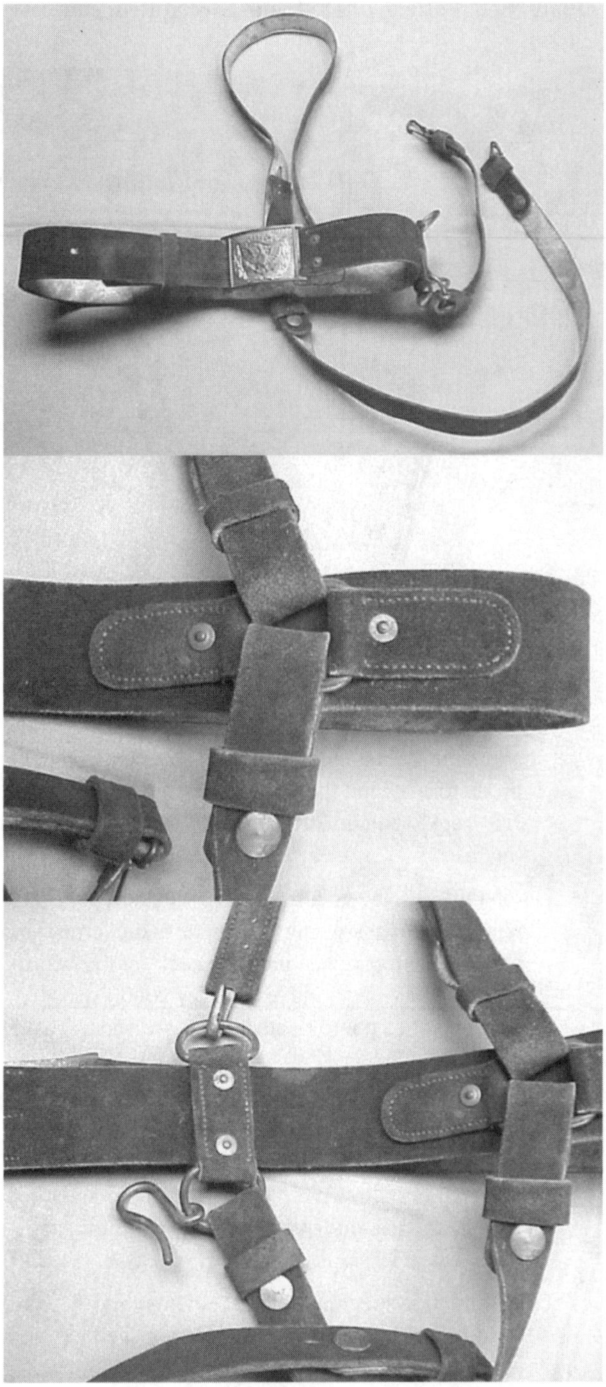

This complete and maker-marked sword belt was part of an 1863 contract filled by Joseph Davy & Company of Newark, New Jersey for 60,000 sets of cavalry accouterments.

Sharpsburg Arsenal

This excellent condition, buff leather sword belt was manufactured by, "Joseph Davy & Co., Newark, NJ." On Sept. 11 and 12, 1863, Davy received four contracts for a total of 60,000 sets of cavalry accoutrements. This features a M1851 Sword belt plate w/applied wreath. Rig is complete with over-the-shoulder straps, absolutely mint condition. **2,500.00**

Plate, Belt, Pattern of 1851, and Sword Belt, cont.

The belt plate and buckle hook have matching "39" stamps on this officer's sword belt.

This is a wonderful Civil War officer's sword belt and buckle. The belt is 1-5/8" wide and has the original adjustment ring and hook and leather uniform protectors behind the hook and behind the buckle. The buckle and hook both have the number "39" on them................................ 325.00

Union Officer's sword belt with 1851 Pattern plate still retains its scabbard rings.The plate is die-struck solid brass with no part silvered. The neck for the sword scabbard has a tear, the rest is very good. Also included are a pair of leather strips for spurs. . .175.00

Plate, Belt, Pattern of 1851

A fine, attractive, rectangular officer's-grade eagle buckle with fine detail to the face and solid wreath integrally cast into the plate. Shows light age, pretty patina, and has mid-war, medium-width tongue. 279.00

Fine, attractive specimen of the rectangular officer's-grade eagle buckle with fine detail to the face, and solid wreath integrally cast into the plate. Shows light age, pretty patina, and has mid-war, medium-width tongue. 295.00

Perfect example of the enlisted saber belt plate also used by N.C.O.s with one-piece silver wreath and narrow tongue. 345.00

Buckle is marked deeply on the back, "Evans and Hassel." Outstanding in all respects. 350.00

Cast brass with applied German silver one-piece wreath, standard-issue buckle, shows use. 245.00

Eagle belt plate recovered from a fire pit at Stafford Court House, Virginia. The wreath is missing, but the plate is still nice for a dug piece and is hallmarked "806." 175.00

Excavated, this Pattern of 1851 plate still retains 100% of its silver wreath.

Middle Tennessee Relics

Excellent condition, non-excavated, cast-brass, pattern of 1851, Union eagle sword belt plate with a nice, uncleaned patina. The applied silver wreath is 100% intact, it is marked on the reverse, "832." ... 375.00

Excellent condition, non-excavated, cast-brass, Union eagle sword belt plate with three-piece applied silver wreath. The benchmark on the reverse is "645." The width of the plate is 2", and the length is 3-3/8". 395.00

Pattern of 1851 plate with only traces left of the applied wreath.

Middle Tennessee Relics

Excellent, dug, cast-brass Union eagle sword belt plate from Stones River, crisp detail, nice body curve, and a smooth chocolate-brown patina. Traces of where applied wreaths once were............... 225.00

Nice, dug plate, part of wreath missing, narrow tongue on the back and is benchmarked "121." 195.00

Officer's-quality, rectangular eagle buckle with early war narrow tongue, good gilt mixed w/aged patina. 275.00

Officer's-quality with detail, 95% original gilt, mid-war, medium-width tongue on back............ 325.00

Perfect, non-dug specimen, super color, great die detail, proper narrow tongue, and perfect one-piece silver wreath on the face. **325.00**

Perfect, non-dug specimen buckle used by cavalry, artillery, and N.C.O.s. Super color, great die detail, proper narrow tongue, and perfect, one-piece silver wreath on the face. **345.00**

Regulation brass rectangle, with integral wreath and medium-size tongue, patina shows use. **245.00**

Regulation eagle plate with early-war narrow tongue, made thinner than most, being a cast plate hit with a die & counter die to make a super-crisp strike, and leaving a faint reverse impression in the back. Eagle is fierce and color is exquisite. **350.00**

Standard rectangular eagle buckle with silver wreath, slight damage to the wreath, some light cleaning on the plate. **245.00**

This one is the earlier pattern with tips of silver wreath extending above the eagle's wings. **345.00**

Regulation eagle plate with early-war narrow tongue, made thinner than buckles usually encountered, cast plate hit with a die and counter die to make a super-crisp strike, leaving a faint reverse impression in the back. **350.00**

U.S., State Issue

Plate, Belt, New York, and Sword Belt, identified to George Vail, Union Continentals. The belt has two suspension straps with scabbard hooks and a rectangular cast-brass *N.Y.* buckle with wreath and old English letters *N.Y.* Belt has a small area of scuffing, condition is still fine. **300.00**

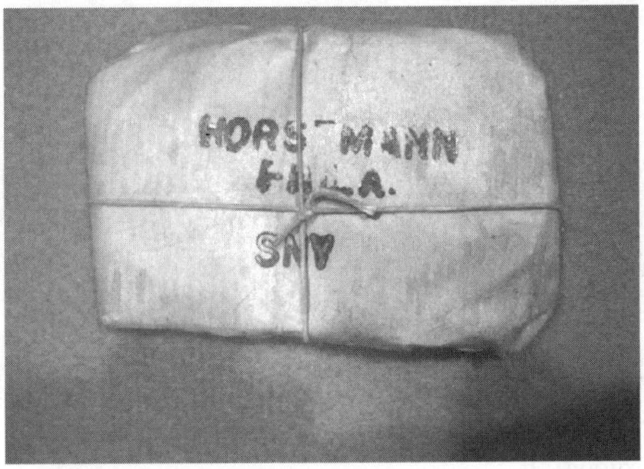

State of New York plate, "still wrapped in its original brown paper."

Drumbeat Civil War Memorabilia

Plate, Belt, New York

"Horstmann Phila.," paper-wrapped SNY buckle. Wrapped in brown paper with original string and marked, "Horstmann, Phila. SNY," this original buckle is fascinating, appears completely original. **750.00**

1851 Pattern, sword belt plate in fine, non-dug condition with pleasant light patina, has wreath encircling "NY" cast as the face design. **550.00**

State of New York plate still attached to a buff enlisted man's belt (originally white and then dyed brown).

Drumbeat Civil War Memorabilia

Extremely mint, buff-leather enlisted man's belt, originally white (inside), dyed brown for Civil War use, brass adjusting loop, with an SNY double arrow buckle. The rear catch hook is broken off, although still present. **650.00**

Good condition with minimal wear, lead back, measures 1-1/2" x 2-3/4". **303.00**

New York plate designed as a sword belt plate.

The Civil War Relicman

Non-dug, New York sword belt plate, solid brass casting, cast tongue, benchmarks on back and keeper bar, beautiful plate, no problems. **750.00**

State of New York shoulder belt plate made for the City Guard, a volunteer militia unit from the late 1850s.

Sharpsburg Arsenal

NY Militia shoulder belt plate of the City Guard, ca. 1855-1865. Gilt-rolled brass plate displaying a die-struck, white metal motif secured by three wire loops through plate. Attachment pin is there. In addition to the 9th Regiment (10th prior to 1859), N.Y.S.M., this style may have been worn by Brooklyn's 23rd Regiment (City Guard Reserve), which was formed from portions of the 9th and 10th in 1859, and reorganized in 1862. .... 475.00

Regulation State of New York large-sized waist belt plate with letters "SNY" on the face. Full solder-filled back with two arrow hooks and single prong. A great specimen that has been polished, giving it a very pretty shine. 495.00

Made for use in the Civil War, this plate is part of a surplus stock that was never issued. Rather, it was sold to Mexico in 1866. The ship carrying these plates sunk before unloading the goods. In recent years, several SNY plates have been recovered from the wreck site.

The Civil War Relicman

Stamped brass, solder filled with the early wire hooks. These buckles were manufactured well before the Civil War, were stored in a warehouse in New York, but, due to a classic case of bureaucratic bungling, were forgotten and missed the fighting entirely. Discovered during 1866, they were sold as surplus stock, and loaded on an old merchant steamer enroute to Mexico. The ship sank off the coast of South Carolina in a storm. The wreck was scattered over a large distance, in international water, and many of these plates have been discovered along with muskets, cannons, and other military items. Most of the plates, so discovered, have been in very poor condition as the salt-water environment is extremely harsh on any small metal objects buried on the ocean floor. The brass skin and iron hooks are entirely missing leaving the solder filling fully intact and clearly bearing the motif, "SNY." This one is in relatively good condition. 200.00

State of New York large-size waist belt plate, letters "SNY" on the face. Full, lead-filled back with two arrow hooks and single prong. This great specimen possesses a rich patina and just the right amount of wear. 495.00

This plate has a lighter patina and a small crimp at the left plate edge. Fine with stud hooks and prong. 495.00

Dug SNY plate with puppy-paw studs from northern Virginia.

Dug, SNY buckle that came out of northern Virginia. The face is in good condition, the rim is rough in spots, the back has all the hooks and they are puppy paw in style, the lead around the rim is rough, the back is in good condition. 250.00

Puppy-paw SNY plate recovered in a New York camp near the Antietam Battlefield. All hooks intact. 495.00

Because of their rarity, Ohio Volunteer Militia (OVM) plates can be the centerpiece of a Civil War collection. This plate was dug in West Virginia.

Sharpsburg Arsenal

Plate, Belt, Ohio Volunteer Militia, plate was found in 1990 at Camp Jones in Southern Raleigh County, Huffs Knob, West Virginia, hooks are missing, beautiful brown patina. **1,895.00**

Plate, Belt, Ohio

Very scarce Ohio Volunteer Militia buckle being the medium-size variety. This was disposed of a few years back by a museum in the Midwest with verbal history that it was dug at Antietam. Edges are chipped, and hooks intentionally removed when displayed decades ago, but a good solid buckle with much appeal. **595.00**

Oval "OVM" plate with a .44-caliber-sized "half-moon" taken out of the top edge. Fine smooth brown patina overall, retains both back hooks. This plate was found in the 1960s by a local Virginia relic hunter on the Cedar Mountain Battlefield near Culpepper, Virginia. **2,250.00**

Plate, Cartridge Box Sling, Ohio

An excellent, excavated Ohio breastplate, found in an Ohio camp in Franklin, Tennessee. This plate has a pleasing chocolate patina with a clear face and both loops attached and present on the reverse. . **2,150.00**

Considered by many to be the rarest and most beautiful of all Federal plates, this Ohio state seal breastplate is a non-excavated example in absolutely gorgeous condition. The face has nice patina and super detail. The reverse has full lead and both brass loops perfectly intact. **3,850.00**

Round Ohio state seal plate in near-perfect condition. Front is a deep, chocolate-brown patina, lead-filled back retains both wire loops for attaching to sling. This plate was found in the late 1960s at Tabler's Mill (Martinsburg), West Virginia. This is the place to where Stonewall Jackson's Corps withdrew after the battle of Sharpsburg in 1862. This plate, along with an Ohio Belt Plate and Box Plate, was found in a depression along with 35 other sets of "Yankee" accoutrement plates. **3,000.00**

Volunteer Militia of Maine (VMM) plates are relatively rare.

The Civil War Relicman

Plate, Cartridge Box, U.S, Volunteer Militia of Maine, constructed of stamped brass, solder filling is missing as expected for this plate, pattern of plate is distinguished by shoddy workmanship. Hooks missing, outstanding example is still dirt covered. **700.00**

Plate, Cartridge Box, New Jersey, lead-filled, oval brass plate with large "NJ," has two iron loops on the back to attach to the box flap. This is the early model, 2-3/4" diameter that actually pre-dates the Civil War, nice heavy patina. **185.00**

Miscellaneous

Buckle, Belt, Snake

English manufacture, sometimes referred to as a "duck's head buckle." Nice patina. Excavated in Winchester, Virginia. **367.50**

Excavated brass frame buckle with split "snake tongue" keeper, dug and cleaned many years ago. . . . **600.00**

Snake buckle with adjuster manufactured in England for use by both the Union and Confederacy, complete. **475.00**

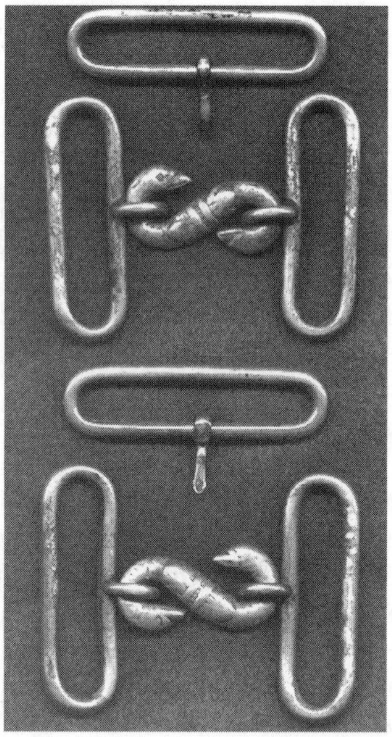

Some dealers will want to represent snake buckles as Confederate pieces. Unless there is strong provenance associated with a particular example, a collector should recognize that these plates were worn by soldiers of both sides during the war, as well as soldiers of the United Kingdom.

Sharpsburg Arsenal

Plate, Belt, Clipped Corner, stamped brass, excavated at Winchester, Virginia. Missing bar and tongue on back, dark black-brown patina. **325.00**

Plate, Belt, Militia, oval, looks like a small U.S. buckle but has a plain face, two hooks, dug near Gettysburg, very good condition. **275.00**

Plate, Belt, Militia, and Belt, 1850-era, two-piece militia buckle on a C.S.-style brown leather belt. Belt and buckle are from a southern estate. **1,250.00**

Plate, Belt, ca. 1840, this is a dug, 1840 vintage-stamped brass buckle with early-style spread-winged eagle on the face surrounded by a decorative frame pattern around the eagle, rich deep ground patina. **385.00**

Produced in the 1850s, it is easy to believe the possibility of this plate and belt being worn during the Civil War.

Middle Tennessee Relics

Plate, Belt, U.S.

Two-piece interlocking eagle with magnificent patina, and a sturdy, solid, cast buckle, rich, full patina. . . .**395.00**

Two-piece interlocking U.S. for the artillery short sword belt of the Mexican War era and used early into the Civil War, non-dug example with great detail and patina. **395.00**

Plate, Belt, ca. 1840 Rectangular and Belt, really an outstanding example, being a stamped brass rectangular buckle with spread-winged eagle in center (small star shield top on his breast), and this eagle surrounded by a scalloped rectangular panel outside of which forms an edge border on the plate which incorporates a vine and 12 stars. Buckle has a drop-bar on the back and narrow tongue. It is still attached to its original black-tarred leather waist belt with the original iron wire keeper. This is the type of buckle worn by militiamen during the period of the Mexican War. **550.00**

Plate, Belt, Militia, adopted in the 1840s and universally worn by militia of all states from the Mexican War and well into the Civil War. Heavy, sheet-brass stamping with fine detail. Belt loop and narrow sheet brass tongue soldered on back. Features spread eagle within a border enclosing 13 stars, brass tarnished dark, otherwise fine.........**295.00**

Plate and Buckle Terminology

Belt plate: Intended for wear on a leather belt, and generally has a decorative face.

Cartridge box plate: Similar to belt plates, cartridge box plates are decorative and generally have loops for fastening to a cartridge box flap. Though decorative, a cartridge box plate provided weight that kept the box flap closed.

Cartridge box sling plate: Intended to be worn on the shoulder sling of the cartridge box strap. Its function was strictly decorative.

Frame buckle: This is simply a utilitarian buckle that was not intended to have any decorative value. Often associated with Confederate accoutrements, these buckles come in a wide variety of styles.

Keeper: A brass fitting that accepted the belt plate's hook.

Puppy paw: Consisting of two studs, this is a style of attachment found on some U.S. belt plates.

Saber belt: An enlisted man's grade leather belt fitted with straps for attaching a saber and often, also fitted with a shoulder strap.

Sword belt: An officer's grade belt fitted with straps for carrying a sword. Often, there will be provisions for a shoulder strap.

Tongue: On a two-piece buckle, the "tongue" is the male half.

Also see: Accoutrements, Groupings.

Chapter 5

Bullets, Cartridges, and Projectiles

When one considers the sheer volume of lead and iron that was fired during the Civil War, it is not surprising that an extensive variety of projectiles existed. A single armory, or even a system of armories, simply could not provide all of the bullets, balls, shells, and projectiles required by the armies. Therefore, governments on both sides turned to any source they could find to fulfill the demand. In many cases, the companies that supplied contracted weapons also were required to supply the ammunition, thereby, increasing the chain from the Ordnance officer placing the order and the manufacturer producing the product. It is no wonder that standardization was not achieved.

All of this is good news for collectors of bullets, cartridges, and projectiles. Entering this field of Civil War collecting is not going to be mastered with a few key purchases. Rather, there are several extensive studies that have been published identifying thousands of varieties. Further attempts have been made to classify projectiles into "Union," "Confederate," "Western Theater," "contracted," "carved," "imported," "dropped," "fired," or many other categories. The derivatives are so vast, a collector can focus on .58-caliber rounds, carbine bullets, Confederate-used, or any one of several other paths that this field offers.

Cartridges are an extremely interesting area of collecting. The Civil War was the last time the United States issued paper-wrapped cartridges to its infantry soldiers. Intended to be bitten off at the end and rammed into the musket, the survival of paper cartridges was small. Most that are available to collectors were leftovers found in cartridges boxes. The same is true for the paper or linen combustible cartridges used in many revolvers and carbines.

On the other hand, metallic-cased rounds have survived in decent quantity to make it possible for novice collectors to easily assemble extensive collections. Dealers will often have both dug and non-dug examples for sale.

Another area of projectile collecting enters a larger scale. Collecting artillery rounds offers some unique challenges. First, and foremost, a collector has to bear in mind that most artillery projectiles (besides solid shot and rifled bolts) were intended to explode. Before lifting one out of a freshly dug hole, a collector should pause to consider why the round he just uncovered did not explode. The second question he should ask is, "will it explode when I handle it?" Disarming artillery rounds is best left to experts. If, however, you decide to collect artillery rounds, you might be best served by buying rounds from reputable dealers that are already disarmed.

The other consideration when collecting artillery rounds is the weight. If you choose to specialize in 32 lb. projectiles, don't count on friends to help you move your collection when the time comes!

Collecting projectiles, whether dug bullets or artillery rounds, unfired cartridges, or original, unissued packages can be a hobby all in itself. But, if you are more generalized in your Civil War collecting focus, these items are great compliments to a display of weapons, artillery implements, or accoutrements.

Collecting Hints

Pros:

- Collecting bullets or projectiles allows a collector to become peripherally involved in the study of Civil War weaponry for a fraction of the cost of collecting firearms. Consider, for example, a bullet for a .56-caliber Colt Revolving Rifle will sell for about $7.50, a complete cartridge for around $125, an unopened package of cartridges for $600, and the actual rifle for $2,750. It becomes apparent that, for the novice at least, bullets and cartridges are a much more affordable way of becoming engaged with the Colt Revolving Rifle.
- There are a lot of excavated bullets and projectiles available for collectors and new ones are being unearthed every year. The supply will certainly keep up with the demand for many years.
- Both bullets and artillery rounds are relatively stable and do not require a lot of room for storage making it easy for a collector with limited area for storage and display to enjoy the collection.
- Projectiles and cartridges are wonderful adjunct items to display with accouterments, weapons, or artillery items. The projectiles help put the rest of the items into context for the viewer.
- Excellent references are available in several facets of this area. Standardized numbering has been established within the hobby enabling collectors to effectively sort and categorize their projectiles.

Availability ★★★★
Price ★
Reproduction Alert ★

Collecting Hints, cont.

Cons:

- Many cartridges and artillery rounds are live! That is, they can explode. Know what you're acquiring before you take it home. If you are out digging, bear in mind that the artillery round you are unearthing could explode. Exercise extreme caution. Only allow experts to disarm a projectile. There isn't much of a learning curve that allows for mistakes.
- You need to decide a purely ethical question before you begin: Should battlefields be mined for the relics they retain? Some consider a battlefield a sacred area and digging at such a site is considered to be a desecration of it. On the other hand, plenty of relics are dug at non-battle sites, such as camp and bivouac sites.
- Displayed on their own, outside of the context of the associated weapons, projectiles are not the most impressive items. It might be difficult to convey your enthusiasm for a tray of bullets to a viewer that is not intimate with the various idiosyncrasies that so enthrall an expert.

Individual Cartridges

.28 Plant Revolver, in brass casing, non-dug, used in Plant Revolver, .28 caliber. **18.00**

.30 Teat Fire, brass cartridge is cylindrical, open at one end exposing the bullet, which is seated down inside the cartridge, rear is rounded with teat protruding. **29.00**

.31 Volcanic Self-Contained

.31 caliber, very-fine condition, brass base. **95.00**

.31 caliber, brass base, very fine condition. **95.00**

Brass base, fine condition. **95.00**

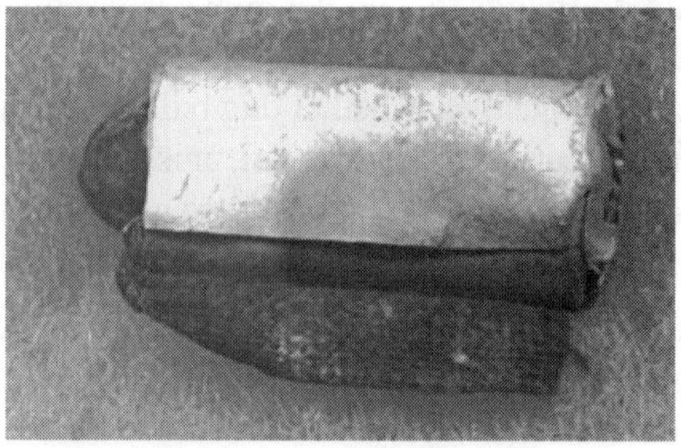

Made for use in Moore's Pat Firearms Company's Front Loading Revolver, these .32-caliber teat-fire cartridges were specially designed by Daniel Moore and David Williamson. They date to circa 1864-1870.

Battleground Antiques

Made for use in the First Model Maynard Carbine, the .35-caliber cartridge has been called the "top hat" style because of its distinctive shape. Since Mississippi, Florida, South Carolina, and Louisiana are known to have purchased significant numbers of the .35 First Model Carbine right before the outbreak of the war, these cartridges are often considered as "Confederate."

Middle Tennessee Relics

.32 Moore's Revolver, original cartridge for Moore's Teat-fire revolver, .32 caliber. **35.00**

.32 National Revolver

Teat-fire cartridge in brass casing, very fine. **18.00**

.32 caliber, round teat, in brass casing, VF. **18.00**

.32 Smith & Wesson Revolver, .32 long (1857-1860), dish-based, non-dug, in brass casing, very fine condition. **35.00**

.35 Maynard Carbine

Excellent condition and quite rare, .35, non-excavated Maynard sporting carbine cartridge. **65.00**

.35-caliber "top hat" cartridge with conical lead projectile. Most of the .35-caliber First Model Maynard Carbines "went South," so this has a good chance of being a Confederate cartridge. Excellent condition in a glass-fronted Riker case. **95.00**

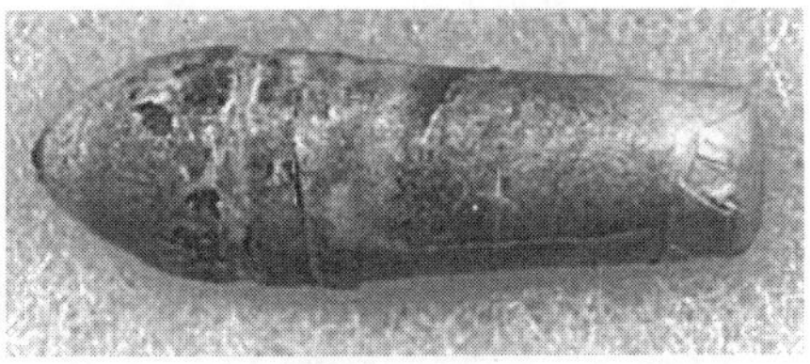

This .36-caliber cartridge was made by Colt using combustible paper. This allowed the loader to place the entire round in a chamber and seat it without having to measure and pour powder.

Sharpsburg Arsenal

.36 Colt Pocket Revolver

Manufactured by Colt with combustible paper. . . . **110.00**

This combustible cartridge for a .36-caliber revolver was made with Ely Hays, English Patent Paper.

Sharpsburg Arsenal

Manufactured by Eley Hays, English Patent Paper sleeve with orange label. **95.00**

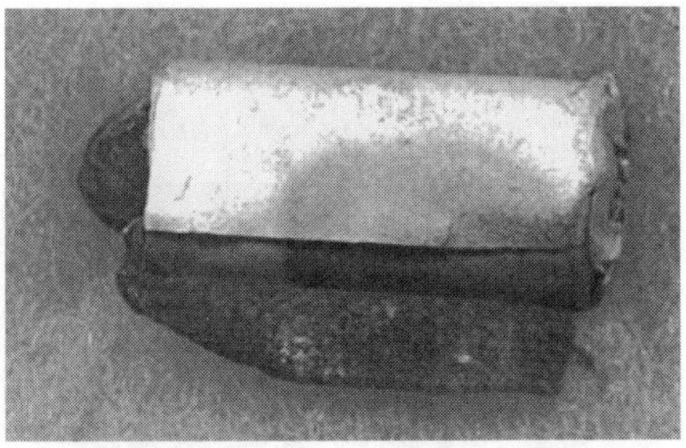

Though this .36-caliber round was marketed directly to Colt owners, it could have been used in any .36-caliber cap-and-ball revolver. This cartridge was made with orange Ely Hays, English Patent Paper.

Sharpsburg Arsenal

Manufactured by Eley Hays, English Patent Paper sleeve with orange label. **85.00**

.36 Revolver, paper-wrapped cartridge of revolver size, entirely closed in by paper wrapping. One end has tiny "Ely London" label, other end has a cloth pull-strip. **15.00**

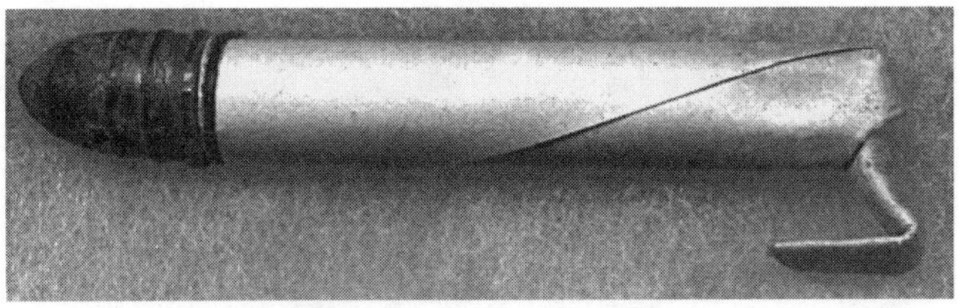

Made specifically for the .36-caliber Sharps Model 1851 Sporting Carbine, these cartridges are as rare as the weapons.

Sharpsburg Arsenal

.36 Sharps Carbine, Model 1851 Sporting Rifle. . . **275.00**

.41, identity of this cartridge is unknown. It is made something like a Smith carbine cartridge but is a .41-caliber conical bullet. This has a pasteboard cylindrical powder container attached with a small hole in the back end, about perfect condition. **65.00**

.42 Plant Revolver, brass casing, non-dug, very fine condition, used in .42 Plant Revolver. **25.00**

.44 Colt Revolver, a perfect "skin" cartridge being a .44-caliber conical bullet with nitrated paper powder bag still attached and full. **65.00**

.44 Henry Rifle

"H" on bottom, non-dug, very fine condition. **26.00**

Coppery brass cartridge with snow white, flat-nosed lead projectile, excellent condition, in a glass-fronted Riker mount. **35.00**

Excellent, non-dug cartridge with heavy patina, embossed "H" head stamp. **35.00**

.44 Revolver, formed conical bullet with shaped propellant covered with nitrated paper, fine condition. **125.00**

.45 Whitworth Rifle

Cardboard casing, .45/85-caliber. **325.00**

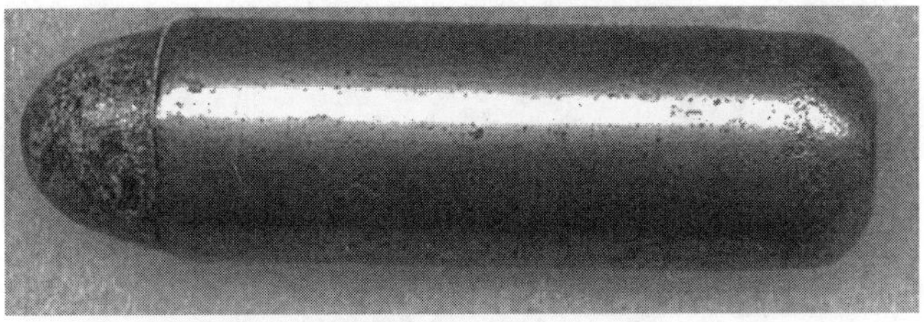

A hole in the back of this .50-caliber Gallager cartridge permitted the spark to travel through the brass casing to ignite the charge.

Sharpsburg Arsenal

.50 Gallager Carbine

Drawn brass. **165.00**

.50 caliber, in paper and foil, manufactured by Poultney, nice condition. **48.00**

Fine condition, unusual cartridge, not the standard brass foil and paper wrap, in Riker mount. **110.00**

In paper and foil casing by Poultney, nice condition. **48.00**

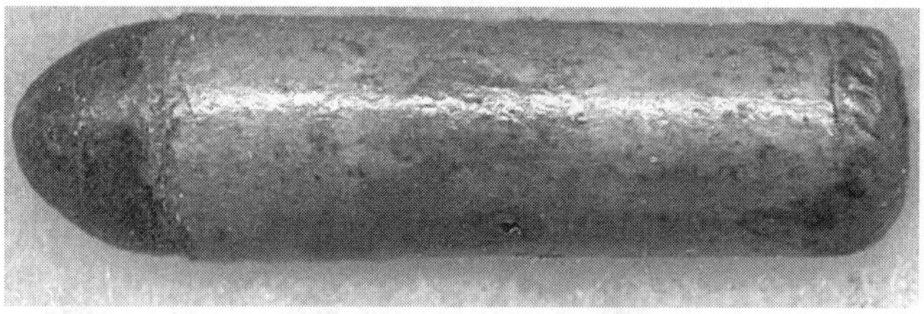

Following Jackson's Patent, this .50-caliber Gallager cartridge is made of combustible materials, rather than housed in a brass casing.

Sharpsburg Arsenal

Jackson Pat. #45,830. .... **350.00**
Perfect non-dug cartridge for use with the Gallager breech-loading carbine. **59.00**
Poultney's Pat. #40,988.. .... **85.00**

.50 Maynard Carbine

Brass casing, non-dug, .50 caliber, very-fine condition, ... **25.00**
Brass casing, non-dug, very fine condition. **25.00**
Made by Poultney. Paper and foil, .50 caliber, fine condition. **55.00**
Perfect condition, non-excavated, .50 Maynard carbine cartridge. **45.00**

.50 Smith Carbine

A single complete cartridge, excellent with light handling age. **95.00**
Cartridge in rubber casing, .50 caliber, very-good condition. **145.00**
Fine condition in paper and foil casing. **85.00**
Perfect, complete, non-dug, with the paper covering the metallic foil cartridge. **105.00**
Cardboard casing, made by Moore for Smith Carbine, fine condition, .50 caliber. **95.00**

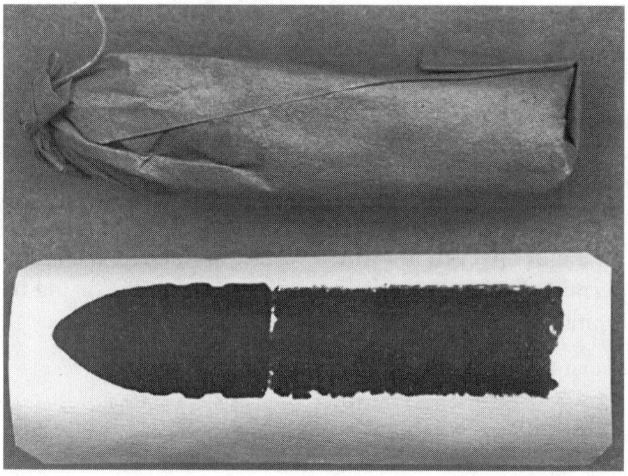

X-ray proved that a Confederate-style, .52-caliber Sharps bullet was inside this tied salmon paper cartridge.

Sharpsburg Arsenal

.52 Sharps Carbine, salmon paper, X-ray shows Confederate Sharps-style bullet. **250.00**

Most cartridges for the Sharps carbines and rifles were made of combustible paper or chemically treated linen as these three. More than 16 million cartridges for Sharps weapons were delivered during the war.

Sharpsburg Arsenal

.52 Sharps

Nice condition, complete .52 linen cartridge for the Sharps carbine or rifle. **125.00**
A perfect example of the .52 caliber Sharps linen cartridge as issued with the rifles and carbines. **135.00**

.52 Spencer

Non-excavated .56/.52 round, head stamped "S.A.W.," excellent shape. **29.50**
Excavated cartridge (whole, unbroken). **35.00**
Fine, non-dug, rimfire Spencer cartridge with copper case and lead bullet. **16.00**
Nice excavated Spencer cartridge is complete and the bullet has a whitening patina. **20.00**
The earlier pattern with two rings exposed on the lead bullet. **29.00**

.54 Ball

.54 caliber, used in Harpers Ferry rifles, cavalry pistols, and various other rifles. In paper casing, very-fine condition. **95.00**

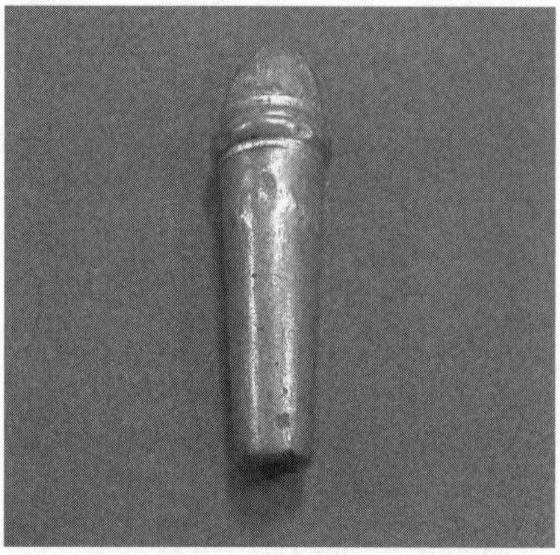

Up until a few years ago, it seemed that the odd-shaped cartridge for the Burnside Carbine was in abundant supply. The cartridges are becoming increasingly harder to find.

Middle Tennessee Relics

.54 Burnside Carbine

Excellent condition, non-excavated, .54 Burnside carbine cartridge, very-good condition. **75.00**

A complete brass cartridge and bullet for the Burnside carbine. Once common, now quite hard to find. .. **65.00**

.54-caliber Burnside carbine cartridges.

Sharpsburg Arsenal

Excellent condition. **75.00**

In brass casing, dug in Louisiana, good condition, .54 caliber. **35.00**

In brass casing, non-dug, very-fine condition, .54 caliber, deep cavity base. **55.00**

Reportedly, the United States purchased 21 million cartridges for the Burnside's Carbine. It is no wonder that there seemed to be an endless supply. Nevertheless, that supply is dwindling.

Drumbeat Civil War Memorabilia

Mint, unfired Burnside carbine cartridge with a lovely mellow tone to brass. Approximately 55,567 Burnside carbines were purchased by U.S. during the Civil War, along with 21,000,000 cartridges. **60.00**

.54 Enfield, Macon, Georgia Enfield Cartridge in paper casing, green bottom, fine condition, .54-caliber. **195.00**

.54 Hall Rifle, .54-caliber round ball along with a folded paper cartridge, ball is loose and just sits on top of the cartridge. **135.00**

.54 Hunt & Jennings Self-Propelled, .54-caliber, also known as the "Rocket Ball," very-fine condition. **145.00**

.54 Merrill Carbine, .54-caliber, in paper casing, fine condition. **85.00**

.54 Model 1841 Rifle

Three-ringed bullet in paper casing, fine condition. **95.00**

Pinkish-brown, paper-tied, .54-caliber Minié ball, excellent condition, in glass-fronted Riker mount. **145.00**

Three-ring bullet made for the Model 1841 "Mississippi" rifle in paper casing, non-dug, fine condition. **95.00**

.54 Model 1842 Pistol, mint condition. **135.00**

.54 Starr Carbine

.54 caliber, linen casing, very-good condition. ... **85.00**

A perfect complete cartridge for the Starr breech-loading carbine, bullet with nitrated linen powder bag. **135.00**

Very good condition, linen casing. **85.00**

This brass-cased .56-caliber round was for use in the 25-barrel Requa Battery built in 1861 by the Billinghurst Company.

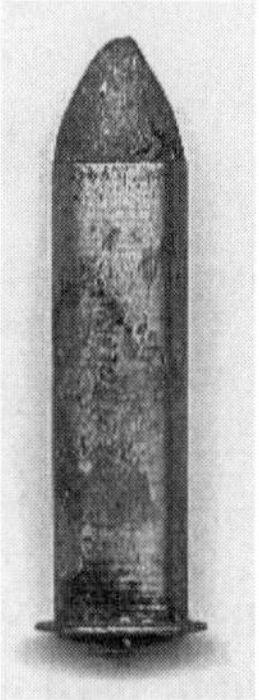

.56 Billinghurst & Requa Battery

In brass casing, non-dug, fine condition. **96.00**

In brass casing, non-dug, very-fine condition. .. **115.00**

.577 Rifled Musket

.577 caliber, fine condition, in paper casing, non-dug. **115.00**

.577 caliber, in paper casing, fine condition, marked "Eley Bro's-London." **175.00**

Perfect paper-tubed .577 Enfield rifle musket cartridges, came out of an 1860-dated packet of 10. .... **140.00**

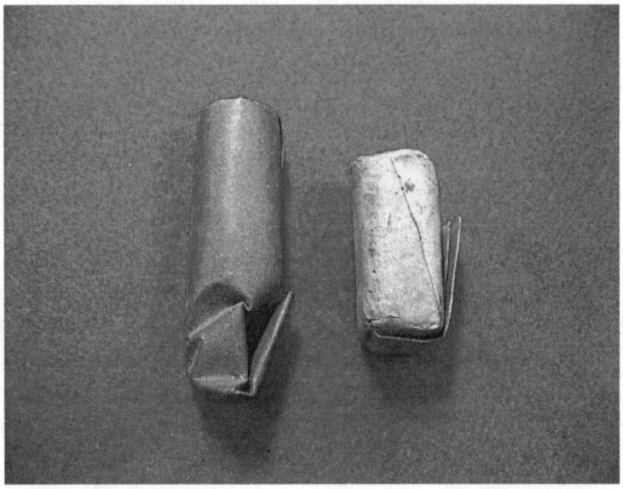

Original blanks should more closely resemble the shape and form of the full cartridge that they replace.

Middle Tennessee Relics

.58 Musket Blank, .58 Union blank cartridges used for training purposes, especially in training cavalry horses to become accustomed to the sound of gunfire, brown paper wrap. **45.00**

.58 Rifled Musket

An original paper wrapped .58-caliber musket cartridge just as was issued, excellent condition. **125.00**

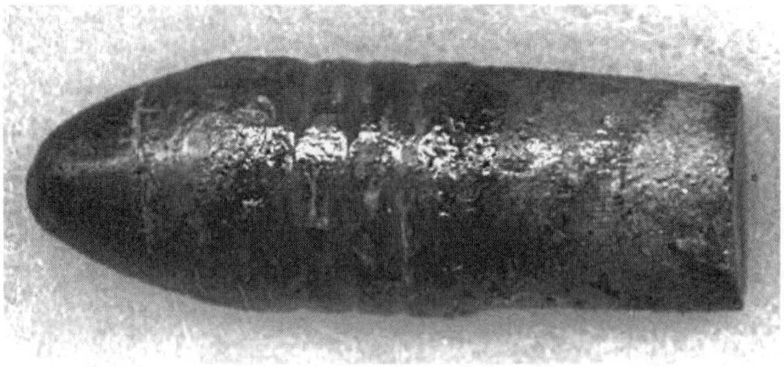

Bartholow's patent provided for a combustible cartridge to be used with the .58-caliber rifled musket. This innovation allowed for a soldier to combine the whole process of tearing a cartridge, pouring the powder, and placing the bullet in the muzzle into one step. The rounds are extremely delicate and their survival rate is small.

Sharpsburg Arsenal

Bartholow's Pattern #36,066 (repaired). **450.00**

Dug Johnston & Dow combustible .58 cartridge. The combustible envelope is still present on this bullet—sort of petrified and varnished. **49.00**

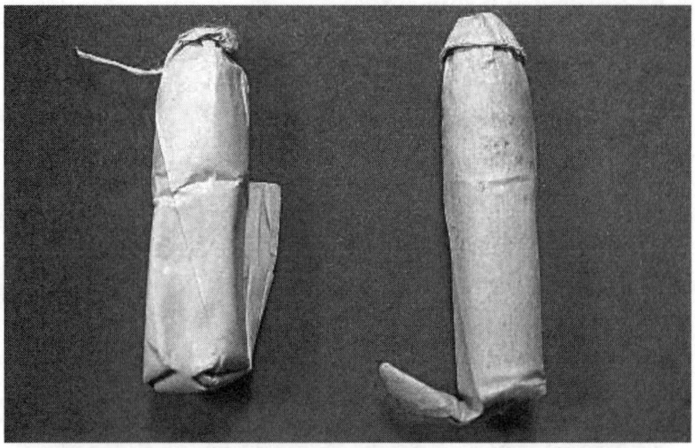

The most common cartridge of the war was the paper-wrapped .58-caliber Minié bullet. Issued in bundles of ten, a soldier would tear the end off with his teeth, pour the powder down the bore, and manually insert the bullet before ramming it home with his ramrod.

Middle Tennessee Relics

Excellent condition, authentic .58 Minié ball complete in original brown paper wrap. **95.00**

Has a tiny crack in part of the paper wrapper, still sound. **100.00**

In paper casing, fine condition, non-dug. **95.00**

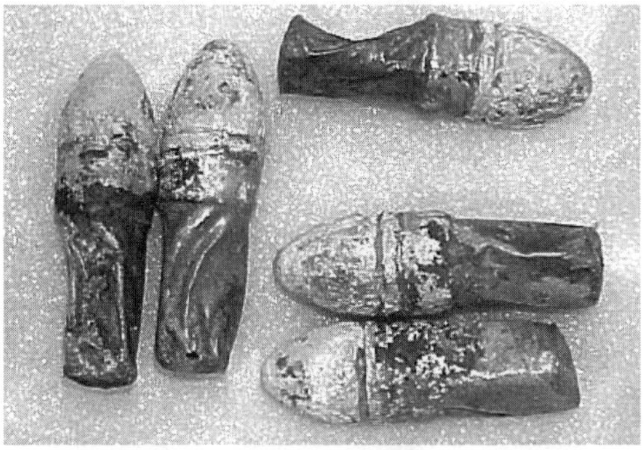

All that remain of these .58-caliber combustible cartridges are the bullets and the skins.

Sharpsburg Arsenal

Just the .58 bullet and the skins remain. **65.00**

Removed from an original package of ten rounds, absolutely perfect .58-caliber paper cartridge complete in all respects. **89.00**

Tied paper .58 Minié projectile, comes with dissertation from the fellow who found the original damaged pack of Confederate cartridges, excellent condition in a glass-fronted Riker case. **165.00**

Tied paper cartridge with the standard .58 Minié ball projectile, from a torn 10-pack of musket cartridges with the St. Louis Arsenal label. Slightly dirty, otherwise in fine condition, with Riker mount. . .**85.00**

.58 Sharps Shotgun. Linen casing, very-good condition. **90.00**

.60 Sharps Shotgun. .60 caliber, linen casing, very-good condition. **90.00**

.69 Ball, Musket

Found in a Confederate cartridge box and appears to be homemade. Heavy course paper is all there and has been emptied of all powder. **385.00**

.69 caliber, very fine condition. **105.00**

The standard Civil War cartridge as issued to all troops equipped with the .69-caliber musket. **65.00**

Beige paper and .69-caliber round ball tied with red and white string around the top and ball, excellent condition. **125.00**

Long cartridge, very-good condition. **125.00**

Very fine condition. **105.00**

.69 Buck and Ball, Musket

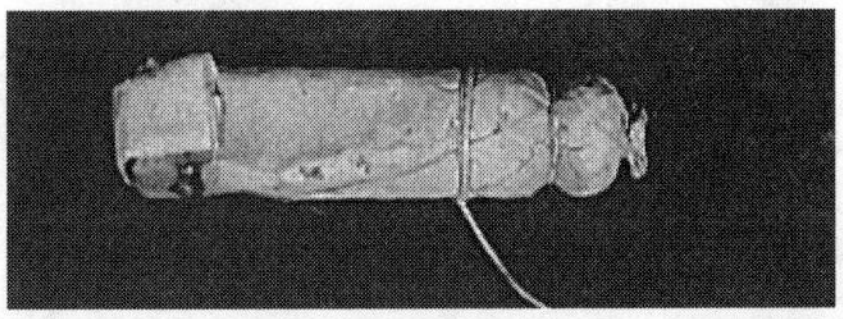

The .69-caliber "buck and ball" round, consisting of a one-ounce lead ball and three smaller buckshot, was the main cartridge used by the U.S. Military through the 1840s. It also was a staple of early Civil War issues to both Union and Confederate troops.

This is an original cartridge, in great overall condition, has one small repair. **101.00**

One large .69-caliber ball with three small buckshot tied on top, slight paper missing exposing shoulders of the buckshot, otherwise excellent, in Riker display. **150.00**

Perfect early-war cartridge that came inside a cartridge box. **185.00**

7 mm Pinfire, non-dug, in brass casing, very-fine condition. **14.00**

9 mm Pinfire

Excellent condition, non-excavated, Civil War-era 9 mm French pinfire cartridge, nice clear "FUSNOT" French base marking. **15.00**

Brass casing, non-dug, very-fine condition. **16.00**

Non-dug in brass casing, very-fine condition. **16.00**

Non-excavated, head stamped "BB 9," excellent condition. **27.50**

Marked "Fusnot" on the base, this pinfire cartridge was for use in a 9mm weapon, most likely the LeFaucheux Navy. The U.S. Government purchased a total of 12,374 of the pinfire revolvers.

Middle Tennessee Relics

12 mm Pinfire

Brass casing, as used in the LeFaucheaux Revolver, very-fine condition. **19.00**

Copper cartridge for use in such revolvers as the LeFaucheux, this has a short casing, excellent, and complete. **22.00**

The 12mm pinfire round was used in the larger LeFaucheux Army revolver, a weapon that the U.S. government purchased to the sum of 12,374.

Middle Tennessee Relics

Excellent condition, non-excavated, 12 mm-long pattern French pinfire cartridge, has a crisp "Paris" base mark. **15.00**

Has the longer casing. **22.00**

In brass casing, very fine. **19.00**

Large 12 mm (roughly .43 cal) copper cartridge for use in such revolvers as the LeFaucheux. This has a short casing, excellent and complete. **22.00**

Cartridge Packages

.31 Colt Pocket Revolver, Package, near perfect condition, label reads, "6 Combustible Envelope/ Cartridges/Made of Hazards Powder/-Expressly for/ Col. Colt's Patent Revolving/Pocket Pistol/Address/ Colt's Cartridge Works/Hartford Conn/USA America." **275.00**

.35 Maynard Carbine, Package, .35 caliber ammo (10 rounds), which is proper for display with the Confederate-used 1st Model Maynard carbines, still tied with the original string, couple of minor tears in wrapper. **575.00**

.36 Colt Pocket Revolver, Package, great unopened package (drilled wood with fine paper label) reading, "6 Combustible Envelope Cartridges/Col Colts Patent Revolving POCKET PISTOL/Colt's Cartridge Works Hartford," perfect unopened package. 285.00

.36 Colt Police Revolver, Package, paper cracked on top, otherwise in fine condition. Label reads, "5 Combustible Envelope/Cartridges/Made of Hazards Powder/ Expressly for/Col. Colt's Patent/New Model/Revolving/ Police Pistol/.36/100 Inch Caliber/Address Col Colts Works/Hartford Conn/US America." 295.00

.36 Colt Revolver, Package, a mint unopened package of six .36-caliber skin cartridges with a wonderful label which reads, "6 Combustible Envelope Cartridges Made of Hazards Powder For Either Colt's or Whitney's Revolving Belt Pistols 36/100 inch Calibre Warranted Superior Quality." This label is around the interior wooden block that holds the cartridges. 365.00

.36 Revolver, Package, wooden block with affixed label reads, "Six Seamless Skin Cartridges with percussion caps For Colt's, Whitney, or Remington's Navy Pistol 36/100 Caliber Hotchkiss Patent Feb. 11, 1862/Manufactured for W.J. Syms & Bro./300 Broadway NY/by D.C. Sage Middletown, Conn." Package is worn and roughed up a bit, with the top section open to expose the bullet tops, and portions of the label edges are worn away. 135.00

.36 Whitney Navy Revolver, Package, two packages, one that is a perfect pack (wood block covered with paper label). Label reads, "Six Seamless Skin/CARTRIDGES/ for Whitney's/Navy Pistol/36/100 calibre/Hotchkiss Patent Feb 11th 1862/Manufactured by/D. C Sage Middletown Conn." The second package is identical, but has had one cartridge removed and that small end section of the package broken off, still has fine label.. . . . .475.00

.44 Colt Revolver, Package

A perfect empty package with spectacular label reading, "Six Johnston & Dow Waterproof & Combustible cartridges/For Colts Army Revolvers Cal 44-100 Patented Oct 1st 1861 and June 24th 1862/New York." Perfect for display. 135.00

No label remains, just the wooden block and four bullets-the cartridges themselves have disintegrated. 35.00

This is a near-perfect package (wood block covered with paper label), which is empty. Label reads, "6 Combustible Envelope CARTRIDGES Made of Hazard's Powder Expressly For Col. Colt's Patent NEW MODEL REVOLVING HOLSTER PISTOL 44/100 Calibre Address Colts Cartridge Works Hartford, Conn USA." 249.00

Unopened box of six cartridges and percussion caps marketed at people who owned .44 Colt or Remington Army revolvers.

Sharpsburg Arsenal

.44 Revolver, Package, complete, unopened box of Lane's Cartridges for Colt and Remington Army Revolvers, contains six cartridges and seven percussion caps. 350.00

.50 Gallager Carbine, Package

A fine, empty package with great label on the box's top giving all the data and date. 125.00

Just the empty box with nice label and Civil War date. Excellent with lid neatly opened, looks like a full package. 125.00

Pack remnants with most of the label. 45.00

Unopened package with label that reads, "10 Poultney's Metallic Cartridges Patented December 15th 1863 For Gallager's Breech Loading Carbine 50/100 Calibre." 675.00

This wooden block was part of the packaging for .50-caliber Gallager Carbine cartridges.

Sharpsburg Arsenal

Wooden block of cartridges for a Gallager Carbine, from Corinth, Mississippi. 225.00

A complete box (empty) with label that reads, "10 Poultney's Metallic CARTRIDGES Patented December 15th 1863: 12 Caps For Gallager's Breech Loading Carbine 50/100 Calibre.". 125.00

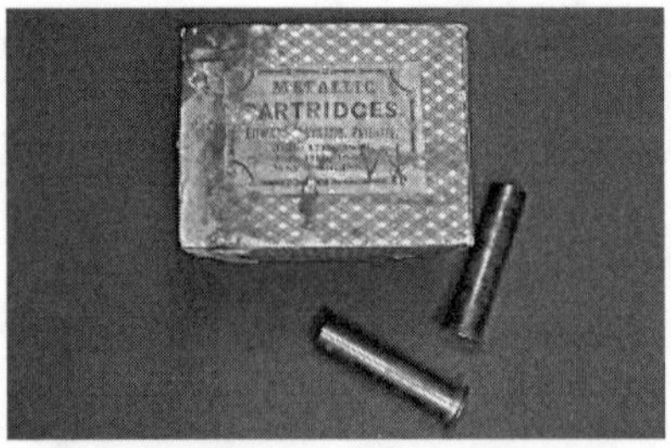

Package of .50 cartridges for the Maynard Carbine.

Middle Tennessee Relics

.50 Maynard Carbine, Package, unopened and wrapped in the plain paper wrapper still tied with original string. Some light tears in wrapper. Contains 10 cartridges. 495.00

.50 Smith Carbine, Package

A perfect empty box with full Smith carbine data on the top label. 135.00

Perfect, unopened specimen. Label reads, "10 Poultney's Patent Metallic CARTRIDGES Patented Dec 15th 1863 12 caps, For Smith's Breech Loading CARBINE 50/100 Calibre/Address Poultney & Trimble Baltimore, MD." **1,150.00**

.52 Sharps Carbine, Package

Package with one complete linen cartridge for the Sharps military .52-caliber rifle and carbine. **85.00**

This pasteboard box contains nine complete cartridges and the pack of caps (one cartridge gone). The box's left end is cut off to open the package, the rest of the box is intact and displays very well. The box's top is labeled, "TEN/LINEN CARTRIDGES/For Sharps Carbine/Cal. 52-100/With Percussion Caps/ WATERVLIET ARSENAL/1864." The box and label are brown with age but very sound. **895.00**

.52 Sharps Rifle, Package, near perfect box (empty) with label which reads, "10 Cartridges 12 Caps For Sharps Improved Rifle 52/IW Calibre A Superior Quality of Powder is used made by A G Fay, Potter & Tolman Boston Mass. Address Sharps Rifle Manuf'g Co. Hartford Ct." Just one small label scuff. **275.00**

.52 Spencer, Package

An original cardboard box still containing seven original Spencer cartridges, excellent with one end of the box open. **95.00**

Complete box of 42 rounds. On the lid is a label that reads, "42/Metallic Cartridges/for the/Spencer and Joslyn Carbine/No. 56 Navy and Infantry Size/ Manufactured by/Crittendon & Tibbals Mfg Co./ Coventry Conn US." Label has small section torn off through name "Crittendon" and town "Coventry." **675.00**

Just the way this ammo was issued: six cardboard packages of seven rounds per package, all bound in a larger cardboard box with super green paper label which reads, "Forty Two/METALLIC CARTRIDGES/For Spencer Carbine/Cal. .50 Model 1865/Manufactured by/Sage Ammunition Works/ Middletown Conn." **595.00**

Original brown cardboard packet containing seven Spencer cartridges. **175.00**

.54 Burnside Carbine, Package

Complete unopened package with label "10 Cartridges/ with 12 Caps/For The Burnside Breech Loading Rifle Patented March 25, 1856 Burnside Rifle Co. Providence RI." **895.00**

The full wrapper with fantastic label which reads, "10 CARTRIDGES with 12 Caps for the Burnside Breech Loading Rifle Patented March 25th 1856 Caliber.54/100 Made By The Burnside Rifle Co. Providence R.I." Package is empty. **145.00**

.54 Starr Carbine, Package, complete, unopened package in the proper St. Louis arsenal paper wrapper without label. Still wrapped with the original string, contains 10 rounds. **950.00**

.56 Colt Revolving Rifle, Package, wooden block package (empty) with label reading, "5 Combustible Envelope CARTRIDGES/for/Col. Colt's Patent REVOLVING RIFLE 56/100 inch Caliber. Address Colt's Cartridge Works Hartford Conn. US America." The package also has an illustration of the revolving rifle on each side of the label. **595.00**

.58 Rifled Musket, Package

Exactly as issued, perfect, unopened package of 10 paper cartridges, still tied with the original string. **975.00**

This lot consists of a near-complete wrapper with fine logo from the St Louis Arsenal in 1864 with date, and likeness of Minié ball on it. Also included are four original .58-caliber paper cartridges in excellent condition. **495.00**

.64 Hall Carbine, Package, 10 rounds in original plain paper wrapper for the Model 1836 Hall Breech Loading Carbine. Perfect condition, still wrapped with the original string. **1,475.00**

12 mm Pinfire, Package, for the LeFaucheaux pinfire revolver, small cardboard box with label that reads, "Cartouches/12 Millimetr/Houllier-Blanchard/ Arqubusier Brevete/Paris/A Longue Portee," excellent condition. **165.00**

Package, .69 Buck and Ball, package of Confederate Columbus Depot .69 buck and ball cartridges. **6,500.00**

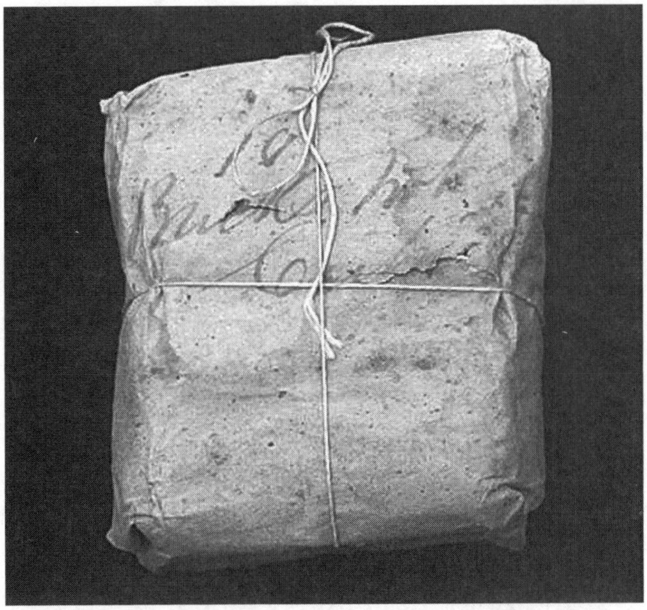

Bundle of 10, .69 "buck and ball" cartridges packaged at the Confederate Columbus Depot.

Old South Military Antiques

Caps, Percussion

Sampling of original musket and revolver percussion caps.

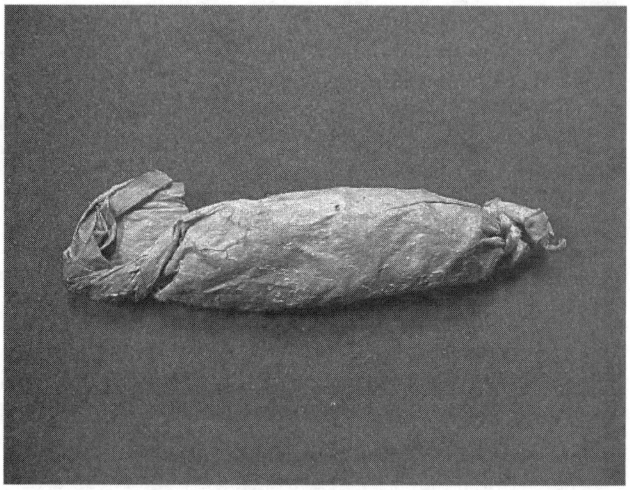

In every bundle of ten rifled musket cartridges, there was an eleventh tube containing percussion caps.

Middle Tennessee Relics

Civil War period musket and pistol caps all in non-excavated condition. **3.25**

Lawrence Pellet Primers, little copper or brass tube with a small wooden block holding in what appears to be 25 of the small, wafer-thin fulminates for the Lawrence Pellet Priming assembly on the Sharps Carbine and some other Lawrence equipped firearms, excellent condition. **.65.00**

Maynard Priming

One original roll of paper caps for use with the Maynard tape priming devices on the 1855 rifles (and others), still in wrapper. **35.00**

Roll of the famous Maynard caps unwrapped from the original, waxed tissue paper, displayed in a Riker display case. **80.00**

Musket, Package

Paper-rolled package of 12 percussion caps that came out of a package of musket or carbine ammunition. **38.00**

Pasteboard container that is labeled on the top, "UNITED STATES ARMY CAPS-WATERPROOF-100" and has a picture of an eagle. Inside box is labeled "PRESENTED TO ARGUS OGBORN BY HIS GRANDFATHER JOHN CHRISTOPHER MENKE." Menke was a veteran of the 7th New York Infantry, promoted to corporal and was wounded on April 2, 1865, at South Side Railroad, Virginia. The box's bottom is labeled, "ORIGINAL CIVIL WAR PERCUSSION CAPS FOR MUZZLE-LOADING ARMY RIFLED MUSKET—COLLECTION OF ARGUS E. OGBORN. COL. SVR 258 N. 22 ST RICHMOND, IND." Argus was a noted collector who passed away several years ago. The box's top must have come loose as someone has taped it down, but it's still in good condition. **65.00**

Original, string-tied, brown paper packet of musket percussion caps. **48.00**

Revolver

Mint pasteboard circular container with label on each side. Top label bears date of 1858 and, "American Manufacture Anticorrosive Percussion Caps by J. Goldmark" along with pictures of two medals awarded for excellence. Other side has label with crossed muskets and a ribbon and is written in French saying 100 caps American Made, etc. **49.00**

Tin pistol percussion cap can with lid. **25.00**

"When daylight came we could see two men chopping at a tree, about 400 yards distant. Brother Mifflin and I shot several times at them, but they continued chopping. Finally we doubled our cartridges and fired. When the smoke cleared, the tree was standing, but the men were missing."

—Mifflin Jennings
11th Iowa Infantry
Battle of Peach Tree Creek, Georgia
July 20, 1864

Bullets

Ball, .69 Musket. Found in Potomac Creek. 7.00

.36 Teardrop Revolver, very attractive little bullet in perfect condition. 9.50

This .44-caliber bullet was for use in the Adams' Patent Deane & Adams 5-shot revolver. The U.S. Government bought 500 of these from the Massachusetts Arms Company during the period of 1857 to 1861. Another 1,049 imported English-made Adams revolvers were purchased on the open market from 1861-1866. Furthermore, at least 1,000 Adams are known to have run the blockade into the South.

Middle Tennessee Relics

.44 Deane & Adams, non-excavated, spike-base, bullet, rare caliber, still has the leather washer intact on spike. 45.00

The .45 Whitworth round is considered to be a rarity of import ammunition often employed by Confederate troops.

Middle Tennessee Relics

.45 Whitworth, mint, flawless condition, freshly dug drop 45 cal. cylindrical Whitworth projectile. This beauty was dug from General John Bell Hood's sharpshooter positions at the Battle of Nashville, Tennessee; it has smooth, perfect white patina. 275.00

.50 Carbine, .50 Union carbine, perfect dropped example with good patina. 7.50

This .50 Smith Carbine bullet was dug in the early 1960s during the Civil War Centennial, a period when digging first gained widespread popularity.

.50 Smith Carbine, dug in 1960s. 4.00

.52 Joslyn Carbine, perfect dropped example with nice white patina. 7.50

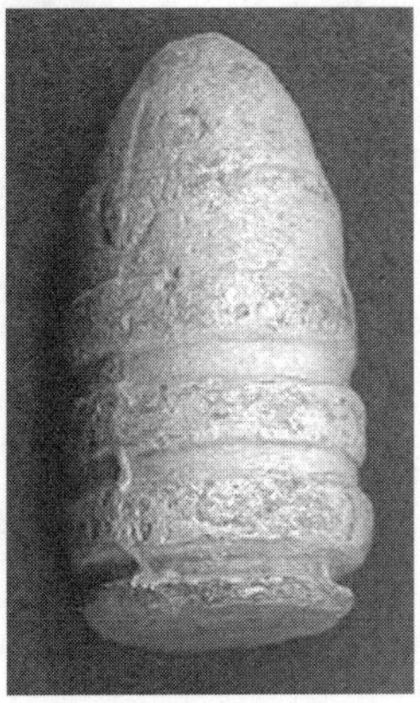

The four-ring Sharps bullets are generally attributed to being used exclusively by Confederate troops.

Sharpsburg Arsenal

.52 Sharps, 4-ring as used with Confederate Sharps Carbines. 75.00

"Regular" .52 Sharps bullet.

.52 Sharps, dug, good, dropped bullet with some nicks. 3.00

.54 Burnside Carbine

Flat-based. 7.50

Dished-base. 7.50

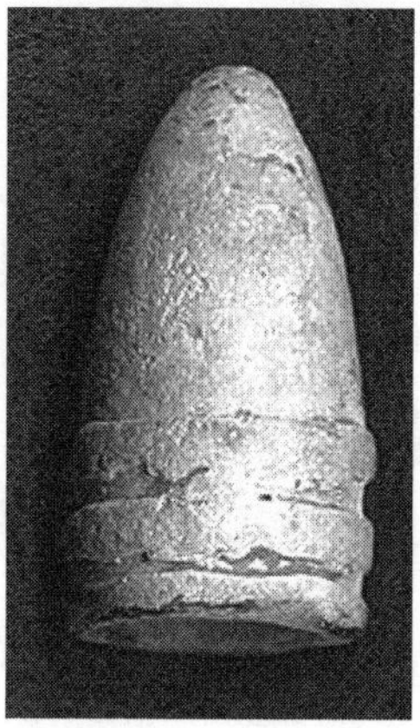

The Carcano .54-caliber bullet is often called the "Garibaldi."

Sharpsburg Arsenal

.54 Italian Garibaldi. **40.00**

.54 Merrill Carbine

Merrill carbine bullet in non-excavated condition. ... **3.00**

Called a "Richmond-style" .54 Merrill Carbine, this bullet is often considered to be a Confederate-made product.

Sharpsburg Arsenal

Richmond-style bullet. **47.00**

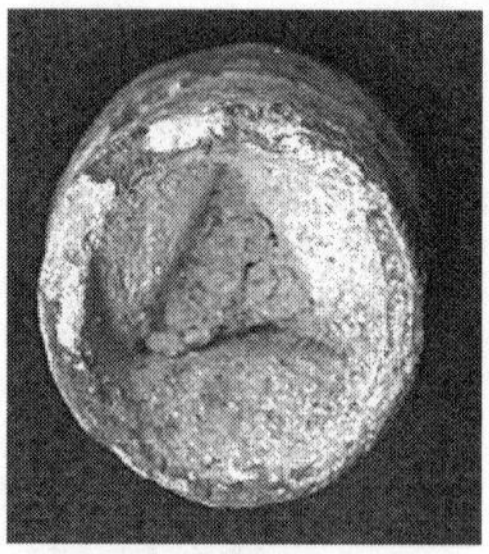

This view shows the triangular imprint in the base of a .54 Prussian bullet.

Sharpsburg Arsenal

.54 Prussian Rifle. **25.00**

Though unidentified, this .54-caliber bullet was unearthed near Corinth, Mississippi.

.54 Rifle, dug at Corinth, Mississippi, good patina and not damaged. **7.00**

.54 Suhl, .54 German Suhl. This is a nice dropped example. These were used almost exclusively by Southern cavalry. **10.00**

This .56 bullet was most likely dropped by a soldier loading a Colt Revolving Rifle.

Middle Tennessee Relics

.56 Colt Revolving Rifle, nice, dropped example with smooth white patina. **7.50**

.577 Rifle

Nice white and brown patina with no dig marks, dug at New Hope Church, Georgia. **4.50**

Looks like an Enfield, but has one ring toward the bottom, and a base like a Sharps (hole in the bottom), dug in a C.S. Texas camp. **35.00**

.577 Rifle, remnants of powder in base, large base that tapers off at the nose, has ring around nose, drop, fine condition. **20.00**

The "Gardner" bullet is the only Civil War smalls arm projectile that can conclusively be called "Confederate." Frederick J. Gardner from Hillsboro, North Carolina, was issued C.S.A. patent No. 12 on August 17, 1861, for his projectile and that originally made at the CSA Arsenal Richmond, Virginia.

Sharpsburg Arsenal

.58 Gardner, the one bullet type used exclusively by the Confederate Army during the Civil War. It is recognized by the two grooves at the base of the bullet. This bullet was found in the Shenandoah of Virginia. It had been fired and in very good condition. **7.00**

.58 Shaler

Three-piece bullet, comes in a nice Riker case. ...**110.00**

An excellent example of this terrible missile that separated into three pieces after being fired. ..**85.00**

The Williams cleaner bullet was rolled into cartridges that were issued by Federal arsenals at the rate of one per bundle of 10 cartridges until 1863, when it was increased to three per bundle. The Williams cleaner bullet was believed to help keep the bore cleaner by scouring the barrel of black powder residue.

.58 Williams Bullet, this is .58 Williams Cleaner. ... **7.00**

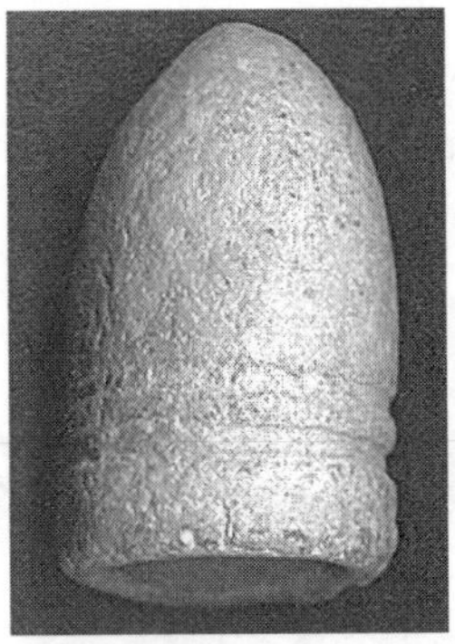

This .69 Confederate-issued Gardner bullet sold for $325.00.

Sharpsburg Arsenal

.69 Gardner

Deep base. **325.00**

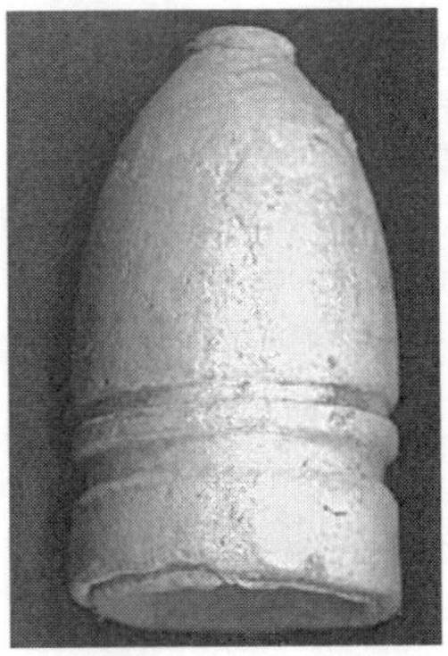

Called a "bulb-nose" Gardner for obvious reasons, this Confederate .69 is the more common of the Richmond-produced bullets.

Sharpsburg Arsenal

Bulb nose. **125.00**

Gardner insert-dug at Salem Church. This fired Gardner insert bullet was found in the battlefield along Old Orange Plank Road. **6.00**

A Confederate soldier probably dropped this .69 Gardner. Dug by a relic hunter.

Middle Tennessee Relics

Very rare to dig, this is a dropped .69 Confederate Gardner bullet. **85.00**

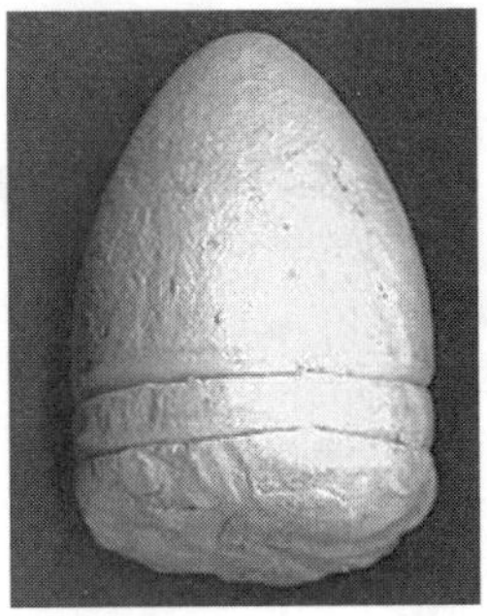

This .69-caliber bullet has been labeled a "Hall" by collectors.

Sharpsburg Arsenal

.69 Hall, by Merrill. **80.00**

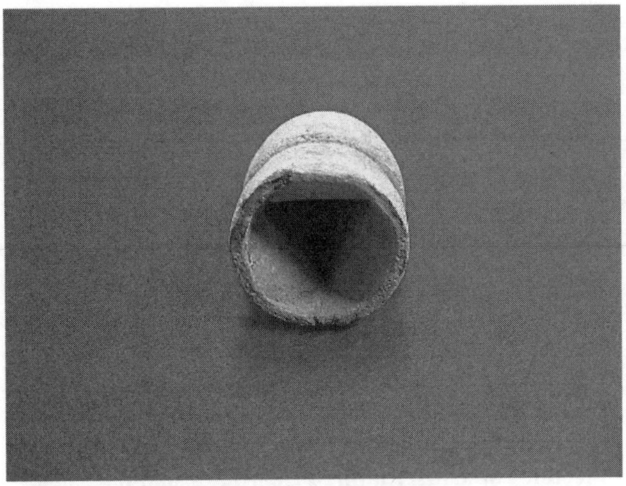

This view shows the triangular impression in the base of a dropped, one-ring .69 Minié bullet.

Middle Tennessee Relics

.69 One Ring, nice dug .69, one ring, triangle base French Minié; this is a dropped example. **15.00**

.69 Rifled Musketoon, .69 caliber, very-fine condition, dropped bullet, dug in a camp used by C.S. and U.S. troops in Texas,. **25.00**

Shotgun

Double-end slug. **75.00**

Nice condition, dug, Confederate shotgun slug, dropped example. **55.00**

.54 Prussian Rifle, two Prussian .54 bullets found near Vicksburg, Mississippi. **6.00**

Collecting small arms projectiles does not have to be expensive to be interesting. This group of "pulled" 3-ring Miniés were dug at Petersburg. The hole in the nose and spiral groove around the cone indicate that, for one reason or another (probably due to misfire), the soldier had to use his worm to extricate the bullet from his rifle.

.58 Rifled Musket, four pulled three-ring bullets. These had probably been stuck in the barrel and pulled with a ball puller, found near Petersburg, Virginia. **6.50**

For just a few dollars, a person can become a bullet collector. These three unfired .58 Miniés sold for $5.50.

Group

A collection of three dropped .58-caliber Minié balls in very-good condition. 5.50

Group of five bullets dug in the 1940s from the area of the first battle at Manassas, Virginia.

Collection of five bullets found on private property near First Manassa battlefield. These are from a collection that was started in the 1940s. These are all fired and include a swage-based Sharps, some Sharps that were carved, and one that must have hit a rock or something very hard. 4.50

"War Logs"

This war log was penetrated with a .52 Sharps bullet.

Middle Tennessee Relics

12" piece of heartwood pine from the Battle of Chickamauga; bullet appears to be a .52 Sharps. 55.00

Large 28" piece of heartwood pine with Minié ball embedded inside of it, came from the battle area of Chickamauga. The Minié ball, entrance wound, and vapor trail have been carefully milled out to show the bullet's path to its final resting place. Most "bullet-in-wood" examples are a few inches long, this one is over two feet. 125.00

Small-size bullet in wood, 3-ring Minié in a pine knot. 25.00

This .58 bullet was embedded in a pine when it was fired during a Civil War engagement. The tree subsequently healed around the bullet.

Middle Tennessee Relics

.58 caliber

Three-ring Minié ball embedded in a small knot of wood. This is from the Battle of Chickamauga and would at one time have been embedded in a tree. The tree eventually healed and knotted around the Minié ball. After many years, the tree died and rotted away except the hard knot around the Minié ball. . . . 30.00

This bullet-in-wood was recovered from the area of the Battle of Chickamauga. The wood was carefully removed to expose the bullet within the branch.

Middle Tennessee Relics

Three-ring Minié ball embedded in a 25" piece of heartwood pine. This artifact was recovered from the Battle of Chickamauga. For display, the wood has been carefully removed to expose the Minié ball inside. **150.00**

Three-ring Mini-ball imbedded in a 12" piece of heart wood pine. This bullet in wood is from the Battle of Chickamauga, Georgia. The Minié ball can be clearly seen. **75.00**

Artillery Fuses

Fuse and Wood Plug, from a siege shell. Very-fine condition, length- 2-1/4" x 1-2/5". **25.00**

U.S.

Fits a 30 lb Parrot shell, very-good condition, dug near Vicksburg **35.00**

10-Second

An original, paper, time fuse for an exploding artillery projectile, nicely displayed in a Riker case with description. **20.00**

This original, paper, time fuse was used for exploding an artillery projectile. Nicely displayed in a glass case with description. **20.00**

Naval, marked "ORD 1862." Made of brass. **65.00**

5-Second, Package

Brown paper-wrapped package stenciled in large black letters on paper "5.S." Mint surplus example. . **59.00**

Frankford Arsenal. **195.00**

8-Second, Package

Marked "8.S.". **59.00**

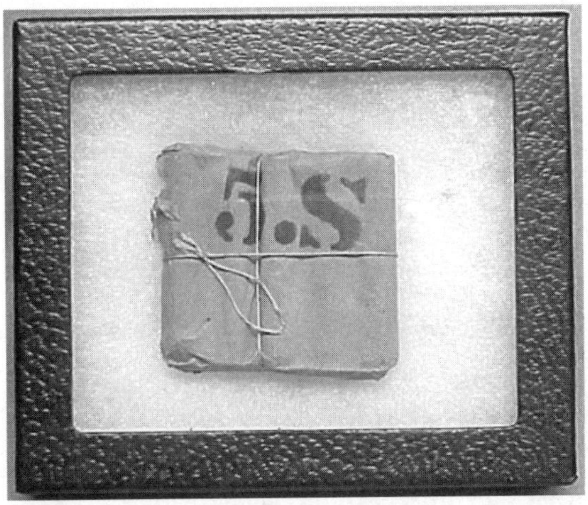

Simply labeled "5.S," this pack of artillery fuses have been attributed to the Frankford Arsenal.

Sharpsburg Arsenal

Paper time fuses from Frankford Arsenal, untied. . . .**150.00**

> **"So unaccustomed were they to the whistling sounds, that they began to question among themselves as to what they were, some saying that they were the sounds of flying bullets; others that they were not. An officer hearing the talk said: 'Boys those are bullets as sure as you live'."**
>
> ***—William Hewitt***
> ***12th West Virginia Volunteer Infantry***

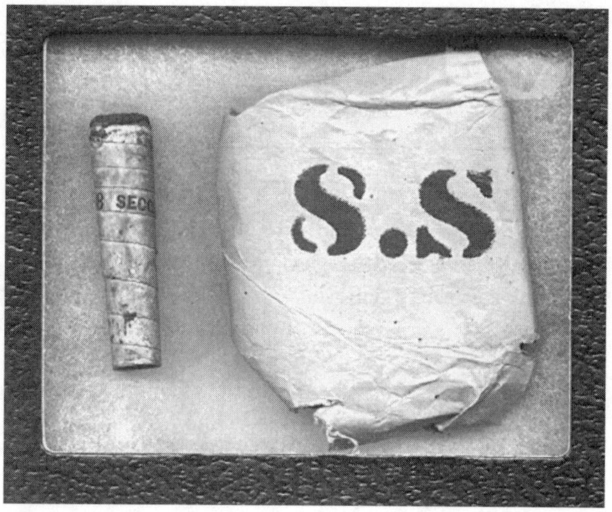

Bundle of Frankford Arsenal fuses marked, "8.S," and a sample fuse.

Sharpsburg Arsenal

10-Second, Package, pack of 1864-dated Frankford Arsenal fuses complete with label, tapes, and fuses in Riker display. **80.00**

12-Second, Package, box of 12-second fuses in their original blue case from the Frankfort Arsenal, 1863. Instructions say "To take a fuse from the package, tear the paper at the top by raising the piece at tape, and press against the small end of the fuse [sic] with the finger," intact and never opened. **115.00**

Pack of Frankford Arsenal 20-second fuses perfect to display with larger artillery projectiles.

Sharpsburg Arsenal

20-Second, Package, Frankford Arsenal fuse pack in mint condition. **135.00**

Bundle of 25-second fuses probably packaged at the Frankford Arsenal.

Middle Tennessee Relics

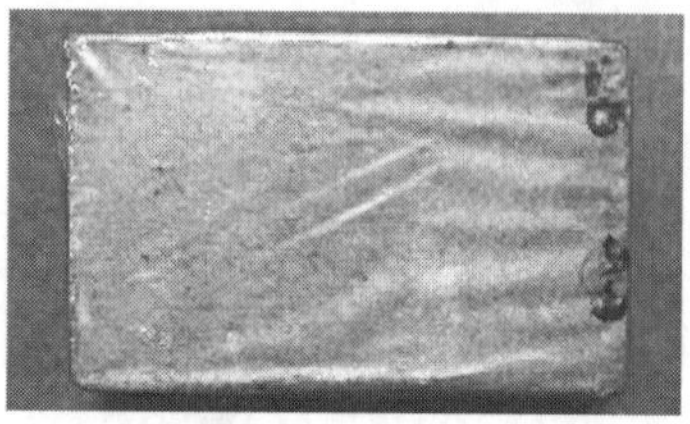

25-Second, Package, original, unopened, brown-wrapped packet containing two 25-second artillery time fuses. **45.00**

14-Second, Package, Confederate fuse pack labeled, "10 paper fuses 14 Sec. to an inch." **365.00**

Artillery Projectiles, Confederate

A "bolt" is an artillery round that is solid. That is, it contains no explosive material that would fragment the projectile. They were best used in counter-battery fire and against fortified positions. They are also the safest artillery rounds to dig and collect. This Confederate 3" Archer bolt was dug at Shiloh.

Middle Tennessee Relics

Bolt, Confederate

Nice, excavated 3" Archer bolt, projectile was dug at Shiloh many years ago. For the past several years, it has been on display at the Lotz House Civil War Museum in Franklin, Tennessee. The museum's accession number still remains on the projectile. It is cleaned, coated, and ready for display. **650.00**

3.3" round-nose Selma disc, fine condition, with sabot, cloverleaf design. **1,250.00**

In case shot, the bursting charge was usually located in a thin tin or iron container and placed in the center of an internal cavity that was surrounded by smaller, iron or lead shot.

Middle Tennessee Relics

Case Shot, Confederate, 12 lb, excellent condition, wood, drive-in fuse-type cannon ball. Not only is this projectile in nice condition, but it also has a couple of unusual and rare characteristics. First of all, the wooden fuse plug is petrified and remains 100 percent intact. And secondly, this is a case shot, rather than being a shell, which is typically the case with this type projectile. This was determined by its unusual heavy weight and case-shot ball cuttings during drilling, quite rare C.S. ball. **295.00**

Grape Shot, Confederate, 2" used in Confederate canister, fine condition, dug at Port Gibson, Mississippi. **19.00**

Grape Shot, Confederate, large, lead-covered marbles, fine condition. **9.00**

Shell, Confederate

Read Parrot, shell shows ground action, but is stabilized and mounted to a display board with brass plaque that says "BATTLE OF MOBILE, ALABAMA." **285.00**

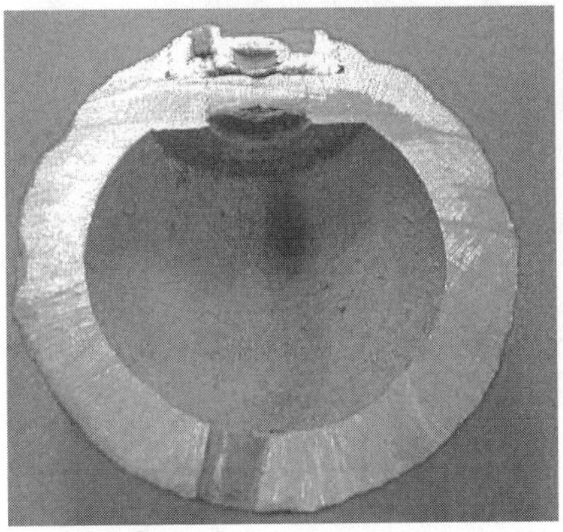

This 12 lb Confederate cannon ball has been cut in half to reveal the powder cavity and to display the cross-section of the brass Bormann fuse.

Middle Tennessee Relics

12 lb Bormann-Type, this 12 lb Confederate Bormann cannon ball has been nicely sectioned in half to show the powder cavity, brass C.S. underplug, and Bormann fuse. This ball was recovered at Shiloh, and is a great visual aid in showing how Civil War explosive cannon balls worked. **150.00**

Interestingly, this 12 lb ball was a veteran bring-back. George Frazee, a soldier in the 12th Indiana Infantry, is credited with preserving this non-dug projectile. It is possible that this was actually a souvenir that Frazee purchased after the war.

Caldwell and Company Civil War Antiques

12 lb Mortar, an excellent item that was brought back after the war by George Frazee of Grant County, Indiana, who was in the 12th Indiana Infantry. This mortar shell is in mint, non-dug condition and measures about 5-1/2" across. This type took the wooden drive-in fuse, mold seam around the middle of the cannonball that indicates Confederate use. **275.00**

12 lb Side-Loading

Excavated Confederate cannon ball with brass paper fuse plug and leaded loading hole for adding the explosive, fine plum patina. **575.00**

This is Confederate cannon ball is referred to as a side-loader case shot, because it has a hole in the side of the body through which the case shot material could be added. This cannon ball has the copper fuse that held the paper time fuse. It also has the lead side plug that was used to fill the ball with the iron shot.

Nice C.S. side-loader case shot, cannon ball has copper fuse that held the paper time fuse. It also has the lead side plug that was used to fill the ball with iron shot. The ball has a few little chips missing from the side, but that doesn't take away from the total appearance of the cannon ball. The ball has been cleaned and disarmed and is completely safe. It was recovered in north Georgia. **265.00**

12 lb

Dug at Jones Creek in Texas, still has nice wood fuse that is seldom seen, very-good condition. ... **225.00**

Confederate 12 lb shell recovered from the battlefield at Franklin, Tennessee.

This iron shell was most likely a Confederate projectile, as the United States had phased these out of the arsenals by the time of the Civil War.

12 lb, cont.

Hollow iron cannon ball pierced for the wooden fuse plug that had been phased out by the Union artillery. Excellent condition, non-fired, appears to be non-dug, smooth, plum-brown patina overall. . . . **375.00**

Recovered from the battlefield at Lookout Mountain, this Confederate 12 lb projectile had long been part of a museum collection.

Middle Tennessee Relics

Nice condition, Confederate, wood, drive-in fuse-type 12 lb cannon ball. This projectile came off Lookout Mountain and had been on display at the now-closed "Tennessee Civil War Museum" at Chattanooga, Tennessee. **275.00**

Wood plug shell dug at Jones Creek in Texas, seldom seen nice wood fuse, very-good condition. . . **225.00**

Wood plug shell dug at Jones Creek in Texas, no wood plug, very-good condition. **195.00**

Dug at Jones Creek in Texas, no wood plug, very-good condition. **195.00**

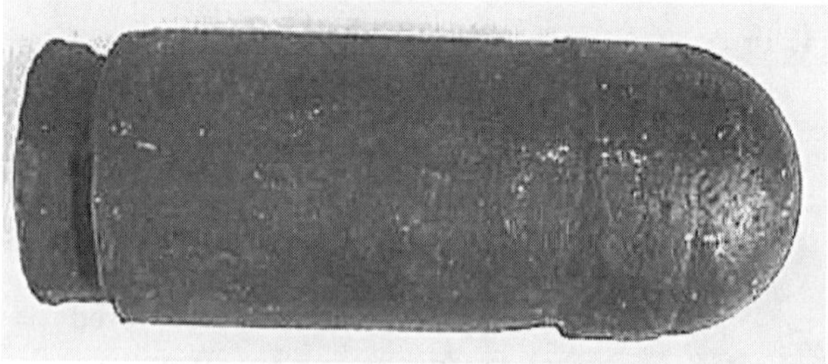

2.94" Broun shell named after Confederate Lieutenant Colonel of Ordnance William Le Roy Broun.

Military Antiques & Museum

2.94" Broun, shell is 7-1/2", very crude machine work on this shell, very clean shell. **625.00**

24 lb

No fuse, but still has brass underplug, nice iron shell, dug near Vicksburg. **245.00**

A 24 lb Confederate shell dug near Vicksburg, Mississippi.

Middle Tennessee Relics

Wood drive-in fuse cannon ball dug at Vicksburg, Mississippi, it has been cleaned, coated, and is ready for display. The surface is about average with normal ground action, one of the most affordable types of all C.S.-manufactured cannon projectiles. **295.00**

3" Read

Excavated from the Battle of Stone's River, Tennessee. Missing a portion of one side of nose section, but doesn't detract from the shell. Fuse grooves strong and visible, missing the copper sabot, good shape, professionally cleaned and coated. **295.00**

Exceptionally nice, dug, 3-inch Confederate Read shell that has a smooth shell body and a complete brass sabot with deep clean rifling. **475.00**

Confederate 3" Read shell with the sabot still intact.

Middle Tennessee Relics

Nice condition, dug, Confederate Read shell with a perfect rifled brass sabot intact, as is, a nice brass C.S. time fuse. Good metal, but was not cleaned well before being coated, the clear coat is actually over rust build-up that needs to be removed. This will be a very nice Read once properly cleaned and coated. **350.00**

Complete Confederate Read projectile dug near Richmond, Virginia, nice condition, good metal and has been nicely cleaned and coated. The copper sabot remains intact with deep clear rifling. The copper time fuse still remains intact as well. **425.00**

Shell has exploded, probably a ground burst. These two pieces fit together perfectly, has copper sabot, found at Petersburg. **165.00**

3" Read-Broun

Exceptionally nice condition, dug Confederate Read-Broun projectile. This shell was dug at Petersburg, Virginia. It has already been cleaned and coated and is ready for display. This type Confederate shell usually is quite pitted due to the poor-quality iron from which it was cast. The brass sabot is intact with deep sharp rifling except for one small 2" section that was thrown when fired. **450.00**

This is the short pattern shell and shows general pitting, but is in good condition, has original wood fuse and full sabot. Sabot is stamped with large capital "A," good solid Confederate shell found near Globe Tavern. 975.00

3" Read-Parrot

This projectile has a nice smooth shell body and has been cleaned, coated, and is ready for display. It is a wood drive-in fuse-type and was dug at Petersburg, Virginia. About a quarter of the iron sabot is intact, and the remainder was thrown when fired. It has the characteristic C.S. lathe dimple in the base. . 295.00

Shell was dug near Richmond, Virginia, and has already been cleaned and coated, copper Confederate time fuse still intact. This is the pattern with the copper sabot, and the sabot is 100 percent intact with deep sharp rifling. The shell's base is chipped out as is the case with many Reads and Read-Parrotts due to a sabot attachment design flaw. 295.00

3" Tredegar Reed, the Tredegar Reed was found near Union Fort Weed, Bermuda Hundred, Virginia. The Tredegar Reed derives its name as it was manufactured at Tredegar Iron Works, Richmond, Virginia. Shell has some chipping on one side above the base as was common with Confederate shells. 425.00

3.67" J.P. Schenkl, this is a Marshall Arsenal rounded, short-nose Schenkl. In excellent condition, this C.S. Schenkl still retains the bottom iron plate designed to hold the wood sabot in place. This shell used the wood drive-in fuse. Minimal ground action with no major pitting or flaking, cleaned and coated, found near Provencal, Louisiana. 1,500.00

32 lb

Fine iron shell with wood plug dug near Vicksburg. . 250.00

Wood plug shell, fine iron, dug near Vicksburg. . 250.00

4.6" Read, unlisted Confederate 4.6" Read Shell. Only about 6 of these shells are known to exist, great condition with absolutely no pitting, cleaned and coated. 3,500.00

Archer, excellent condition Confederate Archer shell with some of the original wooden drive-in fuse still visible. Minimal ground action with no major pitting or flaking. Nice example, cleaned and coated, found near Shiloh, Tennessee. 645.00

This 8 lb solid shot was attributed to the Confederate Augusta Arsenal.

Solid Shot

Confederate, 8 lb, it came from the Augusta, Georgia, Arsenal. 585.00

Confederate, 12 lb, solid shot with a very pronounced seam mark, has traces of gold paint on it, display base. 165.00

Artillery Projectiles, U.S.

Bolt, U.S., 2.35-inch Pattison, extremely rare short version, measuring only 5-1/4". 1,550.00

Fired from the 20 lb Parrot Rifle, this bolt was found at Vicksburg, Mississippi.

Middle Tennessee Relics

Bolt, U.S., 20 lb Parrot, 3.67" "bottlenose" Parrott bolt dug at Vicksburg, Mississippi, has been nicely cleaned and coated. As was commonly the case, this projectile threw the copper sabot when fired. 225.00

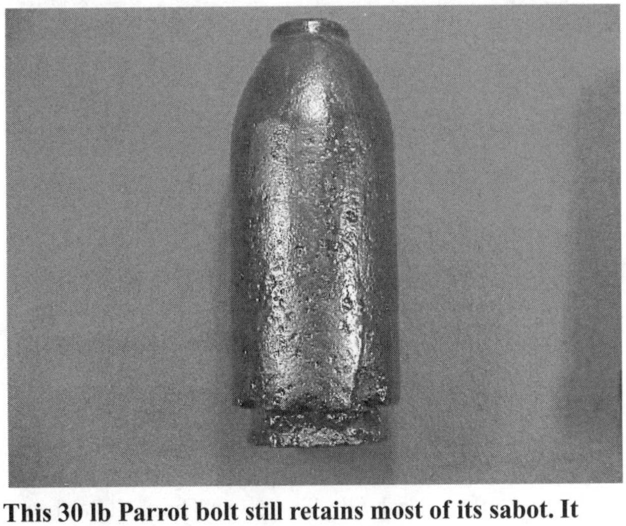

This 30 lb Parrot bolt still retains most of its sabot. It was recovered at Vicksburg, Mississippi.

Middle Tennessee Relics

Bolt, U.S., 30 lb Parrot, Vicksburg-dug "bottle nose" Parrott bolt. This projectile has been cleaned, coated, and is ready for display. It has nice condition iron with only a typical amount of pitting in areas. The rifled brass sabot is 100% intact. This is somewhat rare in that 30 lb. Parrott bolts often threw all, or part, of their sabot. **350.00**

Bolt, U.S., 60 lb Parrott, extremely rare, as this Navy caliber was primarily fired over water. This bottlenose bolt hit something hard and dead-on as the nose is chipped and the shock sheared a portion of the sabot mount. Some cosmetic work on the nose and the base has been done to allow it to stand. **1,350.00**

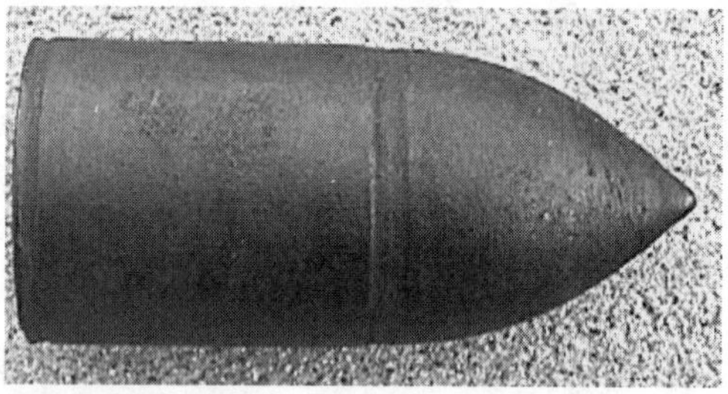

Only 20 Ellsworth Rifled Cannons were acquired by the U.S. Government in late 1861. This projectile is the type used in the pieces.

Military Antiques & Museum

Bolt, U.S., Ellsworth, extremely rare bolt for the Ellsworth Steel Rifled Cannon. Only 20 of the cannon were purchased by Abraham Lincoln on November 29, 1861. Five of the guns have survived, the bolt is 3-1/4" x 1-7/16" and is in very-fine condition. **1,500.00**

Case Shot, U.S., 20 lb Parrott, iron sabot, good dug condition, remnant of zinc fuse, cleaned and disarmed. **275.00**

This 3" Hotchkiss was complete when dug, retaining the cup, rifled lead sabot, nose, and brass time fuse.

Middle Tennessee Relics

Case Shot, U.S., 3" Hotchkiss, complete, dug, 3" flame groove Hotchkiss case shot projectile excavated from the Battle of Nashville, Tennessee. The shell has been cleaned and coated and consists of cup, rifled lead sabot, nose, and brass time fuse. Only about one Hotchkiss out of 10 are dug with all parts intact. **250.00**

Grape Shot, U.S., Stand, recovered from a well in Vicksburg many years ago. An extremely fine specimen, with little sign of its great time buried. Clearly the ground was very dry. Could be cleaned much more or left as is. Has a thin rust patina, but solid and stable, measures 6-1/4" in diameter, and 8-1/4" high. Weight is approximately 35 lbs. Consists of cast-iron discs top and bottom, each of which has on its inside face, three depressions which hold the balls in position. There are levels of 3 balls, held into position by two iron rings. There is a heavy bolt top to bottom. On firing, the bolt and the rings break, and the entire thing comes apart. **1,950.00**

When dug near Kennesaw Mountain, Georgia, this 10 lb Parrot shell retained the brass sabot and the pewter fuse.

Middle Tennessee Relics

Shell, U.S.

10 lb Parrot, very nice condition, dug, 10 lb Union Parrott projectile. This shell was dug at Kennesaw Mountain and has smooth clean iron, a complete excellent brass sabot, and a complete, pewter time fuse intact. **250.00**

Shell with a Bormann fuse made for use in a 12 lb smoothbore gun.

Military Antiques & Museum

12 lb

12 lb smoothbore shell with Bormann time fuse. This is a very clean specimen showing signs of the four tin wood sabot straps and the fuse collar. The Bormann fuse is perfect. The ball is 4.52" d. **450.00**

12 lb shell with an extremely rare Bormann-type variant fuse. This projectile was recovered from Williamsburg, Virginia, area. **450.00**

Bormann-fused cannonball from Honey Hill, South Carolina, near where the 55th Massachusetts was in battle. The top of the fuse has been broken off but is otherwise intact, display base included. **165.00**

Very nice 12 lb cannon ball with Bormann fuse from the Shiloh battlefield. It is equipped with a 5-second fuse. **515.00**

2.94" Absterdam, marked “Patented S & Co. August 12, 1862,” this is a 2.94" diameter shell and is 7-1/2" l, lead sabot and front bearing surface, very clean. **450.00**

2.94" Hotchkiss, length is 6-5/8", it has a lead Hotchkiss 14-second fuse. Screw-in percussion fuse missing, excellent condition. **575.00**

20 lb Parrot

Early variety with the high brass Parrots, these sabots almost always threw their sabots and most are recovered without the sabot intact. Rare variant of the 20 lb Parrott projectile, missing threaded fuse.. . . . . **375.00**

This projectile was dug from the Siege of Vicksburg, Mississippi, and has been cleaned and coated, making it ready for display. The iron surface is good with about a typical amount of pitting. The complete rifled iron sabot is intact. The pewter time fuse still remains intact as well. **275.00**

This 20 lb Parrot round came from area near the Kennesaw Mountain battlefield in Georgia.

Middle Tennessee Relics

This shell has been cleaned, coated, and is ready for display. It was dug at Kennesaw Mountain, Georgia. It has a smooth shell body, and 100% rifled iron sabot remains intact. **275.00**

3" Dyer, artillery shell has been cut in half and put in a wooden plaque, has a brass nameplate with the shell’s name. This is very nice in that the lead balls (case shot) and a cut away of the fuse are visible, the shell was dug in the Richmond area. **275.00**

3" Hotchkiss

Excavated and still retains nice flame grooves. Has brass fuse intact, but missing the lead band. Good shape, professionally cleaned and coated. **215.00**

Complete with cup and sabot, the rifling marks on this 3" Hotchkiss does show signs that it was fired and not simply discarded.

Caldwell and Company Civil War Antiques

Hotchkiss shell complete with sabot, cup, and brass fuse plug. Shell is completely inert and measures 3" w and about 7" l. The lead sabot shows signs that it has been fired due to the rifling impressions in the lead but it’s complete and looks great. **250.00**

Just the nose did not completely blow up! The shell blew off this part of the nose that was dug near Vicksburg. **45.00**

3" Hotchkiss shell retaining the sabot and fuse.

Drumbeat Civil War Memorabilia

Shell with sabot and fuse. This fired, non-exploded 3" shell is in great dug condition with the original sabot intact and with the original paper fuse adapter that can be unscrewed. An extremely fine example. **300.00**

Unfired, brass fuse intact. **245.00**

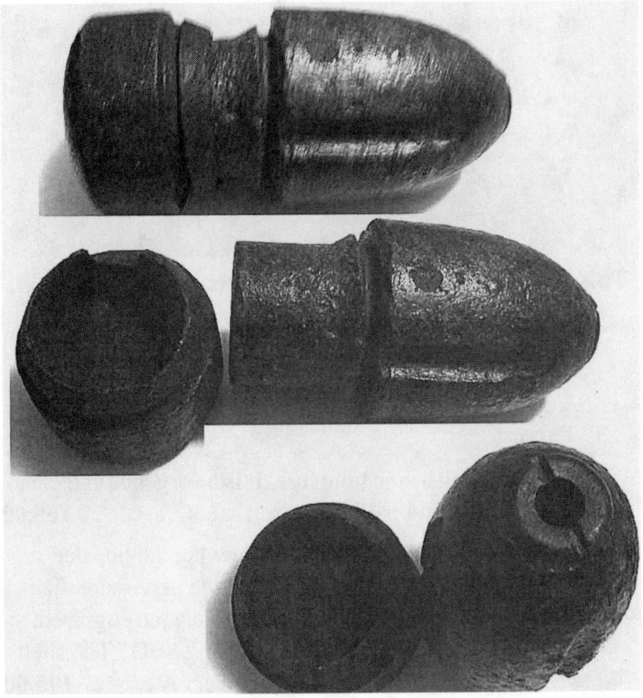

This 3" Hotchkiss still had its fuse holder intact when it was recovered.

This shell is in very good shape, also has the fuse holder. 195.00

Recovered from the battle lines around Nashville, Tennessee, this Union 3" Schenkl shell still retains most of its brass fuse. The patent date of October 10, 1861, is still legible on the fuse.

Middle Tennessee Relics

J.P. Schenkl projectile excavated from the second day's battle line at the Battle of Nashville, Tennessee. The shell body has been cleaned and coated and has about average pitting. The brass J.P. Schenkl fuse is intact and is marked "J.P. Schenkl-Oct. 10, 1861." Someone apparently tried to remove the fuse and scarred the edges a bit. This projectile for many years has been on display at the Lotz House Civil War Museum in Franklin, Tennessee. It still retains the museum's accession number...................... 425.00

This 10 lb Parrot has a zinc fuse still in place.

Middle Tennessee Relics

3" Parrott

This one took a zinc time fuse. It is a very nice and clean shell, missing half of the iron sabot. 165.00

A 10 lb Parrot shell cut in half showing the powder compartment and a cut away of the percussion fuse. Mounted on a board with a brass plaque engraved, "3 IN. PARROT/PERCUSSION FUSED." The shell was dug in the Richmond area. 195.00

3.25" J.P. Schenkl, about 3-1/4" d, still has most of its lead Bormann fuse. Nice crusty brown patina. 175.00

3.67" Hotchkiss, wood drive-in fuse that has small section out of the side, but still has legible markings on base, fine sabot, and unfired. 495.00

Recovered at Drewry's Bluff, Virginia, in 1974, this 3.67" Schenkl round retains the brass Schenkl fuse holder.

Military Antiques & Museum

3.67" J.P. Schenkl

Federal Schenkl shell is 8-5/8" l with Schenkl brass percussion fuse. The shell was found at Drewry's Bluff, Virginia, many years ago. It was marked by the finder, "Found 4 Jan, 1974. Drewry's Bluff. U.S. 3 1/8 in Schenkl." Nice shell in very nice condition. 700.00

Dug at Stone's River, Tennessee, this raised-rib 3.67" Schenkl retained its brass fuse holder.

Middle Tennessee Relics

Football-shaped, raised rib-type projectile with the Schenkl brass percussion fuse still intact. This one was dug at Stones River. It has been drilled but remains rusty and uncleaned exactly as dug. 425.00

Complete with brass percussion fuse. Very-fine iron dug near Vicksburg. 475.00

3.67" Sawyer, great condition flanged Sawyer percussion shell. This one has more lead reaming than most after firing. No fuse remains on this one though. Some amount of the lead was lost on the initial firing of this shell. 1,800.00

7" Dyer, great excavated condition, excellent rifling with flame groove hacked by gunner to improve ignition. Remnants of fuse plug, weight 90 lbs. 550.00

8" Mortar, no tong holes, very-fine iron shell, dug near Vicksburg. 275.00

9" Experimental, this shell has a large brass concussion fuse and appears to be a variant of the George P. Ganster Concussion Fuse. About 1-1/2" w with a groove or channel in the middle which goes all the way across the fuse, very-good condition. **950.00**

J.P. Schenkl, shows plenty of ground action, but stabilized and mounted to a display board with brass plaque. Plaque says, "BATTLE OF MOBILE, ALABAMA." **325.00**

Solid Shot, U.S.

4 lb, very-early-type solid shot made for smoothbore gun, 3-1/8" d and weighs a bit over four pounds. From the Battle of Lexington, Missouri, September 18-20, 1861. Early pick-up, very-good shape. **115.00**

12 lb

Nice condition, dug 12 lb solid shot cannon ball. This was an early find here at Stones River and has already been cleaned, coated, and is ready for display. **150.00**

Very-fine condition, iron, with original wood sabot. **395.00**

18 lb, shell has mold seam, sprue on top, very good example, found in Pennsylvania, and painted black. **225.00**

24 lb

Fine condition, found at Vicksburg. **225.00**

5-5/8" d, an extremely clean shot. **240.00**

32 lb, very good condition. **235.00**

Miscellaneous

Bolt, English, 12 lb Whitworth

These were used by both the Union and Confederate Forces, but apparently more by the South. This specimen came from an old collection of artillery ammunition and is 2.73" across the flats, and about 13 pounds in weight. Its length is a little shorter than some at 9-3/8". Pitting is not too bad with nothing over 1/32" deep, and much of the projectile is covered in very old, possibly original, black paint. It is a solid shot and was never loaded with any sort of explosive filler. . . **763.00**

9" h cast-iron shell about 2-3/4" in diameter. Has the distinctive hexagonal twist grooves for the Whitworth rifling system. Threaded nose with deep narrow powder chamber, no fuse or fuse assembly. Outside of shell is a dark, plum brown with a lightly corroded patina. Not excavated, but sitting outside for some time. . . **1,000.00**

Solid iron projectile or bolt with the distinguishing hexagonal cuts or loops used in the Whitworth system of rifling. Smooth plum patina overall, about 2-3/4" d, from an imported Whitworth gun. . **650.00**

Bolt, English, 2.5" Blakely, this projectile was recovered from the 2nd Manassas Battlefield area and came out of the legendary Beverly DuBose collection in Atlanta. Fired from a 2.5" Blakely rifle. **1,100.00**

As removed from a cartridge box, this tin still retains one .58-caliber paper cartridge and the wrapper from the bundle in which it was issued.

Sharpsburg Arsenal

Canister Balls, standard Union and Confederate canister balls, iron, from eastern North Carolina sites. . . . **12.00**

Cartridge Box Tin with Cartridges, original tin has one full .58-cal cartridge with powder and percussion cap that was left with extremely rare, original cartridge pack wrapper. **225.00**

Grenade, Confederate, Selma, 3" hollow iron ball with hole for fuse, known to be Confederate and most of them came from a river near the Confederate Selma Arsenal, very good condition. **475.00**

Gun Clip, Billinghurst and Requa Battery, excellent condition original gun clip. Only a few hundred of these were ever produced, this one still hinges perfectly. **275.00**

Shell Fragments, 5 lbs of artillery shell fragments from area around Fort Fisher, North Carolina. **10.00**

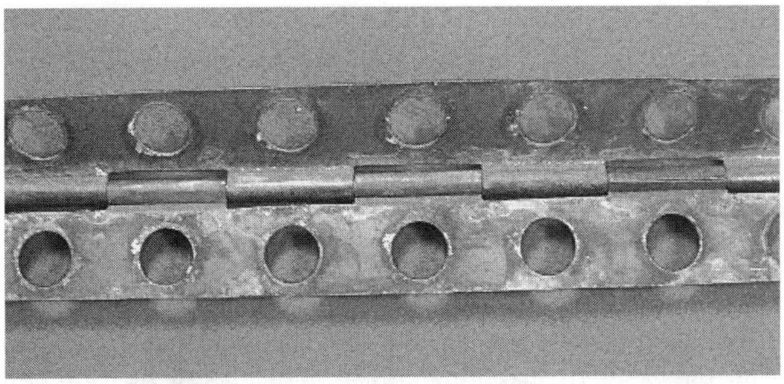

This clip was made for use in the 25-barrel Requa battery. The hinged clip held 25 of the .56-caliber brass cartridges. Fired all at once, a three-man crew could supposedly discharge 175 rounds via seven volleys in just one minute.

Middle Tennessee Relics

Bullets, Cartridges, and Projectiles Terminology

Blank cartridge: A cartridge filled with powder, but having no projectile.

Blind shell: A projectile with a hollow cavity that was plugged and not intended to have been fitted with a fuse. This projectile weighed less than a solid shot of the same caliber, thereby increasing its velocity when it was fired.

Bolt: An elongated, solid, rifled projectile that contains no explosive material that would fragment it. They were best used in counter-battery fire and against fortified positions. Because there are no explosives involved, they are also the safest artillery rounds to dig and collect.

Bormann fuse: This fuse is the invention of an officer of the Belgian service. The case is made of an alloy of tin and lead, cast in iron molds. Its shape is that of a thick circular disk. A screw thread is cut upon the edge, allowing it to be fastened into the fuse-hole of a projectile.

Bundle: Period term to describe a sealed package of cartridges.

Canister: A metal cylinder made of tin, iron, or lead, with a removable thin iron top. A heavy iron plate is usually located between the canister balls and the wooden sabot at the bottom. The cylinder contains iron or lead balls that are arranged in rows with sawdust packed between them. The top edge of the vertical cylinder wall is bent over the iron top plate to help keep the canister contents in place, and the bottom edge is nailed to the wooden sabot. Canister was designed to be used against infantry at close range.

Case shot: Also known as spherical case shot. Similar to the co mmon shell except that the walls of the projectile were thinner. In both spherical and rifled projectiles, the bursting charge was usually located in a thin tin or iron container and placed in the center of the internal cavity. The case shot was placed around this container. The Confederates usually drilled into the case shot to form the bursting charge cavity. Due to the shortage of lead needed by the Confederates for small arms ammunition, iron case-shot balls were often substituted for lead.

Combination fuse: Combination of the time fuse and percussion fuse system. The inertia of firing caused the plunger in the fuse to strike a chemical composition, thereby, igniting the powder train. The fuse was designed to act as a percussion fuse if it struck an object before the pre-set time.

Concussion fuse: A chemical fuse designed to activate from the shock of striking an object. The chemicals were kept separate until impact when the action of the chemicals upon each other caused a flame.

Drop: This is a collector term to describe a bullet that was dug and found to be in unfired condition. The idea is that the soldier who originally handled the round somehow dropped it and never recovered it.

Fixed ammunition: A pre-assembled (or fixed) combination of a smoothbore projectile, sabot, and powder bag. This assembly allowed an increase in the rate of fire of the artillery crew by eliminating two steps in the process of loading and firing.

Friction primer: A small brass or quill tube, known as the priming tube, filled with gunpowder and used to send a flame to the powder charge inside the bore. An artilleryman used a lanyard to pull the wire, which ignited the fuse.

Fuse: Fuses for projectiles are classified as time fuses, percussion-fuses, and combination-fuses. The time fuse serves to explode a projectile during flight, or at the end of a given period of time after its discharge from the gun. The percussion-fuse, rifled guns, serves to explode a projectile either during flight or on impact. The combination fuse involves both of these elements.

Grapeshot: Iron balls that, when bound together, formed a stand of grapeshot.

Minié bullet: Perfected by Captain Claude Etienne Minié of the French Army in 1848. The U.S. Army adopted the design in 1855. The bullet was elongated, but was hollow at the base for about one-third of the length. When fired, gasses forced the lead into the rifling grooves in the barrel.

Percussion cap: A slightly conical copper cap, shaped like a top hat, which contained fulminate of mercury. The cap was placed on the nipple of the fuse slider in the percussion fuse or simply the nipple of a musket. When struck, it sent a spark to the charge.

Ring: On the base of a conical bullet, "rings" will often be found. The idea is that, when fired, these rings would expand and engage the rifling grooves in the barrel.

Sabot: The sabot served as the driving band for an artillery projectile. Generally, a sabot was made of wood, brass, copper, lead, or wrought iron. The sabot for a rifled projectile was attached directly onto the projectile. When the weapon was fired, the gases from the explosion caused the sabot to expand into the rifling grooves of the barrel.

Shell: A hollow projectile, cast iron, containing a bursting charge that was ignited by means of a fuse.

Solid shot: A solid projectile cast without a powder chamber or fuse hole. Also known as a "shot" or "cannon ball."

War log: The term "war log" was first used in the early days of the Grand Army of the Republic and United Confederate Veterans to describe souvenir pieces of wood recovered from battlefields that showed the impact of bullets or artillery pieces. These early specimens served as reminders of the perils the veterans had faced. Today, "war logs" are reemerging on the market. No longer the branches or stumps stripped of bark, these are battlefield-recovered specimens where the tree had actually "healed" around the projectile. Split open, these branches reveal the bullet, and often, the path it took to enter the wood. Definitely possessing a different feel than the earlier veteran-acquired specimens, they are, nonetheless, a true testament of the deadliness the soldiers had faced.

Also see: Accoutrements, Artillery and Accessories, Carbines, Muskets and Rifles, and Revolvers and Pistols.

Chapter 6
Buttons

Collecting uniform buttons can be very satisfying to a collector, whether beginner or expert. Without the expense of collecting cloth items, a Civil War enthusiast can feel a link to individual soldiers by assembling a collection of buttons. The variety of issues, as well as manufacturer's, provides for a wide field of available items with a price scale ranging from a couple of dollars for a common U.S. General Service button to several thousands of dollars for a Confederate locally-made Staff Officer's button.

Like so many areas of Civil War collecting, it is important to specialize if you decide to focus your attention on buttons. Pick a branch of service, a state, (or better, a manageable combination) as opposed to simply buying what comes along. There are far too many buttons available, and you will soon become overwhelmed if you don't narrow the field a bit. Simply collecting Confederate buttons will soon empty your financial resources, whereas a collection of Virginia buttons will provide a wide variety of items at a more affordable collecting pace.

Button collectors have the opportunity to collect non-dug or dug items. Whereas dug items lend a greater sense of authenticity, their usual dull patinas are not the most attractive. Non-dug buttons, on the other hand, can be very expensive for rare examples, and are easier to reproduce. Collecting on the high end of the field should only be done after exhaustive research and examination of buttons in other collections.

As is the case in so many areas of Civil War collecting, the button field has been inundated with reproductions and fakes. The same dies that were used to stamp buttons during the 1860s still exist and, in many cases, are used to produce buttons primarily for the reenacting market. It takes very little campaigning to give a newly struck brass button a warm, rich patina.

High prices have prompted some forgers to actually bury or artificially age buttons to achieve a dug appearance. Inspect any button, but especially those priced over more than a few dollars, with attention to detail. Use a high-powered magnifying glass and bright light to make your inspection.

Button Types

Figure 1. Type I style button consists of a single, die-struck or cast face with a shank.

Figure 2. Type II buttons have a convex, stamped shell crimped onto a flat back plate. The shank is attached to the back plate.

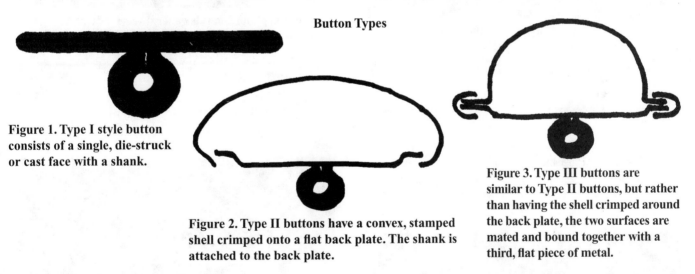

Figure 3. Type III buttons are similar to Type II buttons, but rather than having the shell crimped around the back plate, the two surfaces are mated and bound together with a third, flat piece of metal.

During the Civil War, three button styles were in use: the one-piece button (figure 1); the two-piece button (figure 2); and the staff button (figure 3). It is important to note that the style of button is *not* an indicator of rank, but rather is a result of different manufacturing techniques.

The one-piece button was very popular during the eighteenth century and the first half of the nineteenth for both uniforms and civilian clothes. It can be found in cast, molded, or die-struck form. The shank, in earlier examples, is often part of the same casting as the face. On later, struck examples, the shank was made of a separate loop of wire and brazed onto the back of the face.

Two-piece buttons were first introduced around 1813 by an English inventor, Benjamin Sanders. The button consists of a front "shell" on which the design is struck and a back "plate" on which the shank is attached. The front shell is attached by rolling it over the edge of the back plate.

The third style is often referred to as a "staff" button. It was first produced in the United States in the 1830s, and became the mainstay of uniform button style through the twentieth century. It is similar to the two-piece button except that the front shell and back plate are held together by a separate rim piece.

Collecting Hints

Pros:
- There is a huge variety of buttons available for collectors.
- It is easy to assemble a large collection and not require a lot of space.
- Buttons display well and are not adversely affected by long-time exposure.
- Many buttons can be purchased for under $30 each.
- Good references are available.

Cons:
- Many buttons have been restruck, reproduced, and faked.
- Variety is virtually unlimited and a collector can easily become overwhelmed.
- Because of the size, buttons do not easily command a lot of attention when displayed.

Availability ★
Price ★★★★
Reproduction Alert ★★

Buttons, Part I: Confederate, Branch of Service Buttons

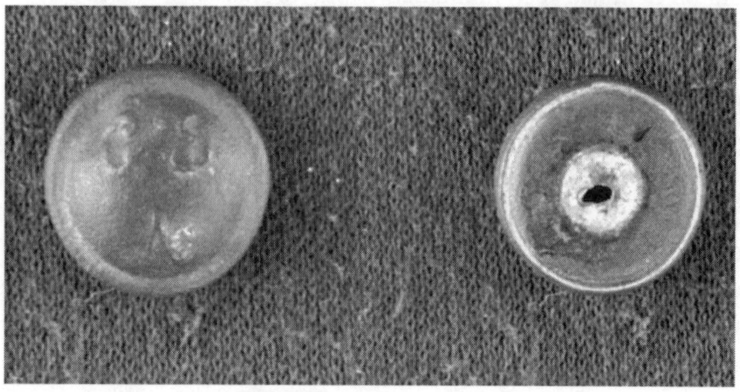

General service button bearing the unusual pyramid-style stamped "C.S.A."

www.civilwarbuttons.com

General Service

"CS over A." Rare and unusually nice! Smooth, without shank; most of this variety are dented or heavily pushed, very minor place above the "C" and is an especially fine example, 17 mm. **600.00**

Another general service button, similar condition to the previous example.

www.civilwarbuttons.com

"Superior Quality," 23 mm. **200.00**

Sold as a kepi button, this general service "C.S.A." button is more correctly considered as a "cuff-sized" button.

Middle Tennessee Relics.

Scarce kepi "CSA" button, "Treble Rich/Standard," 13 mm. **450.00**

Solid, non-dug condition button.

This is a non-excavated, 23 mm, coat-size "CSA." Beautiful condition with "Superior Quality" backmark and shank intact. **225.00**

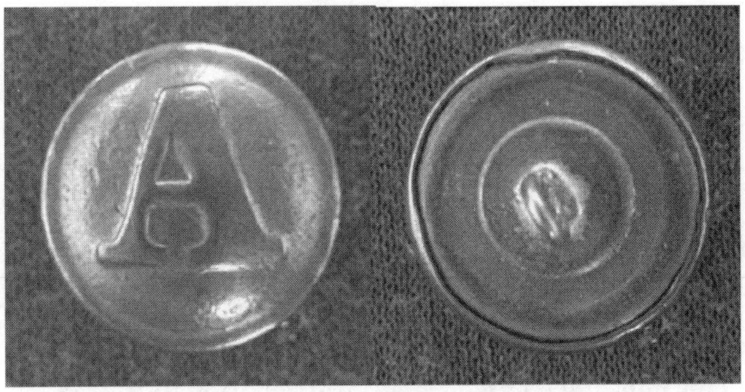

The tinned back of this button gives it a distinct, locally-produced feel and certainly distinguishes it from other imported examples.

www.civilwarbuttons.com

Artillery

Block "A" local tinned iron back; copper face, 23 mm. **775.00**

Block "A" with a tin back, a crudely-made local, beautiful chocolate patina. **750.00**

The Confederate "lined A" buttons like this example do not command the price of the more elaborate looking script variety.

www.civilwarbuttons.com

Lined "A" "Superior Quality," 23 mm. **200.00**

A London-import, "script A" button.

www.civilwarbuttons.com

Script "A" "Isaacs & Campbell/London/71 Jermyn St.," 23 mm. **950.00**

Another import artillery button, this time in the "stippled" style.

www.civilwarbuttons.com

Stippled "A" "HT&B/Manchester," 25 mm. **675.00**

A very nice example of the block "A" button with backmark, "E.M. Lewis & Co./Richmond." Small face dent, back is slightly pushed in, still really great-looking artifact with super character, complete with the shank. **135.00**

"Stippled A" English import with slight push in the face.

www.civilwarbuttons.com

Stippled "A" "HT&B/Manchester." Slight push that hides along the "A" and is not distracting, 25 mm. **550.00**

This excavated two-piece "block A" artillery button was dug in Tennessee.

Middle Tennessee Relics

This is a two-piece, coat-size button with a brass face and an iron back. Attractive Confederate Block A button excavated from General Bragg's artillery camp four miles south of Shelbyville on Lewisburg Pike. . . **125.00**

Simple "lined C" cavalry button.

www.civilwarbuttons.com

Cavalry

Lined "C," blank, 23 mm. **650.00**

Lined "C," backmark blank, beautiful copper face. **625.00**

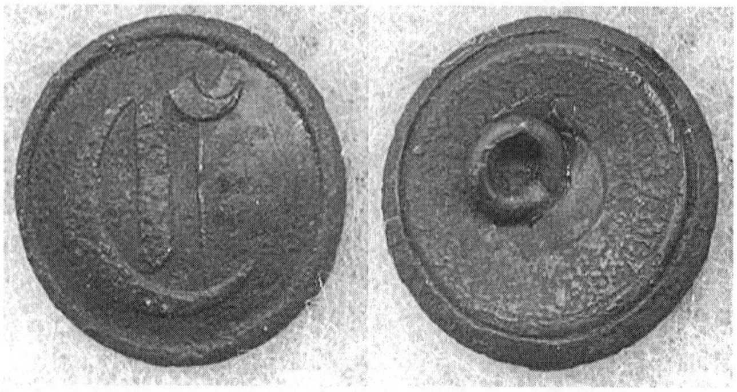

Old English "lined C" with double border.

Sharpsburg Arsenal

Lined Old English "C," two-piece with border. . **900.00**

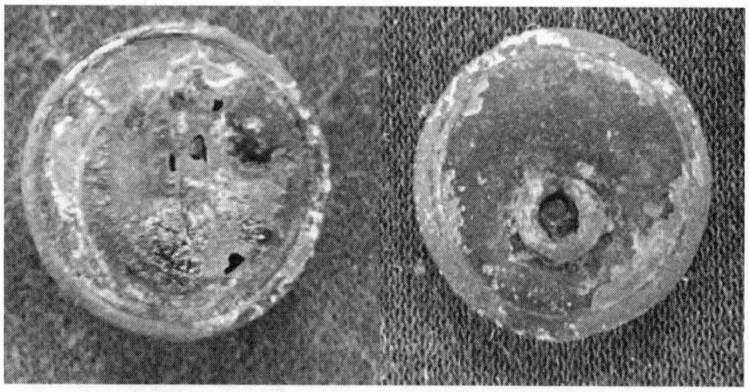

Confederate Cavalry button in rough condition.

www.civilwarbuttons.com

Script "C": "Isaacs & Campbell/London/71 Jeremyn St." Dug from low country South Carolina, condition rough, 23 mm. **85.00**

Outstanding example of large blouse-sized button, being a lined "C" on a plain background, backmark of "Superior Quality," non-dug. **495.00**

Stippled "C," "HT&B/Manchester," 25 mm. . . . **725.00**

This non-dug Confederate Cavalry button possessed a warm, convincing patina and an English exporter's mark.

www.civilwarbuttons.com

Engineer, manuscript, "E" ".S. Isaacs Campbell & Co./ London/St.James .St.," 26 mm. **3,000.00**

The Confederate Engineer button is rarely encountered.

www.civilwarbuttons.com

When groups of buttons are found with a provenance that links them together, prices will soar. These three dug Confederate Infantry buttons were dug in the same location, indicating that they probably all were on the same jacket.

Middle Tennessee Relics

Infantry

Beautiful set of three, two-piece Confederate block "I" coat-size buttons. These buttons were dug only a few inches from each other off the same jacket. All three have beautiful faces, full back, and shank intact. **250.00**

A beautiful, dug example of a solid cast "I" button with rich chocolate patina.. **125.00**

A fine, dug example of an Old English "I" button with S. Isaacs Campbell backmark, excellent dug condition with pretty patina, good detail, and very legible backmark. 135.00
A perfect non-dug example, "Superior Quality" backmark. 265.00
Lined "I" button, nice dug example, very nice age patina, good detail, nice color, complete with shank (bent) and having a blank backmark. 135.00

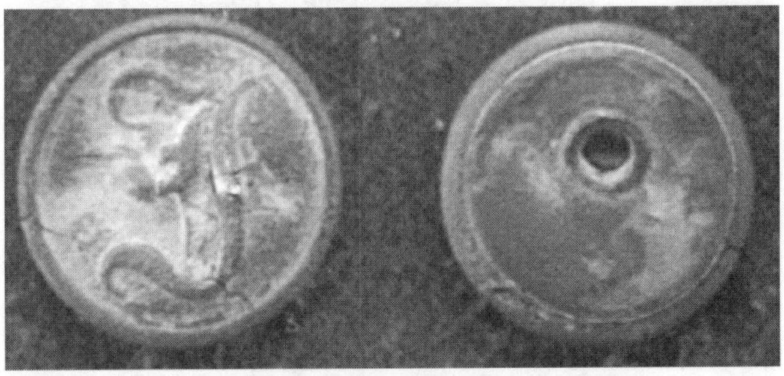

Even though this button has been flattened while underground, it still displays well.

www.civilwarbuttons.com

Blank back, dug and flattened; display-worthy example, 23 mm. 65.00
Block "I," no shank, nice face, dug at Morton, Mississippi. 65.00
Block "I," pewter, no shank, very fine condition. . 75.00
Block "I," Richmond, Virginia backmark, fine condition. 95.00

Non-dug, tin-backed "Block I" button.

www.civilwarbuttons.com

Block "I" local, tinned iron back, 22 mm. 575.00

Even though this "Block I" has been heavily pitted, the shank is still intact and the backmark is nearly legible.

Military Antiques & Museum

Brass "I" button, backmark is unreadable, but probably "E.M. Lewis Richmond, VA." 75.00

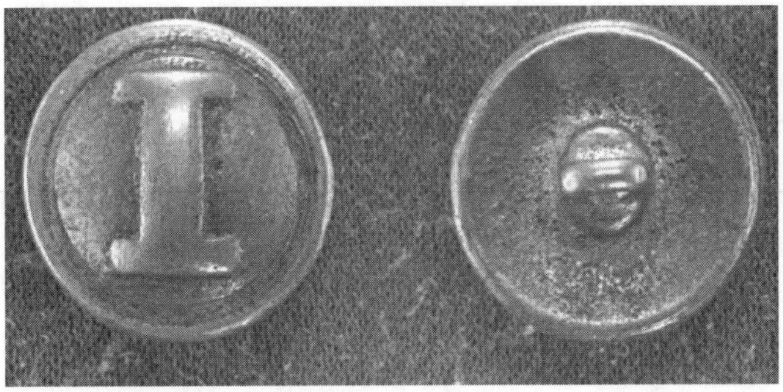

Non-dug and complete, cast Confederate "I" button.

www.civilwarbuttons.com

Cast "I," nice, guaranteed non-dug and real, 23 mm. 600.00
Coast-size, solid cast-brass Confederate block "I." It is very rare to find this button in non-excavated condition, 23 mm-button with shank intact. . . 495.00
Confederate infantry button, solid cast-brass "I." Nice dug example, 100% authentic in every respect, from a Georgia camp in Northern Virginia, uncleaned patina overall. 190.00

Damage to the back and the missing shank did not detract from the sale of this Confederate infantry button.

www.civilwarbuttons.com

Confederate lined "I" coat "Superior Quality*," missing shank, back has break and some damage, superb face, dug in Petersburg, Virginia, 23 mm. 100.00

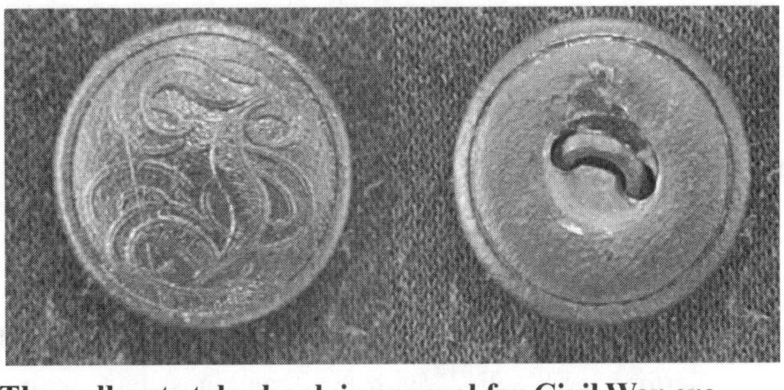

The pull-out style shank is unusual for Civil War-era buttons.

www.civilwarbuttons.com

Infantry, cont.

Confederate manuscript "I" blank, (P. Tait-style pull-out shank), dug, light ground action; very slight flaw on reverse, 23 mm. **250.00**

Confederate script "I," non-dug button, nice example with blank back and shank, 100% guaranteed authentic in every respect, from a house yard sale in Northern Virginia, uncleaned patina overall. . **145.00**

C.S. block "I" button with no shank, nice face, dug at Morton, Mississippi...................... **65.00**

C.S. Block "I" button, fine condition........... **95.00**

Top condition button.

www.civilwarbuttons.com

Excellent condition, non-dug, 7/8" d with tin back. **396.00**

Lined "I," shank bent and back difficult to read, but is an import from England. **145.00**

Looks like pewter with a brass shank, unusual example to find with only very light pitting to face, 24 mm. **195.00**

"Manuscript I" infantry button with an Alabama maker's mark.

www.civilwarbuttons.com

Manuscript, "I" "Halfmann & Taylor/Montgomery," 23 mm. **325.00**

Non-excavated, coat-sized, script "I, backmark, "Halfmann & Taylor/Montg*" excellent condition." **395.00**

Perfect dug block "I" with shank and brass back with series of tiny dots........................ **95.00**

Pewter "I" with no shank, very-fine condition, gorgeous face. **75.00**

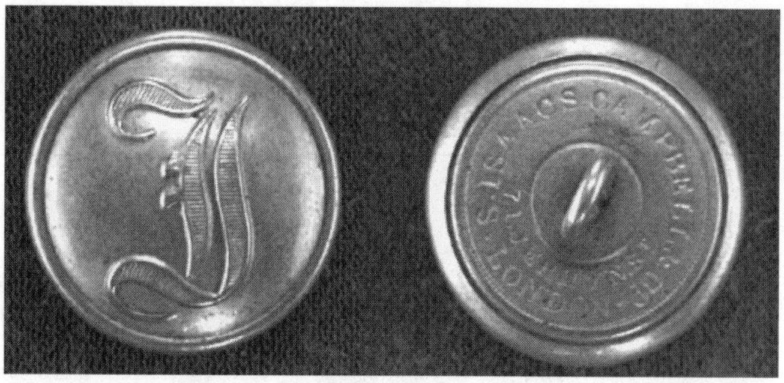

Immaculate condition with a backmark not known to be reproduced will ensure a high price.

www.civilwarbuttons.com

Script "I", "Isaacs & Campbell/London/71 Jermyn St," 23 mm.. .... **275.00**

Script "I" blank, shows nice patina, 23 mm. **275.00**

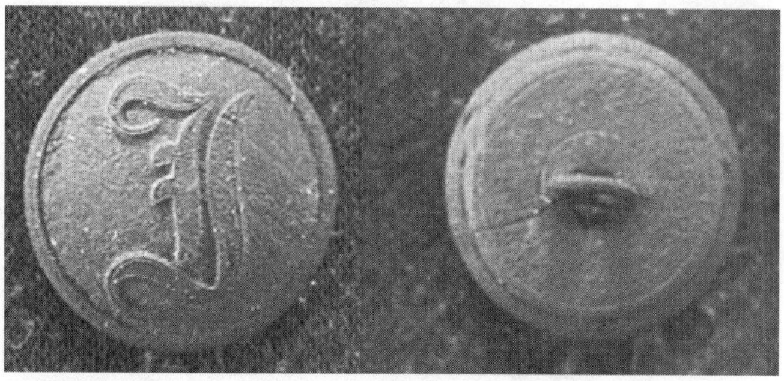

Dug button with a hairline crack.

Middle Tennessee Relics

Script "I" Isaacs & Campbell/London/71 Jermyn St.," dug, hairline flaw on reverse, 23 mm....... **135.00**

All brass button in excellent condition, backstamped, "Courtney & Tennent." **461.00**

Excavated, 23 mm, coat-size old English "I." Button has brass Confederate C.S. local back, smooth brown patina, no dents, and the shank has rusted away long ago, a very scarce button. **295.00**

"Block I" is probably one of the most common Confederate buttons.

Middle Tennessee Relics

Dug, two-piece Confederate Block "I" coat-size button, iron back, face has attractive smooth brown patina. The back is rusty but intact, and the iron loop is rusted away as usual. A good, solid example of probably the most frequently encountered marked Confederate button in the western theater. **85.00**

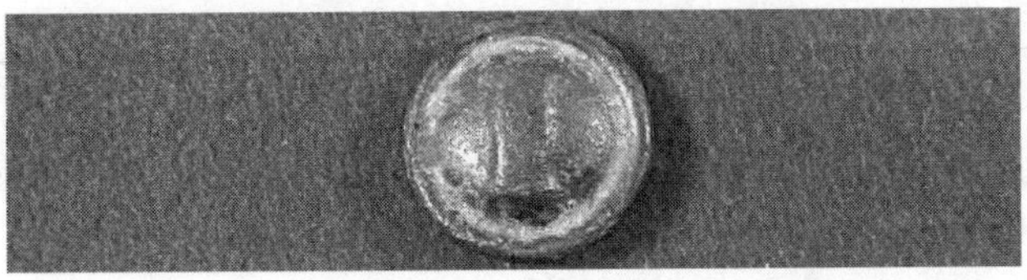

Collectors refer to the heavy edge on the "Block I" button as a "puff rim." Really not more than a variation, the puff rim does not add any significant value to a button.

Middle Tennessee Relics

Very nice condition freshly dug two-piece, coat-size Confederate "puff-rim" block "I" button. Face is solid with brown-green patina and no dents. Iron back is rusty, but totally intact. This button was dug from Polk's Corp Confederate camps along Duck River near Shelbyville, Tennessee. **95.00**

Even with the more common Confederate infantry button, condition is a large determining factor for price. The missing shank kept the price of this button down.

www.civilwarbuttons.com

"E.M.L & C./Richmond. Va." rmdc, dug example, excellent face, no shank, 22 mm. **75.00**

Navy

A very fine hard rubber or black plastic-type of material. Very attractive Confederate button, backmark, "Courtney & Tennent/Charleston S C/Manton's Patent.". **1,200.00**

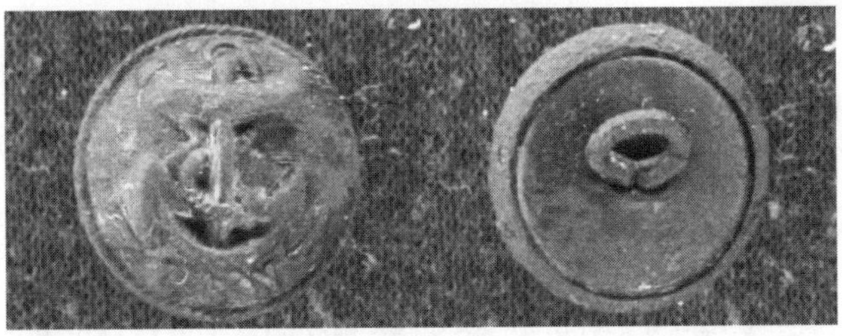

Confederate Navy buttons are very rare. Existing in both hard rubber and brass, this two-piece example is of the latter material.

www.civilwarbuttons.com

Confederate Navy medium size. Blank, stand up shank intact, chocolate-brown patina, 18 mm. **500.00**

Confederate Navy button in excellent condition with a very clear London maker's mark

www.civilwarbuttons.com

CS Navy, coat size; "Firmin & Sons/153 Strand London/& 13/Conduit St," 23 mm. **1,450.00**

The "rifleman's button was adopted by the Army of the Confederate States in 1861.

www.civilwarbuttons.com

Rifleman

German Text "R" "Van Wart Son & Co.," 23 mm. . . **450.00**

This is a two-piece, non-dug, coat-size button with a stippled Roman "R" with an "H T & B Manchester" backmark, 25 mm d, complete with shank. **645.00**

Staff

1-1/6" d with backmark "Halfmann & Taylor Montgomery." Truly the best-struck and most handsome button that was made for the Confederacy. . . . **2,250.00**

The Confederate staff button was worn by general officers and officers of the general staff. They were prescribed for wear by an order issued June 6, 1861.

Middle Tennessee Relics

Staff, cont.

Beautiful condition, non-excavated, Confederate, droop-wing eagle, staff officer's button, 19 mm size, "Treble Gilt Extra Rich" backmark, 100% bright gold gilt and nice straight shank intact on the reverse...... **225.00**

Coat-size, droop-wing eagle, Confederate staff officer's button dug from General Leonidas Polk's winter camps along Duck River following the Battle of Stones River, smooth, uncleaned, brown patina. Button does have a slight dent, but still looks great, iron shank remains intact on the reverse..... **125.00**

CS staff officer with stars, local backmark, with shank, very-good condition, small push on face. Dug at Morton, Mississippi. **165.00**

Dug, very fine condition with shank, backmark "Extra Rich/Treble Gilt" loaded with gilt, vest-size.. **275.00**

Has shank, non-dug, loaded with gilt, "Extra Rich" backmark, vest size. **195.00**

Dug off Charleston, South Carolina, 15% bright background gilt, shank half broken off by digger, very nice example of the "droop-wing" eagle button. **395.00**

Shank present, non-dug, vest-size with lots of gilt, "Extra Rich" backmark. **195.00**

Staff officer's button, with shank, dug, very fine condition, Extra Rich/Treble Gilt B/M, loaded with gilt, vest size. **275.00**

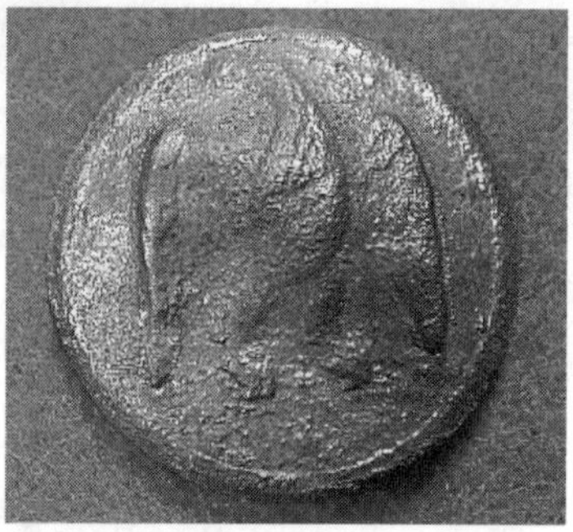

The "Droop-Wing" is a rare general staff button.

Middle Tennessee Relics

Extremely rare, excavated 16 mm, cuff-size, Confederate, droop-wing eagle, staff officer button. This button has a brown patina with typical ground action, no dents and intact shank. **225.00**

Coat-sized army officer's eagle button.

www.civilwarbuttons.com

"Extra Rich/Treble Gilt," 24 mm. **185.00**

Button with a dented face and a missing shank.

www.civilwarbuttons.com

"Extra Rich/Treble Gilt," dented, no shank, 24 mm. **100.00**

This 13mm diameter general service button is a small-sized example that could be used for any application such as uniform cuffs, vests, and yes, even kepi side buttons.

www.civilwarbuttons.com

"HT & B/Manchester," kepi-size and rare, 13 mm. **675.00**

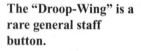

General service button with a backmark that describes the construction technique, this "Rivet'd & Solder'd" is marked with "C.S.A." on the eagle's shield.

www.civilwarbuttons.com

"Rivt'd & Solder'd/(lion, unicorn, & coat of arms)." Rarest backmark found on CS1s, 26 mm. ... **2,000.00**

Large-sized staff button with eagle surrounded by stars and blank backmark. Complete with the shank, and is very solid, patina is heavy red-brown. Detail on the button is good with a slight push. **245.00**

Because the eagle does not bear a shield with "C.S.A.," this general service is not as desirable as the previous button (even though it, too, is marked "Rivet'd & Solder'd").

www.civilwarbuttons.com

"Rivt'd & Solder'd/(lion, unicorn,& coat of arms)" quite rare, seldom found on the coat-sized CS5s, 24 mm. **550.00**

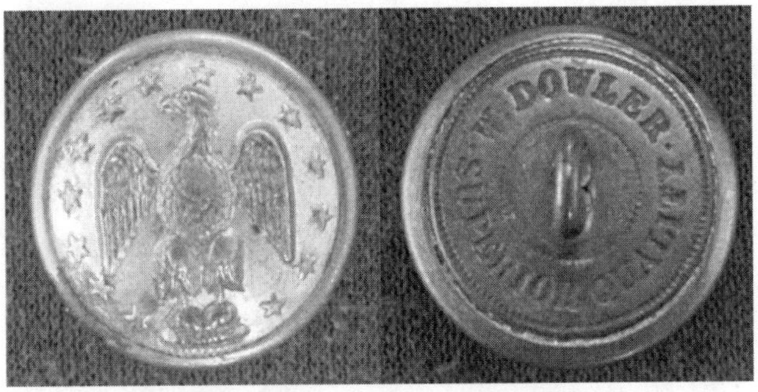

Button authority Alphaeus Albert notes this style of general service button as not being significantly rare.

www.civilwarbuttons.com

"W. Dowler/Superior Quality" 23 mm. **1,375.00**

The position of the eagle and the eleven surrounding buttons lend a distinctly early martial appearance to this rare general service button.

www.civilwarbuttons.com

Confederate general officers, rare, "*HT&B/ Manchester," choice example with patina providing excellent contrast to this nicely gilted button, 24 mm. **2,600.00**

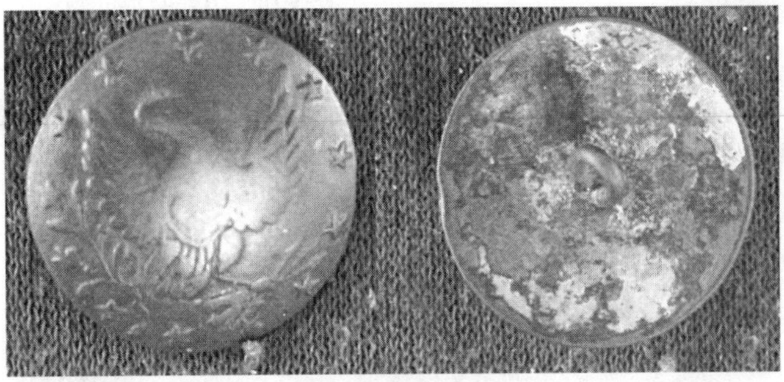

General service button with "C.S." marking the shield on the eagle's chest.

www.civilwarbuttons.com

Confederate officers, one-piece, rare "CS" in the shield, extra smooth patina and shows genuine wear, 24 mm. **600.00**

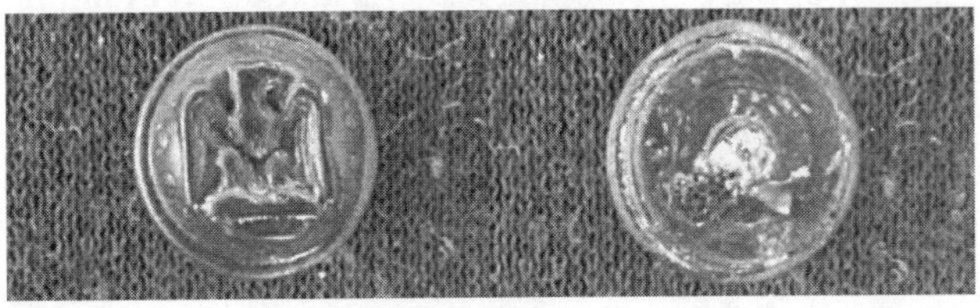

This style of general service cuff-sized button is rarely, if ever, found as a backmark.

www.civilwarbuttons.com

General officers, local, very rare cuff size. Dug with a small push; no shank, nice smooth patina and great eye appeal, 13 mm. **250.00**

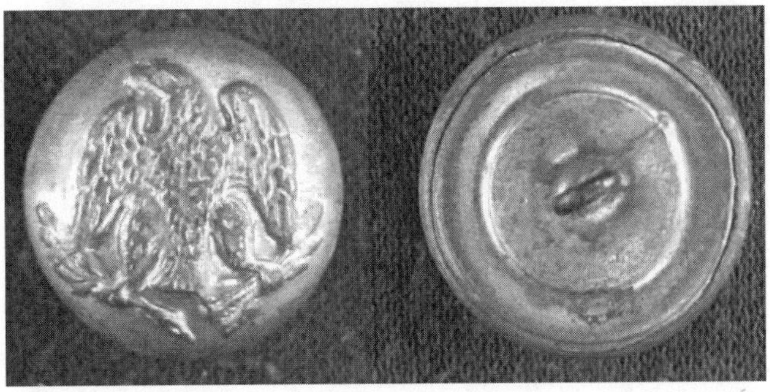

Made as a two-piece rather than a three-piece, staff-style button, this general service button can be considered rare.

www.civilwarbuttons.com

Non-dug, local C.S. officer's button, loaded with gilt, 21 mm.. .... **1,850.00**

Confederate, State-Issued Buttons

The distinction is rarely made by button dealers between buttons produced with state seals before the war and buttons produced during the war. Though rarely priced accordingly, it is safe to assume that a button bearing a southern state seal and possessing a northern manufacturer's mark were produced before or after 1861-1865. Whereas, it is likely that these buttons produced prior to 1861 found their way to Confederate uniforms, one should consider place of manufacture before expending large sums of money.

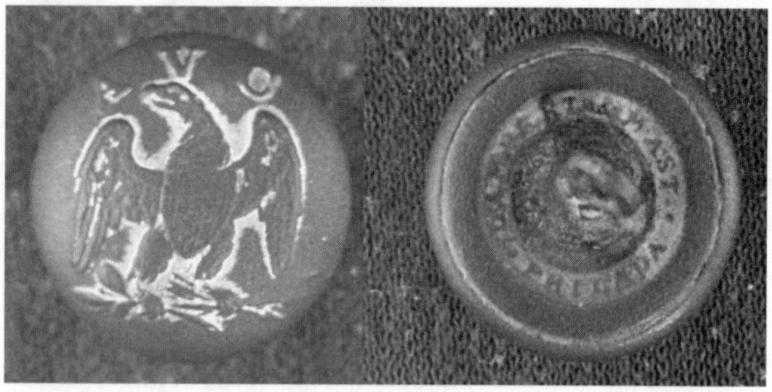

Because of the Philadelphia maker's mark, this example was probably produced before the Civil War for the Alabama Volunteer Corps.

www.civilwarbuttons.com

Alabama

"AVC, has rare, "Lambert & Mast/Philada" rmdc, unusual and desirable mark is easily readable, smooth patina, device is highlighted with gilt, 21 mm." **400.00**

Attributed to the Alabama Cadet Corps, this button is considered a reasonable Confederate piece. The strong patina gives it a good period feel.

Sharpsburg Arsenal

Alabama (University) Cadet Corps. **250.00**

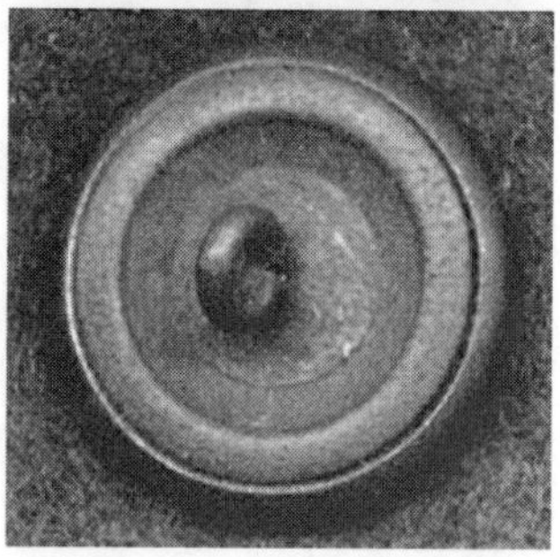

Alabama Volunteer Corps button with no backmark and a strong push to the face.

Sharpsburg Arsenal

Alabama Volunteer Corps. **425.00**

State seal, non-dug, coat-sized, straight, solid shank with a couple of stains on the back, marked, "Horstman Bros. & Allen N.Y." **494.00**

This AVC was found in Caroline County, Virginia, touch of gold gilt above the eagle's head, inside the "V," and front has light touches. The front has light ground action typical of many dug buttons. The backmark is "R W Robinson Extra Rich." The shank is slightly bent which put pressure on the back and slightly kinked it. **230.00**

London manufacturer Van Wart and Son supplied thousands of buttons to the Confederacy.

Middle Tennessee Relics

Georgia

Beautiful condition, non-dug, coat-size Georgia state seal, Van Wart backmark, 100% bright gold gilt with shank intact. **95.00**

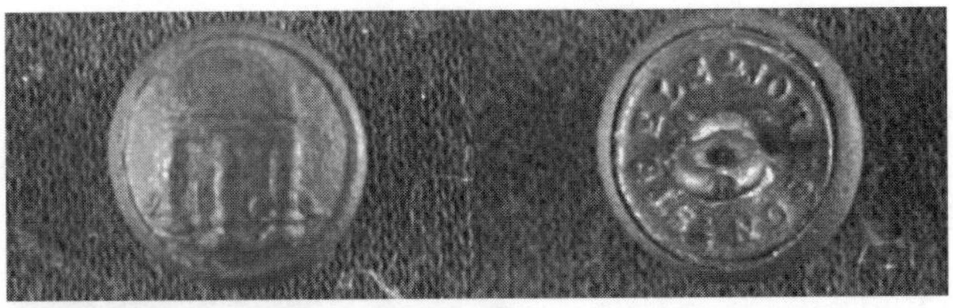

Dug example of a Georgia state seal button made by Steele and Johnson.

www.civilwarbuttons.com

Georgia cuff, rare with Steele and Johnson backmark, dug, 15 mm. **100.00**

Georgia seal button.

www.civilwarbuttons.com

Georgia seal, "*Van Wart. Son & Co.," 24 mm. . .**125.00**

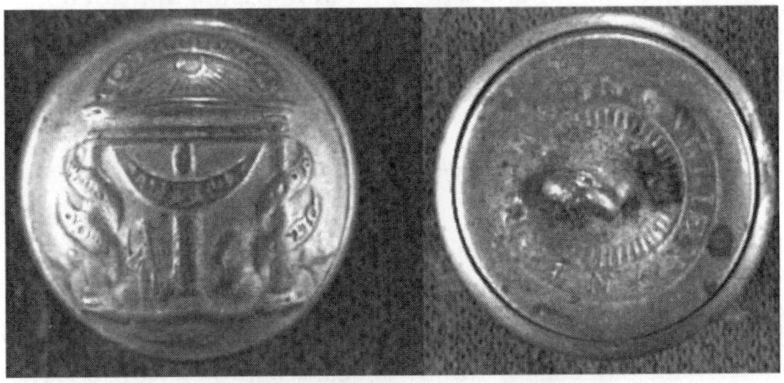

Horstmann and Allien were New York manufacturers. Because this button bears their hallmark, it is most likely that this button was delivered prior to the outbreak of the war.

www.civilwarbuttons.com

Georgia seal, "Horstmann & Allien/NY" with rays, 24 mm. **200.00**

Group. Nice little Georgia state seal cuff button with small piece of rebel cloth still clinging to the back. Face is decent with Georgia state seal, back pushed in and deteriorated, no gilt, overall dark-brown patina. Dug in Tennessee. Also included is large eagle "I" button (excellent w/ shank) with cloth clinging, small eagle "I" with some gilt and some cloth, nice eagle enlisted button with cloth, one smashed eagle "I" button with cloth, and a plain button with cloth covering. All dug in "the Valley" in Virginia except the Georgia button. **79.00**

Again, produced before the war, this rare silver-plated version probably adorned a militia officer's uniform.

www.civilwarbuttons.com

Scarce silver-plated Georgia seal, "Horstmann & Allien/N.Y." with rays, 23 mm. **550.00**

This is a brass, one-piece button with a rattlesnake and the words, "Don't Tread On Me," on the face. This button was dug in a Civil War camp in Savannah, Georgia. It has a perfect straight shank and a backmark, "Double Gilt." This button is believed to have been used by the Chatham Artillery. **450.00**

When a dug example of a Confederate button bears a northern maker's mark, the secessionist history of the item seems to easily reveal itself.

www.civilwarbuttons.com

Very fine, dug, Georgia seal with nice gilt highlighting the device, "*W. H. Smith & Co*/New-York" rmdc, 24 mm. **275.00**

Dated backmarks are extremely rare. Solid provenance is the best protection against forgery and price deflation.

www.civilwarbuttons.com

Georgia, cont.

Very fine, Georgia seal with dated backmark, "*W. G. Mintzer/Phila 1861," rmdc. This is one of the very few backmarks which includes a Civil War date, 24 mm. **200.00**

In spite of providing troops to both the Union and the Confederacy, most collectors like to believe that their Kentucky buttons have solid ties to the South's rebellion. Kentucky items with solid Confederate provenance should command premium prices.

www.civilwarbuttons.com

Kentucky

Kentucky cuff, "*Extra*/Quality," 15 mm. **250.00**

Kentucky-seal button.

www.civilwarbuttons.com

Kentucky seal, "Horstmann & Allien/NY," mint, 23 mm. **750.00**

Again, this is a state seal button with a Yankee backmark. Without additional history, it is impossible to say that it is 100% certain that this button adorned a Confederate uniform.

www.civilwarbuttons.com

Kentucky state seal, "*Superior*/Quality," rmdc, 23 mm. **750.00**

A legitimate, battlefield-dug Louisiana button retaining some gilt like on this one, is an added bonus.

Middle Tennessee Relics

Louisiana

Dug, coat-size Confederate local Louisiana state seal, smooth brown patina with 80% bright beautiful gilt and dent-free. The back is very solid, but the wire loop is rusted away. **350.00**

When compared to the previous button, even though this one is non-dug and retains a lot of its visual appeal, it bears a northern maker's mark.

www.civilwarbuttons.com

Louisiana seal, "Horstmann's/N.Y.& PHI," 23 mm. **450.00**

A cuff-sized example "Pelican" button, pelican has her head to her left, Scovill backmark, rich dug patina, nice detail, no shank. **95.00**

Nice dug example of a "Pelican" button, having a Hyde & Goodrich New Orleans backmark. This retains about 30% gilt with the balance a pleasing patina, and some light wear. **185.00**

Possessing a New Orleans' manufactured hallmark, this button has to be considered a solid, good buy.

www.civilwarbuttons.com

Louisiana seal; "Hyde & Goodrich/N-O," rmdc, unusual variant with LA2 marking on LA3 face design, no shank; very nice mellow patina, 23 mm. **300.00**

Dug, cuff-sized Louisiana button with no backmark.

Middle Tennessee Relics

Quite rare, dug, cuff-size "sideways pelican" Louisiana state seal button, it has a smooth brown patina, crisp detail, and a nice straight shank. **175.00**

Though most collectors automatically consider buttons from border states as "Confederate," an astute collector will recognize that state seal buttons may have just as likely been used by pre-war militia or even troops raised for the Union.

www.civilwarbuttons.com

Maryland

Maryland cuff, marked, "*Extra*/Quality."15 mm. **175.00**

A striking anomaly such as the double-struck backmark on this button, usually does not add any value to a button. Indeed, it will often detract from the value.

www.civilwarbuttons.com

Unusual Maryland with double-struck backmark, "*Extra*/Quality," 23 mm. **375.00**

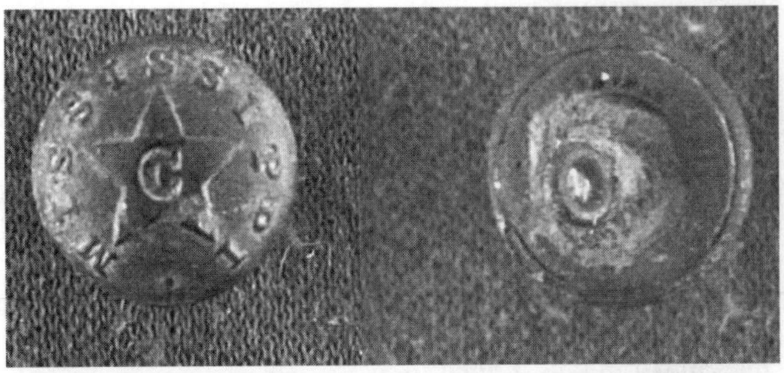

Branch-marked Mississippi buttons are very attractive and display a strong degree of martial spirit. Therefore, they are highly sought-after by Confederate collectors. The New Orleans backmark on this example seems to cinch its Dixie connection.

www.civilwarbuttons.com

Mississippi

Dug, Mississippi "C" cuff, "Hyde & Goodrich/N.O.," 16 mm.. .... **375.00**

Dug, Mississippi Infantry "I" "local" cuff blank, probably produced by C. Rouyer, no shank, attractive patina, 16 mm.......................... **125.00**

Non-dug Mississippi infantry button with a tin back and no hallmark. True Confederate pieces are hard to find, and even harder to buy!

www.civilwarbuttons.com

Exquisite local Mississippi "I," 22 mm....... **2,500.00**

Perhaps not possessing some of the detail as the previous Mississippi button, this one does have a New Orleans maker mark.

www.civilwarbuttons.com

Mississippi, cont.

Mississippi "I", "Hyde & Goodrich/N-O,"rmdc, stippling still present on the star, 22 mm..... **975.00**

Dug, Mississippi "I" cuff button with heavy patina, no gilt, "Hyde & Goodrich N.O." backmark. Worn condition with heavy patina.. .... **65.00**

A button like this Mississippi infantry with New Orleans backmark makes it hard to understand why dug buttons tend to command less price than similar buttons with doubtful provenance. Dug on a Southern battlefield, this button almost certainly was part of some Johnny Reb's uniform.

Middle Tennessee Relics

This is a coat-size button with a Hyde & Goodrich New Orleans backmark, button was dug in northern Mississippi and has a chocolate-brown patina with gold in the "I," and traces around the star and letters. This is a good solid example with no dents and shank intact. **275.00**

Like so many state seal buttons from border states, this Missouri example appears, for all practical purposes to be produced for prewar militia or northern state volunteers. Regardless, dealers like to represent and price them as legitimate Confederate pieces.

www.civilwarbuttons.com

Missouri, Missouri state seal, "Scovill Mf'g Co./ Waterbury," 23 mm. **350.00**

North Carolina

Perfect specimen, 65% plus gilt, tiny push at 7:00. .... **265.00**

Sunburst button with no shank, fine condition, dug in Tennessee. **95.00**

Described as non-dug, this button certainly appears to be extremely crude. It sold for $475.00.

Middle Tennessee Relics

Absolutely beautiful, non-dug, coat-size Confederate local North Carolina state seal, 100% bright gold gilt front and back, huge crude shank intact but leans to one side. This button has brilliant sparkling bright gilt. ...**475.00**

Backmark blank. 95% gilt. **650.00**

Local NC Seal, "W. Wildt & Son/Richmond VA," unusually readable and fine example, backmarks are usually obscure and unreadable, 23 mm.. .... **800.00**

Though dug and missing its shank, this button displays well. And for only $75.00, it was an inexpensive Confederate relic.

www.civilwarbuttons.com

Local NC seal, dug, blank channel with star, shankless, smooth patina, 22 mm. **60.00**

This button appears to be a local variation on the North Carolina state seal theme.

www.civilwarbuttons.com

Local, this die is not pictured in Albert's or Tice's books, blank channel, 23 mm. **750.00**

Excellent, Richmond, Virginia-produced North Carolina button.

www.civilwarbuttons.com

NC state seal, local, five-pointed star in channel with Wildt & Kline punched through shank, 23 mm. **675.00**

Nice, dug, state seal example with shank from a North Carolina camp in Northern Virginia, uncleaned patina overall. 185.00

Nice, dug, sunburst example missing shank (as usual for this pattern). 110.00

North Carolina state seal, half of shank broken off, 5% silver gilt in center, moderate ground action. 125.00

Missing shank, deep chocolate patina. 110.00

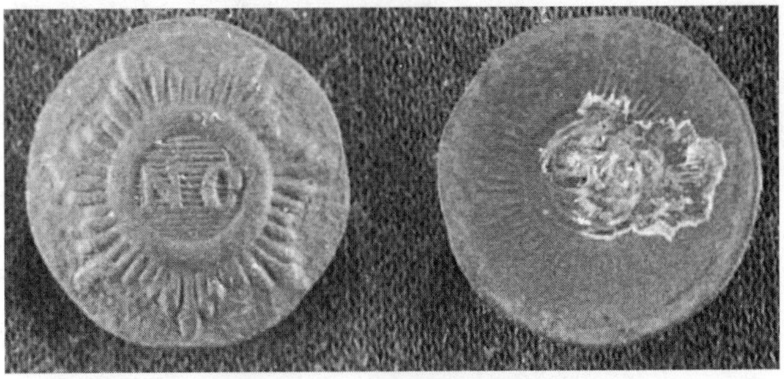

Being a one-piece, locally struck North Carolina example found on a Virginia battlefield speaks as much to the Confederate origins of this button as one could hope.

www.civilwarbuttons.com

North Carolina sunburst, high-relief variant with good color and look, found near Tenth Legion, VA, 23 mm. 100.00

Sunburst with no shank, fine condition, dug in Tennessee. 95.00

In spite of being dug and bearing the appearance of a locally made button, appearance *does* count for a button. This two-piece North Carolina button simply didn't display well.

Middle Tennessee Relics

Very crude, dug, Confederate local North Carolina state seal, button has an attractive brown patina with a couple small rim dents. 65.00

South Carolina

State seal, non-dug, vest size with shank. 75.00

Though sold as a South Carolina pin, this could very well have been a poncho button.

75% original guilt remaining, carved lead Palmetto Tree w/metal pin. 385.00

Beautiful dug, coat-size, South Carolina state seal button that has 90% bright gold gilt with shank intact, "Horstmann and Allen" backmark . . 185.00.

Coat size, dug, with shank, good, very-good condition. 68.00

Cuff-sized button dug in Charleston, South Carolina.

www.civilwarbuttons.com

Dug South Carolina seal, medium size, ".Extra./Rich" rmdc, gilted, from Charleston, S.C., 19 mm. . 125.00

Fine, medium-sized, non-dug button with Horstmann & Allien backmark. 45.00

Local South Carolina seal, blank channel with star, no shank, dented, but smooth, chocolate brown. Old-time find from Virginia, 23 mm. 65.00

Nice, dug example with shank, uncleaned patina overall. 140.00

Nice, dug, coat-size South Carolina state seal, seldom seen, "Young and Smith" backmark, 30% gold gilt with brown patina and shank intact. 275.00

Non-excavated vest size South Carolina state seal, 100% bright gold gilt with rare "Schuyler, H. G." backmark, intact shank. 125.00

Non-dug, coat size with shank, extra fine. 85.00

Non-dug, vest size with shank, extra fine. 75.00

Exquisite, non-dug, South Carolina button produced in New York.

www.civilwarbuttons.com

Rare, low-convex South Carolina, "*Wm. H. Smith & Co*/New-York" rmdc; light push. Heavily silver-plated. Rare and very hard to find non-dug, 23 mm. 450.00

South Carolina, cont.

An excellent example of the large SC state seal button with backmark of "Van Wart & Co." **69.00**

South Carolina state seal produced in New York.

www.civilwarbuttons.com

South Carolina seal, "Schuyler. H.& G./New-York.," rmdc, excellent condition, 23 mm.......... **250.00**

It might be easier to make a case for Confederate usage for this South Carolina button bearing no backmark than it would be for the earlier illustrated New York-produced examples.

www.civilwarbuttons.com

South Carolina seal, blank depressed channel, 23 mm. **225.00**

Bearing the Van Wart mark, this London-made South Carolina button retains a strong visual appearance.

Military Antiques & Museum

South Carolina state seal brass coat button backmark "Van Wart." **140.00**

Vest-size, dug north of Vicksburg, shank present, lots of gilt on face, very-fine condition. **95.00**

Texas, Confederate local, has "CS" in a circle in the middle of the button, with shank, made of pewter, very-fine condition. **450.00**

Nice two-piece Virginia button was probably produced in the years prior to the Civil War.

www.civilwarbuttons.com

Virginia

Virginia staff, "Horstmann & Allien/N.Y." flat back, 23 mm.. .... **225.00**

Northern-produced Virginia coat-sized button.

www.civilwarbuttons.com

Virginia staff, "Horstmann & Co/NY&Phi.," 23 mm. **250.00**

"Extra Quality" backmark, very good with about 50% gilt.. .... **100.00**

A collection could focus solely on Virginia buttons.

www.civilwarbuttons.com

"Swords-Up," Virginia, "*Scovill Mfg.Co.*/Waterbury" rmdc, super condition, 22 mm. **300.00**

Dug, large, blouse-size Virginia staff button with the state seal and having a backmark of "Extra Quality." 70% gilt and a light patina, small spot to the left of Virtue. **150.00**

Cuff-size militia/Confederate-used button bearing the Virginia coat of arms, generic "Extra Quality" backmark, shows age. **95.00**

Cuff-size with shank, dug in a CS camp in Texas, very-good condition. **75.00**

Cuff-size, no shank, very fine face, dug in Texas. **65.00**

Dug, one-piece button, recovered on private property just outside Harpers Ferry, West Virginia. Shank is intact and has "Young. Smith & Co. New York" backmark. **123.50**

Horstmann backmark, dug, Virginia state seal, chocolate-brown patina with gold outlining the detail, no dents, intact shank. **150.00**

New York-made Virginia button.

www.civilwarbuttons.com

Low convex, Virginia, "*Wm. H. Smith & Co*/ New-York" rmdc, 23 mm. **350.00**

Low convex, Virginia, "+Canfield & Brother+/ Baltimore" rmdc, 75% plus silver plate remains, 23 mm. **450.00**

Minor ground action with frost burn, nice shank. **125.00**

Nice, dug, has shank, uncleaned patina overall. . **120.00**

Non-excavated, pre-Civil War, one-piece coat button, "Superior Quality" backmark, fine. **350.00**

Virginia button probably locally produced during the war.

www.civilwarbuttons.com

Rare, local high-dome Virginia with blank channel back, nice brown patina, 23 mm. **375.00**

Scarce early example, minor push at central 3:00; 15%+ rose gilt on face; rare Baltimore backmark, tiny rim damage on reverse. **165.00**

State seal cuff-sized, with shank, very-good condition, dug in a C.S. camp in Texas. **75.00**

State seal, cuff-sized, no shank, very-fine face, dug in Texas. **75.00**

Cuff-sized Virginia button.

Middle Tennessee Relics

This is a non-excavated, 15 mm, cuff-size Virginia state seal, flawless condition, "Extra Quality" backmark, shank intact. **195.00**

"Extra Quality" backmark, very good though something sticky was spilled on the left side, really pretty with about 50% gilt. **100.00**

New York-produced, Virginia coat-sized button.

www.civilwarbuttons.com

Virginia, "*Horstmann*/N.Y.& Philada," 23 mm. **425.00**

Coat-sized Virginia button produced in Baltimore, and thereby, a bit more plausible that it was produced for the Confederacy.

www.civilwarbuttons.com

Virginia, "Canfield Bro & Co/Baltimore" rmdc, 23 mm. **300.00**

Virginia , cont.

Virginia button clearly produced in New York.

www.civilwarbuttons.com

Virginia, "Horstmann & Allien/NY," with rays, 22 mm. **250.00**

Virginia Military Institute brass button with Virginia state seal, backmarked, "D. Evans Attleboro." **125.00**

Buying cadet buttons has to be done with a bit of willingness to believe their military association. Unless dug or accompanied by solid written material, it is just too much of a leap of faith to rely on backmarks to guarantee Civil War association.

www.civilwarbuttons.com

Virginia Military Institute, "R&W Robinson" in ribbon with eagle above, spearhead passes between the "D" and the "E" of "Cadet," 22 mm. **200.00**

Virginia staff, "Scovill Mf'g Co./Waterbury," 23 mm. **250.00**

Most likely an 1840s button, it would have been helpful to know where it was dug. Many of these one-piece Virginia state seal buttons have shown up in Texas and northern Mexico being remnants of the 1847 campaign of the 1st Virginia Volunteers.

www.civilwarbuttons.com

Virginia state seal, one-piece construction, "Young.Smith & CO./New-York," dug with shank, smooth patina, 23 mm. **175.00**

Virginia state seal, brass button, tiny bit of gold remaining, backmarked "Scovill," battlefield-excavated. **80.00**

Virginia state seal, brass uniform button, backmarked, "Scovill MFG Co. Waterbury." **100.00**

Cuff-sized VMI button.

www.civilwarbuttons.com

Virginia Military Institute cuff, "*Robinsons*/Extra," 15 mm. **200.00**

Confederate, Miscellaneous Buttons

Buttons, Confederate, beautiful antique museum card containing two Confederate buttons (one Virginia and one North Carolina) picked up on the battlefield of Cedar Mountain, Virginia. Card and the buttons have untouched age patina. **750.00**

Part II:
U.S., Branch of Service Buttons

General Service

Dug Union buttons have to be the bargain of Civil War collecting.

Two nice, dug buttons with different backmarks, "Scovill Manufacturing Co. Waterbury," and, "Waterbury Button Co." Both are rmdc with stand-up shanks. 7.00

13/16" d, backmark, "Schuyler H.&G., N.Y." 75.00

Coat-sized and Scoville-marked general service eagle button. 15.00

Dug, large-sized eagle button with dark, aged patina. Back is slightly pushed in and still has the shank and Scovill backmark. 15.00

Excellent condition, non-excavated, gilt, cuff-size Union eagle, Scovill backmark, intact shank. 17.00

Union overcoat-sized button.

www.civilwarbuttons.com

Infantry, Civil War, overcoat size, "*D. Evans & Co.*/ Attleboro," 23 mm. 25.00

This silvered example general service button probably dates before the Civil War.

www.civilwarbuttons.com

Infantry, silvered, 21 mm, low convex, two-piece, ".Young. Smith & Co./New York." 45.00

A second silvered general service button.

www.civilwarbuttons.com

Infantry, low convex, two-piece, "Scovills/Waterbury," silvered example, 21 mm. 45.00

Non-dug, cuff-size eagle button. 6.00

Non-dug, with shank, extra fine. 28.00

Non-excavated U.S. Eagle coat button, Scovill backmark, fine condition. 20.00

Heavily gilted overcoat-sized button.

www.civilwarbuttons.com

Scarce overcoat-size eagle button; heavily gilted, "*Scovill Mf'g Co*/Waterbury," 23 mm. . . . 35.00

Seven, dug, cuff eagle buttons and two blouse-sized large coat buttons. All are excellent condition except for a small one, which is squashed. 35.00

Standard pattern eagle button, size is midway between the small "shell jacket size" and the standard "blouse size" (20% larger than the small-size button). This size is sometimes seen on infantry pattern shell jackets, and is a very scarce variant. 15.00

With shank, dug in a Union camp in Texas. 4.00

Artillery

Eagle "A," dug in Central Mississippi, shank present, fine condition. 29.00

Artillery, cont.

Dating to the 1850s, this artillery button could just as easily have seen Southern as Union service.

Military Antiques & Museum

U.S. Officer of Artillery brass eagle button. Shield has "A" in center of eagle's chest. Backmark is "Superior Quality." 50.00

Two-piece, non-excavated, gilt, cuff-size Eagle "A" with the D. Evan's backmark. 23.00

A fine example of a federal artillery button.

www.civilwarbuttons.com

Artillery, ".W.H.Horstmann & Sons /Phi.," rmdc, heavily gilted, 21 mm. 55.00

Coat-sized Federal artillery button.

www.civilwarbuttons.com

Artillery, ".W.H.Horstmann & Sons/Phi.," rmdc, 21 mm. 45.00

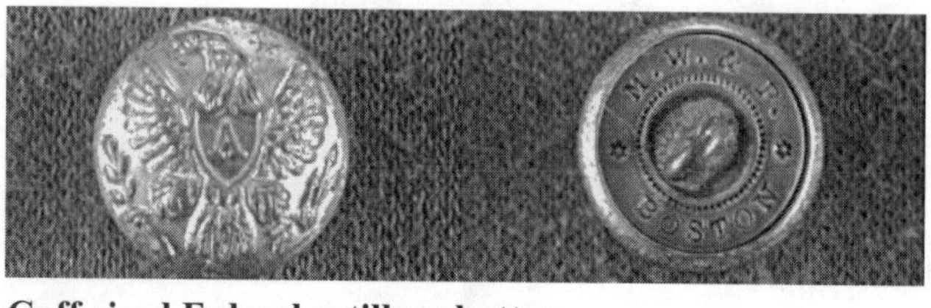

Cuff-sized Federal artillery button.

www.civilwarbuttons.com

Artillery, Civil War, cuff, "*M.W.P.*/Boston." 15 mm. 45.00

Overcoat-sized Federal artillery button.

www.civilwarbuttons.com

Artillery, Civil War, overcoat size, "*Scovill Mf'g Co*/ Waterbury," 23 mm.. .... 55.00

Coat-size button with shank, "Extra Quality" backmark, non-dug, lots of gilt, very fine. 28.00

Federal artillery button, cuff-sized, Scovill backmark.

Sharpsburg Arsenal

Cuff-sized button. 50.00

Coat-size Eagle "A," with shank, non-dug. "Extra Quality" backmark, very-fine condition....... 28.00

Cuff-size, Eagle "A," non-dug, with shank, very fine. 19.00

Eagle "A" cuff button by Waterbury. 25.00

Federal artillery button, coat-sized, Waterbury backmark.

Sharpsburg Arsenal

Eagle artillery button. 40.00

This nice, early overcoat-sized artillery button dates closer to the Mexican-American War of 1846-1848.

www.civilwarbuttons.com

Early overcoat-size Eagle"A" with rare backmark: "-Horstmann Sons & Druker-/New-York," dates 1845-1849, gilt, 23 mm. 75.00
Non-dug artillery button with desirable Horstmann & Allien backmark. 30.00
Union "A" artillery button dug in central Mississippi, with shank, fine condition. 29.00
Union "A" button in cuff size, non-dug, with shank, very fine. 19.00
Very fine, war date vest- or jacket-sized artillery button. 29.00
Very fine, non-dug, coat-sized artillery button with war date backmark. 35.00

A coat-sized cavalry button. Though relatively common, these general service buttons with branch of service initial on the shields have been reproduced for many years.

Military Antiques & Museum

Cavalry

Backmarked "Waterbury Button Co. Waterbury Con." 55.00
Civil War cavalry button set of 12 with history, 10 are a bit under 23 mm and the two cuff buttons are just over 16 mm. Larger button backs all say, "Extra Quality," cuff button backs say, "Waterbury Button Co." They all have the very articulated eagle with the "C" in the shield or center area. Excellent condition with just a couple having bent shanks. The consigner included the following information: "These buttons were from the uniform of William McKendree Snyder. He served in the Civil War enlisting at the age of 12 as a drummer boy for the Union (Indiana Volunteers) side. After the war he became a noteworthy painter. He is a listed artist and his work can be found on the art search sites online. He was born in 1848 and died in 1930." 385.00
Civil War cavalry cuff size with rare backmark, "A.C.M. & Co./Phil'a.," 15 mm. 55.00

Overcoat-sized cavalry button bearing the mark of A.C. Marien & Co. Because of the vast number of extant examples, collections of general service buttons can focus on gathering a variety of backmarks.

www.civilwarbuttons.com

Civil War cavalry overcoat-size with rare backmark, "*A.C. Marien & Co.*/Philadelphia." 23 mm. . .100.00
Cuff size. 35.00

Dug example of an overcoat-sized cavalry button.

www.civilwarbuttons.com

Overcoat-size, nice, dug, Civil War cavalry button, "*Extra*/Quality," 22 mm. 75.00
Pair of large-sized and small-sized eagle "C" buttons, both perfect with 60% gilt, dug in 1960s. 59.00

Dragoon

Beautiful condition, non-excavated, coat-size eagle "D," 100% bright gold gilt, button has the WG Mintzer backmark and shank intact 125.00
Dug, dragoon cuff button, perfect dug condition, "Scovill" backmark. 55.00
Dug in Texas, with shank, very-good condition, cuff size. 35.00
Eagle "D," coat size with shank, very-good condition. 35.00
Eagle "D," dug in Texas, cuff-size button with shank, very good condition. 35.00
Cuff-sized officer with "Horstmann" backmark. . 95.00
Officer eagle button, battlefield-excavated, backmark, "Scovills & Co Superfine." 100.00

Engineer buttons are one of the rarer branch of service buttons to find.

www.civilwarbuttons.com

Engineer

"Scovill Mf'g. Co,/Waterbury," 23 mm........ **225.00**
"Horstmann.Bros.&.Allien/N.Y." 23 mm. **225.00**
Engineer's coat size, "Scovill Mf'g Co,/Waterbury," near mint, 23 mm.. .... **200.00**
Engineer's cuff, "Robinsons/Extra" 15 mm..... **125.00**

Infantry

"D. Evans & Co.," backmark. Eagle I coat button, lots of gilt left, small push to back at shank. **20.00**
Two-piece, non-excavated, gilt, cuff-size eagle "I." Horstmann and Co. backmark and intact shank. **20.00**
A standard, large-sized eagle "I" button as worn on the frock coats and blouses, fine condition....... **18.00**
A very fine example of the cuff-sized eagle "I" button with traces of gilt and lovely patina.......... **12.00**
Backmark: "Thomas N. Dale New York," coat size. **25.00**
Eagle "I" coat button, Scoville Mfg. Co. Waterbury. **25.00**
Civil War Infantry, "*Extra*/Quality," 21 mm. .. **25.00**
Dug, eagle "I" coat button, nice chocolate patina with shank bent to one side. Steel-back button with no backmark, dug near Richmond, Virginia...... **20.00**
Dug, eagle "I" coat button, lot of shine, backmark is not readable, nice shank, no pushes. Dug east of Richmond, Virginia. **20.00**
Dug, Eagle "I" cuff button from Richmond, Virginia, full shank steel back, no backmark.......... **15.00**
Eagle "I," backmark: "R&W. Robinson/Extra Rich," 85% gilt. **30.00**
Eagle "I," backmark: "Scovill MF'G Co/Waterbury." brass patina. **30.00**
Eagle "I," backmark: "Scovills & Co/Waterbury." 100% gilt. **30.00**
Eagle button with "I" in shield, no backmark. ... **20.00**
Eagle "I' coat button from Horstmann & Allien New York. **20.00**
Eagle "I" dug coat button, backmark, "Scovill." ...**20.00**
Excavated Union infantry brass button, no backmark. **18.00**

Retaining a lot of its gilt, this dug infantry button looks as good as several non-dug examples.

Middle Tennessee Relics

Excellent, dug, eagle "I" coat-size Union infantry officer's gilt button, 70%-80% bright gold gilt with shank intact. **25.00**
Hand-chased Infantry officer's button, eagle and "I" are tooled (decorated), "*Horstmann Bros & Co*/Phil," 23 mm.. .... **45.00**

Hand-chased buttons are seldom encountered. The tooling defines details of the button.

www.civilwarbuttons.com

Infantry, low convex, two-piece, "Young Smith & Co./ New York," excellent silvered example, 21 mm. ..**55.00**
Non-excavated, coat-size eagle "I," "Extra Quality" backmark and intact shank. **35.00**
Non-excavated, gilt, great coat-size eagle "I," Horstmann Bros. & Allen backmark, intact shank. **35.00**
One-piece, eagle coat button, backmark: "Young Smith Co. NY." **35.00**
Regulation Union infantry large-size coat button, excellent condition. **14.00**
Cuff-size infantry button with war date backmark. ..**10.00**
T W & W backmarked eagle "I" cuff button. **20.00**
Three infantry officer's eagle "I" coat buttons. ...**95.00**
Union officer gold-over-brass button, mint condition, backmark, "Horstmann & Allien N.Y."....... **40.00**

Marine Corps button with slight face dent.

www.civilwarbuttons.com

Marine

"*Extra Quality*" in ribbon, slight dent, 23 mm. . . **75.00**

Horstmann Bros & Allien, New York. **75.00**

Looking as though a new shield has been applied to the front of a staff officer's button, the "N.G." probably stands for "National Guard." This would be for use by a local volunteer militia unit.

www.civilwarbuttons.com

National Guard, "NG" on breast of eagle, 1850s "*Waterbury Button. Co.*/Extra" (in small letters around outside edge of button back), condition excellent, 23 mm. **100.00**

U.S. Navy button measuring 23 mm across.

www.civilwarbuttons.com

Navy

".Scovill Mf'g. Co/Waterbury." rmdc, 23 mm. . . **40.00**

The inclusion of an eagle in the backmark stamp added to the appeal of this button.

www.civilwarbuttons.com

"R&W. Robinson" with eagle, 22 mm. **75.00**

Another U.S. Navy design used during the Civil War.

www.civilwarbuttons.com

"Scovills & Co/Waterbury," rmdc, 23 mm. **65.00**

Backmarked, "D. Evans & Co." **25.00**

Coat-size, non-excavated, two-piece button with 100% bright gold gilt, backmarked, "Waterbury-Scovill," intact shank. **45.00**

Coat-size, brilliant gilt, perfect condition, "Evans & Hassell" backmark. **40.00**

Cuff-size with shank, tin back, gorgeous face, dug in Texas. **25.00**

Cuff-size example, "Scovill Mfg Co." backmark.. . .**12.00**

Eagle facing to his left, perched on horizontal anchor, backmark "Treble Gilt London," non-dug with blotch of green patina on button's left half. **20.00**

Cuff-sized Navy button measuring only 15mm in diameter.

www.civilwarbuttons.com

Low convex Navy cuff ".Robinsons./Extra.," 15 mm. **35.00**

Navy vest button with backmark, "Scovill Mfg Co." **25.00**

Non-excavated, U.S. Navy officer's coat button, "Evans & Hassal/Phila" backmark, brilliant.. . . . . **40.00**

Non-excavated, cuff size, Union Navy, perfect condition with Scovill backmark, shank intact. **28.00**

One-piece button with backmark, "Treble Gilt/Standard Colour.," 100% gilt back and front. **145.00**

Navy, cont.

Cuff-sized Navy button with an unusual backmark.

www.civilwarbuttons.com

Scarce mark, odd die design, "R&W Robinson/Extra Rich," 23 mm. **55.00**

Eagle perched on upright small anchor, eagle facing to his right, backmark, "Young Smith and Co NY." perfect, non-dug, button. **75.00**

Vest-size Navy, non-excavated Union Navy with Scovill backmark, 100% gold gilt, intact shank. **35.00**

Similar buttons as this example have been attributed to the diplomatic corps, though there is some speculation that they were used as military uniform buttons. Regardless, it is a rather rare button.

www.civilwarbuttons.com

Official, U.S. official, beautiful, applied device, "G&Cie/Paris/20/(coat of arms)," 21 mm. **275.00**

Ordnance Corps buttons can be tricky to collect as they closely resemble buttons used by several countries including the United States. This example, however, is beautifully hallmarked, "US Ordnance Corps."

www.civilwarbuttons.com

Ordnance

Ordnance Corps, three-piece, "US/Ordnance Corps" tight button, non-dug, 21 mm.............. **395.00**

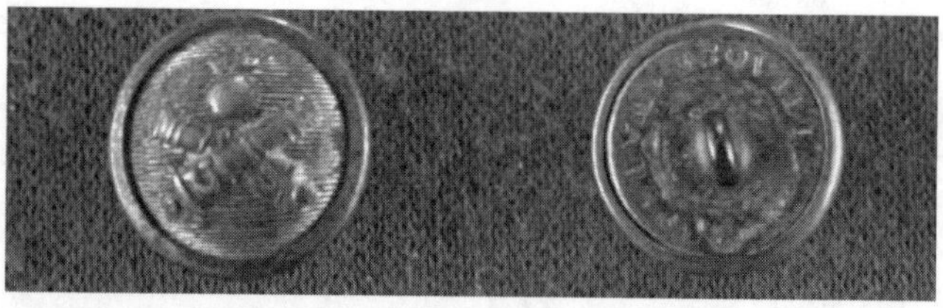

Scovill-marked, cuff-sized ordnance button.

www.civilwarbuttons.com

Ordnance Corps, three-piece, "Scovills/Waterbury," 15 mm.................................. **200.00**

Ordnance Corps, coat-sized uniform button with full shank and a minor front stain, generous gilt remains. **125.00**

Part of the Treasury Department, the Revenue Service had its own uniform. Its buttons are quite difficult to locate.

www.civilwarbuttons.com

Revenue Cutter service, ".Scovills & Co./Waterbury," rmdc, 23 mm. **200.00**

Rifleman

Dug, eagle "R" Rifleman's cuff button from Richmond, Virginia, full shank, illegible backmark....... **50.00**

Fine pre-war eagle "R" button, rmdc Horstmann maker's mark on back, excellent, non-dug example. ... **45.00**

Sharpshooter, perfect, cuff-sized, enlisted, hard-rubber eagle button from the 1st USSS Berdan, sharpshooter's green frock coat. **135.00**

Buttons bearing this device date between 1831 and 1863 when the Topographical Engineers were abolished on March 3.

www.civilwarbuttons.com

Topographical Engineer, two-piece "*R&W. Robinson*/ Extra Rich." 23 mm. **700.00**

Staff

"Extra Quality" backmark. **45.00**

Backmark, "Extra Quality," 100% gilt. **45.00**

Backmark, "Scovill MF'G Co/Waterbury," 100% gilt. **45.00**

Dug, somewhat squashed, standard U.S. staff officer's button. **10.00**

Eagle staff button, "W.G.Minter-Phila.," backmark. **45.00**

Excavated brass button, backmark illegible, button filled with glue to preserve. **15.00**

Excellent, non-excavated, cuff-size, Union staff officer with 100% bright gold gilt, has the Scovill backmark, intact shank. **25.00**

Non-dug, large-sized staff button. **16.00**

Non-dug, with shank, XF condition. **28.00**

Non-excavated, gilt, cuff-size Union staff officer button, rare backmark, "G&B/Extra," no dents, intact shank. **23.00**

The general service staff button was used from 1832 until 1902. The variety of marks and slight variations in design require a discerning eye to detect actual Civil War examples.

www.civilwarbuttons.com

"*Extra*/Quality," 23 mm. **35.00**

The R&W Robinson backmark guarantees that this staff button dates to the Civil War period.

www.civilwarbuttons.com

"**R&W. Robinson**/Makers/*Attleborough*/Mass," 23 mm. **55.00**

The Horstmann backmark is another desirable Civil War period imprint.

www.civilwarbuttons.com

"*Horstmann Bro & Co*/Phila," rmdc, silver plated, 23 mm. **85.00**

General staff button made by Evans and Hassall.

www.civilwarbuttons.com

Federal officer's button with scarce backmark, "*Evans & Hassall*/Phila.," great condition, 23 mm.... **55.00**

Young, Smith and Co.-made buttons are a bit harder to find.

www.civilwarbuttons.com

General staff officer's button, ".Young.Smith & Co./ New York," 22 mm. **75.00**

General staff officer's button, "Horstmann & Co./N.Y.& Phi.," 23 mm. **55.00**

State-Issued Buttons

California buttons bearing a wartime manufacturer's mark are very scarce. The difference between an example made during the Civil War and one made after can be several hundred dollars.

www.civilwarbuttons.com

California, state seal, wartime and increasingly hard to find, "Scovill Mf'g Co./Waterbury," 23 mm. ... **225.00**

This dug, two-piece Connecticut state seal button retained its full shank.

Military Antiques & Museum

Connecticut

Battlefield-excavated, state seal button, backmark "Scovill Waterbury." **35.00**

"Connecticut National Guard" is what the initials denote on this button.

www.civilwarbuttons.com

C.N.G. "Scovill Mf'g Co,/Waterbury." 23 mm. .. **30.00**

C.N.G., staff cuff, "*Superior*/Quality," low convex relief, 15 mm. **25.00**

The Scovill backmark ensures that this Connecticut state-seal button was produced during the war years.

www.civilwarbuttons.com

Connecticut seal, "*Scovill Mf'g Co./Waterbury," 23 mm.. .... **60.00**

Very attractive, excavated large-sized blouse button with 80% gilt and backmark "Scovill Mfg Co. Waterbury," excellent. **35.00**

The Richmond maker's imprint on this Connecticut state-seal button indicates that it was probably manufactured before 1861.

www.civilwarbuttons.com

Connecticut seal staff, "Mitchel & Tyler/Richmond," 15 mm.. .... **100.00**

Non-dug, cuff-size with backmark, "Scovills & Co. Extra." **29.00**

This dug Connecticut state-seal button is good documentation of the Scovill mark being a wartime imprint.

Middle Tennessee Relics

Dug, coat-size, Connecticut state seal, button slightly dented, smooth, attractive brown patina and intact shank, has an early rmdc, Scovill backmark. ...**30.00**

Connecticut, cont.

The Hartford City Guards were a prewar volunteer militia unit. This button is from one of their uniforms.

www.civilwarbuttons.com

Hartford City Guard, "Scovill Mf'g Co./Waterbury," 23 mm. **145.00**

Cuff-sized Hartford City Guard button.

www.civilwarbuttons.com

Hartford City Guard, cuff, "Scovill Mf'g Co./ Waterbury," 15 mm. **60.00**

Button from the New Haven Grays, another Connecticut pre-war volunteer militia unit.

www.civilwarbuttons.com

New Haven Grays, ".*.W. B. Co.*./Waterbury" rmdc, 23 mm. **375.00**

Maine

Backmark, "Waterbury Button Co. Waterbury." . . **40.00**

Large-size, coin-style, one-piece button, five-pointed star surrounded by 17 tiny stars on lined field, Imperial Standard backmark, perfect non-dug with shank. **59.00**

What would appear to be a generic militia button has been long attributed as being specifically used by Maine units.

www.civilwarbuttons.com

Maine "R&W. Robinson/Attleborough/***Extra***/ Rich." 22 mm. **68.00**

Cuff button bearing the state seal of Maine.

www.civilwarbuttons.com

Maine cuff, "*Extra*/Quality," 15 mm. **45.00**

Maine cuff, "Scovill Mf'g Co./Waterbury," 15 mm. **40.00**

Maine seal, "Scovill Mf'g Co./Waterbury," some staining, 23 mm. **75.00**

Staff-styled Massachusetts button impressed with a Robinson, Attelboro, Mass. backmark.

Sharpsburg Arsenal

Massachusetts

Staff button. **40.00**

Massachusetts, cont.

Non-dug Massachusetts coat-sized button.

Middle Tennessee Relics

Beautiful non-excavated, gilt, coat-size Massachusetts state seal with "Extra Quality" backmark, 100% bright gold gilt, no dents, and shank intact. . . . 45.00

Though attributed to the pre-Civil War volunteer militia Boston City Guard, two-piece buttons bearing "CG" could have been sold to any group where the initials would be appropriate (for example, the Charleston Guard, Cincinnati Guard, etc.).

www.civilwarbuttons.com

Boston city guards, "Draper & Sandland/Extra," 23 mm. 150.00

Two-piece, cuff-sized CG button.

www.civilwarbuttons.com

Boston city guards, cuff "*Robinsons*/Extra," 15 mm. 55.00

Prewar button attributed to the Boston Light Infantry. The best way to document the use of such volunteer militia buttons is to examine actual uniform pieces that have these buttons attached.

Boston Light Infantry; one-piece convex, "*R&W. Robinson*/Attleborough/***Extra***/Rich." Scarce and nice, early example, 21 mm. 250.00

Cuff-size staff button with rim, nice prewar backmark, "Robinsons Makers," excellent, non-dug example.. 25.00

. Cuff-size staff button with rim, nice prewar backmark, "*D. Evans & Co.* Extra." 25.00

Independent Corps of Cadets "*Robinsons*/Extra." Mint, 15 mm. 35.00

Large, blouse-sized MVM staff button with raised hand holding sword, Scovill backmark, non-dug, and excellent. 29.00

Any military button bearing a figural representation is going to command a high price.

www.civilwarbuttons.com

Mansfield Cadets, one-piece convex, "*Robinsons, Jones, & Co/Attleboro/.*.*.*.Extra.*.*.*./Rich," 22 mm. 375.00

The arm-with-saber motif is the most common Massachusetts design. This button is cuff sized.

www.civilwarbuttons.com

Massachusetts cuff, "*W.Button Co*/Extra," flat, early mark, 15 mm. **20.00**

Example of a coat-sized button.

www.civilwarbuttons.com

Massachusetts seal, "*Extra*/Quality," 23 mm. .. **30.00**

It is not known why the saber has been removed from the face of this button. In spite of the defacing, the button bears a nice wartime Boston maker's mark.

www.civilwarbuttons.com

Massachusetts vol. militia, "*L.B. Horton & Co.*," rmdc, sword intentionally removed, 23 mm. .. **55.00**

Massachusetts vol. militia, ".Steele & Johnson" (rmdc with lined channel), 23 mm. **40.00**

This example bears the Massachusetts state seal (notice that the arm-and-saber is above the shield).

www.civilwarbuttons.com

Massachusetts vol. militia, low convex, two-piece, ":*V*ICC*G*/Perfectionne," rare, 23 mm. ... **75.00**

Massachusetts vol. militia, low convex, two-piece, "*R&W. Robinson*/Extra Rich," 23 mm. **40.00**

Massachusetts vol. militia, low convex, two-piece cuff, "Robinsons/Extra," 14 mm. **30.00**

Massachusetts vol. militia, low convex, two-piece cuff, "Robinsons/Extra," heavily silvered, 14 mm. ...**40.00**

Massachusetts volunteer militia, brass state seal button has all gold, backmark, "Scovill MFG Co. Waterbury." **45.00**

This dug example of a Massachusetts button bears an unusual variation on the state seal in that the Indian is depicted holding up the saber.

Military Antiques & Museum

Massachusetts volunteer militia, brass state seal excavated button, backmark, "Extra Quality." ...**35.00**

Massachusetts, one-piece, "Rich Quality (OE)/London/ (circle of stars)," super, gilt example, 25 mm. **100.00**

As a general rule, cleaning a dug button detracts from the value. Dug (and cleaned) example of the flat, one-piece button.

www.civilwarbuttons.com

Massachusetts, one-piece, "Rich Quality (OE)/London/ (circle of stars)," dug, cleaned, no shank, 25 mm. **50.00**

Massachusetts, one-piece, "Rich Quality/London," silver plated, 17 mm. **100.00**

Massachusetts, one-piece, "Warranted/(wreath)/Treble/ Plated," silver plated, 25 mm. **100.00**

Massachusetts, cont.

As is the case with many Civil War-era buttons, the convex one-pieced Massachusetts button was reproduced in the early 20th century.

www.civilwarbuttons.com

Massachusetts, authentic, 20 mm, one-piece, high convex, "Warranted/(wreath)/Treble/Plated," silver plate, fabulous button; Bannerman chose it to replicate. **200.00**

Though an attractive variant on the Massachusetts state theme, this one-piece button was a prewar piece.

www.civilwarbuttons.com

Massachusetts, one-piece, plain field; "(16 asterisks in depressed channel)," scarce Peasley-made variant, distinctive die, 22 mm. **185.00**

New England guards, cuff, "R&W. Robinson/Extra," 15 mm. **35.00**

New England guards, low convex, two-piece, "R&W. Robinson," in ribbon with eagle, 21 mm. **55.00**

Nice, pre-war, large, blouse-sized button with desirable "R&W Robinson" backmark designed with raised arm, sword, and motto, beautiful button, great gilt. **39.00**

Nice, pre-war, blouse-sized button with R&W Robinson backmark. Nice, light age patina. **45.00**

Non-excavated, state seal, gilt, cuff size, "Schuyler Hartley & Graham--New York" backmark, no dents, intact shank. **30.00**

Attributed to the Norfolk (Massachusetts) Guard. The initials are common enough that the maker undoubtedly tried to sell the button to other units as well.

www.civilwarbuttons.com

Norfolk Guards, low convex two-piece, "D. Evans & Co./Attleborough," 23 mm. **300.00**

With the initials "R.L.G." on its face, this button has been attributed to the Richardson (Massachusetts) Light Guard.

www.civilwarbuttons.com

Richardson Light Guard, nice, rmdc marking, "Scovill Mfg Co./Waterbury CT.," outstanding, 23 mm. **200.00**

Small-size staff MVM button, non-dug, one with Waterbury backmark and one with D. Evans back. **22.00**

Dug, staff button, backmark of "Treble Gilt," 30% gilt, small face dent, very solid and attractive. **35.00**

Union Massachusetts volunteer militia button with shank, non-dug, loaded with gilt, very-fine condition. **28.00**

Bearing a bugle with regimental designation, this Massachusetts volunteer militia button has an overpowering Civil War appeal.

www.civilwarbuttons.com

Vol. Militia 1st Regiment, "Scovill Mf'g Co./ Waterbury," 23 mm. **100.00**

Vol. Militia 1st Regiment cuff, "Robinson/Extra," 15 mm. **75.00**

The same design as the previously illustrated button, this example bears the number "4" denoting the 4th Regiment of Massachusetts Volunteer Militia.

www.civilwarbuttons.com

Vol. Militia 4th Regiment, "*R&W. Robinson*/Extra Rich," 23 mm. **350.00**

Vol. Militia 4th Regiment, "Robinson/Extra," 15 mm. **150.00**

Volunteer militia, shank present, non-dug, loaded with gilt, very fine. **28.00**

Michigan cuff-sized staff button.

www.civilwarbuttons.com

Michigan

Michigan cuff, "Scovill Mf'g Co,/Waterbury," 15 mm. **45.00**

Dug, "Extra Quality" backmark, quite a bit of gilt, slight push in back, nice looking, found on Civil War site. **39.00**

Handsome coat-sized Michigan staff button with stags.

www.civilwarbuttons.com

Michigan seal, "Scovill Mf'g Co,/Waterbury," 23 mm. **200.00**

Coat-sized New Hampshire buttons bearing a, "D. Evans & Co.," backmark.

Military Antiques & Museum

New Hampshire

Gold-over-brass state seal button, backmark, "Scovill MFG Co Waterbury." **60.00**

Nice, non-dug pair, war date, no shanks, glue remnants where mounted in button display. **20.00**

Enhanced by a design that incorporates the phrase, "New Hampshire Vol. Militia."

New Hampshire, "D. Evans & CO. Attleboro' Mass," in ribbon, 23 mm. **65.00**

New Hampshire, blank (one depressed ring) 23 mm. **65.00**

Cuff-sized version of the New Hampshire Volunteer Militia button.

www.civilwarbuttons.com

New Hampshire cuff "*D. Evans & CO.*/Extra," 15 mm. **35.00**

New Hampshire cuff "Steele & Johnson," 15 mm... **75.00**

Nice, non-dug, pair with war date, no shanks, glue remnants where once mounted in button display. **20.00**

State seal cuff button with Scovill backmark. **60.00**

New Hampshire, cont.

Cuff-sized, example with the seal, and "Vol Militia" on the face, backmark, "D. Evans & Co. Superfine." **35.00**

New Jersey

Nice, war-date button with thin rim and small cuff size, has "Extra Quality" backmark. **75.00**

Coat-size with backmark, "Waterbury Button Co./ Waterbury Con." **10.00**

Because the state produced several famous regiments, New Jersey buttons are wildly sought.

www.civilwarbuttons.com

New Jersey cuff, "*Extra*/Quality," 15 mm. ... **150.00**

New Jersey state seal, "Scovill Mf'g Co./Waterbury," 23 mm............................. **375.00**

New York

A fine, non-dug, cuff-size example, "Scovill Mfg Co" backmark, excellent with nice gilt........... **15.00**

Backmark, "Waterbury Button Co./Extra," 100% gilt. **30.00**

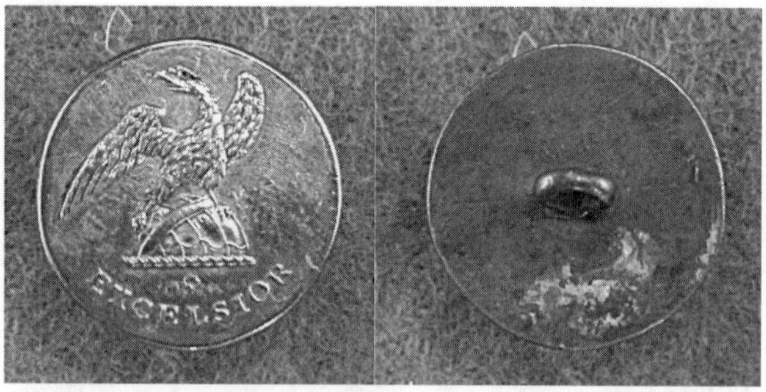

Undoubtedly, this button predates the Civil War by about 30 years. Still, collectors seem eager to add examples to their Civil War collections.

www.civilwarbuttons.com

Big, flat, New York one-piece, silver-plated, blank, 24 mm. **145.00**

Brass, state seal button excavated from Sharpsburg battlefield, 7/8" d, backmarked, "Goddard & Bro Extra." **25.00**

The style of New York button most often encountered on original uniforms is the Excelsior staff-style button as seen here. This example was dug on a Tennessee battlefield.

Middle Tennessee Relics

Coat-size state seal, non-dug, Goddard & Brother backmark, perfect with shank intact. **45.00**

Dug, NY cuff button from Richmond, Virginia, backmark, "A T.N.Dale & Co. N.Y." **10.00**

Probably dating to the late 1850s, this 13th Regiment button has been attributed the 13th New York National Guard.

www.civilwarbuttons.com

New York 13th Regiment, "*Scovill Mf'g Co*/ Waterbury," 23 mm...................... **75.00**

Slightly dented New York City Guard button.

www.civilwarbuttons.com

New York City guard, "Scovills & Co:/Waterbury" rmdc, slight push, 23 mm................. **200.00**

Cuff-sized Excelsior button.

www.civilwarbuttons.com

New York cuff, ".*.G & B.*./Extra" nice mark, 15 mm. **25.00**

New York cuff, "Scovills & Co /Waterbury," early and quite unusual, 15 mm. **25.00**

New York seal, "Horstmann & Allien/N.Y.," flat-back example, 23 mm. **40.00**

New York staff officers, "*Extra*/Quality," 15 mm. **45.00**

A Wm. H. Smith backmark places this button back to the 1850s.

www.civilwarbuttons.com

New York staff officers, "*Wm. H Smith & Co*/ New York," flat mark, 1850s, scarce, 23 mm. **100.00**

A variation on the Excelsior button theme, this specialized sample was used by artillery units.

www.civilwarbuttons.com

New York State, artillery, "Horstmann Bro & Allien/ N.Y.," rmdc, 21 mm...................... **40.00**

Cuff-sized New York artillery button.

www.civilwarbuttons.com

New York State, artillery cuff ,"*Horstmann*/ N.Y.*Phila," 15 mm. **30.00**

This one-piece New York button dates to the mid-1830s. Occasionally, examples do turn up on Civil War battlefields.

www.civilwarbuttons.com

New York, one-piece, "Superior /Strong Plated," heavily silver plated, 23 mm...................... **45.00**

Again, this one-piece button pre-dates the Civil War by at least 30 years. Nevertheless, Civil War collectors seem eager to add these one-piece buttons to their collections.

www.civilwarbuttons.com

New York, one-piece, "Treble Gilt./Orange," 15 mm. **150.00**

New York, cont.

A cuff-sized Excelsior button pre-dating the Mexican War.

www.civilwarbuttons.com

New York, one-piece, "Treble Gilt/Gold Colour," 15 mm. **75.00**

The variety of New York state buttons made before the Civil War present a wide range for collecting possibilities.

www.civilwarbuttons.com

New York, one-piece, slightly convex, "*Plated*/L&T," heavily silver-plated, 21 mm. **65.00**

Though the same design as earlier state buttons, this two-piece brass New York button probably dates to the mid-1840s. It would be appropriate in either a Mexican or Civil War display.

www.civilwarbuttons.com

New York, two-piece, low convex, "Imperial/Standd. Colr," 21 mm. **85.00**

Non-dug, coat size, with shank, lots of gold gilt, very fine. **29.00**

One-piece staff button with backmark "L & T Plated." **85.00**

State-seal cuff button with "Boyland" backmark, bent shank.. . . . . **15.00**

Cuff size, attractive eagle on lined field, shield on breast, and "Excelsior" below, shank crushed together and clipped at the top to leave a stud, Scovill backmark. **20.00**

Cuff-sized button marked, "U.C.C.," this button has been attributed to the Utica Citizen's Corp.

www.civilwarbuttons.com

Utica Citizen Corps "Scovill Mfg Co/Waterbur," 15 mm.. . . . . **60.00**

Very pretty, dug, coat-size New York state seal, solid button with 80% bright gold gilt, Scovill backmark, intact and straight shank. **35.00**

With shank, front gilt, fine condition, dug at Port Hudson, Louisiana. **28.00**

This button was adopted by the 83rd Pennsylvania Volunteers, a unit uniformed in a Chasseur outfit.

www.civilwarbuttons.com

Pennsylvania

Chausseur's button cuff, "Cordier Freres/Paris,"17 mm. **75.00**

Inspite of the large number of troops supplied by Pennsylvania, buttons bearing the state's logo are rather scarce.

www.civilwarbuttons.com

Pennsylvania seal, cuff, "*Extra*/Quality,"15 mm. **75.00**

Pennsylvania staff button bearing the wartime "Superior Quality" backmark.

www.civilwarbuttons.com

Pennsylvania seal, "*Superior*/Quality," 23 mm. **235.00**

Pennsylvania seal, "Horstmann Bro & Allien/N.Y.," rmdc, 23 mm. **325.00**

Pennsylvania seal, flat "Horstmann & Allien/N.Y.," excellent condition, 23 mm. **275.00**

This button was used by the Pennsylvania Grays, a long-standing volunteer militia unit.

www.civilwarbuttons.com

Washington Greys, "Scovill & Co /Waterbury," rmdc, 23 mm. **275.00**

A one-piece convex example bearing a very early style Rhode Island state seal.

www.civilwarbuttons.com

Rhode Island

One-piece, blank, earliest Rhode Island seal, known in 13 mm size. **250.00**

Coat-size, non-excavated, three-piece staff officer's button, 100% bright gold gilt, intact shank. **75.00**

Cuff-sized, backmarked, "Robinson Maker." **35.00**

Excavated sate seal brass button, backmark "Scovill MFG Co. Waterbury." **40.00**

Fine, non-dug, coat-sized state seal with war date, Scovill backmark. **45.00**

Coat-sized button attributed to the Newport (Rhode Island) Artillery.

www.civilwarbuttons.com

Newport Artillery, "*Scovill Mfg Co*/Waterbury," 23 mm. **200.00**

Rhode Island Seal cuff, "*Treble*/Gilt,"15 mm. **35.00**

Rhode Island state-seal adorned coat-sized button.

www.civilwarbuttons.com

Rhode Island, state seal, "Scovill.Mfg.Co./Waterbury," 23 mm. **60.00**

Attributed to the United Train of Artillery, this Rhode Island button may date to the postwar period. It may also be fraternal.

www.civilwarbuttons.com

Rhode Island, United Train of Artillery, "*D. Evans & Co.*/ Attleboro Mass." A beautiful 23 mm button whose time of origin is still unclear (possibly postwar). **75.00**

Sold as Civil War era, this button is said to have been worn by the Rhode Island Washington Cavalry.

www.civilwarbuttons.com

Rhode Island, Washington Cavalry, "*R & W. Robinson*/ Extra Rich," 23 mm. **175.00**

State seal brass button with backmark, "D. Evans Attleboro Mass." **40.00**

State seal button marked, "D. Evans." **50.00**

Though unidentified, the similarity to a U.S. staff button is striking. Without the lines found on the regular staff button, this example has a solid wartime feel.

www.civilwarbuttons.com

Unidentified, "Horstmann Bro & Allien/N Y." rmdc, 23 mm. **300.00**

Vermont, nice cuff-sized example of the Vermont state seal button, nice, non-dug light patina and one tiny face dent, desirable rmdc backmark "Scovill Mfg Co Waterbury." **55.00**

Non-dug, coat-sized Vermont button.

Sharpsburg Arsenal

Coat-sized, excellent. **60.00**

The striking stag's head of the Vermont state seal made this an attractive button.

Middle Tennessee Relics

Excellent condition, non-excavated, cuff-size, two-piece Vermont state seal, 100% gilt, intact shank, "Scovill" backmark. **45.00**

Non-dug, cuff-sized Vermont state seal with Waterbury Button Co backmark, excellent. **25.00**

Near mint, cuff-sized, design of a stag's head on a lined field and "Vermont." Scovill Mfg Co backmark. **39.00**

Non-excavated, two-piece, coat-size Vermont State seal, excellent condition, 90% bright gold gilt intact shank, Waterbury/Scovill backmark. **85.00**

Cuff-sized, Scovill-marked, Vermont state seal button.

www.civilwarbuttons.com

Vermont cuff, "Goddard & Bro. Mfg Co." 15 mm. **38.00**

Vermont cuff, "Scovill./Mfg. Co." 15 mm. **35.00**

A second variety of Vermont state seal button is often encountered.

www.civilwarbuttons.com

Vermont state seal, ".Scovill Mf'g Co./Waterbury," rmdc, 23 mm. **60.00**

The heavy wear to this one-piece Vermont Volunteer Militia did not detract from its sale price. Though dating at least 20 years prior to the Civil War, it found its way into a new collection.

www.civilwarbuttons.com

Vermont Volunteer Militia, light infantry; one-piece, "R&W. Robinson/Attleborough/.*.*.*.Extra.*.*.*./ Rich." Shows honest use and genuine wear, 22 mm. **125.00**

Wisconsin

Very scarce, coat-sized, non-dug, nice patina, some face wear and a tiny dent, backmark, "Extra Quality." **95.00**

Dug, large-sized button, large fragment of Union blue uniform wool still clings to the back. **95.00**

Actual wartime-produced buttons bearing the Wisconsin state seal are quite rare. Nevertheless, gray uniforms produced in 1861 for members of the 1st Wisconsin Volunteer Infantry did sport them. This is a cuff-sized example.

www.civilwarbuttons.com

Wisconsin cuff, "Scovill.Mfg.Co./Waterbury." 15 mm. **75.00**

Wisconsin state seal, cuff button, Scovill backmark **100.00**

Non-dug, nice patina, some face wear and a tiny dent, backmark, "Extra Quality"............... **100.00**

Coat-sized Wisconsin button.

www.civilwarbuttons.com

Wisconsin state seal, "*Extra*/Quality," 23 mm. ...**225.00**

U.S. Miscellaneous

Button, Poncho, 1862-patented eagle button, spring hook on back for securing the poncho or shelter tent, marked. These were patented by Abel Putnam, Jr. in November 1862. .... **79.00**

Though not specifically martial in origin, hard rubber buttons were used on woolen M1851 shirts.

Button, Utility, four shirt buttons, "Goodyear 1851 Patent" markings, other \button is marked, "DICKINSON H.R.CO." **4.00**

Button Terminology

B/m: "Backmark."

Dug: Any item that has been excavated, usually using a metal detector. Many collectors prefer dug items because such pieces are more difficult to fake.

Face: The front of a button on which the design is stamped or cast.

Gilt: The gold wash applied to the face of a button.

Push: Slight dent, usually used to describe damage to a dug button.

Rmdc: "Raised mark depressed channel."

Rm: This refers to a "raised mark" maker's mark.

Shank: The loop on the back of a button for attaching to material.

Also see: Uniforms, Groupings.

Chapter 7
Carbines

The carbine, a shorter-than-normal shoulder arm, was the essential weapon of the Civil War cavalry trooper. Never in large supply before the Civil War, manufacturers rushed to meet the demand of both the Northern and Southern force. By War's end, no fewer than 17 different makes had been adopted by U.S. troops. Secessionist troops were not as fortunate and adopted a wide variety of captured carbines, sawed off shotguns and muskets, imported musketoons and breechloaders, in addition to a few thousand Southern-produced carbines.

Carbine collectors can focus on a variety of areas. For example, one could collect just breechloaders, metal cartridge weapons, Southern-produced, imports, or even variations of one specific make like Sharps or Spencer. Collecting carbines can also be just a facet of a larger collection such as cavalry-related items, or highlighting a photograph or accouterment collection. One should not be intimidated by the wide variety and price range of these weapons.

J.C. Devine Inc.

Middle Tennessee Relics

Collecting Hints

Pros:

- There is a wide variety of Civil War carbines still available to collectors at reasonable prices.
- Reproductions have been marketed to reenactors and skirmishers, and therefore, are appropriately marked as being reproductions.
- Carbines take a relatively small amount of space to store and are stable if kept in a low-humidity environment.

Availability ★★
Price ★★★
Reproduction Alert ★★★★★

Cons:

- Firearms are always prime targets for thieves. Civil War carbines are easily sold and not easily traced. Having a weapons-based collection presents new concerns and responsibilities to collectors.
- Actual, documented, Confederate-produced and/or used carbines are scarce. The price range limits these items to advanced collectors.
- A lot of muskets shortened after the Civil War are marketed as "cut-downs" or "Confederate."
- The market for firearms is a bit more fluid than other collectibles. There can be steep peaks and cavernous valleys based on supply and demand.

Carbines

Confederate

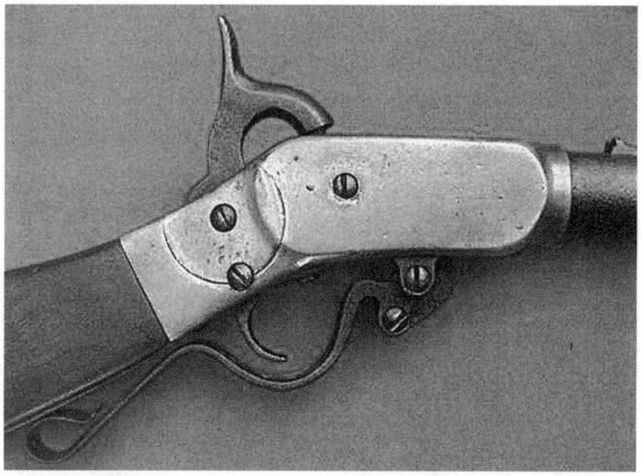

Keen, Walker & Company made 282 of these carbines. Collectors often refer to them as "Confederate Perry" or Tilting Breech Keens."

Old South Military Antiques

Keen, Walker & Co.

Brass-framed, breechloading carbine, estimated that fewer than 25 currently exist. Very good condition, barrel has brown patina and a good sharp "P" proof mark, very good rifling, saddle ring and bar are replacements. The brass frame has a beautiful mellow patina, excellent walnut stock with only minor chips and abrasions, breech and lever action is smooth and tight......... **24,500.00**

Extremely rare Confederate carbine (one of only 286 made between May and September 1862, in Danville, Virginia). Gun is 100% original in very good attic condition, has uncleaned, beautiful brass receiver with a rich patina. The barrel has a dark-brown patina with light salt and pepper pitting, "P" marked barrel, which is a proof mark, walnut stock is fine with the letters, "R.H. Harris" carved in it. Complete history of R.H. Harris comes with this extremely well-researched carbine. Lieutenant R.H. Harris was a member of the "Nottoway Reserves," Company F, 1st. Regiment of Virginia Reserves under the command of Captain Benjamin L. Farinholt. **24,000.00**

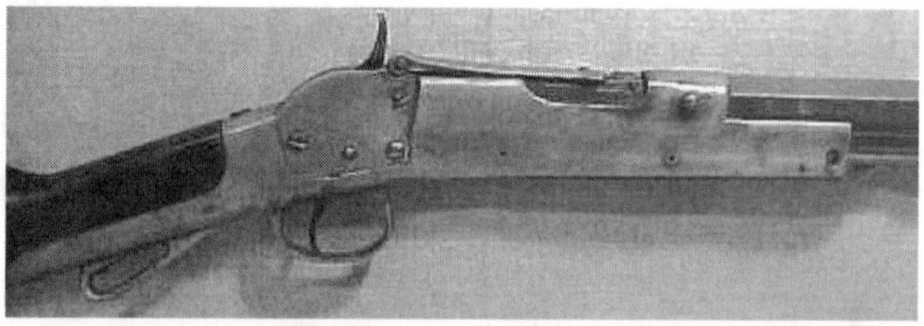

At some point, someone exchanged the original barrel of this Morse Carbine for a rifled octagonal barrel chambered to .58 caliber. The supposition is that this was done due to shortages of the .50 Morse cartridge.

Battleground Antiques

Morse, interesting period adaptation of this brass-framed carbine, manufactured in South Carolina. Weapon is number "374," at some point, the carbine barrel was removed and a rifled octagonal barrel added. The gun turned up in Florida in the mid-1980s without much history. Unquestionably original, typical Confederate "make-do" to compensate for lack of the Morse cartridges—musket barrel has nipple threaded at rear of breech to take a percussion cap. **3,500.00**

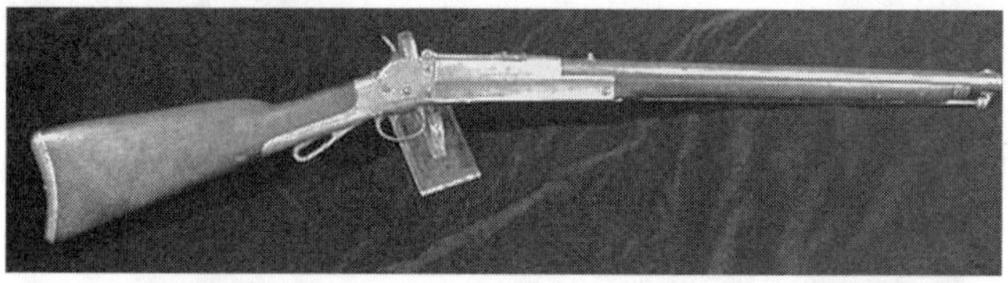

Contracted by the South Carolina State Militia, Morse Carbines were made at the Greenville Military Works. Less than 1,000 examples were completed.

Old South Military Antiques

Morse, Type III, serial no. 437. .... **17,100.00**

Marked with a "JS" over an anchor, this musketoon was probably made by the London Armory Company.

Old South Military Antiques

Musketoon

Confederate carbine marked, "J S"-over-anchor. **5,500.00**

Confederate Richmond cavalry carbine dated 1863, excellent and mellow example with all original parts and beautiful patina to the brass mounts. Nice bore, perfect "pinch" front sight, superb wood. **11,500.00**

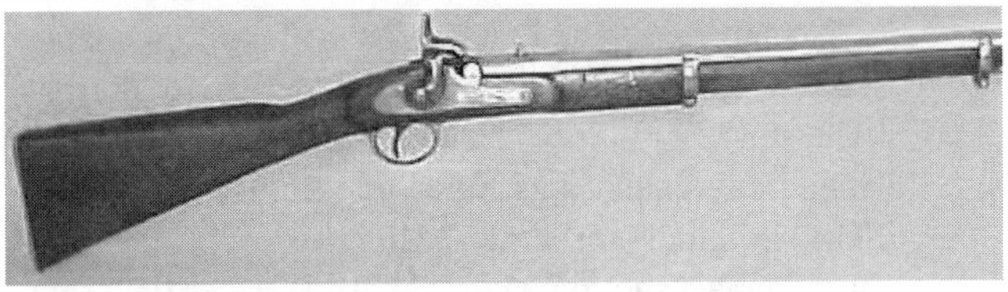

Dated 1863, this Richmond Armory-produced musketoon was one of about 5,000 produced.

Battleground Antiques

Richmond percussion carbine, cavalry pattern, dated 1863. Fine wood and clean metal overall, scattered light pitting, mainly at the breech area. Clear lock markings, strong action, missing butt swivel and ramrod, brass lightly cleaned on nose cap and buttplate. **7,500.00**

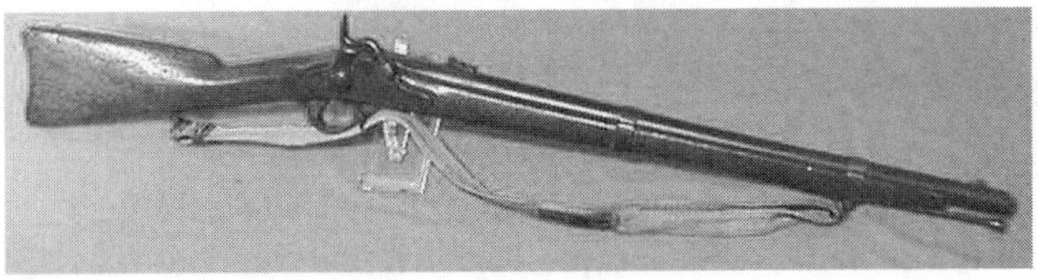

Confederate two-band Richmond Armory musketoon.

Old South Military Antiques

Richmond two-band carbine. **9,900.00**

Sharps, Richmond Pattern

Serial no. 2,812 on the lock, tang, and barrel, very-good condition and rates a fine grading. Smooth metal uniformly covered with a plum-brown color, patch of barrel pitting on the right side near the brass barrel band, and another small patch to the right of the rear sight. No other appreciable pitting except on the lever and bottom of the frame, marked "Richmond Va.," 100% complete including the rear sight, butt sling swivel, sling ring, and bar that are frequently missing. The wood to metal fit is outstanding, and the bore is fine. **13,500.00**

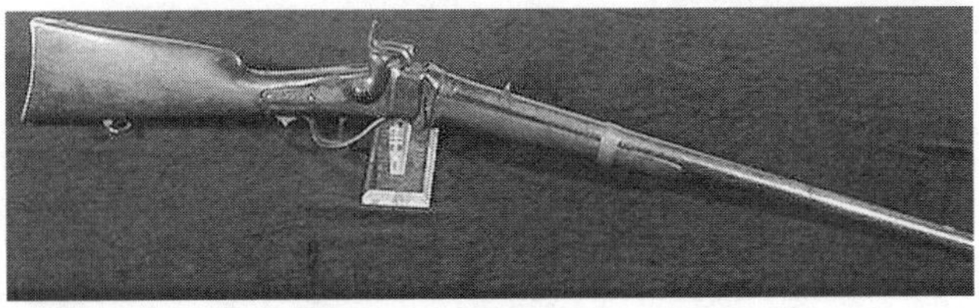

Collectors refer to these Confederate copied Sharps carbines as the "Richmond Pattern." Made by S.C. Robinson Company, more than 5,000 of these were issued before the war's end.

Old South Military Antiques

Samuel Robinson began making Sharps model carbines for the Confederate government in December 1862. Robinson completed just over 1,900 guns before the C.S. government bought him out in March 1863. The C.S. Government continued Robinson's serial no. range and produced roughly another 3,500 carbines by the spring of 1864, when production ceased. The guns are nearly identical, distinguished only by the change in markings (the C.S.-produced models do not retain Robinson's stamp). This .52-caliber carbine bears serial no. 2785. Its manufacture date, based on production figures and time of operation, would place this carbine's manufacture in June or July 1863. The metal is smooth and dark, the wood has only minor dings, and the rifling is strong. It has a brass blade set into the pinched front sight. **12,500.00**

S.C. Robinson, South Carolina. **14,500.00**

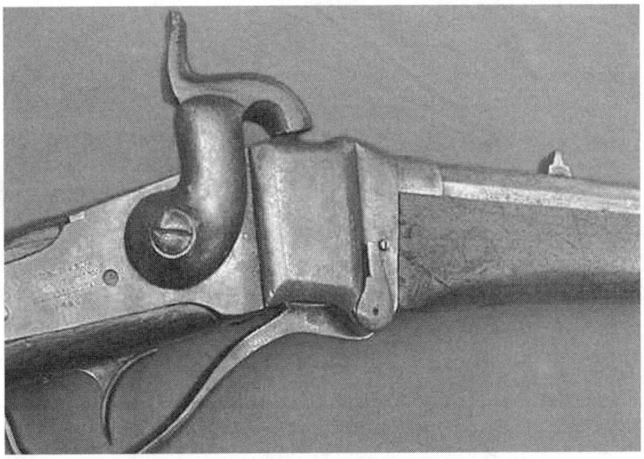

The "Richmond Pattern" carbines bear the S.C. Robinson imprint just behind the hammer.

Old South Military Antiques

S.C. Robinson Sharps carbine, serial no. 1265. .... **15,500.00**

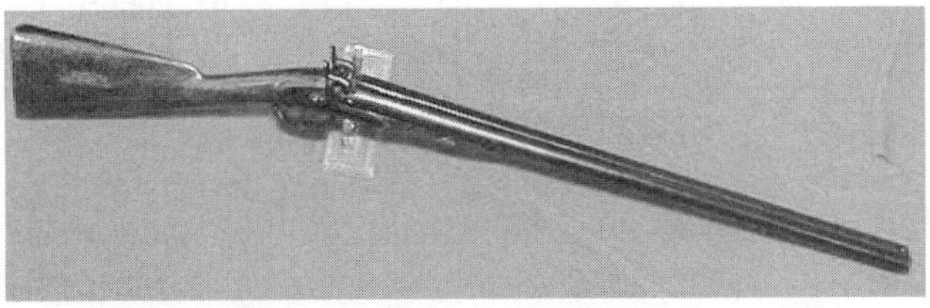

Supposedly a favorite among Confederate cavalry troopers, sawed-off, muzzle-loading shotguns are hard to document. This example, fortunately, has Richmond, Virginia, markings.

Old South Military Antiques

Shotgun

Confederate, Richmond, Virginia-marked double barrel. **1,150.00**

Shotgun, cont.

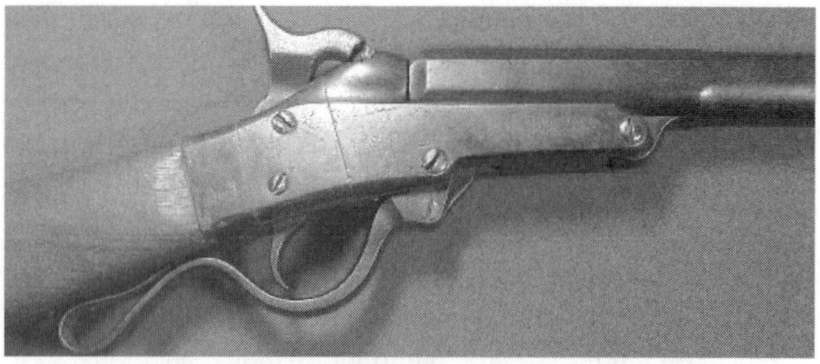

The states of Georgia, Florida, and Mississippi purchased more than 2,300 Maynard carbines from the Massachusetts Arms Company in 1860 and early 1861. This rare shotgun gauged Maynard was probably part of this purchase.

Middle Tennessee Relics

U.S., extremely rare, Confederate-carried lst Model Maynard, .64-caliber, 26" barrel shotgun. A number of Maynard rifles and carbines were purchased by Florida, Georgia, and Mississippi, and even more were confiscated out of southern arsenals. This particular weapon came out of central Mississippi. The metal on this weapon has a thick, dark, never-cleaned patina. The Maynard markings all remain crisp and clear. The bracket for the long-range tang site remains present, but the site itself is not present. The stock is in nice condition, but does have numerous small dings and marks from actual service. The shotgun is serial no. 7020. This particular weapon is a shotgun (longer barrel) rather than a carbine. **1,250.00**

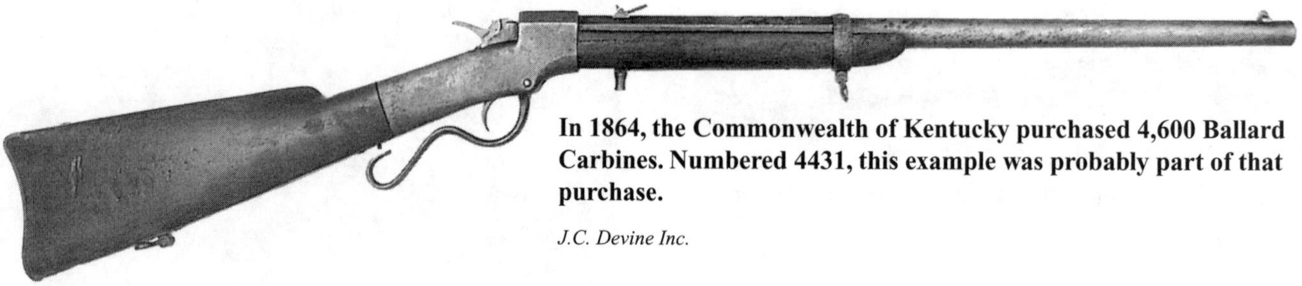

In 1864, the Commonwealth of Kentucky purchased 4,600 Ballard Carbines. Numbered 4431, this example was probably part of that purchase.

J.C. Devine Inc.

U.S.

Ballard

Serial no. 4431, .44 rimfire, 22-3/8" part round/part octagon barrel, good bore. Gray patina on metal, negligible faint pitting. The forend has a repaired grain crack and the stock shows some normal handling marks. The mainspring is weak, good-plus condition overall. **600.00**

"Presented to Cap't D.L. Wilcox, Jr. by the Officers, on Morris Island 1863." Captain Wilcox was the youngest officer in the Navy during the Civil War. At the age of 17, he was assigned as First Officer of the Warship, General Burnside, under the command of Rear Admiral Dahlgren. This carbine was displayed in the Bruce Museum, on loan by Mrs. Lee H. Crittenden, a family descendent. At the exhibit's close, it was purchased by Mr. Norm Flayderman. Captain Wilcox's records and purchased documentation accompany the carbine. **9,500.00**

Burnside, 2nd Model, very scarce, early production that includes 1st Model barrel. These 2nd Models were manufactured without forend wood, and without a hinged breechblock lever. Only about 2,000 of these models were produced, and of that number, roughly one third to one half incorporate parts from two different 2nd Models, or combinations of 1st and 2nd Models with mixed serial nos. This gun has a 1st Model barrel bearing serial no. 333. The frame and breechblock bear serial no. 402 (early 2nd Model), and the butt plate bears number 981 (mid-production 2nd Model). This gun was produced in 1860 or 1861, "good" to "very good" condition, walnut butt stock has good lines and color, shows normal age and use. The metal is uniform, smooth steel mixed with a light-brown patina, and no appreciable pitting (some scattered salt and pepper tiny pits on the frame's front left and barrel breech. The markings are crisp and clear "Bristol Firearm Co." on lock, "G.P. Foster Patent April 10th 1860" on lever, and "Burnside's Patent Nov. 25th 1856" on the breechblock. The sling ring and bar were removed with the screws being left in the frame. A small piece of steel is chipped off of the breechblock where the block itself joins the floating small block that carries the nipple (very minor). It is otherwise complete and functional. **2,150.00**

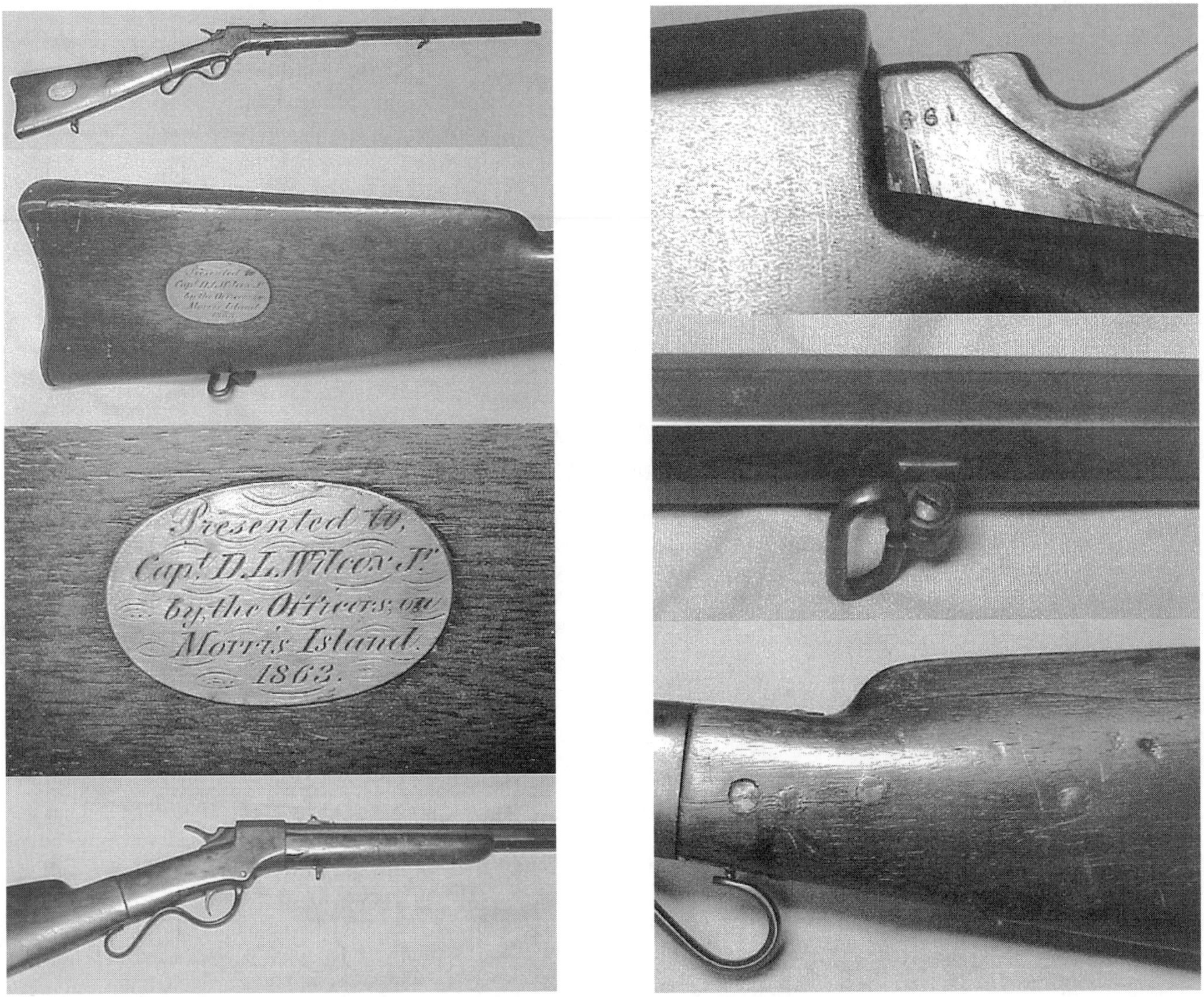

In 1863, officers stationed on Morris Island presented this Ballard Carbine to Captain D.L. Wilcox, the youngest officer in the U.S. Navy at the time.

Sharpsburg Arsenal

Burnside 3rd Model

Serial no. 1463, .54 caliber, standard military configuration, fair condition. Mottled gray metal shows pitting, buttplate has heavy pitting, missing the frame screw and cock. Action needs adjustment, wood has scattered dents, scratches, and bruises. **400.00**

Serial no. 13826, .54 caliber, 21" barrel, walnut stock and forend. Wrist with two inspector's cartouches, good condition. Metal has dark patina, some patches of heavy pitting. Stock with scattered light dents and bruises. **575.00**

Serial no. 16392, .54 caliber, standard military configuration. Right side of buttstock incised with large initials "HM," fair to good condition. Metal with dark-brown patina showing areas of spotting and light pitting, missing sling ring. Stock with numerous dents, scratches, and bruises and with 1 silver missing between upper tang and back plate. **515.00**

The first Burnside that utilized a wooden forend on the gun, otherwise virtually identical to the 2nd Models including the breechblock lever having no hinge in the middle, very good condition with even steel-gray color on the metal parts, very light surface pitting. It has attractive wood on both the butt and fore stock with good lines and edges showing normal handling and age. There were approximately 1,500 of this pattern produced. This one has all matched serial nos. of 3,320 (the number on the block is nearly illegible due to some nicks and dings in that area.) The gun is 100% original and complete, and is mechanically perfect. The lock is marked, "Burnside Rifle Co. Providence RI," the breechblock has a partially legible 1856 patent marking. and the lever has the Foster's patent stamping. **1,650.00**

Burnside 3rd Model, cont.

Serial no. 16420, .54 caliber, standard military configuration, very good to fine condition. Barrel with smooth, brown patina showing some minor spotting. Frame retains much darkened casehardening, stock has fine cartouches, scattered dents, and bruises. . . **1,725.00**

Serial no. 17497, .54 caliber, 21" round barrel, very good bright bore, wood forend and barrel marked "CAST STEEL 1862," good to very good condition. **700.00**

Serial no. 15477, .54 caliber, 21" round barrel marked, "CAST STEEL 1864," very good condition. Dark patina on all the metal mixed with traces of blue on the barrel, metal should clean leaving only a little light pitting on the buttplate, light handling marks and several scored marks on the side of the buttstock and the comb, the wrist has a sharp inspector's cartouche, "R.K.W." **1,100.00**

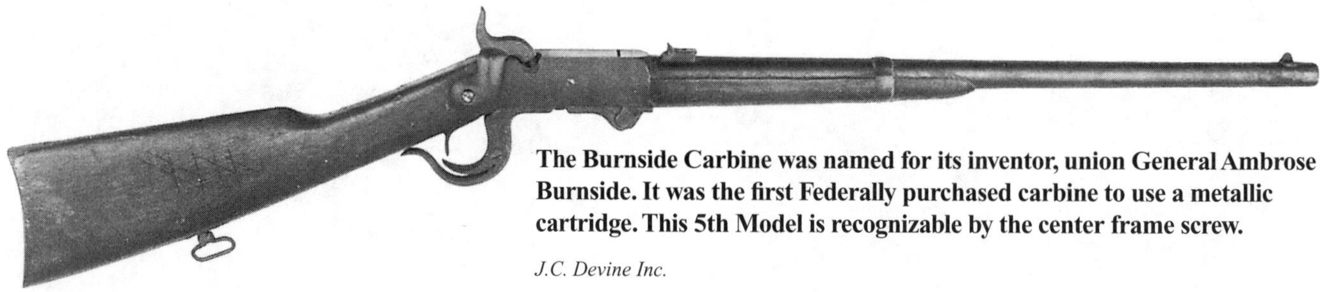

The Burnside Carbine was named for its inventor, union General Ambrose Burnside. It was the first Federally purchased carbine to use a metallic cartridge. This 5th Model is recognizable by the center frame screw.

J.C. Devine Inc.

Burnside, 5th Model

.52 caliber, breech-loading, percussion carbine, serial no. 15221. The third most used carbine of the Civil War, the 5th Model (Model 1864) Burnsides started production during April 1863. Fine condition, the barrel retains 90-95% bright original blue, crisp markings. Frame retains 70-80% bright, vivid case color hardening with swirls of blues, blacks, and purples. Tang and lever retain 80-90% brilliant charcoal fire blue. Excellent bore and mechanics. Stock and forend have several service and storage dings, but still rate very good with a crisp "RKW" cartouche at the left flat. Complete with sling swivel at the butt and sling ring and bar at the left frame. **3,250.00**

Serial no. 15454, .54 caliber, 21" round barrel, very good bore. The lockplate is not marked and has an incorrect hammer and screw. Clear markings on the frame with "BURNSIDE PATENT/MODEL OF 1864." Traces of mottled dark case colors on the frame, the barrel has an old reblue that has turned dark plum, the lever has been cleaned and shows scratches. The forend is in fine condition, but is missing the screw. The buttstock has an old oil refinish with partially legible cartouche. The hammer does not stay cocked. Good condition. **550.00**

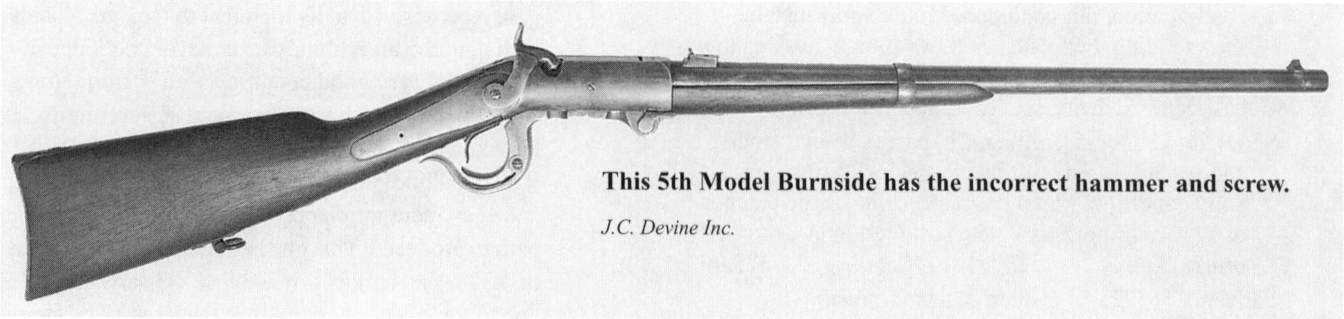

This 5th Model Burnside has the incorrect hammer and screw.

J.C. Devine Inc.

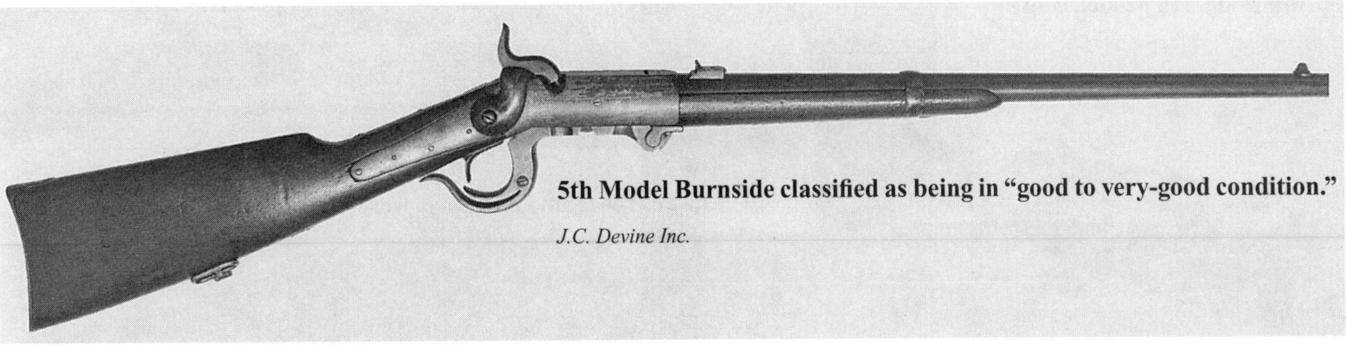

5th Model Burnside classified as being in "good to very-good condition."

J.C. Devine Inc.

Serial no. 15850, .54 caliber, 21" round barrel, some pitting on bore, otherwise bright. The 5th Model had a center frame guide screw. The stock shows two oblong cartouches on the left side above the trigger. One is faint, the other is possibly "RHKW" (Robert Henry Kirkwood Whitley, Capt. U.S.A. 1838-75). The breechblock is marked, "BURNSIDE PATENT MODEL OF 1864." Traces of blue/case color remain on the outside lever and breechblock with considerably more visible when the lever is lowered. The balance of exterior metal is a gray-brown color. Inspector's marks "B" and "MM" appear in several places. Good to very-good condition........ **850.00**

Serial no. 16518, .54 caliber, 21" barrel, good bore. The frame and lock are a smooth dark grey, the barrel has a lot of original blue mixing with plum patina. The tangs and sling ring bar have light pitting. Frame markings are clear but lockplate markings are worn. The stocks show the usual handling marks, there are two 3/8" circular depressions in the buttstock near the buttplate (purpose unknown), and two very-good cartouches, "E.P.K.," and, "R.K.W." Good condition.................. **1,250.00**

Serial no. 38724, .54 caliber, 21" barrel, good bore. The Burnside is entirely gray with even dark freckling overall. The wood has many old handling marks, particularly a large gouge on the comb of the buttstock and several deep marks on the forend. Cartouches still visible under an added oil finish. Fair/good condition. **700.00**

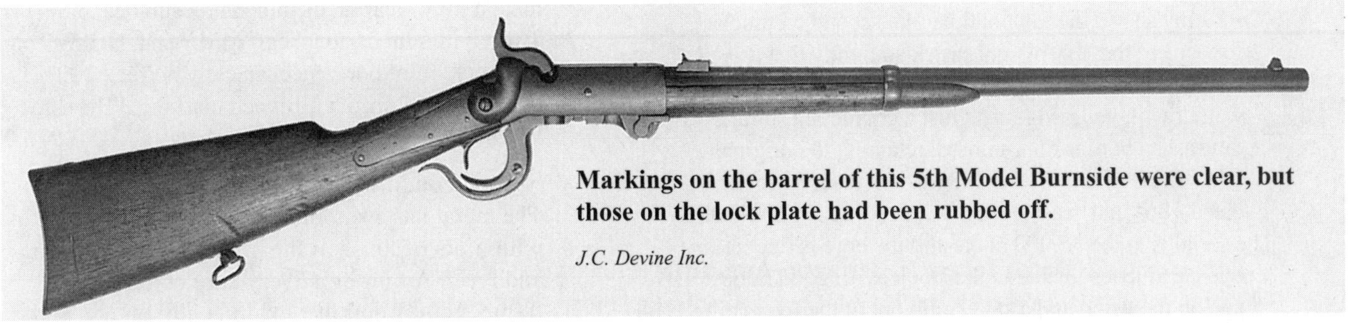

Markings on the barrel of this 5th Model Burnside were clear, but those on the lock plate had been rubbed off.

J.C. Devine Inc.

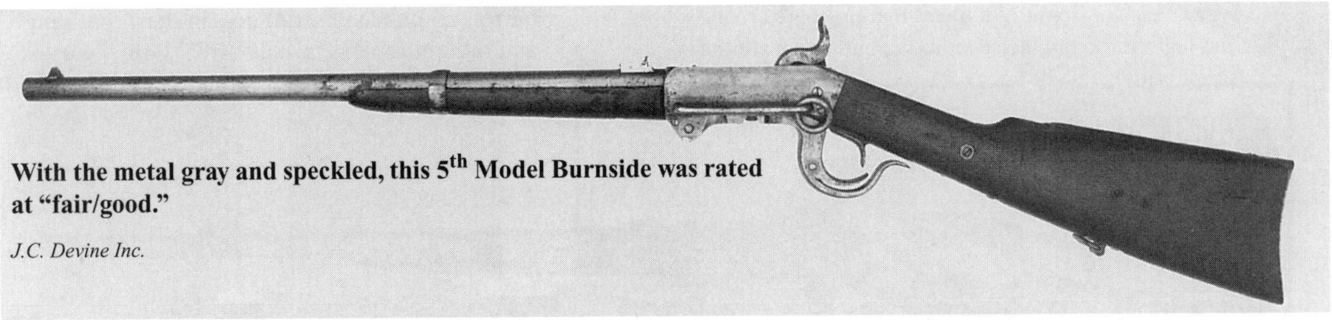

With the metal gray and speckled, this 5th Model Burnside was rated at "fair/good."

J.C. Devine Inc.

Burnside, 5th Model, cont.

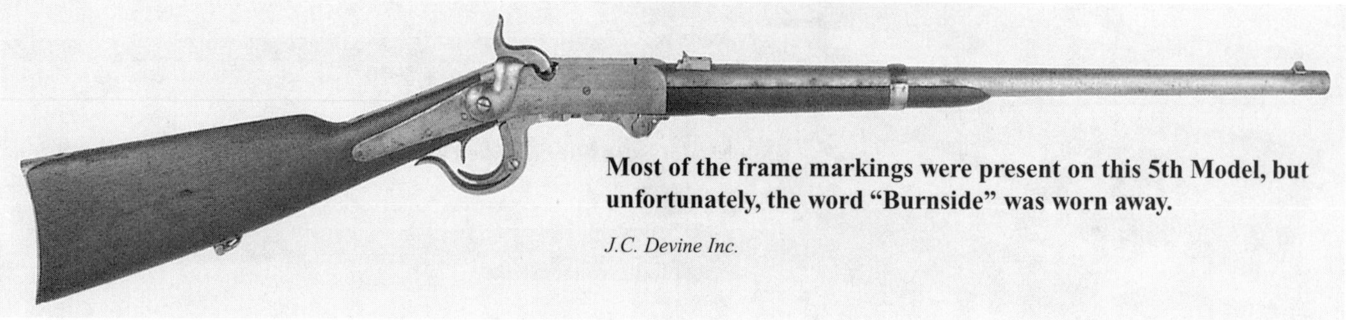

Most of the frame markings were present on this 5th Model, but unfortunately, the word "Burnside" was worn away.

J.C. Devine Inc.

Serial no. 3897, .54 caliber, 21" round barrel, good-plus bore may clean to very good. Gray patina on all the metal with scattered patches of fine pitting, most of the frame marking is clear, but "BURNSIDE" is worn or missing, refinished stocks. Good condition. **700.00**

Serial no. 5437, .54 caliber, 21" barrel, fair bore. Metal is dark with even light pitting, stock shows normal handling marks and a worn cartouche. Fair overall condition. **450.00**

Standard 5th Model Burnside in unfired condition. Nearly factory new with slightest fading to the barrel blue, and faint rumors of handling signs on the wood. Barrel has 99% blue slightly faded, frame has 99% vivid bright case colors, hammer has 80% vivid case, lock has 75% vivid case colors, tang at wrist has 70% vivid blue, top of breechblock has 85% vivid blue, stock has vivid deep cartouche "RKW" in a rectangle. Close scrutiny shows the faint outline of a second cartouche forward of the "PKW," but struck so lightly that it hardly shows. The stock is beautiful straight grain walnut with vivid edges and just a couple old storage dings. The bore is mint-unfired, retaining the original blue. The frame bears the 1864 patent date, barrel is dated 1864 and "cast steel." **3,950.00**

The serial is in the 35,000 range and the bore is fine. Has two cartouches visible in the stock, with good honest age on the wood and a small chip out of the forearm's tip. The metal is overall gray-steel color with evidence of light cleaning, 1856 patent stamping (very clear) on frame. All metal markings are crisp and legible. Neatly incised into the butt stock are the script initials, "JV." **975.00**

Approximately 45,000 Burnsides were produced in their own serial range. They are nearly identical to the 4th Models (improved hinged lever and having a wood forend) but also have a guide screw in the frame's right side to help the breechblock function smoothly. Very-good condition and is 100% original and complete. The metal has both a smooth gray and light plum patina with hints of silvery case color on the frame, good wood that exhibits normal age and handling wear, eroded cartouche. The metal markings are all clear, 1864 patent mark on frame, "Burnside Rifle Co." stamp on lock, and "New Model 1864" on barrel, all matched serial nos. in the 15,000 range, and mint bore. Initials "RB" lightly carved in the stock. **1,050.00**

Near mint, unissued condition, 95% barrel blue with little fading, 95% vivid case color on the frame and lock, a little wear on the blued breechblock and lever. Two vivid mint cartouches, "MM," and, "RKW," on the stock, mint bore, mechanically perfect, 100% complete and original. Breech marking, "Burnside Patent Model of 1864." **3,975.00**

Very good condition, 100% original and complete. The metal has a smooth gray and light-plum patina with hints of finish at the breech and on the tang and lever. A hint of silvery case color on the frame, good wood that exhibits normal age and handling wear, faintly visible cartouche, "Burnside Rifle Co." stamp on lock, and "cast steel" on barrel, all matched serial nos. in the 7,900 range, and mint bore. Has initials "JPP" lightly carved in the stock. **1,295.00**

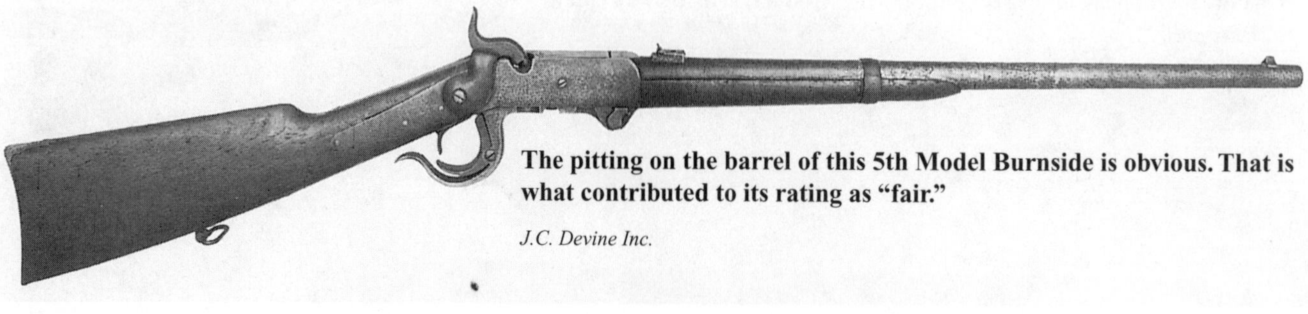

The pitting on the barrel of this 5th Model Burnside is obvious. That is what contributed to its rating as "fair."

J.C. Devine Inc.

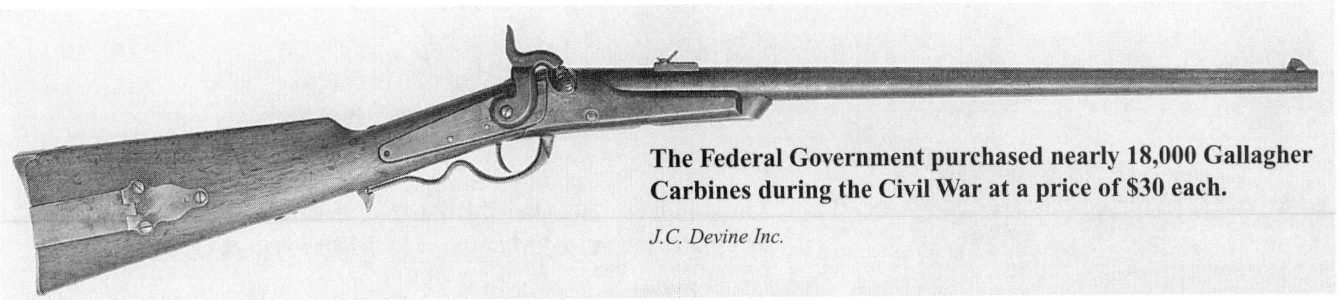

The Federal Government purchased nearly 18,000 Gallagher Carbines during the Civil War at a price of $30 each.

J.C. Devine Inc.

Gallagher

Serial no. 1149, .50 caliber, 22-1/4" round barrel, fine bore, manufactured circa 1861, all original, good-plus condition, stock has no finish and many dings and dents, clear markings. **800.00**

Serial no. 133xx, .50 caliber, barrel shows 80% original blue with no pitting, bore is very good to excellent. Frame and lock show sharp markings and 40% original color. Patch box and butt plate show equal amounts of color. Walnut stock is in very good condition. Overall a very nice gun. **2,795.00**

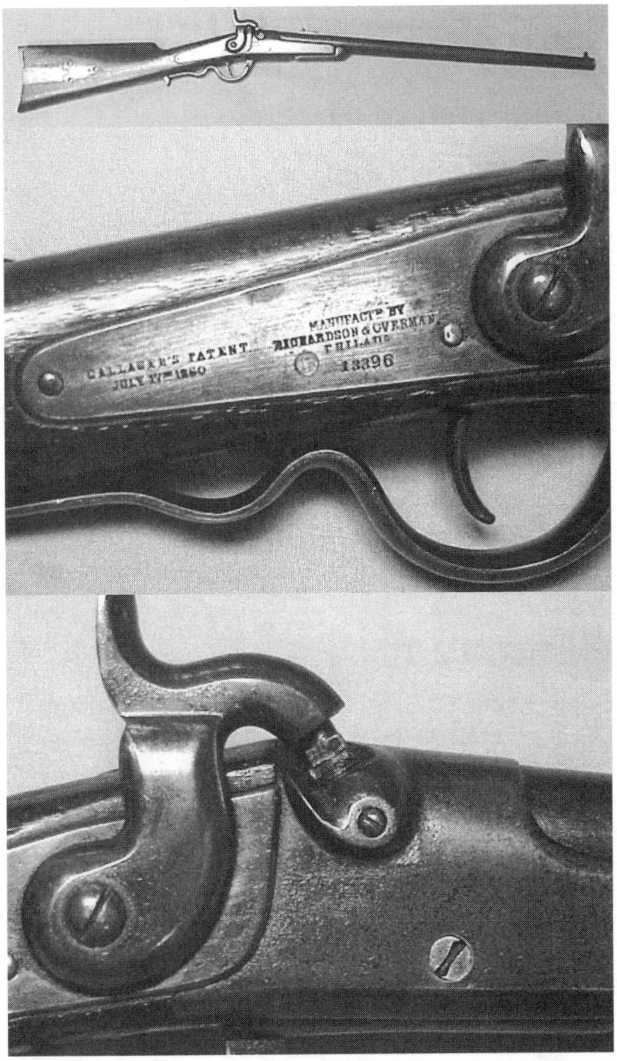

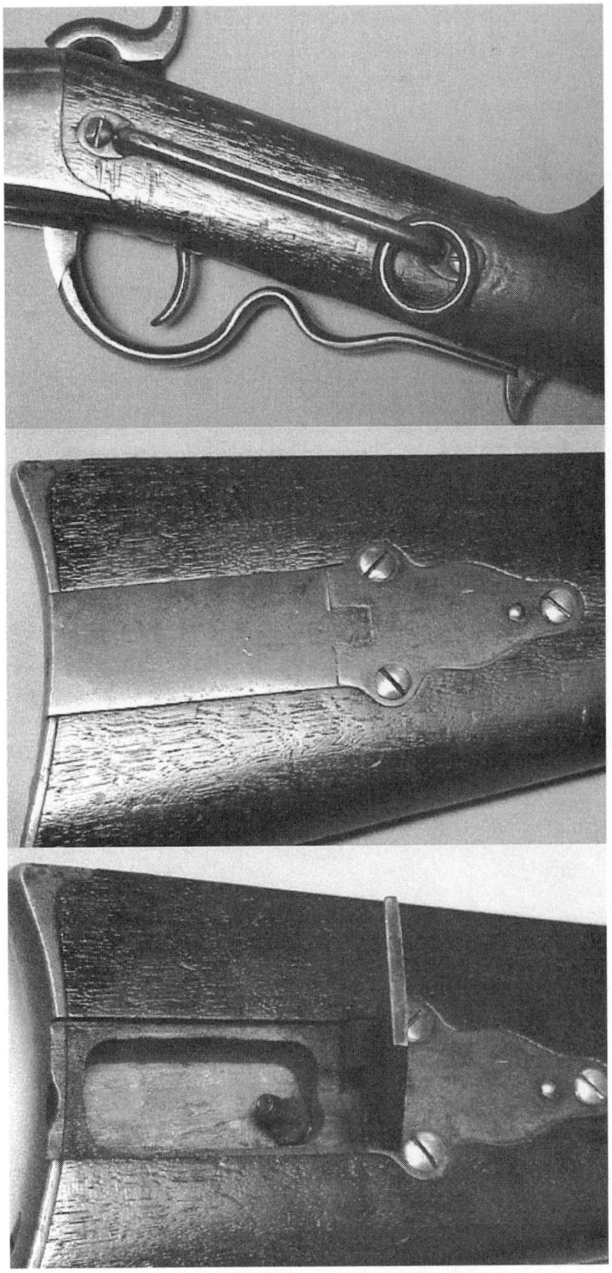

Gallagher possessing great color, sharp stampings, and even a spare nipple in the patchbox.

Sharpsburg Arsenal

Gallagher, cont.

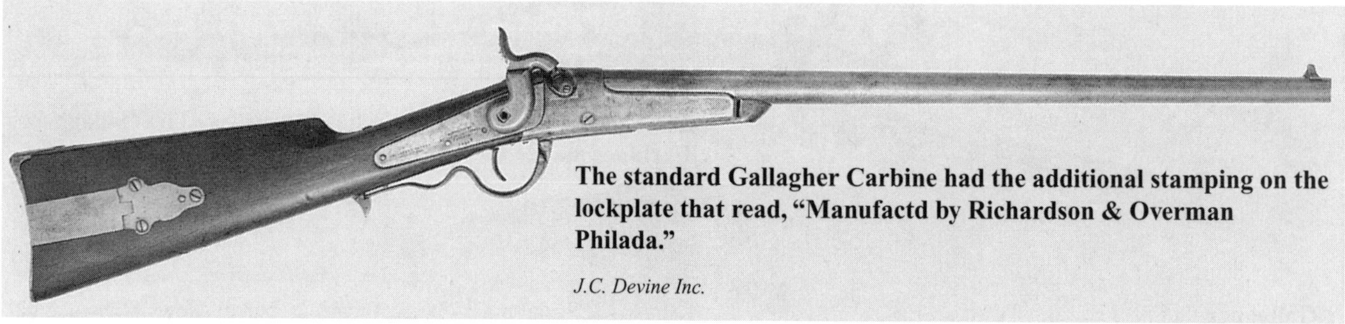

The standard Gallagher Carbine had the additional stamping on the lockplate that read, "Manufactd by Richardson & Overman Philada."

J.C. Devine Inc.

Serial no. 14518, .50 caliber, 22-1/4" round barrel, fine-plus bore. This is the standard model with lockplate having additional marking, "MANUFACTD BY/ RICHARDSON OVERMAN/PHILADA." Buttstock has several narrow age checks and wear from the sling ring, the left side has the scratched initial, "W." Overall condition is very good.. . . . . **650.00**

Serial no. 15745, .50 caliber, 22" round barrel, bright bore with minor pitting. standard model, marked, "Manufactd By/Richardson & Overman/Philada." Traces of light case color remain, most have turned silver/gray. The barrel blue has turned a plum patina. Negligible pitting, light surface rust on the buttplate, several minor dents in the metal, sharp markings. The stock finish is worn, the inspector's cartouche is legible. Very-good overall condition. **1,200.00**

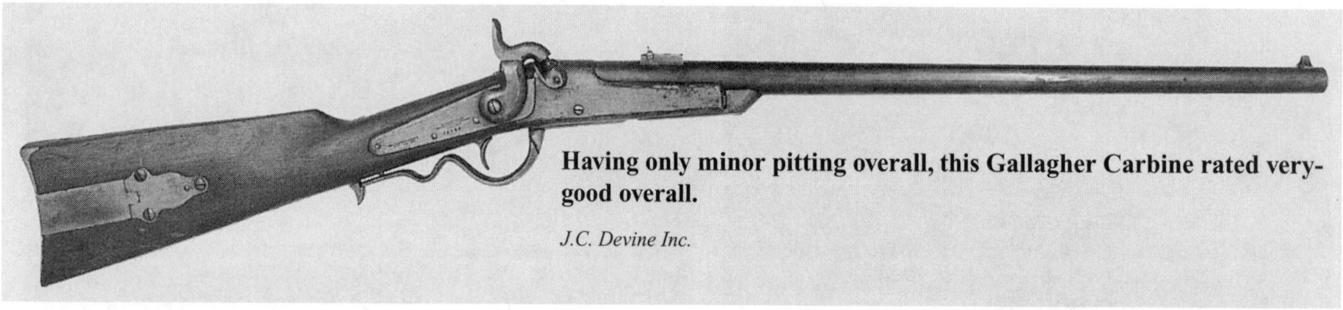

Having only minor pitting overall, this Gallagher Carbine rated very-good overall.

J.C. Devine Inc.

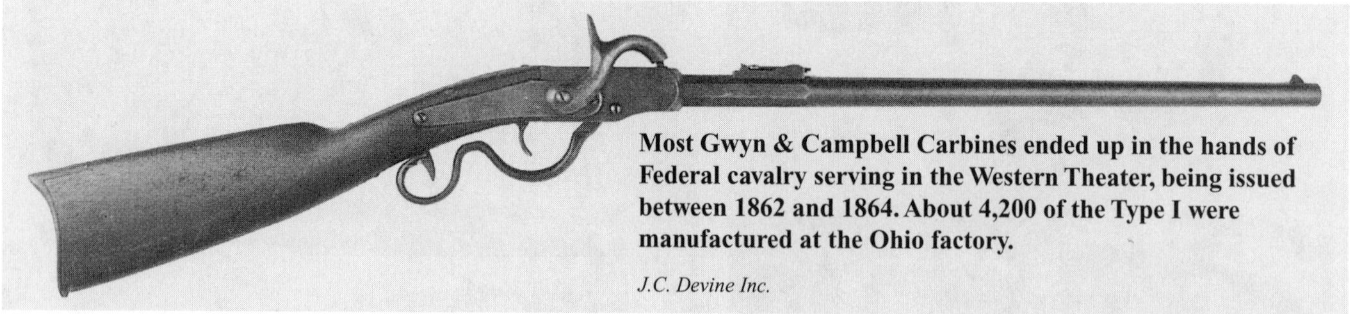

Most Gwyn & Campbell Carbines ended up in the hands of Federal cavalry serving in the Western Theater, being issued between 1862 and 1864. About 4,200 of the Type I were manufactured at the Ohio factory.

J.C. Devine Inc.

Gwyn & Campbell, Type I

Serial no. 1274, .52 caliber. This has a 20" round barrel, good-plus bore, dark patina on all metal, clear markings, pitting near muzzle, removed sling ring, sanded and refinished buttstock has a small chip missing at the toe. Overall good condition. **1,300.00**

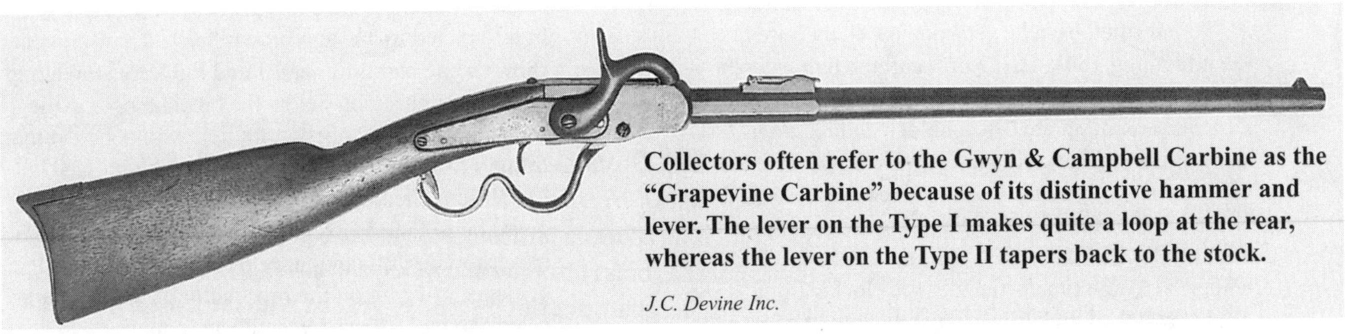

Collectors often refer to the Gwyn & Campbell Carbine as the "Grapevine Carbine" because of its distinctive hammer and lever. The lever on the Type I makes quite a loop at the rear, whereas the lever on the Type II tapers back to the stock.

J.C. Devine Inc.

Serial no. 1744, .52 caliber, 20" barrel, fair bore, dark-brown patina on all metal, good markings on lockplate with clear "UNION/RIFLE" on frame, breechblock and frame top are pitting, broken nipple. The rear sight leaf is slightly bent and the slide and stop screws are missing. The buttstock has a large splinter missing on the right side of the trigger, crack at same place on the left side, sanded and refinished stock. Fair-plus condition. **600.00**

Serial no. 734, .52 caliber, 20" barrel, good bore, frame and barrel have old reblue that turned dark plum, "UNION/RIFLE" partially legible, lockplate was not refinished, but weak markings. The stock has an old refinish in varnish, "E.C. RODIMON" stamped on the right side, good condition **950.00**

A near-mint carbine, 95+% original blue on barrel, strong case colors on lockplate and hammer, lots of purple! All markings are crisp, mint bore, beautiful grain walnut stock. Crisp cartouche, serial no. 4430. .... **3,650.00**

Serial no. 4499, .52 caliber, 20" barrel, fair bore, lever end and rear sight leaf missing, cracked hammer nose, dark patina on all metal, scattering pitting, refinished stock, about good overall condition. **800.00**

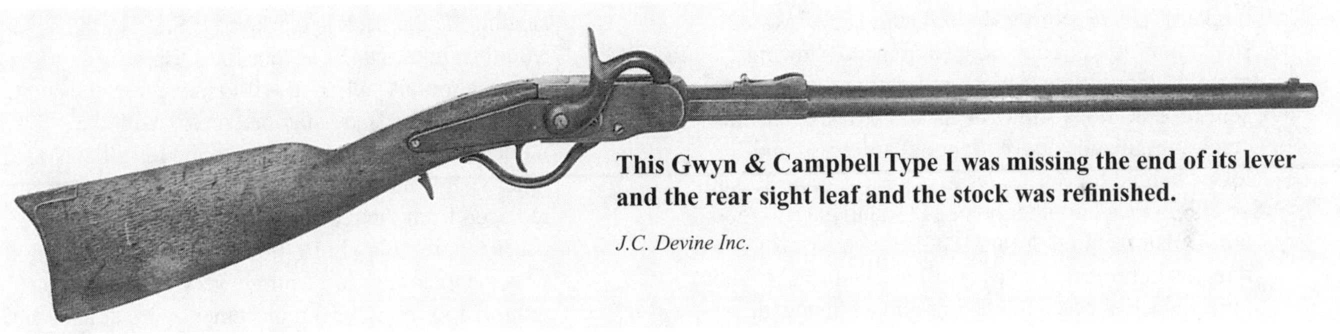

This Gwyn & Campbell Type I was missing the end of its lever and the rear sight leaf and the stock was refinished.

J.C. Devine Inc.

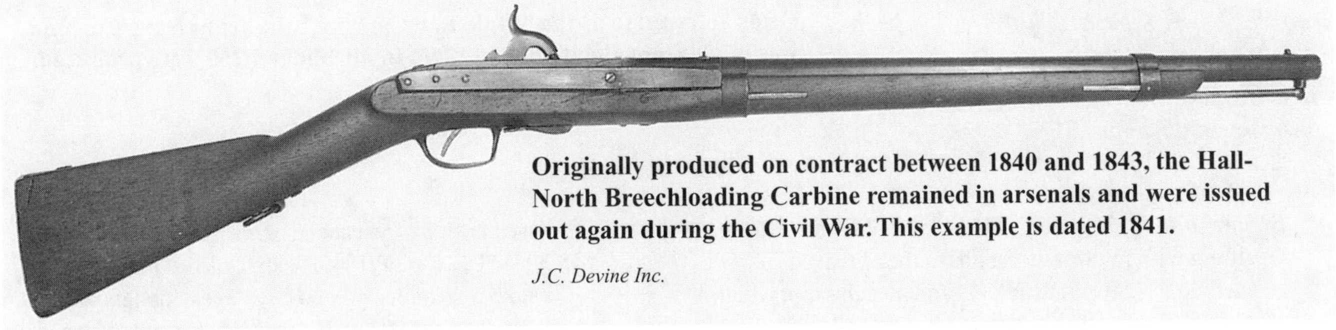

Originally produced on contract between 1840 and 1843, the Hall-North Breechloading Carbine remained in arsenals and were issued out again during the Civil War. This example is dated 1841.

J.C. Devine Inc.

Hall, Model 1840, Type II, serial no. 134, .52 caliber, 21" round rifled barrels, very fine/excellent bores, manufactured 1841, Hall/North carbine retains 95% smooth, brown lacquer finish on the barrel and frame, with 50% on buttplate. Breechblock and hammer show a mottled dark-blue finish with scattered areas of light-brown spotting, and the block marked, "U.S. North Midlin Conn. 1841." Barrel breech stamped with small "EB" and a "B" at frame's left rear. The letters "HA" are punched under the block's front, "134" scratched under the trigger and punched into both barrel bands. One-piece trigger guard with ring, fishtail opening lever and both barrel bands are lightly rusted to a rough brown finish. The wood shows some handling marks and light bruising along with minor chipping below the breechblock on the right side. Two cartouches are lightly punched at the frame's rear, one on either side, with the initials "WB" scratched into the wood at rear of the trigger guard tang. Fine to excellent condition, with a bright bore showing little evidence of use, no pitting or evidence of firing on the breechblock face. A scarce rifled Model 1840 carbine with a production estimate of 6,000 pieces. **3,650.00**

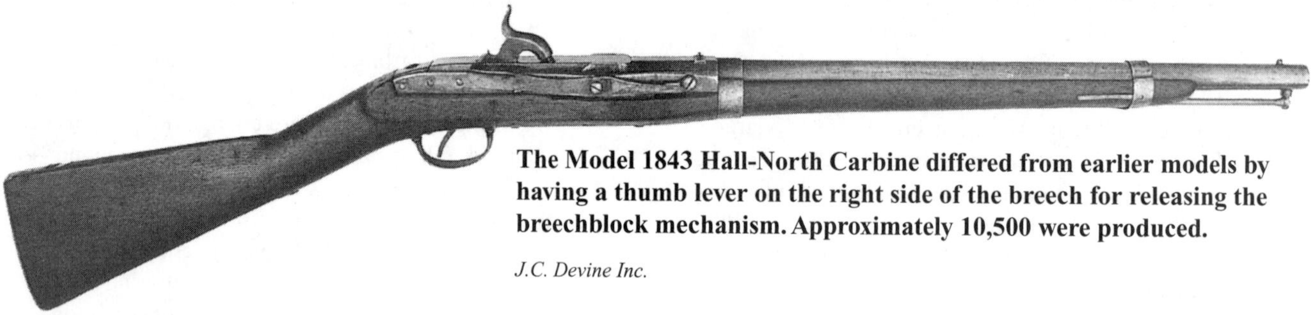

The Model 1843 Hall-North Carbine differed from earlier models by having a thumb lever on the right side of the breech for releasing the breechblock mechanism. Approximately 10,500 were produced.

J.C. Devine Inc.

Hall, Model 1843

Standard model, .52 caliber, 21" barrel, breechblock marked, "U.S./S. North/Midltn/Conn/1852." Walnut stock, poor to fair condition. Gray metal showing areas of light pitting. Sling ring missing, hammer spur broken, stock shows dents and bruises, hairline crack to right side above trigger guard, chips and losses behind breech. **850.00**

NSN, .52 caliber smoother bore, 21" round barrel, good bore, manufactured during 1845. Brown varnish remains in protected areas on all metal surfaces. The breechblock shows a mottled fire blue finish with pitted areas near the percussion nipple, stock has some gouges, dings, and bruises and apparent sanding. The breech is marked, "U.S.S. North Midlton Conn. 1845" in four lines. Barrel is marked with the initials "J.H.," at left to the rear of the sight, both barrel bands are stamped on top with the number "1" and number "40" on the left side. No other visible marks. A piece of wood has been neatly replaced from the rear band back to the left stock cheek, approximately 10-1/4". The wood grades good with the metal grading antique very good. The ramrod appears to be a replacement. **700.00**

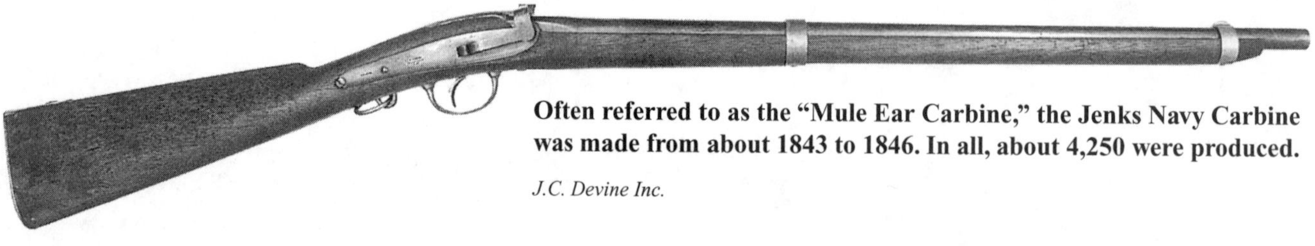

Often referred to as the "Mule Ear Carbine," the Jenks Navy Carbine was made from about 1843 to 1846. In all, about 4,250 were produced.

J.C. Devine Inc.

Jenks, Navy

Serial no. 417, .54 caliber, 24-1/4" round barrel, strong rifling with minor pitting. Sharp metal markings include, "U.S.N./JCB/P/1843" on breech's top, which has an oval loading aperture, 50-60% original barrel browning, attractive mustard-brown patina on the brass furniture, the case colors on the lock and hammer turned to a blue patina. Very thin stock crack between the lockplate and top tang, nothing is loose, light handling marks to an old oil refinish and two worn inspector's cartouches. Very-good overall condition. **1,400.00**

Browned 24-1/2", .54 caliber, barrel marked at breech, "W. Jenks//USN/RC/P/1846." Casehardened mule ear lock marked, "Wm. Jenks" and "NP Ames/Springfield/Mass." Brass furniture and walnut stock of standard pattern, faint inspector's cartouche opposite lock, fine to excellent condition. Barrel retains 90% brown finish, light spotting, wear at muzzle, and area of wear and light pitting behind lever barrel band. Lock retains 80% faded casehardening colors. Stock with scattered light blemishes and one deep dent to right side of buttstock. **3,163.00**

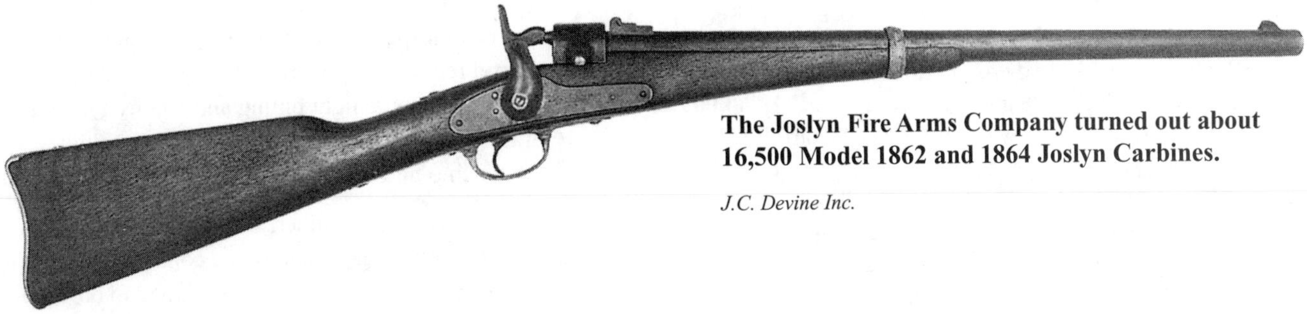

The Joslyn Fire Arms Company turned out about 16,500 Model 1862 and 1864 Joslyn Carbines.

J.C. Devine Inc.

Joslyn, Model 1862

Serial no. 1849, .52 rimfire caliber, 22" round barrel, good bore, hook-type latch on the breechblock and brass furniture. Dark-plum patina on iron, small patches of light corrosion, metal markings are clear. The brass is dark, sanded stock has been sanded, inlet for a band spring at the tip that is missing. The tip has a 1" crack, thin crack between the breechblock and sling bar, good overall condition. **1,300.00**

This piece is 100% original and complete, barrel retains 60-70% barrel blue thinning and turning plum color. Lock exhibits 25-35% case color, as does the base plate under the sling ring bar. Brass barrel band and butt plate have delicate age patina, stock has very strong edges and some expected handling bruises, near mint cartouche "VP" in rectangle, serial in 2,500 range......................... **2,450.00**

Joslyn, Model 1864

Serial no. 15759, good condition, .52 rimfire caliber, 22" round barrel, good-plus bore. The barrel has a dark patina with even light surface corrosion; the lock case colors have gone dark with a large patch of very light surface corrosion. Firing pin hood has a piece missing at the bottom. Sanded stock with an old refinish in oil, no visible cartouche, buttplate heel marked "U.S." There is a 1" long crack behind the upper tang and the name, "BREADON," has been stamped numerous times into the butt......................... **700.00**

Serial no. 16432, .52 rimfire caliber, 22" round barrel, air bore, U.S. marked on heel of buttplate. Dark patina on all metal, scattered fine pitting, clear markings, stock has an old refinish and shows very few handling marks, good-plus condition. ... **750.00**

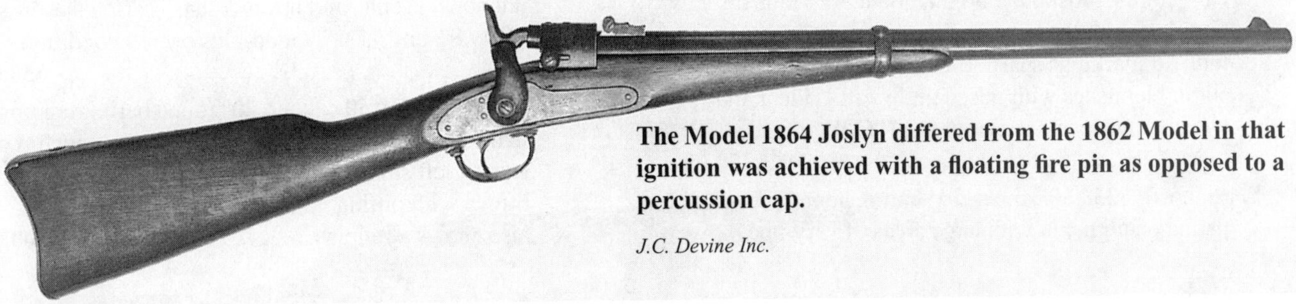

The Model 1864 Joslyn differed from the 1862 Model in that ignition was achieved with a floating fire pin as opposed to a percussion cap.

J.C. Devine Inc.

Excellent stock with sharp edges and vivid, near mint "FDL" cartouches, dried linseed oil on the butt stock, barrel retains 75% factory blue turning plum mixed with light areas of surface rust. The lock has faint traces of case color, the bar under the sling ring bar has much vivid case color. The bore is as dark and filthy as a West Virginia coal mine. The action is crisp as new, serial is 6,xxx range and matched. Attic brown condition with a whole lot of original factory finish mixed with the age, 100% original and complete except for the bar ring. **1,950.00**

.52 rimfire, serial no. 9969, metal has a smooth, gently aging, gray-brown patina with traces of case colors still visible on the lockplate. The markings are, "Joslyn Firearms Co.-Stonington, Conn.-1864," and are clear and easily legible, good bore, very nice stock shows a few small use marks, but remains quite crisp with readable inspector marks. **1,695.00**

This close-up shows the pullout latch for the breechblock on the Model 1864 Joslyn.

Middle Tennessee Relics

Maynard, 2nd Model

Carbine has 100% blue on the barrel. Very good case colors on the frame and very fine bore, light dings on the walnut stock. Two crisp cartouches and serial no. 14193, a strong, 90% gun. **2,700.00**

.50 caliber, well marked with cartouche, "Victor Reis" on stock, very-fine condition............ **2,450.00**

Serial no. 17971, .50 caliber. Standard military configuration, good condition. Barrel with smooth mottled patina retaining generous traces of thin blue finish. Frame shows scattered minor pitting. Stock has scattered minor blemishes, series of small dents to right side, hairline cracks to lower-left side and with abrasion marks removing the cartouches. **575.00**

Serial no. 22984, .50 caliber, standard model with 20" blued barrel, casehardened frame and walnut stock with two inspector's cartouches, fine condition. Barrel retains 95% blue finish, frame shows gray metal with some light pitting and retains generous traces of casehardening colors. Stock has fine cartouches and scattered scratches....... **1,610.00**

Serial no. 23121, .50 caliber, standard military configuration, very good to fine condition. Barrel retains 95% blue finish partially turned to brown and showing scattered light pitting overall. Frame has dark-brown patina. Fine wood, with scattered small dents and scratches and excellent cartouches. **1,380.00**

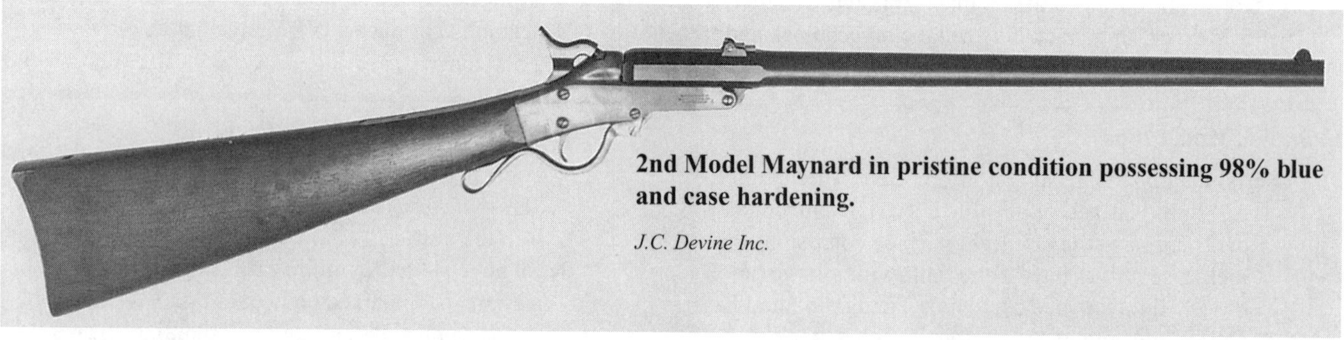

2nd Model Maynard in pristine condition possessing 98% blue and case hardening.

J.C. Devine Inc.

Serial no. 22381, .50 caliber, 20" round barrel, perfect bright bore. Carbine shows 98% blue on barrel, 98% case colors, most quite bright, about 50% blue on buttplate with the balance flaked, no metal pitting with all markings sharp. Buttstock shows only a few slight blemishes with raised grain still evident and two sharp inspector's cartouches, "G.W.S." and "J.M." **3,250.00**

Serial no. 24833, .50 caliber, 20" barrel, good bore, dark patina on all metal with large areas of very fine pitting, buttstock shows very little wear, has sixteen notches cut into the wrist area to commemorate some unknown events, and has two sharp cartouches, "G.W.S." and "J.M." Good-plus overall condition. **850.00**

Serial no. 25145, .50 caliber, 20" round barrel, fair bore, manufactured in 1865, remains of two cartouches on stock's left side. The metal is now gray and dark brown with pitting, missing chip from stock's toe, also shows a refinish.................... **300.00**

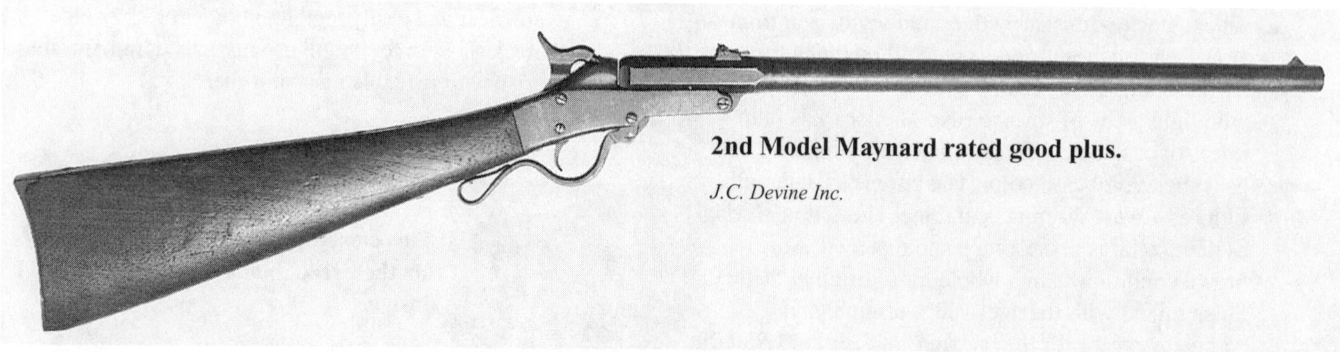

2nd Model Maynard rated good plus.

J.C. Devine Inc.

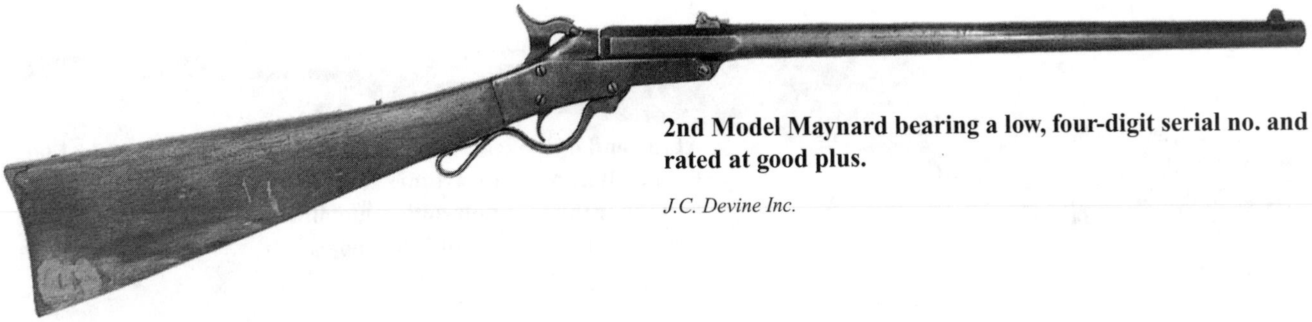

2nd Model Maynard bearing a low, four-digit serial no. and rated at good plus.

J.C. Devine Inc.

Serial no. 3536, .50 caliber, U.S. purchase during the Civil War, has "G.W.S." inspector's initials breech's left side and two faint, but legible, stock cartouches. 20" round barrel, octagonal at the breech, dark bore, dark patina on all metal, scattered pine pitting, buttstock shows normal handling marks, good-plus overall condition. **800.00**

Serial no. 879, .50 caliber, 20" round barrel, fair bore. This carbine shows two inspector's cartouches on left side of stock. The metal is brown overall with an antique overall grade of good/very good, screw head damage, saddle ring is attached with the ring removed. **800.00**

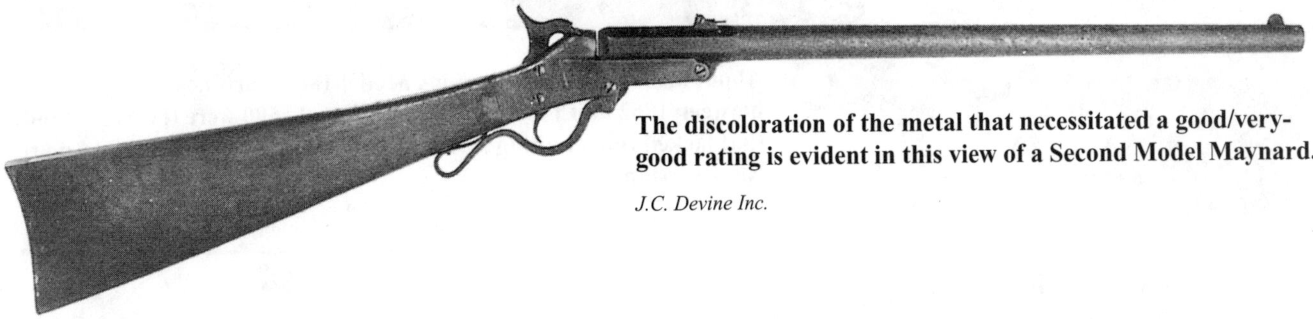

The discoloration of the metal that necessitated a good/very-good rating is evident in this view of a Second Model Maynard.

J.C. Devine Inc.

Merrill, 1st Type, serial no. 6676, .54 caliber, 22-1/8" round barrel, dark bore, brass furniture, including patchbox. Hammer nose and nipple are chipped, iron dark with scattered pitting, the stock with cracks (not broken) at the wrist with the grain, fair-plus condition. **800.00**

1st Model Merrill Carbines had a patchbox in the stock that was not found on Second Models. The Federal Government purchased about 14,495 First and Second Model Merrills.

J.C. Devine Inc.

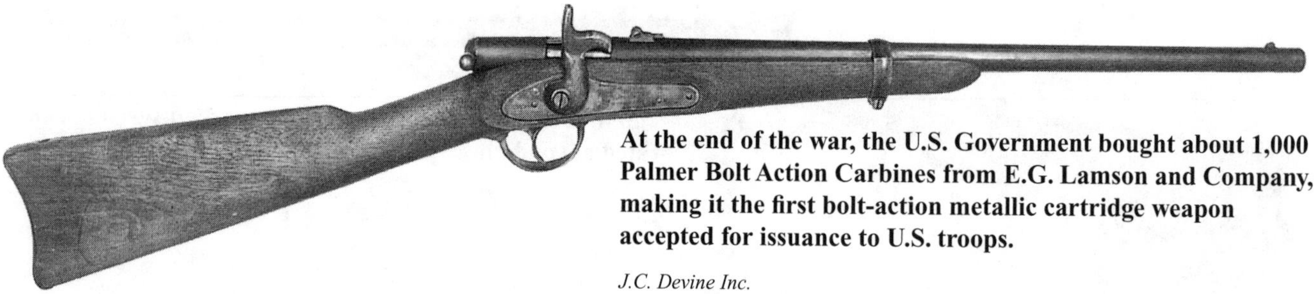

At the end of the war, the U.S. Government bought about 1,000 Palmer Bolt Action Carbines from E.G. Lamson and Company, making it the first bolt-action metallic cartridge weapon accepted for issuance to U.S. troops.

J.C. Devine Inc.

Palmer, Bolt Action, .50-rimfire caliber, 20" round barrel, bright, excellent condition bore, outstanding carbine (probably never issued). Sharp inspector's marks, "M.M." on the stock and barrel, sharp manufacturer's marking on barrel and lock. Bright case colors remain on the lock and barrel band. The case colors are just a little duller on the trigger guard, buttplate, and sling ring with well over 90% remaining. The buttplate has slight heel corrosion, the barrel and action retain 99% original blue that has a little dried grease and a small area of light rust at the muzzle. Sharp-edged stock with raised grain evident, the forend has three small nicks, and a couple of shallow scratches have been sanded on the buttstock. **3,100.00**

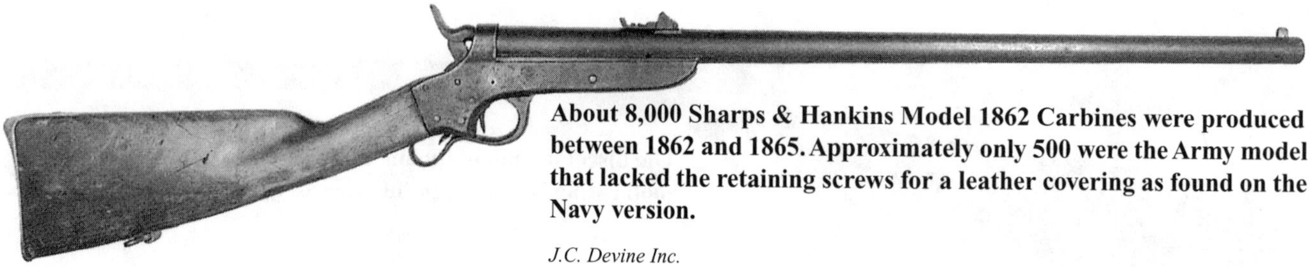

About 8,000 Sharps & Hankins Model 1862 Carbines were produced between 1862 and 1865. Approximately only 500 were the Army model that lacked the retaining screws for a leather covering as found on the Navy version.

J.C. Devine Inc.

Sharps & Hankins, Model 1862, Army

Serial no. 2487, .52 rimfire, 24" round barrel, fair bore, saddle ring, brass buttplate. Dark patina on all metal, scattered fine pitting, missing safety lever. Stock with two short grain cracks at the frame, epoxy filler at the broken lower tang, about-good overall condition. **750.00**

Only 500, 24" barrels made, overall very good condition with plum color on all metal parts and hints of Schuyler Hartley and Graham blue finish on the frame. Very solid, mechanically perfect, decent bore, and very representative, no firm markings on the frame, very fine wood on butt stock. **995.00**

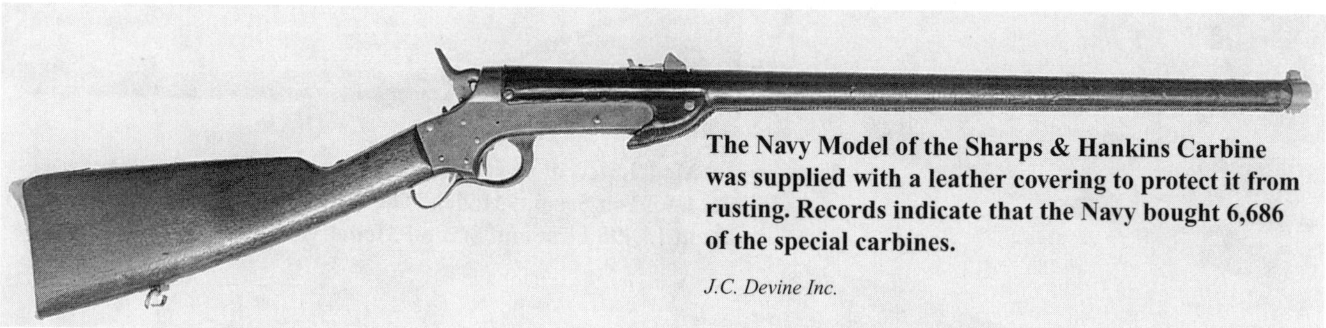

The Navy Model of the Sharps & Hankins Carbine was supplied with a leather covering to protect it from rusting. Records indicate that the Navy bought 6,686 of the special carbines.

J.C. Devine Inc.

Sharps & Hankins, Model 1862, Navy

Serial no. 11933, .52 rimfire, 24" leather covered round barrel, very good bore, manufactured circa 1864, carbine retains almost all the leather covering on barrel. Muzzle right side missing small piece from 1/2" crack. Leather separated where action enters leather covering. Some case color is visible on action and hammer, all markings crisp. The stock has had some added shellac, overall this carbine is nearly fine. **1,350.00**

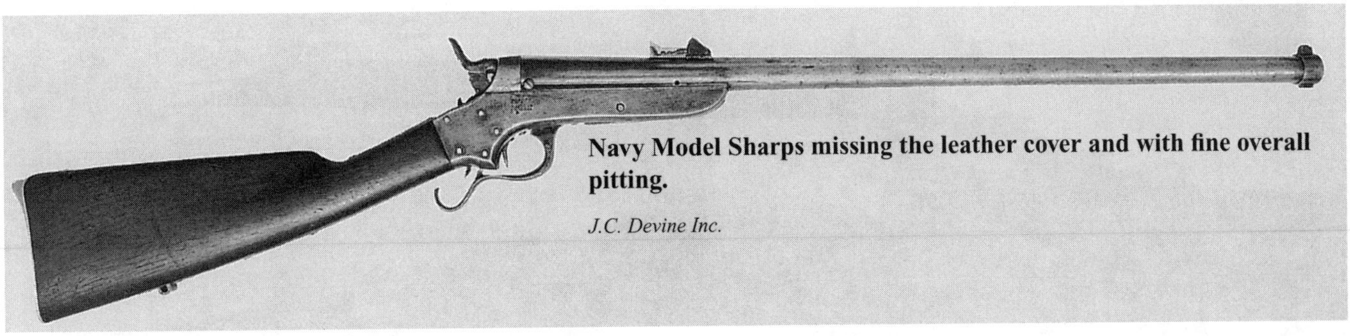

Navy Model Sharps missing the leather cover and with fine overall pitting.

J.C. Devine Inc.

Serial no. 3270, .52 rimfire caliber, 24" barrel, very good bore, missing leather barrel cover, iron has gray patina with faint pitting, clear factory markings. The brass buttplate is stamped, "PHIL" on the heel (Philadelphia Navy Yard?). The walnut buttstock has the base only for the swivel and shows several small circular dings the size of a nail head. The lever catch needs adjustment. **350.00**

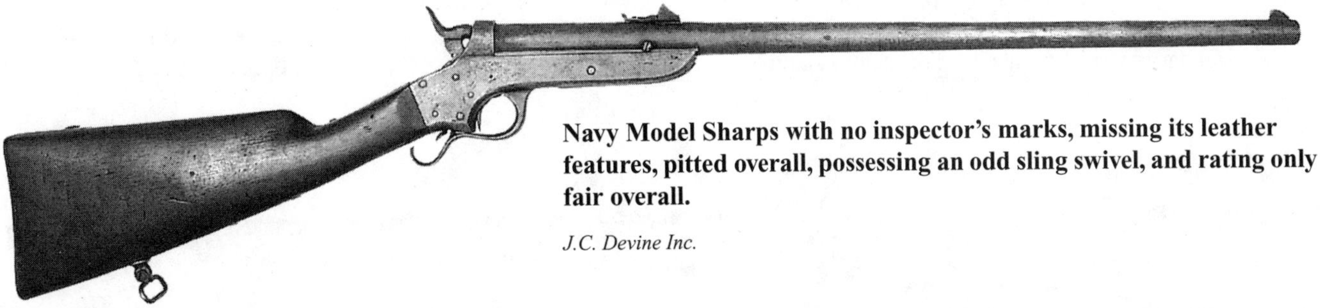

Navy Model Sharps with no inspector's marks, missing its leather features, pitted overall, possessing an odd sling swivel, and rating only fair overall.

J.C. Devine Inc.

Serial no. 5117, smooth 23-7/8" barrel, .55 caliber, removed leather covering and muzzle ring. Metal is gray with scattered fine pitting, metal markings are fair, no inspector's marking, the safety has been removed, the stock has an unusual sling swivel and shows only normal handling marks, fair overall condition............................. **175.00**

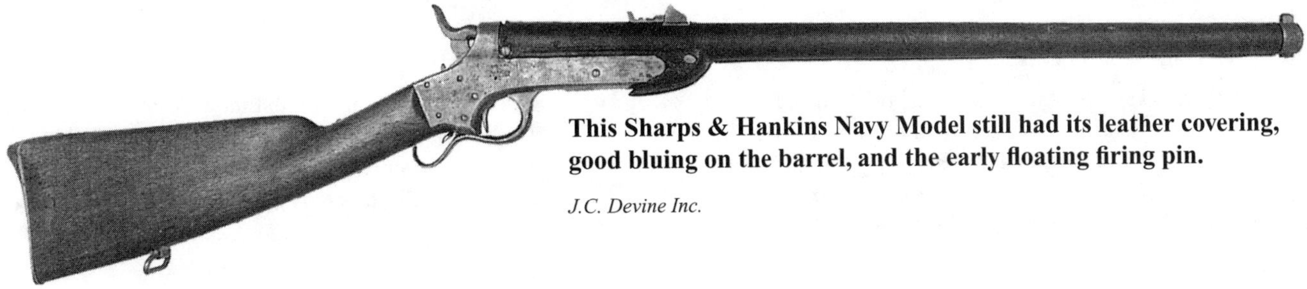

This Sharps & Hankins Navy Model still had its leather covering, good bluing on the barrel, and the early floating firing pin.

J.C. Devine Inc.

Serial no. 8237, .52 rimfire, 24" round barrel, good bore, leather barrel covering has a couple of small holes near the muzzle, and is torn at one of the rear screws, otherwise it is in good condition with most of the surface intact. Second model with floating firing pin, one of the early ones without an inspector's stamp on the metal. The frame is gray with scattered pitting on the right side, the walnut buttstock shows only a few light handling marks, very-good overall condition. **750.00**

Serial no. 3158, .52 rimfire, 24" barrel, missing leather covering, walnut stock with brass buttplate, fair condition. Mottled gray metal shows areas of light pitting, frame/barrel juncture slightly loose. Stock with scattered light blemishes and crack extends 5-6" back from upper tang.................... **517.00**

Sharps, Model 1853, Slanting Breech

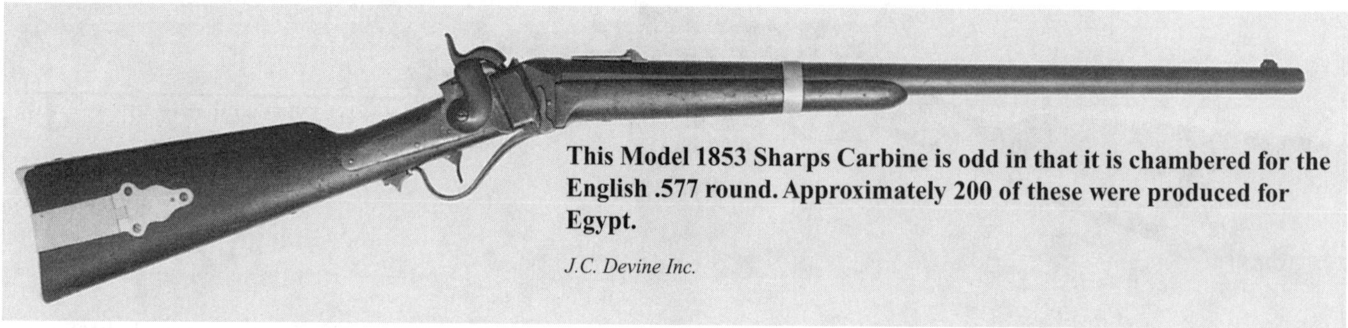

This Model 1853 Sharps Carbine is odd in that it is chambered for the English .577 round. Approximately 200 of these were produced for Egypt.

J.C. Devine Inc.

Serial no. 21649, .577 caliber, 25" round barrel, good bore. This carbine was never equipped with a sling ring bar, although the frame has a factory-plugged hole for one. The caliber is relatively unusual in a Sharps. There are no foreign proof marks or government marks, barrel has matching serial no. Standard markings except small factory stamped number "319" on the top tang in addition to the serial no. All markings are clear with iron having a dark patina and the front half of the barrel showing pinprick pitting. Oil-finished walnut stocks show extensive handling marks with the brass patchbox, buttplate, and barrel band having a light patina. Good-plus condition. **1,900.00**

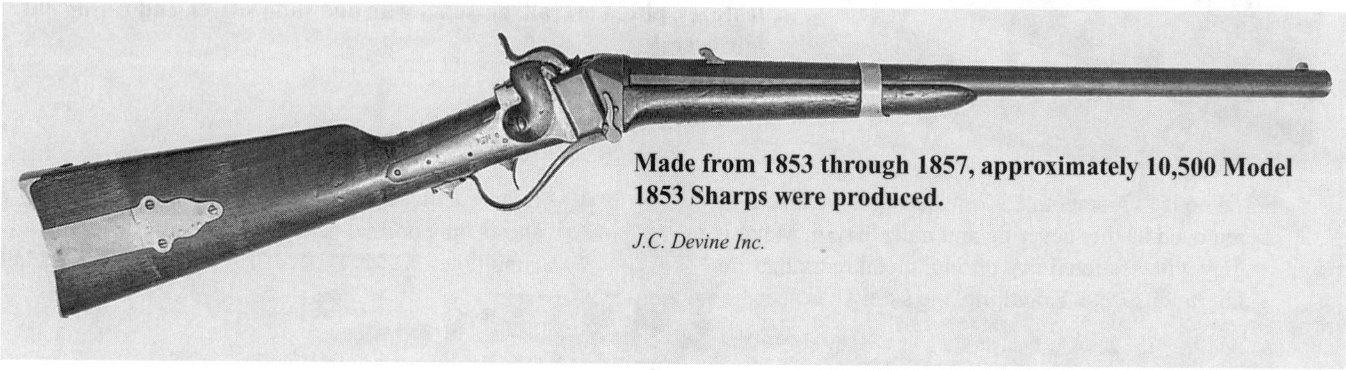

Made from 1853 through 1857, approximately 10,500 Model 1853 Sharps were produced.

J.C. Devine Inc.

Serial no. 9134, .52 caliber, 21-1/2" round barrel, good bore, early production gun with brass patchbox, buttplate, and barrel band. Early long sling swivel bar, but the bar is a well done replacement. Rear sight is missing the leaf, the nipple is a replacement. The iron has a smooth, dark patina with good markings, the barrel has a couple of small dings, negligible faint pitting. The stocks show only normal handling marks on an old oil refinish. A nice looking Sharps in good-plus condition. **1,500.00**

"We are marched into Vicksburg by merry music and cheers from the lusty throats of the boys. It is a glorious celebration of old Independence Day and one that every participant will ever remember."

— Arthur J. Robinson,
Co. E, 33rd Wisconsin Volunteers

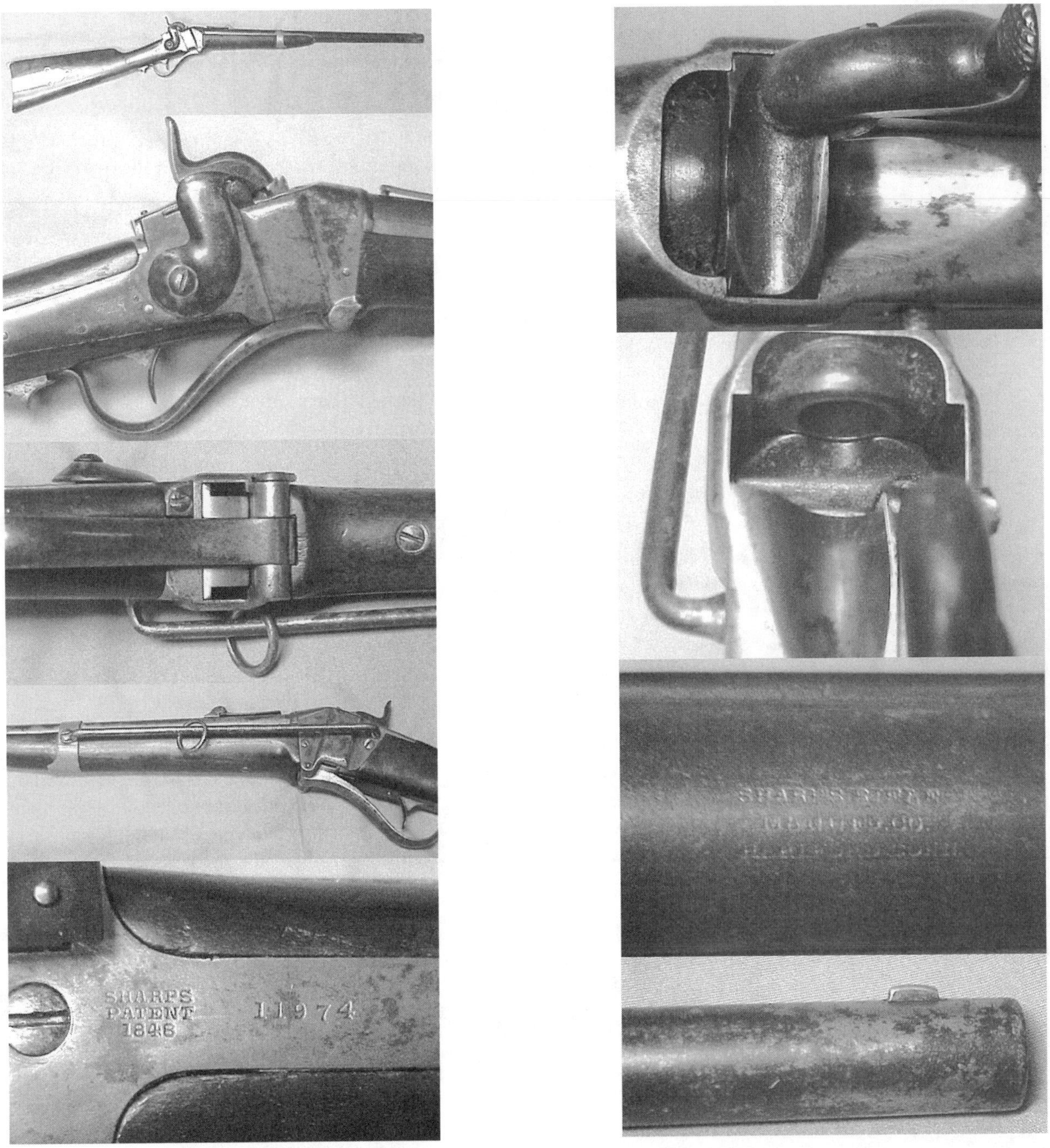

Though advertised as a "John Brown" Model, this Model 1853 Sharps bore a serial no. not within the range shipped in 1855-1856 to Kansas abolitionists.

Sharpsburg Arsenal

"John Brown Model," .52 caliber, serial no. 119xx, good condition barrel with brown patina and original bright finish. Long-range leaf ladder site with slide missing. Saddle sling bar and ring are original with brass barrel mounting band, intact pellet primer. Breech retaining pin has ear broken, wood is in very good condition, normal handling marks, initial "LRD" carved in left stock flat. Brass patch box is original with letters "MD" carved on mounting brass and door. **4,695.00**

Solid and complete, rare martial example with faint cartouche and sub-inspector's initials at the breech. Overall very-good to fine condition, sharp edges on all metal parts, crisp metal markings showing no wear at all, mint bore, and strong stock edges. Steel is bright, 100% original exception for elevator slide on rear sight. **3,600.00**

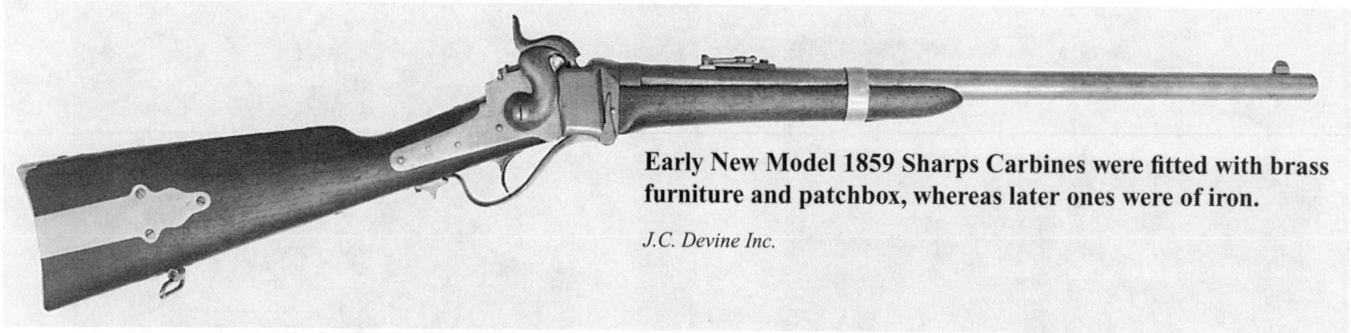

Early New Model 1859 Sharps Carbines were fitted with brass furniture and patchbox, whereas later ones were of iron.

J.C. Devine Inc.

Sharps, New Model 1859

Serial no. 31535, .52 caliber, 21-5/8" barrel, very good bore, early model with brass patchbox, buttplate, and barrel band. Iron has smooth gray patina, only minor scattered faint pitting, Lawrence patent sight shows quite a bit of blue. Brass has been cleaned in the past, metal markings are good. The stocks show moderate wear with what appears to be an arsenal-style toe repair, overall condition is very good. **3,500.00**

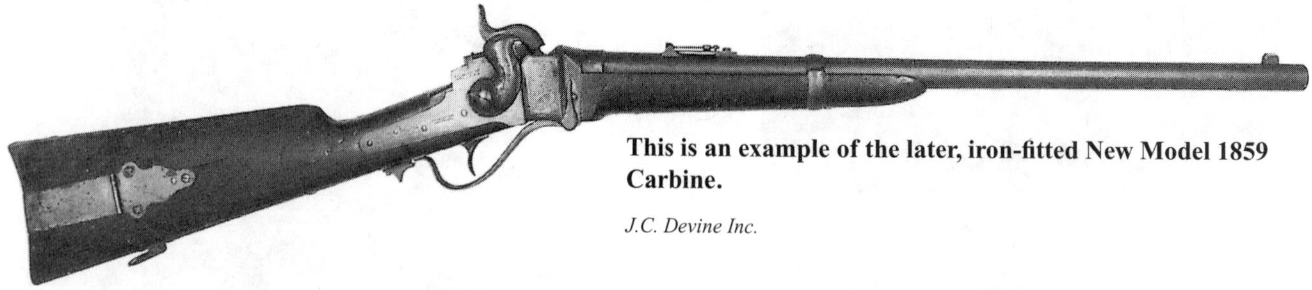

This is an example of the later, iron-fitted New Model 1859 Carbine.

J.C. Devine Inc.

Serial no. 39315, .52 caliber, 22" barrel, very good bore, carbine has iron furniture and patchbox, single sling swivel in buttstock and does not have a sling bar, this is the proper configuration for a U.S. Navy carbine, and it is in the right serial no. range. All factory metal markings are excellent, barrel has a good deal of original blue mixed with plum patina and some light surface rust. The frame and lock are a mixed dark gray and silver with a trace of case colors on the lock. The stocks have a couple of short age cracks, show numerous light handling marks, and over 70% original finish. **2,350.00**

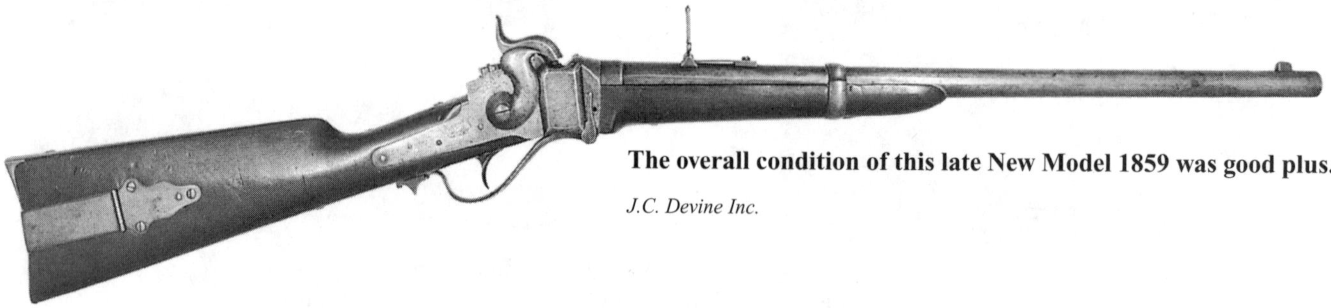

The overall condition of this late New Model 1859 was good plus.

J.C. Devine Inc.

Serial no. 70941, .52 caliber, 22" round barrel, good bore, iron patchbox and furniture, the sling ring bar base has inspector's initials, "E.C.B.," replacement ring. The stock has two legible inspector's cartouches, "E.C.B." and "F.T." The pellet primer mechanism has the cover and feed arm, but is missing a couple of small parts. The detent stud for the hinge pin is missing. All the metal has a gray patina, pitting is negligible. The buttstock has a break between the bottom of the lock plate and the trigger plate with a missing chip at the same location. The stock otherwise presents a fine appearance with a dark oil finish and normal handling marks. Overall condition is good plus.. . . . . . **1,750.00**

Overall good to very-good condition, 100% original and complete, shows nice honest signs of wartime use, classic saddle wear line on butt stock's left side. The metal is overall clean steel color with good markings including the "New Model 1859" stamp on the barrel (all metal markings are deep and legible), barrel has 1,000-yard rear sight and the serial no. is in the 58,000 range. The wood shows handling and bruises, yet has attractive deep-brown walnut color. The cartouche is barely visible under the sling ring bar. The bore is very good with deep rifling. . . . **1,650.00**

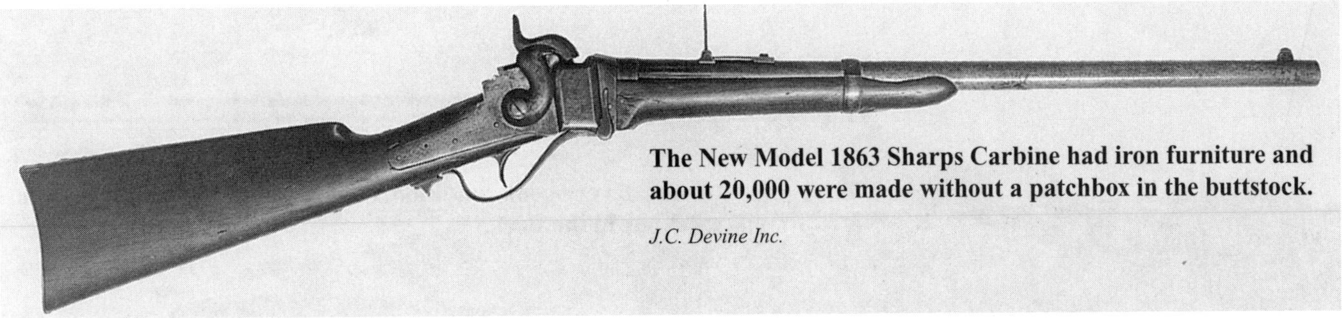

The New Model 1863 Sharps Carbine had iron furniture and about 20,000 were made without a patchbox in the buttstock.

J.C. Devine Inc.

Sharps, New Model 1863

Serial no. 98876, .52 caliber, 22" barrel, fair bore. Missing the cover and feed arm for the pellet primer mechanism, sling bar removed, stock base ground flush. Dark patina on frame and lock with light pitting on the block's top and hammer nose. Barrel has mottled gray patina, stocks without patchbox have a nail repair to a wrist splinter and a crack at the rear of the forend. Good overall. **800.00**

Overall very-good condition, 100% original & complete (serial C4, 9xx range). The metal is uniformly smooth, brown age patina with good strong markings. Bore rifling is deep and sharp, faint silvery case color along the edge of the lock and lever. The rear sight is the standard 700-yard carbine sight. The stock has the faintest light crack in the forearm, standard 1863 with no patchbox in the butt stock. There are two visible cartouches under the sling ring bar, a great-looking gun with character. **1,795.00**

Overall very-good condition and 100% original & complete (serial C18,000 range). The metal is uniformly smooth, brown age patina with good strong markings. Bore rifling is deep and sharp with patches of pitting, silvery case color along the edge of the lock and lever. Standard 700-yard carbine rear sight. The stock has faintest indication of saddle wear on the butt stock's left side. There is a visible cartouche under the sling ring bar. **1,650.00**

Overall very-good to near fine condition and 100% original and complete (serial C8,1xx range). The metal is uniformly smooth, brown age patina with hints of finish in protected areas and really good strong markings. The bore rifling is deep and sharp, faint silvery case color along the edge of the lock and lever, standard 700-yard carbine rear sight. The stock has sharp edges and a rich antique luster. Standard 1863 with no patchbox in the butt stock. Faint cartouches under the sling ring bar, microscopic stress fracture in the steel on the left side of the frame and consequently should never be fired, 100% complete except for internal pellet primer feeder. **1,975.00**

Serial no. 65511, .52 rimfire, barrel reduced to 12", no rear sight. Stock with period canvas cover, very good condition, as altered during period of use. Gray metal showing areas of light pitting, wood has minor blemishes. **978.00**

Serial no. C4905, .52 caliber, standard configuration with 22" barrel and oil-finished walnut stock and forend. Very good condition, barrel has smooth brown patina. Frame with generous traces of casehardening colors. Wood with scattered light blemishes, buttstock with 6" hairline crack extending from buttplate's lower section.. .... **2,300.00**

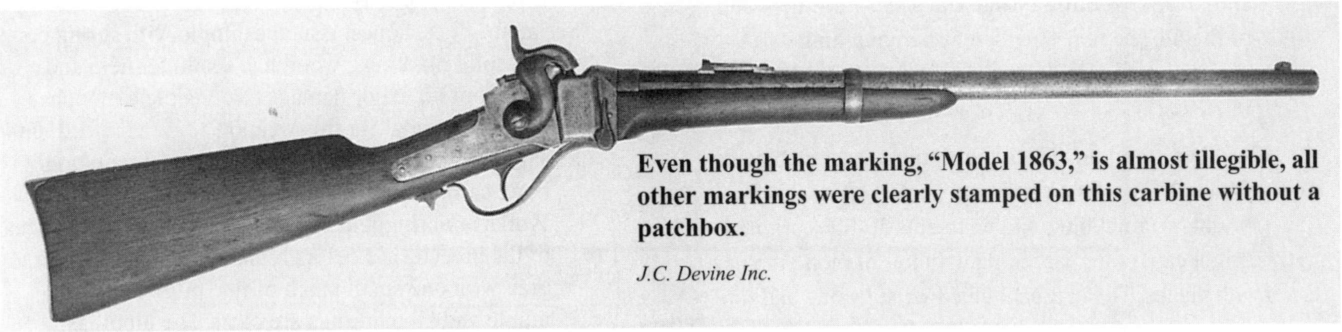

Even though the marking, "Model 1863," is almost illegible, all other markings were clearly stamped on this carbine without a patchbox.

J.C. Devine Inc.

Serial no. C28542, .52 caliber, 22" round barrel, very good bore. The Lawrence patent rear sight is missing the slide and stop screw, the front trigger plate screw is also missing. All metal is mottled gray with scattered faint pitting, the "Model 1863" marking is almost illegible, all other markings are good. The heavily sanded stocks have an old oil refinish, good condition. **1,150.00**

Sharps, New Model 1863, cont.

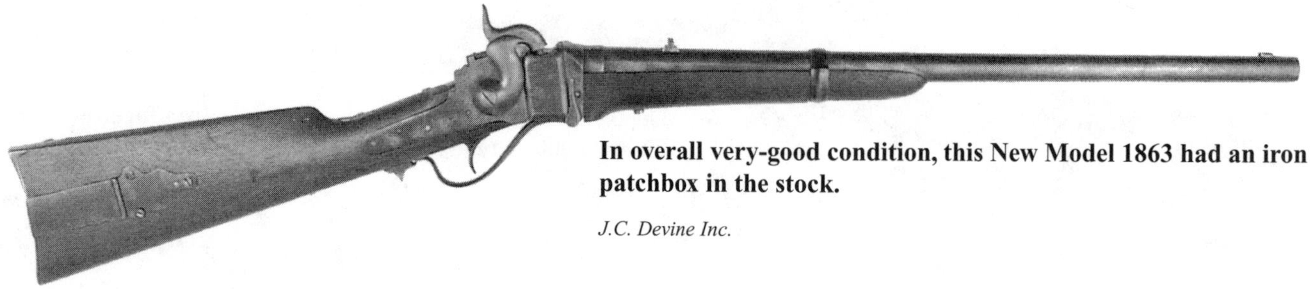

In overall very-good condition, this New Model 1863 had an iron patchbox in the stock.

J.C. Devine Inc.

Serial no. C22949, .52 caliber, 22" barrel, good bore. Rear sight altered to a fixed blade utilizing the original sight base. The front sight base is missing the blade. Dark patina on all metal with scattered fine pitting (light pitting on the top of the hammer) and clear lettering. Both of the stocks are factory made replacements and show very few light handling marks. The buttstock has an iron patchbox with some light pitting and a single inspector's initial. The barrel breech has the inspector's initials, "E.A.W." The top tang and patchbox screws stand proud of the wood. Overall very good condition with an original Civil War carbine snap hook and swivel. **1,300.00**

Serial no. C8383, .52 caliber, 22" round barrel, dark bore, iron patchbox with an iron buttplate that is not factory cut for a patchbox. The pellet primer mechanism is missing internal small parts, but does have the cover. The lever spring is missing, 60% of an old reblue remains, light pitting on the patchbox, otherwise negligible pitting, refinished stock shows only a few light handling marks, but the forend has a long crack on the bottom, good overall condition. **900.00**

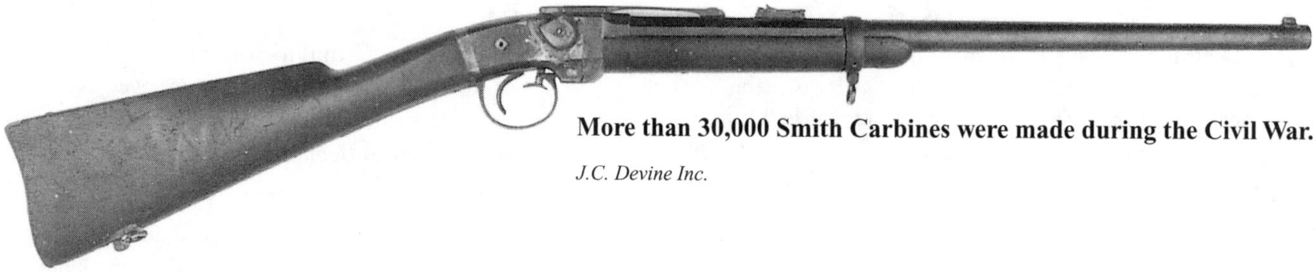

More than 30,000 Smith Carbines were made during the Civil War.

J.C. Devine Inc.

Smith

Mass Arms, serial no. 10681, .50 caliber, 21-5/8" octagon to round barrel, fair bore. Manufactured between 1861-1865, has the barrel bands and no sling ring. No military markings show on the wood or metal. The rear tang screw, hammer and percussion nipple are missing. Overall condition is fair. **650.00**

.50 caliber, serial no. 3716, fourth most-used carbine of the Civil War. Fine condition, barrel retains 95-98% bright, original blue. Frame retains 50-60% original bright case color hardening with lots of mottled blues and blacks. The charcoal blued wrist ferrule and top spring strap retain 70-80% of this fragile finish. Crisp maker's marks and patent markings on left side of frame. Buttplate retains 80-90% blue, but trigger guard and band have faded to mostly plum. Excellent bore and mechanics, fine stock and forend with crisp "JH" in oval cartouche at the left flat. Complete with sling ring and bar. **3,250.00**

100% blue on the barrel and strong case colors with a lot of purple on the frame. A fine walnut stock with a couple of small use or storage dings and a good cartouche, mint bore, serial no. 5524. . . . . **3,350.00**

Serial no. 3221, honest issued example with strong bore and solid markings, wood has a splinter here and there, but no major damage. No visible cartouche, which is normal for this weapon. **1,250.00**

Serial no. 6936, .50 caliber, 21-5/8" barrel, fine bright bore, carbine was made by the American Machine Works in Springfield, Massachusetts, only faint traces of the breech case colors remain, most have faded to gray with one small patch of fine pitting near the nipple and all markings are clear. The nipple is broken, the barrel and latch have traces of blue mixed with dark plum, very little minor faint pitting. The stocks show very little wear with several small dings in the butt. The buttstock does have two 1-1/4" long line cracks at the frame with two clear inspector's cartouches. Very-good condition overall. **900.00**

Serial no. 8739, .50 caliber, standard military configuration with Poultney & Trimble and American Machine works markings, fine condition. Retains 98% blue finish, shows some thinning and light spotting. Frame with smooth mottled patina retains traces of faded casehardening. Wood with sharp markings and showing light dents, scratches, and bruises. **2,070.00**

Mechanically perfect, 100% original and complete, investment grade condition. This has 95% factory barrel blue, 75% case color on frame, vivid inspector's cartouche, mint bore. **1,950.00**

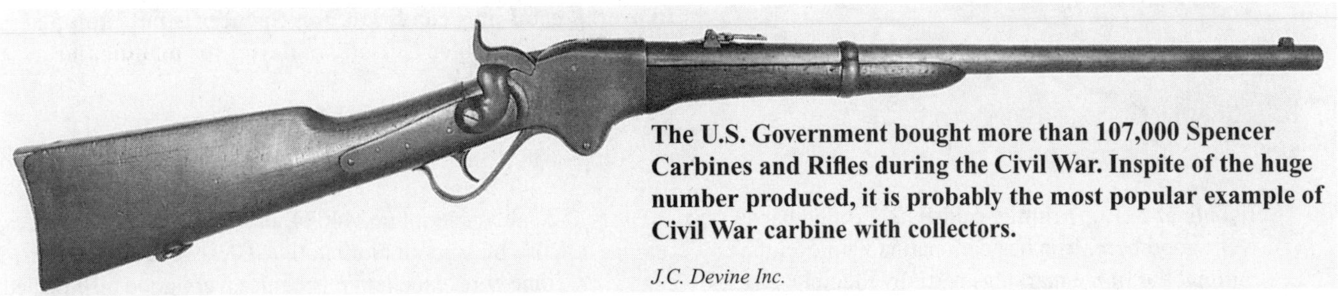

The U.S. Government bought more than 107,000 Spencer Carbines and Rifles during the Civil War. Inspite of the huge number produced, it is probably the most popular example of Civil War carbine with collectors.

J.C. Devine Inc.

Spencer

Serial no. 30307, .52 caliber rimfire, 22" round barrel, good bore. Barrel's breech shows vise marks, the metal with a dark patina and fine pitting on the frame and front portion of the barrel, the frame address partially illegible on the top line. The original stocks show normal handling marks, a 5" grain crack in the buttstock at the magazine tube, traces of two cartouches, and has had a little extra oil rubbed on through the years, good overall condition. **1,500.00**

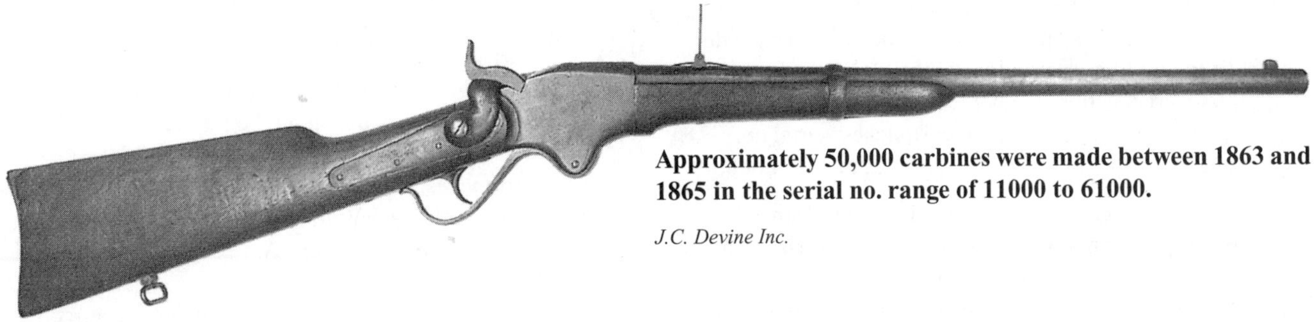

Approximately 50,000 carbines were made between 1863 and 1865 in the serial no. range of 11000 to 61000.

J.C. Devine Inc.

Serial no. 35590, .52 rimfire, 22" round barrel, fair bore, dark patina on all iron with scattered patches of light pitting, frame markings are legible. The walnut stocks show light handling marks and a trace of a cartouche, good plus. **1,100.00**

Serial no. 8308, .50 caliber, 19" barrel, folding rear sight, casehardened frame, saddle ring, walnut stocks with inspector's cartouche, sling mounts, excellent condition. Retains approximately 85-90% finish overall, with scattered wear throughout. Wood has a few minor marks present. **3,450.00**

Serial no. 35483, .52 rimfire, 22" barrel, walnut stock and forend, good condition, gray metal showing areas of light pitting, refinished wood with scattered dents and bruises. **1,495.00**

Serial no. 44909, .52 rimfire, 22" barrel, walnut stock and forend, fair condition. Metal with dark-brown patina shows scattered dents and areas of light pitting. Wood with numerous dents, scratches, and bruises, 5" crack from buttplate's center. **1,495.00**

Serial no. 39533, .52 rimfire caliber, 22" round barrel, fair bore. Metal is a dark gray with even pitting, the stocks have several thin age cracks and show normal handling marks on an old refinish, several screws are replacements. Fair to good condition. **900.00**

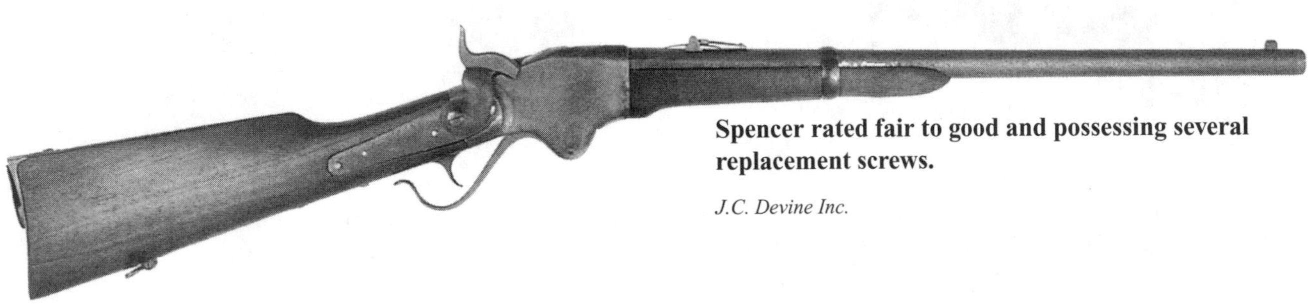

Spencer rated fair to good and possessing several replacement screws.

J.C. Devine Inc.

Spencer, cont.

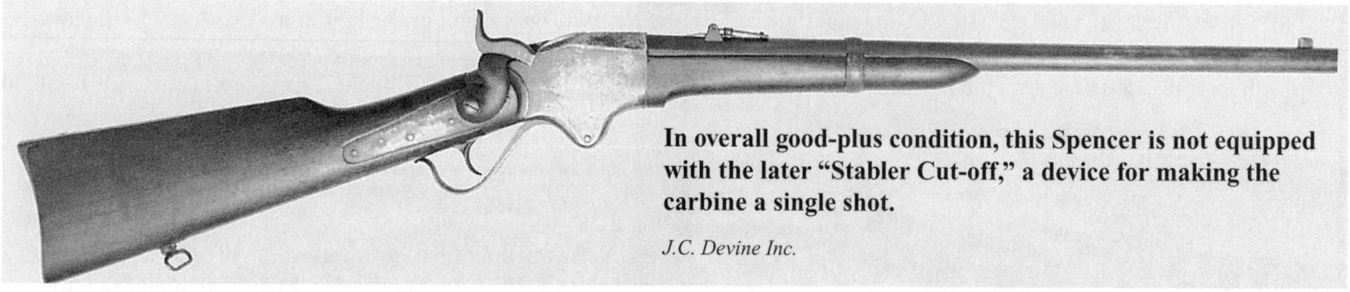

In overall good-plus condition, this Spencer is not equipped with the later "Stabler Cut-off," a device for making the carbine a single shot.

J.C. Devine Inc.

Serial no. 58237, .52 rimfire caliber, 22" round barrel, very good bore. Iron has dark patina with even fine pitting, the frame markings partially illegible. Stocks are in fine condition with two legible cartouches, this is an un-altered Civil War carbine without the Stabler cut-off and with groove rifling, good-plus overall condition. **1,100.00**

This carbine has original blue finish on the barrel, a lot of blue in the area around the rear sight, and it tapers to light blue to plum around the front sight. The barrel metal is very smooth with no pitting. There are light case colors on the frame on the saddle ring side. There are light case colors on the block and butt plate, crisp action, the bore is very fine. The walnut stock is fine, with two clear cartouches, serial no. 54236. .... **4,600.00**

A very good specimen with attractive light-plum age patina uniformly distributed on the metal parts. This one is in the 38,xxx serial range, frame marking legible, bore is good with sharp rifling, stock has nice antique walnut color and faintly visible cartouche, one light surface crack in the butt running about 5" up from the buttplate (very minor and nearly invisible). Very tight and solid with outstanding wood to metal fit. The previous owner installed the center fire conversion pin in the breechblock and was shooting blanks out of this at a reenactment. This is absolutely complete and 100% as issued (except for the center fire pin). **1,695.00**

.52 caliber, serial no. 44034, barrel and receiver are a bright, smooth plum patina. Clear breech markings, fine bore, excellent mechanics, very good oil-finished stock and forend with visible cartouche at the left flat. Two small slivers out of forend, where the forend joins the receiver. These are ancient and do not detract. Complete with butt swivel and sling ring and bar. **2,850.00**

Better than average, good plum color on the steel parts, hints of silvery case color on the lock, frame, and hammer, and some case colors on the internal breechblock. Barrel is a mixture of plum and steel gray with just a very nice uniform tone to it. Very, very tight and solid with outstanding wood to metal fit, crisp firm marking on the frame, excellent bore, fine wood with very good edges, two faint cartouches, and no chips or bad bruises, save for one bang on the face of the butt stock 100% original and complete in all respects. A nice mid-production gun in the 30,000 serial range. **2,450.00**

Spencer, Model 1860, very good specimen, attractive, light-plum age patina uniformly distributed on the metal parts, serial range 53,xxx, crisp frame marking, fine bore with sharp rifling, stock has nice antique walnut color and very faintly visible half cartouche. No cracks or bad dents, very tight and solid with outstanding wood to metal fit, one small patch of pitting on the frame's side that is exactly the size of a thumbprint. The balance of the steel has a very nice plum patina. **1,850.00**

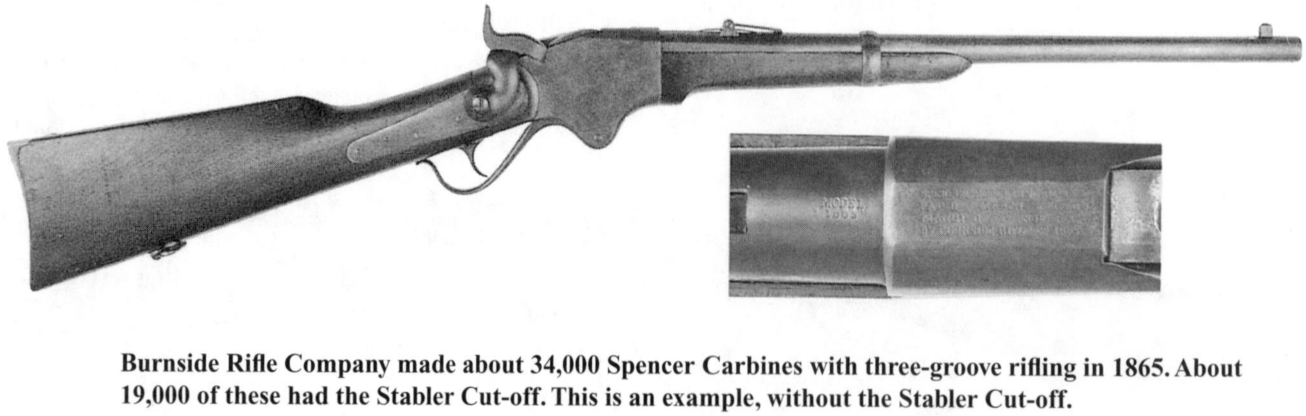

Burnside Rifle Company made about 34,000 Spencer Carbines with three-groove rifling in 1865. About 19,000 of these had the Stabler Cut-off. This is an example, without the Stabler Cut-off.

J.C. Devine Inc.

Spencer, Model 1865

Serial no. 426, .56-50 caliber, 22" barrel, strong three-groove rifling with a little scattered pitting. Made without the Stabler cutoff, metal has a plum patina, a little scattered faint pitting on the barrel, several small barrel breech dings, lettering is clear on the metal. The stocks show relatively few light handling marks, retains most of the original finish, has a 2-1/2" grain crack in the forend (easily glued), and has two very-good to fine inspector's cartouches. Also with the carbine is a Civil War snap hook and swivel for the carbine shoulder sling. Fine condition. **1,350.00**

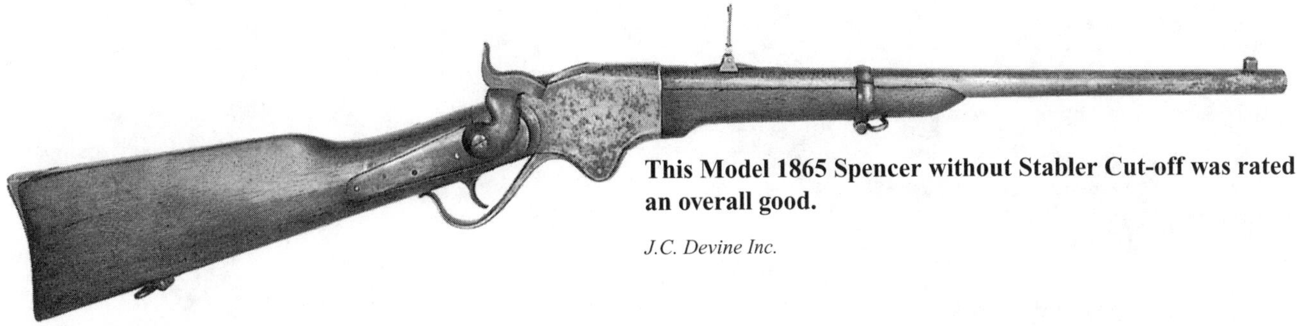

This Model 1865 Spencer without Stabler Cut-off was rated an overall good.

J.C. Devine Inc.

Serial no. 7329, .50 rimfire, 20" barrel, made without a Stabler cutoff. Dark-gray patina on the barrel, mottled-gray frame, frame has areas of fine pitting and scattered faint barrel pitting. The buttstock has a 2" grain crack at the magazine tube, otherwise the stock shows light wear and handling marks. Good overall condition. **850.00**

Excellent condition, barrel has virtually all the original blue, which is only lightly faded. The frame, hammer, butt plate, and lock have 80% vivid case color, breechblock has 98% color, excellent bore. Beautiful stock with two vivid cartouches, sharp edges, and good color, just shows light handling age and a couple storage dents. **2,950.00**

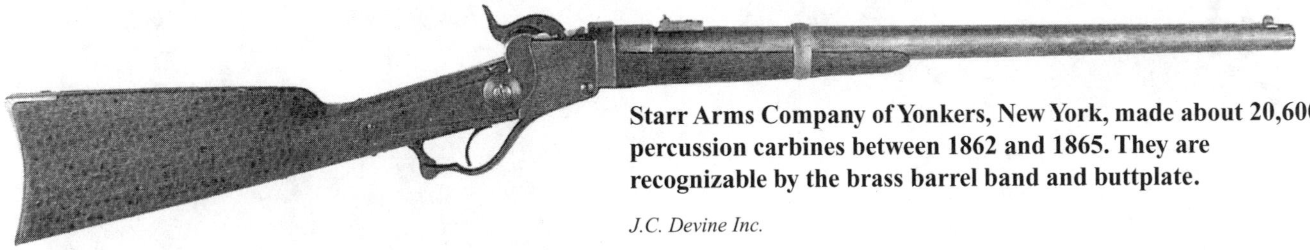

Starr Arms Company of Yonkers, New York, made about 20,600 percussion carbines between 1862 and 1865. They are recognizable by the brass barrel band and buttplate.

J.C. Devine Inc.

Starr

Serial no. 2473, .54 caliber, 21" round barrel, good bore, dark-gray patina on all the iron with scattered pinprick pitting, metal markings are clear with inspector's initials "L.A.B." on breech's side. The buttstock has an illegible name stamped into it and the forend shows heavy wear. Good condition. **1,400.00**

Factory new condition except for a couple minor surface scratches. **12,500.00**

54 caliber, 30% blue on barrel, all markings are clear. Smooth metal is plum brown where it is not blue, no pitting. The walnut stock is in very-good condition with the usual usage marks, no cartouches, serial no. 19786. Very crisp action and a very-good bore. The brass has a smooth, uncleaned patina. **2,295.00**

Starr, cont.

Starr Carbine numbering in the 12000 range.

Sharpsburg Arsenal

Fore stock and stock are in beautiful condition with two sharp cartouches. Brass mountings are inspected with wonderful mellow patina. Barrel retains 90% original color. Iron breech and lock plate light, but showing case color throughout. Excellent condition breech and bore, sharp metal markings, serial no. 12xxx. **. 4,750.00**

Serial no. 12824, .54 caliber, 21" barrel, bore has strong rifling with scattered pitting. Clear markings on metal include "FDL" inspection mark on breech's side, 60% of an old reblue remains with minor scattered pitting, stock shows a few light handling marks on an old oil refinish. Good overall condition. **1,000.00**

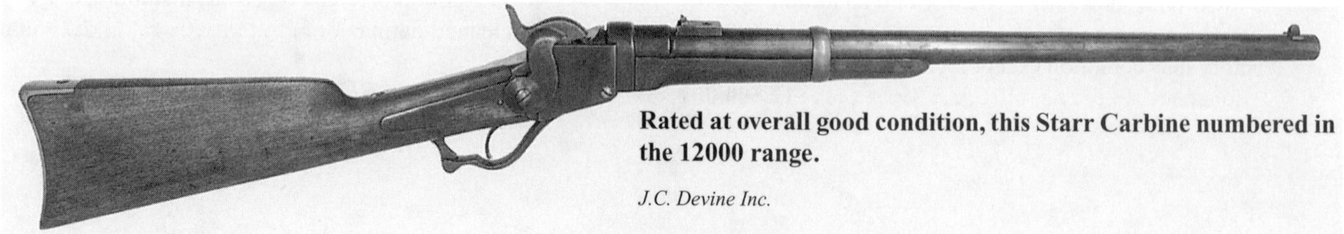

Rated at overall good condition, this Starr Carbine numbered in the 12000 range.

J.C. Devine Inc.

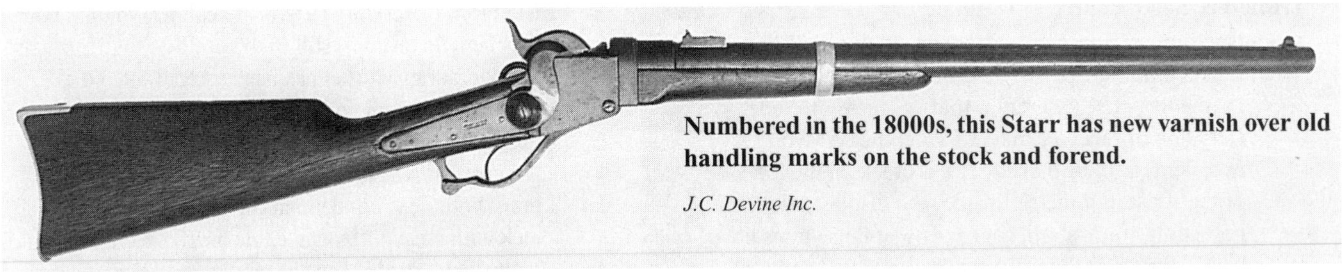

Numbered in the 18000s, this Starr has new varnish over old handling marks on the stock and forend.

J.C. Devine Inc.

Serial no. 18175, .54 caliber, 21" barrel, dark bore, overall plum-brown patina and patches of light to moderate pitting on the action and breech end of the barrel. The brass barrel band and buttplate have tarnished to ochre. The buttstock and forearm have an added varnish finish over mild handling marks, good condition Starr. **950.00**

Serial no. 4898, .54 caliber, 21" round barrel, fair bore. Brass buttplate and barrel band, dark patina on all iron with fine pitting on frame and barrel, metal markings are good. The buttstock has an age check behind the lockplate and at the toe with a short crack from the top tang to the rear lock screw. The stocks show light wear and fewer than normal handling marks with a clear inspector stamping, "H.G.S.," above the buttplate's heel. Overall good condition. **1,050.00**

First pattern percussion gun with brass butt plate and barrel band, 100% original and complete, 60% rich barrel blue, 20% silvery case color on frame and hammer. Very crisp, sharp stock edges inspector's initials, "LAB," stamped just forward of the buttplate tang. Breechblock has generous amounts of color case hardening visible when the lever is opened and the block "dropped." The bore is like a mirror, all markings are deep and crisp, and the action is as crisp as new. The only major blemish on this fine gun is a small chunk of wood that was chipped out of the right side of the butt (about below the butt plate tang and directly next to the butt plate) and a small dent in the butt plate at the same place. This small bit of damage occurred over a century ago and is not a major detraction. The missing sliver is about 1/8" d, 1/2" w, and 2" l. A really strong condition Starr with great appeal, serial no. in the 19000 range. **2,250.00**

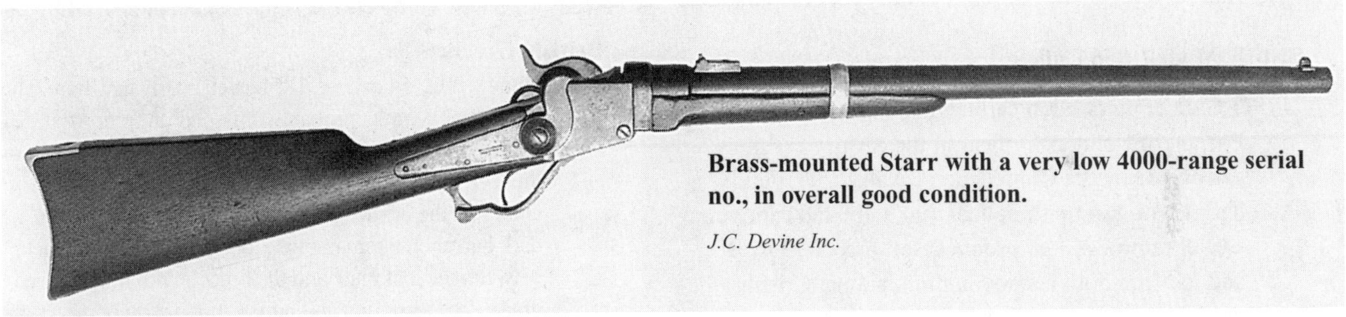

Brass-mounted Starr with a very low 4000-range serial no., in overall good condition.

J.C. Devine Inc.

Triplett & Scott

Serial no. 1719, .50 rimfire caliber, 22" round barrel, good bore. The rear sight leaf is broken, as is the spring on the cartridge stop. The top swivel is missing from the heel of the buttplate, as is one small screw at the front of the frame. Smooth dark-gray metal with sharp markings, minor faint muzzle pitting, light buttplate pitting, several small breech dents. Clear metal markings with "KENTUCKY" marked on left side of breech. Forend has a large piece of replaced wood, the buttstock has a replacement strip of wood over part of the magazine tube and two line cracks. Overall condition is good. **700.00**

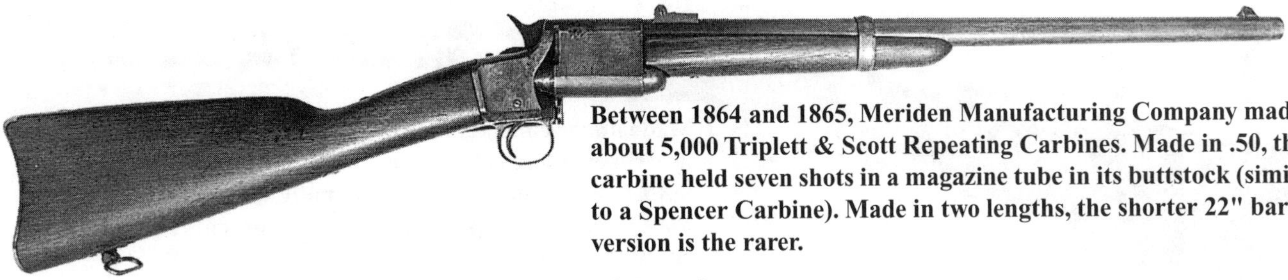

Between 1864 and 1865, Meriden Manufacturing Company made about 5,000 Triplett & Scott Repeating Carbines. Made in .50, the carbine held seven shots in a magazine tube in its buttstock (similar to a Spencer Carbine). Made in two lengths, the shorter 22" barrel version is the rarer.

J.C. Devine Inc.

Triplett & Scott, cont.

Outstanding example of long barrel version (30" barrel). Barrel exhibits 95% vivid blue as does the receiver. Frame has 40% case color that is starting to fade. Left side of receiver marked, "Kentucky." Wood is excellent, faintest hairline stress crack on the left side of the wrist, but the right side (the display side) has no visible crack at all. Since 90% of these guns have bad fractures at the wrist (caused by the design flaw of running the magazine tube too close to the sides of the wrist) finding one with nice wood is a great bonus. Very fine to excellent. **2,850.00**

Musketoon, U.S., Model 1816, .69 caliber, smooth bore, excellent mechanics, still in the original flintlock configuration. Musket has been arsenal-altered to musketoon length with a 38" barrel with top muzzle mounted bayonet lug. Barrel retains 60-70% bright "armory brown" lacquer finish. Crisp eagle head/"P" proof with deep condemnation mark at breech. Superb lock with crisp horizontal eagle head over "Springfield" in the lock's center. Fine brown-lacquered finish iron furniture with both sling swivels and button tipped ramrod. Excellent oil-finished stock with super edges around the lock, flats, and barrel and ramrod channels. This musket was obviously arsenal shortened, because the double band and spring were set back the proscribed distance as was the bayonet lug and ramrod. Fine, overall condition. **2,750.00**

Imports

Austrian, Froewurth, imported weapon, commonly called the "Froewurth" carbine. Short, .71 caliber percussion conversion carbine, George Schuyler imported 10,000 in 1861. Fine, smooth metal with a blue hue. Austrian proofs along the barrel channel. Smooth lock with huge percussion hammer. Iron ramrod and trigger guard with extended pistol grip. Fine bore and mechanics. Excellent stock has been tongue oiled. Double iron ring hooks at left flat for sling belt. **650.00**

British, Model 1856 Enfield

.577 Caliber percussion carbine manufactured by Barnett of London. Typical of the cavalry carbines so coveted by the Confederate cavalry, 20" round barrel with flip up three-leaf rear sight and captive swivel ramrod. Clear proofs at left breech. Barrel and lock are both a smooth, plum patina. Crisply marked lock, "Crown/Tower" to the rear of the hammer and "Barnett/London" under the bolster. No British military marks which is typical of imported Civil War arms. Good bore and mechanics. Brass furniture is a deep umber patina. Fine oil finished stock with sharp edges around lock and flats and along the ramrod and barrel channel. Sling ring and bar at the flats. **1,995.00**

Confederate imported Tower Enfield percussion carbine. Crisp overall with all original parts, clear markings, 1859 dated lock, strong action. Bright metal and solid wood. **2,650.00**

P-1856 .577 Caliber British-produced percussion carbine. No British military markings. Metal is a bright smooth plum overall. Crisp Birmingham proofs at breech and "Barnett" markings on the lock. Good bore, excellent mechanics, fine stock, missing yoke on swivel ramrod, otherwise complete . . . . **.1,895.00**

British, Greene

Serial no. 1602, .54 caliber, 18" barrel, nearly new bore. This is a great example, probably unissued/unfired. All metal and wood markings are sharp. Case colors have faded on the lock and breech to a mottled, dark patina with the colors on the primer door a little more prominent, 80% dark barrel blue remaining. Stock has a repaired crack between the lockplate and the breech with much raised grain, shows no wear and only minor handling marks, the barrel has one small ding. The metal has several British inspectors' markings and a broad arrow with release marking and "S." The stock is stamped with a 5/16" high numeral "1" in front of the patchbox and on the left side near the heel is stamped in 1/8" high letters "U.S." These stock markings appear to be of the period and are evidence of the Union purchase of British Green carbines during the Civil War. **3,000.00**

Made under contract to the British government in 1855 for use in Crimea, there is a great deal of conjecture as to whether or not English Greene Carbines actually saw service in the Civil War. This example possessed a "U.S." surcharge lending some credibility to the idea.

J.C. Devine Inc.

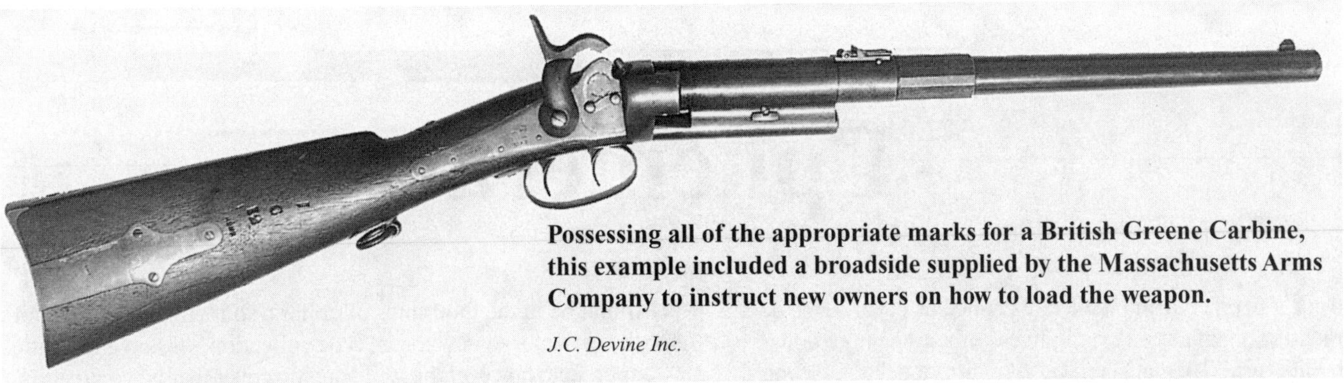

Possessing all of the appropriate marks for a British Greene Carbine, this example included a broadside supplied by the Massachusetts Arms Company to instruct new owners on how to load the weapon.

J.C. Devine Inc.

Serial no. 928, .56 caliber, 18" barrel, near mint bore. Metal markings are excellent with "Crown/VR" on lockplate and British government marks on barrels. Some faded case colors remain on lockplate and frame, the barrel and receiver apparently were both originally blued, the receiver finish is now a dark gray/blue patina with most of the barrel blue turned plum. Barrel has areas of very fine pinprick pitting, as does the iron patchbox. Stock has a few light handling marks and clearly marked British inspection stamps behind the trigger guard. The buttstock's right side has sharply marked unit markings, "1/C/12/ RDMR." Some British Greenes are believed to have been imported for the American Civil War, overall condition is fine on this scarce carbine. Included is a rare original broadside *Directions For Using Greene's Carbine*, 5-1/8" x 8", with "MASSACHUSETTS ARMS COMPANY/ CHICOPEE FALLS, MASS./T. W. Carter. Agt." at the bottom. The document is chipped at the edges and has several oil stains. Still rates very good.. **2,300.00**

Carbine Terminology

Carbine: A breech or muzzle-loading shoulder arm having a smooth or rifled bore, using externally primed ammunition. Originally designed for horse-mounted troops.

Cartouche: A marking impressed on a firearm, usually denoting an inspector's initials.

Cartridge: A complete unit of ammunition for small arms consisting of a cartridge case, primer, propellant, and projectile(s), which is inserted into the firing chamber.

Musketoon: A muzzle-loading shoulder arm having a smooth or rifled bore and a maximum barrel length of 26.5".

Receiver: The housing for a firearm's breech (portion of the barrel with chamber into which a cartridge or projectile is loaded) and firing mechanism.

Repeating firearm: A firearm that may be discharged repeatedly by recharging through means of deliberate, successive, mechanical actions of the user.

Rimfire: A rimmed or flanged cartridge with the priming mixture located inside the rim of the case.

Chapter 8

Ephemera

Ephemera can be loosely defined as paper items documenting a generation's daily lives without the intention of being saved. By that standard, our current ephemera would range from the nightly newspaper to the wrappers on our fast-food hamburgers. In the context of the Civil War, ephemera is the group of items that allows us to peer deeply into the everyday existence of the soldiers. This could range from a set of general orders intended to be read at a morning inspection to a parole, granting a secessionist the right to return to his home in return for a pledge of allegiance. Civil War ephemera is the group of written snapshots of the soldier's life.

Collecting ephemera is a very broad category. It is not as easy as assembling a type collection that includes one of everything. That approach may leave a collector overwhelmed, and eventually, low on funds. Rather, many collectors of ephemera take a thematic approach. Perhaps, a single regiment is the focus of their collection, or a battle, or even, a political theme such as President Lincoln or slavery. The thematic approach imposes a discipline that many collectors desperately seem to need to rein them in from buying every piece they encounter. More importantly though, thematic collecting starts to define a particular idea.

Take for example, a person who is interested in the role a sutler played during the Civil War. Perhaps this interest began by acquiring a rare and expensive broadside touting a regimental sutler's availability of goods. The price of such an item might be in the thousands of dollars, so it will be difficult for the collector to develop a "type collection." Using a thematic approach, however, he will soon discover that he could add sutler's tokens, soldier's letters describing visits to the sutler, documents that tabulate a soldier's accounts, autographs of regimental sutlers, handbills, or even newspapers advertising the availability of goods for sutlers to sell to soldiers in the field. Soon, the collector has assembled a variety of items that afford a much better understanding of the regimental sutler's role than the line or two that most published histories provide.

There is, however, an ethical dilemma associated with ephemera collecting, and it relates directly to manuscript material such as diaries, letters, and other handwritten documents. Though it is with great pride that a collector obtains an original diary or pack of soldier's letters, this does pull the items out of their effective role as historical documents. When stored in a private collection, these items are withdrawn from access to scholarly research. Perhaps, one day, when the collection comes back to the market, a public archives will be able to acquire the pieces, making them accessible once again. But, private ownership does, in many cases, remove important records from a generation's access. It is an issue that only individual collectors can decide for themselves. As with any historical item, we are just the caretakers until the items pass to the next generation or are deposited into the public's trust.

Collecting Hints

Pros:

- Ephemera stores in very little space. It is easy to accumulate hundreds of pieces and store them in only one box.
- Ephemera is extremely available. Ephemera dealers, stamp dealers, numismatists, newspaper handlers, and antiquarians are all possible sources.
- Ephemera can be very affordable. Though, like all areas of Civil War collecting, items associated with the Confederacy, President Lincoln, or African-Americans in the service will always be pricey, other items pertaining to less recognizable themes are within the means of a novice.
- Other than autographs, stamps, a few poorly reproduced broadsides, and Confederate notes, there are very few reproductions of documents on the market. This makes ephemera a safer venue for novice collectors. Unfortunately, apart from the above-named collector areas, though, there are very few published references available.

Cons:

- Unless you have lots of wall space, it will be difficult to display much of the ephemera you collect. Most collections are relegated to flat, acid-free boxes, or slipped into archival sleeves and tucked into three-ring binders. It requires lots of flat space to visually enjoy a collection. Furthermore, long-term exposure to light is extremely detrimental to paper items.
- Paper items are susceptible to fluctuations in temperature and humidity. A collection will require a very stable environment.
- Document collecting promotes the dissolution of manuscript collections and removing valuable primary sources from public access. This is one of those ethical issues you have to deal with on your own.

Availability ★★

Price ★★★★★

Reproduction Alert ★★★★★

Autographs

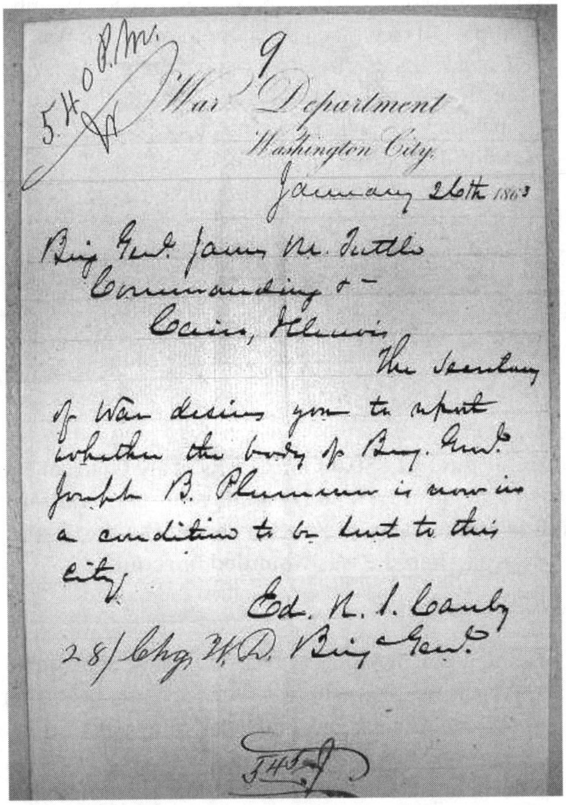
5408 M.
9
War Department
Washington City.
January 26th 1863
Brig. Genl. James M. Tuttle
Commanding &c
Cairo, Illinois
The Secretary of War desires you to report whether the body of Brig. Genl. Joseph B. Plummer is now in a condition to be sent to this city.
Ed. R. S. Canby
28/Chg. W.D. Brig. Genl.

This is a one-page letter on War Department letterhead signed by General Edward S. Canby.

Frohne's Historic Military

Canby, Edward S., general, U.S.A., one page, autographed letter signed with rank by General Edward R. S. Canby. Fine condition, written in period ink on "War Department, Washington City" letterhead. Great content about the condition of the body of General Joseph B. Plummer, and whether it can be transported to Washington City. Edward Canby was the only U.S. Army general to die at the hands of Indians, when he was brutally murdered by the Modoc Indians in 1873. . . . . **375.00**

Cockrell, F. M., general, C.S.A., fine condition. . . **145.00**

Davis, Jefferson, President, C.S.A., fine signature penned as "JeffersDavis" on a federal War Department document from 1854. His signature appears just above his printed title, "Secretary of War." The document itself is 7" x 13" and is handsomely framed with a CDV engraving of Davis and a beautiful brass plate with the details of his life. Overall size of the frame, constructed from red burled wood, is 21" square. **1,250.00**

Davis, Varina, first lady, C.S.A., wife of Confederate President Jefferson Davis. Charming letter written and signed by Varina Davis in 1904 to Colonel L. P. Yerger of Mississippi, concerning all sorts of personal affairs and her own opinions and observations, including her troubles with "the whole race of pepper and mustard under the guise of Reporters…" Especially interesting are her comments regarding the "War in Manchuria," referring to the Russo-Japanese War of 1904-1905. She writes, "I do not love either side, but it is a weak power struggling against a powerful and unscrupulous adversary and I hope the Righteous God of Battles will help the worthy helpless ones." One back page smudged but legible, otherwise very good and with the original envelope. Signed "V. Jefferson Davis." **560.00**

DeKay, Drake, lieutenant colonel, U.S.A., Union officer, brevetted lieutenant colonel for gallantry. De Kay served on the staffs of Generals Mansfield, Pope, and Hooker during the Civil War. Partially printed pass from the Headquarters of the Military Department of Washington, dated August 6, 1861, just a few weeks after the First Battle of Bull Run, allowing passage "over the bridges & within the lines" of defense of Washington, DC. Reverse has a printed loyalty oath that includes "and if ever hereafter found in arms against the Union, or in any way aiding her enemies, the penalty will be death." Signed on the front by De Kay as aide-de-camp with his famously enormous signature—the signature alone measures 1-1/2" x 6"! De Kay's colossal autograph was well remembered by many people moving within the capital boundaries during the early days of the war. "That fearful signature," one contemporary journalist wrote, "could be read as far away as the Sandwich Islands." Professionally de-acidified and backed. **265.00**

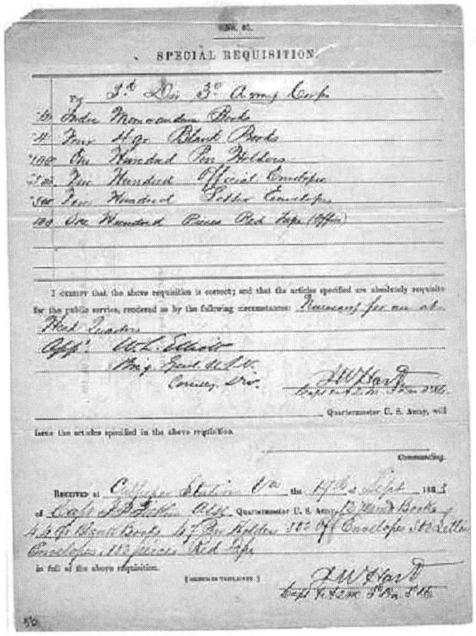
SPECIAL REQUISITION.
For 3d Div. 3d Army Corps
Indorsement Books
Four Hd. Blank Books
One Hundred Pen Holders
Five Hundred Official Envelopes
Five Hundred Letter Envelopes
One Hundred Pieces Red Tape (Office)
I certify that the above requisition is correct; and that the articles specified are absolutely requisite for the public service, rendered so by the following circumstances:
W. L. Elliott
Brig. Genl. U.S.V.
J. W. Hart
Quartermaster U. S. Army, will issue the articles specified in the above requisition.
Commanding.
Received at Culpeper Station Va the 19th Sept 1863
in full of the above requisition.
J. W. Hart

General Washington Lafayette Elliot signed this requisition.

Frohne's Historic Military

Elliott, Washington Lafayette, general, U.S.A., war date document signed (endorsed) by Union General Washington Lafayette Elliott. "No. 40 SPECIAL REQUISITION" dated Sept. 19th, 1863, and signed boldly by Elliot with rank. Also signed by Captain J.W. Hart as acting quartermaster for the 3rd Division of the 3rd Army Corps. Very-fine condition. **195.00**

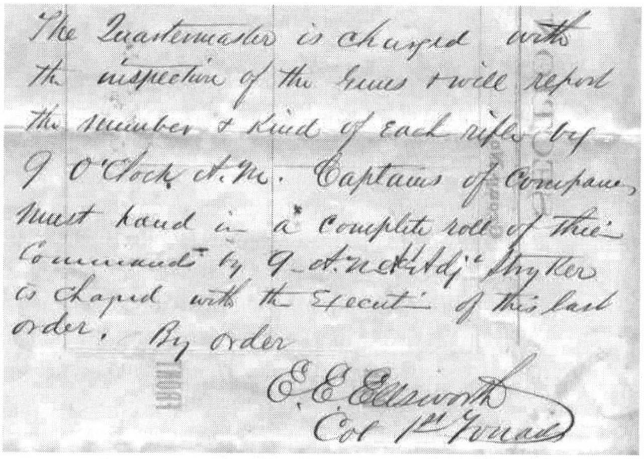
The Quartermaster is charged with the inspection of the Guns & will report the number & kind of each rifle by 9 O'Clock A.M. Captains of Companies must hand in a complete roll of their Commands by 9 A.M. Adjt Stryker is charged with the Execution of this last order. By order

E.E. Ellsworth
Col 1st Zouaves

Wartime signatures by Colonel Elmer Ellsworth are exceedingly rare, since the officer was killed on May 24, 1861. This signature is on the back of a fire department form.

Antebellum Antiques

Ellsworth, Elmer Ephraim, colonel, U.S.A., one legal page autographed document signed, Head Quarters, 1st Zouaves, Capital Buildings, May 6, 1861. Special Order giving orders to Lieutenant Barry, Company E. as Officer of the Day, Sergeant Leary as Officer of the Guard and telling him to post the Police Guard with positive orders that no one shall pass unless by order of the Colonel, ordering the Quartermaster to inspect the guns and report the number and kind of each rifle, and finally ordering the Captains of the Companies to hand in a complete roll of their command, more content. Signed "E.E. Ellsworth, Col 1st Zouaves." He wrote this on the back of what is thought to be a fire department form that makes it an extremely rare manuscript. Ellsworth war-dated items are extremely rare, because his war service lasted from April 12 (firing on Fort Sumter) to May 24, 1861, when he was shot at the Marshall House in Alexandria, Virginia, in the process of removing a Confederate flag from the roof. . . . 11,950.00

Farragut, David Glasgow, admiral, U.S.A. Civil War naval hero, first U.S. admiral, victor of the Battle of Mobile Bay, where he uttered his famous line "Damn the torpedoes! Full speed ahead!" Original copy of General Orders concerning the sending of requisitions within the West Gulf Blockading Squadron. Signed as Rear Admiral, "D. G. Farragut." 950.00

Forrest, Nathan Bedford, general, C.S.A., clipped signature from a Selma, Marion & Memphis Railroad bond. Signature is on a panel of the bond which measures 4-1/2" h x 8" w, and is darkly penned in brown ink. Railroad bonds are now basically the most affordable format for obtaining an authentic Forrest signature with no risk of deception. Forrest served as president of this railroad and then resigned as a result of the Panic of 1873. The Selma, Marion and Memphis Railroad had been started by Confederate general Gideon Pillow and thus this enterprise was strongly imbued with the energy and vision of southern military men whose role in the war had reduced their wealth, status and opportunities. 1,695.00

Grant, Ulysses, general, U.S.A., letter, dated December 2, 1865, is a recommendation for former Civil War Colonel S.S. Curtis while visiting Europe. The letter is in the hand of Grant and is signed boldly by him, including his rank. Letter measures 5" x 6-1/2". .762.00

Hamlin, Hannibal, vice-president, U.S.A., Lincoln's first vice-president, fine condition. 65.00

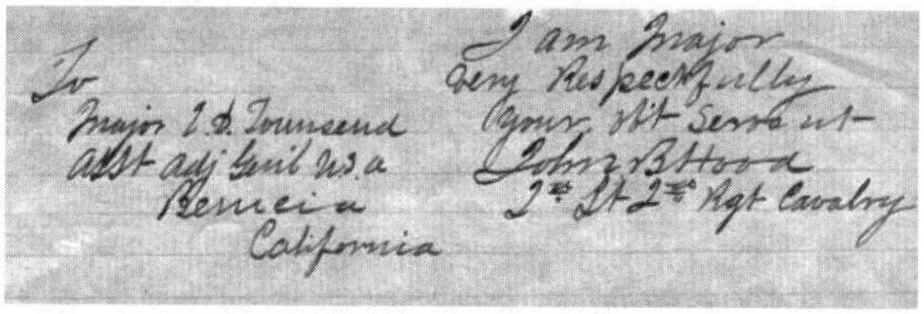
To Major E.D. Townsend
Asst Adj Genl U.S.A.
Benicia
California

I am Major
Very Respectfully
Your Obt Servant
John B Hood
2nd Lt 2nd Regt Cavalry

A collector paid $2,850.00 for Confederate General John B. Hood's signature. Hood is possibly most famous for his handling of a division of Southerners at the Battle of Gettysburg (where he was wounded in action).

Antebellum Antiques

Hood, John Bell, general, C.S.A. who fought at 2nd Manassas, Sharpsburg, Fredericksburg, Gettysburg (WIA), Atlanta, and Tennessee campaigns. ALS, one page on blue-lined paper, about 8" x 10". Fort Reading, California, July 4, 1855, to Major E.D. Townsend, assistant adjutant general, U.S.A., Benicia, California, pertaining to being relieved from an expedition to join his unit (2nd U.S. Cavalry). Extra fine and a most desirable ALS, comes with a transmittal panel prepared by a clerk. 2,850.00

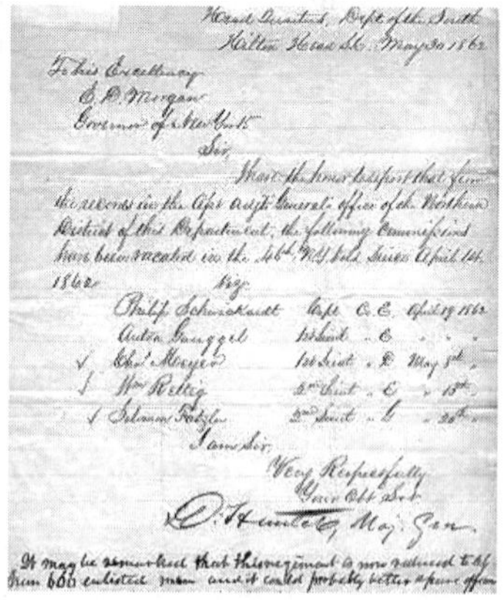
Head Quarters, Dept of the South
Hilton Head SC. May 30 1862

To his Excellency
E.D. Morgan
Governor of New York
Sir,

I am Sir,
Very Respectfully
Your Obt Servt
D. Hunter Maj. Gen.

This letter, signed by General David Hunter, also contains interesting information about the size of regiments under his command. This sort of content adds to the value of a wartime signature.

Frohne's Historic Military

Hunter, David, general, U.S.A., war-dated letter signed by General David Hunter, as commander of the Department of the South. "Head Quarters, Dept. of the South, Hilton Head S.C. May 30, 1862." To the governor of New York pertaining to vacated officers from the 46th New York Infantry. Signed boldly "D. Hunter, Maj. Gen." Hunter adds below his name, "It may be remarked that this regiment is now reduced to less than 660 enlisted men and it could probably better spare officers for staff duty than any other in this command." Full margins and in very-fine condition. 185.00

I Certify, that the articles within enumerated have been received, and the services performed: that they were necessary for, and have been or will be applied in the construction or repairs of Fort La Fayette and that the prices are reasonable and just.
R.E. Lee
Capt Engrs

Fort La Fayette
Voucher No. 13

Probably the most sought-after Confederate signature is that of Robert E. Lee. But that does not mean his signature commands the highest prices. Being the commander of the Army of Northern Virginia, his name will appear on many documents, so look closely! This R.E. Lee signature is on a document from Fort Lafayette.

Antebellum Antiques

Lee, Robert E., general, C.S.A., document signed and dated May 31, 1842, from Fort La Fayette. Two 8" x 10" pages with two check-size attachments, printed and filled in with Lee's bold blue signature on back of 8" x 10" sheet. Listing of supplies to do repairs on Fort and Lee is certifying that it is correct and that the prices are reasonable. Main document completed by a clerk, other receipts by two different other people. **4,650.00**

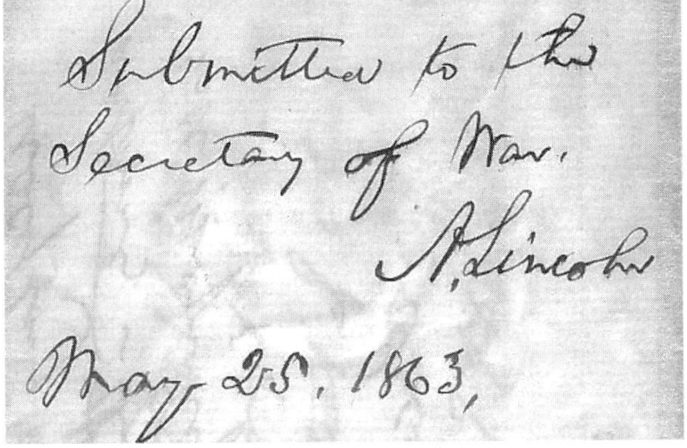
Submitted to the Secretary of War.
A. Lincoln
May 25, 1863,

No signature commands more admiration and respect than that of President Abraham Lincoln.

Lincoln, Abraham, president, U.S.A., an extraordinary document, hand-signed and dated with notation by Abraham Lincoln on May 25, 1863. The document is a letter on Head Quarters, Department of the East letterhead written by prominent Californian, James McDougall, and dated March 31, 1863. McDougall wrote President Lincoln recommending Major Lawrence Kip for promotion to brigadier general. The text, in part: "Mr. President: Major Kip, recently On General Sumner's Staff, and now on the Staff of Genl Wool, I have known and now know he is proposed as a proper person to command a brigade...If you would be pleased to accept my judgment I will expect his appointment ordered as Brigadier Genl. Respectfully, J. McDougall." The letter takes up the first page. The next two pages are filled completely with numerous additional recommendations. In addition, General Winfield Scott writes and signs entirely in his hand, "I have taken an interest in Major Kip's career since he first entered the Service...He would make an excellent brigadier general of volunteers. Winfield Scott." Finally Abraham Lincoln adds his endorsement fully in his hand and on the back page: "Submitted to the Secretary of War, A Lincoln May 25, 1863." The paper is heavy grade, folded into 7 1/2" x 10" pages and in excellent condition. **6,750.00**

Logan, John A., general, U.S.A., fine one-page ink "autograph letter signed" (written and signed entirely in the hand of the writer) by Union General John A. Logan. Written in the field, the letter is headed "Head Quarters 3d Division 17th Army Corps On Big Black River, Miss. May 5th 1863." It reads, "Mr. L.I. Cist, Dear Sir, Your favor of April 15th is received, inquiring the date of my commissions as Brig and Maj General. I take rank of Brig General from March 21, 1862 and accepted my commission as Maj General April 19, 1863 to take rank from Nov 29, 1862." It is boldly signed "Very Respectfully/Your Obt Servt/John A Logan". Written on lined paper 8" x 10" in size, entirely on the front of the sheet. **595.00**

Meig, Montgomery, admiral, U.S.A., Civil War-date autograph letter signed, two pages, quarto on "Quarter-Master General's Office" letterhead stationery, dated November 25, 1861. Written to Captain Andrew H. Foote, a Union naval officer then in command of the Western flotilla. Meigs pens (in part), "Dear Captain, When I laid these matters before the Asst Sec[retar]y the reply was that Gen. Halleck had special instructions in regard to the gunboats. I appreciate your endeavors & can readily imagine your difficulties. Whatever I can do to assist you in gaining final success which as you say 'is with the public the test of merit' I will gladly do. Final success I do not doubt for you. All who have carried on the great & complicated affairs of war have had similar difficulties to encounter…Wellington Napoleon Marlborough did much more than merely fight. A commander must be some thing more than a bulldog. He has to weld the wills & minds of men of all kinds…Having faith in the people & believing that right will triumph in the end I know a glorious conclusion is within reach. Truly your friend, M.C. Meigs" A stirring message from Meigs to this Navy captain. In fine condition. **2,500.00**

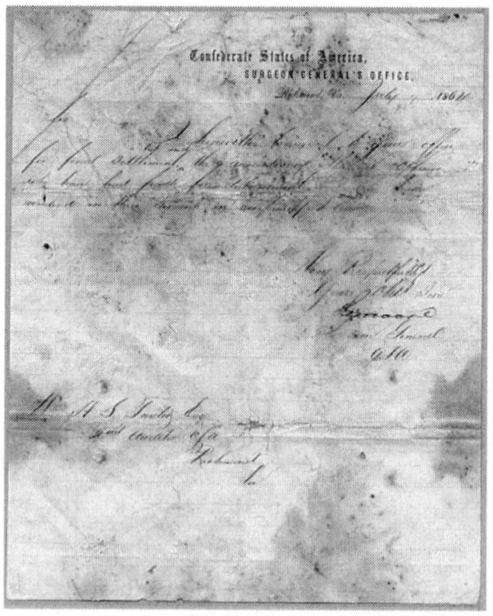
Confederate States of America,
Surgeon General's Office,

Two things contributed to the price of this signed document: First, it is written on very rarely encountered Confederate States of America Surgeon General's Office stationery. And second, it is signed by the Confederate Medical Department's director, Samuel Moore.

Drumbeat Civil WarMemorabilia

Moore, Samuel, medical director, C.S.A., original handwritten letter signed by "Samuel P. Moore, Medical Director of the CS Medical Department" on Confederate States of America Surgeon General's Office stationery. The letter is dated "Richmond, Va. 1864" and describes transfer of officer's pay vouchers. Approximately 8" x 11", some foxing of this paper, but no tears. **550.00**

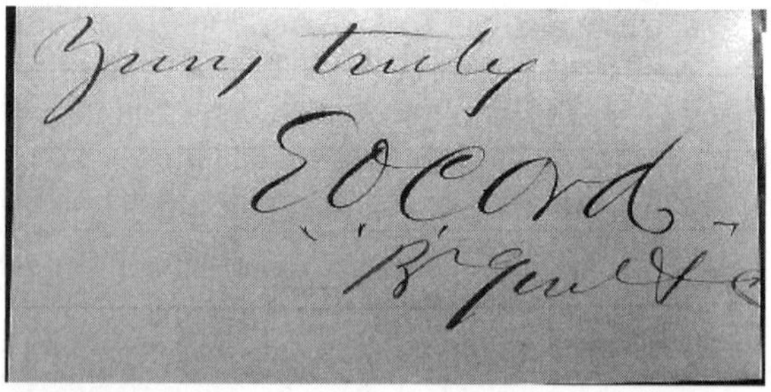

General E.O.C. Ord is best known for participating in the capture of Harpers Ferry in 1859, and his participation in the Vicksburg campaign.

Middle Tennessee Relics

Ord, E.O.C., general, U.S.A., nice condition wartime signature of General Ord. In 1859, General Ord participated in the capture of John Brown at Harper's Ferry. General Ord served throughout the entire Civil War. **75.00**

Picket, George E., general, C.S.A., extremely rare Civil War-date autograph letter signed, four pages, quarto, dated "July 4" [1864], from the Howlett Line (near Fort Walthall, north of Petersburg) during the Bermuda Hundred Campaign. Written to his wife La Salle Corbett Pickett ("Sallie"), then at Richmond and nine-months pregnant with child. On July 17, less than two weeks after the date of this letter, Sallie gave birth to a son, George Jr. Pickett wrote (in part): "I got your sweet long letter darling of my heart. Does not your husband wish, pray and sigh to be with his Sallie, his only only love. Dearest I like very much the tone of your letter, it seems healthy, your bountiful trust in our Giver of life, the Great Being, is so like you, so holy, so humble and like a Christian in the true sense of the word…This lemonade is most delicious every body has had a share, it makes the most delightful punch its so strong my pet that it only takes two spoons ful to season a whole glass. Auld Dearest we have just taken a 'fourth of July' to your sweet self while the Enemy fired their usual salute at 12 m[idnight]. The national salute to day they fired with solid shot. Darling I am so much obliged to you for thinking of me, but 'suffer' I sent after commons to you, for you and for nobody else, certainly not for myself and these miserable fellows here–…Kiss my little sis–What did that Rascal Hal Heth [General Henry Heth] write you? He is my favorite cousin and he loves me like a brother. Bye Bye my own darling, every & always & 'forever', your George." Pickett is extremely rare in Civil War-date correspondence. This full handwritten letter is especially desirable. Archival repair, and some chipping; on the whole, in fine condition. **15,000.00**

Porter, David D., admiral, U.S.A., amazing autograph statement signed, one page, quarto, on Navy Department letterhead, dated August 14, 1865, from Washington, D.C. Written to an unknown correspondent, in the form of a patriotic statement of belief, Porter pens (in full): "In fighting for a Country like ours, all personal Considerations should be lost sight of, it is so necessary for the good of mankind that this union should live, that we should give our lives freely to maintain the present form of government under which we have attained a prosperity unparalleled in the annals of history. David D. Porter, Rear Admiral" Mounting remnants on verso; otherwise in fine condition. **6,950.00**

The addition of an image of the person will greatly enhance both the esthetic and monetary value of an autograph.

Middle Tennessee Relics

Schofield, John McAllister, general, U.S.A., beautifully matted and framed full standing pose CDV and autograph of Schofield. General Schofield is famous for his roles in the Battles of Spring Hill and Franklin, Tennessee. **295.00**

Soule, Pierre, general (honorary), C.S.A., French-born Louisiana politician, served as U.S. Senator, and Minister to Spain. He followed his state into the Confederacy during the Civil War, and worked to establish a colony of Confederate veterans in Sonora after the war. Served for a time as an honorary Brigadier General on Beauregard's staff. Signature on paper, "Pierre Soule." Includes a fine Civil War period carte de visite of Soule by Charles D. Fredericks of New York. **125.00**

Terry, Alfred H., general, U.S.A., signed "Alfred H. Terry, Brig. General" in ink on a 3" x 1-3/4" piece of paper. The ink is a little smudged, but the signature is still clear. Terry served in the Civil War as a Colonel and then as a Brigadier General. He captured Fort Fisher, fought at First Manassas, Fort Pulaski, Bermuda Hundred, Petersburg, and the March to the Sea. He was George A. Custer's superior officer in the Little Big Horn Campaign. **125.00**

Thomas, George H., general, U.S.A., known as "The Rock of Chickamauga" for his feat at that battle in holding the Union left wing against tremendous odds. Civil War-date autograph letter, signed, one page, octavo, dated July 3, 1862, from Tuscumbia, Alabama. Written to General James Birdseye McPherson Thomas pens (in full): "Mr. A.H. Russell who will hand you this was sent here by Genl [Don Carlos] Buell's order with an Engineer & firemen to take charge of the Engine sent round from Nashville. As the engine was disabled before his arrival I send him to you for instruction what to do. The Engineer informed me this morning that you had sent him word to return to Nashville. I therefore let him go up to Dublin this afternoon. Respectfully, Geo. H Thomas, Maj Genl" A superb one-page letter from one of the Union's finest field-grade officers to another. In very fine condition. War-dated letters of Thomas are quite uncommon. **1,500.00**

Welles, Gideon

Secretary of the navy, U.S.A., a journalist and Connecticut legislator, Welles served with great skill and ability as Secretary of the Navy during the Civil War. Manuscript letter dated October 7, 1861, from the Navy Department in Washington, addressed to P. J. Woodbury, Judge Advocate, New York. The letter concerns Commodore Pendergrast being unable to comply with a summons until his duty as a member of a Navy Board of Inquiry concludes. **225.00**

Secretary of the navy, U.S.A., beautifully penned on fancy printed letterhead "Navy Dept./Washington," and dated February 4, 1864. Addressed to "Col. John Harris, Comd't Marine Coprs, Hdq. Wash." Instructs him to, "send Marine Band to President's house this evening 7 ëoclock." Signed, "Gideon Welles, Sec' Navy." Entirely written by Welles and has his distinct full autograph signature. Notation at the top that this was sent as a "telegram at 11:35 a.m." with a stamped surcharge at bottom "U.S. MILITARY TELEGRAPH." **1,200.00**

Printed Matter: Books and Manuals

Bible, Pocket

Standard pocket bible, bears desirable 1863 date, some spine chipping, but very solid. **59.00**

1863 presentation bible to "John K Byrne, of the U.S.S. Port Royal." Bible has color imprint of Federal Eagle above the National Shield with the motto, "God Bless Our Countrys Defenders" in a crescent below. Byrnes inked name is in the bible twice, along with the name of his ship. The *Port Royal* was at Mobile Bay with Farragut, very-good condition. **650.00**

2" x 4" New Testament dated 1861 with leatherette cover. Closing tab is torn on the cover, but otherwise in very-good condition. **95.00**

Both Old and New Testament, in a red leather wrap-around binder. Has fancy stenciling "J.J. Murphy Co. F. 31 Me. Regt." on inside back cover. No title page. **125.00**

Classic pocket-size testament with 1863 printing date, inscribed in brown ink is "This book was presented to William Augustus Lay By his Father while soldiering in the Army of the Potomac, Hazel Run April 24th 1864." Lay saw fighting service with the 177th Pennsylvania Volunteers in the hard fights with Grant in the last two years of the war. Very nice with old leather repair to the spine **225.00**

Dated 1861 and printed by The American Bible Society in New York. Inscribed in brown ink inside the cover "John H Drum/Brasier/August the 2nd 1862," nice condition. **95.00**

Fine, leather-bound pocket testament bearing desirable 1861 date as issued to the Union volunteers as they left for the front. Owner's name "M.A. Wheeler" written inside, excellent in all respects. **69.00**

New Testament Bible published by the American Bible Society in 1865, 316 pages, cloth binding. Belonged to "Benj. Libey Warren Me. Co. B 24th Me. Regt." with his fancy upper and lowercase stenciling on the inside front cover, shows wear and use. **125.00**

Old and New Testament with black leather wrap-around binding. Printed in New York in 1847. It has the soldier's name, "D.M. Kelly Qtr. Master Sergeant" barely visible on inside front cover. Kelly was in the 50th Massachusetts Volunteers, leather weak on folds, but intact **85.00**

Old and New Testament, published in New York in 1845, red leather wraparound binding, marked on flyleaf, "M. Scott Hebron" and, "A gift from Mother Aug. 12th 1864." **75.00**

Printed in 1844, Old and New Testaments, two names, one of which is "E.A. Sadler Troop 18th Cavalry," in fancy stenciling, bound in black leather, embossed in gold. **85.00**

Red-leather bound bible with closing strap, dated "1861" and printed by The American Bible Society in New York. Very nice condition and great quality, includes a multicolor card with image of Grant on horseback and wording "In Memory Gen Grant," mounted on a calling card of "George L. Bradford." **75.00**

Standard clothbound style printed in New York during 1861, entirely in German. Pasted inside the front cover is a beautiful colorful presentation label with waving flag and printed wording, "To The Defenders of Their Country. Presented by The New York Bible Society July 1861." Truly excellent condition. **135.00**

Book

The Soldier From Home. Published by the American Tract Society, unusual rather slick-waxed or enameled cover, back cover has U.S. Christian Commission motif. **95.00**

1864 Annual Report of the Bureau of Military Statistics. Published in Albany in 1864, 212 pages, clothbound, it covers everything for New York troops, such as descriptions of regimental flags, religious tract titles distributed to troops, descriptions of battles, etc. Includes a list of men serving by country and town and much more. **85.00**

About The War Plain Words to Plain People By a Plain Man. Published by the Union League with cover illustration of an old man talking to children. A very nice 8" x 5" pro-Union pamphlet. **40.00**

Annals of the Army of the Cumberland. By John Fitch, 1864, cover good with some minor watermarks, was recovered in 1960. Author was Provost Judge for the Army of the Cumberland; illustrated with steel portraits, wood engravings, and maps. Includes descriptions of departments, accounts of expeditions, skirmishes, and battles, as well as the records of spies, smugglers, and prominent Rebel emissaries. Also has the official reports of the Battle of Stone's River and the Chickamauga campaign. **95.00**

Army Hymns Written for the First Regiment New England Cavalry. Written by their chaplain, Reverend Friederich Denison. Printed in Providence, Rhode Island, in 1861. Denison served with the regiment until 1863, 16 pages, pocket size. . . . **85.00**

Bunyan's Glad Tidings For Sinners. Soldier's religious tract published by the American Tract Society. It warns soldiers about, "A healthy young mans interest in matters of the flesh," and other matters for soldiers. Pocket size, 64 pgs., stiff paper covers. This belonged to "Benj. Libby Warren Me. Co. B 24th Me. Regt.," identified by fancy inside cover stenciling. . . . **115.00**

Directory of Soldiers. Register of Wayne County, Indiana. By J.C. Power, 1865, some water staining and the spine has been attached with tape. Cloth, 8vo. A primary historical source of information on the citizens and soldiers of Wayne County, Indiana, at the conclusion of the Civil War. The 484-page volume not only contains information about the citizenry of Wayne County, but gives a sketch of every Civil War soldier from the county. The directory was sold by subscription about a year after the war ended. The hundreds of pages are also illustrated by charming, elaborate advertisements for Wayne County businesses, in 1865. **245.00**

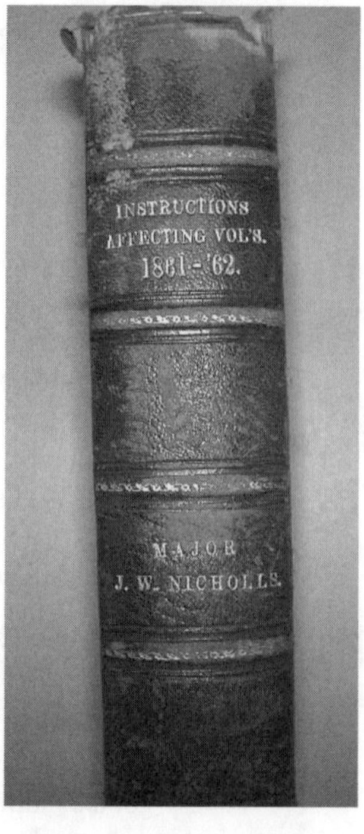

General orders are often bound into a single volume. This particular binding included 111 orders.

Frohne's Historic Military

General Orders Affecting the Volunteer Force. Five different Civil War publications, all bound together in one volume by Major J. W. Nicholls, Paymaster, U.S.A. **Section 1:** *General Orders Affecting the Volunteer Force, 1861*. Printed at Washington Printing Office in 1862, 111 orders, 60 total pages. **Section 2:** *General Orders Affecting the Volunteer Force, 1862*. Printed at Washington Printing Office in 1863, large Index, 216 orders, 158 total pages (not including index). **Section 3:** *Instructions for Making Muster-Rolls, Mustering Into Service, Periodical Payments and Discharging From Service of Volunteers or Militia (Revised)*. Washington Government Printing Office, 1863, 55 pages. **Section 4:** *Rules for Keeping the Principal Record Books used at Department and General Headquarters and at the Adjutant General's Office.* Washington Government Printing Office, 1862, many pullout forms. **Section 5:** *Regulations for the Recruiting Service of the Army of the United States*. Washington Government Printing Office, 1863, 99 pages. Edge wear to some pages, spine leather has wear as well as marbled cover. Nicely identified on the spine to "Major J. W. Nicholls." **115.00**

The years 1861-1863 were covered by this bound volume of general orders affecting volunteers.

Frohne's Historic Military

General Orders for 1863. Covers all the General Orders for the volunteers for that year. Printed in 1864, it is inscribed on the first page "Colored Troops Div. Russell." General Charles Russell commanded the 28th U.S. Colored Infantry. Contains seven sections on colored troops, spine edges weak........ **200.00**

General Orders for Volunteer Forces. Issued by the Adjutant General's Office, in 1861-1863. A large, clothbound volume, compiling all of the orders related to the Volunteer Regiments and Militia, inscribed, "Adjutant's Office 9 N.Y. Cavalry December 29 1864." **165.00**

Set of general orders covering the time immediately after the Battle of Gettysburg.

Frohne's Historic Military

General Orders, July 1 to Dec. 31, 1863. Collection of authentic period imprinted orders bound into a book, 2-1/2" thick. Identified on spine to "Major J. W. Nicholls." Some cover wear and a very tiny amount of insect damage to first few pages in one area. The rest of the pages are in very-good condition. **495.00**

General Orders, U.S. Army for 1862. Published by the Adjutant Generals Office, contains all 217 General Orders for 1862. Leather-bound volume is 1-3/4" thick. **195.00**

Hymn Book for the Army and Navy. Classic soldier's hymnbook, front cover illustrated with flag and, "Hymn Book For The Army and Navy." Back cover worded, "Presented by the United States Christian Commission Phila." Published by The American Tract Society, excellent condition. **95.00**

Hymn Book for the Army and Navy. Extra nice condition tract book, black and white front cover emblazoned with waving flag, back cover has U.S. Christian Commission information, overall fine with a couple of minor scuffs. **145.00**

Journal of the Senate of the State of Georgia 1861. Paper slip case, 351 pages, a large section on the "military," "war tax," and other wartime topics. **225.00**

> **"I could see a long line of our old fellows (Winchester prisoners) who had been sent off in October to be exhanged. Each man was signing his name in a book."**
>
> ***— Archibald Atkinson, Jr.***
> ***Surgeon, 10th Virginia Cavalry***

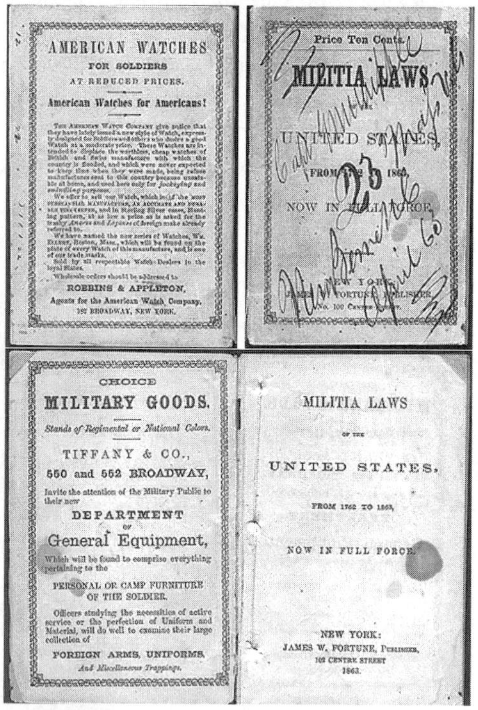

When a manual or a book can be associated to a particular soldier, the value will increase. This book of militia laws was owed by G.M. Whipple who served in the 23rd Massachusetts Infantry.

Sharpsburg Arsenal

Militia Laws of the United States from 1792-1863. Identified to G.M. Whipple, Company F, 23rd Massachusetts Infantry. Includes the Act approved on May 8, 1792, stating "that each and every able-bodied white male citizen of the respective states...who is or shall be of the age of eighteen years, and under forty-five years...shall, severely and respectively be enrolled in the militia." Booklet is completely intact and in very-good condition. Identification is on the front cover. . . . **285.00**

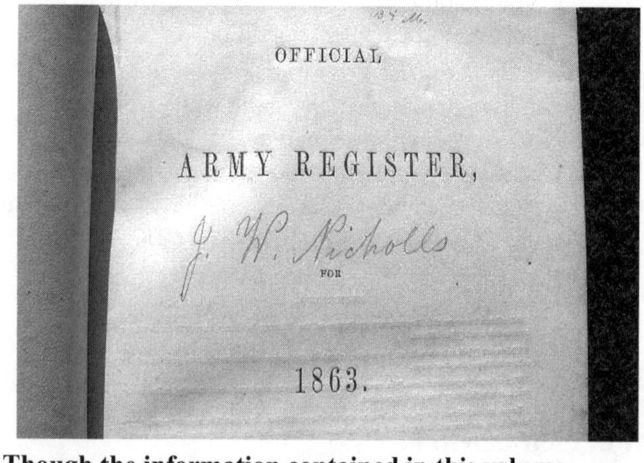

Though the information contained in this volume, *Official Army Register for 1863*, is readily available in various other, more-recently published sources, owning an original edition is always very attractive.

Frohne's Historic Military

Official Army Register for 1863. Nicely bound by the owner, Brevet Lieutenant Colonel J. W. Nicholls, who was a paymaster in the regular army from February 1863 until 1875. Nicely signed in pencil on the title page. Cover shows much wear, but the internal pages are all in very-good condition, with minor water stains on the right lower page corners. This book has 151 pages, and was published on April 1, 1863, in the Adjutant General's Office. Full of information, including all promotions, transfers, deaths, resignations for the regular army. **125.00**

Reports from the Committee on the Conduct of the War—Fort Pillow Massacre & Returning Prisoners. Published 1864, very-good condition, illustrated, gilt lettering on faded cover, binding is hardbound. **150.00**

Soldier's Hymn. Published by the Boston YMCA and distributed by the U.S. Christian Commission, has upper and lowercase period stencil of, "Benj. Libbey/ Warren Me./Co. B 2th Me. Regt." on the first page. **95.00**

Soldier's Hymns. Published by the American Tract Society and presented by the Christian Commission of the Young Men's Christian Associations, ca. 1862, 96 pages, soft cover book with period ink identification to "Chas. Evans, 10th Mass Reg. Vols." The 10th Massachusetts was a 3rd Division, Sixth Corps regiment. The 10th was involved in the actions at Gettysburg and the Bloody Angle at Spotsylvania and the entire Wilderness campaign. This book has seen hard use and is typical of private items that a soldier would carry in their knapsack or haversack. **190.00**

Soldier's Trust. Mint book embossed with military trophies on cover and "Soldier's Trust." Inscribed in ink, "Rev. Dr. Ellis with respects of J.B.M." This is a discourse addressed to The Putnam Blues, published in Boston. **69.00**

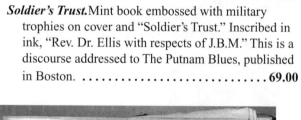

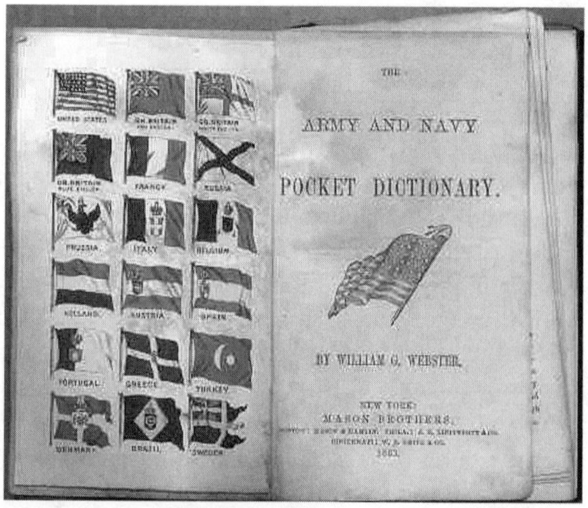

The Army and Navy Pocket Dictionary **was published in 1860.**

The Army and Navy Pocket Dictionary. Published in 1863, 319 pages, some pages have stains, none of which affects text legibility. Most of the pages are clean and all have gilt edges on three sides. The outside wraparound cover is in very-good condition with clear embossed gold letters. It measures 4-5/8" x 3-1/2" x 7/8". **460.00**

The Soldier's Pocket Book. This is a clothbound, pocket-size tract published in Philadelphia in 1864, by the Presbyterian Board of Publication. It is inscribed by the soldier on the inner flyleaf, "Mr. James Swartwoody Central Park Hospital N.Y." Embossed in gold, "Presented by The United States Christian Commission" on the back cover. .. **115.00**

The Soldier's Hymn Book. Inscribed on flyleaf, "Louis Mc Fahe Charlestown, Mass." Words and music published by the Boston YMCA and distributed by the U.S. Christian Commission. Worn but intact. **85.00**

War Pictures From the South. By B. Estvan, Colonel of Cavalry in Confederate States. Appleton, 1863, New York, 352 pages. First edition. Estvan, a Hungarian soldier of fortune, wrote about Charleston before its bombardment, Montgomery, Pensacola, the First Battle of Manassas, the siege of Richmond, North Carolina, and Savannah. Yellowing pages with a worn cover. **75.00**

Welcome to Jesus. Standard clothbound tract book with embossed military panoply on the cover. Published by the American Tract Society. **125.00**

Manual

Army Regulations, 1861. An excellent copy of the standard blue-bound 1861 U.S. Army Regulations book printed by the Government Printing Office. Almost perfect condition, just showing the lightest handling age. **135.00**

Casey's Infantry Tactics Vol. II. Published in 1865, it is the tactics for the soldier, company line skirmishes, etc. 183 pages, plus advertisements, bound in bottle-green cloth. Missing front and back flyleaves (blank pages), otherwise in excellent condition. Has stenciled identification, "J.J. Murphy Co.F 31. Me. Reg." on inside front cover. **125.00**

Casey's Infantry Tactics, Vol. II. Worn and ratty, manual published by Van Nostrand in 1865. Both covers are loose with the back cover actually separated from the book, but still present. **45.00**

Casey's Infantry Tactics, Vols. I, II, and III. The complete three-volume set by Silas Casey, all in very good and solid condition, show light wear and use. **225.00**

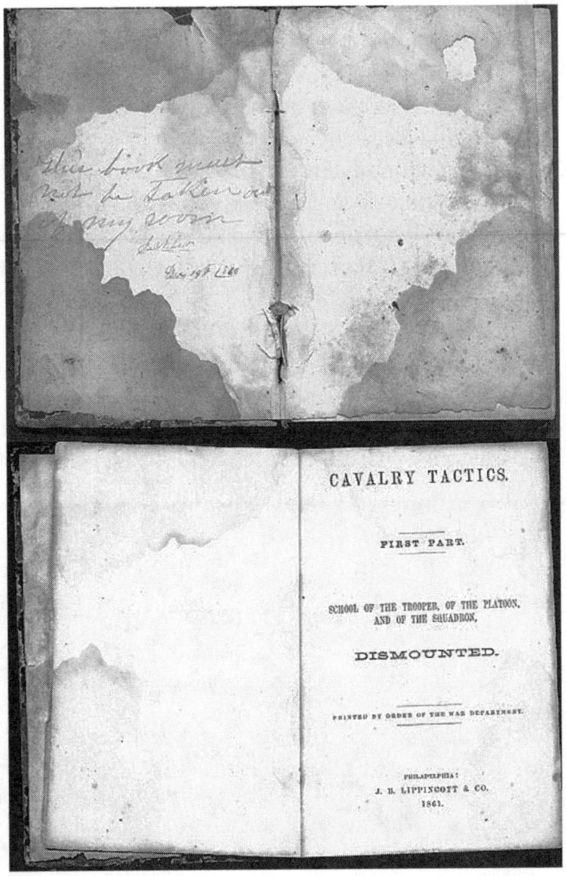

This copy of cavalry tactics belonged to Confederate Captain Junius Law, 1st Battalion Alabama Artillery.

Sharpsburg Arsenal

Cavalry Tactics, First Part. Identified to Junius A. Law, Captain, Alabama 1st Artillery Battalion, Company D. Inside cover has a note stating, "This book must not be taken out of my room. J.A. Laws Dec. 14th, 1860.". **325.00**

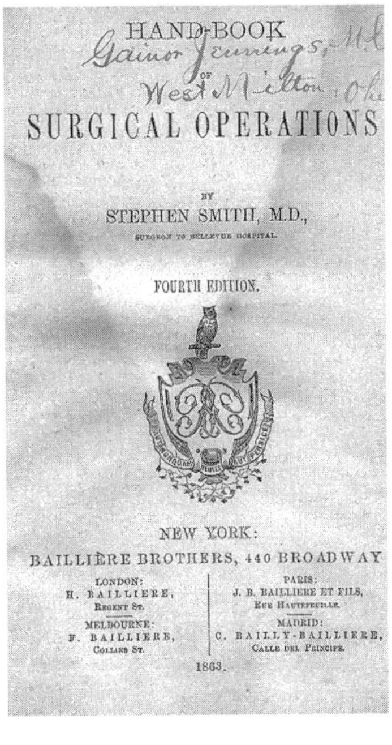

Surgical manuals are extremely pointed in their coverage of war-related wounds. These items, though of interest to general Civil War collectors, are of premium value to medical collectors.

Drumbeat Civil War Memorabilia

Handbook Of Surgical Operations. One of the finest-known surgical texts of the Civil War, published in 1863. The handbook details all of the instruments and surgical operations as used during the Civil War. Specific instructions for treatment of wounds, amputations, and resections with dozens of illustrations, being a complete manual for the military surgeon. Condition is excellent with minor staining. The covers and binding are tight, overall a fine example. **1,250.00**

Hardee's Infantry Tactics, Vol. I. Volume I only, decent condition showing light wear, printed in 1861. This is the standard U.S. army infantry tactic's manual written by William Hardee, front plate torn out, otherwise fine.. . . . . **49.00**

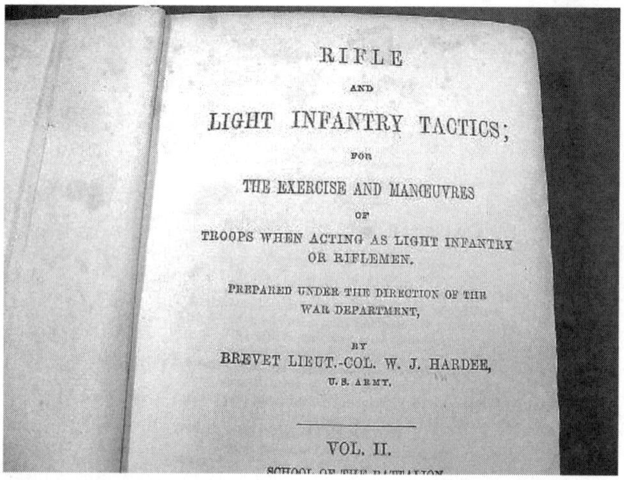
RIFLE
AND
LIGHT INFANTRY TACTICS;
FOR
THE EXERCISE AND MANŒUVRES
OF
TROOPS WHEN ACTING AS LIGHT INFANTRY
OR RIFLEMEN.
PREPARED UNDER THE DIRECTION OF THE
WAR DEPARTMENT,
BY
BREVET LIEUT.-COL. W. J. HARDEE,
U. S. ARMY.
VOL. II.

An inscription on this copy of *Hardee's Tactics* indicates that this manual was owned by a Lieutenant Marshall. It was presented to him very early in the war on April 24, 1861.

Middle Tennessee Relics

Hardee's Infantry Tactics, Vol. II. Dated 1861, identified in old brown ink to "Lieut. Marshal-Camp Harrison-April 24, 1861." Displayed for the past several years at the Lotz House Civil War Museum in Franklin, Tennessee. **275.00**

Hardee's Infantry Tactics. Excellent condition, 1861-dated copy, penciled in a period hand on the flyleaf and inside the text, "H.D. Tiffany, G Co., 7th Regt NYSG/Washington, Dist. Co. April 1861." . . **250.00**

Hardee's Infantry Tactics.The full infantry tactics in one volume published by Joseph H. Riley, Columbus, Ohio, 1863. Solid and tight with leather repair on the spine. Several names written inside, as well as reminder notes written on and near the plates by the original officer who owned this. **135.00**

Infantry Tactics, Vol. III. By Casey, 189 pages, printed in 1865, it has, "J.J. Murphy Co. B 31 ME. Reg.," stenciled on the inside cover. **95.00**

Instruction for Field Artillery. Rare, nice manual published by Lippincott in 1863, prepared by a board of artillery officers, 348 pages, plus plates, plus bugle music plates. Brown cloth hardbound covers with eagle embossed on cover, and gilt title on spine. Autographed by owner on flyleaf, "M.D. Norton Brimfield, Portage Co. Ohio.". **375.00**

Instructions and Forms to be Observed in Applying for Army Pensions Under the Act of July 14, 1862. Near-perfect condition with fold where it put in a pocket, printed in 1863. . . . . **65.00**

Manual of Bayonet Exercise Prepared for the Use of the Army of the United States. Written by George B. McClellan, printed by Order of the War Department Philadelphia, 1862. The book is in great shape showing spine wear and cover corners. The blue-green covers have a patriotic eagle on front and back. There are 118 pages of text and 24 plates in this fine book. **250.00**

Manual of Gunnery Instructions. Pocket-size, leather manual with brass closing clasp. Front cover embossed in gilt, "Manual of Gunnery Instruction." Title page reads, "Manual of Gunnery Instruction for the Navy of the United States/Compiled from the Ordnance Instructions for the US Navy. For the use of The United States Naval Academy New York Van Nostrand 1864," 180 pages, numerous illustrations of cannons and equipment. Has a lengthy inscription inside the front cover from one midshipman to another in 1865. Shows honest wear, but no abuse. . . . . **.295.00**

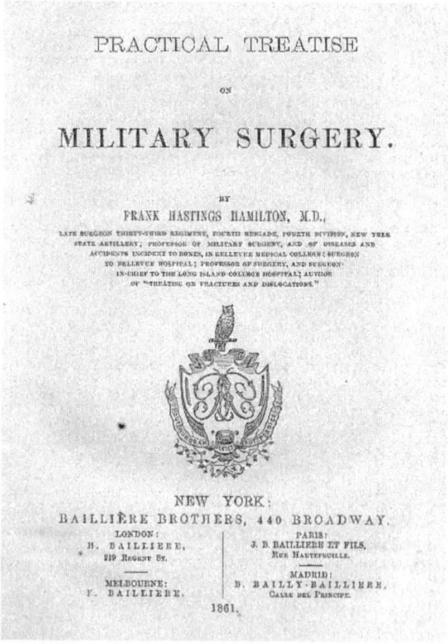
PRACTICAL TREATISE
ON
MILITARY SURGERY.
BY
FRANK HASTINGS HAMILTON, M.D.,
NEW YORK:
BAILLIÈRE BROTHERS, 440 BROADWAY.
1861.

***The Practical Treatise on Military Surgery* is prized for its coverage of bullet wounds, amputations, and the treatment of other war-inflicted wounds.**

Drumbeat Civil War Memorabilia

Practical Treatise On Military Surgery. By Frank Hamilton, 1861, original, first edition of the classic military surgery text of the day containing all the details for military surgery and duties of military surgeons, including preparations for the field, hospitals, conveyance of sick and wounded, gunshot wounds, and amputations. This copy with perfect covers and spine is in mint condition. **1,250.00**

Regulations of the Army of Confederate States. By J.W. Randolph, Richmond, 1863, hardcover, penciled inscription, "Arthur Huger, Dec, 1863—Savannah" (minor stains). **550.00**

Scott's Infantry Tactics, Vols. I, II, and III. All solid and good showing just honest light wear. Vols. I and II printed in New York in 1854, and Vol. III printed in New York by the same company in 1840. Has the owner's name, J.B. Donalson, written inside in ink. **195.00**

Scott's Infantry Tactics, Vols. I and II. In excellent condition, printed in New York during 1860. ..**110.00**

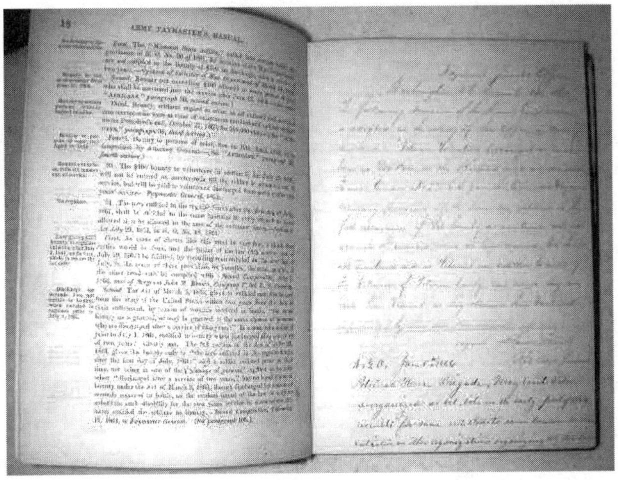

***The Paymaster's Manual*, dated 1864.**

Frohne's Historic Military

The Army Paymaster's Manual For the Information and Guidance for Officers of the Pay Department. Dated June 30, 1864, compiled by J. H. Eaton. This rare manual has both imprinted pages and blank note pages intermixed. Nicholl's has written several pages of notes (they make interesting reading) in each different section. There are probably almost 200 total pages to this book, it measures about 1-1/4" thick. Interior in very-fine condition, the cover is good with the exception of the spine, which is chipped..**175.00**

Treatise on Field Fortifications. Authored by D. H. Mahan, dated 1861, all folding maps intact. Inside page signed in ink, "Frank Wheaton Col nd R.I.V." This would have been signed between July 21, 1861, when Wheaton succeeded to the command of the 2nd Rhode Island Infantry upon the death of its Colonel at First Bull Run (Manassas) and November 29, 1862, when he was promoted to Brigadier General. He later commanded the 6th Corps, Army of the Potomac and retired as a Major General in 1897. ....**434.00**

U.S. Army Regulations, 1857. Published in 1857 and inscribed on flyleaf, "Capt. S. P. Johnston AQM 2nd Div. 3rd Corps" and in the back "John Brown AQM Harpers Ferry." This book is fine, solid, and tight, but the cloth covering on the spine is about 50% worn away................................. **95.00**

U.S. Infantry Tactics, 1861-1862. Identified to Captain S. Rooker, possibly Sam Rooker from Indiana. The front pullout has part missing, otherwise this is in good condition with green cover. Over 450 pages with all the other pullouts present. **145.00**

U.S. Infantry Tactics. Book is 400+ pages, 3.5" x 5.5", published by J.B. Lippincott, 1861.Outer binding worn, some tearing at seam of cover, warping and slight staining to inner pages, some foldouts have creasing and wear. Its full title is the *U.S. Infantry Tactics for the instruction, exercise and maneuvers of the United States Infantry, including Infantry of Nine, Eight and Riflemen, authorized by Secretary of War, School of Soldier, Company, Skirmishers, General Calls, School of Battalion, Dictionary of Military terms* and it has fold-out drawings showing Army formations. **96.00**

United States Infantry/Infantry of the Line, Light Infantry, and Riflemen. "Authorized by the Secretary of War, May 1, 1861." Book was used and carried by David I. Finch, "Co. I, 10th Reg't.," shows use.. ....**260.00**

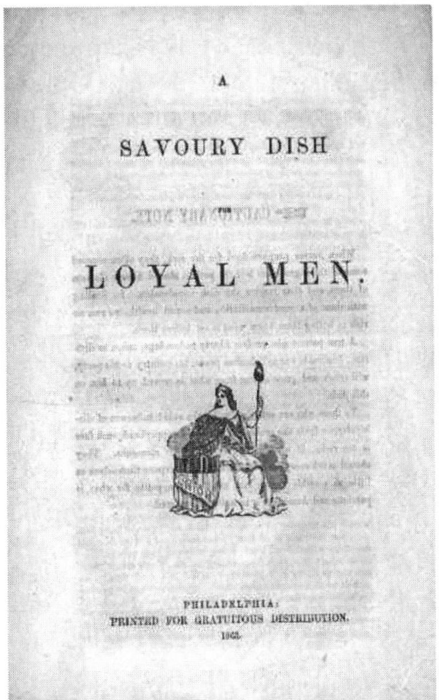
A

SAVOURY DISH

LOYAL MEN.

PHILADELPHIA:
PRINTED FOR GRATUITOUS DISTRIBUTION.
1863.

***The Savoury Dish* was a tract published in 1863, decrying pro-South sentiments.**

N. Flayderman & Co., Inc.

Pamphlet

A Savory Dish for Loyal Man. Published in Philadelphia in 1863. Virulently anti-Copperhead document, light aging, cover and back page loose. **40.00**

The Coming Contraband: A Reason Against the Emancipation Proclamation Not Given by Mr. Justice Curtis. Fancy bold title on paper cover, 21-page pamphlet dated 1862, "By An Officer In The Field." A bitter caustic anti-Emancipation diatribe, light aging; cover partially loose at hinge but still attached; some faint damp stains but all intact. **165.00**

Monetary-Related

Bonds

Confederate, 7% cotton loan of the Confederate States of America for 3 millions Sterling or 75 millions Francs. Coupons redeemable March 1, 1864 thru September 1, 1883. There is a hole about 3mm and another hole/tear is at the top of the bond right between and below the "c" and the "o" in the word "cotton." **435.00**

C.S.A., 4% Registered. Ships in battle at sea. 4 percent registered bond. (Geo. Dunn & Company, Richmond), Fine+. **525.00**

C.S.A., $50

Two females (Commerce & Agriculture), Montgomery issue, thick paper, "Douglas, Engr., N. Orleans," extra fine condition, minor folds. **145.00**

Two females (Commerce & Agriculture), Montgomery issue, thick paper, "Douglas, Engr., N. Orleans," thin paper, extra fine. **145.00**

Vignette of Thomas Bragg, the second C.S.A. attorney general, ("B. Duncan, Columbia, S.C.") 3,614 issued, very fine. **85.00**

C.S.A., $100

C.S.A. officer by tree, center; steamboat, lower, pink-tint paper. (Archer & Daly, Richmond). Full coupons, very fine. **85.00**

Liberty holding C.S.A. flag, ships in background (Evans & Cogswell, Charleston, S.C.), 614 issued, very fine. **185.00**

R.M.T. Hunter, dog and safe on lower bottom, fine. **75.00**

Stephen R. Mallory, C.S.A. Navy secretary, three females ("B. Duncan. Columbia, S.C."), 2,414 issued, extra fine. **95.00**

Symbolic representation of the historic Battle of Shiloh, with C. G. Memminger at center, very fine. **225.00**

Thomas Bragg, females, ships. ("B. Duncan, Richmond, Virginia") 2,964 issued, extra fine. **95.00**

Two females, thick paper, "Douglas-New Orleans," Montgomery issue, extra fine, folds probable. **145.00**

Vignette of R.M.T. Hunter, C.S.A. Secretary of State. (B. Duncan, Richmond), extra fine. **95.00**

Vignette of Thomas Bragg, C.S.A. attorney general (B. Duncan, Columbia), fine. **95.00**

Vignette of Thomas Bragg ("B. Duncan, Columbia, S.C."), 14 coupons, 1,615 issued, extra fine. **95.00**

Confederate bonds, though not a primary focus of many collectors, are an affordable and attractive representation of the South's attempts to finance their war machine.

Middle Tennessee Relics

Confederate, $500, nice condition, pink 1863 Confederate $500 issued B-121 with the steamboat at the bottom, and the Confederate soldier warming his hands at the top. There are seven coupons remaining, with the last one redeemed January 1, 1865, and the next one due (and remaining) July 1, 1865. . . . . **95.00**

C.S.A., $500

C.G. Memminger, very fine. **80.00**

J.P. Benjamin, with maids, extra fine. **145.00**

Ornate green scroll with Arabic "500," Montgomery issue (American Bank Note Company, New Orleans; no imprint), extra fine. **145.00**

Ornate green scroll with Arabic "500," Montgomery issue (reverse, endorsement: "Sinking fund for the Confederate Loan" in blue ink.), extra fine. . **225.00**

Stephen R. Mallory, three female figures ("B. Duncan, Columbia, S.C."), 1,397 issued, extra fine. . . **145.00**

Vignette of C. G. Memminger, first C.S.A. secretary of the treasury. Ornate, cotton plant at bottom. (Evans & Cogswell, Columbia). Full coupons, uncirculated. **245.00**

Vignette of C.S.A. soldier by the fire. Steamboat at bottom. (Archer & Daly, Richmond). Full coupons, uncirculated. **225.00**

Vignette of Howell Cobb, GA governor and C.S.A. Maj. Gen. (B. Duncan, Columbia) Extra fine. **165.00**

Vignette of Thomas H. Watts, third C.S.A. attorney general and Alabama governor. (B. Duncan, Columbia) Extra fine. **165.00**

C.S.A., $1,000

"Stonewall" Jackson, center; steamboat, lower, pink-tint paper, full coupons, very fine. **495.00**

Four cherubic children with sheaves of wheat (Hoyer & Ludwig, Richmond), extra fine. **175.00**

J.A. Seddon, Secretary of War, cotton with historic coupons, (Evans & Cogswell, Columbia), full coupons, uncirculated. **235.00**

Mythical female figure, cornucopia, ships, factories ("Hoyer & Ludwig, Richmond"), very good. . **165.00**

Ornate green scroll with Arabic "1000" (American Bank Note Company, New Orleans; no imprint) very fine. **135.00**

President Davis overlooks the city of Richmond. Liberty at bottom (Evans & Cogswell, Columbia), very fine. **195.00**

Confederate Currency, By Year

Notes

Though only peripherally related to Civil War memorabilia, Confederate currency does cross the paths of many collectors.

Middle Tennessee Relics

This 1861 $5 note was in circulated condition when it sold.

Middle Tennessee Relics

C.S.A., $5

1861, early issue note, dated September 2, 1861, pictures Ceres seated on a cotton bale, a sound but circulated C.S. note. **48.00**

1861, sailor seated beside bales of cotton, center; C.G. Memminger, left; Justice & Ceres, right. Dated: Richmond, September 2, 1861, good condition. **50.00**

1861, sailor at left with allegorical Peace sitting on strongbox at top. Double signed and hand serial numbered, fine condition. **38.00**

This $10 note bore an incorrect date of "1862" when, in fact, it was an 1861 bill.

Middle Tennessee Relics

C.S.A., $10

1861, this popular note pictures Ceres reclining on a cotton bale, printing error by Hoyer & Ludwig. It should be dated, "Sep. 2, 1861," and is dated in error, "Sep. 2, 1862." This is a circulated note in solid condition with good print color. **65.00**

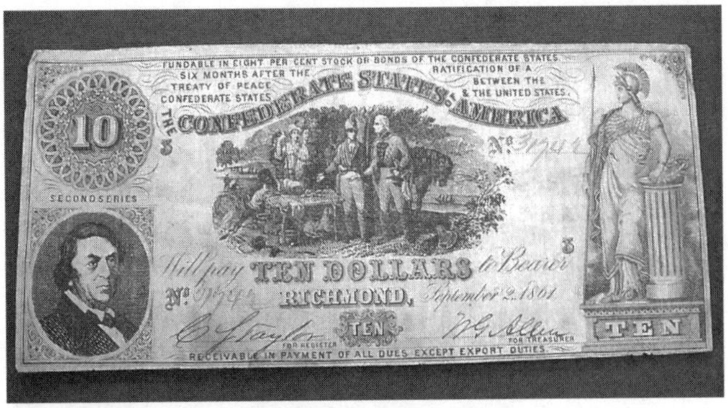

1861 $10 note featuring General Marion.

Middle Tennessee Relics

1861, quite rare, early-war Confederate note pictures General Francis Marion's Sweet Potato Dinner. This is a good solid circulated note, dates September 2, 1861. .... **55.00**

It is thought that the bust shot on this 1861, $20 note is A.H. Stephens.

Middle Tennessee Relics

C.S.A., $20

1861, nice circulated condition, issue date September 2, 1861, Industry is seated between cupid and a beehive, it also has a bust shot of A.H. Stephens. **45.00**

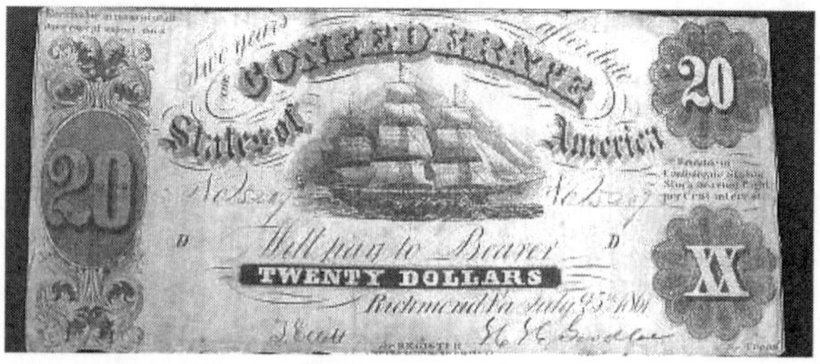

$20 note dated July 25, 1861.

Middle Tennessee Relics

1861, this is the note with the large sailing vessel dated July 25, 1861. This is a circulated, but quite sound, note. **65.00**

C.S.A. $50, 1861, sailors on the left, lady in the center, Richmond, Virginia, fine condition. **65.00**

C.S.A., $1

1862, steamship, Lucy Pickens, uncirculated, tight margins, bright white paper. **265.00**

C.S.A., $2

1862, South strikes Union, circulated. **325.00**

1862, Judah Benjamin at top left, Justice triumphs over tyranny in center, very-good condition. **33.00**

1862, personification of South striking down Union, center; J. P. Benjamin, left, date: Richmond, June 2, 1862, good condition. **45.00**

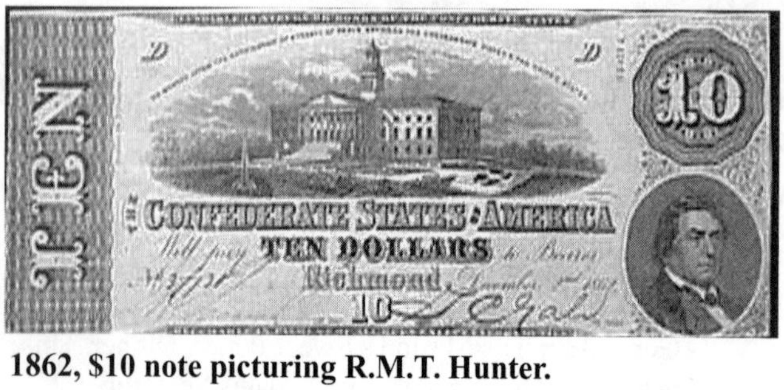

1862, $10 note picturing R.M.T. Hunter.

Middle Tennessee Relics

C.S.A., $10, 1862, nice circulated condition, issue date December 2, 1862, fancy blue back with the state capitol at Columbia, South Carolina, and has R.M.T. Hunter at right. **45.00**

1862 $20 note featuring the capitol building in Nashville.

Phillip B. Lamb, Ltd./Col. Lamb's Antiques

C.S.A., $20, 1862, capitol building in Nashville, Tennessee, blue reverse, extra fine. **195.00**

This $50 note displayed the likeness of Confederate President Jefferson Davis.

Phillip B. Lamb, Ltd./Col. Lamb's Antiques

C.S.A., $50, 1862, Jefferson Davis, C.S.A. president, green tint, very fine. **395.00**

The image of Negroes hoeing in the field makes this a desirable piece.

Phillip B. Lamb, Ltd./Col. Lamb's Antiques

C.S.A., $100

1862, Negroes hoeing cotton, J.C. Calhoun, orange "HUNDRED," circulated. **125.00**

Dated June 23, 1862, this note features a locomotive.

Middle Tennessee Relics

1862, nice circulated condition. The issue date is June 23, 1862. Railway train with diffused steam from the locomotive with a milkmaid at the left. **60.00**

1862, Richmond, Virginia, train in center, lady on the left, fine condition. **59.00**

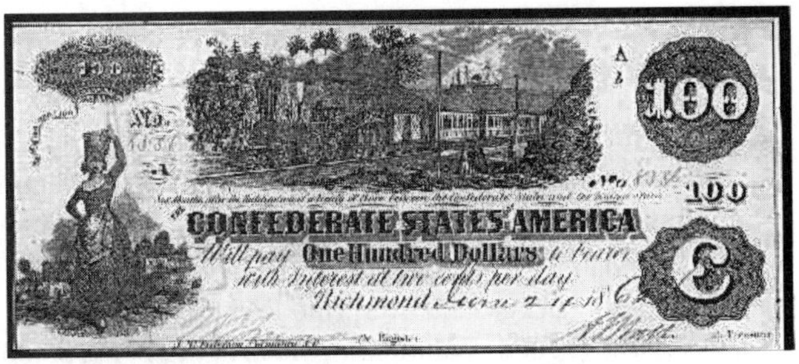

This 1862, $100 note in uncirculated condition.

Phillip B. Lamb, Ltd./Col. Lamb's Antiques

1862, train, straight steam, milkmaid, by Patterson, two Charleston stamps, uncirculated. **195.00**

1862, train, straight steam, milkmaid, by Patterson, two Montgomery stamps, very fine. **85.00**

1862, train, diffused steam, extra fine. **85.00**

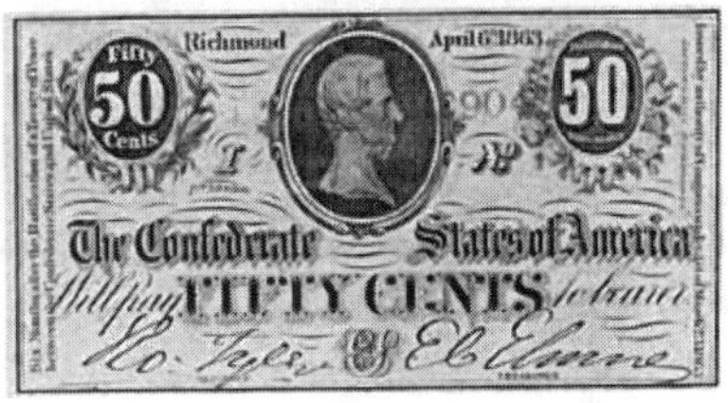

This 1863, 50¢ note features a bust of Jefferson Davis.

Phillip B. Lamb, Ltd./Col. Lamb's Antiques

C.S.A., 50¢, 1863, bust of Jeff Davis, circulated. ... **49.00**

C.S.A., $1

1863, Clement C. Clay Center, April 6, 1863, fair condition. **55.00**

1863, Clement C. Clay center, Richmond, April 6, 1863, fine condition. **60.00**

Uncirculated, 1863, $1 note.

Phillip B. Lamb, Ltd./Col. Lamb's Antiques

1863, Clement C. Clay, pink paper, plain black, uncirculated. **225.00**

C.S.A., $2

1863, Judah P. Benjamin, right, Richmond, April 6, 1863, good condition. **60.00**

J.P. Benjamin is illustrated on this uncirculated 1863, $2 note.

Phillip B. Lamb, Ltd./Col. Lamb's Antiques

1863, J.P. Benjamin, pink paper, plain reverse, uncirculated. **475.00**

The capitol at Richmond, Virginia, was illustrated on this circulated $5 note.

Phillip B. Lamb, Ltd./Col. Lamb's Antiques

C.S.A., $5, 1863, Capitol-Richmond, blue reverse, circulated. **125.00**

C.S.A., $10, 1863, Capitol-Columbia R.M.T. Hunter, blue reverse, circulated. **125.00**

1863, $20 note featuring the capitol building at Nashville, uncirculated example.

Phillip B. Lamb, Ltd./Col. Lamb's Antiques

C.S.A., $20, 1863, Capitol-Nashville, blue reverse, uncirculated. **245.00**

Jefferson Davis was featured on the 1863, $50 note.

Phillip B. Lamb, Ltd./Col. Lamb's Antiques

C.S.A., $50, 1863, Jefferson Davis, fancy green reverse, uncirculated. **265.00**

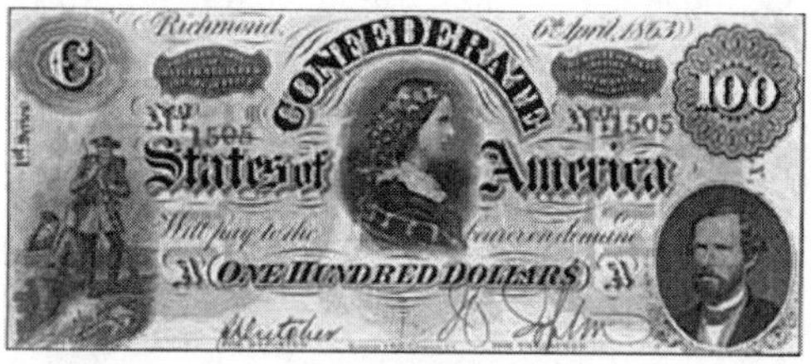

Lucy Pickens and soldiers adorned the 1863, $100 note.

Phillip B. Lamb, Ltd./Col. Lamb's Antiques

C.S.A., $100

1863, Lucy Pickens, soldiers, green reverse, uncirculated. **895.00**

1863, Lucy Pickens, soldiers, G.W. Randolph, green reverse, circulated. **375.00**

1864, 50-cent note sold in circulated condition.

Middle Tennessee Relics

C.S.A., 50¢

1864, circulated condition but remains solid. **38.00**

1864, bust of Jefferson Davis, pink paper, small format, circulated. **45.00**

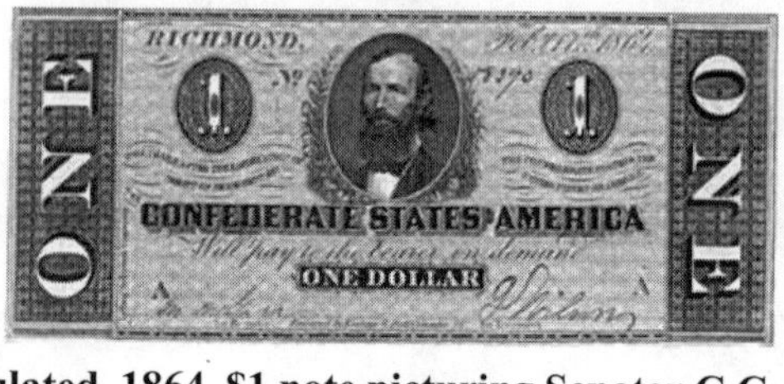

Uncirculated, 1864, $1 note picturing Senator C.C. Clay.

Phillip B. Lamb, Ltd./Col. Lamb's Antiques

C.S.A., $1

1864, C.C. Clay, C.S.A. senator, uncirculated, dark red. **225.00**

1864, Clement C. Clay, center, black with red-orange overprint, Richmond, February 17, 1864, fine condition. **68.00**

1864, Clement C. Clay, center, Richmond, February 17, 1864, fine condition. **72.00**

J.P. Benjamin's likeness was on this uncirculated, 1864, $2 note.

Phillip B. Lamb, Ltd./Col. Lamb's Antiques

C.S.A., $2

1864, J.P. Benjamin, plain reverse uncirculated, medium pink. **135.00**

1864, Judah P. Benjamin, right, black with reddish network background overprint, Richmond, February 17, 1864, good condition. **55.00**

C.S.A., $5

1864, Capitol-Richmond, C.G. Memminger, blue "FIVE," uncirculated. **49.00**

This $5 note pictures C.G. Memminger and the Capitol of the Confederacy.

Middle Tennessee Relics

1864, nice circulated condition, issue date is February 17, 1864, reddish network overprint background, state capitol at Richmond, Virginia, and C.G. Memminger at the right. **45.00**

C.S.A., $10

1864, fine notes with a battery of Confederate Horse Artillery featured in the center, hand-signed and serial numbered. **25.00**

A scene depicting a battery of artillery rolling into action adorned this 1864, $10 note.

Phillip B. Lamb, Ltd./Col. Lamb's Antiques

1864, horses pulling cannon (Mexican War scene), R.M.T. Hunter, blue "TEN" reverse, uncirculated. 45.00

C.S.A., $20

1864, capitol-Nashville, blue reverse, circulated. . 55.00

$20 note issued on February 17, 1864.

Middle Tennessee Relics

1864, nice circulated condition, issue date is February 17, 1864, note has a reddish network background overprint, intricate blue back with "Twenty" in large letters. A.H. Stephens at the right. 45.00

C.S.A., $50

1864, Jefferson Davis in center, fine condition. 50.00

1864, $50 note decorated with an image of President Davis.

Middle Tennessee Relics

1864, this is the February 17, 1864, issue with Jefferson Davis pictured. Strong, attractive, but circulated. 55.00

1864, Jefferson Davis, blue "FIFTY." 115.00

Combining the images of George Washington, the Confederate flag, and Stonewall Jackson, this 1864, $500 note is a solid representation of southern pride.

Phillip B. Lamb, Ltd./Col. Lamb's Antiques

C.S.A., $500

1864, equestrian view of Washington, C.S.A. flag, Gen. T.J. (Stonewall) Jackson, light red, very sharp. 740.00

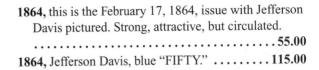

Example of a circulated, $500 note.

Middle Tennessee Relics

1864, February 17, 1864, solid, circulated note with a pretty pink color, face of the note is very nice, serial #2142. The note's reverse has "$3,000" written in old brown ink and has a spatter where a drop of ink fell. 375.00

1864, handsome note with the "Stainless Banner" above the Seal of the Confederacy and a handsome profile of General "Stonewall" Jackson at the right. . 225.00

1864, February 17, 1864, Confederate $500 Stonewall Jackson note, attractive circulated note with nice pink color, couple of small stains in the upper-right corner, but otherwise very respectable. 375.00

> **"The pay was almost nominal from the depreciated nature of the currency."**
>
> ***— Phoebe Yates Pember***
> ***Reminiscences of a Southern Hospital by its Matron***

Confederate Currency, State-Issued

Alabama

50¢, 1863, State seal in the center, lady on the right. 20.00

$1, 1863, note issued out of Montgomery, Alabama, January 1. The note is in sound circulated condition, serial #89585. .... 45.00

$1, 1863, state seal, capitol building in center, very-good condition. 25.00

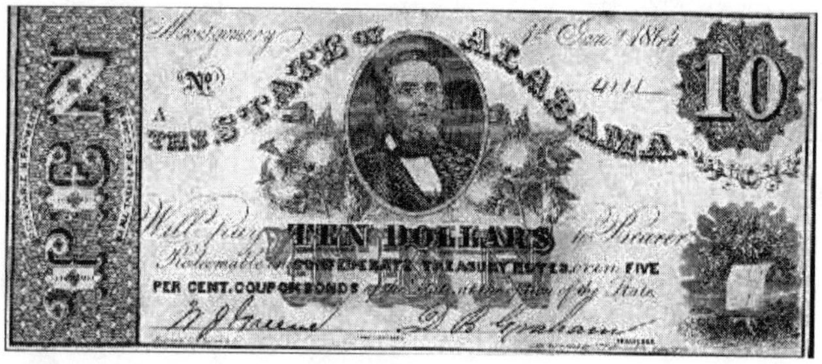

$10 note issued by the State of Alabama.

Phillip B. Lamb, Ltd./Col. Lamb's Antiques

$10, 1864, Governor Watts, cotton bolls, green "10," uncirculated. 100.00

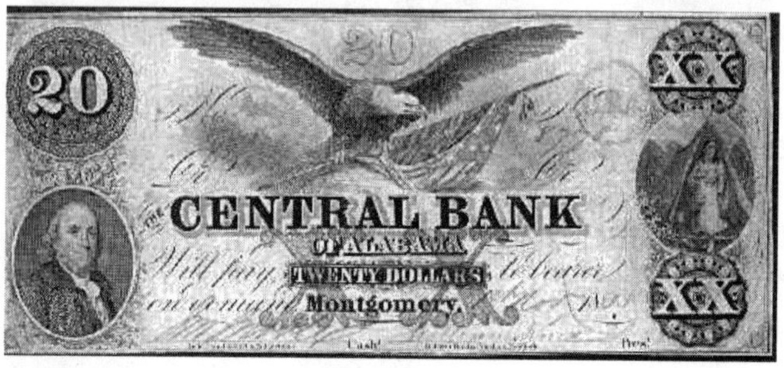

Originally issued in 1853, the "CSA" red circular stamp signifies that the Confederacy recognized this Alabama $20 note.

Phillip B. Lamb, Ltd./Col. Lamb's Antiques

$20, 1853, Central Bank of Alabama, Montgomery, beautiful, spread-wing eagle holding American flag, Ben Franklin, left. Indian maiden in tent, rare, historic "C.S.A." red circular stamp documenting this state note as Confederate-issue currency, fine. 105.00

Georgia

5¢, 1863, Milledgeville, Georgia,fine condition. . 21.00

10¢, 1863, Augusta, Georgia,very-good condition. 18.00

10¢, 1863, Milledgeville, Georgia, fine condition. 20.00

50¢, 1863, Augusta, Georgia, very-good condition. . 19.00

50¢, 1861, Savannah, very-fine. 25.00

50¢, 1863, very-good condition. 25.00

$1, 1863, train center, January 1, 1863, good condition. 50.00

$1, appealing note on the Timber Cutters Bank, Savannah, Georgia, with lithographs of slaves working at cutting timber, carrying cotton, and also a sailor sitting on a bale of cotton. Worn, ca. 1857-1861, roughly 7" x 3". 18.50

$2, 1863, steamship at sea. Dated January 1, 1863. Good condition. 75.00

$2, 1864, warship in center, very-fine condition. . 28.00

$5, prewar Georgia bank note, some wear, shows slaves working. 19.00

Louisiana

$5, 1862, soldier striking down Lady Liberty in the center, pelican on the left, Baton Rouge, Louisiana, very-fine condition. 39.00

50¢, 1864, Eagle on the left, Navy ship in the middle, Shreveport, Louisiana, very-good condition. . . 35.00

$1, 1861, New Orleans/Jackson Railroad, train in the center, lady and eagle on the right, fine condition. 39.00

$20 Louisiana note issued by the Canal Bank.

Phillip B. Lamb, Ltd./Col. Lamb's Antiques

$20. Canal Bank, unsigned, three maids in the center, red reverse, circulated. 25.00

Maryland, $5. The Valley Bank of Maryland. 28.00

Mississippi

$2, 1863. Fine, Holly Springs, Mississippi. 35.00

Mississippi $50 note bearing an Indian, train, and a maiden.

Phillip B. Lamb, Ltd./Col. Lamb's Antiques

$50, Faith of the State Pledged, red, Indian, maiden, left; train center, red "50," beautiful note, extra fine. 115.00

$1 North Carolina note dated October 12, 1861.

Middle Tennessee Relics

North Carolina

$1, 1861, dated October 12, 1861, $1 North Carolina note, nice circulated condition. **45.00**

$1, 1863, January 1,1863-dated $1 North Carolina note, nice circulated condition. **40.00**

$1, 1863, ladies in the center, very-good condition. **25.00**

$3 North Carolina note picturing Liberty and Ceres.

Phillip B. Lamb, Ltd./Col. Lamb's Antiques

$3, 1863, Liberty and Ceres center, extra fine. ... **45.00**

$5, 1862, steamship at sea, uncirculated. **60.00**

$5, "Miners & Planters Bank." Indian in full headdress at left with allegorical print of Commerce and Peace overlooking a field of slaves picking cotton with a train off in the distance, fine condition. **58.00**

South Carolina

15¢, 1863, good condition. **18.00**

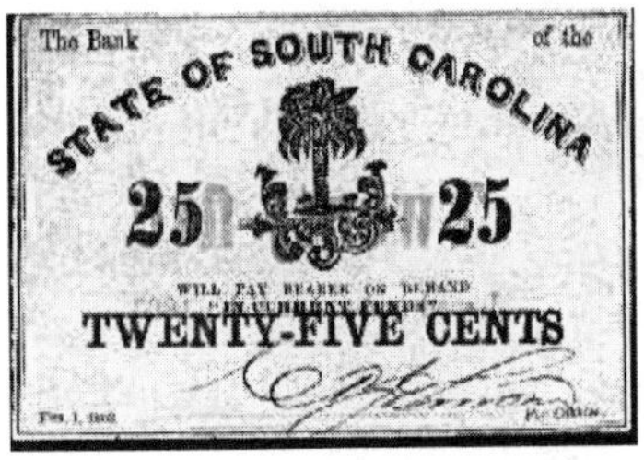

Palmetto-emblazoned twenty-five-cent note issued by the State Bank of South Carolina.

Phillip B. Lamb, Ltd./Col. Lamb's Antiques

25¢, 1863, Bank of the State of South Carolina Palmetto, no watermark. **30.00**

Tennessee ten-cent note issued on December 4, 1861.

Middle Tennessee Relics

Tennessee

10¢, 1861, quite rare 10-cent Bank of Tennessee at Nashville, dated December 4, 1861, complete but circulated. **35.00**

50¢, 1861, December 1, 1861, war date, 50-cent note from the Bank of Tennessee at Nashville. When this note was issued, Nashville was under Confederate control, quite scarce, complete circulated note. **45.00**

50¢, 1863, train in center, Nashville date, very fine condition. **48.00**

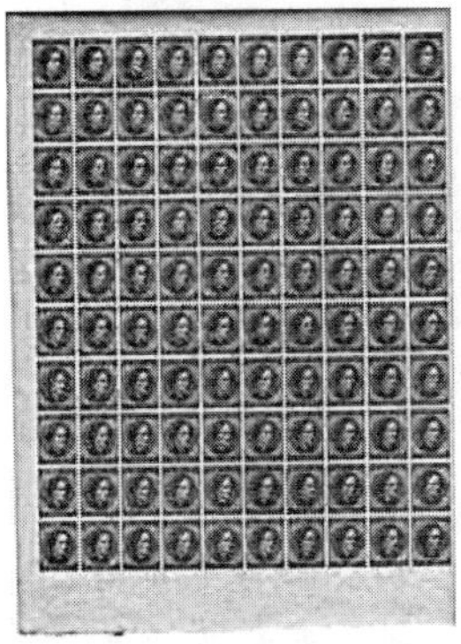

This $1 Virginia Treasury note was issued on July 21, 1861.

Middle Tennessee Relics

Virginia

$1, 1861, Virginia Treasury note in nice, circulated condition, issue date is July 21, 1861, note has a red overprint, Ceres is seated, bust of Governor John Letcher on left. **45.00**

Corporation of Fredericksburg, $2, train and ship center; woman in field right, November 1, 1861, good condition. **55.00**

Miscellaneous

Postal Receipt, C.S.A., Post Office at Canton, Mississippi, labeled to Jackson & Vicksburg, very-good condition. **45.00**

Stamp, C.S.A., No. 6., sheet of 100 stamps, light blue, London-print with gum, sheet has at least a 1/2" border on every edge. **665.00**

Token, Bread

Charles L. Pascal collected this item soon after the Civil War. He corresponded with most major military figures of the day, asking for autographed pictures and whatever they would send. These bread "chits" come from Fort Dalles, in Oregon Territory. The Fort was named as an Indian war supply base, ca. 1850-1867. In order to make the issuing of rations more manageable and convenient (a soldier could take them or save them), the soldiers were given a number of colored, printed chits for each item. When he needed something, he turned in the chit. Dark-orange, thick paper ticket approximately 1-1/8" x 2", has narrow, decorative border around "FORT DALLES/POST BAKERY/GOOD FOR/1 RATION BREAD." Reverse signed in ink by post official, legible. **20.00**

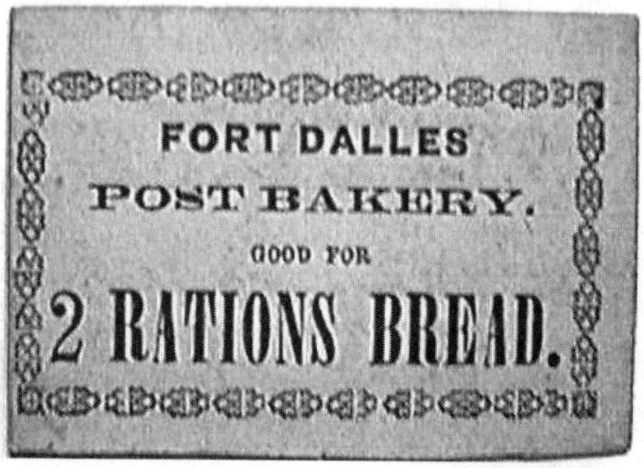

The chances of a "bread ration" chit surviving is rare indeed! This paper ticket was issued at Fort Dalles in Oregon Territory.

Dale C. Anderson Co.

Mint, 1-3/8" x 2", in pale buff-orange heavy paper printed with narrow decorative border around, "FORT DALLES/POST BAKERY/GOOD FOR/2 RATIONS BREAD," unused and perfect. **22.00**

Token, Sutler

1st Mounted Rifles, nice, dug sutler's token about the size of a nickel for, "JJ Benson Sutler 1st Mounted Rifles." It is a ten-cent denomination and has a rich, deep-brown patina. **95.00**

Though tokens were minted by the thousands during the Civil War, very few were aimed specifically at the soldiers for distribution. Sutler tokens are the exception, though. This token was distributed by the sutler of the 41st Illinois Volunteer Infantry.

Sutler, 41st Volunteer Infantry, issued by J.C. Benton, the sutler for the 41st Regiment of Illinois Volunteers. The token has been in the ground and is dark and lightly corroded. The token says, "Good For Twenty Five Cents in Goods at Sutlers Store," on one side and says, "Forty First Reg't Ill V. J.C. Benton," on the other side. **91.00**

Printed Matter: Broadsides, Circulars, and Newspapers

Broadsides

"Instructions for Provost Guard, 8-1/2" x 13", interesting rules for soldiers on guard duty, among them are: 4) "Will arrest all intoxicated soldiers, sailors, citizens, or Negroes, and carry them to the guard house;" 13) "Riding on sidewalks prohibited (Enlisted men to be arrested, officers to be notified that it is against orders)." Signed "By Command of Brig. Gen. Harland." Has small tears at center, displays well. **275.00**

This broadside rallied volunteers to the 6th New Jersey Volunteer Infantry in late 1862.

Antebellum Antiques

6th New Jersey Volunteer Infantry, printed after November 1862, when Capt. William H. Hemsing was promoted from first lieutenant. Hemsing's name is printed at the bottom and with the broadside comes a pass for Hemsing to find a lost train and a ribbon from Hooker's Brigade. This broadside is one of only eight known to exist (as of 1956) and came from the family of Edwin V. Snyder. It supposedly once graced a rostrum when Abraham Lincoln made a speech in Camden, New Jersey. **29,500.00**

6th Pennsylvania Reserves, flyer measures 8" x 10", with bold heading, "Union Christian Association of the Sixth Regiment Pennsylvania Reserve Volunteer Corps." It is a printed oath for a soldier to state, along the lines of a prayer, affirming the soldier's faith in God and Jesus as Savior. Issued by Samuel Jessup Chaplain. Also included is a manuscript roster of the organization listing John Harrison and 40 others as members. **85.00**

Delaware, illustrated, political broadside satirizing the nomination of Charles Brown to political office in Delaware. The broadside states that by voting for Charles Brown, "you are voting to cut Delaware loose from her moorings; blot her Star from the Old Flag of the Union, and make her the battleground of Rebellion." Broadside presents an illustration in upper portion that satirizes a secret society meeting of the Knights of the Grand Confederacy and equates Jefferson Davis with Benedict Arnold and Judas Iscariot. Large amounts of text portray the shortcomings in a tongue-in-cheek manner if one votes for Charles Brown. Bottom portion of broadside is officially designated "By Order of the Democratic Confederate State Committee." Broadside measures 29" x 43-1/2" and exhibits some chipping on fold areas with some text loss. Broadside also exhibits some off-setting and has been reinforced with archival paper. **3,000.00**

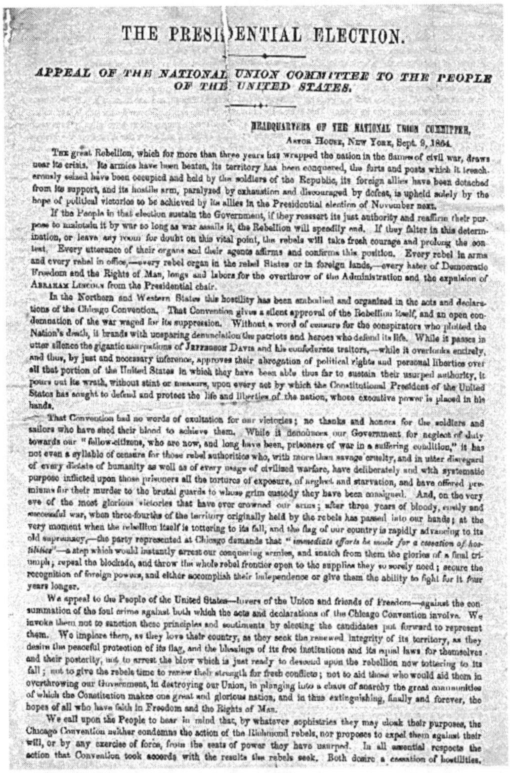
THE PRESIDENTIAL ELECTION.

APPEAL OF THE NATIONAL UNION COMMITTEE TO THE PEOPLE OF THE UNITED STATES.

HEADQUARTERS OF THE NATIONAL UNION COMMITTEE,
Astor House, New York, Sept. 9, 1864.

The great Rebellion, which for more than three years has wrapped the nation in the flames of civil war, draws near its crisis. Its armies have been beaten, its territory has been conquered, the forts and posts which it treacherously seized have been occupied and held by the soldiers of the Republic, its foreign allies have been detached from its support, and its hostile arm, paralyzed by exhaustion and discouraged by defeat, is upheld solely by the hope of political victories to be achieved by its allies in the Presidential election of November next.

If the People in that election sustain the Government, if they reassert its just authority and reaffirm their purpose to maintain it by war so long as war assails it, the Rebellion will speedily end. If they falter in this determination, or leave any room for doubt on this vital point, the rebels will take fresh courage and prolong the contest. Every utterance of their organs and their agents affirms and confirms this position. Every rebel in arms and every rebel in office,—every rebel organ in the rebel States or in foreign lands,—every hater of Democratic Freedom and the Rights of Man, longs and labors for the overthrow of the Administration and the expulsion of Abraham Lincoln from the Presidential chair.

In the Northern and Western States this hostility has been embodied and organized in the acts and declarations of the Chicago Convention. That Convention gives a silent approval of the Rebellion itself, and an open condemnation of the war waged for its suppression. Without a word of censure for the conspirators who plotted the Nation's death, it brands with unsparing denunciation the patriots and heroes who defend its life. While it passes in utter silence the gigantic usurpations of Jefferson Davis and his confederate traitors,—while it overlooks entirely, and thus, by just and necessary inference, approves their abrogation of political rights and personal liberties over all that portion of the United States in which they have been able thus far to sustain their usurped authority, it pours out its wrath, without stint or measure, upon every act by which the Constitutional President of the United States has sought to defend and protect the life and liberties of the nation, whose executive power is placed in his hands.

That Convention had no words of exultation for our victories; no thanks and honors for the soldiers and sailors who have shed their blood to achieve them. While it denounces our Government for neglect of duty towards our "fellow-citizens, who are now, and long have been, prisoners of war in a suffering condition," it has not even a syllable of censure for those rebel authorities who, with more than savage cruelty, and in utter disregard of every dictate of humanity as well as of every usage of civilized warfare, have deliberately and with systematic purpose inflicted upon those prisoners all the tortures of exposure, of neglect and starvation, and have offered premiums for their murder to the brutal guards to whose grim custody they have been consigned. And, on the very eve of the most glorious victories that have ever crowned our arms; after three years of bloody, costly and successful war, when three-fourths of the territory originally held by the rebels has passed into our hands; at the very moment when the rebellion itself is tottering to its fall, and the flag of our country is rapidly advancing to its old supremacy,—the party represented at Chicago demands that "*immediate efforts be made for a cessation of hostilities*"—a step which would instantly arrest our conquering armies, and snatch from them the glories of a final triumph; repeal the blockade, and throw the whole rebel frontier open to the supplies they so sorely need; secure the recognition of foreign powers, and either accomplish their independence or give them the ability to fight for it *four* years longer.

We appeal to the People of the United States—lovers of the Union and friends of Freedom—against the consummation of the foul crime against both which the acts and declarations of the Chicago Convention involve. We invoke them not to sanction these principles and sentiments by electing the candidates put forward to represent them. We implore them, as they love their country, as they seek the renewed integrity of its territory, as they desire the peaceful protection of its flag, and the blessings of its free institutions and its equal laws for themselves and their posterity, not to arrest the blow which is just ready to descend upon the rebellion now tottering to its fall; not to give the rebels time to renew their strength for fresh conflicts; not to aid those who would aid them in overthrowing our Government, in destroying our Union, in plunging into a chaos of anarchy the great communities of which the Constitution makes one great and glorious nation, and in thus extinguishing, finally and forever, the hopes of all who have faith in Freedom and the Rights of Man.

We call upon the People to bear in mind that, by whatever sophistries they may cloak their purposes, the Chicago Convention neither condemns the action of the Richmond rebels, nor proposes to expel them against their will, or by any exercise of force, from the seats of power they have usurped. In all essential respects the action that Convention took accords with the results the rebels seek. Both desire a cessation of hostilities.

This "Presidential Election Appeal," dated September 9, 1864, is a fine addition to a collection focusing on the Lincoln-McClellan struggle.

N. Flayderman & Co., Inc.

Lincoln-Related, "We appeal to the people of the U.S...lovers of the Union & friends of freedom against the foul crime (by the Democrats) by their 'Declaration of the Chicago Convention'." Large bold headlines, "THE PRESIDENTIAL ELECTION/APPEAL OF THE NATIONAL UNION COMMITTEE TO THE PEOPLE OF THE U.S." from "Hdqtrs Nat'l Union Committee/NY, Sept. 9, 1864." Age browning, small chips in margin, and tear top center, measures 8" x 10". **425.00**

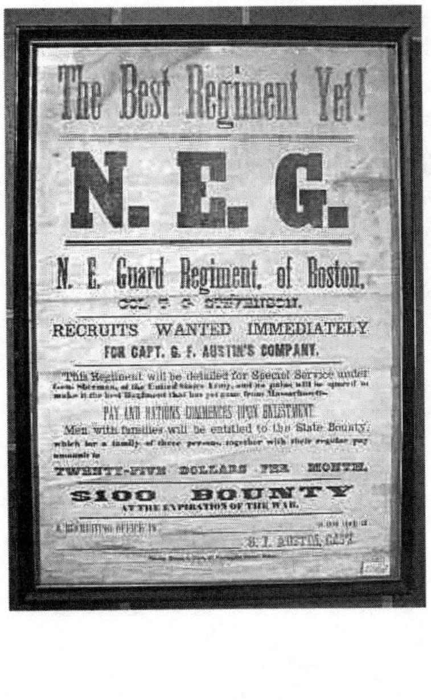

Framed recruiting broadside for the New England Guards.

N. Flayderman & Co., Inc.

New England Guards, superb December 1861 recruiting poster for the New England Guards, measuring 17" x 24". Reads, "THE BEST REGIMENT YET!/Of Boston/Col. T. G. Stevenson/ Recruits wanted immediately for Capt. Austin's company...regiment will be detailed for Special Service under General Sherman and no pains will be spared to make it the best regiment that has yet gone from Mass...pay and rations upon enlistment...men with families entitled to state bounty which for a family of three persons together with their regular pay amounts to . . . 25.00 per month...$100 bounty at expiration of the War." Light aging; minor faint damp staining; all intact; tiny piece out extreme edge of corner (very minor), handsomely framed. . . **1,900.00**

Broadside, calling for recruits for New England recruits is dated, September 12, 1861.

Recruiting, broadside printed in Portland, Maine, on September 21, 1861, measures 12" x 9-1/4" and reads, "ATTENTION VOLUNTEERS Seventy-Five Men must be enrolled at once, for a Company to join one of the New England Regiments of VOLUNTEERS, called for from this State. GOVERNMENT WANTS AND MUST HAVE 150,000 More Men Immediately to bring this WAR TO A CLOSE. This is a favorable opportunity for all intending to reenlist, to join a Good Company. W.W. Deane, Recruiting Officer, Saccarappa, Sept. 12, 1861." Published at Ira Berry & Son, Printers, 177 Fore St., Portland. **819.00**

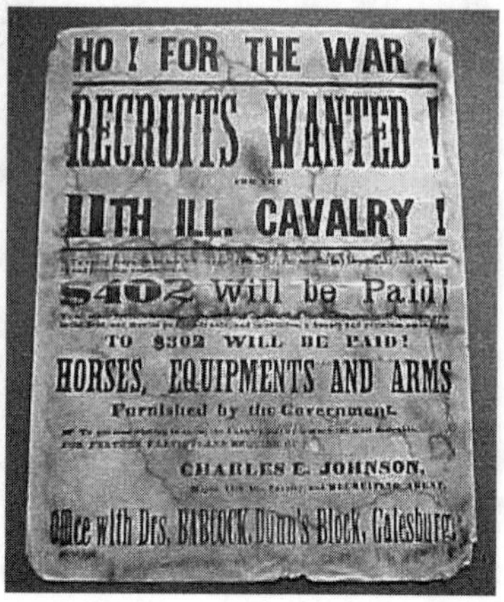

Recruiting for the 11th Illinois Cavalry, this is one of two broadsides that emerged from the rafters of a midwestern building.

Recruiting, Poster 1. "Volunteers wanted" is dated at bottom by Watertown printer: "Watertown, April 20, 1861 Ingalls, Brockway & Beebee, Printers, Reformer Office, Watertown." The poster has "WM. C. BROWNE, Col. Comd'g 35th Regiment." printed at bottom. **Poster 2.** Exact same size and paper thickness, but has been folded at one time. No printer listed and no date. This one is for the 11th Illinois Cavalry. Much more water spotting on this one. Both have torn corner edges. Paper is approx. 1/64" thickness, 10-7/8" x 13-7/8" **637.00**

Union Meeting, 13" x 10" in size matted to 19" x 15". Great appeal with spread-winged eagle at top and large bold type, "UNION MEETING." States that the meeting will be held "at Saranac Village Thursday Evening 29th Inst. Hon J S Adams of Burlington Vt., Geo L Clark, and other speakers will be present." **475.00**

Envelope

Connecticut, state seal, fine condition. **20.00**

Florida, "Florida Secession" and eagle on front, fine condition. **95.00**

Georgia, state seal on the front, fine condition. . . **45.00**

Missouri, state seal on the front, very-fine condition. **95.00**

Patriotic, picture of a Zouave soldier holding an American flag and sword while trampling on the Confederate Stars and Bars flag. Printed in blue and red ink. **35.00**

Virginia, state seal on the front, fine condition. . . **65.00**

Map, North Carolina, used by Major Leyden, 3rd New York Volunteer Cavalry. The colored map measures roughly 18" x 18". Printed at the top is "Colton's North Carolina" and the map shows all the railroad lines, common roads, canals, and cities. Inscribed in tiny brown ink script along the top edge of the reverse side is "New Bern, North Carolina June 1862." **350.00**

Memorial, Soldiers', 137th Regiment New York Volunteer Infantry, very colorful roster of soldiers from Broom County, New York, lithographed by Ehrgott, Forbinger & Co. in 1863. Nicely matted in old wood frame, 19" x 25". The paper has some light water stains, condition is very good. **125.00**

Newspaper

Boston (November 10, 1862), removal of Union General McClellan, very-good condition. **15.00**

Boston (November 28, 1863), advance of General Meade. **15.00**

***Boston Daily Journal* (July 23, 1864),** occupation of Atlanta, very-good condition. **15.00**

Intelligen

PRIL 17, 1865.

FROM SATURDAY'S EDITIONS.

SECOND EDITION.

THE PRESIDENT IS DEAD!

With profound sorrow, we announce the death, by the hands of an assassin, of the President of the United States. He expired this morning at 30 minutes past 7 o'clock.

In the agony of grief into which we are plunged by this horrible tragedy, we feel the inadequacy of words to express the deep and saddening emotions of the heart. As we write, the murky clouds above and the rain-drops falling around us—as if the very Heavens wept over the dark and bloody deed—are emblematic of the gloom and tears of the popular heart.

God grant that our People, thus sorely afflicted, may bear, with Christian fortitude, this great calamity, that our beloved Country may triumph over the machinations of her enemies; that our glorious Union may outlive the storms that beset it; that our noble form of Government may forever endure; and that peace, prosperity, and happiness may again visit our stricken land.

Announcing the death of President Lincoln, this second edition of the *Daily National Intelligencer* is dated Monday, April 17, 1865.

N. Flayderman & Co., Inc.

Daily National Intelligencer (April 17, 1865) "From Saturday's Edition's/Second Edition/The President Is Dead!" Very bold headline on front-page, huge headlines inside as well; almost entire edition devoted to the tragic event and those that followed. Light aging; some brown spotting; overall exc.; tattered blank right margin; all readable. **400.00**

New Orleans (May, 19 1863), lots of war news. . . .**50.00**

NEWBURYPORT HERALD.

EXTRA.

SATURDAY EVENING, APRIL 13, 1861; 10 O'CLOCK.

THE WAR BEGUN!

LATEST FROM CHARLESTON

BOMBARDMENT OF FORT SUMTER!

APPARENT SIGNALS OF DISTRESS!

FEDERAL FLAG AT HALF-MAST.

EXPLOSION Of Maj. Anderson's Batteries

Barracks of Fort Sumter in flames!

SURRENDER OF FORT SUMTER.

This framed copy of the April 13, 1861, issue of the *Newburyport Herald* proclaims the bombing of Fort Sumter by boldly broadcasting, "The War has Begun!"

J.C. Devine Inc.

***Newburyport Herald* (April 13, 1861),** "An Extra Edition For Saturday Evening, April 13, 1861; 10 o'clock.The headlines read, "THE WAR BEGUN!/ LATEST FROM CHARLESTON/ BOMBARDMENT/OF FORT SUMTER!" Measures 8-1/2" x 12-1/2", ink stained on the upper right corner, otherwise very good condition with very good account of the opening battle of the Civil War, framed copy.". **150.00**

Daily Morni

VOLUME III. WASHINGTON, MONDAY

SHERMAN.

THE ORDER HE ISSUED TO HIS ARMY

SUSPENSION OF HOSTILITIES ANNOUNCED.

MEMBERS OF THE N. C. LEGISLATURE AT NEWBERN.

Movements of Lieutenant General Grant.

THE NATIONAL SORROW.

MEMORABLE DAYS IN PHILADELPHIA.

The Remains of the Late President in Independence Hall.

200,000 PERSONS BEHOLD THEM

IMPRESSIVE SCENES AND INCIDENTS.

Tasteful Mourning Drapery Throughout the City.

BOOTH.

THE ASSASSIN REPORTED WOUNDED.

IN HIS FLIGHT HE FRACTURES A LEG.

HIS FACE DIVESTED OF A MOUSTACHE.

PIRACY ON THE LAKES.

ANOTHER SCHEME FRUSTRATED.

ONE OF THE TORONTO COUNCIL IMPLICATED.

Published the morning after President Lincoln was shot, this issue of the *Sunday Morning Chronicle*, dated April 16, 1865, included an engraving of Lincoln, along with the black-bordered details of the assassination.

N. Flayderman & Co., Inc.

Sunday Morning Chronicle (April 16, 1865), "THE ASSASSINATION OF THE PRESIDENT/THE TERRIBLE DETAILS/WHEN, WHERE, HOW THE DEED WAS DONE/THE ROOM IN WHICH THE PRESIDENT DIED," all in very large bold headlines front page single sheet; two pages; two minor holes center columns (general info) light aging. **325.00**

Sheet Music

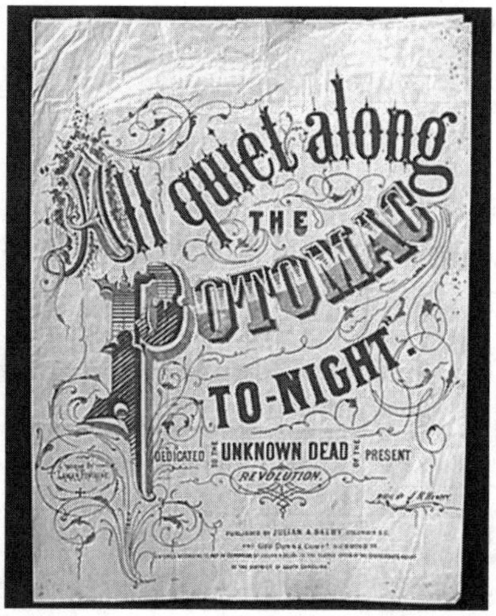

Published in Richmond, Virginia, this piece of sheet music entitled, *All Quiet Along the Potomac Tonight* tells the mournful tale of a Confederate soldier who was thinking about his wife moments before being killed while on picket duty. Truly Southern, wartime sheet music is quite desirable.

Dale C. Anderson Co.

All Quiet Along the Potomac To-night. "Dedicated to the unknown dead of the present revolution. Published by Julian Selby, Columbia, S.C. and Geo. Dunn & Co., Richmond and so marked. Copyright in clerk's office of the Confederate Court, District of South Carolina." Clean, thin paper printed in dark blue, 9" x 11-3/4", single fold, with four sides. Words and music inside, terribly maudlin words about a picket on the Potomac dreaming of wife and home, suddenly shot. Excellent condition, some fly specks on edge.. . . . . **225.00**

Funeral March Dedicated to the Memory of Abraham Lincoln. "By/Bvt. Major General J.C. Barnard/ Played at the obsequies of the late/President of the United States/by the/U.S. Marine Band." Published by Wm. A. Pond, N.Y. Fine condition, dated 1865. . . . . **175.00**

Rally Cry of Freedom. These were issued as advertising for sheet music, and produced a marvelously handsome item. The entire face of a folded piece of letter paper is printed in red, white, and blue, giving all the words to "The Rally Cry of Freedom," surrounded by pillars supporting an arch, enclosing a battle scene, a panoply of flags, rampant eagle, and soldiers standing guard, 5" x 8", mint condition. **95.00**

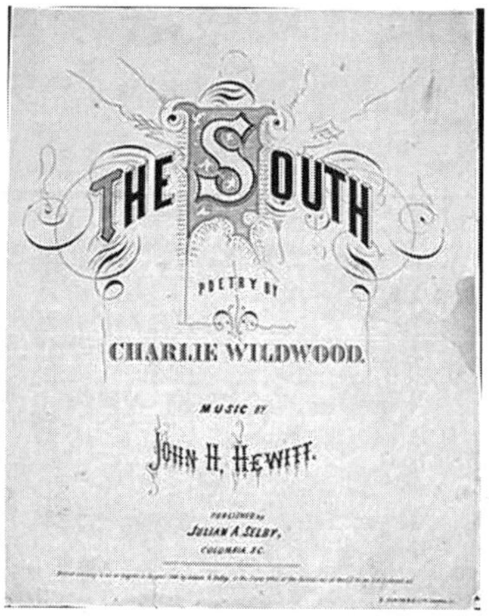

This patriotically titled piece of sheet music, *The South, is* dated 1863, and was published in Columbia, South Carolina.

Dale C. Anderson Co.

The South, dated 1863, published by Julian Shelby of Columbia, S.C. Ornately lettered cover, black on cream-colored paper 9-1/2" x 12". Stirring words: "Like swarms of foul demons, his minions come down, and their war-rusted weapons unsultingly [sic] frown; to fright thy fair fields with their bloody alarms, and rob the, dear land of all of thy charms. The tyrant with shackles would manacle thee, would strangle thy spirit, dear land of the free..." Very good overall. Few tears on the edge. Old excellent repair on the right edge that doesn't touch print. **195.00**

Seemingly prophetic, *Wait till the War, Love, Is Over,* was published in Richmond, Virginia during 1864.

Dale C. Anderson Co.

Wait till the War, Love, Is Over. Published by West & Johnston, Richmond, Virginia. 1864 copyright in the District Court of the Confederate States, 9-5/8" x 12". Single fold giving four sides, very light off-white/beige with pale foxing (light brownish age spotting), deep maroon print. Words and music inside, excellent. **225.00**

Manuscript-Related

Commission

7th Regiment Pennsylvania Reserve Corps, official 14" x 18" printed document naming Joseph G. Holmes First Lieutenant of Company I, 7th Regiment of the Pennsylvania Reserve Corps. Dated September 25, 1861, and signed by Eli Slifin, Secretary of the Commonwealth. Yellow state official seal at the top. Slight tears at folds, but framed and displayed very nicely. **150.00**

Officer's commissions can often be worth more than what one might think. Ordinarily this commission for a hospital chaplain might not be considered too desirable. A medical collector might be vaguely interest, but because the chaplain did not have combat or regimental affiliations, this commission might go unnoticed. But when a collector paid $4,500.00 for it on an online auction, he knew exactly what he was buying: The chaplain's commission was signed by both Secretary of War Edwin Stanton and Abraham Lincoln!

Hospital Chaplin, document that commissioned James Tuttle Smith to Hospital Chaplain on March 20, 1863. "Signed by his own hand, Abraham Lincoln, President of the United States, and by his own hand, Cabinet Member, Secretary of War, Edwin M. Stanton." The overall size of this document is 16" x 20". Excellent condition, Lincoln's signature is very clear and a bit lighter than Stanton's bold, crisp signature. **4,500.00**

108th Illinois Volunteer Infantry, three service documents of Mr. Albert Attebery. He served in the 108th Illinois Volunteers. The 108th saw service and much bloody action in Sherman's Yazoo expedition, Vicksburg & Corinth, Mississippi, Champion Hill, Black River & Memphis Tennessee to name a few. **Document #1** is Mr. Attebery's promotion to corporal. **Document #2** is Mr. Attebery's promotion to sergeant. **Document #3** is Mr. Attebery's commission to first lieutenant of Company K. Signed by Richard Yates, Governor of Illinois on October 26, 1864. . . . . **785.00**

12th Missouri State Militia Cavalry, standard federal eagle masthead, NCO commission appointing Joseph Mattingly 1st corporal in Company F, 12th Missouri State Militia Cavalry. Dated at Jackson, Missouri, February 9, 1863, and signed by "B.F. Lazean Lt. Col 12th MSM Cav.," fine condition. **125.00**

130th Ohio Militia, a fine and vivid war-date document with fantastic screaming eagle masthead at the top (very large and ferocious) and signed at the bottom by Ohio Governor, David Tod. This commission is filled out in brown ink and appoints George Carson as a lieutenant in the 1st Ohio Militia. This unit would become the 130th Regiment Ohio Volunteer Infantry one year later in 1864. This document is signed and dated August 4th 1863, measures roughly 10" x 12", excellent condition, small stain on the right side. **135.00**

"I met Capt. John R. Dickens who was raising a company for the war. He said he wanted one hundred picked men ready to go at a minute's warning. I gave him my name and there became a member of the 'Sardis Blues'."

— Robert Joseph Walker Matthews
12th Mississippi Volunteers

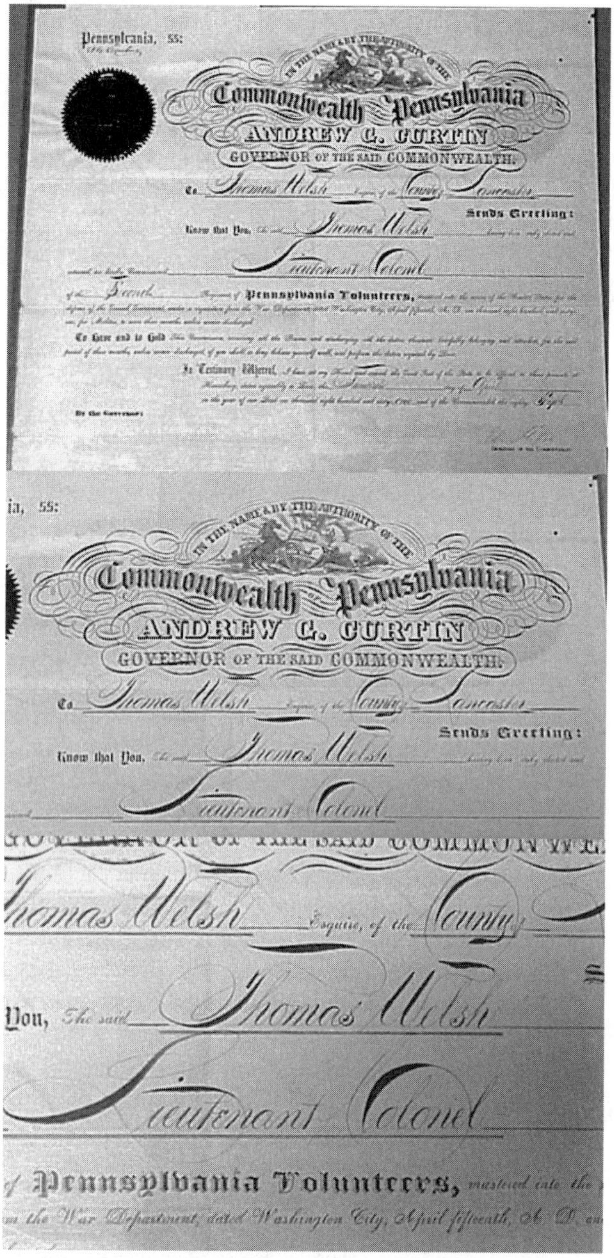

2nd Pennsylvania Volunteer Infantry, promotion of Thomas Welsh of Lancaster County to lieutenant colonel, signed by Andrew G. Curtin, April 20, 1861. Welsh served during the War with Mexico, and for gallant conduct in the battle of Buena Vista was promoted to lieutenant. At the commencement of the Civil War, he entered the service and was commissioned in the 2nd Pennsylvania Infantry. He was later promoted to colonel of the 45th Pennsylvania Infantry and went on to become brigadier general of volunteers. General Welsh died at Cincinnati, Ohio on August 14, 1863, of congestive fever acquired during the campaign in Mississippi. **650.00**

Thomas Welsh served in the Mexican War, and with this commission, was made a lieutenant colonel of the 2nd Pennsylvania Infantry in 1861. He went on to command a regiment and was subsequently made a brigadier general. All of these factors—prewar service and subsequent military promotions all contribute to the value of a commission. This 1861 document appoints Welsh a lieutenant colonel.

Sharpsburg Arsenal

4th Arkansas African Regiment, 8" x 10" pre-printed document notifying Charles Norton of the 4th Arkansas African Regiment that the president has appointed him a captain. Signed by General Lorenzo Thomas, August 1, 1863. . . . . **65.00**

Diary

10th Regiment, United States Colored Troops, plain paper, 48 pages and stiff paper covers. Belonged to Captain George Torrey of the 10th U.S.C.T., and signed by him. Also several other signatures. Lists the enlisted men in his command and other info for 1863, written in brown ink. **325.00**

All of the value of a diary lies in its content. First, it must be readable. Non-English language diaries that are not translated generally do not sell for the same price of a comparable English language diary. Second, unit affiliation is crucial. A railroad-guarding private's diary from the one hundred and something infantry is not going to be worth a fraction of a diary written by a soldier in the Stonewall Brigade. And finally, content is the final factor contributing in a large worth to value. If a diary simply chronicles the weather and distances marched, the reading becomes dull. On the other hand, a diary filled with vivid battle accounts or engaging anecdotes about camp life will bring top dollar.

120th Ohio Volunteer Infantry, this diary is for the year of 1864, the year rebel forces captured most of the 120th. Simon M. Bott enlisted when 29 years old on August 15, 1862, as a private. On October 14, 1862, he mustered into Company E, 120th Ohio Infantry. Diary covers are loose, as are many pages, all but 10 days are there; shows the wear of being in a soldier's pocket. 5" x 3-1/2" inscribed, "Simon M. Bott, Company E 120 Regt Ohio." Commercially made diary with oilcloth covers; first page reads, "Daily Pocket Remembrances of 1864, For the Trade." The daily entries begin January 1 and has 176 days with entries. There are some additional entries that he apparently put in 1866 through 1869, but the 176 entries are while he was still in the 120th Ohio. **1,026.00**

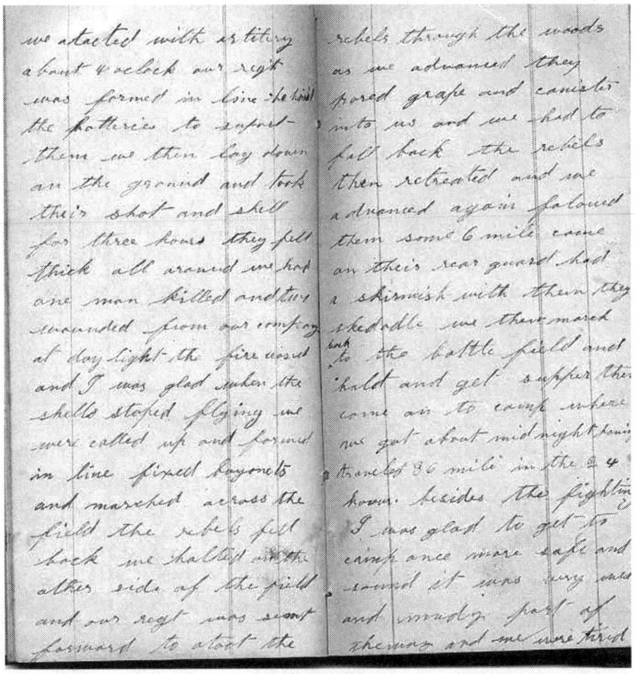

we atacted with artilery about 4 oclock our regt was formed in line to hoist the batteries to support them we then lay down on the ground and took their shot and shell for three hours they fell thick all around we had one man killed and two wounded from our company at day light the fire ceased and I was glad when the shells stoped flying we were called up and formed in line fixed bayonets and marched across the field the rebels fell back we halted on the other side of the field and our regt was sent forward to atact the

rebels through the woods as we advanced they pored grape and canister into us and we had to fall back the rebels then retreated and we advanced again folowed them some 6 mile came on their rear guard had a skirmish with them they skedaddle we then marched to the battle field and halt and get supper then come on to camp where we got about mid night having traveled 36 mile in the 24 hours besides the fightin I was glad to get to camp once more safe and sound it was very cold and muddy part of the way and we were tired

Written by a member of the 1st New York Dragoons, this three-volume diary recounted the soldier life of Sergeant V.M. Babbitt. The pages were filled with battle accounts, stories about his buddies, and the exploits of this very unique outfit that began as the 130th New York Infantry.

1st New York Dragoons, three really nice Civil War diaries from a soldier in the 1st New York Dragoons (which started out as the 130th NYVI, then became the 19th New York Cavalry and finally, the 1st NY Dragoons) and other related items. The diaries are typical, black-covered (about 3" x 6") booklets. They all belonged to Sgt. Vernon M. Babbitt, who lived in Allegany County, New York. These diaries were on loan to Alfred University, as Babbitt was an 1871 graduate. Diary #1 covers August 14, 1862, until November 13, 1863. The diary is very legible and the daily entries are in ink. Inside the front cover is "Sergt. V.M. Babbitt's Book Co. H 1st N.Y. Dragoons." This diary is unlined and was apparently a blank pocket ledger. Included are 67 typed pages transcribed of this first book. The following entry is the continuation of the Jan 30, 1863, entry about the Deserted House, Virginia battle, in which the 1st NY Dragoons had an officer and six men killed and two officers and 18 men wounded, plus two captured: "We came on the rebel camp which we atacted [sic] with artilery [sic]. About 4 o'clock our reg't. was formed in line. We hoist the batteries to support them. We then lay down on the ground and took their shot and shell for three hours. They fell thick all around. We had one man killed and two wounded from our company. At daylight, the fire ceased and I was glad when the shells stoped [sic] flying. We were called up and formed in line, fixed bayonets and marched across the field. The rebels fell back...As we advanced, they pored (sic) grape and canister into us and we fell back. Diary #2 is the same style blank ledger booklet and covers January 1, 1864, to December 31, 1864. A few pages at the back are blank. Good battle content continues Diary #3 is a commercial "Diary for 1865" produced by William Perry, Manufacturing Stationer of Philadelphia. Again, some wonderful entries including the surrender at Appomattox. Each diary has Babbitt's name and unit in the front. Diary #3 covers the whole year and appears to have an entry for every date. It also has miscellaneous entries in the back such as "Captured by the rebs on March the 5th, 2 horses, 2 saddles, 2 blankets, 2 bridles, 2 holsters, 1 carbine." There are a few pages loose in this diary and all three show normal wear and minor age discoloration. The lot also includes his GAR calling card, a funeral card, a photo of him with his wife, plus original obituaries from the paper, a funeral card, several other minor related items and the Alfred University research on Babbitt and his family. **3,167.00**

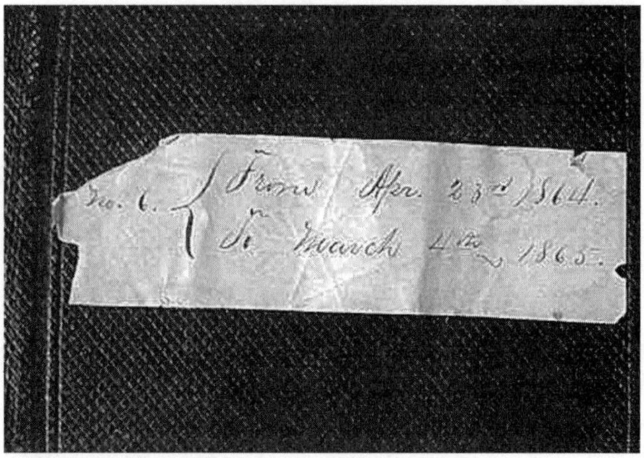

More than 100 pages are filled in this diary written by a soldier in the 25th Massachusetts Infantry.

25th Massachusetts Volunteer Infantry, museum quality, Civil War soldier's handwritten diary with entries dating between April 23, 1864, and March 4, 1865. The diary's writer is unidentified, but the entries are specific with names and battle locations. From that, it has been determined to have belonged to an enlisted soldier from the 25th Massachusetts Regiment of Infantry. The diary is 6.5" x 4" and has 100+ pages completely filled with sepia-toned hand-written entries. The writer took great effort to record all aspects of his war experience—the weather, the food consumed, the military details of important battles at Drury's Point, the Siege of Richmond, the gruesome details of the diphtheria epidemic that killed many of his fellow soldiers and the frolicsome activities of a young man intent upon continuing his religious studies and entertaining young ladies during off-hours.................... **2,750.00**

33rd Missouri Infantry, written in German by a member of the 33rd Missouri, kept from August 2, 1862, to August 12, 1865, includes translation. **950.00**

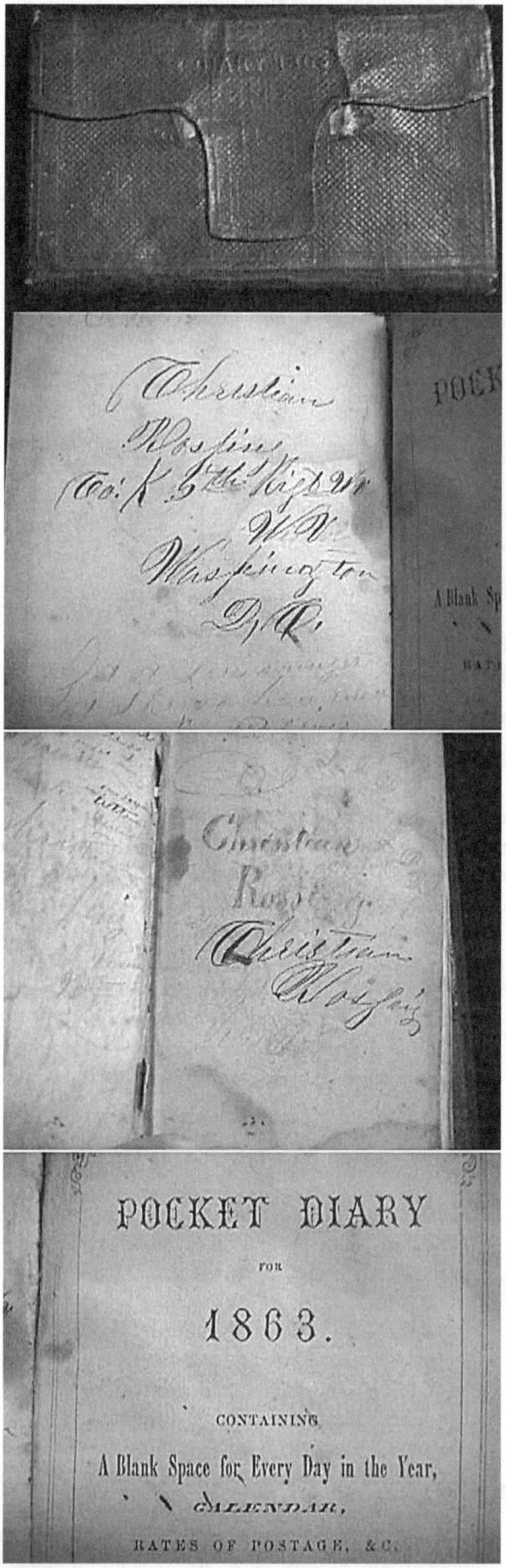

Though it is entirely written in German, this diary kept by a member of the 5th Wisconsin Infantry of the Sixth Corps famous "Light Brigade" did include a full translation.

5th Wisconsin Volunteer Infantry, very nice diary of Christian Rossings, Company K, 5th Wisconsin from January 1, 1863, through August 1863. Diary is written in untranslated German, comes with records. **1,300.00**

8th Regiment United States Colored Troops, kept by William P. Woodlin, Musician of the 8th Regt. U.S.C.T. 2nd Brigade, Army of the James, begins in November 1863, and ends on October 31, 1864. .... **2,200.00**

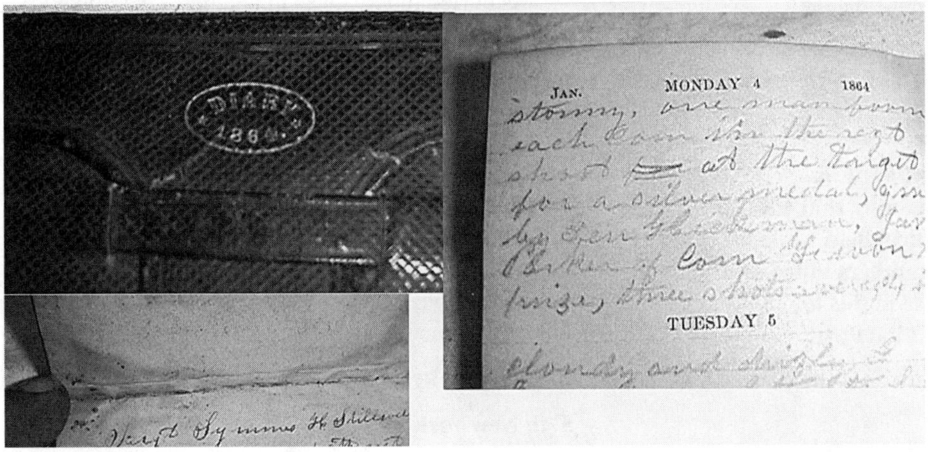

Although Symmes Stillwell alludes to some interesting occurrences during his service in the 9th New Jersey Infantry, his entries were short and not too detailed. Nevertheless, an online bidder paid $975.00 to acquire the original diary.

9th New Jersey Volunteer Infantry, diary written by Symmes H. Stillwell. First page reads, "Symmes H. Stillwell book Company A 9th Regiment New Jersey Volunteers Nearby Fort Monroe Encamped at Newport News, Virginia Jan 18, 1863." First entry is dated January 1, 1864. Some entries made in diary as follows: "April 12, 1864 execution of private Cumbton reprieved by President; April 28, 1864, files ordered to be destroyed; May 2, 1864, Sgt of Guard at Hosp; March 3, 1864, Alfred Nutt killed along Dismal Swamp Canal and left in the rebel hands. Armed forces got his body. The rebs had stripped him of all his clothes except drawers, shirt & stockings. Rebels laid in ambush & shot him." The diary also has names of men killed, wounded, and taken prisoner. **975.00**

Independent Battery of New York Volunteers, small pocketsize paper notebook inscribed on front cover "Independent Battery/NY Vols/Notes Book/1863." Inside are names and comments, also included is an old scrapbook with some notes from 1861. .... **35.00**

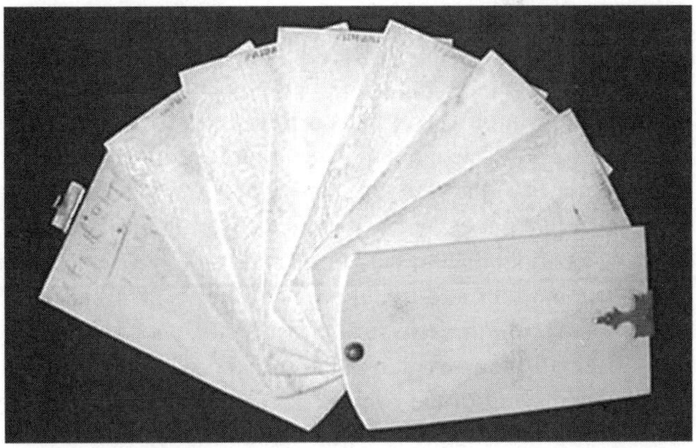

Victorian ivory day planners have long been acquired by Civil War collectors as the type of diary a soldier might carry. As such, they were only useful as daily reminders, because at the end of a week, the owner would have to erase what he wrote to begin the new week.

Dale C. Anderson Co.

Ivory, an all ivory pocket notepad of distinct design. Basically, a flat rectangular pack of thin ivory sheets, pinned at the base so they hinged out like a hand of cards. Has front and back covers of ivory and six pages, each headed with the day of the week except Sunday. Has a small decorative clasp at top, fine condition, 2" x 3-5/8". **195.00**

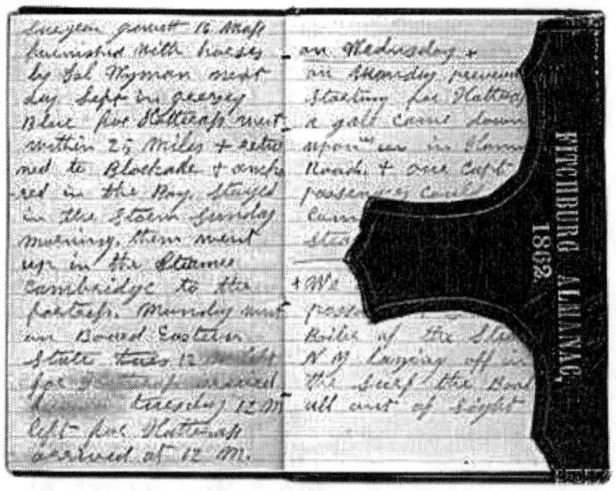

Belonging to a person simply identified as "E.K. Hewett," this log was sold on the probability that Hewett was somehow connected with the medical field while in the service. Though he recorded the numbers killed and wounded over time, there was little else in this log to associate him with field service or hospital duty.

Surgeon, this 1862 diary/booklet belonged to "E. G. Hewett" who may have been a doctor. The beginning of the booklet starts with two pages of handwritten names of soldiers along with their regiment and the date of their death (all in February and March 1862). This is followed with the notation "52K 222 wounded." Then there are five additional pages of names, apparently soldiers. Following this is five pages of diary entries covering a trip to Roanoke Island via Fortress Monroe. There are then some four additional pages of diary entries also covering this trip further back in the booklet, and finally four written pages in the back containing some additional names, etc. The diary entries for the trip to Roanoke indicate that the writer was apparently making the trip to exhume a soldier's body: "Went to the battlefield on Roanoke Island N.C. disinterred Randal Man to remove his body home." This small, diary-style book is titled *The Fitchburg Almanac Directory and Business Advertiser for 1862* (Fitchburg, MA: R. Wallace & Co., 1862). It measures approximately 3" x 6" with a pocket at the rear and a flap on the back cover wraps around to the front some 170 pages in length (approximately 20 pages have the above-mentioned handwritten notations). It is made of leather or leatherette over cardboard, and is embossed with gilt lettering. **385.00**

Union Infantryman, small pocket diary of John Adams who enlisted at Leavenworth on December 1, 1861, missing one side of its leather cover. Wartime entries are written from both sides of the book with the center functioning as a ledger used up until 1868.There are about 34 wartime pages, most with accounts of activities. The entries mention Springfield, Missouri, the movements of the army through Arkansas including Roseville, Clarksville, and Fort Smith. Skirmishes with "Bushwhackers" and a larger confrontation on April 4, 1864, are mentioned. Most entries are in pencil and some pages are difficult to read. Sample entry: "Mar 22 1864: John E Brooks of D co. died last night and was buried today. I was in charge of the funeral escort we buried him with the honors of war that is due to every soldier and the last tribute that we can give the dead." **809.00**

Discharge

139th Pennsylvania Volunteer Infantry, Private John Uplinger of Company B, 139th Pennsylvania Infantry was born in Pennsylvania and was of "dark complexion, gray eyes and dark hair," has bounty, and pension surcharge is stamped. **200.00**

27th Kentucky Infantry, William Lockwood. ... **65.00**

57th New York Volunteers and 7th Veteran Reserve Corps, two standard eagle masthead papers for same soldier, Hugh O'Connell, plus a pension paper, one is excellent condition from the 7th VRC, other is lightly worn from 57th New York. **110.00**

8th New Jersey Volunteer Infantry, given to Private John B. Engle of Company G, 8th New Jersey Volunteers. Engles was a farmer who was mustered in at Trenton, New Jersey. He was discharged on a surgeon's certificate of disability in May 1862.. **95.00**

115th New York Volunteer Infantry, made out for James Fielding (African-American) from Company H, 115th New York Infantry and dated 1864 when he re-enlisted in the U.S. Navy, in excellent condition. **75.00**

Document

104th Pennsylvania Volunteer Infantry, a large ink furlough filled out for Sergeant John S. Hartley, 104th Regiment, Pennsylvania Volunteers, granting him leave for late February and early March 1862. Signed and issued by a captain in his company and dated February 26, 1862. The back is endorsed and autographed by Colonel Davis, 104th Pennsylvania, as well as what appears to be Brigadier General Silas Casey. **100.00**

115th Regiment, United States Colored Troops, List of Stores No. 45, received from the Assistant Quartermaster at Indianola, Texas, by Lieut. Stephen P. Jocelyn of the 115th U.S.C.T. **50.00**

124th Regiment, United States Colored Troops, pay voucher issued to "Capt. A.R. Mills, 124 U.S.C.T." in June 1865. An 11" x 17" printed document, filled out in browned ink. **65.00**

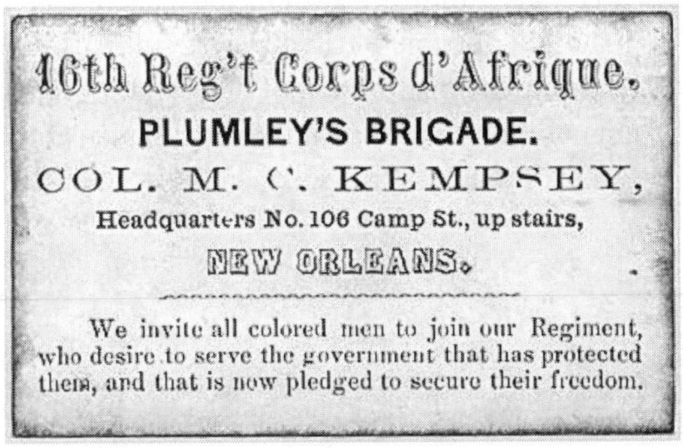
16th Reg't Corps d'Afrique.
PLUMLEY'S BRIGADE.
COL. M. C. KEMPSEY,
Headquarters No. 106 Camp St., up stairs,
NEW ORLEANS.
We invite all colored men to join our Regiment, who desire to serve the government that has protected them, and that is now pledged to secure their freedom.

Ever since the movie *Glory* appeared, anything associated with African-American troops in the Civil War have become extremely popular. This recruiting card for 16th Regiment, Corps d'Afrique was no exception.

16th Regiment Corps d' Afrique, recruiting card that reads,"16th Reg't Corps d' Afrique. Plumley's Brigade. Col. M. C. Kempsey, Headquarters No. 106 Camp St., upstairs, New Orleans. We invite all colored men to join our Regiment, who desire to serve the government that has protected them, and that is now pledged to secure their freedom." Measures 3-1/2" x 2-1/4", and imprinted on shiny card stock. Very small glue stain on the reverse and slight foxing on the edges of the stock, otherwise in outstanding condition. **650.00**

17th Massachusetts Volunteer Infantry, 1863 appointment of Soloman Martin to corporal in the 17th Massachusetts Volunteer Infantry. Includes his carte de visite photo in civilian clothes. **85.00**

1st Cavalry Corps, manuscript ink on 8" x 3" slip of paper from Mossy Creek, for 1,450 pounds of beef for use by the 2nd Brigade, 1st Cavalry Corps, signed "Thos A Bates, Butcher." **12.00**

1st Pennsylvania Rifles, furlough that looks like a discharge paper with the masthead of "To All Whom It May Concern" but is printed with furlough data instead of discharge data. It is for a soldier in the 1st Pennsylvania Rifles, giving him permission to take a furlough to Mansfield, Pennsylvania, from December 16, 1864, to January 15, 1865. Issued at Camp Parole, Maryland (he must have been an exchanged POW), and signed by "Col. A.R. Root 94th NVY." Has some old tape repairs to the folds and a couple minor separations but very solid, very legible. **75.00**

1st Regiment U.S. Artillery, final statement of Pvt. James Ahern, a member of Company L, lst Regiment of U.S. Artillery, was born in Cork, Ireland, and enlisted at Boston. He entered for five years in 1860 and discharged to reenlist on 1864. .... **50.00**

29th Alabama Volunteer Infantry, list of goods at quartermaster's stores Captain Watts (CS Army Quartermaster), 29th Alabama Regiment, Atlanta-Georgia, 1864, fine condition. **85.00**

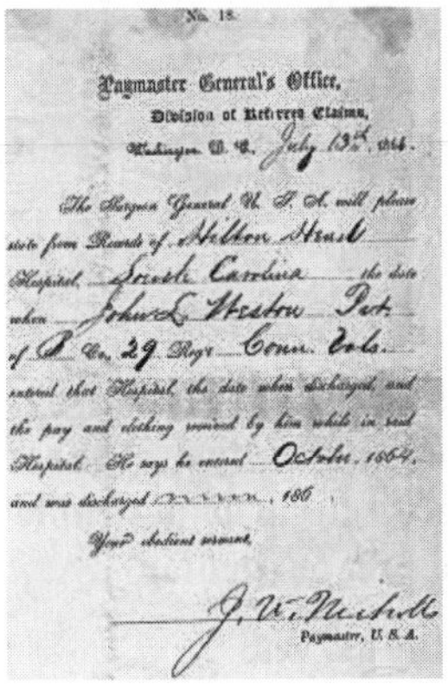
Paymaster General's Office,
Division of Referred Claims,
Washington, D. C., July 13th 18
The Surgeon General U. S. A. will please state from Records of Hilton Head Hospital, South Carolina the date when John L. Weston Pvt. of B Co. 29 Regt. Conn. Vols. entered that Hospital, the date when discharged, and the pay and clothing received by him while in said Hospital. He says he entered October 1864, and was discharged , 186 .
Your obedient servant,
J. W. Nicholls
Paymaster, U. S. A.

Official documents are collected more for the units represented than the information they contain. This communication was issued by a paymaster and a hospital surgeon for a soldier in Connecticut's only African-American unit, the 29th Volunteer Infantry.

Frohne's Historic Military

29th Connecticut Volunteer Infantry, document for Private John L. Weston of Company B, dated July 13, 1866, and signed at Hilton Head Hospital by J.W. Nicholls, Paymaster, and on the back by Surgeon Charles Page. Great Hospital imprints attached on back of document, rare to find anything to do with Connecticut's only Negro regiment. **29.00**

2nd Virginia Volunteer Cavalry, 10" x 23-1/2" muster roll, printed and filled in with ink, with typical tape reinforcing on the folds. This one is for the officers and staff. **55.00**

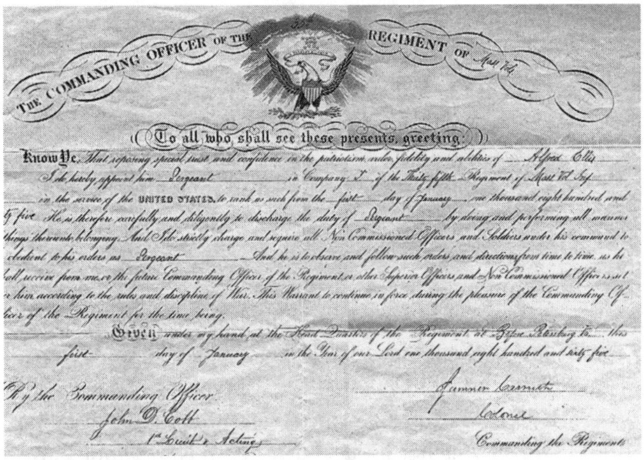
The Commanding Officer of the Regiment of Mass. Vol.
To all who shall see these presents, greeting:
Know Ye, That reposing special trust and confidence in the patriotism, valor, fidelity and abilities of Alfred Ellis I do hereby appoint him Sergeant in Company I of the Thirty fifth Regiment of Mass. Vol. Inf. in the service of the UNITED STATES, to rank as such from the first day of January one thousand eight hundred and sixty five. He is therefore carefully and diligently to discharge the duty of Sergeant by doing and performing all manner of things thereunto belonging. And I do strictly charge and require all Non Commissioned Officers and Soldiers under his command to be obedient to his orders as Sergeant. And he is to observe and follow such orders and directions from time to time, as he shall receive from me, or the future Commanding Officer of the Regiment, or other Superior Officers and Non Commissioned Officers set over him, according to the rules and discipline of War. This Warrant to continue in force during the pleasure of the Commanding Officer of the Regiment for the time being.
Given under my hand, at the Head Quarters of the Regiment at this first day of January in the Year of our Lord one thousand eight hundred and sixty five.
By the Commanding Officer
John D. Cobb
1st Lieut. & Acting
Sumner Carruth
Colonel
Commanding the Regiment

This document conveyed the promotion to sergeant onto Alfred Ellis of the 35th Massachusetts Infantry. It was signed by his lieutenant and the unit's colonel.

35th Massachusetts Volunteer Infantry, promotion for "Alfred Ellis, 35th Ma. Infantry promoted to Sergeant as of January 1, 1865." Promotion is signed by "John D. Cobb, 1st Lt. 35th Mass." and by Colonel Sumner Carruth. **275.00**

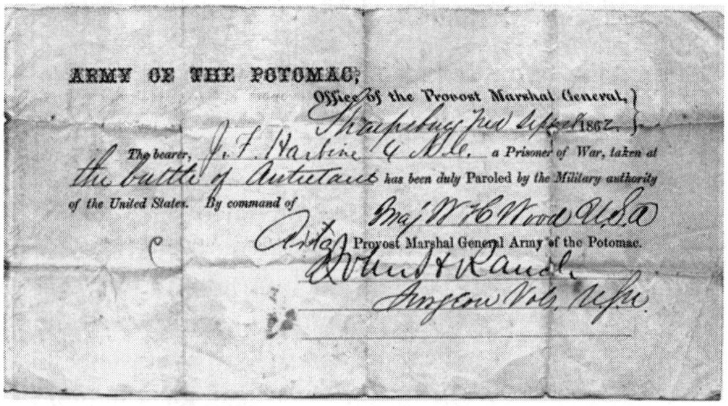
ARMY OF THE POTOMAC,
Office of the Provost Marshal General,
Sharpsburg Md Sept 28 1862.
The bearer, J. F. Harbine 4 N.C. a Prisoner of War, taken at the battle of Antietam has been duly Paroled by the Military authority of the United States. By command of
Maj W H Wood U.S.A.
Provost Marshal General Army of the Potomac.
John H Rauch
Surgeon Vols. USA

This parole was given to a soldier from the 4th North Carolina Troops after his wounding and capture at the Battle of Antietam. Such paroles are extremely desirable for the information they reveal about a particular soldier.

Sharpsburg Arsenal

4th North Carolina Troops, Antietam parole of North Carolina Private. James F. Harbine, 4th NCT dated, "Sharpsburg, Md. Sept. 28, 1862" and signed by John H. Rauch, Surgeon, Volunteers, USA. Harbine enlisted on February 2, 1862, at Iredell County, North Carolina, as a Private and was mustered into Company C. Harbine is listed as, "wounded (left cheek), captured and paroled—Sharpsburg, Maryland. He later rejoined his company and was wounded again at Chancellorsville, Virginia, which resulted in amputation of his right arm. Harbine retired to the Invalid Corps on December 12, 1864, by reason of total disability." **5,895.00**

57th Indiana Volunteer Infantry, muster roll for Company B, for the period of December 31, 1864, to February, 28, 1865, Captain Thomas D. Ridge, commanding. Names and information of 78 soldiers on place of enlistment, home, battles and service, death, taken prisoner, disease and other info. The 57th Indiana were involved in numerous bloody battles such as Corinth, Shiloh, Franklin, Perryville, Nashville, Stone's River, Chickamauga, Chattanooga, Atlanta, and Dalton, 31" x 21". **158.00**

5th New Hampshire Volunteer Infantry, 1862-dated travel voucher for a soldier in 5th New Hampshire allowing him $53.72 to travel from Virginia to New Hampshire upon discharge. **70.00**

5th New Hampshire Volunteer Infantry, general orders instructing the regiment to proceed to Washington, D.C., on October 26, 1862. .... **110.00**

60th New York Veteran Volunteer Infantry, enlistment document of Charles Waymouth dated February 20, 1864. He signed up in Alabama, nicely matted and framed ready to hang. **75.00**

63rd Illinois Volunteer Infantry, dated May 1862, this document is for muskets, bayonets, cartridge boxes, belts, and belt plates. It was issued to Colonel J. B. McCown of the 63rd Illinois Infantry. **45.00**

63rd Illinois Volunteer Infantry, excellent condition, 10" x 15" document dated December 31, 1863, outlining the distribution of thousands of rounds of ammunition issued to various companies of the 63rd Illinois Infantry. **45.00**

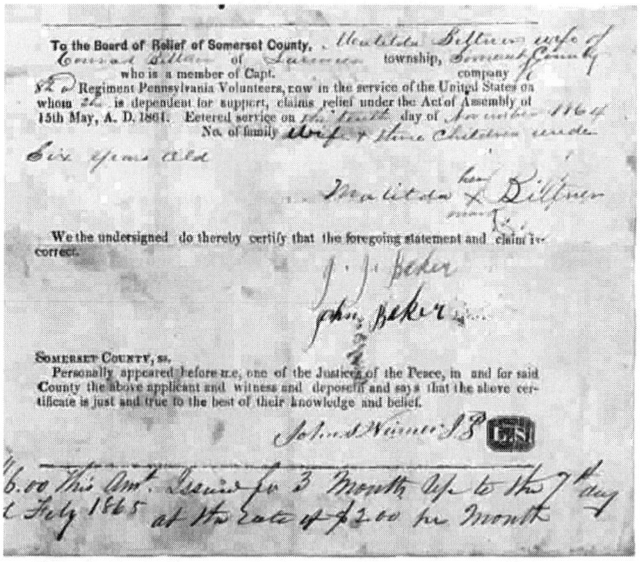
To the Board of Relief of Somerset County, Matilda Biltner wife of Conrad Biltner of township, Somerset County who is a member of Capt. company 82 Regiment Pennsylvania Volunteers, now in the service of the United States on whom she is dependent for support, claims relief under the Act of Assembly of 15th May, A. D. 1861. Entered service on the day of November 1864. No. of family Wife & three Children under six years old
Matilda her mark Biltner
We the undersigned do thereby certify that the foregoing statement and claim is correct.
J. J. Beker
John Beker
Somerset County, ss.
Personally appeared before me, one of the Justices of the Peace, in and for said County the above applicant and witness and deposes and says that the above certificate is just and true to the best of their knowledge and belief.
J.P.
6.00 This Amt. Issued for 3 Months up to the 7th day of July 1865 at the Rate of $2.00 per Month

Dated 1865, this note was a request for relief for the family of a member of the 82nd Pennsylvania Infantry.

82nd Pennsylvania Volunteer Infantry, 1865 Somerset County, Pennsylvania, part-printed, part-manuscript soldier's family relief request for Matilda Biltner, wife of Conrad Biltner, "a drafted man, 82nd Reg't Penn. Vol's." Size 8" x 6-1/2", age toned, has been folded, and has several minor stains and tiny hole along the fold, otherwise good condition. **5.00**

84th Illinois Volunteer Infantry, a large pre-printed document (roughly 16" x 10") filled out in ink for "O.B. Price private 84th Illinois." Lists his statistics as well as a list of all clothing he has drawn, that is, "2 blankets, 1 frock coat, 2 shirts, 3 pr drawers, 1 cap, 2 pr shoes, etc." Signed by "CB Cox Capt Comdg" on December 24, 1862, at Nashville, Tennessee. **45.00**

84th Regiment, United States Colored Troops, 1865-dated ordnance return for Company G. Printed document, just post-war. Completely filled out down to the last tumbler spring. Excellent condition. **150.00**

8th United States Infantry, printed card the size of a small postcard, with the likeness of woman's face in a flower petal and a poem printed on the front. The back is stenciled four times by soldier with his army stencil "Aaron Bond Co "A" 3rd Bat. 8th USI" and inscribed also "Martha Jane Badt." **25.00**

99th Pennsylvania Volunteer Infantry, this pay document refers to two soldiers' enlistment. On the front is the pay account of John Welsh, Company K, 99th Pennsylvania Volunteers, dated March 11, 1864. On the reverse is the pay account of Isaac Weller, Company K, of the 99th. Accounts of clothing and equipment drawn upon enlistment such as pants, coats, haversack, cap shoes, socks, shirts, etc. Measures 15" x 10", in very good shape with no tears or tape repairs. **88.00**

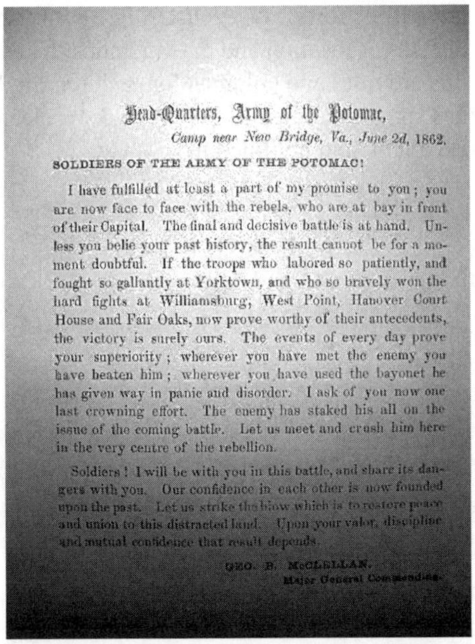

Head-Quarters, Army of the Potomac,

Camp near New Bridge, Va., June 2d, 1862.

SOLDIERS OF THE ARMY OF THE POTOMAC!

I have fulfilled at least a part of my promise to you; you are now face to face with the rebels, who are at bay in front of their Capital. The final and decisive battle is at hand. Unless you belie your past history, the result cannot be for a moment doubtful. If the troops who labored so patiently, and fought so gallantly at Yorktown, and who so bravely won the hard fights at Williamsburg, West Point, Hanover Court House and Fair Oaks, now prove worthy of their antecedents, the victory is surely ours. The events of every day prove your superiority; wherever you have met the enemy you have beaten him; wherever you have used the bayonet he has given way in panic and disorder. I ask of you now one last crowning effort. The enemy has staked his all on the issue of the coming battle. Let us meet and crush him here in the very centre of the rebellion.

Soldiers! I will be with you in this battle, and share its dangers with you. Our confidence in each other is now founded upon the past. Let us strike the blow which is to restore peace and union to this distracted land. Upon your valor, discipline and mutual confidence that result depends.

GEO. B. McCLELLAN,
Major General Commanding.

This official communication from General McClellan asks the Army of the Potomac to make one final push.

Frohne's Historic Military

Army of the Potomac, General George McClellan asks the "Soldiers of the Army of the Potomac" to fight the "The final and decisive battle... ." As the Army of the Potomac rested after the Battle of Fair Oaks and was in position in front of Richmond, Virginia, McClellan tried to stir his men with a patriotic announcement. This item is dated June, 2, 1862, mounting traces from previously being bound in an orders book, measures 7-1/2" x 4-1/2". **65.00**

Army of West Mississippi, soldier's pass issued from Provost Marshal General Andrews, Army of West Mississippi, on April 25, 1865, in Mobile, Alabama and signed by Brig. General L. Andrews. **85.00**

Confederate Oath, superb Confederate oath issued in Montgomery, Alabama, on November 14, 1862. Executed on a preprinted form and signed in medium-brown ink, this fine document was one of a number of legal and legislative formats used in the south during the Civil War to enforce Confederate laws and provide security for civilian and military operations, 7-1/2" x 9-1/2". Text: "I, George D. Purdue, do solemnly swear that I will bear true allegiance to, observe and support the Constitution of the Confederate States of America, and that I will serve them honestly and faithfully against all their enemies or opposers [sic] whatsoever. Subscribed and sworn to/before me, this14th day of November, 1862." Excellent condition. **225.00**

Confederate Parole and Oath of Allegiance, the parole measures roughly 5" x 8" and is pre-printed with federal eagle and heading "Certificate of Release Prisoner of War/Head Quarters Point Lookout, Md." It is dated at the Provost Marshal's office June 26, 1865, and carries a black ink stamp from the Provost Marshal. It is filled in for Virgil S. Cavin of North Carolina and reads "I hereby certify that Virgil S. Cavin, Prisoner of War, having this day taken the Oath of Allegiance to the United States, as prescribed by the President in his proclamation of December 8th 1863, is hereby in conformity with instructions from the War Department hereby released and discharged... A.G. Brady Major and Provost Marshal." Attached to the back of this parole is Cavin's Oath of Allegiance. It is preprinted "United States of America" as well as having all the legal wording printed and is filled in for, and signed by Cavin. Very fine piece of Confederate prisoner history. **795.00**

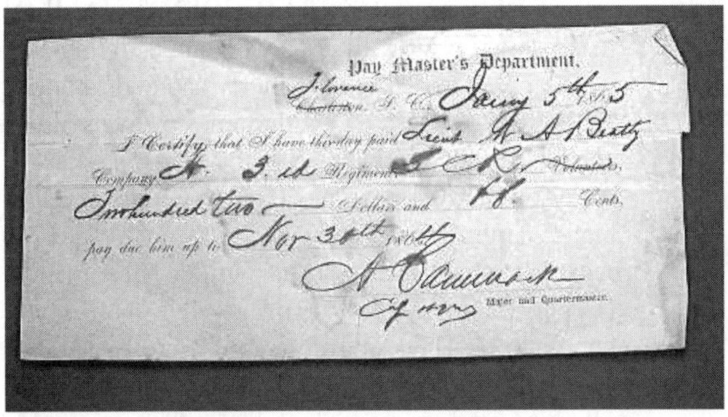

Pay Master's Department.

Confederate paymaster's document originally issued to a soldier in the 3rd South Carolina Infantry.

Middle Tennessee Relics

Confederate Paymaster, this document is from Florence, South Carolina, and dated January 15, 1865. It is for $202 payable to "Lieut. W. A. Beatty of Co. A, 3rd Regiment South Carolina Volunteers" for services rendered through November 30, 1864. The document is in good condition. **175.00**

General Order, Civil War U.S. Army Uniform, Clothing and Garrison Equipage General Order No. 2, dated January 7, 1865. It lists all uniform parts and insignias and their cost, 8 pages (including fold outs). **45.00**

General Orders, a nice lot of five printed General Orders from the effects of Captain John W. Hort, Company C, 57th Indiana Volunteers. **29.00**

Headquarter Troops, Department of the Gulf, enlistment certificate filled out for L.E. Hartford at New Orleans, August 6, 1863, Hartford, a seaman from Maine, was 23 years old and enlisted for three years into Company B, Headquarter Troops, Department of the Gulf. **75.00**

Indiana Volunteers, "Bounty of Volunteers for $50, No. 1832" and dated April 24, 1865. This piece was given to Ferdinand Rosen from Miami County, Peru, Indiana, and is partially printed and signed in ink. There is also a 5-cent revenue stamp affixed, the piece measures 4-1/2" x 8-1/2". **95.00**

Indiana Volunteers, Indiana bounty voucher for $100 to the bearer for "Expense of Volunteering," dated February 14, 1865. The strange thing about this check-sized voucher is that it is written on the back "Presented and not paid for want of funds this 14th day of February 1865. EH Richard." **45.00**

Lincoln-related, 1864 campaign piece, "National Union Ticket/For President Abraham Lincol/V.P. Andrew Johnson, etc." all in very bold large print with 5 "electors from San Francisco/Eldorado/ Alameda/Santa Clara/Siskiyou" listed. Small 3" x 4-1/2". Light aging. **195.00**

Lincoln-related, small hand-out broadsheet, "REPUBLICAN TICKET/LINCOLN & HAMLIN," in very bold print with large woodcut of flying eagle with large American flag, Liberty cap and ribbon. "LIBERTY & UNION" with names of five state electors. Light aging; small chips extreme outer edges of margin; small piece out extreme corner blank margin, very showy, 3" x-1/2". **175.00**

Provost Marshall, furlough pass written for James Harper for 10 days from February 7, 1864, to February 17, 1864, and signed by the Provost Marshall at Norwich Headquarters. Printed form filled in with browned ink, 3-1/4" x 8". **35.00**

Steamer *E.B. Hale,* large printed form for clothing allowances, "Duck, Nankin, Calfskin shoes, Kipskin shoes, Blue Cloth Caps," Several sailors are named and places and dates of their transfer or joining, excellent condition.. .... **95.00**

Pennsylvania Volunteers, (A) Paperwork used to document expenses accrued while recruiting troops, 7-3/4" x 9-3/4". White paper, printed in black (not filled in). Top line headed with ornate large letters "THE UNITED STATES." Center of form has lines and columns in which to enumerate expenses and amounts. Certified below by Recruiting Officer. Reverse has oath for further attesting to charges, a bit rumpled. (B) This is the form for listing new recruits by name, whether veterans or new recruits, regiment selected, by whom presented, and remarks. Top has large title "ROLL OF VOLUNTEERS," followed by blanks for location and date in Pennsylvania. Below this are lines and columns for each recruit, bottom has signature lines, 10-3/4" x 16-3/4", clean, excellent, and not filled in. **25.00**

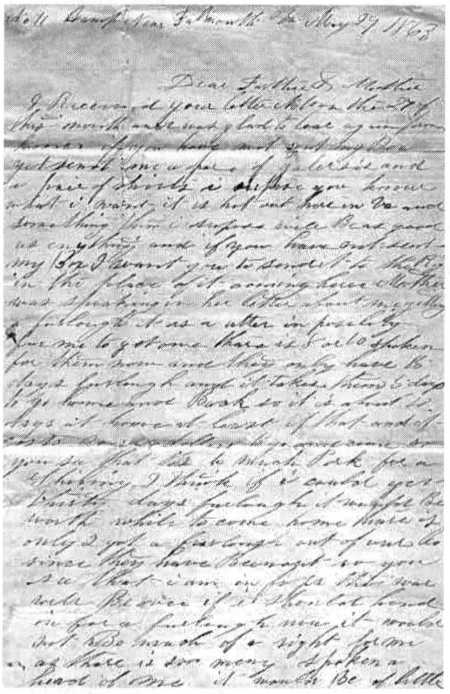

Similar to diaries, the value of a soldier's letters depends on the unit represented, content, and legibility. This letter, written by a member of the 2nd Corps 17th Maine Infantry talks about Generals Grant and Hooker's abilities to lead.

Frohne's Historic Military

> **"In writing this little book, I have endeavored to make it as interesting as possible without any false coloring. It is made up from memoranda that I kept during my service of three years in the Civil War."**
>
> ***—Arthur J. Robinson, Co. E, 33rd Wisconsin Volunteers***

Letter

17th Maine Volunteer Infantry, four-page letter written by Arthur Harmon, Company E, 17th Maine Infantry. Nice content, comes with typed transcript. He writes, "I guess there is no doubt that Hooker and General Grant is Bricks and got a good deal of cheek to them But the Rebels have got still more than they. Is reported here that there is going to be the greatest fight was ever known they think the Rebs will attack our forces and try for Washington if this is true it will be a Fight indeed..." Signed boldly "Arthur A. Harmon, Esq." **150.00**

17th Maine Volunteer Infantry, letter written by Arthur Harmon, Company E, 17th Maine Infantry. Harmon was shot in the bowels on July 2nd, 1863, in the Wheatfield at Gettysburg. Two page ALS on beautiful "United States Capitol" letterhead. Written in period ink, and in very fine condition. A gruesome excerpt, "...I have got the diarrhea the doctor is giving me something for it. I have had to turn out 2 and 3 times in one night from 8 o'clock last night till 8 this morning I had to go to the privy 4 or 5 times. Since they have moved me to this place I see those that have been wounded in the ankles and shoulders and arms, fingers shot off and some with one leg and half to go round on crutches!" Signed, "from your Son A. A. Harmon" Comes with typed transcript. **150.00**

21st Illinois Volunteer Infantry, excellent letter from Lt. John A. Freeland to Lt. Col. McMackin, dated February 22, 1862, suggesting that several soldiers would be suitable to fill the spots of officers that have resigned. The 21st Illinois was mustered into the States service for 30 days by Captain U.S. Grant. It was later mustered into service for three years with U.S Grant as commander and he remained as such until he made General. **95.00**

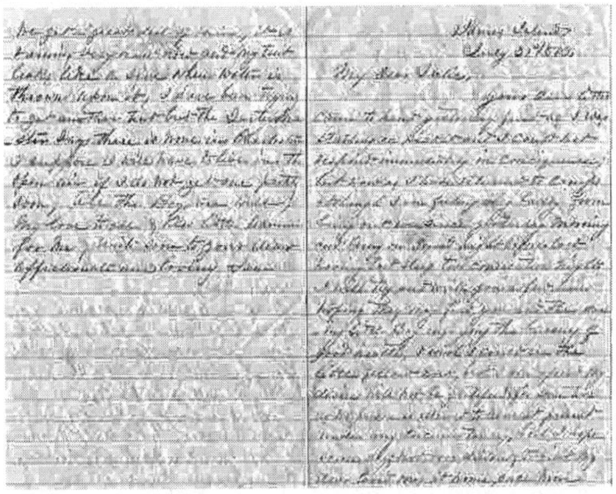

Confederate-written letters, just like diaries, are very desirable. Still, the value depends on content. This 3-1/2-page letter from a soldier in 25th South Carolina Infantry describes quiet times, but then concludes with lamenting the lack of tents and proper rain gear.

Frohne's Historic Military

25th South Carolina Volunteers, written by Lieutenant Sam Kennerly, 25th S.C. Volunteers. Kennerly later died at Globe Tavern on the Weldon Railroad with 70 percent of his brigade. Signed "Sam," comes with a photocopy of covers he has addressed in ink to his wife. 8vo., 3-1/2 pp., ALS, James Island, July 21, 1863. It reads, in part, "My Dear Julia, Your dear letter came to hand yesterday just as I was starting on picket and I could not respond immediately in consequence, but now as I have returned to camp although I am feeling very badly from being out ever since yesterday morning and being on guard night before last having lost sleep two consecutive nights...We have comparatively quiet about Charleston now, but I am afraid it is an omen of another desperate effort to get Charleston, the Yankees are making preparations for that event. We can see them building batteries on Morris Island and before very many days I apprehend a stormy time...We get a great deal of rain. It is coming very hard now and my tent leaks like a sieve when water is thrown upon it. I have been trying to get another tent but the Quartermaster says there is none in Charleston. I suppose I will have to live in the open air if I do not get one pretty soon. All the boys are well. Give love to all & kiss little Sammie for me. Write soon to your dear, affectionate, loving Sam." **575.00**

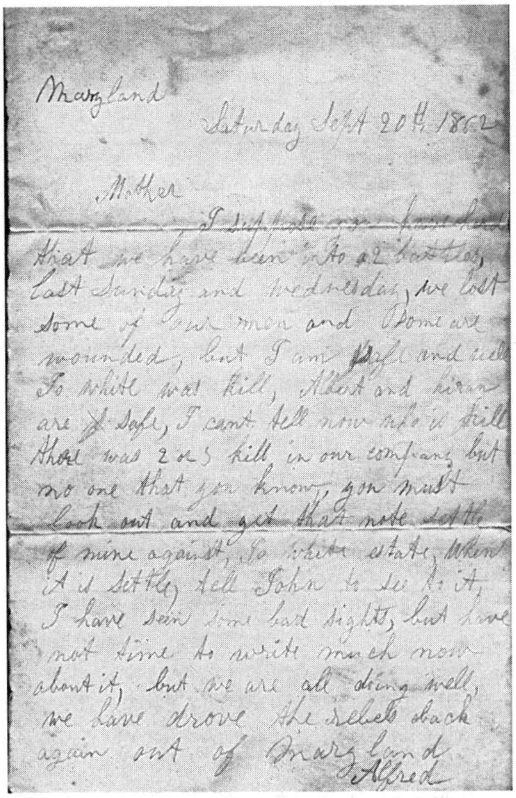

Maryland
Saturday Sept 20th 1862

Mother

I suppose you have heard that we have been into 2 battles last Sunday and wednesday, we lost some of our men and some are wounded, but I am safe and well, Jo White was kill, Albert and hiram are safe, I cant tell now who is kill There was 2 or 3 kill in our company but no one that you know, you must look out and get that note settle of mine against Jo White estate, When it is settle tell John to see to it, I have seen some bad sights, but have not time to write much now about it, but we are all doing well, we have drove the rebels back again out of Maryland

Alfred

In this letter, a soldier in the 35th Massachusetts Infantry relates a few details about the two recent battles in which he participated, one of them being the contest at Antietam.

Sharpsburg Arsenal

35th Massachusetts Volunteer Infantry, letter from Alfred Ellis, Private, 35th Massachusetts Infantry, Company I. Letter is dated, "Maryland Saturday, Sept. 20th, 1862." Ellis writes, "Mother, I suppose you have herd that we have been into 2 battles, last Sunday and Wednesday, we lost some of our men and some are wounded, but I am safe and well. Jo White was killed, Albert and Hiram are safe, I can't tell now who is killed. There was 2 or 3 killed in our company but no one that you know...I have seen some bad sights, but have not time to write much now about it, but we are all doing will, we have drove the rebels back again out of Maryland. Alfred."....... **225.00**

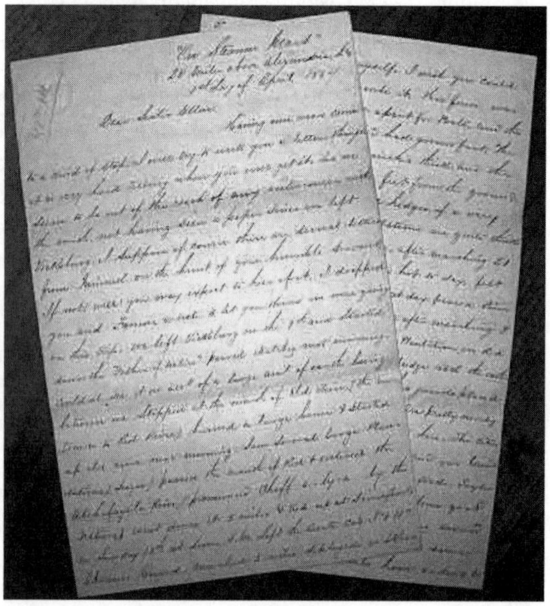

This 8-page letter from a member of the 47th Illinois Infantry contained an in-depth description of the Red River Campaign.

Frohne's Historic Military

47th Illinois Volunteer Infantry, excellent condition 8-page, Red River diary/battle letter written by David McGowan of the 47th Illinois Infantry. This letter goes into great detail from day to day, battle to battle. A few minor center seam splits, but very legible and very easily read. McGowan was a very educated man and it shows in his writing. **395.00**

51st New York Volunteer Infantry, William Chapman of the 51st New York Infantry writes about a box of blankets, a visit to Boston and applying for a discharge. One sheet, two pages written in pencil, from camp. **30.00**

5th Michigan Volunteer Cavalry, letter written by Corporal George A. Clarkson. Company, H, 5th Michigan Cavalry Volunteers. Written from Camp Copeland, East Capitol Hill, Washington, Feb. 26th, 1863 to his wife. Tells her about how his "regiment went on a raid into Virginia and to be gone for three days. The artillery and six Companies of the 6th Cavalry have gone with them. (However, due to a bad back, Clarkson was told to remain at camp by Lt. Starky.) All Milford men are gone, they expect to raise Cain with the rebels." He goes on about camp life, arrivals and departures, returning to his profession as a sash and door maker, talks of this children and personal business. In closing he states, "I hope as soon as the fine weather comes and the mud dries up we will be able to do something and whip the rebels." Interesting letter written over a couple of days, the archival information. Letter is written on paper with print of Vicksburg on the back. Very good condition with one small area of fading. **50.00**

75th New York Volunteer Infantry, a short, one-page letter in ink headed "Camp Stevens La. Jan 3 1863." It reads, "Dear Father, Enclosed is $25 please put it out where it will draw me interest providing you do not wish to use it. We are well and ready for action. Yours in haste Jno H Smith. PS I write you twice per week & hope you receive the same JHS." **20.00**

Aide-de-camp to J.E.B. Stuart. R.C. Price served as major and aide-de-camp to the J.E.B. Stuart and was killed at Chancellorsville, during the opening stages of the battle whilst Stuart and "Stonewall" Jackson were conferring. Rare Civil War autograph letter signed, four pages, octavo, in pencil, dated August 1, 1862, from "Howitzer Camp," Yorktown, Virginia, and written to his sister. Price reports on the game of cat-and-mouse then being played by J.E.B. Stuart's cavalry and the Union forces then at Hampton, Virginia. In part, "For several days there have been rumors in Camp that we were to move shortly, & this morning on returning from Drill we found that orders had been received from our Company to march to morrow morning at day break for a place called Mulberry Island which is just between Warwick & James. The troops returned Monday evening from their expedition towards Hampton. They met with no enemy, though they expected on several occasions to have a fight. One night they went within a short distance of Hampton, & the enemy retreated after burning some of the houses. They however reoccupied it after our forces, which were nothing more than a scouting party, had returned. They also went over one night after a party of Yankees on Back River who had been burning vessels, but they got there too late. Since they got back, we have been drilling & leading a quiet life. I have been washing & fixing up to move to all day & now am just about ready. Give my love to all & believe me your loving brother, R. Channing Price." At the start of the war, Price joined the 3rd Company of Richmond Howitzers, then joined Stuart's staff in August 1862, becoming an aide-de-camp. Price accompanied Stuart and the cavalry on many of their most famous expeditions, including the Second Ride Around McClellan in October 1862. An excellent war-date letter written from Yorktown, just one week before Price was promoted to lieutenant to begin one of the most valuable staff careers of the Confederate service. In fine condition. **3,950.00**

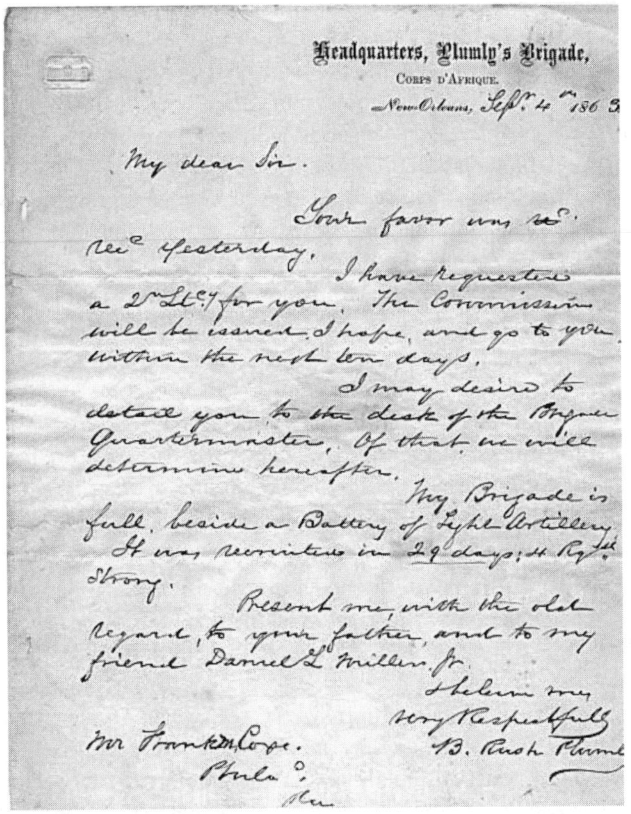
Headquarters, Plumly's Brigade,
Corps d'Afrique.
New Orleans, Sept. 4th 1863

My dear Sir.

Your favor was rec'd yesterday. I have requested a 2nd Ltcy for you. The Commission will be issued, I hope, and go to you within the next ten days.

I may desire to detail you to the desk of the Brigade Quartermaster. Of that, we will determine hereafter.

My Brigade is full, beside a Battery of Light Artillery. It was recruited in 29 days; 4 Rgts strong.

Present me, with the old regard, to your father, and to my friend Daniel L. Miller Jr.

& believe me very Respectfully
B. Rush Plumly

Mr Frank M. Coxe.
Phila P.

Written on one page, this letter announces the support for an appointment to lieutenant in the Corps d'Afrique.

Frohne's Historic Military

Corps d' Afrique. Excellent, one page ALS from ardent abolitionist D. Rush Plumly, to Frank M. Coxe, telling him he has secured a commission in the "Corps d' Afrique" for him. Rare letterhead. Content reads, "Headquarters Plumly's Brigade, Corps D'Afrique. New Orleans, Sept 4th, 1863. "My dear Sir, Your favor was rec'd yesterday. I have requested a 2 Ltcy for you. The Commission will be issued I hope, and go to you, within the next ten days. I may desire to detail you to the desk of the Brigade Quartermaster, of that, we will determine hereafter. My Brigade is full, beside a Battery of Light Artillery. It was recruited in 29 days; 4 Rgts strong. Present me, with old regard to your father, and to my friend Daniel L. Miller, Jr. & believe me very Respectfully B. Rush . Mr Frank M. Coxe. Phila Pa." 225.00

Lady's Aid Society,"Mass. Military State Agency" letterhead in Washington D.C. Dated July 12, 1864, written by Priscilla Lewis to her parents describing Washington with "thousands and thousands of soldiers." Includes original postmarked envelope. 75.00

Pennsylvania Bucktails, headed, "Bucktail City, Jan. 24th 1862." A nice two-page ink letter to James Morrison from "Sam." Says he received a letter from James, has been unwell, expect the rebels to attack every night, Beauregard has advanced to Centerville, and the unit keeps an extra guard every night. Says of Beauregard, "Oh I wish he would come, if he did he would have to go back quicker than he came..." Nice soldier letter better than average with great manuscript Bucktail heading on front. 69.00

U.S. Ordnance Corps, October 1861, letter to the Colt Factory superintendent for a certificate of inspection, signed by "Lt. George T. Balch US Ordnance Corps," excellent condition. 145.00

U.S. Volunteers, November 1864 letter from Amos Russell to Thomas Brayton thanking him for sending stamps and asking if the money he sent was received. On printed Sanitary Commission Stationery. Tintype included that shows young soldier in Union Army Frock Coat, excellent condition. 145.00

Sold as a group, nine letters from a member of the 13th Vermont Infantry recounted his service from September 1862 until right after the Battle of Gettysburg in July 1863.

J.C. Devine Inc.

13th Vermont Volunteer Infantry, written by Corporal John J. Hill of Company G. This was a 9-month regiment and Hill served from Sept. 11, 1862, until July 21, 1863. These letters written between November and March and detail camp life, picket duty and small engagement with the enemy—one of which resulted in the capture of their Brigadier General. The letters are inked in an easily legible hand, with the Vermont farmer turned soldier being very inventive in spelling. The letters are in excellent condition in their original envelopes with stamps. Included are several pages of information from Civil War data bases, including detailed accounts of the Regiment's participation at Gettysburg and a photocopy of a CDV of Corporal Hill with his Springfield musket. 200.00

19th Michigan Volunteer Infantry, really great group of nine ink letters. Eight of the letters written by S. Halstead, and one, a note by the Chaplain, telling that Halstead was wounded at Thompson's Station on March 3rd, 1863 and died in a rebel hospital. The eight letters by Halstead are sewn together to form a booklet. They cover September 1862 thru March

1863, all written in ink. Tops and bottoms have some minor mouse chews, not affecting content. Good content about army life, one really good letter (January 17, 1863) with story about soldier and darkie finding a "dud" artillery shell and "...tride to open it by twisting the cap with a cold chisel the niger held it between his knees while the other tride to turn the cap when the shell burst killing the nigro and wounding the white man." Another letter tells of Fort Donalson and arriving the day after a hard fight and describing the scene "...the rebs got fed canister and grape to (their) hearts content. The battlefield shode the effect of shot and lead, our men was busy hiding the rebs beneath the sod." **275.00**

28th Connecticut Volunteer Infantry, group includes an envelope addressed to Wolcott in the service with great note on front; cover from him; a great ink letter to him with cover addressed to him in 28th Conn. from his dad; a postwar family letter; two partial war-date letters from Eben while in the service, covering a few days' events; a family contract paper; an 1852 invitation from his dad; two more envelopes (war period); plus a couple other family letters and papers. **25.00**

Letters

Lot Of Two Civil War Soldier's. 1) Three pages on patriotic stationery with envelope, from a Vermont Lieutenant, Charles C. Gregg, to his friend in Vermont. Dated June 30, 1861, with good content about the troop buildup in Washington, D.C. Rebels lurking near camp and firing into it, his unit preparing to march to the White House to see "old Abe." 2) Letter from "camp near Harrison's Landing, Virginia, July 31st" from a Union artilleryman to his brother and sister. The four-page letter is signed only with initials, but has good content about his unit's retreat from battle and the care given to wounded soldiers in the hospital. All in fine condition...................... **150.00**

Pennsylvania Bucktails. First is a nice two-page ink letter written by John F. Pond dated April 8, 1863, to his sister telling of being sick, misses letters from home, stands soldiering first rate, and hopes "we shall whip the Rebs out this Summer." Second is a letter to his brother telling him that he is well, getting paid, that he received the bucktail that his brother sent, and that he wants papa to send four prs. of gloves & he will pay $2 a pair for them as it is cold handling a gun. **85.00**

Poem, Battle of Shiloh, a contemporary copy, nine pages, quarto, on U.S. Congress-embossed stationery. Composed by an unknown author, this touching poem about the Battle of Shiloh (fought April 6-7, 1862), in fine condition. **495.00**

Telegram

14th Indiana Volunteer Cavalry, great letterhead "US Military Telegraph" pre-printed on the top of the sheet. Two-page telegram dated April 15, 1863, reads, "Gen Manson, Reed your dispatch/pickets fired on tonight, 13 shots exchanged, 20 of 4th Indiana Cavalry came in at six o'clock this evening & camp with us tonight/we are quartered in Court House out of rations but will subsist off citizens/ forage scarce/shall advance in direction of picket firing in the morning & leave Provost Marshall Lieut Cherry and make my headqrs until I get further information./This is a good stockade/let me know by 4 o'clock in morning/the rebels have not crossed at Burksville not have they at Greelsboro They are in this vicinity/I will reconnoiter tomorrow. Respectfully A.S. Hamilton Capt Comdg Scouts." **125.00**

4th Indiana Volunteer Cavalry, "US Military Telegraph" pre-printed on the sheet top. Reads, "April 15th 1863 Columbia to Gen Manson/Sir. I arrived here this morning all quiet, no intelligence more than the 4th Indiana Cav have cut off the retreat to Burksville. They are arriving to cross river at Creelsboro. Shall we stay until tomorrow? Or return to camp immediately." "We may get news tonight dispatched to me immediately. A.G. Hamilton Comdg Scouts." **115.00**

7th Kentucky Volunteer Cavalry, this has the letterhead "US Military Telegraph" pre-printed on the sheet top. It reads, "April 15th 1863 Louisville To Capt Little AAG/I am suffering with neuralgia/May I remain here until 17th?/JC Brent Maj. 7th Ky Cav." Has note that this was answered in the affirmative. **65.00**

General H.G. Wright, "US Military Telegraph" pre-printed on the sheet top. Dated April 15, 1863, Louisville, 11:30 PM and addressed to General Manson: "In holding your force ready to move it need not be kept under arms but only hold ready with all preparations made for marching./Carter may be able to take care of any force crossing the Cumberland without your aid./Have your operator ready to send any news at any time on night./Office here always open. HG Wright Brig Genl Cmdg." **125.00**

Military Detective, "US Military Telegraph" preprinted on the sheet top. One page that reads "April 19th 1863 from Louisville to Commander of Post (Manson). You will arrest or cause to be arrested if found in your dept George Hoarn. He represents himself as being a discharged 1st Lieut Co "F" 3rd Ky. Infantry and drew pay on papers supposed to be surreptitiously obtained and send him to Col M Mundy that justice may be done. Capt SL Demarest Mil Detective." **95.00**

Ephemera Terminology

ADS: "Autograph document signed."

ALS: "Autographed letter signed."

Broadside: Single-sheet notices or announcements printed on one or both sides, intended to be read unfolded.

Chipped: Used to describe where small pieces are missing or where fraying has occurred on a dust jacket or the edge of a paperback.

DS: "Document signed."

DuoDecimo: A book or document approximately 7" to 8" t.

Edges: The outer surfaces of a book's leaves.

Ephemera: Items that were intended to be used for a short period of time, then disposed.

Flyleaf: A blank leaf, sometimes more than one, following the front free endpaper, or at the end of a book where there is not sufficient text to fill out the last few pages.

Folio: Has several meanings: (1) a leaf numbered on the front; (2) the numeral itself; and (3) a folio-sized publication. When used as this third definition, it refers to the largest size of printed material. By the mid-1800s the normal folio size had increased to about 17" x 21", the size that is still standard to this day.

Foxing: Brown spotting of the paper caused by a chemical reaction, generally found in 19th century books, particularly in steel engravings of the period.

Imprint: A term that can refer either to the place of publication or to the publisher.

LS: "Letter signed."

Obverse: The right-hand page of a book, more commonly called the recto.

Octavo (8vo): A book or document of about 5" w and 8" t to about 6" x 9". Octavo is the most common size for current hardcover books. To make octavo books, each sheet of paper is folded to make eight leaves (sixteen pages).

Pamphlet: Published, non-serial volumes with no cover or with a paper cover; usually five or more pages and fewer than 49.

Paper boards: Stiff cardboard covered in paper.

Provenance: The history of ownership or possession of a given item.

Quarto (4to): A book or document between octavo and folio in size; approximately 11" to 13" t. To make a quarto, a sheet of paper is folded twice, forming four leaves (eight pages).

Recto: The front side of a printed sheet or the front side of a leaf in a bound book; in other words, the right-hand page of an opened book. Also called the obverse.

Sextodecimo (16mo): A small book or document, approximately 4" w and 6" t. To make it, each sheet of paper is folded four times, forming sixteen leaves (32 pages).

Spine: The book's backbone. The spine is covered with a "backstrip."

Verso: The backside of a printed sheet or the rear side of a leaf in a bound book; in other words, the left-hand page of an opened book. Also called the verso.

Waterstained: Discoloration and perhaps actual shrinking. A greater degree of "dampstained."

Wraps (a.k.a. Wrappers): The outer covers of a paperbound book or pamphlet. Not to be confused with "dust wrapper" which protects a hardcover book.

Also see: Groupings, Personal Items, and Photographs.

Chapter 9

Flags and Musical Equipment

Early in the war, each regiment was mustered with a band. The belief was that playing martial tunes would elevate the soldiers to tasks they normally would not consider. Furthermore, each infantry company assigned a drummer and fifer. In addition to eliciting a military spirit, these two individuals performed the important business of communicating a commander's desire to the company by playing particular "calls" on their instruments. By mid-1862, regimental bands were, for the most part, eliminated. At the same time, the bugle began to replace the drum and fife as the preferred method of communicating calls on the battlefield.

In addition to the musicians, a regiment also assigned men to function as the color guard. In the field, each regiment carried a stand of colors consisting of the National flag and the regimental flag. A color guard of four men—two to carry the colors and two to act as guards—were given the task of safeguarding the regiment's flags. These banners were as treasured and protected *after* the war as they were during the war, so very few have ended up in private hands. The vast majority of regimental flags that have survived reside in museums or other public collections.

Regimental colors, though, are not the only variety of flag that existed during the Civil War, and therefore, the prospect of collecting flags does become better. In addition to headquarter flags, recruiting flags, garrison flags, and other miscellaneous military-associated flags, there are all the civilian expressions of patriotism that were created in many different sizes and shapes. Usually, a person who specializes in collecting flags looks for them in a variety of forms and sizes. At the outbreak of the Civil War, the United States flag had 33 stars. Though the arrangement of the stars varied greatly, the most common arrangement was of five horizontal lines of stars, from top to bottom in these numbers: 7-7-5-7-7.

Nevertheless, the ultimate in this area of collecting is a regimental banner. Because of the extremely fragile nature, flags that haven't been stored properly over the years should be handled and stabilized only by a professional textile conservator. Should you happen to stumble onto a rolled or folded banner that has been forgotten since the 1800s, resist the urge to open it yourself. You will be amazed at how fast a silk flag can turn to crumbs and dust if not handled properly. On the other hand, the variety of small, personal flags that were made on wool, cotton, or linen bunting will withstand light handling, but still, it would be best to have a conservator evaluate any flag before displaying it.

A final thought in regard to flag collecting: Flags possess the ability to evoke strong emotional responses from viewers. After all, that is the very reason of a flag's existence. The political and social environment may have changed since the Civil War, but one can be surprised how soon old emotions of our ancestors are drug to the surface.

Collecting Hints

Pros:

- Original Civil War flags are extremely impressive when on display.
- It is extremely difficult to create an appropriately aged reproduction Civil War flag.
- Brass musical instruments (and some wood) can still be played today.
- The folk-art crossover of a painted drum or Civil War-era instrument is large, lending credibility to interior decorating with martial items.

Cons:

- Original Civil War flags carried or utilized by the military of either side are exceedingly rare to find in private hands. When they do become available, the cost can be prohibitive.
- Proper storage for flags will require special, rolled storage in a humidity-monitored environment. Silk flags are especially sensitive to their environment and will literally crumble if not care for properly.
- To actually display a flag without contributing to its decay, the lowest of light levels should be used. Dark viewing isn't real conducive to enjoying the pride awarded by ownership.
- Much controversy surrounds the ownership and repatriation of flags, particularly those once flown over Confederate soldiers. Several museums have been involved in litigation over ownership. It is only a matter of time before private collectors are impacted.
- Very little has been published on musical instruments that will aid the collector. The most wanting area for quality research is almost the most popular area collected: military drums.
- Other than regimentally-marked drums or fifes, it is very difficult to ascertain whether an instrument was actually used by soldiers or is simply a civilian item of the era.

Availability ★★★★★
Price ★
Reproduction Alert ★★★★★

Flags and Guidons

Flag, Confederate

Texas, "Lone Star" flag, 24" x 39", made of hand-sewn flag bunting. This flag would have been appropriate as an infantry flanker flag, a main unit battle flag, or equally as a cavalry flag, as many were rectangular, rather than of the swallow-tail design. Double-sided with large white linen or cotton star hand sewn to each side of the blue canton. Narrow hoist binding of white sailcloth with hand-sewn grommet top and bottom. White/red stripe section is a single piece, the red being dyed brilliantly giving a bit irregular rough edge between red & white. Overall clean, excellent, with several small holes scattered, yet having a very clean, solid appearance. White stripe is actually a pale beige.........................**4,750.00**

These two swatches were removed from the flag that flew over the Confederacy's capitol in Richmond, Virginia, on April 3, 1865. It is accompanied by an 1888 statement signed by the Christian Commission member who made the acquisition.

Hendershott Museum Consultants

Flag that flew over the Capitol of the Confederacy—"I certify that this is a piece of the large flag taken from the State House in Richmond, Virginia, on the morning of April 3, 1865, by a detachment of General Witzell's Command the day of the evacuation of the Confederate Capitol. It has been in my possession until this date, Chicago, Illinois, March 8, 1886. John O. Foster, late delegate, U.S. Christians Commission." One can only imagine this soldier's excitement at tearing down and cutting up the Confederate flag that flew over the capitol of the Confederacy. Two large swatches approx. 2" x 3". Accompanied by a small swatch from the Fort Sumter white Flag of Truce, Charleston Harbor, 1862..............................**2,500.00**

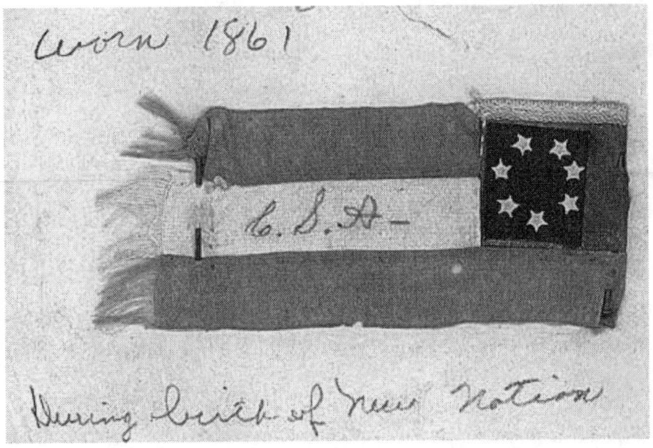

Collectors sometimes refer to these small, homemade flags as "Bible Flags." In spite of the name, these were often worn expressions of patriotism and were quite popular in the early days of the Confederacy.

Hendershott Museum Consultants

Hand-sewn measuring 2-3/4" x 1" with period identification CSA across the white bar. The canton has a field of seven stars in a concentric design. It is attached to card stock with identification "worn 1861-during birth of new nation." An excellent example of a Confederate Stars and Bars bible flag. **2,500.00**

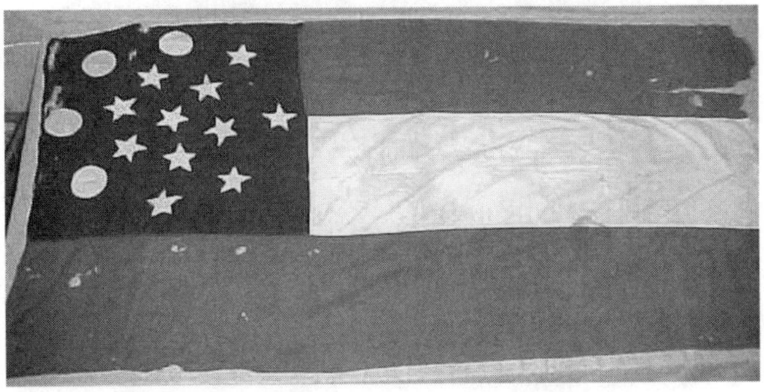

Supposedly, the meaning of the four "moons" on this 11-star First National represent the four slaves states that had yet to secede from the Union, June 1861.

Original and rare, 33-1/4" on the hoist and 67" on the fly, eleven stars appliquéd on both sides, as well as four "moons", which represent the four slave states that had not seceded as of June to November 1861. Flag is likely from Tennessee, Kentucky, or Missouri, according to evaluation by H. Michael Madaus, made in 1998. Fonda Thomsen, Textile Preservation Associates, performed a full textile authentication evaluation in 1998. .... **15,000.00**

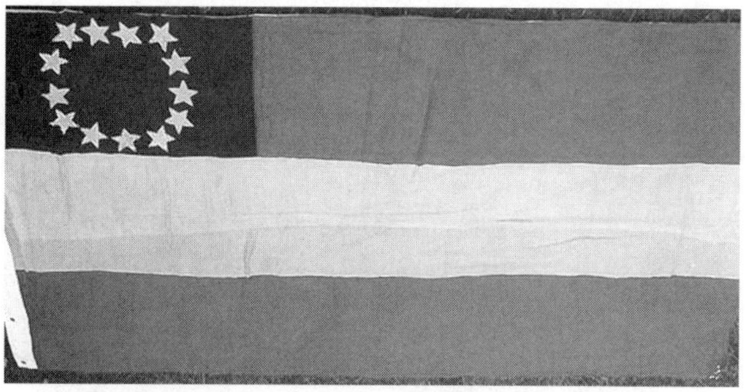

The Confederate "First National" flag was authorized for use from March 1861 to May 1863, this example bears 13 stars.

Old South Military Antiques

1st National

1st National flag. **20,000.00**

1st National pattern flag, very early 11-star example (1861). All-wool bunting construction with hand-sewn polished cotton stars, large field size 51" on the hoist by 130" on the fly. Associated history with the area surrounding Galveston, Texas. Exceptional condition with very little damage—but does have a few weak seams and some minor use-associated wear, retains vivid, strong colors, hoist has whipped eyelets. **16,000.00**

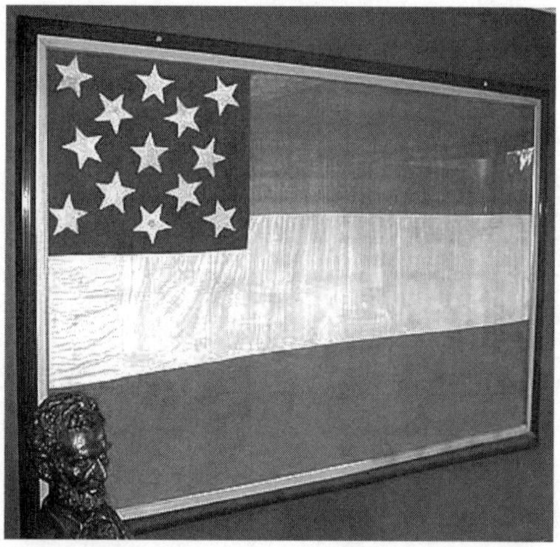

It is exceedingly rare to find a Confederate First Pattern National flag that can be assigned to a particular maker. James A. Cameron was commissioned in 1861 to make this flag for a Tennessee regiment.

Hendershott Museum Consultants

Very rare and attractive Confederate First National Flag made by famed sail maker James A. Cameron of Memphis, Tennessee, who became one of the most trusted and sought after sail and taurpin makers in the south. In the summer of 1861 he was commissioned to make this richly colored Confederate flag for a volunteer regiment from Nashville. Although records are unclear which regiment or company it was, Mr. Cameron was a talented craftsman and it is certain that his skills were well known throughout Tennessee. This flag is made of cotton sailcloth and is in excellent condition. Very rarely does one see such a remarkable flag identified to its maker. In addition, James A. Cameron signed his masterpiece by embroidering "JAC" into the hoist so that all who gazed upon the flag would know it was his handiwork. Only a few Confederate flags are actually identified by their maker. This Confederate First National flag was made in the summer of 1861 and has 13 stars in the blue canton. Accompanied by Howard Madaus' authentication. Size: 60" x 84" framed. **45,000.00**

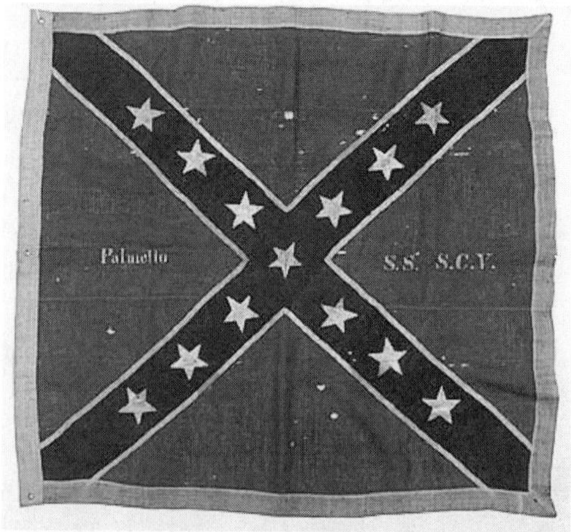

The Palmetto Sharpshooters of South Carolina Volunteers surrendered this flag to the 27th Michigan Volunteer Infantry at Appomattox Court House in 1865.

Hendershott Museum Consultants

Regimental

The very rare and historical Regimental Battle Flag of the famous Palmetto Sharpshooters, South Carolina Volunteers. They surrendered this flag to Michigan troops in 1865. The men of the Palmetto Sharpshooters marched at the front of Bratton's Brigade during the Surrender Ceremony at Appomattox and laid down their arms and surrendered their Confederate regimental battle flag, ironically, in front of the same Michigan regiment which they had fought a bloody battlefield duel with during the Battle of Gaines Mill. Of the 1,400 men and officers that served in the Palmetto Sharpshooters since its formation in 1862 until it surrendered at Appomattox with Lee in 1865, the overwhelming majority were volunteers. Over 470 men lost their lives fighting under this flag, most of which laid down their lives on the battlefield. It is interesting to note, however, that during the Surrender at Appomattox, the Palmetto Sharpshooters was the largest single Confederate regiment to be surrendered, with 356 men and 29 officers who stacked their weapons and surrendered this flag (recently purchased from Lieutenant John P. Anderson's descendants (27th Michigan), accompanied by Howard Madaus' letter of authenticity). This is one of the finest and most historical battle flags to have ever come on the market. It is a Richmond Depot issue, Army of Northern Virginia Battle flag with bold fresh color. It has several bullet holes, size 48" x 48". **250,000.00**

A unique Confederate 1st National flag with eleven stars in the blue canton and interesting salmon-colored bars made of silk indicating that it was likely made in the Western Theater. The star arrangement is unique to Confederate First National, as originally there were 13 stars, but two were removed during 1861 in conjunction with Missouri and Kentucky refusing to "officially" secede. This flag was discovered in Louisville, Kentucky, with an oral tradition of having been made for a Kentucky regiment. Superb with unique star design within the canton, accompanied by Howard Madaus' authentication, size: 84" x 38" **35,000.00**

Department of South Carolina, Georgia, and Florida regimental battle flag has the "Richmond Clothing Depot" pattern.

Battleground Antiques, Inc.

South Carolina regimental battle flag........**65,000.00**

Beautiful, handmade Confederate battle flag presented to the 47th Georgia Infantry by the Ladies of Charleston, South Carolina in June 1862, just after the Battle of Secessionville during the first siege of Charleston. The flag's aesthetic value is only superceded by its historical significance in that the 47th Georgia fought valiantly and rendered outstanding service to the citizens of Charleston, as well as to the Confederate Army. It was bloodied during the Battle of Chickamauga and Missionary Ridge and the Atlanta Campaign and then consolidated with the 46th Georgia and was engaged in the campaign of the Carolinas under General Joseph Johnston. Prior to that, however, during the Battle of Secessionville outside Charleston, South Carolina, the 47th Georgia displayed courage and chivalry in turning the Yankee tide and saving the city from the Union onslaught. A period article in the *Charleston Mercury* stated that the, "Ladies Charleston Association in aid of their volunteer soldiers presented four battle flags that they had prepared locally for the four Georgia units that had been called to Charleston during the crisis," that culminated in the Battle of Secessionville on June 16, 1862. The 47th Georgia was one of these regiments along with the 46th Georgia, the 51st Georgia, and the 32nd Georgia. This particular flag was handmade from a red cotton flannel with a dark blue wool and cotton mixture dress material making up the blue cross portion of the St. Andrew's cross. There are 13 white cotton, five-pointed stars appliqued to each side of the cross. Significantly, on one side of the hoist is an ink inscription reading "Col. A.C. Edwards." Edwards was the hard fighting Lieutenant Colonel of the 47th Georgia. The overall size of the flag is 72" x 72" and it is beautifully framed in a museum quality exhibition frame. Flag is accompanied by Howard Madaus' and Fonda Thomson's authentication and research...............**125,000.00**

Basically a 2nd Pattern National Flag, this variant was captured in Louisiana by members of the 3rd Massachusetts Cavalry.

Hendershott Museum Consultants

This historically important Confederate 2nd National flag is a variant pattern that was used by Confederates primarily in the Trans-Mississippi Department. It has a red cotton St. Andrews cross in the blue canton with 13 white 3-3/4" stars machine-stitched within the cross. This flag is a unique variant of the Confederate 2nd National Flag in many respects although there are examples that are somewhat similar to its design. This flag was captured by the 3rd Massachusetts Cavalry during its service in Louisiana. Eventually disembarking in Louisiana, the 3rd was in a constant fight battling small Confederate contingents, guerrillas, and full-blown engagements with the enemy. During the latter days of the siege of Port Hudson, the 3rd Massachusetts Cavalry was in front of the Union siege lines of battle and served as one of the main antagonists leading to the surrender of the fort. Colonel Chickering of the 3rd Massachusetts, was made Provost Marshall of the captured city and it is at this time that this flag was most likely captured. This rare and historically important Confederate 2nd National flag measures 48-1/2" x 62-1/2" and bears holes and rust marks in the hoist where the flag was undoubtedly nailed to a staff. The blood-red St. Andrews cross stands out against the dark blue canton. The red and white bars are striking in their color and there is evidence of battle usage and wear. Accompanied by Howard Madaus' authentication.. .... **55,000.00**

Georgia silk regimental battle flag. **30,000.00**

A variant on the "General Richard Taylor Battle Flag, Trans-Mississippi Department," this style of flag is often called a "reversal" flag due to the coloration. General Taylor flew this style of flag in operations in West Louisiana in 1864 and 1865. Though several Texas regiments are known to have flown similar flags, this particular silk flag has history that points to Georgia.

Battleground Antiques, Inc.

Flag, U.S.

A large, regimental-size Civil War flag with 36 stars. Nevada was the 36th state to join the Union on October 31, 1864, authorized by Congress for statehood, so they could vote for President Lincoln's, "Emancipation of Slaves being the 13th Amendment to the United States Constitution." A superb flag of red, white, and blue wool bunting with bright fresh color. The five-point cotton stars measure 6" across. A few minor rips and tears as one might expect on a flag of this size that was flown during the Civil War, 90" x 138"... **3,500.00**

Painted and stenciled 36-star flag from November 1864. Polished cotton, excellent condition, no tears. Perfect framable size, approximately 36" x 20-1/2", nice, aged look, colors have faded slightly, banner on parade flag. **725.00**

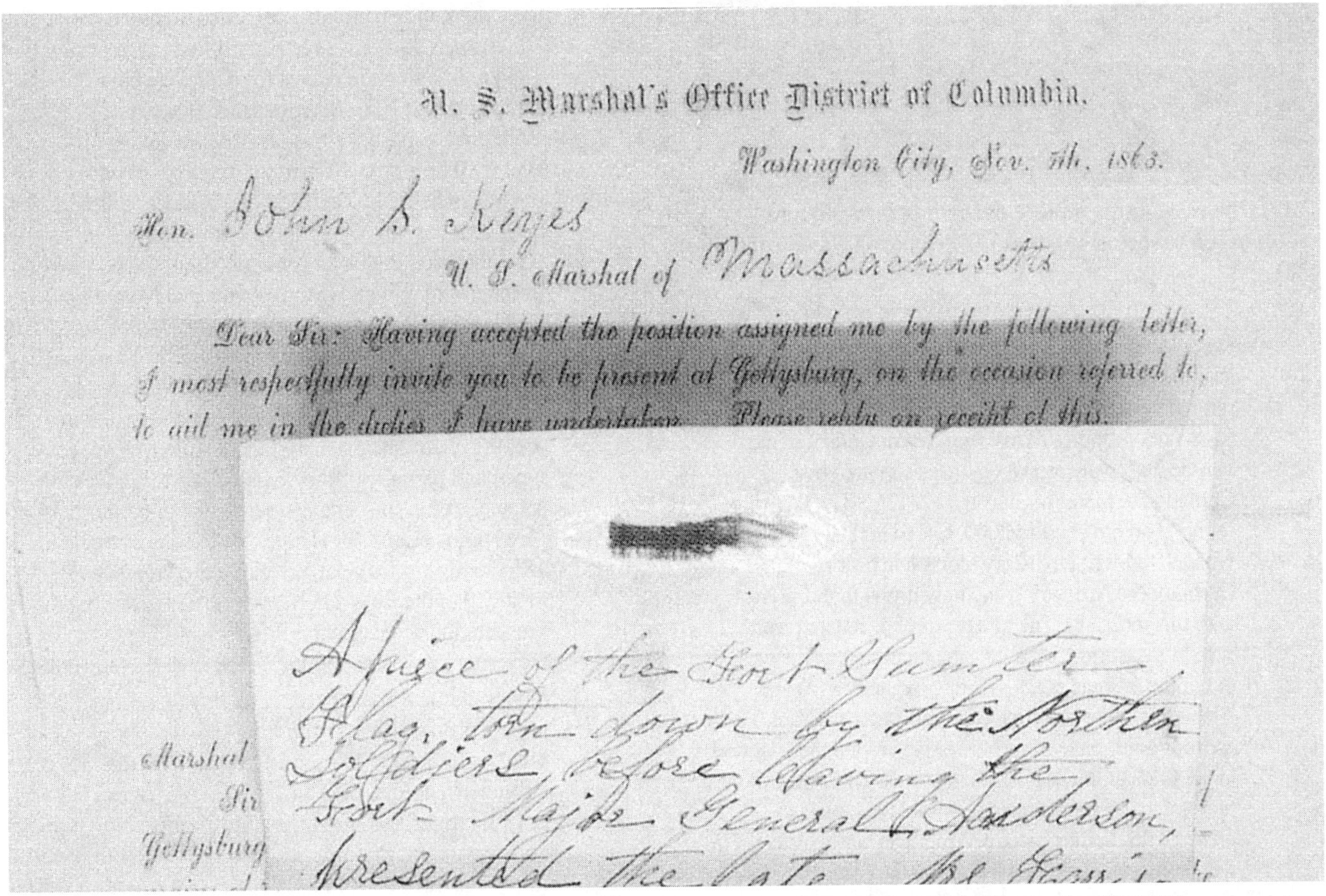
U. S. Marshal's Office District of Columbia.
Washington City, Nov. 7th, 1863.
Hon. John S. Keyes
U. S. Marshal of Massachusetts
Dear Sir: Having accepted the position assigned me by the following letter, I most respectfully invite you to be present at Gettysburg, on the occasion referred to, to aid me in the duties I have undertaken. Please reply on receipt of this.

A piece of the Fort Sumter Flag, torn down by the Northern Soldiers, before leaving the Fort. Major General Anderson, presented the late

Purported to be a scrap of the flag that flew over Fort Sumter when it surrendered to Rebel forces in 1861, this remnant comes with strong supporting paperwork.

J.C. Devine Inc.

Scrap of the flag flown over Fort Sumter during the opening engagement of the American Civil War. Removed from the Fort by Major Robert Anderson after the surrender of the Fort on April 14, 1861. The fragment of the flag is pasted at the top of a handwritten note signed by Lavinia B. Bates of Concord, Massachusetts, who writes, "Major General Anderson presented the late Mrs. Garrison Gray Otis with a piece of the flag and the staff which she divided with me." This fragment given to Lavinia Bates by Mrs. Otis was later given to Judge Prescott Keyes of Concord, Massachusetts. It was recently found among the effects of Prescott Keyes and of his father, John S. Keyes. Colonel John Keyes was also present by invitation to Gettysburg, and a Lincoln inauguration program is also included in this rare offering... **1,100.00**

36-star flag (1864), 23"x 31" with printed stars and stripes, faded... **245.00**

This large remnant is a piece of the flag lowered and surrendered to secessionists at the Pensacola Naval Yard in 1861.

Naval, Civil War U.S. Naval Commodore's silk flag with stars from Pensacola Naval Yard, 1861. This very large remnant is part of the silk Naval Flag lowered by Commodore James Armstrong, Commandant of the Pensacola Naval Yard when it was captured by Confederate forces on January 12, 1861. The flag was found in an old chest in 2000, folded up in a canvas bag with a hand-written history (complete history of flag, Commodore Armstrong and how it was found, comes with this remnant). The remains are the red and white stripes, measuring 32" x 28", the blue canton area was cut out of the original 6' x 9-1/2' flag by the Florida and Alabama militia units that captured the Naval Yard. There are four gold stars with a blue circle around them (found in the folds of the flag) on each corner. This remnant was professionally framed using non-acid materials to preserve this unique piece of American Naval history. The flag has been passed down through the Armstrong family after Commodore Armstrong "liberated" it from its Confederate captors, just before he was released to return to Washington. Also included, is a carte de visite of Commodore Armstrong taken in 1862 after his return home to Pennsylvania upon his retirement. **2,330.00**

Regimental

Fantastic collection of Civil War documents and a rare remnant from a regimental flag all dealing with one soldier's service history. This grouping of items deal with the Civil War service of one Charles B. Newcomb who served as Sergeant in the 4th Battery of Light Artillery Massachusetts Volunteers. The centerpiece of this collection is a remnant (the letter "O") from one of the two original regimental flags of this battery. The silk letter is framed and penned on the back is, "Letter ('O' from the 4th Battery Co. flag used during the Rebellion. Father was Sergeant in this Battery." The remnant itself measures approximately 1-1/2" x 1-3/4" and is quite beautiful. It is nicely matted and framed (framing done ca. 1900), with three original documents relating to the enlistment and discharge of Charles Newcomb, including a "Form for Examining a Recruit," filled out upon Newcomb's examination by a doctor at the time of his enlistment. It states that he has had no serious sicknesses or symptoms of diseases—that he is a farmer, age 24, from Salem, Mass, and under "Remarks" it states, "Has Wife and two Children in Salem." This form was filled out at Camp Chase on October 4, 1861, a short time after Newcomb's enlistment in September 1861. Also included are Newcomb's two discharge papers—one dated January 1864 and stating the reason for discharge being "Reenlistment." The other is dated October 13, 1865. Both documents are signed by officers in the 4th Battery. The earlier discharge is quite worn with tape repairs to the folds. The 1865 discharge is a bit wrinkled and has a few small stains, but is still in nice condition. Also included in this lot is a booklet produced by the Soldiers and Sailors Historical and Benevolent Society for Newcomb in *Portfolio of Personal Military and Civil History* that details the service of Charles Newcomb and contains two photographs of Newcomb in old age—one in his G.A.R. uniform and one seated in a rocking chair. The extensive and detailed two-page typed and partially printed personal history gives the sequence of events, engagements, and appointments of Newcomb and the 4th Battery from his enlistment in 1861 to his discharge at the end of the War. Also included in the lot is a newspaper article detailing the presentation of the second Regimental Flag to the Governor of Massachusetts.. .... **905.00**

Remnant that is affixed (tied, actually) to a piece of paper (probably a section of an old scrapbook). The notation in period ink reads, "Portion of the battleworn color of the 11th Inf. USA." The 11th was at Gettysburg and that means it's highly likely these colors were there, too. Condition of the cloth is still fairly decent. **310.00**

This 9' x 15' flag flew at the headquarters of the 23rd New Jersey Volunteer Infantry, a hard-fighting 6th Corps unit of the Army of the Potomac. It was sent home in 1863 by the unit's quartermaster.

Battleground Antiques, Inc.

Flag of 23rd New Jersey Infantry, all-wool bunting construction with polished cotton stars. This is the 9' x 15' headquarters flag of the unit, as sent home by its Quartermaster, Lieutenant Abel H. Nichols (name on hoist). Retains great, vivid original color and shows just a few field repairs. Hoist is tattered in some places, as is bunting. All hand-sewn stars and brass grommet construction in the style of the Philadelphia Depot. Originally constructed with 34 stars; has two additional ones sewn on (pretty obvious, and definitely of the era) indicating use into 1863. This unit served from September 13, 1862, until June 27, 1863, and saw heavy action in the 1st Brigade, 1st Division, 6th Corps, Army of the Potomac, suffering 90 casualties, primarily at Fredericksburg and Chancellorsville, very historic item, with sterling provenance. **2,000.00**

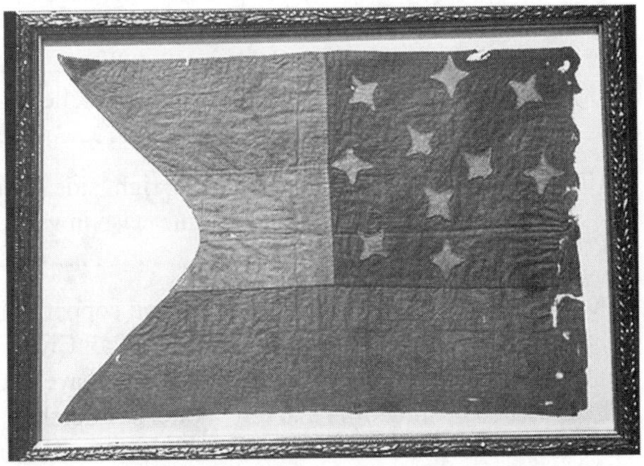

This swallowtail first National Pattern guidon was most likely used by a Confederate mounted unit.

Old South Military Antiques

Guidon, Confederate

First National, cavalry guidon. **12,200.00**

Texas, attributed to Texas cavalry unit, Civil War-era swallow tail. **2,100.00**

Guidon, U.S.

Regimental

Beautiful hand-painted gold stars, 35-star silk cavalry guidon carried by the 8th Ohio Cavalry throughout the battlefields of Virginia. The 8th Ohio Cavalry was organized March 28, 1864, from the veterans and recruits of the 44th Ohio Infantry. The newly outfitted regiment proceeded to West Virginia to join General Averll's raid on Lynchburg, Virginia where they met with heavy resistance from the Confederates. This cavalry guidon floated proudly above the regiment as it fought the Rebels throughout West Virginia and into the Shenandoah Valley. U.S. Cavalry guidons are rare, especially in this superb condition. Beautifully made of silk with hand-painted gold stars. The red strips have slightly bled over to the white, yet it is in remarkable condition and the silk is in fresh condition, size 42" x 28". Accompanied by Howard Madaus' letter of authenticity. **25,000.00**

Mounted and preserved, this U.S. guidon of Battery E, 3rd New York Volunteer Artillery bears three battle honors earned in December 1862, while campaigning in North Carolina: Kinson, Whitehall, and Goldsoro. At that time, the battery was on unattached duty in the Department of North Carolina. **8,500.00**

The guidon of Battery E, 3rd New York Light Artillery, dates to early 1863, right after it participated in the battles around Kinston, North Carolina.

Battleground Antiques, Inc.

Virginia, 33 White Stars, 26" x 26" blue silk guidon that still retains the ties on either corner. Few nips and some slight fraying, but otherwise in fine condition. Old typewritten tag glued to guidon states, "Flag of the 55th Virginia Cavalry/This flag was made for Co. A. 55th Va./ in 1858. It was carried at the/capture of John Brown at Harpers Ferry in 1859." **5,500.00**

Musical Instruments

Bugle

8th Wisconsin Light Artillery, bugle is in near perfect condition and free from any major dents or damage, it is 100 percent regulation Union army having a single twist, copper body, brass bands and mouthpiece, and the reinforced bell. Family legend on this bugle is that it was given to Lieutenant Stiles, 8th Wisconsin Light Artillery, after being captured from Confederate troops at the Battle of Lookout Mountain. **2,450.00**

Cavalry

Very pretty "Turner Ashby" Yeager hunting horn configuration cavalry bugle. This bugle is out of the personal collection of Mark Elrod, author of, *A Pictorial History of Civil War Bands and Band Instruments*. The bugle comes with full-page letter from Mark authenticating the bugle. **850.00**

It is 16" l with a 4-1/4" reinforced bell with a floating rim, there are double loops 12" l and 6" h, has a few dings. **685.00**

Small, triple loop model, 11" l with a 4-1/2" d bell with reinforced floating rim (indicative of Civil War period). There is a tightening screw on the mouthpiece holder, has been professionally restored to remove dents, cleaned, and is in excellent, playable condition. **485.00**

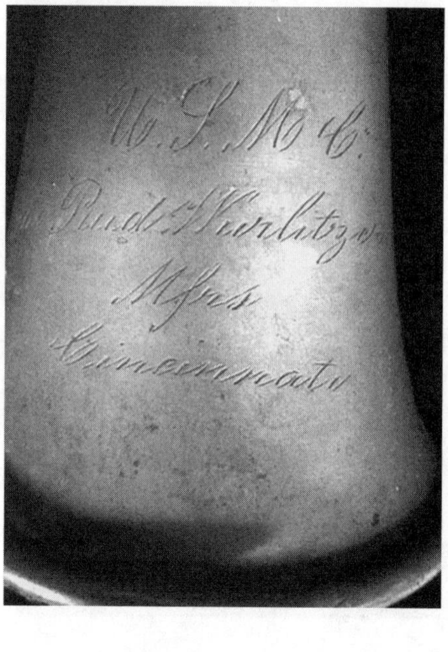

This bugle was inscribed designating it as having been used by the U.S. Marines.

Dale C. Anderson Co.

U.S.M.C., the product of a contract from the U.S.M.C. to the Wurlitzer Co of Cincinnati. Inscription in fancy script hand-engraved on the bell by the contractor. It reads "U.S.M.C./The Rud. Wurlitzer Co./Mfgs./ Cincinnati," double loop, had two lanyard rings, one gone from the rear. Thick reinforcing band around the bell, tongue and groove seam goes all the way to the bell's edge, some crinkling around the edge of the bell, about half way. Wonderful, untouched storage film and patina evenly dulls the surface, some small dings on the rear tube bends, otherwise excellent. **3,750.00**

10" brass bugle with brass mouthpiece, right side of bell was crumpled and straightened, otherwise in very nice condition. **400.00**

A very attractive bugle, made of brass and copper, it is seamed the entire length, as is typical of all Civil War-era instruments, the brass and copper have a soft uncleaned patina. It is marked "Potter's Aldershot/ LP." **995.00**

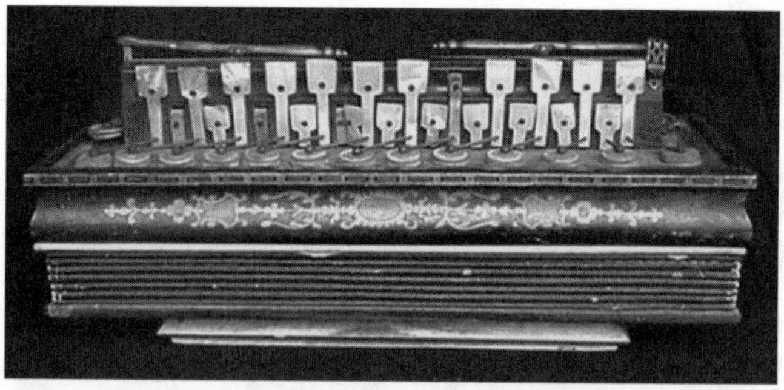

Concertinas were certainly a favorite camp instrument among soldiers on both sides. Nevertheless, it is difficult to associate a particular instrument as having been on campaign with the troops.

Dale C. Anderson Co.

Concertina, could easily date from the 1830, 14" l x 4-1/2" w. Edges of the box frame almost entirely inlayed with lighter wood in rococo sprays and scrolls, plus line borders, 26 circular mother-of-pearl valve caps, 23 keys also capped with mother-of-pearl, four keys need new caps. Bellows faced with pretty colored print paper, does not seem to leak, finish lightly worn/rubbed.... **335.00**

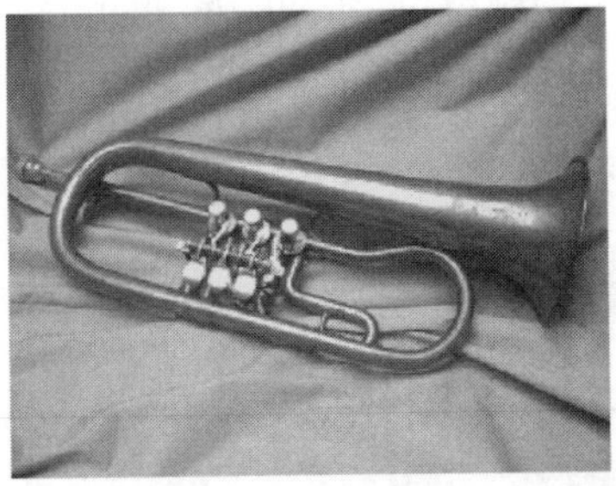

All brass, three-valve cornet.

Drumbeat Civil War Memorabilia

Cornet

All-brass cornet with nice aged patina, three valves, no visible maker's markings, no breaks in the seams. **995.00**

Civil War-era-rotary cornet in excellent condition, there are no dents, and only a few very minor dings, no missing parts. There is a small patch on the bow near the bell, the valves work great and are lightning fast. This cornet is made of nickel silver, also known as German silver, it comes with two shanks. One puts it in B-flat, the other in A-flat. On the bell is engraved "yon & Healy Chicago." This horn was made somewhere between 1860 and 1880. ...... **2,095.00**

Civil war, side-rotary-valve, E-flat cornet, unknown maker. Valves are airtight and is playable, but slides are stuck. There is evidence of many early bell solder repairs, a great horn for a restoration project. **$1,000.00**

Civil War-period E-flat top-rotary cornet. This is a German silver horn made by "J.H.F., NYC." It is missing its lead pipe and two of the top valve keys, intact rotors, slides are stuck. **520.00**

European made, all-brass cornet.

The markings on the horn are "J M Burger, Strasburg I/ E." It is raw brass and has recently been buffed. All slides and valves are free and it really does sound great when played by a cornet player. **635.00**

Drum

23rd Connecticut Volunteer Infantry, exquisite United States eagle drum made by Horstmann Brothers of Pennsylvania and presented to Drummer Boy James W. Skidmore of the 23rd Connecticut Volunteers. This beautiful drum is in excellent condition. It is hand-painted in bold patriotic colors and detailed flourishes around each head with the Horstmann Bros. label still evident through the peephole. The presentation on a solid silver plaque attached to the top rim reads, "Presented to Julius W. Skidmore, The Drummer Boy aged 15 years of the 23rd C.V., Aug 25, 1863." The drum was ceremoniously given to Pvt. Skidmore by the citizens of Bridgeport, Connecticut who were led by famed showman P.T. Barnum in appreciation for his bravery in the line of battle, this drum survives as a superb tribute to the battles in Louisiana in which Union troops were forced to hold their ground deep on Southern soil, 20" tall. **25,000.00**

2nd Ohio Volunteer Infantry, drum was made by, and still retains the label of, "George Kilbourn, Drum Maker, Albany, New York." Accompanying this instrument is the original museum tag from the Civil War Centennial display where it was last publicly shown. The tag is a 40-year old cardboard label which reads, "Carried by A.S. Reeder 2nd Regt. O.V.S. Civil War 1861-65." The drum has damage to the heads; a nice brass tack design on the shell, and it comes with the original drum sling and one broken drumstick. It is dirty and grungy and the ropes are old replacements from the 1960s. **1,608.00**

4th New York Heavy Artillery, superb, identified drum carried by E.B.A. Miller, drummer boy of Company A, 4th New York Heavy Artillery. Miller enlisted on August 27, 1862, and served in the 4th New York Heavy Artillery throughout the entire war being discharged June 3, 1865. The drummer boy signed his name on the bottom head, which is broken and is also accompanied by an old museum tag that further identifies this drum. A superb piece with its original walnut drum sticks. **4,500.00**

Painted on the side, "Co. E-7th Miss-CSA," this drum accompanied the "Franklin Beauregards" when they left Mississippi in 1861.

Hendershott Museum Consultants

7th Mississippi Infantry, homemade with a tin shell and crude wooden hoops put together with iron rivets. The vellum drumheads are in perfect condition and the regimental designation is hand-painted in large red letters on either side of the drum, "Co. E-7th Miss-CSA." The 7th Mississippi Infantry was raised in Franklin County, Mississippi, in May 1861, were it was known as the Franklin Beauregards. The history of this drum is quite clear. It was discovered in 1967 by the original owner of the Old Country Store Museum in Jackson, Tennessee, who acquired it from a family near Corinth, Mississippi. It has a leather harness shoulder strap still attached, and while the original red paint has faded to a medium brown, it is a most attractive Confederate rarity, size 21" around x 8" d. **$27,500.00**

A note written on the vellum head of this drum establishes a wonderful provenance: "I received this on January 1, 1863 at Adairsville, Georgia."

Hendershott Museum Consultants

This typical drum does not possess any distinctive markings.

Dale C. Anderson Co.

16-3/4" d x 13-3/8" h, dark walnut body; red rims. Roped through the rims. Original heads, ropes, and white buff leather tugs, one replaced. Heads intact with no splits. Fairly light, showing moderate use and grime. Rims show paint wear, tugs tanned from age, snare fasteners in place, but the snare strands were cut off. The thumbscrew missing from the adjuster, unusually fine overall condition. **1,195.00**

Though Civil War period in origin, this drum was probably modified in the immediate post-war era.

Dale C. Anderson Co.

17-1/4" d x 12" h, mahogany-colored body with attractive light and dark wood multi-pointed star inlay around the vent hole. Slightly lighter brown rims with heavy traces of gilt band on the faces. Original heads, no tears, iron hook suspension—the alternate mode of roping adopted in the 1850s. Drum was modestly updated during the Indian War period. The rope and tugs were added later and should be replaced, the snare adjuster may also be replaced, but may be original. Gut snares probably Indian War. Overall excellent, shows use, finish shows typical effects of age (some crazing), and some rubs. **675.00**

A very-fine drum manufactured with brass-headed tacks along the seam of the shelf. It is a pretty maple body drum with intact heads, ropes, and tighteners, all of which are original to this piece. This stands roughly 14" tall and 16" diameter. **1,295.00**

Civil War-era drum (tack design), about 15" tall x 16" diameter. Top of the drum has a 3" tear with old tape repair. Wear to rope holes, though rope is not present. There is a paper label inside that reads, "William Kilbourne, Bass and Snare Drums, Albany NY." There is other writing on the label, but it is too small to read. Overall light wear, comes with a pair of 16-3/4" black drumsticks............... **$545.00**

Labeled on the interior, "Noble & Cooley/ Manufactures of/ Military and Toy Drums/East Granville, Mass."

Dale C. Anderson Co.

A magnificent specimen with red, white, and blue striped rims splendidly framing brilliant red shell bearing a side-view rampant eagle upon a rolled American flag and holding in its beak a blue ribbon with the national motto, "E. Pluribus Unum." There is a red, white, and blue label inside approximately 3" x 4", with a standing figure of Miss Liberty holding a flag, and pictures of several drums, with the text, "Noble & Cooley/ Manufactures of/Military and Toy Drums/East Granville, Mass.," 16-1/2" d x 13-1/2" h, original heads, some paint wear to edges of rims. Snare adjuster may be slightly later replacement or may be original, lacks one tug. A few are period replacements. Top rim has three small holes that may have held a sling hook. **4,995.00**

Fine regimental size Civil War drum measuring about 15" tall and about the same in diameter. It has a nice brass-headed tack design on the drum's shell. Also present is an old piece of tape from the Civil War centennial with the simple note, "Civil War/100 Years Old/Bud Fonda." Apparently it was displayed somewhere during the centennial and loaned by Mr. Fonda. The drum retains the original red painted hoops, the flesh hoops, and the shell. Both heads and the ropes are disintegrated. **875.00**

Made by "John C. Hayes and Co." of Boston.. . . **625.00**

Drumsticks, good condition showing use and age, and one stick as a small crack, made of ebony.. . . . . **49.00**

Fife

23rd Ohio Infantry, fine regulation maple fife with brass end ferrules in excellent condition. It is accompanied by a note from a previous owner detailing that it was purchased from a family estate sale, and was carried by Alfred Paton (aka Patton) of the 23rd Ohio Volunteer Infantry. The note details family stories about Alfred, including his being wounded and carried from the field at Cedar Creek by his brother. **159.00**

16-1/2" overall. Standard fife with the turned and border decorated brass ferrules at the end, excellent condition. **210.00**

Classic fife made of maple with brass end ferrules. Neatly penned in script brown ink on the body is "Chas Reiters/Fife," wonderful patina and color. **169.00**

Constructed of ebony wood with long silver end ferrules.. . . . . **129.00**

Constructed of ebony wood with long silver end ferrules, "Crosby" maker's mark. **129.00**

Constructed of rosewood with a long silver end ferrule, and one ferrule missing. **59.00**

Dark fruit wood, 14-5/8" l with 3/4" German silver ferrules at each end, without manufacturer's or regimental marking.. . . . . **85.00**

Hickory with nickel silver ferrules. **225.00**

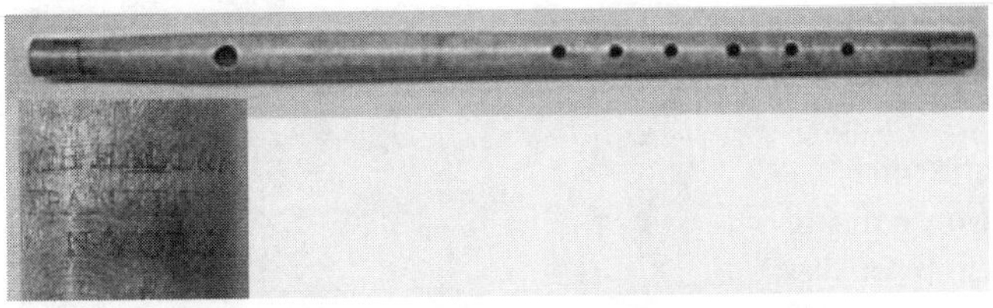

Marked "Furth, Hall & Pond, New York," this fife is a good representative of a Civil War-era instrument.

This fife was made by "Furth, Hall & Pond, New York." It appears to be burl maple, overall condition very-good, 15". **208.00**

This includes a "dummy's" mouthpiece shaped like a pipe stem to facilitate ease in playing, and has the standard mouthpiece where you have to blow air over a hole in the body. Appears to be made of cherry wood, with silver ferrules, and German silver keys, in excellent condition. **$165.00**

This one constructed of rosewood wood with pretty silver end ferrules. **139.00**

This brass, upright, baritone saxhorn is probably a postwar instrument.

Middle Tennessee Relics

Saxhorn, Upright Baritone, beautiful horn was manufactured by "C.G. Conn-Elkhart, Ind." and is nicely maker marked. This horn is equipped with three Berliner "pumpen" valves. **295.00**

> **"We had a splendid string band, and some of the best music I ever heard was in camp, at night."**
>
> ***— Robert Joseph Walker Matthews***
> ***"Sardis Blues," 12th Mississippi Volunteer Infantry***

Miscellaneous

This extremely unusual tree-shaped flagpole top was excavated from a former Confederate camp in West Virginia.

Sharpsburg Arsenal

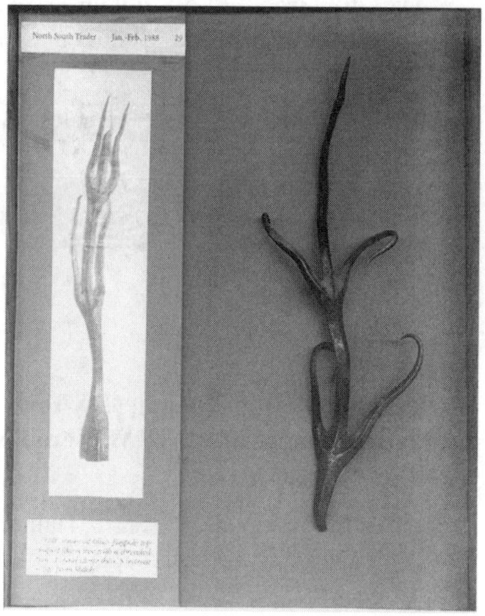

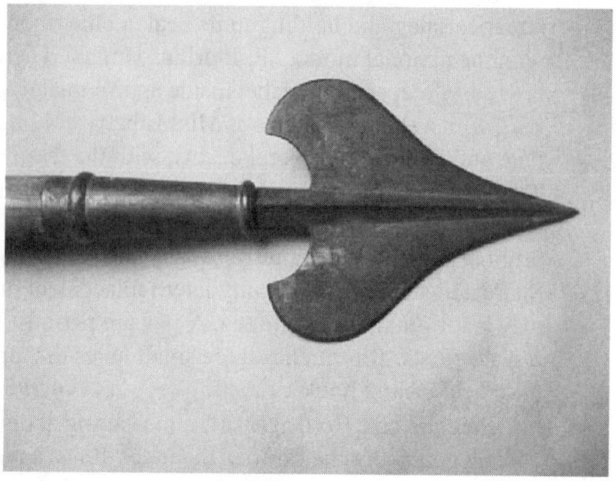

Brass-tipped, original 10' flag mast.

Drumbeat Civil War Memorabilia

Flagpole Tip, unusual brass flagpole tip shaped like a tree, recovered on Rt. 11, south of Bunker Hill, West Virginia, in a former Confederate camp. Framed in a wood shadow box. **795.00**

Staff, Flag, original 10' Civil War flag staff with brass finial and end cap. It still has most of original maker's label that reads, "A Ertle -Artillery Reg't Colors New York maker." Also has the original long gold and red tassle cord. This is an authentic Civil War flagstaff. **1,250.00**

Flag Terminology

Battle honors: The names of battles or engagements in which the unit fought; honors are sewn or painted onto the flag or attached by streamers.

Bunting: The woolen fabric from which flags were traditionally made.

Canton: Any quarter of the flag, but commonly refers to the upper-left corner. On the U.S. flag, it is the blue section.

Charge: An emblem or design added to the basic flag.

Color: During the Civil War, this was the national, state, or regimental flag carried by dismounted units.

Ensign: A flag flown on ships or boats.

Ferrule: A metal tip at the bottom of a staff used to plant the flag in the ground or rest the flag in a sling around the neck.

Field: The background color on a flag.

Finial: An ornamental device attached to the head of a flagstaff.

Flank Markers: Small flags carried at each end of an infantry regiment's line of battle to mark the flanks.

Fly: The part of the flag furthest from the staff.

Guidon: A small flag or banner carried by military units to identify their origin or affiliation.

Hoist: The part of the flag nearest to the staff or flagpole.

Pennant: A flag made in the shape of an isosceles triangle, which has two equal sides.

Standard: This was the national, state, or regimental flag carried by mounted units.

Chapter 10

Groupings

Groupings can provide a virtual window into the lives of individual Civil War soldiers. Whether a grouping consists of simply an identification disc and a couple of letters or a trunk field with every piece of a soldier's uniform and equipment, groupings place the collector one step closer to the Civil War experience.

There is no exact formula that will determine whether or not several items constitute a grouping. Generally, any items that were together during the Civil War and have survived together until today are considered to be a "grouping." Premium value and historical significance is placed on groupings that still retain an identified association with a particular soldier. Holding a cartridge box and Springfield rifle that were found together is interesting, but add to that the knowledge that Corporal Stephen Page of the famous Iron Brigade's 6th Wisconsin Volunteer Infantry wore the cartridge box and carried the rifle at the Battle of Gettysburg instantaneously multiplies interest, appeal, and monetary value of the two items.

Collecting groupings can involve a lot of homework. Not too many fresh groupings emerge anymore, but occasionally items do emerge from attics, barns, or other long forgotten storage places. When a grouping does come to market, the competition to own it is high. Both collectors and museums place a premium value on associate, identified collections. Be prepared to spend a lot more for a grouping than you would for the same type of items without any known provenance or association.

Collecting groupings, though, does not necessarily have to be expensive. Excavated relics that came from the same trash pit, breastwork, battlefield, or even state, are all "groupings." A handful of buttons and a carte de visite that passed down through family hands are a "grouping." Groupings come in all sizes and forms. The crucial point is to record the information about the items origins so that the sense of the grouping is not lost to the next generation of collectors.

Collecting Hints

Pros:

- A group of items that belonged to an individual soldier imparts a direct sense of the Civil War to a collector. Groupings allow personality to emerge from the pages of history.
- Groupings tend to tell a more complete story of Civil War soldier than just a single, identified object.

Cons:

- Most groupings are expensive. One pays extra for the fact that the items have remained together since the Civil War. A premium price is paid when an item is "identified," that is, when the original soldier who used the item is known.
- Groupings require special care and handling to insure that the known history of the items is not lost. Often, groupings consist items made of dissimilar materials that require different storage environments, such as leather goods requiring humid storage and firearms requiring dry climates.
- Groupings are only as good as the documentation that accompanies them. It is easy, and often tempting, to assemble groupings. As an example, accouterment sets are often assembled (many right after the war by the veterans themselves) and represented as always having been together.

Availability ★★★★★
Price ★★
Reproduction Alert ★★★★

1st Pennsylvania Volunteer Grouping, identified to Private John F. Shawmon, Company F, 1st Pennsylvania Cavalry, this grouping consists of his leather ammunition pouch, maker-marked bull's-eye canteen with original blue cover, and a superb lock-blade knife, includes a family history, military records, and even a rubbing from the monument at Gettysburg which has his name on it. **1,150.00**

3rd Massachusetts Heavy Artillery Grouping, consists of a canteen, an accouterment set, and stencil that once belonged to Daniel O. Hovey, 3rd Massachusetts Heavy Artillery. The grouping includes Hovey's Model 1858 canteen, complete in all respects, has the cover, shoulder strap, stopper, chain, and it bears Hovey's name in ink on the cover. Also includes Hovey's .58-caliber cartridge box with the sling, both plates, and tin liners—all in exceptionally nice condition with a pretty russet-brown box finish, and sling in matching condition, maker-marked box, "Chillingworth/Maker/Greenfield, Mass." The sling is marked, "A.W. Decrow/Maker/Bangor, Me." The box and sling are near perfect except for the missing small tab on the inner implement pouch. All other straps and buckles are firmly in place. Other pieces are his waist belt, U.S. buckle, and cap box with his name nicely stenciled with his full name inside the belt. The belt is complete with the leather loop adjuster, and the cap box bears the same maker's stamp as the cartridge box sling, "A.W. Decrow/ Maker/Bangor, Me." Finally is Hovey's original large clothing stencil and brush in the original blue pasteboard box, the stencil is filled out, "Daniel O. Hovey." The box is nicely inscribed in period ink script with his name and the unit of "7th Co." The original ink brush is still inside the box along with a length of twine that Hovey saved for some reason. A really superb lot of gear really owned and carried by one Yankee soldier. Mr. Hovey served in two units; the 7th Company of Heavy Artillery, and the 3rd Regiment of Heavy Artillery, that was organized by consolidating several of the independent companies (including the 7th) in August 1864, and using them as infantry in the defenses of Washington. The Massachusetts rosters show him as O.D. Hovey instead of D.O. Hovey and represent him as having served in both 7th Company and 3rd Regiment of artillery. **2,850.00**

7th South Carolina Volunteer Cavalry Grouping, nice condition Confederate linen haversack, match safe, and combination spoon-fork that came out of United Daughters of the Confederacy (U.D.C), Chapter 2048, Georgetown, South Carolina, and belonged to one of two brothers who were both members of Hampton's Legion, 7th South Carolina Cavalry. The two brothers were Benjamin and Paul Fraser. With the haversack comes an old three-page U.D.C. letter detailing the lives and service of both brothers. The group remains in the original old box marked "Bessie Fraser-Personal" that it was in when given to the U.D.C. This is a fine South Carolina Confederate grouping. **1,850.00**

10th Maine Volunteer Infantry Grouping, material was owned by Lieutenant William Davis of the 1st and 9th USCT and formerly of the 10th Maine. First is a fine period framed 8" x 10" albumen portrait of Davis in line officer's frock. Next is his cdv album which contains seven soldier photos including 1) Full view of Davis in uniform with sash and sword belt; 2) Bust view of Davis in uniform; 3) Standing view in uniform and sword with belt and sash of E. Winter 12th Maine (signed in ink); 4) Bust view of C.C. Richardson, 12th Maine; 5) Standing view with sword, belt, and sash, of same C.C. Richardson, signed in ink; 6) Bust view in uniform of W. Hodson, 12th Maine (signed in ink); and a group photo cdv of seven men in uniforms with caps. In addition to these, there are views of, "The Prince of Wales with Victoria," Tom Thumb and wife, and numerous family views including some great shots of kids. The album itself is an outstanding leather-bound affair. The last piece is the engraved seal (for making wax seals on letters) from the U.S. Mint at New Orleans. It has a rosewood handle, and brass seal beautifully engraved with an eagle's head and ribbon that reads "US Br. Mint N.O" (US Branch Mint New Orleans). It is likely that this is something that Davis brought home with him.......................**975.00**

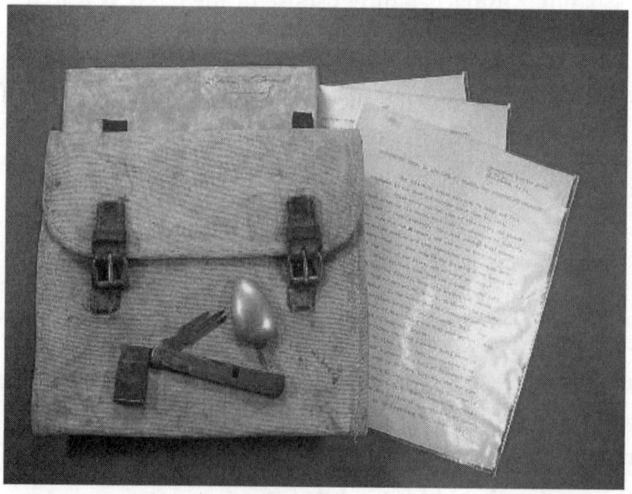

Adding a Confederate grouping to a collection can be like setting the crown jewel in place. This interesting haversack and mess equipment belonged to one of two brothers who served together in the 7th South Carolina Volunteer Cavalry, a unit in the famous Hampton's Legion.

Middle Tennessee Relics

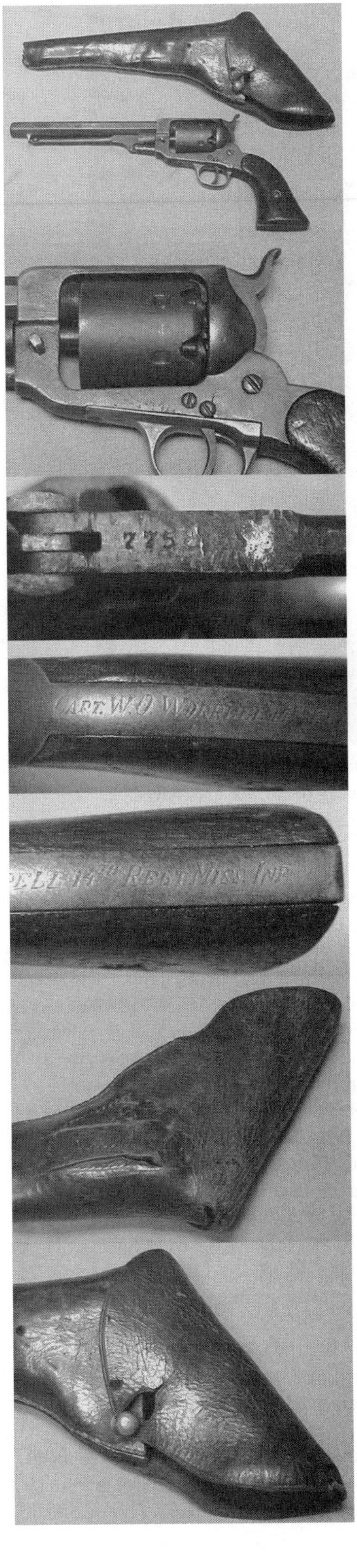

This .36 revolver and holster was carried by Captain William Worrell, 14th Mississippi Volunteer Infantry.

Sharpsburg Arsenal

14th Mississippi Volunteer Infantry Grouping, Whitney .36-caliber revolver with holster identified to Captain William Worrell, 14th Regiment Mississippi Infantry. Worrell's residence was in Lowndes County, Tennessee. According to records included, Worrell was mustered in on May 25, 1861. He was captured at Fort Donelson on February 16, 1862, and listed as escaped on July 4, 1862. Worrell was promoted to Captain on September 25, 1862. He is listed again as captured at Franklin, Tennessee, December 17, 1864, and later released in accordance with General Order No. 109. War Department records also have William Worrell as being transferred from "Military Prison" to "No. 2 (New), U.S.A., Gen'l Hosp. Nashville, Tenn." on June 24, 1865, with a diagnosis of "G.S.W. [gunshot wound] right chest." **12,795.00**

A grouping of items from a member of the 15th New Hampshire Volunteer Infantry included his identification disc, carte de visite, and letters concerning his death.

15th New Hampshire Volunteer Infantry Grouping, first in this group is a "War of 1861" identification disc, the reverse of which is stamped: "J.E. Garland Co. I, 15th REG NHV Rochester." Next is a letter with cover written by Private John Garland from General N.P. Banks Expedition Camp Parapet New Orleans, Louisiana, dated March 3, 1863. There is also an original photo of Private Garland in uniform. In addition, there is a period photo of Mrs. Lizzie Garland (Garland's wife) and a widow's letter with cover to family members discussing "particulars" of the soldier's death from typhoid fever dated January 25, 1864, and a second one dated May 8, 1863. All items are in excellent condition. **1,135.00**

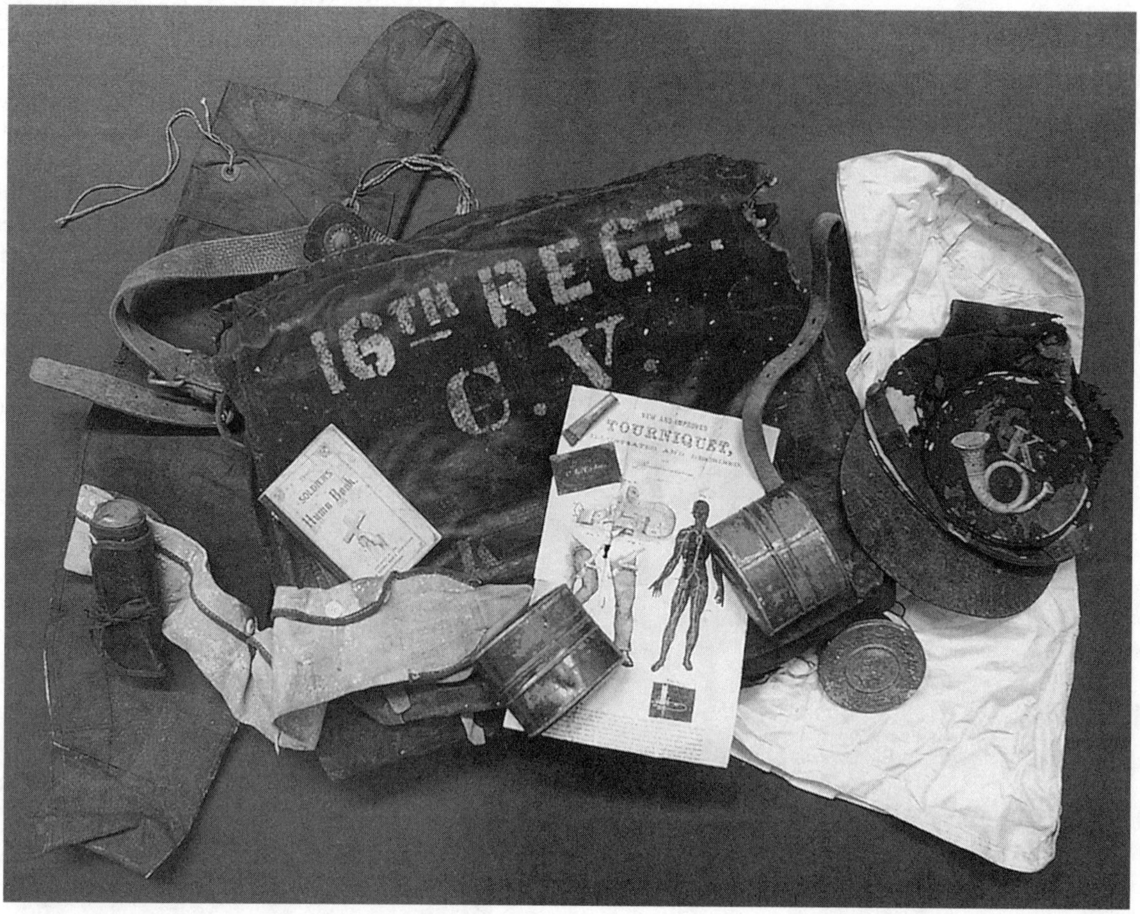

Charles L. Taylor sent a box of his Civil War belongings to a family member before he passed away. It contained several mementoes of Taylor's service in the 16th Connecticut including his forage cap, havelock, knapsack, and several personal items.

J.C. Devine Inc.

16th Connecticut Volunteer Infantry Grouping, the 16th Connecticut was a three-year unit and Charles L. Taylor enlisted as a Sergeant on July 29, 1862, and served until June 24, 1865. This regiment suffered heavy losses at Antietam, participated in the battle of Fredericksburg, narrowly escaped shipwreck off Roanoke Island, and was overwhelmed at the siege of Plymouth with losses, including many captured, of 436 men. These effects were consigned by Taylor's descendants. Included is the original, large, colorful receipt from, "Adams Express Company," in Newbern, North Carolina, dated April 11, 1865, that Charles Taylor received when he shipped the box home to his mother. This receipt is in excellent condition. Contents of the box include: an issue black tarred cloth knapsack and associated straps, the flap marked, "16th REGT/C.V./K," with attached tag with Taylor's name and address, fair to good condition; Taylor's forage cap in relic condition, with brass "K" and infantry bugle on the top; his white cotton havelock, stained, but showing no wear; 3" d shaving mirror in stamped metal case with bust of Napoleon on the cover, good; small stencil and brush with Taylor's name, very good; tinned iron spoon, fair; small *Soldier's Hymn Book*, very good; 1861-patent tourniquet in original tin case with instructions, good; extra case for tourniquet with bandage, very good; housewife with sewing supplies, very good; sheet of emery paper used to keep metal musket parts bright, marked by the London maker, "Manufacturers To Her Majesty's Honorable Board of Ordnance;" box with 23 assorted brass eagle buttons, very good; leather money belt, good; small burlap shot bag with N.Y. City and Newbern, N.C. address, good; three G.A.R. stamped metal hat devices and a small medal for the 1899 encampment, all in fine condition; several small flag scraps, believed to be from the Regimental colors that were torn into shreds at the fall of Plymouth to prevent their capture when the town was surrendered; several large sheets of paper used to wrap parcels received by Taylor; Feb. 22, 1864 dated, "Account of Pay and Clothing," 11" x 21" for Taylor, very good; a bundle of approximately a dozen post-Civil War newspapers. As Taylor was detached for a time to act as a clerk at headquarters he managed to accumulate a large assortment of original documents which included: seven passes; 25 general orders; 14 special orders (many of which mention Taylor by name); eight clipped autographs of military men; and three cabinet photos. All the paper is in excellent condition. Also found in the box was an unusual period rubberized cloth case for a carbine, the condition is good. **5,500.00**

16th and 62nd North Carolina Troops Grouping, .36-caliber, single action Remington Beales Revolver, serial number 14119, with smooth plum-gray finish overall. Old repair on loading lever catch. Back strap professionally engraved in old English letters, "Col. R. G. A. Love." Pommel engraved in same style, "62nd Regt. N.C.T." The engraving appears to be ancient and is totally in keeping with the rest of the piece's condition. Black, thin saddle-leather, Confederate-style holster with lead closing finial, in very good condition with only moderate crazing, very supple leather. Love joined the Confederate Army in 1861 as captain of Company L, 16th North Carolina. He was elected lieutenant colonel of that regiment in late 1861, but was not re-elected after the reorganization of the Army of Northern Virginia in the spring of 1862. He was reassigned to the 62nd North Carolina, then being formed in Western North Carolina. He was elected colonel and formed the Regiment into, "a war-like set of men." Love led the regiment in several forays against Union sympathizers, catching several and disbanding other units. In doing this, his health declined so badly that he was forced to resign from the Army on August 13, 1863, 60 pages of documents accompanies the group. **6,500.00**

17th Indiana Volunteer Infantry Grouping, a grouping that belonged to John W. Ryan of Indiana who was in both the 17th Indiana of Wilder's Brigade fame and of the 34th Indiana Infantry (who dressed in Zouave uniforms). There are two promotional documents for John W. Ryan, both signed by the Indiana Wartime Governor, Oliver P. Morton. The first one is for the 17th Indiana (Wilder's Brigade) dated January 17, 1862, in which he was second lieutenant (John joined this regiment as a sergeant). This document is also signed by the Secretary of State and the Adjutant General Indiana Militia. There are tape repairs to the back of the document that have bled through, but all is easily read. The second promotional document is dated March 20, 1862, in which John Ryan was named first lieutenant and adjutant of the 34th Indiana Regiment. This document has some tape residue, but not badly, and a hole in the document's center that doesn't affect any text. Regimental histories of both the 17th and 34th Indiana are included with the grouping. Also included in this grouping are two later civilian photographs of John W. Ryan, one bust shot and one full shot, as well as a postcard of his home in Anderson, Indiana, after the turn of the century. There is also an early photocopy of his original service memorial listing his military service in both outfits. This is a large document measuring about 15 x 20 inches. John was wounded at the battle of Shiloh and was involved in several campaigns. Finally, there is a handwritten letter by John dated April 8, 1915, and seems to be his life history or his obituary that he wrote himself. **450.00**

23rd New York Volunteer Infantry Grouping. This is a collection of the Civil War-related personal effects, photos, and personal papers of Jarius Lamouree, who enlisted as a private in K Company, 23rd New York Volunteer Infantry on December 27, 1861, and mustered out Friday, May 22, 1863. He survived to become a member of the G.A.R. Mr. Lamouree lived in the Elmira New York area, and was buried in Woodlawn National Cemetery in Elmira. The collection includes a tintype in gold-plated embossed mat of Jarius as a civilian; a hand-tinted tintype of Jarius in his Civil War uniform including his caped coat (the tintype is in half of a gutta-percha case); two later carte de visites apparently of Jarius later in life as a civilian, one with a Treasury stamp on the back taken in New York, the other taken in Elmira by Moulton; two handwritten letters, one from the Sergeant Major of the 23rd NY Volunteers dated 1870 attesting to Jarius' service record, another written by George Clute, Binghamton, New York also attesting to his service record; his discharge papers dated 1863, and signed by the Captain of the 14th Infantry; his pension papers; his wife's various pension payments; a G.A.R. postcard announcing an 1898 encampment reunion in Elmira, New York; plus numerous papers including his marriage license, mortgage, and others. The most poignant piece is a handwritten letter to his wife from "Ebneyser Hospital," on November 15, 1862, in which he tells her, "I am no better and I don't think I will be til it gets warm." There is also the family Bible in fragile condition with the family birth records including Jarius' and his family. There is a small, pocket-sized bible also included is his 8-1/4" original brass-embossed powder flask with hare and game birds in high relief on both sides, with some dinging from use, but in very nice condition. In addition, also included is Jarius' lap desk 13-7/8" x 9-1/4" x 4-1/8", with a round brass medallion top inset, a brass key escutcheon, working lock and key, and his original, mother-of-pearl and gold-plated dip pen in its own fitted, black leatherette box.............. **1,500.00**

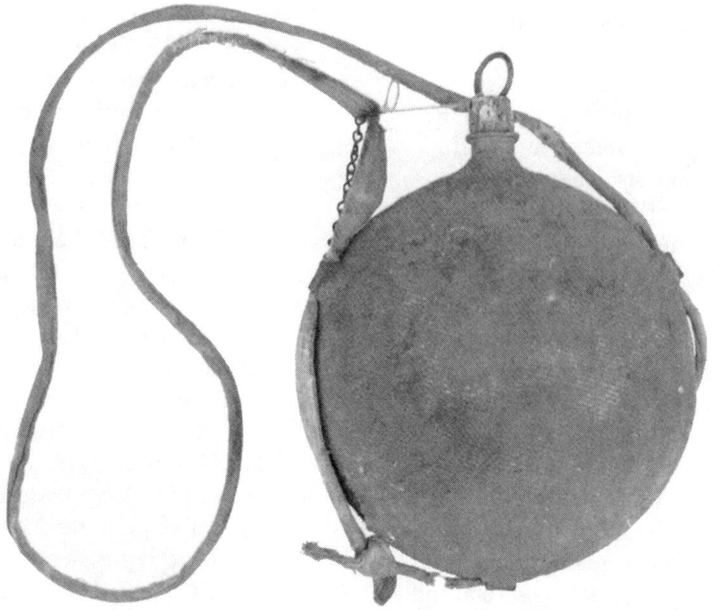

This complete Model 1858 smooth-sided canteen was part of a group of items that belonged Lieutenant H.A. Darling of the 25th Connecticut Volunteer Infantry.

J.C. Devine Inc.

25th Connecticut Volunteer Infantry Grouping, highlighting this grouping is a Model 1858 canteen with cloth cover, sling, and original cork stopper. The cover has faded to gray with three moth holes, the sling shows a few frayed spots, but is sound, only part of the chain remains for the stopper. With the canteen is the former owner's brass stencil marked, "Lt. H.A. DARLING/CO.B.25, REG't CT. V," his gold bullion hat cord, a reunion ribbon for the 25th Connecticut Volunteers for 1904; a G.A.R. medal for the 31st Encampment in Buffalo in 1897; a stencil brush, and two additional brass stencils for other members of Darling's family. Lieutenant Darling served with the 25th from August 20, 1862, until the unit was mustered out on August 26, 1863, with active service in Louisiana. On September 15, 1863, Darling was mustered in the U.S. Volunteer Commissary Department as a captain, and made lieutenant colonel by brevet in March 1865, serving until June 23, 1886. .... **450.00**

44th Wisconsin Volunteer Infantry Grouping, canteen, relic haversack, and framed memorial of the Wipf brothers. The canteen is the standard Model 1858 smooth-side variety complete with full tan wool cover, full shoulder strap, and stopper. Excellent condition, shows honest use and storage age, but no damage or defects, also present is a commercial, officer's grade haversack in torn and worn condition without the shoulder strap. Finally, there is an excellent framed color Company Roster of Company E, 44th Wisconsin, which carries the names of the Wipf brothers (Jacob and Conrad). The company roster-memorial is beautiful red, white, and blue with eagle killing a snake, drum, ships, and patriotic motifs that bears an 1862 copyright by Samuel Martin of Wisconsin. **675.00**

56th New York Volunteer Infantry Grouping, saved by a Union army officer and his family, all in superb condition, includes a fine Model 1850 foot officer's sword (Horstmann signed) with great etched blade and engraved on the top mount, "Presented to Lieut. Vanderburgh by the members of Co "B" 56th Regt. N.Y.S.V. as a mark of esteem." The sword is housed in its original, unbroken leather scabbard, full sharkskin grip and most of the wire is intact. Also included is Effingham VanDerBurgh's regulation M1858 smooth canteen complete with perfect full tan wool cover, strap, stopper, and painted on the front cover with his initials "E.V.B." Also present in this lot is his large brass stencil reading, "E. VanDerBurgh/Lieut." Additionally, his officer's belt with eagle buckle is included, but no saber hangers are present. The group includes a superb sixth plate tintype of him in frock with this sword, sash, and cap on table. There is also a sixth plate tintype of his child, aged three or four. A rather uneventful bound roll book (size of a diary) is included, as is a rectangular militia shoulder belt plate (prewar?). The brass plate has a separately applied silver bust of George Washington over matching silver numerals, "76." This unit was organized near Newburgh, New York, in the summer of 1861. The regiment was sent to Washington in November and was assigned to Silas Casey's division serving in the areas surrounding the capitol. The regiment served with distinction in the 7 Days Battles, and later in the 18th Corps, but Lieutenant Vanderburgh saw fit to leave the service in the early part of 1862. ..... **4,500.00**

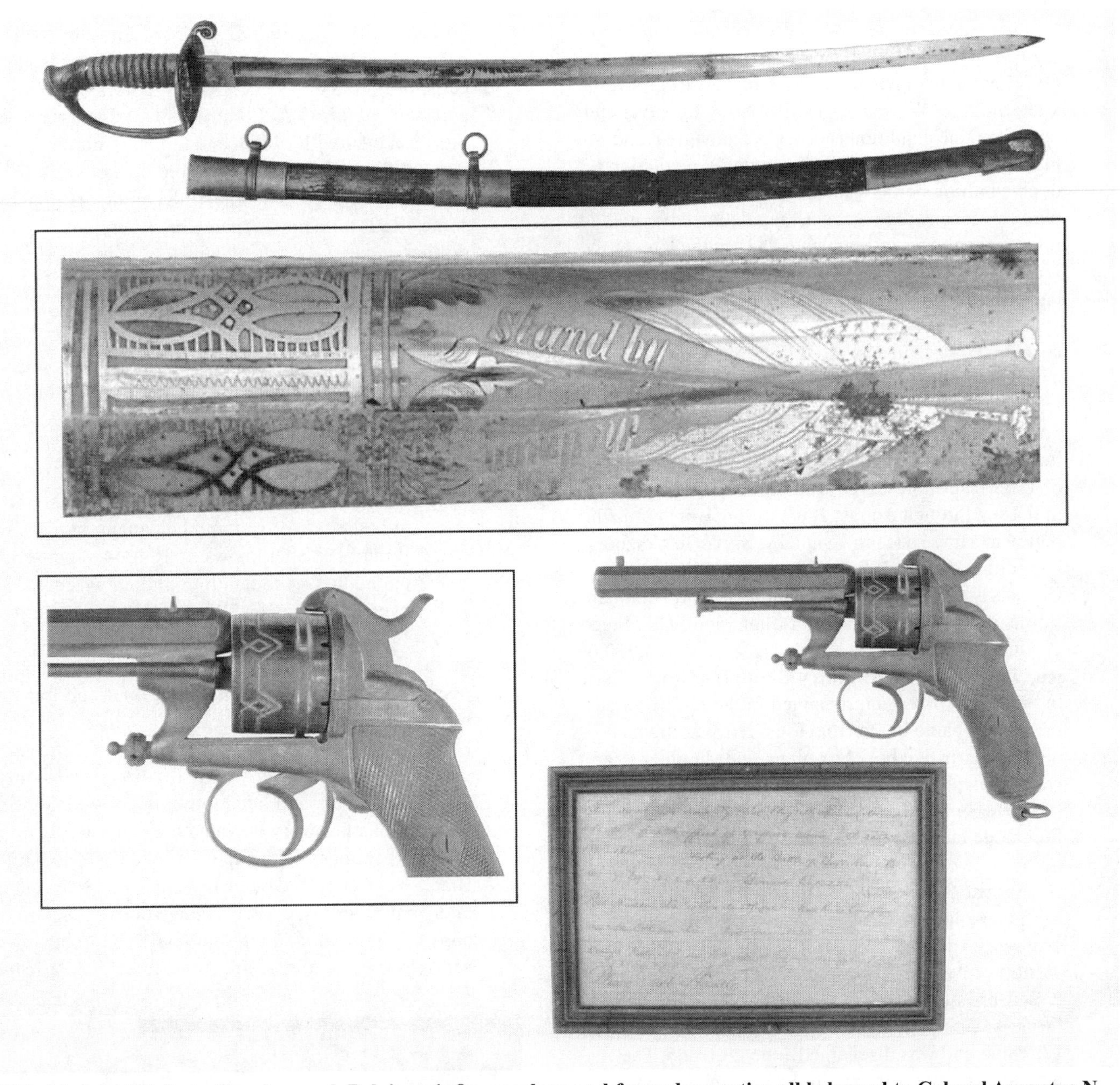

This Model 1850 foot officer's sword, Belgian pinfire revolver, and framed narrative all belonged to Colonel Augustus N. Thomas of the 71st New York Infantry.

J.C. Devine Inc.

71st New York Volunteer Infantry Grouping, consists of the sword and revolver that belonged to Colonel Augustus N. Thomas, 71st Regiment of New York Infantry. The 1850 foot officer's sword has a 31-1/4" blade etched on the reverse ricasso with the name of the retailer, "Schuyler/Hartley/+Graham/New York." Beautiful etching done with each side having floral scrolls, an American eagle with rib, a Liberty cap, and a stand of flags with the motto, "Stand by the Union." The brass guard and pommel retain traces of gilt and have mostly a mustard-brown patina; the fish skin wrapped grip is in fine condition, but is missing almost all of the wire. The brass-mounted black leather scabbard has an open seam and a complete break between the middle band and the drag. The blade shows very little wear, but does have many small patches of surface rust. The revolver is a Belgian-made pinfire, double action Chamelot-Delvigne, 11.2mm cal.. with a 5-3/8" l octagon barrel. The revolver has inlaid silver frame borders and inlaid silver hands on the cylinder. The cylinder retains much original blue with many small spots of surface rust; the barrel has a dark patina, frame case colors have turned dark, the checkered wood grips are fine. The lot includes a framed handwritten narrative of Colonel Thomas's participation in the Civil War and a notarized letter from his great grandson. **1,600.00**

83rd Ohio Volunteer Infantry Grouping, includes the following items owned by Albert Thornton: his regulation 1850 foot officer's sword and scabbard (excellent with one bend in scabbard); officer's sword knot; Smith & Wesson .32 caliber Army Revolver and holster in fine condition (holster is really great and marked "Kittridge and Co. Cincinnati"); regulation double bullion border captain's shoulder straps with blue velvet centers (excellent); regulation embroidered infantry hat bugle insignia with "83" in the loop of the horn insignia (excellent with brown, polished cotton back over metal insert complete with loops); eyeglasses, a wonderful war-date embroidered pin cushion, G.A.R. medals, MOLLUS medal (numbered), a neckerchief, a postwar crystal inkwell, a postwar leather cigar case full of ammo for the revolver, a postwar silver match safe, and miscellaneous other items including his resignation document from August of 1863. Thornton served with the 83rd Ohio from mid-1862 through August 1863, during which time the regiment saw service in Kentucky, Sherman's Yazoo Expedition, Millike's Bend, Chickasaw Bayou, Chickasaw Bluff, assault and capture of Fort Hindman, Battle of Port Gibson, Battle of Champion's Hill, Siege of Vicksburg, and more. **4,950.00**

178th Ohio Volunteer Infantry Grouping, from a barn in Southern Michigan, remained in the family since the soldier came home from the Civil War. Items include: cartridge box, box plate, and shoulder strap with breastplate; belt, buckle, and cap box; canteen (no cover or strap); tin box with five eagle "I" and four eagle buttons; bayonet and scabbard (tip is in the tin box); two powder horns, one small, one large; tin shaving mug; and sixteen letters with envelopes (14 from the soldier, one of which is on Sanitary Fair stationery and four on patriotic stationery (one patriotic envelope). The soldier's name was Benjamin F. Beavers and he was in the 178th Ohio Volunteer Infantry, Company D. He entered service on August 17, 1864, and was discharged June 29, 1865. The letters have little war news or battle content; however, they are interesting nonetheless. The items in this grouping are untouched, not cleaned, and as found. The leather is in rather poor shape, yet it is complete, there are cracks and breaks in some of the pieces. **2,706.00**

207th Pennsylvania Infantry Grouping, accoutrements and letters of James Morrison that turned up in central Pennsylvania in a small storage box full of Civil War letters from the Morrison-Harrison family. First is his .69-caliber U.S. cartridge box in good solid worn condition (latch tab broken) with a small silver star affixed to the front flap. Inside the box's inner flap is an old brown ink tag, which reads, "James Morrison/1831-1904 Civil War Veteran." Next is a nice, brown leather cap box marked by Gaylord with some old .32-caliber center fire shell casings inside for some reason. Also present is his eagle breastplate (decent with some storage dings). In addition, are his G.A.R. hat wreath insignia, G.A.R. pewter medal with ribbon and top bar from the 27th Annual Encampment, a rusted old pocket knife of unknown vintage, some late 19th century eyeglasses, some 1850s note books (name on cover), his discharge paper, G.A.R. documents, some pictures, and a hundred family papers and letters from 1812 to 1880s. Finally, in this grouping is his collection of 35 war date letters he wrote home in 1864 and 1865 with some excellent content covering the heated contest over Virginia during Grant's final assaults on Lee. Some selections include March 5, 1865 on regimental letterhead, "...have been in two hard fights and have not been hit by a ball yet, Andrew Floyd is killed and so is brother Wm Harrison/dear wife you must not worry, it is the fate of war and how many more of us will fall the Lord only knows..." 10/6/64 super letter near Appomattox river detailing trading w/reb pickets and conversation they had "... the Johnnys hollerd over to us hello thair yanks air you all dead over there? We told them no and we told them it was a poorty ruff nite... they come to our lines and traded tobacco for sugar and coffee and jackiniase(?)..."Needless to say, this is an historical grouping from a soldier who really was there, really saw the elephant, and lived to tell the story. The material displays very well and the war letters are really great, many with super letterheads (one with Black-Negro boy and poem) There is a pile of related later family letters, a 1920 vintage photo negative copy of Civil War soldier photo believed to be Morrison, and more. **2,250.00**

Though bearing no soldier's identification, this set of infantryman's accoutrements had "SNY" plates on the belt and cartridge box.

Accouterment Grouping, Unidentified

A fine New York soldier's accoutrement set in overall very good to fine condition, has both the "SNY" (State of New York) plate (stud back variety) and the "SNY" cartridge box plate. All of the leather is solid and strong with good finish, just showing light age from use. The cap box has a faint inspector's cartouche on the front flap, and maker's stamp of "Storms NY Maker" on the inner flap (some flaking on finish of inner flap). The belt is solid and has had the brass adjuster removed as is seen on nearly all "actually used" belts. The cartridge box has one in liner inside and bears the maker's stamp of "L.S. Baker NY." Both plates have a beautiful untouched age patina.......................... **1,195.00**

Grouping consists of a Civil War period U.S. belt, belt plate and cap box. Belt leather is 36" from end to end, 1-3/4" wide and 1/8" thick. Cap box and belt leather are soft and pliable. Cap box is solid with all stitching in good shape, and a good amount of fleece inside. There are no maker marks on the belt or box, U.S. belt plate has a few front dents. **333.00**

Grouping consisting of a belt (no plate), cartridge box, and scabbard.

J.C. Devine Inc.

Grouping consists of a U.S. infantryman's waist belt with a Model 1864 cartridge box and socket bayonet scabbard.The .58 caliber box is marked on the inside flap, "WATERTOWN/ARSENAL/1864 / US." The box has one tin, the belt no longer has the oval plate, and the scabbard has a partial seam opening. The dark-brown leather accoutrements show surface crazing and wear, overall condition is good. **275.00**

Remnants of a waist belt and a very tired cartridge box with "red rot." The U.S. oval buckle is spectacular with magnificent age patina. It has an arrow hook back and is very pretty................... **245.00**

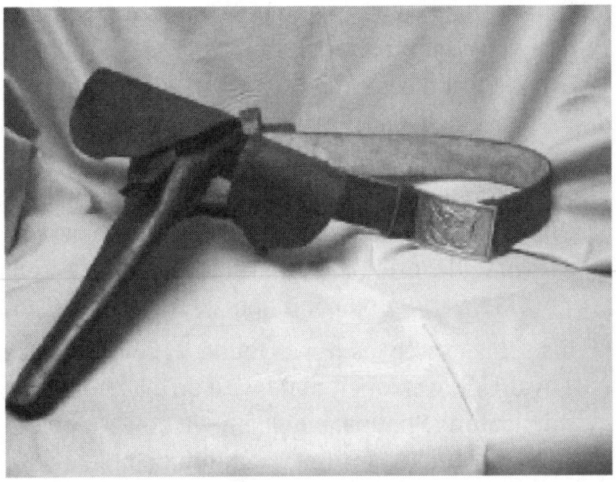

An interesting cavalryman's rig consisting of belt, Model 1851 plate, cap box, and right-draw holster.

The grouping consists of a holster belt rig with cap pouch and pistol cartridge box (arsenal-marked). An exceptional NCO-type Eagle buckle is Allegheny Arsenal marked as is the matching keeper. There is also a modified right-hand-draw military holster. All in excellent condition with great eye appeal. **1,750.00**

This excellent set consists of a U.S. oval buckle with arrow hook back, fine U.S. regulation infantry waist belt complete with the brass adjuster, regulation Civil War infantry cap box with bold "Haedrich" maker's stamp, and a Model 1864, .58-caliber infantry cartridge box with clear Woodbury inspector's cartouche on the outer flap and crisp maker's stamp of "W. H. Wilkinson Maker Springfield Mass" on the inner flap. All of the leather is fine condition with good finish and honest handling wear. Everything is complete (all straps and buckles firmly in place). The only things missing are the tin liners inside the cartridge box......................... **795.00**

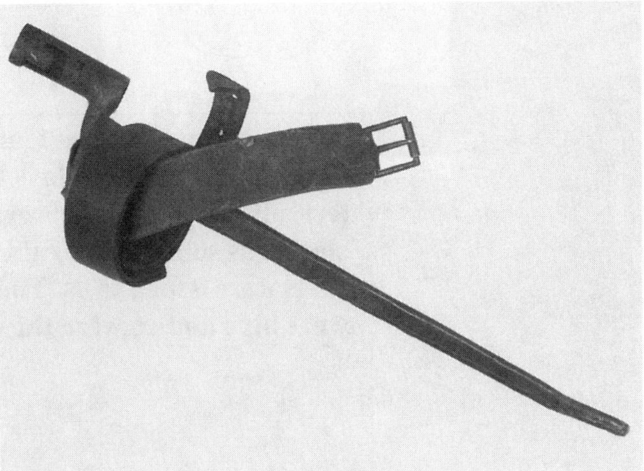

Model 1816 bayonet, scabbard, and belt with roller buckle.

J.C. Devine Inc.

This grouping consists of a U.S. Model 1816 socket bayonet with scabbard and belt. The blade is U.S.-marked and basically bright with spotty light corrosion, the socket with a dark patina. The scabbard is slightly longer than necessary, but from a partial break at the end of the bayonet it is evident that they have been together a long time. The scabbard frog is sewn to the original belt, which has a black iron roller buckle, very-good condition. **200.00**

This set is exactly as it was found. It consists of a nice oval U.S. waist belt plate with arrow hooks and delicate age patina; a fine, brown buff leather infantry waist belt in near mint condition complete with the brass adjuster; and a regulation cap box with clear maker's and inspector's stamps and the full complement of sheep wool inside as well as the vent pick. The leather on the front of the cap box is somewhat crackled with small areas of loss to finish. Also in this grouping is a Model 1864 infantry cartridge box with embossed "US" on the front flap complete with the tin liners inside. The leather on this box matches the cap box exactly (in terms of condition) with some crackling and slight loss to areas of finish, but totally stable and solid with no flakes or flaking. **795.00**

U.S. buckle with arrow hooks in solid, but "cleaned and polished" condition attached to the original soldier's waist belt (that has the owner's name "HERL" inked on it). The belt is full length and very good, but lacks the brass adjuster. Also comes with Herl's cap box that is pretty beat up with both belt loops broken (but present) and a ripped latch tab. **225.00**

Confederate Grouping, Kenansville D-guard Bowie knife, CDV, and a button board used by E. L. Hopkins. **7,950.00**

Dug Artifact Grouping, nice Civil War camp-dug knapsack hooks—all different. Nice brown patina on all and in excellent dug condition. **3.00**

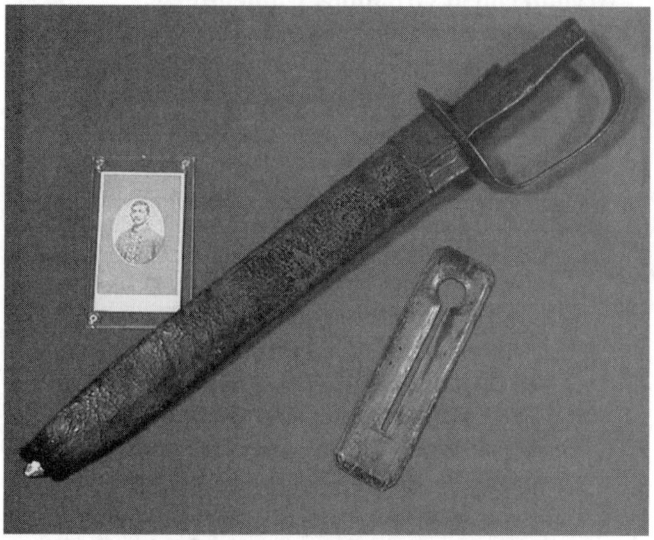

The D-Guard Bowie knife, button board, and carte de visite of Confederate E.L. Hopkins.

Old South Military Antiques

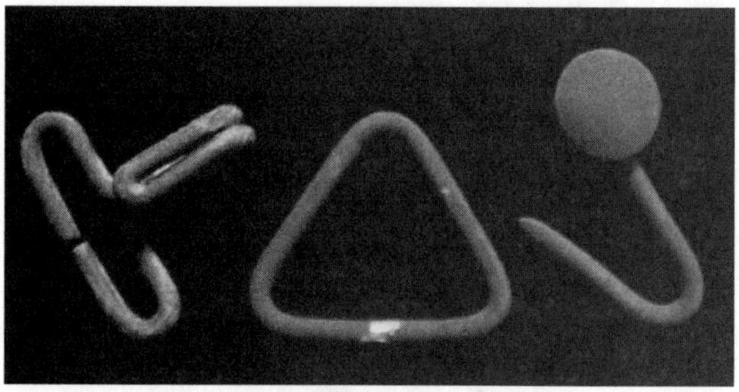

Groupings can come in all sizes and prices. These three knapsack hooks were dug together.

"We went into camp at Camp Texas with much better clothes than common. A few days before leaving our old winter quarters, all the men of our regiment drew uniforms of gray. The cloth was solid and durable. Only trousers and roundabout coats were issued to us. The cuffs or wrist bands on the sleeves were blue and so were the collars."

— Private Silas Turnbo
27th Arkansas Infantry (C.S.A.)

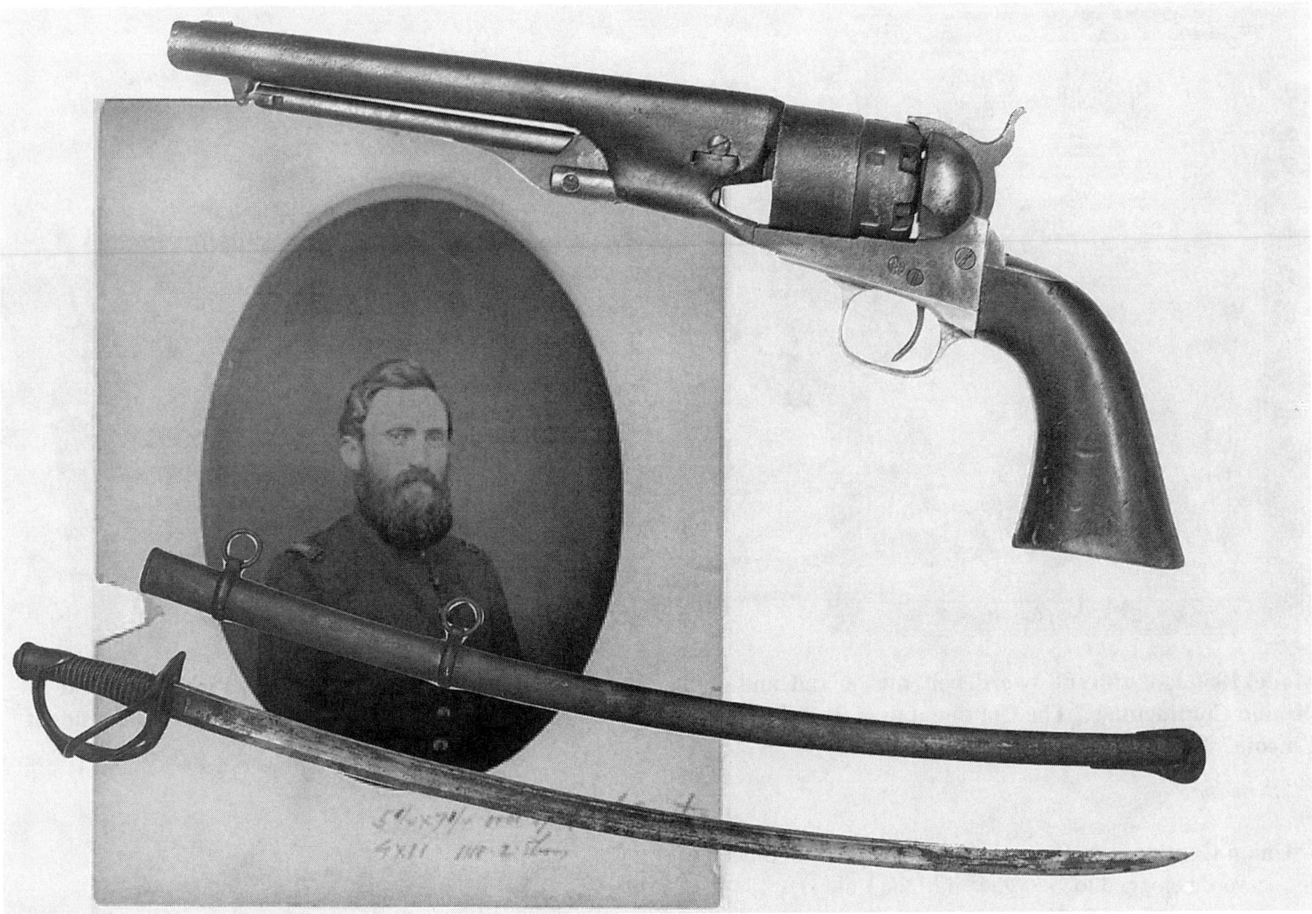

Model 1840 cavalry saber, Model 1860 Colt Army revolver, and large albumen photograph of Union Brigadier General Samuel Graham.

J.C. Devine Inc.

Purnell's Legion Grouping, items belonged to Samuel A. Graham of Purnell's Legion. Graham was born in Ireland and was a prominent Maryland lawyer who enlisted on September 15, 1861, as the captain of Company D of Purnell's Legion. The Legion was comprised of nine infantry companies, two cavalry companies, and two batteries of light artillery. In early 1862 they were engaged in driving armed Confederate bands from the eastern shore of Virginia and later served under General Pope in his campaigns in Virginia. The Legion participated in the Battle of Antietam and Graham wrote in one of his letters that is part of the grouping, "I was present on the 17th of September at Antietam and for seven hours the whistling of bullets and the roar of cannon sounded in my ears. I saw sights that time cannot efface from my memory." On January 12, 1863, Graham was commissioned into the Field and Staff of Purnell's Legion as Colonel. In 1864, the Legion took part in the Wilderness and Petersburg campaigns. On August 18, 1864, Graham was transferred into the U.S. Army, Second Brigade, Second Division. Information indicates that Graham later had a horse killed under him and was wounded in the hand while a brigadier general serving as the commander of the 5th Army Corps. The grouping is comprised of: Graham's Colt 1860 Army revolver, his Model 1840 heavy cavalry saber, his bible, his ebony and bone domino set, five letters to his sister, his framed commission as captain from the State of Maryland. The 1860 Colt is serial number 64940, .44 caliber. It has a three-screw frame cut for shoulder stock and has traces of military inspector's cartouches on both sides of the grip. All numbers match, the wedge is not numbered and about 30 percent of the cylinder scene remains. All the iron has a dark patina with scattered light pitting, the frame having a couple of large shallow dents. The grips show wear at the butt, retains most of the original oil finish. The 1840 saber is made by Ames, "U.S." marked and inspected, dated 1847. The blade has rust freckling and age spots with much of the original polish visible, should clean to excellent. The grip shows light wear to the leather and retains all the wire. The pommel bears the inspector's stamp, "J.W.P.," the scabbard is dark with light pitting on the lower half. Graham's bible has an inscription from his mother that begins, "A dying gift from his mother to Mr. Samuel A. Graham." Also included are a newspaper obituary of Graham, copies of research from Internet databases, and a statement about Graham's history. **3,500.00**

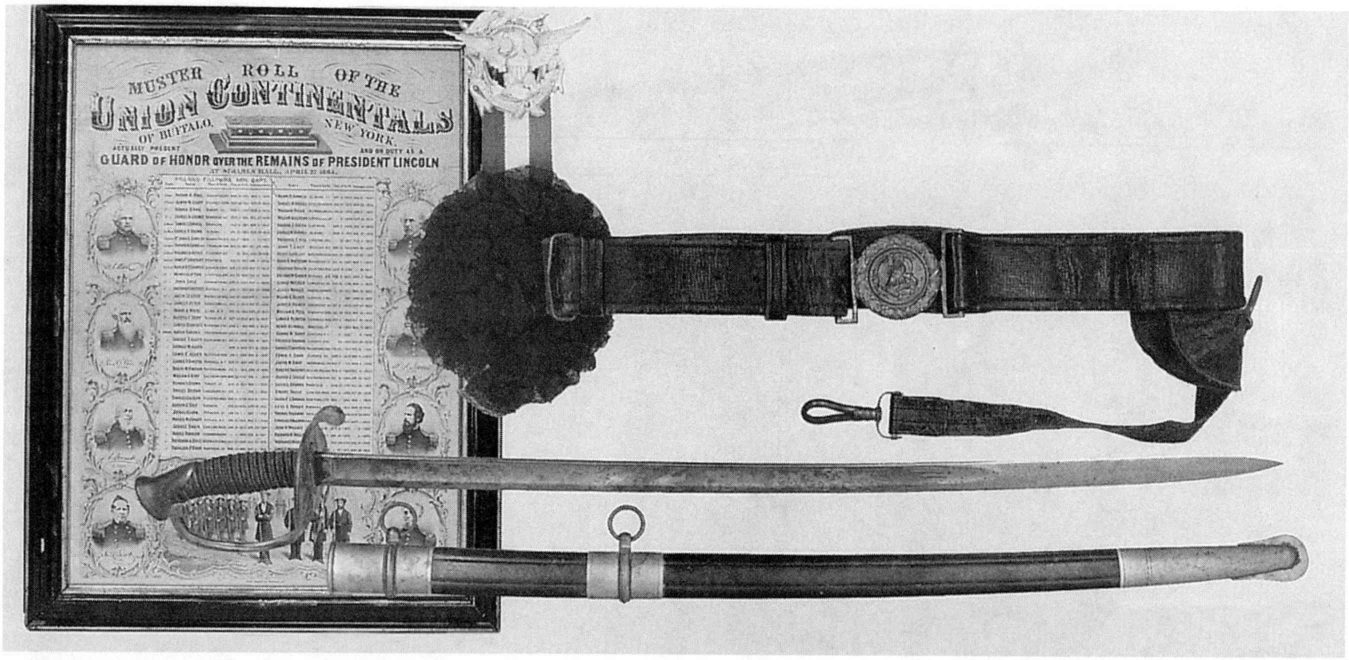

Model 1850 foot officer's sword, belt, muster roll, and mourning badge all belonged to George Vail, a member of the "Union Continentals." The Continentals, a Buffalo, New York, militia unit functioned as the honor guard for President Lincoln's remains.

J.C. Devine Inc.

Union Continentals Grouping, Model 1850 foot officer's sword belonged to George Vail of the Union Continentals of Buffalo, New York. A militia unit that formed it the 1850s, the Continentals were the honor guard for the remains of President Lincoln on April 27, 1865. The sword is a standard pattern with a 30-1/2" l blade, brightly etched on both sides with floral scrolls, the reverse with U.S. and the obverse with an American eagle and shield that oddly does not have a riband with motto. The blade shows age spotting and one tiny nick, with a little, very light tarnish/rust near the hilt. The blade's etching shows no wear to the gray frosting. The grip retains all of the wire and shows only the lightest wear on the fish skin wrap, the brass guard and pommel retain at least 50 percent of the gilt, and a careful cleaning may reveal much more. The brass-mounted black leather scabbard is in fine-plus condition. The scabbard drag is missing a screw; at least 70 percent of the gilt remains on the fittings. Included with the sword are a large (24" x 33") *Muster Roll Of The Union Continentals* in an old frame. This muster roll lists George O. Vail as a second lieutenant who was born in Danby, Vt. and has small oval vignettes of all of the unit's officers, including Vail. Also part of this lot are: a black cloth mourning badge for the assassinated President suspended by a ribbon from a metal eagle clasp; a framed black and white photograph of Vail in civilian clothes with a white beard; several photocopied sheets of information on Vail, copies of *Harpers Weekly* and *Leslie's Illustrated*; several hand written sheets of onion skin paper on Lincoln's funeral. **2,800.00**

Medical Grouping, Unidentified, superb Civil War asst. surgeon's cased fringed epaulets with bullion "MS" insignia on each, housed in the original japanned tin storage box. Overall fine to excellent condition with rich gilt bullion fringe, undented crescents, though there is a little damage to one "S" (in the "MS" bullion) on one of the epaulets. Also included is the high quality green medical sash with large tasseled knots and wide body. Excellent with a couple inconsequential nips in the body. **4,250.00**

Naval, Grouping, hockey puck-shaped gutta-percha shaving dish with raised U.S. Naval Insignia and the banner, "Don't Give Up The Ship." Darkened mirror inside, dish in perfect condition. Well-used stag-handled folding knife with single blade stamped "Sailors Knife/John C. Cowry/ Warrented" on the ricasso. Additionally a fine, man's leather wallet, strapped like the period wallets, embossed on both sides with the 1840s' period Naval eagle that is clutching an anchor within an oval. Nice set which came out of a North Carolina Family. .... **.675.00**

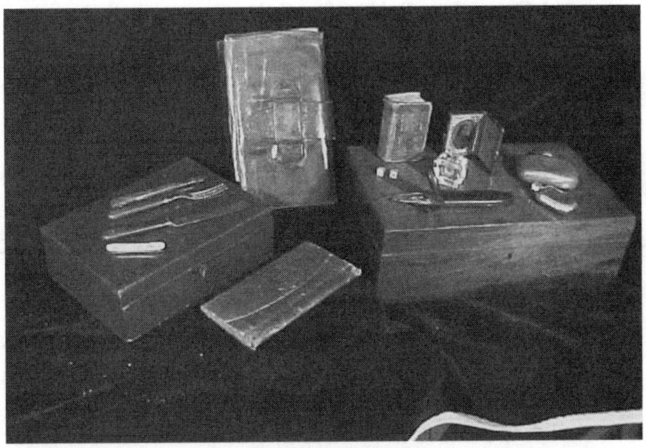

This is a grouping of items assembled by a collector, rather than by a single soldier who preserved them. "Married" groupings such as these do not curry much favor with ardent collectors, however, they do serve the purpose of demonstrating what a private soldier may have used.

Soldier's Personal Belongings, Unidentified, 16, 19th century pieces, The first item is a solid walnut lap desk with original writing surface. Except for a repair to the cloth hinge on the inside it is in very-good condition. It measures, 9" x 15" x 5". The walnut box still has its original decoration. Inside is a removable tray that measures 7-1/4" x 10" x 3" and is in perfect condition. One of the best items in this collection is a dark-green-leather personal paper carrier. It is made similarly to the wallets from the Civil War period, and is in very good usable condition. It measures, 6" x 10-1/2". The folding wallet is still soft and supple, and aside from two wear spots in the corner, is in very good, usable condition. It measures, 4" x 8". There are two flasks, the pewter flask is made by "Dixon" and holds a quarter pint, one side is dented, but it doesn't affect its use. The smaller, silver-plated, flask would have been used for medicine. It holds one ounce and measures 1-1/2" x 2-3/4". The knife and fork are made of steel and hard rubber and were made in Providence, Rhode Island. Both pieces are in very good condition. The rosewood-handled ink scraper is marked "CSO." The small book is the *Psalms of David* and was published in 1838. It is in very good condition. There is a small ambrotype and case of a young woman who could easily have been the girlfriend or wife of a Civil War soldier. The solid brass eyeglasses need a little cleaning up but are in very good condition. They come in their original, hard papier-mâché case that is in very good condition. The ivory-handled knife has two blades and a personal fingernail-grooming blade. The two knife blades have been sharpened to a very small size and the ivory is stained but not chipped or broken. Last, are two bone dice to be used only on payday. **280.00**

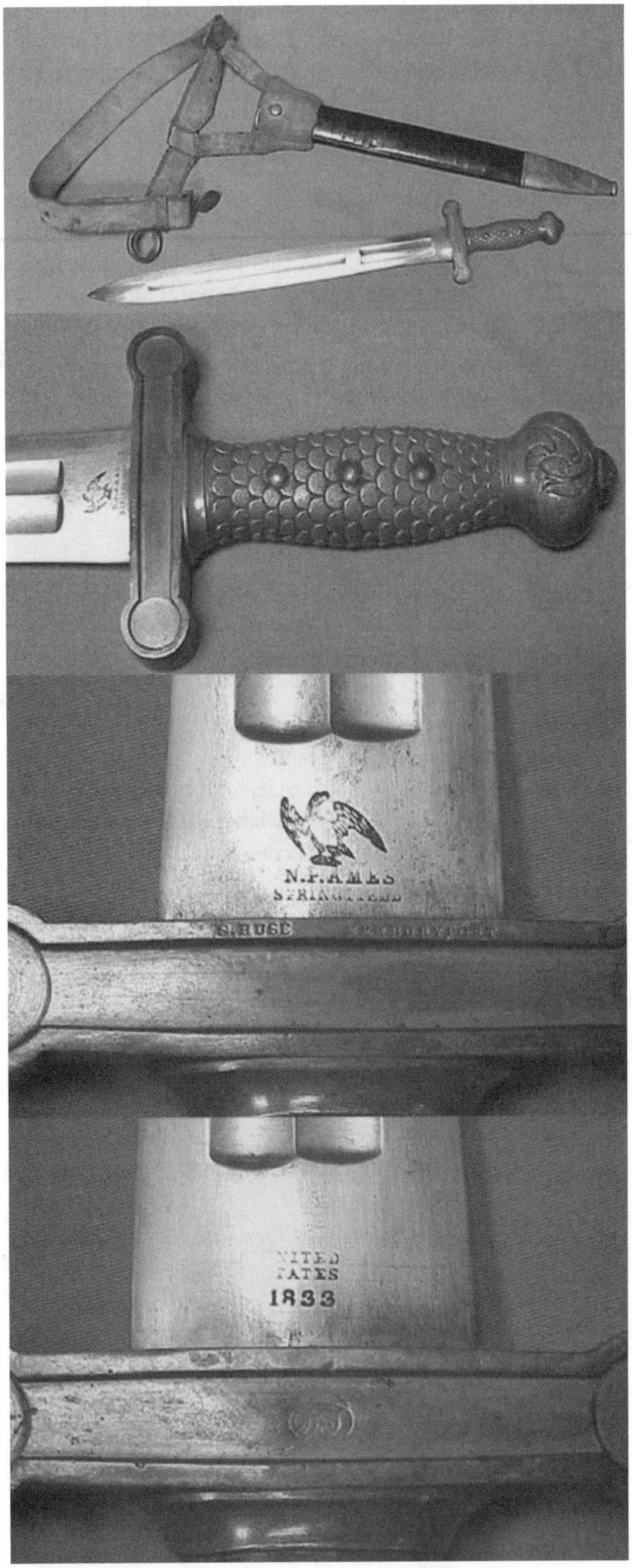

Though no identification accompanied this Model 1832 Belt and Sword, it was apparent that it had spent many years as a set.

Sharpsburg Arsenal

Sword and Accoutrement Grouping, Unidentified, M1832 foot artillery sword complete with belt hanger and scabbard manufactured by N.P. Ames and dated 1833. Stamped on the guard is, "S. Huse Newburyport" (a variant foundry for Ames). Inspected by "D.T." (Lieutenant Daniel Tyler, Ordnance Officer). Belt and buckle are in excellent condition with a very old repair where frog was cut and then put back together. Scabbard is in excellent condition with minor crazing on leather. This very desirable, early dated sword with accoutrements is 100 percent correct and in excellent condition. **3,795.00**

Sword Grouping. Pair of Confederate swords fully identified to a Confederate cavalry soldier. Swords come with a notarized statement and military service records. Both swords came from the old pre-Civil War family home in Edenton, North Carolina. Both swords show hard field use and honest-as-they come wear; neither has any grip covering left, but one has some wire. Both have original scabbards. One sword is a blockade-run English Pattern 1822 made in Solingen, Germany, by W. Walscheid, known exporter to the Confederacy. The other is a Confederate "Dog River" type, with a fantastic crudely cast alloyed copper hilt, unstopped fuller blade, and lap seam soldered scabbard. All original rings and bands are intact, nothing tampered or altered in any way. **4,550.00**

Grouping Terminology

Grouping: The term used by collectors to identify items that are historically associated.

Identified: When a collector or dealer refers to an "identified" item, that means that the name of the soldier associated with the item is known.

Married: Items that were not historically together, but rather, put together some time after the Civil War are referred to as being "married."

Provenance: This is the known history pertaining to the origin of an item.

See also: Accoutrements, Swords, Revolvers, and Insignia.

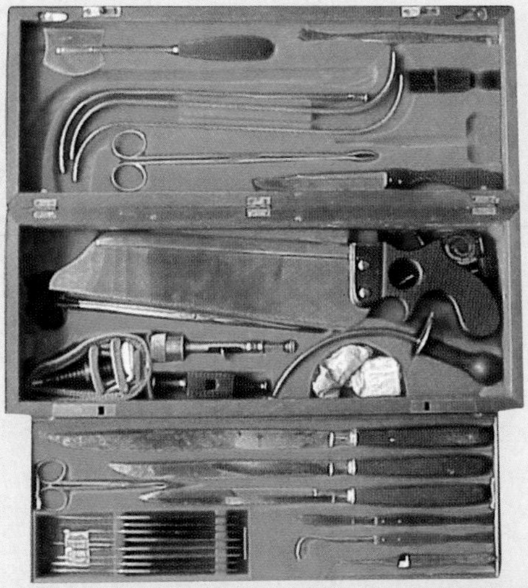

Gemrig capital military medical sets contained instruments for field surgery, amputation, urology, and bullet removal. Sets will sell for $4,500-$5,500 depending on completeness, condition, and provenance.
Dr. Michael Echols

Many buttons used on Confederate uniforms were actually produced in the North before the Civil War. These early sales were for use on by state militias. This South Carolina state seal button bears the backmark of the New York firm, Schuyler, Hartley and Graham. It sold for $125.

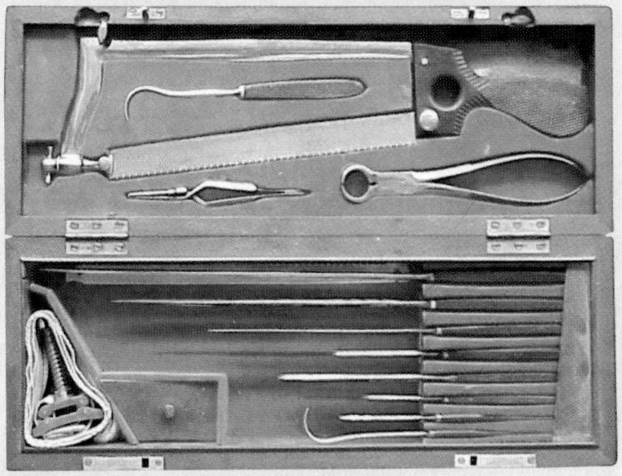

The Hernstein military amputation set was intended strictly for field amputation. The tools in these bear U.S. Hospital Department markings. Sets like these will sell for $3,500-$6,500, depending on condition and completeness. Any provenance linking the set to a particular surgeon will increase the price substantially.
Dr. Michael Echols

Manufactured in 1862, "Henry Rifle Serial Number 654" was decorated by New York city engraver, L.D. Himschke, probably for the purposes of presenting the weapon as an award to someone. The highly desirable Henry Rifle sold for $35,000.
J.C. Devine Inc.

Dug in northern Tennessee, a relic collector bought this U.S. Model 1851 belt plate for $275.
Middle Tennessee Relic

Called by collector's the "Swords Up" button, this Confederate Virginia state seal example sold for $300.
J.C. Devine Inc.

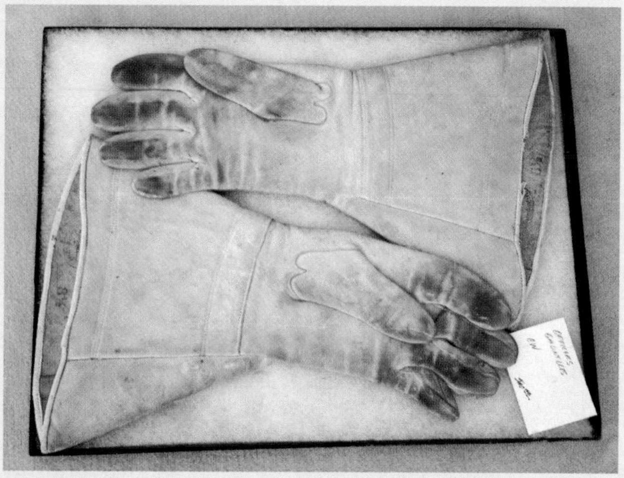

Though lacking an identification, this pair of gauntlets is typical of those favored by officers and mounted soldiers. A collector picked them up for $500.
Battleground Antiques, Inc.

Collectors refer to this style of Confederate enlisted man's plates as the "Clipped-Corner C.S. plate." Distinguished by its sardine-can shape, these plates will fetch between $2,000 and $5,000. A plate similar to this non-dug example on original belt sold for $4,850.
Battleground Antiques, Inc.

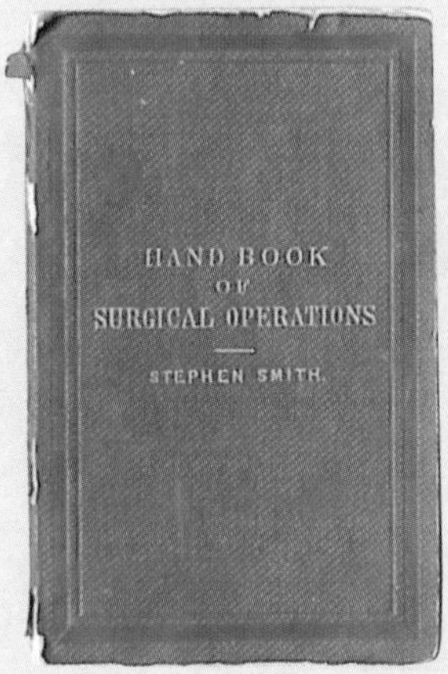

Published in 1863, the ***Handbook Of Surgical Operations*** is one of the finest known surgical texts of the Civil War. Detailing all of the instruments and surgical operations as used during the Civil War, this volume is prized by medical collectors. A similar volume to the one pictures sold for $1,250.
Dr. Michael Echols

Artillery projectiles are sought after by collectors of both excavated and non-dug relics. These dug, Confederate 3" bolts sold for $295 each.
Battleground Antiques, Inc.

Weapon collectors can easily branch out to other arenas of Civil War memorabilia. For example, nothing sets off a Remington New Model Army like an original set of accouterments such as this enlisted man's belt and cap box.
Battleground Antiques, Inc.

The value of officer's epaulettes depends on condition, rank, and provenance. A set similar to this 11th Infantry lieutenant's pair sold for $450.
Battleground Antiques, Inc.

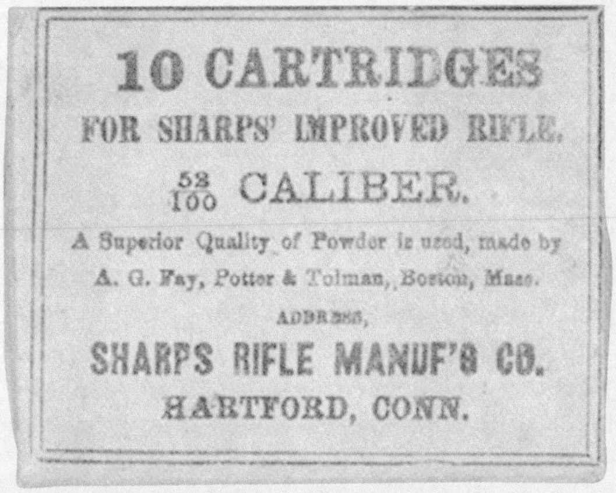

An original package of cartridges is a prominent addition to either a weapons or a projectile collection. Because of their rarity, though, few can specialize in unopened bundles of Civil War ammunition. This pack of cartridges for the Sharps rifle sold for $700.
J.C. Devine Inc.

The "snake" buckle was a common import from England and was worn by both Confederate and Union troops as evidenced by original photographs and excavated examples. A buckle similar to this one on its original belt sold for $485.
Battleground Antiques, Inc.

Although it was the most common belt plate worn during the Civil War, the enlisted man's oval U.S. plate can sell for as high as $500. This excavated example sold at auction for $200.
J.C. Devine Inc.

Collections of material that belonged to one soldier are widely sought by collectors. Simply referred to as "groupings," the greater the variety of items, the more insight that is gained into the daily life of an individual soldier. A large group of material related to Major Henry L. Swords of Rhode Island included letters, documents, commissions, and a large, ink-washed photograph of the major. The lot sold for $1,300.
J.C. Devine Inc.

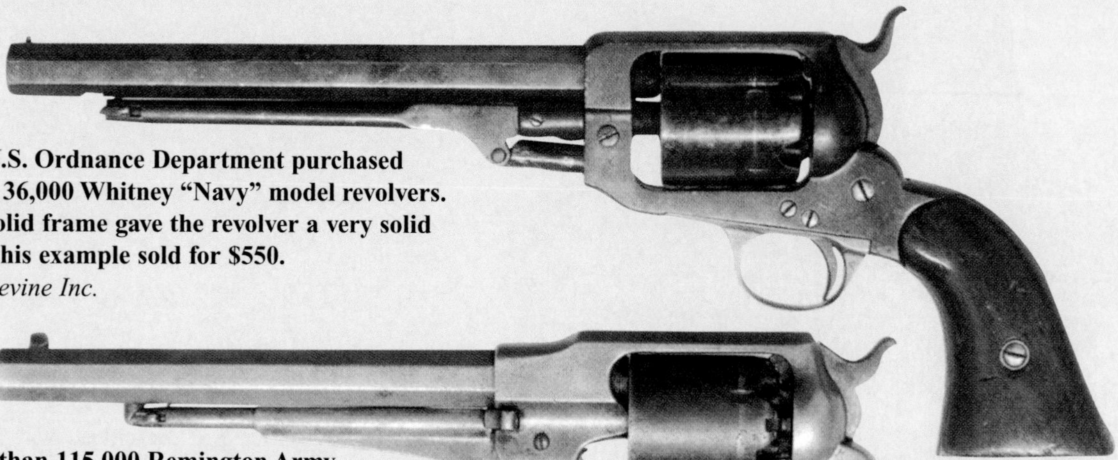

The U.S. Ordnance Department purchased about 36,000 Whitney "Navy" model revolvers. The solid frame gave the revolver a very solid feel. This example sold for $550.
J.C. Devine Inc.

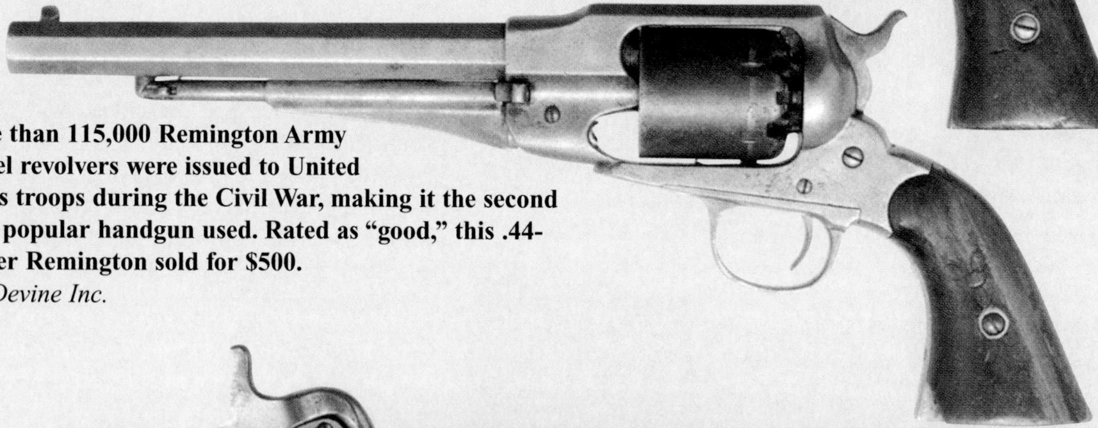

More than 115,000 Remington Army Model revolvers were issued to United States troops during the Civil War, making it the second most popular handgun used. Rated as "good," this .44-caliber Remington sold for $500.
J.C. Devine Inc.

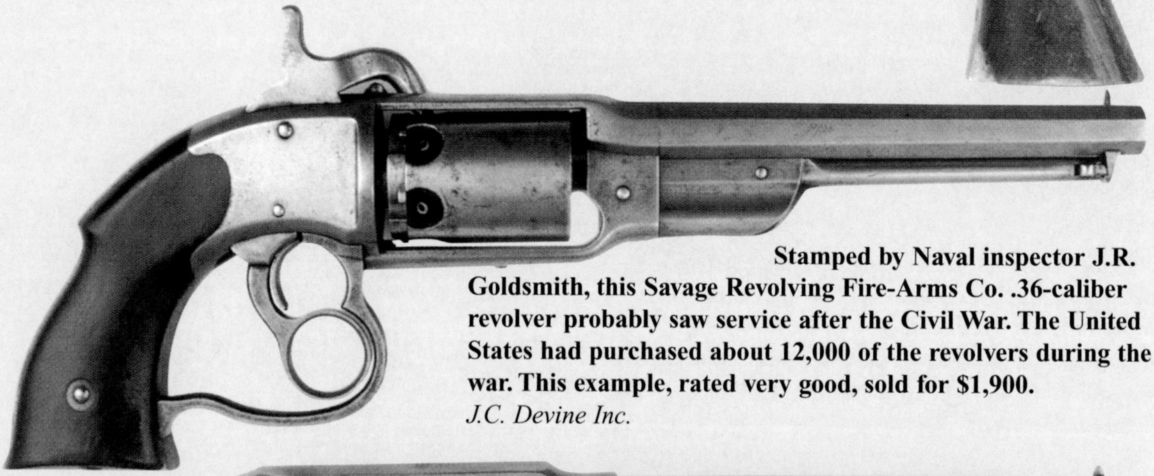

Stamped by Naval inspector J.R. Goldsmith, this Savage Revolving Fire-Arms Co. .36-caliber revolver probably saw service after the Civil War. The United States had purchased about 12,000 of the revolvers during the war. This example, rated very good, sold for $1,900.
J.C. Devine Inc.

The U.S. government purchased 2,001 C.S. Pettengill Army Model revolvers during the Civil War. This survivor in good condition sold for $1,300.
J.C. Devine Inc.

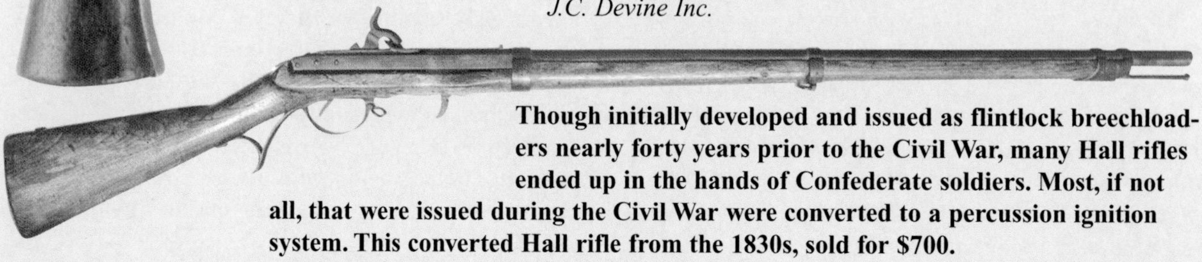

Though initially developed and issued as flintlock breechloaders nearly forty years prior to the Civil War, many Hall rifles ended up in the hands of Confederate soldiers. Most, if not all, that were issued during the Civil War were converted to a percussion ignition system. This converted Hall rifle from the 1830s, sold for $700.
J.C. Devine Inc.

The Colt Model 1862 Police revolver was chambered to fire five, .36-caliber rounds. Designed as a civilian weapon and never sold on government contract, it did emerge as a popular choice of many officers during the war. This example in fair condition sold for $500.
J.C. Devine Inc.

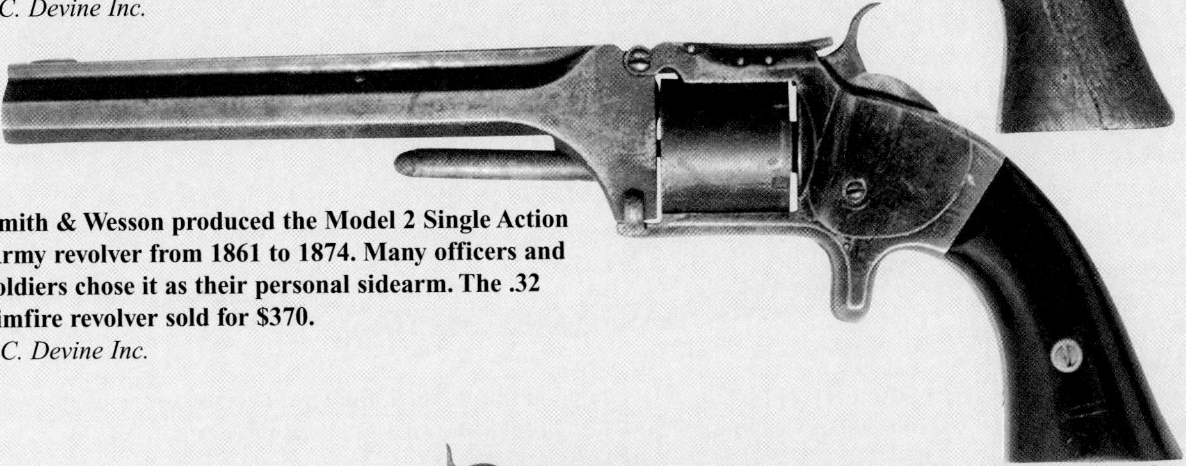

Smith & Wesson produced the Model 2 Single Action Army revolver from 1861 to 1874. Many officers and soldiers chose it as their personal sidearm. The .32 rimfire revolver sold for $370.
J.C. Devine Inc.

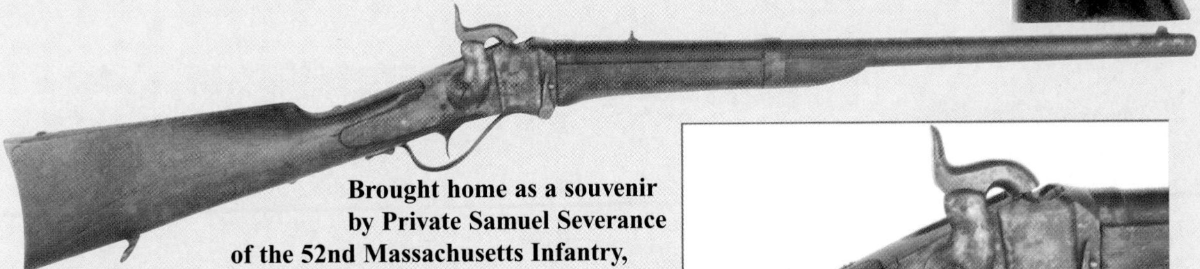

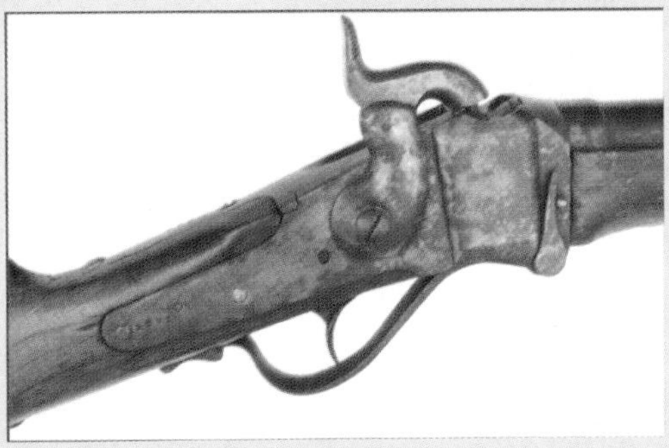

Brought home as a souvenir by Private Samuel Severance of the 52nd Massachusetts Infantry, this 2nd Model Richmond Sharps-type carbine sold for $8,500.
J.C. Devine Inc.

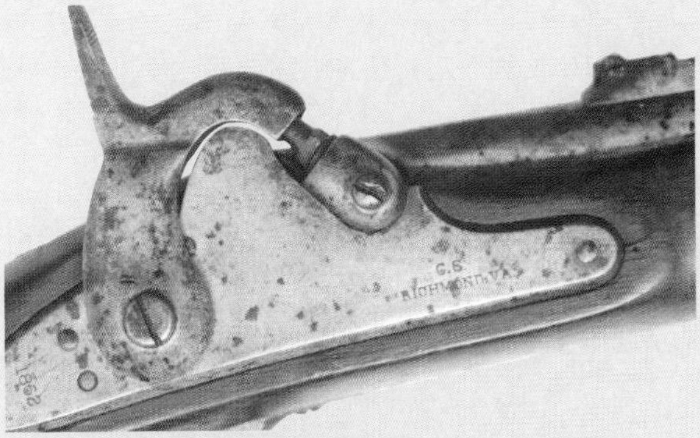

This close-up of the lockplate of a Confederate Type II Richmond Armory musket shows the unusual, high-hump blank where a Maynard-type priming system would have been installed. The .58-caliber rifle went to a high bidder for $17,500.
J.C. Devine Inc.

The Colt factory presented this Colt's Model 1862 revolver to Obadiah Clough. Factory presentation-grade Colts are beyond the means of a lot of collectors. Clough's Colt sold at auction for $16,000.
J.C. Devine Inc.

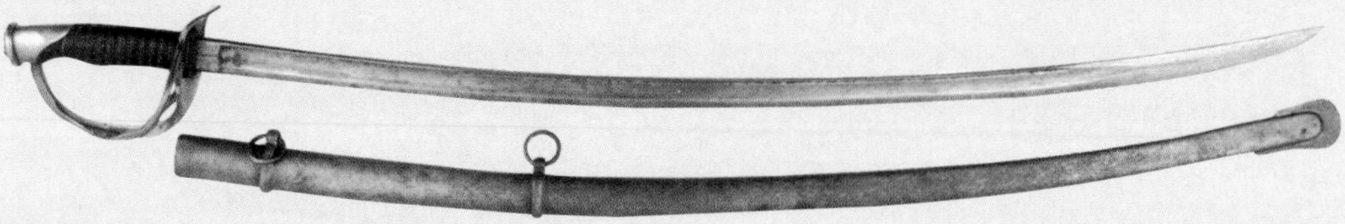

Collectors pay close attention to the manufacturer's name and date when examining U.S. Model 1860 Cavalry sabers. Early blades made by companies such as Tiffany's or Providence Tool can sell for as much as $1,500. This 1864-dated Ames saber sold for $550.
J.C. Devine Inc.

Marked 1861 on the ricasso, and, "Made by Ames Mfg. Co. Chicopee Mass.," on the reverse, this saber bayonet for a Sharps New Model 1859 rifle sold for $2,800.
J.C. Devine Inc.

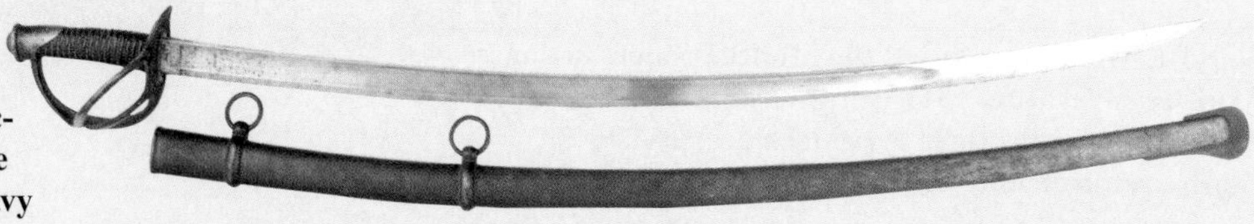

Historians and collectors often refer to the U.S. Model 1840 Heavy Cavalry saber as "old wristbreaker" because of its heavy 36" blade. Early dated examples fetch the most because of the likelihood that they were used in both the Mexican and Civil Wars. This 1849-dated Ames example sold for $700.
J.C. Devine Inc.

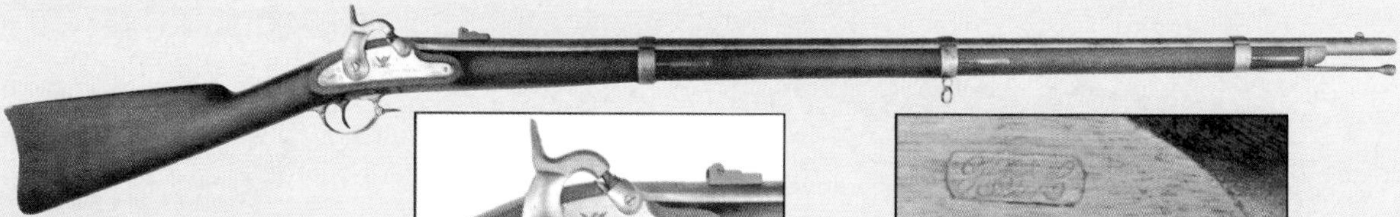

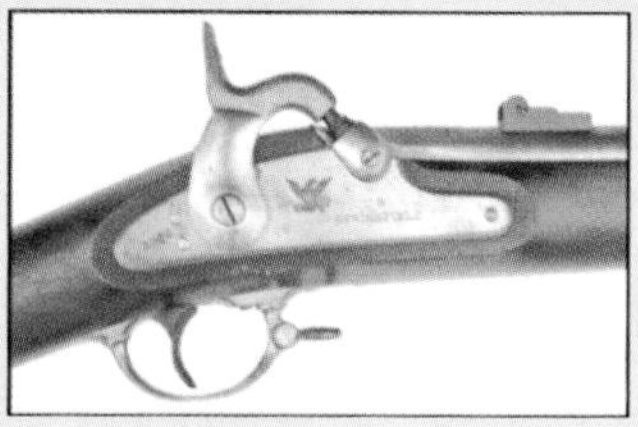

With a lockplate stamped "1862," and two very crisp inspector's cartouches on the stock, this Springfield Model 1861 rifled musket appeared to have never been issued. Rated excellent overall, the rifle sold for $4,000.
J.C. Devine Inc.

A group of materials that belonged to Samuel A. Graham, a captain in Purnell's Legion of Maryland volunteers included his 1847-dated Ames Model 1840 saber, Colt Model 1860 Army revolver, Bible, and a set of ebony and bone dominos. A collector won the grouping with a top bid of $3,500.
J.C. Devine Inc.

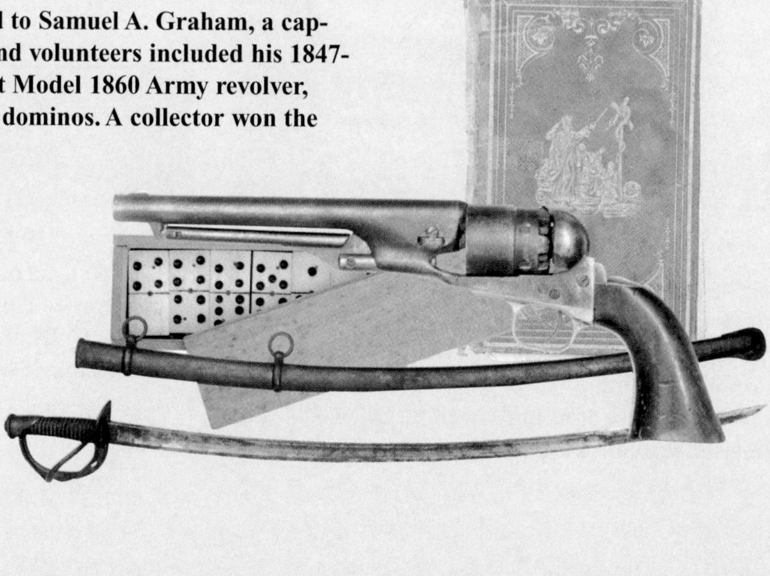

This Union cavalry trooper posed for his 1/4-plate tintype wearing an overcoat and his forage cap and holding his saber. The lightly tinted image sold for $235.
J.C. Devine Inc.

A Union cavalry corporal posed with his saber for this 1/4-plate tintype. Also barely visible is the butt of his revolver. Collectors refer to this as a "double-armed" image. It sold for $200.
J.C. Devine Inc.

This captain sat for his 1/4-plate tintype holding his officer's quality saber and an overcoat draped over one shoulder. The clear image sold for $200.
J.C. Devine Inc.

This 1/6th-plate image contains several elements that made it a prize for a collector with the top bid of $175. The seated cavalry trooper is wearing an oilcloth cover on his forage cap, is holding his saber, his belt plate is visible, and to top it all, there is a U.S. flag behind him.
J.C. Devine Inc.

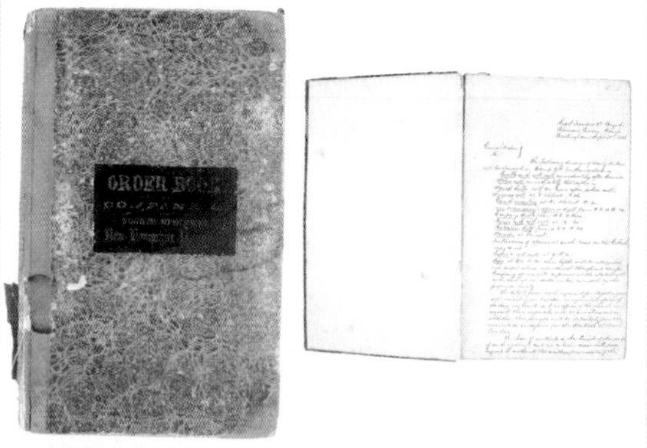

The original, "Order Book, Company G, Fourth Regiment New Hampshire Volunteers," sold at auction for a top bid of $2,000.
J.C. Devine Inc.

George Vail of the Buffalo, New York, militia unit the Union Continentals wore this New York belt plate on April 27, 1865, when he served as an honor guard for President Abraham Lincoln's remains. The plate and sword belt sold for $300.
J.C. Devine Inc.

Never issued, this Union enlisted artilleryman's shell jacket was probably one of thousands saved by surplus dealer Francis Bannerman in the early 1900s. Once common and inexpensive, these jackets sell for as much as $4,000 today. This example sold for $2,450.
Dave Taylor Civil War Antiques

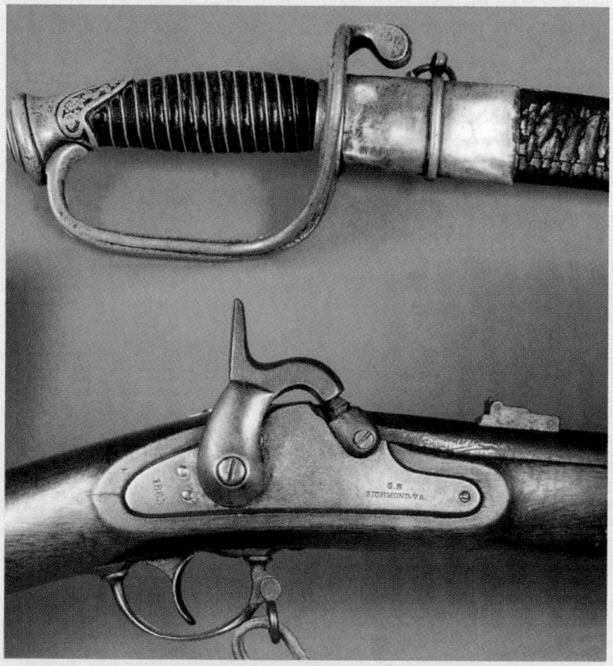

The Confederate Boyle & Gamble officer's sword and scabbard sold $8,900. The 1863-dated Richmond rifled musket with a low-hump lockplate sold for $11,500.
Dave Taylor Civil War Antiques

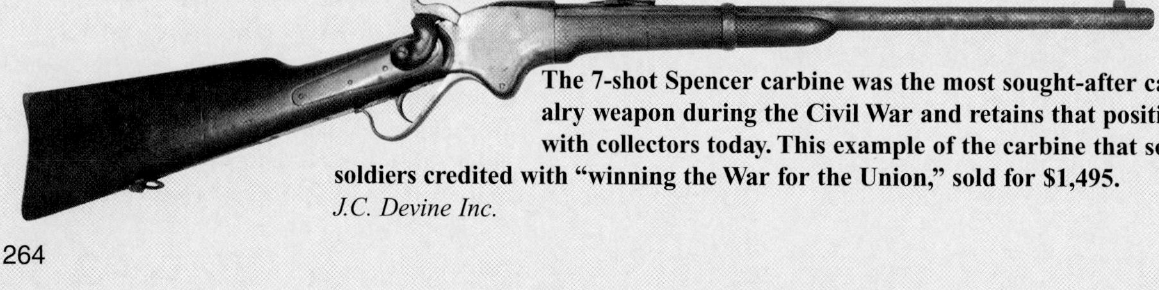

The 7-shot Spencer carbine was the most sought-after cavalry weapon during the Civil War and retains that position with collectors today. This example of the carbine that some soldiers credited with "winning the War for the Union," sold for $1,495.
J.C. Devine Inc.

Chapter 11
Insignia

When one doesn't have the resources, either monetarily or physically, to collect Civil War uniforms, the next best thing is to collect insignia. Not taking up nearly the space or the capital that uniforms do, a person can spend a lifetime assembling a collection of shoulder boards, chevrons, corps badges, hatpins, or any number of other items intended to adorn a uniform.

One of the ironies of insignia collecting is that dug examples will often sell for more than non-dug examples. Take Union infantry hatpins, for example. A non-dug example from 1861-1865 with some patina is very hard to distinguish from a reproduction that spent ten years on a reenactor's cap. This is because the insignia on the reenactor's cap was struck from exactly the same dies as the original! Made from the same material, in the same design, only 150 years separates the original from the restrike. Now consider an excavated example of the same insignia. Resting underground for 150 years has some pretty noticeable affects on a brass hat pin that are awfully hard to replicate (apart from burying a reproduction for 150 years). Therefore, many collectors are willing to pay *more* for an item they *know* is original, rather than take a chance on a non-dug item.

Collecting Hints

Pros:

- Because most of it is nearly two-dimensional, insignia items do not take up much space.
- Due to the volume of items available, insignia collecting is a great entry-level to Civil War relics.
- To help avoid the problem of unknowingly purchasing reproductions, a lot of dug relics are available. There are enough excavated items available as a sole focus to keep a collector busy for years.

Cons:

- Civil War brass insignias have been reproduced for many years. Made from the original dies, it is extremely difficult to discern reproductions from originals.
- Cloth insignias have not survived in great numbers. A simple pair of chevrons or shoulder boards is expensive.
- Adequate published material is not presently available to help a new collector discern between Civil War insignias and those of the 1870-1890 period.
- Confederate insignias are extremely rare. They are available only to serious collectors. Obtaining even a representative piece will be difficult for a novice collector.

Availability ★★
Price ★★★★
Reproduction Alert ★★★

Corps Badges

U.S., 2nd

A red clover leaf (1st Division) with twisted gold wire borders and a blue wool backing. **475.00**

The three-leaf clover was adopted as the insignia of the Union Army's 2nd Corps. This silver 2nd Corp Badge belonged to Private Henry Swineford of the 184th Pennsylvania Volunteers.

Civil War corps badge, three-leaf-clover shape, identified to Henry Swineford, 184th Pennsylvania Volunteers, Company E., acquired from Snyder County Pennsylvania, appears to be made of German silver and is hand-inscribed, as found, untouched condition. **800.00**

When corps badges were initially instituted, the army handed out cloth badges to the various corps. This example is a cloth 2nd Corps badge.

Drumbeat Civil War Memorabilila

Original 2nd Corps badge, all wool with just enough mothing to assure authenticity. Approximately 2" x 2". **300.00**

U.S., 3rd

A silver-plated diamond, red enamel center, twisted wire border, pin backed, excellent condition. **350.00**

Army of the Potomac silhouette corps badge, brass diamond with red wool center; tin-backed with a T-bar pin extending below the badge, excellent condition. **425.00**

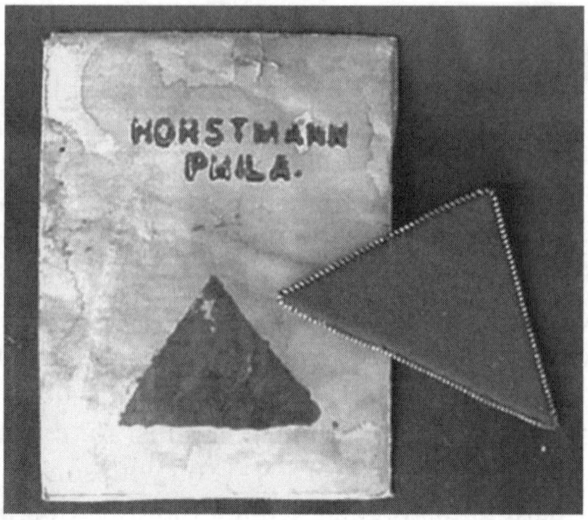

This unissued 4th Corps Badge is still in its brown paper package from Civil War insignia manufacturer Horstmann.

Dale C. Anderson Co.

U.S., 4th

A Civil War 4th Corps, 3rd Division cloth corps badge still in its original paper packet from Horstmann's, 2-3/4" w, dark blue wool pyramid with internal stiffener, spun brass wire edging, brown fabric backing. Meant to be sewn to coat or hat, unused and good as new. Only the brass has toned a bit. Comes with 3" x 4" dark-tan paper envelope in which it was sold. Has ink-stamped, "HORSTMANN/PHILA" and black stamped corps badge design on one side. Shows some age stain only, first ever encountered. **595.00**

Red wool (1st Division), triangular in shape with twisted gilt wire edging and tan polished cotton backing, 2" high, the 4th Corps were in the Department of the Cumberland. **385.00**

U.S., 5th, a German silver bar with T-bar pin, engraved "52 Mass. Reg." from which hangs a Maltese Cross in a circle with a large "E" (Company E) in the center, 2-1/2" h. **400.00**

U.S., 6th

German silver cross, 1" h, indented center with dark blue cross (3rd Division) in center, T-bar pin on back. **350.00**

Gilt 1-3/8" cross in red enamel with a 5/8" cross in center, T-bar pin on back, excellent condition. **450.00**

Often, a soldier would resort to making his own corps badge to adorn his uniform. This 6th Corps badge was hand cut from brass and punched with holes enabling the soldier to attach it to his headgear or jacket.

Dale C. Anderson Co.

Hand-cut sheet brass, 1-3/4" across, small hole in the end of each arm, for sewing to the coat or hat. Deep chocolate-brown patina, guaranteed original, rare and extremely desirable dug badge. Came from Virginia. **195.00**

White wool center with heavy gold bullion borders, almost 2" h. A superior corps badge, excellent condition. **475.00**

U.S., 7th, rare army corps badge stamped, "7th A.C." The pin attachment is still intact and sweated onto the reverse.. .... **395.00**

U.S., 9th

Gilt brass, 1-1/2" h, die-struck crossed cannons and anchor with twisted rope, very sharp profile, T-bar pin. **385.00**

Original wool and bullion 9th Corps badge, approximately 2"x 2", dark-red wool background with bullion crossed cannon and anchor with bullion border, minor moth damage, dark color to bullion with great aged patina. **350.00**

The dark red wool backing on this 9th Corps badge indicates that it was intended for a soldier of the Corps' 1st Division.

Drumbeat Civil War Memorabilia

U.S., 10th, white metal, dark-blue wool center (3rd Division), tin backed, T-bar pin extends below the badge, excellent condition. **425.00**

U.S., 12th or 20th, metal five-pointed star with American shield in center, two soldered back wires. **225.00**

U.S., 12th, good condition, dug in Texas camp. **150.00**

U.S., 14th

Three-dimensional brass acorn, 1-1/2" h, two affixing loops on back, worn by the men who fought and marched with Sherman and Thomas. **275.00**

White wool with twisted wire borders, black paper over gauze back, 2-1/4" h, three tiny moth holes, otherwise excellent condition............. **400.00**

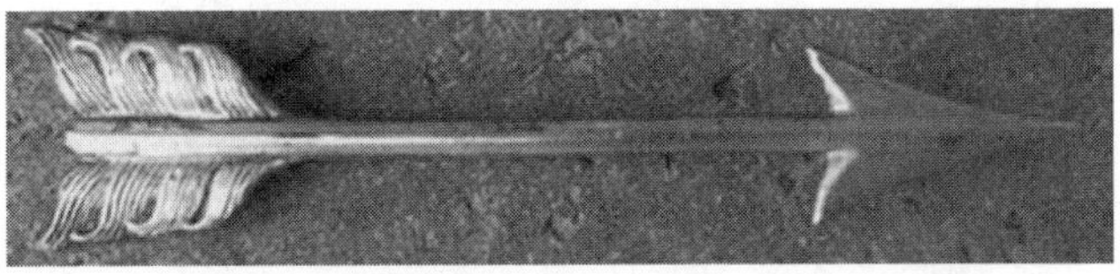

This officer's quality badge was for a soldier of the 17th Army Corps.

Dale C. Anderson Co.

U.S., 17th

2-3/8" l, three-dimensional face contours, hand-engraved feather detail, flat back, T-bar pin with "C" clasp. Touch mark on back appears to read "M & S." Fine condition, private purchase, officer-quality corps badge.. .... **695.00**

Sterling silver arrow, 2-1/4" l, pin backed, marked "Sterling," maker's name on the feather's back. . **.285.00**

U.S., 18th, high-quality corps badge, identified to Josiah M. Crocker of the 23rd Massachusetts Regiment of Volunteers. Josiah was a private of Co. F. Excellant condition with T-bar remaining intact on back, beautifully engraved. **950.00**

U.S., 19th

A silver-colored badge, cutout circle engraved, "H. Alford (of) Lyons NY, 2nd Brigade Vol., 19th Army Corps, Co. C 160 Reg. N.Y.," pin backed, unusual named corps badge. There are also "sew-on" holes on right and left arm, a real beauty. **485.00**

Red wool four-pointed star, twisted brass wire border, black cloth backing; 2-1/2" h, scarce 1863 version, as the badge was changed to a fan leaf cross in 1864, dirty.. .... **425.00**

U.S., 22nd, nickel-plated "foliated" cross (five arms), "27 Maine" on face, hung from a purple-blue silk ribbon, nickel-plated pin bar with T-bar pin, excellent condition. **325.00**

U.S., 23rd, except for a bit of age toning to the spun brass wire edging, this badge is good as new. Almost certainly this one came from Horstmann's, dark-blue wool shield with internal stiffener, spun brass wire edging, and brown backing fabric.. .... **495.00**

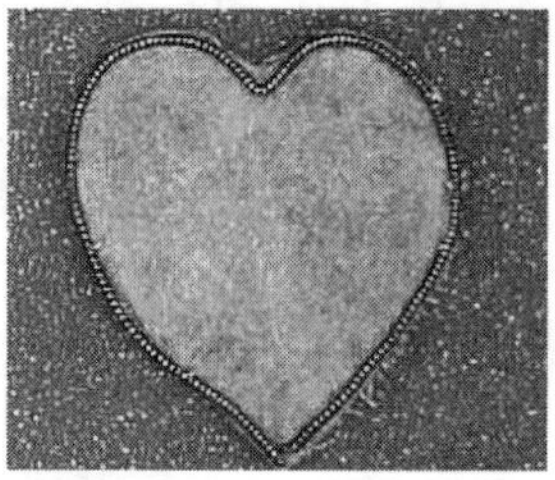

Shaped like a heart, this white cloth cops badge was for a soldier of the 2nd Division, 24th Army Corps.

Sharpsburg Arsenal

U.S., 24th

24th Corps, 2nd Division badge, twisted wire border. **595.00**

German silver heart with scalloped edges and white enamel center, T-bar pin extends below badge, usual age crackling to enamel, but otherwise excellent condition............................ **450.00**

U.S., 25th, brass silhouette-type badge with scalloped edges, red cloth center, T-bar pin extends below badge, some cloth wear, but in excellent condition.................**450.00**

Insignia of Rank

Chevrons, U.S.

Corporal, new condition, intended for an artilleryman, made of bright scarlet wool stripes sewn to dark navy-blue wool, thread is light tan stripes are 11/16" w and 7" across the top. **435.00**

Sergeant, pair of infantry sergeant chevrons, three classic sky-blue worsted stripes sewn to the dark-blue woolen backing, excellent condition overall, shows just the right amount of age, with virtually no moth damage............................ **650.00**

Quartermaster Sergeant, light-blue herringbone tape stripes, three going down in a "V" and three straight across the top. These are applied to almost blue-black wool backing. Stripes are slightly faded and have some brown water stains, still exceptionally good condition. **450.00**

Epaulettes, U.S.

This pair of enlisted man's epaulettes was for a soldier of the "10th Volunteer Corps," probably a late 1850s or early 1860s militia unit.

Sharpsburg Arsenal

Enlisted Man, 10th Volunteer Corps dress epaulettes, Civil War-era or earlier, gold bullion embroidery in excellent condition..................... **425.00**

Pair of epaulettes, backed in green, designed to be used with the Chasseur-style uniform.

Drumbeat Civil War Memorabilia

Enlisted Man, Chasseur, pair of green woolen chasseur epaulettes as imported from France and worn by Massachusetts and Pennsylvania Chasseur or Zouave units during the Civil War. These troops wore uniforms imported from France, distinctive jacket and kepi, as well as the 1855 Rifleman's saber belt, extremely rare. Brown, polished cotton backing is perfect. **400.00**

Officer

Dug in northern Mississippi, fine condition...... **85.00**

Comes with original tin box, embroidered cloth with gilded finish, buttons marked, "G and cie. Paris," by Schuyler, Hartley and Graham, cased in tin box with worn japanning, 6-1/4" x 7-1/2" x 9-1/4"..... **165.00**

George Vail, a member of the Buffalo, New York, Continental Guards, wore these epaulettes when he was a member of Lincoln's funeral color guard.

J.C. Devine Inc.

Gold bullion epaulettes that belonged to George Vail, Union Continentals. 2-3/4" fringe, excellent condition. **175.00**

Civil War, field-grade officer's epaulettes made of gold bullion with gold-plated crescents and heavy gold bullion fringe (denoting colonel, lieutenant colonel, or major). Complete with hinged and padded mounting strap, super set in excellent condition. **285.00**

Horstmann-produced epaulettes for an artillery officer still housed in the original japanned tin box.

Early pair of Civil War epaulettes, all original in original tin container, made by "The Horstmann Co.," marked on the back. One of them is missing its letter "A" eagle button. The original tin retains most of its original japanning. **288.00**

This pair of epaulettes were for a lieutenant of the 5th Infantry. Whether or not it was the 5th regiment of a state's volunteers or of regular U.S. Infantry is not known.

J.C. Devine Inc.

Lieutenant, in original japanned tin case, silver bars of a first lieutenant, the insignia of the 5th Infantry Regiment, probably of Massachusetts, since that is where they were found. One of the buttons is a replacement naval button, fine condition..... **450.00**

Colonel, mushroom-shaped brass gilt epaulettes with cloth of gold inside, topped with magnificent silver-embroidered eagle. Edges are bound with bright, gold-gilt binding, 3-1/2" brilliant gold bullion ringlets, red silk padding underneath. Red Moroccan leather under the connecting straps, left and right connecting straps are brilliant gilt, superb condition. **1,100.00**

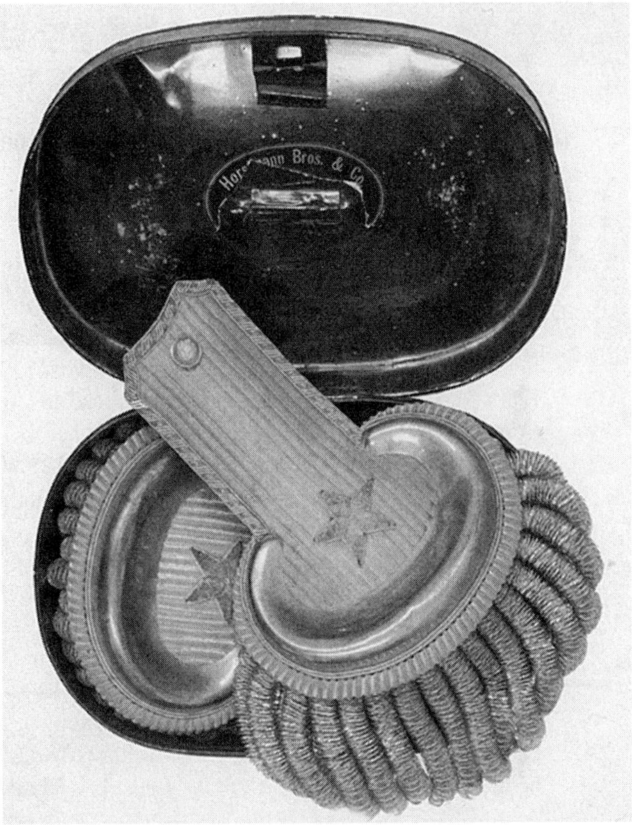

The star affixed to each of these epaulettes denotes that they were for a general's uniform.

J.C. Devine Inc.

General, japanned tin box with paper label that reads, "Horstmann Bros. Co./Fifty Cherry Sts./ PHILADELPHIA/MILITARY SOCIETY GOODS." The epaulets are in fine condition with gold bullion fringe and a single silver bullion star. The tin case has remnants of a paper label inside, and has a large dent on the bottom front.................... **425.00**

Patch, Rating

U.S., Navy, black printed on white duck of eagle perched on coiled anchor, white, five-pointed star on top of all, fine condition.................. **40.00**

Sash, U.S.

Officer

Union officer's sash made of maroon silk.

Middle Tennessee Relics

Beautiful condition maroon officer's sash. **795.00**

Burgundy officer's sword belt sash, retains both knots and tassels, body remains, but is quite tattered and fragile. Reliable oral tradition identifies the officer who used this as Captain William Reuben Rowley who served as a 1st lieutenant in the 45th Illinois in 1861, a captain and aide-de-camp for General Grant in 1862, and as major when he served as Provost Marshal of the important Federal staging base at Cairo, Illinois beginning in November 1862, he resigned in 1864. . . . . **225.00**

Infantry, burgundy officer's sword belt sash retains both knots and tassels, body remains, but is quite tattered and fragile. Reliable oral tradition identifies the officer who used this as Captain William Reuben Rowley who served as a 1st lieutenant in the 45th Illinois in 1861, a captain and aide-de-camp for General Grant in 1862, and as major he served as Provost Marshal of the important Federal staging base at Cairo, Illinois beginning in November 1862, he resigned in 1864. . . . . **225.00**

Shoulder Straps, U.S.

Second Lieutenant, Artillery, red cloth fields and heavy gold bullion borders, partial dark-blue wool undersides. Sewn together with crossed stitches, showing strap interiors, pair is in excellent condition. **385.00**

Second Lieutenant, Cavalry, Smith's Patent shoulder straps with false embroidered (ribbed brass) borders, yellow velvet field with yellow wool undersides, but with dark blue edging where sewn to coat, excellent condition. **385.00**

Lieutenant, Cavalry, Smith's Patent strap with a bright-yellow wool field, gilt brass false embroidered borders, and silver oak leaves in false embroidery at either end. Blue wool underside, in excellent condition (a single). **195.00**

Major, Cavalry, single shoulder board insignia in excellent condition with mustard-color velvet backing, and oak leaves in fine gold bullion. **245.00**

Lieutenant Colonel, Cavalry, Smith's Patent with gilt brass borders, a bright-yellow field, and metal oak leaves at either end, blue wool undersides, this pair is in excellent condition. **425.00**

Second Lieutenant, Infantry

Heavy gold bullion border on an Infantry blue field, uniform blue backing, shows some wear and fraying at one end. **95.00**

Dark-blue wool fields with heavy gold-bullion borders, blue undersides go only partly across the back, dome gold bullion missing, but still a great set of straps. **225.00**

Lieutenant, Infantry

Designed to reduce the high casualty rate among front-line combat officers, rank insignia was made smaller, without bullion, and often worn in less conspicuous ways. This is a unique and important example of the subdued strap in marvelous condition. The borders instead of being bullion embroidery, are contoured navy-blue felt, tightly edged by spun-brass wire, that also outlines the lieutenant's bars against the black velvet facings. Backsides are navy-blue uniform fabric folded over and hand sewn, still shows a bit of stiffener at center. Condition is clean and excellent. Backside of one has a few moth holes, 1-1/2" x 3-11/16". **875.00**

Non-excavated shoulder strap of a Federal commissioned officer, great, solid brass, only about half of dark-blue wool, as it has seen a bit of moth damage or heavy wear. **315.00**

Gilt ribbed frame (false embroidered), medium-blue wool field and dark-blue wool backing. Marked, "Jas. Smith Pat. June 16 1861 16 Dutch St. N.Y.," a single. **115.00**

Captain, Infantry, single, dark-blue velvet with heavy gold-bullion border and gold-bullion captain's bars, shows use.. . . . . **135.00**

Second Lieutenant, possibly used by a Zouave unit, this pair of straps has red cloth undersides (open in the center) intended for use on a red uniform. Centers are black velvet with fancy gold bullion borders, size is 1-3/8" x 3-1/2", shows wear and age. **475.00**

Captain, Assistant Surgeon, ribbed brass (false embroidered) borders and captain's bars on a blue velvet field (assistant surgeons were captains of staff), tin backed (a single). **145.00**

Second Lieutenant, Rifleman, Smith patent with ribbed metal frames (imitation gold embroidery), rifleman green field, pair marked, "Jas. Smith Pat. June 18, 1861 15 Dutch Sts. N.Y.," on the blue backing, excellent condition. **425.00**

Hat/Cap Insignia

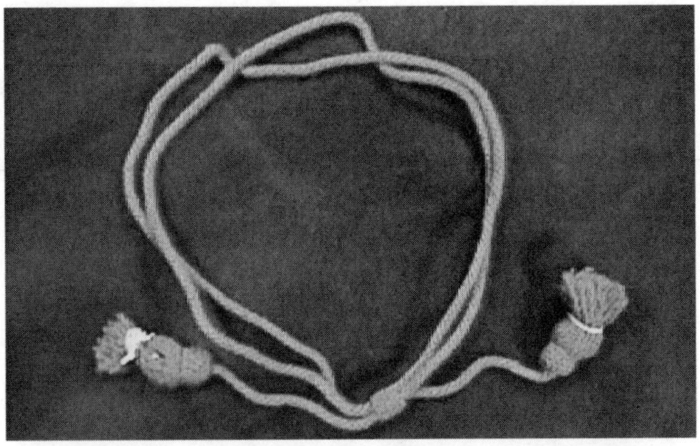

The red cord for the Model 1858 hat denoted artillery.

Middle Tennessee Relics

Hat Cord, U.S.

Enlisted Man, Artillery

Bright red hat cord, great condition, no moth damage. **60.00**

Original, Civil War red artillery cord........... **45.00**

Perfect surplus example of red, worsted-wool artillery hat cord for use on the Hardee hat........... **45.00**

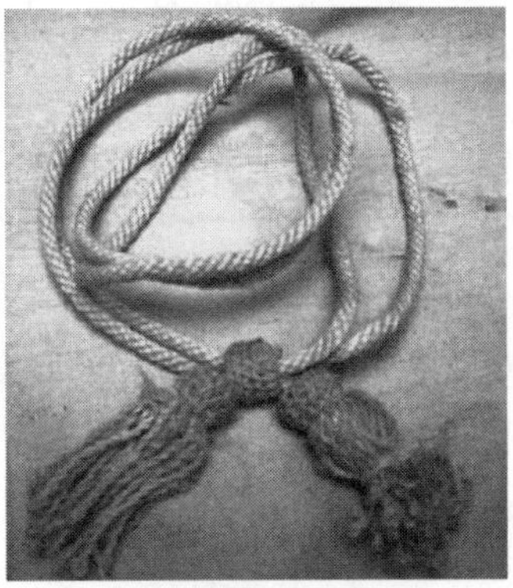

Absolutely pristine, yellow cavalryman's hat cord.

Drumbeat Civil War Memorabilia

Enlisted Man, Cavalry

Mint condition, yellow cavalry hat cord, absolutely the best.................................. **185.00**

Yellow, worsted-wool cord with tassels and adjustment slide, original unissued Civil War cord with storage wear only. **80.00**

Enlisted Man, Infantry

Solid condition with good color................ **59.00**

Medium-blue worsted wool hat cord for the Model 1858 Hardee hat, tassels retain original cord ties, unissued example from old Bannerman's Island stock. . . .**45.00**

Solid condition with some fading to blue color. . . **49.00**

Original, Civil War, blue infantry cord.......... **65.00**

Officer, original hat cord, single strand that goes around the hat in black and gold and has a black and gold slide, acorns are also gold with black webbing. **125.00**

Hat Insignia

This extremely intriguing hat plate was excavated from a campsite used by General Tom Green's Texas Cavalry. It is quite possible that it denotes the 3rd Dragoons.

Confederate, rare 3rd Dragoon hat pin, dug in a camp of C.S. General Tom Green's Texas Cavalry from the Red River Campaign in western Louisiana, made of heavy cast brass, not the thin stamped variety, and is fashioned to look like a rectangular belt plate such as the 1851 sword belt plate. All four hooks are present on the reverse, very fine brown patina with green bits of patina on the edge. Measures 1-1/4" l x 7/8" h x 1/8" w. **600.00**

South Carolina, rare palmetto tree with two shields propped up against the base, represents the early state seal of South Carolina. Excellent condition, intact T-Bar pin. The device is made of brass with the applied shields of stamped brass, exquisite detail work in the tree leaves.......................... **1,250.00**

Confederate, Enlisted Man, Louisiana, very rare hatpin dug in a Louisiana camp in middle Louisiana during the early 1980s, very good condition, pin retains about 40 percent of the gold gilt. Loop attached to the back is still present and seems to imply that this pin was made to be a hatpin. Pin is 5/8" w x 3/4" h....................... **1,600.00**

This letter "S" was dug at an Army of Tennessee site. It was probably used as a hat insignia.

Middle Tennessee Relics

Letter "S," large-size, cast letter "S," dug from a Confederate Army of Tennessee winter camp. . . **.65.00**

Non-dug letter "T" made of stamped brass.

Middle Tennessee Relics

Letter "T," Excellent condition, non-dug, lead-filled, stamped brass letter "T." **65.00**

Stamped brass regimental numeral "1" dug in central Tennessee.

Middle Tennessee Relics

Number "1," nice condition, dug, large-size, stamped brass Union cap, smooth brown patina.......... **38.00**

U.S., Enlisted Man, Artillery

Bannerman's surplus Civil War headgear insignia, never had the attaching wires attached to the back, but were added later by the Francis Bannerman Military Surplus company........................ **85.00**

Pair of enlisted man's crossed cannons insignia with a bend that was present when it was dug.

Middle Tennessee Relics

Dug, Union crossed cannons artillery hat insignia, very attractive set of crossed cannons with a brown-green, uncleaned patina. When dug, the insignia had a bend and crack near the center which has been tastefully straightened and strengthened............ **175.00**

Hat insignia for artillery soldier, two wire loops on back and stamped brass..................... **260.00**

Large crossed cannons in brass, 3-1/2" across, heavy trunions, and smaller horizontal intersection angles than the more common specimens. Complete with four flat, original wires attached to the back...**250.00**

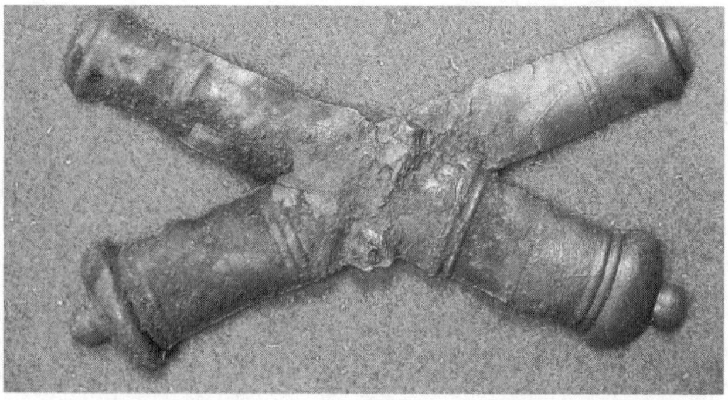

Though a lot of people like to believe that Union troops in the west didn't go in for lots of brass and decoration on their uniforms, this pair of crossed cannons should give them pause. It was excavated at the Stones River battle site.

Middle Tennessee Relics

Large-size, crossed cannons, stamped brass hat insignia has a slight ripple in the center from an old bend. **195.00**

Stamped, sheet brass, crossed cannons, excellent condition with most of the original shellac and all four soldered attaching loops.............. **185.00**

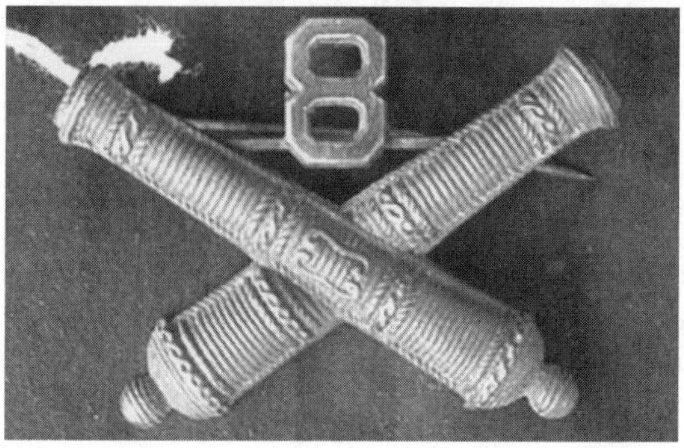

Officer's quality pin-on hat badge denoting the 8th Battery.

Dale C. Anderson Co.

U.S., Officer, Artillery

2-1/2" w, stamped brass, crossed cannons with embossed surface simulating bullion embroidery. Wide, wire pin-back fastener, number "8" soldered to a horizontal bar above center, for 8th Artillery, dark, even coppery patina, very-fine condition..... **295.00**

Brass, crossed cannons on black felt.......... **425.00**

Brilliant gilt artillery insignia that retains all four brass mounting wires on the back, near perfect condition. **360.00**

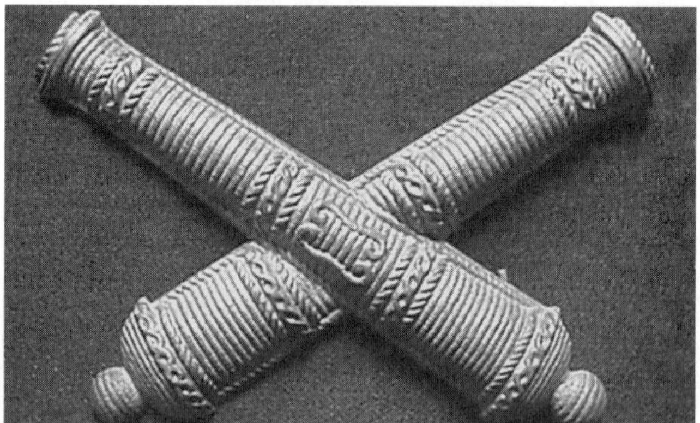

Pair of crossed cannons stamped in brass to simulate an embroidered insignia.

Dale C. Anderson Co.

Exactly as purchased, stamped sheet brass with surface design to simulate bullion embroidery, 1-3/4" x 2-1/2" w. Has three of four wire fasteners on back, excellent medium patina................. **250.00**

False embroidered, stamped brass "crossed cannons" with 90-99 percent bright original heavy gilt finish, retains all four mounting pins on the back, super condition........................... **360.00**

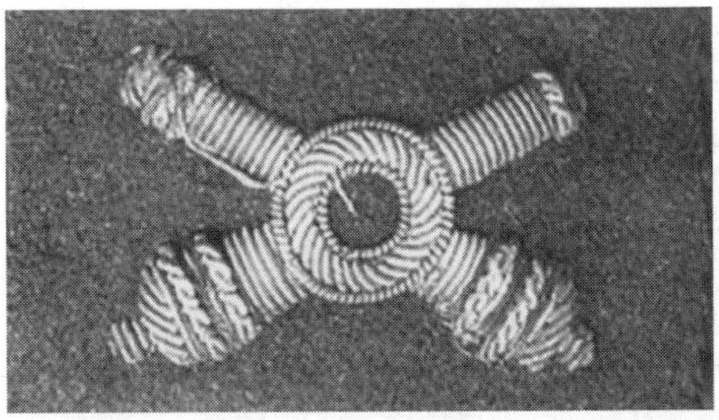

The gold-embroidered insignia was a favorite with Union officers.

Dale C. Anderson Co.

Gold bullion crossed cannon embroidered on a rectangle of black wool with a fabric stiffener on back. Fine condition with minor tarnish, 1-3/8" x 2-3/16", has a brush of residual adhesive on back from having been in an album. **265.00**

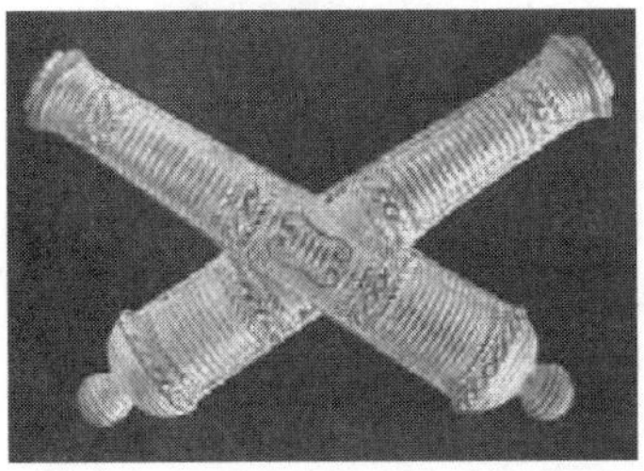

All four attaching wires were still intact on this set of false embroidered, stamped-brass cannons.

Original Civil War period artillery officer's false-embroidered, crossed-cannon headgear insignia. Retains its original gilt, except raised edges. All four original attachment wires present with old light gray solder, cannon barrels measure about 2-1/2" across at the muzzles. **150.00**

Stamped sheet brass insignia, very fine strike with much detail, near-perfect condition, it still retains all of the mounting loops on the back.............. **195.00**

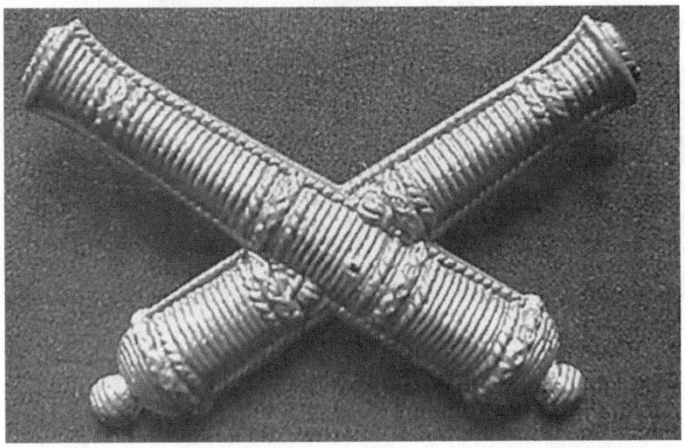

The false embroidered stamped insignia held up better to wear than an embroidered insignia. Often, dealers will describe a false embroidered brass insignia as being officer quality. While that is true, this style of insignia was readily available from sutlers, jewelers, and other insignia peddlers to any soldier, either an enlisted man or an officer.

Dale C. Anderson Co.

Superbly detailed, heavy-stamped brass, crossed cannons, with high-relief embossed surface texture meant to simulate bullion embroidery. This form was adopted to better stand up in the field where bullion insignia was soon snagged, frayed, and destroyed. Good as new with three out of four wire fasteners on back, fairly light tarnish or patina, 1-3/4" x 2-1/2" w. **250.00**

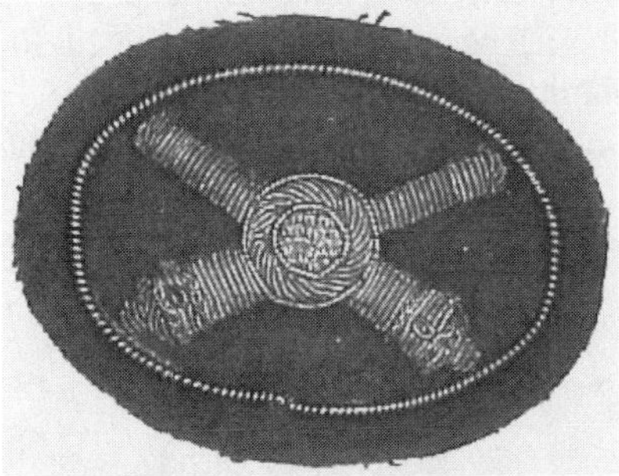

Set of embroidered cannons originally intended for use by the New York State Militia.

Sharpsburg Arsenal

New York Militia artillery officer's hat insignia. **595.00**

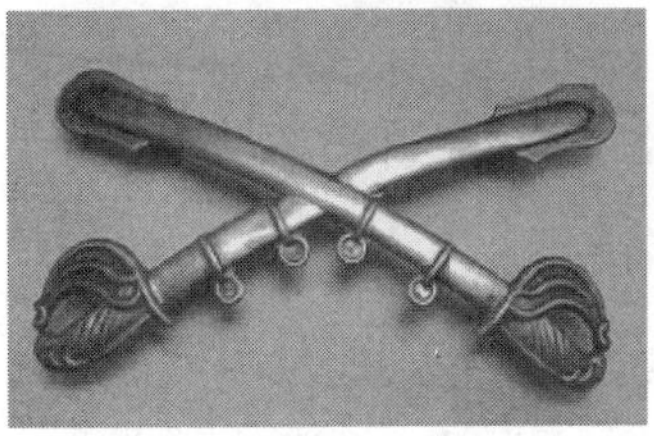

The crossed sabers insignia denoted cavalry troops.

Drumbeat Civil War Memorabilia

U.S., Enlisted Man, Cavalry

Original and mint example of the Civil War cavalry hat badge with the stand up attachment loops on the back. **275.00**

Bannerman's surplus Civil War headgear insignia, never had the attaching wires attached to the back, but they were added later by the Francis Bannerman Military Surplus company. **150.00**

Came from a 50-year-old collection, very nice... **325.00**

Stamped-brass crossed sabers, fine umber patina, retains one iron mounting pin on the back. Comes in Riker display case.......................... **260.00**

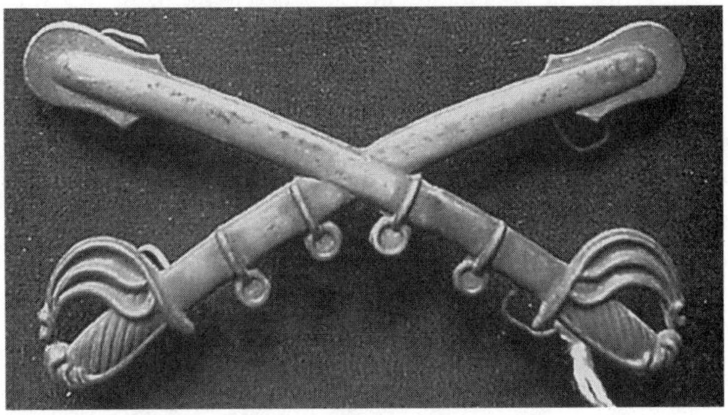

This set of crossed sabers still has the four attaching wires intact.

Dale C. Anderson Co.

U.S., Enlisted Man, Cavalry, cont.

Stamped-brass, crossed sabers, 3-3/8" w, four thin-brass wire loops soldered on back, light patina, fine example. **325.00**

Stamped sheet-brass insignia, deep mustard-color patina and fine striking, perfect with all back retaining loops. **260.00**

U.S., Officer, Cavalry, false embroidered, stamped-brass "hunting horn," beautiful condition with 20-30 percent original gilt and both back mounting pins. **285.00**

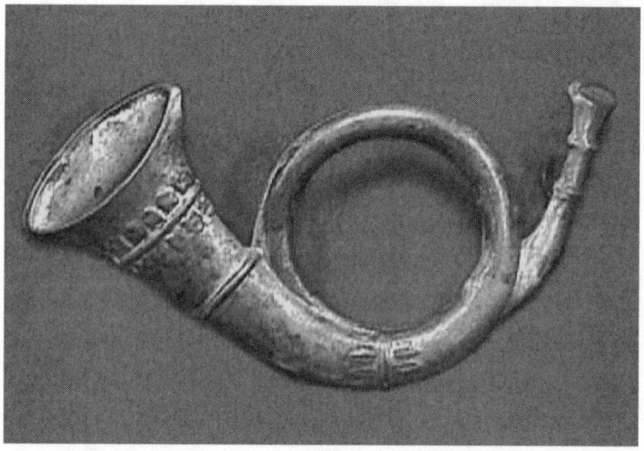

The Union infantry used a brass-stamped hunting horn as their insignia. This is a non-dug example.

Middle Tennessee Relics

U.S., Enlisted Man, Infantry

Excellent condition, non-dug, stamped-brass bugle infantry hat insignia, both loops intact. **95.00**

Dug, large-size Union infantry bugle hatpin with brown-green patina, very solid, but does appear to have an old repair to the mouthpiece tip. **125.00**

Hooks present, non-dug, excellent condition..... **85.00**

Bannerman's surplus Civil War headgear insignia, never had the attaching wires attached to the back, but were added later by the Francis Bannerman Military Surplus company. **45.00**

Federal infantry cap/hat emblem in shape of horn, excellent condition, two wire loops on back intact. **90.00**

Gilt, sheet-brass stamped in the false embroidered pattern. Very fine strike with beautiful detail, bugle retains almost all its original gilt, which is slightly tarnished to a gold patina. Perfect attaching wires on the back, excellent condition. **285.00**

Mint, unissued stamped brass infantry bugle insignia from the Wm. H. Horstmann stock, excellent condition just lacking one attaching loop. **49.00**

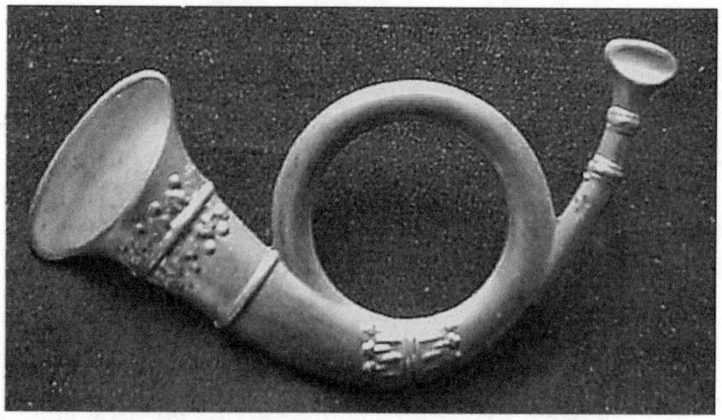

Non-dug infantry insignia with only two attaching wires on the back.

Dale C. Anderson Co.

Stamped brass hunting horn, worn by nearly all infantry, 3-1/2" w, two brass wire loops on back to fasten to hat, untouched, dull patina to brass, not a dug relic. **99.00**

With hooks, non-dug, excellent condition. **85.00**

Mint, unissued stamped-brass infantry bugle (hunting horn) insignia from the Wm. H. Horstmann stock. Excellent condition just lacking one attaching loop. **49.00**

U.S., Officer, Infantry

Hat insignia, embroidered cloth, rectangular with tufted area with a silver "18" in the crook of the horn, fine quality gold embroidery, 2" x 3-3/8". **138.00**

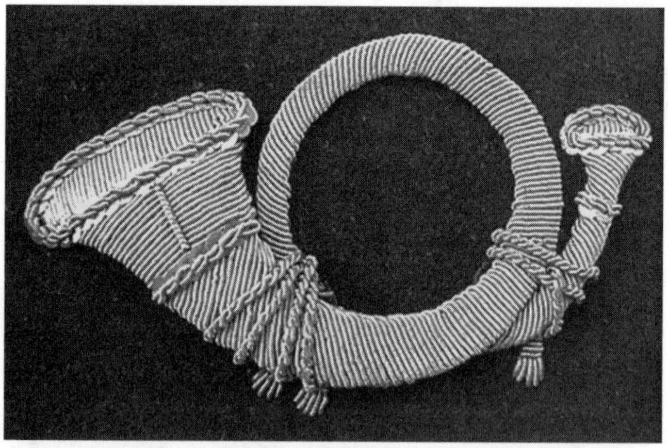

Extremely large, embroidered infantry hat insignia.

Dale C. Anderson Co.

Mint and unused, this embroidered bugle is in the exact state it was sold to an officer, still untrimmed for sewing to a hat. Large and impressive, the bugle is on a 3-1/8" x 4-1/4" rectangle of prime-quality black wool with stiffener layer behind. The gold bullion infantry horn is embroidered in unbelievable three-dimensional, high relief. It is almost as if the horn were laid on the backing. Gorgeous condition with the slightest, even muting. **495.00**

U.S., Officer, Infantry, cont.

Rounded oval 2-5/8" w, black velvet facing over internal stiffener, affixed to the face is a stamped sheet-brass infantry horn, with embossed surface raised to simulate bullion embroidery. Nice toned patina, fastening wires bent over on back. Within the horn's loop is a false embroidered, silver number "5." The entire thing is bordered by a line of thin spun brass wire...this now aged to a coppery tone. Reverse faced with thin black wool, excellent overall. **545.00**

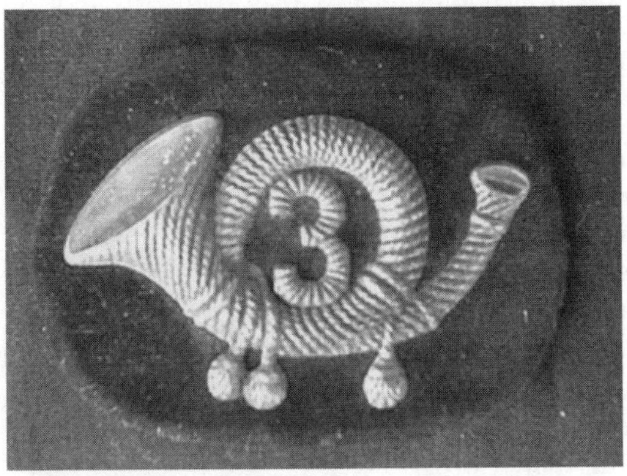

Embroidered infantry bugle with the numeral "3" denoting the 3rd Regiment.

Dale C. Anderson Co.

Stiffened black velvet oval with very rare-sized officer's stamped-brass infantry horn applied at center. The surface is embossed with a detailed texture simulating bullion embroidery. Within the turn of the horn is the silvered number "3" for 3rd Infantry. It also has false embroidery, brass and silver both have even coppery-toned patina, condition excellent, backing 2-3/16" w, horn 1-7/8" wide........ **445.00**

This is the regulation officer's velvet, embroidered, hunting horn infantry hat insignia with metal stiffener inside, brown polished cotton back, and beautiful gold bunion embroidered hunting horn insignia. This has the applied numerals "54" inside the horn's loop. Excellent condition just lacks the twisted wire outer border................. **495.00**

Typical of that seen on the front of slouch hats and tall forage caps, 3-1/2" w black wool oval, stiffened by a piece of backing fabric, entirely hand embroidered in a professional manner, with gold bullion and sequins, forming the traditional infantry horn around the number "1." All this is surrounded by two narrow rows of spun brass wire. Bullion is tarnished dark brown, overall condition fine with no damage. **495.00**

U.S., Enlisted Man, Regimental, Irish-American regimental badge consisting of a shamrock of German silver with a harp, elkhound, and tower cut out of the same material and affixed to the shamrock, T-bar pin on back, 1-1/4" h............................ **385.00**

U.S., Enlisted Man, Corcoran's Legion, uncovered in a small insignia lot from a Maryland historical society, familiar harp insignia (as shown in Lord's *Civil War Collector's Encyclopedia*) is embroidered in silver bullion and sequins, approximately 2-1/4" h and unused. Embroidered on thin, stiff paper on which it was sold, shows slight tarnish...................... **110.00**

U.S., Officer, Engineers

A silver anchor with a ribbon running from fluke to fluke and with crossed oars overlay, T-bar pin on back, very scarce badge, excellent condition.. **350.00**

Appears to be silver, or more likely, silver-plated sheet brass, has dark silvery-gray tarnish distinctive of silver or silver plate. A most handsome insignia worn by a very small, select group of army engineer officers before and during the Civil War period. Also by officers at West Point since 1842, 3-1/4" w, 2-1/4" h. Classic engineer's castle bent a bit to take the hat's contour, two original wire fasteners soldered on back. Fine overall, and very rare. **645.00**

U.S., Officer, Ordnance, a flaming bomb embroidered in gold bullion on black wool, unused. **150.00**

U.S., Officer, Rifleman, consists of a bugle standing vertical with the cords forming the letter "R," all embroidered in gold bullion on a rectangle of black wool, very fine condition, minor tarnish, fabric stiffener on back and a bit of adhesive residue from album display.................................. **535.00**

The embroidered "US" in the wreath was used by officers of the Union general staff.

Sharpsburg Arsenal

U.S., Officer, embroidered General Officer's hat insignia. **495.00**

U.S., Enlisted Man

Eagle hat plate for the Model 1858 "Hardee" hat, classic stamped-brass eagle with loop and "fish hook" loop on the reverse, non-dug, beautiful. **295.00**

Sometimes referred to as a "Jeff Davis" hatpin, non-excavated, absolutely genuine and complete with a nicely aged patina....................... **465.00**

Shako Plate

U.S., Model 1851, New York, brass shield almost 4" h, eagle on a demiglobe above and "Excelsior" on a ribbon below. Worn on the shako into the Civil War and pictured in *General Regulations for the Military forces of the State of New York*, excellent condition. **385.00**

Personal Identification

Identification Disc

Andrew Howard of the 2nd Delaware Infantry wore this identification disc. It was generally thought by soldiers, that if they fell wearing identification of some sort, their remains would be properly cared for, and even, possibly returned to their loved ones.

Enlisted Man

Delaware, exact measurements are more than a quarter, brass, excellent condition, marked on one side is an eagle clutching arrows, and "The War of 1861/The United States." On the other side, the soldier's name is engraved, "Andrew Howard, Company H, 2nd Regiment Delaware Volunteers." **863.00**

Ohio. Pewter dog tag embossed edge, "War of 1861." Wreath is marked, "Engaged in the above Battles." Filled in here with, "Enlisted Jan 26th 1865 under Capt Green at Fremont, Ohio." Reverse marked, "Henry Spade Co "E" 186th O.V.I. Fremont Ohio." Tag is cast with a small nib (drilled with hole) protruding above the disc's edge (designed to pass a neck cord through). Attached to this nib is a small link of chain attached to a stamped German silver shield (pin back) with bust of Grant and words "Lt. Gen. Grant." **475.00**

Vermont, War of 1861-style, made of brass, 28mm diameter, non-excavated specimen, mellow patina, disc marked, "G.C. Richardson Co. H. 6th Reg Roxbury, VT. Vol." George C. Richardson, was a private in the 6th Vermont Infantry. He enlisted August 8, 1861, into Company H and was discharged December 6, 1862. He died three days later on December 9, 1862. The 6th Vermont had been engaged in battle at Williamsburg, Malvern Hill, Alexandria, and Antietam just prior to Richardson's death. **855.00**

Bearing the likeness of General Grant, this late-war identification disc was worn by F.H. Oliver, a soldier in the Unattached Maine Volunteers assigned to the 19th Army Corps.

Dale C. Anderson Co.

Maine, 1-5/8" diameter, neatly cast in a lead alloy, face has side-view bust of General Grant surrounded by three narrow rings of decoration, the inner reads, "LIEU. GEN. U.S. GRANT," within a wreath, with a gnarled edge. The other side has a splendid, complex design of a shield at center, flanked by a panoply of U.S. flags on staffs, under a spread eagle. Stamped in tiny letters is, "F. H. OLIVER/UNATTACHED/ MAINE/VOLS/19/ARMY CORPS." Fine detail, tarnished to dark gray, minor wear......... **675.00**

One side of an 1861 disc worn by Sergeant J.T. Gordon of the 15th New Hampshire Volunteer Infantry bore the impression of an eagle. On the reverse, it was personalized for Gordon.

New Hampshire, stamped, "Sergeant J.T. Gordon, Company A, 15th Regiment, New Hampshire Volunteers, Lake Village. War of 1861."..... **725.00**

"Against Rebellion" declares this patriotic 1861 identification disc that once belonged to James Smith, an artilleryman in Company F, 3rd U.S. Artillery.

Dale C. Anderson Co.

Silver-plated brass disc, 1-3/16" diameter, crisply minted coin with finely detailed American shield at center with "UNION" across center, surrounded by the raised lettering, "AGAINST REBELLION 1861." Stamped on reverse side, "JAMES SMITH/CO. F. 3D/U.S./ARTY." Bright crisp condition, slight wear to plating on edge. **595.00**

Whereas this metal "ladder tag" was represented as a wartime product, it could very easily be a postwar purchase by the veteran. It is inscribed with the name, "J. Standring." Standring was a member of the 124th Pennsylvania Volunteer Infantry.

Identification Tag

U.S., Enlisted Man

Pennsylvania, "J. Standring" is engraved on the badge's top. Standring was a member of the 124th Pennsylvania Volunteer Infantry, measures 2" x 1-1/4" and appears to be silver, but is unmarked. **464.00**

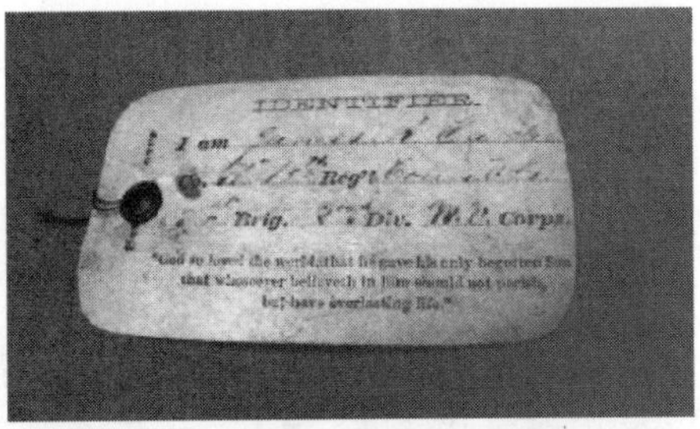

Paper tag was filled out by a member of the 18th Connecticut Volunteer Infantry. This Christian Commission tag was intended to be attached to the soldier's uniform in order to identify him if wounded or to know to whom the remains belonged if killed.

Drumbeat Civil War Memorabilia

Connecticut, identification tag made of reinforced paper, handed out to soldiers by the Christian Commission to wear in case they were killed or wounded. Many soldiers simply wrote a note and kept it on their person in case of injury or death. This one has been filled out by a private in Company K, 18th Connecticut Volunteers. They saw extensive service in the Shenandoah Valley against Jackson. Extremely rare as this is paper and few survived. Complete with its original carrying envelope. **1,300.00**

"As I went into line a man approached me having as a prisoner a Confederate colonel mounted. The man asked me where headquarters were. I pointed ou the corps flag in a field to the rear. The colonel then addressed me as follows: "For God sake, how big is this Catholic corps? (Having reference to our corps badge, a Greek cross.)"

— Colonel William H. Penrose
15th New Jersey Volunteer Infantry

Shoulder Scales

Though not exactly a badge of insignia, shoulder scales were worn only by soldiers who ranked as non-commissioned officers or lower. Therefore, just by glancing at a soldier who had on a pair of scales, one would immediately be able to determine that the soldier was not of a "gentleman's rank."

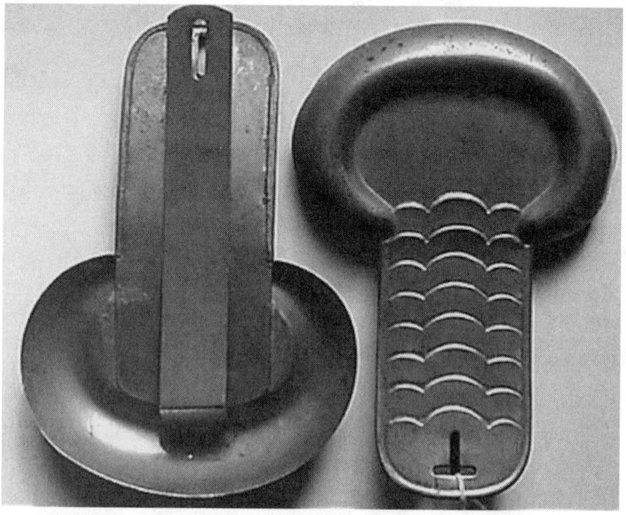

Rather than an insignia, shoulder scales were more a form of body armor. The idea was that if a soldier wearing these was struck down by a swordsman, the blow would be diminished by the protecting scales. Good in theory, but there are few accounts of the scales actually serving successfully in the role.

Dale C. Anderson Co.

Shoulder Scales, U.S., Enlisted Man

Exact style worn by the U.S. Marines, but these are nickel plated, which suggests wear by a fancy militia unit. Excellent, complete, and untouched, with haze of storage grime and patina. **275.00**

Excavated, pieces are separated, but fit nicely together. Comes displayed in Riker mount. **48.00**

Nice and near-mint matched pair of brass shoulder scales, seen being worn in early war photos. **350.00**

The brass fish-scale epaulette worn by cavalry and mounted artillery to protect the shoulders from saber cuts. These are the type with hollow backs and brass attaching tongues. **275.00**

Excellent set of private's scales as worn on the shoulders of the enlisted men's coats to ward off saber blows, fine with delicate patina. **295.00**

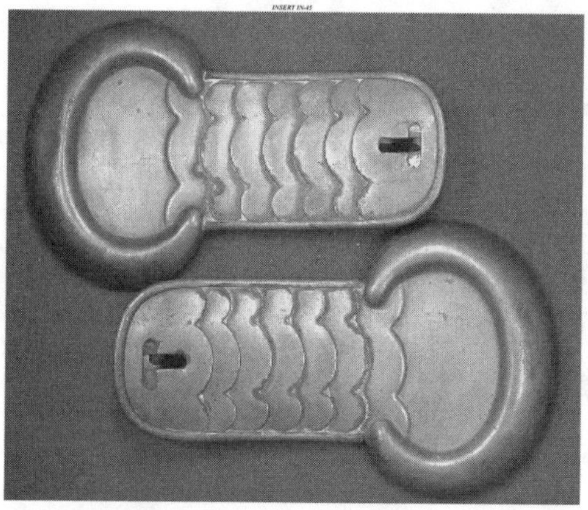

Matched pair of shoulder scales still retaining the tabs for attaching to a uniform.

Middle Tennessee Relics

Nice condition matching pair of brass Union enlisted man's shoulder scales with an attractive, aged patina. This set has both attachment tabs intact. **275.00**

Perfect set of private's scales or epaulets, as worn on the shoulders of the enlisted men's coats to ward off saber blows, fine with delicate patina. **325.00**

These have the original turnkeys to sew to the uniform. **325.00**

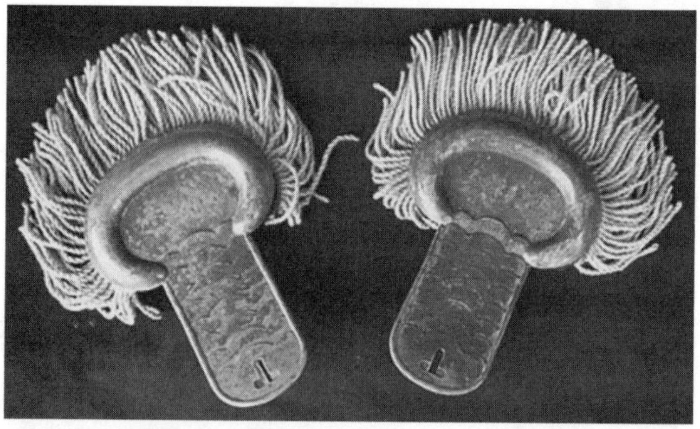

With provisions for attaching fringe, this style of shoulder scales was used by the Marines.

Dale C. Anderson Co.

This model was used by enlisted men of the U.S. Marine Corps, and some militia units also adopted them. They are distinctly different from U.S. Army models in that they are a bit larger, and the undersides of the crescents are open allowing a removable second plate that carries a corded fringe to slip into place. Thus, the epaulets can be worn with fringe, or without. A very excellent, complete set, no dents on crescents. Medium brass patina that can be polished good as new, fringe is yellow (cavalry), excellent, lightly faded. Retains springs on back, marked, "HORSTMANN/PHILA." **370.00**

Miscellaneous

Baldric Insignia, U.S., Officer, beautiful, about-mint condition, stamped brass insignia still on the simple wood plaque on which it was mounted when offered for sale by Bannermans & Stokes Kirk in the early 1900s. Consists of high-relief lion's head supporting three parallel lengths of brass chain that attach below to the top of a shield with the American eagle emblem. Brass wire fasteners on back, go through thin wood plaque. **195.00**

Insignia Terminology

Bannerman's: Francis Bannerman was an early surplus dealer, beginning his business in the late nineteenth century. He bought vast supplies of Civil War goods direct from the government and manufacturers for resale to early Civil War buffs. Bannerman was also the first individual to reproduce Civil War items on a large scale.

Corps badge: In 1863, the Union Army instituted a system of denoting corps affiliations by displaying specific symbols. These symbols, cut of wool felt, were initially issued to soldiers. Enthusiasm caught on for the idea, and soldiers soon began buying commercial corps badges to decorate their hats, caps, coats, and jackets.

Epaulette: Worn on the shoulder and fringed, epaulettes are part of a dress uniform. Rarely would they ever be worn in a combat situation.

Identification disc: These are the precursors to the issued "dog tags." These items were not issued during the Civil War. Rather, soldiers purchased and made a variety of identification tags to wear while in service.

Sash: A sash was worn by officers and NCOs wrapped around their waist and under the sword belt.

Shoulder scale: Not actually an insignia (though they were worn only by NCOs and lower ranks), shoulder scales were more of a form of "body armor." The idea was that if a soldier wearing these was struck down by a swordsman, the blow would be diminished by the protecting scales.

Chapter 12

Medical Instruments

These items, probably won't come cheap. Solid, identified, surgeon sets will easily run in excess of $5,000. An engraved surgeon's sword will go for at least $2,500. Understandably, a lot of your competition will come from twenty-first-century doctors and surgeons. They may just be in a better financial position for acquiring these top-end collectibles.

Even if your funds don't abound, you can still succeed by acquiring knowledge. In all the different aspects of Civil War relics and memorabilia, medical items are perhaps the most misunderstood and misrepresented items. In most cases, this is not a result of trying to take advantage of an unknowing customer, but simply because the dealer doesn't know the hobby. It is a very intricate hobby requiring a deep study to understand the nuances of what makes a particular item "of the period" or not. Time and money invested in acquiring and studying as many books as possible will be the second best thing to having lots of money to just, "learn as you buy."

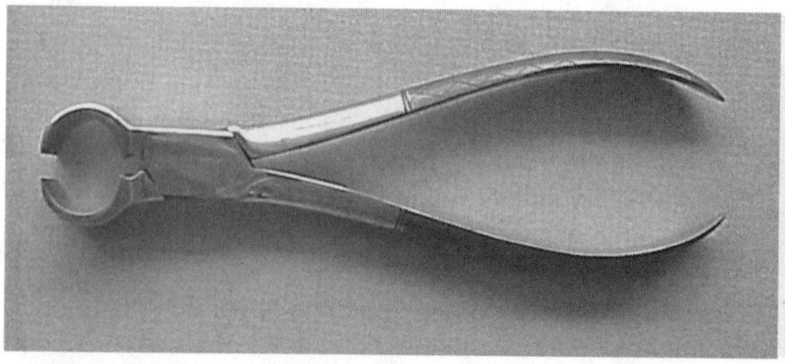

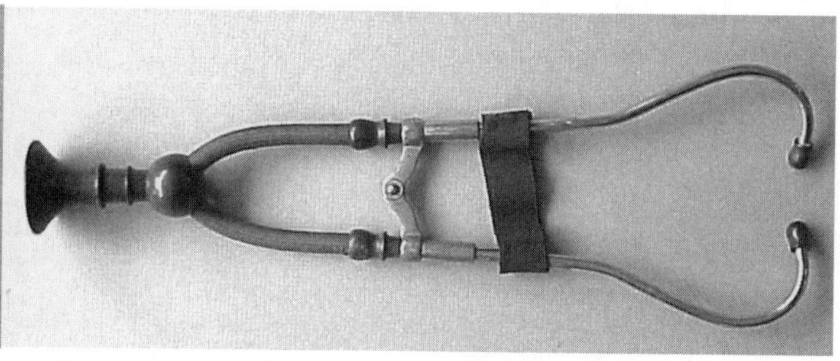

Collecting Hints

Pros:

- Nineteenth-century medical tools have been popular for many years. Therefore, there are several excellent references available to guide one in developing a collection.
- The survivability rate is rather high for medical tools. Generally, if you are ready to begin collecting these items, they are readily found.

Cons:

- Many surgical sets and tools are represented as being "Civil War," when, in fact, they are simply late nineteenth-century items. In most cases, these misrepresentations are not so much intentional as they are wishful. Medical collecting is highly specialized, and most folks simply don't have a general understanding of its nuances.
- Though many items may indeed date to the Civil War, or even pre-date it, this does not mean that the items were actually used in the treatment of war-related injuries. To be sure of actual Civil War surgeon-used items, one must limit themselves to pieces with solid provenance. This severely limits the number of collectible items and greatly increases the cost involved.
- As a subject, medical items are not for everyone. You may be greeted with less than enthusiastic responses when showing off your collection to the squeamish.
- Collecting Civil War medical items can be its own specialty. The key is to learn to look beyond the obvious. For example, while it is relatively easy to recognize a surgeon's set on a table, you will have to look deeper for other medical-related items. For example, highly prized among advanced medical collectors are period photographs of hospital stewards, surgeons, and doctors. Don't forget to look at the swords—an engraved surgeon's model may become the standout of a Civil War medicine collection. Doctor's commissions, receipts, and letterhead may be found in stacks of Civil War ephemera. A surgeon's shoulder straps, hat insignia, or even the special green sash may be found displayed with insignia. Medical bottles may be found on shelves with various nineteenth-century glass. The successful medical collector will learn to look everywhere for related items.

Availability ★★★★
Price ★★★
Reproduction Alert ★★★★★

Civil War-Era Instruments

A visual directory to instruments typically found in or associated with Civil War-era surgical sets and their values, based sales catalogs, Internet auctions, and private sales (add 20% for handles made of real ivory and not bone)—*Dr. Michael Echols, Ft. Myers, Florida.*

Excellent = no rust, no cracked handles, no problems
Good = about average, but serviceable
Marked = maker name on instrument

PRICES ARE GIVEN IN TWO GRADES EX G

EX G

Amputation Knife, large, unplated, composite handle with crosshatching.................... **80-120.00** **70.00**

EX G

Artery Forceps, unplated, olive-tip forceps for holding and tying off arteries.......................... **60-65.00** **35.00**

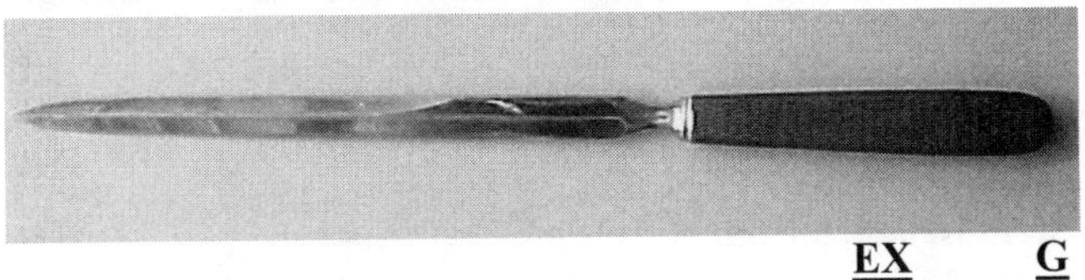

EX G

Amputation Catlin, large, double-sided blade, composite handle with crosshatching................ **80-120.00** **70.00**

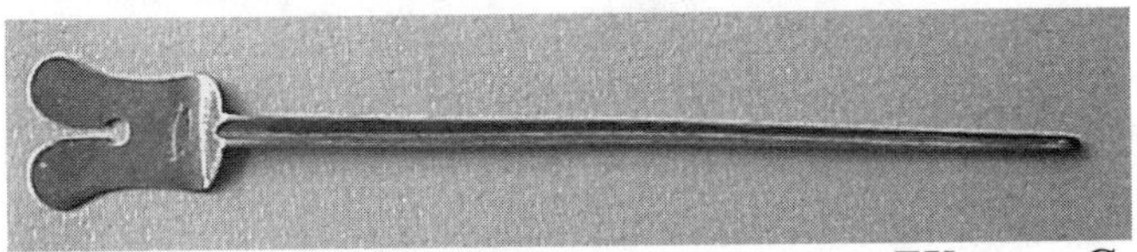

EX G

Blade Director, to direct knife blade. **18-20.00** **10.00**

EX G

Bistoury Knives, unplated, curved blade with blunt tip or curved blade and sharp point...................... **40-45.00** **25.00**

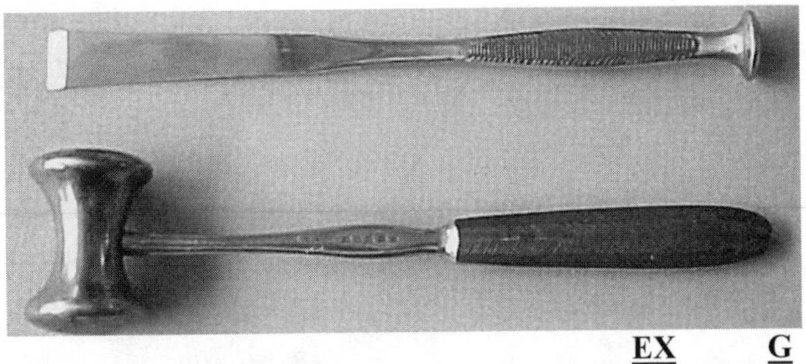

EX G

Bone Hammer and Chisel, hammer..... **55-75.00** **40.00**

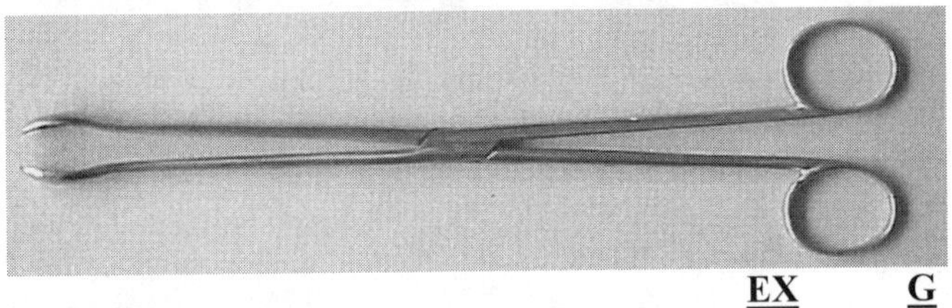

EX G

Bullet Forceps, long shank, serrated tips, marked.................... **190-230.00** **150.00**

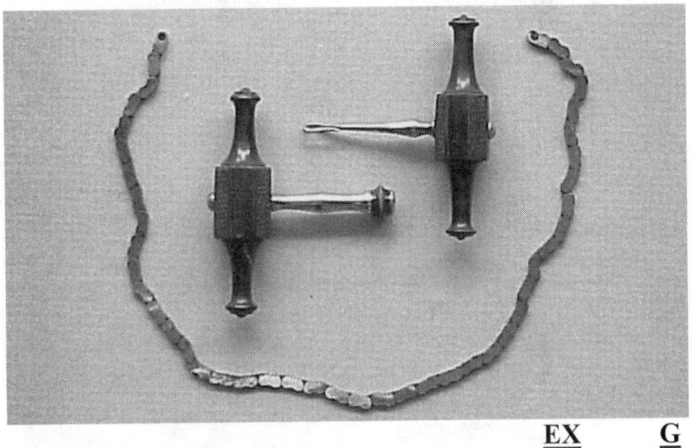

EX G

Chain Saw, both handles, unmarked, no rust on chain................. **180-200.00** **100.00**

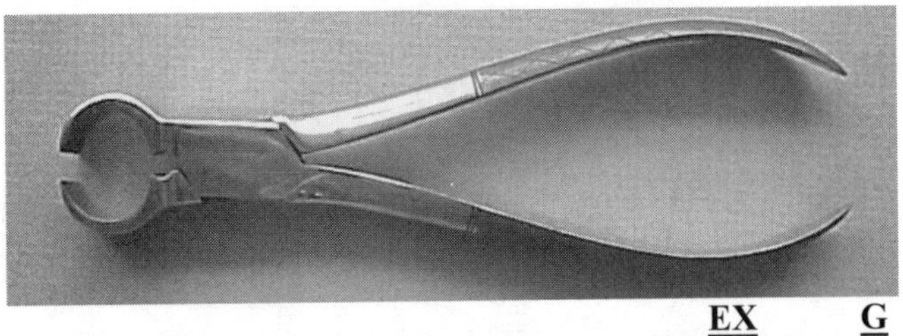

EX G

End Cutting Bone Forceps, marked.... **140-150.00** **75.00**

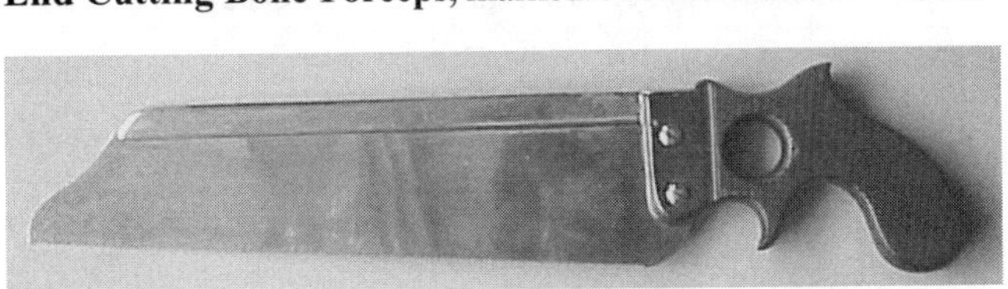

EX G

Gemrig Amputation Saw, early, marked........................ **200-250.00** **100.00**

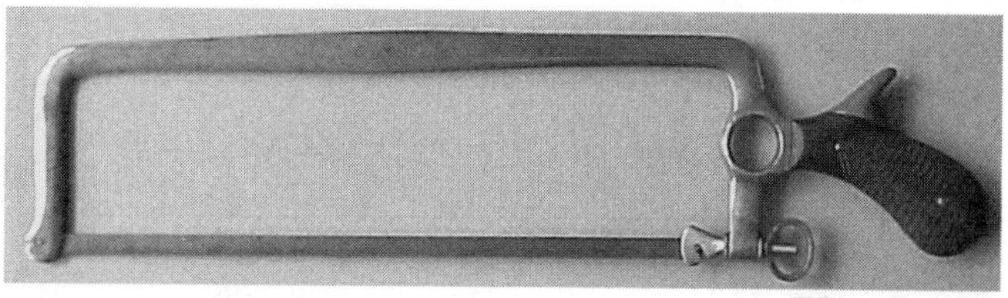

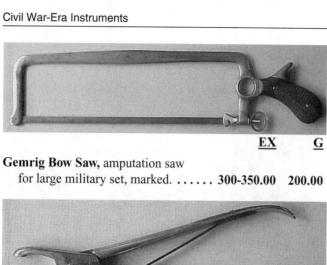

EX G

Gemrig Bow Saw, amputation saw
for large military set, marked. **300-350.00** **200.00**

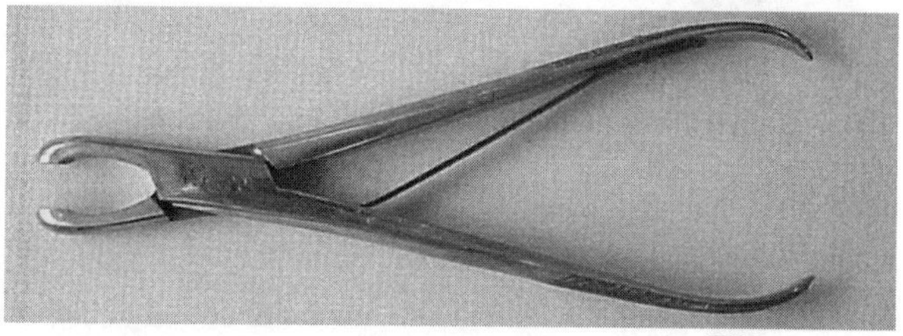

EX G

Gnawing Bone Forceps,
round tip, marked. **125-150.00** **60.00**

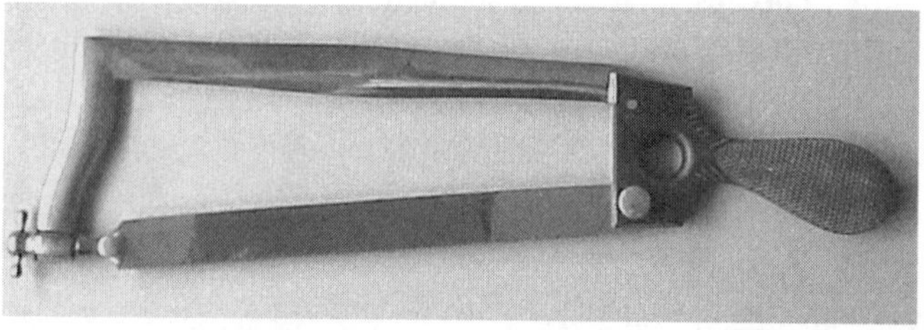

EX G

Hernstein Amputation Saw,
military, marked. **250-300** **150.00**

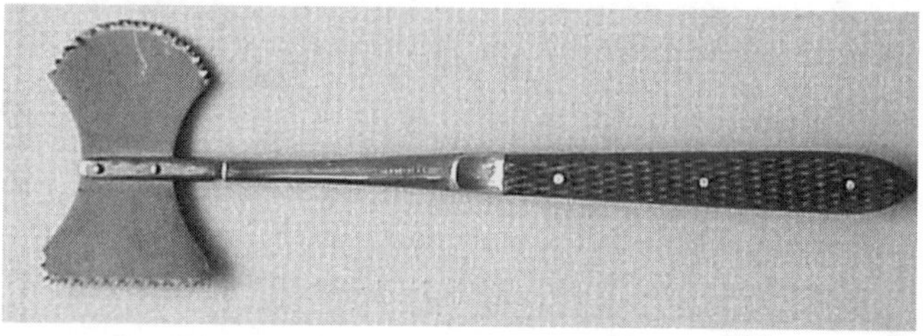

EX G

Hey Saw, skull-trepanning saw, marked. . **75-120.00** **90.00**

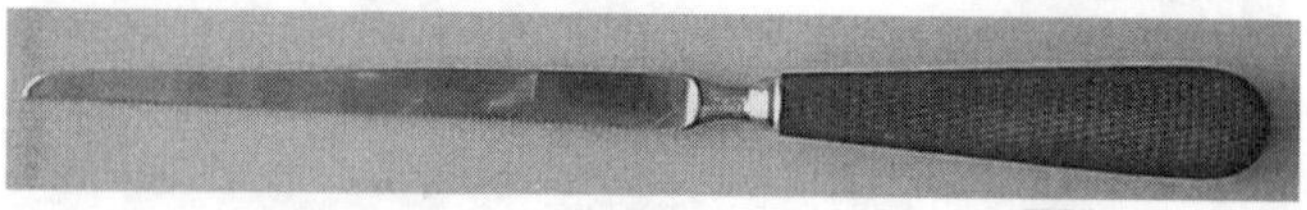

EX G

Metacarpal Saw, for small bones, marked,
composite crosshatched handle. **110-120.00** **75.00**

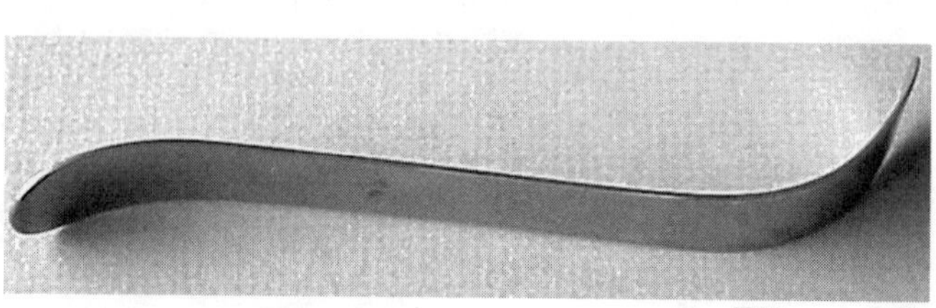

EX G

Muscle Retractor, unmarked. **20-25.00** **15.00**

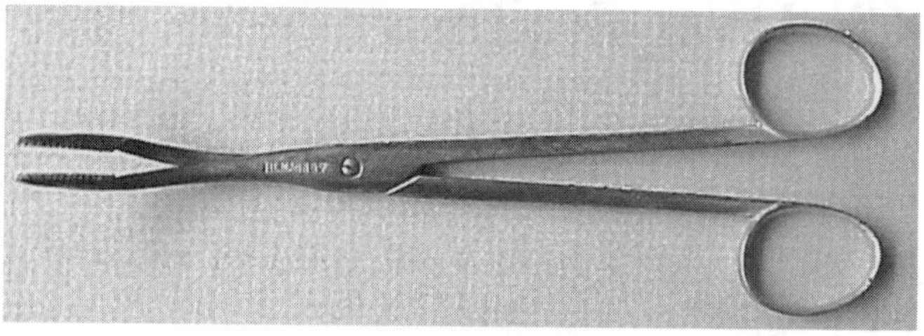

EX G

Sequestrum Forceps, for bone fragments,
holding tissue, shallow bullets, short
shanked, marked. **80-85.00** **50.00**

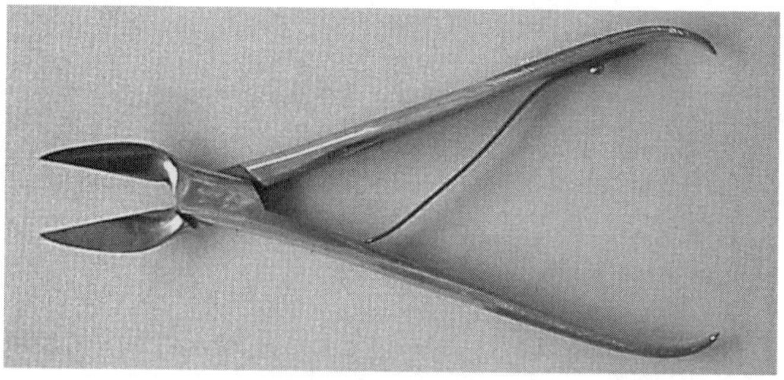

EX G

Side-Cutting Forceps, for bone, unplated,
marked. **170-180.00** **75.00**

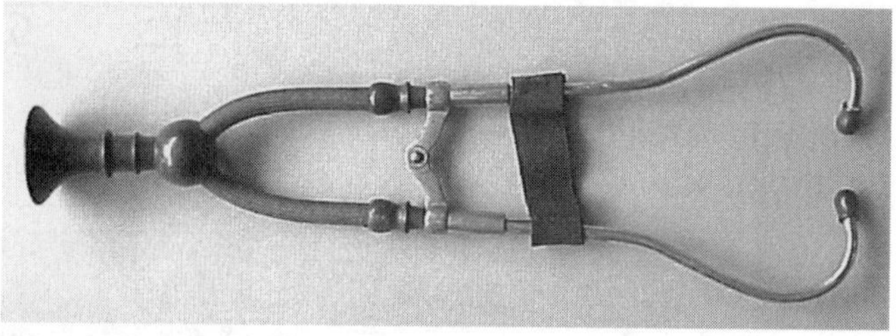

EX G

Stethoscope, uncommon during Civil War;
marked, early elastic band. **400-500.00** **200.00**

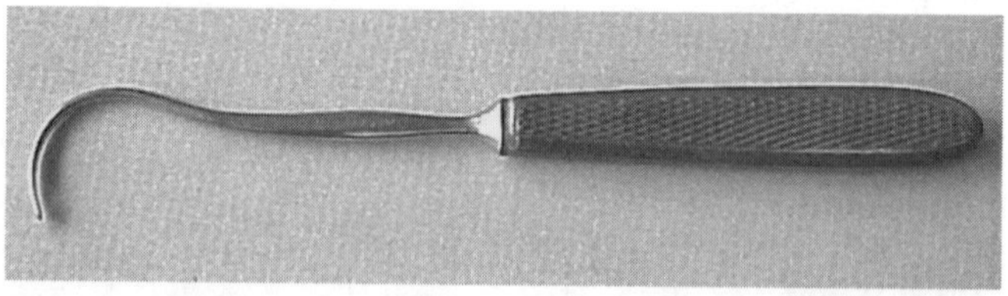

EX G

Tenaculum, for artery traction during suturing, marked,
composite crosshatched handle. **50-60.00** **35.00**

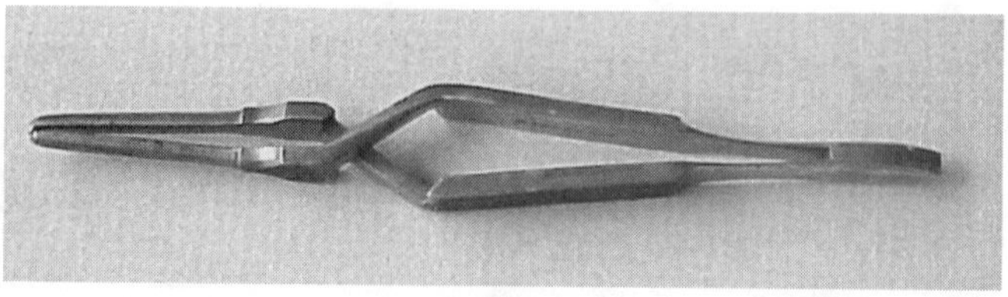

EX G

Tissue Forceps, to clamp off artery or holding tissue,
unplated, unmarked. **40-50.00** **20.00**

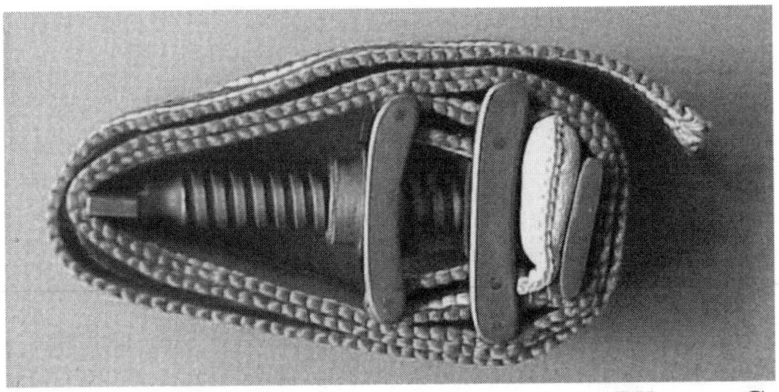

	EX	G
Tourniquet, petit brass screw frame, fabric strap, marked.	**270.00**	**200.00**

	EX	G
Tourniquet Strap, belt type for field use.	**170.00**	**100.00**

	EX	G
Trepanning Bone Brush, to remove bone dust, unmarked.	**95.00**	**50.00**

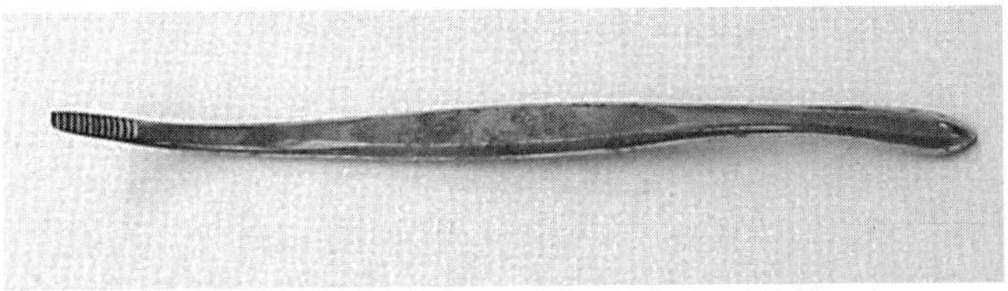

	EX	G
Trepanning Bone File, for smoothing edge and elevating tissues of skull, marked.	**75.00**	**55.00**

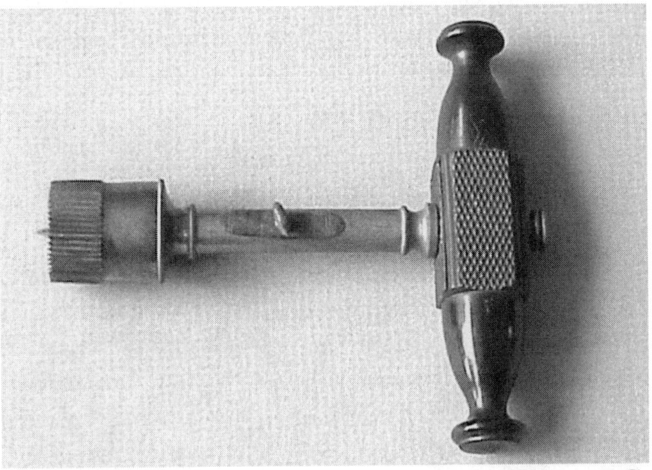

	EX	G
Trepanning Trephine, for boring hole in skull, unmarked.	**150.00**	**90.00**

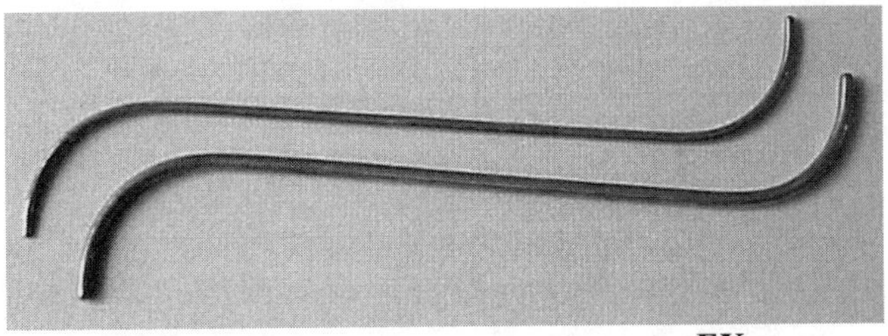

	EX
Urinary Staves or Sounds, urethral dilators, common to military sets, unplated: exc.	**20.00 ea.**

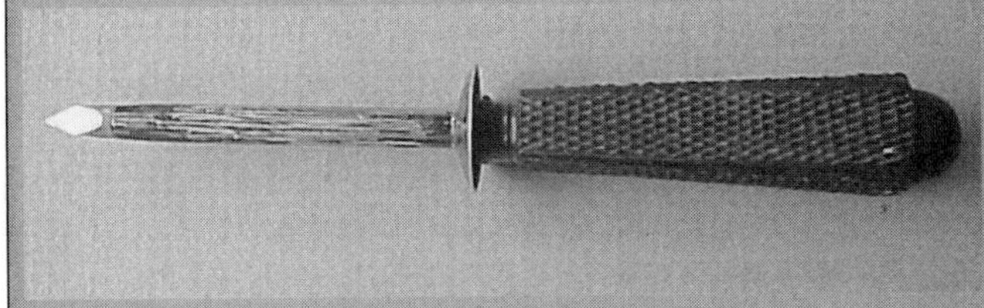

Trocar, for draining fluids, unmarked, small, ex. **65.00**; large, ex. **85.00**; good **40.00**

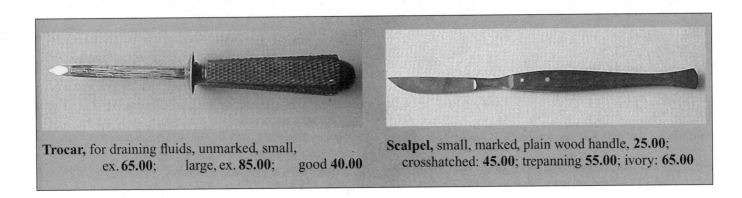

Scalpel, small, marked, plain wood handle, **25.00**; crosshatched: **45.00**; trepanning **55.00**; ivory: **65.00**

Civil War-Era Surgical Sets

Civil War surgical sets, which were made or used during the war, generally come in three variations: civilian, U.S. Army Medical Department, or U. S. Army Hospital Department. Civilian sets that existed prior to the war may have been used during the war. The prices shown here are for sets made during, or specifically for, the military during the Civil War.

As a general rule, military sets usually have double sliding latches and no keys. Civilian sets usually have only a central key (note: for extensive information on identifying Civil War surgical sets, see Dr. Michael Echols' Web site, Pre-1870 American Surgical Sets, at: www.braceface.com/medical).

Values vary greatly due to condition, maker, presence of correct and original instruments, maker or military markings, inscriptions on the case brass plaque, and proven ownership by a Civil War surgeon. The prices included in this visual directory are derived from sales catalogs, Internet auctions, and private sales.

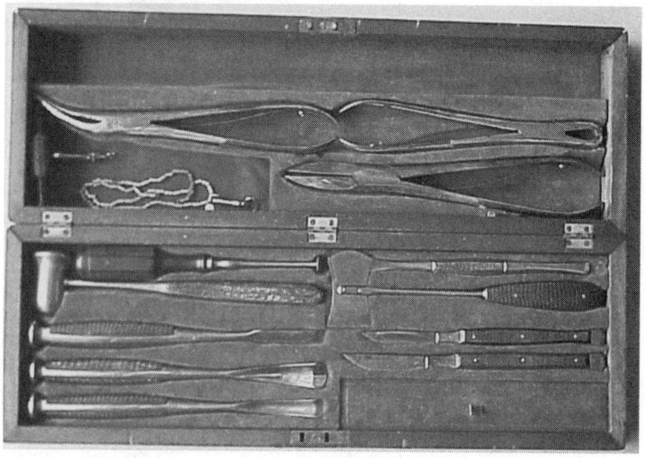

Gemrig Bone Surgery Set, a specialized surgical set issued to military surgeons for bone resection or removal. J. H. Gemrig was a supplier of military and civilian surgical sets both before and during the war, excellent condition. **3,500.00-4,000.00**

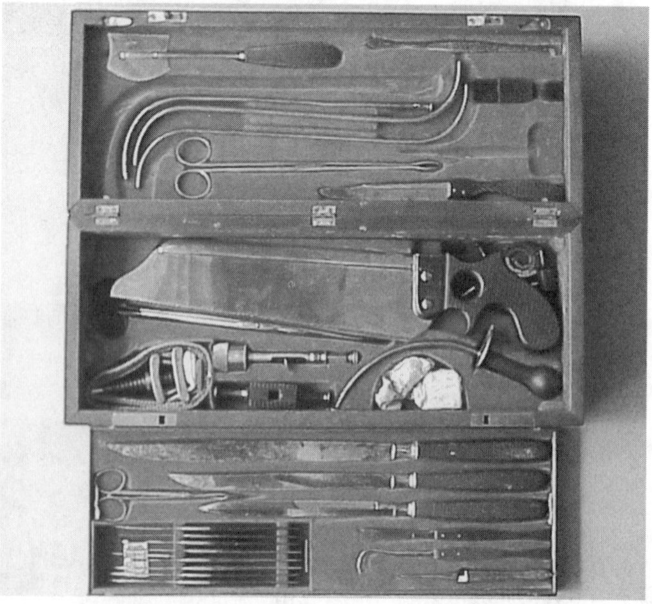

Gemrig Capital Military Set, instruments for field surgery, amputation, trepanning, urology, minor surgery, bullet removal; type issued to Union Army surgeons, excellent condition. ... **4,500.00-5,500.00**

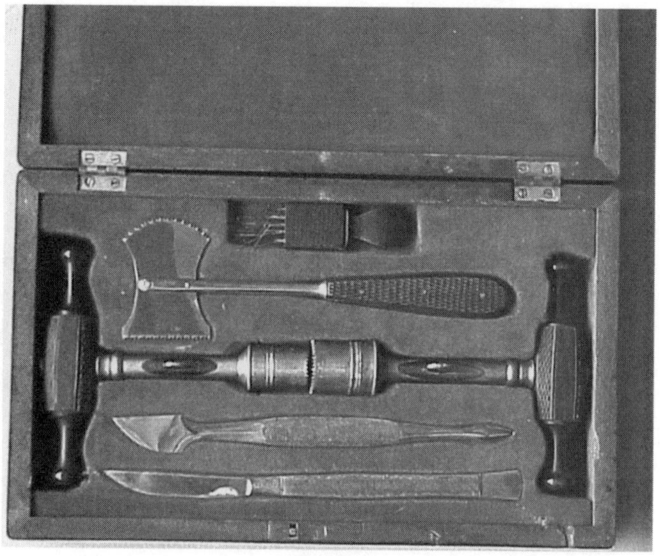

Kern Trepanning Set, civilian set for surgery of the skull. H. Kern was a supplier of military and civilian surgical sets before and during the war, in excellent condition.................... **1,800.00-2,800.00**

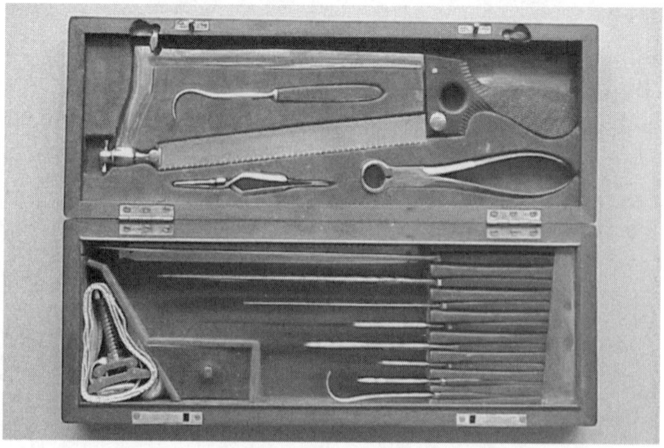

Hernstein Military Amputation Set, strictly for field amputation, marked instruments for U.S. Army Hospital Department. H. Hernstein was a supplier of military and civilian surgical sets both before and during the war, excellent condition.
.............................**3,500.00-4,500.00**

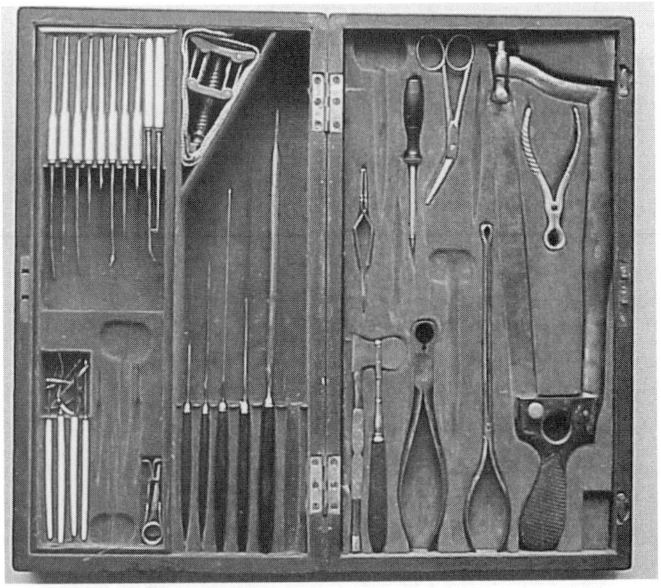

Hernstein Military Set, intended for field surgery, amputation, trepanning, urology, minor surgery, bullet removal; owned by a documented Confederate surgeon, purchased the year before the war, excellent condition. **3,800.00-4,800.00**

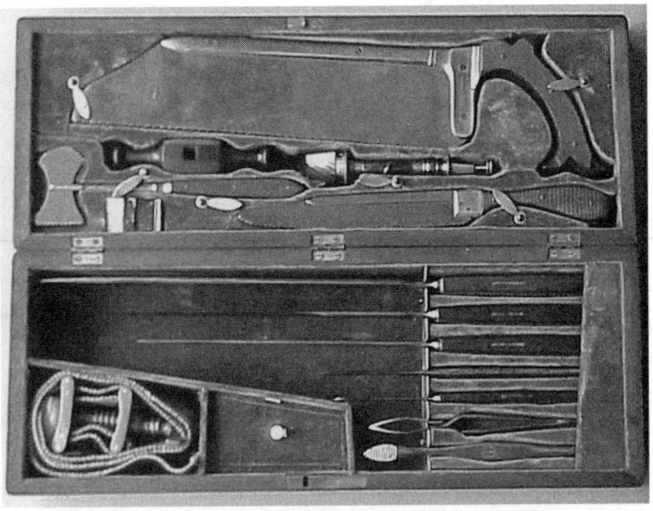

Shepard & Dudley Civilian Set, intended for amputation and trepanning, made during the war years and typical of sets owned and used by civilian contract surgeons. Documented set in various catalogs as having been produced ca. 1862. Shepard and Dudley were suppliers of civilian surgical sets before and during the war, excellent condition. ....**3,500.00 to 4,200.00**

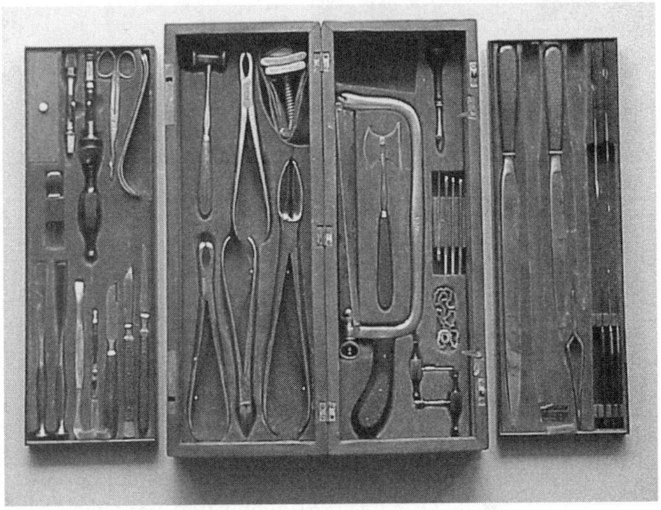

Kolbe Military Set, intended for major bone surgery, trepanning, amputation, a specialized set for bone resection or removal. Marked for U.S. Army Medical Department. Date of manufacture determined by label address of maker. D. Kolbe was a supplier of military and civilian surgical sets both before and during the war, excellent condition. **5,000.00-6,000.00**

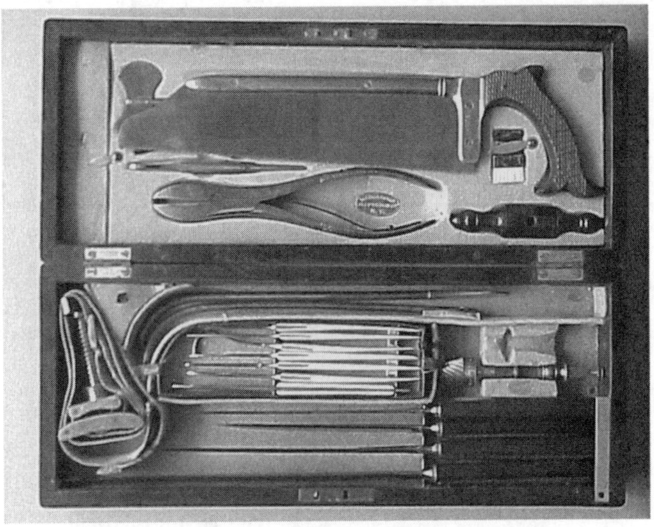

Wade and Ford Civilian Set, documented and inscribed brass plaque on set shows it was owned by a Civil War Union Navy surgeon, purchased in 1861. Pictured in Smith's Manual of Surgery. Used for amputation, trepanning, urology, minor surgery, and eye surgery. Wade & Ford was a supplier of military and civilian surgical sets both before and during the war, excellent condition. **5,000.00-6,000.00**

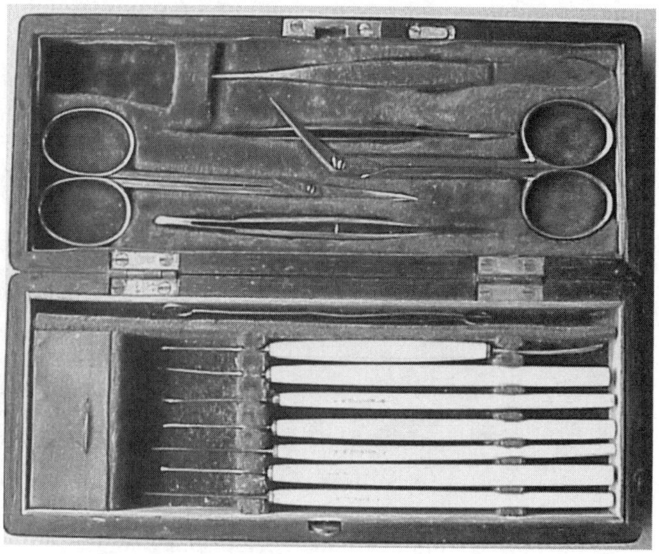

Tiemann Eye Surgery Set, small civilian set for eye surgery, dated ca. 1860 by maker label address. Tiemann was a major maker and supplier of military and civilian surgical sets both before and during the war, excellent condition. 300.00-500.00

Books and Manuals

Book, Medical, a very interesting clothbound book titled, *The Actions of Medicines on the System,* by Frederick Headland, MD, printed in Philadelphia during 1863. Front has inked inscription, "Merrel H Macken Feb 25th 1863." Contents include Haematica, Catalytica, Neurotica, Stimulantia, Narcotica, Sedantia, and other medical topics. Very solid and tight with an old repair to the front cover hinge and some edge wear on the binding. . . . **95.00**

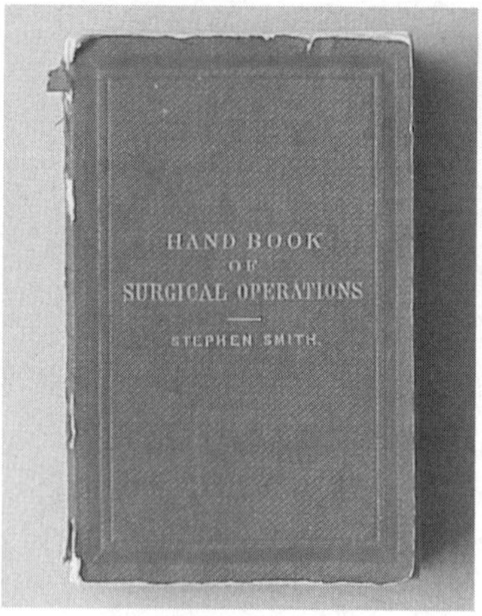

Manuals and medical books published during the war or carried by military surgeons are great complements to a medical display. Pictured is such a treatise on medical procedures.

Photo courtesy of Dr. Michael Echols

Manual, Medical

The Hand-Book of Surgical Operations, title embossed in gold on the front cover. Hardbound with brown cloth covers, missing the front papers including flyleaf, title page, copyright page, and first two pages of text. Starts on page three, and is complete from that point, 122 pages long, plus appendices and charts. The gilt title on the cover makes this an ideal display item with surgeon's effects. **395.00**

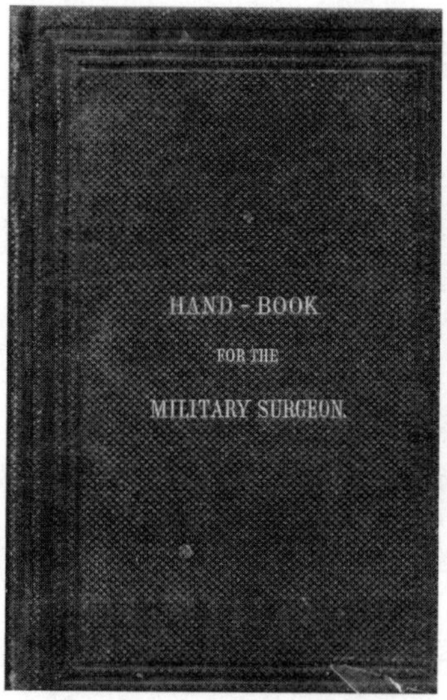

Published in 1861, *Hand Book for the Military Surgeon,* gave explicit instructions on how to deal with war-related wounds.

Drumbeat Civil War Memorabilia

Hand Book for the Military Surgeon by Tripler & Blackman. Original 1861 publication, contains instructions for medical officers, plus a section on war surgery, detailing treatment of gunshot wounds, amputations, wounds of the chest, abdomen, arteries, and head, plus the use of chloroform. Book in fine condition. **1,250.00**

Manual, Surgical, *Hand Book for the Military Surgeon,* title gilt-embossed on the green front cover. It measures roughly 8" x 5", and is just under an inch thick. Published by Robert Clarke & Co. of Cincinnati in 1861, 121-pages long with appendices, including medical inventories and equipment needed, instructions on filling out government medical forms, etc. This is autographed inside the front cover, "J.H. Seaton MD/Keokuk June 24th 1861." Seaton was a surgeon from the 21st Missouri regiment. Near-mint condition and very rare. **1,150.00**

Containers

Bottle, Medicine

USA Hospital Department bottle recovered at Point of Rocks, Maryland, in excellent condition with no cracks or chips, small flaw on bottle neck made during manufacture, measures 9-1/2" x 3-1/2". **895.00**

Original and near perfect Jacob Dunton bottle marked, "Ext. Cinch. Arom. Fl/US Army Medical Supplies/ Jacob Dunton, Philadelphia," original glass stopper, 2" x 2" x 5." Excellent label is intact. The interior is stained from the original contents. **850.00**

Box, Pill, mint condition, circular cardboard container exactly the size & shape of a pistol percussion cap tin. Lid is deep blue with gold lettering, "Dr. Chilton Manufactured by Comstock & Brother New York/ One Dollar/Per Box/Fever and Ague Cure." . . . **49.00**

Canteen, Medical

This one carried quinine, and is identical to one in Sylvia's *Civil War Canteens*. The only difference is this one has the design painted on the cover, not the metal body, standard M1858 smooth-sided canteen with coarse medium-brown original cover, no holes. Painted in faded white, on one side is the large word, "QUININE," with shell-like decorations above and below. Lacks sling, lip of spout trimmed off for unknown reason. **675.00**

Because of the relative rarity of Medical Department-marked containers, an excavated bottle is just as desirable as a non-dug specimen.

Sharpsburg Arsenal

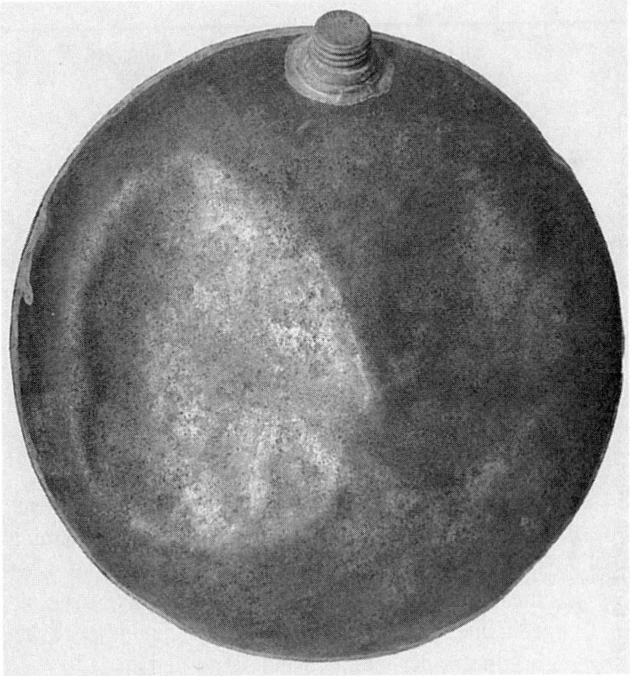

Canteens with screw tops are generally thought to date after the Civil War. This medical canteen, however, clearly bears a patent date, "Oct. 25 1857." Whether or not it is indeed a "medical" canteen, though, is not clear.

J.C. Devine Inc.

This tin canteen has the basic shape of the Model 1858 canteen, but is 13" d, has no sling loops, and has a spout at the top edge of one face with a metal screw top. Though screw tops are very unusual on Civil War canteens, this one is marked with a patent date of, "Oct. 27, 1857." The canteen has scattered surface rust and is dented. It comes with a well-worn carry bag/cover made of multicolored carpet. **100.00**

Chest, Medical, a large walnut Medical Chest with Brass end-handles, measuring 12" x 8" x 7" (closed) and containing 26 period medicine bottles, some with contents. Interior is fitted for various-sized bottles from very small to very large, and is full. The case and bottles are all in excellent condition. ... **722.00**

Container, Medicine, original Edward Squibb, "Stronger Ether for Anesthesia," one-pound tin with original labels, extremely rare, excellent condition, labels are clearly readable and original. ... **1,000.00**

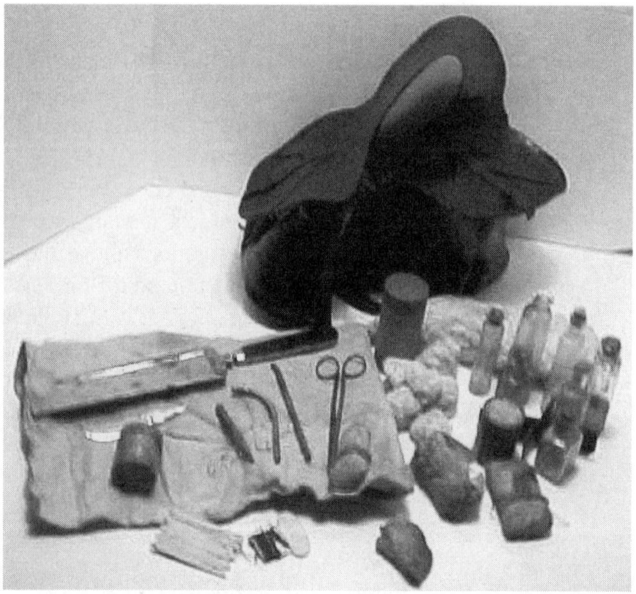

Though nothing clearly pointed to this saddlebag set of medical implements as being carried by a surgeon during the Civil War, it was sold as such.

Saddle Bags, Medical

"Crow-foot" strap design, black leather, even the straps and roller-buckles. The leather was hardened and brittle, but has been treated with a museum leather restorative and is now supple as original. One strap is broken, but all there. There is an assortment of medicine bottles (some still with contents), two tin containers, one wood container and a number of the original paper-wrapped and string-tied dry medications (some never opened). A leather instrument roll contains an amputation saw and knife with interchangeable handle, complete urethral catheter, small bullet forceps, assorted suturing needles, suturing material, old cotton, etc. . **2,500.00**

Provenance indicated that this pair of saddlebags were used by Hospital Steward Howard Wigglesworth of the 45th Massachusetts Volunteer Infantry.

J.C. Devine Inc.

These medical saddlebags were used by Hospital Steward Edward Wigglesworth, Jr., of the 45th Regiment, Massachusetts Volunteer Militia. These unusual saddlebags are constructed of brown leather with each side having 10 compartments to hold medicine bottles, an inner flap to secure the bottles in their compartments, and an outer flap of tarred black leather. Each of the flaps, inner and outer, has a compartment for storage. The other flaps are missing the ends of the small securing straps, the central strap is missing a small buckle. The overall condition is good plus. Wigglesworth was a 21-year-old student from Boston when he enlisted on Oct. 28, 1862, and mustered into the Field and Staff of the Regiment. On November 5, the regiment embarked on the steamer Mississippi for Beaufort, North Carolina and then traveled by train to Newbern. At Kinston on December 14, 1862, the regiment suffered 58 casualties in its first engagement with the enemy. Two days later at Whitehall, it lost four killed and 16 wounded. Included are photocopies of information on the 45th Massachusetts and Edward Wigglesworth. **200.00**

Medical Instruments and Devices

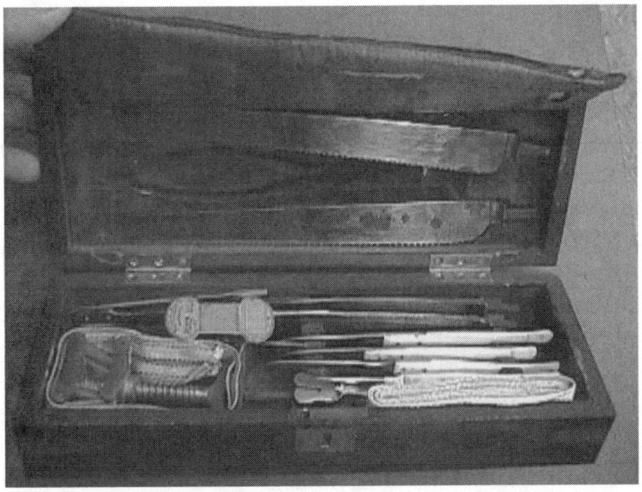

Though this kit contained a few post-Civil War tools, the bulk of the contents were wartime.

Amputation Set

A beautiful and 90% complete Civil War era surgeon's amputation set in a fitted rosewood case, with brass hardware measuring 12" l x 4-1/2" w x 2-3/4" t. Case and hardware, in excellent condition. The green velvet lining has some minor damage. Instruments include the following: Petit Tourniquet with brass screw and original linen strap; 6-1/2" scalpel marked, "Spangenbere," ivory handle; 5-3/4" scalpel marked, "Coxeter London," ivory handle; 6-1/2" knife marked, "Coxeter London," ivory handle; 6" tenaculum marked, "Tiemann," ivory handle; 8-3/4" amputation knife blade marked, "Rose & Sellers," has some pitting and nick in blade; 8" amputation knife blade marked, "Rose & Sellers," some pitting and nick in blade; 10-3/4" amputation saw blade, unmarked, some pitting; 9-1/2" amputation saw blade, unmarked, light pitting; rosewood handle measuring 3-1/2" l and marked, "Dodel S.F. Cal. pat sept 5 99" and two tools that fit into the handle both marked, "Dodel;" 5-3/4" long forceps marked "35095;" 5-1/2" hollow funnel-shaped probe; 5-3/4" scalpel guide; extra and unused tourniquet strap; "J. Satlee" surgeon's silk. The Dodel instrument and the forceps are later additions to this set, but were with it when it was found. Missing handle for amputation saw blades and knives, and an instrument that was housed between the two saw blades in the upper compartment, appears to be bone nippers that are gone. The scalpels and knives with the ivory handles are definitely Civil War period. Use of ivory handles by Tiemann and other manufacturers ended in 1865. The case is definitely Civil War period, as are the amputation saw blades and knives. A beautiful and attractive cased amputation set worthy of display in any venue. Came from a Kentucky estate. . . **1,250.00**

Absolutely wonderful surgical kit. This set is housed in a beautiful mahogany-veneered box with red velvet lining, and each instrument is nicely marked, "H.G. Kern/Phila." The set is nearly complete, but does lack the rongeur, one small scalpel, and a bone scraper. It has a fine, large amputation saw, a fine smaller saw, which resembles a hacksaw in terms of its design (this one rests in a hidden spot under the larger saw), the original tourniquet with strap, three large amputation knives, and the small hooked tool that supports blood vessels during cutting. Inside the case is still present a typed note which reads "Amputation set used by Dr. A. W. McClure during the Civil War." Dr. McClure is listed as the surgeon of the 4th Iowa Cavalry. He received his commission on October 20, 1861, and served with the regiment until April 1863. During this time frame the 4th was attached to the Army of Southwest Missouri and the Department of Missouri, and saw action at such battles as Talbot's Ferry, Little Red River, White River, Jones Lane, Helena, Lick Creek. Marianna, and St. Francis River. A very attractive and appealing set with a wonderful Civil War history. **2,950.00**

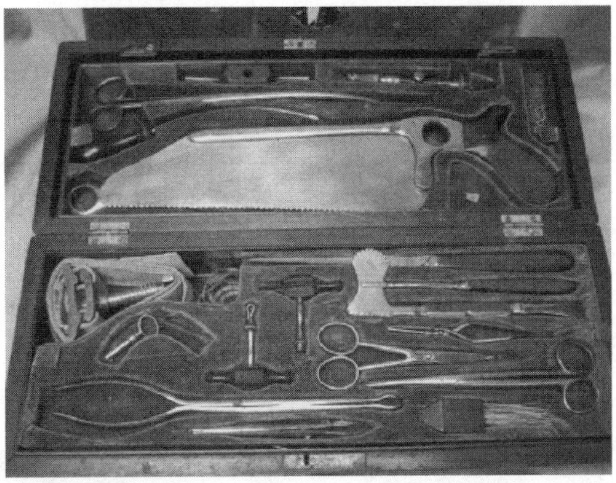

Kit perfectly marked, "USA Hospital Department," and nearly complete.

Drumbeat Civil War Memorabilia

Authentic U.S.A. Hospital Department-marked, four-tier major amputation set by Brinkerhoff, N.Y. This outstanding set is 99% complete, excellent condition. Most of the major pieces are marked and all are matching. The maker's label is present in two places. **6,900.00**

Amputation Set, cont.

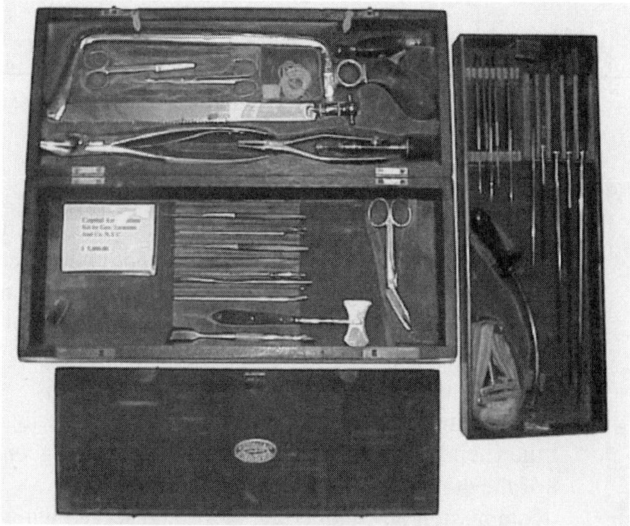

This amputation set made by George Tiemann may actually postdate the Civil War.

Sharpsburg Arsenal

By George Tiemann, near-mint condition, missing three small scalpels, two small tweezers, all major pieces intact, in excellent condition. Wooden box with tray in excellent condition. **5,800.00**

Scales, Apothecary

Cased set of scales with weights of the type used during the Civil War. The case is green with a patriotic eagle embossed on the top. The scales are made of brass, case is 3" x 5-7/8", fine condition. **250.00**

Civil War-era, eagle-marked, cased set of apothecary scales. The scales are complete and still work perfectly. **250.00**

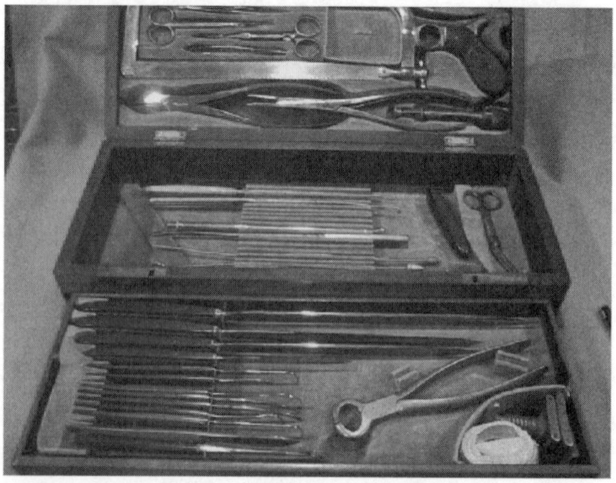

Marked "U.S.A. Hospital Department," this three-tier medical set has more than 30 matching tools. It is maker marked, "Tiennken, New York."

Drumbeat Civil War Memorabilia

Surgical Set

Three-tier USA Hospital Department-marked surgical/amputation set that is military issue, as evidenced by inscribed plate on front. Maker is Tiennken, New York. Over 30 original instruments, most marked. All major instruments matching, few minor pieces missing. **5,900.00**

7" l x 3" w, has all the tools, fine condition. ... **375.00**

Outstanding item in near-perfect condition, leather book-shaped device measures 7.5" x 4" x 1-1/2" thick when closed, and roughly double that length and width when open. It is designed to hold 48 vials of medicine, of which 43 are still present (a few with contents). The body is made of tooled leather with impressed gilt scrolls and designs like on the cover of an expensive book. Inside are two areas or compartments with two dozen leather loops in each, the loops holding the glass vials in place. The vials are covered by a pair of leather flaps lined in red velvet. The cover of this miniature pannier is equipped with a German silver lock that consists of a rotating pin on the body and a key-slot hasp on the closing flap, superb condition. **225.00**

Cased set contains 20 tools including tourniquet, pliers, trepanning tool, three saws, nine scalpels and knives, silk thread, needles, probes, etc., all but a few with checkered ebony handles and some with, "W.F. Ford," and, "Caswell Hazard," marks, fitted in rosewood veneer case with brass oval-engraved, "J.R. Roberts, M.D." Case is 6" x 13-3/8" x 4". **2,090.00**

Civil War field surgical instrument set with instruments encased in a wooden/leather box. The case is in excellent shape for its age. It contains numerous instruments used for saving lives in the field during the war. There are several styles and shapes of scalpels that remain very sharp. A large, very sharp knife, bone clippers, several retractors, including hinged bullet retractors, forceps, probes, etc. The instruments are in excellent shape and have very minor, if any, blemishes. **930.00**

Contains eight tools, including scissors, tweezers, three scalpels, pick with bone handle and a probe, by J. Teufel, Philadelphia, mahogany case, 2-7/8" x 7-1/4" x 1-1/2". **385.00**

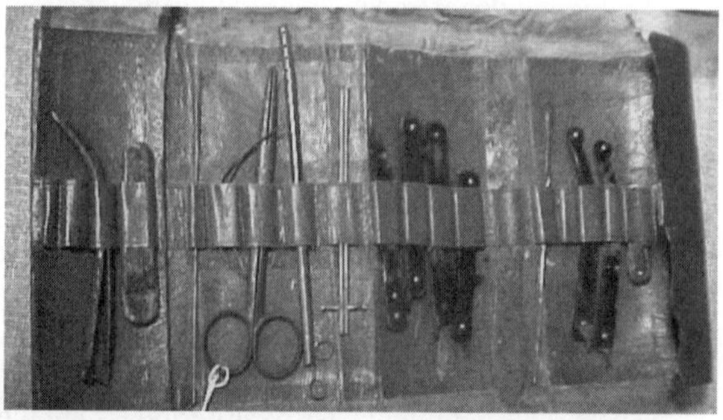

Benjamin T. Green, a surgeon for the 14th North Carolina Infantry, owned this surgical set. It is quite possible that Green acquired this set after the war.

Great example of a roll-up case circa 1850-60, maybe even run in via the blockade to Rebel forces. Family history notes that it belonged to Benjamin T. Green of Lincoln County, North Carolina. Green served as surgeon of the 14th North Carolina Infantry from April 1864 until captured and imprisoned at the Old Capital Prison in Washington, D.C. until paroled on April 19, 1865. Great Russian red leatherette with iron locking clasp, and full of surgical instruments by Rogers, an English tool maker. Some handles of the folding instruments are fancy, artistic patterned faux tortoise shell. 950.00

Manufactured just like the surgical roll up kits is this roll-up medicine kit. It is roughly the size of a large manís fist when rolled up, and it unrolls to a length of roughly 20". Inside are numerous brown paper wrappers nicely identified in brown ink as to what medicines were inside. There is also one large glass via] inside. There are nine packages of medicines present and spaces for about nine more. Very fine condition, and makes a great display item with surgeonís effects. 395.00

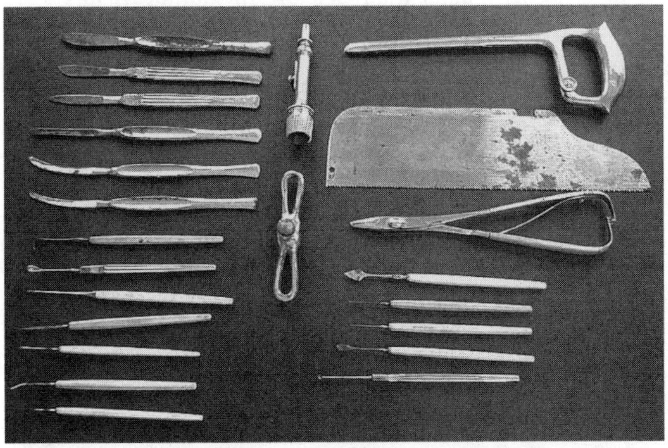

Described by the seller as a "ca. 1860 medical set," in actuality, this is a set of tools dating to the late 1890s.

This ca. 1860 surgical case was made by, "The McDermott, Inst. Co. Ltd., New Orleans, La." Case in worn condition, 3-1/2" x 12" x 5", with handle and original key. As you open case, there are two sides that hold approximately 23 medical pieces, including six fixed scalpels ("Made in Germany"); 10 small instruments, seven of which are approximately 5-1/4" l, made in Germany by G. Tiemann & Co.; three tools 5" l, made by Traux & Co.; two metal instruments with no maker's mark; seven metal scalpels approximately 7" l; one surgical saw that breaks down, 9-1/2"; one Ratchet release catch #38 approximately 7-1/4" l; and one Trephine "T" Skull Drill. Scalpels have surface rust, appears that it can be cleaned off. 400.00

Note: This set, sold as Civil War period, more likely dates from around 1890.

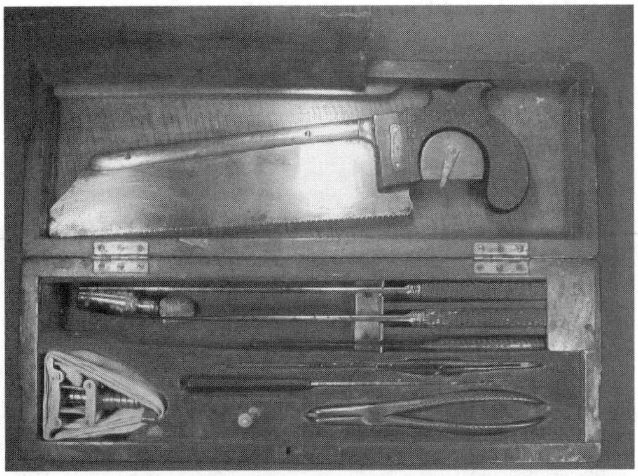

Circa 1860 English-made kit marked, "S. Maw & Son-London Master Surgeon's Kit."

Very attractive 1860 "S. Maw & Son-London Master Surgeon's Kit," consists of master amputation saw, tourniquet, and an array of knives, probes, tweezers, and pliers. The case itself is red velvet lined, and in nice solid condition. 2,250.00

Though bleeders are an intriguing bit of nineteenth century medical history, their use by surgeons during the Civil War is suspect. Nevertheless, many surgeons probably had the devices among their tools.

Tool, Bleeder

This scarificator was a device made and used in the 19th century for bleeding. This one is made of solid brass with 12 steel blades that pop out and cut. It is in very good condition, works perfectly. It cocks in the center position, which shows the blades extended, upon doing some research, this must have been made around 1830. . . . . 332.00

Two-blade, folding bleeder. 125.00

Brass handle, iron bleeders marked, "Joseph Rodgers/No 6/Norfolk St/Sheffield." All three blades are intact and freely swing out. 125.00

This brass scarificator, or "bleeder," was used by medical personnel to open wounds to permit cleaner blood-flow and reduce the chance of infection. The item is in superb original condition in that it has never been cleaned or polished. It functions as well as when it was made, and the five blades are still razor-sharp. The cock and release mechanism is extremely crisp. 154.00

Tool, Dental Elevator, Civil War-era elevator in excellent condition. Has a wood handle and an unplated steel shaft. The angulated tip has a serrated edge, measures 4-3/4" l. **91.00**

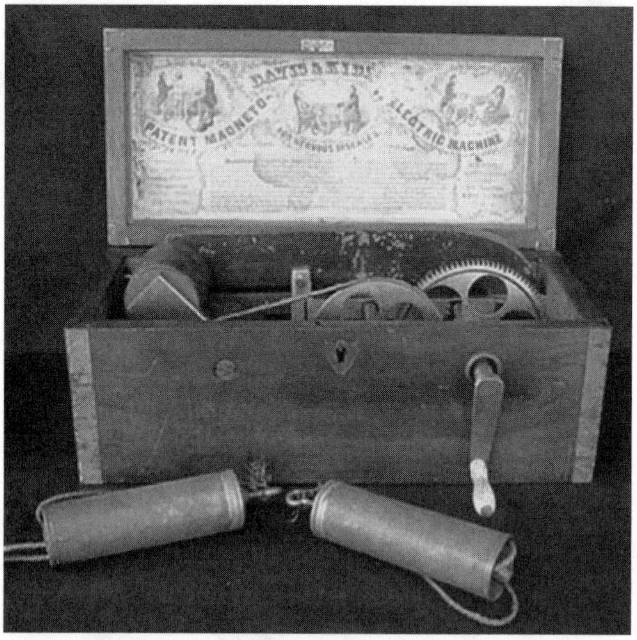

Antique medical oddities have enough collector appeal that hanging the "Civil War" handle on them doesn't really do much for the item, nor for the study of military medical history. Whereas this "Magneto" was patented in 1855 and may well have been constructed before the Civil War, it is a fanciful notion to consider that a surgeon may have carried this as part of his personal equipment. The period description does imply that it is ideal for the treatment of "Nervous Diseases," so whether or not it has any military provenance, the story-telling opportunities abound.

Dale C. Anderson Co.

Tool, Electric Magneto, patented in 1855, "Davis & Kidder's Patent Magneto-Electric Machine For Nervous Diseases," so states the illustrated label/ instructions inside the lid. A fine, working piece of handsome machinery that actually puts out a strong pulsing electric charge designed to apply to the diseased parts of the body. It was so popular in its time that it was copied extensively in this country and in Europe. Comes in a fine mahogany case with hinged lid 10" x 4 –1/2" x 4 –1/2". Has brass corner reinforcements. Inside, there is a large horseshoe magnet, a spinning coil, and heavy brass framework and gears. The front has a handle to turn. Two probes at the end of wires come from each end. Handle of probes are housed inside, all original and working. Case finish is excellent with some wear. Label stained and 95% intact. **445.00**

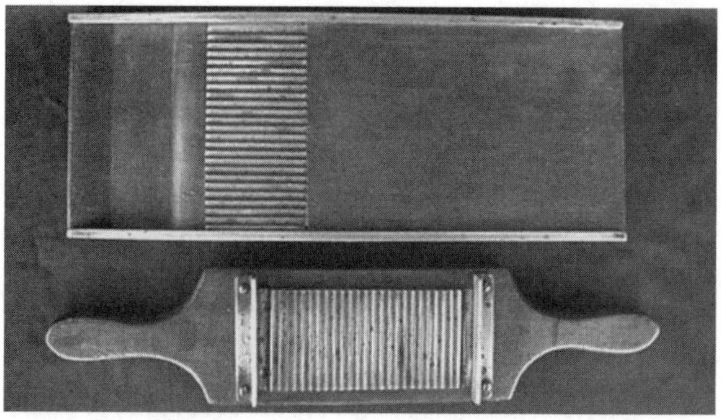

Chemist's tool described as a "pill roller."

Dale C. Anderson Co.

Tool, Pill Roller, a physician would first combine the powdered dry mixture and then add a binding agent. He next dampened the batch and spread a wad onto the brass, channeled base. He would then place the moveable top over the mass and move it back and forth on its brass railed track. The medicine would thereby be divided and rolled into spherical pills. The roller consists of a solid walnut base 4-5/8" x 11-7/8", and a top piece also of walnut, which moves over the base. Top piece is 13-1/2" long and 7/8" thick. Both top and bottom have a channeled brass plate, which rides over each other, forming the pills. Excellent condition, showing some use..... **395.00**

Tool, Saw, blade 12-1/2 " l, with teeth on one side and a cutting edge on the other. Blade has a nice dark patina to it, but is not badly pitted or rusted, not missing any teeth, some very small nicks in the knife's edge. Has a nice solid handle, and a hole bored in the end (this was probably for a lanyard). Nice mellow patina to the wood, never cleaned. **178.00**

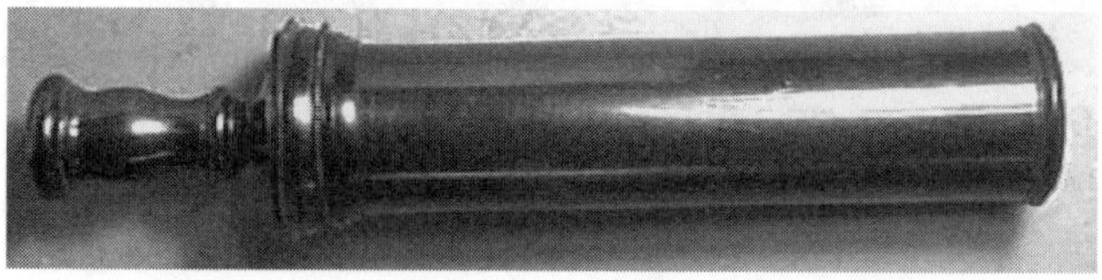

Hard rubber syringe bearing a "Goodyear 1851."

The Civil War Relicman

Tool, Syringe

This hard rubber syringe bears the Goodyear 1851 patent mark. **75.00**

About 4" l, typical of the hard rubber syringes of the period. **39.00**

Hard rubber syringe measuring roughly 5" l, excellent overall. **69.00**

This type of syringe was used by doctors to irrigate wounds. The hard rubber is complete with both leather washers intact, overall length is 5-3/4" l (closed), barrel tube is 3/4" d, unmarked, no chips or cracks.....**235.00**

Tools, Surgical, included in this lot is a standard size (small) scalpel and a small hook-like instrument both signed "Helmold Phila", with ivory handles. ..**85.00**

Miscellaneous Medical Items

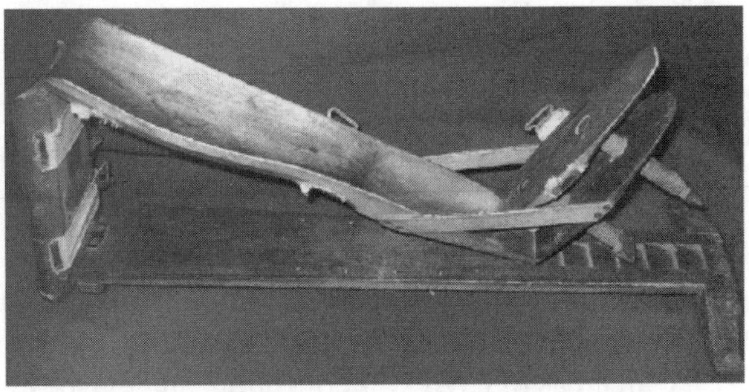

Unmarked splint identical to a Day's Patent splint.

Drumbeat Civil War Memorabilia

Splint, Day's-Type Wooden Adjustable Leg, folding, adjustable wooden leg splint. This particular one is unmarked, but is exactly like the ones marked, "Day's Patent." Originally, there were canvas straps to hold the leg in place, most of which are only partially intact. **400.00**

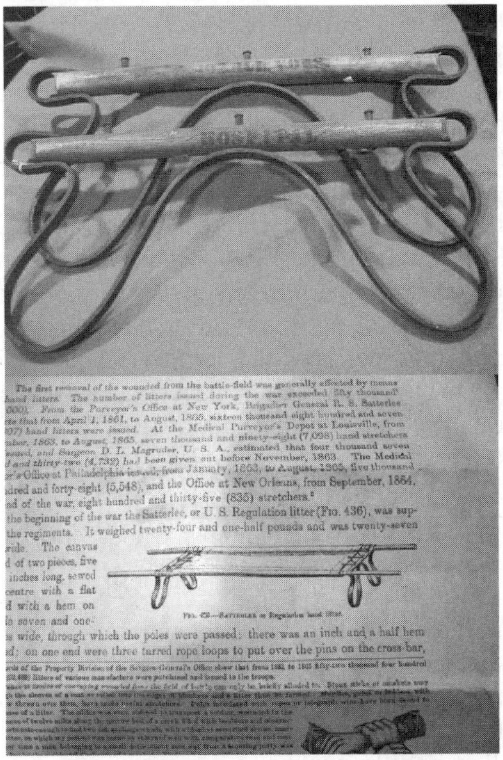

A pair of "Satterlee's Patent Stretcher Legs" marked, "102nd Illinois Hospital," and accompanied by a period diagram of the items in use.

Drumbeat Civil War Memorabilia

Strecher Legs, Satterlee's Patent, as illustrated in the *Medical and Surgical History of the War of the Rebellion*, this is a pair of wood and steel stretcher legs. The handles of the stretcher pass through these handles and act to keep the stretcher off the ground. These are stenciled, "102nd Illinois Hospital." **1,000.00**

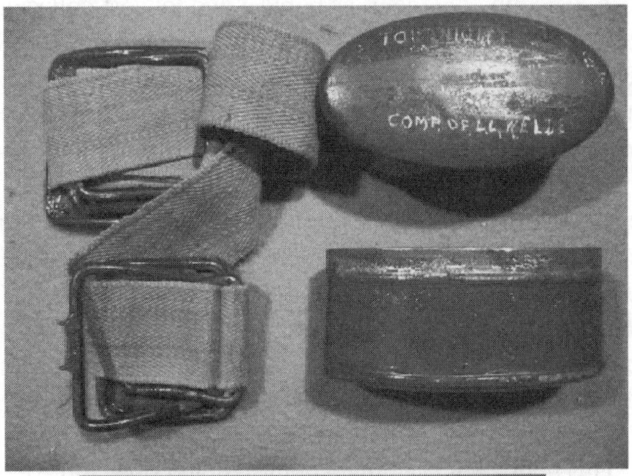

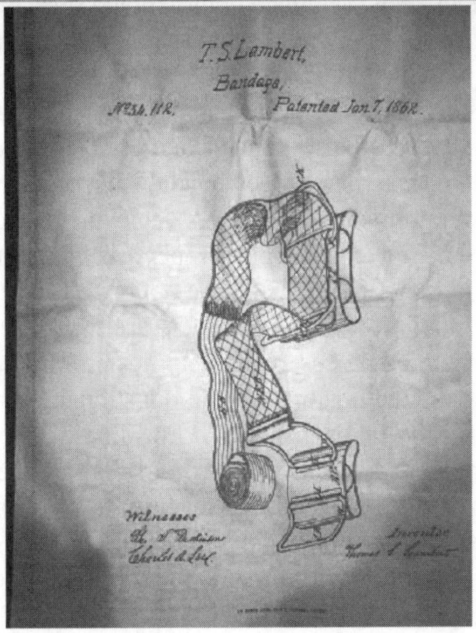

Stored in its original tin and accompanied by a set of instructions for use, this Lambert-Patent tourniquet had an old, handwritten label stating, "Used in Civil War, 1864."

Drumbeat Civil War Memorabilia

Tourniquet, original, cased and mint condition Lambert Patent Tourniquet with copy of patent document. In original tole tin case marked, "Used in Civil War 1864." **795.00**

Also see: Groupings, Accoutrements, Swords, Uniforms, Photographs, and Ephemera.

Chapter 13

Muskets and Rifles

Undoubtedly the most popular and longest-collected item of Civil War memorabilia has been the very tool used to decide the war's outcome, the muzzle-loading long arm. Immediately following the war, a booming business emerged wherein dealers readily supplied souvenir muskets, rifles, and other weapons to a public fascinated by war. No longer regarded as the implements of carnage, these firearms were regarded as historic relics. Holding the ancient Springfield or Enfield rifle, the sense of purpose and honor seemed to transmit from the old walnut and iron into the collector's sense of self. The weapon of war became a relic worthy of devotion. Soon, collectors covered their walls with weapons and continued to look for variations and rarities.

This hobby has continued uninterrupted since those early days when a collector could actually approach veterans of the war. The search continues for rarities, oddities, and variations. Simultaneously, research has dug deep into armory records, military archives, and personal collections of correspondence to piece together new interpretations and statistics about firearm production, deployment, and usage.

A person should not feel that there are not quality weapons out there to be had. The opposite is true. Actually, now more than ever, there are well-researched and documented pieces available. Furthermore, long-held traditions and suppositions about questionable arms have been either proven or dispelled. Guns that were once attributed as being Confederate or arsenal-adapted into one form or another have been revealed as something else. In the best case, simply misidentified. In the worst, clear misrepresentations with the intent to deceive. The collector of today is more informed and better equipped to assemble quality collections and to avoid the many costly pitfalls that often entrapped earlier collectors.

Like all areas of Civil War collecting, and maybe even more so because of the prices involved, if you intend to collect long arms, decide *how* you are going to collect before making your initial purchase. For example: Do you simply desire a representative weapon from both sides? If so, a Model 1861 Rifle Musket and a Model 1853 Enfield might suffice. But, perhaps you want to collect weapons used by a certain regiment? Through three years of service, several units may have carried a variety of weapons ranging from Potsdam imports to Austrian Lorenz rifles to .58-caliber rifled muskets. This sort of approach will provide for a limited variety and also help develop a feel for the arming of one particular regiment.

Collecting long arms can be addictive. Perhaps you will begin collecting by buying a nice Trenton-marked Model 1861 at a show. Pretty soon, you might think, "Hmm, it might be fun to collect one of each of the Model 1861 contractors." After time, and several thousand dollars spent, your habit might blossom into, "Now that I have those, I will need to have a representative of all the U.S. martial .69-caliber muskets." Before you know it, you have branched out into "breechloaders of the sharpshooters" and you are mortgaging your house to buy a Henry repeater! As pointed out earlier, formulate a plan before you begin to buy. There are too many weapons out there, and you simply can't buy them all. Choices will have to be made to form a meaningful and valuable collection.

Collecting Hints

Pros:

- Muskets are great visual aids for learning or teaching about the Civil War. The Civil War soldier's existence came down to the weapon he carried. Collecting long arms places your hands on the very tools that made history.
- Firearms tend to hold their value, making them a tangible hedge against inflation.
- Civil War long arms are in plentiful supply, so it is fairly easy enter the hobby.

Availability ★★

Price ★★★

Reproduction Alert ★★★★

Cons:

- Guns draw attention, both welcome and unwelcome. They are a prime target of thieves.
- Muskets and rifles are cumbersome to display and collect. As your collection grows, you will find that wall space fills quickly.
- You must answer the question, "Do I restore a weapon to the way it appeared when issued, or keep it in the condition as I found it?"
- Because of the quantity and variety of weapons available, unless you are independently wealthy, you will be faced with a limited collection.

Confederate Muskets and Rifles

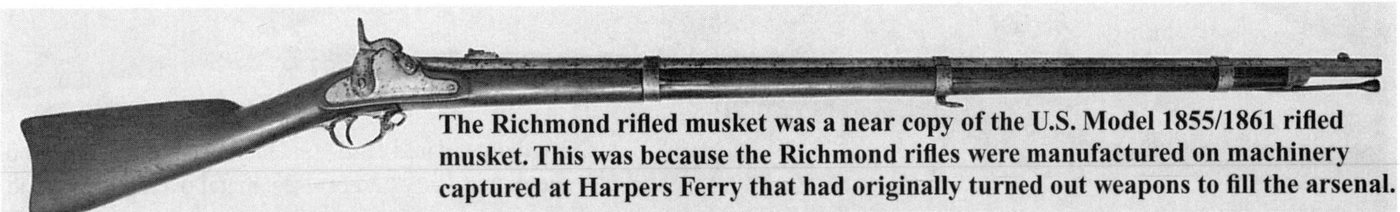

The Richmond rifled musket was a near copy of the U.S. Model 1855/1861 rifled musket. This was because the Richmond rifles were manufactured on machinery captured at Harpers Ferry that had originally turned out weapons to fill the arsenal.

J.C. Devine Inc.

Rifled Musket, Model 1861, pristine Confederate "High-Hump" 1861-rifled musket, one of the first made in Richmond using parts and machinery captured at Harpers Ferry Arsenal. Beautiful specimen, all matching, complete with the original Confederate linen sling, initials "WHH" carved deeply in stock. Weapon from the family of William H. Hutcherson who served in Company D, 38th Virginia Infantry—Picketts Division, present at the infamous charge at Gettysburg. Comes with full documentation and family affidavit. **27,500.00**

Rifled Musket, Richmond, an 1863 example, barrel has a clearly visible "VP" and eagle, but the date is not visible. The rear sight is the proper "stepped" 1855-1861-style held in place by an old copper disc rivet. The front band's "U" stamping is classic Confederate workmanship stamped at an angle on the wrong edge of the band. The middle and lower band have the "U"s hit off center as well. The stock has strong edges, and the lock inlet is absolutely Richmond done, with no provision for the Maynard tape "arm" as found on the 1855 muskets, and no cartouche mark. Straight ramrod channel, not milled for the swelled ramrod on the U.S. guns. Classic Richmond brass buttplate with rich undisturbed patina and color that melds with the butt, Federal steel nose cap. The patina and wear are uniform and wonderful overall, never improved or gunsmithed. **11,500.00**

Rifled Musket, Richmond Armory, Type II, exceptional condition, 58 caliber, 40" barrel, good bore. Barrel dated "1862" on top, marked with "V/P" over eagle head on the top left flat, lock marked "C.S/RICHMOND, VA," and dated 1862. Barrel date's first digit is weak, other barrel markings are clear, lock markings are sharp, iron nose cap and unmarked buttplate. All the iron has a natural gray patina with evenly scattered black age spots, very faint pitting near the nipple and heel of the buttplate. Stock has a small repaired chip behind the tang and an age crack at the rear lock screw escutcheon. The stock has an old, well done oil refinish and has the faint initials "WR" scratched on the left flat, correct lock recess, rear sight and sight dovetail, and iron ramrod. Rear sight leaves are missing and the base has a couple of dents. Overall condition is very good. **17,500.00**

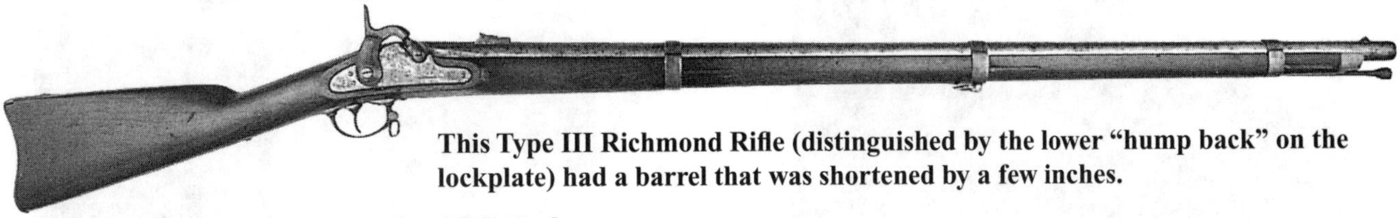

This Type III Richmond Rifle (distinguished by the lower "hump back" on the lockplate) had a barrel that was shortened by a few inches.

J.C. Devine Inc.

Rifled Musket, Richmond Armory, Type III
.58 caliber, lockplate dated "1863" and marked "C.S./RICHMOND, VA," barrel shortened to 38" and has a good bore. Breech dated 1864 and marked with "V/P/(eagle head)." Gray patina on all iron, minor light pitting, vise marks on barrel breech, clear markings on lock and barrel proofs, barrel date legible. Stock has a nice older refinish, a few light handling marks, and a small forend cap chip. The brass buttplate and forend cap have an ochre patina, good-plus condition with ramrod. **1,600.00**

Rifled Musket, Richmond Armory, Type III, cont.

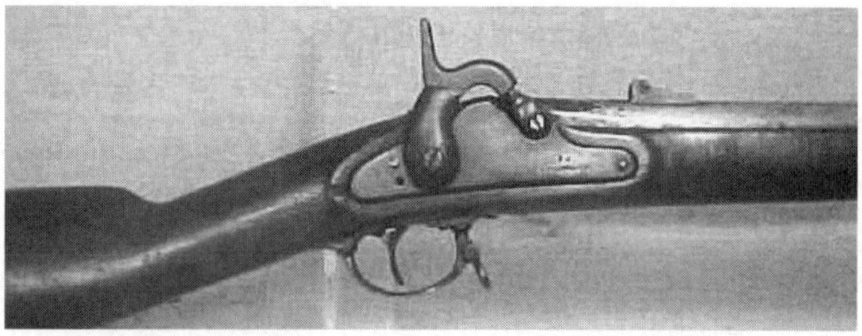

Type III Richmond dated 1863, and having a replaced nose cap and ramrod.

Battleground Antiques

Confederate, dated 1863, replaced nose cap and ramrod, stock has dings and bruises, metal overall very good, clear markings. **5,850.00**

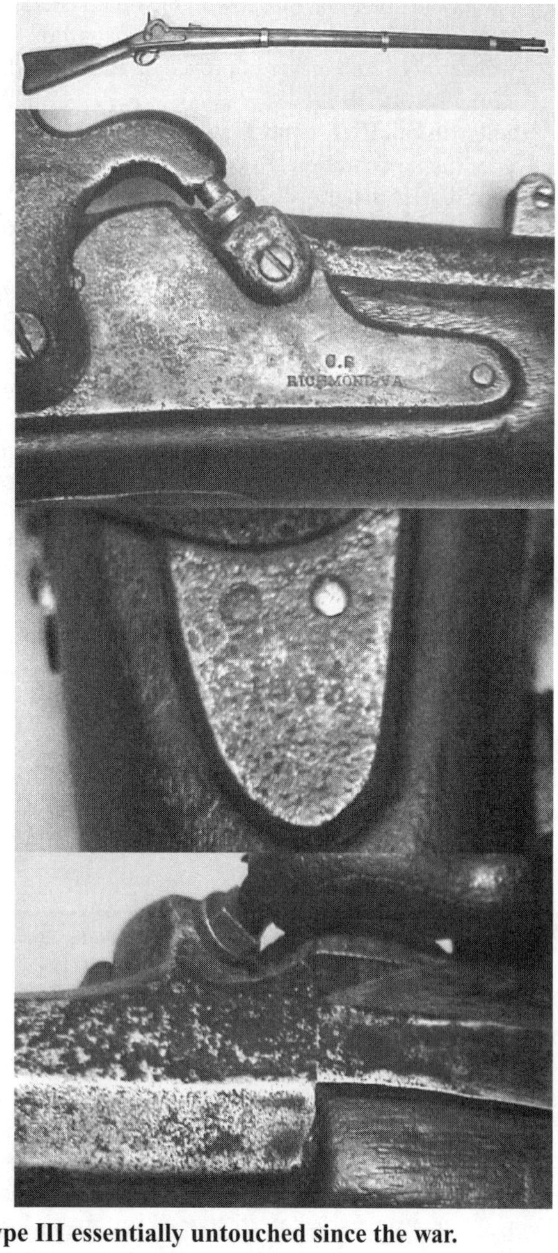

Type III essentially untouched since the war.

Sharpsburg Arsenal

Gun shows good field usage, but not abuse. Sling swivels are missing and appear to have been that way for a long time. Original Richmond ramrod, barrel bands, and buttplate. Lockplate has good markings with some pitting around the 1863 date. Wood is feathery on the surface due to lack of fine finishing equipment you find on federal guns. Truly an untouched Richmond. **12,500.00**

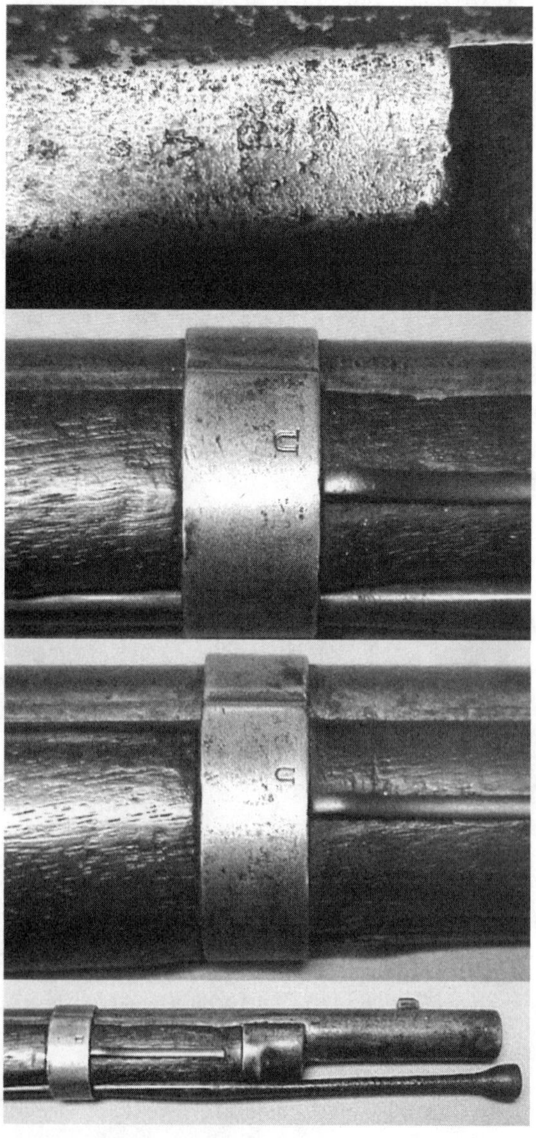

Fayetteville Rifles were assembled at the Fayetteville Arsenal from parts captured from the Harpers Ferry Arsenal and those found within the Fayetteville works. Nearly 9,000 were completed.

Battleground Antiques

Rifle, Confederate, Fayetteville

Manufactured on machinery captured at the Harpers Ferry Arsenal. Rare transitional model with features including an iron nose cap, filled in muzzle slot (for the saber bayonet, discontinued in early 1863), and the stamped inspector marking of "P.B." (Philip Burkhart, Master Armorer). Rear sight altered during the time of actual use to a simple V-notch type; ramrod not the typical Fayetteville pattern, same color as the rest of the weapon, and likely used with it; sling swivels are modern additions. Weapon is a pleasing deep-brown patina overall with brass bands and buttplate (stamped "C.S.A."). Clear lockplate markings of Confederate eagle, "Fayetteville" and "C.S.A." as well as date of 1863. Rich, deep-colored walnut stock is free of defects such as cracks or deep gouges. **16,500.00**

.58-caliber percussion Confederate manufactured long arm dated "1863" at lock and barrel flat. Crisp markings include the proofs at left breech and lock, "1863" to the hammer's rear and an eagle/"CSA" and "Fayetteville" in the center and right of the lock. Barrel and lock are a smooth, deep, plum patina with only some light salt and peppering around the bolster. Lock has no hump and the distinctive S-shaped Fayetteville hammer, rear sight removed, simple military-style post sight is dovetailed to the barrel. Bayonet lug has been removed from right of muzzle, but this may be a factory alteration, because this rifle falls right on the cusp of the Confederate authorities' decision to go from an unwieldy saber bayonet to an easier-to-produce socket style. Good bore, fine mechanics, transitional-style iron stock cap, fine brass furniture with deep, deep umber patina. Crisp "CSA" on tang of buttplate. Ramrod is Confederate-produced, champagne-glass-shaped rod. Fine stock with very crisp edges around the lock and both the barrel channels and ramrod channel. Sharp "PB" inspector's cartouche at the left flat. **19,500.00**

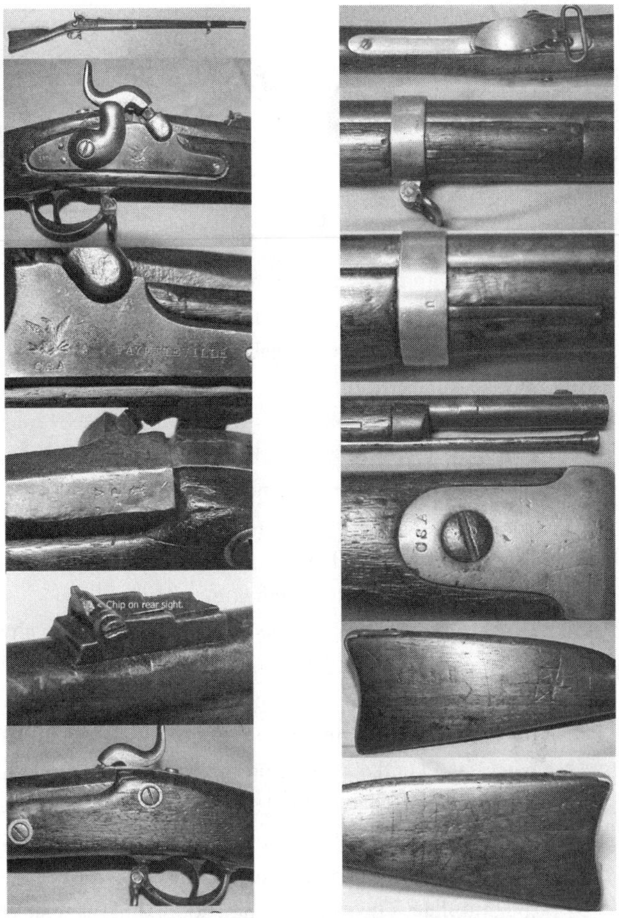

Collectors have divided the Fayetteville production into four distinct groups. This example is classified as a Type III because the lockplate does not have a hump, it is fitted with a bayonet lug, and has the distinctive S-shaped hammer.

Sharpsburg Arsenal

Rifle, Fayetteville, Type III, .58-caliber percussion Confederate rifle with 33" round barrel with iron blade front sight and three-leaf rear sight. Fair bore with mostly visible rifling. Top flat dated "1863" as is the lock. Barrel is a smooth plum-brown patina with clear "V/P"/eaglehead proofs at the left of the breech. The saber bayonet lug has been milled off flush with the curve of the barrel, probably to facilitate the use of a socket bayonet. The clean-out screw at the bolster has been peened over a new nipple. Very fine salt-and-pepper pitting around the bolster. Excellent lock with crisp markings, "1863" to the rear of the hammer and a small crisp eagle/"C.S.A." in the lock's center, "Fayetteville" is stamped on the right of the lock. Mellow brass buttplate is stamped "C.S.A." on the tang. Golden patina on brass trigger guard with iron sling swivel. Lower brass barrel band stamped with a "U." The brass top band with iron sling swivel, iron stock cap, fine oil-finished stock with two small patches, one under the lock about 1/2" x 1/4" and another about the size of a fingernail above the lock bolt on the off side. Name "Charle" carved at right of the butt with two St. Andrews crossed in front of them. Several names scratched on the left butt. ..**19,500.00**

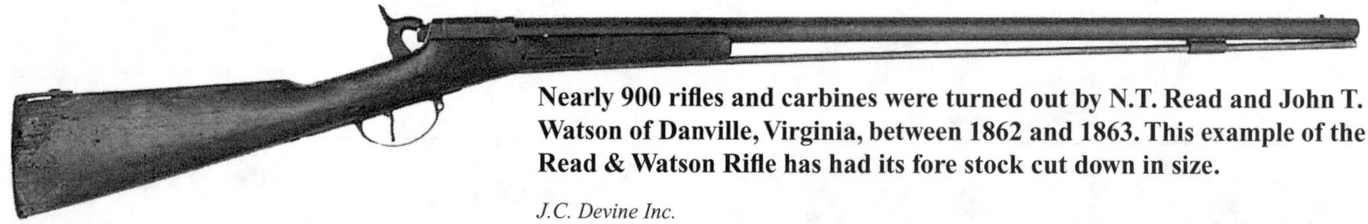

Nearly 900 rifles and carbines were turned out by N.T. Read and John T. Watson of Danville, Virginia, between 1862 and 1863. This example of the Read & Watson Rifle has had its fore stock cut down in size.

J.C. Devine Inc.

Rifle, Read and Watson, recovered from the Hanging Rock Battlefield in Virginia, early studies believed that these arms were made by J.B. Barrett of Wytheville, Virginia, from parts captured at Harpers Ferry. Authorities on these arms recently discovered that they were alterations of Hall rifles and carbines belonging to the Virginia militia and that the work was performed by N.T. Read and John T. Watson of Danville, Virginia. This arm is classed as a Type 1 and is almost identical to the one pictured in *Confederate Rifles and Muskets* by Dr. John Murphy and Howard M. Madaus. The rifle is 48-1/2" overall with a 32-5/8" long barrel of .54 caliber. The rifle is half-stocked in walnut with a single spring retained barrel band and a single iron ramrod ferrule beneath the barrel. The barrel band and spring are missing. All of the iron is dark and evenly pitted. The stock has old repairs to a wrist break and shows erosion at the buttplate. The stock has had some oil added since its recovery from the field. The ramrod is a replacement. The stock has fourteen notches carved behind the trigger guard and the left side is carved in 5/8" high letters "B. Mc. C." over a 3/4" high "A." It is believed that these initials may be those of one of several related individuals by the name of McClung who participated in the battle with the 14th, 16th, 17th, 22nd, and 23rd Virginia Cavalry. Includes a copy of the book *Civil War Tales* by Gary C. Walker, that has a chapter on this rifle written by Col. William Terry Slusher who found this rifle as a seven-year-old boy. This chapter includes the names of several of the McClungs and the cavalry units with which they served, and also has a picture of Col. Slusher holding this rifle. Few Confederate arms have such interesting provenance. **3,500.00**

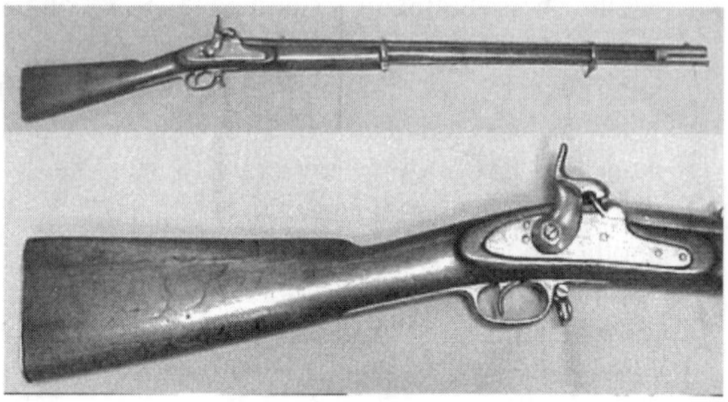

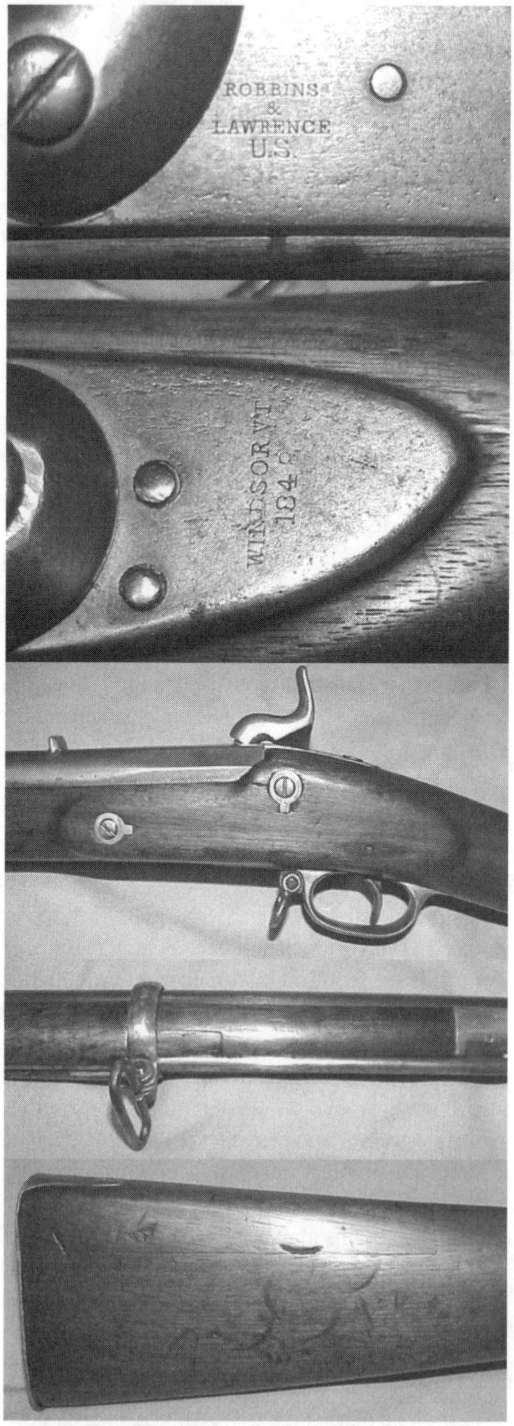

Fewer than 300 rifles were produced by L.G. Sturdivant at his works in Talladega, Alabama. This example is numbered 109.

Sharpsburg Arsenal

Rifle, L. G. Sturdivant, .58 caliber, serial no. 109. Less than 300 produced by Lewis G. Sturdivant of Talladega, Alabama. In March 1862, he had a contract for 2,000 Mississippi Type Rifles. Overall in very good condition with a forend repair and buttstock repair both look to be period and done at the factory. Stocks very cheaply made, lock marked, "Robbins, Kendall & Lawrence, U.S. Windsor, Vt., 1848." **5,500.00**

U.S. Muskets and Rifles

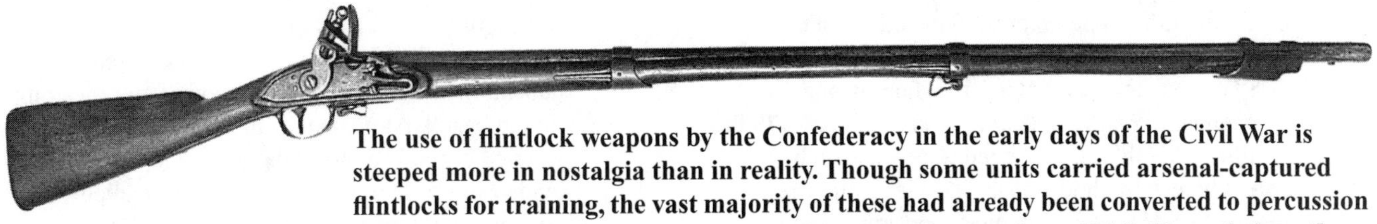

The use of flintlock weapons by the Confederacy in the early days of the Civil War is steeped more in nostalgia than in reality. Though some units carried arsenal-captured flintlocks for training, the vast majority of these had already been converted to percussion ignition systems (a program that started in arsenals as early as 1844). Nevertheless, the flintlock is part of the "bedraggled South" image and is therefore, popular with collectors.

Musket, Model 1808, no serial no., .69 caliber, 42-5/8" round barrel, fair bore, manufactured in 181?. A contract musket by Rudolph and Charles Leonard, shows traces of the eagle with the U.S. in circle. The last digit of the date is illegible. The hammer is the correct Harpers Ferry-type with a straight hammer spur. No other marks appear on metal or wood. The metal is a gray-brown with darker spotting and pitting near the breech and lock area. The frizzen has been re-faced and a few screws appear to be older replacements. The wood shows a well-done repair forward of the trigger guard. Missing ramrod, and overall fair to good condition. **1,100.00**

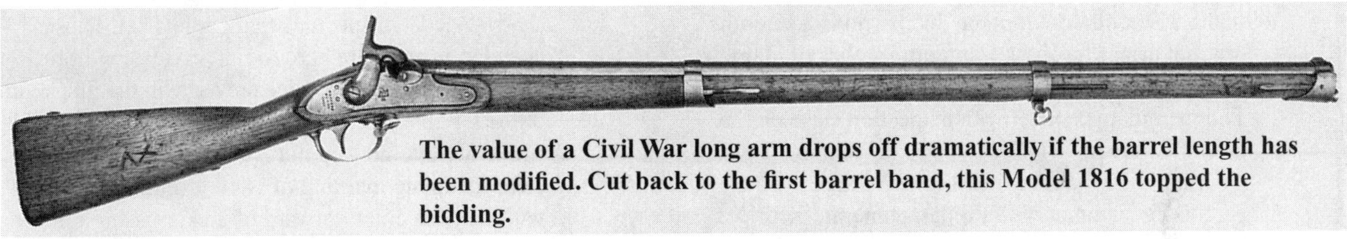

The value of a Civil War long arm drops off dramatically if the barrel length has been modified. Cut back to the first barrel band, this Model 1816 topped the bidding.

Musket, Model 1816, Conversion

.69-caliber smoothbore, 37" shortened barrel is almost flush with the front band that has been altered by removing the front strap. Lockplate has clear standard Harpers Ferry markings and is dated 1837. The percussion conversion was done by the addition of a new bolster with a clean-out screw and is almost identical to one done by M.A. Baker of Fayetteville, North Carolina, shown in *Confederate Longarms And Pistols,* by Hill and Anthony. Barrel's bottom is struck with Roman numbers "LLXXXXIII." The new percussion bolster, barrel, lockplate, hammer and trigger are all marked with a 5 over 74, with the sideplate marked only 74. The metal has been cleaned in the past and is now mostly a smooth gray with light pitting on the breech's top. The stock's right side has a carved "XV," refinished wood with a glued joint under the rear band, the ramrod is a modern replacement, good condition. **350.00**

The ramrod on this Springfield-produced Model 1816 was not correct for the musket, otherwise it was rated in fair condition.

J.C. Devine Inc.

.69 caliber, 42" barrel, smooth bore, clearly marked, "Spring/Field/1839," the barrel date is illegible and the stock cartouche is faint. Arsenal-style cone conversion, all metal has dark patina, scattered fine pitting with the breech heavily pitted, missing hammer screw, replacement ramrod, overall fair condition. **600.00**

Musket, Model 1816, Conversion, cont.

.69-caliber smoothbore contract musket converted by the firm of Hewes and Phillips to percussion by the patent breech method, smooth steel-gray barrel, two-leaf flip-up sight, bore unrifled. Crisp "1862" date for breech conversion, "H&P" stamped on bolster face, converted from an 1826-dated Springfield Model 1816 Flintlock Musket. Smooth lock with superb markings, fine iron furniture with smooth steel patina. Complete with original sling swivels and original button tipped ramrod. Fine oil-finished stock, very good edges around lock and flats, clear "LS" cartouche in oval at left flat, fine, strong mechanics. **1,075.00**

.69-caliber smoothbore converted to percussion by the patent breech method, bolster has clean-out screw, looks like a Hewes and Philips conversion, but is not marked as such. Leman also converted arms in this manner. Bright barrel with the remnants of the original "US" and "NWP" inspector's proof in front of the new breech, bright lock and hammer. Clear "1839" date and "US/D. Nippes/Phila.," bright iron furniture including sling swivels and original button-tipped ramrod. Excellent oil-finished stock with crisp cartouche and "2" category number for dividing the guns in order of conversion. Bright smooth bore and excellent mechanics. **1,850.00**

.69-caliber smoothbore musket, 36" barrel is a smooth original bright finish with smooth patches of plum patina. Bayonet lug on top of the barrel, large Thomas Adams bolster with inspection slash on the flat, "Richmond/1817" marked to the hammer's rear. "Virginia/Mfry" in the lock's center. Large percussion hammer with Roman numeral "XII" chiseled into the back of it, (as it is on the inside of the lock, side plate and under the barrel). Fine smooth iron furniture with original sling swivels and button-tipped ramrod. Smooth bore, fine mechanics, oil finished stock has slash inspection behind trigger guard along with a large "B" for James Burton who was overseeing the alteration of Virginia Arms early in the Civil War. Very good stock with a drying crack on either side of the barrel channel. These have not separated and do not detract from this desirable Confederate long arm. Almost all of the parts bear the old Virginia Manufactory number "66." Arm is complete with original linen and leather Confederate-issue sling. **9,500.00**

.69-caliber, smoothbore converted to percussion by the arsenal with the "Belgian" method of putting a nipple in the barrel. Almost all of these conversions were carried out in U.S. arsenals starting in the late 1840s and going right until the Civil War. Excellent example with bright, smooth barrel and superb proofs at the breech along with "S/96" inspection marks directly under the hammer from the conversion. Tang dated "1833." Superb lock marked, "Harper's/Ferry/1833" to the rear of the hammer and has a large Eagle/"US" in the center. Percussion hammer is still vividly case color hardened. Bright, smooth iron furniture. Original ramrod and sling swivels. Smooth bore, perfect mechanics. Fine, oil-finished stock with good crisp edges around the lock and flats and along the ramrod and barrel channels, sharp "AR/V" inspector's mark at left flat. These conversion arms are hard to find in this condition because of the hard service they saw in the first years of the Civil War, excellent condition. **1,995.00**

Confederate-altered Virginia Manufactory Musket, very clear lockplate marking of 1819, overall brown gun with hairline crack forward of lock, missing ramrod. These early weapons were altered at the Richmond Armory and saw service in both the Mexican War and the Civil War. **2,400.00**

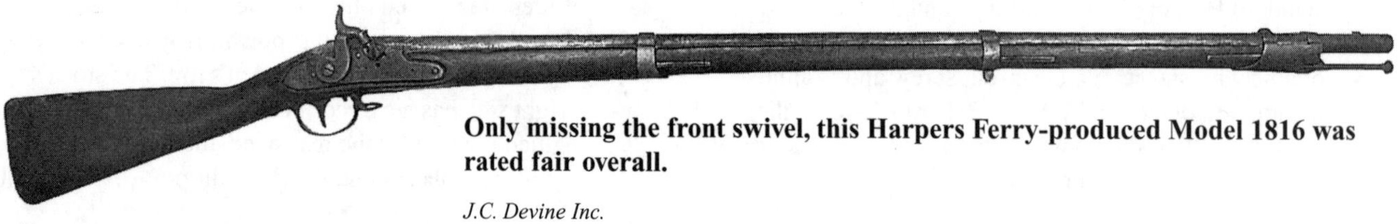

Only missing the front swivel, this Harpers Ferry-produced Model 1816 was rated fair overall.

J.C. Devine Inc.

No serial no., .69 caliber, 42" barrel, dark bore. Manufactured in 1829. A standard Type III Waters-made musket with cone-type conversion. Heavy pitting on barrel, heaviest on the breech. Hammer is a replacement. Wood has been sanded and refinished, fair condition overall. **250.00**

Model 1816 Harpers Ferry Musket dated 1838, excellent, smooth brown patina overall, arsenal converted to percussion via a bolster; rear sight added at that time. **1,050.00**

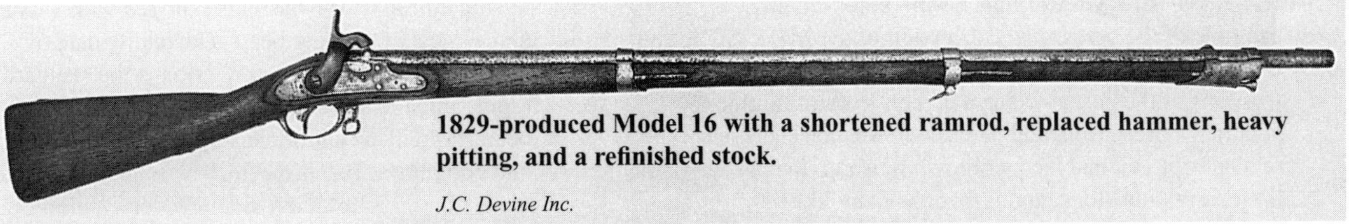

1829-produced Model 16 with a shortened ramrod, replaced hammer, heavy pitting, and a refinished stock.

J.C. Devine Inc.

Musket, Model 1816, Conversion, cont.

Converted to percussion ignition, .69 caliber, 42" barrel, smooth bore. Lock marked "Harpers/Ferry/1828," no breech date, but proof marks are good, side of breech marked "S.M. Co." and the conversion uses a crude drum and nipple. The metal is dark with scattered areas of light pitting, the stock is refinished with an old repair to a large crack from the wrist through the lock recess. The front swivel is missing, but the original ramrod is present, overall fair-plus condition. **400.00**

Overall very good condition being 100% original and complete. Metal is overall gray steel and uniformly colored with areas of light pitting. Lock stamped with an eagle and "Springfield 1837." Barrel has a breech with a cast bolster and cleanout screw. There is moderate pitting at the breech obliterating the markings. The stock is very nice with two legible inspector's cartouches. Action is crisp. Comes with original button-tip ramrod. **895.00**

100% original and complete, lock marked, "US/P.& E.W. Blake," and, "New Haven/1826." The stock's left side bears two cartouches as well as a deep "OHIO" stamp. There is a small hairline crack over the word "OHIO." The conversion is the standard cone-style with the nipple being threaded directly into the barrel. The metal has a deep-brown patina overall with areas of pitting around the nipple. The stock is nice and shows normal expected wear, with a little burnout near the nipple. It is mechanically perfect and totally complete including the ramrod. **695.00**

Very good condition, E. Whitney contract Model 1816 Musket converted with "cone in barrel" conversion. All metal markings crisp with matching lock and barrel dates. Barrel is profusely marked "1835," "JM," "P," and "MS" (Massachusetts State), and with a rack number of 16. All metal parts are mottled steel color mixed with brown. The stock is fine with good edges, color, and nice cartouche. Boldly stamped into the escutcheon plate opposite the lock is the name, "H.A. Hills." Henry A. Hills served with the 9th Massachusetts Battery during the second half of 1862, and was discharged for disability at Washington, D.C., in December 1862. 100% original and complete including ramrod, and very nicely inscribed with a real identification. **1,150.00**

Rifled Musket, U.S., Model 1816, Conversion

.69-caliber rifled weapon, "1857" dated lock and breech, fine overall condition, clear "NJ" surcharge on left breech, complete with both sling swivels and coned button-tip ramrod, fine oil-finished stock with clear cartouches at left flat. **1,950.00**

.69-caliber, originally manufactured as a smoothbore flintlock, but rifled and converted to percussion by the Arsenal with the cone-in-the-barrel method after the Mexican War. Excellent, bright barrel with crisp "US/JC/P" proofs along with the conversion inspection, "19-H I." Tang dated "1830" and has the inspector's initials "H I." Crisp lock marked, "New Haven/1830" to the hammer's rear and "US/P. &E.W. Blake" in the center. Excellent, bright smooth furniture, including the original sling swivels and the button-tipped ramrod that has been "cupped" for the new Minie projectile. Excellent bore and mechanics, fine oil-finished stock with very fine edges around the lock, flats, and along both the ramrod and barrel channels. Two discernible oval cartouches at the left flat, very-fine condition. **1,995.00**

Rifle, Model 1817, Conversion, no serial no., .54 caliber, 33" octagon to round barrel. This rifle is marked on the lockplate, "S. Cogswell Troy." The barrel is marked "SNY" (State New York) and "AWP" who was most-likely the barrel maker. "AWP" is also stamped under the barrel and can only be seen when the barrel is removed from the stock. The only reference found for an AWP was Allen W. Page, listed as working in New York City in 1801. The under rib, rod pipes, trigger guard, oval patchbox and buttplate are of brass. The percussion conversion was done with a drum and nipple threaded into the barrel. Part of the removable brass pan remains, as do the holes for the frizzen and spring. The walnut stock has a cheek rest and is also stamped "SNY" behind and below the rear lock bolt. No U.S. marks or stamps appear on the rifle, suggesting it was a state and not a U.S. contract rifle. In appearance, the gun appears to be the Model 1803, but the oval patchbox and removable brass pan suggest a later model. The iron ramrod has no brass tip. The stock is single wedge fastened and shows a recent oil-type finish applied. The barrel flats measure 11-3/4" transitioning to round with a single wedding band. The overall rifle length is 49", an interesting gun that has both 1803 and 1814 features, the antique grade is fair. **900.00**

Rifle, Model 1819, Conversion, a superb, top-quality example of the percussion conversion of the M1819 Hall Rifle. The Hall was one of the most advanced weapons of the period, being a breech-loading flintlock, and then a breech-loading percussion weapon. This one retains 98% original lacquer brown finish on the barrel, has nearly mint stock, and is mechanically like new. **3,450.00**

Musket, Model 1822, Conversion, Whitney contract percussion conversion musket with 42" .75-caliber barrel with tang dated "1828." Lock with Belgian alteration to percussion. Lockplate marked "U.S./P/ & E.W. Blake" and "New Haven/1828." Stock and furniture of standard pattern. Gray metal has been cleaned and shows scattered areas of light pitting and some heavy pitting at the breech. Sound wood with scattered dents, scratches, and bruises. **460.00**

Musket, Model 1840, Conversion

.69-caliber smoothbore converted to percussion at the Leman Rifle Works facility in Lancaster, Pennsylvania, by the patent breech method. Flintlock barrel was cut off at the breech and a new percussion breech with bolster was fitted on. No proof or inspection marks, most of the work done by Leman was for the State of Pennsylvania. Barrel is bright and smooth, head on the bolster's clean-out screw slightly buggered. Lock marked, "Mill/Creek/Pa/ 1845," to the hammer's rear and "D. Nippes/US" in the lock's center. Smooth bore, excellent mechanics, excellent iron furniture all in the bright with the exception of the trigger guard, which appears to be armory brown. Musket is complete with original sling swivels and champagne-glass ramrod. Fine stock with very good edges. One old chip out at back of lock, two very clear cartouches at the left flat, overall fine condition. **1,350.00**

Brilliant .69-caliber rifled martial long arm, converted to percussion by the Arsenal by adding a cone in the barrel. Brilliant barrel with very crisp proofs, "US/ EB/P.," date of "1842" on barrel tang. Brilliant lock dated "1842" to the rear of the large percussion hammer, and has the big eagle/"US" in center. Bright original iron furniture, original sling swivels, ramrod is a blacksmith shop copy of a Model 1855 tulip-tipped rammer with a straight shank. Near perfect stock with superb edges around the lock and flats and also along the barrel and ramrod channels. Two extremely crisp cartouches at the left flat and tiny sub-inspectors cartouches on other parts of the stock. Excellent rifled bore and perfect mechanics. **2,750.00**

Overall very good (near "fine") condition example of the scarce Model 1840 Springfield (only 30,000 produced), that is 100% original and complete, and has matched dates on the lock and barrel. The metal is all-clean steel color with strong markings. The lock is marked "Springfield 1841" as well as "US" and having an eagle. The barrel is stamped with a "VP" and eagle and the tang bears a matching date of "1841." The percussion conversion is the standard nipple threaded directly into the barrel. The stock is beautiful with a rich-brown antique walnut patina, and good lines. Two inspector's cartouches are faintly visible on the stock's left side. The lock action is as crisp as new. The ramrod is original and proper having the trumpet-shaped head. **1,195.00**

Rifled Musket, Model 1840, Conversion, fine condition example, barrel is light nicotine-brown over steel with some deep-brown rust patina at the breech. The lock is smooth brown, all metal is uniformly light-brown patina. Stock is outstanding with sharp edges and two vivid cartouches, "WAT," and, "NWP." Lock marked with eagle/"US, L. Pomeroy 1844." Barrel has much nipple pitting obliterating the markings. This has the cone-in-barrel conversion and is complete with the trumpet-head ramrod. **1,450.00**

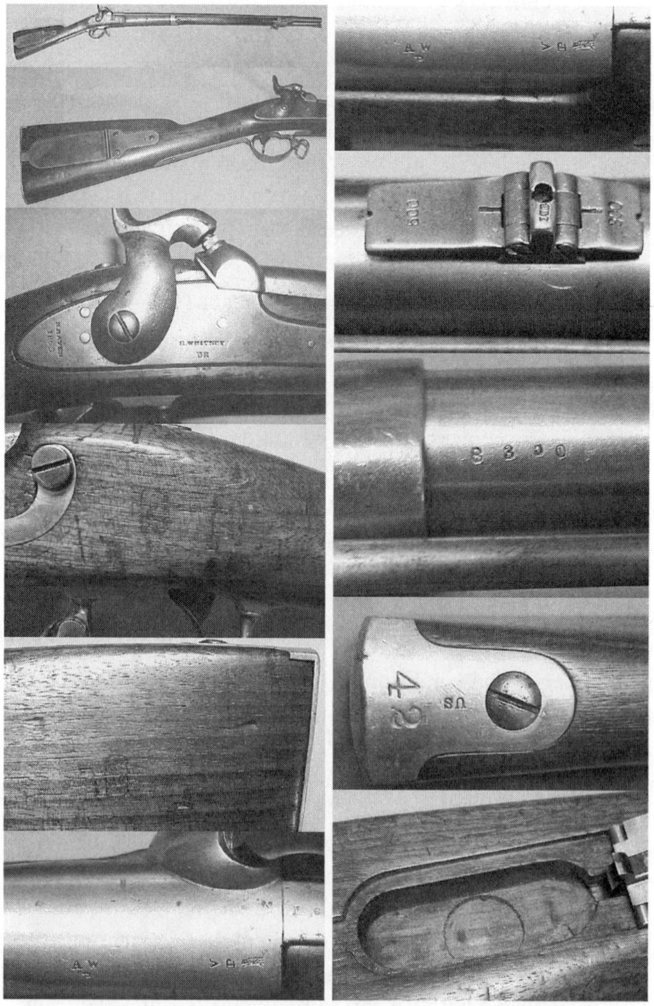

More than 70,000 Model 1841 Rifles were produced by the Harpers Ferry Armory and several other contractors between 1846 and 1855. Originally chambered for .54, this example was rechambered to .58 at the Colt Factory in 1861.

Sharpsburg Arsenal

Rifle, U.S., Model 1841

Colt factory alterations performed late in 1861 by reboring to .58 caliber, fitting Colt-style folding-leaf rear sight, and having trumpet-head ramrod without brass tip. Barrels were serial numbered by Colt with matching sabre bayonet and Colt adapter ring. This gun is serial no. 8350, metal is in excellent condition with sharp markings overall with an 1853 lock date. Brass furniture is in excellent condition, with buttplate having "US" and "42" stamped. Walnut stock has two original cartouches on stock flat with a Colt factory cartouche on butt. Bore is very good, an excellent example. **3,950.00**

.54-caliber percussion rifle dated "1850" at the lock and barrel tang. Barrel is a bright smooth plum mixture of original lacquer brown and patina. Simple post rear sight, brass blade front sight. Crisp markings at the breech, "US/SA/VP." Smooth plum lock marked, "New Haven/1850" to the rear of the hammer and "E. Whitney/US" in the center. Hammer has chip in the striking part. Wonderful brass furniture with handsome golden patina. Rifle has the original brass-tipped iron ramrod and sling swivels. Fine oil-finished stock with very defined edges on the lock, flat, barrel and ramrod channel. Very fine gun in exceptional condition. **3,650.00**

.54-caliber percussion weapon in good to very good condition overall. Two-leaf flip-up carbine rear sight appears to have been put on during the period of use. Moderate pitting around the breech, but clear, "JPC/P," proofs at the left. Barrel and lock have been cleaned to bright steel. Crisp lock marked, "Windsor VT./1849," to the hammer's rear and "Robbins/&/Lawrence/US" in the center. Fine bore, excellent mechanics, bright, golden brass furniture including the large, distinctive Mississippi patchbox. Retains both sling swivels, and has an original Austrian Lorenz ramrod as a replacement for the original rod. Fine, oil-finished stock with two clear cartouches at the left flat. **2,100.00**

.58-caliber percussion rifle with a smooth, plum brown mixed with original lacquer brown armory finish to the barrel. Original brass blade front and post sights. Slight salt and peppering around bolster from use. Barrel inspected by, "JCP/VP." "Steel-sk" stamped at left barrel flat. Date "1850" just discernible on tang, fine, smooth black, casehardened lock crisply marked, "N. Haven/1849" to the hammer's rear and "E. Whitney/US" in the center. Fine .58 altered and rifled bore. Excellent mechanics. Type II iron ramrod. Fine deep umber brass mounts at bands, trigger guard, patchbox, and buttplate. Excellent oil-finished stock with very slight burn out behind the bolster. Otherwise excellent edges along the barrel channel, flats, and ramrod channels. Clear "WAT" cartouche at the left flat. **3,450.00**

E. Whitney contract, unmarked 33" barrel in .58 caliber. Lock marked "E. Whitney" and at tail "N. Haven." Brass furniture, walnut stock, condition: very good. Gray metal showing scattered light pitting with heavier pitting at breech, missing rear sight, excellent wood. **863.00**

Harpers Ferry Percussion Rifle, standard model with 33" .54-caliber barrel, Harpers Ferry lock dated 1850 and brass furniture. Condition is poor, gray metal showing areas of pitting, bayonet lug and sights missing, wood shows heavy use and cleaning. **460.00**

Super nice Model 1841 Mississippi Rifle by Whitney, rare one with original brass-tipped ramrod, still in the factory, .54 caliber. Barrel is dated 1850, and marked "STEEL," lock is dated 1851 (typical of Whitney Arms). Nothing replaced or added to this one; very mellow finish to metal and wood, crisp markings, tight as new-virtually no pitting and a fine bore. **3,250.00**

The metal on the barrel is a smooth gray patina. There is some very light salt and pepper pitting around the nipple. Very good and smooth action, lockplate is marked, "E.WHITNEY/US," and at the rear at the lock "N. HAVEN/ 1850." The barrel is dated 1850, also, "US/S.K/VP," and, "Steel," on the barrel's side. Very fine bore with strong lands and grooves. The walnut stock has the usual dings for a used gun, two clear cartouches, original ramrod, .54 caliber. **2,500.00**

Very-fine walnut stock with two clear cartouches, barrel has a very smooth brown patina. There is light pitting around the nipple. Very good to fine bore, it is semi bright with strong rifling, not converted to .58, as so many were. Original ramrod present, lockplate marked, "E. WHITNEY/U S," and to the rear of the hammer is, "N.HAVEN/1851." The brass was cleaned many years ago, and now has an aged-brass patina. **3,100.00**

Whitney 1855 contract Model 1841 Percussion Rifle. The 33" .54-caliber barrel with saber bayonet lug, long-range rear sight and marked at the breech, "US/A.D.K./VP," with the date, "1855," on the tang. Lockplate has standard markings for this model, the 1855 date with mismatched five dies, brass furniture including variant front barrel band. Walnut stock has two cartouches and initials, "WCK." Overall very good condition, barrel shows scattered light pitting, sound wood with numerous small dents and bruises. **1,725.00**

Nearly 275,000 Model 1842 Muskets were produced from 1842 to 1855. This example, bears a 1842 date on its lockplate and a sanded stock.

J.C. Devine Inc.

Musket, U.S., Model 1842

.69 caliber, 42" barrel, Harpers Ferry lockplate dated "1842," last digit on breech date is illegible. Dark gray patina on all metal, fine pitting on the buttplate and breech. The stock has been sanded and has a 3" long crack at the front band. Good-plus condition with original ramrod. **500.00**

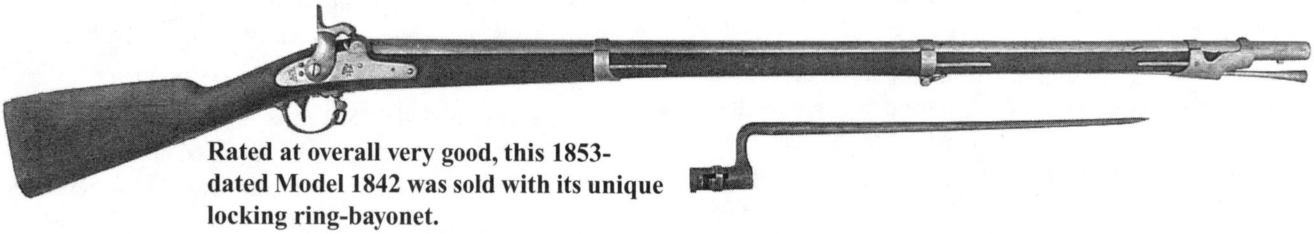

Rated at overall very good, this 1853-dated Model 1842 was sold with its unique locking ring-bayonet.

J.C. Devine Inc.

.69 caliber, 42" round barrel, excellent bore, Springfield Armory lock and tang both dated "1853," the heel of the buttplate with a rack number "3A3/3." Sharp markings on all metal, which is still in the white, showing tarnish and a little very light rust that should clean without a trace. The stock has been sanded and has no cartouche, shows several dings and dents, and an incipient chip behind the lockplate. With an original ramrod and matching condition bayonet. Overall very-good-plus condition. **1,200.00**

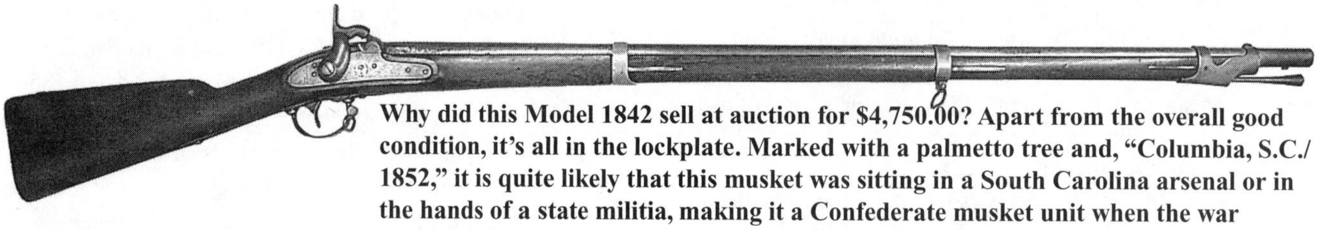

Why did this Model 1842 sell at auction for $4,750.00? Apart from the overall good condition, it's all in the lockplate. Marked with a palmetto tree and, "Columbia, S.C./ 1852," it is quite likely that this musket was sitting in a South Carolina arsenal or in the hands of a state militia, making it a Confederate musket unit when the war commenced in 1861.

J.C. Devine Inc.

.69-caliber, 42" round barrel, marked on the breech's side, "W.G. & Co.," and on top of the breech, "V/P/(palmetto tree)." The lockplate is marked vertically behind the hammer, "Columbia/S.C. 1852," and in front of the hammer is the palmetto tree encircled by, "Palmetto Armory S*C." The heel of the buttplate is marked, "SC." All the iron has a gray patina with pitting on the breech and bolster and only minor pitting elsewhere. The brass bands have a light-ochre patina. All of the metal markings are clear. The stock is in fine condition with sharp edges and some raised grain evident, relatively few light handling marks, but has probably had a little extra oil wiped on through the years. The original ramrod is about 1" short. **4,750.00**

.69-caliber smoothbore musket, evidently B. Flagg took over the Asa Waters Contract and machinery and parts and produced very few of these arms under his own contract and many more under the guise of "The Palmetto Arsenal." Excellent condition, crisp "V/P"/ eagle at left breech, inspector's stamp, "12," and, "1849," date on the tang. Barrel has old dried coat of grease, but would certainly clean to brilliant. Lock crisply marked with eagle/"US" in center under the bolster and "B. Flagg & Co/Millbury/1849" to the hammer's rear. Shadow of an earlier date shows, "Waters," lockplate. Excellent iron furniture with old coat of dried grease would also clean to brilliant. Original sling swivels and ramrod. Excellent oil-finished stock with superb edges around the lock, flats, barrel, and ramrod channels. **5,250.00**

.69-caliber smoothbore, barrel cleaned back to the original armory bright color. Very fine salt and peppering around the breech, crisp "V/P"/eagle at left breech, "1853" date on tang, very good lock and hammer also cleaned to bright with very crisp eagle/"US" in the center and "Spring/Field/1852" to the hammer's rear. Original iron furniture has been brightened, but other than the rear sling swivel is original. Fine oil-finished stock with shadow of cartouche at the left flat, smooth bore, fine mechanics. **1,775.00**

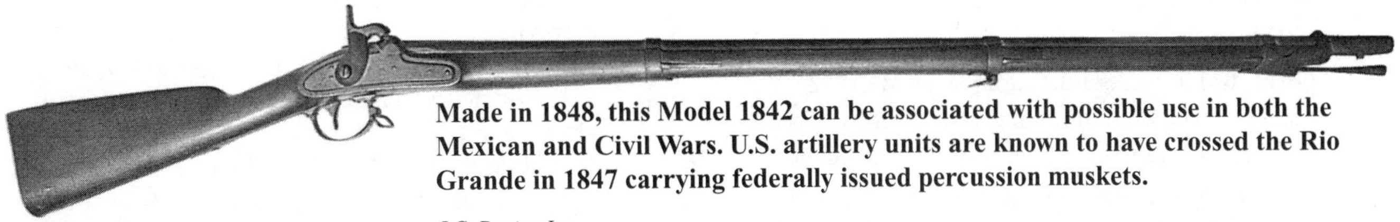

Made in 1848, this Model 1842 can be associated with possible use in both the Mexican and Civil Wars. U.S. artillery units are known to have crossed the Rio Grande in 1847 carrying federally issued percussion muskets.

J.C. Devine Inc.

42" round barrel .69-caliber, this musket was made by Springfield Armory and has an "1848" dated barrel and lock. The musket probably was never issued with the stock having sharp edges, raised grain, crisp "R.C." inspector's cartouche and New Jersey surcharge. The stock has a small nail hole behind the middle band and shows several fine scratches and small dings. Metal has a dark-brown patina with very light surface roughness, will probably clean with very little, if any, fine pitting remaining. Barrel date is lightly struck, all other metal markings are good, has the correct ramrod. **1,625.00**

With an 1848 dated lock and an 185?-dated tang, it is likely that this musket was repaired at one time. It is missing the bayonet lug.

J.C. Devine Inc.

Harpers Ferry, .69-caliber, 42" smoothbore barrel, 1848-dated lock, 185? dated tang, all other metal markings are legible. The stock has only a trace of the inspector's cartouche. Metal has been cleaned in the past, now has a light gray patina with scattered light pitting. The bayonet lug has been removed. The stock has only normal handling marks, good condition, with original ramrod. **600.00**

Harpers Ferry, percussion, .69-caliber musket with a 34" barrel bored out to smoothbore, lock dated 1850. Stock shortened to 9" in front of lock. Condition is poor, barrel with later browned finish and areas of pitting, lock with dark patina, stock cleaned and modified. **127.00**

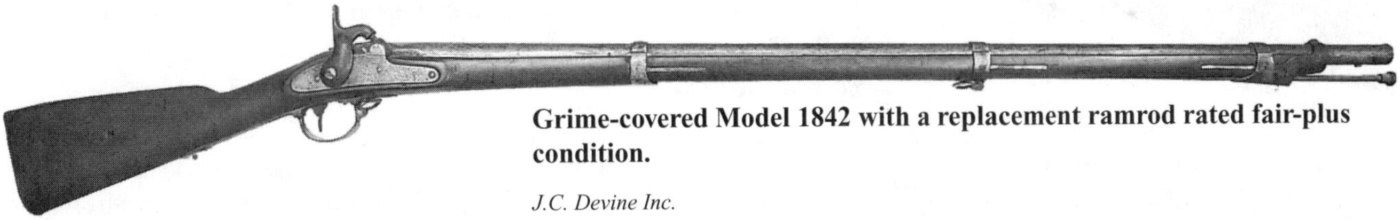

Grime-covered Model 1842 with a replacement ramrod rated fair-plus condition.

J.C. Devine Inc.

Made by Springfield Armory, .69-caliber, 42" smoothbore barrel, 1848-dated breech with clear, "V/P," proof mark, 1849-dated lockplate. Dark patina with areas of light pitting, the refinished stock has a legible cartouche and normal handling marks, good condition. **700.00**

Musket by Springfield Armory, .69-caliber, 42" long barrel, lock and barrel dated 1851, the lock and breech markings are good, no markings on bands. Most metal is gray with light pitting, the stock has been refinished and has a hole in the butt and two forend cracks, replacement ramrod, fair-plus condition, the musket is covered in grime and needs a good cleaning. . . **350.00**

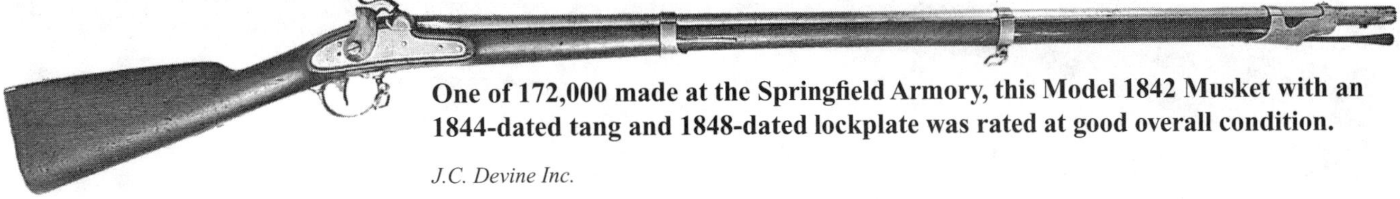

One of 172,000 made at the Springfield Armory, this Model 1842 Musket with an 1844-dated tang and 1848-dated lockplate was rated at good overall condition.

J.C. Devine Inc.

Percussion musket by Springfield Armory, .69-caliber smoothbore, 42" round barrel, 1848-dated lockplate, 1844-dated barrel tang, all metal markings are good. The stock has two illegible inspector's cartouches. All metal is gray, light pitting at muzzle and buttplate, faint pitting over most of the remaining barrel. Stock shows normal handling marks on an old oil refinish, original ramrod, good condition overall. **950.00**

Musket, U.S., Model 1842 , cont.

Rare Palmetto Armory Model 1842 Musket by William Glaze, Columbia, South Carolina, dated "1852," and equipped with brass furniture, barrel marked, "WG& Co.," crisp lock. This is a secondary Confederate weapon made under contract for the use of the state of South Carolina. Moderate pitting at breech from use and hairline-crack on forestock between upper two bands. **7,500.00**

Standard configuration, 42" .69-caliber barrel, and 1849-dated Springfield lock, condition is good to very good. Mottled gray metal showing scattered light pitting with some heavy muzzle pitting. Stock cleaned and shows dents, scratches, and bruises. Ramrod is an incorrect replacement. **403.00**

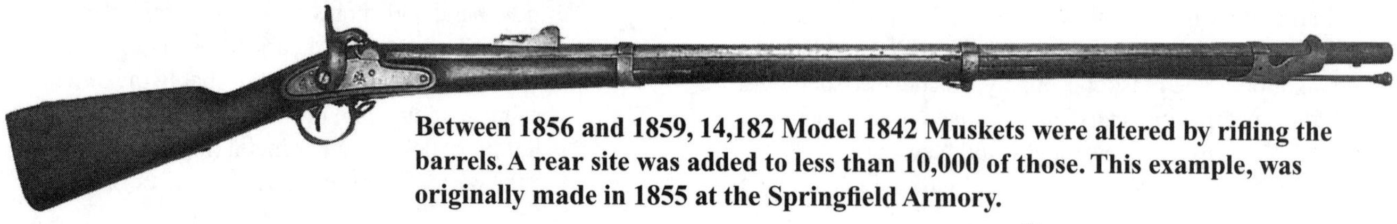

Between 1856 and 1859, 14,182 Model 1842 Muskets were altered by rifling the barrels. A rear site was added to less than 10,000 of those. This example, was originally made in 1855 at the Springfield Armory.

J.C. Devine Inc.

Rifled Musket, Model 1842, .69 caliber, lockplate marked, "Springfield," and dated 1855. The 42" rifled barrel fitted with a long-range sight, dark bore. Good metal markings, no visible stock cartouche. The ramrod is a replacement and the front band spring is missing the tip. The gun is covered in grime, after cleaning this should grade good-plus to very-good condition. **1,000.00**

Rifle, Model 1853, Sharps, Sporting, serial no. 8375, .44 caliber. The 25-3/4" octagon barrel has a dark bore, a legible Hartford address, a fixed-leaf rear sight, and added markings on the breech's side, *40-.90-420*. The rifle has double set triggers and plain walnut stocks with a pewter forend tip and an iron patchbox. Missing lever spring and the tip of the takedown lever. All of the metal has a dark patina with extensive fine pitting, a little heavier around the breech. The stocks are sound, but have several short grain cracks and show wear with the pewter forend tip missing a small piece. This old Texas Sharps is in fair condition and has great character. **1,100.00**

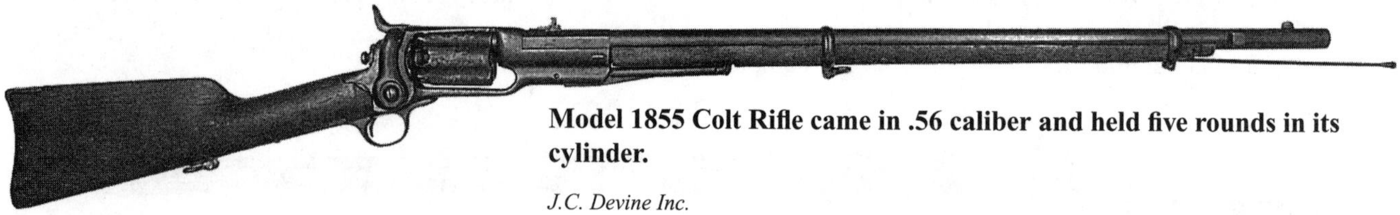

Model 1855 Colt Rifle came in .56 caliber and held five rounds in its cylinder.

J.C. Devine Inc.

Rifle, U.S., Model 1855, Colt Revolving

Serial no. 3449, .56 caliber, 31-1/8" round barrel, good bore, fitted with a lug for a saber bayonet. Dark patina on all metal, patches of light pitting, the cylinder battered with several broken nipples. The fore stock has a large piece missing at the left side of the loading lever, the butt has a 3" crack with the grain at the top tang. The ramrod is a replacement, fair to good overall condition. **2,750.00**

Root Military by Colt, serial no. 131, .56 caliber, unmarked 31-9/16" barrel. Lower tang with sling swivel mount, walnut half-stock forend and varnished walnut buttstock, poor to fair condition. Metal has been cleaned to gray metal showing areas of light pitting. Fore stock replaced, refinished buttstock shows dents, scratches, small hairline cracks and pinned wrist repair, action not functioning. **1,150.00**

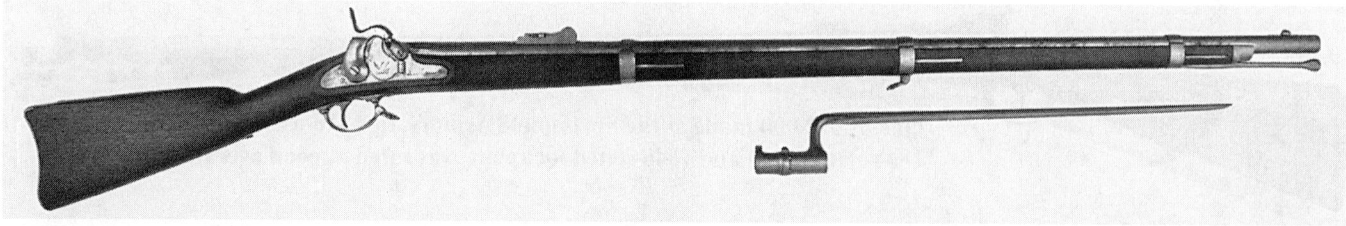

Made by both the Springfield and Harpers Ferry Armory, 59,273 Model 1855 rifle muskets were stockpiled between 1857 and 1861. The distinctive feature of this weapon is the humped hammer and the Maynard priming system. Harpers Ferry Model 1855 rated at good-plus and sold with an original bayonet.

J.C. Devine Inc.

Rifled Musket, U.S., Model 1855

.58-caliber, 40" barrel, fair bore, "1858"-dated on lock and breech, the lock cleaned in the past and the "HARPERS" a little weak, all other metal markings are clear. Gray patina on all the metal with scattered areas of fine pitting. The stock has an old refinish and shows very few light handling markings with two legible oval inspector's cartouches and a clearly stamped set of inspector's initials on the wood and metal "W.C.K." Made by Harpers Ferry Armory. Good-plus condition with an original ramrod and matching socket bayonet. **2,400.00**

.58-caliber, 40" barrel, fine bore, 1858-dated lock and breech, excellent stampings on all metal including, "V/P(eagle head)," on breech. No stock cartouche is visible, and it does not appear there ever was one, the stock does not show much wear and most edges are good. The stock does show normal light scratches and dings with two small splinters at the barrel and ramrod channels. The barrel is fitted with a long-range rear sight with leaf graduated to 800 yards, the forend has a brass cap. All of the metal is a steel gray with light tarnish and dried grease on barrel, will clean to near excellent with several minor dings, but no pitting. Made by Springfield Armory, fine condition with correct ramrod. **2,250.00**

58-caliber percussion, Maynard primed U.S. martial long arm with long-range rear sight, 1858-dated barrel flat, crisp, "V/P/eaglehead," proofs. Bright barrel, cleaned finish, fine salt and peppering on the flat. Fine, bright lock with crisp markings including the eagle on the Maynard primer door. Priming system missing mechanism, lock works perfectly, but caps won't function in the lock. Excellent bore, bright iron furniture is complete with the original sling swivels and the original Model 1855 swollen-end ramrod. Very good original oil-finished stock with good edges around the lock and flats and along the barrel and ramrod channel. Discernable cartouche at left, brass stock cap. **2,950.00**

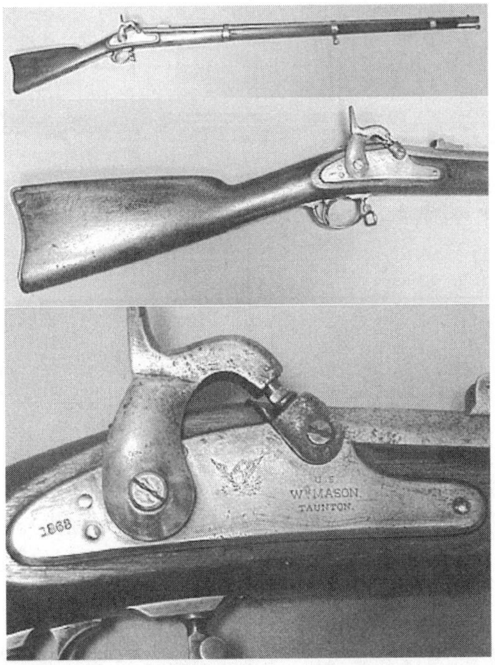

Though advertised as a Model 1855, this is actually a Model 1861. The absence of the Maynard priming system and the lockplate indicating that it was made by William Mason. A good rule to remember is that only the armories at Springfield and Harpers Ferry delivered Model 1855 Rifle Muskets.

Sharpsburg Arsenal

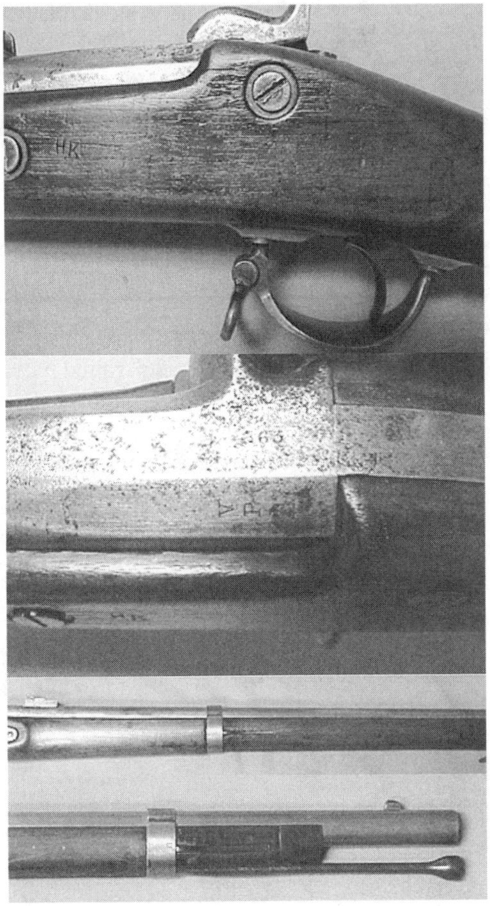

Contract musket by William Mason, Taunton, Massachusetts. Barrel has nice gray patina and appears to have been cleaned some years ago, good barrel marks, "D1863." Standard three-leaf sight and original nipple, lockplate dated "1863" with sharp markings, barrel bands and buttplate have sharp markings with inspector's initials. Wood is very good with minor handling marks and two sharp cartouches. Bore is average with good rifling grooves. . . **2,395.00**

Rifled Musket, U.S., Model 1855, cont.

Exceptional Model 1855 Harper's Ferry Rifled Musket dated "1860." Brown and untouched patina with fine bore and wood, original sling, tompion, and musket tools in patchbox. **2,650.00**

Harpers Ferry Percussion-rifled Musket of standard configuration, the 1860-dated barrel tang and lock. Breech with additional stamping, "W. Raubs/N.Y." Comes with brown leather sling, condition is very good, gray metal shows light spotting and areas of minor pitting. Barrel with light scratches overall, wood with numerous dents and bruises, chipping along ramrod trough and to both forend sides. **1,619.00**

Maynard-primed, percussion-rifled musket with 40", .58-caliber barrel with standard proofs at breech, dated 1860 and additionally stamped, "W. Raurs/ N.Y." Harpers Ferry lock dated 1860, stock and furniture of standard pattern. Comes with brown leather sling, condition is good, gray metal showing areas of light pitting, wood with scattered dents and bruises, and slivered losses at forend. **805.00**

Springfield Maynard-primed, percussion-rifled musket, standard model with 40" .58-caliber barrel, 1858-dated lock and barred, walnut stock, black leather sling. Overall very good condition. Gray metal with scattered light pitting, wood with light dents, scratches, and finish loss. **2,070.00**

Rifled Musket, Model 1855, Type II, 1857-dated lockplate, "U.S./SPRINGFIELD," and a nice crisp national eagle on primer door that opens to reveal complete Maynard tape primer system with feeder paw, spring, and catch. The hammer is correct Model 1855 pattern with tape cut-off. Barrel retains only traces of rifling and second pattern short rear sight was missing its leaves. Barrel is unmarked except for possible company and regimental tang stamps, "H/ 34." Dark walnut stock has buttplate with "US" stamp, trigger guard with swivel, barrel bands with "U" stamp and middle band with sling swivel. Steel Type II nose cap is retained for display with a replacement screw; there is small damage to the stock right under the nose cap (and completely covered by it) that doesn't affect the display of the musket. Reverse of stock has nice clear cartouche. Musket is complete with original Model 1861 ramrod. Metal surfaces appear to have been cleaned to their wartime appearance. **1,395.00**

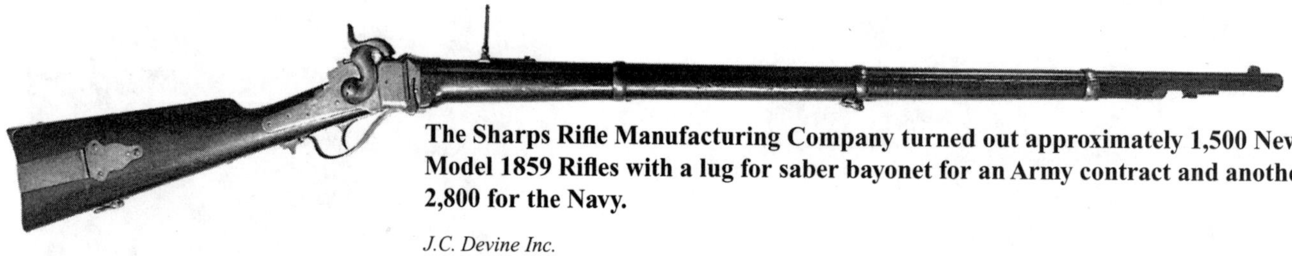

The Sharps Rifle Manufacturing Company turned out approximately 1,500 New Model 1859 Rifles with a lug for saber bayonet for an Army contract and another 2,800 for the Navy.

J.C. Devine Inc.

Rifle, New Model 1859, Sharps

Serial no. 36794, .52 caliber, 36" round barrel with bayonet lug on the bottom, good bore. Breech-loading rifle, Lawrence patent rear sight, single trigger, iron patchbox, frame and lock case colors have turned gray with large areas of pinprick pitting, all markings are very good. Barrel has a smooth dark patina with no visible markings. The head of one frame screw is marred and the primer feed arm is missing. The buttstock has a 3/8" high letter "H" stamped into the left hand side and has a legible "W.W." cartouche. The stocks show normal handling marks on an old oil refinish with a 1/2" age crack behind the lock, overall good-plus condition. **3,000.00**

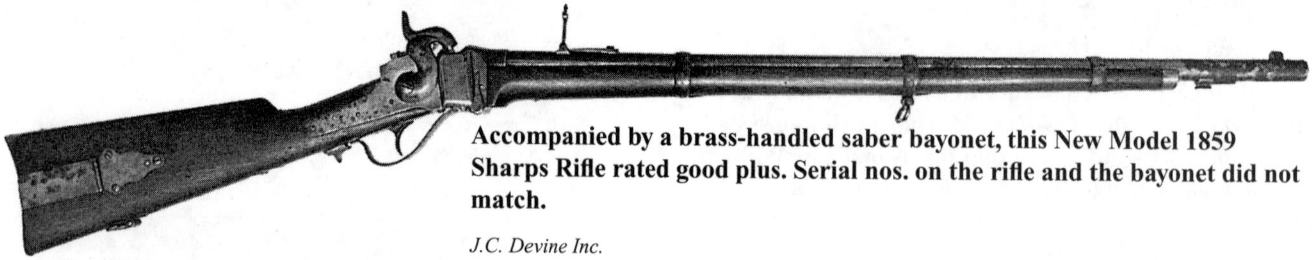

Accompanied by a brass-handled saber bayonet, this New Model 1859 Sharps Rifle rated good plus. Serial nos. on the rifle and the bayonet did not match.

J.C. Devine Inc.

Serial no. 40520, .52 caliber, 30" barrel, very good bore. Model has bayonet lug for a saber bayonet, and a bayonet with serial no. 40911 accompanies the rifle. All metal markings are clear, all metal is a dark gray with small spots of corrosion on the lock, patchbox, and rear of the trigger plate. The front 5" of the barrel and top two bands have large patches of light pitting. The stocks show normal handling marks and do not appear to have ever had a cartouche, although a rack number "44" appears on the wood in front of the heel of the buttplate. Overall condition is good plus to very good. The brass-handled saber bayonet has a very good 20"-long blade marked, "COLLINS CO/HARTFORD," on the ricasso, unfortunately the muzzle ring is broken. **3,000.00**

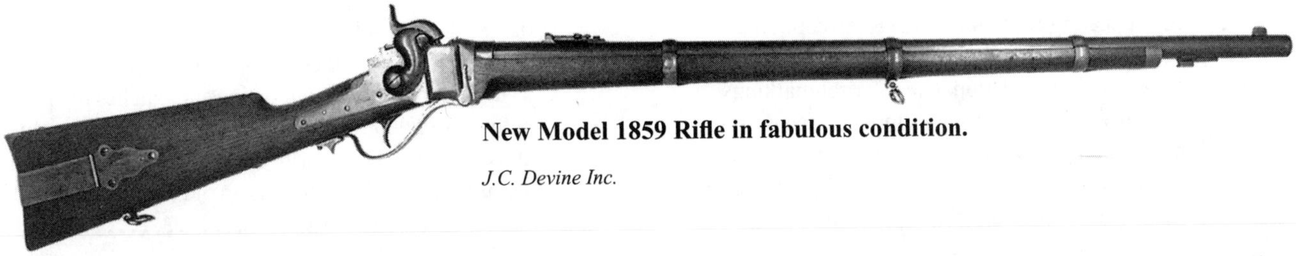

New Model 1859 Rifle in fabulous condition.

J.C. Devine Inc.

Serial no. 40570, .52 cal, 30" barrel has bottom lug for saber bayonet, bore is bright and appears to be unfired. The rifle shows no wear and has only minor storage blemishes. All metal markings are sharp, 95% vivid case colors remain with most of the loss due to fading on the lever and bands, 99% original barrel blue, minor scattered age spotting, some of which should clean. The wood has sharp edges with raised grain, a very small ding at the front of the comb and other minor small handling marks. An outstanding Sharps Rifle. **10,000.00**

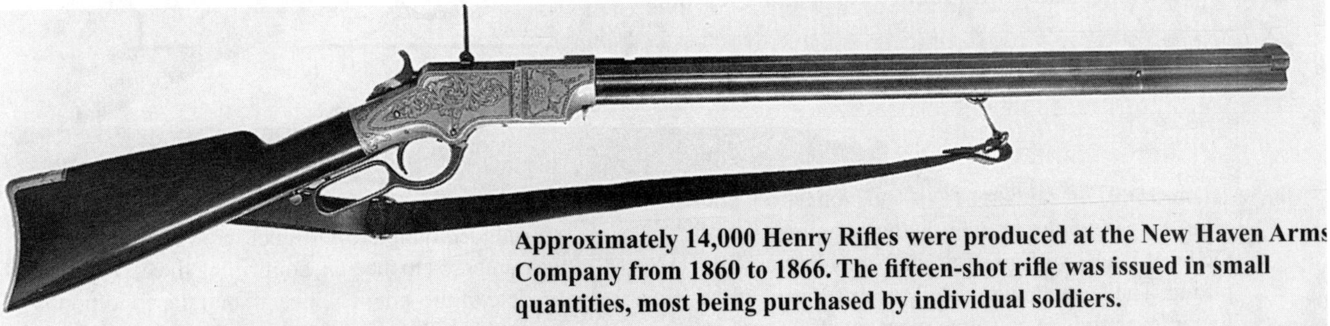

Approximately 14,000 Henry Rifles were produced at the New Haven Arms Company from 1860 to 1866. The fifteen-shot rifle was issued in small quantities, most being purchased by individual soldiers.

J.C. Devine Inc.

Rifle, Henry, Factory-Engraved With Rosewood Stock, serial no. 2384, .44 rimfire caliber, 24" barrel, good bore, manufactured in 1863. Early, rare, Samuel Hoggson engraved, rosewood-stocked Henry is all original. All serial no.s match, including the screws, all assembly numbers match, letter "R" for rosewood is forward on lower tang and buttplate. Beautiful Hoggson engraving has extra coverage making this rifle special. The rifle is in fine condition overall with 30% original silver plate on buttplate, about 15% original silver on receiver. Stock is fine with old extra coat of finish and hairline crack. Bronze parts have a smooth, aged patina. Barrel has aged even brown patina, original sights. Sling is old and contemporary to the rifle, sling hook may be a replacement. **23,000.00**

Rifle, Henry, Nimschke-Engraved, serial no. 654, .44 rimfire caliber, 24" integral slotted tube magazine barrel, good bore, manufactured in 1862. In earlier issues, the Henry Rifle was serially numbered on many parts. Serial numbers are found on the rear top of the barrel, on the lower tang under the stocks, on the stocks under the upper tang and on the inside of the buttplate, all of these numbers are correct and match. On rifles as early as this, the serial number is found on the screws holding the stocks and buttplate. In addition to the serial numbers an assembly number is found on the barrel under the loading sleeve and on the rear end of the loading sleeve. This rifle has assembly number 166 on these parts. Barrel markings as well as all assembly numbers and serial nos. are correct, unaltered, and matching. Walnut was favored for stocking Henry Rifles, and the stocks on this rifle are in excellent condition, with the original color of the wood and some of the original finish remaining. Front sights on these rifles were a blade of lighter metal inlaid into the loading sleeve retaining band. Rear sights were of adjustable style, and both of these sights are original. Rifles in earlier serials such as this often have a rear sight seat in the top of the receiver. Traces of the original blued finish remain on some of the iron and steel parts, with the balance having a smooth aged patina. All of the bronze parts are also in excellent condition, with some signs of use, but no signs of abuse. The bronze parts are also in excellent condition, with some signs of use, but no signs of rifle. Nimschke, an engraver in New York City, was probably the most popular engraver of his time, and his marks have been copied extensively, both in his time and at present. On number 654 the engraving is by this master's hand. Scrolls, sculpture of scrolls, borders and backgrounds, and the shading all show Nimschke's fine engraving. Overlaid scrolls, especially as seen on the front of the receiver sides, are one of the more outstanding Nimschke motifs. On the left side of the receiver is a running buck, and this animal is typical of the master's perfect engraving. An inscription banner on right side balances the animal. Tulip-style filler seen on various panels are typical of early Nimschke work. We see somewhat more extensive engraving coverage on this rifle. Every screw, pin, and other part of this Henry is original and have not been altered in any way. **35,000.00**

Rifle, U.S., Henry

Fine Henry repeating rifle number 8718, exceptionally nice brass and wood (a few tiny patches of filler in buttstock), very crisp action. Clear barrel markings and very nice bore. Extremely minor surface pitting. Original cleaning rod in butt and has the original sling. Rear sight ladder is a replacement, as is upper bracket of sling (not the barrel attachment). **15,000.00**

Serial no. 12755, .44 caliber, 24" barrel. Sling swivels. Varnished walnut stock. Condition is fair to good. Barrel with heavy brown patina and patches of spotting/pitting overall. Front sight blade missing. Rear sight dovetail filled. Frame with dark age patina and scattered dents and scratches. Stock is an old replacement and showing dents and bruises. **10,350.00**

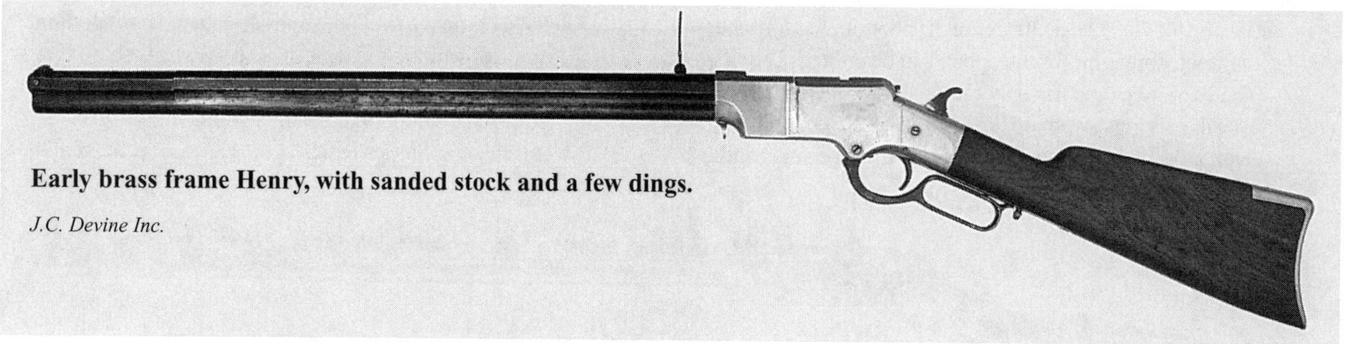

Early brass frame Henry, with sanded stock and a few dings.

J.C. Devine Inc.

Serial no. 1569, .44 caliber, 24 3/8" octagon barrel, poor bore. An early brass frame rifle that is equipped with the lever latch. All iron parts show gray brown with pitting. The lever shows a weld repair forward of the finger lever and the cartridge magazine follower is a modern replacement. The receiver top is dovetailed but the sight is installed on the barrel. The early rounded buttplate and steel screws are correctly numbered to the gun, confirming the early production date of the rifle. The overall antique condition is good. With a sanded stock and some dings in the frame. **9,000.00**

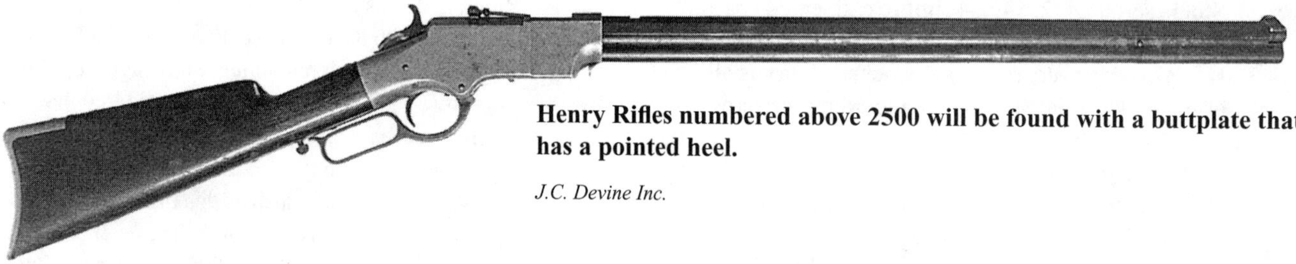

Henry Rifles numbered above 2500 will be found with a buttplate that has a pointed heel.

J.C. Devine Inc.

Serial no. 2916, .44 rimfire, 24 1/4" octagon barrel, the bore has strong rifling with scattered pitting. The rifle has the early rounded buttplate usually not found on rifles over serial no. 2500. The buttplate and screws are numbered to the gun, with one of the screws having transposed digits, 2169. The rifle is equipped with a lever catch, sling fittings, adjustable leaf sight on the frame and an extra factory sight dovetail on the barrel's rear. The frame has very good edges and an attractive mustard-brown patina with a few tiny dings. The barrel has a dark patina with scattered fine pitting, a few light dents on the loading sleeve, and very good factory markings. The walnut buttstock shows light handling scratches and scrapes on old varnish, about 60% of this good-looking refinish remains. The tip of the lever is slightly short and does not engage the catch. The rifle is in good-plus condition overall. This Henry was made in 1863, during the height of the Civil War and undoubtedly was privately purchased by a soldier for use in that conflict. **12,000.00**

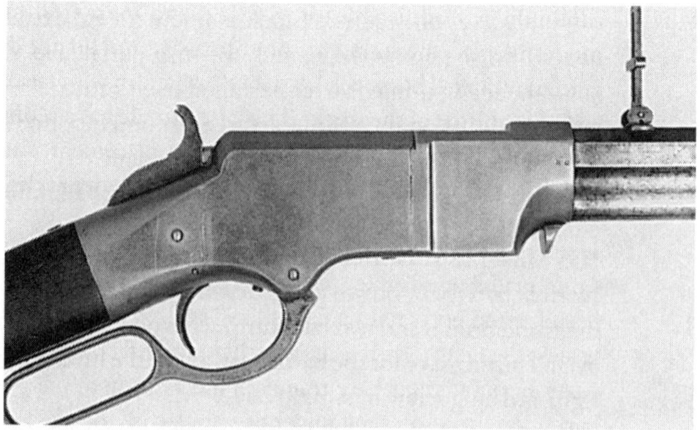

Late, brass-frame model of the Henry made in 1863.

J.C. Devine Inc.

Serial no. 3272, .44 rimfire, 24" octagon barrel with integral magazine tube, good bore. Manufactured in 1863. This rifle is all original with buttplate and screws, numbered 3272 barrel at receiver. Right side marked "C.G.C." frame "HC" barrel "C." The barrel and magazine have no finish and have been lightly cleaned. Strong, crisp maker's mark and serial no. The bronze is smooth with sharp edges. Adjustable leaf barrel sight with no dovetail on receiver. Silver blade front sight, wood is fine with lots of original finish with jackknife star on left side. A. Henry that certainly saw service during the Civil War. **11,000.00**

Serial no. 9561, .44 caliber, 24" barrel, sling swivels, varnished walnut stock, fair condition. Barrel cleaned and showing patches of light pitting. Front sight blade altered, frame cleaned and showing scratches, dents, and dovetailed for rear sights, action needs adjustment. Wood with numerous deep dents and bruises. **8,625.00**

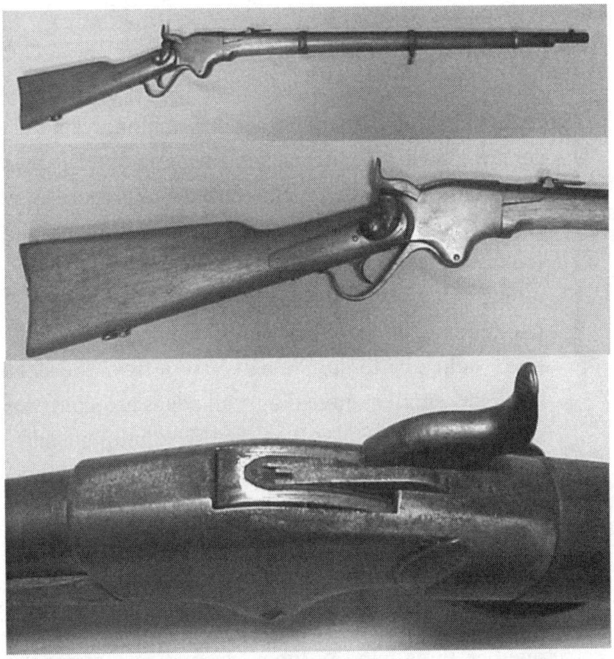

The seven-shot Spencer Rifle fast became a favorite of those who were lucky enough to be issued one or who could afford buying one on their own. Those produced for Army contracts were in .52 caliber and numbered from 700 to 11000 with another small group in the 28000 range.

Sharpsburg Arsenal

Rifle, Spencer

Barrel, band and receiver all have a dark-brown patina on this unaltered rifle. Bore is average, but needs cleaning. Wood appears to have been cleaned, but not refinished small sliver out of the fore stock on both sides where it meets the receiver (a week spot for most Spencers). Inspector marks in front of butt tang "E.M.W." Rifle is 100% complete and in good working condition, serial no. 8xxx. **4,195.00**

Very-fine walnut stock with two very clear cartouches. The metal on the barrel is very smooth with a little blue around the rear sight, the rest is a soft plum-brown patina. The bore is bright with strong lands and grooves, very crisp action. The markings on the barrel are, "SPENCER REPEATING/RIFLE CO. BOSTON MASS/PAT'D.MARCH 1860." A fine untouched Spencer Rifle with serial no. 24026. . . . . **4,100.00**

NRA "very good" Spencer 3-band infantry rifle. Totally honest and 100% original and complete. All metal surfaces are uniformly discolored with a mixture of steel color mixed with light brown aged patina. The stock is a pretty deep walnut-brown with good edges, and excellent wood to metal fit. Decent bore, has complete rear sight, swivel in butt, etc. The firm name on the frame's top is clear and legible. **2,850.00**

Serial no. 3215, .52 rimfire caliber, 30" round barrel, good bore. Dark patina on frame with even faint pitting, legible, "Spencer Repeating Rifle Co.," marking. The barrel has a smooth dark patina with a few small dings, only minor faint muzzle pitting. The stocks show normal handling marks and dings with a 1" age crack at the frame and a 2" age crack at the buttplate. The right side of the stock has a large "S" carved into it. An old, yellowed paper label with a printed history of this rifle is pasted to the right side of the stock. The label appears to have come from an old inventory list and states that this rifle was captured by Private Thomas G. Henshaw of the 9th Virginia Cavalry, during a cavalry battle at Ream's Station on the Petersburg & Weldon Railroad. During the battle, the Virginians were engaged with a company of Union cavalry from Troy, New York. According to the label, Private Henshaw used this Spencer for the rest of the war and finally sold it on November 30, 1888, to whomever compiled the inventory. Very good condition overall. . . . **3,500.00**

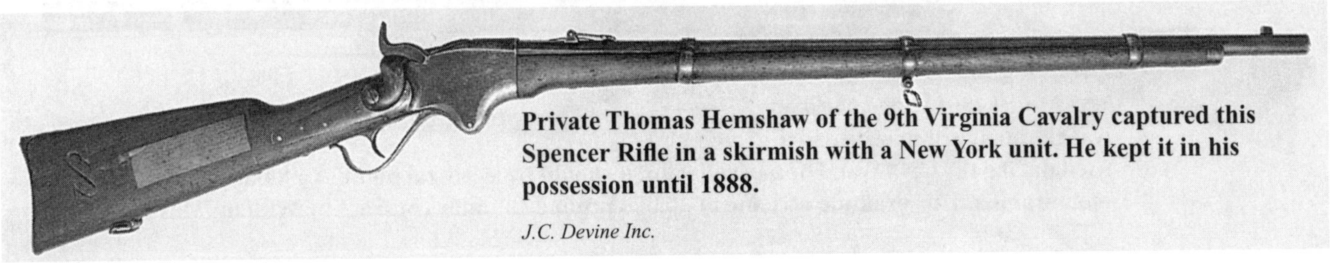

Private Thomas Hemshaw of the 9th Virginia Cavalry captured this Spencer Rifle in a skirmish with a New York unit. He kept it in his possession until 1888.

J.C. Devine Inc.

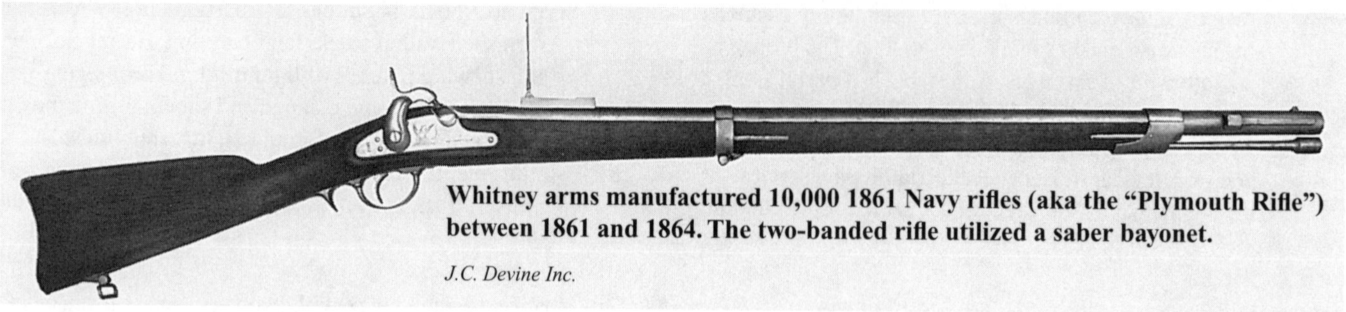

Whitney arms manufactured 10,000 1861 Navy rifles (aka the "Plymouth Rifle") between 1861 and 1864. The two-banded rifle utilized a saber bayonet.

J.C. Devine Inc.

Rifle, Model 1861, Navy, serial 34247, .69 caliber, 34" round barrel, bright bore with sharp rifling and minor fine pitting. Made by Whitney, dated "1863" on the breech and lock, double-stamped inspector's initials "F.C.W." on left side of breech. The lock has the first-style large eagle-shield-flag stamping, and all metal markings are excellent. All of the iron still has the arsenal bright finish, shows light tarnish. Stock has been lightly sanded and shows a few light scratches and small dents, the inspector's cartouche, "FCW," is still legible. Very-good to fine condition, with original ramrod. **2,000.00**

Rifle, Model 1861, Sharps & Hankins, Navy

.52-caliber breech-loading U.S. Naval long arm. Barrel is bright steel with bottom mounted bayonet lug. Frame and tang retain traces of the original blued finish. Fine bore, excellent mechanics. Crisp markings, complete with both sling swivels. Very good oil-finished buttstock and forend. Comes with a fine brass-hilted, 1861-dated Collins' saber bayonet, serial no. 495. Very scarce rifle with a rare bayonet. **3,950.00**

Serial no. 240, .52 rimfire, barrel has been cut to 27-15/16" in length and ends just in front of the forend, which appears to be original length, bore is dark. The barrel has dovetailed front and rear sights with the original sight dovetail filled by a blank. The safety device is missing and the lever catch is broken. Dark patina on all metal, scattered fine pitting, frame markings are legible, stocks show normal handling marks on an old refinish with several age cracks at the butt. About good overall condition. **400.00**

Rifled Musket, Model 1861

Rifled musket by William Mason of Taunton, New Jersey, .58-caliber, 40" barrel, fine bore may clean to excellent, 1863-dated lock, 1862-dated breech. Gray patina on all the metal, a patch of fine pitting on the lock and pinprick pitting on the breech near the nipple. All metal markings are sharp, the stock never marked with an inspector's cartouche, as this was likely delivered to the State of New Jersey. The stock has a few small storage dings, all edges are sharp and some raised grain is still evident. The buttplate and tip of the comb have the rack number "20" and in front of the trigger guard is a small shallow hole made for some obscure purpose. Fine-plus condition, original ramrod, fine socket bayonet in a later scabbard. **1,000.00**

.58-caliber, three-band William Mason Co. contract rifle. In 1862, Mason received a government contract for 30,000 muskets. The vast majority of muskets produced to fill this contract have lockplate markings of "U.S. Wm. Mason." Mason did, however, produce a small number of muskets for this contract that have a plain lockplate, marked only with the date. This is a good solid middle-grade example of this unusual contract. The metal has a smooth gray-brown patina, lockplate marked, "1863." The stock is complete and attractive. It does have a small 1/2" wood chip out just behind the nipple. Only faint traces of rifling remain, and the stock inspector cartouches are worn too dim to see. The ramrod, both swing swivels, and long-range site are intact. **1,150.00**

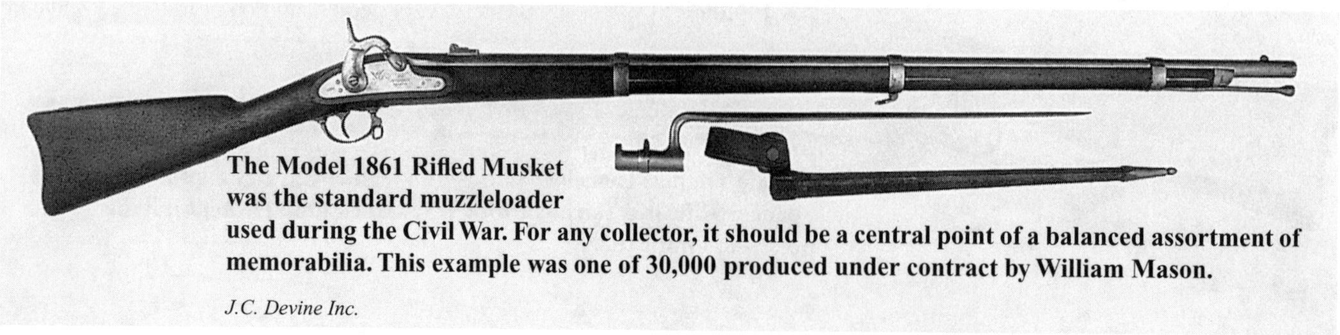

The Model 1861 Rifled Musket was the standard muzzleloader used during the Civil War. For any collector, it should be a central point of a balanced assortment of memorabilia. This example was one of 30,000 produced under contract by William Mason.

J.C. Devine Inc.

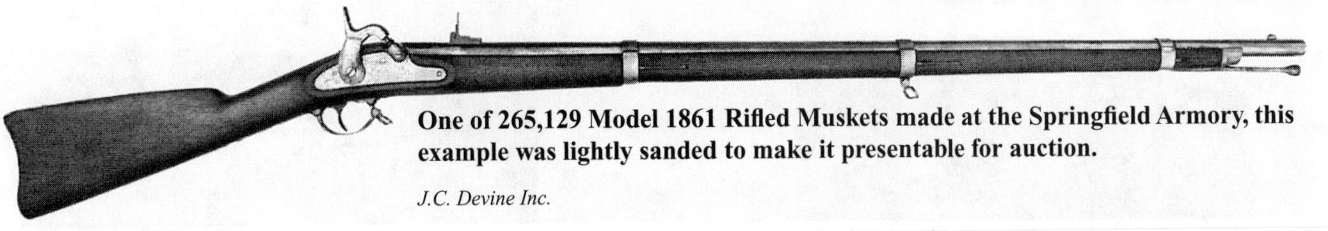

One of 265,129 Model 1861 Rifled Muskets made at the Springfield Armory, this example was lightly sanded to make it presentable for auction.

J.C. Devine Inc.

.58-caliber, 40" barrel, fine bore, lock is marked, "U.S./ SPRINGFIELD," and dated, "1862," and the breech markings are not visible. All the metal is a mottled dark gray with faint pitting, one small patch of light pitting on the barrel, and light buttplate pitting. Stock has a short age crack at the rear lockplate screw and has been lightly sanded and refinished in oil, showing only a few light handling marks. The correct ramrod has been slightly altered by forming a worm on the end, overall condition is good-plus. **700.00**

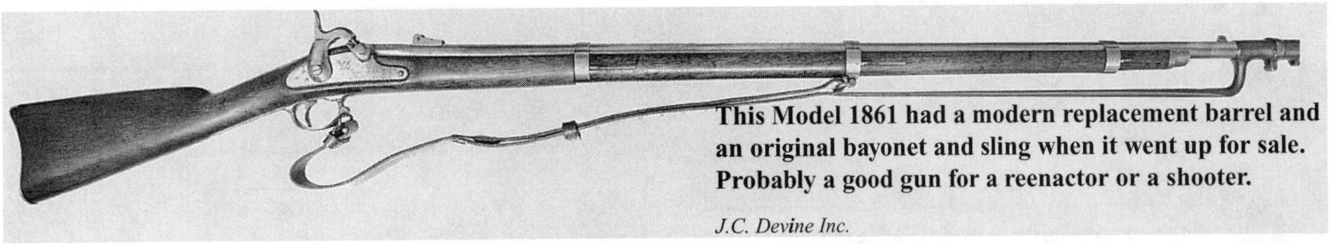

This Model 1861 had a modern replacement barrel and an original bayonet and sling when it went up for sale. Probably a good gun for a reenactor or a shooter.

J.C. Devine Inc.

.58-caliber, 40" barrel, fine bore. The lockplate and barrel of the musket are both dated 1861 with light lockplate freckling and scattered areas throughout the gun. The barrel is of modern manufacture with "U/P" eagle head proofs. Traces of a thin varnish wash are visible on the hammer and areas of the barrel. Sanded and oil-finished stock with added initials "T.C." carved on the left side of the butt. The bayonet has a thick coat of brown varnish over lightly freckled metal, an old military sling is provided, overall good condition. **700.00**

Superb condition just showing some storage and handling age and dings. Metal is bright and shiny with bold crisp markings. Lock has full Colt firm name and crisp date of 1863, and survives in original polish. Barrel has crisp eagle on the bolster, bold 1862 date. State proof mark, "P," and state ownership/acceptance stamp of, "NJ" (New Jersey). It also shows evidence of recent light cleaning of surface rust. The stock is likewise near mint with a crisp "NJ" stamping on the flat opposite the lock. All edges are sharp with some occasional storage nicks and dings and a couple scratches, excellent bore, shiny ramrod shows evidence of pitting. **2,350.00**

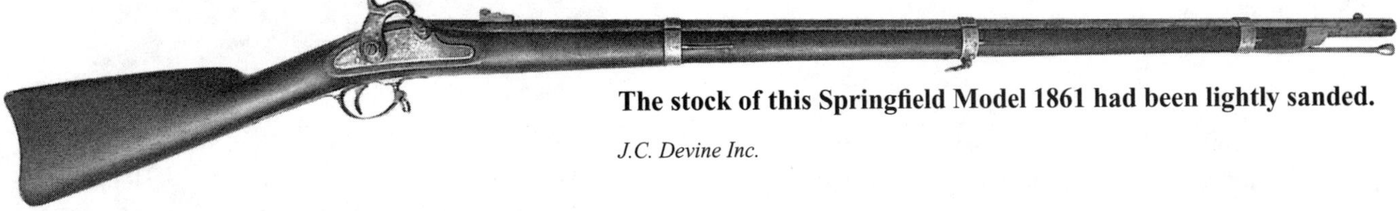

The stock of this Springfield Model 1861 had been lightly sanded.

J.C. Devine Inc.

.58 caliber, 40" barrel, very good bore, lock marked, "U.S./SPRINGFIELD," and dated, "1862." The breech markings are not visible. The barrel and bands are gray metal and show fine scratches from an abrasive cleaning. The rest of the metal is gray and shows scattered fine pitting. The correct ramrod is slightly short. Stock has been lightly sanded and refinished in oil, there is a storage crack at the buttplate and very few light handling marks. A German silver shield has been inlaid on top of the wrist. Overall condition is good-plus. **700.00**

Rifled Musket, Model 1861, cont.

All the metal on this Springfield Model 1861 had been cleaned bright, thereby, weakening all markings. The stock was clearly marked and had the addition of a previous owner's initials.

Sharpsburg Arsenal

.58 caliber 40" round barrel with standard proofs at breech dated "1862" on barrel flat. Lock dated "1862" behind hammer; marked below bolster, "U.S./ SPRINGFIELD," with eagle between hammer and bolster. "U.S." on buttplate tang, cartouche on the flat opposite the lock and above the trigger guard tang, initials, "LWF," scribed opposite the lock. Overall condition is very good, all metal surfaces have been cleaned bright with weakened markings. Sound stock has good eagles, weak visible cartouche. **3,250.00**

1863-dated, .58 caliber by Trenton, an historical Gettysburg-related item. The name "J. Hodge" is neatly carved in wood opposite lock. Hodge served in Company H, 142nd Pennsylvania Infantry and saw action at Fredericksburg and Gettysburg, dying in November 1863. Weapon is missing ramrod and rear sight, and is a very honest brown patina overall. **1,750.00**

.58-caliber percussion long arm, barrel dated, "1863." Fine bore, 1863-dated Bridesburg lock. Superb stock with two crisp cartouches, fine furniture. **1,650.00**

.58-caliber percussion, smooth plum barrel patina, crisp proofs, light-to-moderate pitting on top flat around nipple. Fine 1862-dated lock with crisp markings and mechanics, complete iron furniture including ramrod and sling swivels. Excellent oil-finished stock with crisp edges around the lock and flat, and clear, "ESA," cartouche at the left flat. **1,650.00**

100% original and complete, mechanically perfect, with matched dates of 1862 on lock and barrel, and overall very good condition. Metal is clean steel color with crisp marks and no rust or pitting. Lock has good eagle, "US Springfield," and, "1862." Barrel has very clear "1862," as well as "VP" and eagle's head. The stock has good edges showing just honest age and handling with a couple bruises and one bang in front of the lock. The proper two cartouches are still legible including the Springfield "ESA" (Erskin S. Allin, master armorer). The bore is crisp with great rifling, and the ramrod is original and matches the rest of the gun. **2,450.00**

1861 Norfolk, dated 1863, scarce tinned example (sea service Marines or coastal defense troops), with original matching tinned socket bayonet. Nice markings and wood, smooth action. **1,150.00**

A much better-than-average example of the contract Springfield made by Savage. Lock and barrel carry matched dates of 1863, all metal markings are crisp and clear, all metal is smooth steel with gunmetal gray patina. The wood has excellent edges, great color, no bad bruises, and two visible inspector's marks opposite the lock. This is 100% complete including the proper swelled ramrod, and very good bore. **1,895.00**

Contract-rifled musket by Alfred Jenks & Son. 40" .58-caliber barrel, lock marked, "U.S./Bridesburg," and, "1863," with steel furniture and walnut stock of standard pattern. Overall condition is very good. Gray metal showing dark patina and areas of light pitting, rear sight missing. Stock with few light blemishes. **748.00**

Matched dates of 1864 on the lock and barrel, and federal inspector's cartouches on the stock's left side, no pitting, stock is mint with razor sharp edges and raised grain. Metal is perfect and the barrel is a mixture of bright steel and gunmetal gray, handful of minor storage dings in the wood. **3,950.00**

A near fine example of the true Model 1861 Springfield Rifled Musket. This one is 100% original and complete, really nice state of preservation, mechanically perfect. Lock and barrel have matched dates of 1862. The barrel proof marks are clearly legible, as is the inspector's cartouche "ESA" on the left side of the stock. The metal is overall clear steel color with some scratches and light wear. The stock is very nice with good edges and color. The most interesting aspect of this gun is a carving in the right side of the buttstock. Nicely done, and definitely from the period, wonderful five-pointed star executed in good quality on the stock's face. The design is that of a star within a circle. The background behind the star (and inside the circle) is stippled in an artistic fashion. This star is the emblem of the 12th corps, which fought at Gettysburg and was later transferred west to become the 20th corps, which utilized the same corps insignia. **2,495.00**

Top-notch, fine-excellent condition, 100% original and complete, mechanically perfect, sharp edges on the wood and metal, and all markings are crisp. The lock and barrel bear matched dates of 1863, the stock and bbl have "NJ" cartouches clearly visible, and the bore is super. **2,250.00**

An unfired example of the Colt Special Model 1861 Musket with matched dates of 1863 on lock and barrel. With the exception of some light surface pits in a couple small areas on top of the barrel, the weapon is nearly mint. The stock has crisp edges and a raised grain. Metal is bright and shiny, all markings are crisp and appear like new, barrel is surcharged "NJ" for New Jersey, and the stock has the "NJ" cartouche. The rear sight has all the blue on it, the bore is mint. **3.950.00**

Lock marked "Wm Muir & Co./Windsor Locks, Ct.," and dated 1863. The rear sight has a base only and the 40" barrel has been bored smooth to .60 caliber. The rifle is covered in grime, but the exterior should clean to fine or better, most metal is gray and covered in light rust. Stock has two very good inspector's cartouches, "H.J.," and, "E.C.B.," has good edges and shows fewer than normal light handling marks. Gun has original ramrod showing pitting, a poor condition original leather sling, and a very-good condition original bayonet. . . . **.550.00**

Marked, "Wm. Muir & Co.," this Model 1861 was part of a 30,000-gun contract fulfilled between 1863 and 1864. Rated "poor," with a broken, original sling and an original bayonet.

J.C. Devine Inc.

Rifled Musket, Model 1861, cont.

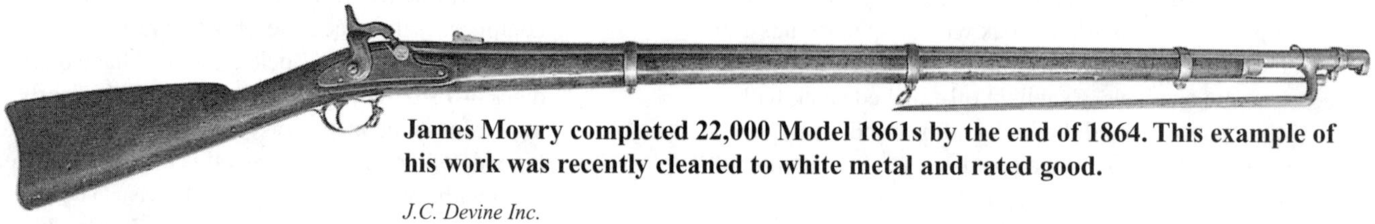

James Mowry completed 22,000 Model 1861s by the end of 1864. This example of his work was recently cleaned to white metal and rated good.

J.C. Devine Inc.

James D. Mowry, .58 caliber, 40" barrel, 1864 manufactured, barrel has been cleaned to white with moderate pitting visible on bolster and breech, light pitting on barrel bands and at the muzzle. Lockplate and hammer have a darker patina with pinprick pitting visible around the bolster. Stock has a thick coat of added varnish over many small handling marks and blemishes. Cartouches are still visible, bayonet has a matching patina to the musket with a band of deep pitting around the base of the blade above, "US," overall good condition. **600.00**

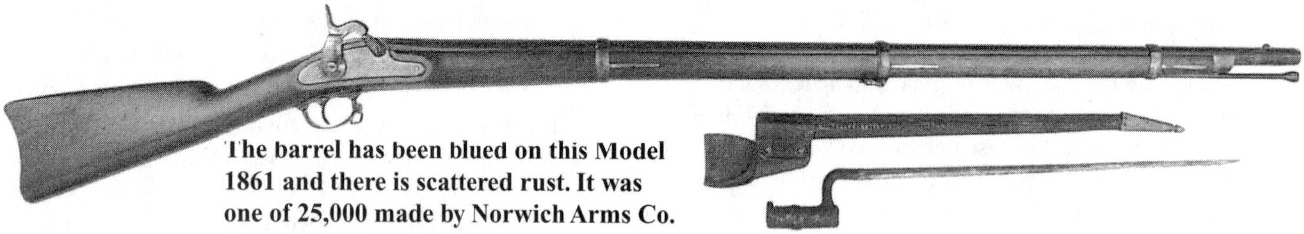

The barrel has been blued on this Model 1861 and there is scattered rust. It was one of 25,000 made by Norwich Arms Co. between 1863 and 1864.

J.C. Devine Inc.

Norwich, 40" barrel bored smooth to .60 caliber, no breech date visible, but "V/P" and eagle head proof marks are legible. The 1864-dated lockplate has been lacquered and has some faint case colors remaining with clear markings. The breech's side and the buttplate's heel have clearly marked inspector's initials, "E.P.R.," as do all the bands and the trigger guard. The stock has three excellent inspector's cartouches, "EPR," "WHR," and, "GKJ." The stock has had some oil added, but shows only a few light handling marks. The blued barrel has scattered light surface rust, missing mainspring, original ramrod, and has a good condition socket bayonet with leather scabbard. **425.00**

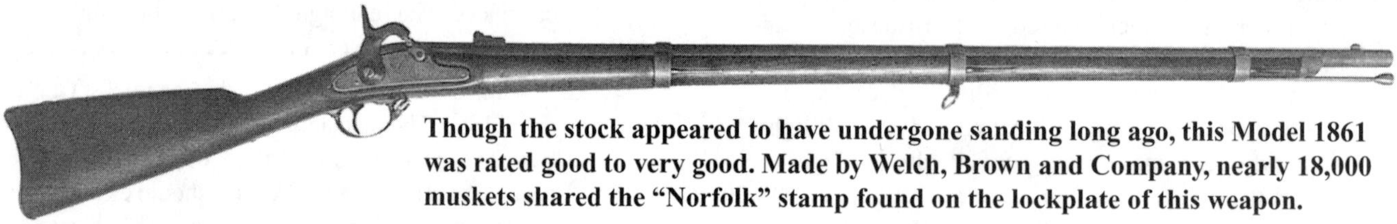

Though the stock appeared to have undergone sanding long ago, this Model 1861 was rated good to very good. Made by Welch, Brown and Company, nearly 18,000 muskets shared the "Norfolk" stamp found on the lockplate of this weapon.

J.C. Devine Inc.

No serial no., .58 caliber, 40" round barrel, very good bore. Manufactured sometime during 1862-1863. Made by Welch, Brown & Co., Norfolk Connecticut, 1863-dated lock shows the correct eagle, "U.S. Norfolk." The barrel is marked with the standard "VP" over eagle and is dated 1863. The bolster has the correct clean-out screw. Stock appears to have undergone an old sanding and no inspector's marks are present. The metal is a gray-brown color with pitting near the breech. The stock shows repairs on both sides of the tang and some bruising and dings. The overall condition is good to very good. **675.00**

Overall very good condition and 100% original and complete. This example is quite scarce bearing the 1862 date on the lock, that was the first year Providence Tool Company produced any Springfield contract muskets. The metal is overall steel color with light patina. The lock is clearly marked "US Providence Tool Co. Providence R.I." and having an eagle stamp as well as the date of 1862. The buttplate has the double-lined, "US," stamp showing that it is the correct buttplate for this contract. The barrel markings at the breech are vaguely visible, but largely obscured by light pitting around the bolster. The clean-out screw in the bolster is fine with a nice clean slot still present. The stock is very nice with good edges and a clear inspector's cartouche, "WP," inside a rectangular box. The bore rifling is very sharp and deep. **1,295.00**

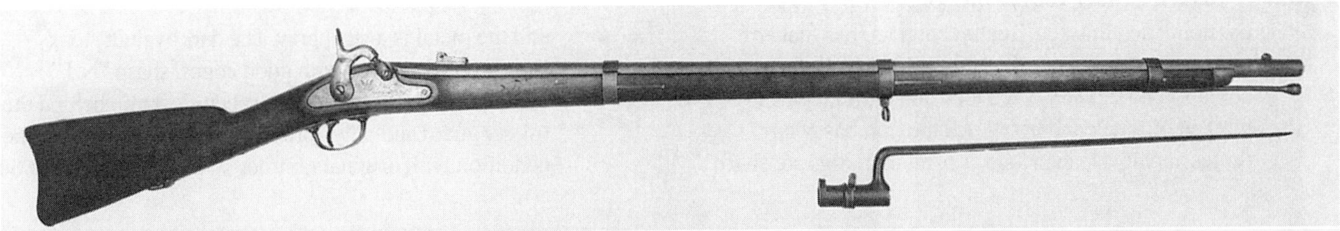

Weapons actually made at the Springfield Armory are the favorites of collectors. A weapon bearing the armory's hallmark will always sell for more than another Model 1861 in similar condition made under contract.

J.C. Devine Inc.

Percussion-rifled musket by Springfield Armory, .58 caliber, 40" barrel, bore has strong rifling with scattered light pitting, 1861-dated barrel, 1864-dated lock. The lockplate has clear markings, gray patina on metal with minor scattered pinprick pitting, the breech with light pitting and legible markings. The dark walnut stock has an old refinish and shows light handling marks. Good-plus condition with the original ramrod, and an original bayonet in fair condition. **1,000.00**

Percussion-rifled musket by Welch, Brown and Co., .58 caliber, 40" barrel, excellent bright bore. Lockplate marked, "US/NORFOLK," and both the lockplate and breech are dated 1863. All lettering on metal is in excellent condition, with only the eagle on the lockplate showing light wear. The stock opposite the lock is marked "W.WELCH" (in an arc), "NORFOLK CT." This mark is worn, but legible, and the inspector's cartouche is visible, but illegible. All of the metal has been professionally cleaned to bright, the stock shows only minor small handling marks. Several years ago about three dozen of these muskets were sold at a country auction in New Hampshire by descendents of the original manufacturers. These muskets were un-issued and showed varying degrees of storage wear. This one was bought by Navy Arms and they had it cleaned before selling it. Overall condition is about fine with the original ramrod. **1,800.00**

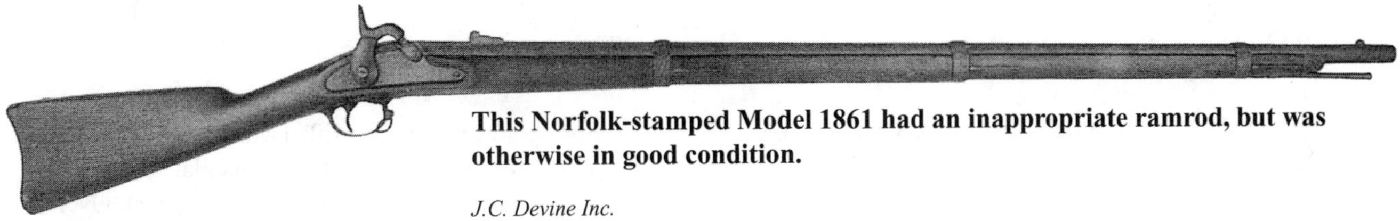

This Norfolk-stamped Model 1861 had an inappropriate ramrod, but was otherwise in good condition.

J.C. Devine Inc.

Percussion-rifled musket by Welch, Brown and Co., .58 caliber, 40" long barrel, strong rifling in dark bore that should clean to good. The lockplate has legible markings, "U.S./NORFOLK," eagle, and, "1863." No breech markings are visible by the left stock flat still has stamping, "W.W. WELCH/NORFOLK CT." The rear sight leafs are missing, all of the metal has a dark-brown patina with even light pitting on most surfaces. The stock shows only light handling marks and the steel ramrod is from a .45/70. ...... **550.00**

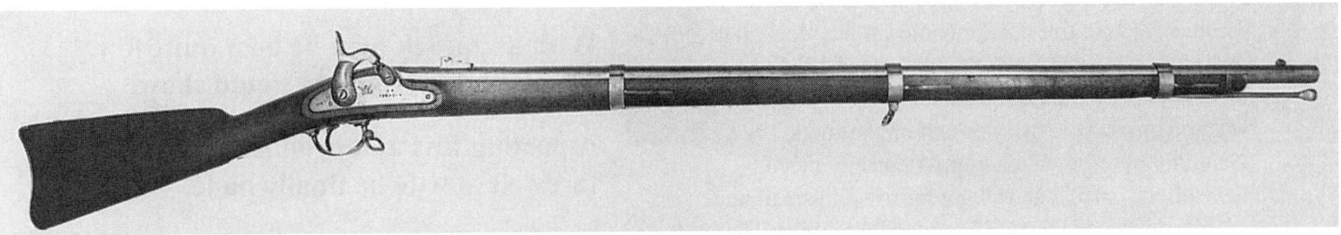

Made at the Trenton Locomotive and Machine Company in Trenton, New Jersey, this Model 1861 coincidentally also has State of New Jersey surcharges on it. Though often touted as part of a New Jersey purchase for issue to its own troops during the war, most New Jersey-surcharged weapons received their distinctive marks after the war when New Jersey made large purchases of surplus weapons from the Federal government.

J.C. Devine Inc.

Rifled Musket, Model 1861, cont.

Percussion-rifled musket, Trenton contract, has State of New Jersey markings, .58 caliber, 40" barrel, fine condition bore, 1863-dated lock and barrel, "N.J." marked on stock and barrel. All the iron has been professionally cleaned long ago, all markings are sharp and the metal is a steel gray. The dark-walnut stock shows very little use with good edges, sharp "N.J." opposite the lock, clear "S" inspector's stamp behind the trigger guard and only normal light handling marks, fine condition with original ramrod. **1,750.00**

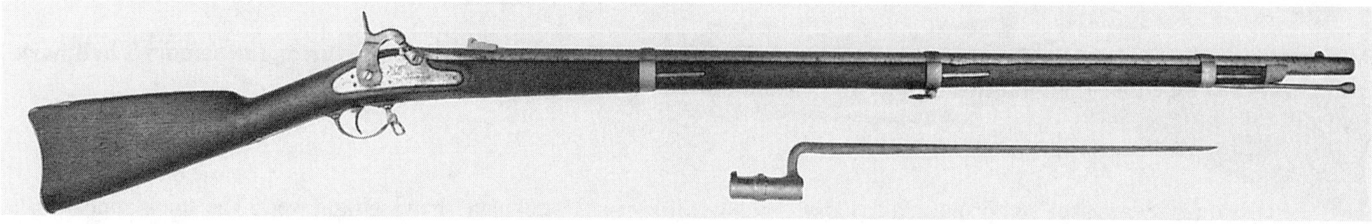

The stock had been refinished and several chips filled giving a rating of "fair" to this Springfield Model 1861.

J.C. Devine Inc.

Rifled musket by Springfield Armory, .58 caliber, 40" barrel, fair bore, 1862-dated lock with all markings legible, the breech with light file marks has no legible markings. Gray metal, extensive light pitting. The stock has been refinished and has some small chips missing at the buttplate. In fair-plus condition with an original ramrod and an original bayonet in good condition. **450.00**

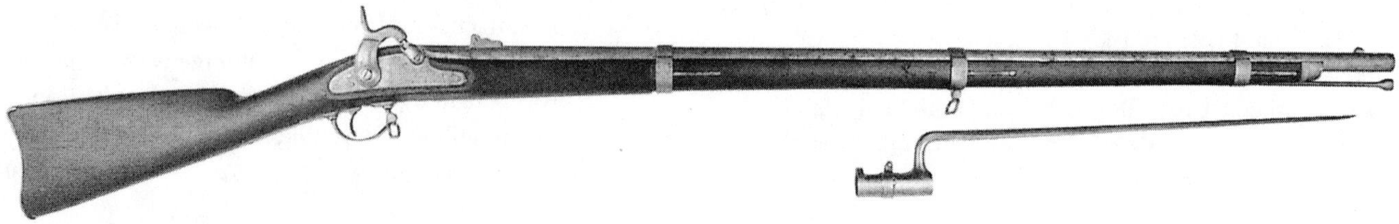

Though it was equipped with an inappropriate reproduction ramrod, this Springfield Model 1861 rated good plus and sold with a correct bayonet.

J.C. Devine Inc.

Rifled musket by Springfield Armory, .58 caliber, 40" barrel, dark bore, 1862-dated lock and breech. Gray patina on all metal with extensive fine pitting, lock markings are good, breech markings are faint. The stock shows light handling marks, but not much wear with two very good cartouches. Good-plus with incorrect reproduction ramrod and a very good original bayonet. **850.00**

Rifled musket with State of New Jersey markings, .58 caliber, 40" barrel, bright bore is very good and may clean to better. Made by Hodge and Burton at the Trenton Locomotive and Machine Co., the lockplate is marked, "U.S./TRENTON," and dated 1864, the breech with 1863 date and standard proof marks. Marked on the breech's side and on the stock, "N.J." Genuine "attic-mint" exterior with bright metal beneath the barrel bands, light tarnish and small age spots on exposed metal, sharp metal markings. The stock shows no wear, has sharp edges, and minor storage bruises, the "N.J." partially illegible due to a small bruise. Fine-plus condition with ramrod. A hard Civil War musket to find as only 11,495 were made. **2,000.00**

Springfield Percussion-rifled Musket of standard military configuration with lockplate dated 1861. Together with associated socket bayonet. Overall condition is poor. Metal with dark patina showing spotting/light pitting overall, worn markings, stock has numerous dents, scratches, bruises, silvered losses along forend and with two wrist cracks showing unusual bound repair. **460.00**

Clad in blue and standing tall,
he was the proudest one of all.

With knapsack high he bent quite low,
for his childs', his love would show.

A parting kiss and promises made,
farewell to wife he finally bade.

Shouldering musket he joined the ranks,
while marching off, the crowd gave thanks.

— Matthew L. Roberson
19th Iowa Volunteer Infantry

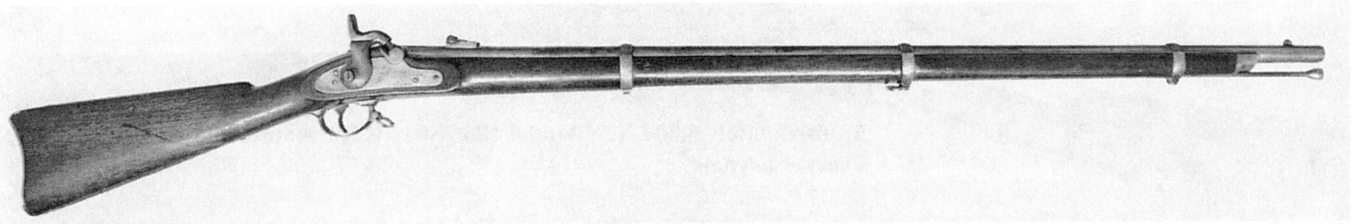

More than 152,000 rifle-muskets were made under a special 1861 contract. Though they look similar to a Model 1861, Model 1861 Special Contract Rifle-Muskets are distinctly different. The most immediate distinguishing feature is the shape of the hammer and lockplate. Furthermore, very few parts actually interchange between the Model 1861 and the Special Model 1861 weapons.

J.C. Devine Inc.

Rifled Musket, Special Model 1861

Lamson, Goodnow & Yale Of Windsor, Vermont, .58 caliber, 40" round barrel, very good bore, 1863-dated lockplate and breech, lock marked, "L.G.&Y./ Windsor." Almost illegible "VT" marking, all the metal has a light gray patina with some tarnish, faint pitting near the nipple. The eagles on the lockplate and bolster are faint. The stock has good edges, no cartouche, has had a little oil added through the years. Buttstock has a 1" high cross-scratched into it near the buttplate, otherwise the wood shows only light handling marks. Overall condition is very good with original ramrod that is 1/4" short. **1,100.00**

Special contract musket by Colt, 28" barrel dated 1862 and bearing surcharge, "NJ," for New Jersey, very-good condition, barrel and stock shortened. Gray metal has light pitting, wood with scattered dents and bruises, forend cap missing................ **460.00**

Special contract-rifled musket by Colt, 32" barrel with standard government proofs, dated 1862. Lock, furniture, and stock of standard pattern, left side of stock stamped, "N.J.," fair condition. Barrel and stock shortened, smooth gray metal has been cleaned overall and shows areas of light pitting. Wood with light dents and scratches. **518.00**

Special musket made by Colt, .58 caliber, 40" barrel, very good bore, 1864-dated lock and breech. All metal has been cleaned sometime in the past and now has a steel-gray patina with scattered pinprick pitting, all markings are clear. Refinished stock, shows light wear and handling marks with only traces of two cartouches. Good-plus with an Enfield socket bayonet in very good condition and an original ramrod. **750.00**

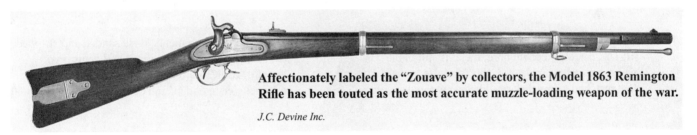

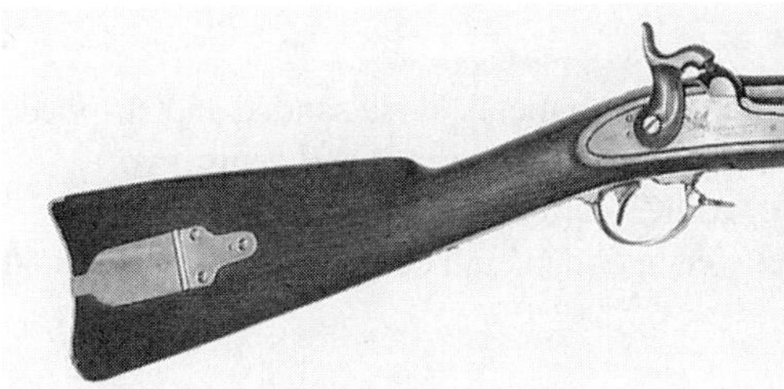

Affectionately labeled the "Zouave" by collectors, the Model 1863 Remington Rifle has been touted as the most accurate muzzle-loading weapon of the war.

J.C. Devine Inc.

Rifle, U.S., Model 1863, Remington

No serial no., .58 caliber, 33" round 7-groove barrel, fine bore, manufactured in 1863. This "Zouave" retains most blue with case color grading 90% on lockplate and hammer with some fading to gray. All marks are correct with lock and barrel dated 1863. The barrel inspector is, "M.S.L.," with the stock cartouches for, "H.D.J.," and "R.H." The wood shows a light sanding with both cartouches very readable and the brass has been cleaned. **2,000.00**

Manufactured by Remington, Ilion, New York. .58 caliber. Total quantity made was 12,501. Lockplate and hammer retain case-hardening with excellent markings. Barrel has 98% of its original deep blue finish. Brass nose cap, barrel bands, patchbox, buttplate and trigger guard have nice mellow patina. All have inspector marks. Wood is in excellent condition with minor handling marks and two sharp cartouches. Small sliver missing at barrel tang (looks original from factory). Bore is very good with minor pitting. **4,795.00**

Standard model with 33", .58-caliber barrel. Lock and barrel dated 1863, brass furniture, stock with two inspector's cartouches. Condition: Fine to excellent, possibly an arsenal refinish, stock with scattered dents and bruises. **3,163.00**

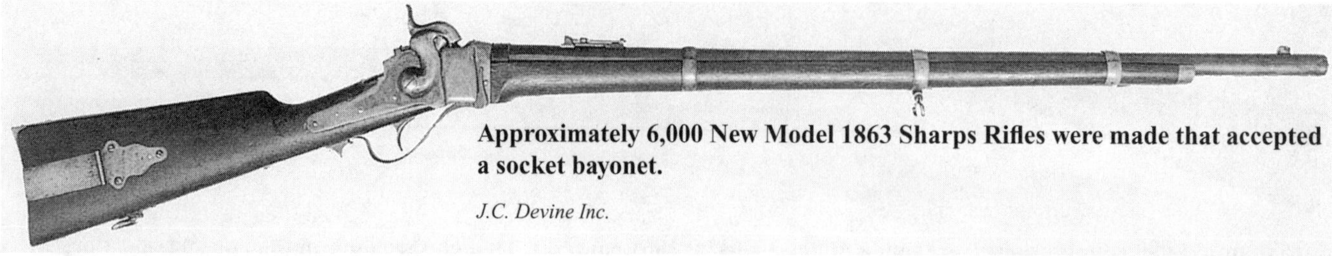

Approximately 6,000 New Model 1863 Sharps Rifles were made that accepted a socket bayonet.

J.C. Devine Inc.

Rifle, U.S., New Model 1863, Sharps

Serial no. C33300, .52 caliber, 30" barrel, good bore, adapted for a socket bayonet, has iron patchbox, 20% fading case colors remain on frame, 50% case colors remain on lock, balance faded to gray. All metal markings are clear, 95% dull blue on barrel, small patch of faint pitting, 50% bright blue on pellet primer cover with more on some screw heads. Forend shows no wear, legible, "A.W.M.," inspection stamp. Buttstock shows light handling marks, two very good, "F.W.R.," cartouches with most of the oil finish remaining. The buttplate and patchbox have turned silver/gray while the bands have some faint case color. A great three-band rifle in fine-plus condition. **3,350.00**

Serial no. C38175, .52 caliber, 30" barrel, poor bore. The breech-loading rifle is missing the rear sight leaf and lever pin stud, but has an iron patchbox in the butt. The barrel bands are replaced and have a lot of original case colors, all other metal is dark with light corrosion, most of the metal markings are clear. The forend is also a replacement in excellent condition with clear inspector's initials, "M.N.M." The buttstock shows normal handling marks, good overall. **2,200.00**

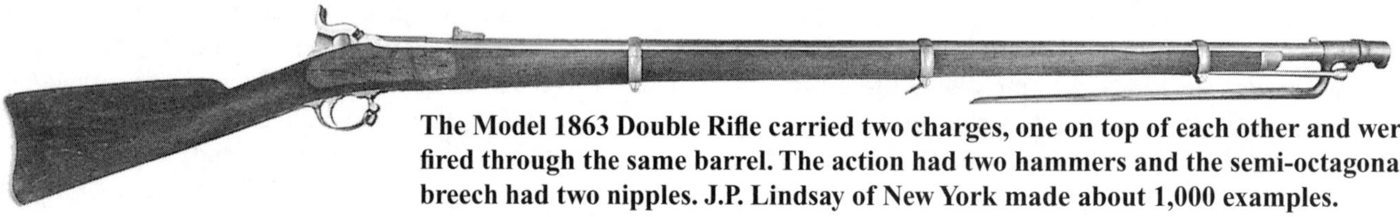

The Model 1863 Double Rifle carried two charges, one on top of each other and were fired through the same barrel. The action had two hammers and the semi-octagonal breech had two nipples. J.P. Lindsay of New York made about 1,000 examples.

J.C. Devine Inc.

Rifled Musket, Model 1863, Double, .58 caliber, 41-1/8" barrel, excellent bore, metal is still in the white, has not been cleaned, shows a little tarnish, fine rust, and grime that should clean without a trace. Sharp markings on metal, stock sanded and stripped of finish, shows handling dings and dents, two legible, "ADK," cartouches, correct ramrod and bayonet, very-good overall condition. **2,000.00**

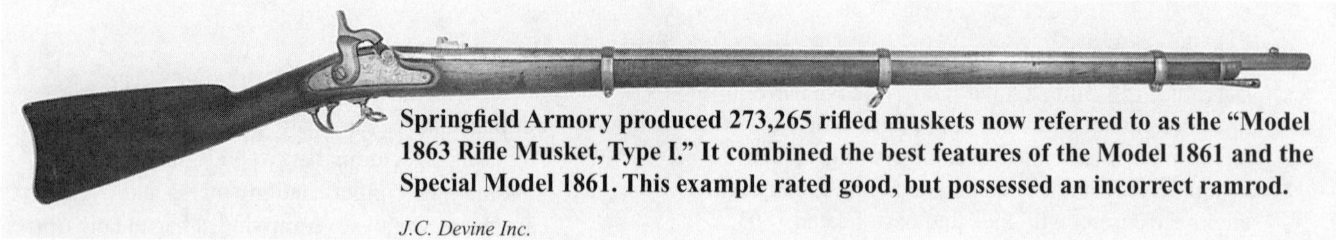

Springfield Armory produced 273,265 rifled muskets now referred to as the "Model 1863 Rifle Musket, Type I." It combined the best features of the Model 1861 and the Special Model 1861. This example rated good, but possessed an incorrect ramrod.

J.C. Devine Inc.

Rifled Musket, Model 1863, Type I

No serial no., .58 caliber, 40" round barrel, good bore, manufactured in 1863, correct two-leaf sight and barrel, lock dated 1863. No marks show on wood, all metal is gray with brown spotting and appears to have had an old cleaning. Split barrel bands with no retaining springs. Overall condition is good with an incorrect ramrod. **700.00**

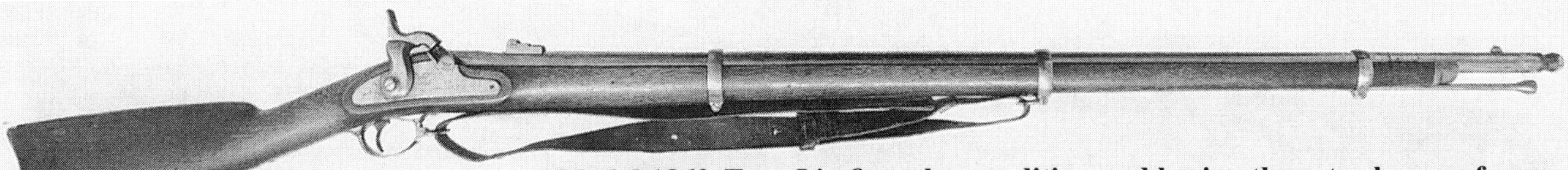

Model 1863, Type I in fine-plus condition and having the extra bonus of an owner's initials carved into the buttplate.

J.C. Devine Inc.

Made by Springfield Armory, .58 caliber, 40" round barrel, excellent bore, 1863-dated on lock and breech. All metal is bright including exterior of the lockplate with an old layer of dried grease or lacquer, all metal markings are sharp, no pitting. The stock has good edges, two clear inspector's cartouches, "W.T.T.," and, "E.S.A.," only normal light handling scratches and a shallow imprint of a vise jaw forward of the lock. With the original tulip-head ramrod, tompion, and an issue leather sling in sound condition. The buttplate has the initials "W.S." neatly formed with small punch dots, the sling has a partially legible name scratched into the surface. Fine-plus condition. **2,400.00**

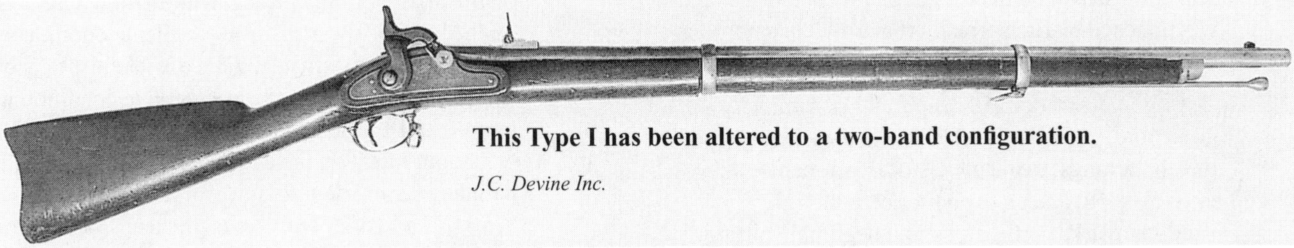

This Type I has been altered to a two-band configuration.

J.C. Devine Inc.

This has been altered to two-band style with a 32" long barrel, fine bore, lock dated 1864, all metal markings are clear. The barrel is gray with light surface rust, the stock has been refinished with a legible, "E.S.A.," cartouche and a partially legible second cartouche, small chips and dings. Stock has a rack number stamped onto an aluminum washer on the left side opposite the lock, tulip-head ramrod, very good. **350.00**

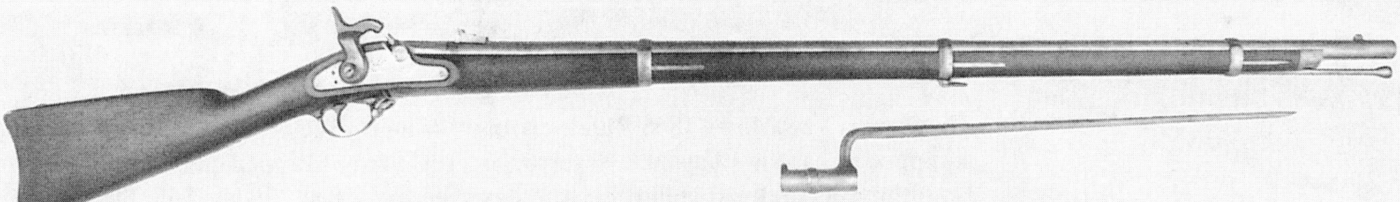

Model 1863 Type IIs are identical to Type Is except that they will bear lock dates of 1864 or 1865, have a single leaf rear sight, solid barrel bands held in place by flat springs, tulip or knurled and slotted ramrods, rounded cone shoulders, and some bluing eliminated. The Springfield armory produced 255,040 Type IIs.

J.C. Devine Inc.

Rifled Musket, Model 1863, Type II

58 caliber, 40" barrel, very good bore, lockplate marked, 1864-dated "US/SPRINGFIELD," the breech with an 1864 date and "V/P(eagle head)" proof marks. Light gray patina on all the iron, sharp markings, a couple of patches of very faint nipple pitting on the muzzle, the hammer with some mottled case colors remaining. Stock shows relatively few light handling marks and a paint splatter on an old refinish with two legible inspector's cartouches. Overall condition is very good, very nice looking Civil War musket, complete with correct ramrod. **1,500.00**

.58 caliber, 40" barrel, bright bore, strong rifling with a couple of rings. 1864-dated lock and breech, sharp markings. The stock has a small piece of wood replaced at the toe, nicely refinished, legible, "E.S.A.," cartouche, and an only partially legible second cartouche. The bands and band springs are incorrect, the ramrod has been repaired. The buttplate has an extra hole, good-looking musket with clean gray barrel and lock, only minor marks on the wood. **600.00**

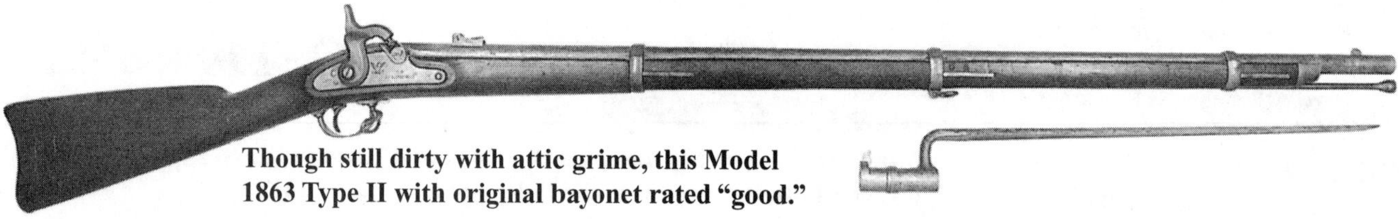

Though still dirty with attic grime, this Model 1863 Type II with original bayonet rated "good."

J.C. Devine Inc.

A really outstanding condition example, but one assembled out of parts on Bannerman's Island. Stock is superb with crisp edges and vivid cartouches including the "ESA" mark, it has the retaining springs for the barrel bands. The lock is near mint with hints of case color and date of 1863, the barrel has crisp markings "1864" and "VP" and an eagle's head (the bore has been reamed out... no rifling). The rear sling swivel on the trigger guard is incorrect and was attached by Bannerman's that way. The ramrod is a homemade device of no consequence. **895.00**

By Springfield Armory, .58 caliber, 40" barrel, very good bore, 1864-dated on lock and barrel, very good metal markings, two legible stock cartouches, dirty musket, should clean to about fine with light handling marks on the stock and negligible pitting. Complete with the original ramrod and original bayonet, good condition. **1,900.00**

No serial no., .58 caliber, 30" barrel, dark bore, manufactured in 1864, standard musket modified to cadet length and refinished. Metal mostly gray with dark overall freckling, incorrect trapdoor cleaning rod is present, good condition overall. **225.00**

Percussion-rifled musket by Springfield Armory, .58 caliber, 40" barrel, very good bore may clean to fine, 1863-dated lock, 1865-dated breech, steel gray patina on metal, minor faint pitting, with shallow vise marks on the breech. The stock is in excellent condition with sharp edges and only negligible tiny blemishes, stock was never marked by an inspector. Fine condition with ramrod and a bayonet in good condition. **900.00**

Very smooth metal on the entire musket, no pitting. The patina is semi-bright to gray, barrel is marked, "1864," and, "VP," with the eagle head, lockplate is crisp and marked, "U.S./SPRINGFIELD," and dated, "1864." A very fine walnut stock, all wood lines are very sharp, two crisp cartouches, light original blue on the sight and nipple, very fine bright bore, original ramrod present. **2,595.00**

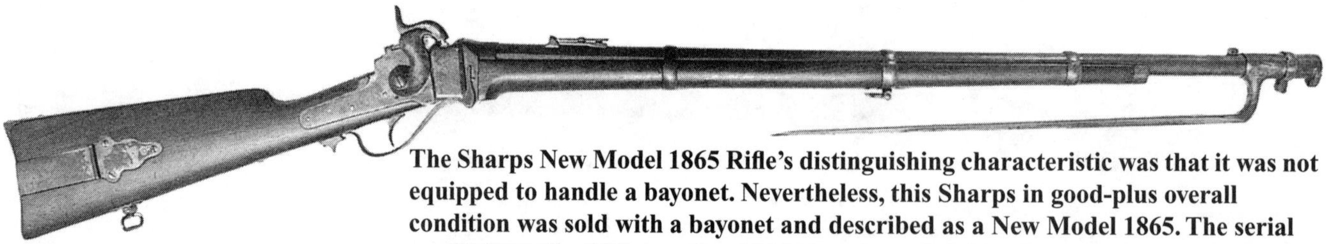

The Sharps New Model 1865 Rifle's distinguishing characteristic was that it was not equipped to handle a bayonet. Nevertheless, this Sharps in good-plus overall condition was sold with a bayonet and described as a New Model 1865. The serial no, C30287 (the "C" denoting 100,000 and not "carbine") would place this weapon in the New Model 1863 series, making it one of 6,000 made to handle a socket bayonet.

J.C. Devine Inc.

Rifle, New Model 1865, Sharps, serial no. C30287, .52 caliber, 30" barrel, very good bore. This rifle has a single trigger and an iron patchbox, clear markings on lock and frame, legible barrel markings. The frame and lock are mottled-gray with patches of faint pitting. The barrel has a dark patina with light corrosion, some original blue visible in protected areas and at the muzzle where the bayonet was affixed. The forend has a surface ship at the rear, the butt has one legible cartouche and a trace of the second. Both stocks show very few light handling marks and have had a little oil added through the years. The nipple is a replacement, good-plus overall with correct unmarked socket bayonet that has remnants of nickel plating. **2,500.00**

Rifle, Greene, .54 caliber percussion, under hammer, bolt-action weapon. The first bolt-action long arm that the U.S. military adopted. Doomed by its component ammunition and a silly, unworkable underhammer. The arm still had some very forward-looking ideas with a streamlined look and breech-loading bolt and gas seals. Brightly blued barrel retains 90-95% original finish. Bottom two bands retain 90-95% brilliant charcoal blue. Top band was held and sweat probably rubbed most of the blue off. Hammer retains 70-80% vivid case color hardening, excellent oval bore and mechanics, fine solid stock with typical storage dings on butt. Complete except for a replacement ramrod. **2,650.00**

Rifle, C.B. Holden, serial no. 142, .44 rimfire caliber, 24" octagon barrel, good bore. Less than 200 of these open frame rifles were made from 1862 to as late as the early 1870s. Barrel shorter than standard length, but appears to have been made this way. The barrel is marked on top, "HOLDEN'S PATENT/APRIL 1862." All of the metal has dark gray patina, the walnut stocks show normal handling marks on an old refinish and have a 2" long grain crack on the left side of the forend. This rifle (with a unique action) was made by a former employee of Frank Wesson, and it is easy to see some similarity in the rifle's lines. Good-plus condition. 300.00

Rifle, Joslyn, produced by Springfield, serial no. 863, .50-.60-.450 Joslyn rimfire caliber, 35-1/2" barrel, fair bore, manufactured in 1864. This Joslyn breech-loading rifle has dark freckling overall, which has turned to moderate pitting with the heaviest pitting on the breechpiece, hammer, and lockplate. The stock has an added oil finish over many small handling marks and blemishes. Included with the rifle are a modern leather sling and a non-matching socket type bayonet. Fine overall condition. 550.00

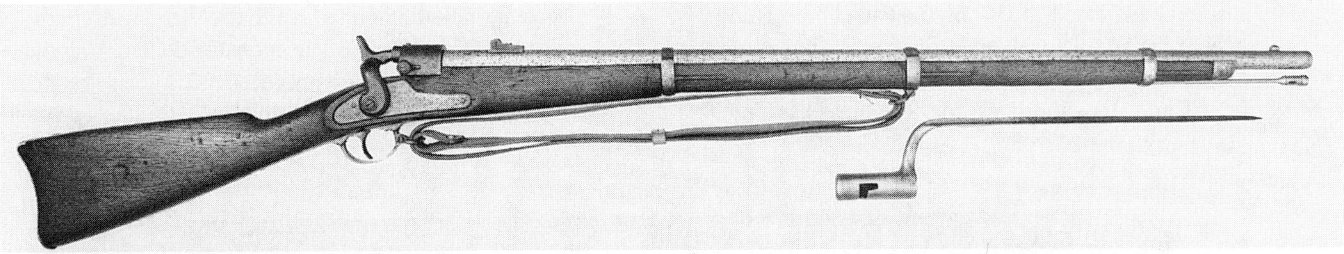

In early 1865, the Joslyn Firearms Company delivered their carbine actions to the Springfield Armory. There, gunsmiths fitted them to 3,007 infantry rifles that were chambered to accept the Joslyn 50-60-450 rimfire cartridge.

J.C. Devine Inc.

Rifled Musket, P.S. Justice, overall very good condition being 100% original, complete, and mechanically perfect. Metal is all clean steel color and free from rust or pitting except for some moderate barrel pitting between the front and middle bands. Lock is nice, "P.S. Justice PHILAd," marking. Barrrel has same stamp and is .69 caliber, rifled. Stock has great color and good edges showing just honest handling age and use. Has the early "stepped" 1855-1861-style rear sight, and double curve-style trigger guard. These guns were made from refurbished 1816 parts and issued almost exclusively to Pennsylvania troops during the Civil War, very nice example, with a good look. There are numerous variations on these Justice rifles and muskets, this is one of the more scarce and desirable with the brass furniture (most are found with iron in this pattern). 1,595.00

Rifle, Whitney-Enfield, very rare Whitney "Enfield" pattern musket, circa 1861, that has the odd .69-barrel with pewter nose cap, and is marked "E. Whitney" on lock. Has very nice wood and a totally attic-brown patina overall. One of the models rejected by the U.S. Government for "good and serviceable arms" that Whitney promptly sold on the open market, many of which ended up in the hands of Southern troops. This one is missing the hammer screw and has some initials carved in the buttstock. 975.00

Rifle, Maynard, First Model, no serial no., .50 caliber, 26" round barrel, octagonal at the breech, poor bore. This breech-loading rifle has the Maynard tape primer, factory barrel sights, factory long-leaf tang sight, iron patchbox. Made without a sling swivel, but one has been added by notching the stock under the lower tang. The frame case colors have turned to dark mottled patina, the barrel is a dark blue/black, scattered light pitting and rust freckling. The hammer will not engage, we suspect the action is gummed up with dirt and grease. The stock shows relatively few handling marks, and has a few small paint spots. Many of these were southern state purchases, this is likely one of them. Came from an old Texas collection, very-good overall condition. 4,200.00

"I was never a strong robust boy, and having only past my 16th birthday about four months when I went into service, it required just a little more physical strength than I possessed to handle a big old smooth bore mussel loading musket."

— Kingman Porter Moore
3rd Battalion of Georgia Volunteers

Import Muskets and Rifles

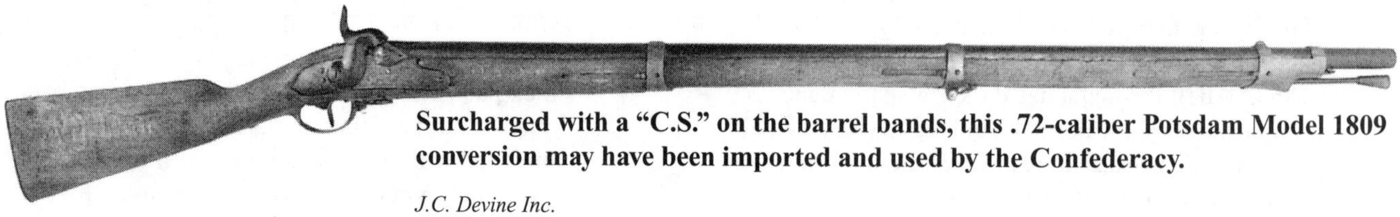

Surcharged with a "C.S." on the barrel bands, this .72-caliber Potsdam Model 1809 conversion may have been imported and used by the Confederacy.

J.C. Devine Inc.

Musket, Model 1809, Conversion

.72 caliber, smoothbore, 41-1/2" round barrel. *Potsdam* marked lock, dated "1830" on the barrel breech and heel of the buttplate, all brass furniture. All the iron has a dark patina with the barrel having pitting at the breech and along the stock line. The brass has a nice mustard-brown patina. All the metal markings are clear, including on the rear barrel band the letters "C.S." These were unquestionably done during the period of use and are not recent additions. The stock is sound and shows little finish. **900.00**

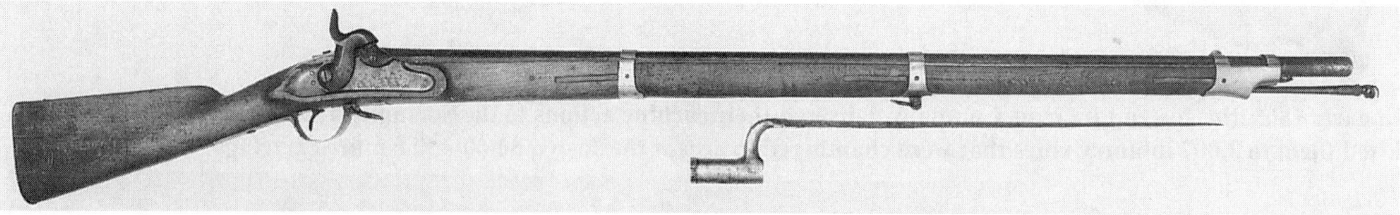

In fair condition, this Model 1809 Potsdam conversion is roughly .75 caliber, though that could simply be from metal depletion in barrel. Originally, the Model 1809 was chambered to fire a .71 caliber ball.

J.C. Devine Inc.

No serial no., .75 caliber, 41" barrel, dark bore, manufactured in 1819 in Potsdam. This musket (likely one of thousands imported during the Civil War) has dark metal, pitted heavily around the nipple. Brass furniture has been cleaned, stock has an added finish and reduced comb, but is still in good condition. A correct socket bayonet in poor condition fitted. Fair overall condition. **300.00**

German Potsdam Model 1809 converted to percussion. This is approximately .70 caliber. The lockplate is marked, "DANZIG 1835," and has a crown over the Danzig name. The wood is in very good condition, with some buttstock markings. All brass fittings are present as well as the sling swivels. The barrel has some pitting near the end, but not too bad. There are markings on the barrel with the rear sight present. The ramrod is present as well., the mechanics work fine............ **650.00**

Rifled Musket, Model 1815, Conversion, .69-caliber rifled percussion conversion of a French standard military long arm, 42-1/2" round barrel with French proofs and date, "1820." Good bore with shallow rifling, iron ramrod cupped for the new pointed projectile. No sights except for the standard brass blade on the top band. Bayonet lug mounted under the muzzle. Barrel was brown lacquered and still retains 20-25% of this fragile finish. Lock is blank with a blackish patina. Large, proofed percussion hammer. Rifle retains both iron sling swivels. Fine iron furniture with 20-25% original armory brown finish as well. Fine oil finished stock with one or two drying cracks at the lock mortise. **950.00**

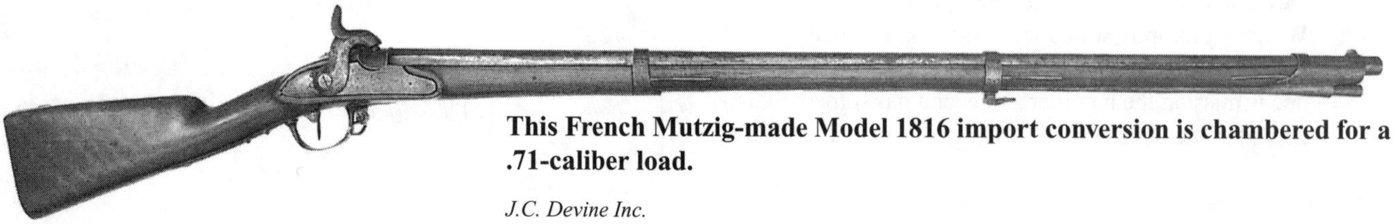

This French Mutzig-made Model 1816 import conversion is chambered for a .71-caliber load.

J.C. Devine Inc.

Musket, Model 1816, Conversion, no serial no., .71 caliber, 41" smoothbore barrel, dark bore. This Mutzig-made musket has a massive bolster conversion with slightly shortened barrel. All metal has a dark-brown patina with pitting around the breech. The stock has a dished-out comb and many small handling marks under an added finish. It is likely that this musket was imported during the Civil War. Fair overall condition. **300.00**

Musket, Model 1842, Conversion, .71-caliber smoothbore French military Musket with right barrel with crisp proofs and "Mdle 1848" at the tang and "1844" manufacture date at the bolster. Bright smooth back action lock marked, "Mre Rle/de St. Etienne." Complete, bright iron furniture with original sling swivels and ramrod. Excellent stock with sharp French manufacturing marks at the right butt. Smooth bore, excellent mechanics. ... **1,350.00**

Rifled Musket, Model 1816, Conversion, maybe a Model 1816 French pattern. It is roughly the same as the U.S. 1816 conversions. Very good to fine condition, metal surfaces are smooth steel with light-brown patina. The barrel is marked "1818." The lock has a tiny proof mark incorporating a cipher, script "R," and numeral "17." This has a long-range rear sight (elevation slide missing). The stock has good edges and shows only honest use (no abuse). Carved into the back of the buttstock is "M.S." Stamped into the buttstock are "AR 1840." "NR," and two other script cartouches. This comes with a modern U.S. 1816 pattern ramrod. **750.00**

Musket, Model 1842, classic back-action lock French 42, three-band infantry musket in overall very good condition being 100% original and complete (except for the missing ramrod), with great color, nice stock, and great patina. **650.00**

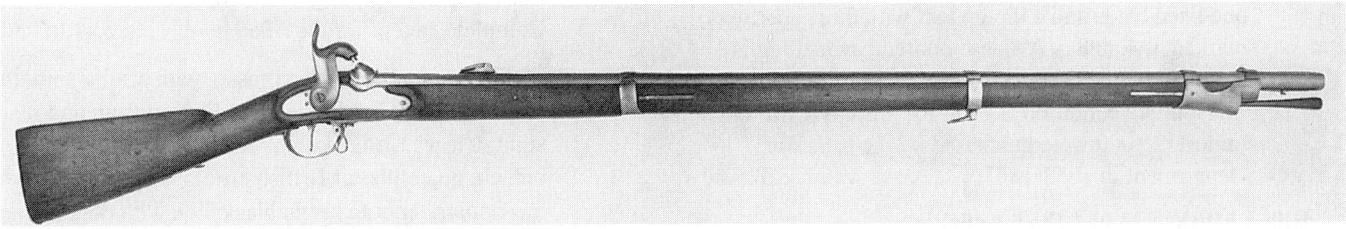

The Austrian Model 1842 was originally developed as a "tubelock" firearm. Those imported to the United States to meet the demands of suppliers were altered to percussion as is this one.

J.C. Devine Inc.

Rifled Musket, Model 1842, Conversion, Austrian Model 1842, .69 caliber, 42-1/2" barrel is smooth bored and has a long-range rear site, metal cleaned to bright with scattered fine pitting. The refinished stock shows relatively few handling marks. Good condition with replacement ramrod. **800.00**

Musket, Model 1848, Conversion, .71-caliber smoothbore French military musket. Thousands of these were imported during our Civil War. Bright barrel with crisp proofs and "Mdle 1848" at the tang and "1844" manufacture date at the bolster. Bright smooth back action lock marked, "Mre Rle/de St. Etienne." Complete, bright iron furniture with original sling swivels and ramrod. Excellent stock with sharp French manufacturing marks at the right butt. Bright, smooth bore and excellent mechanics. **1,350.00**

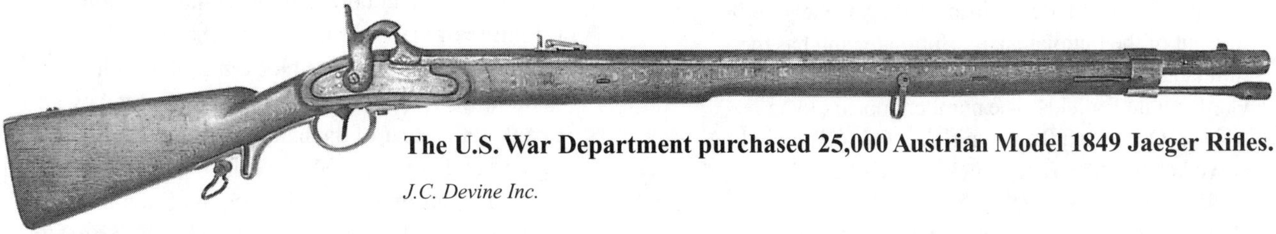

The U.S. War Department purchased 25,000 Austrian Model 1849 Jaeger Rifles.

J.C. Devine Inc.

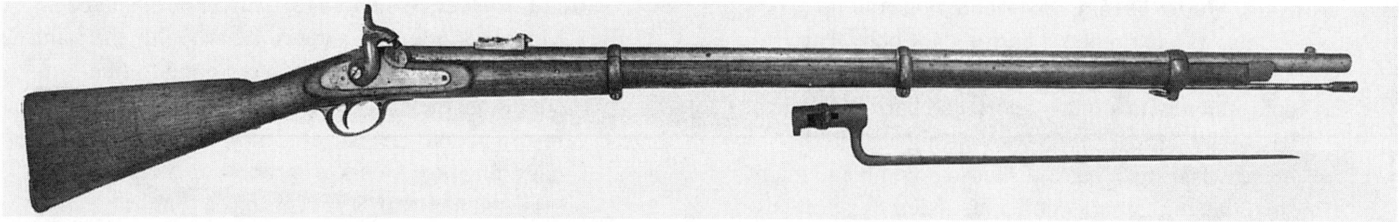

During the early months of the war, the United States purchased 428,000 Enfield Muskets. By the end of 1862, the Confederacy had taken delivery of nearly 400,000. This Model 1853, or "P1853" as it was known to the British, is an example of those weapons purchased early in the war.

J.C. Devine Inc.

Rifled Musket, Model 1849, Austrian Jaeger with no serial no., .71 caliber, 33" octagon to round barrel, fair bore. Manufactured circa 1850. A large caliber rifle/musket showing no marks other than the number 70 punched into the trigger guard and lock bolt plate. All furniture is brass with steel sling swivels, ramrod and barrel band. The barrel is also fastened to the beech stock with a rear wedge. The cheek rest is for a right-hand shooter. The sight is a two-leaf affair with one fixed blade and a flip-up leaf with three apertures marked 3, 4, and 5. A side-mounted bayonet lug is mounted on the barrel 2 7/8 inches from the muzzle. The antique condition is good for this Civil War era import. 25,000 were purchased by the U.S. War Department in 1862-1863. . . . . **325.00**

Rifled Musket, Model 1853, Enfield

.577 caliber, 39" barrel, rifled bore is dark, lockplate is marked with a crown and "1862/TOWER." The gun is dirty, should clean to good plus. Complete with correct ramrod and a U.S. socket bayonet that does not fit. **800.00**

.577-caliber British manufactured and Confederate-imported percussion-rifled musket. Smooth plum barrel with light salt and pepper pitting around bolster. Clear Birmingham proofs along with the "25-25" bore-size markings. Smooth blackish lock engraved with a crown to the hammer's rear and "1862/Tower" under the bolster. Fine mechanics, dark, but very good bore. Mellow brass trigger guard, buttplate, and stock cap. Iron bands and original ramrod, complete with both sling swivels. Smooth oil- fine condition finished stock, very slight burnout for 1/8" in front of bolster, "JS"/anchor, Confederate inspector's cartouche right in front of the buttplate tang. Buttplate tang has the remnants of the lot number so often found on Confederate Enfields. The number appears to be "4212." On the left flat the initials, "C.C.C." are lightly carved above "Co. B." A quick search of *The Roster of Confederate Soldiers 1861-65* edited by Janet B. Hewett, shows only one Confederate soldier with those initials in a Company B was Second Sergeant C.C. Camp, Company B, 26th Alabama Infantry. Very-good condition. **4,250.00**

.577-caliber British manufactured weapon, bored smooth. Fine dark patina on metal, light to moderate pitting around bolster. Clear proofs and "24-24" caliber markings. Crown and "Tower/1862" crisply marked on the lock. No British military markings, so this is most probably one that was brought in to the U.S. during our Civil War. Complete with sling swivels, ramrod, and brass-chained nipple protector. Mellow brass trigger guard, buttplate, and stock cap. Complete except for the rifled bore. **1,050.00**

.58-caliber percussion-rifled musket with bright, smooth plum 39" barrel and a standard Enfield front and rear sight. Clear "EL/G" Liege proof in oval at left breech, no caliber or British proofs. Fine bore and mechanics, smooth bright black lock with double line border engraving, and no other markings. Hammer is engraved in the typical Enfield style. Iron mounts with original sling swivels and ramrod. Brass buttplate and trigger guard have turned almost black or have a thin blackish paint applied to them. Fine stock has wonderful edges along the flats, barrel channel and ramrod channel. Stock is unmarked except for a script inspector's marking on the right butt. **1,950.00**

.58-caliber percussion musket manufactured under contract by J.P. Moore & Sons of New York City. Moore manufactured these arms from a mixture of imported and domestic parts. Fine 39" barrel has English Proofs and "25-25" bore diameter at left breech. Enfield-style rear sight graduated to 400 yards. Excellent bore and mechanics, barrel is a mixture of original blue and bright, smooth plum patina. Crisp 1863-dated lock in center with a federal shield with "M" in the top half surmounted by an eagle to the rear of the hammer. Mellow brass trigger guard and buttplate. Missing the top sling swivel, but has the bottom one and the original Enfield-style ramrod. Excellent dark oil-finished walnut stock with sharp edges around the lock and both barrel and ramrod channel. Small "V" viewing cartouches at the left flat and behind the trigger guard. **3,500.00**

This close-up of a Confederate-imported Enfield shows the large crown stamping found on the lockplate of the English weapon.

Battleground Antiques

Confederate imported English Tower Enfield Rifled Musket, .577 caliber, and exceptionally brown example with clear maker and inspector marks in wood and metal. Complete throughout with rare Sinclair Hamilton importer mark as well as the Isaac Campbell proof cartouche. ... **2,450.00**

Extremely rare .577 Confederate Sinclair-Hamilton import three-band Enfield Rifle complete with sling, bayonet, tompion, and nipple protector with chain. Sinclair, Hamilton and Company imported Enfield muskets through Wilmington, north Carolina, for the Confederacy. The musket is marked "SH" over "C" behind the trigger guard. The markings have been cleaned out with a needle to make them more visible. This musket is out of a central North Carolina estate. The metal has a smooth brown uncleaned patina with lockplate markings of "1861 Tower." The wood is pretty with normal small marks and dings from use. The stock has the soldier's initials "O.P.L." and name "Betty" carved into the left-hand side...... **2,850.00**

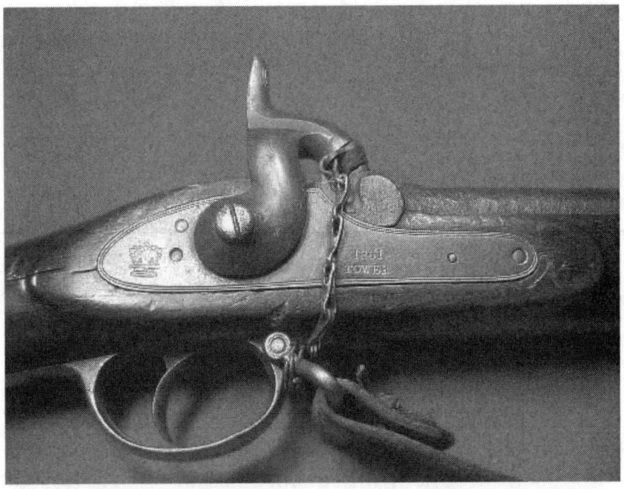

Just behind the trigger guard are the markings of "SH" over a "C" indicating that this Enfield was imported by Sinclair, Hamilton and Company for the Confederacy.

Middle Tennessee Relics

Imported and fully marked Enfield Rifled Musket. Isaac & Campbell marked sling, engraved lot number on buttplate, "J.S." anchor cartouche, and dated 1862, this weapon even has the matching engraved ramrod! Overall shows light use and honest wear. This is one of the second lot of 10,000 Enfield Rifled Muskets purchased by Caleb Huse for the Confederacy under direct Navy contract. **12,500.00**

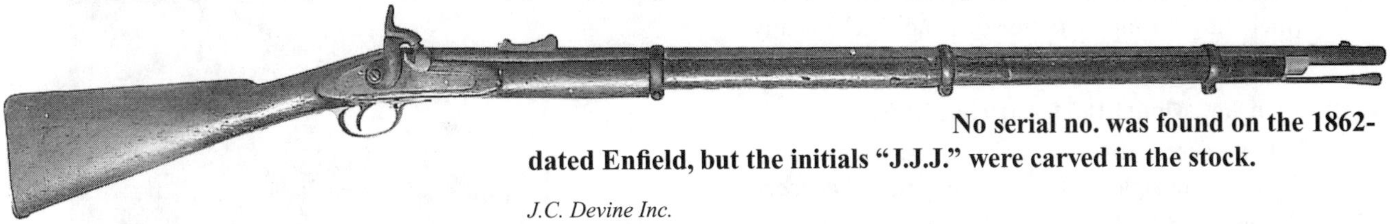

No serial no. was found on the 1862-dated Enfield, but the initials "J.J.J." were carved in the stock.

J.C. Devine Inc.

Lock marked, "1862/Tower," with a crown at the rear. No serial no.. .577 caliber, 39" barrel, poor bore. The rear sight is missing its leaf. Dark patina with light pitting on lock and barrel, markings are clear. The brass buttplate and trigger guard have a light patina. The stock shows heavy wear, dings, and an old refinish. In front of the trigger guard are 1/2" carved initials "J.J.J." There is an age crack at the rear lock screw escutcheon. Musket is in fair condition with period replacement iron ramrod. **600.00**

Original Enfield in overall good condition. Lock is marked, "Tower 1863," barrel has proper proof marks "25-25" (with part of it obliterated). Metal is cleaned steel being somewhat over cleaned. The stock is very nice with good lines and shows only honest wear no abuse, "Isaac Hollis & Co:" stamped into the bottom of the butt, stamped into stock ahead of the buttplate is an anchor over an "S", and there is a smaller stamp behind the trigger guard tang which may be the, "JS"/ anchor mark (usually associated with southern import guns). It is complete with both swivels, and the original rear sight. The ramrod is a perfect replacement, crisp lock action. The bore is of no consequence, there are a couple screws that appear to be replaced (tang screw, buttplate screw). ... **750.00**

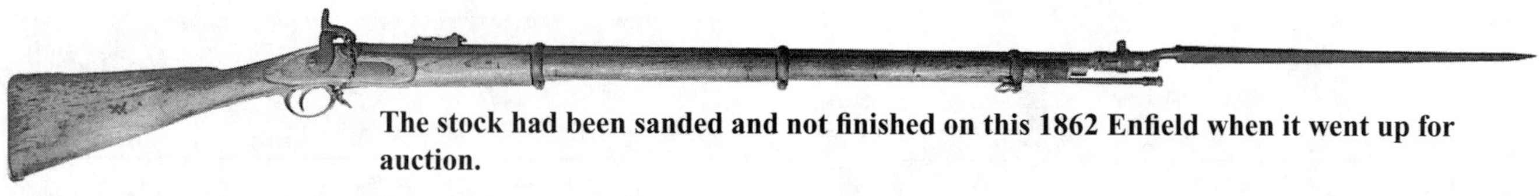

The stock had been sanded and not finished on this 1862 Enfield when it went up for auction.

J.C. Devine Inc.

Smooth plum barrel with light to moderate pitting around nipple and bolster. Crisp Birmingham proofs at the left breech. No caliber or bore markings. Smooth black lock simply marked "Barnett/London." Very good bore and mechanics, original iron Enfield ramrod and sling swivels. Mellow brass trigger guard and buttplate. Fine oil-finished stock with very fine edges around the flats, and both ramrod and barrel channels, no British martial markings. **1,650.00**

Tower-marked 1853 Enfield Pattern Musket, .577 caliber, 39" barrel, dark bore. Manufactured in 1862. This musket is dark brown overall with light pinprick pitting throughout. The socket bayonet has rusted tight to the muzzle. The stock has been sanded and is dry without any wood finish at present. Fair condition overall. **750.00**

Truly handsome in all respects with the highest degree of appeal in the color and lines. The stock has crisp, sharp edges with vivid Birmingham Small Arms. Trade circular stamp in the butt. The wood color is exquisite. The metal is a superb homogeneous mixture of blue and plum with sharp import proof marks of "25-25," outstanding bore. The lock has generous hints of case color and crisp 1863 date, tower, and crown. It is 100% original, complete (including the nipple protector), and mechanically perfect. **1,695.00**

Rifled Musket, Model 1854, Austrian Lorenz

.54-caliber percussion Austrian arm, really typical Confederate-style Lorenz with the original caliber, simple block post rear sight, and raised cheek rest. Rifle is in outstanding condition, overall a smooth, dark black patina. Crisp proofs and date on barrel flat, "859" match those on the lock, every part is numbered and inspected alike. Excellent bore and mechanics, original sling swivels. The ramrod is brass tipped and appears period, but it is not one usually associated with Lorenz Rifles. The stock is superb, like new and inspected everywhere. **1,650.00**

.58-caliber percussion Austrian military rifle has cleaned metal, a good bore and mechanics. Repro leaf style rear sight, missing ramrod, but otherwise complete. **750.00**

.58-caliber percussion Austrian military rifle, one of the hundreds of thousands imported for both sides during our Civil War. Metal has been cleaned back to bright. Reproduction Grislyn flip-up leaf-style rear sight, "859," date on lock. Original sling swivels, missing ramrod. Good sound stock with the large cheek rest at left, good bore and mechanics. **795.00**

The two-banded Enfield Rifle, known to the English as the P-56, was equipped to handle a saber bayonet.

Sharpsburg Arsenal

Rifle, Model 1856, Enfield, P-56, 1861 tower with sharp barrel proof marks. Lock marked, "Tower 1861." Barrel has nice plum patina with only very minor breech pitting, original chain and nipple protector. Wood is in very good condition, but appears to have been lightly cleaned. Rear sling swivel is missing screw, bore is average. **2,495.00**

Rifled Musket, Model 1858, looks very much like an Austrian Lorenz, but this 1858 Bavarian has interesting patent breech. Metal is smooth with overall light-brown patina. The stock is the reddish blonde wood just like on the Lorenz. Good edges, various parts are marked with "1675" assembly or inventory number. Interestingly, this has a U.S. Springfield two-leaf rear sight that has been with this gun. This is complete with the tulip-tipped ramrod drilled with a hole for cleaning rag. Overall very good condition, only defect is a piece of wood knocked out behind the tang, it has been reglued in place. Front sight has had a taller silver blade added presumably by a shooter. **595.00**

Rifle, Model 1858, Enfield

.577 caliber manufactured between 1857-1860. Barrel retains 98% original blue with sharp markings. All metal parts have sharp markings, bore is very good. Walnut wood stock is in very good condition with minor handling marks, stock and barrel both marked "VII." This rifle was probably one of the arms purchased early in the war by Major Huse and shipped to the south. **3,995.00**

Overall "very good" condition and 100% original and complete with the exception of the bayonet lug that was removed long ago. The steel parts are all gun-metal gray color with strong markings. The lock is stamped "1861 Tower" and has a crown. The barrel has the British "25-25" marking indicating manufacture for shipment to North America in .577 caliber. The wood is a deep-brown English walnut with excellent lines and free from any major nicks or bruises. This gun is 100% steel mounted including the buttplate, trigger guard, and nose cap. It has the 1,000-yard long-range rear sight firmly in place, and still retains its original ramrod. Both sling swivels are present. **950.00**

This is the classic Belgian Enfield patterned directly from the British two-band infantry rifle. The metal is wonderful with smooth light-brown age patina, and the stock is excellent with great line and super color, and no bangs or bruises of consequence. The lock is marked only with a "DC" and anchor stamp. The barrel has the well-known Liege proof mark at the breech. The buttplate, and trigger guard are brass with a beautiful untouched age patina, and the trigger guard is stamped with the "DC" and anchor mark. **550.00**

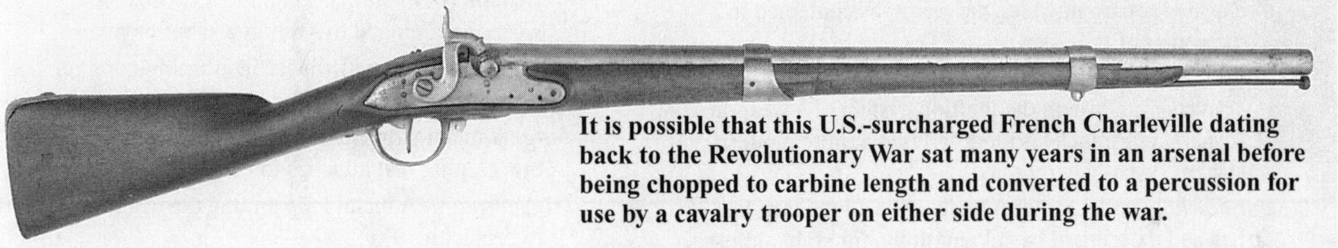

It is possible that this U.S.-surcharged French Charleville dating back to the Revolutionary War sat many years in an arsenal before being chopped to carbine length and converted to a percussion for use by a cavalry trooper on either side during the war.

J.C. Devine Inc.

Musket, Charleville, Conversion, .69-caliber "1771" marked barrel tang, "US" surcharged at rear of lock and on top of the breech. The barrel is cut to 27-3/4", and the stock altered to two-band-style with band springs removed and their recesses filled. Drum and nipple conversion, all metal cleaned to gray with scattered pitting. The stock is missing several large splinters at the barrel channel, fair-plus condition. **850.00**

Rifle, Augustin Pattern

48" long rifle, all metal has deep, rust-brown patina with integral pitting. The wood is quite nice. Buttplate and trigger guard are brass with deep, rich patina. Mechanically perfect and very displayable. Just lacks the rear sight and ramrod (a rod is included, but not the right one). **395.00**

This one is in a really nice condition, and has the bayonet. Overall very good condition with clean steel and attractive blonde wood as seen on the Lorenz Rifles. This one has the original ramrod with bulbous tulip-head drilled with hole to accept a cleaning rag. The brass buttplate and trigger guard are "mellow yellow" brass. Various proofs and assembly marks are present on various parts. This comes with the original long saber blade socket bayonet. The rear sight has been modified by filling in the dovetail and fashioning a fine v-notch. **695.00**

"The recruits were furnished with a lot of Belgian muskets with a kind of saber bayonet. They were a short gun with a caliber which made up in 'width' what the gun lacked in 'length' and in kicking proclivities. They were as energetic as the most vicious army mule."

— John H. Stearns
Company K, 5th Kansas Cavalry

Musket and Rifle Terminology

Armory brown: A term used today to describe a soft even discoloring of a weapon's metal. Originally, bright metal was treated at the arsenals with a protective coating of brown lacquer.

Armory: The place where firearms are built.

Arsenal: A government location where weapons are stored. May also contain an armory where weapons are built.

Barrel band: A metal band, either fixed or adjustable, around the for end of a gun that holds the barrel to the stock.

Breechloader: A long arm that is loaded from the area nearest the ignition system, rather than down the muzzle of the weapon. Most often involves a premade cartridge.

Cap: Short for "percussion cap," the primer that when placed on the nipple and struck with the hammer, provides the fire to ignite the gunpowder charge.

Cartridge: A case usually made of paper for muzzleloaders and of copper, brass, or combustible paper for breechloaders that contains the powder charge, bullet, and sometimes, the primer.

Centerfire: A case in which the primer is contained in the center of the base.

Conversion: In terms of Civil War firearms, a conversion is where the ignition system of a weapon (usually a flintlock) is modified into a more modern system (usually percussion).

Cut-down: A collector term to describe a long arm that has had its original barrel length modified. In almost every case, a cut-down will not be worth as much as an original full-length weapon.

Flintlock: A firing mechanism used primarily on martial firearms prior about 1848. It uses a shower of sparks created when a piece of flint strikes a steel frizzen to ignite a priming charge, which in turn ignites the main powder charge.

Hammer: The part of a gun's mechanism that, after being cocked, flies (usually) forward to strike the percussion cap or primer, thus, firing the gun.

Import: In Civil War terms, any weapon not produced in a northern or southern armory.

Lock: The firing mechanism of a muzzle-loading firearm.

Musket: A muzzle-loading, smooth-bore long arm that is equipped to support a bayonet.

Nipple: A small metal tube extending through the breech of a percussion firearm also called the "cone."

Ramrod: A wood or metal rod used to force a bullet down the barrel of a muzzle-loading firearm.

Rifled musket: A muzzle-loading, rifled long arm that is equipped to support an angular bayonet.

Rifle: In terms of Civil War weaponry, a two-banded weapon (or of similar length to a two-banded weapon) equipped to support a saber bayonet.

Rimfire: A cartridge in which the priming compound is contained in the rim at the base of a cartridge.

Tang: A metal strip extending rearward from a the breech plug that attaches to the stock of the weapon.

Trigger guard: A metal loop around the trigger designed to protect it.

Also see: Bullets, Cartridges, and Projectiles, Groupings, Accoutrements, and Carbines.

Chapter 14

Personal Items

Looking at a Civil War dealer's list or perusing the Internet often leaves one with the impression that personal items carried or used during the Civil War abound and are available for minimal investment. That is only partially true. There are many items that were made or used during the time period of 1861-1865. That does not mean that a soldier used the item, or carried it in his knapsack.

This is a frustrating area to collect, and even more so, to describe. Many of the items that can be loosely tossed into this category rely on imagination and very little on documentation. Selling personal items, or "smalls," is a profitable business. Simple utilitarian antiques can often be found for a few dollars at an antiques show or flea market. With some wishful thinking and some clever writing, an average mid-nineteenth-century item can immediately become a soldier's item. Unfortunately, this wishful thinking is infectious, and soon, plenty of customers believe the romantic yarns spun by a dealer.

Playing cards from Belgium; matches out of Mexico; toothpaste jars from England—a lot of antiques are currently being imported that look period appropriate and are being sold as Civil War items. Again, it cannot be emphasized enough: Buyer Beware! If you are in the market for items typical of the period, or simply that look good, then you will have no shortage of available items to purchase. On the other hand, if you stick with items that have a known provenance linking them to a soldier, or the time period of 1861-1865, be prepared to pay for them. Personal items that were actually carried or used by a soldier are actually quite rare, because they were used. The items were, by their very intent, expendable and 150-year-survival was not the goal when these items were manufactured.

The best defense is patience and study. Limit yourself to known entities—items with a strong provenance or documented period use. Look over the items in this chapter. You will notice that the items that have a known association with a Civil War soldier sold for strong prices. The rest of the items are low-level collectibles. Resist the temptation to say or believe, "a soldier could have used it." Just saying it doesn't make it so. Visit museums and study books on utilitarian antiques to determine a sense of construction and use of items from the Civil War era.

Personal items might seem, at first, the easiest arena in which to begin collecting. It is, in fact, the most difficult. Because civilian-produced and used items followed no "regulation" pattern or order, the variety is endless. Notice the number of "folding mirrors" listed below. It's easy to say, "Sure! A soldier would have needed this to shave!" Yet, not one of them has a solid provenance linking them to a soldier. Are they Civil War? Who is to say?

To successfully collect in this area, a person must first familiarize himself with the material culture of mid-nineteenth-century United States. A lot of time and effort can be spent on studying decorative arts to hone the skill of recognizing a period-appropriate civilian ware. It is a lot easier to recognize a Model 1858 cartridge box or a Fifth Model Burnside carbine, than it is to determine whether a coffee pot or an ginger beer bottle dates to the Civil War.

Collecting Hints

Pros:

- Genuine articles identified to a soldier are a very immediate link to the soldier's life.
- Items with a strong, proven provenance are solid investments. The prices of these items keep going up.
- Collecting personal items allows a Civil War enthusiast to inject a bit of their own personality into the hobby by collecting items that appeal directly to themselves.

Availability ★★★★★
Price ★★★
Reproduction Alert ★★

Cons:

- Very few items with solid provenance have survived. Personal items that are identified as having belonged to a soldier are extremely rare. Those that do exist are often part of a larger grouping of items associated with the soldier further driving the price beyond a beginner's reach.
- This area is inundated with items represented as "Civil War" when, in fact, there is no provenance to support the claims.

Collecting Hints, cont.

Cons:

- Civil War experts are not usually experts in decorative arts. Therefore, a lot of items that look time appropriate are represented as typical of items from the Civil War era.
- Provenance for items is often "created" by a dealer looking to increase the value of a relatively common Civil War-era item. Many items that never had any association can suddenly become part of a group, or in the worst case, sprout markings that identify them to a soldier. In a rare instance, a dealer is known to have used an original soldier's stencil to mark a variety of personal items.
- Personal items do not follow any set of regulation designs or patterns so it is very difficult to clearly identify an item as having been made or used before or during the war.

Bottle, Ink, Gutta-percha, Shaffer Rosewood ink bottle with an 1858 patent date. **85.00**

Box, Pen Tip, made like a tintype case, measures 3" x 2", has great silk label inside which reads, "Palmer and Batchelders Extra Fine GOLD PENS 162 Washington St. Boston." A super personal item with great appeal . .**89.00**

Can, Sardine, dug in New Orleans, Louisiana, still has brass foil label, excellent condition. **45.00**

Candlesticks, complete set of two screw-apart, donut-shaped dishes with screw-on candle holders. When not in use, candle sockets unscrew and store inside of the dishes that screw together, looking like a brass donut, excellent condition. **195.00**

Cane, Wooden, a lovely example of a classic folk-art carving, obviously by the soldier himself as a souvenir record of his personal and regiment's history. Carved 1865 date, obviously the exact period that it was made, 35" overall, with the wood having acquired a lovely, mellow age patina. Upper section is carved in high relief with a primitive, yet very quaint depiction of bearded head wearing the standard wide-brim hat. Above that in large letters, "Cpl. David E. Jones/4th Oneida" (his regiment was known as the "4th Oneida Regiment"), also a large U.S. shield. The entire lower section below the carving of head is incise-carved in a wide, large spiral manner almost full length of cane with his regiment, "117 N.Y. Vol. F Co," with many corps insignias. Also carved in large letters in spiral fashion all battle honors of the regiment from, "DRURY'S BLUFF, COLD HARBOR, PETERSBURG, FORT FISHER." Quite likely made during the last days of service during their campaigns in North Carolina. **1,750.00**

Carpetbag, Identified

Officer's personal carpet bag Captain Samuel F. Willard, Company G, 14th Connecticut Infantry. Killed at Antietam on September 17, 1862. The 14th were deployed on the Roulette Farm, later moved to the Mumma Farm, and then moved again to the advance on Bloody Lane. Losses at Antietam—20 killed, 98 wounded, 48 missing. During the war the 14th suffered the greatest losses of all Connecticut regiments. This carpetbag is engraved with his name on the lock and has the original shipping labels on the bottom from when his effects were shipped home after his death. Records included. **1,500.00**

A large-size bag, 16" square with leather bottom and handles, brass lock and key with fancy stenciling on the flap lining, "J.J. Murphy Co. F 31st ME. Regt." Murphy was the Quartermaster Sergeant of the 31st Maine Infantry, excellent condition. **225.00**

Carpetbag

Belonged to, "D.M. Kelly Qtrmaster Serg't. 50th Reg't. Mass. Vols." (Stenciled inside the flap.) **275.00**

Traveling bag made from carpet. Lined with a linen material, it has remnants of leather handles. Brass plate 3-1/4" x 13/16" around the keyhole lock. The bag is 16-1/2" x 14", bottom is 16" x 5-1/2" and it has four brass button feet 7/8" each in size. **225.00**

Sold as an "eyeglass case," this pewter box is probably not that, but rather a simple snuff box, or even more accurately, a "pewter box." Whatever it is, the presentation inscription is what makes it special. Given to Lieutenant Ross Black by the men of the 50th Pennsylvania Infantry in August 1863, this box is a standout piece of personal goods.

N. Flayderman & Co., Inc.

Case, Eyeglasses, Presentation, quite beautifully made, 2-1/2" x 5" with hinged lid; 60 percent original silver finish remaining on the pewter box. Very beautifully engraved entirely filling upper and lower sides; large oval, fancy bordered panel in center inscribed in five fancy lines in the most professional manner, "PRESENTED TO LIEUT A. ROSS BLACK BY CO. B., 50'TH REGT. P.V.M. AUGUST 15, 1863." Original velvet covering inside shows normal aging and wear, intact. The Pennsylvania Volunteer Militia outfit was organized at Harrisburg July 1863, for the protection of Pennsylvania to repel Lee's invasion. It served until its mustering out, August 15 (the date of the inscription). .... **.375.00**

Officers enjoyed a bit of comfort when garrisoned. These two civilian chairs are typical of camp furniture that was available during and after the War.

N. Flayderman & Co., Inc.

Chairs, Folding, classic style seen in many Civil War photographs used by officers as a normal part of their personal field equipment. Especially nice as a matched pair and identified. Made of pine wood with original painted and dark-stained finish that has acquired a lovely old patina. Chairs fold very flat to a small 16" x 26" for easy portability; each weighs about 3 lbs. The top bar acts as a handle for easy carrying. A typical-type seat of red carpet-like material with a tan edging (worn threadbare, but very sound). Authentic stenciling in large black letters along top of each chair, "ROBINSON," has faded and has same patina as the painted finish to the chairs. Original maker markings neatly stamped on cross slat of each, "B. J. HARRISON CO./ARKVILLE, N.Y." Chairs found in upstate New York; although no documentary supporting evidence, suspect they were owned by Surgeon Joseph W. Robinson who served with the 141st and 179th New York Infantry; his home in upstate New York near Elmira. **550.00**

Nothing other than the description says this checkerboard is Civil War vintage, let alone used by a soldier. This is a very popular antique and is quite often forged. The dealer felt confident that this was indeed a mid-19th century game board.

Dale C. Anderson Co.

Checker Board, hugely popular items eagerly sought by folk-art collectors who have pushed the average price for these up to $750-$850. Seen in all Civil War camps and many were made by soldiers in the field. Most are made from scrap board with the checkered board painted on. 17-1/4" x 21". Made from a single board 17-1/4" w, with a border piece added to the narrow ends. Drying over the years has produced a few edge cracks making it seem that border pieces are on all sides, but a careful look shows it is all one board. The checkered area has squares in maroon red and dark tan. Everything has a wonderful mellow look, edges are smoothed by wear. There is a hole on one end to hang it from a nail. **495.00**

> **"In the fiercely raging conflict at the time, I had no time to look out for my haversack, and lost the little provision there was in it for sustaining the physical man. Indeed, in such times of carnage and sadness, none of us cared anything about eating."**
>
> ***— Kingman Porter Moore***
> ***Scogin's Battery, Georgia Light Artillery***

This chess set bears a nice prewar date and a couple of signatures.

Chess Set, hand-carved chess set, identified and dated to two different soldiers. On the inside of the box is the name John H. Kimball, Topsham, Maine, and date of 1849. On the under side of the lid is printed, "1846 Chess Box for N." Also printed in ink is the date 1860. There is also writing in lead pencil that is too faint to read. On the bottom of the box is the name "John H. Kimball" and "Washington D.C. 1846." Below that is the name (in different handwriting), "Denver A. Hawkins," and the date, "April 16, (the year is illegible)." These names and dates are all in period ink with some wear and are obviously authentic. There are 32 pieces with the set, but looks like the reddish-colored ones are two different shades. The box has dovetailed joints and the lid slides on and off. Oral tradition is that John H. Kimball became a soldier in the Union Army and carried the set with him until somehow it ended up in the hands of a Confederate soldier named Denver A. Hawkins who was with the 7th South Carolina Cavalry. **515.00**

Chest, Wood, inscription stenciled on the chest reads, "Major Thos B Dewees/St James Station USA/ Washington Co MD/C No 1/Depot, Quartermaster." Above is painted over the following inscription, which is weak, "Col Thos B Dewees/Co [?] 2nd US Cav.," chest measures 40" x 22" x 22". Joints are dovetailed, the sides are single pieces of old pine, not pieced together. The double inscription suggests this soldier may have had an extended career in the U.S. military. **750.00**

Coffee Pot, Presentation, beautiful Brittania metal gallon-size coffee server. Very decorative with pewter-like patina, hinged lid with acorn finial, grapes-and-leaves motif on handle, and lined engraving on body. Finely engraved inside an escutcheon on the front in classic 1860s script, in four lines is, "Presented/To/Capt. A.A. Powers/Co. "I" 5th Regt. MVM." Cursory background data shows that the recipient was Captain Andrew A. Powers of Bolton, Massachusetts. Records show he served two terms in the unit, first in Company I, 5th Massachusetts, Department of North Carolina from 1862 to 1863, and then again in Company I, 5th Massachusetts hundred days service in 1864. Duty included Williamston, New Berne, Kinston, Goldsboro, and more.............................. **1,250.00**

Coffee Pot

12" h with detachable lid, tinned iron construction with flat soldered. Wire bale handle at top and tinned iron flat handle on the back away from the spout, excellent condition. **65.00**

A classic camp-size example that would hold a gallon or so of coffee. Complete with lid and wire bail handle for hanging over the campfire. Excellent condition with nice patina. **69.00**

Big enough for just one good cup of coffee, but just like the full-size pots, 5" tall, including the knob on the lid. Tapered larger toward bottom, couple rings about the middle. Spout on one side, loop handle on other, 3" in d at top, 4-1/4" at bottom. Flat bottom with edge curled up around the side and neatly soldered, overall smooth gray, not dented. **110.00**

Same style as the pots used by one or two soldiers, except this one holds two gallons as used by a unit mess, 13" h x 7-1/2" d at top, 12" across the bottom. Reinforced loop handle on one side, with spout on the other. Sheet metal fittings riveted to the rim to hold wire bale handle over top. Hinged lid, raised ring design around the middle area, and even, dark gray. Some speckled raised rust texture on some areas. **150.00**

Comb, Folding, a folding pocket-size hair comb made of horn material, very good with some teeth missing, rare personal item. **49.00**

Compass, Traveling, classic pocket-size Civil War-era brass compass, measures 2" d, very good condition. **89.00**

Compass, Wooden, this is a classic compass being a wooden square-shaped affair measuring roughly 2-1/2" x 2-1/2" and having a hinged wooden lid that lifts to expose the compass dial. Nicely inscribed in brown ink on the bottom of the compass is, "H.R. Campbell to Capt. J.B. Campbell 4th Artillery." Campbell was a West Point graduate in 1857, and he was also a US regular who served throughout the Civil War. He received his commission as 1st lieutenant in the 4th Artillery in June of 1861. He received his commission to captain in May of 1862, then he was mustered out of the volunteer service in July of 1865. He was brevetted to the rank of captain for gallantry at Bull Run, and was further brevetted to major for gallantry at Antietam. Campbell commanded Battery B, 4th US Artillery from the period of October 1861, succeeding General John Gibbon who had previously been the captain and battery commander. At the battles of South Mountain and Antietam, the battery was heavily engaged and Captain Campbell was severely wounded at Antietam. **4,950.00**

Cork Screw, steel screw, finely made wood handle, with a brush to clean off the neck at one end. Belonged to E.A. Sadler, Troop 18th Cavalry (unmarked). Typical, but seldom found. **50.00**

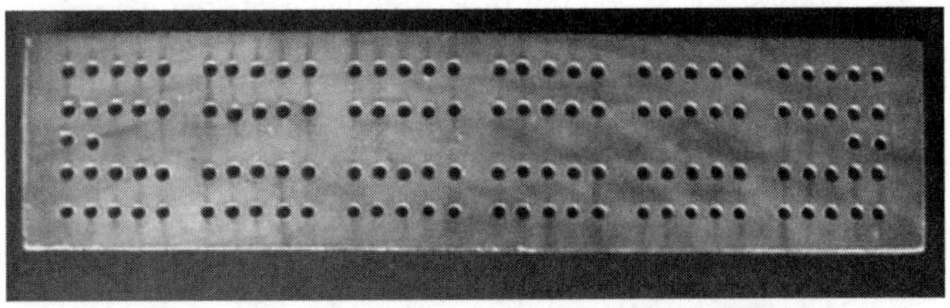

Cribbage board made from a piece of mahogany.

Dale C. Anderson Co.

Cribbage Board, Civil War period, made from a solid mahogany board, 3-1/2" x 14-7/8" x 1-1/8" thick. Very nicely finished and mellowed. Simple board with holes drilled on top, wonderful color, bottom faced with thin leather. **45.00**

Crucifix, in a tin slip case, this is typical of the religious figure carried by many troops, both North and South. **85.00**

Cup, Boiler

Tin with handles, fine condition. **95.00**

Variant issue cup made as a coffee boiler, with two ears riveted in place on each side of the cup with a stout wire bail connected to the ears and running over the top of the cup to hang in the camp fire. This is the type with large handle held in place with rivets, super condition with even green/brown patina, and no rust or pitting. **345.00**

Cup, Folding

Classic pewter drinking cup that collapses into itself for traveling, in excellent condition, just the cup (no carrying case). **49.00**

Nice personal item in excellent condition, collapsible pewter-style in japanned tin carrying case. . . . **79.00**

Pewter, marked "US 1861," in a tole tin case with "D. Ferguson" scratched on the base. Daniel Ferguson served both Company F, 1st New Jersey Infantry, and the 1st U.S. Veteran Volunteer Infantry. **125.00**

Standard style with collapsible pewter cup designed for use in travel. Excellent with some scraping to the japanned finish on the tin carrying case. **69.00**

Cup, Issue, Variant, large quart-size issue cup identical to the ones with the wire loops around the handles, but this one does not have the wire loops. This style cup is the second most common type found in archaeological excavations from U.S. army posts of the 1860s period, and is unquestionably Civil War issue. Excellent condition with some small vines painted on it years ago as folk art. **135.00**

Cup, Issue

Regulation-issue cup, wire reinforcement loops from handle to lip of cup, very solid, shows use, and is overall brown in color with some rust and a couple tiny holes in bottom. **245.00**

Regulation issue cup with wire reinforcement from handle to lip of cup. Very solid, used, brown example with dents showing real war date use. **235.00**

Civil War, regulation-size issue soldier's cup that measures 4-1/2" x 4-1/2". Very nice condition with no holes and terrific aged surface rust/patina. Flat bottom and tapered mouth, came from a grouping of items belonging to Private Charles O. Davison of Company G, 4th Vermont Infantry. Research shows that he enlisted on September 21, 1861, and served through the entire war until July 13, 1865. He was wounded at the Battle of Wilderness on May 5, 1864. This item shows uncleaned honest wear. **150.00**

Standard regulation-issue cup, wire reinforcement wires attach handle to lip of cup, some light pitting, but no dents. Good color and very solid with a couple small rust holes in the bottom. **225.00**

Standard pattern 4" t, made of heavy gauge tin with large loop handle secured to the body by rivets and rolled reinforced loops running from the handle around lip of cup, excellent condition with some light surface pitting. **259.00**

Cup, Tin

4-3/8" d, 4-3/8" t, flat bottom with edge rolled up against the side and soldered. Loop handle soldered to the side, some rolled, raised ridges for strength. Dark gray sheet iron with traces of brighter tin, some speckled brown stain on bottom. Typical cup carried by many soldiers. **115.00**

This cup is a fine variant of the Civil War period, virtually identical to the so-called "type 3" issue cups, and is 4-1/2" d with a large tin handle at the side. It is constructed with folded and soldered construction (no rivets used), has the flat (not recessed) bottom, and exhibits a nice undisturbed tin patina overall. **79.00**

Dice, Civil War era pair of bone dice. **60.00**

Dominoes

A fine wood box 5-1/2" x 8" x 1-1/2", with name of owner D.M. Kelly (50th Massachusetts Volunteers) on inside lid, 45 bone-ivory and ebony dominoes, few rim nicks or dings in chest. **145.00**

Comes in a redwood box with sliding top, 28 tiles made of bone and ebony, all are in fine condition. . . **135.00**

Ebony and ivory, each is 2-3/16" x 1-1/6", 28 pieces. **170.00**

Made of bone ivory and ebony affixed with a single brass rivet. This complete set is in a dovetailed wood box with sliding cover marked, " J.J. Murphy." He served Company F, 31st Maine Volunteers. . . **125.00**

Twenty-seven ivory and ebony pieces (with two rivets) in a finely made wood box with "A. Sadler" and regimental markings stenciled on the sliding cover's top. **145.00**

Eyeglasses and Case

A quaint pair of finely made steel frame spectacles with delicate wire ear pieces, glasses are in excellent condition. These are housed in an 1860 Parker's Patent tin carrying case (this one is not marked or dated). Case is lined in a beautiful blue velvet in excellent condition.. . . . . **65.00**

Brass-framed specs with extendible earpieces, and semi-rectangular lenses. Housed in the original velvet-lined tin carrying case, which is boldly marked, "PATd Jan. 20, 1860 PARKER.". **89.00**

Flask, Glass, about 7" h, bottom is covered in glove leather. Top has a pewter cap that comes off to form a cup. Pewter cap on top of flask, excellent condition. **135.00**

Flask, Pewter, pocket 1860s vintage whiskey flask with screw-on pewter cap and removable pewter cup from the bottom, excellent condition. **65.00**

This flask is impressed with an 1865 patent date.

Flask, Rubber, body is glass that is coated with a beautiful flame-pattern design of hard rubber. Refer to Woshner's, *India-Rubber and Gutta-Percha In the Civil War* for a similar flask. The two-piece body has a removable bottom section that can be used as a cup. The screw cap with a cork liner has the following embossment on the top, "IND. RUBBER COMB CO. GOODYEARS PAT 1865." The India Rubber Comb Company was a well known manufacturer of various rubber products during this period. The approximate overall dimensions are 3-1/2" w at the shoulders and 7" h. The capacity is about 1/2 pint. The cup fits firmly to the flask's body, and yet can be easily removed. There are no cracks or chips in either the hard-rubber coating or the glass body. The surface is smooth and the overall condition of the flask is excellent. **128.00**

Fork and Cork Screw, Folding, has three-tined metal fork that folds into a bone ivory handle. There is also a fold-out cork screw, has a small chip in handle. **75.00**

Fork and Knife Set

Fork marked, "Perry & Co-Limited;" knife marked, "W.H. Wragg-Patentee." **160.00**

Marked "3 Vt. inf." on the knife blade. This is the type where the metal utensils slip into the wooden handle of the opposite part. **185.00**

Marked "U.S." on the fork, both have riveted wood handles. The type where knife and fork slide into handle of the opposite utensil. **175.00**

Oak handles, knife marked, "ANCS." Set interlocks and is in great condition. **175.00**

Fork, Knife, and Spoon Set

Nice combination sliding fork and knife set that slides past each other to put together. The handles are dark hardwood and has a small chip on one end with brass bands holding two halves together as made, one replaced with an iron band. The blade of the knife is marked, "E. BROOKES SHEFFIELD." **165.00**

This folding knife, fork, and spoon may have been British manufacture.

Dale C. Anderson Co.

All-metal construction, including grip facings. Looks exactly like a clasp knife all closed, and is 3-7/8" l. It comes apart lengthwise into three separate pieces, and each has the tool-portion which hinges open like a blade. There is a fork, knife, and spoon. Grips, spoon, and fork are German silver, knife is steel, appears to be British import. Very nice condition, shows use. **550.00**

Knife, fork, and spoon with ivory handles, a beautiful set. **225.00**

Stamped metal combination eating utensils made to connect and fit together for ease in carrying in the soldier's haversack. Boldly marked, "Worman & Ely/ Phila./Pat'd. Feb. 4, 1862." Fine condition, just shows age patina and normal evidence of use. **450.00**

When closed, this looks like the standard folding knife, fork, and spoon-style sets, but that is where the similarity ends. This set is made with a rosewood handle that contains a folding knife. Into each side of the rosewood grip, a slot is milled-out into which fits a folding hallmarked silver fork on one side and a folding, hallmarked silver spoon on the other. The spoon and fork have thin silvered handles that slide into the rosewood grips of the knife for storage. When used, this set is far superior to other designs as the diner has use of three separate utensils, just like real tableware. The knife blade is signed, "Crookes Brothers Sheffield" in classic mid-nineteenth-century style. **375.00**

Fork, Knife, and Spoon, Folding Combination, wooden handled folding utensils come apart in the middle, so you have a knife on one side and either a spoon or fork on the other. Excellent condition. **325.00**

Fork, Knife, and Spoon

Worman and Ely Patent. Three utensils made of steel with metal handles, with the spoon and fork together. The knife and spoon are marked, "Worman & Ely Phila. Patd. Feb. 4, 1862." **265.00**

Wood handle with steel knife blade, folding two-prong fork and a large, white-metal folding spoon. Blade marked, "Ulster Knife Co." **175.00**

Fork, a simple, three-tined fork with worn bone handle. **5.00**

Gauntlets, Leather, reportedly used by an officer from Maryland (Union), but no supportive history strong enough to prove it, very high quality overall. **575.00**

Heel Plate, Star Pattern, dug in Confederate camp in Texas. **65.00**

Housewife

3" glove leather, roll-up sewing kit. Hand-stitched flaps inside for pins and needles. Velvet bumpers on either end of the roll up tube to be used as pin cushion. Tube is hollow and probably stored thimble, two silk ties act as closures. **265.00**

Typical black-leather covered roll-up sewing kit, with various-size needles in the two cloth needle flaps inside and pins in the pincushion ends. Stenciled, "D.M. Kelly Qtrmaster Sergt." He served in the 50th Massachusetts Volunteers. **85.00**

Similar to the Brooks and Hathaway's patent roll-up kits. Unquestionably a Civil War kit, this specimen is a roll-up pattern with a tin cylinder at one end to hold pencils or paper. This cylinder has a small hatch or door on it to keep the contents from spilling out (an improvement over the above mentioned patterns where the cylinders had open tops exposed when the body was unrolled). This cylinder is attached to a leather body that is lined in a wonderful checkered-pattern material with leather straps to hold sewing materials or toiletries in place. Measures roughly 12" x 7" when unrolled, and 7" l x 2" d when rolled up for carrying. **395.00**

Constructed of black oilcloth in a wrap-around configuration like the pocket testaments, opens to expose patching cloth, needles, and thread. **139.00**

Ink Bottle, clay with short, low neck. **25.00**

This inkwell was clearly designed for traveling, and as such would be a fitting item to display with an officer's belongings. It does have an anchor and a caduceus engraved on it, so it is likely that this belonged to a person in the medical field.

Inkwell, Glass, leather covering still intact. Wonderful Civil War-era traveling inkwell with spring-latch top. This has an anchor/medical caduceus mark on it. Inkwell bottle intact, all latches perfect and functioning and all leather intact. **305.00**

Inkwell, Gutta-percha, black cylindrical inkwell with screw-on cap in excellent condition with dried remnants of ink still inside. **25.00**

Inkwell, Rosewood

Rosewood cylinder with screw-off cap that exposes the glass vial inside to hold the ink. **69.00**

Very nice, just having a small crack in the wooden lid. **65.00**

Inkwell, dug out of a Civil War trash pit in Virginia. . **4.25**

Jar, Toothpaste, white ceramic jar with transfer label on top, "Cherry Tooth/Paste/specially prepared/by Breidenbach & Co./London/for/Francis & Son/Brixton," fine condition. **145.00**

Lamp, Tin, in rough terms, it is a japanned tin cylinder of 5" l and 2" d. This cylinder extends to 9" with an extendible brass pedestal base, so that it will stand on its own. The cylinder top has a hinged cap which opens to allow heat to escape, and it has a pair of brass hooks in the cap that are intended to hook into the wall of a canvas tent, should the user want a wall lamp. The body of the cylinder rotates to expose a glass cylinder and mirror-finish cylinder inside which acts as the lantern. Stamped into the back of this portion is, "E. P. NORTH / MAKER," in classic mid-19th century die stamps. When closed, the glass is perfectly protected making this item perfect for use by a military man. Affixed to the outer body's bottom is an embossed brass maker's plate, which is emblazoned with an English coat of arms and the word "PATENT." **225.00**

Lantern, stands roughly 14" h with a large bail handle at top, tin base with removable burner, large glass globe protected by four substantial wire rods, a tin cap, and brass top (above the cap). It looks something like an early railroad lantern in terms of its design. Affixed to the base of the lantern just above a sliding tin door that allows access to the burner is a fine, embossed-brass plaque which reads, "S. Sargents Patent Sept. 17th 1861." The kerosene burner inside the lamp is a slightly later replacement and has a brass knob with three patent dates on it, ranging from 1862 to 1867. The lantern is definitely pre-1865. . . . . **395.00**

Lap Desk, traveling-type, mahogany, rectangular, with lift top, carved name on bottom, "Maj. A.B. Parkell, 4 Iowa," with copies of book discussing Parkell's action in a battle (reglued age crack in top). **248.00**

Matches

Five rows of match strips, each match has fulminate at the top just like the kitchen matches of today. One simply snapped off the one at the end of the row. This pack has five rows of about 20 matches each, in the original tissue paper pack. **95.00**

Typical strip of 17 wood matches, marked "US 1861." See Lord's *Civil War Encyclopedia*, in excellent condition. **15.00**

Mirror, Folding

3" d, circular zinc shaving mirror with cover boldly embossed with profile bust of George Washington and words, "George Washington." The back is embossed, "Brevette 1844," has a heavy brass hinge and small loop so that the mirror can stand up on its own, or be hung from a nail. **375.00**

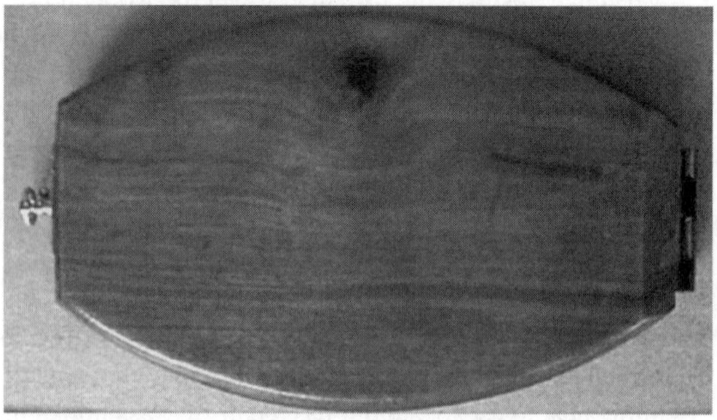

Example of a zinc mirror.

Dale C. Anderson Co.

4-1/2" x 8" closed; hinges on the end to open, and for it to sit, continues to hinge one end until it stops, forming an "L" with the other end. Has a circular ring on one end for hanging. Two mirrors inside; one a regular, one a magnifying mirror. The silvering has some crazing along edges and a few speckles, mostly on the smaller magnifying mirror, very nice display item, and still usable. **245.00**

8" x 5" in size and having two mirrors inside. When the lid is swung open, there is a smaller circular mirror inside the bottom half, and a large mirror inside the lid. A great personal item that displays very well. **169.00**

Disc-shaped pocket mirror folds out to form a small platform to set on something for shaving. Outside is embossed tin, excellent condition. **135.00**

Large 3" d standard shaving mirror, embossed with floral vines, still has wire hinge and loop. . . . **65.00**

Roughly 5" x 3" shaving mirror, hinged lid, wooden case, most often encountered Civil War period mirror having a wooden body and a lid that swings away to expose the looking glass. Perfect condition with great patina on the wood. **139.00**

Typical 1860-period circular traveling shaving mirror made something like a woman's compact. This measures about three-plus inches diameter, overall very good condition. **65.00**

Typical type that pulls apart and has a ring on the zinc back from which it could hang. This one is almost twice as large as usually seen, being 3-1/2" d. . **65.00**

Pen, Traveling, brass body pen which measures roughly 6.5" l when extended for writing. When not in use the business end of the pen pulls out of the brass cylinder and can be reinserted backwards, so that the pen is ready for traveling. Nice patina, comes with two nibs that are later. **69.00**

Pencil, old pencil (never sharpened) with vegetable ivory ball on one end and black painted body, plus a CW era unused yellow envelope, pencil marked, "AWF". . **15.00**

Pipe, Carved Soldier's Head, burl, the bowl carved as the head of a Civil War solider wearing a kepi, well-executed, found in Ohio (couple of age cracks). **550.00**

Pipe, Clay

Excavated at Fort Craig, New Mexico, a few decades ago. Fort Craig was the site of a major Civil War battle. This one is complete, fired red clay with a reeded surface design. It took a reed stem, now gone. **25.00**

Fouled anchor design on one side and sailors' knots on the other, 7" l. **75.00**

Wood, tree branch bowl and stem, typical period pipe, fine specimen. **50.00**

Pipe, Gutta-percha

Gutta-percha (thermoplastic) molded stem with bird-claw base holding a briarwood bowl, scarce but typical piece. **125.00**

Boot-shaped bowl, stem and bowl all one piece, and almost 7" l. A typical, yet unusual, soldier's item. **125.00**

Pipe, Presentation, carved burl, with an American eagle and, "Union-From W. Keech, Capt. Co. B., 61st Regt. NY S.V. To E.M. H., Oxford, N.Y.," carved around top of bowl in relief, "Camp Mars, Va.—Feb. 21, 1863," fine brown patina (stem missing). **1,045.00**

Plate, Tin, a great personal item to display with mess gear of the common soldier. Roughly 8" d and stamped with a dished out area in the center 6-1/2" area is recessed 1/2" deep, leaving a raised flat surface of 1-1/2" around the border of the plate. This has a rolled edge and is identical to known tin plates of the period. **89.00**

Playing Cards

"Great Moguls," American deck, perfect condition. **150.00**

A plain white card with red heart or diamond, or black club. When held to the light they reveal a nude woman in an engraving under the card face. Considered very pornographic for this period, in excellent condition, three cards. **150.00**

Imported from Belgium, complete deck in wrapper. **75.00**

Made by A. Dougherty of 78 Center Street New York. The Jack of Hearts has been replaced by joker or title card of the deck, and two cards are damaged, otherwise in excellent condition. **185.00**

The classic deck with face cards being ranking officers and Liberty, and suits being stars, shields, eagles, and flags. Housed in the complete box with patriotic label and revenue stamp on it. **1,350.00**

Razor Strop, 14" l with wood handle. The handle pulls out to expose the strop that also has a sliding drawer compartment inside for storing the straight razor, nice printed label with a small eagle on one end and directions for use. **65.00**

Razor

"Co. A 4th N.H. Vols." engraved on an escutcheon on the shell handle, blade marked, "Joseph Rogers & Sons Sheffield." A beautiful, engraved piece. **185.00**

A good, solid example of the typical soldier's straight razor, heavy wide blade, nicely stamped on the neck, "Wade & Butcher/Sheffield." **22.00**

A good solid example of the typical soldier's straight razor, has heavy, heavy blade, and is nicely stamped on the neck with a French maker's name. **22.00**

Ribbon, Patriotic, worn on and dated, "July 4, 1861." Sold to raise money for the Young Men's Association and offered to take advantage of the patriotic fervor of the country, just after the war's beginning. This is a white silk ribbon 2" w x 6-3/4" l, printed in red and blue. Top has the block letters in blue, "Y.M.A." over a red/white/blue billowing flag on a staff (flag is 34 stars in form of five-pointed star), this over the date in red/blue "July 4th, 1861." **150.00**

Ring, Bone, a classic piece of Civil War camp or prisoner art. The ring is carved from a piece of bone and into the top is carved "C.N.R." with the letters filled in with red sealing wax. **59.00**

Shaving Mug, Tin

The classic mid-nineteenth-century shaving mug, nice tin patina in excellent condition. It measures about 5" t and 3" d and has a tin handle on one side and a razor compartment on the other (no tin soap insert as usual). **89.00**

Tin, has removable soap cup, 4-3/4" h, very good condition.............................. **75.00**

When this mug was put up for auction it was referenced to an identical mug illustrated in Francis Lord's *Civil War Collector's Encyclopedia.* A quick check of that reference, though, proved that the mug illustrated therein was simply a representative mug not firmly attributed to use by a soldier.

J.C. Devine Inc.

Shaving Mug, made of "tinned" sheet steel with a strap handle and a rectangular soap compartment. **95.00**

> **"We were on the picket line just before the Poplar Grove fight and that evening you ought to have seen the gambling. If you was a looking for a fight, you had one if you tried to stop the card playing."**
>
> ***— Henry Fitzgerald Charles***
> ***21st Pennsylvania Cavalry***

This Civil War-era shawl had a wonderful period handwritten note pinned to it describing it as, "Papa's Army Shawl Civil War 1863."

Sharpsburg Arsenal

Shawl, Hand Woven, measures 54" w x 124" l. Hand-woven shawl with fringe showing signs of being southern manufactured. Picked up at a southern estate sale with old tag reading, "Papa's Army Shawl Civil War 1863." Very minor moth holes. **995.00**

Snuff Box, Gutta-percha, molded circular snuff box 2" d, looks like a hard rubber tintype case in terms of color and design. Lid lifts off to expose the container for the snuff. Lid has geometric pattern and inset frame with small painting of a flower, bottom has molded design of a woven checkerboard pattern. Included with this is a tiny 1860-era gem type of a lady, which came with it at the auction. **65.00**

Snuff Box, Horn, made of horn with a hinged cover, the box measures 1-1/2" x 2" x 3/4", belonged to Lieut. Joseph Flint of the First Dragoons. **65.00**

Snuff Box, Tin

3" l, oval, tin snuff box with hinged lid and stamped with Parker's patent, "Jan 1860," marking on the catch, excellent condition, nice age patina. **59.00**

Circular tin container, measures roughly 3" d and 1/2" thick. Lid consists of a cover that rotates to allow access to the inside. Marked in tiny letters in the top is, "Patented July 3rd 1860 / ED." Uncleaned with deep patina, in excellent solid condition. **135.00**

Soap Dish and Mirror Set, Goodyear's patent (1851) hard-rubber shaving item that is a combination soap dish and mirror. The top lid is embossed with an anchor "USN" and the motto "Don't Give Up the Ship." The bottom carries the full firm (Novelty Rubber Co) and patent (Goodyear 1851) information embossed in small letters. When opened, there is a shaving mirror inside the top lid, this one being totally cloudy, excellent condition. **275.00**

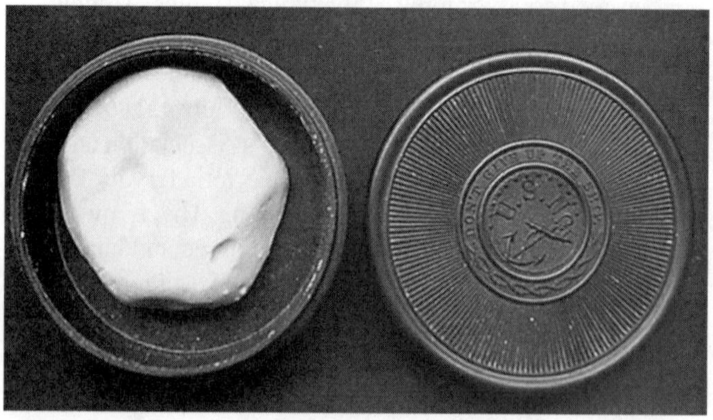

This soap dish was designed to hold a mirror inside the lid. Bearing a maker's reference to manufacture under the provisions of Goodyear's patent of 1851, several of these have recently come onto the market. A similar one bearing army motifs is documented as having been a part of a soldier's kit. This example bears a naval motif.

Dale C. Anderson Co.

Soap Dish, black gutta-percha; 3-1/4" d, 1-1/2" h, with lift-off lid. Still has piece of original soap inside. Top of lid has splendid, crisp design, center has anchor with "USN" and an arc of stars at center, surrounded by a decorative band bearing the motto, "DON'T GIVE UP THE SHIP," plus a twisted rope design. Surrounding this is a radiating sunburst design of grooves, covering the balance of the lid, within a raised border. Inside the lid is a circular glass mirror (original) with minor gray speckling. The ring border bears the tiny raised inscription, "Manufactured by the Novelty Rubber Co. New Brunswick, New Jersey, under Goodyear's Patent May 6, 1851." Lacks little metal ring on outer edge, and tiny bit of gutta-percha material, otherwise very fine. 275.00

Spoon and Knife, Folding, typical type with wooden handles, a large fold-out spoon and 3-1/2" knife blade (tiny part of point missing) made by the CamLilis Cutlery Co. of New York, shows use. 125.00

An identical religious statuette to this one is pictured in Francis Lord's *Civil War Collector's Encyclopedia*, but this one has no firm attribution to a Civil War soldier.

Sharpsburg Arsenal

Statuette, Religious

Pocket-sized religious statues were often carried by soldiers during the war. 95.00

Statute of St. Anthony holding a child. Made of pewter, it is in a brass slip case. 85.00

Virgin Mary housed in a japanned tole tin slip case. 85.00

Stencil Kit, a small brass stencil with fancy lettering (1-1/8" x 2-3/4"), a glass bottle for, "Hichcock Indelible Ink," to mark clothing, a stencil brush, a set of printed instructions and a half pasteboard box which has a terrific label for, "Down's Vegetable and Balsamic Elixir." 50.00

Soldier stencils are identified by their very design, making them an excellent choice of personal gear to acquire. This stencil was used by D. Bickford of the 15th New Hampshire Volunteers to identify his personal belongings.

Dave Taylor Civil War Antiques

Stencil

Large, 4-1/2" w, format with rich patina, pierced to read, "D. Bickford/Co. I. 15th N.H.V." This unit was organized in 1862, and fought at Port Hudson Louisiana with quite heavy casualties, very appealing. 475.00

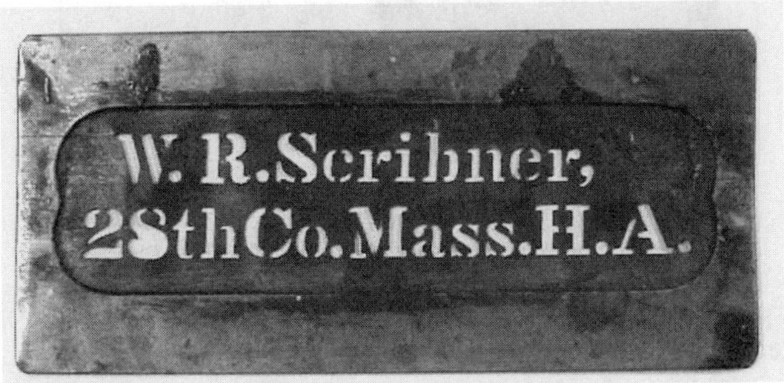

W.R. Scribner of the 4th Massachusetts Heavy Artillery used this stencil.

Dave Taylor Civil War Antiques

A large format measuring roughly 4" w, and is filled in to read, "W.R. Scribner/28th Co. Mass. H.A." Unit was formed in August of 1864, and transferred to the 4th Regiment Heavy Artillery, where it served in DeRussey's division in the defenses of Washington, D.C. Very striking with great patina and size. .. 485.00

Filled out to read, "M.H. Neville/Co. G 22d Me. Regt. Littleton, Me." This unit served at Baton Rouge and Port Hudson Louisiana, very-fine condition. .. 485.00

J. Green of the 187th Pennsylvania Volunteers owned this stencil.

Dave Taylor Civil War Antiques

Measures roughly 3-1/2" w, and is pierced to read, "J. Green / Co. D. 187th P.V.", very rich patina. Unit was organized near Philadelphia in the spring of 1864, and served with the Army of the Potomac at the terrible battles of Cold Harbor and Petersburg. **495.00**

Stove, Sibley, this thin-sheet iron stove is 28-1/4" h and 18" d at its base. It utilized a four-inch stove pipe that served also as the mail tent pole for the Sibley Tent. Stove has no rust or damage and has an excellent finish on the metal. **999.00**

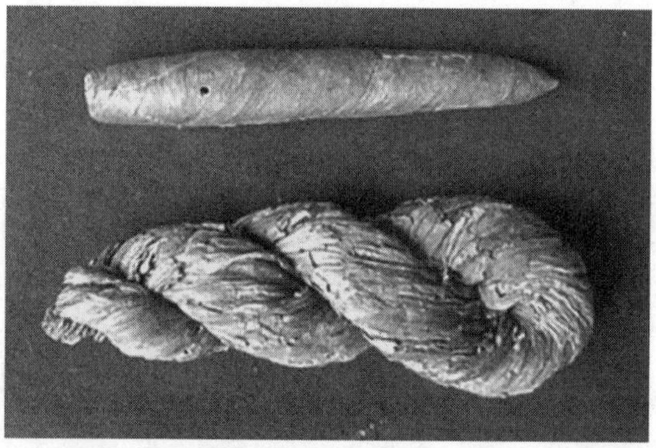

Tobacco was a soldier's favorite, so a twist or a pack of leaves would certainly fit into a display of typical soldier belongings.

Dale C. Anderson Co.

Tobacco Twist and Cigar, twists are how tobacco was frequently sold, and they were often brought home as souvenirs. This one is 1-3/4" x 4-1/2", very good, very dry, comes with original cigar, 4" l.. . . . . **55.00**

Tobacco, yellow paper wrapped with wording, "Queen of the West James River Sweet Leaf Tobacco Manufactured by H. L. Tickner Anoka, Minn." . . **65.00**

Toothbrush and Case, bone ivory, complete with brush, case is 6-1/2" l, and 1" d, it screws apart at the middle, both ends are perforated to allow brush to dry, belonged to Surgeon Herman H. Gillett of the 8th Vermont Veteran Infantry. **125.00**

Toothbrush

Bone handled toothbrush with boar hair bristles, excellent condition. **40.00**

Civil War period bone toothbrush. **35.00**

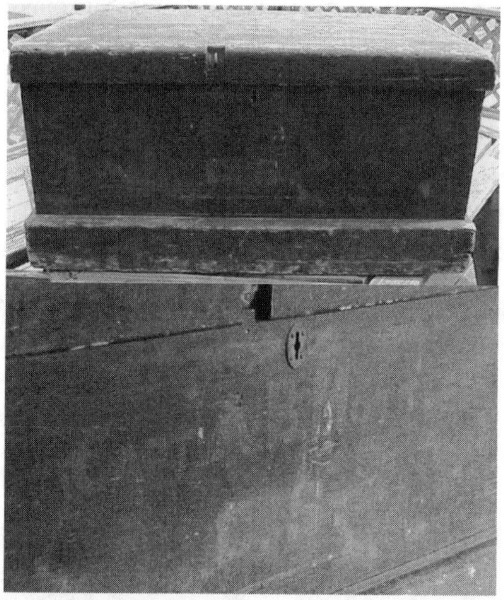

This trunk belonged to Captain A.B. Mott of the U.S. Volunteers. It was sold with documents belonging to Captain Mott.

Sharpsburg Arsenal

Trunk, Officer, identified to, "Capt. A B Mott." Papers included, Amos Mott was appointed as a captain in the US Volunteers (Commissary and Subsistence) on April 14, 1862. He would accept his commission on April 29, 1862, and be assigned to the Army of the Potomac. He was honorably discharged on February 20, 1865.The trunk is all-wood construction measuring 37" x 19" x 18-1/2". **1,250.00**

Wallet, Leather and Steel, outstanding condition embossed leather accordion-style wallet or change purse with metal frame and metal-hinged closing clasp, measures roughly 5" x 3" when closed, inside is lined and made of red Moroccan leather and opens to expose four compartments and a small folder for postage stamps. **125.00**

Wallet, Leather

Embossed with scrolls and a small, mounted rider jumping a fence, excellent condition. **75.00**

Four compartment wallet made of soft brown glove leather, lined with red silk, "Israel R. Berry," stamped on the inside cover flap six times. **95.00**

Embossed with anchors and crests with a pseudo-military flavor. **75.00**

Large flat billfold measuring 7" x 4" closed. When opened, the wallet reveals a fantastic maker's stamp with spread-winged American eagle and shield perched upon an oval containing the words, "A.A.Hotchkiss Maker Watertown Conn," perfect condition. **125.00**

Wallet, Leather, cont.

Standard roll-up design in excellent condition and complete with the closing strap, fine and solid. . . **49.00**

Measures roughly 6" x 3-1/2" when closed and opens to expose two inner compartments. It is made of plain, smooth brown leather. Accompanying this is a modern ink note that identifies it to Humphrey H. Bittrick of the 5th Massachusetts Volunteers. **75.00**

Typical wallet as carried in the Civil War, unquestionably 1860s or earlier, measures roughly 6" x 2-1/2" when closed, and beautifully embossed with dogs and scrolls, magnificent condition. **75.00**

Watch Chain, full-length, 10". At one end is a cross "T" bar for securing through a buttonhole, and the other end has a clip for attaching to the watch. The chain is comprised of nice small "coins" linked together. The "coins" are brass counterfeits of 1864 $1 gold pieces. The face of each coin has Liberty's head surrounded by stars. The reverse of each has stars, a wreath, the numeral "1", and date of 1864. . . . . **175.00**

Possibly a postwar item, this watch chain displays a 9th Corps badge.

Dale C. Anderson Co.

Watch Fob

11-1/2" l, brass watch chain with traces of gilding. Standard cross stud for buttonhole on one end, and a snap swivel on the other to attach to the watch. Hanging from the chain as a fob is a custom, jeweler made silver 9th Corps badge, 1-3/8" tall shield, deeply and expertly engraved on its face with classic 9th Corps insignia of crossed cannon and anchor with number nine in front of the anchor as formed by the chain or rope. Decorative border, hanging with the badge is a watch key. Badge bright as new, reverse side shows some tool marks from when it was made. **575.00**

Fob has an identification badge for a soldier of the 29th Mississippi Infantry. **8,800.00**

Watch, Pocket

A definite wartime example made by William Ellery of Boston (one of the Waltham makers) and having a serial number of 76,388 (this dates the watch to 1863 or 1864). Ellery advertised in the newspapers of the Civil War as a supplier of watches for soldiers. Very nice condition with full silver hunting case (lid that covers the face), and complete with an old watch chain and fob. **275.00**

Inscribed and dated 1862 with the owner's name, Joseph Lawton, this watch was a solid investment. Research showed that Lawton served in the 27th Massachusetts Infantry.

Civil War watch made of solid gold, "not plated." Owned by Joseph W. Lawton, 27th Regiment Massachusetts Infantry. Comes with a piece of gold jewelry, presented to his wife along with his watch. Plaque is made of solid gold, inscribed on it, "ROANOKE JOS W. LAWTON MARCH 14TH 1862 NEWBERN." Plaque was off a bracelet she wore, the watch is 2-3/16" d, 3-1/8" from top to bottom. Front is engraved with an American eagle clutching arrows and a shield. Back is engraved with a church overlooking a valley with mountains. Case has gold hallmarks and the number 12601 stamped on it. Movement is marked "Josh Johnson # 12601," watch runs. **962.00**

Personal Item Terminology

Attributed: This term is used to associate an item to a particular soldier, even though it is not marked as having belonged to him.

Housewife: A small, usually roll-up, portfolio for storing sewing supplies.

Identified: Collector term referring to a firm attribution of an item to a particular soldier.

Provenance: The history of an item. Usually, provenance will identify the original owner and in some cases, subsequent owners of an item.

See also: Grouping, Accoutrements, Medical, and Ephemera.

Chapter 15

Photographs

Image collecting is a great way to pursue all sorts of Civil War interests including: swords, firearms, uniforms, particular regiments and famous personages. While it is relatively inexpensive to assemble a collection of interesting carte de visites, collecting the "hard" images—ambrotypes, tintypes, and even daguerreotypes—of soldiers, runs into some serious money. It is best to develop a focus for your collection. Perhaps you are interested in collecting only identified images, images of soldiers from a particular state, soldiers of a particular branch of service, or even images in which weapons are displayed. By narrowing the field from the beginning, you will be able to assemble a meaningful collection that will grow in value.

Be cautious about buying every cheap image you see—you will soon be overwhelmed. Soldiers by the tens of thousands sat for their likenesses. Many received six copies or more of their carte de visites and tintypes. That means there are hundreds of thousands of images out there. All of them are not going to be strong in content. Try to resist placing that bid or buying that straggler when you see it. You may very well need the cash you spent when that absolutely stellar image does come up for sale.

So what exactly makes an image "stellar?" There are several factors, and it can almost become formulaic. First is the view itself. A full-length view is more desirable than a bust shot because more of the soldier's uniform is visible. A weapon of any sort will immediately increase an image's value, as will any visible accoutrements. If the soldier is wearing a corps badge, that will also add a few dollars to the price. Outdoor shots, just by their rarity, tend to sell for more than a comparable indoor shot. Finally, for many collectors, it is all about identification—do you know the name that goes with the face in the photo? If so, research can begin tracing the soldier's unit and history of service.

An area not mentioned, but widely collected, is famous faces—the generals, politicians, and public speakers of the day. Many photographic enterprises printed quantities of images of the likenesses of people like President Lincoln, General Grant, and even a wide selection of Confederate leaders. The public read about these people everyday, and they wanted to see how the heroes and enemies looked. These likenesses were collected much as a young person today will collect bubble gum cards of their sports heroes. When the historic images of these folks are available with the sitter's signature, the price will jump dramatically.

If you do decide to collect Civil War photography, do take the time to learn proper handling and storage methods. Even though the images have survived for more than 100 years, they are fragile documents. Simply handling them with bare fingers can speed their deterioration. Humidity is also a villain to all historic photographs. There is nothing as sad as seeing an image disappear as the emulsion flakes off a tintype or ambrotype. Purchase a basic guide to care and handling of historic paper and photographs and study it. The image you save will be available for future students of the war.

Collecting Hints

Pros:

- The human connection with the Civil War has the strongest potential through studying images.
- The crossover to other areas of Civil War collecting is strong. For example, a weapons' collector may want to embellish his displays with a few images of soldiers holding weapons similar to those in his collection. Or, an historian of uniforms will rely on photographic evidence to support the conclusions their research produced.
- Though there are some current photographers working in the style of 19th century artists, very few do it with the intent to deceive or produce forgeries. A few spectacular images have hit the market that turned out to be newly produced photographs of reenactors, although this is still the exception to the rule.
- Image collecting is relatively inexpensive. A decent cdv of a Union soldier still can be purchased for under $50.

Cons:

- As with most arenas of the Civil War hobby, anything Confederate is going to be expensive. Images are not without exception. If you want to collect images of both sides of the War, be prepared to pay dearly.
- Internet auctions have become a dumping ground for images. Prices paid often are not in line with the rest of the hobby. Also, many spurious and questionable images are sold via the Internet.
- One type of forgery has emerged in image collecting and it involves using a laser color copier to produce copies of albumens and then gluing them to old cdv stock. In years past, this same form of forgery was perpetrated by soaking off mundane images from desirably marked cards and replacing the image with a soldier. In this way, many "Confederates" were created. A lot of these cdvs are still out there, so study each image before you buy.

Availability ★★
Price ★★★★
Reproduction Alert ★★★★★

Albumen Photos (except carte de visites)

Frederick Scott Archer's invention of sensitizing glass plates with collodion (wet plate) in 1851 revolutionized photography. Within ten years, it had replaced almost all other processes. The use of glass negatives instead of paper made a far better image, as well as the ability to make multiple copies of consistent quality. This hailed the beginning of the Golden Age of photography when everything and anything was possible to photograph, both in the studio and out in the furthest reaches of the world.

Prints, Confederate

General Robert E. Lee, rare oval photograph, approximately 6-1/2" x 7". It is a handsome and distinguished head and shoulder portrait by Vannerson & Jones, Richmond, Virginia, late 1863 (ca. December 9-21, when Lee was in Richmond conferring with C.S.A. President Jefferson Davis). Lee is shown wearing his Confederate uniform, posing in profile. Supposedly, Vannerson took four poses, though only three exist: The left profile, the standing view, and the three-quarter view from the left. The famous Vannerson portraits were widely circulated, and eventually appeared in London newspapers and periodicals in the form of lithographs and engravings. This handsome portrait of Lee is signed (on the image), "R E Lee." **25,000.00**

Prints, Union

Outstanding 10" x 12-1/2" image of Union General Thomas McParlin. Large format albumen photos, for some unexplainable reason, don't seem to command the high prices of the smaller carte de visites or hard images.

Frohne's Historic Military

General Thomas A. McParlin, medical director of the Army of the Potomac 1864 to 1865. McParlin enjoyed a long and exciting career in the 19th century army. Appointed acting assistant surgeon in 1848 at Vera Cruz, Mexico, he served out west in the 1850s and became the director of the Army of Virginia for John Pope in 1862. He was assigned to be the medical director of the Army of the Potomac by the president himself in January 1864. McParlin was given a brigadier general's brevet for his actions in New Orleans against cholera and yellow fever in 1866. He was Post Surgeon at Fort Leavenworth from 1873 to 1875 and chief medical officer, District of New Mexico from 1875 to 1877. Mid-1860s albumen, measures approximately 10" x 12-1/2" including the mount, incredible detail and contrast. **150.00**

Colonel David Stricker, 2nd Delaware Infantry, was killed during the Battle of Spotsylvania in 1864. This is a large albumen print of him in uniform.

Frohne's Historic Military

Lieutenant Colonel David L. Stricker, 2nd Delaware Infantry, killed at Spotsylvania, May 12, 1864. Very fine condition, top and bottom of mount trimmed. **375.00**

Lieutenant, vintage photograph of a Union lieutenant. The photograph measures approximately 6-3/4" by 8-1/8". The corners of the photograph have been trimmed apparently to accommodate an oval frame. **301.00**

Officer, Outdoor, spectacular large albumen photo showing a bearded colonel, one of his officer's, and a well-dressed man seated in wooden chairs inside of the colonel's tent that has the tent flaps open to expose the entire interior. The colonel wears his regulation frock and trousers. The younger officer wears a jaunty bowtie and blouse. Visible inside the tent are a desk, table covered with writing implements, and two huge American flags draped from the tent's ceiling.. . . **395.00**

Officer, nice 8" x 10" format albumen photo of a worldly looking Union officer in the uniform of a major of lieutenant colonel. He is shown from the waist up with a good view of the coat and straps, very nice condition. **135.00**

Officers, 12th New York Volunteer Infantry, Outdoor

Artistic pose of a seated captain wearing a fancy kepi with "12" in wreath insignia, frock with straps, sash in the "officer of the day" fashion, and holding his sword. Next to him, and standing in the open flap of a tent door is the assistant surgeon wearing a line officer's frock with straps, kepi with "NY" in wreath insignia, sword belt with clearly visible "NY" buckle, he is leaning on his Model 1840 medical staff sword. **245.00**

The photographer positioned himself outside the tent flap and took the picture of the tent's interior. There are eight officers and one lady seated at a table inside the tent with numerous bottles, dishes, and condiments in the table's center. One fellow is smoking a cigar, so I assume they have just finished their meal, and one gentleman appears to be the colonel. **225.00**

Officers, superb 8" x 10" albumen photo showing a Colonel and eight other officers seated in a studio view. Perfect clarity and contrast, believed to be a New York artillery unit. **425.00**

Soldiers, 12th New York Volunteer Infantry, Outdoor

A horizontal format albumen showing a small company of men standing in front of Sibley tents, some armed, some seated, some standing, the drummer with his drum visible, one soldier displaying a newspaper. Roughly 40 soldiers posing, excellent condition. **245.00**

View of roughly 40 men standing in line (double row) armed with muskets (at least two are Harpers Ferry Model 1855 muskets with the patchboxes visible), and the drummer (a first sergeant) is standing with his drum at the left side of the line. The men have their bayonets attached, a flagpole is visible, and a couple others are shown standing around watching the photo being taken. The men are holding their guns at the "present arms" position. **265.00**

Soldiers, 1st Rhode Island Volunteer Infantry, Outdoor, very fine 9" x 11" albumen photo from the early days of the war showing 16 soldiers wearing the Rhode Island blouse and lounging around camp. One fellow wears a smoking cap, one fellow has his musket, others wear different caps and shirts and there are 3 barracks buildings running back away from the camera. **350.00**

Soldiers

Fine 8" x 10" albumen photo by Gardner showing four well-worn Yankee cavalrymen sitting on a pile of debris near the camera, with a railroad train on the tracks to their left, and a group of mounted riders in the distance. Superb clarity and contrast taken in March 1862. . . . .**495.00**

Soldiers

Unmounted image, 3" x 3" showing Federal soldiers repairing the bridge over the Chickahominy River and so marked on the reverse. Some edge chipping on two sides of the image. The image has been placed on acid-free board and is shrink wrapped. Shows good detail and quality. **110.00**

Stereo Views, Confederate

Stereo views were sold commercially to a public hungry for news and views of the war. View of Confederate dead, originally distributed by Anthony and Company.

Frohne's Historic Military

Dead, head bloody; lying stiffly on ground, this Rebel met his fate at Petersburg, Virginia in April 1865. Very fine condition, with minor mount wear. **225.00**

Part of a series of Anthony stereo views entitled, "War for the Union."

Frohne's Historic Military

Torpedoes, early view (CR 1865), "E. & H.T. Anthony & Co." "Group of relics in Charleston, S.C., Arsenal, showing Rebel torpedoes, shot, shell, and breach of the 600 lb. Blakely Gun." This near-mint condition view has great stereo effect. **95.00**

Stereo Views, Union

View of Professor Lowe's balloon on an Anthony-produced card.

Frohne's Historic Military

Balloon, great close-up view, "Prof. Lowe observing the Battle of Fair Oaks, Va. From his Balloon. No. 2348." "Published by "Anthony, NY. Negative by Brady." Very-good condition, with wear, excellent contrast and clarity. **275.00**

Images that depict African-American soldiers will command premium prices. This is an Anthony-made stereo view of a black Union cook.

Frohne's Historic Military

Cook, Anthony Stereo View in very good condition, of a black soldier cooking near City Point, Virginia, minor wear. . **225.00**

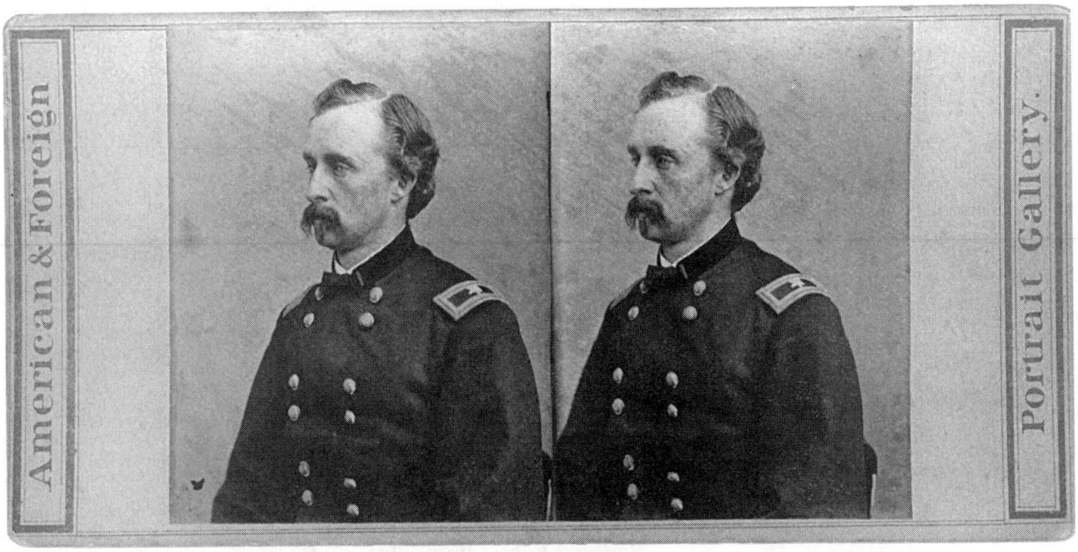

General George A. Custer is just as popular today as he was during and right after the Civil War. Images that depict the flamboyant Union general or members of his command are competitively bought and sold.

Frohne's Historic Military

General George A. Custer, beautiful Anthony late-war stereo view of the Custer, excellent contrast and clarity. **3,500.00**

Taken aboard the U.S.S. Colorado, this stereo view depicts sailors, a drummer, and black members of the ship's crew.

Frohne's Historic Military

Sailors, superb Civil War-date stereo view of "the Sailors and Drummer Boy of U.S. Naval ship the *Colorado*." Sharp focus, very minor center crease, "C. W. Woodward, Rochester, NY." **250.00**

Cartes de Visite

The Carte de visite, another use of collodian, was invented by the famous French photographer Andre Disderi in 1854. Their similarity to a visiting card and their relatively easy production, made them hugely successful. People not only wanted to have their own cartes de visite, they wanted cartes of famous personalities from royalty to actors, which they put in albums alongside of their family portraits. When a person sat for their likeness in carte de visite form, they generally received six images. Because a negative existed, reprints were easily made as well. This lent itself ideally to selling and collecting images of famous personages.

Image of Confederate General A.P. Hill distributed by New York photographer Fredericks.

Frohne's Historic Military

Confederate, Generals

General Ambrose Powell Hill, lieutenant general, Confederate States of America, Hill was one of the South's most famous fighting generals. He was also a graduate of the West Point class of 1847. Hill was killed by two Union 6th Corps soldiers on April 2, 1865, while riding to rally his men. Excellent view of Hill, minor foxing and soiling, "C. D. Fredricks, New York" backmark with a tax stamp. 350.00

General Braxton Bragg, shows Bragg in C.S.A. general's uniform................................ 59.00

Image of Confederate General Van Dorn bearing no backmark.

Frohne's Historic Military

General Earl Van Dorn, imprinted name on bottom front of mount, no backmark. 65.00

General Fitzhugh Lee, bust view with fine ink inscription on front "Fitz Lee Cav Div," and great backmark of "Vannerson & Jones Richmond, Va." Image is yellowed and has a small hole below the image, and a small pinhole at top and bottom.................. 150.00

General Joe Johnston, perfect cdv-litho by, "Gurney NY," bust view of Joe Johnston in prewar U.S. uniform. ...59.00

Matthew Brady distributed this photo of Confederate John Hunt Morgan and his wife.

Middle Tennessee Relics

General John Hunt Morgan, image of the Confederate cavalry general and wife, Mattie Ready Morgan. This is an Anthony-backmarked photograph and has, "John Morgan & Lady," in old brown ink on front below image. 350.00

General Nathan Bedford Forest

Nice, clear image in good condition with some foxing. The tax stamp is dated 1865 in pen, published by, "E. & H.T. Anthony."...................... 330.00

E. & H. Anthony distributed this photograph of the guerilla and Confederate General Nathan Bedford Forest immediately after the war.

Phillip B. Lamb Ltd./Col. Lamb's Antiques

Superb E. & H. Anthony view of Forrest printed immediately after the war. This so-called "common" view of Forrest is still the mainstay for the average collector who cannot obtain or afford photos of Forrest with extremely rare southern backmarks. This particular view is exceptionally clean and crisp, with no damage anywhere on the card. Sharp, mid-chest-up image with a hand-cancelled, two-cent federal tax stamp. 1,350.00

View of General N.B. Forest, probably dating to around 1866.

Phillip B. Lamb Ltd./Col. Lamb's Antiques

Unusual and scarce postwar cdv of an engraving of Forrest. This view probably dates from late 1865 to early 1866, though it may have been published earlier by one of the five photographic entities, which bore the Bingham name in Memphis. This view is imprinted on the front with the name, "Bingham Bros. Memphis, Tenn." Some soiling around the cameo oval, along with handwriting in red at bottom of card, otherwise clear and historic. 325.00

General P.G.T. Beauregard, vignette bust view retouched photo, showing Pierre G.T. Beauregard in prewar U.S. uniform. J Gurney NY backmark. **75.00**

Postwar view of General Robert E. Lee previously unpublished.

Old South Military Antiques

General Robert E. Lee

Previously unpublished, signed cdv of General Robert E. Lee. **7,400.00**

Stylized view of General Lee produced during the war by a Richmond, Virginia, photographer.

Phillip B. Lamb Ltd./Col. Lamb's Antiques

Rare, fantasy view of General Lee with his right hand on the headstone of General Stonewall Jackson. Front mark of "Geo. O. Ennis, Richmond, Va." Essentially a mint card representing the bond between two of the greatest C.S.A. generals. George O. Ennis is a known Confederate photographer and is listed in the *Catalogue of Civil War Photographers*. **995.00**

Stunning wartime view of General Lee.

Middle Tennessee Relics

Large, wartime shot in his Confederate uniform, in nice condition, but is chipped just slightly on two corners. **275.00**

General Sterling Price, bust portrait from a retouched negative showing prewar uniform. Notated in period hand front and back as "Price" and "Gen Price." **. 69.00**

General T.J. "Stonewall" Jackson

Clear image, no backmark, excellent condition. **75.00**

Classic early war bust portrait (mass produced variety) of old Stonewall wearing prewar U.S. uniform, corners of card lightly trimmed. **45.00**

Cdv of General "Stonewall" Jackson probably reproduced from a daguerreotype taken c. 1846.

Middle Tennessee Relics

Mexican War era-bust shot, in nice condition with strong sharp corners, slightly faded from light exposure. **150.00**

General T.J. "Stonewall" Jackson, cont.

Somewhat faded view of General Thomas J. Jackson in his Confederate uniform.

Middle Tennessee Relics

Bust view in Confederate uniform, photo, unfortunately, has faded and is somewhat light. For this reason, the price is much, much more reasonable than it would otherwise be for this rare cdv, has no backmark. **195.00**

President Jefferson Davis

Handsome portrait of the President of the Confederacy, negative slightly re-touched, but good clarity and photo contrast. Shows him in a fine suit of clothes circa 1861. .... **49.00**

Image of Confederate President Jefferson Davis.

Middle Tennessee Relics

Perhaps the Louisville, Kentucky, photographer's imprint or the personalized message on the back of this image reading, "Jefferson Davis Pres. Confederacy—Mrs. Hart's mother and Jeff Davis were intimate friends—1861" pushed the price of this image higher than usual for a Davis photo.

Middle Tennessee Relics

Photo has some yellowing from age, but is complete and sound, has a rare "Webster & Bro. Louisville" photographer's mark. On the back is written "Jefferson Davis Pres. Confederacy—Mrs. Hart's mother and Jeff Davis were intimate friends—1861." **275.00**

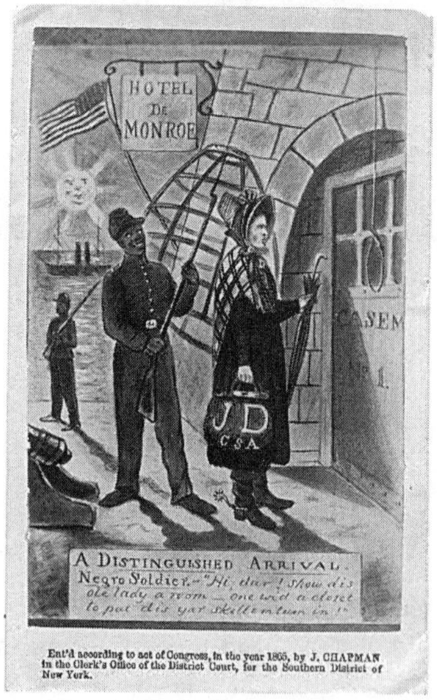

The story of the Confederate President attempting to elude capture by wearing a woman's dress was popular fodder for postwar caricatures.

1865 cartoon depicting Confederate President Jefferson Davis, and his ill-fated attempt to escape Union forces by dressing in women' clothes. Shown here escorted by a Union soldier to a prison cell at Fort Monroe.............................. **130.00**

Confederate, Other

Confederate carte de visites are actually quite rare. Many of those that exist were actually made of Confederate prisoners of war by northern photographers. This stunning image of Captain John C. Underwood, 9th Tennessee Cavalry Battalion, was probably made while a captive at Fort Warren.

Frohne's Historic Military

Captain John C. Underwood, 9th Tennessee Cavalry Battalion, armed Confederate Captain prisoner-of-war John C. Underwood. He was a prisoner of war at Fort Warren, Boston Harbor, during 1863-1865. Note the very unusual pleated Confederate uniform, as well as the two-piece belt buckle. Underwood is holding a sword, obviously a photographer's prop. Image is in very-fine condition. This image was part of the large album of confederate prisoner of war images that included many officers from the Confederate ironclad *Atlanta*. **1,500.00**

Dated on the back, "June 12, 1862," it is quite likely that this image of Confederate Captain R.F. Ford is the exception to the rule and was produced by a southern photographer.

Frohne's Historic Military

Captain R.F. Ford, rank insignia boldly shown on his collar. No backmark, but written in pencil on the back is "June 12, 1862." Very minor crease in bottom right corner. **595.00**

This postwar copy of a wartime image depicts Colonel Edward Dillon of the 2nd Mississippi Cavalry. Like all Confederate images, this one was immediately snapped up by a collector.

Frohne's Historic Military

Colonel Edward Dillon, 2nd Mississippi Cavalry, 2nd Mississippi Cavalry, formed in the Spring of 1863 from soldiers originally destined for the 47th Mississippi Infantry. They fought in Mississippi and Georgia and probably served under Forrest at one time. A number were captured at Selma, Alabama, in 1865. A strong, sharp postwar image in his colonel's uniform. **500.00**

First Assistant Engineer Thomas Morrill served aboard the rebel ironclad *Atlanta.*

Frohne's Historic Military

First Assistant Engineer William Thomas Morrill, served aboard the Rebel ironclad *Atlanta*. Image taken while a prisoner of war at Fort Warren, Boston Harbor, black, Boston backmark. Signed in period ink on the front. **1,500.00**

Image of Quantrill raider "Bloody Bill" Anderson.

Frohne's Historic Military

Lieutenant William Anderson, absolutely wonderful cdv of Quantrill Raider William Anderson (also known as "Bloody Bill"). Noted for riding into battle with a necklace of Union scalps around his horses neck and encouraging his men to scalp and mutilate their corpses. Image taken in death, no photographer's backmark. Anderson had been shot twice in the back of the head. Very-fine condition! **3,500.00**

Officer, Armed, full standing view crisply contrasted with fine clarity. Officer is short of stature wearing regulation C.S. cap, frock coat with vivid galloons on sleeves, sword belt with two-piece interlocking buckle, and holding his foot officer's sword directly in front of him. Edges have been trimmed to round the top and bottom, some edge scuffs on the extreme right not touching the subject at all. **575.00**

Officer, knees-up seated pose of an officer with heavy long beard. Wears regulation C.S. double-breasted frock, knee-high boots, and holding a regulation C.S. officer's kepi in his lap. Excellent with bottom edge trimmed and some yellow toning. **350.00**

Water Battery at Yorktown, very good condition, Brady's Album Gallery. **275.00**

Union, Generals

Images of General Abner Doubleday are popular with both Civil War collectors and baseball enthusiasts (though he didn't really invent the game in spite of his claims).

Frohne's Historic Military

General Abner Doubleday, fought at Gettysburg, but most famous for the false attribution that he had founded the game of baseball. A beautiful 1863 cdv in fine condition, Brady imprint. **750.00**

Noted for organizing a regiment of Zouaves (the 5th New York Infantry), Abram Duryee was wounded five times during the war.

Frohne's Historic Military

General Abram Duryee, wounded 5 times during the war (twice during the 2nd Bull Run campaign, and three more times during the South Mountain and Sharpsburg battles), Duryee was the Colonel of the "Duryee's Zouaves" (5th New York Infantry). This is an outstanding image, with superb contrast and clarity. Anthony by Brady backmark. **275.00**

Alexander Pennington received his general's brevet for his support of Custer's cavalry brigade at the Battle of Gettysburg.

Frohne's Historic Military

General Alexander C.M. Pennington, very boldly signed image of Alexander C. M. Pennington as Colonel of the 3rd New Jersey Cavalry (the famous "Butterflies") and brevet Brigadier General. Pennington was an 1860 graduate of West Point and a very famous artillery officer during the early part of the war. He was an extremely active commander of Battery M, 2nd U. S. Artillery until his promotion to Colonel of the 3rd New Jersey Cavalry. He was given a brevet promotion for his gallantry in supporting Custer's Brigade at Gettysburg. Faint hint of shoulder board can been seen on what appears to be a civilian coat. Tax stamp, New York backmark. **1,100.00**

General Alexander Hays was killed during the Battle of the Wilderness in 1864.

Frohne's Historic Military

General Alexander Hays, killed in action on May 5, 1864, at the Wilderness. Anthony backmark, stunning contrast and clarity. **550.00**

Clear view of General Alfred Pleasanton.

Frohne's Historic Military

General Alfred Pleasanton, very sharp and clear, minor foxing and staining as shown, and the contrast is superb. Fredricks, New York, backmark. **175.00**

General Alpheus Williams, a rare bust pose of a young looking Alpheus Williams in a brigadier's frock with straps. The backmark reads "Photographed by AR Henwood 46th Regt PV Gen Williams Division 12th Army Corps." Bottom edge of carte is irregularly trimmed. **190.00**

Wartime view of General Alvin Gillem.

Frohne's Historic Military

General Alvin Gillem, not only a great civil war general, but his postwar career as Colonel of the 1st U. S. Cavalry included duty during the Modoc War. Very minor corner crease on lower left-hand bottom of image that affects nothing and is difficult to notice. Merritt's National Portrait Gallery, Nashville, Tennessee, backmark. Also a period ink id. of "Brig Genl Gillem" on verso. **495.00**

Once the commander of the Army of the Potomac, General Ambrose was elected governor of Rhode Island following the war.

Frohne's Historic Military

General Ambrose Burnside, one-time commander of the Army of the Potomac, Burnside was also Governor of Rhode Island after the war, very-fine condition, Anthony by Brady backmark. **185.00**

Brevetted a general during the Civil War, Andrew Jackson Smith was appointed Colonel of the 7th U.S. Cavalry in 1866.

Frohne's Historic Military

General Andrew Jackson Smith, appointed to be the first colonel of the 7th U. S. Cavalry in 1866, a command he held until he resigned it in 1869. Smith had an excellent civil war service record, receiving three brevet promotions for Pleasant Hill, Louisiana, Tupelo, Mississippi, and Nashville, Tennessee. Fine condition with soiling, no backmark. **200.00**

General Benjamin Prentiss was recognized for his gallant defense in the Hornet's Nest at the Battle of Shiloh in 1862. Example shown is an Anthony image.

Frohne's Historic Military

General Benjamin Prentiss, Prentiss was the colonel of the 10th Illinois Infantry, and was promoted to General in May 1861. "He commanded the 6th Division of U. S. Grant's Army of the Tennessee on April 1, 1862, at Shiloh where he gallantly defended the celebrated Hornets Nest. After holding off the Confederates for six hours, his position, an eroded lane with a field of brambles in front, was overrun and he was compelled to surrender." He also commanded the District of Eastern Arkansas and successfully defended Helena from Confederate attack. Minor spots in background top (part of the image), otherwise, superb condition and contrast, Anthony backmark **250.00**

An 1843 graduate of West Point, General C.C. Auger was wounded at the Battle of Cedar Mountain.

Frohne's Historic Military

General C. C. Augur, 1843 West Point graduate, on active duty until 1885, severely wounded at the battle of Cedar Mountain, and was General N. P. Banks requested second in command during the Port Hudson campaign. Augur also commanded the Department of Texas during the Indian Wars. A stunning photograph of Augur, with superb tones and sharp contrast, no backmark. . . **195.00**

General Charles Albright began his military career as the Colonel of the 132 Pennsylvania Volunteer Infantry.

Frohne's Historic Military

General Charles Albright, colonel of the 132nd Pennsylvania Infantry, 34th Pennsylvania Militia, and the 202nd Pennsylvania Infantry. Excellent condition. "Henszey & Co., Photographers, 812 Arch Street, Philadelphia" backmark. Remnant of previous (small) price label on verso, along with blue tax stamp. . **195.00**

General Charles Bradley Stoughton, Stoughton was the colonel of the 4th Vermont Infantry and Brevet Brigadier General. (Shown in the Brady bust photo as a colonel). A scarce Brady General's photo. **250.00**

Charles Devans went to war as the Colonel of the 15th Massachusetts. He swiftly rose through the ranks to earn general's stars. This image of him has a period ink signature.

Frohne's Historic Military

General Charles Devens, Jr., colonel of the 15th Mass. Infantry, almost killed at Balls Bluff, but bullet was stopped by uniform button. Also wounded at Seven Pines (Fair Oaks) and Chancellorsville. Commander of the Army of the Tennessee under Sherman. J. W. Black, Boston backmark. Blue two-cent tax stamp, some foxing spots on verso, as well as those shown on the front, nice period ink id. **295.00**

General Charles Stone carte de viste.

Frohne's Historic Military

General Charles P. Stone, Brady backmark, very minor trim near bottom of image, stunning contrast and quality. **195.00**

Clinton Bowen Fisk soon rose from the colonelcy of the 33rd Missouri Infantry to the rank of Major General.

Frohne's Historic Military

General Clinton Bowen Fisk, appointed as the colonel of the 33rd Missouri Infantry. Soon a major general, Fisk commanded the Department of Southeast Missouri and later the Department of North Missouri. He successfully defended the state from raids led by Price, Marmaduke, and Joe Shelby. Fisk was an avowed abolitionist who neither drank nor swore. He was the founder of Fisk University for Negroes in Nashville, Tennessee. Gutekunst, Philadelphia backmark. **295.00**

The famous commander of the 3rd Corps, Dan Sickles is also noted for writing the music of "Taps."

Frohne's Historic Military

General Daniel Sickles, scarce variation on the normal view of Sickles, he is turned to his left slightly and gazing off in the distance. Very-fine condition with a very minor smudge on the very bottom of the card stock front, under the albumen. This is a great image of the general who lost his leg at Gettysburg, Anthony backmark. **360.00**

General David Birney led the 3rd Corps at Gettysburg after Dan Sickles fell wounded.

Frohne's Historic Military

General David Birney, beautiful Brady, New York, image of this Union general. Birney led the Third Corps at Gettysburg after Sickles was wounded. He died of Malaria in 1864, an outstanding image. **300.00**

General David Hunter, image taken when he was the Colonel of the 1st U.S. Cavalry, bust portrait, published by "A. Winchof Phila." **100.00**

Originally the commander of the 7th Massachusetts Infantry, David Russell was given the command of the Union VI Corps.

Frohne's Historic Military

General David Russell, Russell, a West Point class of 1845 graduate, was promoted in 1862 to be the Colonel of the 7th Massachusetts. November 1862, Russell was promoted to General and given a brigade command in the VI Corps. At the battle of Winchester, Russell was killed instantly by a shell fragment that tore through his heart. Exceptionally fine condition, Anthony backmark. **395.00**

E.R.S. Canby was the only general officer killed during the Indian wars.

Frohne's Historic Military

General E.R.S. Canby, sharp clarity and content, excellent mount, blue tax stamp on verso. Anthony backmark. Canby had a long, successful career in the army, only to have it cut short by the treachery of Captain Jack and the Modoc Indians in April 1873. He is the only General officer to be killed by Indians. **450.00**

This outdoor view of General Edwin Sumner was originally marketed by Matthew Brady.

Frohne's Historic Military

General Edwin Sumner, Sumner standing outside of his headquarters near Yorktown in May 1862. Brady's Album Gallery image, No. 408, outstanding contrast and clarity, minor clipped corners. **295.00**

This image of General Ely Parker is signed with both his given and Indian name.

Frohne's Historic Military

General Ely S. Parker, image taken by Gutenkunst, Philadelphia. Previously framed, you can still see a slight discoloration caused by the mat around the image. Signed with both his military rank, and his Indian Nation name of "Do-ne-ho-ga-wa" (translated as "Open Door"). **3,200.00**

This is an 1862-dated image of General Franz Sigel.

Frohne's Historic Military

General Franz Sigel, superb condition, image of the famous German general dated 1862, Anthony by Brady backmark, M.B. Brady frontmark. Sigel was soundly defeated by the cadets from VMI at the battle of New Market in 1864. . . . . **275.00**

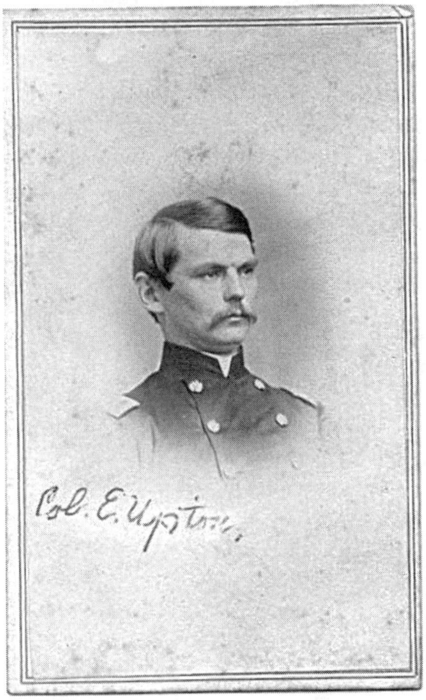

General Emory Upton was once the commander of the 121st New York Infantry.

Frohne's Historic Military

General Emory Upton, Addis, Washington D.C. backmark. **595.00**

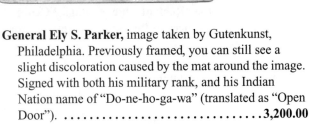

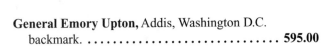

Image of General George McCall.

Frohne's Historic Military

General George A. McCall. Brady backmark, good condition, with some foxing and soiling. **210.00**

George Day Wagner was promoted to general on April 4, 1863.

Frohne's Historic Military

General George Day Wagner, Wagner began the war as Colonel of the 15th Indiana Infantry, and was promoted to General on April 4, 1863. Wagner is best known for his attempted stand at the battle of Franklin, Tennessee, in front of Schofield's army, in which he was routed by Hood and the charging rebel army. Excellent period identification of Wagner, with wear and stains as shown. **250.00**

General George Gordon Meade

Classic bust portrait in uniform of General George G. Meade. The reverse bears the highly desirable imprint of "Tyson Brothers Gettysburg, Pa."......... **79.00**

George Gordon Meade is best known for commanding the Union forces at the Battle of Gettysburg.

Middle Tennessee Relics

General Meade is famous for commanding Union forces at the Battle of Gettysburg. The image is displayed in a paper holder possibly out of a period photo album. The photo is a little shorter than normal, probably cut to fit the holder. **85.00**

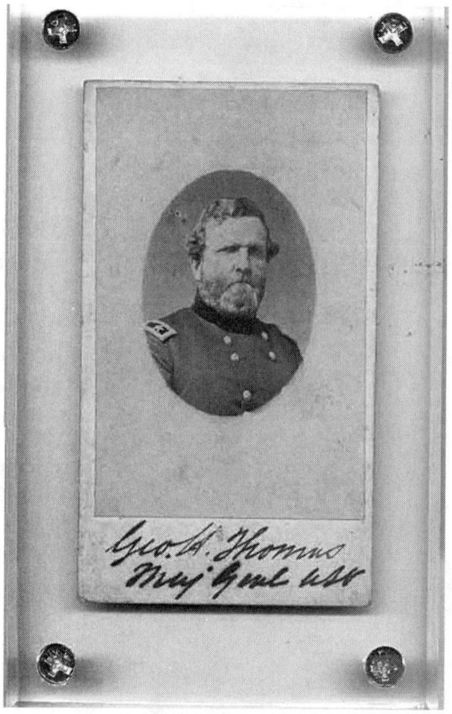

Made famous as the "Rock of Chickamauga," George H. Thomas became the hero of thousands of western troops.

Frohne's Historic Military

General George H. Thomas

Superb, period, ink signed image of "The Rock of Chickamauga." Thomas is one of the most famous western union generals, and his signed cartes de visite are highly sought after. **1,250.00**

Truly pristine, mint, magnificent seated portrait of "The Rock of Chickamauga" boldly autographed in brown ink on the bottom front of the mount. The image has impeccable contrast and depth showing him in Major General's frock and straps. The autograph is likewise bold and strong and dark: "Geo H Thomas/Maj. Gen'l. USV." **1,595.00**

Once the commander of the Army of Potomac and probably second in popularity only to General Grant, George McClellan made an unsuccessful bid for the presidency in 1864. His images, though, were successfully distributed throughout the Union.

Middle Tennessee Relics

General George McClellan, bust-shot view shows his general straps on the double-breasted frock coat. No backmark. **65.00**

George Stoneman commanded the 3rd Corps during the Fredricksburg Campaign.

Frohne's Historic Military

General George Stoneman, looking directly at the camera, Rockwood, Philadelphia, backmark. Wonderful contrast and clarity to the image, minor browning of areas on the mount, not affecting albumen. **175.00**

Anthony-marked image of General Stoneman.

Frohne's Historic Military

General George Stoneman, sharp Anthony backmarked view of this famous Union cavalry officer, fine condition. **185.00**

General Gordon Granger

Very handsome bust portrait bearing Brandy/Anthony imprint showing this famed Western Campaign general in his Major General's coat and straps. . .**24.00**

Gordon Granger rose from being the Colonel of the 2nd Michigan Cavalry to earn a general's brevet. After the war, he was appointed Colonel of the 25th U.S. Infantry.

Frohne's Historic Military

Colonel of the 2nd Michigan cavalry in the early part of the war, Granger had a fine record while in the army, and at the end of the war he was appointed to be the Colonel of the 25th U.S. Infantry. This superb image has an Anthony by Brady backmark, and is in exceptional condition. **195.00**

Governor Warren adeptly commanded the II Corps during the Battle of Gettysburg.

Frohne's Historic Military

General Governor K. Warren, at Gettysburg he handled the 2nd Corps after Hancock was wounded. Brady, Washington backmark, minor corner clips, superb contrast and clarity. **195.00**

Green B. Raum commanded the 2nd Brigade, 3rd Division, 15th Army Corps.

Frohne's Historic Military

General Green B. Raum, beautifully signed cdv of Illinois General Green B. Raum, signed while a Colonel commanding the "2 Brig 3rd Div 15th AC." Fine condition with minor wear and foxing. **595.00**

General Henry Slocum, rare image bearing the backmark of "Goldin Wash DC." This shows Slocum seated (knees up) wearing his regulation major general's frock coat with shoulder straps. Excellent near-mint image. **125.00**

General Hugh Kilpatrick, from life, clear uniformed photo of cavalry general "Kill Cavalry." Picture has been removed from its original CDV backing. **110.00**

Irwin McDowell is most noted for his mishandling of Union troops at the First Bull Run and his appetite for watermelons.

General Irwin McDowell

C. D. Fredricks & Co. New York backmark, minor foxing, soiling. **95.00**

Commander of Union Forces at Bull Run. a bust portrait, taken from life by Hallet & Brothers of New York. He wears the General's frock coat with velvet collar and shoulder straps with two stars. ... **185.00**

Nice bust portrait, "McClees Wash DC" backmark, top and bottom edges of carte trimmed.......... **69.00**

Photo of General Joseph B. Carr.

Frohne's Historic Military

General J.B. Carr, image was owned by General Eugene A. Carr, no backmark, almost the size of a cabinet card. **195.00**

General J.D. Webster, bust pose in brigadier's uniform with straps. Carte dramatically trimmed to 1/9th plate size. **59.00**

A Civil War General, James Garfield rose to the Presidency of the United States after the Civil War. This is a stunningly clear image of Garfield in his General's uniform.

Frohne's Historic Military

General James A. Garfield

Clarity and crispness are outstanding. Every wrinkle in his uniform is evident and you can actually count whiskers. There is minor wear to top left corner as you look at the image, no photographer's mark. **495.00**

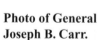

Wartime view of General James Garfield taken by "army photographer" J.W. Campbell.

Frohne's Historic Military

Very sharp view of assassinated President James A. Garfield, taken during the war when he was a Union Army General. Outstanding contrast and clarity. "J. W. Campbell, Army Photographer, 20th Army Corps, Army of the Cumberland" backmark, trimmed. **295.00**

General James B. Ricketts, great standing view by Brady of Ricketts in Brigadier's uniform coat and straps. Nicely notated on back in brown ink "Ricketts commanding division 6th Corps Army of Potomac." **95.00**

General James McPherson was the only Union Army commander killed during the Civil War.

Frohne's Historic Military

Minor foxing on this image of General McPherson may have contributed to keeping the price down.

Frohne's Historic Military

General James Birdseye McPherson
McPherson has the unlucky distinction of being the only Union Army commander to be killed in the Civil War. This 1863 image is in fine condition, with very minor foxing on albumen and mount. Photographers imprint on bottom front of carte reads "Maj. Gen. J. B. McPherson. Entered according to Act of Congress, A.D. 1863, by Barr & Young, in the Clerk's Office of the District Court of the U.S. for the So. District of Ohio." Also imprinted "Barr & Young" on verso of image. **300.00**

General James Birdseye McPherson, nice view of the only Union Army commander to be killed during the war. Minor foxing as shown, "J. Carbutt, 131 Lake St., Chicago" backmark, orange tax stamp. **175.00**

Image of General McPherson.

Frohne's Historic Military

Image once owned by General Eugene A. Carr. St. Louis backmark. **375.00**

James Shackelford rose from his original rank of Colonel of the 25th Kentucky Volunteer Infantry to eventually capture his general's stars.

Frohne's Historic Military

General James M. Shackelford, began the war as colonel of the 25th Kentucky Infantry, he then raised to the 8th Kentucky Cavalry, the unit credited for capturing the Rebel General John Hunt Morgan during his famous raid. A beautiful image with wonderful contrast and clarity. Period ink writing on the back reads "Brig. Gen. Shackelford Morgan's Capturer." Schleier, Nashville, backmark. **375.00**

General James S. Jackson gave his life for the Union at the Battle of Perryville in 1862. This image was produced after his death.

Frohne's Historic Military

General James S. Jackson, Jackson began the Civil War as colonel of the 3rd Kentucky Cavalry and was promoted to Brigadier General in July, 1862. At the battle of Perryville on October 8, 1862, Jackson and both his brigade commanders were killed on the field. Image is in fine condition with one bottom (right) corner clip and very minor soiling to Jackson's. Broadbent, Philadelphia backmark. **295.00**

James Shields commanded a brigade of volunteers during the Mexican War. He was made a general of volunteers in 1861, but resigned his rank in 1863. Images of Shields in uniform are scarce.

Frohne's Historic Military

General James Shield, the only man to represent three different states in the U. S. Senate. Shields almost fought a duel with future president A. Lincoln (Lincoln wrote an insulting article about him) and he also was a Mexican War General of Illinois Volunteers. Appointed a brigadier general by his now close friend Lincoln in 1861. He resigned his commission in 1863. Superb condition, Fredricks' backmark. **495.00**

General James Wadsworth took a bullet to the brain at the Battle of the Wilderness in 1864.

Frohne's Historic Military

General James Wadsworth

Absolutely superb war date image of Wadsworth with his sword. "At the Wilderness on May 6, 1864, while leading his men in an attempt to repel an assault, he was shot off his horse, a bullet entering the back of his head and lodging in his brain." Very minor wear to image, striking contrast **325.00**

Wartime, outdoor view of General Wadsworth.

Frohne's Historic Military

Absolutely superb war date image of Wadsworth with his sword, standing outside. Very minor wear to image, good contrast, Anthony by Brady backmark. **250.00**

General John Buford served with distinction while using his cavalry troops to delay the Confederate advance on Gettysburg on July 1, 1863.

Frohne's Historic Military

General John Buford, very fine condition cdv of famous Gettysburg General John Buford. Brady backmark, he died in late 1863. .... **850.00**

General John G. Foster, very nice knees-up standing view with Brady/Anthony imprint showing the general standing in his regulation Brigadier's frock and straps and holding his kepi. **89.00**

General John "Black Jack" Logan was credited with beginning the celebration of Memorial Day.

Frohne's Historic Military

General John Logan, excellent contrast and clarity, minor trim as shown, no backmark. **225.00**

This albumen print of General John McArthur is a bit larger than a normal cdv.

Frohne's Historic Military

General John MacArthur, albumen measures 5.5" x 4". Minor stain on thin paper mount as shown, otherwise very good condition. Good contrast and clarity. Facsimile signature near bottom of mount. Authentic period albumen, not a modern reproduction. . . . **195.00**

General John Milton Brannon, excellent with Brady-Anthony backmark. This shows Brannan seated (waist up) with his stupendous beard wearing the regulation frock of a brigadier with brigadier's shoulder straps. **115.00**

General John Newton, "He was conspicuous in storming Marye's Heights at Fredericksburg during the campaign of Chancellorsville, and at Gettysburg he was selected by George G. Meade to direct the I Corps after the death of John F. Reynolds, even though he belonged to a different corps." Brady backmark, some foxing and staining. **200.00**

Having commanded the 1st Colorado Infantry at the Battle of Glorietta Pass, John Potts Slough was awarded general's stars. After the war, he perished in a billiard hall.

Frohne's Historic Military

General John Potts Slough, "For Gov. & Mrs. Mitchell" written on verso in period ink. Hoag & Quick Cincinnati backmark, image in very fine condition. Slough became the Colonel of the 1st Colorado Infantry and won glory at Glorieta Pass in direct defiance of orders from his superior officer. Promoted to General in August 1862, served as military governor of Alexandria, Virginia. Appointed Chief justice of New Mexico Territory in 1865. Killed in an 1867 billiard room fight in New Mexico. **350.00**

General John Reynolds

Beautiful and rare image of this famous killed-at-Gettysburg general. Trimmed at top, but the image in superb condition with strong contrast and clarity. **750.00**

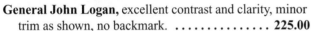

A hero of the Mexican War, John Reynolds fell on the first day of the Battle of Gettysburg while commanding the First Corps.

Frohne's Historic Military

General John Reynolds, cont.

Commander of the 1st Corps killed in action on July 1, 1863 at Gettysburg. McClees, Philadelphia, backmark. **350.00**

Famous for his cavalry exploits, General Judson Kilpatrick embodied the romantic notion of the mounted soldier.

Frohne's Historic Military

General Judson Kilpatrick

Anthony by Brady backmark. Minor foxing on verso of this excellent view of the famous Union cavalry general. **195.00**

Unusual pose of General Kilpatrick.

Frohne's Historic Military

Unusual pose of this famous Union cavalry commander, wear and foxing, Bogardus, New York backmark. **195.00**

A rare view of Kit Carson in uniform, this image of the famous western hero and Edwin Perrin was taken in 1862.

Frohne's Historic Military

General Kit Carson and Edwin Perrin, a rare image of Carson in his Army frock coat with Edwin Perrin, taken in Albuquerque, January 1862. Perrin was a government expediter, sent to New Mexico by the Secretary of War to help arm New Mexican troops for conflict in the Southwestern theater. Imprint of Anthony. Rich tones, very slightly clipped corners. **3,000.00**

General Lorenzo Thomas was known as the "Rock of Chickamauga."

General Lorenzo Thomas, Frederick's & Co., New York, backmark. Image in excellent condition. **135.00**

General Lovell H. Rousseau, seated 3/4-length pose bearing Giers, Nashville backmark, showing him seated at table with slouch hat next to him. He wears his brigadier's coat and straps. **39.00**

Carte de viste of General Mitchell taken by a New York photographer.

Middle Tennessee Relics

General Mitchell, bust view image of Union General Mitchell. This is a nice condition image with a "D. Appleton, N.Y." backmark. **85.00**

Before earning the rank of General, Morgan Lewis Smith was the Colonel of the 8th Missouri Infantry.

Frohne's Historic Military

General Morgan Lewis Smith, superb image of the former Colonel of the 8th Missouri Infantry and General, Morgan L. Smith. Armstead & Taylor, Corinth, Mississippi, backmark. Very-fine condition with very minor wear. **495.00**

Later to be promoted to General, Colonel Mortimer Leggett and Lieutenant Owen posed in their field uniforms for this appealing image.

Dave Taylor Civil War Antiques

General Mortimer Leggett, shows Mortimer Leggett as Colonel and Lieutenant Owen, A.A.G. both in actual field garb including dirty boots and spurs, slouch hats, gauntlets, and ratty swords posed in a very striking studio pose. Boldly signed on the reverse by each of the men, "M.D. Leggett Col. Comdg 2d Brig.," and, "Lieut. E.N. Owen AAA Genl 2nd Brigade." **1,450.00**

As the Colonel of the 30th Massachusetts Infantry, Nathan Dudley earned the brevet rank of general while campaigning in Louisiana.

Frohne's Historic Military

General Nathan Augustus Monroe Dudley, Nathan Augustus Monroe Dudley joined the 10th U.S. Infantry in 1855 and served until his retirement as Colonel of the 1st U.S. Cavalry in 1889. "He was an overbearing, quarrelsome man and a heavy drinker" is how he was described. Dudley became the colonel of the 30th Mass. Infantry and earned brevets for Baton Rouge and Port Hudson during the war. As lieutenant colonel of the 9th Cavalry, Dudley refused to send troops to keep the peace during the famous "Lincoln County War." No backmark, but superb period ink identification along the edges of the image. Small pin holes in upper corners. . . . **450.00**

After being promoted to General, Oliver Otis Howard lost his right arm at the Battle of Seven Pines.

Frohne's Historic Military

General Oliver Otis Howard

Excellent view of this famous Gettysburg commander. Colonel of the 3rd Maine Infantry, Howard was quickly promoted to Brigadier General. He lost his right arm at the battle of the Seven Pines. Howard was given the thanks of Congress for his actions during the battle of Gettysburg. "Gutekunst, Phila." backmark. Minor ink stain and very minor soiling. **195.00**

General O.O. Howard lost his arm at the Battle of Seven Pines.

Frohne's Historic Military

O. O. Howard served his country for over 40 years. He lost his arm at the battle of Seven Pines in 1862 and was awarded the Medal of Honor for his actions there. Image in fine condition with outstanding contrast and clarity. Minor chip to lower left corner, no backmark. **225.00**

The value of a signature on a carte de visite is demonstrated by this image of O.O. Howard.

Frohne's Historic Military

Spectacular signed view of Union General Oliver Otis Howard. Clear and crisp 1/2 view, signed boldly by Howard in the top background of the albumen. Minor trim to bottom of the card, Anthony backmark. **950.00**

General Orlando B. Wilcox, a pristine seated view showing Wilcox wearing the uniform and straps of a major general. A splendid, beautifully composed image taken at the war's end. **175.00**

General Ormsby Mitchell, a clear from life standing view circa 1862 showing Ormsby Mitchell with his large full head of hair wearing a brigadier's frock with straps, buff general's sash, sword belt, sword, and holding his forage cap. A very obscure view taken by Hoag & Quick in Cincinnati, Ohio, and bearing their backmark. . . . **95.00**

The flamboyant Phil Sheridan is just as popular today as he was during the war.

Frohne's Historic Military

General Philip H. Sheridan

A super crisp image of the Union's famous cavalry commander. Minor wear at very bottom of the mount, not affecting the image, no backmark. **375.00**

Uniformed steel engraved portrait of Union Cavalry General "Little Phil" Sheridan. "New York Photographic Co." Broadway backmark. **110.00**

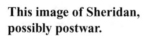

This image of Sheridan, possibly postwar.

Frohne's Historic Military

Might be postwar, but similar views taken in May and June 1865. Very fine condition, with great contrast and clarity. Hartford, Connecticut, backmark. **350.00**

The capture of Morris Island is considered to be General Quincy Gilmore's greatest achievement during the war.

Frohne's Historic Military

General Quincy Gillmore, commanded the Department of the South, and the capture of Morris Island, his greatest accomplishment, Anthony backmark. **110.00**

Having distinguished himself at the head of the 8th Illinois Infantry at the battles of Forts Henry and Donelson, Richard Ogelsby was promoted to general.

Frohne's Historic Military

General Richard Oglesby, colonel of the 8th Illinois Infantry, he distinguished himself at Forts Henry and Donelson. Promoted to general, he was so severely wounded at Corinth he was out of action for over a year. Elected governor of Illinois in 1864, he also served as a senator. Excellent half-view with minor wear, Decatur, Illinois, backmark. **225.00**

General Robert Anderson

Absolutely pristine image (richly contrasted and incredibly clear) showing Major Robert Anderson, the hero of Fort Sumter, seated in the uniform of a major general. He has his frock coat with shoulder straps, a cape draped over his left shoulder, a pair of reading glasses in his right hand, a book in his left hand, and his kepi with "US" in wreath insignia on the table next to him. Best of all the bottom front of this rich card is boldly autographed in brown ink "Robert Anderson" making this a truly historic piece of photo history. The left and right sides of the card have been slightly trimmed, not affecting the photo or signature at all. **1,150.00**

Best known as having sustained the bombardment, but eventually surrendering Fort Sumter, Robert Anderson eventually achieved the rank of general.

Frohne's Historic Military

"Hero of Fort Sumter." 3/4-view, in uniform with hat, backmarked, "J. Gurney & Son, New York.". . **185.00**

The hero of Fort Sumter shown from his left rear standing in a 3/4-length pose. Viewer can see back of Anderson's coat, one brigadier's strap, and the left side of his face, as well as his McDowell cap on the table next to him. Great clarity and contrast, taken by Fredricks of New York. **175.00**

Promoted to General, Robert Mitchell served as Chief of Cavalry for George H. Thomas.

Frohne's Historic Military

General Robert B. Mitchell, badly wounded at the battle of Wilson's Creek as commander of the 2nd Kansas Infantry. Mitchell served as Chief of Cavalry to General G. H. Thomas during the Chickamauga campaign. Mathew Brady, New York backmark, minor corner clips, otherwise sharp contrast and clarity. **275.00**

Before becoming a general, Robert Cameron was the colonel of the famous Iron Brigade unit, the 19th Indiana Volunteer Infantry.

Frohne's Historic Military

General Robert Cameron, lieutenant colonel of the 19th Indiana Infantry (Iron Brigade) before becoming the colonel of the 34th Indiana Infantry (Zouaves). Tax stamp, New Orleans backmark. **650.00**

Robert S. Foster advanced through the ranks to eventually achieve the brevet rank of major general.

Frohne's Historic Military

General Robert S. Foster, born in Vernon, Jennings County, Indiana on January 27, 1834, where he received a common school education. Joining the Union army at the outbreak of the war he fought to the close, being advanced from rank to rank until, on March 31, 1865, he received the brevet of major general of volunteers for gallant conduct in the field. He resigned September 25, 1865, and was offered a lieutenant-colonelcy in the regular army, but declined and took up his residence in Indianapolis. Anthony backmark, blue two-cent cancelled tax stamp. **275.00**

General Rufus Saxton was awarded the Medal of Honor for his defense of Harpers Ferry, Virginia, in 1862.

Frohne's Historic Military

General Rufus Saxton

Rare Gurney view of Rufus Saxton, Medal of Honor winner. **225.00**

This image of Rufus Saxton is a bit more common, but did possess a nice period identification (not in his own hand).

Frohne's Historic Military

Saxton was awarded the Medal of Honor for defending Harpers Ferry in 1862. Great period ink identification on front. Minor wear and foxing. Anthony by Brady backmark. **145.00**

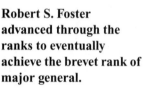

Early image of General Samuel Carroll with just a shoulder strap barely visible.

Middle Tennessee Relics

General Samuel S. Carroll, early photo with visible shoulder straps. **85.00**

Stephen Hurlburt commanded the 4th Division at the bloody Battle of Shiloh in 1862 before being involved in some unsavory handlings at the head of the Department of the Gulf.

Frohne's Historic Military

General Stephen A. Hurlburt, "He commanded the 4th Division of the Army of the Tennessee at Shiloh and in the ensuing campaign against Corinth." He also commanded the Department of the Gulf, and was recommended for arrest for his very corrupt practices. These charges were silenced. Hurlburt was the first Commander-in-Chief of the G.A.R. Morse's Gallery of the Cumberland, Nashville, Tennessee, backmark. **145.00**

Thomas Rowley commanded the 102nd Pennsylvania Infantry before being promoted to general.

Frohne's Historic Military

General Thomas Algeo Rowley, superb view of this very scarce Union general. From an album of 102nd Pennsylvania images, Rowley was their colonel, and this image is not the one published in *Generals in Blue.* Pittsburgh, Pennsylvania backmark. **450.00**

General Thomas L. Crittenden

Crisp and sharply contrasted view of the General who is full length seated and close to the camera. His hair is long and pulled behind his ears. Beard is full and covers only the mustache and chin areas leaving gaunt cheeks showing. His major general's frock has huge, ultra-rich grade shoulder straps with 2 stars in each. He sports a sword belt, gauntlets, and holds his 1850 pattern staff sword in his left hand. **325.00**

Image of Thomas L. Crittenden bearing the appealing back mark of the Army of the Cumberland photographers' Schwing and Rudd.

Frohne's Historic Military

Minor foxing and wear. "Schwing & Rudd, Photographers, Army of the Cumberland" backmark. **195.00**

First achieving notoriety at the Battle of Buena Vista during the Mexican War, Thomas Sherman rose to command a division of the Army of Ohio during the Civil War.

Frohne's Historic Military

General Thomas W. Sherman, excellent 3/4-view of the scarce Union general. Commanded a division of the Army of Ohio during the march upon Corinth, Mississippi, after the battle of Shiloh. Sherman was wounded while leading an assault against the rebel works at Port Hudson on May 27, 1863, resulting in amputation of his right leg. Sharp contrast and clarity, nice early Anthony backmark. **195.00**

General U.S. Grant and Confederate General Lee. Nice cdv-lithograph showing Grant and Lee seated at a table, cdv is of a larger lithograph, circa 1865. .... **35.00**

Today, as in 1865, images of General Grant are only second to images of President Lincoln in popularity. Produced in mass, they are relatively common.

Middle Tennessee Relics

General U.S. Grant

Nice condition image of Ulysses S. Grant. "Gen. Grant" is printed at the bottom of the photograph. ... **85.00**

General U.S. Grant, cont.

A wonderful waist-up seated photo of a pensive looking Grant posed with his eyes cast downward. He is wearing the coat and shoulder straps of a major general (2 stars). The clarity, contrast and condition are all superb. Boldly autographed on the front is Grant's distinctive signature "U.S. Grant/Maj. Gen. USA" executed in deep-brown ink. The photo bears an imprint, "T.F. Saltsman, Nashville," which would date this photo to late 1862 or 1863. ...... **2,500.00**

Fine "from life" bust view in uniform with three stars on shoulder straps. Short hair, well-trimmed beard, Brady copyright printed on bottom front with date of 1865. .... **150.00**

It is a fine bust portrait of Grant with longer hair, fuller beard, and wearing the coat of a major general, imprint on the reverse is from McClees Gallery in Philadelphia. **165.00**

Posed in his uniform, waist up view, fine. **45.00**

Image bearing an ink identification, but not in Grant's hand.

Frohne's Historic Military

Super sharp, period-ink identified image of General U.S. Grant, contrast and clarity are outstanding, no backmark. **195.00**

Wesley Merritt received his brevet to general for his actions at the Battle of Brandy Station. This is an image of General Merritt, made with outstanding contrast and clarity.

Frohne's Historic Military

General Wesley Merritt, John Goldin, Washington backmark, minor foxing, superb contrast and clarity. **650.00**

Commanding the 2nd Cavalry Division at the Battle of Kelly's Ford, Virginia, in 1863, William Averell achieved notoriety as a superb horseman.

Frohne's Historic Military

General William Averell, colonel of the 3rd Pennsylvania Cavalry. "His 2nd Cavalry Division won the first claimed victory of the Federal horse over the Confederates at Kelly's Ford, Virginia, in March 1863-an action said to be the turning point of cavalry fighting in the Eastern theater." Has rubber stamped numbers "13166" near bottom verso. R. W. Addis backmark. **185.00**

General William F. Arny, full standing view of Arny wearing a frontiersman's fur hat and clothed in buckskins and hides, standing next to a chair, which is draped with an Indian blanket. The image bears a Brady/Anthony backmark, but was taken by Alexander Gardner, who was a personal friend of Arny. The view is in excellent condition, and there is some color tinting on some of the buckskins. **395.00**

General William F. Bartlett

Wounded four times and taken prisoner, wartime images of General William F. Bartlett are rather scarce.

Frohne's Historic Military

Rare image of amputee 4-time wounded General W. F. Bartlett, not long after his release from Libby Prison. Taken by Black & Case in Boston in March of 1865. Wonderful photographer's proof stamp on verso, minor corner clips. Images of Bartlett as a General are extremely rare, as he received his commission towards the end of the war (June 1864) and spent most of the time in prison. **495.00**

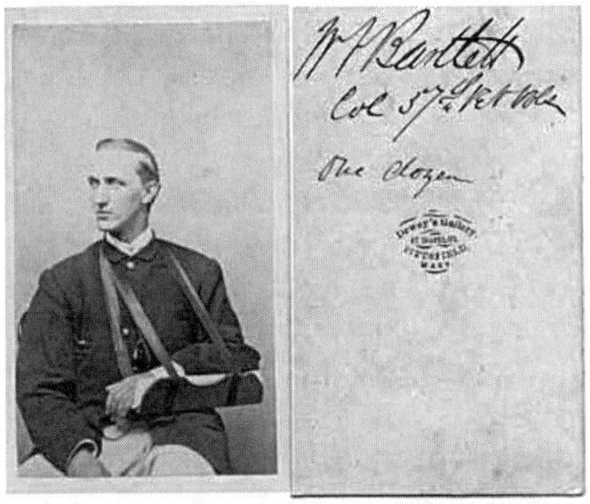

Image of William Bartlett taken while recovering from an arm wound and as the Colonel of the 57th Massachusetts Infantry.

Frohne's Historic Military

Signed image of Bartlett, taken as colonel of the 57th Massachusetts Infantry. Boldly ink signed on the verso. Excellent view of this often wounded general actually wearing a sling for his wounded arm, Pittsfield, MA backmark, very-fine condition. **1,250.00**

General William Barry was General W.T. Sherman's Chief of Artillery.

Frohne's Historic Military

General William Barry, General Sherman's chief of artillery, he served in all actions of the Atlanta campaign, as well as the subsequent Georgia and Carolinas campaigns resulting in the surrender of Johnston's army. A very rare view, minor foxing. **275.00**

Achieving fame as an artilleryman in Mexico at the Battle of Buena Vista in 1847, William French went on to become a corps commander in the Civil War.

Frohne's Historic Military

General William French, Brooklyn, New York backmark, trimmed at top, excellent 1/2 view. **199.00**

William Hays assumed command of the Union Second Corps on the third day of the Battle of Gettysburg.

Frohne's Historic Military

General William Hays, William Hays was a graduate of West Point, Class of 1840. Captured at Chancellorsville, he was delivered at Fortress Monroe on May 15th. On the third day of Gettysburg, Meade assigned Hays to command the II Corps in place of the wounded Hancock and Gibbon. A superb view with period ink identification, Fredrick's New York backmark. . . **295.00**

William Hazen had a military career that spanned nearly forty years.

Frohne's Historic Military

General William Hazen, long outstanding career in the U.S. Army spanned over 30 years. Wounded severely by Indians in 1859, Hazen was appointed colonel of the 41st Ohio Infantry in late 1861. Superb contrast and clarity, no backmark. **375.00**

General William Henry Lawrence, pristine bust portrait, Fredericks NY, shows Lawrence wearing the frock coat of a Colonel and shoulder straps of a Brigadier General (he was brevetted to the rank of Brigadier on March 13, 1865). He served as adjutant of the 1st Massachusetts Volunteers, and then as aide-de-camp to General Joe Hooker. **145.00**

A West Point graduate, William Carlin entered the Civil War as Colonel of the 38th Illinois Infantry and eventually rose to the rank of general.

Frohne's Historic Military

General William P. Carlin, West Point graduate, class of 1850. Began the war as colonel of the 38th Illinois, and was promoted to general in late 1862. Carlin had long successful career in the regulars. Image has some foxing and stains, and the mount has some slight separation along the edges from previous exposure to moisture, no backmark, superb contrast and clarity. **275.00**

This image of William Brooks has a great period ink caption, not in his own hand, identifying him as the commander of the Vermont Brigade.

Frohne's Historic Military

William T.H. Brooks, led a brigade of Vermont Regiments (the back of the image has a great period ink identification "Brig. Gen Brooks, Com Vt Brigade Oct 1st 1862") and was wounded during the Seven Days Campaign in the leg and was wounded again at Antietam as his brigade repulsed a Confederate counterattack. McClees, Philadelphia backmark. Slight trace of old label on the back, otherwise fine condition, with very small corner clips. **225.00**

General William Tecumseh Sherman

Superb signed Civil War-date Brady image, light sepia-tone. This is a head-and-shoulders portrait of the general wearing his dress uniform. Signed at the lower margin, "W.T. Sherman, General." Verso is printed, "Brady's Nation Photographic Portrait Galleries, No. 627 Pennsylvania Avenue, Washington, D.C." Image is in mint condition. **2,500.00**

Rich and deeply contrasted waist-up seated pose of Sherman giving the camera his best "stare." Wears frock and straps of major general. Excellent image with some damage to the cardstock along the right edge and bottom right corner, canceled revenue stamp on the reverse. **69.00**

Sherman as he looked in 1862, taken by "Peplow & Butch" in Memphis, though there is no backmark. It shows "Uncle Billy" in a bust portrait wearing the coat and straps of a major general. His hair is shorter than normal and not combed. His beard is a little messy and his eyes are younger not the hardened eyes in the more common later images. **135.00**

William Tibbits achieved the rank of general late in 1865.

Frohne's Historic Military

General William Tibbits, Rockwell, New York backmark, very-fine condition, and a very, very rare image. Tibbits became a general late in 1865. .... **275.00**

William Burns was the General of the Philadelphia Brigade consisting of the 69th, 71st, 72nd, and 106th Pennsylvania Volunteer Infantry Regiments.

Frohne's Historic Military

General William W. Burns, of the Philadelphia Brigade. **275.00**

Known to his soldiers as "Hancock the Superb," Winfield Scott Hancock was popular in the field and at homes throughout the north.

Frohne's Historic Military

General Winfield Scott Hancock, almost three-dimensional, this is a very nice Hancock image. The contrast and clarity are almost perfect. As to condition, it is very-fine overall, with minor wear to the Brady mount (a small amount of softness to the bottom corners). The albumen has a minute amount of chipping near the bottom in two areas. Also two small rubbed areas. Someone long ago wrote "Hancock" in pencil above his head in the background, this appears to have been erased, leaving a very, very faint background smudge. **395.00**

Less-than-formal portraits of generals are extremely desirable to collectors. This is a group portrait of Generals Phil Sheridan, Wesley Merritt, and George Forsyth.

Frohne's Historic Military

Generals Phil Sheridan, Wesley Merritt, and George "Sandy" Forsyth, posed with two other staff officers, one of whom may be General George Getty. Minor (very minor) bottom trim to mount. Excellent contrast and clarity, "Bendann Bros. Baltimore" backmark. **695.00**

This group portrait that includes General Stoneman and General Naglee.

Frohne's Historic Military

Generals Stoneman and Naglee, outdoor view of Generals Stoneman and Naglee sitting on chairs in front of a tent with four staff officers and enlisted man. Among the staff officers are two future generals: Brevet Generals Andrew J. Alexander and Edwin V. Sumner Jr. A dog is visible in front of the group lying on the ground. Other tents, men, and horses are just visible in left background. Backmark is, "Brady's Album Gallery. No. 438. Generals Stoneman And Nagle and Staff, Richmond, June, 1862." Nice period-ink identifications on image. **625.00**

President Abraham Lincoln and Cabinet , nice composite with 9 oval portraits, Lincoln in the center oval, surrounded by Seward, Chase, Stanton, Blair, Hamlin, Bates, Wells, and Caleb Smith. NY photo company imprint, circa 1862. .... **59.00**

President Abraham Lincoln and Family

Clear image, fine condition. **45.00**

Mass produced cdv-lithograph of Lincoln and his family seated around a table in a fine family setting, circa 1864. .... **39.00**

Nice mid-war lithograph-cdv view being an artist's rendition of the Lincoln family at the White House showing Lincoln reading to Tad, Robert standing behind Abe, Mary off to the other side of the table, etc. Each likeness being based on known Brady photo views.. .... **35.00**

President Abraham Lincoln and Wife, cdv-litho showing the family reading at a table, circa 1864. .... **39.00**

President Abraham Lincoln, fine, 1864-era, mass-produced cdv-lithograph view of Lincoln in the five-dollar bill pose. **35.00**

Published in 1862, this Anthony view of President Abraham Lincoln has a period ink identification, but not in the Lincoln's hand.

Frohne's Historic Military

President Abraham Lincoln, published in 1862 by E. Anthony from a "Photographic Negative in Brady's National Portrait Gallery." Period ink identification on verso, minor back stains. The rich tones and clarity of this image are what separates it from the normal Lincoln images available. **1,500.00**

President Andrew Johnson

Crisp, near full-seated view in the famous Brady chair. Excellent with one tiny scuff at the top of image. Beautifully inscribed in ink on the back, "President Andrew Johnson Inaugurated Apr. 15th 1865. Seventeenth President of the United States. Bought of Brady N.Y. June 5th 1865." **125.00**

No backmark, very-good condition. **65.00**

Though a famous statesman, Edward Everett is probably best remembered for his two-hour speech delivered at the dedication of the National Cemetery at Gettysburg.

Frohne's Historic Military

Presidential Elector Edward Everett, beautiful contrast and clarity, best known for his famous (and lengthy!) Gettysburg oration, given before Lincoln's famous speech. Fredricks' New York backmark, blue tax stamp. **75.00**

Presidents George Washington and Abraham Lincoln, engraving, fine condition. **39.00**

Union, Other

U.S.S. Monitor and C.S. Virginia, Engraving, shows the battle between the Monitor and the Merrimac (Virginia). This is an engraving, but looks more like a real photograph. Backmark is, "James S. Earle & Son, Philadelphia." **45.00**

"Hero of Gettysburg" John Burns

Called the "Hero of Gettysburg," 70-year-old John Burns is known for having taken his gun and joined the Union lines to defend against the Rebel invasion on the first day of the Battle of Gettysburg.

Frohne's Historic Military

Beautiful signed cdv of the famous 70-year-old John Burns who grabbed his gun on July 1, 1863, to help the Union fight on the first day of Gettysburg. A couple very tiny tears in bottom of albumen, otherwise in very fine condition and boldly signed. "Bogardus, New York" backmark. **875.00**

This old War of 1812 veteran, who lived in Gettysburg, was furious about the Confederate invasion of Pennsylvania, so left his farm with musket in hand and fought valiantly with one of the Pennsylvania infantry regiments during the battle of Gettysburg. After the battle he was heralded as a true hero. This photo is near full-length showing old John Burns standing with a bayoneted musket at his side. Brady/Anthony backmark, crisp clarity and contrast, bottom of carte lightly trimmed. Fine piece. **275.00**

Assistant Surgeon Joseph Heaton, 29th Indiana Volunteer Infantry, signed on the front in browned ink, "Yours Truly Jos. Heaton." Heaton was an assistant surgeon in the 29th Indiana Infantry. **150.00**

Captain Abner Heald, 1st Wisconsin Volunteer Infantry, was killed at the Battle of Chickamauga.

Frohne's Historic Military

Captain Abner O. Heald, 1st Wisconsin Infantry, killed in action at the battle of Chickamauga on September 19, 1863, identified on front of image as "Uncle Abner," also on verso as "A. O. Heald, killed in the battle of Chickamauga." Tax stamp, "Harmon, Sheyboygan, Wis." frontmark. **275.00**

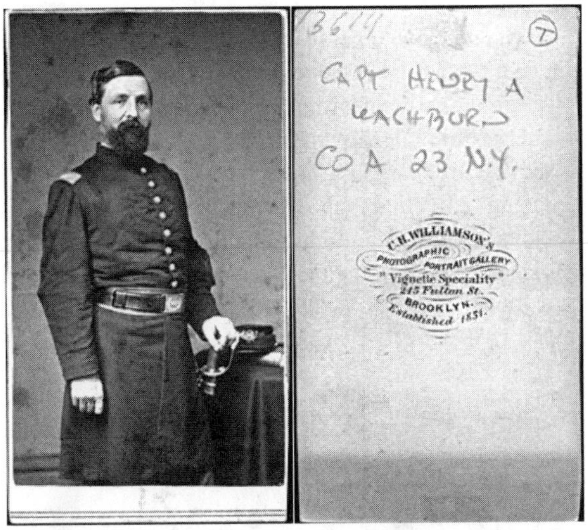

Image identified as Captain Henry Washburn, 23rd New York Militia.

Sharpsburg Arsenal

Captain Henry A. Washburn, 23rd New York Militia, C.H. Williamson's backmark. **175.00**

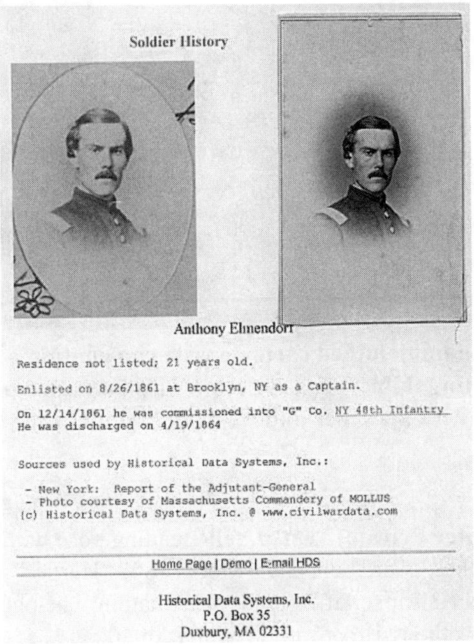

Soldier History

Anthony Elmendorf

Residence not listed; 21 years old.

Enlisted on 8/26/1861 at Brooklyn, NY as a Captain.

On 12/14/1861 he was commissioned into "G" Co. NY 48th Infantry
He was discharged on 4/19/1864

Sources used by Historical Data Systems, Inc.:

- New York: Report of the Adjutant-General
- Photo courtesy of Massachusetts Commandery of MOLLUS

(c) Historical Data Systems, Inc. @ www.civilwardata.com

Home Page | Demo | E-mail HDS

Historical Data Systems, Inc.
P.O. Box 35
Duxbury, MA 02331

Image of Captain Anthony Elmendorf, 48th New York Infantry.

Frohne's Historic Military

Captain Anthony Elmendorf, 48th New York Infantry, served from 1861 to 1864 in the 48th. Brooklyn, New York, backmark, minor trim to bottom of image and some tiny scuffs near bottom. **95.00**

Captain Charles H. Morton, 58th Massachusetts Volunteer Infantry, wearing his nine-button frock coat with captain's shoulder straps. Morton was taken prisoner at Poplar Grove Church, Virginia, on September 30, 1864, and exchanged February 23, 1865. .... **125.00**

Captain J.W. Sligh, 1st Michigan Engineers and Mechanics, died of injuries in 1863.

Frohne's Historic Military

Captain J. W. Sligh, 1st Michigan Engineers & Mechanics, great period ink identification on front and rear of carte. "Died at Tullahoma, Tenn., Nov. 15, 1863, of injuries received in a railroad accident, while train was being attacked by rebels." **195.00**

Captain Roger Jones, "Hero of Harpers Ferry," Lieutenant Roger Jones, cousin of Robert E. Lee and son of General Roger Jones (the former adjutant-general of the army), commanded the U.S. Arsenal at Harpers Ferry in April 1861. Through his intelligence sources and the pickets he sent out, he was apprised of the approach of 2,500 Virginia troops sent out by Governor John Letcher. Jones knew the recently seceded Commonwealth would try to capture the 15,000 rifles and machinery at Harpers Ferry, and also knew that the

Captain Roger Jones, cont.
town and the arsenal workers would not resist in the event of an attack. He touched off the powder as the Virginians were nearing Harpers Ferry, and was successful in destroying nearly all the rifles. He and his garrison retreated toward Chambersburg, Pennsylvania, losing only three men. Jones achieved the rank of captain for his action. In November of that same year, he was promoted to major. After the war, Jones went on to achieve the rank of brigadier general. He died January 16, 1889. . . . . **295.00**

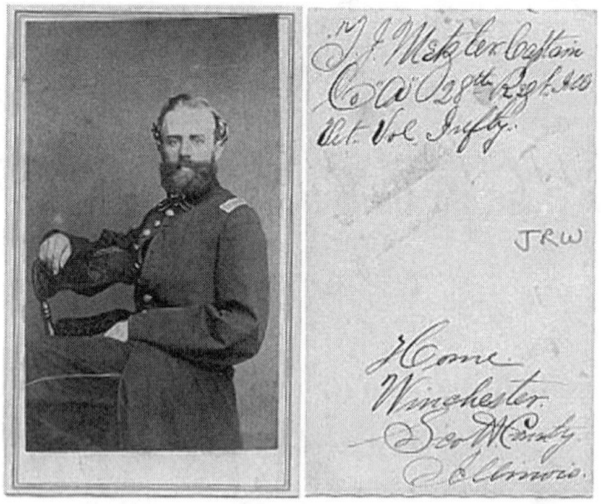

Carte de viste bearing an ink identification of Captain Thomas Metzger, 28th Illinois Volunteer Infantry.

Frohne's Historic Military

Captain Thomas J. Metzger, 28th Illinois Volunteer Infantry, excellent view with period ink identification on rear. The 28th was severely punished at the battle of Shiloh, Tennessee on April 6-7, 1862. Metzger enlisted on August 18, 1861, as a corporal. He reenlisted on February 15, 1864, he was mustered out at Brownsville, Texas, March 1866. . . . . **185.00**

Captain W.H. Gibbs, 15th Illinois Volunteer Infantry, very-fine bust portrait of Capt. W.H. Gibbs 15th Illinois wearing his line officer's frock coat and shoulder straps. Nicely signed in ink on the front "WH Gibbs" and bears a Memphis backmark. Gibbs served his entire term of enlistment being mustered out on the expiration of his term. **125.00**

Captain William David Porter, U.S.S. Essex, "A worthy member of a distinguished military family: Brother of Admiral David D. Porter, cousin of General Fitz John Porter, and adoptive brother of Admiral David G. Farragut." Scalded while commanding the *Essex* during the attack on Fort Henry. He died in 1864, nice 1862 imprint on front, Anthony by Brady backmark. **. 125.00**

Captain, Armed, standing-view bearded, frock with Smith's Patent captain's straps that may have "MS" in center. Sports sash, sword belt, and officer's sword, very good, no backmark. **79.00**

Captain, knees-up, seated profile pose, freshly combed and slicked hair, frock with straps, sword belt with eagle buckle, forage cap artistically placed between the subject and the camera. "Gonrel Boston" photographer's backstamp. **69.00**

Even an unidentified carte de viste can contain a lot of interesting tidbits for a collector. This unnamed private is armed with his saber and wearing a Model 1858 hat.

Middle Tennessee Relics

Cavalry Private, Armed, full-standing pose with cavalry saber, sword belt, and a Model 1858 "Hardee" hat with a nice clear set of crossed sabers hatpin. The photo has an "Anthony Broadway, N.Y." backmark. **85.00**

Captain of the U.S.S. *Essex*, William Porter died from injuries in 1864.

Frohne's Historic Military

Images of clergyman that actually served with field troops are quite desirable. This is one of Chaplain John J. Hight.

Frohne's Historic Military

Chaplain John J. Hight, excellent ink-signed image of Chaplain John J. Hight, taken in his Chaplain's uniform. Minor corner clips and slight trim to top of the image. **195.00**

Chasseur, possibly a view of a "New England Guard" (has Boston photographer's backmark). View shows determined federal wearing classic chasseur jacket with Russian pattern shoulder knots, waist belt with two-piece interlocking buckle, baggy trousers, gaiters, and sporting a light color kepi with dark band. Note on reverse indicates soldier's name was Bradley Dean. **125.00**

Chief Engineer, Union Naval officer with sword in complete uniform with hat. His rank is the pre-1862 Chief Engineer, card has been slightly trimmed, but doesn't affect the quality of the image at all. **95.00**

Colonel Alex Fowler, 99th Indiana Volunteer Infantry, standing pose showing Fowler with black slouch hat, regulation double-breasted frock with full colonel shoulder straps (eagles are visible), belt with eagle buckle, and holding his sword in his left hand. Signed on reverse in ink, "Alex Fowler Col. 99th Ind." ... **260.00**

Colonel John Zagonyi was aide-de-camp to General John Fremont.

Frohne's Historic Military

Colonel Charles Zagonyi, made famous in the beginning of the war for his famous cavalry charge at Springfield, Missouri. Colonel of General Charles Fremont's bodyguard of Missouri Cavalry, and asst. aide-de-camp. from 1861 to 1864, Anthony by Brady backmark. **195.00**

Colonel Dudley Donnelly of the 28th New York Infantry was mortally wounded at the Battle of Cedar Mountain.

Frohne's Historic Military

Colonel Dudley Donnelly, 28th New York Infantry, fine condition with "Albion, NY" backmark. Two one-cent "Express" tax stamps on the back. Donnelly was mortally wounded at the battle of Cedar Mountain in August 1862. The 28th, the "Niagara Rifles," was composed of five companies from Niagara county, two from Orleans county, one from Ontario, one from Genesee and one from Sullivan, and was mustered into the U. S. service for two years on May 22, 1861, at Albany. A month was spent in camp at Camp Morgan and on June 25, the regiment left the state for Washington. In the battle of Cedar Mountain, the loss of the 28th was 213 killed, wounded, and missing out of 339 engaged, and of these 41 men were mortally wounded. "Historical Society" written near bottom back in black ink, as well as "Col. Dudley E. Donnelly" written in what looks like modern ink just above it. **250.00**

There are, perhaps, no Union regiments more famous than the 2nd, 6th, 7th Wisconsin Infantry, 19th Indiana Infantry, and the 24th Michigan Infantry—the "Iron Brigade." Images of soldiers from these units bring a premium price. This is an image of Edward Bragg, a colonel of the 6th Wisconsin.

Frohne's Historic Military

Colonel Edward Bragg, 6th Wisconsin Volunteer Infantry, Fredricks, New York backmark, Tax stamp. **895.00**

When a Virginia hotelkeeper fired his shotgun into the chest of Elmer Elsworth in early 1861, he immediately immortalized the flamboyant Colonel as a martyr for the cause of preserving the Union. Images of Elsworth were mass produced and distributed.

Frohne's Historic Military

Colonel Elmer Elsworth, nice clear image, the first man killed in the Civil War. This is a full-standing view with his name in old brown ink at the picture's bottom. The photo has a nice Brady backmark, it appears to have been trimmed a little across the top to fit into a photo album. **95.00**

Colonel George Clarke, 11th Massachusetts Volunteer Infantry, very-fine standing view, autographed, "George Clarke, Col. 11th Mass Infantry," shows his kepi, non-regulation frock with two rows of nine buttons each, shoulder straps, sword belt with clear eagle buckle, sash, and his Model 1850 staff and field officer's sword. **195.00**

Image of Colonel Bryant of the "Marching Twelfth" Wisconsin Infantry.

Frohne's Historic Military

Colonel George E. Bryant, 12th Wisconsin Volunteer Infantry, from Madison, Wisconsin, served as a captain in the 1st Wisconsin Infantry and later, as colonel of the 12th Wisconsin Infantry. Bryant had a superb war record, and served as a brigade commander twice during the war. This is a published image of Bryant, and has no backmark. Carte has been trimmed, which has removed most of the identification. **275.00**

Colonel George W. Roberts, 42nd Illinois Volunteer Infantry, outstanding image with the contrast and clarity almost perfect. Identified in period ink on the front and signed boldly on the back, "Your friend & fellow soldier GW Roberts Col 42nd RIV." Backmark is, "J. Carbutt, Chicago." Roberts lost his jaw and part of his head when struck by a rebel shell on December 31, 1862 at the battle of Stone's River, Tennessee. His early war record shows that he was highly thought of by his superiors and led many dangerous missions. . . . **450.00**

Colonel James C. Clarke, 7th Regiment Corps de Afrique, standing view, "James C Clark Col 7th Regt Corps de Afrique," wears kepi with bugle insignia, frock with colonel's straps, sash, sword belt, huge gauntlets, and holding cavalry saber. Blauvelt, Port Hudson backmark, signed in ink. **295.00**

Image of Colonel of the 1st Rhode Island Cavalry, R.B.Lawton's image.

Frohne's Historic Military

Colonel R.B. Lawton, 1st Regiment Rhode Island Cavalry, Brady, Washington image with photographer's imprint on front bottom. Identified in period brown ink. Minor corner clips and a few minor scuffs to image. Lawton was the colonel of the 1st Rhode Island Cavalry. **175.00**

Colonel Samuel J. Jackson, 3rd Kansas Infantry signed the back of this image.

Frohne's Historic Military

Colonel Samuel J. Crawford, 3rd Kansas (Colored) Infantry, period ink signed (on verso), "S. J. Crawford," Leavenworth, Kansas, backmark. **295.00**

Colonel Stewart, 2nd Indiana Volunteer Cavalry, photo of Colonel Stewart showing him seated in a waist-up pose wearing the frock coat and straps of a full-bird Colonel. What makes this image so striking is the subject himself. The Colonel has long hair pulled behind his ears and a long mustache and chin whiskers—really a dangerous looking character. The photo bears a Nashville imprint, and is in excellent condition except for a small amount of glue stuck to the top and right edge where this was once mounted to a piece of paper. **235.00**

Photo of Colonel Thomas Morris, 80th Ohio Infantry.

Frohne's Historic Military

Colonel Thomas C. Morris, 80th Ohio Volunteer Infantry, excellent period-ink identified image. **195.00**

Colonel, Armed, full-standing, full-bird colonel with visible straps, gauntlets, sword belt, sash, and hilt of sword visible. Outstanding clarity and contrast, some age spotting, no backmark. **125.00**

Union artillery corporal's image seated with a hat on his knee.

Middle Tennessee Relics

Corporal, Artillery, seated wearing an artillery shell jacket with clearly visible corporal stripes, wide brim hat on his knee, photo has a, "Stansbury & Co. Louisville, Ky," backmark with a 5-cent revenue stamp remaining intact. **75.00**

Corporal C. Hammond, waist-up seated pose of a bearded soldier wearing four-button with very visible seams and crisp corporal's chevrons. Ink signed on back, "Corp. C. Hammond May 1865." **49.00**

Corporal Charles Black's (12th Kansas Infantry) signed carte.

Frohne's Historic Military

Corporal Charles A. Black, 12th Kansas Infantry, boldly identified in period ink on the mount, no backmark. Contrast and clarity are outstanding, black served in the 12th from August 1862 until June 1865. . . . .**225.00**

Identified images of Zouaves are highly sought after. This is an image of Corporal Guinn of the 34th Indiana Infantry in his Zouave uniform.

Frohne's Historic Military

Corporal Harvey Guinn, 34th Indiana Infantry, Guinn is wearing his distinctive Zouave uniform. He served from October 1861 until February 1866. Very fine condition, image is signed in period ink, and has a New Orlean's backmark. **475.00**

Drummer Boy, with his drum and sticks, wearing his kepie, four-button blouse, and a belt with oval U.S. buckle. It is interesting to note the drum has metal rope hooks, a super image. **350.00**

Drummer Robert Hendershot, 8th Michigan Volunteer Infantry

Fine, from-life photo showing young Hendershot with his presentation brass drum. Shows him wearing bummer cap, short jacket, dark trousers, and having his drum slung in front of him with his hands holding the sticks as if playing the drum. Hendershot began the war with the 8th Michigan. Legend says his drum was destroyed by a rebel artillery shell at Fredericksburg though there was some controversy after the war, when another drummer claimed the title and event as his own. A fine clear view with great contrast and light toning, ca. 1863. . . . . **450.00**

Crisp and clear-standing view of Robert H. Hendershot with forage cap, shell jacket, and holding his drum with sticks. Bottom-edge-trimmed and printed identification pasted there, very fine. **395.00**

Ensign, excellent knees-up view of a full uniformed Civil War Naval Ensign with his cap on a stand. He is shown with his hand inside his coat and is sporting a very nice Model 1852 Naval Sword in scabbard, as well as full chin whiskers. The insignia is clearly seen on his epaulettes and on his cap, no backmark. **125.00**

First Lieutenant Charles F. Tucker, 29th Indiana Volunteer Infantry, signed on background, "C.F. Tucker." This view shows Lt. Tucker holding his kepi with quatrefoil on the top. Taken by A.R. Miller of Indianapolis. **150.00**

George Augustus Marden was a member of the famous 1st U.S. Volunteer Sharpshooters.

First Lieutenant George Augustus Marden, 1st U.S. Volunteer Sharpshooters, enlisted on November 9,1861, as a sergeant. On December 12, 1861, he mustered into Company G, 2nd US Volunteers Sharpshooters He was discharged for promotion on July 10, 1862; the same day he was commissioned into the Field and Staff of the 1st U.S. Volunteers Sharpshooters He was discharged on September 22, 1864. . . . . **147.00**

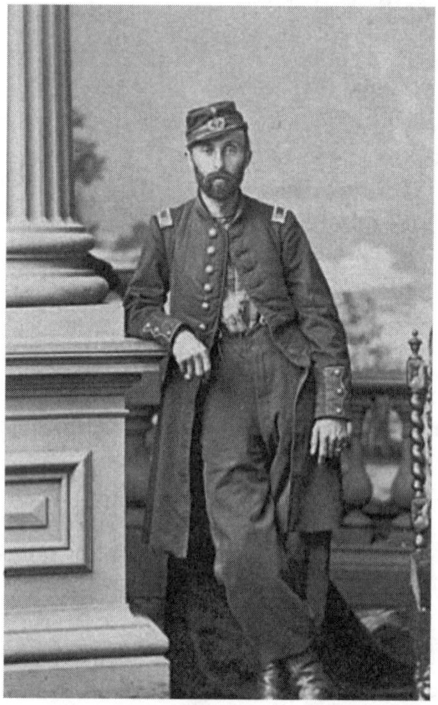

Image of Lieutenant Edmund Green, 83rd New York Infantry.

First Lieutenant Edmund Randall Green, 83rd New York Volunteers, carte de visite of a Civil War era officer from the Ninth New York State Militia (83rd N.Y. Volunteers), by Charles D. Fredericks & Co. of New York City, circa 1860. The portrait view, identified in the album as Ed Green, shows a young man with a full beard and mustache posing for his likeness in a photographic studio. He is dressed in the distinctive uniform worn by the officers of the 9th N.Y.S.M. at the beginning of the Civil War. A "9" is visible on the front of his cap. Edmund Randall Green, born in 1829, served as first lieutenant in Company D of the 9th N.Y.S.M. (83rd N.Y. Infantry) from May 27, 1861, to May 22, 1862, when he was discharged. Superb image in very-good or better condition overall, a few very minor pinprick spots of damage at the right and top edges of the card. The photograph exhibits very-good to excellent tonal range. **157.00**

First Lieutenant Edwing Humphrey, 11th Massachusetts Infantry, killed at Gettysburg, enlisted and commissioned on June 13, 1861, as a first lieutenant of Company G, 11th Massachusetts Infantry. He died of wounds on July 3, 1863, at Gettysburg, Pennsylvania. **94.00**

Lieutenant Newland was a member of the 34th Indiana Infantry, a Zouave regiment.

Frohne's Historic Military

First Lieutenant Sanford W. Newland, 34th Indiana Infantry, wearing his distinctive officer's Zouave uniform. He served from October 1861 until his death in May 1865, very-fine condition, image is signed in period ink and has a New Orlean's backmark. . . **325.00**

First Lieutenant William J. Miner, 34th Indiana Infantry, Miner is wearing his distinctive Zouave officer's uniform, he served from October 1861 until October 1864, very fine condition, image is signed in period ink, and has a New Orlean's backmark. . . **475.00**

Paschal Forbis was a sergeant in the 28th Illinois Infantry.

Frohne's Historic Military

First Sergeant Paschal F. Forbis, 28th Illinois Volunteer Infantry, excellent view of a 28th Illinois' First Sergeant. Period ink identification on rear of carte. Forbis enlisted on August 17, 1861 as a private. He reenlisted on February 13, 1864, and was mustered out at Brownsville, Texas, March 1866. He was prompted to First Sergeant on January 1, 1864. .... **185.00**

Flag, 44th New York Volunteer Infantry, rare Brady, New York, "The Tattered Flag of the 44th Regiment NY Volunteer Infantry." Listed as one of Fox's "Three Hundred Fighting Regiments," the 44th New York was among the first units to seize and hold Little Round Top at Gettysburg. At that battle, the 44th met their heaviest losses: 111 killed, wounded and missing. Very good condition, slight wear to edges, small spot at bottom edge of albumen. The text "44th Regt. N.Y." seen at bottom of image is written in the negative. **750.00**

Edward McAtee was a hospital steward for the 60th Illinois Infantry. Medical images have their own following that will drive up the price of any photograph of a surgeon, steward, or other medical-oriented position.

Frohne's Historic Military

Hospital Steward Edward A. McAtee, 60th Illinois Volunteer Infantry, backmark, "T.M. Scheier's Carte de Viste Photograph Gallery, Nashville, Tenn."..... **250.00**

Hospital Steward, unidentified

Image of an unidentified hospital steward.

Frohne's Historic Military

Excellent 3/4-view showing insignia on both sleeves of his uniform. Minor wear and foxing, no backmark. **195.00**

He is wearing a four-button blouse with hospital steward's diagonal chevron on each sleeve. His forage cap with small wreath enclosing "MS" is visible on a table at his side. Taken in Indianapolis, came from a 29th Indiana Volunteer Infantry album. .... **.350.00**

Image of Lieutenant Colonel George Evans. Evans served with the 60th Illinois Infantry.

Frohne's Historic Military

Lieutenant Colonel George Evans, 60th Illinois Volunteer Infantry, backmark, "T.M. Schleier's Carte de Visite Photograph Gallery , Nashville." **250.00**

Lieutenant Colonel of the 14th Maine Infantry, John Laing signed this carte de visite.

Frohne's Historic Military

Lieutenant Colonel John K. Laing, 14th Maine Infantry, spectacular image of Laing as a captain. He joined the 14th on December 11, 1861, and rose from the rank of sergeant to that of lieutenant colonel late in the war. Bangor, Maine, photographer's imprint. Boldly signed in period ink on the back. 175.00

Lieutenant Colonel Robert Lyon of the 102nd Pennsylvania Infantry.

Frohne's Historic Military

Lieutenant Colonel Robert Lyon, 102nd Pennsylvania Volunteer Infantry. Pittsburgh, Pennsylvania, backmarked, wear on image. 175.00

Wounded twice, Lieutenant Colonel Thomas McLaughlin served in the 102nd Pennsylvania.

Frohne's Historic Military

Lieutenant Colonel Tom McLaughlin, 102nd Pennsylvania Volunteer Infantry, beautiful image of twice-wounded McLaughlin. Pittsburgh, Pennsylvania, backmark. 175.00

Lieutenant Colonel, Unidentified

A crisp, seated pose of a bearded Union lieutenant colonel wearing double-breasted frock with straps and having a black silk mourning ribbon on his left arm. Excellent in all respects with Washington, D.C., backmark. 95.00

Full-standing view of an intriguing gent with a great deal of facial hair, standing with hand tucked in coat. Trim and fit looking in his late 40s apparently. Photo taken by Landy in Cincinnati, Ohio. Crisp, clear, and finely contrasted. 69.00

Lieutenant Commander Robert Cushing achieved fame for sinking the Confederate ram *Albemarle*. This is a stunning, Brady image of him.

Frohne's Historic Military

Lieutenant Commander William Barker Cushing. A very sharp image of this famous Civil War Naval hero. He received the thanks of Congress for his actions at the sinking of the rebel ram *Albemarle*, that led to the recapture of Plymouth. He was promoted to lieutenant commander for this action. Near-mint condition with an outstanding contrast and clarity. Anthony by Brady backmark. 795.00

Image of Lieutenant George Leslie of the 14th U.S. Infantry.

Frohne's Historic Military

Lieutenant George Leslie, 14th U.S. Infantry, beautifully-tinted image of George Leslie Browning, first lieutenant, 14th U.S. Infantry. Browning served in the famous 7th New York Militia from April to June 1861. He was a private and sergeant in the 1st Battalion of the 14th Infantry from September 1862 until his promotion to second lieutenant in February 1863. Promoted to first lieutenant in August 1864, transferred to the 23rd Infantry in 1866, and then to John Gibbon's famous 7th U. S. Infantry in 1871. Browning is written up in several books for his heroic actions at the battle of The Big Hole, Montana in August 1877. A beautiful image of a regular army officer with a great record! San Francisco, California, backmark. 175.00

Lieutenant Henry Hidden, 1st New York Volunteer Cavalry, fine bust portrait of Lieutenant Henry Hidden of the 1st New York Cavalry who was killed in action at Sangster Station, Virginia, on March 9 1862. View shows him in bust portrait wearing a line officer's frock and first lieutenant's shoulder straps. Backmark is a Brady-Anthony. 89.00

Likeness (probably a copy of a hard image) of John T. Gregle, the first graduate of West Point to be killed in the Civil War.

Frohne's Historic Military

Lieutenant John T. Gregle, 2nd U.S. Artillery, killed June 10, 1861, at the battle of Big Bethel, Virginia. One of only 18 men killed, and considered West Point's first Civil War killed-in-action officer. Excellent view with period ink identification, Boston backmark. **95.00**

Lieutenant Marvine, 144th New York Volunteer Infantry, knees-up bearded officer in frock with straps, holding cap, wearing sash, belt with eagle buckle, sash, and sword at his side. Brady backmark, signed in brown ink, "Lieut Marvine Co "B" 144th N.Y. Vols." Nice view, some age toning. **125.00**

Lieutenant, Armed, great full-standing pose of a bearded officer wearing slouch hat, short jacket with lieutenant's straps, sword belt, sash, sword at his side, and holding a Colt Army revolver up across his chest, Carlisle Pennsylvania backmark. **195.00**

Lieutenant, Naval

Unidentified image of a naval lieutenant.

Middle Tennessee Relics

Full-length, seated pose of a Union Naval lieutenant. Insignia on his coat is clearly visible. **95.00**

Though signed, the writing is too light to indentify this image of a naval lieutenant.

Middle Tennessee Relics

The sailor's name is written at the bottom of the photograph, but has faded so dim that it is not readable. "Chas. Hart Watertown, N.Y." backmark. **85.00**

Not identified, the New York state buttons are discernible on this image of a lieutenant.

Middle Tennessee Relics

Lieutenant, New York, crisp, of a first lieutenant backmarked "Kertson & Barker New York. The photo is clear enough that you can actually see the State of New York motif on a couple of his buttons. **75.00**

This crisp image of an unidentified lieutenant was taken in the famous studio of Gurney and Son, New York.

Middle Tennessee Relics

Lieutenant, Unidentified

Crisp, of a standing Union second lieutenant. He is wearing a nine-button officer's frock coat, and his shoulder straps are clearly visible, card is marked, "Gurney & Son N.Y." **75.00**

Lieutentant, Unidentified, cont.

Full-length image of a Union lieutenant with no identification.

Middle Tennessee Relics

He is wearing an officer's nine-button frock coat, and has his hand tucked in "Napoleon style." **85.00**

Image of Charles Pruyn, 118th New York Infantry signed on the back.

Frohne's Historic Military

Major Charles E. Pruyn, 118th New York Volunteer Infantry, killed in assault on Petersburg, beautiful ink identification on rear (signed "Ch. E. Pruyn 1st Lieut & adjt 118th NYV") and on the front as shown. Abbott, Albany New York backmark, some creases and minor wear on image. **275.00**

Unidentified, this officer can be determined to serve in the 5th Infantry regiment of some state, simply by the insignia on his cap.

Middle Tennessee Relics

Nice, clear, seated Union lieutenant wearing an officer's nine-button frock coat and officer's waist sash. His forage cap is sitting on the table beside him and has an embroidered infantry bugle and number "5." **95.00**

Lieutenants B.F. Ryer and J.L. Mast, 2nd U.S. Artillery, crisp and well contrasted view showing (full length) two seated artillery officers. Both wear frock coats with shoulder straps, both have their kepis with crossed cannon insignia on their knees, and the man on the right has a swagger stick or thin cane between his legs. Beautifully identified on the back in brown ink, "Lieuts B.F. Ryer, J.L. Mast, 2nd US Arty." Brooklyn, New York, backmark, records shows Ryer served in the 20th NY Battery from 1862 to 1865 and then served in the 2nd US in 1866. Mast's record shows service in the 25th Pennsylvania Volunteers in 1861, then service in the Pennsylvania artillery from 1861 to 1865, then service in the 2nd U.S. Artillery in 1866. . . . . **225.00**

James McDonald was the major of the 60th Illinois Infantry.

Frohne's Historic Military

Major James H. McDonald, 60th Illinois Volunteer Infantry, backmark, "T.M. Scheier's Carte de Viste Photograph Gallery, Nashville, Tenn." **250.00**

E.J. Brunner was a musician in the 4th Ohio Infantry.

Frohne's Historic Military

Musician E. J. Brunner, 4th Ohio Infantry, finished the war as a member of the band for two different Maryland regiments, "Renezvous of Distribution, Va." Backmark, very-fine condition. **185.00**

Musician, soldier holding his three-valve trumpet and wearing a musician's frock coat with fancy sleeve facings, hat with "LCB" on the front, sits at his side. **185.00**

Officer , bust portrait of a lieutenant colonel or major wearing a regulation double-breasted frock with straps. Has "Cross & Childs Forts Richardson & Lyon Va." backmark. **75.00**

Officer A.W. Brown, highly appealing, full-standing profile pose of officer holding his left hand to his chin, wearing frock with straps, dark trouser, kepi poised on studio banister, and holding binoculars in his right hand. Signed in ink on front, "AW Brown US Army" and the back is inscribed with a full letter in brown ink, "To William, Hope you are all enjoying yourself in the North. Weather here fearfully warm but no fevers with us. AWB. Miss Fletcher has left Cincinnati for Europe A.M." Philadelphia backmark. **225.00**

Charles Waterman was a cadet at West Point when he had this picture taken in 1864. He later died as a result of imprisonment in a Confederate camp.

Frohne's Historic Military

Officer Cadet, Charles Douglas Waterman, sharp view of West Point cadet Charles Douglas Waterman, class of 1864, died on active duty as an engineer just three months after graduation. Waterman was captured by a Confederate privateer on a voyage to New Orleans and held prisoner for two months (June-July 1864). He was paroled and went to New Jersey, where he died of illness contracted in a Confederate prison. Identified in pencil on verso "Mer Waterman at West Point" and gone over again in ink, no backmark, very-fine condition. **195.00**

Officer, very fine, near full-length, seated view of handsome mustached Union officer wearing a custom made eight-button short jacket with huge Smith's Patent shoulder straps, and holding his kepi. On his left breast is a large oval badge made in silhouette form. Small trim on left corner, Utica NY backmark. **69.00**

Officer, Armed

A pristine full-standing view of bearded officer wearing bummer cap with bugle insignia, frock coat with straps, sword belt with eagle buckle, waist sash, and he is cradling his Model 1850 foot officer's sword (with knot dangling from it) in his left arm. . . **115.00**

Posed in frock with straps, gauntlets, knee-high boots, sash, sword belt, Model 1860 staff sword (not the common 1850 pattern), sword knot, and his kepi with U.S. staff wreath on the front clearly displayed on a studio table next to him. Mint clarity and contrast, superb Brady image. **165.00**

Officer, Cavalry, Armed, pristine, full-standing view of mustached Union officer wearing short jacket with straps, holding kepi, wearing saber belt with visible eagle buckle, and having his cavalry saber with knot held at his side. New Orleans backmark. **135.00**

Officer, Massachusetts, fine, knees-up, seated portrait of Union captain wearing frock, straps, and belt with eagle buckle. Boston "Gonrel" backmark and comes with an 1890s photo of a G.A.R. vet who does not appear to be the same man. **69.00**

Officer, Naval, Armed, pristine standing pose of a US Naval officer wearing his officer's frock with straps, sword belt with navy buckle, and holding his naval officer's sword at his side. He has his visor-cap sitting on a studio table next to him. The cuffs of the coat have a single row of bullion braid. Photo has Plattsburgh, New York, imprint on the back. **85.00**

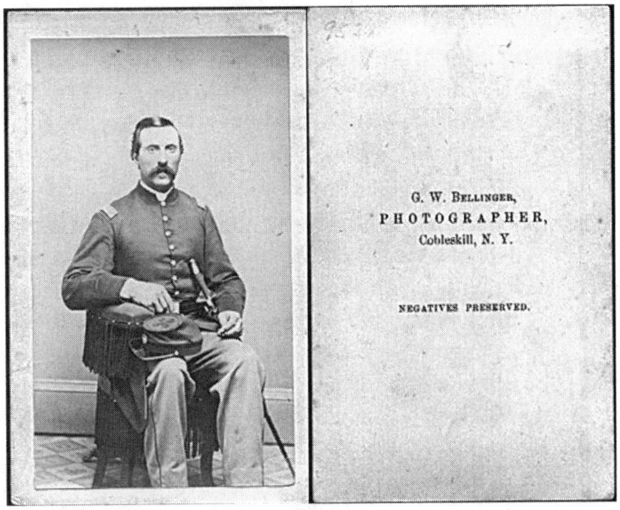

This unidentified, armed Union officer may have served in a New York regiment.

Sharpsburg Arsenal

Officer, New York, Armed, G.W. Bellinger backmark. **145.00**

Officer, bust view of line officer wearing frock and straps. Barely visible at the edge of the vignette is a two-piece suspension medal with a 20th Corps badge. **39.00**

Officers, Cavalry, Armed, full-standing view, two mustached Yankee officers wearing short jackets with straps, gauntlets, kepis with crossed saber insignia, sword belts, sashes, and each holds his cavalry saber in front of him, backmark of Lytle/Baton Rouge. A near-mint carte with great contrast and clarity. **235.00**

Image of Sergeant William Merry, 27th Massachusetts Infantry boldly signed in ink.

Frohne's Historic Military

Orderly Sergeant Willard, Merry, 27th Massachusetts Volunteer Infantry, excellent period ink identified image of Willard Merry who died in North Carolina in early 1862. Pittsfield, Massachusetts, backmark, very-good condition. **250.00**

Outdoor Scene, shows five army clerks at Alexandria, Virginia, near their desks in front of the headquarters tent. Taken by G.Y. Rosenberry of Alexandria. **185.00**

Paymaster Mark Hollingshead, superb bust portrait in double-breasted frock with major's straps. **65.00**

Private Caleb Mott, 2nd Wisconsin Volunteer Cavalry, Caleb Mott enlisted on February 2, 1864, as a Private. On February 2, 1864, he mustered into Company M, 2nd Wisconsin Cavalry, he mustered out on November 15, 1865, at Austin, Texas. **144.00**

Private David H. Brady, 35th Ohio Volunteer Infantry, full standing view of soldier in front of a camp scene patriotic backdrop. Soldier wears regulation frock coat and trousers and holds his cap in his left hand. Nicely signed in brown ink on the back, "David H. Brady Co. "B" 35th Regt. OVI," very clear with a slightly yellow tone. **95.00**

Private David Snavely, 35th Ohio Volunteer Infantry, very faded, seated view of soldier wearing slouch hat and four-button blouse. Nicely signed on the reverse in brown ink, "David Snavely Co. "G" 35th Regt. O.," great signature. **49.00**

Private E.W. Edson, 8th New York Artillery, fine standing view of 8th New York artilleryman wearing forage cap, regulation frock, U.S. belt and buckle, cap box, and brass-handled saber bayonet in scabbard clearly displayed. Signed in ink on front, "Yours Truly E.W. Edson," and noted on the back, "Compliments of the substance here shadowed faith." **185.00**

Private Fred Dunn, Pennsylvania Cavalry, full-standing in tight-fitting shell jacket, saber belt, and displaying his cavalry saber in front. Inscribed in brown ink on the reverse, "Mr. Fred Dutton of Delaware Co Penn in the War of '63," as well as other notes, photographer's backmark from Wilmington, Delaware, very fine with great contrast and clarity, bottom edge trimmed.. **175.00**

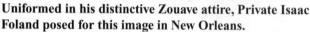

Uniformed in his distinctive Zouave attire, Private Isaac Foland posed for this image in New Orleans.

Frohne's Historic Military

Private Issac P. Foland, 34th Indiana Infantry, wearing the unit's distinctive Zouave uniform. He served from October 1861 until February 1866. Very fine condition, image is signed in period ink and has a New Orlean's backmark.............................. **475.00**

Private James F. Upham, 26th Massachusetts Volunteer Infantry, Near-mint bust portrait in uniform. Autographed in ink, "Very Respectfully Jas F Upham," on front. Lowell photographer's imprint. This unit had 64 men killed or mortally wounded while fighting in Louisiana and Virginia. **79.00**

Private John Bonner, 34th New York Volunteer Infantry, Brady/Washington showing yank wearing classic Zouave fez with tassel, sky blue or gray shell jacket open to expose issue shirt, U.S. buckle on belt, sky blue (or gray) trousers tucked into gaiters. Signed by soldier on back three times "John Bonner" (or Bonnie?) and collector's note indicating "Co I 34th NYV." ... **450.00**

Private John Davis, 6th Pennsylvania Reserves, bust view of a Union soldier wearing a black slouch hat and regulation infantry frock coat. With it is modern typed history indicating that the man is John Davis Co. "E" 6th PVR, and that he served in 20+ battles...... **40.00**

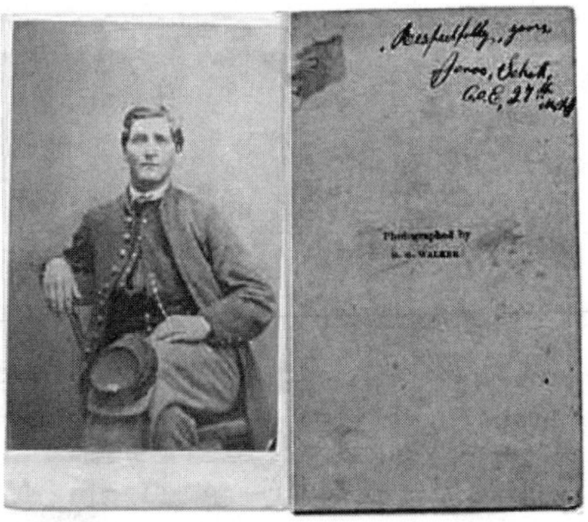

Jonas Scott, a private in the 27th Massachusetts Infantry fell at the Battle of Drewry's Bluff in 1864, and was taken prisoner. He died of his wounds three weeks later.

Frohne's Historic

Private Jonas Scott, 27th Massachusetts Volunteer Infantry, excellent period ink identified image of Jonas Scott, who was wounded and captured at Drewry's Bluff, Virginia, on May 16, 1864 and died while a prisoner in Richmond, Virginia, just three weeks later. **250.00**

Patriotic painted backdrops can add a lot of interest to an image. This is a clear photograph of an armed Private Milton Ritter of the 164th Ohio Infantry (a regiment organized in 1864).

Frohne's Historic Military

Private Milton Ritter, 164th Ohio Volunteer Infantry, great armed shot of Ritter in front of a painted patriotic backdrop. No backmark, period pencil identification on the verso. **260.00**

Private Nathan Smith, 1st Rhode Island Volunteer Infantry, wearing nine-button frock coat in an almost full-length portrait. Taken in Providence, R.I., signed in ink on front, "Yrs. Truly N. A. Smith." Smith later served in the Independent Hospital Guards, Company A. **135.00**

Private Orin G. Gilloway 1st New Hampshire Battery, served from Aug. 1861 to June 1865. He wears an artillery shell jacket with a rosette, possibly a corps badge just above the breast pocket. A super signed and identified image. **125.00**

Private Samuel Bricker, Armed, very crisp full-standing view showing a bearded Yankee wearing a forage cap with insignia, regulation frock coat, regulation trousers, U.S. belt, buckle and cap box, and having his cartridge box sling with eagle plate across his chest. Upright at his right side is his Model 1861 Springfield musket with bayonet. This one is signed on the reverse "Samuel Bricker." **145.00**

Private Sylvester Chesbrough, 10th New York Volunteer Cavalry, luckily this view is finely inscribed on the back in brown ink, "Mr. Sylvester Chesbrough Suspension Bridge NY. He belonged to the 10th Regt. N.Y.S.V. Cav. Dide (sic) August 30th 1864". A really great inscription. Records show he died of gangrene of the leg. **59.00**

Carte de viste of Private Thomas Dayton, 61st Illinois Infantry dated September 24, 1865.

Frohne's Historic Military

Private Thomas H. Dayton, 61st Illinois Volunteer Infantry, backmark, "A.C. Townsend, Springfield, IL," dated September 24, 1865, on the verso and bearing a three-cent revenue stamp.................. **185.00**

Carte de viste identified as Private William Barnes of the Iron Brigade's 7th Wisconsin Infantry.

Sharpsburg Arsenal

Private William Barnes, 7th Wisconsin Volunteer Infantry, identified on the back, "William Barnes Comp. A 7th Wisc Inf." **295.00**

Private William H. Cossart, nice full-standing pose of soldier in front of a patriotic backdrop. He wears an infantry frock coat, issue trousers, military vest, and is holding his bummer cap at his side. On the crown is visible a very large star corps badge with cutout center (silhouette type) and a couple numerals. Inscribed on the reverse is, "William H. Cossart July 1864." Very fine with bottom edge trimmed and a little foxing, Nashville backmark. **89.00**

Private, 2nd Corps, knees-up view of a soldier wearing a frock coat with a 2nd Corps badge attached to the breast. He also wears his bummer cap and he stands in front of a painted camp scene, wonderful condition with no backmark. **85.00**

Private, Armed

Full standing yank with Hardee hat with bugle and cords, four-button blouse, belt, buckle, cap box, scabbard, cross belt with eagle plate, and Enfield musket upright at his side posed before a patriotic camp backdrop. Image has military backmark from Fort Reno in Washington, D.C. The photographer mounted this image on card stock that was printed with a gilt oval frame design on the face (designed for use with a bust portrait) mounting the albumen paper over the gilt design, and faintly visible through the albumen paper is the outline of this gilt frame underneath. **95.00**

Full-view standing of soldier in slouch hat, frock coat, leather gear, and holding his musket with bayonet upright at his side. The image is nice but about 35% faded (still very viewable,). **65.00**

Superb contrast & clarity, full-standing, bearded infantryman in slouch hat, four-button blouse, full leather accoutrements, Enfield musket at side, bayonet on musket, Colt Navy revolver tucked in belt right up front, and clearly visible. **245.00**

This New York soldier sports the piped state-issue 1863 New York jacket and matching state-issue piped forage cap. Musket appears to be an 1863 Springfield. Belt and buckle at waist, pom-pom on kepi front with brass insignia, very good to fine. Troy photographer's mark. **125.00**

Private, Artillery, soldier wears an enlisted man's frock coat with brass epaulets, belt with oval US buckle, and gauntlets, sports a Hardee hat with Battery H, 4th Artillery insignia. **125.00**

Private, Cavalry, nice full-standing view of clean-shaven Yankee trooper wearing an unpiped shell jacket and mounted trousers (reinforcement seams clearly visible on inside of each leg). Posed in front of a photographer's painted backdrop. Very nice image showing just light handling age and very little soiling. **39.00**

Image of a Union private not identified, but bearing an Ohio backmark.

Middle Tennessee Relics

Private, Ohio, full-standing view with his coat partially open showing his military vest. His hat is on the table beside him, "C. Hempstep Newark, Ohio" backmark. **75.00**

With reference to the Army of the Cumberland, the Nashville photographer's back mark on this image of a Union private reads, "Gallery of the Cumberland."

Middle Tennessee Relics

Private, Unidentified

Crisp, clear image of a young western theater Union private. This is a bust view with coat open showing the military vest. This photo has a "Gallery of the Cumberland No. 25 Cedar St. Morse & Peaslee Nashville" backmark. **125.00**

No identification or backmark kept the price of this Union private's lower.

Middle Tennessee Relics

This is a seated pose with his enlisted man's frock coat open showing his military vest. The photo does have a couple 1/4" age spots, but is, otherwise, clear and in good shape. **55.00**

Quartermaster Sergeant Dorland, 29th Indiana Infantry, signed in brown ink, "Yours Truly George C. Dorland Q.M. Sergt. 29th Ind. Inf." Taken by J.F. Nice, Lewisburg, Pennsylvania. two-cent tax stamp present on the back. **150.00**

Quartermaster Sergeant H. Haskins, fine bust portrait of a handsome soldier with commercial frock, autographed on front, "QMS H Haskins." **69.00**

Famous for his exclamation, "Damn the torpedoes! Full steam ahead!" David Farragut made an impression on the public during the war, so much so, his likeness was sold by photography dealers.

Middle Tennessee Relics

Rear Admiral D.G. Farragut, clear bust view, corners have been nipped to fit in a photo album. **85.00**

Samuel Godfrey, Jr., a black sailor aboard the U.S.S. Pensacola had this image made after the war.

Frohne's Historic Military

Sailor, ink identified black Union sailor from the ship *Pensacola*. Beautifully identified on the verso as "Samuel M. Godfrey Jr," as well as the ship name. Fine contrast and clarity, slight minor crease to lower-right corner, no backmark. Appears to be slightly postwar, around ca. 1870. .... **2,900.00**

Second Lieutenant Charles Shepley, 19th Illinois Volunteer Infantry, nice image signed, "Charles H. Shepley - Co. J., 19th regt., Illinois volunteers." Photographer imprint on back of card as well. The card is in good condition with some spotting. **305.00**

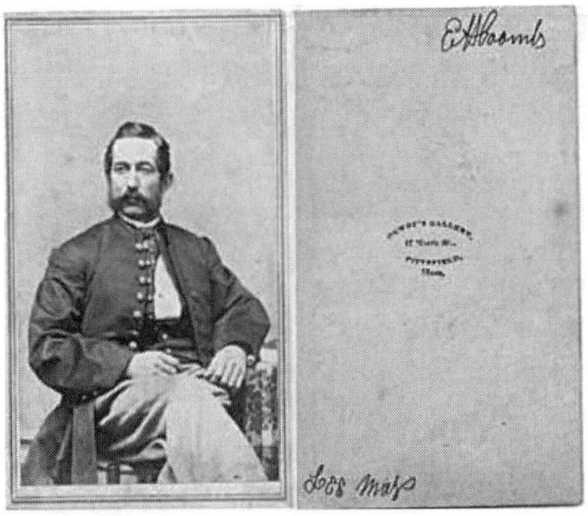

Lieutenant E.A. Coombs, 27th Massachusetts Infantry was killed in an assault at Cold Harbor, Virginia, in 1864.

Frohne's Historic Military

Second Lieutenant E.A. Coombs, 27th Massachusetts Infantry, ink-signed image of Coombs, who was killed in one of the assaults at Cold Harbor on June 4, 1864. .... **250.00**

Sergeant Adison Dwiggins, 34th Indiana Infantry, posed in his distinctive Zouave uniform for this New Orleans-made image.

Frohne's Historic Military

Sergeant Adison Dwiggins, 34th Indiana Infantry, Dwiggins is wearing his distinctive Zouave uniform. He served from October 1861 until February 1866. Very-fine condition, image is signed lightly on front mount in period pencil, and has a New Orlean's backmark, minor corner chip in mount. **475.00**

Sergeant George Bower, 27th Massachusetts, was killed in action at the Battle of Petersburg.

Frohne's Historic Military

Sergeant George W. Brewer, 27th Massachusetts Volunteer Infantry, excellent signed image of killed-in-action George W. Brewer. Brewer was killed with his brother, in one of the futile assaults by the Union troops at Petersburg, Virginia, on June 18, 1864. Boldly signed in period ink with name and regiment as shown. **250.00**

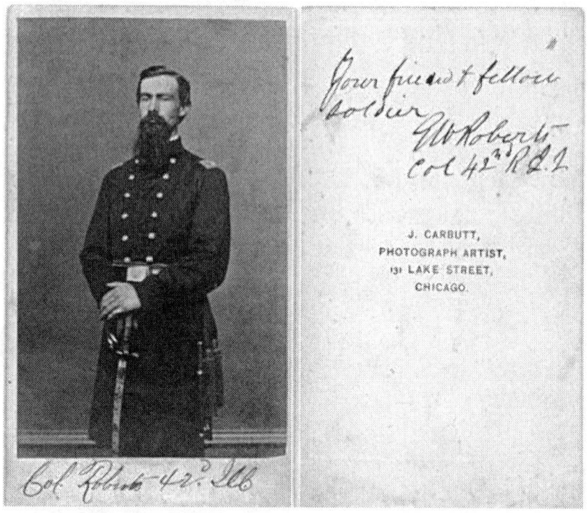

Image of Sergeant Isaac Wilkins, 12th Kansas Infantry signed in ink.

Frohne's Historic Military

Sergeant Isaac J. Wilkins, 12th Kansas Infantry, boldly identified in period ink on the back. Little Rock, Arkansas, backmark, wonderful contrast and clarity, Wilkins served from September 1862 until June 1865. . . . . **225.00**

Renowned as the "Drummer Boy of Chickamauga, images of Johnny Clem were commercially produced and sold. Nevertheless, there are rather rare today.

Frohne's Historic Military

Sergeant John Lincoln Clem, also known as the "Drummer Boy of Chickamauga." Morse's Army of the Cumberland backmark, minor trim to bottom. . . **850.00**

Sergeant Joseph A. Witherow, 5th Illinois Volunteer Cavalry, ink signed on reverse, Witherow has a Remington pistol jammed into his belt and a holster showing under his right arm. He wears his slouch hat at a jaunty angle. There is an ink stain on his lap. Some smudging front and back, and both top and bottom of carte are trimmed slightly. Back reads in ink, "Joseph A. Witherow September 20 1864 Bloomington, Illinois." Photo taken from life. **86.00**

Sergeant Lorenzo Brown, 35th Ohio Volunteer Infantry, very-fine bust portrait bearing imprint of Winder's Gallery in Cincinnati, Ohio. View shows a yank with goatee whiskers wearing four-button blouse and black slouch hat. Signed in ink on the front is, "Yours Truly Lorenzo Brown." His record shows him as commissary sergeant of the 35th OVI. **79.00**

A crisp ink signature identifies Sergeant Milton Buckler of the 12th Kansas Infantry.

Frohne's Historic Military

Sergeant Milton A. Buckler, 12th Kansas Infantry, boldly identified in period ink on the mount, no backmark, wonderful contrast and clarity, Buckler served from September 1862 until June 1865. . . **225.00**

Sergeant Peter De Graff served in Custer's 7th Michigan Cavalry. A bold, ink signature clearly identifies him.

Frohne's Historic Military

Sergeant Peter C. De Graff, 7th Michigan Volunteer Cavalry, identified in period ink on the back, "P C De Graffe Co F 7th Mich Cavalry Post Master Genl Custer's Cavalry Brigade. Stevensburg, Va April 1864." Peter C. De Graff enlisted in the 7th Michigan Cavalry on December 27, 1862, and was promoted to Sergeant on July 14th, 1863. He mustered out at Ft. Leavenworth on December 15, 1865. Signed beautifully in period ink on the rear of the image, as well as a nice pencil identification on the front. Image is in very good condition, with normal soiling and foxing. **425.00**

Simply identified as "Walter Tibbets," this sergeant's regiment is not known.

Middle Tennessee Relics

Sergeant Walter Tibbits, full-standing pose image of a young Union sergeant wearing an enlisted man's nine-button frock coat with his sergeant's stripes clearly visible. He is holding his forage cap in his hand, "Walter Tibbitts," is written in old brown ink. This photo has a nice outdoor river backdrop. **85.00**

Sergeant, 6th New Hampshire Volunteers, wears a frock coat, open to show his vest. His forage cap with "6 NHV" is on a pedestal at his side. His sergeant's chevrons are very clear. **150.00**

Sergeant, Cavalry, Armed, fine strapping standing trooper with mutton chops, shell jacket with sergeant's chevrons, huge gauntlets, saber belt with holstered revolver, holding cavalry saber with sword knot in front, small plug slouch hat with crossed saber insignia on front resting on table. Very clear image with good contrast, a couple scuffs on edge. **135.00**

Sergeant, wearing a frock coat with chevrons and holding his forage cap. Taken by D. Denison of Albany, New York. **125.00**

Soldier on Lookout Mountain, lone officer sits on the edge of a cliff with slouch hat in hand. He stares out at the panorama below, taken by Delong of Fairbury, Illinois. **95.00**

Soldier, Armed

A fine, full-standing cdv showing early war yank wearing four-button blouse with large corporal's chevrons, and dark trousers. He is holding his bummer cap in his left hand. He has his waist belt with oval buckle, cap box, and bayonet in scabbard round his waist. He has his cartridge box with plates on the sling hung so that the box is visible on the front area of his belt and he has a covered canteen hanging down also in front in full view of the camera. Perfect condition with backmark of Leon Van Loo Cinn., Ohio. **325.00**

A full-length image, he wears a four-button blouse and a forage cap with insignia on the front. He is holding his musket. There is a three-cent tax stamp on the back, which has a printed cancellation, "A.K. Josse Mar. 25th 1865." **175.00**

Cap, frock, belt, buckle, cap box, cartridge box and sling, musket with bayonet at side. Superb clarity & contrast. **175.00**

Crisp and well contrasted standing view. Black slouch hat, nine-button frock, belt, buckle, cap box, U.S. buckle, bayonet scabbard, upright Enfield with bayonet at side. Outstanding save for a chunk of albumen paper gone from the upper right. ...**125.00**

Knees-up, 1864 copy of a bearded soldier with kepi, frock, belt, buckle, cap box, and bayonet with scabbard. Backmark from North Bridgewater, Massachusetts. **65.00**

Artillery, Armed, Dashing Yank has donned his saber belt around the outside of his mounted greatcoat. He has a forage cap on his head, sword belt around his waist, and his regulation artillery saber with sword knot clearly visible hanging in front of him on display for the camera. Connecticut backmark, excellent. **295.00**

Cavalry, Armed

A near full-length standing pose of a tough-looking Yankee cavalryman posed with a defiant glare and having his right hand perched on his holster. He sports a forage cap with embroidered crossed sabers insignia on the front (insignia placed with the hilts of the swords "up" on his cap), a regulation 12-button piped shell jacket open to expose his shirt and cravat, regulation mounted trousers, and having a waist belt with clearly visible rectangular eagle buckle, cap box, and bolstered revolver (very large and prominent) on the belt. **285.00**

Knees-up seated view of bearded Yankee trooper, wearing shell jacket, issue trousers, saber belt with clear eagle buckle, cap box, and holding cavalry saber at his side posed very close to camera. Super clarity and contrast, some light soiling. **145.00**

Although dressed in a civilian frock coat, this soldier is wearing his forage cap and a Sixth Corps badge.

Middle Tennessee Relics

Soldier, Sixth Corps, crisp, bust view of a young Federal private wearing his kepi and a nine-button enlisted man's frock coat. On his chest is a clear "Sixth Corp" badge. Photographer is "J.L. Lovell Amherst, Mass." **115.00**

Soldier

Backmark "Mansfield's City Gallery, St. Louis, Mo." **75.00**

Full standing in frock with U.S. belt, buckle, cap box, and bayonet with scabbard. Camp scene backdrop, handsome subject, corners trimmed. **79.00**

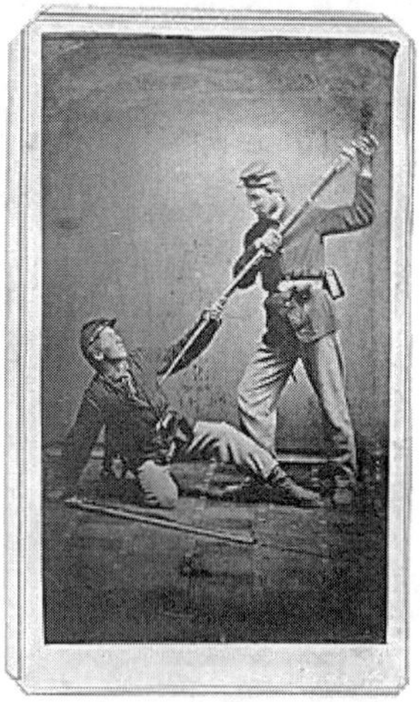

Though probably a copy of a tintype, this amazing carte de viste depicts a bit of soldier theatrics.

Soldiers, combat-posed image of a bayonet about to plunge deeply into another soldier's chest. Both soldiers are fully equipped and appear to be taking themselves seriously. The image is from life and not a retouched or painting image. Appears to be a copy of a tintype, very fine condition with excellent contrast and clarity, minor clipped corners. Dayton, Ohio backmark, with a two-cent orange tax stamp. **550.00**

Dick Turpin,
(a union Spy)
Dept. of the Cumberland

Identified on the front in ink as "Dick Turpin Army of the Cumberland," this image is of a notorious Union spy.

Frohne's Historic Military

Spy Dick Turpin, superb image of one of the shady characters involved in espionage during the Civil War in the Tennessee area. Obviously famous enough to have his image taken and distributed at the time. Ink identified on the front as, "Dick Turpin (a union spy) Dept. of the Cumberland." No backmark. **675.00**

Pauline Cushman is one of the more famous female spies who worked for the Union's cause.

Frohne's Historic Military

Spy Pauline Cushman

Excellent full-view with sword. Wonderful contrast and clarity to this image. Minor scratch in albumen near her head, no backmark. **395.00**

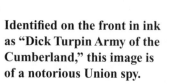

MISS MAJ. PAULINE CUSHMAN,
The famous Union Scout and Spy of the U. S. secret service.
Army of the Cumberland.

Commercially produced and printed on the front, "Miss Major Pauline Cushman."

Frohne's Historic Military

One of the Civil War's most famous females, excellent half-view of Cushman wearing a union major's uniform. This image is from life, minor corner wear, and usual foxing. Stamped backmark "G.W. Thorne Manufacturer of Photo. Albums & Photographs 60 Nassau St. N.Y." Imprinted on front bottom of carte, "Miss Maj. Pauline Cushman, The famous Union Scout and Spy of the U. S. secret service. Army of the Cumberland.". **350.00**

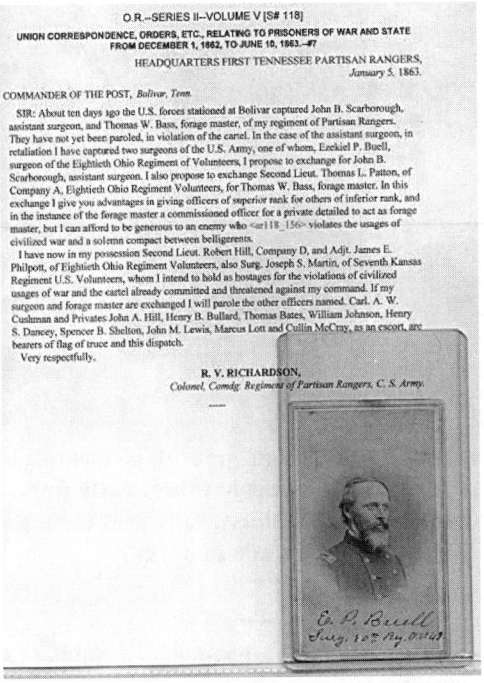
O.R.--SERIES II--VOLUME V [S# 118]

UNION CORRESPONDENCE, ORDERS, ETC., RELATING TO PRISONERS OF WAR AND STATE FROM DECEMBER 1, 1862, TO JUNE 10, 1863.--#7

HEADQUARTERS FIRST TENNESSEE PARTISAN RANGERS,
January 5, 1863.

COMMANDER OF THE POST, *Bolivar, Tenn.*

SIR: About ten days ago the U.S. forces stationed at Bolivar captured John B. Scarborough, assistant surgeon, and Thomas W. Bass, forage master, of my regiment of Partisan Rangers. They have not yet been paroled, in violation of the cartel. In the case of the assistant surgeon, in retaliation I have captured two surgeons of the U.S. Army, one of whom, Ezekiel P. Buell, surgeon of the Eightieth Ohio Regiment of Volunteers, I propose to exchange for John B. Scarborough, assistant surgeon. I also propose to exchange Second Lieut. Thomas L. Patton, of Company A, Eightieth Ohio Regiment Volunteers, for Thomas W. Bass, forage master. In this exchange I give you advantages in giving officers of superior rank for others of inferior rank, and in the instance of the forage master a commissioned officer for a private detailed to act as forage master, but I can afford to be generous to an enemy who <ar118_156> violates the usages of civilized war and a solemn compact between belligerents.

I have now in my possession Second Lieut. Robert Hill, Company D, and Adjt. James E. Philpott, of Eightieth Ohio Regiment Volunteers, also Surg. Joseph S. Martin, of Seventh Kansas Regiment U.S. Volunteers, whom I intend to hold as hostages for the violations of civilized usages of war and the cartel already committed and threatened against my command. If my surgeon and forage master are exchanged I will parole the other officers named. Carl. A. W. Cushman and Privates John A. Hill, Henry B. Bullard, Thomas Bates, William Johnson, Henry S. Dancey, Spencer B. Shelton, John M. Lewis, Marcus Lott and Cullin McCray, as an escort, are bearers of flag of truce and this dispatch.

Very respectfully,

R. V. RICHARDSON,
Colonel, Comdg. Regiment of Partisan Rangers, C. S. Army.

Image of the 80th Ohio Infantry's surgeon, Ezekial Bull, signed on the front.

Frohne's Historic Military

Surgeon Ezekial P. Buell, 80th Ohio Infantry, beautifully signed on front of image, there is a New Philadelphia, Ohio backmark. **175.00**

Surgeon Vanderkief, fantastic full-standing view showing the Army surgeon wearing his kepi with rain cover, commercial double-breasted blouse, and thigh-high boots. He also sports a long riding crop or Model 1860 staff officer's sword. Boldly autographed in ink on the bottom front, " Vanderkief Surgeon USA." Photo taken in Maryland. **275.00**

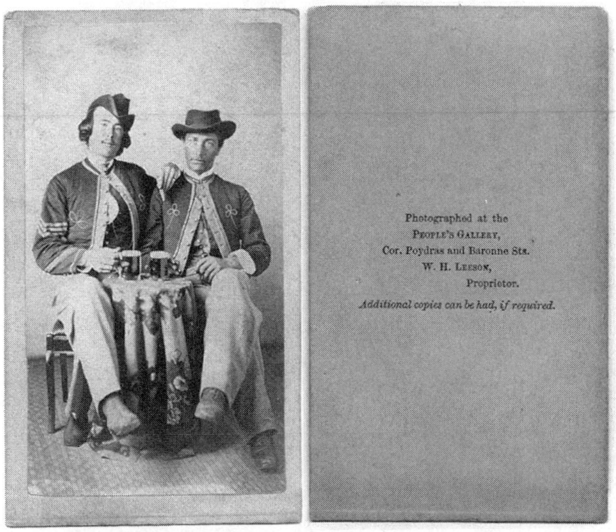

Two Zouaves of the 34th Indiana hoisted a couple of beers and cigars for the photographer.

Frohne's Historic Military

Zouave, Unidentified

He wears the Zouave jacket with fancy braid trim with quarterfoils on the jacket front. A half-length photo. **175.00**

Two 34th Indiana Zouaves in full regalia drinking a couple of beers and holding cigars. Very-fine condition, New Orleans backmark. **950.00**

"Hard" Images (Ambrotypes, Daguerreotypes, and Tintypes)

Ambrotypes

The ambrotype process was used by photographers over a relatively short time period spanning the years of 1854 to 1865. The process relied on sensitized collodion applied to a sheet of glass. A bit muddier in appearance than daguerreotypes, the process was embraced by photographers who no longer wanted to cope with the mercury fumes involved in the daguerreian process.

> **"The patients have begged me for my 'likeness' with the cup in my left hand, and my dressing gown on, a candle in my right hand; this is my 'rig' in the night when I go over the wards to see how the sickest are."**
>
> ***— Hannah Anderson Chandler***
> ***Matron, Union Hospital in Georgetwon, D.C.***

Confederate

Armed with a huge D-Guard Bowie knife, musket, and revolver, this Confederate ambrotype was a collector's dream image.

Old South Military Antiques

Ambrotype, 1/4 plate Confederate Soldier, Armed Ruby ambrotype of well armed and accoutered Confederate. **5,200.00**

The two Confederate soldiers in this 1/4 plate ambrotype display the variety of equipment and uniforms that the South issued early in the war.

Old South Military Antiques

Fully armed and equipped Confederate soldier. **4,200.00**

This fascinating 1/6th plate ambrotype identified simply as "Dillard Boys-38Tn" depicts three early war Confederates in "battle shirts," a type of work smock adopted by some Rebels as a uniform.

Middle Tennessee Relics

Ambrotype, 1/6th plate, Confederate Soldiers, 38th Tennessee Volunteer Infantry. From a Tennessee estate and for several years displayed in a museum. The three subjects have similar facial features and are likely three brothers or cousins. There is a faint notation in the back that says, "Dillard Boys-38TN." All three wear identical battle shirts. One has a holstered pistol on his belt, and another has a musket with bayonet at his side. The photo has a little emulsion halo around the edge, but is still a nice multi-subject Confederate photo. **595.00**

Ambrotype, 1/9th plate, Confederate Soldier, half-length portrait of a Confederate solider, seated wearing a battle shirt with red trim, cased, 2-3/8" x 2-7/8" (small background spots). **385.00**

Ambrotypes, Union

Ambrotype, 1/4 plate

Private Joseph Pierce, 6th New Hampshire Volunteers, posed with his Hardee hat, rifle with bayonet, and frock coat with shoulder scales to make this 1/4 plate ambrotype.

Private Joseph W. Pierce, 9th Regiment of New Hampshire Volunteers, ruby ambro with very good clarity and contrast. Marked in period writing on the original photographer's envelope that it was mailed in, armed holding a fully bayoneted Model 1841 rifle and a pistol tucked into his belt. He is holding a Hardee hat, with a bugle on it. **1,111.00**

This is an example of an unidentified 1/4 plate ambrotype of a New Hampshire sergeant.

Sharpsburg Arsenal

Probably a copy from an albumen print, this is a 1/4 plate ambrotype of President Lincoln's home in Springfield, Illinois.

Dale C. Anderson Co.

Sergeant, New Hampshire Volunteers, Armed, unidentified New Hampshire Volunteer sergeant holding a Model 1842 Musket with bayonet, case is complete, great condition. **795.00**

President Abraham Lincoln's Home, in a double, thermoplastic case, one side enclosing the image, and the other housing two items: (1) a mourning lithograph and (2) a CDV of a litho of Lincoln's home. The image appears to be unknown. The view was taken from across the street, providing a familiar viewpoint. There are no human figures. Changes from the scene from the late 1850s are the tree in front, which is larger, and you can see the new gate in the side fence. It is clearly summer—the windows are open and a vine completely overgrows the trellis in back and reaches the second floor porch railing, and obscures seeing the barn. The image is still sealed with old writing paper glued to the edges. It is a bit light, but crisp, and may be a picture of a picture, taken to provide copies upon his leaving for Washington, or to be given to close friends and family members upon his assassination. Condition is excellent, case measures approximately 4" x 5" and has raised floral and scroll pattern, one little chip to one corner. **1,700.00**

Cavalry soldier's ambrotype shown armed with his saber and wearing his cavalry leather belt.

Middle Tennessee Relics

Ambrotype, 1/6th plate

Cavalry Soldier, full-cased ambrotype of a seated Federal cavalryman with his cavalry saber at his side, wearing a regulation cavalry belt rig. The image has nice content, but is somewhat faded. This photo is in a full red-brown thermoplastic case. **350.00**

Private Francis S. McShane, Illinois Infantry, Armed, bears a wonderful inscription behind the image inside the case, which reads, "Francis S. McShane Taken at Corinth, Miss June 18, 1862/in the 20th year of his age." The image shows him seated from the waist-up wearing a four-button blouse, cartridge box sling, US buckle with belt and cap box, and a Colt navy revolver tacked into his belt. The image is quite nice, but does have some discolored emulsion along the periphery of the mat extending into the image, housed in a full case. . .**325.00**

Unidentified ambrotype of a Union sergeant.

Middle Tennessee Relics

Sergeant, clean-shaven man with tall early war forage cap, sergeant stripes are clearly visible. The photo is in a very attractive brown molded thermoplastic case. . . . **350.00**

Though sold as a Union soldier and a friend, this image may very well be of two civilians. Though the kepi worn by one of the men is distinctly military, it was a cap that was also a favorite with political "support" groups during the 1860 election.

Middle Tennessee Relics

Soldier and Civilian, both are seated, and the soldier is wearing a frock coat and his kepi. The photo is in a half hard case and has nice clarity. **125.00**

Soldier, Armed

Excellent 1/6th plate showing a Civil War soldier in overcoat, forage cap with insignia, and holding a rifled musket with bayonet affixed. Housed in half case. **305.00**

This ambrotype shows a fully-armed, African-American soldier. He is in full uniform and has his Model 1816 musket by his side. He is wearing a U.S. belt with a clear U.S. buckle showing. On the belt is his cap box. Across his chest you can see the eagle breastplate from his cartridge box sling. Very clear image, but has had some flaking to the emulsion as you can see, but everything is clearly visible. It comes nicely displayed in an original thermoplastic case. **1,226.00**

Posed in a civilian frock coat and a kepi with an oilcloth cover, this fellow may be a soldier or a member of the "Wide Awakes," a Republican Party support organization who wore oilcloth capes and kepis for their torch-lit night marches.

Middle Tennessee Relics

Soldier, seated pose wearing a frock coat and his forage cap. The cap appears to have the tarred rain cover on it. There is a small label with the photo that reads "Cary 321 Canal St." which could suggest that the photo was taken in New Orleans. On the reverse side of this picture is a second ambrotype and, no doubt, a relative of the soldier. Both photos and full case. **175.00**

Soldiers, six Civil War soldiers, one is wearing a musician's frock coat. **425.00**

Ambrotype, 1/9th plate

Private George R. Simpson, identified on an old tag in the back as being, "George R. Simpson." The tag states that he was born in 1814 and died on December 19, 1865. He is wearing a regulation Union coat and kepi. This photo is in a half-hard case. **175.00**

Unidentified, 1/9th plate ambrotype of a Union sergeant, the brass insignia displayed on his hat does reveal that he is in Company K of the 8th Regiment—state unknown.

Middle Tennessee Relics

Sergeant, crisp, full-cased 1/9th plate ruby ambrotype of a young Union sergeant wearing a regulation Union frock coat with his sergeant's stripes clearly visible. He is also wearing a brimmed type hat with "K" and "8" insignias. This photo has excellent clarity. **250.00**

Daguerreotypes

The first form of photography, the daguerreotype was popular in the United States from 1839 until about 1859. Even though it went out of favor with most photographers by the time of the Civil War, a few hung on to the old ways of the silver plate. You can recognize a daguerreotype by holding your thumb up to it. If you see a clear, mirror reflection, the image is made on a silver-coated copper plate—a "daguerreotype."

Daguerreotypes

Daguerreotype, 1/6th plate

Union Officer, Naval, seated youthful naval officer wearing uniform coat and holding cap with wreath insignia on the front, shown from the knees-up. Most intriguing is the lengthy inscription in the case behind the image. Written in ancient brown ink is, "Robert Mason - USN Norfolk 1/58-1/63 CSN," and above this is another brown ink inscription that has been crossed out, but is still readable which reads, "Kennedy Rice Hagerstown Washington County Maryland.". . **1,350.00**

Union Soldiers, 3rd New Jersey Volunteer Infantry, rare, brothers Andrew J. Gowrie and Joseph Gowrie with a old ink identification inside case. Andrew died of his wounds received at the battle of Gaines Mills, Joseph was discharged for disability. Andrew wears his nine-button frockcoat and military vest. **650.00**

Tintypes

Tintypes were another version of the use of collodion. In this case, the medium was tin-dipped iron plates instead of glass as in the ambrotype. The advantage of tin was that it was not fragile, could be sent through the mail, and was easily carried. They were also relatively inexpensive, because multiple images could be made on a single plate and cut apart. This provided the sitter with duplicate images. The process came into popular use in the United States during 1856 and was still being used by some photographers as late as 1920.

Confederate

Tintype, 1/4 plate, Confederate Captain John S. Stansell, 52nd Tennessee Volunteer Infantry, 3/4-length seated pose of a very thin and gaunt looking rebel seated next to a studio table. He sports a classic Confederate gray six-button short jacket with three gold stripes on the collar (indicating a rank of captain), and a matching pair of gray trousers. The image is extremely clear and well contrasted and has some light surface "rubs" that only lightly affect the image. It is identified inside the back of the case in classic script, "Capt. John S. Stansell 52nd Regt. Tenn. Vol." This inscription is very nicely done. The regiment fought valiantly at such battles as Chickamauga, Atlanta, and with Hood at Franklin and Nashville. At Chickamauga the unit went into action with 270 men, and suffered a loss of 96 officers and men wounded or killed in the engagement. It surrendered to the Federals at Greensboro, North Carolina, in 1865. Housed in a ratty full leatherette case. **1,175.00**

Tintype, 1/6 plate

Confederate Captain, handsome, 2/3-length seated pose. He is wearing a Confederate officer's double-breasted gray frock coat with three rows of gold braid on each side of the collar indicating the rank of captain. He also wears a waist belt with two-piece interlocking tongue and wreath buckle, which is probably a C.S. plate, but not visible due to light gilt-tinting on the buckle's surface. The clarity, contrast, and condition are all excellent. The image is nice and bright. The only defect is a slight bend running diagonally through the center of the plate with a very slight abrasion in this area on the subject's breast. Housed in a fine gilt mat, frame, and glass. **1,075.00**

> **"April 18, 1863. Got a letter from Mary—all well. Finished a letter to Mary, and sent my likeness in it."**
>
> ***— David B. Arthus***
> ***Company I, 20th Wisconsin Volunteer Infantry***

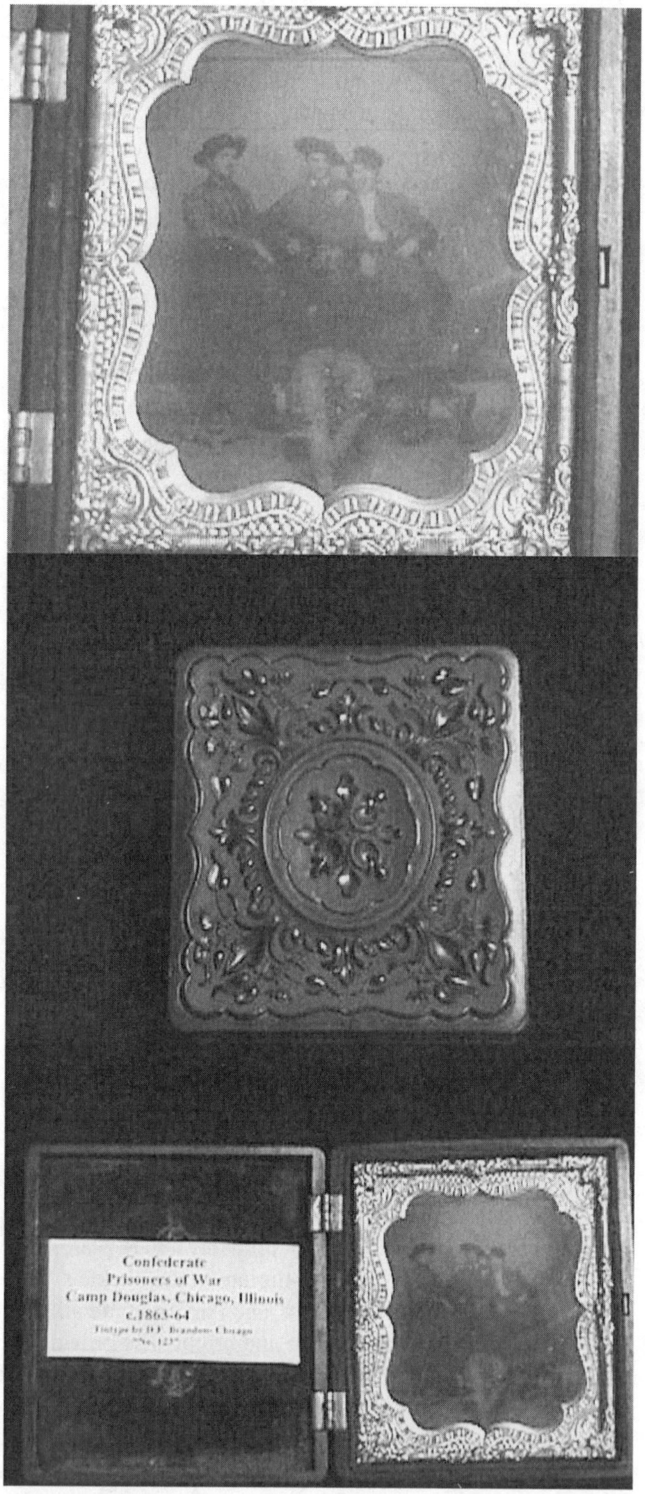

Written behind this image is a note identifying the sitters as Confederate prisoners: "Camp Douglas-Brandon 1863." Camp Douglas was a prisoner of war camp in Illinois.

Confederate Prisoners of War, four Confederates posed at the P.O.W. Camp Douglas near Chicago. Very clean image. At least three of the four appear to be cavalrymen. Image is very clean, just a bit dark. Behind the image is written, "Camp Douglas—Brandon 1863" in pencil Case is ornate thermoplastic. **760.00**

Confederate Private, clear, fully cased tintype of a Confederate private showing his military vest and his gray frock coat. The neatest part of this photo is that there is one large coat-size button visible, and it isn't gilted. The button is a large-size, cast "I" Confederate button with the large letter "I" on the button clearly visible. **425.00**

Tintype, 1/8th plate, Confederate Private, Armed, housed in a nice, embossed, cream paper mat. View shows knees-up standing, bearded, early war Rebel wearing tall top hat, ten-button gray frock coat with fringed epaulets, waistbelt with roller buckle, scabbard, square flat cap box, and the soldier is holding his Enfield musket with bayonet, and has a Colt Root revolver clearly tucked into his belt. Image has great clarity and contrast, with a couple minor bumps and blemishes from not being under glass. Image is apparently a copy view of another tin or ambrotype (subject is not reversed in image) but definitely war date. **395.00**

Tintype, 1/9th plate

Confederate Soldier, young man in "battle shirt" tintype of young Confederate soldier, measures 2" x 2-1/2", condition is good. The image has excellent clarity and some light bubbling in upper right side. The case is crude, but in working order. **350.00**

Confederate Private, crystal-clear fully cased, Confederate soldier wearing a butternut shell jacket open in the center. The buttons are gilted, but one is partially visible and appears to be a drooped wing eagle Confederate button. The photo is mounted in an excellent condition thermoplastic case marked, "Holmes, Booth, and Hayden." **475.00**

Tintypes, Union

Tintype 1/4 plate

Soldiers, Armed, fine view showing four grizzly looking Yankees, two line officers, one sergeant, and an unknown rank. Three of these fellows are wearing M1858 U.S. Army Hardee hats, two with clearly visible infantry horns, company letters "H," and numerals "7" inside the horn. Interestingly these two also have the worsted wool hat cords that are almost never seen in photos, despite the fact that they are called for by regulations. One officer wears a classic round-top slouch hat with officer's embroidered bugle and "7" in the loop. The last fellow (line officer) has no insignia on his hat. Fine clarity and contrast. Good condition, but has two or three tiny chips and two or three minor bends in the tin. The backdrop is distinctive being an outdoor studio with white sheet background actual cut saplings or tree branches laid against the backdrop, housed in full case. **495.00**

Even though discoloring impairs this image to a degree, it is offset by the strong content: A Union soldier holding a bugle with a Colt Army revolver tucked into his belt.

Drumbeat Civil War Memorabilia

Musician, Armed, bugler with a Colt revolver in his belt, wearing a shell jacket with shoulder tabs (possibly a New York issue jacket), and an unusual hat. The bugle and Colt are very obvious. It is tinted and in a gilt frame. Unfortunately there is solarization, but the image itself is extremely sharp and clean. **695.00**

NCOs, four soldiers (one seated three standing) posed in front of a fine camp-scene backdrop. Standing are well-worn, hardened Union soldiers including a corporal and sergeant. These fellows wear forage caps and frock coats, one wears a rectangular eagle buckle on the belt, and two are wearing boots. The seated fellow has no rank showing, and wears a kepi, un-piped infantry shell jacket, regulation trousers, and boots. Crisp clarity and contrast, one inconsequential slight bend, housed in full case. **395.00**

The tinting on this 1/4 plate tintype of a Union cavalryman makes the image leap off the plate.

Dave Taylor Civil War Antiques

Cavalry Private, Armed, super, cased, double-armed cavalry trooper. **595.00**

Cavalry Soldiers, Outdoor, wonderful horizontal format outdoor view showing 14 war-ready cavalrymen posed in their camp in the woods in front of their Sibley tent, and having their national colors standing behind them. There are 13 enlisted troopers wearing shell jackets, bummer caps, sword belts, and holding their sabers—most have large full beards, a couple have high boots, and they are posed looking off to the left as though watching for some rebel cavalry to appear. At the left side of the view, is their company commander wearing his frock coat and holding his sword, also looking off into the distance. It is housed in a full leatherette case (spine split) with a beautiful, rich, green velvet cushion. **3,500.00**

Corporal, Cavalry, Armed, fully cased image of a bearded cavalryman wearing a forage cap, shell jacket with corporal's chevrons, issue trousers, gauntlets, saber belt, Colt Army revolver tucked in belt, saber held upright for all to view. Patriotic backdrop, excellent condition, clarity, and contrast. **675.00**

Officer, Armed, very crisp and close-up view showing a full-seated Union first lieutenant wearing a black slouch hat with clearly visible U.S. staff wreath insignia on the front, frock coat with clearly visible double border shoulder straps, regulation officer's sword belt with stitched designs, light-colored trousers, and gauntlets. He has his Model 1850-foot officer's sword propped upright next to him and proudly displays it to the camera. The image has excellent clarity, contrast, and condition, with a spot of staining on the right side of the image that does not affect the subject at all. This is housed in a full case with frame and glass. **795.00**

Officers, Outdoor, really interesting outdoor image showing five officers and men, and one horse, posed outside a small log cabin. There is an officer and his wife near the doorway, a soldier holding his horse, and three other soldiers to the left of the cabin. Image is 100% solid and stable, but the lacquer coating on the plate has alligatored, leaving tiny lines and crackles in the surface of the lacquer coating. The image is not flaked or flaking in any form. Good contrast and a very appealing outdoor image, housed in mat, frame, and glass only. **395.00**

Private and Painted Backdrop. Very nice, full-cased, young Union infantryman. This is a full-standing view, and he is wearing his forage cap and a regulation four-button sack coat. The photo is taken in front of a patriotic backdrop with a Civil War camp scene in the background. The case is in excellent condition. **295.00**

Samuel Beals, a trooper in the 8th Illinois Cavalry posed for this 1/4 plate tintype.

Frohne's Historic Military

Private Samuel Beals, 8th Illinois Volunteer Cavalry, full-standing soldier in uniform holding his sword. Gilt buckle, painted backdrop of camp scene with American flag. Identified in case as, "Samuel Beals of the Ill. 8th cavalry." Thermoplastic case, some small bends in the tintype. 795.00

1/4 plate tintype of Union soldier seated with a sword across his lap.

Frohne's Historic Military

Private, Armed, bearded soldier wearing a rain tarred kepi and holding his sword across his lap. A gem-sized image of his wife is included, in full case not original to the image. 860.00

When a soldier is seen in an image wearing a great deal or all of his accoutrements, you can be sure that the price is going to go up.

Frohne's Historic Military

Sergeant, Armed, pipe smoking union sergeant, contained in a full leather case. Weapon in hand, wearing all the proper accoutrements, this soldier is shown wearing his bedroll, haversack, and canteen. Great painted backdrop, this image has no flaws. 1,450.00

Sergeant, Cavalry, Armed, subject seated in front of a patriotic camp scene backdrop in his kepi with wreath insignia on the front, a commercially made shell jacket with narrow sergeant's chevrons on each sleeve, one button on the collar, and delicate-fine cuff piping. He wears an officer's sword belt and is cradling his cavalry saber in his lap. Excellent in all respects with some edge chips not visible under the mat, housed in a mediocre half case. 425.00

Soldier, Armed

Full standing with patriotic camp scene backdrop. Shows soldier wearing regulation forage cap, nine-button frock, and holding a Model 1861 Springfield with bayonet in front of him. Very good in all respects, housed in mat, frame, and glass (no case). 235.00

"November 6, 1861. An artist was here and took a likeness of the Regiment while on dress parade."

— Thomas K. Mitchell
Company G, 4th Illinois Cavalry

Sometimes size does matter—especially in the case of outdoor tintypes of Civil War soldiers. This is a 1/2 plate tintype of the 5th Ohio Cavalry with their new 12 lb mountain howitzer.

Drumbeat Civil War Memorabilia

Superb contrast and clarity, fully armed and carrying all the appropriate accoutrements, this soldier is truly ready for war. The condition is almost mint, comes in a full case. **1,500.00**

This well-posed image shows a hardened Union soldier posed in standing profile for the camera wearing his forage cap, frock coat, tall boots, backpack, leather gear, bayonet and scabbard. and holding his Model 1842 musket in front of him also in profile with the lock toward the camera. This subject is posed in front of a studio painted camp scene backdrop. Excellent clarity, very good contrast, fine condition with one little stain. Housed in full case with split spine. **875.00**

Soldier

Full-standing, housed in full case, Yank wears forage cap, frock, trousers, and has rectangular eagle buckle and belt, very good with minor scuff to left of subject. **125.00**

Really superb tintype photo shows a Yankee soldier the way he looked in camp posed in front of a great photographer's painted camp scene backdrop standing next to a studio chair wearing his issue trousers, a large cravat military vest open to expose his homespun shirt, and having a great pair of suspenders. In one hand he is holding a large wine bottle, and in the other he is holding his worn out old black slouch hat. On the studio chair next to him he has laid his uniform blouse, which is draped over the back of the wooden chair. Excellent clarity, contrast, and condition with the edges of the tintype slightly trimmed to fit this in a photo album. No case. **395.00**

Soldiers, Armed, really touching early war photo of one very eager looking bear of a yank, and his serious looking companion, standing side-by-side. Each wears a forage cap (one with insignia), and each is dressed identically in four-button blouses, cartridge boxes with straps and eagle plates, belts, buckles, cap boxes, regulation trousers with cuffs rolled up, and each with his model 1842 musket with bayonet held upright at the "order arms " position. Excellent in all respects in full case with plush velvet liner (hinge split).. ......**395.00**

Soldiers, Sixth Corps, fine, knees-up, seated view, fellow on left is heavily bearded yank wearing frock with sergeant chevrons and clear 6th corps badge on his breast. Fellow on the right is handsome trooper wearing short jacket and knee-high boots. Fine in all respects housed in full case (spine repaired). **225.00**

Soldiers, horizontal format tintype housed in mat, frame, and glass (no case). Shows five Union army soldiers in uniform and two more in shirtsleeves squared off and boxing for the camera. Image has good condition and contrast with the focus being just slightly soft. Fine overall and very rare. **495.00**

U.S. Soldiers, tintype of a first sergeant and a private who have obviously been sharing a bottle of wine. Their facial expressions, as well as the cloth used to cork the opened bottle, give them away. These two soldiers share a rare moment of relaxation during a horrendous war. The first sergeant wears what appears to be a circular belt buckle with a shield and eagle insignia and square framing and loops on one side. A poem is pinned to the velvet mat, entitled "the Blue and the Gray," a portion of which is illustrated here. A modern identification indicates that the private is George Vecks or Veiks of Faugueir City, Virginia. The image has very nice tones and sharp focus and detail. There is some crazing, which is visible only when the image is held at an angle and one small spot of emulsion damage on the private's sleeve. The image is contained in a nice leather case with an unusual star-in-circle motif. **700.00**

This armed cavalry soldier wears a sash over his shoulder. Normally, this would denote "officer of the day." In this 1/6th plate tintype, though, the meaning is not clear.

Sharpsburg Arsenal

Infantry Private, Armed, fully cased, standing Union infantryman wearing a regulation Union waist belt with a cap box and a large oval U.S. waist belt plate. He has tucked his blouse into his trousers. His musket is standing along side, and a nice patriotic camp scene is in the background. A beautiful red, white, and blue tinted U.S. flag can be seen flying in the background. This is a crisp, clear photo with no flaking at all. **450.00**

Sergeant, Armed, fully cased, young Union sergeant, full-standing view, wearing an enlisted man's nine-button frock coat with his sergeant stripes clearly visible. In addition, he is wearing his U.S. belt, cap box, cartridge box, and over-the-shoulder sling. He has an Enfield rifle at his side with fixed bayonet. This is a quality photograph with nice skin-tone tinting. **595.00**

Tintype, 1/6th plate

Private William F. Bowers, 21st Ohio Volunteer Infantry, fine, near-mint tintype in patriotic gutta-percha (thermoplastic) case (also perfect) showing William F. Bower, 21st Ohio, seated with musket and wearing belt with "OVM" buckle. Also comes with his eagle masthead discharge dated June 1865 (Bower served 3 years). Case has liberty cap and patriotic designs.. . . . . **650.00**

Sergeant Benjamin Thomas, New York Volunteers, seated pose shows a New York boy wearing light-color hat, N.Y. state jacket with huge homemade sergeant's chevrons, cross belt with circular eagle plate, waist belt with small-size oval buckle, and issue trousers. Image has dark tonal quality, but very viewable, and otherwise fine. A family note (recent) is on the back of the tin that reads, "Benjamin Thomas MD in civil war was prisoner in Andersonville. Father of Evan Thomas Fess grandmother of Dorothy Fess Herbert." Housed in a nice half case. **185.00**

Soldier, Armed, thighs-up, seated pose of a Union soldier wearing a forage cap, regulation frock coat, issue trousers, and having his cross-belt with circular eagle plate, and a U.S. belt & buckle with cap box and bayonet scabbard clearly visible. Upright at his side he is holding his musket that appears to be a Model 1842. Very nice housed in a full case. **295.00**

Cavalry Private, Armed, good, armed image with cavalry saber, NCO Belt, and holster. Has saber sash tied over the shoulder. Picture has some flaws and creases, but does not detract much from image. **450.00**

Cavalry Private, Double-Armed, fully cased tintype is clear, but just a little dark. The trooper is seated and wearing a cavalry shell jacket, a Hardee hat with a crossed saber hatpin, and a cavalry eagle sword belt rig. His cavalry saber is standing alongside of him, and a Remington Army Model revolver is tucked behind his belt. Although just a little dark, this is a nice photo with excellent content. **395.00**

The case in which a hard image is mounted can often affect the price. This is especially true if the case is thermoplastic. As an example, this 1/6th plate tintype of an armed Union cavalryman would have fetched a decent price on its own. But, because it is housed in a thermoplastic wall frame, it was a great deal.

Frohne's Historic Military

Cavalry Private. An absolutely great of a Union Cavalryman with his drawn saber and Hardee hat sitting on the nearby table. If this is not enough, the image is contained in a very nice wall hanging thermoplastic case. The tin has a slight bend and some light scrapes, but none detract much from the eye appeal of this outstanding image. **800.00**

Corporal, Armed, seated view of a very hardened looking Yankee corporal decked out with his musket and infantry gear. His issue frock sports corporal's chevrons. He wears the regulation forage cap, crossbelt with eagle plate, U.S. belt with oval buckle, cap box, and holds his Austrian rifle upright at his side. He also wears large heavy gloves or gauntlets. A great image, fine condition, clarity, and contrast, full case. **365.00**

Drummer William H. Headly, 10th Vermont Volunteer Infantry, view shows William H. Headley of the 10th Vermont in a 2/3-length seated pose with his drum on a studio table next to him. Headley is posed wearing the elusive infantry musician's frock coat with "grid iron" piping on the breast. He also has his drum sling slung across his chest and a waist belt with eagle buckle clearly visible. The drum next to him is a full-size regimental rope-tension drum and it has the sticks stuck into the ropes for display. The clarity and condition are top-notch, and the contrast is very good with just a slight darkness on the coat and drum. This is not a dark image as his face, buckle, hands are all bright and clear. There is just a slight darkness to the coat and drum. Housed in a gilt mat only. **1,275.00**

Drummers, clarity and contrast are superb, housed in a half case. **897.00**

Militia Soldier, Armed. Very attractive, fully cased, early war Union militiaman. This is a full-standing view with his musket across his chest. He is wearing a tall, early-style shako with plume, a nine-button enlisted man's frock coat, U.S. belt, and cartridge box with sling. The image is bright and clear with no flaking. **450.00**

Armed Union officer's 1/6th plate tintype housed in a full case.

Frohne's Historic Military

Officer, Armed

Excellent, armed Union officer with sword, contained in a full case. **550.00**

Standing view of Union line officer wearing kepi with bugle insignia, frock coat with shoulder straps, belt and sword posed as if he is drawing the sword out of its scabbard. Nice, but has halo effect, dark contrast, half case. **175.00**

Officer, fine image in half case, shows very handsome major wearing double-breasted frock coat, and fine, double border shoulder strap. His hair is slightly long, and his upper lip sports an Errol Flynn pencil-thin mustache. **325.00**

Union Officer, image shows a Union lieutenant seated from the knees-up. He is seated in front of a painted photographer's backdrop that includes tents and a cannon. The officer wears a forage cap with large visor and infantry hunting horn insignia on the front. He also wears a regulation line officer's frock coat with large shoulder straps, and a pair of early-war dark trousers with narrow welt of piping down the outer seam of each leg. This image is perfect in all respects and very appealing, as it is housed in a full case with a fine patriotic gilt mat with flags, muskets, cannon, and ships. **279.00**

Private R.L. Jackson of the 5th New York Heavy Artillery carried his musket to the studio to have this 1/6th plate tintype made.

Frohne's Historic Military

Private R.L. Jackson, 5th New York Heavy Artillery, Private R.L. Jackson (identified on the preserver) stands in full uniform outdoors with his musket and fixed bayonet. Three other soldiers can be seen in the background. One appears to be a black man. . . . **695.00**

Private Silas Laughlin, Ohio Volunteer Cavalry, seated view 18 or 20-year-old soldier wearing regulation US Army forage cap, regulation army fatigue blouse, regulation issue trousers tinted with just a rumor of light blue wash by the photographer, cross belt for cartridge box with circular eagle shoulder belt plate, waist belt with cap box and oval U.S. buckle, and holding his model 1816 conversion musket diagonally across his chest. Excellent in all respects housed in a ratty full case, on the back of which is an inscription that reads, "Presented to Nannie Johnston on the 19th of Feb 1864 by her much-esteemed friend and truehearted soldier Silas Laughlin." Silas Laughlin was in an Ohio cavalry regiment and there is no mention of service in an infantry unit prior or after. **395.00**

The pose should also be considered when determining whether or not to acquire an image. This is a bit more subjective than saying, "add x dollars for a armed, x for outdoor, x for identified, and so forth." This actually requires the art student in you to come out a bit. In the case of this 1/6th plate image of a Union soldier, the unusual (and aggressive) pose of thrusting the bayonet forward pushed up the selling price.

Frohne's Historic Military

Tinted tintype of an armed Union soldier wearing a great coat, pointing his musket with bayonet attached towards the camera. Rich tones to image, full case (repaired professionally along the center seam), pencil inscription dated 1862 behind the image.**650.00**

Private

Bearded Union private seated in a chair, wearing a frock coat, forage cap, belt with oval US buckle, cap pouch, and bayonet. This is image is very sharp, cased and in excellent condition.**185.00**

Crystal-clear image in a half-hard case. He is seated wearing a shell jacket and a military vest beneath.
. .**150.00**

The painted backdrop and the armed private gives this image strong appeal.

Frohne's Historic Military

Housed in a thermoplastic case, these two 1/6th plate tintypes depict an armed officer and an enlisted man wearing an "SNY" belt plate. The unusual belt plate is often enough to make an ordinary image very desirable.

Private, Armed

Beautiful, armed Union soldier, excellent condition, contained in a full case. **575.00**

Private P. Hall Pitcher and Officer, New York Volunteer Infantry, fantastic double Union case with two New York soldiers. The fellow on the left is wearing a nine-button frock coat and a New York script belt plate. His pants are lightly tinted blue. Behind the image is the name, "P. Hall Pitcher." The other image is a Union officer wearing an 1851 sword belt plate and rig, lieutenant shoulder straps and holding an early model dragoon saber. He is also wearing a nine-button frock coat. Behind this image is a neat drawing of a comical general and the phrase, "Don't Disorder." Both images came from a home in Maryland straight from the family. Images are housed in Union case in near-mint condition. **638.00**

Sergeant Augustus Weller, soldier with a pistol under his belt, sword, three chevron stripes on each arm, crossed swords on cap, looks like letter "G" on cap to right of swords. Believed to be Sergeant Augustus Weller of Lawrence County, Pennsylvania. Belt buckle, buttons, stripes, trim on cap all colorized gold or yellow. Under glass in original embossed case with gold-highlighted U.S. flag on front, inside front velvet lined. Case measures 3-1/4" x 4-3/4" x 7/8" and is cloth/paper over what looks like wood. There is a small light scratch at the bottom right of the glass. Front and back of case separated at left. Case still has two closures on right edge, has some wear to fabric/paper cover. Back of case has two cracks, each 3/4" from top/bottom edge; top crack is 2-1/4" long, bottom is 1-1/2" long, measuring from the formerly bound edge. **579.00**

Sergeant, Armed, very fine, seated pose showing a lean, whiskered Union sergeant wearing forage cap, four-button blouse, issue trousers with wide sergeants stripes, leather gear, and holding a long Austrian import musket horizontally in front of him for the camera, and all viewers, to clearly see. Excellent in all respects with just a couple tiny age spots, half case............ **465.00**

Sergeant, nice, clear, seated Union Sergeant wearing a regulation nine-button frock coat with military vest beneath. His sergeant stripes are clearly visible. This photo is beautifully matted and is in an excellent full case. **250.00**

Soldier, 6th Corps, wearing a 6th Corps badge on the right breast of his coat, seated 3/4-length portrait, tinted, and in a full leather-covered case. **150.00**

Soldier, 35th New York Volunteer Infantry, clear, full-cased, young member of Company I, 35th New York Volunteer Infantry. This is a seated pose with his "S.N.Y." belt plate visible. There is an "I" and "35" on his collar. This photo is cased in a perfect condition, geometric pattern, black thermoplastic case. ... **395.00**

Soldier, Armed

Crisp, shows a Federal infantryman with chin whiskers seated in a waist-up pose with a table next to him and a branch of dried leaves leaning from the table to the wall. Subject is wearing a regulation forage cap, a frock coat with piped collar, but no piping on the cuffs (non-regulation), a U.S. buckle with waist belt, cap box, cartridge box (visible at his side), shoulder strap with eagle breastplate, and he is holding his clearly visible Austrian Lorenz rifle with quadrangular bayonet affixed upright at his side. An unusual aspect to this fellow's uniform is the fact that the frock coat appears to have been made with only five or six buttons and is piped only on the collar. Outstanding and bright, housed in a half case with full mat, frame, and glass................. **485.00**

Nice, seated Yankee wearing his forage cap, frock coat, U.S. belt and buckle, and having his cartridge box sling with plate, and canteen strap visible across his chest. Upright at his side is his Model 1816 musket. A couple of bends, a little soiling, and slight darkness of contrast, but still very presentable. Housed in a mat, frame, and glass only. **175.00**

Excellent quality, Civil War soldier holding his rifle, full-standing view. Soldier is standing at attention holding his musket wearing four-button sack coat with tinted blue forage cap hat. You can even see the tinted cheeks. Comes in full case with tape on spine of case. .. **405.00**

Fine, standing view of young fellow around 16-years-old wearing bummer cap, shell jacket, dark trousers, cross belt with circular plate, and holding his Enfield musket in front of him. Patriotic backdrop. Excellent, in a half case. **345.00**

Fine, standing soldier with cap, frock, leather gear, and holding his Model 1816 musket upright at his side. Fine clarity and contrast. Only defect is a small section of the image is fused to the cover glass. Image and emulsion are fine and solid, housed in a half case. **165.00**

Fully cased, young Union soldier, full-standing view with his musket and bayonet across his chest. He is also wearing his shell jacket, forage cap, and belt with cap box and buckle. The photo does have a couple of slight bend ripples, but is otherwise pretty. It is cased in a military motif case. **295.00**

Seated Union soldier in frock coat and dark blue trousers, wearing a baldric with circular eagle breastplate and waist belt with "US" brass plate. He is holding a U.S. Model 1840 NCO sword in the scabbard across his lap, ice-clear image in gilt oval matte, resting in the back half of a pressed wood and leatherette case. **325.00**

A very-fine view showing a lean Union infantryman full standing in front of an elaborate painted camp scene backdrop. The subject wears a regulation Hardee hat with cords and infantry insignia, an infantry frock coat, issue trousers, his leather accoutrement set, and he holds his Springfield musket with bayonet upright at this side. Housed in a full case that lacks the velvet pillow inside the lid. **465.00**

Soldier

Nice waist-up pose showing bearded soldier in his infantry frock coat. Fine overall, full case also very nice. **79.00**

Seated view, excellent clarity and condition. Yank has a mess of chin whiskers and large black wide brim hat. Full case with split spine. **125.00**

Soldiers William and Phillip Letsinger, 14th Indiana Volunteer Infantry, Armed, shows two armed Federal soldiers wearing regulation frocks, caps, and belts with buckles and cap boxes. One fellow is kneeling on the floor with his Model 1842 musket pointed out to the left of the viewer as though he is preparing to shoot, the other yank is standing with his identical 1842 musket at waist level pointing in the same direction. The photographer has posed these two as though they are on picket duty and have just heard the rebs moving into range. These yanks are posed in front of a painted photographer's camp scene backdrop of tents, flag, and troops. The back of the tintype bears the scratched inscription,"Dalrymple, Alma R#1 Mich.," and the previous owner stated that the subjects are William and Phillip Letsinger of the 14th Indiana, and that Phillip was killed at the Battle of Antietam. The tintype has been slightly trimmed and has a small punched hole in the upper-right corner where it was apparently hung on display at one time. The image is very nice with good clarity, contrast, and condition, having some light soiling and age toning. It is housed in a fine case (hinge split) so that the trimmed edges of the tin are not visible under the mat. **485.00**

Soldiers, Cavalry, Armed, wonderful, shows four Federal cavalry troopers with shell jackets with shoulder scales, saber belts with rectangular eagle buckles, issue trousers with the finest, most appealing light blue wash, and all holding their Model 1840 heavy cavalry sabers upright for the camera. Next to these men is a large wooden box, which appears to contain farrier's tools. The upper-right corner of the image shows a cabinet or cupboard of some sort, also visible is what appears to be a stovepipe. The floor is dirt, so it certainly isn't a permanent photo studio. Under magnification, every detail of the sabers, belts, etc. can be clearly seen. **1,650.00**

Soldiers, Outdoor, made by Abraham Cottrell of the 8th Michigan Infantry, image shows a dozen soldiers in greatcoats close to the camera, many more behind, and rows and rows of wedge tents and camp. When Cottrell's estate surfaced many years ago, there were numerous spectacular outdoor tintypes he had taken during the Civil War. He had served on General Stevens' staff. This image is wonderful with excellent clarity and contrast. There is one antique stain on one small spot, and there is some surface crazing in the lacquer only. No emulsion damage—just some surface crazing, housed in a half case. **1,150.00**

Soldiers

Pleasant view of two pards. Left subject wears a regulation forage cap, four-button fatigue blouse, issue trousers, and has his regulation army tarred haversack slung over his shoulder. He is standing next to a friend or relative. Housed in mat, frame, and glass (no case), good condition with some gray tonal quality and a couple tiny tin dents. **169.00**

The two subjects in this photo are apparently 16 or 17-years-old and both are decked out in their government suits. The young man on the left wears a forage cap, frock coat, trousers, and has his U.S. belt and buckle, cap box, bayonet and scabbard, and his cartridge box sling with eagle plate clearly shown. His pard on the right is wearing his cap and frock, but elected not to wear his accoutrements into the photo studio. Housed in the gilt frame and glass only, no case. Excellent clarity, contrast, and condition. **275.00**

Tintype, 1/8th plate

Heavy Artilleryman, Armed, full standing soldier wearing black slouch hat with crossed cannon insignia, letter "M" and numeral "1," enlisted frock coat, U.S. belt with buckle and cap box, and having his cartridge box sling with plate visible across his chest. At his side is a Springfield musket with bayonet. The album that this came with contained all Ohio soldiers from northwest Ohio. The image is very appealing and artistically posed, but it becomes quite dark at the lower-right quadrant. It is housed in a fine mat, frame, and glass. **145.00**

Private, Armed

Standing Union soldier in full case. He is standing at attention with his musket at his side. He is wearing an enlisted man's nine-button frock coat with a U.S. belt plate and cartridge box sling plate visible. . . . **425.00**

Young, well-armed Union infantryman. The photo is in a half case and is quite clear with no flaking or fading. The soldier is holding a Mississippi Rifle and saber bayonet at his side. He is wearing gauntlets, and is also wearing a Model 1858 Hardee hat with one side flipped up and a nice clear infantry bugle hatpin. **450.00**

Sergeant Major, Armed, absolutely pristine-mint tintype housed in a fine full leatherette case. The image shows a dashing looking Federal with Burnside-style "mutton chops." He is shown full-standing wearing a kepi with hunting horn insignia on the front, a commercial frock coat with sergeant major's chevrons, a sword belt with rectangular eagle buckle, a sash, and he is holding his Model 1850 foot officer's sword in front of him, while the scabbard dangles off his belt. This image is pristine mint in all respects with bright contrast, housed in a perfect full leatherette case. **495.00**

Soldier, bright and clear tintype photo showing a soldier wearing a light-colored shell jacket (sky blue or gray?), dark trousers, and standing totally erect. The shell jacket has a ten-button front, cloth shoulder tabs, and piped cuffs and collar. Above the cuff piping is a veteran's stripe on each sleeve, and there is a small "slash" pocket in the right breast. The coat is either a variant Veteran Reserve Corps or state militia jacket, such as was issued by Penna. In any event, it is a very fine image with brilliance and clarity. There is a scratch in the extreme upper-left corner of the tintype, which does not affect, nor detract, from the image in the least, no case. **135.00**

Tintype, 1/9th plate

Private Thomas J. Naylor, 9th Indiana Volunteer Infantry, mint, crystal clear, shows Thomas J. Naylor, Company C, 9th Indiana from the waist up, in a very interesting pose. He is wearing a tall crown forage cap, state-issue shell jacket with shoulder tabs, and has his musket delicately displayed at his side with one hand grasping the fore stock and his other stretched across his body with hand caressing the lower stock. You can see the socket of his bayonet clearly below his belt. This is now housed in mat, frame, and glass, but was found inside the album. The album is beautifully inscribed in brown ink, "Thomas J Naylor Co "C" 9th Regt. Ind. Vet. Vols. Inft. 3rd Brig. 1st Div. 4th Army Corps June 2nd 1865." It is a fine gilt leather 1860s album in very nice condition **495.00**

Cavalry Office, seated, almost full-length pose, he wears the frock coat and holds his slouch hat and a cavalry saber, housed in full leather case. **165.00**

Infantry Lieutenant, he is wearing a forage cap with infantry horn insignia and a frock coat with shoulder straps. Housed in a gilt frame and mat, the ferrotype is a bit smaller than a 1/9th plate. **95.00**

Master Sergeant, fully cased, seated, waist-up shot. He is wearing a regulation nine-button frock coat, and his master sergeant's stripes are clearly visible on both arms. **195.00**

Private, 131st New York Infantry, image of a soldier wearing a bummers cap with "131" on the top and a frock coat, partially open, in leather-covered case. **95.00**

Private, Armed, fully cased, young Union infantry private, seated with a revolver stuck behind his belt. His uniform piping has been trimmed in infantry blue by the artist. The photo is cased in a thermoplastic case with an ornate military scene. **295.00**

Even though there is no identification on this 1/9th plate tintype, it can be determined that the sitter was a New York infantryman from his state-issued jacket and his oval, "SNY" belt plate.

Dale C. Anderson Co.

Private, New York, taken in a field studio where a box is set up with a blanket thrown over it for a seat, and a piece of white canvas is hung up as a backdrop. Fellow looks like an immigrant in his mid-20s. Seated, shown from ankles up, very clear, wearing a forage cap, a New York state-issued short jacket with "muffin" buttons (probably New York state seal). Oval "SNY" belt plate was worn, and clearly seen. He has it on upside-down, typical lighter trousers, 2-3/4" x 3-1/4", matted, with glass, in half case. **365.00**

Private, full-cased, Union soldier wearing his forage cap and also regulation nine-button frock coat. The photo has nice eye appeal with sharp contrast and clarity. The case is red-brown thermoplastic with a flawless, intricate floral motif. **275.00**

Soldier, Fourth Corps, cased, military motive mat, the soldier wears his jacket open to show his uniform vest and a silhouette-style 4th corps badge. **200.00**

Tintype, 1/2 plate, Union 5th Ohio Volunteer Cavalry, rare outdoor image of the men of the 5th Ohio Volunteer Cavalry with their new 12 lb Mountain Howitzer. Image shows cavalrymen, their horses, outbuildings, and the Mountain Howitzer with caisson. This artillery piece was one of two purchased personally by Colonel Thomas Heath, naming one after his wife. . . . **3,000.00**

Tintype, Full Plate

Private, Armed, 6" x 7" image of uniformed and equipped Union infantryman holding a Short Enfield Rifle. Slight flaking to the emulsion at bottom left, otherwise perfectly clear. **525.00**

Views of more than one soldier, or views depicting any unusual insignia, are quite collectible. This particular full plate tintype combines size with a view of three artilleryman, one of whom is wearing an 18th Corps badge on his hat, and the other two who have adorned their forage caps with lots of brass.

Dale Anderson Co.

Artillerymen, shows three soldiers in uniform, two seated, flanking one standing. They wear short jackets, vests, light trousers with stripes, and forage caps. Two hats are shown with crown insignia showing. This is a large, crossed cannon with "7" over top and "I" below. Standing fellow has instead, his 18th Corps badge showing. The photo was taken in studio setting simulating a garden bower. Two seated men rest against a decorative railing. Greens are arched over top. Good clarity for a full plate, which is rarely sharp. This is actually a photograph of a photograph. You can actually see the edges of the original tintype, and the tack heads holding it in place for this shot. **475.00**

Tintype, Gem, Private, postage stamp-size tintype of a young Union private intact in its original paper mount. The image is crisp, clear, and in excellent condition. **95.00**

Tintype, Mammoth Plate, Private Thomas Holton, 6th Maryland Infantry, image is of Thomas Holton of Company G, Sixth Maryland Volunteer Infantry. The oversized 10" x 14", hand-tinted plate shows a 3/4-length seated view of Private Holton in frock, and coat and kepi with a jaunty looking scarf at his throat. The image shows surface crazing, but nothing is missing and condition is fine. A photographer's number is at the bottom of the image, "G.Y. 418841," and each corner has a small nail hole. The original poster board backing has a handwritten identification, "Thomas Holton/ Nandy's Father." Included are archival copies of Holton's service and pension records which show that he mustered in on August 22, 1862, in Baltimore. On June 13, 1863, while engaging the enemy at Berryville, Virginia, Holton was captured and paroled. After his exchange, Holton spent months in the hospital before joining the Veteran Reserve Corp. He apparently never fully regained his health, as he was discharged on a surgeon's certificate of disability. Also includes photocopies of pages from: *The History and Roster of Maryland Volunteers: The Civil War Diary of Lt. William J. Grant. Co. G 6th Maryland Regiment: Cemetery and Census Records.* Also included are three hardcover novels with bookplates from the library of Holton's descendants that came with the tintype. **750.00**

Miscellaneous

Album, Union Soldiers, 25th Michigan Volunteer Infantry, truly a magnificent lot of historical images. First is an oval war-date albumen photo (8" x 6" oval) of the staff officers of the 25th Michigan, including Colonel Moore, Surgeon Barnum, and field officers Brown, Fitch, and Orcutt. Image is full view, showing three seated officers and two standing. Very fine, also included are two fine early hard images. First, is a civilian dress of Kramer and two pards sitting at a table drinking (glasses of ale on table) and smoking. Next is a ninth plate of Kramer in civilian garb with fine patriotic Union rosette on his breast. Also included are six super 1870s cabinet cards as follow: 1) Copy of war-date view of officer in frock with sword. 2) Copy of war-date view of corporal in frock with cap on table with insignia identified on reverse. "Otto Boot Killed by guerrillas near Clarksville, Tenn. Nov 27th 1864." 3) Another identical view not inscribed. 4) Full view of G.A.R. veteran with cup, medals, Civil War accoutrement set hanging next to him, and holding a short import rifle in front of him. 5) Full standing G.A.R. veteran in uniform, belt and holding sword. 6) Standing view of G.A.R. vet in cap, uniform, sword, and medal. Final piece is a great manuscript letter written by "the daughter of the regiment" Mrs. Jesse Moore Loveridge, to Lieutenant Kramer, regarding the death of Kramer's wife, as well as notes about a reunion signed, "daughter of the 25th Michigan." **1,150.00**

Chromolithograph, Union 69th New York State Militia, "Departure of the 69th Regt. N.Y.S.M. Tuesday April 23d. 1861 the Irish Headquarters around St. Patrick's Cathedral Cor. Prince & Moth St." Lithographed by Sarony, major & Knap for D.T. Valentine's, 1862 manual, 7" x 9" with publisher's fold. **65.00**

Drawing, Union Private Addison Burdick, 85th New York Volunteer Infantry, frame measures 27" x 31-1/2", and the pastel shows 15-1/2" x 20". The pastel is on paper with canvas backing. The soldier is Addison Burdick and was done around 1863. Addison Burdick was a Private in the 85th New York Infantry, Company C. He was captured and taken prisoner in Plymouth, North Carolina, in 1863 or 1864, died October 14,1864, at Andersonville Prison and was buried at the National Cemetery. The Burdick family originally settled in Rhode Island, later moving to New York. Both the frame and the pastel are in excellent condition. **384.00**

Drawing, stunning Civil War soldier's art accomplished by Thomas Sugden, a soldier in the 90th New York Infantry, while serving in Florida during the year 1862. The scene is the interior of a paint shed, and you can see the grave markers leaning against the wall, and the cans of paint on the worktable. Beautifully identified on the lower front of the drawing. Measures approximately 4" x 6" and in fine condition. **375.00**

Engraving , Union General John A. Logan, 1865, 8" x 10", full-length engraving in fine condition. **19.00**

Engraving, Union General McPherson, 1865, 8" x 10", full-length engraving in fine condition. **19.00**

Lithograph, Union Admiral David Nixon Porter, black and white lithograph of Porter in uniform, edges trimmed **8.00**

Painting, Union Second Lieutenant Aaron Francis Walcott, 3rd Massachusetts Light Artillery, 30" x 25" painting in 32" x 37" gilt gesso frame. The painting is in good condition with some professional repairs visible on the back. Included are copies of archival records on Walcott and the 3rd Massachusetts Light Artillery. Walcott entered military service on July 31, 1861, with the 2nd Massachusetts Light Artillery as a private, was promoted to second lieutenant on November 28, 1861. In an unusual move he transferred just a few days later to the 3rd Massachusetts Light Artillery as a 1st sergeant. On November 12, 1862, he was promoted to first lieutenant. He was mustered out of service on September 16, 1864. While Walcott was with the 3rd that unit participated in engagements at Yorktown, Richmond, Malvern Hill, Butt Run, Antietam, Fredericksburg, Chancellorsville, Gettysburg, Spotsylvania, and Cole Harbor among others. **1,000.00**

Watercolor, Confederate Soldier, well-executed watercolor of a young Confederate soldier in the original old antique wooden frame. Most watercolors of the era do not seem to capture the detail and life-like qualities that this portrait possesses. This piece is out of a southern Maryland estate. **375.00**

Photograph Terminology

Ambrotype: A positive effect achieved on glass coated with light-sensitive collodion, backed with black paint, fabric, or paper. Patented by James Ambrose Cutting of Boston, 1854. Encased in the then widely available daguerreotype cases, they are often confused with the early daguerrean photographs

Backmark: Wet plate photographers often imprinted their name and address on the cards on which they mounted their photographs. These imprints served as an advertisement and today, can help identify the origin of a particular image.

Carte de visite: Also known as "cdv." A 2-1/2" x 4-1/2" photographic calling card, usually created as one of a number of images on a single photographic plate. Their introduction dates to 1854 by French photographer Adolphe-Eugene Disderi though their popularity in America started in 1860. Their major competition was the lower-cost tintype.

Case: Due to the fragile nature of the photograph, and the familiar practice of housing a painted miniature in a jewel-like case, early photographers packaged daguerreotypes, ambrotypes, and many tintypes in a protective case. First, a thin brass mat was placed over the image, followed by a protective cover glass. After 1849, this sandwich was held together by a thin brass rim known as a "preserver." A miniature case was then selected to house this package. The image was slipped into the right half, opposite a pad, usually of velvet, on the left (some, however, were made to hold photographs on both sides.) The cheapest examples were made of embossed paper applied over a wooden shell. Leather was used as a covering as well, a molded thermoplastic (sometimes called "gutta-percha") "Union" case was the most expensive choice.

Daguerreotype: The first practical system of photography with a positive image produced on copper clad with a layer of burnished (mirror-like) silver, treated in the manner developed in France following successful efforts by Nicephore Niepce and J. L. M. Daguerre; announced to the world in 1839. Without a negative, the superior wet-plate system introduced about ten years later soon brought the daguerreian era to an end.

Plate sizes: Full (whole) plate 6-1/2 x 8-1/2 inches
Half plate 4-1/4 x 6-1/2 inches
Quarter plate 3-1/4 x 4-1/4 inches
One-sixth plate 2-3/4 x 3-1/4 inches
One-eighth plate 2-1/8 x 3-1/4 inches
One-ninth plate 1-1/2 x 1-3/4 inches
One-sixteenth plate 1-5/8 x 2-1/8 inches

Tax Stamp: Images bearing a U.S. postage stamp on the back can be dated as having been produced before or during the period September 1, 1864, to August 1, 1866, when all such photographs transported in the U.S. mail were subject to this form of government tax in order to raise additional wartime revenue. Mainly found on cartes de visite, but also on some tintypes and ambrotypes as well.

Tintype: Also known as "Ferreotype" and "Melainotype" it is a direct-positive (that is, without a negative) photograph on a thin, tin-dipped iron sheet developed by a French process from 1853. Introduced to America beginning in 1856, its tonal range, durability, and low cost made it a popular process that continued in many places well into the early 20th century.

Also see: Groupings, Ephemera.

Chapter 16

Revolvers and Pistols

Though not the source of a great number of wounds or deaths during the Civil War, the revolver or pistol held a mystique for soldiers on both sides. Issued only to mounted troops, thousands of foot soldiers purchased handguns to carry in addition to their government-supplied weapons. In most cases, the only time they withdrew their handgun, though, was for a cleaning or posing in a warlike stance for the photographer.

The Union purchased 373,077 handguns during the Civil War, more than a fourth of which came from Colt. Total Confederate purchases were probably near half of that number. Assuming there were 500,000 government purchases of handguns, this can only be considered a fraction of the weapons carried by soldiers, as period sales of handguns doubled the sales to government agencies.

This is all good news for the collector. Because it takes a good deal of effort to totally destroy a revolver, many have survived. A Civil War collector looking for representative handguns can easily acquire Colt and a Remington New Model Army for a couple of thousand dollars. Be careful though, it is easy to become distracted by the variety of revolvers out there! A Civil War memorabilia collector can become a gun collector in the blink of an eye.

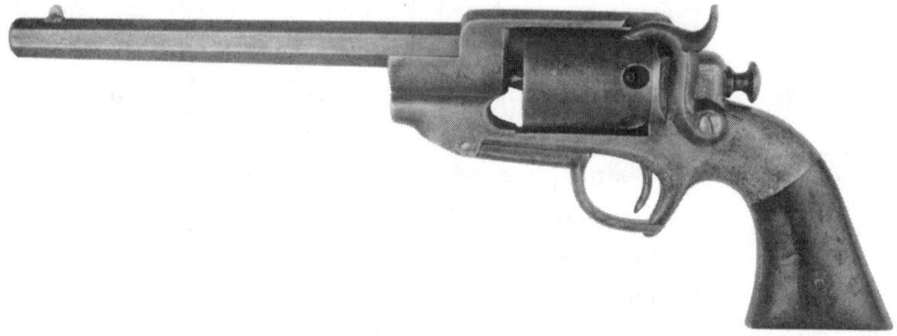

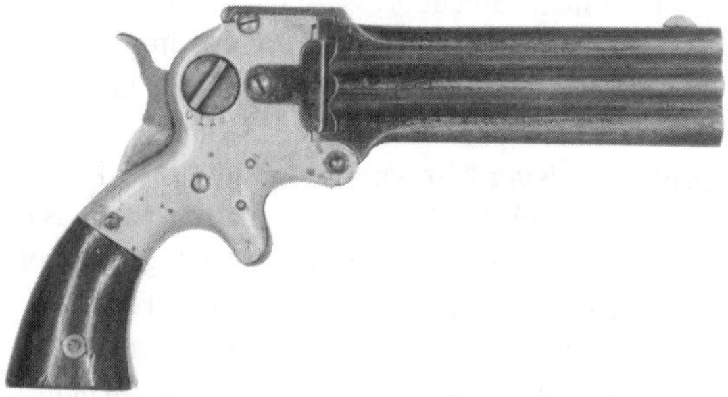

J.C. Devine Inc.

Collecting Hints

Pros:

- Many revolvers from the Civil War period have survived. There is an ample supply available for both beginning and advanced collectors.
- Revolvers and pistols do not take up much space.
- The "wow" factor is high. Most people recognize the lethalness of a handgun, and when they see weapons used during the Civil War, there is a sense of connecting with the past.
- High-end pieces tend to be very stable investments. This is not true for less-desirable makes and conditions of revolvers.
- Reproductions of common arms were produced with reenactors and shooters in mind. Therefore, the reproductions tend to be appropriately marked.
- Plenty of references are available for both beginners and advanced collectors.

Cons:

- Revolvers are probably the most frequently stolen Civil War relics.
- Rare models are often faked or pieced together from parts. High-end purchases should be left to advanced, extremely knowledgeable collectors.
- Though there are plenty of representative pieces available, handguns that have a provenance proving actual use in the Civil War are rather scarce and, therefore, much more expensive. Provenance can add hundreds or thousands of dollars to the price of the most mediocre weapon.

Availability ★★
Price ★★★
Reproduction Alert ★★★★★

Pistols, Confederate

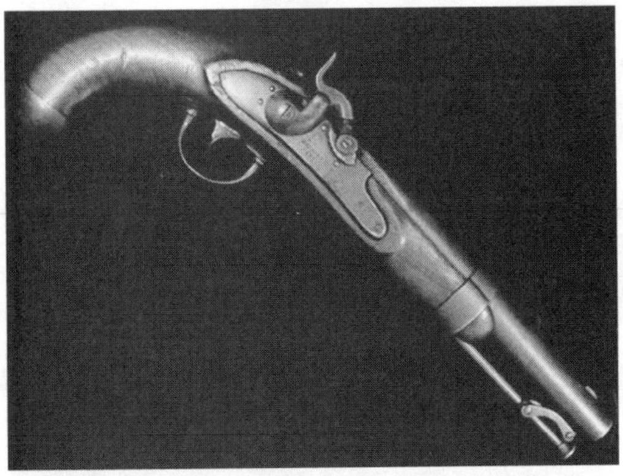

U.S. Model 1836 flintlock conversion pistol.

Old South Military Antiques

Fayetteville Conversion, single-shot percussion pistol started as a flintlock, but with the capture of the Fayetteville Arsenal in April of 1861, the state of North Carolina began converting flintlocks to the percussion system as rapidly as possible. While there were plenty of volunteers to fill the cavalry ranks, the government was unable to arm them. Military Secretary Warren Winslow was pushing the conversions as fast as possible, writing to the commander at Fayetteville on July 24, 1861, "You will please hasten as much as possible the work of changing the flint and steel muskets. As fast as the carbines are ready, send them to Raleigh and also other cavalry weapons." The next day he wrote, "send us the carbines as rapidly as done, but I tremble to think it will take five or six weeks to do them. What shall we do?" Two days later, on July 27, the Confederate Government took over the arsenal as the demand for guns continued to grow. By the middle of October, the armory was still doing conversions, according to the *Richmond Examiner*, "a large force is now engaged in altering old flintlock guns to percussion, making very efficient weapons," referring to Fayetteville. Finally, in November, altered pistols were beginning to trickle out and by the middle of January 1862, 564 had been shipped to the 2nd North Carolina Cavalry. The last 529 of the Fayetteville percussion pistol alterations had been completed and shipped to the 3rd North Carolina Cavalry by March of 1862. Fayetteville converted a total of 1,093 U.S. Model 1836 pistols from flint to percussion, all of which were shipped to the 2nd or 3rd North Carolina Cavalry. The Fayetteville Conversions are quite distinct, having a drum-type bolster with cleanout screw threaded into the barrel. The new percussion hammer is easily recognizable, smaller, but having the same "S" shape as the Fayetteville rifles. This pistol is an untouched example of the 2nd and 3rd cavalry's armament. The lock is marked, "A. Waters Milbury. MS 1839," in three lines with a prominent "F" stamped to the right. The drum bolster with cleanout screw and the Fayetteville hammer clearly identify this as one of the 1,093 alterations issued to the 2nd and 3rd North Carolina Cavalry. The Rebel who carried it carved "SLH" into the left side of the stock and an "A" just below. The only cavalryman in the 2nd or 3rd Company A with the initials "SH" is Solomon Haney. Haney enlisted in June of 1861 at 41 years of age. Despite his age, he served until late 1864. .... **2,800.00**

Revolvers, Confederate

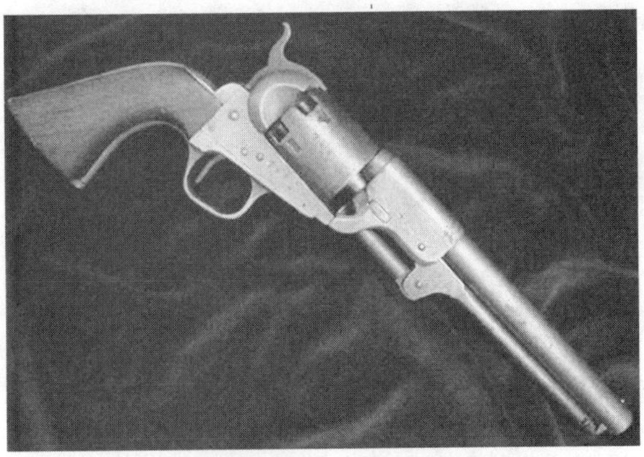

Griswold and Gunnison produced revolver.

Old South Military Antiques

Griswold and Gunnison, when the war broke out in 1861, Griswold began making pikes for the Georgia Government. Arvin Gunnison had begun the manufacture of pistols in New Orleans, Louisiana. When the city fell to the Yankees in the spring of 1862, Arvin and his machinery moved to Griswoldville. He joined up with his old friend Sam Griswold, and together they made handgun history. From July of 1862, until November 22, 1864, when the factory was destroyed by Yankee cavalry, Griswold and Gunnison produced more than 3,600 revolvers on the Colt's pattern. This 1st model is marked with the serial number 766 on the frame, barrel lug and cylinder. The loading lever is secondarily marked, "8". The cryptic "G" appears on the underside of the barrel and "II" on the back of the lug. This revolver is also well marked internally. The cryptic "G" appears on the cylinder back, and "GG" on the back strap, back of frame, and trigger guard. The secondary number "16" appears on the trigger guard, back of frame, back strap, hammer, trigger and even the grips. All screws are original as well. The wedge is probably a period replacement, as it is unmarked. The gun is in very good condition inside and out. The metal has a nice smooth, untouched ashen patina. Both the barrel and cylinder show good twist lines. The cylinder even retains its safety stops. The grips are excellent with the exception of the bottom of the butt. It has been dinged up and its owner carved in the initials "HR." The brass is smooth and uncleaned as well. The action is smooth, strong and tight. **29,500.00**

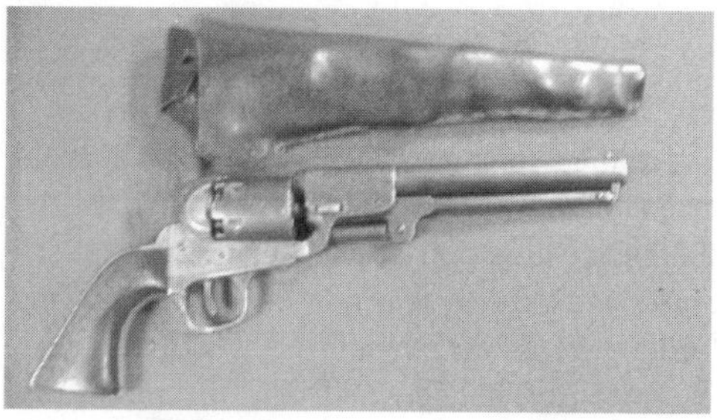

First Model Griswold and Gunnison.

Middle Tennessee Relics

Griswold, absolutely fine condition, original 1st Model Griswold Confederate-manufacture, brass-frame revolver that comes in its original "Slim Jim" Confederate-made, hand-stitched holster. With the exception of the wedge, which is worn too dim to read, all serial numbers throughout the gun are perfectly matching. The revolver is serial number "807." The grips are original and in very nice condition. The metal on this revolver has a very attractive gently graying patina, and the action is excellent. **22,500.00**

Pistols, U.S.

Allen & Tuber, Bar Hammer, percussion firing system, very fine condition, only 400 produced from 1837 to the Civil War period, serial number 260, marked "Patented 1837, Allen's Patent." **475.00**

Allen & Wheelock, action works, single shot, 32 rimfire, fine condition. Only 1,000 produced, serial number 898. . . **425.00**

Model 1836, .54 caliber, smoothbore, single shot US martial pistol converted to percussion by applying a drum bolster and a civilian "mule ear" hammer. Smooth yellowish-plum barrel with crisp, "NWP/P" proofs at the breech. Lock crisply marked, "US/R. Johnson/Middn Conn/1838." Smooth bore, fine mechanics. Iron furniture is a smooth, dove gray, captive ramrod. Excellent stock with fine oil-finished stock. Clear oval cartouche at the left flat. Barrel has standard Federal inspectors' initials underneath. **750.00**

Remington-Elliot, Derringer, 4-barrel pepperbox-style derringer with hard rubber grips, in overall very-good condition. Marked on left side, "Manufactured By E. Remington & Sons Ilion NY," and on the right side, "Elliot's Patent May 29 1860-Oct. 11, 1861.". **365.00**

Three-barreled, 1864, William Marston Derringer.

J.C. Devine Inc.

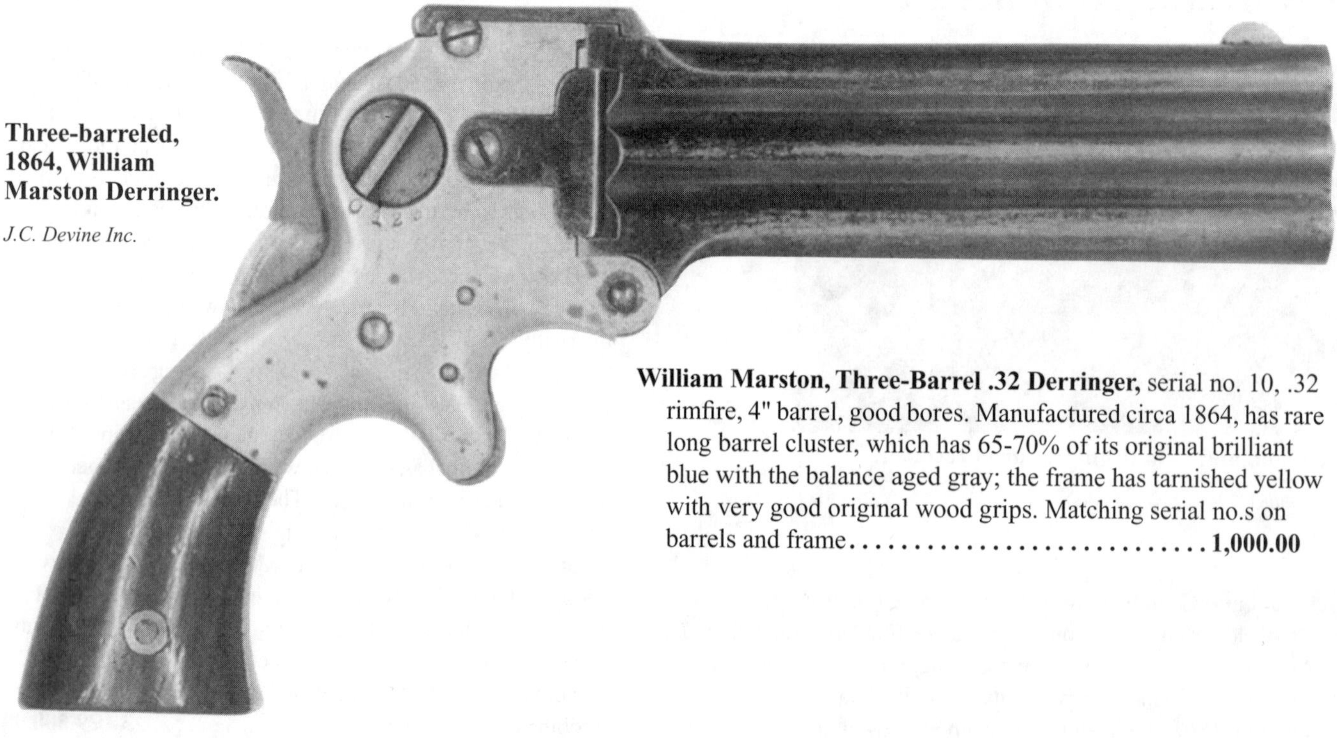

William Marston, Three-Barrel .32 Derringer, serial no. 10, .32 rimfire, 4" barrel, good bores. Manufactured circa 1864, has rare long barrel cluster, which has 65-70% of its original brilliant blue with the balance aged gray; the frame has tarnished yellow with very good original wood grips. Matching serial no.s on barrels and frame. **1,000.00**

Revolvers, U.S.

Adams Patent Percussion Pocket by Massachusetts Arms Co., serial no. 4991, .31 caliber, 3-1/4 inch barrel. Checkered walnut grips, condition: fair to good. Grey metal showing areas of light pitting. Some nipples damaged, one missing. Trigger return spring broke, grips with light wear. **345.00**

Allen & Thurber, Pepperbox, 6-barrel, .31 caliber, nice medium-size pepperbox with straight bar hammer on top of the frame which is stamped "Allen's Patent 1845". This measures roughly 7" in overall length. The barrels are fluted and are marked, "Allen Thurber & Co. Worcester." The frame has some delicate scroll engraving, as does the separately affixed nipple shield. Overall is in very-good condition, with gray steel surfaces and lightly worn walnut bag-style grips. There is light pitting in spots on the barrel and frame. **295.00**

Allen & Wheelock, "Providence Police," made late 1850s thru early 1860s with only 700 produced, 5-shot cylinder, .36 caliber, nice grips, action works, very-fine condition. **595.00**

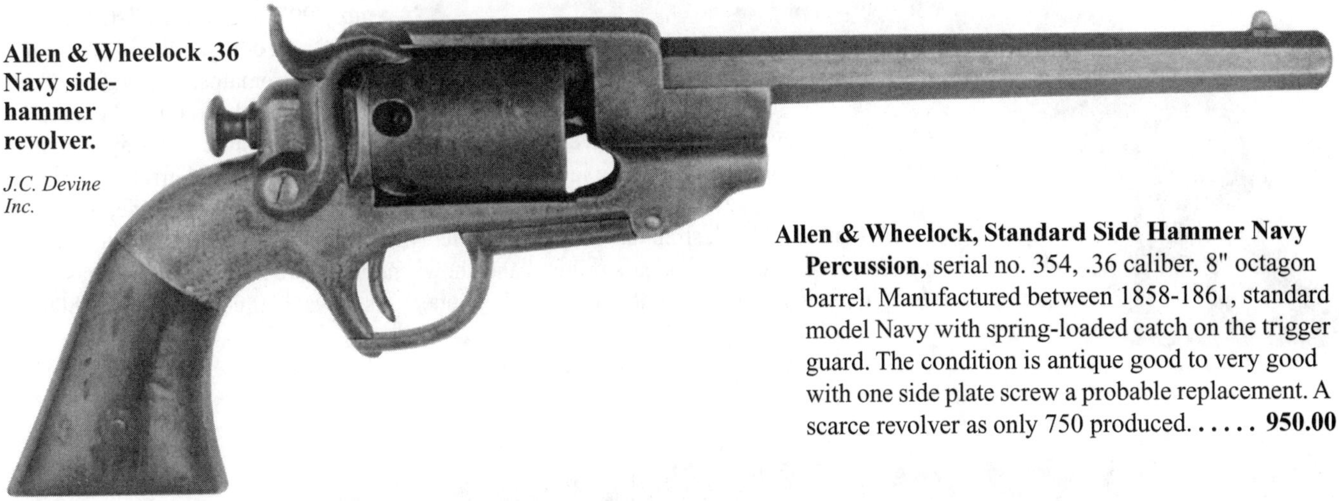

Allen & Wheelock .36 Navy side-hammer revolver.

J.C. Devine Inc.

Allen & Wheelock, Standard Side Hammer Navy Percussion, serial no. 354, .36 caliber, 8" octagon barrel. Manufactured between 1858-1861, standard model Navy with spring-loaded catch on the trigger guard. The condition is antique good to very good with one side plate screw a probable replacement. A scarce revolver as only 750 produced...... **950.00**

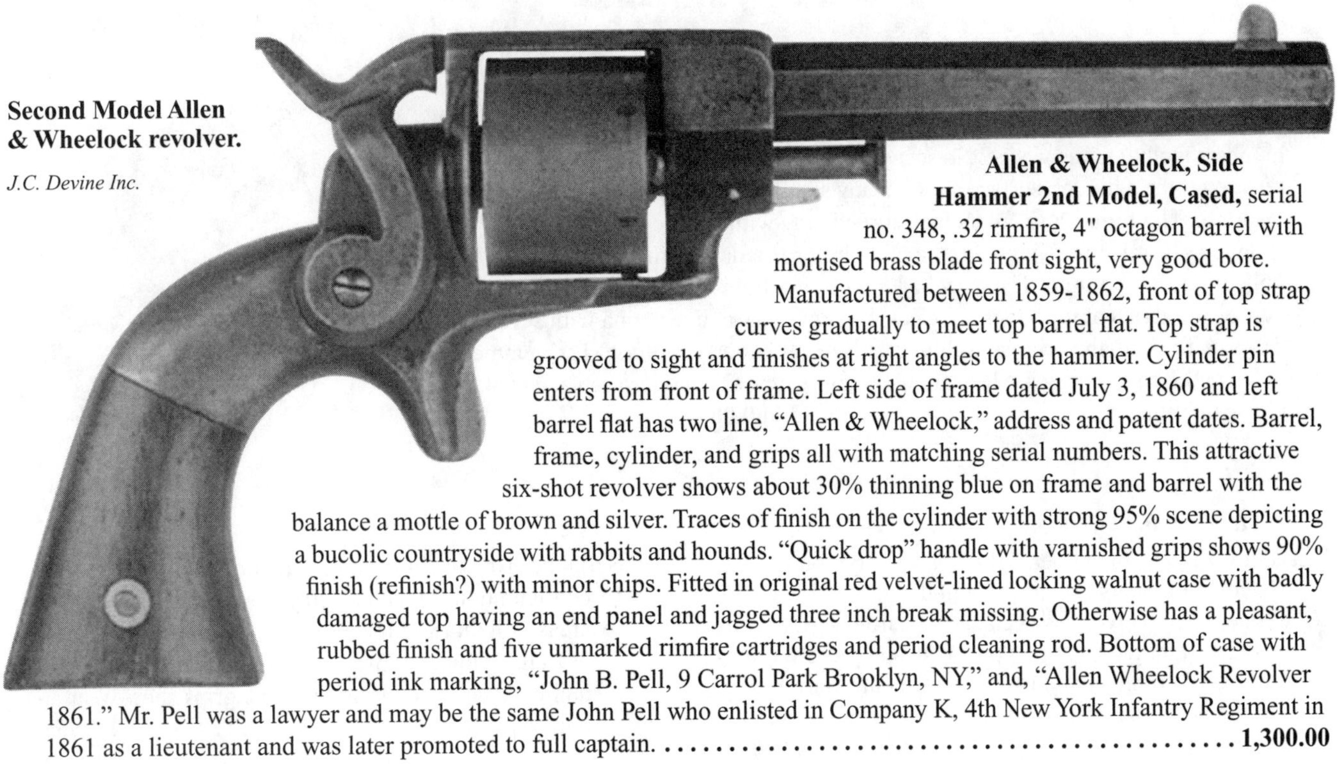

Second Model Allen & Wheelock revolver.

J.C. Devine Inc.

Allen & Wheelock, Side Hammer 2nd Model, Cased, serial no. 348, .32 rimfire, 4" octagon barrel with mortised brass blade front sight, very good bore. Manufactured between 1859-1862, front of top strap curves gradually to meet top barrel flat. Top strap is grooved to sight and finishes at right angles to the hammer. Cylinder pin enters from front of frame. Left side of frame dated July 3, 1860 and left barrel flat has two line, "Allen & Wheelock," address and patent dates. Barrel, frame, cylinder, and grips all with matching serial numbers. This attractive six-shot revolver shows about 30% thinning blue on frame and barrel with the balance a mottle of brown and silver. Traces of finish on the cylinder with strong 95% scene depicting a bucolic countryside with rabbits and hounds. "Quick drop" handle with varnished grips shows 90% finish (refinish?) with minor chips. Fitted in original red velvet-lined locking walnut case with badly damaged top having an end panel and jagged three inch break missing. Otherwise has a pleasant, rubbed finish and five unmarked rimfire cartridges and period cleaning rod. Bottom of case with period ink marking, "John B. Pell, 9 Carrol Park Brooklyn, NY," and, "Allen Wheelock Revolver 1861." Mr. Pell was a lawyer and may be the same John Pell who enlisted in Company K, 4th New York Infantry Regiment in 1861 as a lieutenant and was later promoted to full captain. **1,300.00**

Bacon, Pocket, 5-shot, 4" barrel, and fluted cylinder. Metal is light brown patina, smooth with some extremely fine texture pitting on small surfaces only. Mechanically tight and perfect, very nice grips, markings on top of barrel, "Bacon Mfg Co.," very hard to read. **395.00**

Colt, First Model Dragoon

Serial no. 4966, .44 caliber, 7-1/2" barrel fitted with open rear sight. Walnut grips, condition: fair. Metal has been cleaned and shows areas of light pitting and scattered scratches. Cylinder with no markings remaining except light serial number. Loading lever replaced, grips showing wear, dents, and repairs with copper pins and replaced pieces. **2,300.00**

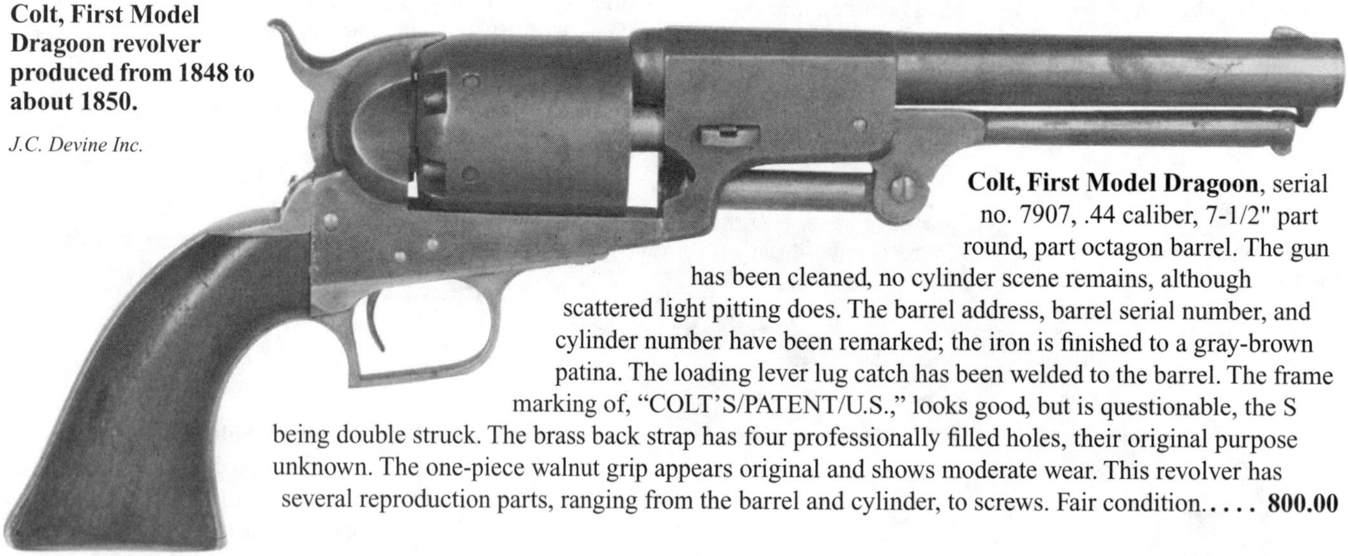

Colt, First Model Dragoon revolver produced from 1848 to about 1850.

J.C. Devine Inc.

Colt, First Model Dragoon, serial no. 7907, .44 caliber, 7-1/2" part round, part octagon barrel. The gun has been cleaned, no cylinder scene remains, although scattered light pitting does. The barrel address, barrel serial number, and cylinder number have been remarked; the iron is finished to a gray-brown patina. The loading lever lug catch has been welded to the barrel. The frame marking of, "COLT'S/PATENT/U.S.," looks good, but is questionable, the S being double struck. The brass back strap has four professionally filled holes, their original purpose unknown. The one-piece walnut grip appears original and shows moderate wear. This revolver has several reproduction parts, ranging from the barrel and cylinder, to screws. Fair condition. **800.00**

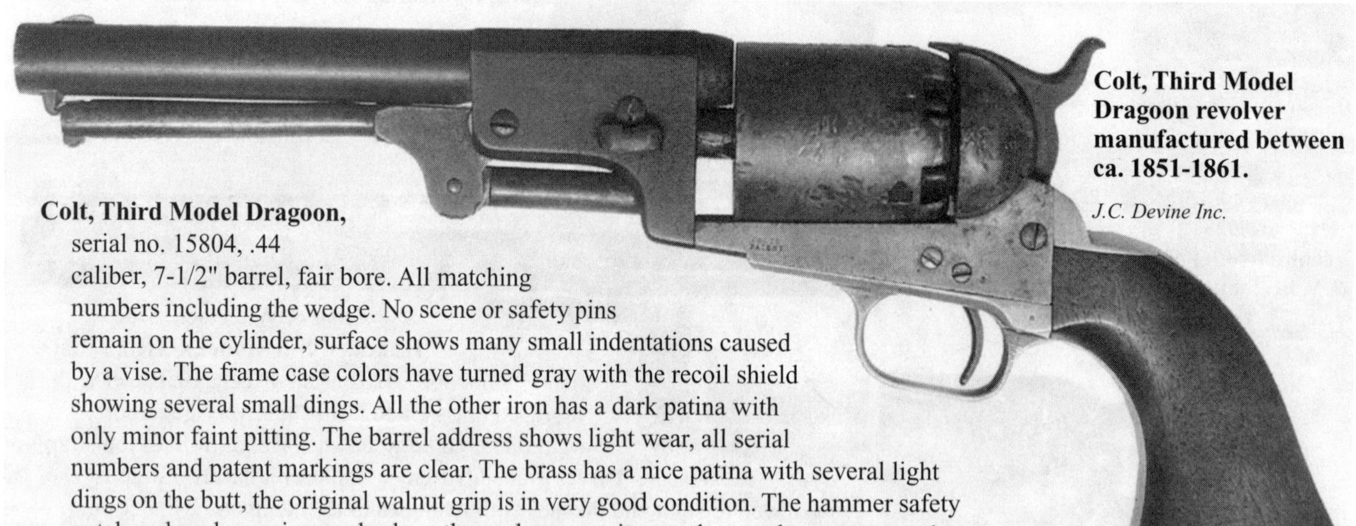

Colt, Third Model Dragoon revolver manufactured between ca. 1851-1861.

J.C. Devine Inc.

Colt, Third Model Dragoon, serial no. 15804, .44 caliber, 7-1/2" barrel, fair bore. All matching numbers including the wedge. No scene or safety pins remain on the cylinder, surface shows many small indentations caused by a vise. The frame case colors have turned gray with the recoil shield showing several small dings. All the other iron has a dark patina with only minor faint pitting. The barrel address shows light wear, all serial numbers and patent markings are clear. The brass has a nice patina with several light dings on the butt, the original walnut grip is in very good condition. The hammer safety notch and wedge spring are broken, the wedge screw is a modern replacement, good-plus condition. **2,800.00**

Colt, Third Model Dragoon

Serial no. 16459, .44 caliber, 7-1/2" barrel, poor bore. Matching numbers except for cylinder and replaced wedge. The revolver has been cleaned, iron is gray with scattered light pitting, brass polished, one-piece walnut grip has old refinish and is worn at the butt. Barrel address is legible, frame patent marking is gone, good overall condition. **1,900.00**

Serial no. 10436, .44 caliber. Standard civilian configuration. Metal has gray chemical patina showing areas of light to heavy pitting, and scattered dents overall. Cylinder of 3rd Model type with indistinct serial number. Hammer spring fatigued, grips show wear and numerous dents at butt. **1,955.00**

Colt Third Model Dragoon, cont.

Serial no. 15751, .44 caliber. Standard civilian configuration with 7-1/2" barrel and walnut grips. Condition: good to very good, smooth gray metal showing some areas of light pitting. Cylinder retaining slight traces of scene. Sound grips showing wear, minor blemishes, and retaining slight traces of varnish. 5,175.00

Colt, Model 1848 Baby Dragoon, serial no. 12424, .31 caliber, 4" barrel with two-line New York markings. Five-shot cylinder with stagecoach holdup scene. Varnished walnut grips, overall fair condition. Barrel, frame, and cylinder showing dark mottled patina with areas of pitting. Barrel markings very worn, cylinder shows slight traces of scene and no visible serial number. Wedge and forward trigger guard screw replaced. Trigger guard/grip strap retain 50-60% silver-plated finish. Grips with 80% varnish and scattered light blemishes. Right grip with deep bruise above butt. 747.50

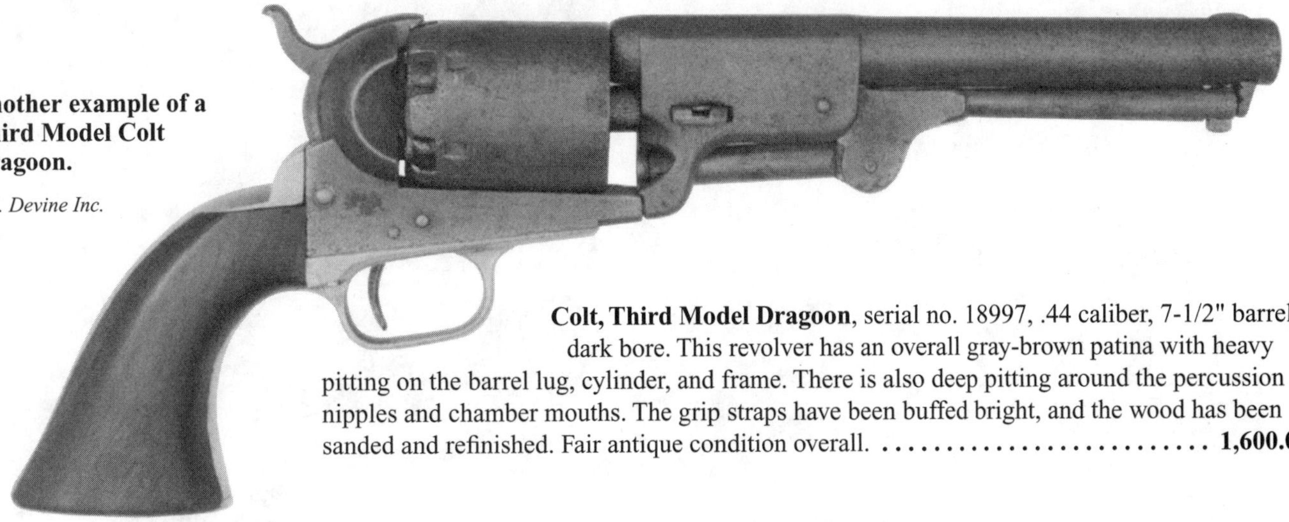

Another example of a Third Model Colt Dragoon.

J.C. Devine Inc.

Colt, Third Model Dragoon, serial no. 18997, .44 caliber, 7-1/2" barrel, dark bore. This revolver has an overall gray-brown patina with heavy pitting on the barrel lug, cylinder, and frame. There is also deep pitting around the percussion nipples and chamber mouths. The grip straps have been buffed bright, and the wood has been sanded and refinished. Fair antique condition overall. 1,600.00

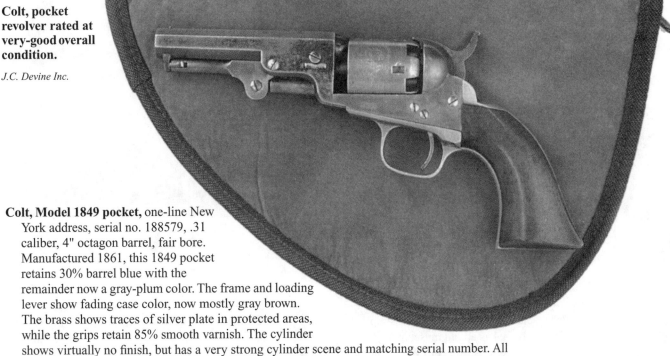

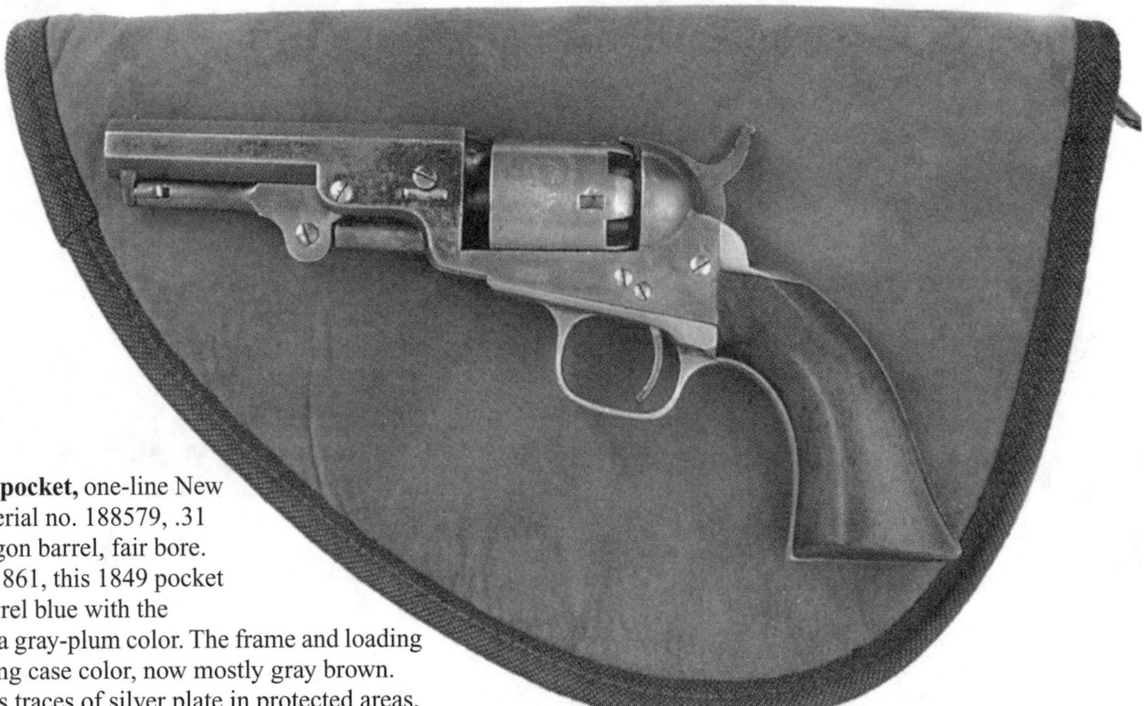

Colt, pocket revolver rated at very-good overall condition.

J.C. Devine Inc.

Colt, Model 1849 pocket, one-line New York address, serial no. 188579, .31 caliber, 4" octagon barrel, fair bore. Manufactured 1861, this 1849 pocket retains 30% barrel blue with the remainder now a gray-plum color. The frame and loading lever show fading case color, now mostly gray brown. The brass shows traces of silver plate in protected areas, while the grips retain 85% smooth varnish. The cylinder shows virtually no finish, but has a very strong cylinder scene and matching serial number. All numbers match except the bottom grip number, which appears to have been removed. The safety pins are now flattened. Very-good overall condition. 750.00

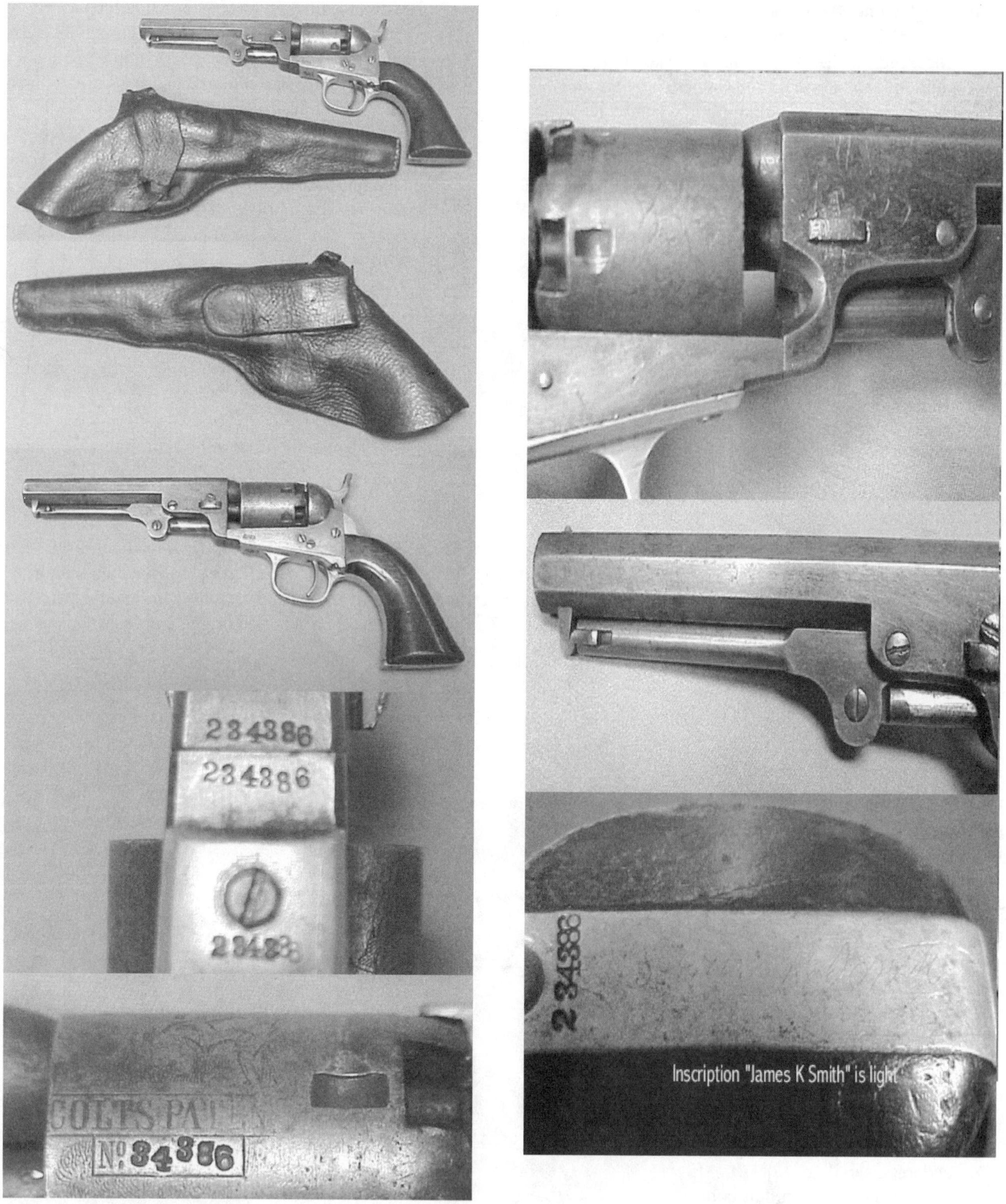

Model 1849 Colt pocket revolver.

The Sharpsburg Arsenal

Brought home by August Hering, 41st New York Infantry, "James K. Smith," "hand-engraved on brass butt strap bottom. Manufactured 1863, has an old museum tag, showing the owner as, "Mrs. A. Hering 340 West Union St." Could have Confederate association, because of single-looped, pigskin holster, which came with weapon. 2,895.00

Model 1849 Colt pocket revolver, cont.

A very good example with 5-inch barrel. 173,xxx serial range, gray steel with strong markings and good edges. Some light surface rust present on a third of cylinder, cylinder scene 80% intact. Good action, excellent grips with much varnish and owner's name very neatly (and attractively) carved into the left grip, "Everitt L. LaClare." Grip straps have nice mellow brass patina and just a hint of silver plate remaining. Mechanically perfect, some buggering on three screw heads, all matched numbers. **750.00**

William W. Squire of Company A, 1st New Jersey Infantry carried the pocket revolver shown below.

The Sharpsburg Arsenal

Model 1849 Colt pocket revolver

Manufactured 1856, .31 caliber, "W.W.S.," William W. Squire, 1st New Jersey Infantry, Company A. Inscription on butt and front of back strap, next to hammer. Gun has a nice even patina overall with sharp markings and showing 85% of cylinder scene. All numbers match, brass has approximately 40% of original silver finish. Walnut grips are in excellent shape with 85% original factory varnish. Squire enlisted as a private and was later promoted to sergeant and further served in the Quartermasters and Commissary Departments. His official records reflect that he was, "in some hard fought battles and proved his patriotism and courage." The 1st New Jersey was a hard fighting unit that engaged C.S.A. troops at many battles including Antietam, Gettysburg, and the Appomattox campaign. Records included. **4,750.00**

Model 1849 Colt pocket revolver, cont.

All matched serial numbers, 100% original and complete, mechanically good with some finicky response in the handspring. The 5" barrel has rich traces of finish mixed with plum patina. Cylinder is gray mixed with splotches of light pitting and retains 50% of the cylinder scene. Frame is gray steel, grips are excellent. Very honest-looking Colt pocket in the 318,xxx serial range, overall very-good condition. **550.00**

Serial no. 45618, made in 1852, has small trigger guard. The back strap has 100% of the silver plate. The grips have 100% original varnish. The metal has a soft, gray patina with touches of original blue. The cylinder scene is very strong, 95% plus. Very crisp action, all matching serial numbers. **1,895.00**

Serial no. 167209, .31 caliber, 5" barrel with two-line New York markings. Five-shot cylinder with stagecoach holdup scene, varnished walnut grips. Barrel retains 70-80% blue finish with some browning, patches of light pitting, and heavy edge wear. Cylinder with very slight wear to scene. Rammer lug retaining much vivid casehardening. Frame with 30-40% vivid casehardening. Trigger guard with 90% plated finish. Grip strap with 15-25% plated finish. Grips with 80% varnish and scattered minor blemishes. Overall condition is fine. **1,380.00**

Serial no. 328113, .31 caliber, 4" barrel with one line New York markings. Six-shot cylinder, varnished walnut grips, condition, good. Grey metal has been cleaned and shows scattered areas of light to moderate pitting. Cylinder retaining 30-40% of scene. Grips with 90% varnish and scattered minor blemishes. **430.00**

Serial no. 77802, .31 caliber, 5" barrel with two-line New York markings. Walnut grips. Grey metal has been cleaned and shows scattered spotting and light pitting. Cylinder with 80% of scene partly obscured by several deep scratches. Grips show wear, minor dents, and bruises with a small chip to the right forward toe. Overall fair condition. **430.00**

Colt, Model 1849 Wells Fargo Pocket, serial no. 164038, .31 caliber, 3" barrel with two-line New York markings. Five-shot cylinder, scarce example with long frame and large trigger guard. Varnished walnut grips. Gray metal with dark patina and areas of light pitting left side of frame and portions of cylinder with numerous dents. Cylinder retaining traces of scene, grips with few minor blemishes. This serial number puts the gun at the end of the serial number range for this model. Overall good condition. **575.00**

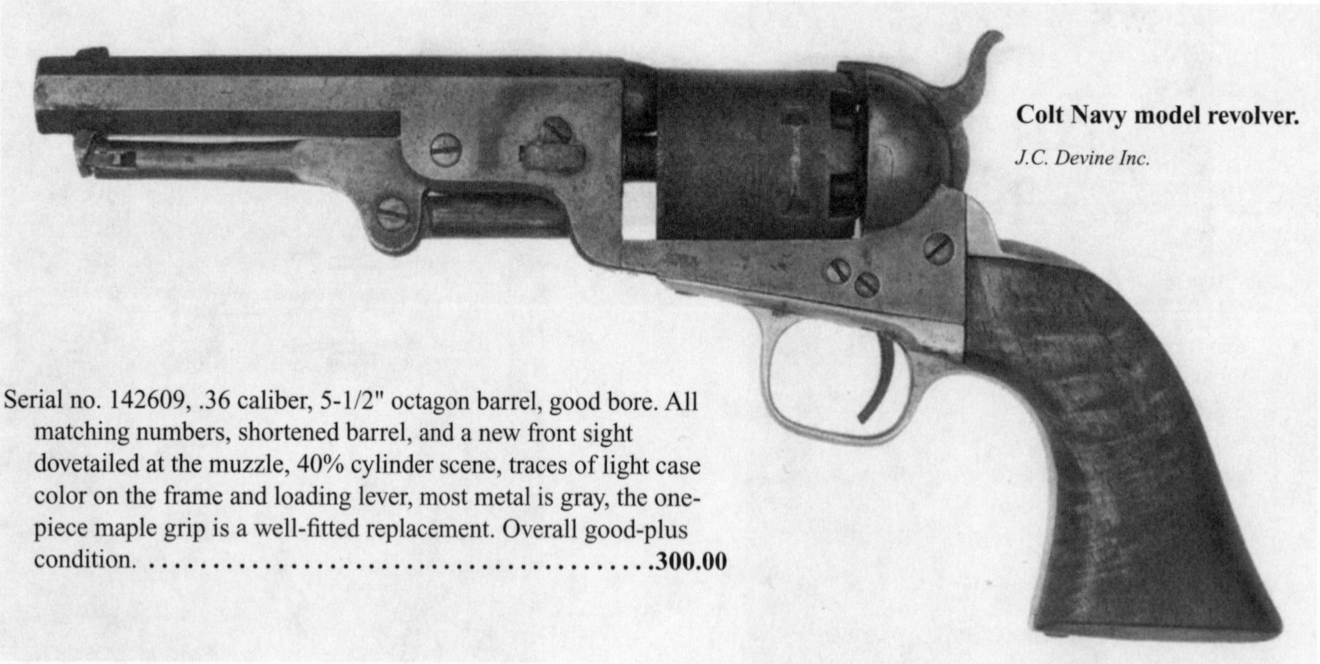

Colt Navy model revolver.

J.C. Devine Inc.

Serial no. 142609, .36 caliber, 5-1/2" octagon barrel, good bore. All matching numbers, shortened barrel, and a new front sight dovetailed at the muzzle, 40% cylinder scene, traces of light case color on the frame and loading lever, most metal is gray, the one-piece maple grip is a well-fitted replacement. Overall good-plus condition. **300.00**

Colt, Model 1851 Navy

.36 caliber, serial 144821, 7.5" barrel; deep untouched plum-brown patina overall; indexes fine, all matching numbers, light cylinder scene; grips show honest use and wear; minor chip on corner of left grip; great barrel marking. **1,125.00**

All matched serials in the 66,xxx range. All original except for the wedge, mechanically perfect, metal is overall uniformly pitted with a gray color. The grips are excellent with a nicely visible cartouche on the right side Aside from the pitted metal this is a pretty decent, martial Navy. The grips fit perfectly and the metal-to-metal fit is good. **975.00**

.36-caliber percussion revolver, all matching numbers 100,782 (early 1861 production), 98% silver on back strap/trigger guard; 35% blue and case; 98% varnish on grips. Incredibly deep and clear Hartford barrel markings and perfect cylinder scene and rotation. **3,950.00**

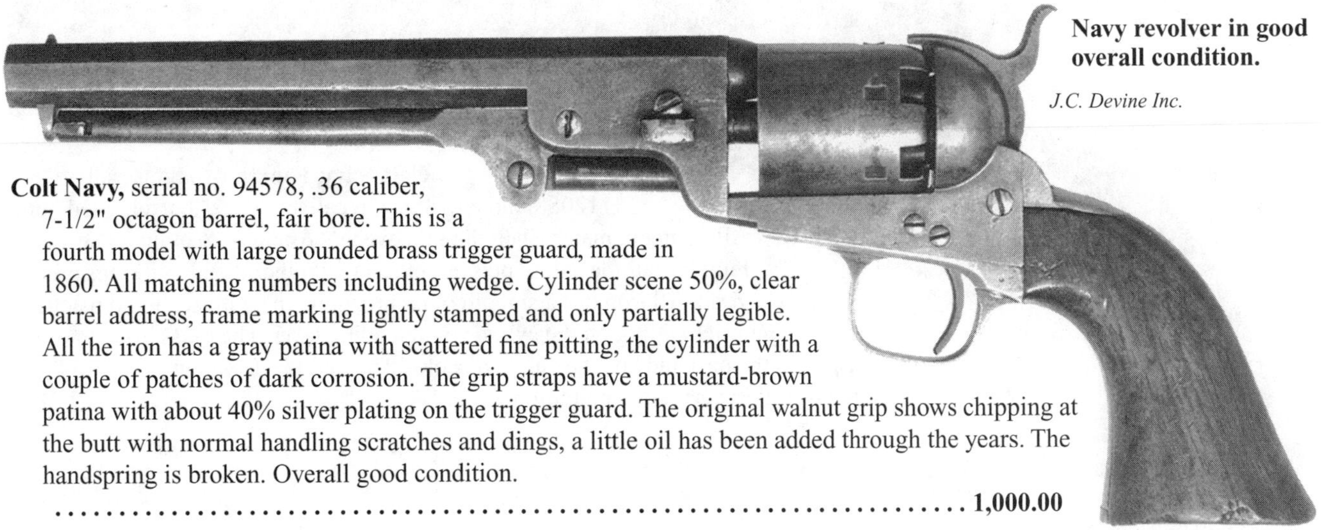

Navy revolver in good overall condition.

J.C. Devine Inc.

Colt Navy, serial no. 94578, .36 caliber, 7-1/2" octagon barrel, fair bore. This is a fourth model with large rounded brass trigger guard, made in 1860. All matching numbers including wedge. Cylinder scene 50%, clear barrel address, frame marking lightly stamped and only partially legible. All the iron has a gray patina with scattered fine pitting, the cylinder with a couple of patches of dark corrosion. The grip straps have a mustard-brown patina with about 40% silver plating on the trigger guard. The original walnut grip shows chipping at the butt with normal handling scratches and dings, a little oil has been added through the years. The handspring is broken. Overall good condition. **1,000.00**

Colt, Model 1851 Navy, Third Model

All matched serial numbers, including the wedge (80492), 100% original and complete. The edges are strong, the grips are fine, with a faint cartouche in the middle of the left grip, and all markings are crisp (barrel marking "Address Saml Colt Hartford CT", sub-inspector's letter "M" on barrel lug and cylinder, letter "C" on back strap, letter "L" on trigger guard, "Colts Patent" and "US" on frame). The octagon barrel has 70% thinning blue on the bottom three flats, 15% thinning blue on the side flats, and traces of blue on the top three flats. The balance of the barrel color mixes with plum. The frame has hints of case color when viewed in the right light, and the balance is plum. The cylinder has no blue, but is a nice uniform patina matching the rest of the gun, and it has 85% vivid cylinder scene. The safety pins on the back of the cylinder are sharp with only one being battered and one showing some wear. There are some "bangs" on the cylinder from period use (numerous small dents). The loading lever has quite a bit of vivid case color in the central area (near the hinge pivot) with the balance being plum and gray, matching the rest of the gun. The number on the loading lever is 0292 (instead of 0492), obviously being a one-digit error struck at the factory, which is seen on about 2% of surviving Colts. Overall fine condition.. .... **3,800.00**

Serial no. 67436, .36 caliber, 4-1/4" barrel with New York markings. Varnished walnut grips. Metal has been cleaned and showing areas of minor pitting. Right side of barrel lug with series of small dents at wedge. Replaced loading lever pitted overall. Cylinder retains 80-85% of scene. Trigger guard/grip straps retain 15-20% silver-plated finish, grips with 60-70% varnish and showing scattered dents and scratches. Overall condition: good. **747.50**

Serial no. 50359, .36 caliber, New York-marked barrel fitted with non-factory German silver blade and open rear sights. Walnut grips, barrel has light gray patina and retaining generous traces of blue finish on underside. Cylinder has good scene partially obscured by several series of dents. Four chambers retaining original charges, grips show wear, small chips at forward toes, possibly replaced. Good to very-good condition. **1,035.00**

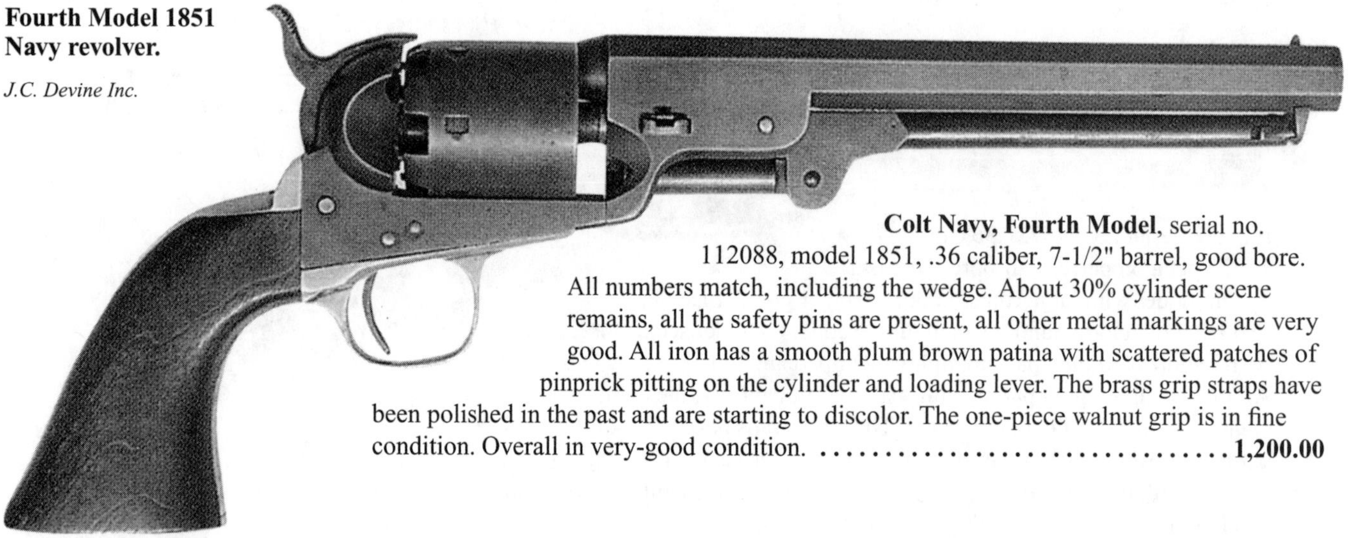

Fourth Model 1851 Navy revolver.

J.C. Devine Inc.

Colt Navy, Fourth Model, serial no. 112088, model 1851, .36 caliber, 7-1/2" barrel, good bore. All numbers match, including the wedge. About 30% cylinder scene remains, all the safety pins are present, all other metal markings are very good. All iron has a smooth plum brown patina with scattered patches of pinprick pitting on the cylinder and loading lever. The brass grip straps have been polished in the past and are starting to discolor. The one-piece walnut grip is in fine condition. Overall in very-good condition. **1,200.00**

Colt, Model 1851 Navy, Fourth Model
Serial no. 104990, .36 caliber, 7-1/2" octagon barrel, manufactured 1861. This 51 Navy has all matching numbers and retains traces of protected barrel blue and case color on the loading lever. The cylinder has six safety pins and shows a naval scene that is 75% complete. A mechanically very tight Navy that grades good to very good. **1,400.00**

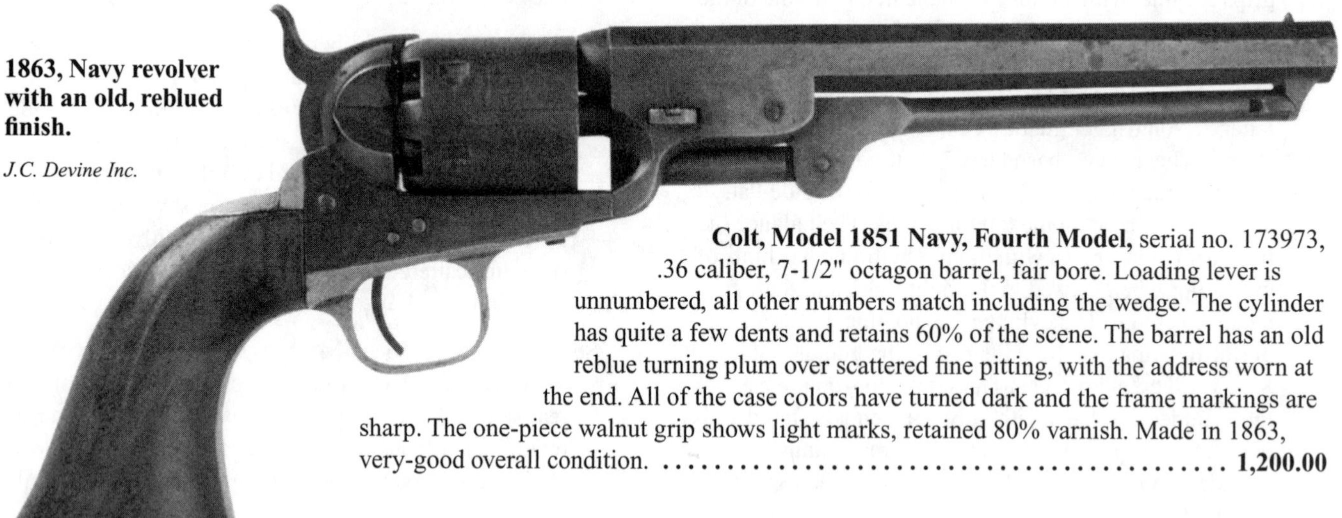

1863, Navy revolver with an old, reblued finish.

J.C. Devine Inc.

Colt, Model 1851 Navy, Fourth Model, serial no. 173973, .36 caliber, 7-1/2" octagon barrel, fair bore. Loading lever is unnumbered, all other numbers match including the wedge. The cylinder has quite a few dents and retains 60% of the scene. The barrel has an old reblue turning plum over scattered fine pitting, with the address worn at the end. All of the case colors have turned dark and the frame markings are sharp. The one-piece walnut grip shows light marks, retained 80% varnish. Made in 1863, very-good overall condition. **1,200.00**

Colt, Model 1855 Root Sidehammer Percussion, serial no. 4496, .31 caliber, 3-1/2" octagonal barrel. Five-shot unfluted cylinder, walnut grips, condition is poor to fair. Mottled gray metal shows areas of light pitting, barrel markings and cylinder scene very worn. Action not functioning, grips show wear and minor blemishes. **315.00**

"Root Model," 1855 was the only Colt revolver built with a solid frame.

J.C. Devine Inc.

Colt, Model 1855 Root, Third Model, serial no. 27796, .28 caliber, 3-1/2" octagon barrel, very good bore. Gray patina on all metal, sharp lettering, fine pitting near the nipples, most of the finish appears to have flaked. Minor scratches on walnut grips with 95% original varnish. Hartford address without pointing hand motif. Very-good overall condition. **600.00**

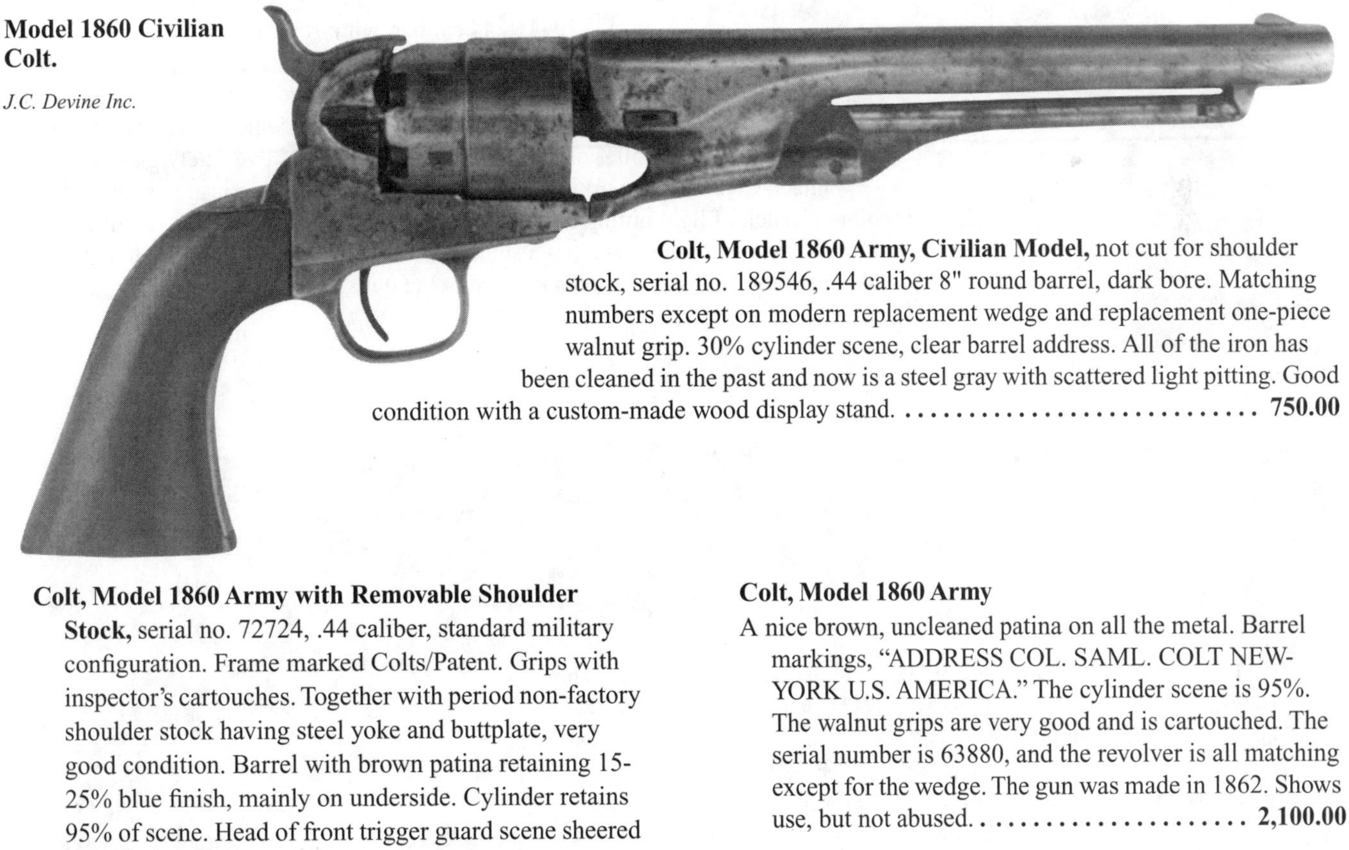

Model 1860 Civilian Colt.

J.C. Devine Inc.

Colt, Model 1860 Army, Civilian Model, not cut for shoulder stock, serial no. 189546, .44 caliber 8" round barrel, dark bore. Matching numbers except on modern replacement wedge and replacement one-piece walnut grip. 30% cylinder scene, clear barrel address. All of the iron has been cleaned in the past and now is a steel gray with scattered light pitting. Good condition with a custom-made wood display stand. **750.00**

Colt, Model 1860 Army with Removable Shoulder Stock, serial no. 72724, .44 caliber, standard military configuration. Frame marked Colts/Patent. Grips with inspector's cartouches. Together with period non-factory shoulder stock having steel yoke and buttplate, very good condition. Barrel with brown patina retaining 15-25% blue finish, mainly on underside. Cylinder retains 95% of scene. Head of front trigger guard scene sheered off. Grips with scattered minor blemishes, the right side with small, neat period repair, the left side with traces of cartouche remaining. Shoulder in very-good condition, but not of Colt manufacture. **1,840.00**

Colt, Model 1860 Army

A nice brown, uncleaned patina on all the metal. Barrel markings, "ADDRESS COL. SAML. COLT NEW-YORK U.S. AMERICA." The cylinder scene is 95%. The walnut grips are very good and is cartouched. The serial number is 63880, and the revolver is all matching except for the wedge. The gun was made in 1862. Shows use, but not abused. **2,100.00**

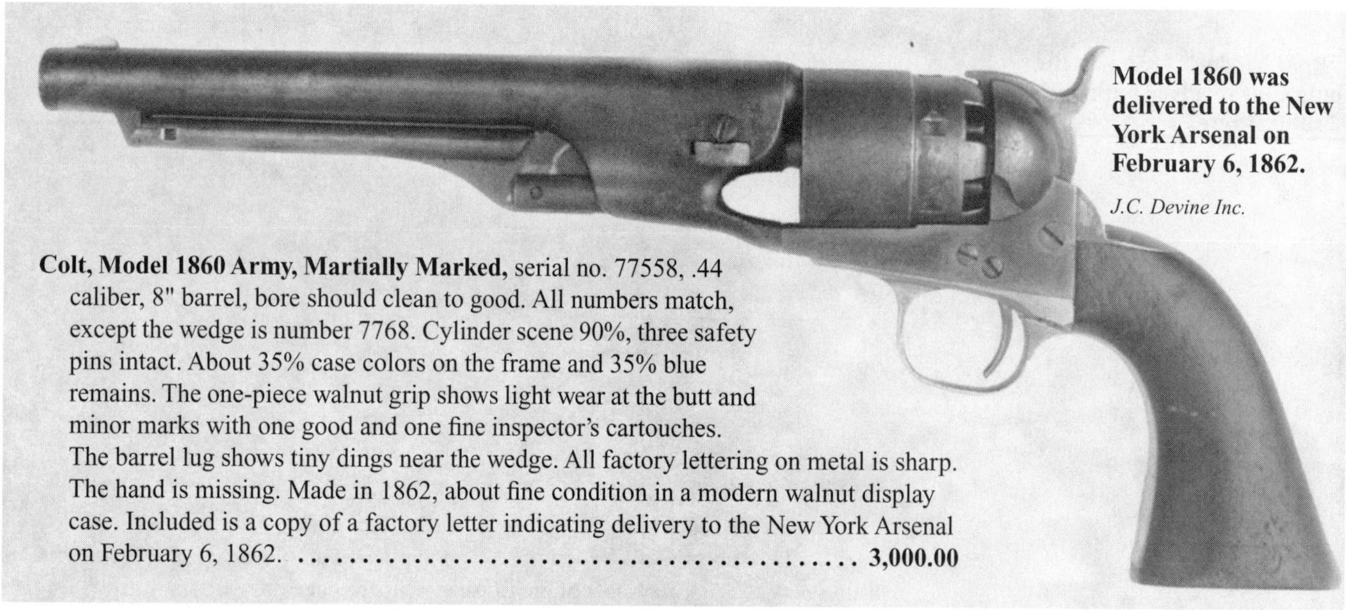

Model 1860 was delivered to the New York Arsenal on February 6, 1862.

J.C. Devine Inc.

Colt, Model 1860 Army, Martially Marked, serial no. 77558, .44 caliber, 8" barrel, bore should clean to good. All numbers match, except the wedge is number 7768. Cylinder scene 90%, three safety pins intact. About 35% case colors on the frame and 35% blue remains. The one-piece walnut grip shows light wear at the butt and minor marks with one good and one fine inspector's cartouches. The barrel lug shows tiny dings near the wedge. All factory lettering on metal is sharp. The hand is missing. Made in 1862, about fine condition in a modern walnut display case. Included is a copy of a factory letter indicating delivery to the New York Arsenal on February 6, 1862. . . . . **3,000.00**

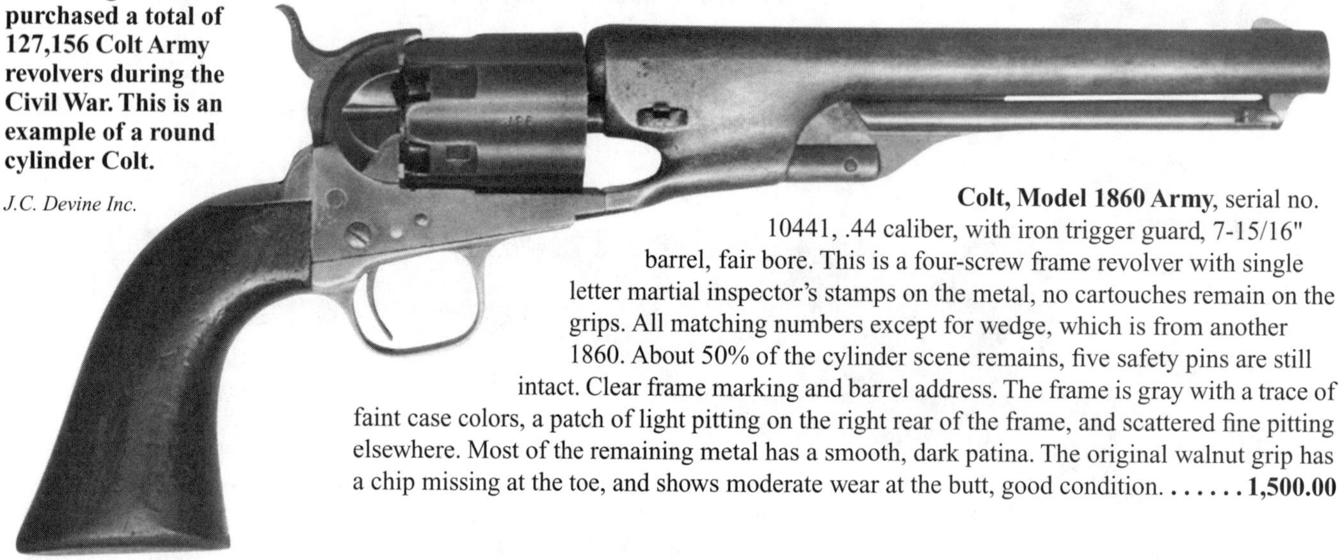

The U.S. government purchased a total of 127,156 Colt Army revolvers during the Civil War. This is an example of a round cylinder Colt.

J.C. Devine Inc.

Colt, Model 1860 Army, serial no. 10441, .44 caliber, with iron trigger guard, 7-15/16" barrel, fair bore. This is a four-screw frame revolver with single letter martial inspector's stamps on the metal, no cartouches remain on the grips. All matching numbers except for wedge, which is from another 1860. About 50% of the cylinder scene remains, five safety pins are still intact. Clear frame marking and barrel address. The frame is gray with a trace of faint case colors, a patch of light pitting on the right rear of the frame, and scattered fine pitting elsewhere. Most of the remaining metal has a smooth, dark patina. The original walnut grip has a chip missing at the toe, and shows moderate wear at the butt, good condition. **1,500.00**

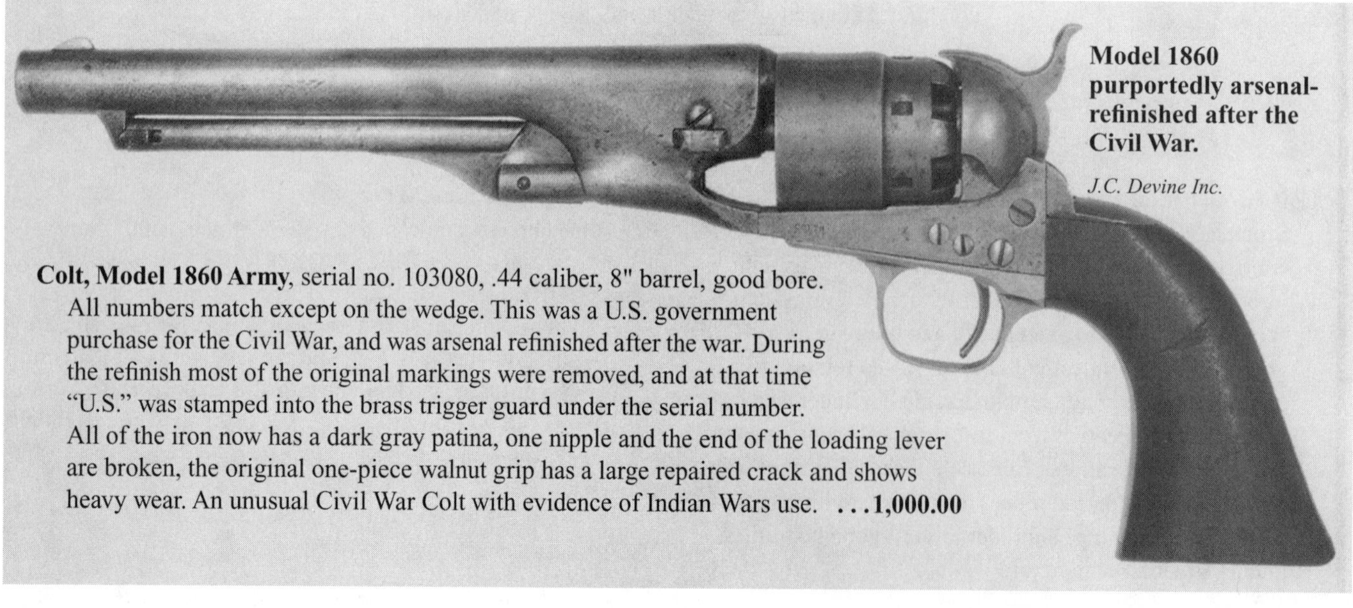

Model 1860 purportedly arsenal-refinished after the Civil War.

J.C. Devine Inc.

Colt, Model 1860 Army, serial no. 103080, .44 caliber, 8" barrel, good bore. All numbers match except on the wedge. This was a U.S. government purchase for the Civil War, and was arsenal refinished after the war. During the refinish most of the original markings were removed, and at that time "U.S." was stamped into the brass trigger guard under the serial number. All of the iron now has a dark gray patina, one nipple and the end of the loading lever are broken, the original one-piece walnut grip has a large repaired crack and shows heavy wear. An unusual Civil War Colt with evidence of Indian Wars use. . . . **1,000.00**

"Round cylinder" Army revolver.

The Sharpsburg Arsenal

Colt, Model 1860 Army, manufactured in 1861, all numbers match including wedge. Barrel, frame, and cylinder have nice dove-gray patina with excellent markings. Cylinder scene appears to be 85%, loading lever has traces of case color. Brass trigger guard has a nice even patina. Walnut grips are in very good shape with a faint cartouche. Good clear inspector's marks on metal parts. Brass front sight appears to be a very early replacement requiring a somewhat higher sight. Overall working condition 100% and tight. An excellent, early example................................ **3,195.00**

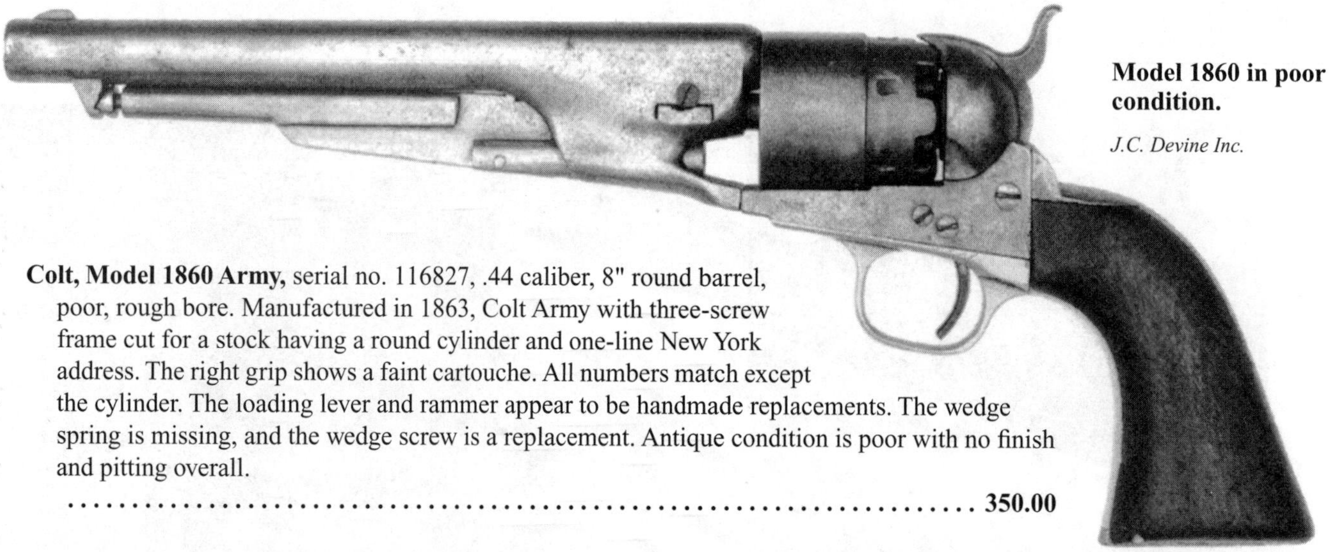

Model 1860 in poor condition.

J.C. Devine Inc.

Colt, Model 1860 Army, serial no. 116827, .44 caliber, 8" round barrel, poor, rough bore. Manufactured in 1863, Colt Army with three-screw frame cut for a stock having a round cylinder and one-line New York address. The right grip shows a faint cartouche. All numbers match except the cylinder. The loading lever and rammer appear to be handmade replacements. The wedge spring is missing, and the wedge screw is a replacement. Antique condition is poor with no finish and pitting overall. **350.00**

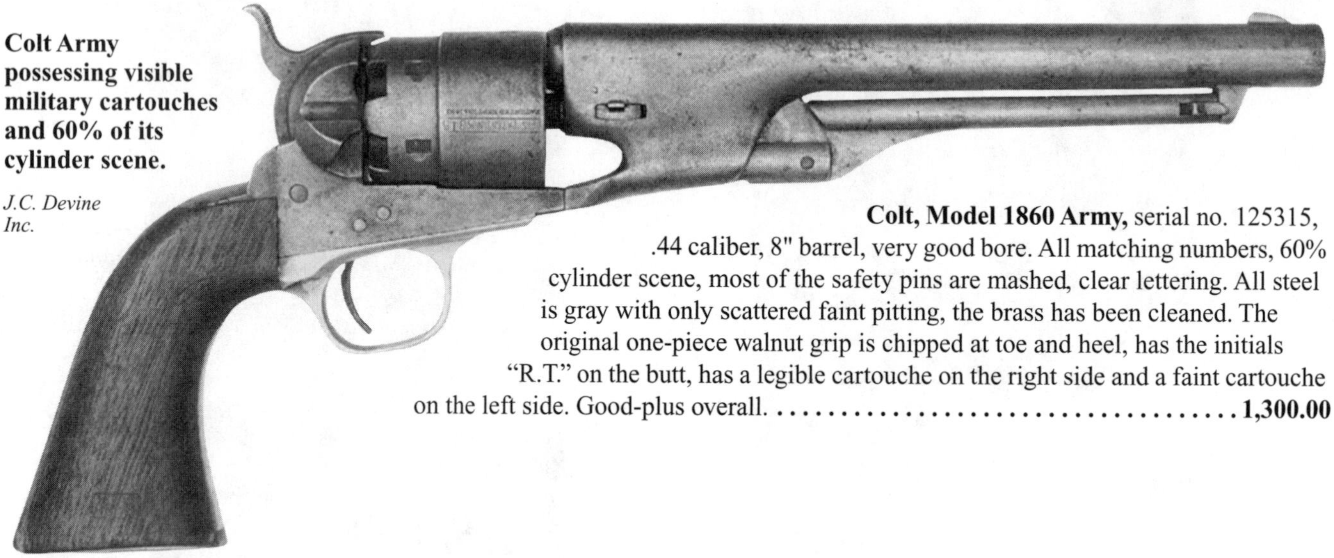

Colt Army possessing visible military cartouches and 60% of its cylinder scene.

J.C. Devine Inc.

Colt, Model 1860 Army, serial no. 125315, .44 caliber, 8" barrel, very good bore. All matching numbers, 60% cylinder scene, most of the safety pins are mashed, clear lettering. All steel is gray with only scattered faint pitting, the brass has been cleaned. The original one-piece walnut grip is chipped at toe and heel, has the initials "R.T." on the butt, has a legible cartouche on the right side and a faint cartouche on the left side. Good-plus overall. **1,300.00**

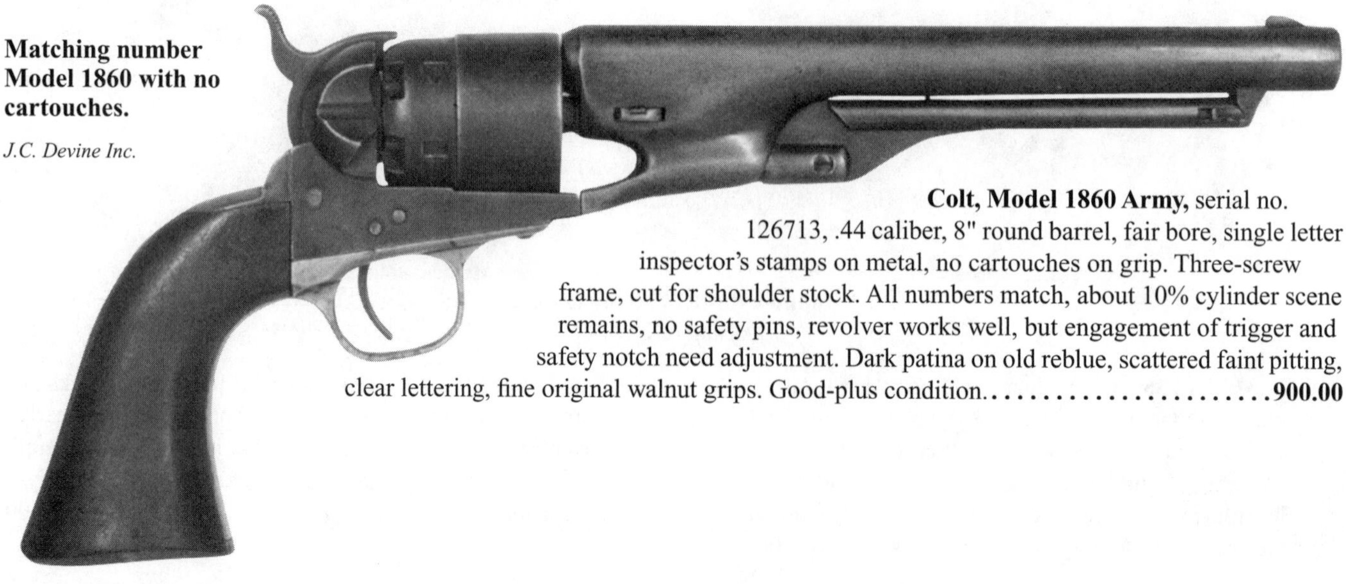

Matching number Model 1860 with no cartouches.

J.C. Devine Inc.

Colt, Model 1860 Army, serial no. 126713, .44 caliber, 8" round barrel, fair bore, single letter inspector's stamps on metal, no cartouches on grip. Three-screw frame, cut for shoulder stock. All numbers match, about 10% cylinder scene remains, no safety pins, revolver works well, but engagement of trigger and safety notch need adjustment. Dark patina on old reblue, scattered faint pitting, clear lettering, fine original walnut grips. Good-plus condition....................... **900.00**

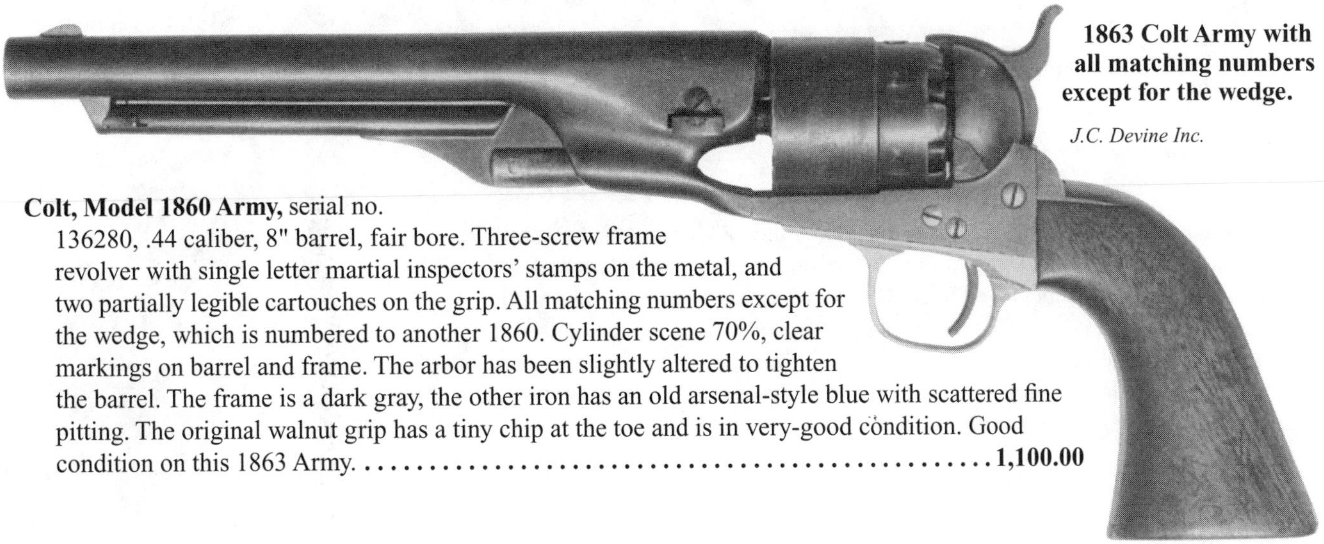

1863 Colt Army with all matching numbers except for the wedge.

J.C. Devine Inc.

Colt, Model 1860 Army, serial no. 136280, .44 caliber, 8" barrel, fair bore. Three-screw frame revolver with single letter martial inspectors' stamps on the metal, and two partially legible cartouches on the grip. All matching numbers except for the wedge, which is numbered to another 1860. Cylinder scene 70%, clear markings on barrel and frame. The arbor has been slightly altered to tighten the barrel. The frame is a dark gray, the other iron has an old arsenal-style blue with scattered fine pitting. The original walnut grip has a tiny chip at the toe and is in very-good condition. Good condition on this 1863 Army. **1,100.00**

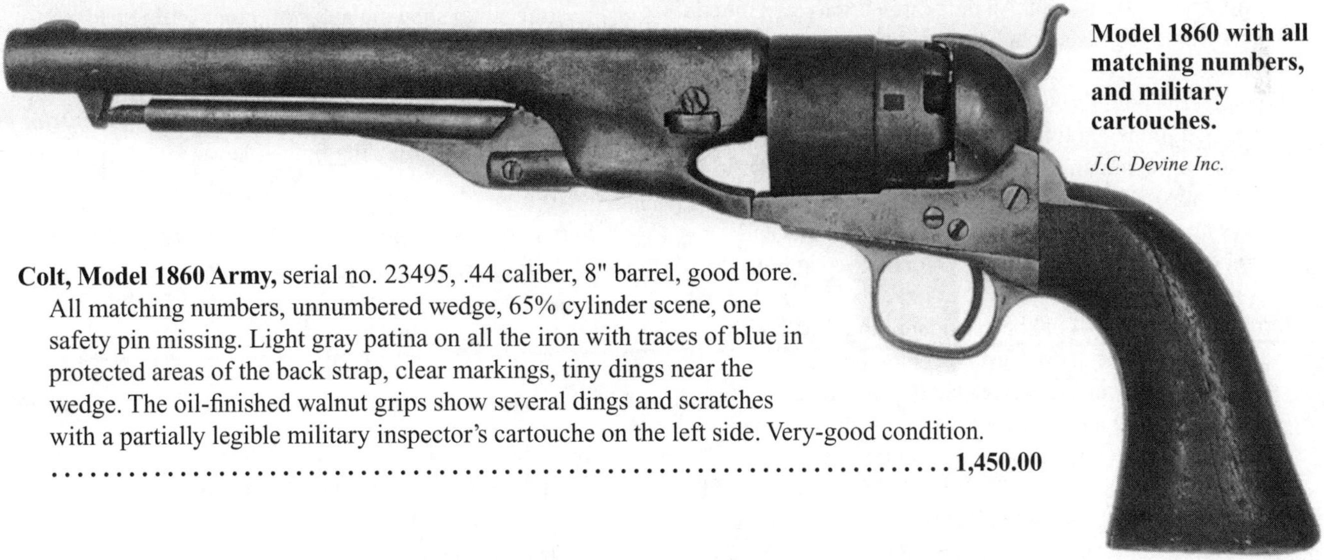

Model 1860 with all matching numbers, and military cartouches.

J.C. Devine Inc.

Colt, Model 1860 Army, serial no. 23495, .44 caliber, 8" barrel, good bore. All matching numbers, unnumbered wedge, 65% cylinder scene, one safety pin missing. Light gray patina on all the iron with traces of blue in protected areas of the back strap, clear markings, tiny dings near the wedge. The oil-finished walnut grips show several dings and scratches with a partially legible military inspector's cartouche on the left side. Very-good condition. **1,450.00**

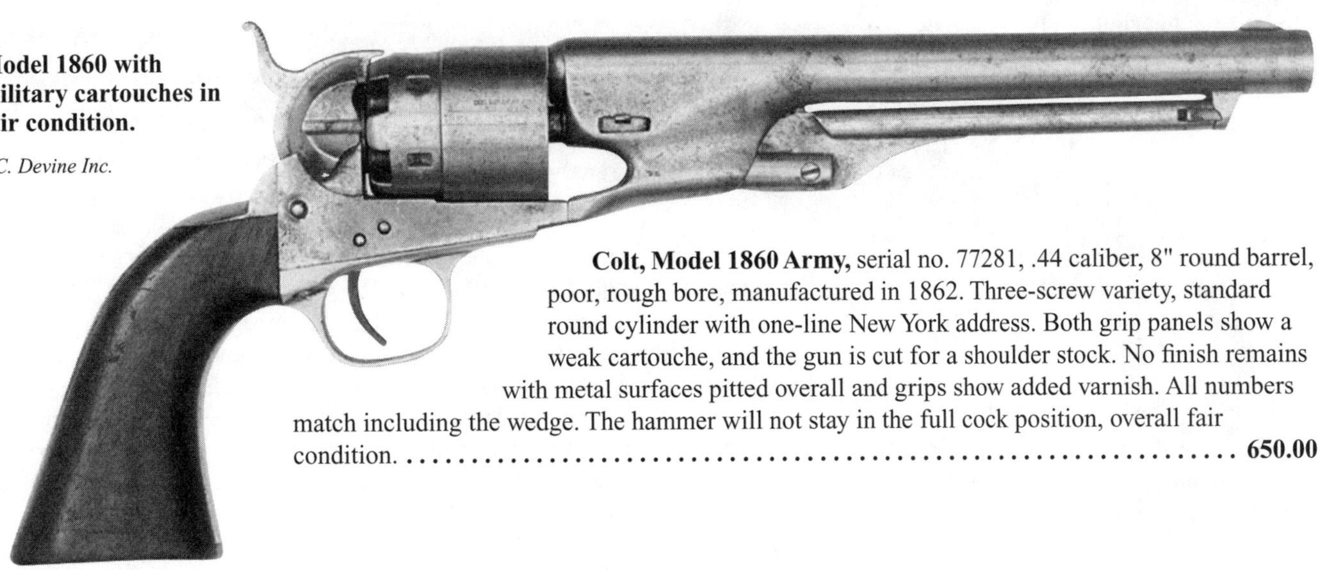

Model 1860 with military cartouches in fair condition.

J.C. Devine Inc.

Colt, Model 1860 Army, serial no. 77281, .44 caliber, 8" round barrel, poor, rough bore, manufactured in 1862. Three-screw variety, standard round cylinder with one-line New York address. Both grip panels show a weak cartouche, and the gun is cut for a shoulder stock. No finish remains with metal surfaces pitted overall and grips show added varnish. All numbers match including the wedge. The hammer will not stay in the full cock position, overall fair condition. **650.00**

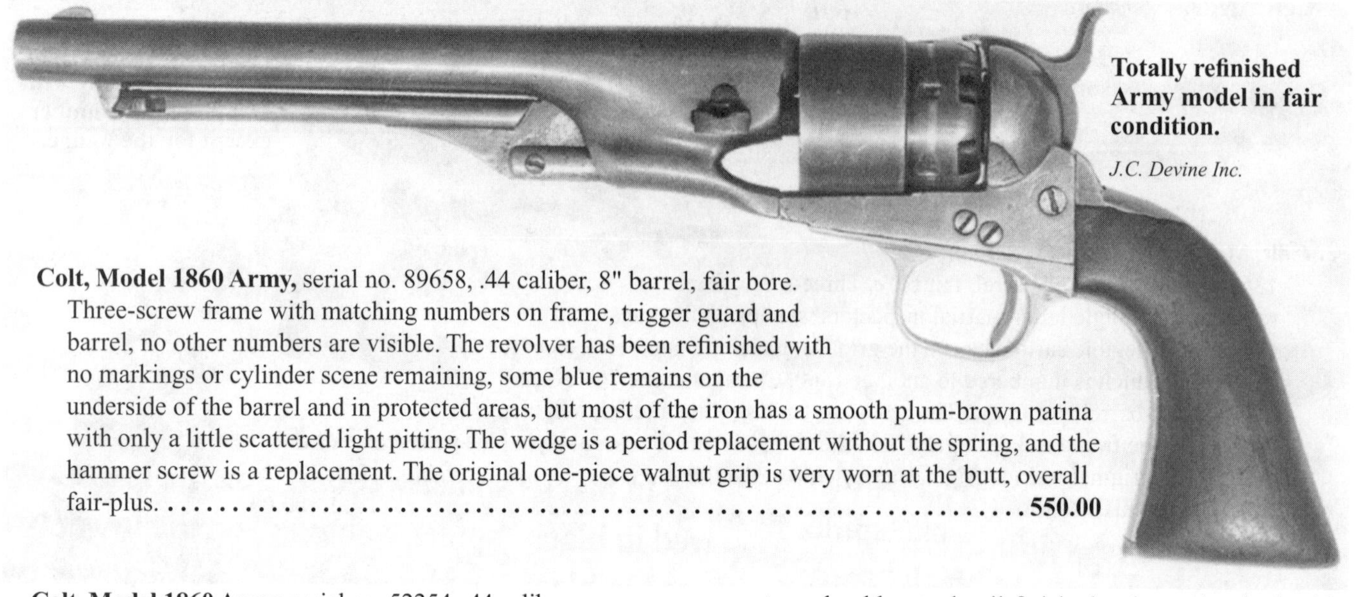

Totally refinished Army model in fair condition.

J.C. Devine Inc.

Colt, Model 1860 Army, serial no. 89658, .44 caliber, 8" barrel, fair bore. Three-screw frame with matching numbers on frame, trigger guard and barrel, no other numbers are visible. The revolver has been refinished with no markings or cylinder scene remaining, some blue remains on the underside of the barrel and in protected areas, but most of the iron has a smooth plum-brown patina with only a little scattered light pitting. The wedge is a period replacement without the spring, and the hammer screw is a replacement. The original one-piece walnut grip is very worn at the butt, overall fair-plus. **550.00**

Colt, Model 1860 Army, serial no. 52254, .44 caliber, missing the loading lever (has the rammer), the wood grip, and the front sight. All of the iron is dark and pitted, the cylinder is frozen, dug relic condition. **200.00**

Serial no. 78433, .44 caliber, 8" barrel, dark bore. This revolver is plum-brown overall with some pitting along barrel, cylinder, and frame. Traces of the roll scene visible on cylinder. Mechanics are functional with the exception of the cylinder, which does not turn. Grips have an old refinish over minor handling marks and bruises. No cartouche visible. Overall good antique condition. **825.00**

Serial no. 118640, .44 caliber, standard model with 8" barrel and frame cut for 3rd-type shoulder stock. Condition is poor. Metal cleaned to gray and showing areas of pitting and scratches overall, cylinder has no markings or scene, replaced grips not of Colt manufacture. **400.00**

Serial no. 143673, .44 caliber, 8" barrel with New York address. Frame marked Colts/Patent. Frame cut for 3rd-type shoulder stock, oil-finished walnut grips, both with inspector's cartouches. Condition is very good. Mottled gray metal showing areas of minor pitting and some scattered small dents. Barrel retains generous traces of blue finish. Frame with traces of light casehardening remaining. Cylinder with fine scene. Hammer spring broken, fine grips, the right side has two deep bruises at butt. **1,955.00**

Serial no. 27154, .44 caliber, 8" barrel with New York address, walnut grips. Good to very-good condition. Metal with mottled brown patina and areas of light pitting and spotting. Cylinder retains slight traces of scene. Sound wood with scattered small dents and bruises. **1,840.00**

Serial no. 66357, .44 caliber, 8" barrel with New York address. Condition is poor. Mottled-gray metal shows areas of pitting. Cylinder heavily cleaned and frozen. Bruised and heavily worn grips replaced. **345.00**

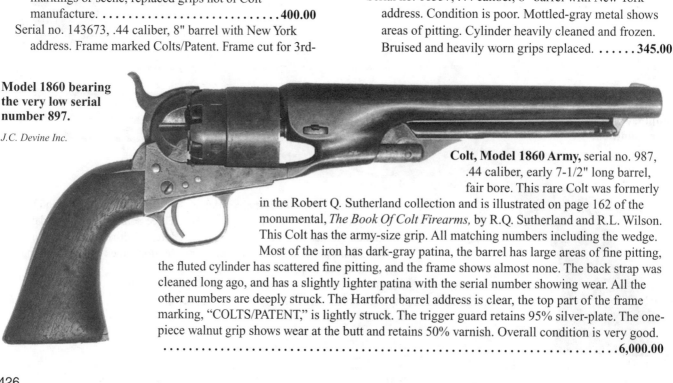

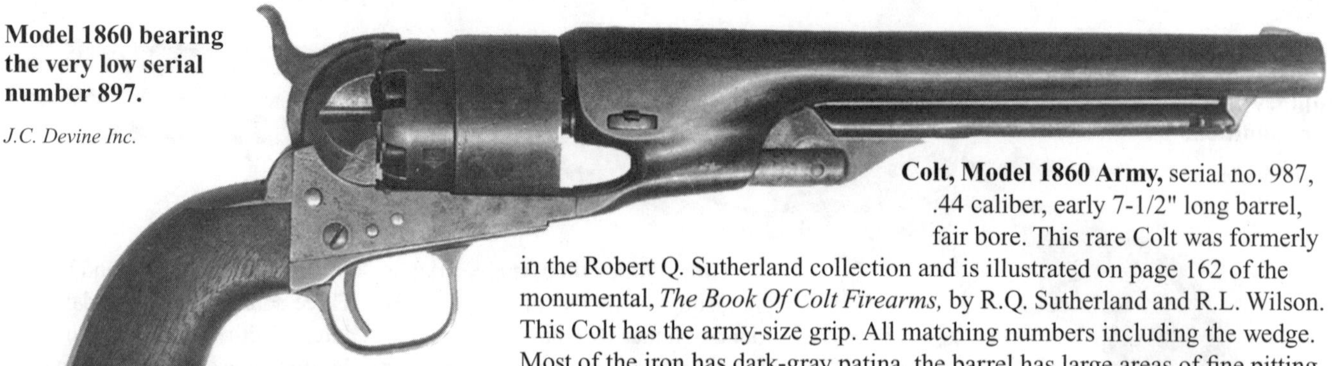

Model 1860 bearing the very low serial number 897.

J.C. Devine Inc.

Colt, Model 1860 Army, serial no. 987, .44 caliber, early 7-1/2" long barrel, fair bore. This rare Colt was formerly in the Robert Q. Sutherland collection and is illustrated on page 162 of the monumental, *The Book Of Colt Firearms,* by R.Q. Sutherland and R.L. Wilson. This Colt has the army-size grip. All matching numbers including the wedge. Most of the iron has dark-gray patina, the barrel has large areas of fine pitting, the fluted cylinder has scattered fine pitting, and the frame shows almost none. The back strap was cleaned long ago, and has a slightly lighter patina with the serial number showing wear. All the other numbers are deeply struck. The Hartford barrel address is clear, the top part of the frame marking, "COLTS/PATENT," is lightly struck. The trigger guard retains 95% silver-plate. The one-piece walnut grip shows wear at the butt and retains 50% varnish. Overall condition is very good. **6,000.00**

Colt, Model 1860 Army, cont.

Serial no. 79890, .44 caliber, 8" New York marked barrel. Frame marked, "Colts/Patent." Oil-finished grips, both with inspector's cartouche. Good to very-good condition. Grey metal has been cleaned and shows scattered areas of pitting, mainly to cylinder. Most cylinder scene remains, but shows wear. Left grip with series of fine notches and illegible inscription. Right side with chipping at butt and series of dents to butt. **1,265.00**

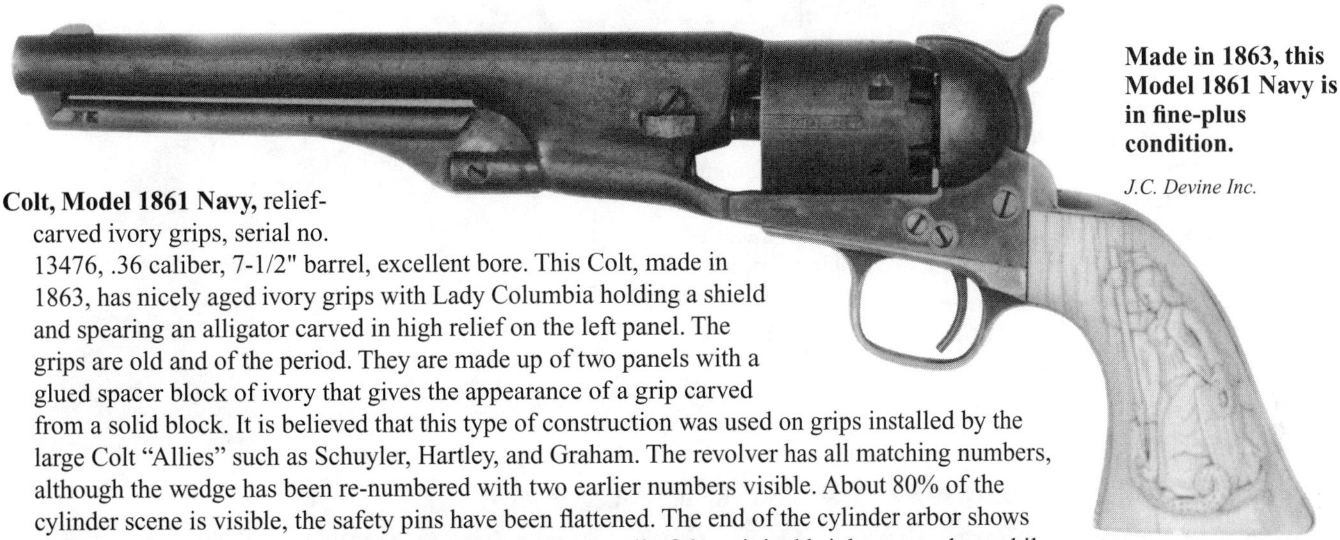

Made in 1863, this Model 1861 Navy is in fine-plus condition.

J.C. Devine Inc.

Colt, Model 1861 Navy, relief-carved ivory grips, serial no. 13476, .36 caliber, 7-1/2" barrel, excellent bore. This Colt, made in 1863, has nicely aged ivory grips with Lady Columbia holding a shield and spearing an alligator carved in high relief on the left panel. The grips are old and of the period. They are made up of two panels with a glued spacer block of ivory that gives the appearance of a grip carved from a solid block. It is believed that this type of construction was used on grips installed by the large Colt "Allies" such as Schuyler, Hartley, and Graham. The revolver has all matching numbers, although the wedge has been re-numbered with two earlier numbers visible. About 80% of the cylinder scene is visible, the safety pins have been flattened. The end of the cylinder arbor shows light file marks. The flat sides of the frame retain almost all of the original bright case colors while the colors on the recoil shield have turned dark. The hammer and loading lever retain about 70% of the case colors, the barrel retains about 70% bright blue with a little scattered fine pitting, most of the blue has flaked from the cylinder leaving a blue/gray patina. The grip straps retain about 70% silver plating, all lettering is sharp. This is a great-looking Colt that was probably fired only a few times, resulting in the blue flaking from the cylinder. Overall fine-plus condition. **8,000.00**

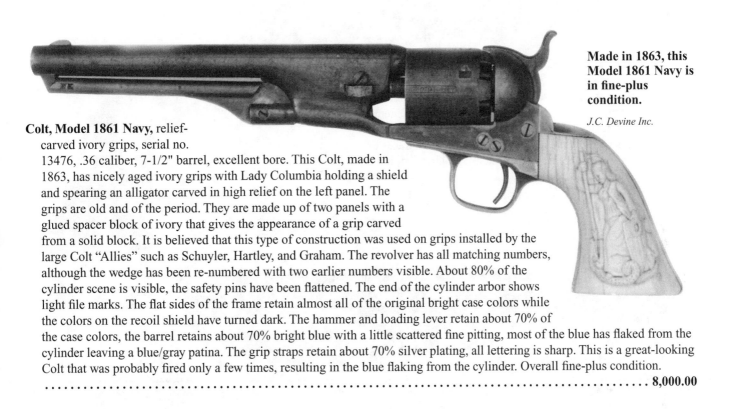

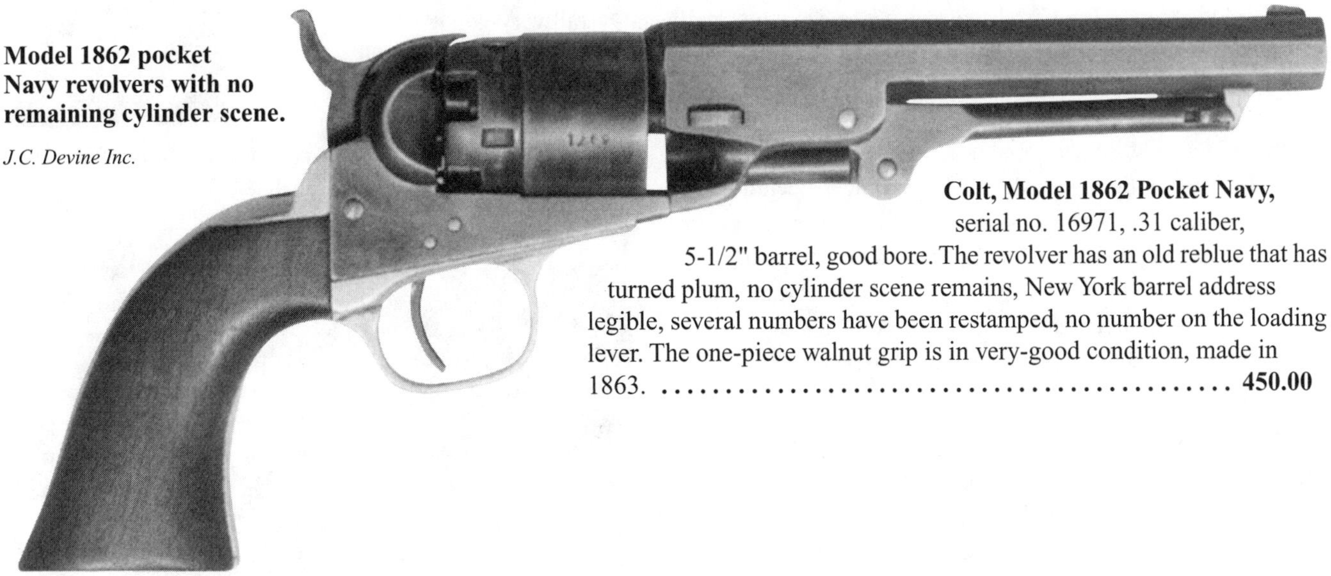

Model 1862 pocket Navy revolvers with no remaining cylinder scene.

J.C. Devine Inc.

Colt, Model 1862 Pocket Navy, serial no. 16971, .31 caliber, 5-1/2" barrel, good bore. The revolver has an old reblue that has turned plum, no cylinder scene remains, New York barrel address legible, several numbers have been restamped, no number on the loading lever. The one-piece walnut grip is in very-good condition, made in 1863. .... **450.00**

Colt, Model 1862 Police

.36 caliber, iron back strap, all matching number 376 (early 1861). A smooth, gray gun with fine walnut stock, clear markings and tight as new. Hangs now and then (weak hand spring). Tip of loading lever has been repaired by professional gunsmith. **1,350.00**

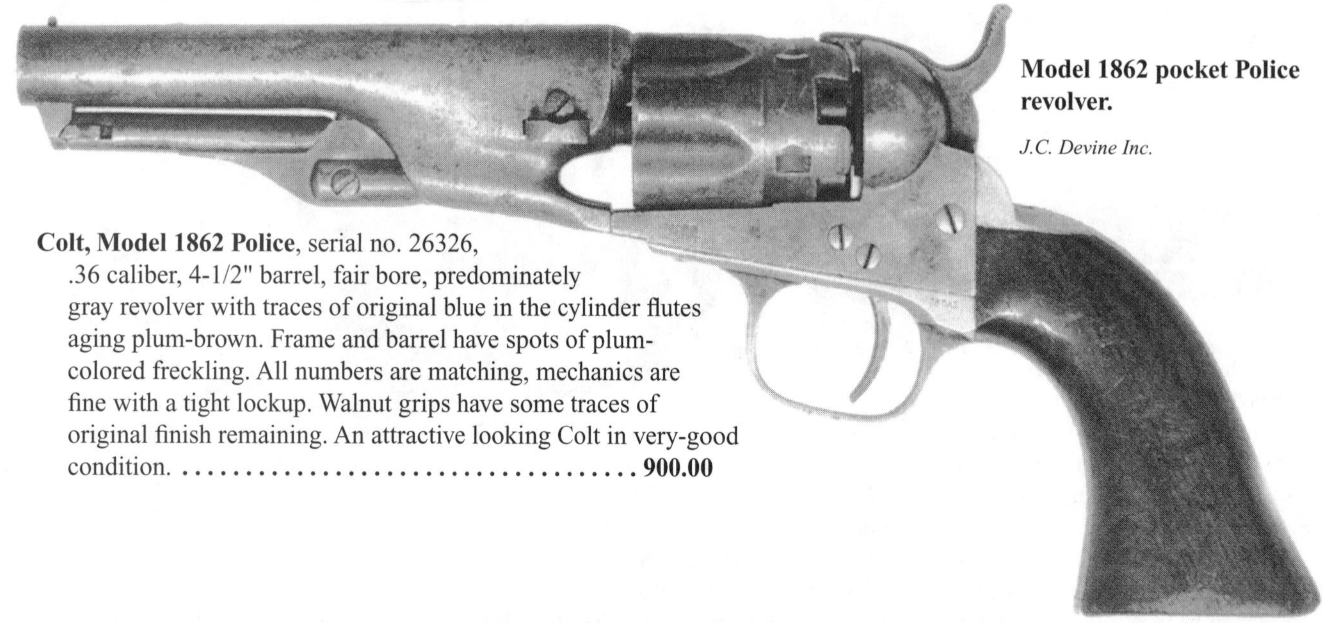

Model 1862 pocket Police revolver.

J.C. Devine Inc.

Colt, Model 1862 Police, serial no. 26326, .36 caliber, 4-1/2" barrel, fair bore, predominately gray revolver with traces of original blue in the cylinder flutes aging plum-brown. Frame and barrel have spots of plum-colored freckling. All numbers are matching, mechanics are fine with a tight lockup. Walnut grips have some traces of original finish remaining. An attractive looking Colt in very-good condition. **900.00**

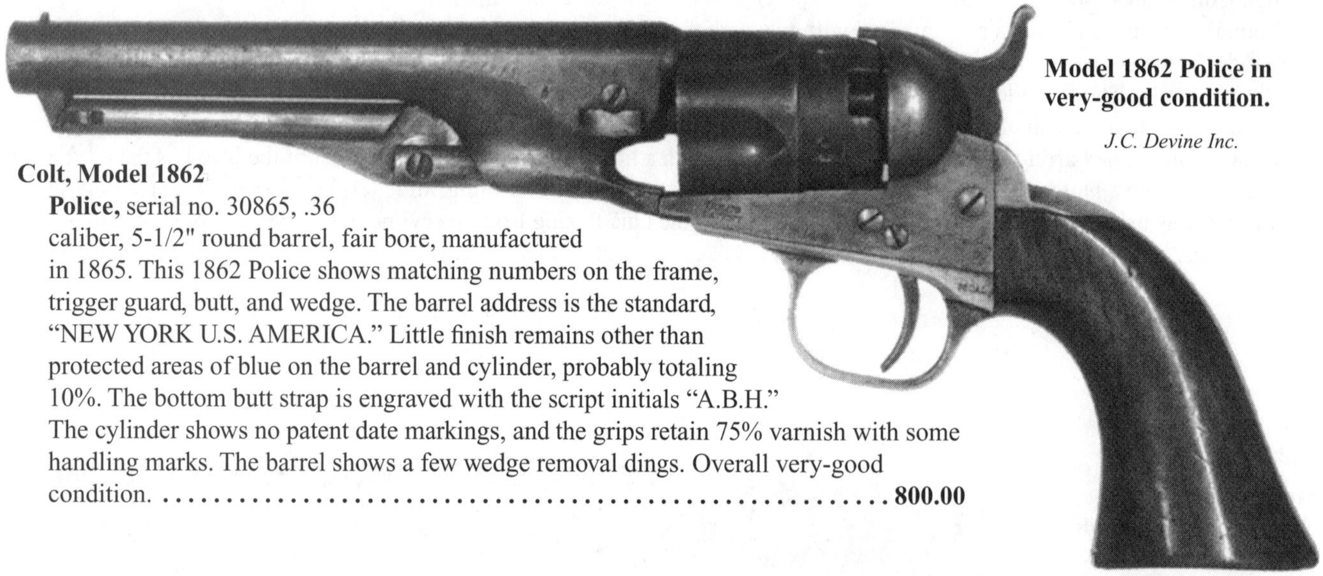

Model 1862 Police in very-good condition.

J.C. Devine Inc.

Colt, Model 1862 Police, serial no. 30865, .36 caliber, 5-1/2" round barrel, fair bore, manufactured in 1865. This 1862 Police shows matching numbers on the frame, trigger guard, butt, and wedge. The barrel address is the standard, "NEW YORK U.S. AMERICA." Little finish remains other than protected areas of blue on the barrel and cylinder, probably totaling 10%. The bottom butt strap is engraved with the script initials "A.B.H." The cylinder shows no patent date markings, and the grips retain 75% varnish with some handling marks. The barrel shows a few wedge removal dings. Overall very-good condition. **800.00**

Colt Model 1862 Police, serial no. 28194, .36 caliber, 6-1/2" barrel, fair bore. All matching numbers including the wedge. The New York barrel address is clear, frame marking is legible. All the iron is a mottled gray with large areas of faint to fine pitting. The original walnut grip has a repaired crack on the left side with four notches carved near the back strap. This 1864-manufactured Colt looks like it saw plenty of service in the Civil War, fair condition. **500.00**

Serial no. 14520, .36 caliber, 6" barrel, varnished walnut grips. Fair to good condition. Mottled-gray metal showing scattered minor pitting and small dents, loading lever loose, grips retain generous traces of varnish with scattered light bruises. **690.00**

Known as the "Dictator," this revolver was one of about 1,000 produced by Hopkins & Allen.

Middle Tennessee Relics

Hopkins and Allen, fully cased, .31 caliber, five-shot pocket model revolver. Hopkins and Allen took over the Bacon Manufacturing facilities in the mid-1860s and produced approximately 1,000 revolvers through 1867. This revolver is clean, well marked, and has full cylinder scene. The revolver is serial number "984". The action is tight, and the walnut grips retain 98% original lacquer. The revolver comes in an original 1860s walnut case complete with powder flask, bullet mold, bullets, percussion caps, and the original key to the case. **1,150.00**

L. Whitney, Navy, 100% original, complete, very tight, mechanically perfect, and well marked. The grips on this revolver are nearly perfect with a crisp cartouche, "SB" (probably Samuel T. Bugbee, armory sub-inspector) on the left grip. The metal is overall plum-brown with traces of blue on the underside of the barrel and lower flats. The cylinder has 60% original scene clearly visible (rare as Whitney scenes are incredibly delicate and almost always worn away), and traces of finish on the cylinder. The top of the barrel is marked, "E. Whitney/N.Haven". There are various sub-inspectors' marks such as letter "D" twice on the barrel and once on the frame, an "S" on the loading lever, and a "DB" on the cylinder. The serial is in the 19,000 range. It shows honest age, but no abuse whatsoever. **2,250.00**

Manhattan Arms Co., serial number 43227, all numbers match, 6-1/2" barrel. The grips are original and the markings are fine. The cylinder scene is 100%, and the words on the cylinder are excellent. Indexes properly sometimes, and other times it needs a little help. There is a little minor pitting on each side of the frame, but not bad. **650.00**

Manhattan Arms Co., Navy, serial no. 3499, .36 caliber, 4" barrel, cylinder with oval panels of military scenes. Varnished walnut grips, very-good condition. Metal with dark-gray patina and areas of light pitting. Cylinder scenes show moderate wear, grips with small dents and scratches. . **.633.00**

Massachusetts Arms, American Adams Pocket, .31 caliber, five-shot, long barrel, pocket revolver in superb condition. Barrel and frame retain 95% high luster factory blue, checkered grips are near mint, action is tight, cylinder has had some touch up on the blue there and is mixed with plum original blue and touch up on the cylinder. Serial is 1,800 range, reference shows that of the 4,500 pocket models made only 100 had round barrels in 4-1/4" **1,250.00**

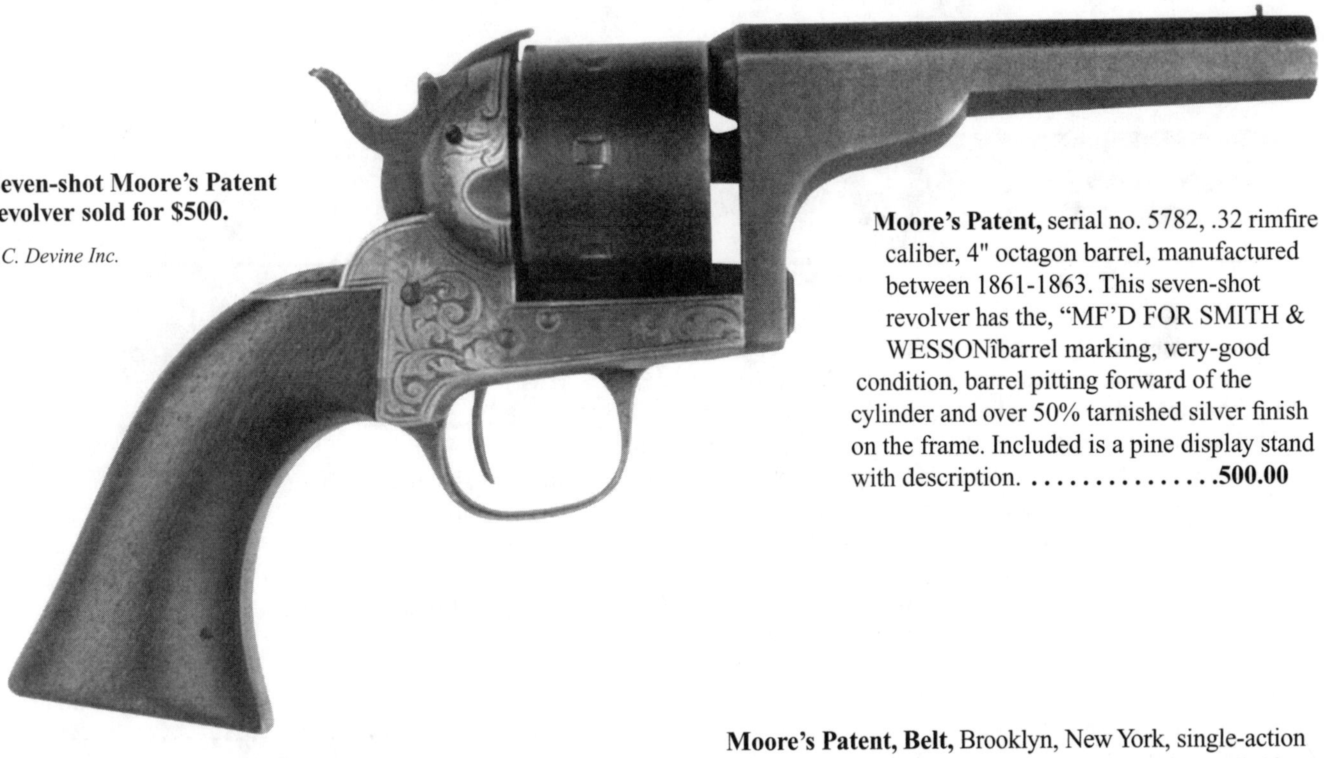

Seven-shot Moore's Patent revolver sold for $500.

J.C. Devine Inc.

Moore's Patent, serial no. 5782, .32 rimfire caliber, 4" octagon barrel, manufactured between 1861-1863. This seven-shot revolver has the, "MF'D FOR SMITH & WESSONîbarrel marking, very-good condition, barrel pitting forward of the cylinder and over 50% tarnished silver finish on the frame. Included is a pine display stand with description. . . . . **.500.00**

Moore's patent revolver with serial number 1075.

Caldwell and Company Civil War Antiques

Moore's Patent, Belt, Brooklyn, New York, single-action belt revolver, also known as the "Seven Shooter." .32-caliber rimfire with 6" octagon barrel. Seven-shot cylinder, removable ejector rod mounted under barrel. Barrel and cylinder swing to right for loading. Brass frame and handle with decorative broad scroll engraving with traces of silver plating remaining. Some blue left on barrel and cylinder. Walnut grips with square butt. A couple of chips on the toe of the left grip are present. Barrel marking is, "D. MOORE PATENT SEPT. 18, 1860" and there is some pitting where the pistol laid on the obverse side, serial number is 107. . . . . **.625.00**

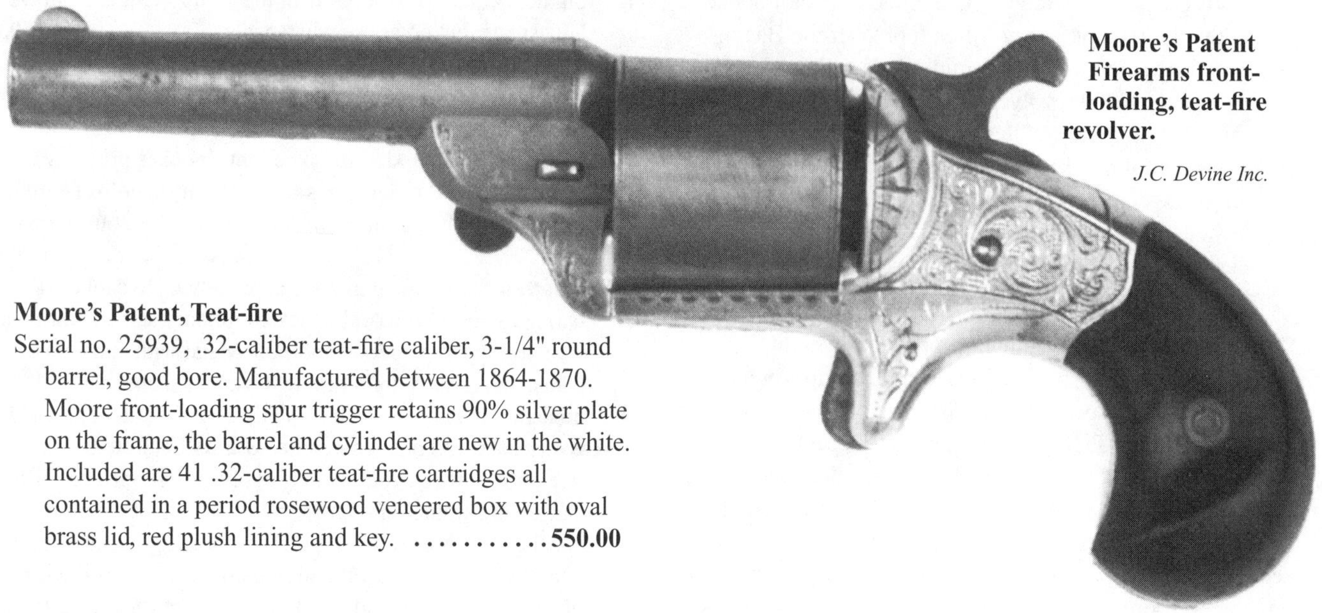

Moore's Patent Firearms front-loading, teat-fire revolver.

J.C. Devine Inc.

Moore's Patent, Teat-fire
Serial no. 25939, .32-caliber teat-fire caliber, 3-1/4" round barrel, good bore. Manufactured between 1864-1870. Moore front-loading spur trigger retains 90% silver plate on the frame, the barrel and cylinder are new in the white. Included are 41 .32-caliber teat-fire cartridges all contained in a period rosewood veneered box with oval brass lid, red plush lining and key. **550.00**

Moore's Patent, Teat-fire
Very nice example of this 1860s hideaway revolver. Overall very-good condition with delicate age patina, and nice engraving, excellent grips. This fired an unusual teat-fire cartridge. **295.00**

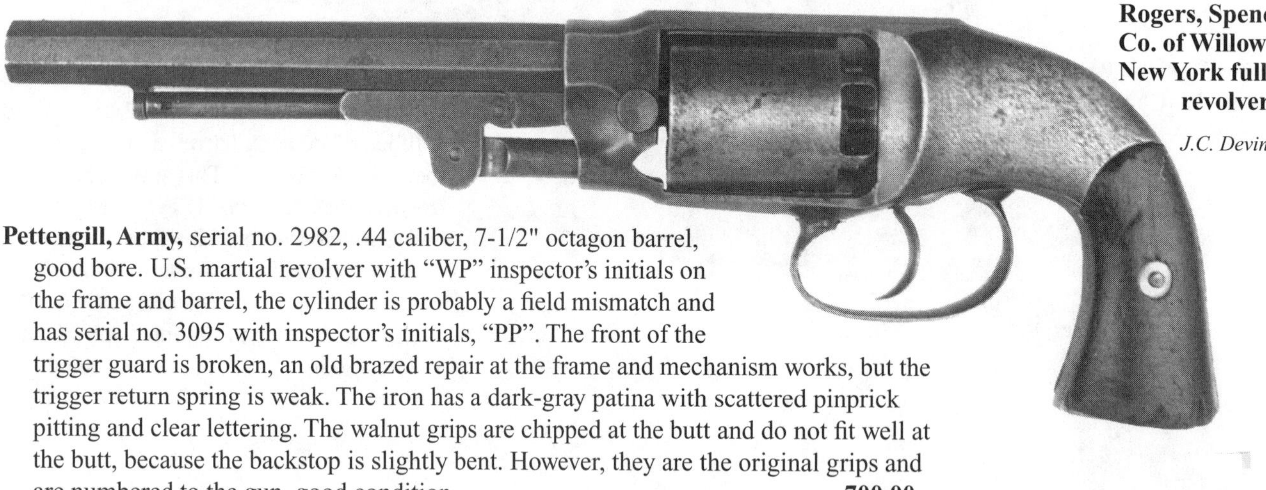

Rogers, Spencer & Co. of Willowvale, New York full frame revolver.

J.C. Devine Inc.

Pettengill, Army, serial no. 2982, .44 caliber, 7-1/2" octagon barrel, good bore. U.S. martial revolver with "WP" inspector's initials on the frame and barrel, the cylinder is probably a field mismatch and has serial no. 3095 with inspector's initials, "PP". The front of the trigger guard is broken, an old brazed repair at the frame and mechanism works, but the trigger return spring is weak. The iron has a dark-gray patina with scattered pinprick pitting and clear lettering. The walnut grips are chipped at the butt and do not fit well at the butt, because the backstop is slightly bent. However, they are the original grips and are numbered to the gun, good condition. **700.00**

Pettingill, Army, scarce, concealed-hammer, double-action revolver with the martial markings, very good with razor sharp edges. It is 100% original and complete in the 3,6xx serial range. Metal is uniformly clean steel color mixed with the lightest of patinas. The markings are crisp and full with 1856 and 1858 dates. The grips are very good with faintly visible inspector's cartouche on the left grip. Proper sub-inspector's markings are boldly visible on barrel, frame, and rammer. **1,850.00**

Philadelphia Cooper, specimen is overall very good, nice plum color with hints and rumors of finish in protected areas. No rust, no pitting, sharp edges, sharp markings, superb grips, mechanically perfect, serial in 2,9xx range, 4" barrel. **675.00**

Remington Beals, Navy, .36 caliber, very-good condition aside from the fact that there is no original finish on this gun, making it closer to fine condition. It is 100% original and complete, and exactly as it was shipped from the factory. All of the edges are sharp, as is the barrel address. The grips are outstanding with virtually no wear or dents. The metal has a uniform light-brown age patina that is quite appealing. It is mechanically perfect, and as tight as a drum. The serial is in the 10,000 range that would indicate manufacture in late 1861 or early 1862 (roughly 14,000 were produced in total). **1,395.00**

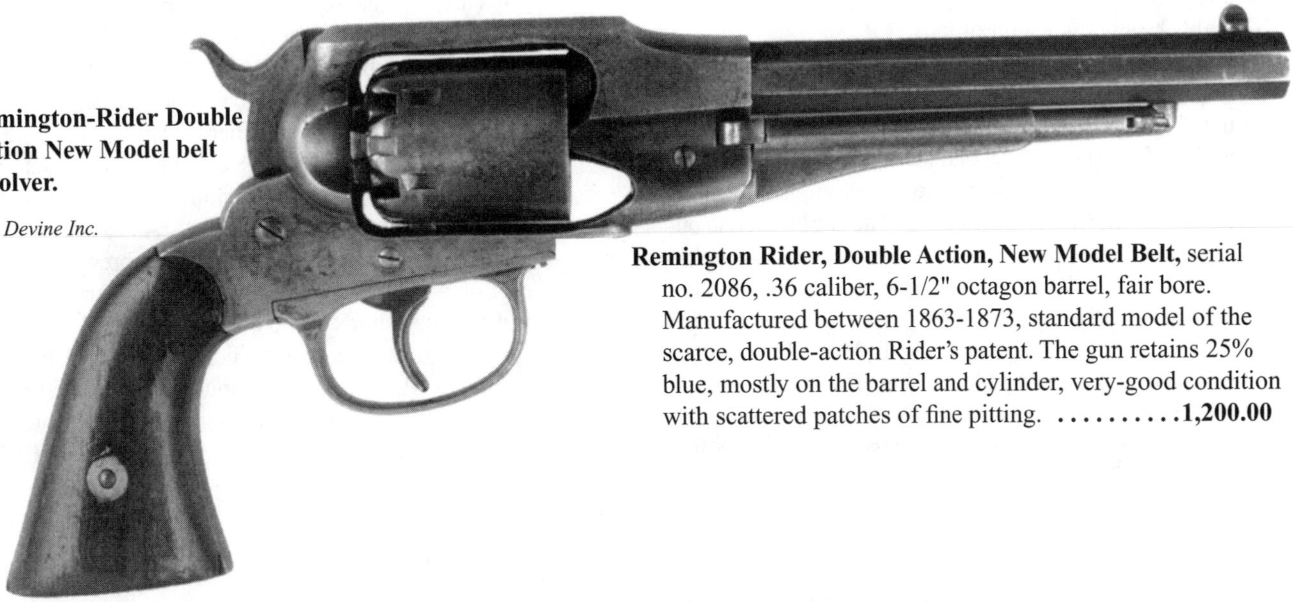

Remington-Rider Double Action New Model belt revolver.

J.C. Devine Inc.

Remington Rider, Double Action, New Model Belt, serial no. 2086, .36 caliber, 6-1/2" octagon barrel, fair bore. Manufactured between 1863-1873, standard model of the scarce, double-action Rider's patent. The gun retains 25% blue, mostly on the barrel and cylinder, very-good condition with scattered patches of fine pitting. **1,200.00**

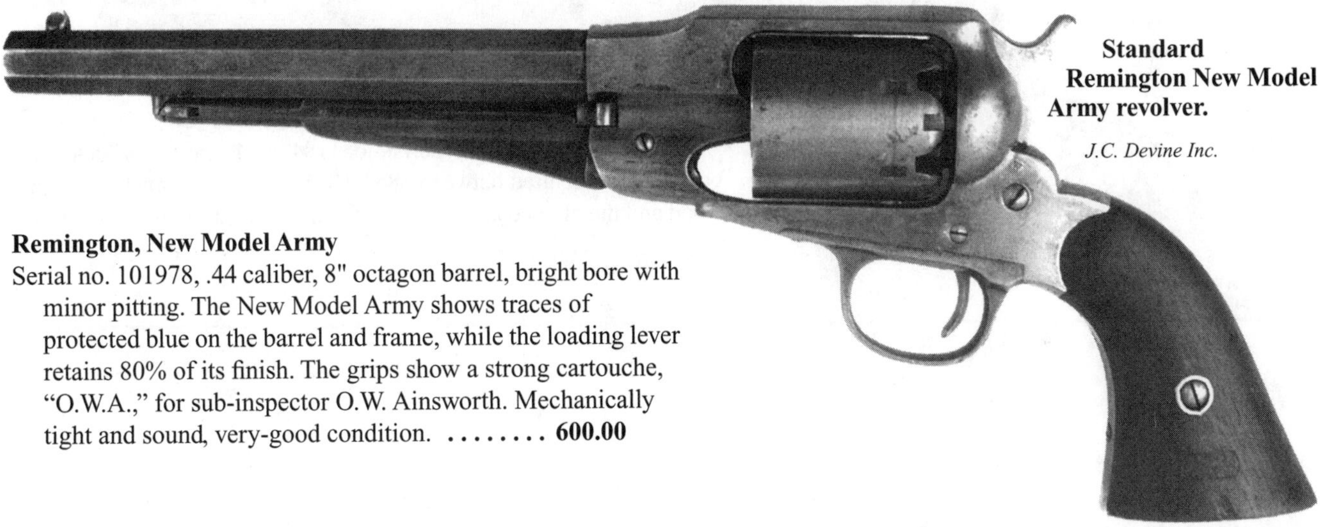

Standard Remington New Model Army revolver.

J.C. Devine Inc.

Remington, New Model Army
Serial no. 101978, .44 caliber, 8" octagon barrel, bright bore with minor pitting. The New Model Army shows traces of protected blue on the barrel and frame, while the loading lever retains 80% of its finish. The grips show a strong cartouche, "O.W.A.," for sub-inspector O.W. Ainsworth. Mechanically tight and sound, very-good condition. **600.00**

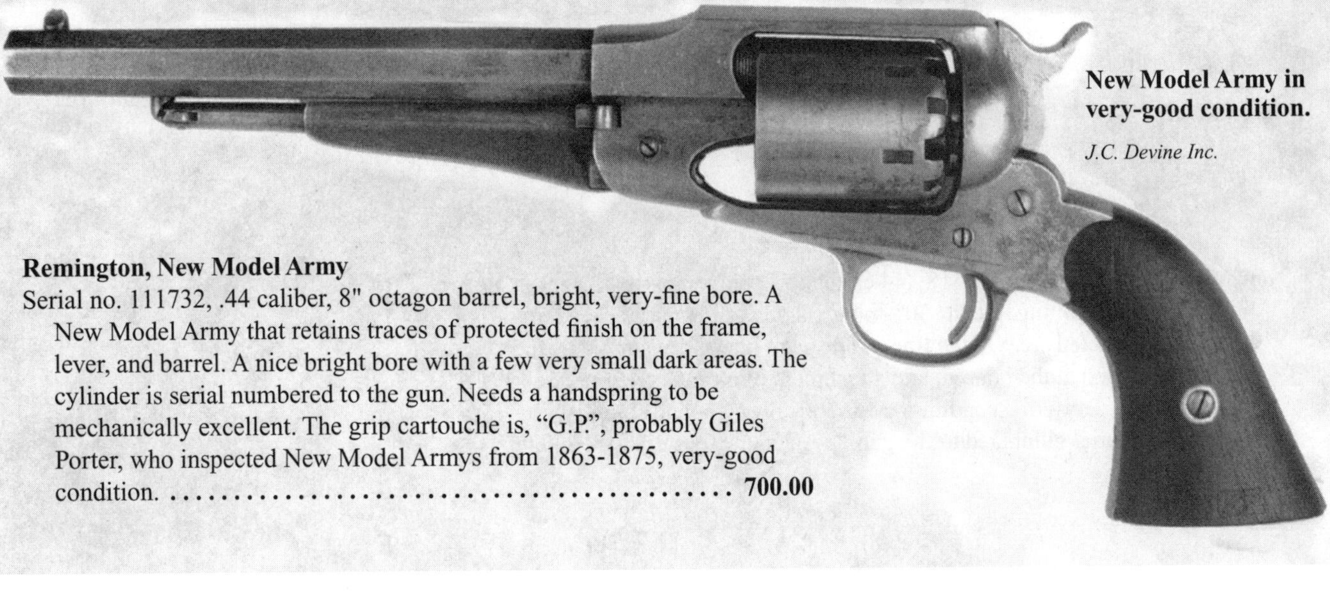

New Model Army in very-good condition.

J.C. Devine Inc.

Remington, New Model Army
Serial no. 111732, .44 caliber, 8" octagon barrel, bright, very-fine bore. A New Model Army that retains traces of protected finish on the frame, lever, and barrel. A nice bright bore with a few very small dark areas. The cylinder is serial numbered to the gun. Needs a handspring to be mechanically excellent. The grip cartouche is, "G.P.", probably Giles Porter, who inspected New Model Armys from 1863-1875, very-good condition. **700.00**

Remington, New Model Army, cont.

.44 caliber, with quite a bit of finish (30%), edges and markings are sharp and crisp. The barrel and frame have thin blue uniformly distributed, with the balance of the metal having a very attractive plum age coloring mixed with a bit of surface rust and the lightest pitting at the muzzle. The proper sub-inspector's markings are present on the barrel, frame, and rammer. The action is crisp and tight and the hammer has generous traces of case color on it. The grips have very nice edges and very legible cartouche, "PH," on the left grip. **1,095.00**

.44 caliber, overall very good, being 100% original and complete and mechanically perfect. The metal has a uniform light age patina overall with strong markings including barrel address and sub-inspector's stamps. The grips are very good, showing only honest wear, and there is a visible inspector's cartouche on the left grip. The serial number is in the 50,000 range. **950.00**

.44 caliber, serial number in the 49,000 range, making this an early production piece. There is slight wear on the barrel address. The sub-inspector's marks are clearly legible, and the inspector's cartouche is faintly visible on the left grip, 100% original. **895.00**

.44 caliber. The metal has a uniform light-brown age patina overall, with strong markings including barrel address and sub-inspector's stamps, very pretty patina. The grips are very good showing only honest wear, and there is a lightly visible inspector's cartouche on the left grip. The serial number is in the 51000 range. It has the old-style cone front sight. **1,050.00**

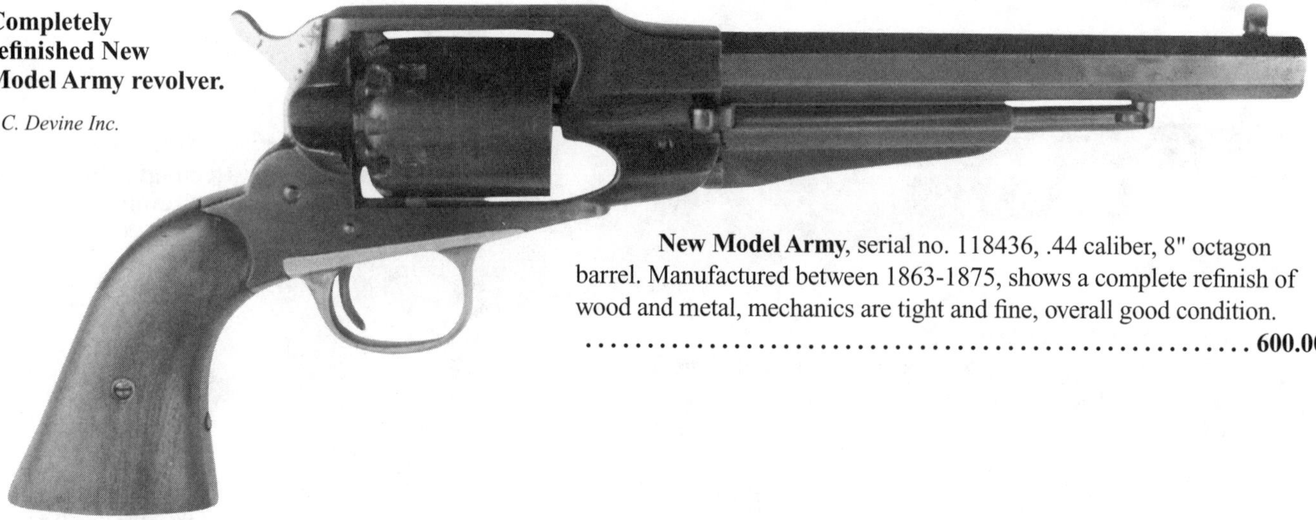

Completely refinished New Model Army revolver.

J.C. Devine Inc.

New Model Army, serial no. 118436, .44 caliber, 8" octagon barrel. Manufactured between 1863-1875, shows a complete refinish of wood and metal, mechanics are tight and fine, overall good condition. **600.00**

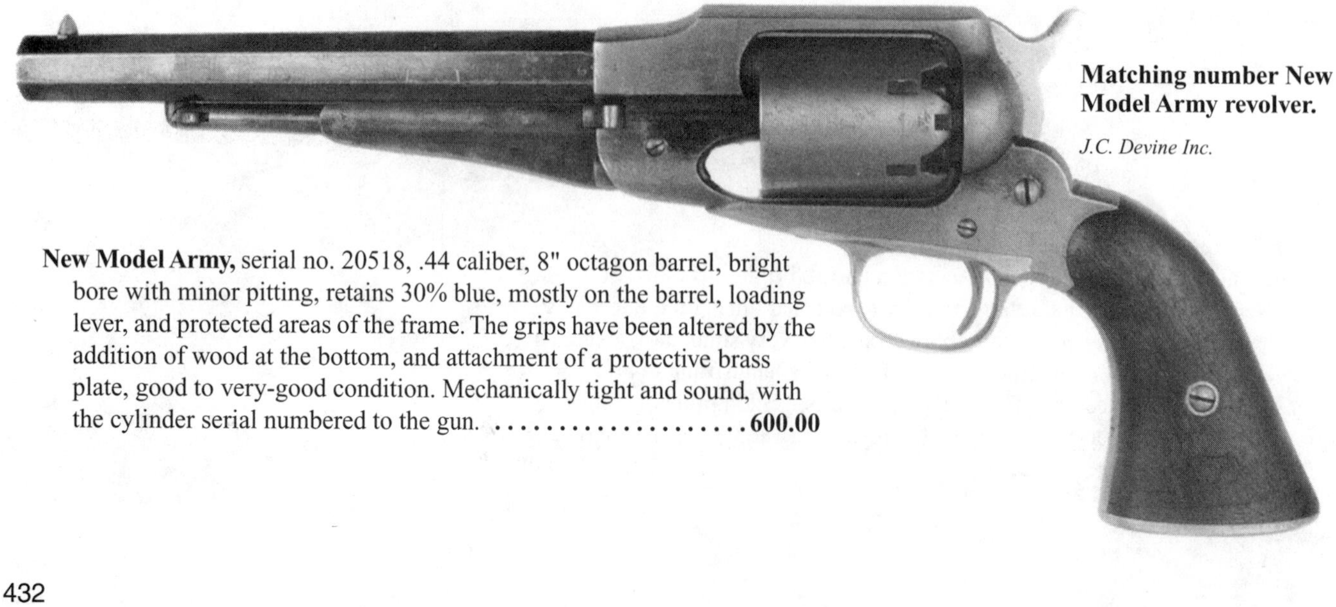

Matching number New Model Army revolver.

J.C. Devine Inc.

New Model Army, serial no. 20518, .44 caliber, 8" octagon barrel, bright bore with minor pitting, retains 30% blue, mostly on the barrel, loading lever, and protected areas of the frame. The grips have been altered by the addition of wood at the bottom, and attachment of a protective brass plate, good to very-good condition. Mechanically tight and sound, with the cylinder serial numbered to the gun. **600.00**

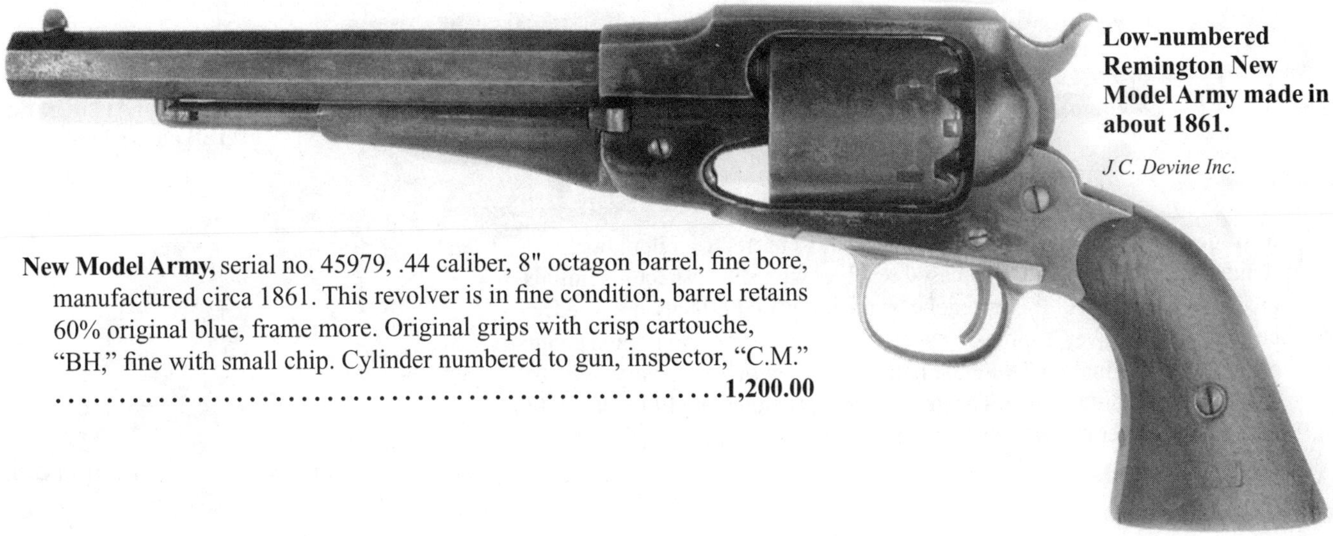

Low-numbered Remington New Model Army made in about 1861.

J.C. Devine Inc.

New Model Army, serial no. 45979, .44 caliber, 8" octagon barrel, fine bore, manufactured circa 1861. This revolver is in fine condition, barrel retains 60% original blue, frame more. Original grips with crisp cartouche, "BH," fine with small chip. Cylinder numbered to gun, inspector, "C.M." **1,200.00**

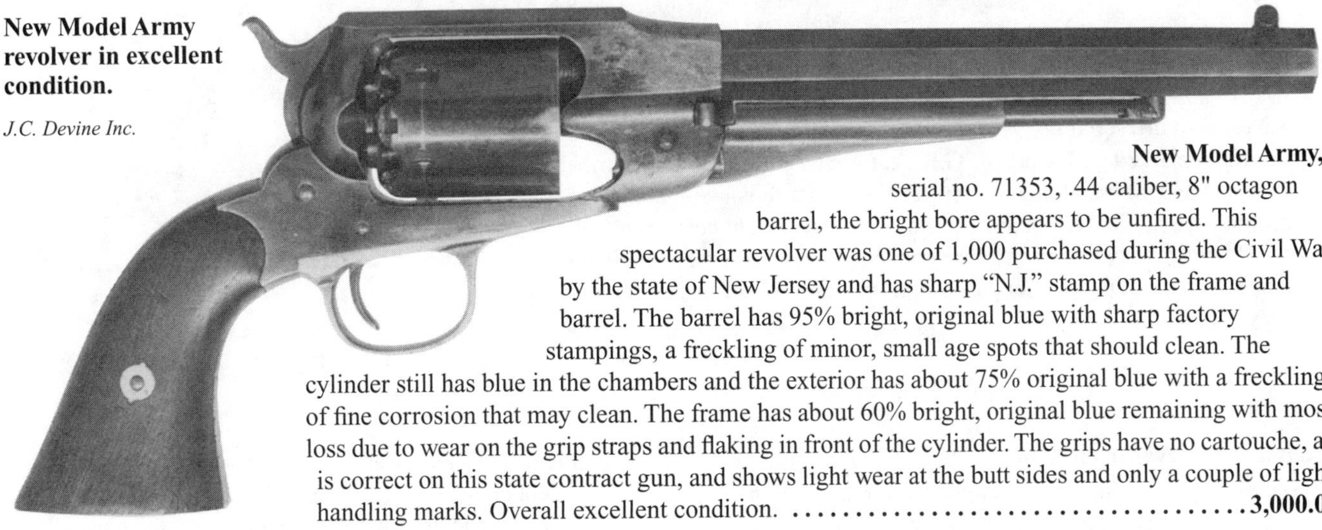

New Model Army revolver in excellent condition.

J.C. Devine Inc.

New Model Army, serial no. 71353, .44 caliber, 8" octagon barrel, the bright bore appears to be unfired. This spectacular revolver was one of 1,000 purchased during the Civil War by the state of New Jersey and has sharp "N.J." stamp on the frame and barrel. The barrel has 95% bright, original blue with sharp factory stampings, a freckling of minor, small age spots that should clean. The cylinder still has blue in the chambers and the exterior has about 75% original blue with a freckling of fine corrosion that may clean. The frame has about 60% bright, original blue remaining with most loss due to wear on the grip straps and flaking in front of the cylinder. The grips have no cartouche, as is correct on this state contract gun, and shows light wear at the butt sides and only a couple of light handling marks. Overall excellent condition. **3,000.00**

Remington New Model Army, serial no. 78271, .44 caliber, 8" octagon barrel, fair bore. Standard model purchased by the Union during the Civil War, has sub-inspector's initials on the metal with the inspector's cartouche visible on the left grip. The barrel and frame are a light gray, the cylinder is probably a replacement with a dark-gray patina. The barrel address is partially legible, the metal has large areas of faint pitting with a few patches of fine pitting. The grips have a repaired crack on the left side with a large chip missing at the toe on the same side. The grips have been refinished with the cartouche legible, good condition.......... **500.00**

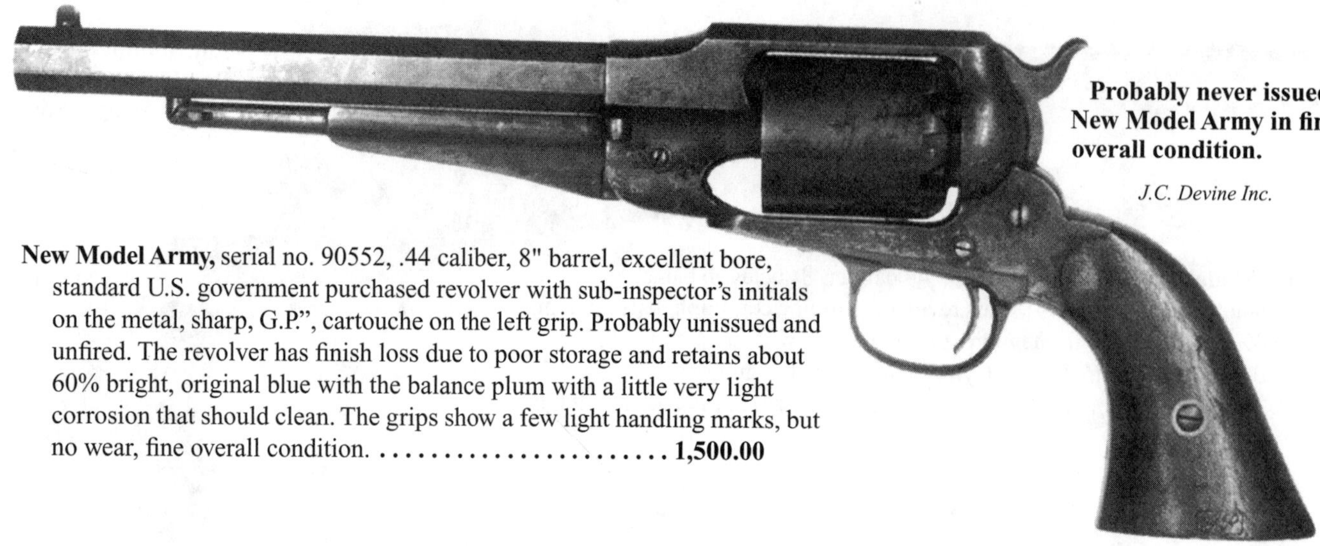

Probably never issued, New Model Army in fine overall condition.

J.C. Devine Inc.

New Model Army, serial no. 90552, .44 caliber, 8" barrel, excellent bore, standard U.S. government purchased revolver with sub-inspector's initials on the metal, sharp, G.P.", cartouche on the left grip. Probably unissued and unfired. The revolver has finish loss due to poor storage and retains about 60% bright, original blue with the balance plum with a little very light corrosion that should clean. The grips show a few light handling marks, but no wear, fine overall condition. **1,500.00**

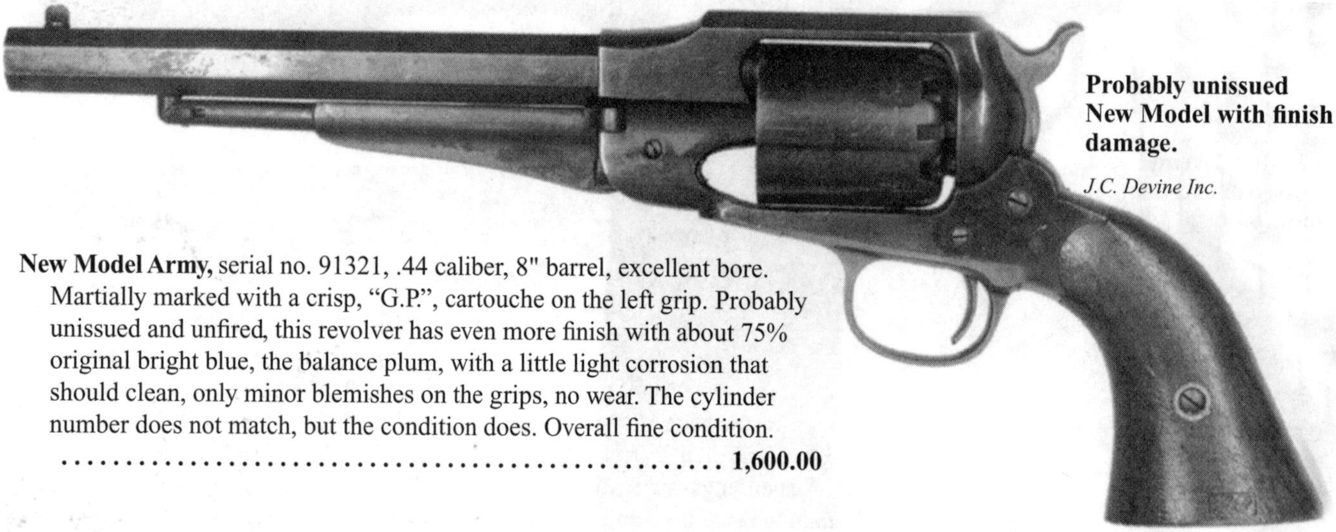

Probably unissued New Model with finish damage.

J.C. Devine Inc.

New Model Army, serial no. 91321, .44 caliber, 8" barrel, excellent bore. Martially marked with a crisp, "G.P.", cartouche on the left grip. Probably unissued and unfired, this revolver has even more finish with about 75% original bright blue, the balance plum, with a little light corrosion that should clean, only minor blemishes on the grips, no wear. The cylinder number does not match, but the condition does. Overall fine condition. **1,600.00**

Remington New Model Army

Serial no. 123267, .44 caliber, standard configuration, the walnut grips with faint inspector's cartouche. Dark, mottled patina with areas of minor pitting and series of dents to the barrel lug. Grips show wear, minor dents at butt and tiny chips at forward toes, good condition. **518.00**

Serial no. 28332, .44 caliber, early example with German silver-cone front sight. Retains 45% blue, traces of case colors and has clear government inspector's cartouche. **1,425.00**

Very crisp action, 60-70% original blue on the barrel frame and cylinder, grips have 95% original varnish, no cartouche. Serial number is 80613. The gun has fancy initials, "W.D.", on the trigger guard. On the inside of the grips is the name, "W. Dunn." **2,000.00**

.44-caliber revolver, edges and markings are sharp and crisp, barrel and frame have thin blue uniformly distributed, with the balance of the metal having a very attractive plum age coloring. The hammer has been cleaned and is a little shiny. The proper sub-inspector's markings are present on the barrel, frame, and rammer, action is crisp and tight. The grips have very nice edges, there is a repaired crack in the right grip only, and no evidence of a cartouche, 100% original and complete......... **975.00**

Remington, New Model Navy

Identical to the .44 caliber revolvers, but slightly smaller and .36 caliber. Overall good to very-good condition. In the 21,000 serial range with all numbers matching. It is all original and complete except for the cylinder pin, that is a proper replacement. There is a factory inspector's mark, "A" on the loading lever, the bottom of each grip has two "R"s. The metal is smooth with a gray-brown patina, except for the loading lever, that has generous amounts of blue finish still present. The grips are beautiful with a nice grain and finish. The barrel marking is worn, but visible. Roughly 28,000 of this model were made with 4,300 being sold to the Navy (these 4,300 were not marked by the government to indicate the fact). **675.00**

Remington, New Model Navy, cont.

Overall very-good condition, 24,000 serial range with all numbers matching, 100% original and complete. The metal is overall smooth, with a deep-brown patina, totally uniform in color and very pretty. Barrel marking is clear three-line new model marking, edges are sharp with only light wear. Good grips with some toe chipping. Front sight is early style cone, and the cylinder is early Beals-style without safety notches between the nipples. **875.00**

Serial no. 23920, .38-centerfire caliber. Standard configuration with factory conversion. Walnut grips, mottled-gray metal with areas of light pitting and series of small dents to barrel lug. Ejector rod missing, trigger return, spring fatigued. Grips showing dents and bruises, series of notches to left butt and chipping at toes, fair condition. **345.00**

Remington's New Model Police was a lightened version of the company's popular New Model Army and Navy revolvers.

J.C. Devine Inc.

Remington, New Model Police, serial no. 8357, .36 caliber, 6-1/2" octagon barrel, fair bore, manufactured between 1865-1873. The lightweight reduced-size version of the Army/Navy Remington's that was popular with civilians and law enforcement people. This one grades very good with a gray-brown metal finish and light bruising on the grips. **400.00**

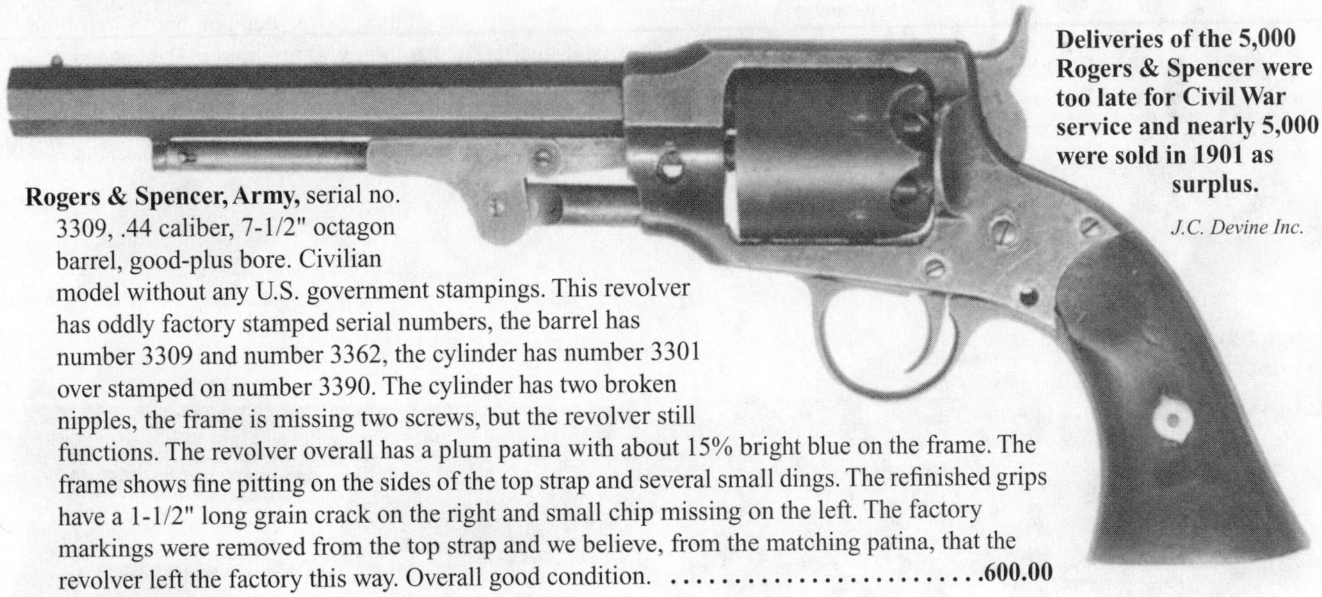

Deliveries of the 5,000 Rogers & Spencer were too late for Civil War service and nearly 5,000 were sold in 1901 as surplus.

J.C. Devine Inc.

Rogers & Spencer, Army, serial no. 3309, .44 caliber, 7-1/2" octagon barrel, good-plus bore. Civilian model without any U.S. government stampings. This revolver has oddly factory stamped serial numbers, the barrel has number 3309 and number 3362, the cylinder has number 3301 over stamped on number 3390. The cylinder has two broken nipples, the frame is missing two screws, but the revolver still functions. The revolver overall has a plum patina with about 15% bright blue on the frame. The frame shows fine pitting on the sides of the top strap and several small dings. The refinished grips have a 1-1/2" long grain crack on the right and small chip missing on the left. The factory markings were removed from the top strap and we believe, from the matching patina, that the revolver left the factory this way. Overall good condition. .... **.600.00**

Rogers & Spencer, Army

.44 caliber, extremely nice example in excellent condition, 100% original, mechanically perfect, tight, solid, and all matched serials in the 1900 range except for the loading lever, which is marked with a number "39." This gun has roughly 75% to 80% original factory blue. The frame has 90% blue, the barrel has some wear to the finish in the center portion of the top five flats. The cylinder retains roughly 50% blue, the hammer and loading lever have generous amounts of case coloring. The grips are super with sharp edges, vivid cartouche "RPB" and a few light bangs on the bottom of the grip. ... **1,450.00**

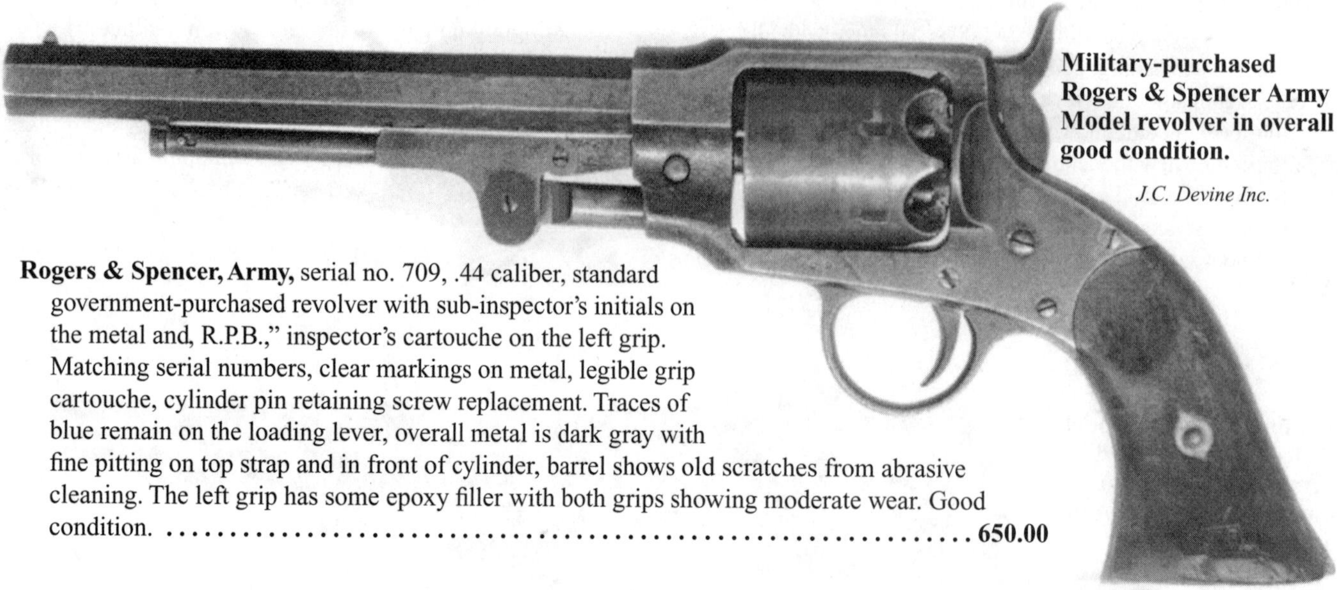

Military-purchased Rogers & Spencer Army Model revolver in overall good condition.

J.C. Devine Inc.

Rogers & Spencer, Army, serial no. 709, .44 caliber, standard government-purchased revolver with sub-inspector's initials on the metal and, R.P.B.," inspector's cartouche on the left grip. Matching serial numbers, clear markings on metal, legible grip cartouche, cylinder pin retaining screw replacement. Traces of blue remain on the loading lever, overall metal is dark gray with fine pitting on top strap and in front of cylinder, barrel shows old scratches from abrasive cleaning. The left grip has some epoxy filler with both grips showing moderate wear. Good condition. **650.00**

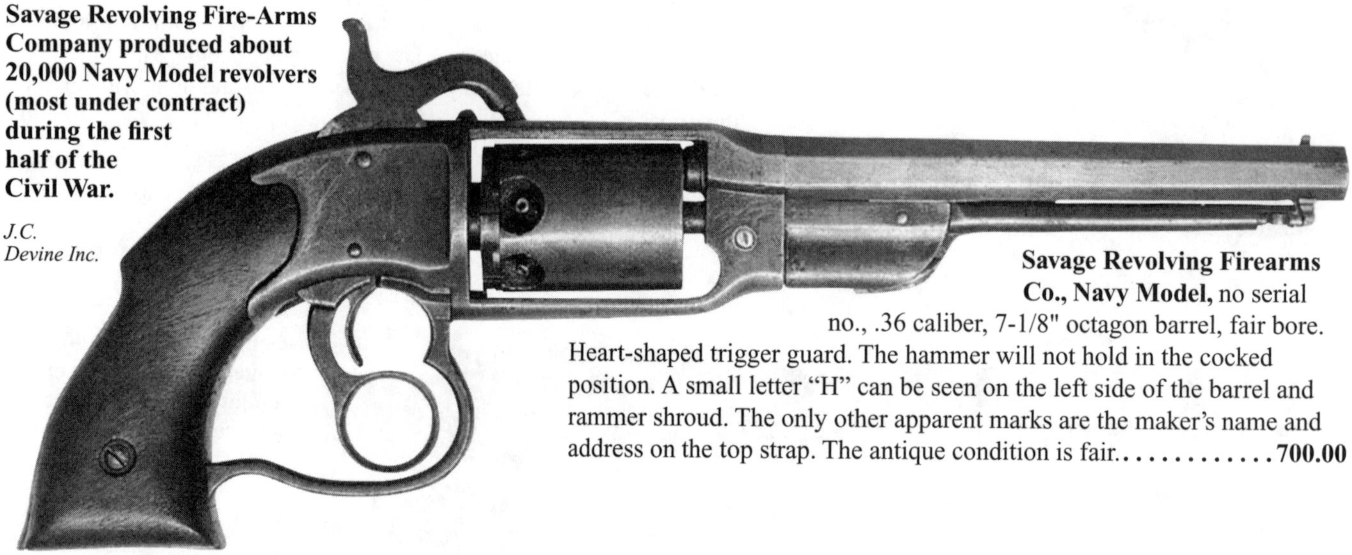

Savage Revolving Fire-Arms Company produced about 20,000 Navy Model revolvers (most under contract) during the first half of the Civil War.

J.C. Devine Inc.

Savage Revolving Firearms Co., Navy Model, no serial no., .36 caliber, 7-1/8" octagon barrel, fair bore. Heart-shaped trigger guard. The hammer will not hold in the cocked position. A small letter "H" can be seen on the left side of the barrel and rammer shroud. The only other apparent marks are the maker's name and address on the top strap. The antique condition is fair............ **700.00**

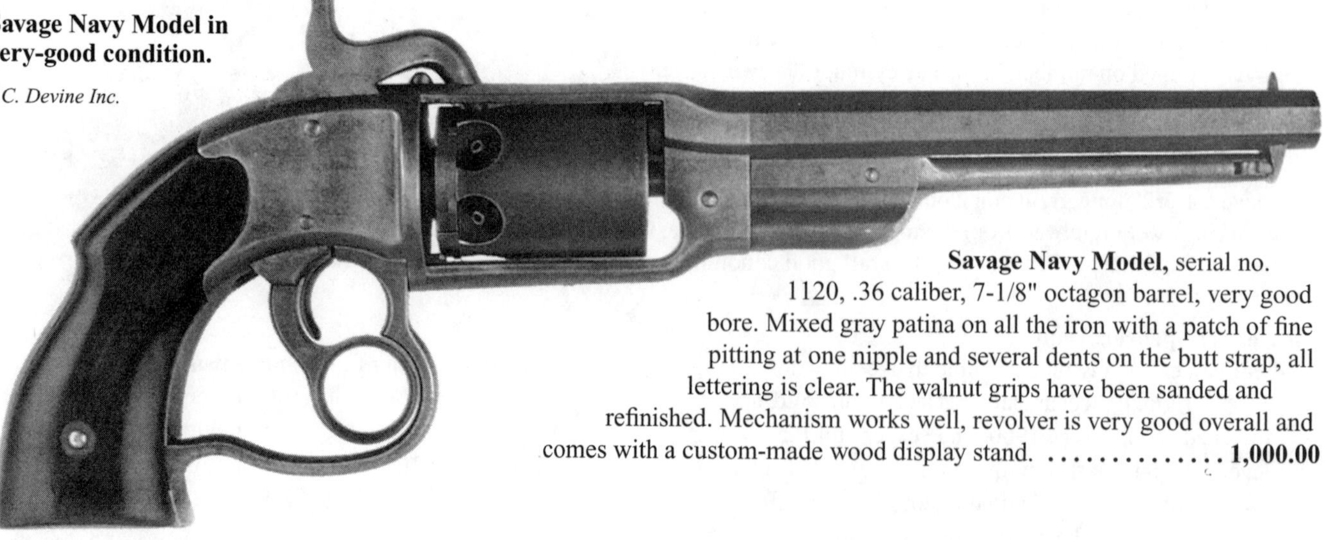

Savage Navy Model in very-good condition.

J.C. Devine Inc.

Savage Navy Model, serial no. 1120, .36 caliber, 7-1/8" octagon barrel, very good bore. Mixed gray patina on all the iron with a patch of fine pitting at one nipple and several dents on the butt strap, all lettering is clear. The walnut grips have been sanded and refinished. Mechanism works well, revolver is very good overall and comes with a custom-made wood display stand. **1,000.00**

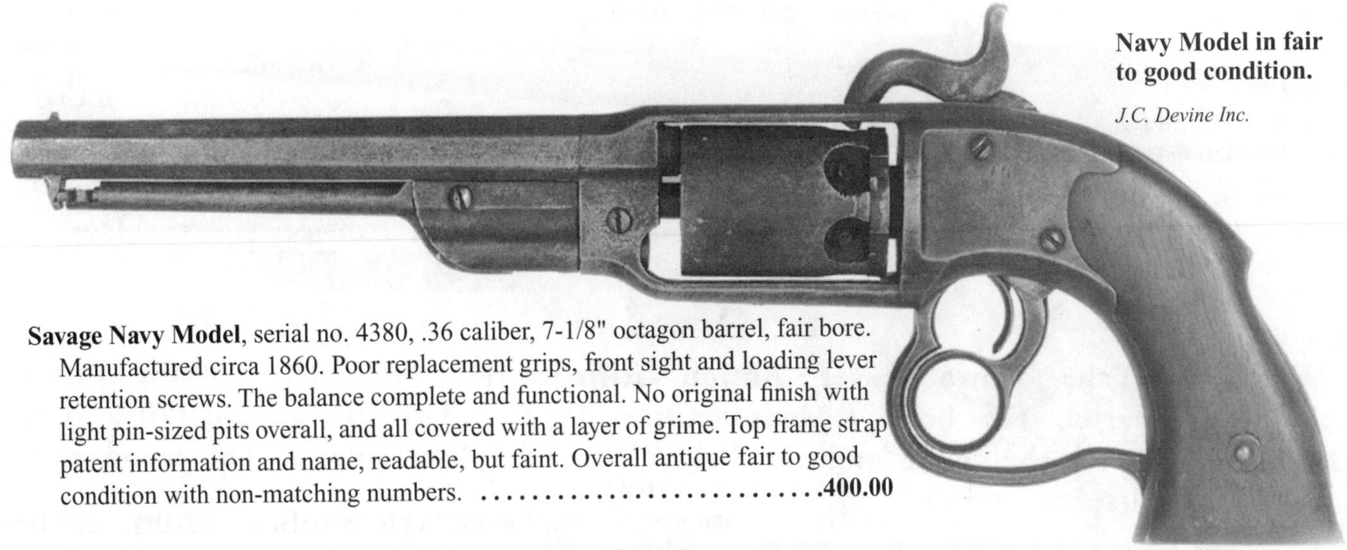

Navy Model in fair to good condition.

J.C. Devine Inc.

Savage Navy Model, serial no. 4380, .36 caliber, 7-1/8" octagon barrel, fair bore. Manufactured circa 1860. Poor replacement grips, front sight and loading lever retention screws. The balance complete and functional. No original finish with light pin-sized pits overall, and all covered with a layer of grime. Top frame strap patent information and name, readable, but faint. Overall antique fair to good condition with non-matching numbers. **400.00**

The Smith & Wesson Fifth Type, had its rifling changed from three grooves to five.

J.C. Devine Inc.

Smith & Wesson, Model 1, 1st Issue, Fifth Type, Single Action, serial no. 4546, .22 rimfire caliber, 3-1/4", 7-sided barrel with rib, fair bore. Manufactured between 1857-1860. A single action Model 1 spur trigger that grades very good. The ejector rod may be an early replacement and the hammer spur screw needs attention. **700.00**

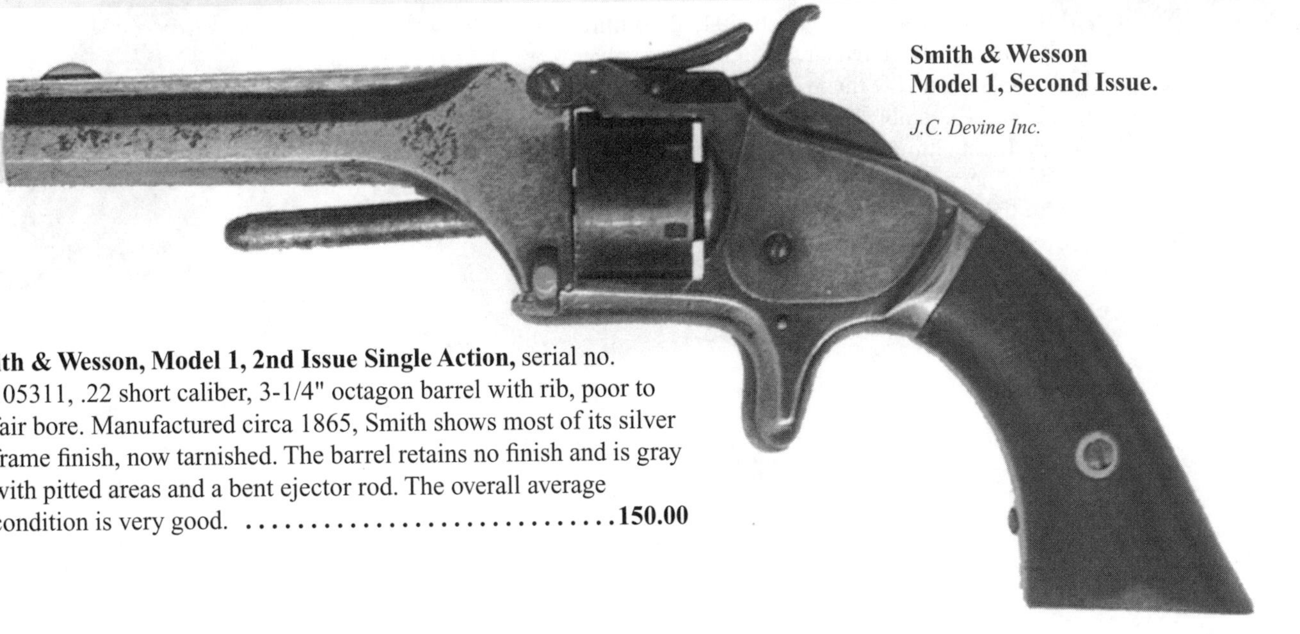

Smith & Wesson Model 1, Second Issue.

J.C. Devine Inc.

Smith & Wesson, Model 1, 2nd Issue Single Action, serial no. 105311, .22 short caliber, 3-1/4" octagon barrel with rib, poor to fair bore. Manufactured circa 1865, Smith shows most of its silver frame finish, now tarnished. The barrel retains no finish and is gray with pitted areas and a bent ejector rod. The overall average condition is very good. **150.00**

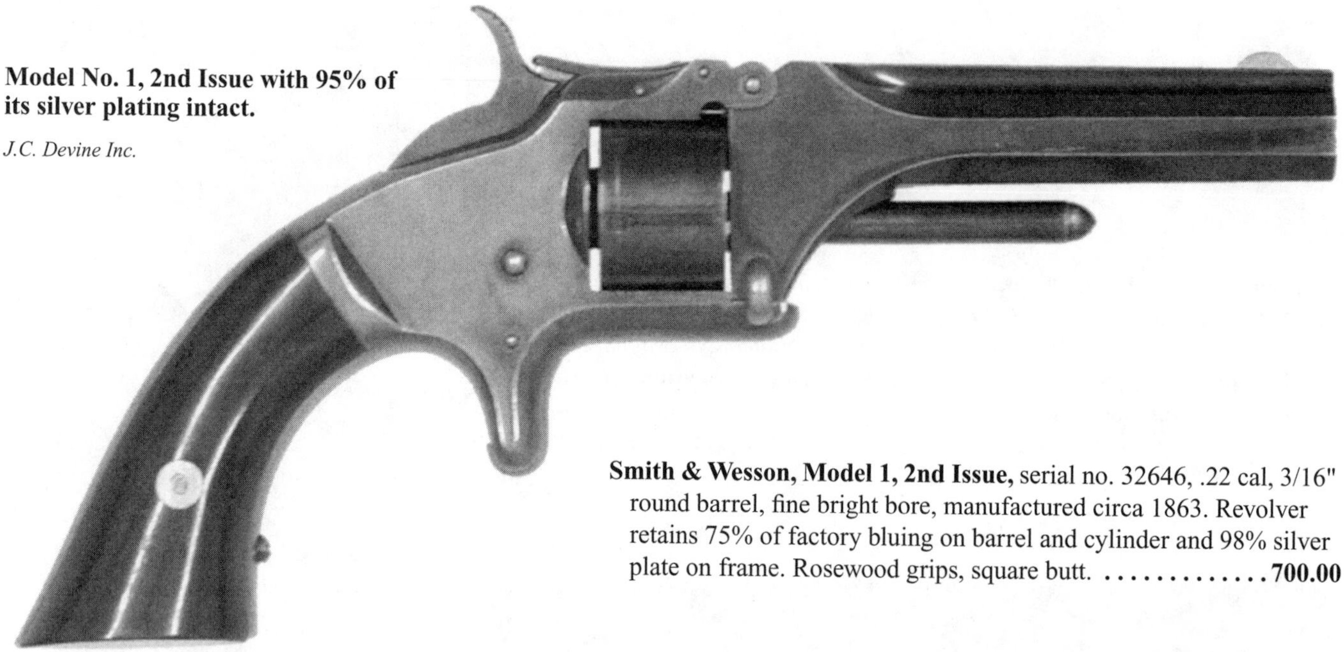

Model No. 1, 2nd Issue with 95% of its silver plating intact.

J.C. Devine Inc.

Smith & Wesson, Model 1, 2nd Issue, serial no. 32646, .22 cal, 3/16" round barrel, fine bright bore, manufactured circa 1863. Revolver retains 75% of factory bluing on barrel and cylinder and 98% silver plate on frame. Rosewood grips, square butt. **700.00**

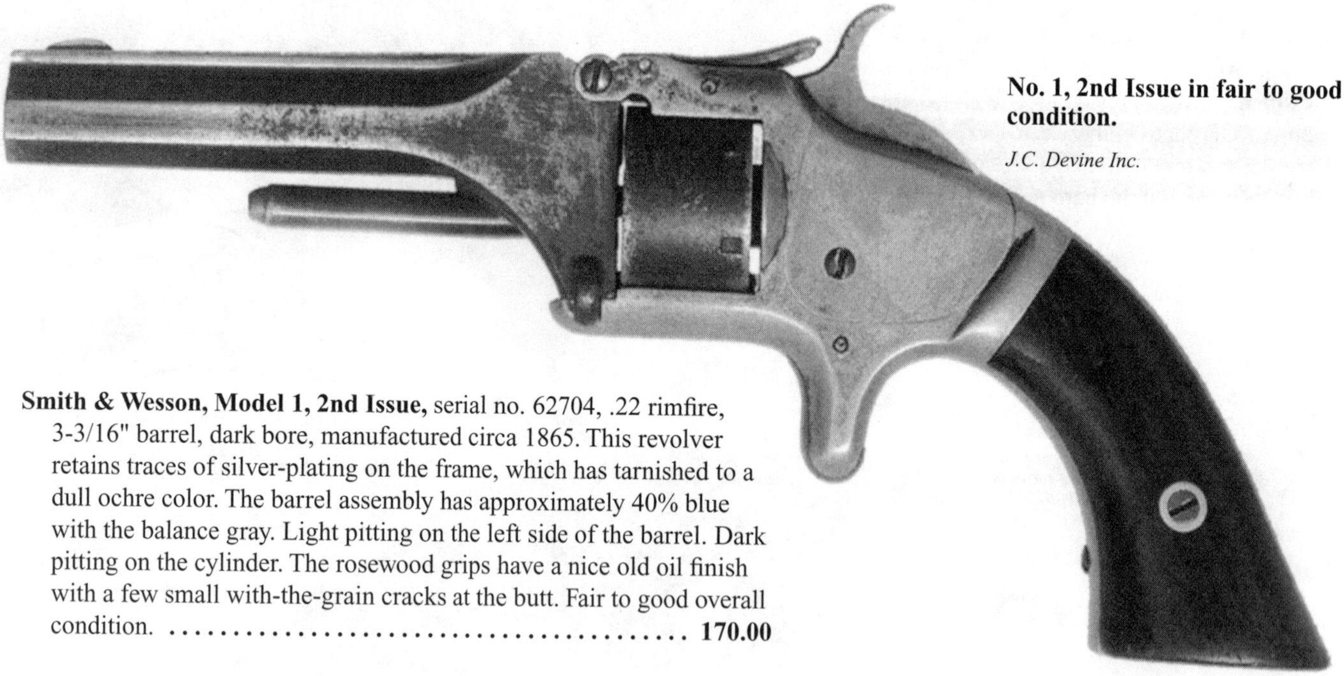

No. 1, 2nd Issue in fair to good condition.

J.C. Devine Inc.

Smith & Wesson, Model 1, 2nd Issue, serial no. 62704, .22 rimfire, 3-3/16" barrel, dark bore, manufactured circa 1865. This revolver retains traces of silver-plating on the frame, which has tarnished to a dull ochre color. The barrel assembly has approximately 40% blue with the balance gray. Light pitting on the left side of the barrel. Dark pitting on the cylinder. The rosewood grips have a nice old oil finish with a few small with-the-grain cracks at the butt. Fair to good overall condition. **170.00**

Smith & Wesson Model No. 1, 2nd Issue with 98% of its nickel plating intact.
J.C. Devine Inc.

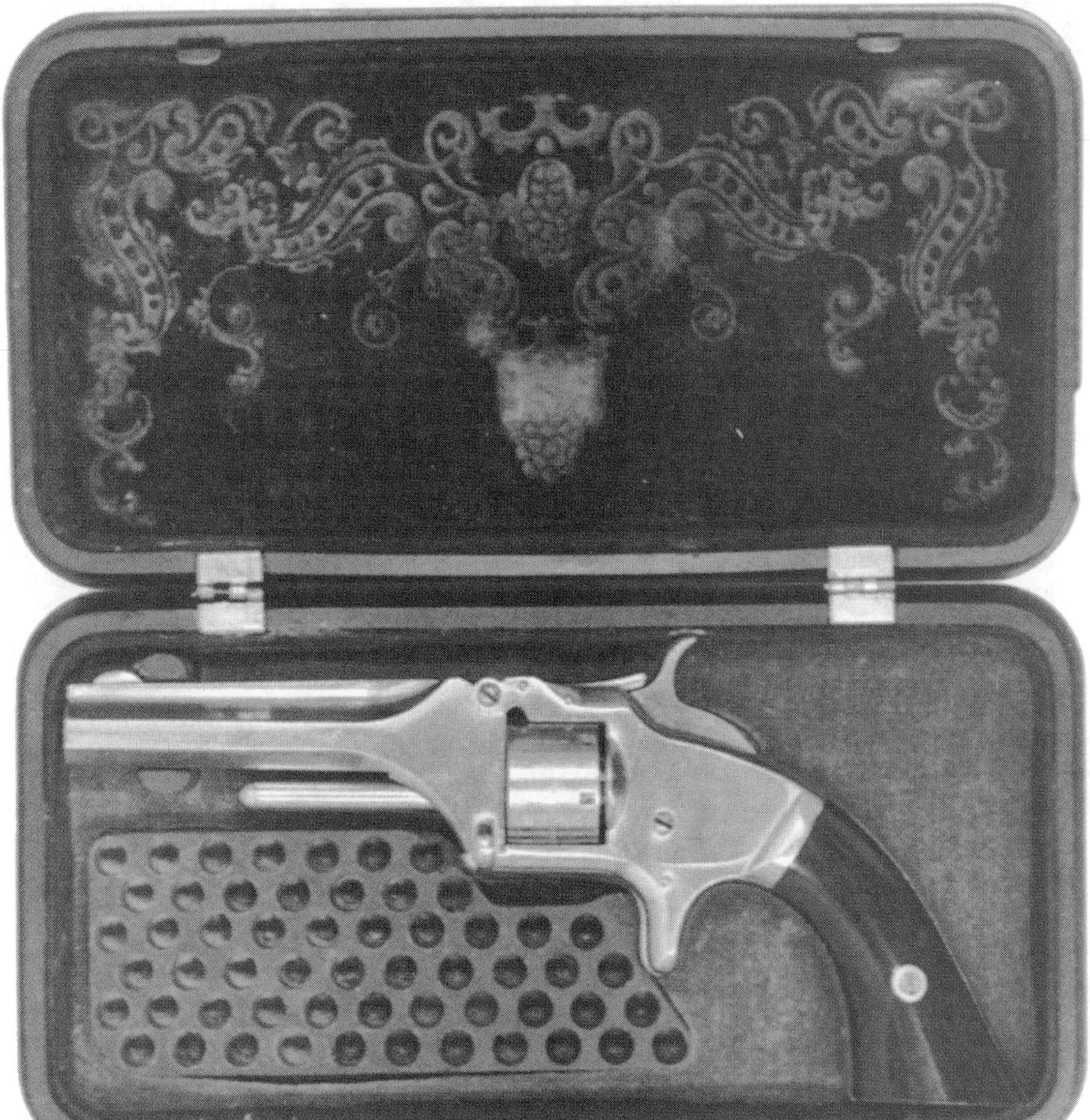

Smith & Wesson Model No. 1, 2nd Issue

Serial no. 83055, .22 rimfire, 3-1/8" barrel, very good bore, fine nickel-plated revolver which retains 98% of its nickel finish with only a few very small peen marks above the trigger on the right side of the frame. Fine case colors on the hammer. The rosewood grips are also fine and are stamped on the interior with the serial number (83055). The revolver is housed in an original revolver lid motif gutta-percha case that has one small chip on the outside edge of the lid and two small chips in the interior shell holder. The interior maroon velveteen lining is in very good condition with some minor fading of the color. A fine cased Smith and a rare accessory. **3,500.00**

7-shot, .22-caliber pocketsize revolver. This one is very good with much silver plate, on the brass frame, fine rosewood grips, nice steel barrel free from pitting, and good strong markings. Cylinder bears the 1855, 1859, and 1860 patent dates. The revolver still cocks and functions perfectly, except the cylinder does not fully lock in place when cocked, and just needs a tiny spring in the cylinder stop device on the top of the frame, 79,000 serial range. **265.00**

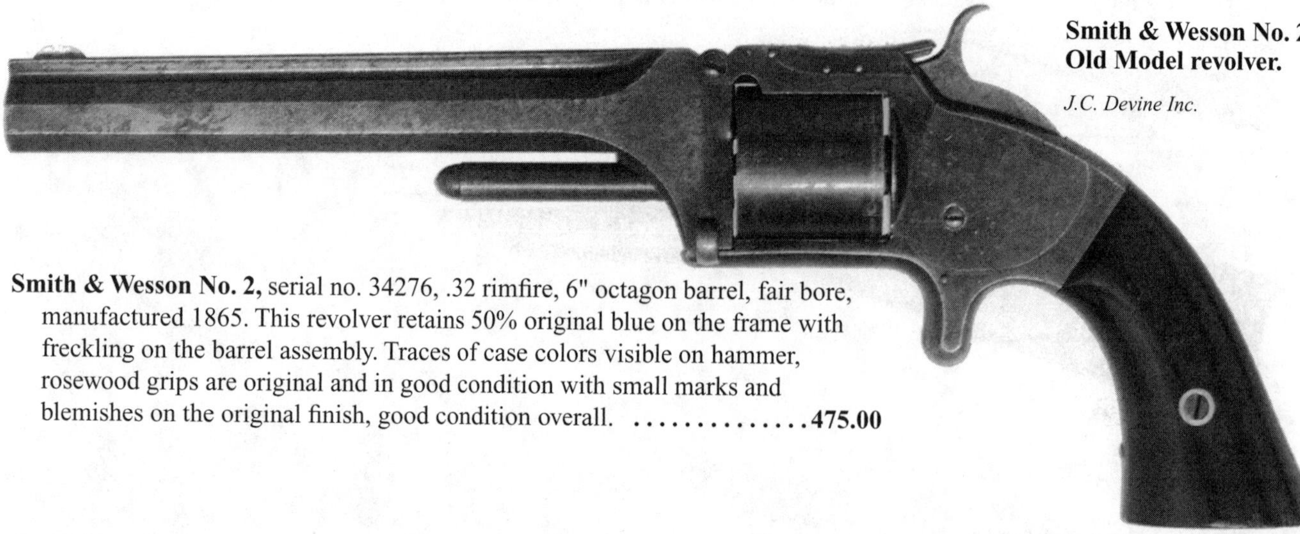

Smith & Wesson No. 2 Old Model revolver.

J.C. Devine Inc.

Smith & Wesson No. 2, serial no. 34276, .32 rimfire, 6" octagon barrel, fair bore, manufactured 1865. This revolver retains 50% original blue on the frame with freckling on the barrel assembly. Traces of case colors visible on hammer, rosewood grips are original and in good condition with small marks and blemishes on the original finish, good condition overall. **475.00**

Smith & Wesson, Model 2, Old Army

Brass framed, serial no. 15, fine condition, action works. **1,200.00**

Serial no. 46726, .32 rimfire long, 6" octagonal with rib barrel, poor bore, manufactured from 1861-1874, three-pin, retains thinning original blue on the frame behind the cylinder. The balance is gray-brown with scattered pitting and dark spotting. The rosewood grips show considerable finish with no chips or cracks. Good condition, the frame latch spring needs attention and the hinge is loose. **370.00**

Long barrel, overall very good condition, complete with a great full flap holster. Gun is overall gray steel with crisp S&W barrel markings. Edges are sharp, all parts original, serial is war date in 25,xxx serial range, action is crisp and solid. Only defect is the spring in the closing catch at the bottom of the barrel lug, which is weak. This revolver comes with its brown-russet leather, full-flap holster with brass closing final and single riveted belt loop on the back in good to very-good condition. **595.00**

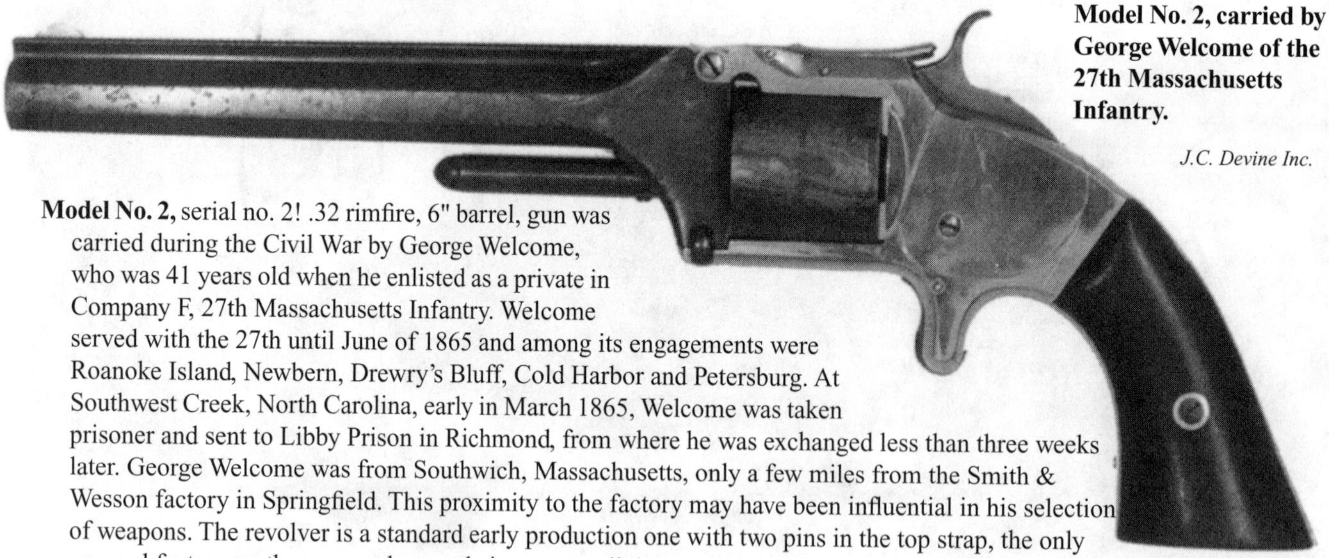

Model No. 2, carried by George Welcome of the 27th Massachusetts Infantry.

J.C. Devine Inc.

Model No. 2, serial no. 2! .32 rimfire, 6" barrel, gun was carried during the Civil War by George Welcome, who was 41 years old when he enlisted as a private in Company F, 27th Massachusetts Infantry. Welcome served with the 27th until June of 1865 and among its engagements were Roanoke Island, Newbern, Drewry's Bluff, Cold Harbor and Petersburg. At Southwest Creek, North Carolina, early in March 1865, Welcome was taken prisoner and sent to Libby Prison in Richmond, from where he was exchanged less than three weeks later. George Welcome was from Southwich, Massachusetts, only a few miles from the Smith & Wesson factory in Springfield. This proximity to the factory may have been influential in his selection of weapons. The revolver is a standard early production one with two pins in the top strap, the only unusual feature on the very early guns being a very slight recess for the cartridge rim at the rear of the cylinder. The frame retains all of a refinish in nickel plate. The cylinder and barrel retain 60% reblue over some light pitting. The rosewood grips have been refinished, fit well, and are each stamped on the inside with the number six or nine. The refinish appears to be of factory quality, although it bears none of the later markings used to denote factory rework. Included are a photocopied picture of George Welcome from the regimental history, and several pages of material on the history of the 27th. **2,500.00**

Springfield Arms, Pocket, .22 caliber, virtually identical to the Smith & Wesson No. I, this brass frame example made by Springfield Arms Co., circa 1863, is in overall very-good condition, being all original and mechanically perfect except for a small catch on the loading gate. **225.00**

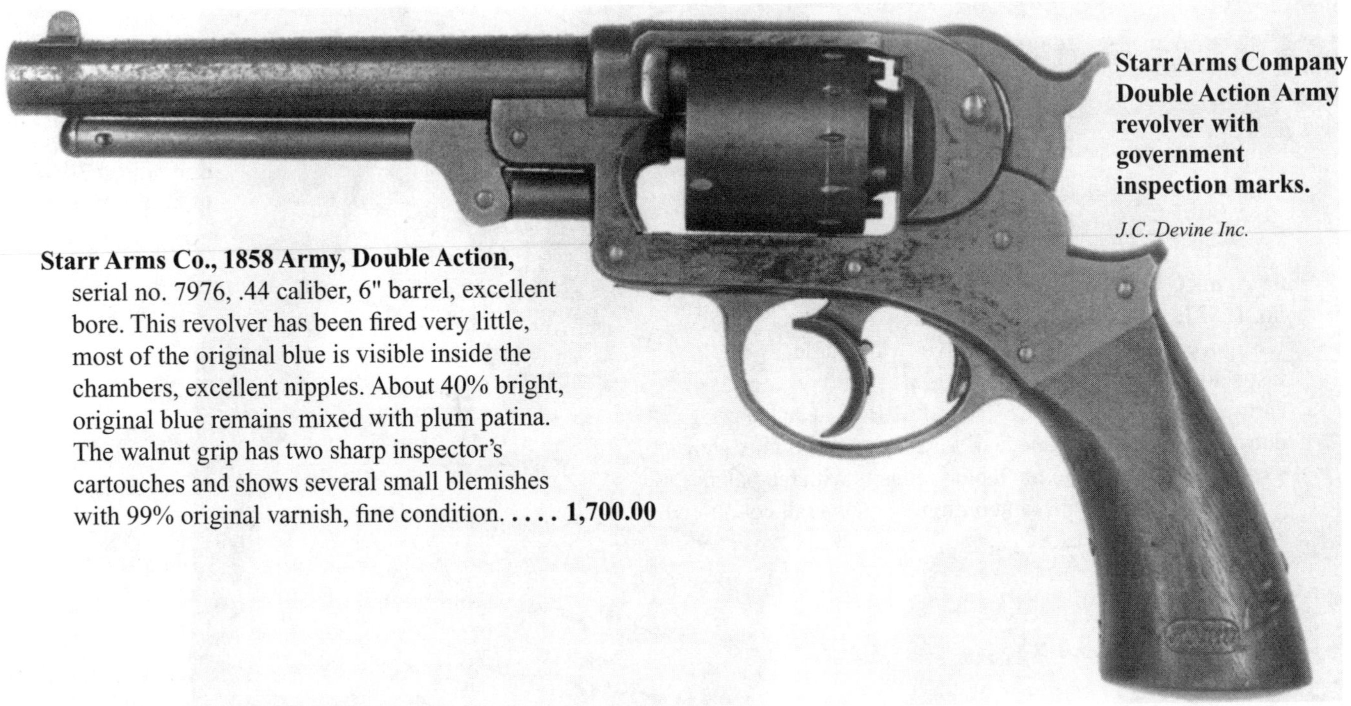

Starr Arms Company Double Action Army revolver with government inspection marks.

J.C. Devine Inc.

Starr Arms Co., 1858 Army, Double Action, serial no. 7976, .44 caliber, 6" barrel, excellent bore. This revolver has been fired very little, most of the original blue is visible inside the chambers, excellent nipples. About 40% bright, original blue remains mixed with plum patina. The walnut grip has two sharp inspector's cartouches and shows several small blemishes with 99% original varnish, fine condition. **1,700.00**

Starr Arms Co., 1858 Army, Double Action
Serial no. 5720, .44 caliber, 6" round barrel, fair to good bore. A Starr Army with a gray-brown metal surface and several dings, mostly on the left side of the barrel. Several areas show file marks and scattered light pitting. Small inspector's "W" is visible on left of barrel and on the cylinder under the serial number. Cartouches show weakly on both grip panels, but the initials cannot be determined with any certainty, good condition. . . .**650.00**

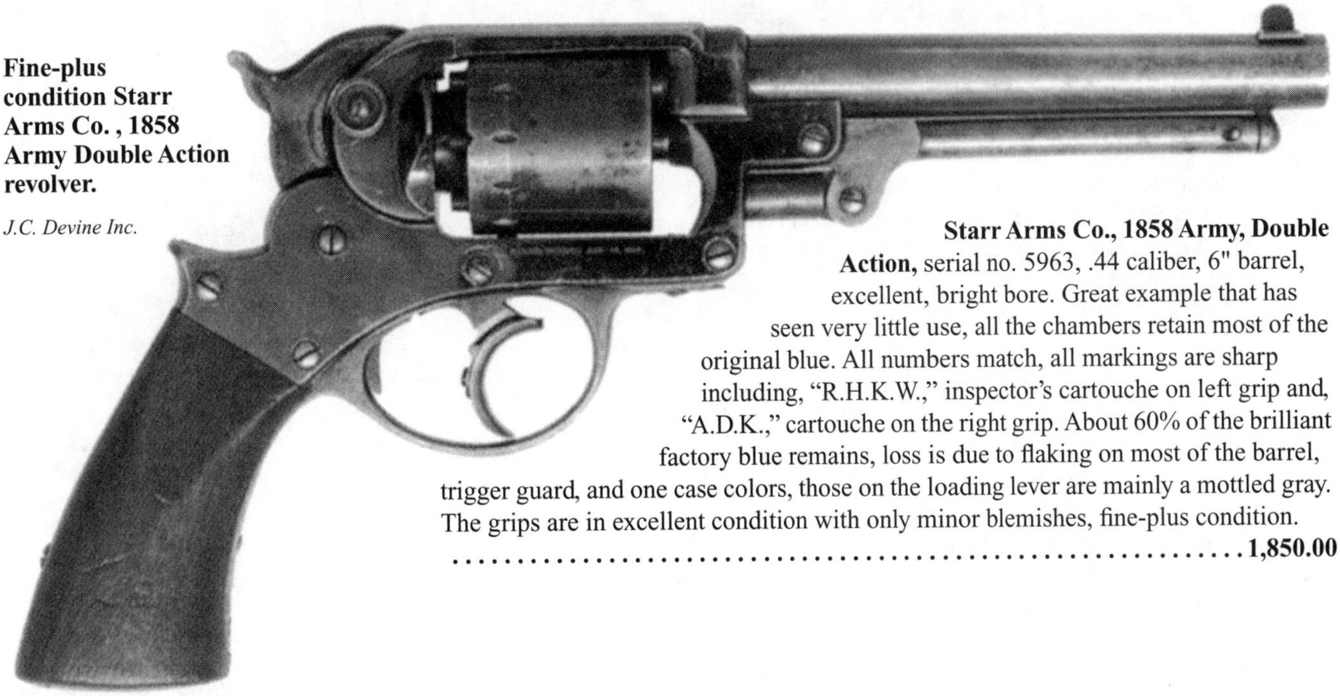

Fine-plus condition Starr Arms Co. , 1858 Army Double Action revolver.

J.C. Devine Inc.

Starr Arms Co., 1858 Army, Double Action, serial no. 5963, .44 caliber, 6" barrel, excellent, bright bore. Great example that has seen very little use, all the chambers retain most of the original blue. All numbers match, all markings are sharp including, "R.H.K.W.," inspector's cartouche on left grip and, "A.D.K.," cartouche on the right grip. About 60% of the brilliant factory blue remains, loss is due to flaking on most of the barrel, trigger guard, and one case colors, those on the loading lever are mainly a mottled gray. The grips are in excellent condition with only minor blemishes, fine-plus condition. **1,850.00**

Starr Arms Co., 1858 Army, Double Action
Serial no. 15603, .44 caliber, 6" barrel, good bore. The cylinder is numbered 11637. The revolver has an old reblue that has turned a dark plum, all lettering on metal is clear. The grip is very good with two illegible inspector's cartouches, good-plus condition.. . . . **650.00**

Serial no. 10980, .44 caliber, standard civilian model, fair condition. Gray metal shows areas of light pitting, non-functioning action. Grips show wear and chipping at butt. **316.00**

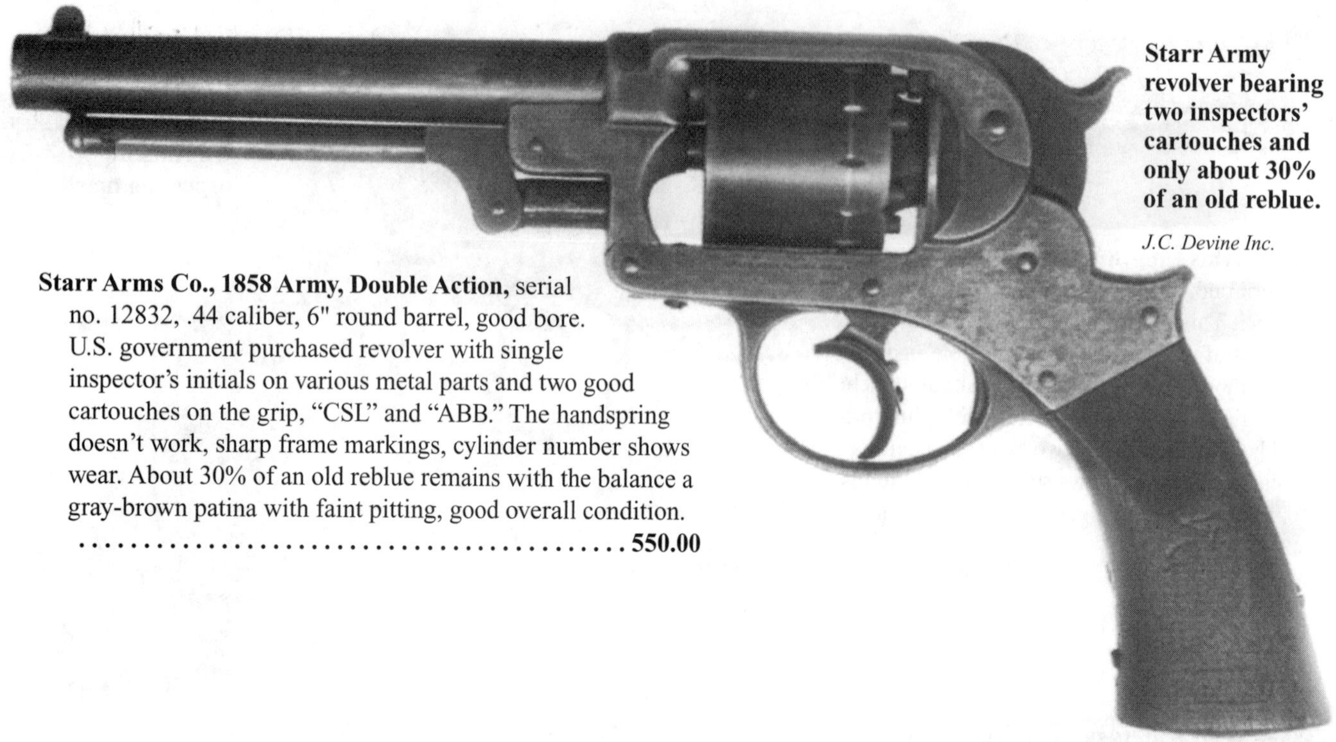

Starr Army revolver bearing two inspectors' cartouches and only about 30% of an old reblue.

J.C. Devine Inc.

Starr Arms Co., 1858 Army, Double Action, serial no. 12832, .44 caliber, 6" round barrel, good bore. U.S. government purchased revolver with single inspector's initials on various metal parts and two good cartouches on the grip, "CSL" and "ABB." The handspring doesn't work, sharp frame markings, cylinder number shows wear. About 30% of an old reblue remains with the balance a gray-brown patina with faint pitting, good overall condition. **550.00**

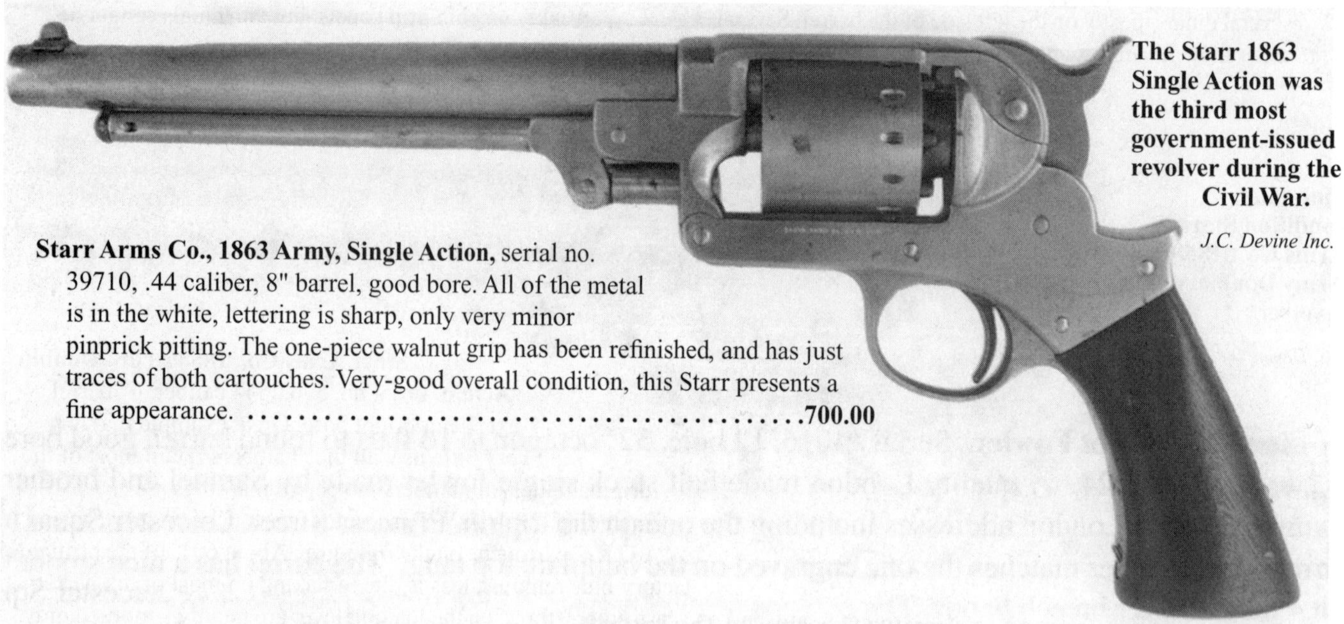

The Starr 1863 Single Action was the third most government-issued revolver during the Civil War.

J.C. Devine Inc.

Starr Arms Co., 1863 Army, Single Action, serial no. 39710, .44 caliber, 8" barrel, good bore. All of the metal is in the white, lettering is sharp, only very minor pinprick pitting. The one-piece walnut grip has been refinished, and has just traces of both cartouches. Very-good overall condition, this Starr presents a fine appearance. **700.00**

Starr Arms Co., 1863 Army, Single Action

.44 caliber, serial no. 27809, 8" barrel, fine action with crisp markings, Civil War inspector cartouches on both grips, 35% original blue, no pitting. Fine example of this handsome and well-balanced revolver. **1,425.00**

Serial no. 39611, .44 caliber, 8" barrel, very good bore. Matching serial numbers, good markings, legible cartouche on right side of stock, partially legible cartouche on left side. Most of the metal has a dark-gray patina with some faint pitting, the frame has quite a bit of old black paint and traces elsewhere, the bottom of the butt with scratched, "USN." Very-good condition. **850.00**

Serial no. 84378, .44 caliber, standard civilian model, mottled gray metal showing areas of light pitting. Barrel with period non-factory modification comprising a band at muzzle with fitting to retain loading lever. No markings visible, but serial number. Grip strap drilled for shoulder stock. Grips show wear and small chips. Good to very-good condition. **374.00**

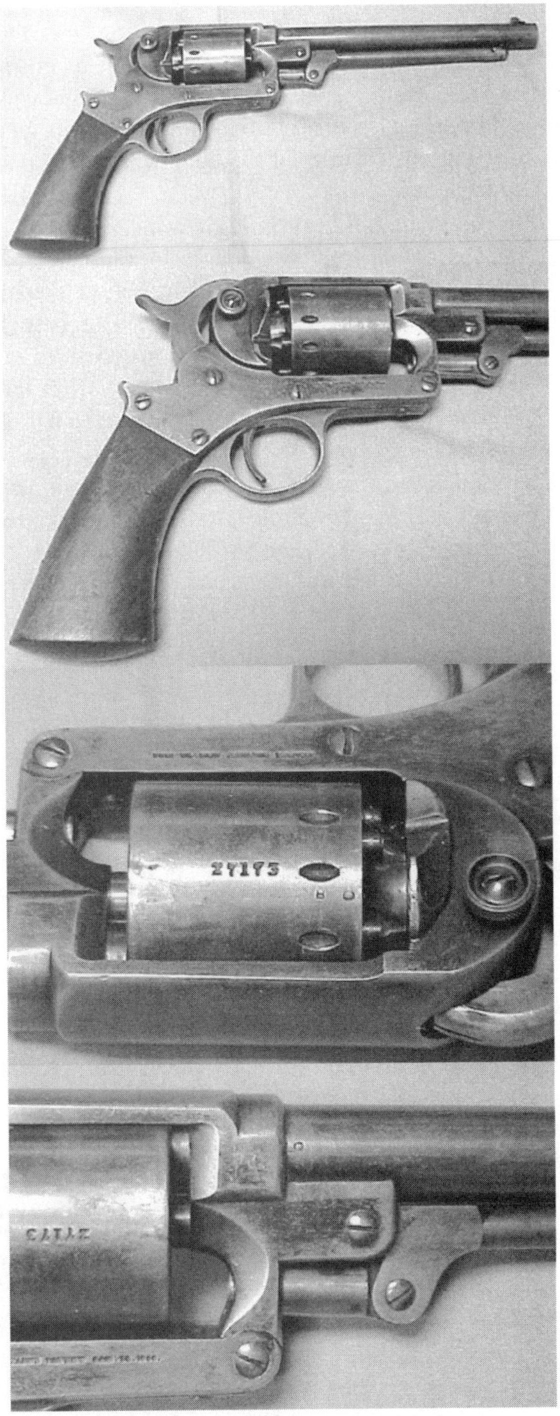

Starr 1863 Single Action revolver.

The Sharpsburg Arsenal

Starr Arms Co., 1863 Army, Single Action

.44 caliber, 8" round barrel, serial no. 27173 matches with cylinder, plus secondary number 26472 on opposite side. There is a cartouche on each side of the grip with sub-inspector's marks on major components. Retains 10-20% bright blue on barrel, 20-30% on frame and hammer with remaining areas a light brown patina, sound grip with good edges and clear, well struck cartouche on left side, right side is weak. Fine mechanical condition, overall very-good condition. **2,695.00**

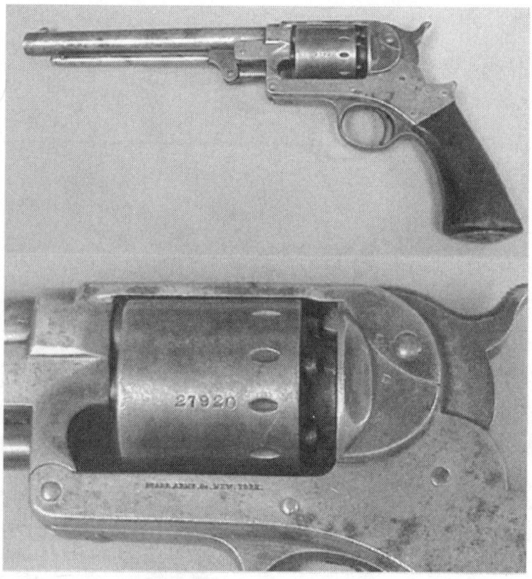

Starr 1863 Single Action with tight action and clear markings.
The Sharpsburg Arsenal

Starr Arms Co., 1863 Army, Single Action, .44 caliber, barrel and frame are in good condition with good markings and inspector's marks. Action is nice and tight with good cylinder nipples. Sharp serial number marking on cylinder, walnut grips are in good condition with coin silver plate added to grip bottom. **1,895.00**

Uhlinger, Pocket, .32 caliber, truly wonderful revolver with mint rosewood grips with high-luster varnish finish, and retaining about 80% original bright factory blue overall. These guns were patent infringements on a patent held by Smith & Wesson. These were usually unmarked except for serial number (as is this one) or marked with fictitious firm names. This one is in 2,300 serial range. About 9" in overall size with a 5" bbl. **795.00**

Warner, Pocket, virtually identical to the Warner percussion revolver, .30-caliber rimfire Warner made in the 1860s. Marked, "Warner's Patent 1857," on the cylinder, 60% barrel blue, balance of metal parts plum, excellent grips and mechanically perfect. **495.00**

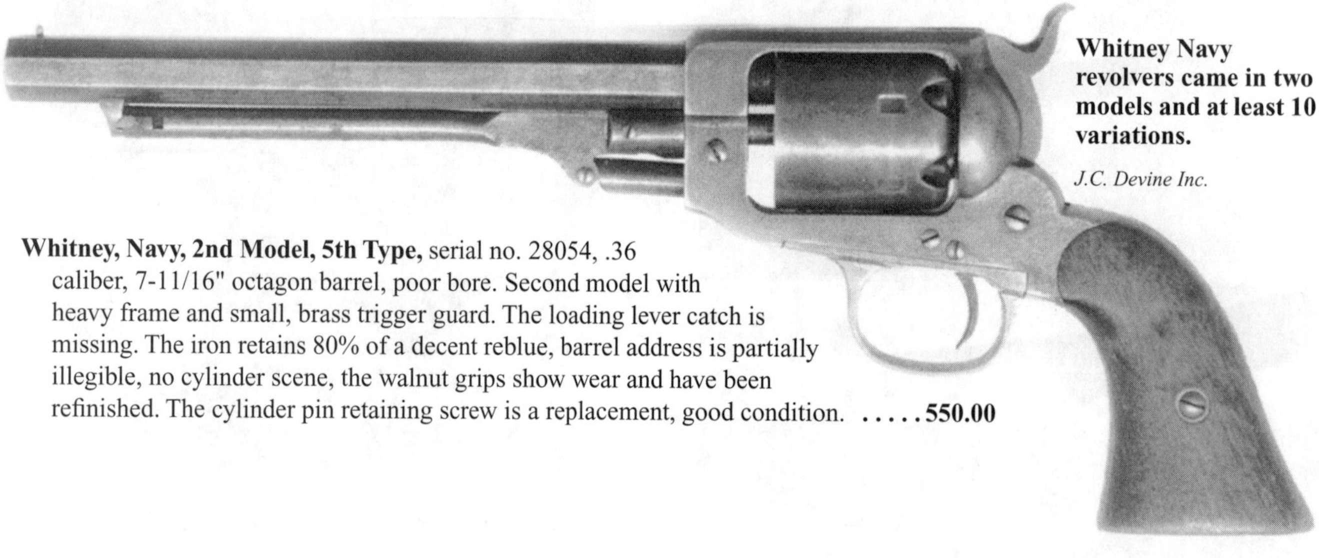

Whitney Navy revolvers came in two models and at least 10 variations.
J.C. Devine Inc.

Whitney, Navy, 2nd Model, 5th Type, serial no. 28054, .36 caliber, 7-11/16" octagon barrel, poor bore. Second model with heavy frame and small, brass trigger guard. The loading lever catch is missing. The iron retains 80% of a decent reblue, barrel address is partially illegible, no cylinder scene, the walnut grips show wear and have been refinished. The cylinder pin retaining screw is a replacement, good condition. **550.00**

Whitney, Navy, 2nd Model, 5th Type

Serial no. 28839, .36 caliber, 7-11/16" octagon barrel, fair bore. Matching serial numbers, clear markings, 2nd Model, 5th type with heavier frame and large brass trigger guard. The cylinder scene was originally applied very lightly on these, and this one is no exception, since 30% remains. Quite a bit of thin blue remains on the barrel's bottom, where it was protected by the loading lever, the balance of the iron has a gray-blue patina with scattered spots of faint to fine pitting. Traces of muted case colors are visible on the hammer and loading lever. The two-piece walnut grips have a repaired crack on the right with surface chips at the butt on the same side, condition is still very good. There are seven shallow notches scribed into the butt, good-plus condition. **950.00**

Whitney, Navy, 2nd Model, 6th Type, .36 caliber, has loading lever with Colt-style catch and five groove rifling in barrel. Serial number in the 30,000 range, all edges and markings are strong, and the metal has a nice, deep plum color (done with "cold blue" or similar coloring agent), which looks very nice. The grips are excellent, the action is as tight and crisp as new, and the gun is 100% original and complete except for a replacement wing-screw, which secures the loading lever and cylinder pin. Overall good to very-good condition. **850.00**

Whitney Pocket Model revolver, 2nd Model, 2nd Type.

J.C. Devine Inc.

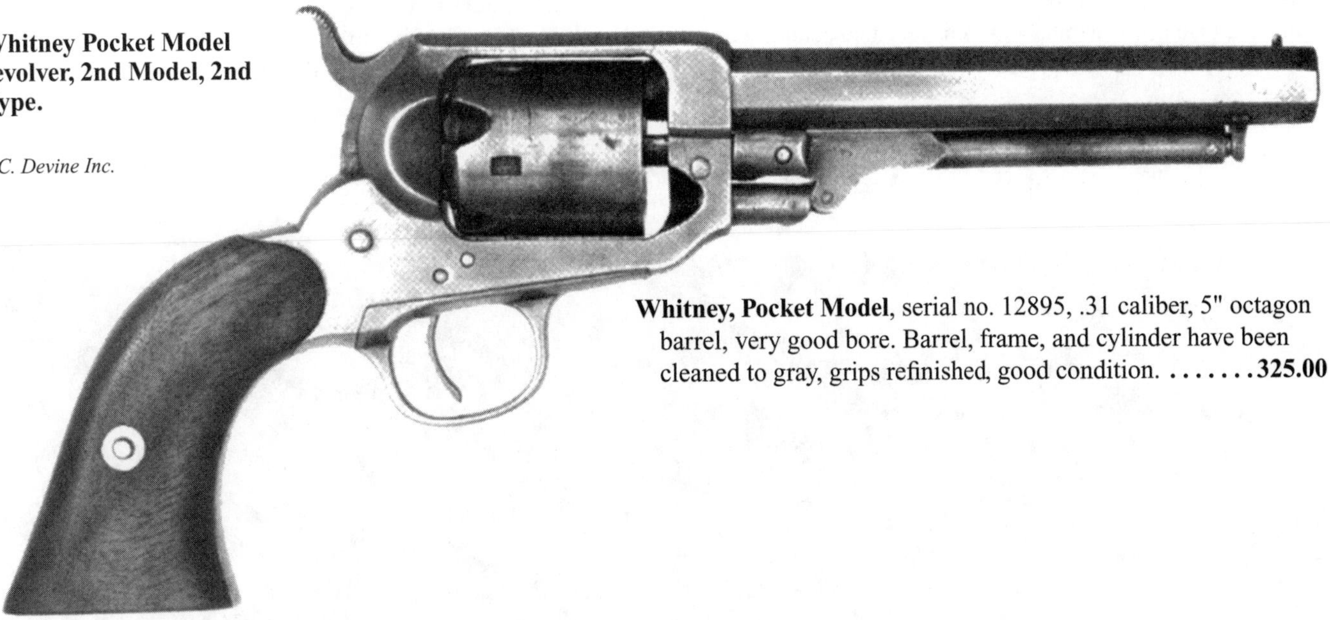

Whitney, Pocket Model, serial no. 12895, .31 caliber, 5" octagon barrel, very good bore. Barrel, frame, and cylinder have been cleaned to gray, grips refinished, good condition. **325.00**

Pistols, Import

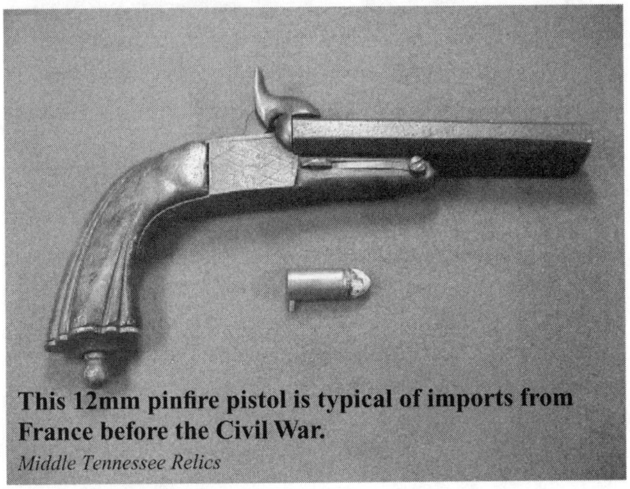

This 12mm pinfire pistol is typical of imports from France before the Civil War.

Middle Tennessee Relics

France, Pinfire, Civil War-era, double-barrel 12mm French import pinfire vest pistol. The pistol has a smooth, brown aged patina and still works perfectly. This one comes complete with an unfired original 12mm pinfire cartridge. **275.00**

Revolvers, Import

England, Kerr

.44 caliber, single-action, serial number 11075, fine condition overall with a smooth steel-gray patina. Traces of original blue under the barrel and in the frame's recesses. Excellent bore and mechanics. Crisp markings, "London Armoury," on the frame and, "LAC," on the barrel. Belonged to Captain Cushman of a New York Infantry Regiment. Excellent diamond checkered grips, complete with lanyard loop and ring. **2,500.00**

Patent No. 202 early type .36 caliber ,5-1/2" octagonal barrel marked, "LONDON," with, "LAC," proofs. Grooved top strap and engraved back action lock marked, "LONDON ARMOURY CO.," Condition is excellent, retains 70-80% bright blue overall with 10% case colors on hammer and lock plate. Grip is sound with strong checkering. **3295.00**

France, Drenotte, ivory grip engraved with the name of an officer of the 3rd Louisiana Volunteer Infantry (CSA). **2,500.00**

France, LeFaucheux, marked on barrel, "Inv. On E. Lefaucheux Brte Paris." **1,200.00**

France, LeFaucheux, 7mm

Import, nice grips, with ejector rod, very fine condition, 7mm pinfire, 6-shot cylinder, marked "LeFaucheux." **275.00**

Nice grips, with ejector rod, very fine condition, 6-shot engraved cylinder, marked, "LeFaucheux.". **275.00**

France, LeFaucheux, 12mm

Holster 6-shot cylinder, Holster in fine condition as is the revolver. Come with six pinfire cartridges and a glass display case. **695.00**

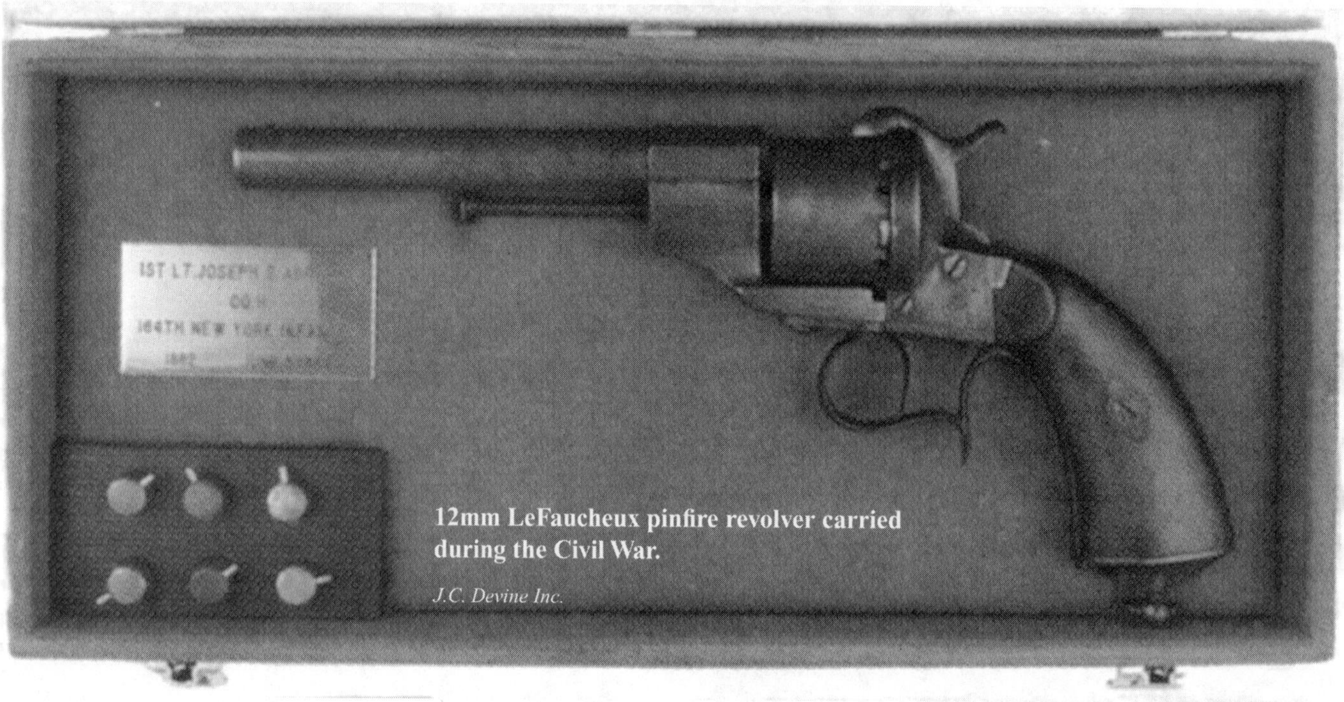

12mm LeFaucheux pinfire revolver carried during the Civil War.

J.C. Devine Inc.

France, LeFaucheux, 12mm, serial no. 19920, 12mm caliber, 6-1/4" barrel. The frame and barrel are marked, "INV on E. Lefaucheux/Brevet SGDG (Paris)." The cylinder has a name neatly engraved in small punch dots, "Lieut. J.S. Abraham 164 Reg.T.N.Y." The hinge on the loading gate is broken. All of the metal has a gray patina, minor fine pitting, very good walnut grips. The revolver is in a modern walnut case with six pinfire cartridges. **1,300.00**

Serial no. 5197, 12mm caliber, 6" barrel, good bore. Appears to be identical to the Model 1854, but does not have a spur on the trigger guard. The only markings on the revolver are, "LF 5197," on the right side of the barrel lug. Missing the handspring, dark patina on metal with very fine pitting, refinished grips in good condition. **175.00**

France, LeMat Percussion, serial no. 1687, .42 and .63 caliber, 6-1/2" octagonal upper barrel marked "Col. LeMat Bte. s.g.d.g. Paris." Checkered walnut grips, condition: fair to good. Gray metal has been cleaned and shows scattered areas of light pitting. Loading lever assembly missing, grips worn. **6,900.00**

Revolver Terminology

Backstrap: The part of the revolver or pistol frame that is exposed at the rear of the grip.

Bluing: The blue or black finish of the metal parts of a gun. Bluing minimizes light reflection, gives a finish to the bare metal, and protects somewhat against rust.

Center Fire: A design of ammunition in which the primer is centrally located in the base of the cartridge case.

Cylinder Scene: Many revolvers of the Civil War era had various pictures, or scenes engraved on the cylinders.

Double Action: A revolver that may be fired by just pulling the trigger to cock the hammer and rotate the cylinder to the next chamber.

Pinfire: The pinfire system is one in which the firing pin is actually a part of the cartridge.

Rimfire: A rimmed or flanged cartridge with the priming mixture located inside the rim of the case. To fire this type of cartridge, the firing pin must impact on this outer rim.

Single Action: The hammer has to be cocked manually on a single action revolver. Depressing the trigger will only fire a fully cocked revolver.

Also see: Groupings; Bullets, Cartridges, and Projectiles; and Accoutrements.

Chapter 17
Swords

During the Civil War, the sword served as both a weapon and a symbol of rank. Among the enlisted men, only cavalry troopers, some artillery soldiers, sergeants, and musicians carried swords or sabers. Officers, both combat and staff, carried swords, more as a privilege entitled by their rank than as a weapon of self-defense.

Though often used interchangeably, the terms "sword" and "saber" denote two very different forms of weapon. A sword is a long, straight-bladed weapon with the primary function to denote rank or status. A saber, on the other hand, is a weapon with a curved blade with the sole function being that of enabling the user to strike a blow. Sabers were most often carried by mounted troops during the Civil War.

Sword collecting offers many areas for the enthusiast. First, one can easily assemble a "type collection" of Civil War swords and sabers. This could include the Model 1850 Staff and Field Sword, a Model 1860 Staff Sword, an 1860 Medical Staff Sword, a Model 1840 and Model 1860 Saber, a Model 1840 NCO's sword, as well as a Musician's sword, a Foot Artillery Sword, a Model 1852 Naval officer's Sword, a Marine NCO sword, and a Model 1860 Naval Cutlass. From this point, a collector might focus on manufacturers or even inscribed presentation swords. The good news is that a lot of these swords have survived and are still available to a person just beginning a collection.

Confederate swords and sabers, however, will present some costly obstacles to collectors. Though many of the Confederacy's blades originated in U.S. arsenals, many were made after secession from the Union by southern manufacturers. These Confederate-produced blades are well beyond the means of an average or beginning collector.

Whatever approach one may decide for assembling a sword collection, one will benefit from years of research that is now available in any number of books on the topic. This is one area of Civil War collecting that is well documented, making it an ideal area for new collectors to safely enter the realm of Civil War relics.

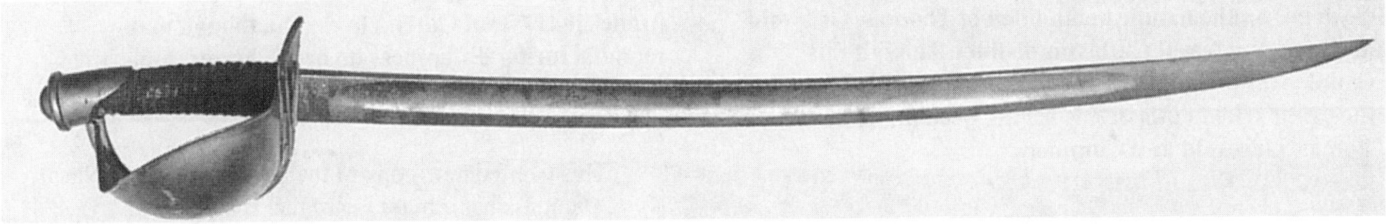

J.C. Devine Inc.

Collecting Hints

Pros:

- Swords are impressive. More so than other relics, a sword will capture the attention of young, old, male, and female. There is a lot of "wow" factor for the dollar when you own and display a sword.
- Swords and sabers are relatively stable. As long as you don't handle the blades and you store the relics in a low humidity environment, deterioration will be minimal.
- Many swords and sabers have been handed down through the ages. There were a wide variety of makes and manufacturers during the war years, so there are plenty of choices for today's collector.
- Research has been intense in this area. Good references are available to assist a collector in determining origin, use, and scarcity.

Cons:

- Confederate swords and sabers sell for very large sums. The high values have lured some into creating swords by assembling pieces or by out-right manufacturing forgeries.
- The attractiveness of high-dollar prices has tempted many dealers to call anything "Confederate" that does not fit the immediate, accepted pattern of a regulation sword or saber.
- This is an area of the hobby where repairs and replacement of missing parts seems to be an accepted norm. It can be difficult to ascertain if the grip on a sword or all of the parts of it were always there, or if they had been expertly replaced in the last twenty years. This sort of alteration does not seem to be regarded as inappropriate within the hobby, so it is up to the collector (and not the dealer) to know exactly what they are examining.

Availability ★★
Price ★★★
Reproduction Alert ★★★★

Confederate Cutlasses

Naval

Copying the grip of the Model 1833 Foot Artillery Sword, this Naval Cutlass is a fine example of the products from Confederate manufacturer, Thomas, Griswold and Company.

J.C. Devine Inc.

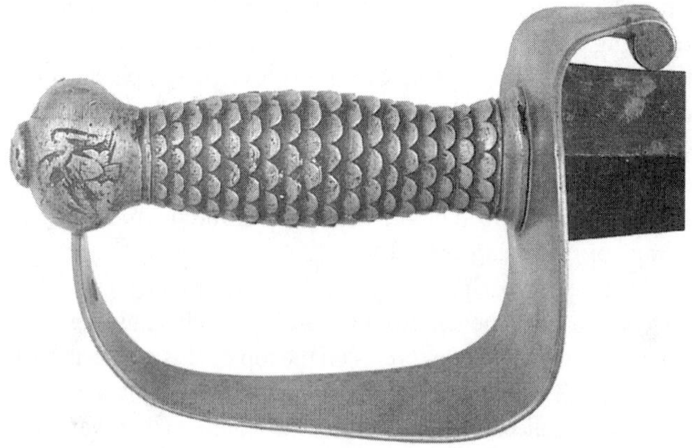

The detail on the handle and quillon of Thomas, Griswold and Company Naval Cutlass is distinct. Though this example was marked, the casting can be used to identify other, unmarked cutlasses as having been made by Thomas, Griswold and Company.

Made by Thomas, Griswold & Company. The 21-1/4" blade is marked, "T.G.&Co./N.O.," and has a dark-gray patina with scattered light pitting, markings are strong and blade is full. The brass hilt has an ocher patina. No scabbard, very-good-plus condition. **2,400.00**

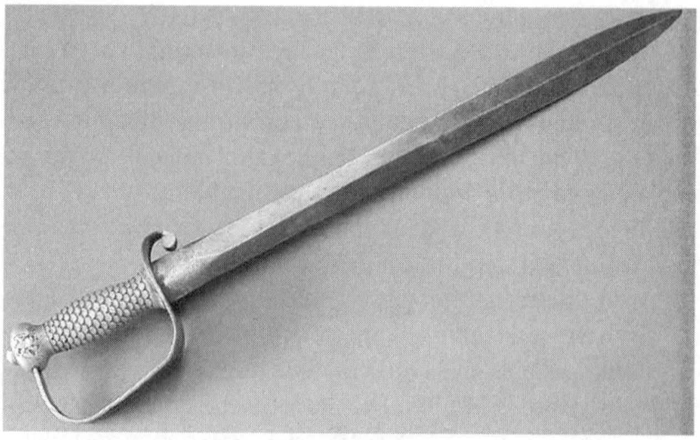

The Confederate Naval Cutlass was a copy of the U.S. Model 1841 Naval Cutlass in design, though many manufacturing differences do occur. For example, the handle of the Confederate version is a solid, single casting.

Richmond Arsenal

This Confederate copy of the U.S. Model 1841 Naval cutlass has a brass guard that is solid cast. A U.S. cutlass had three iron rivets that attach the blade to the guard. The blade is also smaller in width. The overall length is 26", the blade is 21", and the width at the hilt is 1-3/8". The patina is a soft gray and there is no pitting. **3,500.00**

Confederate Sabers

Often referred to as the "Dog River" style of Confederate saber, the blade and scabbard on this example most closely resemble the sabers of the Confederate States Armory at Kenansville, Georgia.

Battleground Antiques, Inc.

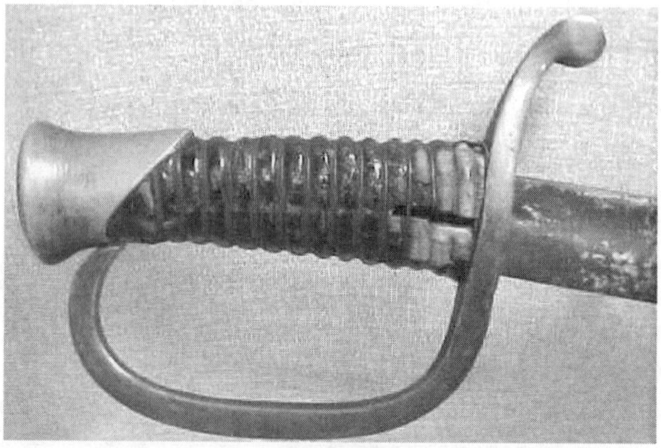

Enlisted Man, Artillery

Incredibly rare example! No import parts here! Single strand wire on grip, which is 95%+ intact. Unstopped fuller blade; crude lap-soldered scabbard with sand-cast brass mounts. Often called a "Dog River" and more recently, a "Boyle and Gamble, Richmond, Va.," pattern. Blade and scabbard most closely resemble the products of the Confederate States Armory at Kenansville, North Carolina, especially the pommel cap construction, fuller on blade, and scabbard construction details. It is documented that Kenansville produced artillery sabers, but nobody can specifically identify them at this point in time. **9,500.00**

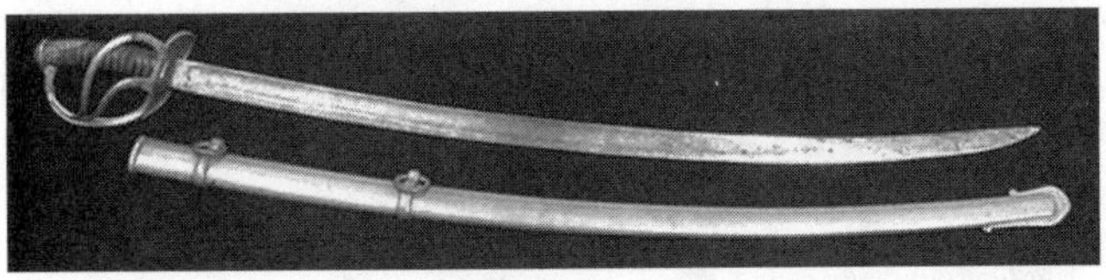

Resembling a U.S. Model 1860 Saber, this Thomas, Griswold & Co. saber was intended for mounted artillery soldiers.

Old South Military Antiques

Thomas, Griswold & Co, New Orleans artillery saber in near-mint condition. **22,000.00**

Model 1840 Light Artillery sword and scabbard, having the very rare early stamp, "Ames, Cabotville, 1845" Fantastic "WAT" script inspector mark in brass guard with full original grip leather and wire. Has initials "PAG" scratched in guard; family history attributes the sword to a relative with the last name of Gallagher, but only verbal provenance. Blade is brown and has light pitting overall; scabbard is correct type for the recessed guard model. . . **1,250.00**

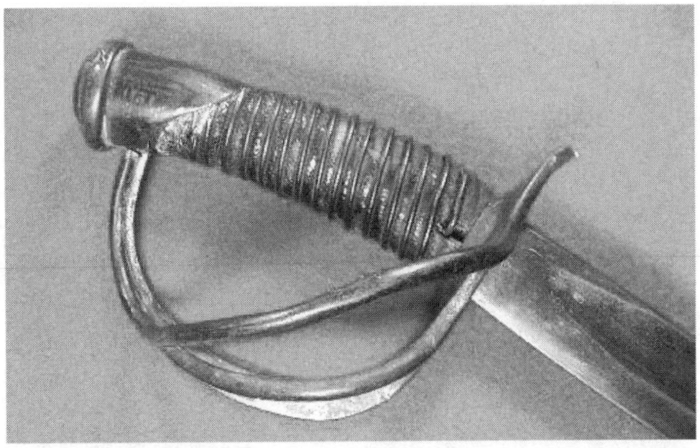

Based on the U.S. Model 1840 Heavy Saber, this Haiman and Brother example came out of their Columbus, Georgia, factory.

Middle Tennessee Relics

Enlisted Man, Cavalry

Civil War cavalry saber manufactured for sale to the Confederate troops between November 1861 and April 1865, in Columbus, Georgia. Haiman and Brother was one of the largest Confederate manufacturers of swords during the Civil War. This excellent example is based on the Model 1840 pattern. This sword has a smooth, even, original patina. The guard is a reddish-umber color showing typical high copper content. There is no pitting on the blade. Casting flaws that are typical of Confederate manufacturers are present. This is an attic example with original iron wire on the grip, and it also maintains complete original oilcloth wrap. **2,950.00**

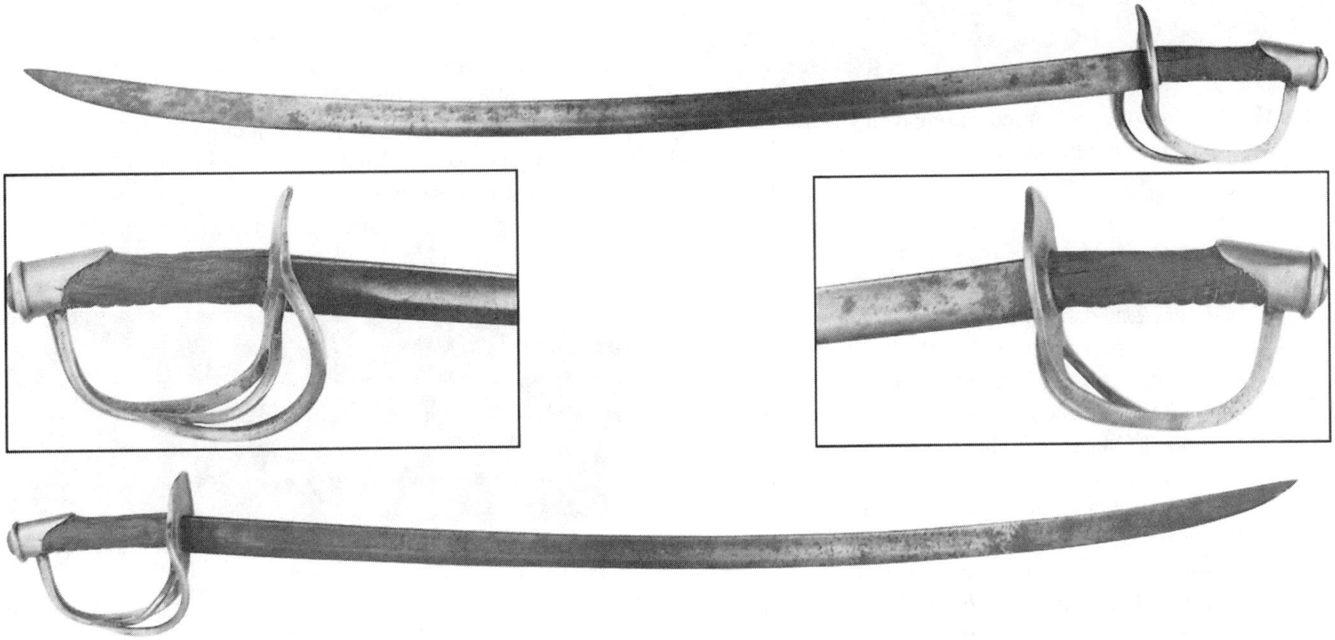

Dog River-style saber missing all of the wrap and wire from the grip (with no scabbard).

J.C. Devine Inc.

Enlisted Man, Cavalry, cont.

"Dog River" style 34-3/4" blade with a wide unstopped fuller on each side of the blade. Sand-cast brass three-branch guard and Phrygian helmet-shaped pommel, very worn wood grip is missing all the leather and wire. Dark patina on the blade with a few patches of corrosion, one branch of the guard is bent, no scabbard. Good condition, likely Virginia made and came from that state with the Reed and Watson Musket. **350.00**

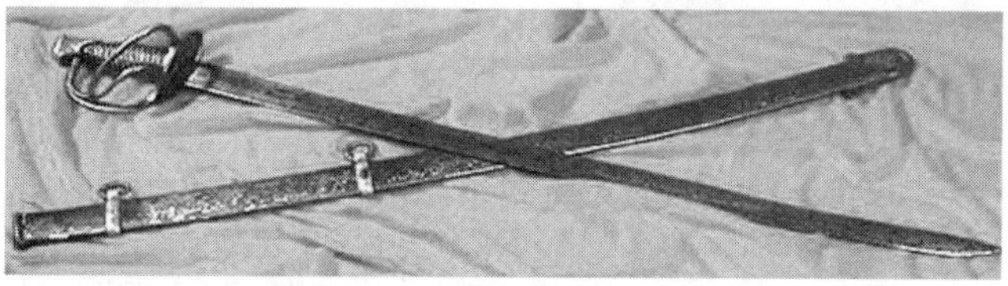

This cavalry saber was made by B. Douglas & Co. of Columbia, South Carolina.

Old South Military Antiques

Cavalry saber made by B. Douglas & Co. of Columbia, South Carolina. **8,500.00**

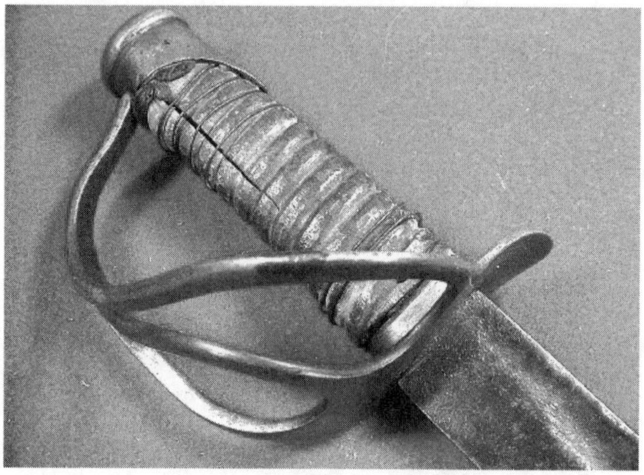

This H. Marshall-made Confederate cavalry saber was housed in a cedar scabbard.

Middle Tennessee Relics

Confederate "H. Marshall" of Atlanta cavalry saber, in absolutely untouched attic condition. The blade has a dark, uncleaned, brown-black patina. The cast-brass guard has a rich, aged patina as well. The grip is down to polished wood, but still retains most of the single strand iron wire and also the distinctive brass ferrule common to Marshall-Atlanta sabers. **2,850.00**

Exceptional Confederate cavalry saber and original scabbard made at the Confederate States Armory at Kenansville, North Carolina, by Louis Froelich. Absolutely fine leather grip (which is correct for this model; not tarred "oilcloth" linen) and full iron wire; smooth unstopped fuller blade with untouched high copper content hilt and smooth pommel cap; fine lapped seam scabbard with 65%+ original black lacquer paint. **7,500.00**

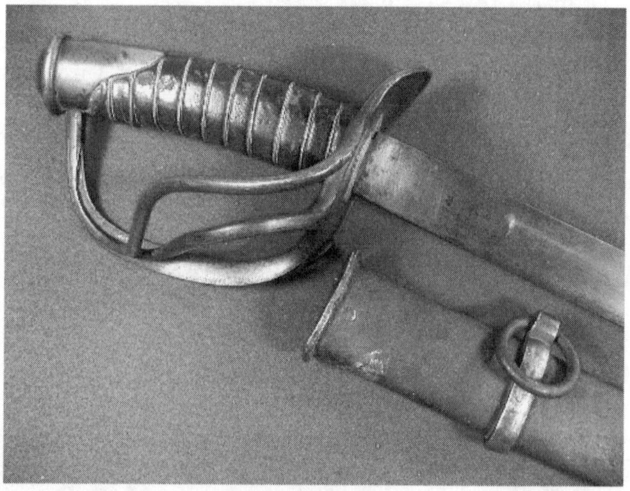

The "flat-blade" Boyle and Gamble cavalry saber used a Confederate States Armory scabbard.

Middle Tennessee Relics

Extremely rare "flat blade" Boyle and Gamble Confederate cavalry saber in original brass-mounted C.S. scabbard. The saber has a nice clean blade and excellent complete original wrap and wire on the grip. The scabbard has an attractive aged-brown patina with numerous small service dents and dings. The scabbard itself is a product of Confederate States Armory and has traces of original red lacquer remaining. This saber and scabbard has a nice rich, uncleaned patina. **4,650.00**

First model Virginia Manufactory cavalry saber and scabbard, 40-1/2" overall with an acutely curved 35-1/2" blade. Huge, classic Virginia saber, blade has heavy patina that would clean to fine. Absolutely no dings or nicks, blade shortened approximately 2". Scabbard original full length, deep-brown "wagon wheel" iron guard and flat pommeled hilt. Grips retain 50% original iron wire wrap and 25% original leather covering. Fine original scabbard with no dings or nicks. Scabbard retains its original frog button. **4,500.00**

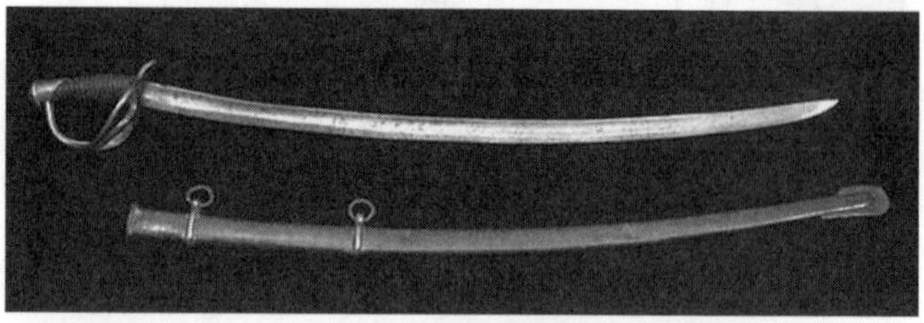

This Haiman Cavalry saber retains about 85% of its original grip.

Old South Military Antiques

Haiman cavalry saber, 85% grip wrap complete, very-good condition. **5,400.00**

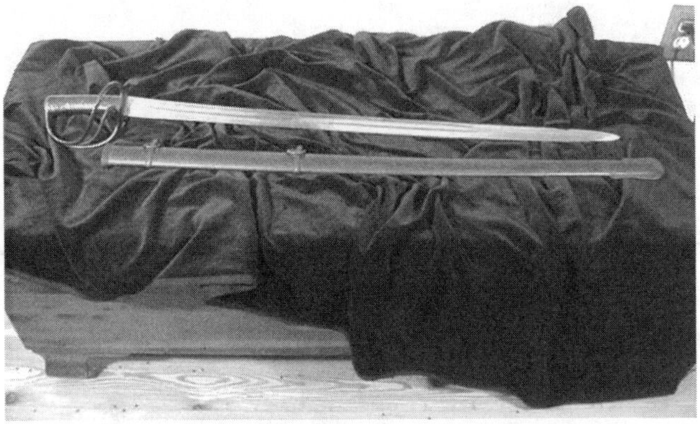

Confederate saber made by Isaacs and Company.

Old South Military Antiques

Isaacs & Co. C.S. cavalry saber. **4,400.00**

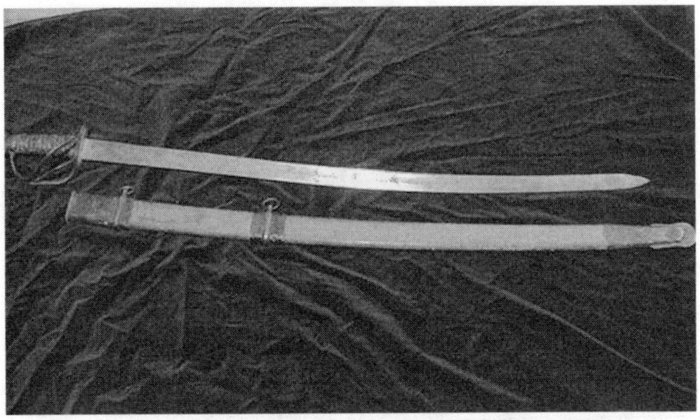

South Carolina manufacturers Kraft, Goldschmidt, & Kraft produced this saber.

Old South Military Antiques

Kraft, Goldsmidt & Kraft, Columbia, South Carolina, saber. **8,800.00**

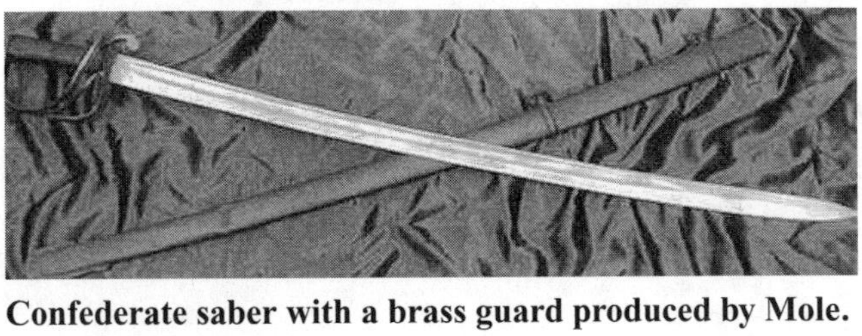

Confederate saber with a brass guard produced by Mole.

Old South Military Antiques

Mole cavalry saber with brass guard. **2,750.00**

Overall very good with full oilcloth grip wrap (wire missing), full scabbard with brass mounts (throat missing), and nice blade. This has traces of ancient silver paint on areas of the scabbard. Classic, unmarked Haimann Georgia saber. **4,250.00**

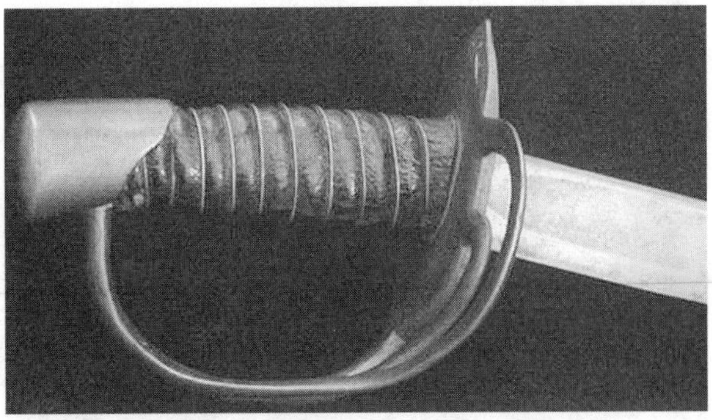

Near-mint condition 2nd Model Kenansville saber.

Old South Military Antiques

Second Model Kenansville saber in mint condition. **9,100.00**

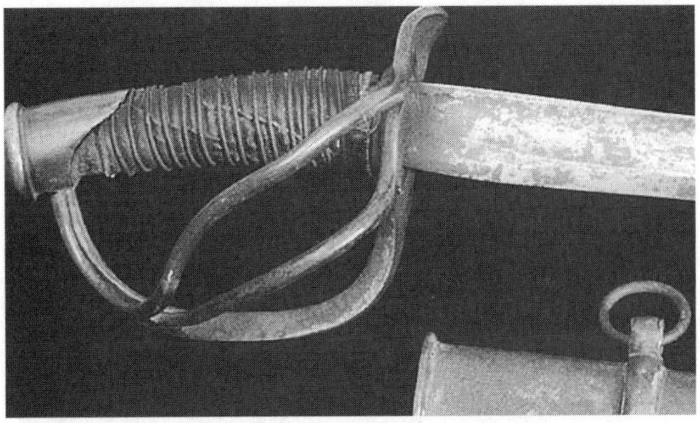

Typical Confederate sword in its original scabbard, possibly made by Louis Haiman.

Old South Military Antiques

The maker of this Confederate-manufactured sword has long been a matter of speculation. It was rumored to have been a product of Louis Haiman & Brothers of Columbus, Georgia. All of Haiman's cavalry swords are nearly identical, thus are easily recognizable. All have the distinct forging flaws at the ricasso. The same style grip tapering down from basket to pommel covered in leather or oilcloth. It is usually wrapped with a single strand of iron wire, though there are some rare examples wrapped with a doubled small gauge copper wire and one has been noted with twisted double strand brass wrap. All scabbards have the exaggerated lapped seam, wide brass mounts, iron carrying rings, flat-topped iron throat, and an iron drag. This example is completely original and has a pleasing, untouched patina. The highly desirable oilcloth grip is 95% complete and the iron wire wrap is 100%. The sword is sheathed in its original scabbard that is perfect except for one small push. . . . **5,600.00**

This Boyle & Gamble flat blade cavalry sword has a fine blade with no nicks or dings. The uncleaned patina is a smooth dark color. It is 34-1/4" long. The grip leather is 98% complete, as is the copper single strand wire. The sword is very tight, and is a fine example of a sword made in the capital of the Confederacy, no scabbard. **3,800.00**

Enlisted Man, Cavalry, cont.

Manufactured by the Memphis Novelty Works was produced between September 1861 and May 1862.

Old South Military Antiques

This Confederate cavalry saber was manufactured by the Memphis Novelty Works, Thomas Leech & Co. Leech began the manufacture of weapons at Main and McCall Streets, Memphis, Tennessee in September of 1861. Shortly thereafter, Charles Rigdon joined him. Leech and Rigdon moved their manufactory to Columbus, Georgia, in May of 1862 when Memphis fell to the Yankees. Thus, the highly desirable three-line address stamped into the quillon clearly shows the time and place of manufacture. It had to be produced in Memphis, between September 1861, when Leech went into the sword business, and May 1862, when Memphis fell. The sword is in excellent condition. The grip wrap and double-twist brass wire is 100% complete. The unstopped blade is smooth and semi bright from ricasso to point and the edge is nick free. The scabbard is correct and original to the sword. It too is in excellent condition. Throat, mounts, and drag are brass. The iron is smooth and nearly ding free. The intials, "J. W.," are cross-hatched into the guard's underside. **13,800.00**

Very fine example of an early Kenansville cavalry sword. The blade is excellent and has no nicks or dings. The patina is a soft, uncleaned gray. It has the original leather washer. The leather grip is as good as you will see on a confederate sword! It has single-strand iron wire. The brass guard has a beautiful uncleaned dark brass patina. The sword is very tight with no wiggle in the guard. The scabbard has 60% original brown paint. The brass sword hangers have a dark green patina. **7,995.00**

Saber, Confederate, Enlisted Man, Cavalry. Believed to be a C.S- salvaged early sword having an early cavalry saber blade marked "P LS (Luther Sage, Inspector) N STARR/US" and it is fitted to an iron cavalry hilt with brown leather grip and double-twisted wire. There is one branch broken on the knuckle bow, but not displaced much. The period repair is done to the area of the guard where the blade goes through. **645.00**

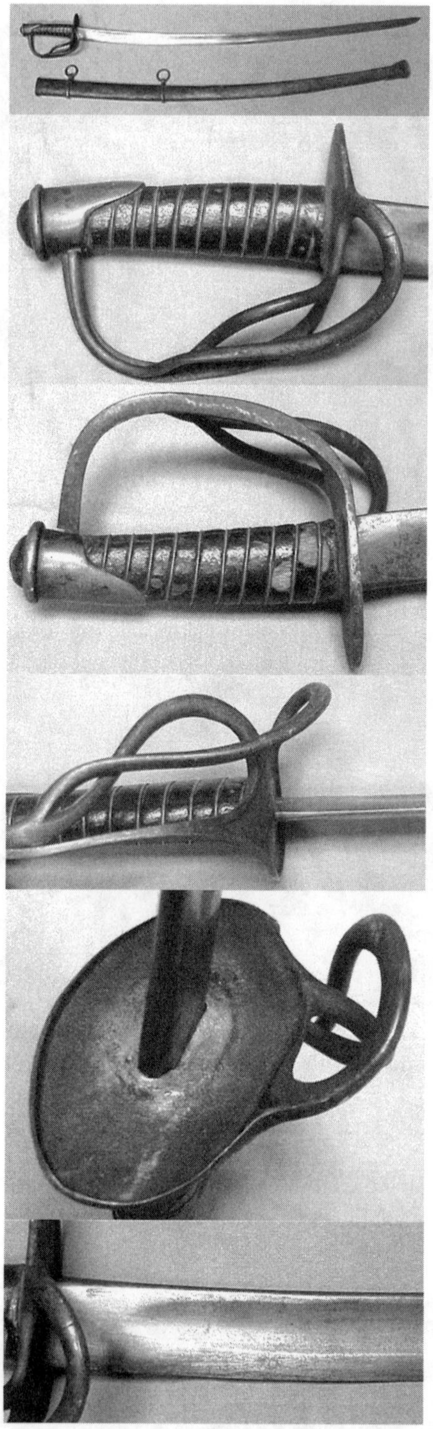

According to family tradition, Thomas Askin of the 40th Virginia Infantry carried this cavalry saber.

Sharpsburg Arsenal

This saber came from a family in Maryland who gave an oral family history of the piece. It was supposedly carried by Thomas Askins, 40th Virginia Infantry. There is no documentation with this sword as to the family history. Full-length blade is in excellent condition with unstopped fuller and only two minor nicks on edge. Ricasso washer is missing, leather grip and single strand copper wire is 90% there and tight. Cast-brass knuckle guard is bent on outer branch.

Brass has a beautiful dark patina—never been cleaned. Scabbard is iron with a heavy lap seam and drag. Brass carrying bands with iron rings. Throat is brass and shows a small buckle in iron. When the sword and scabbard are together, the bend on the branch and scabbard match as to indicate the carrier probably fell on the sword in its scabbard. **6,850.00**

Housed in a prewar scabbard, this Memphis Novelty Works saber hit the market after residing in a Tennessee museum for many years.

Middle Tennessee Relics

This saber carries the rare three-line stamp on the guard's lip, "Memphis Novelty Works-Thos. Leech & Co." The sword originally came from an estate sale in Williamson County, Tennessee, and for many years was on display in the Lotz House Civil War Museum in Franklin, Tennessee. It is in a pre-war 1840-style scabbard. The scabbard has a dark-chocolate patina and a few small dings from use. There is excellent ring wear indicating extensive actual service. The blade is razor sharp and has an aged-brown/black patina overall. The brass guard is perfect and well marked. The grip has been professionally restored using the original wire and antique leather and looks terrific.............**6,500.00**

This sword has a beautiful blade with a soft gray patina and a non-stopped fuller. No nicks or dings, with very smooth metal. It has the original leather washer. The brass guard has an aged-brass patina. The leather on the grip is very fine and is 98%. The twisted fine brass wire is complete and tight. The metal scabbard has a brass throat and brass hangers, the drag is iron. This sword has a lot of features of a Kenansville blade. **5,400.00**

Model 1840 Cavalry saber and scabbard by William Glaze, Columbia, South Carolina, also known as the Palmetto Armory. Borderline fine blade with nice edge and just some scuffs from field use. Grip wire is 100%; grip leather is worn in a few spots, but 75%+ intact. Original matching scabbard. **3,750.00**

Officer's quality Kenansville saber.

Old South Military Antiques

Officer, Cavalry

Kenansville cavalry officer's saber in mint condition. **9,500.00**

Kraft, Goldschmidt & Kraft, Columbia, South Carolina, is best known for their staff officer's swords. They did, however, also produce cavalry sabers. The example shown here is believed to be their product. It is distinguished from its H. Marshall look-alike by the shape of the basket and the brass ferrule at the grip's base. The blade also differs slightly from the Marshall, which has a central ridge for the last 8"or so. The Kraft, Goldschmidt & Kraft is basically flat for the last 8" in length. The tin and brass-mounted wooden scabbards are identical and it is thought that Kraft purchased scabbards from Marshall. The leather grip wrap and wire wrap are 100% intact and original. The blade is bright and nick free. Its original scabbard does not have a single crack in it. It would be perfect, but for the missing top rim of the throat. **8,900.00**

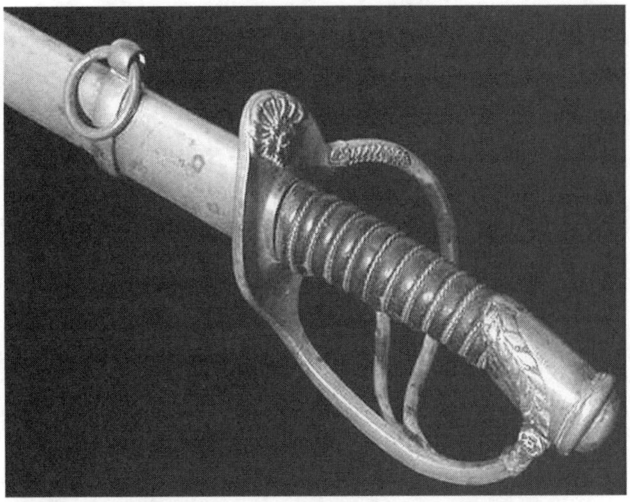

Thomas, Griswold & Co. artillery sabers are made distinctive by their brass scabbards. The same is true for their officer-quality cavalry sabers.

Old South Military Antiques

Officer, Cavalry, cont.

The New Orleans, Louisiana, manufactory of Thomas, Griswold & Co. is well-known for its artillery sabers sheathed in distinctive brass scabbards. Lesser known and much rarer, are their cavalry officer's sabers, also sheathed in distinctive brass scabbards. This is a pristine example of this rare officer's blade. The original leather grip and twisted-brass wire wrap are complete. The guard is tight and the throat washer intact. The semi-bright blade is totally smooth and nick free. The ricasso is clearly marked, "T. G. & Co. N. O." This exceptional sword is still sheathed in its original, all-brass scabbard. The scabbard is completely ding-free and has a lovely golden patina. **22,000.00**

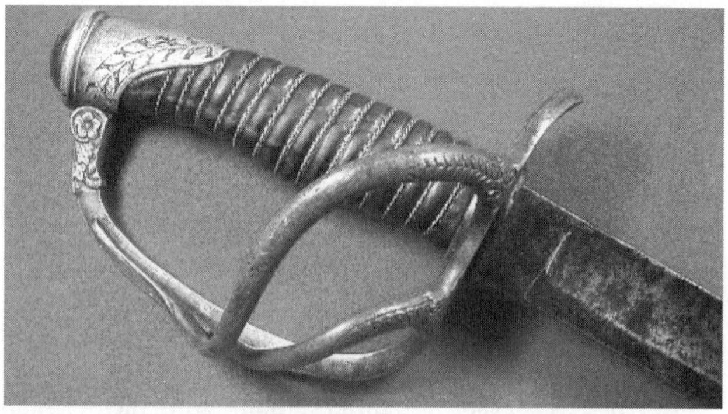

Officer's saber, made by Thomas, Griswold & Co. with a "straight-line" hallmark.

Middle Tennessee Relics

Rare Thomas, Griswold & Co. Confederate cavalry officer's saber with "straight-line" stamp. There are fewer than ten examples known with the rare, straight-line Griswold mark. The blade has an attractive aged-gray/brown patina with a clear, "Thomas Griswold & Co. New Orleans," stamp. The guard is perfect with a rich, dark, aged-bronze/brown patina. The grip has been professionally restored using original Civil War leather, looks absolutely original............................. **8,500.00**

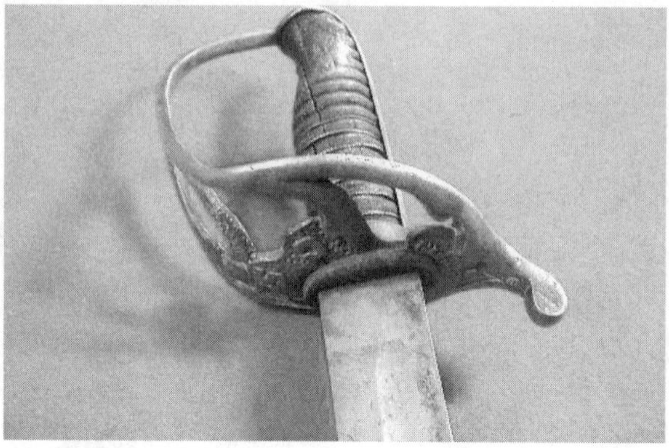

Swords made by the Nashville Plow Works are some of the most popular Confederate blades with collectors.

Middle Tennessee Relics

The reversal of the biblical passage, "turning your swords into plow shares," and the bold "C.S.A." are two of the factors that have contributed to the Nashville Plow Works saber's great popularity. This is the saber only without scabbard. The blade has a smooth, aged-gray patina and is razor sharp. The blade is in nice condition with only one nick. The grip has worn down to polished wood and still retains most of the original wire. The guard is excellent and is the sought after "stippled" variety. The "Nashville Plow Works" casting is clear....... **6,750.00**

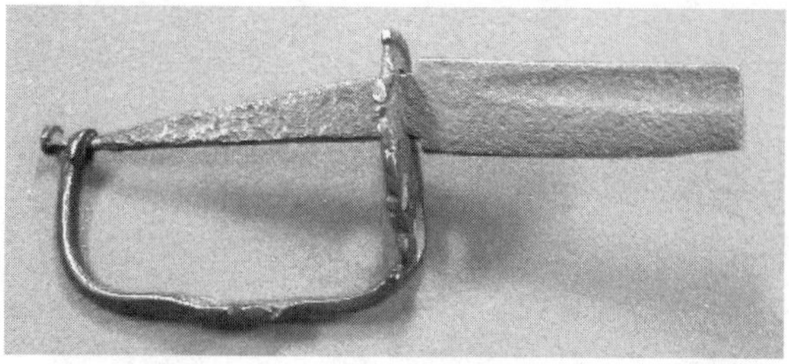

Nashville-produced College Hill saber dug near Shiloh.

Middle Tennessee Relics

Extremely rare battlefield pick-up remains of a Nashville-produced College Hill Confederate cavalry officer's saber. This saber was picked up along the Confederate retreat route from Shiloh towards Corinth, Mississippi. The blade is broken 4" below the brass guard, and a portion of the guard is sheared off. Part of the, "C.S.A.," initials are intact, and remain clearly visible. This blade appears to have taken a severe impact....... **1,250.00**

This exceptionally attractive cavalry officer's saber was made by William J. McElroy of Macon, Georgia. William McElroy is well known for his deep, relief-etched infantry officer swords. This, his cavalry officer's pattern, is much rarer. Rarer still is the etched scabbard. Though it is now faint, the scabbard is etched with an old English script , "CS," crossed cannon, a battle flag and McElroy's vine pattern. The sword's complete and original grip is wrapped with oilcloth and single strand brass wire. The brass guard still retains traces of its original gilt. The sword knot is original to the sword.......... **65,000.00**

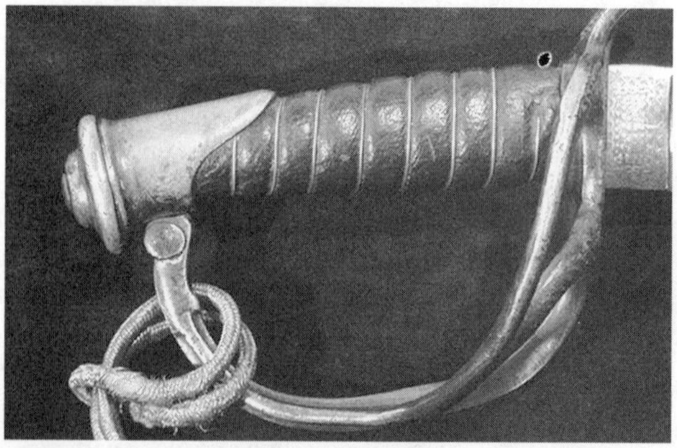

William J. McElroy made this extremely attractive Confederate cavalry officer's saber.

Old South Military Relics

This exceptionally attractive cavalry officer's saber was made by William J. McElroy of Macon, Georgia. William McElroy is well known for his deep, relief-etched infantry officer swords. McElroy's cavalry officer's pattern is much rarer. Rarer still is the etched scabbard. Though it is now faint, the scabbard is etched with an old English script, "CS," crossed cannon, a battle flag, and McElroy's vine pattern. The sword is complete and original grip is wrapped with oilcloth and single strand brass wire. The brass guard still retains traces of its original gilt. The sword knot is original to the sword. **65,000.00**

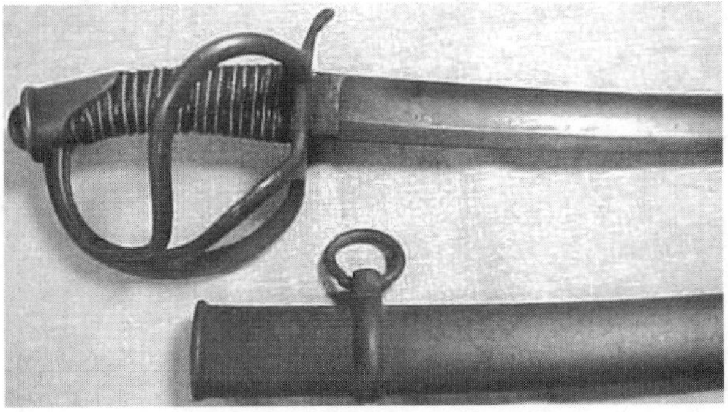

William Glaze & Company made this Palmetto Armory sword.

Battleground Antiques, Inc.

Incredibly honest Confederate Palmetto Armory saber and scabbard. Made by William Glaze & Company of Columbia, South Carolina, totally unaltered, grip is an easy 95% with full wire wrap. **5,000.00**

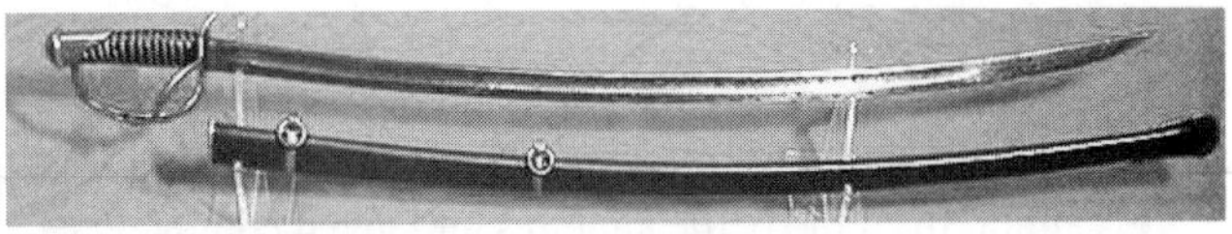

Memphis Novelty Works produced this officer's quality saber.

Old South Military Antiques

Memphis Novelty Works-marked sword. . . . **13,300.00**

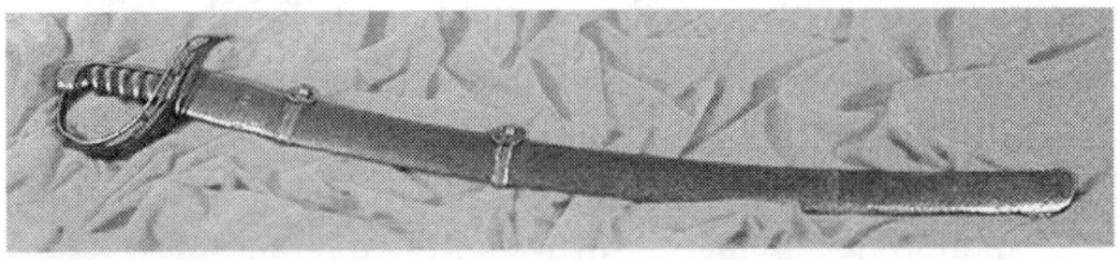

Predating the Civil War, this Virginia Manufactory saber has Confederate alterations.

Old South Military Antiques

Virginia Manufactory sword with Confederate alteration. **5,000.00**

Confederate Swords

Model 1832, Artillery

Artillery sword with tin-mounted, wooden scabbard. **3,400.00**

C.S. copy of the 1832 short artillery sword with crude casting grip with eagle motif just like on the U.S. Model 1832. This one has no rivets and the tang end actually has a small cap on it. The space between the blade and the front of the grip has been filled in with lead to fill the void. The blade shows definite crudeness. There are stampings of "TP" and "127" on the grip. The blade has a dark patina present and some rust. **995.00**

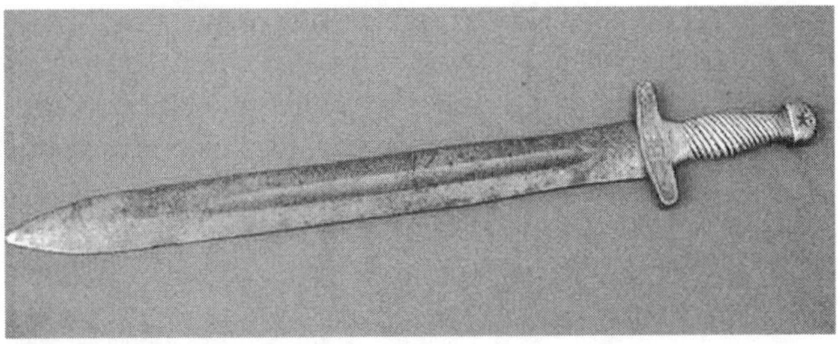

Patterned after the U.S. Model 1832 Short Sword, this Confederate version has a C.S. and star mark.

Old South Military Antiques

CS-and-star-marked short sword. **2,650.00**

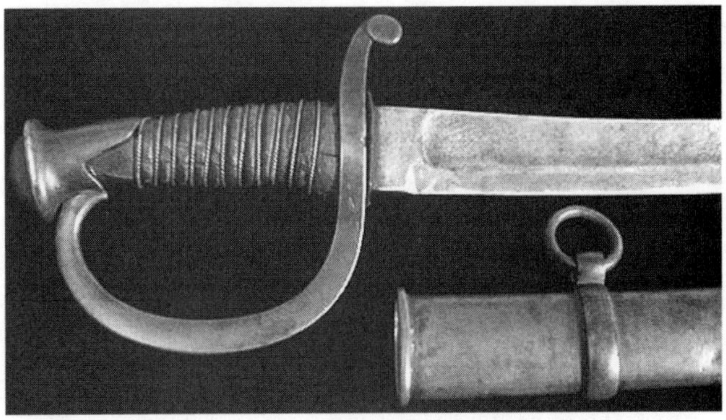

Captain William Carnes, the commander of Carne's Battery, was carrying this sword when he was wounded at the Battle of Perryville on October 8, 1862.

Old South Military Antiques

Officer, Artillery, sword belonged to William Carnes, Captain of Carnes' Battery, C.S.A. Artillery. Captain Carnes commanded his battery at the battle of Perryville, October 8, 1862, where he was wounded in the foot, but remained with his command until after the battle. Though given a medical furlough, rumors of an impending battle sent the Captain back to the front where he effectively commanded his battery at the battle of Murfreesboro. At the battle of Chickamauga, Carnes' Battery lost 38 of 79 men taken into action Saturday afternoon, September

19th. He had 49 horses shot down and his battery captured when his infantry support gave way. When the Confederates counterattacked and retook the guns, Carnes' Battery was so badly cut up it was removed from the field. After the battle, Captain Carnes was highly complimented by General Bragg for his work and given thirty days to recruit his command. As an additional compliment, the young Captain was given his choice of cannon from the battle captures and given command of a battalion of four batteries. He continued in this capacity until 1864, when he was reassigned to the Confederate Navy because of his pre-war naval experience. Carnes had been so effective as a battery commander, General Forrest, specifically requested Carnes as the artillery officer he most desired for service with his command. The sword was purchased from the Carnes family and was later sold to well-known Confederate collector Kent Wall, who did all the subsequent historical research and documentation. The sword is completely original and unaltered. The leather grip wrap is flaking, but it retains all of its twisted-brass wire wrap. The blade and the original brass scabbard are excellent; the maker's name and full New Orleans address are exceptionally good. Captain Carnes' sword comes with full documentation and research done by Mr. Wall, as well as a first edition copy of *The Old Guard in Gray.* **13,800.00**

Foot Officer

Arsenal-produced Confederate foot officer's sword and scabbard that started out life as a standard three-branch Haiman-style cavalry saber. At the C.S. Arsenal, this sword was shortened to foot officer length, and the guard was refashioned to have two branches rather than three. The scabbard was appropriately fashioned to fit the sword. The blade is very nice with a gently aging gray-brown patina. The grip has long ago worn down to wood. The custom-fashioned brass guard has a rich uncleaned patina. The pommel cap has lots of small marks and dings from having been used to hammer something. The scabbard is classic Confederate lap seam, brass mount, and is in very nice condition. **3,850.00**

Confederate Civil War McElroy infantry officer sword and scabbard, clearly marked, "W.J. McElroy Macon Geo.," on ricasso, 95% original tarred leather grip with full wire; scabbard is full length and unbroken (middle mount is unlike the other two, but original to the sword). Clear etching of tobacco vines and "CS" on blade. **23,000.00**

Confederate Civil War officer's sword by Halfmann & Taylor, Montgomery, Alabama, and so etched on ricasso of blade. Noted importers of fine goods from buttons to swords, this firm imported this pattern of sword and etched the blades on site, clear, etched "CS." Guard is unusual, and may have been altered, 95% original ray-skin grip and full wire, fine scabbard............................ **8,500.00**

Exceptionally rare Confederate foot officer sword and scabbard by McElroy, Macon, Georgia, and so marked on the ricasso. Extremely fine, deep etching on blade, "CS," scrolls, cotton plants, more! Beautiful hardwood maple grip never had leather; about 65% original wire remaining, original leather scabbard. **12,500.00**

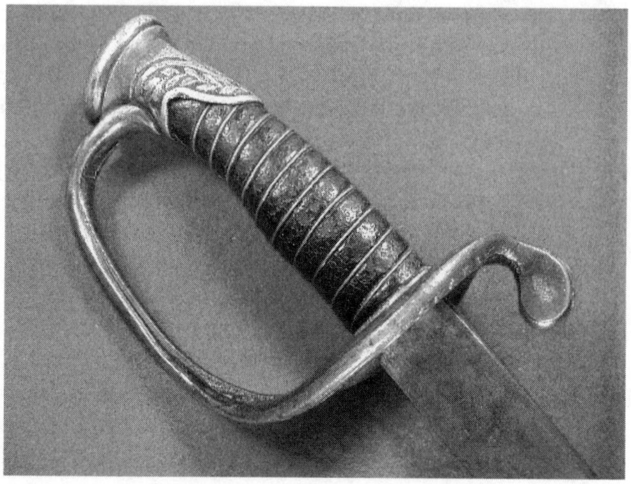

Confederate sword made by Boyle and Gamble.

Middle Tennessee Relics

Made by Boyle and Gamble, beautiful bright blade with excellent engraving, very nice original wrap and wire on grip. **7,500.00**

Nice condition Boyle and Gamble Richmond, Virginia, foot officer's sword without scabbard. The blade has an attractive gently graying patina with faint traces of engraving here and there. The characteristic Boyle & Gamble blade "fault" is clear. The grip is excellent with 100% original wrap and wire. The cast brass guard is flawless as well with deep, rich, uncleaned patina and characteristic Boyle & Gamble casting crudity............................ **5,500.00**

The leather wrap and single-strand brass wire are near perfect, as is the cast brass guard. The blade is fine steel gray color with no edge nicks or rough spots, and has never been cleaned, sharpened, or shined. This is properly unmarked except for batch number "11" stamped into the underside of the guard just above where the spine of the blade meets the brass. The scabbard is a classic Confederate officer's-type with top-stitched seam, crude, flat brass mounts void of decoration and held in place by friction (no screws). It is full length, solid, and complete except for the drag......................... **8,900.00**

This foot officer's sword has a beautiful grip possessing 100% of the leather and original twisted brass wire. The blade has a soft-gray patina. There are a few very small nicks in the blade, no scabbard. This sword was made for Mitchell and Tyler, a fine jeweler in Richmond, who contracted with Boyle & Gamble to make swords for his customers.......... **5,200.00**

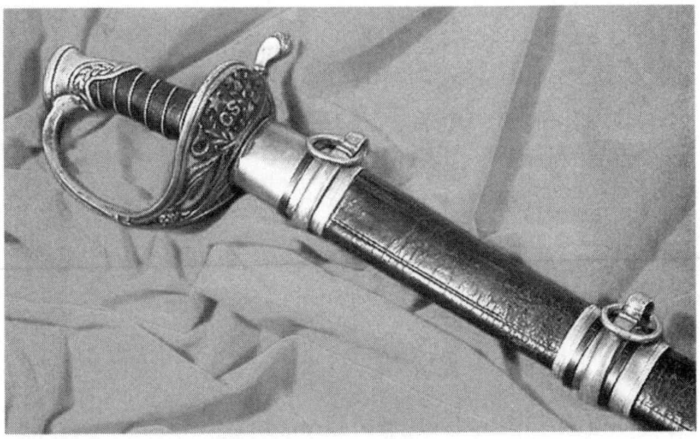

Boyle & Gamble were famous for their highly prized Confederate-made swords.

Old South Military Antiques

Officer, Field and Staff

Boyle and Gamble field and staff sword. **16,500.00**

Extremely rare and beautiful C.S.A. "Kenansville" Field and Staff officer's sword with distinctive cast-brass guard made up of the letters, "C.S.A" The brass has a rich, dark uncleaned patina and has the Roman Numeral "XIX." It has the original blade that has been shortened a few inches. The blade also has a dark never-cleaned patina. The grip was, at some point prior to the 1930s, changed to a polished walnut. This is a beautiful "C.S.A." Kenansville in nice condition. **4,950.00**

Kenansville sword with the cast "C.S.A." standing out clearly and retaining nearly 80% of the paint on its scabbard.

Middle Tennessee Relics

This is the pattern with the backwards "N" in Nashville and the flat-top scabbard with classic baby-size rings. There are only about ten known, complete examples of the short, straight Nashville Plow Works Field and Staff officer's sword. This example has a beautiful clean blade just beginning to gray with age. The brass guard is perfect with a rich, age patina, "C.S.A.," cast around the bottom and, "Nashville Plow Works," cast around the guard's top. The grip has original wrap and wire with approximately 70% of the original leather present and worn through to polished wood in the remaining areas. The grip has a couple normal small age cracks from the shrinkage of the wood with time. The scabbard is the early pattern with the flat brass top. The scabbard retains 80% of its original black enamel. **22,500.00**

Staff officer's sword in original leather scabbard, once in the prestigious Norm Flayderman Confederate Sword Collection (still has the old tag from his collection hanging from the sword). The blade has a gently aging gray patina with original engraving visible in areas. The marking, "Made by Boyle & Gamble & Co. for Mitchell & Tyler Richmond, Va," can be seen faintly etched on the sword's ricasso. The grip is excellent with 100% original wrap and wire. The scabbard is complete and original, but does have some typical leather flaking, and the stitching is open in areas. **15,500.00**

Sword, Confederate, Officer. Confederate Kenansville, North Carolina, Confederate States Armory product with full original grip and wire, and wonderful lapped seam iron scabbard, which retains 65% original black lacquer paint. Smooth blade has some old file marks on cutting edge, but no big dings or nicks. **7,500.00**

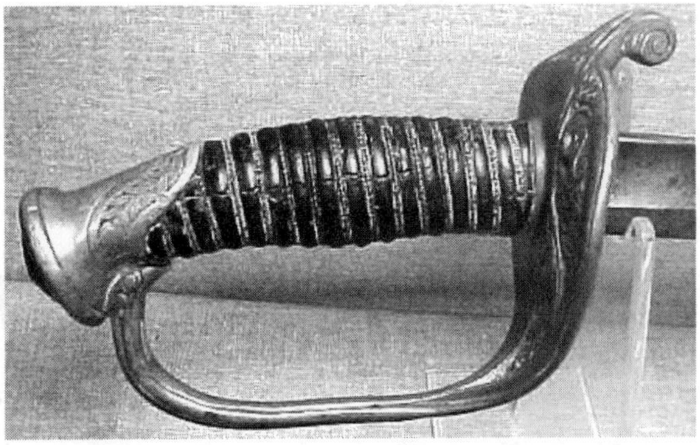

Possibly the product of James Conning of Mobile Alabama, a soldier of the 42nd New York picked up this sword on the Gettysburg battlefield.

Battleground Antiques, Inc.

Officer

Identified Gettysburg Confederate sword that is likely the product of James Conning of Mobile, Alabama, or an unknown Louisiana maker. Full, original, brown leather-covered grip with original wire, top-brazed mounts on leather scabbard, and crudely cast pommel. Stopped fuller blade is plain and devoid of any decoration. Affixed to the scabbard is an old and faded paper tag, 100% genuine, that identifies the sword to a Union soldier in the 42nd New York Infantry. **3,075.00**

Officer, cont.

Full, original, pigskin-leather grip and single-strand brass wire and fine original full-length leather scabbard with top brazed bandless suspension rings, typical of Southern construction. Totally plain blade and simple two-branch, single-knuckle bow guard with evidence of crude sand-casting. This item is totally unmarked, but virtually identical to several known marked, "Hyde and Goodrich, New Orleans, Louisiana," examples. **2,500.00**

U.S. Cutlasses

Model 1860

The 26" blade is marked on the reverse ricasso, "Made by/AMES MFG Co./CHICOPEE/MASS." The obverse ricasso is marked, "U.S.N./D.R./1862." The blade is clean with some age spots, a little fine pitting near the top. The Ames' markings are unusually well defined on this sword. The hilt shows small dents on the brass, the grip retains all the leather, but no wire (the wire was removed from many of these swords by the Navy). The guard is marked, "23M/783." No scabbard, very-good condition. **675.00**

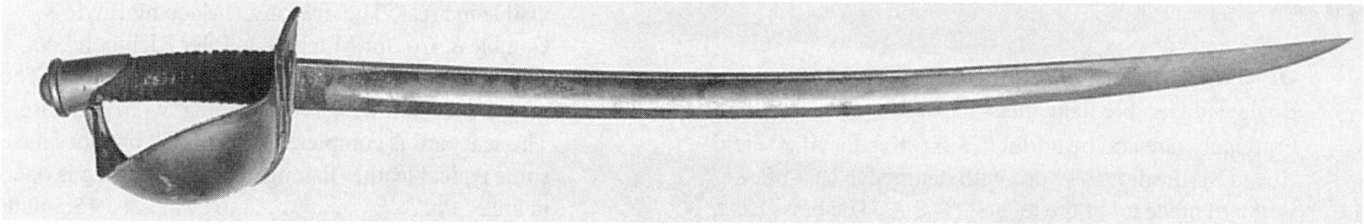

Dated 1862, this Model 1860 Naval Cutlass was missing the wire wrap on its grip and its scabbard.

J.C. Devine Inc.

"Ames Mfg. Co." dated 1862, the 25-3/4" blade is gray with fine pitting near the tip, a couple of patches of corrosion and three very small edge nicks. The handle is missing all the wire and parts of the leather wrap. The brass guard has been cleaned on the exterior long ago, is now starting to discolor. The lip of the guard is numbered, "14M/924," good-plus condition. **400.00**

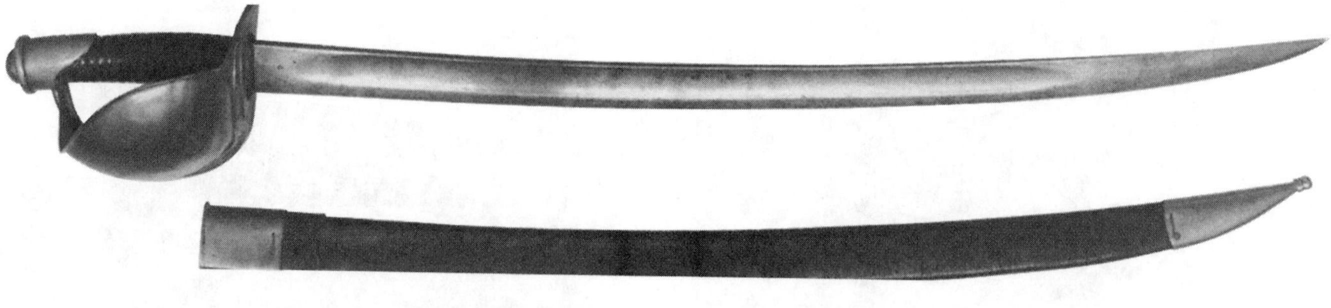

Bearing an 1862 date, this complete 1860 Model Cutlass was a good buy for the collector.

J.C. Devine Inc.

"Ames Mfg. Co.," 25-3/4" blade marked on the obverse ricasso with the naval anchor and date of 1862. The top front of the guard is rack numbered, "6M/125." The Ames markings are notoriously light on these swords, but are distinct on this one, except for a couple of letters. The grip is missing all the wire and has a 1/2" diameter hole in the leather. The brass cup guard shows small dents. The blade is gray with a little pinprick pitting near the tip. Very good with a reproduction brass-mounted, black-leather scabbard and frog. **450.00**

33" overall with a bright 26-1/2" blade, right ricasso worn, but marked clearly, "USN/DR/1864," and over this an anchor over, "P/GG." No discernible markings on the left ricasso. Bright brass bowl-shaped guard and pommel. Grips retain 95-98% black leather and 100% double-twist wire wrap. Original issue tarred black leather scabbard with the copper rivets up the back and at the drag. Scabbard heavily alligatored but in fine, sound condition. **1,250.00**

Regulation enlisted cutlass by Ames, dated 1862, has the Ames firm marking on the ricasso. Blade is plain gray steel in nice shape and free from nicks. The brass basket guard is good with some honest dents and dings. The handle has most of the leather worn away, but still looks good, as the entire grip is a dark-black color. Complete with full and solid scabbard. Still with this is the original belt frog, which is worn and ratty, but still intact. **745.00**

Model 1860 Cutlass housed in a "Navy Yard" style of scabbard.

J.C. Devine Inc.

The 26" long blade is gray and has scattered light pitting, appears to have been plated at one time. The brass basket guard is in fine condition, with the lip of the guard marked, "16M/983." The grip is wrapped in black-enameled canvas (believed to be a Navy yard repair) with twisted wire binding. The black leather scabbard is the Navy yard-style with a row of copper rivets on the back. The leather shows some crazing and about 5% finish loss. **800.00**

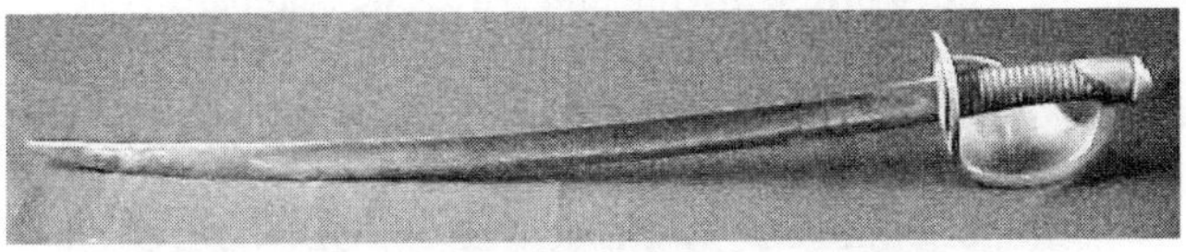

Even though the seller implied that the 1864 date and "USN-D.R." stampings were rare (as opposed to simply an anomaly), it didn't seem to matter much to bidders.

Outstanding 1864 naval cutlass with rare markings, ricasso front has, "USN—D.R. [inspector's initials] 1864—GG" [Guert Ganesvoort], as well as a stamped anchor and, "P." The ricasso back is marked, "Made by Ames Mfg. Co.-Chicopee Mass.," in a scroll. The pommel, cross guard, and solid closed handguard are brass. The handguard has all of the rivets attached, and has some denting and age spots, intact wood grip. The total length is 32" with a 26" blade. The blade is bright in many areas, and has some age spots all over, and pitting toward blade's tip. **495.00**

U.S. Sabers

Model 1833, Enlisted Man, Cavalry, complete leather grip covering and the properly braided piano-style wire wrap. Most 1833 dragoons are found with this delicate piano-style wire broken or missing and current owners have replaced it with new twisted two-strand cavalry-style wire. The leather and wire on this one are perfect and original. The three-branch brass guard is free from bends or dents with, "ORD," and, "HKC," markings near the quillon. The blade is clean and shiny with full-engraved marking, "N.P Ames/Cutler/Springfield," and, "United States." The scabbard is free from dents and has the inspector's initials, "JM," on the drag. It is 50% covered with surface crud and crust. **1,395.00**

Model 1840, Enlisted Man, Artillery

Overall 38" with bright, acutely curved 32" blade with a few tiny nicks, but is overall in fine condition. Crisp, "US/ADK/1863," markings on the right ricasso and, "Ames Mfg./Chicopee/Mass," in a panel on the left ricasso. Blade still retains the scabbard pad. Brass guard and pommel is a deep golden patina. Grips retain 90-98% dry original leather grip wrap and 100% double-twist brass wire wrap. Fine iron scabbard with an old original tin coating. Scabbard rack drag marked, "52". **1,125.00**

Overall 38" with bright, acutely curved 32" blade with a few tiny nicks, but is overall in fine condition. Crisp, "US/ADK/1863," markings on the right ricasso and, "Ames Mfg./Chicopee/Mass," in a panel on the left ricasso. Blade still retains the scabbard pad. Brass guard and pommel is a deep golden patina. Grips retain 90-98% dry original leather grip wrap and 100% double-twist brass wire wrap. Fine iron scabbard with an old original tin coating. Scabbard rack marked "52" on the drag. **1,125.00**

A very, very appealing "as found" condition artillery saber with rich uniform patina overall. The brass D-guard is beautiful with a medium deep age patina and some age spotting. The leather grip is excellent with much original shiny finish and the twisted wire wrap is nicely intact. The blade is smooth (no rust or pitting) with a light-brown surface age patina. There is evidence of edge sharpening long ago. The ricasso is deeply stamped, "1860," no maker's stamp is visible. The brass guard is the early type with recessed area to accept the throat of the steel scabbard. The scabbard is very-good

Model 1840, Enlisted Man, Artillery, cont.

to fine condition and still has the tiny retaining spring still in place inside the throat (this is usually found missing or broken). The scabbard has no dents, a rich, brown age patina spattered with paint flecks. One carrying ring is missing.................... **750.00**

Brass guard and pommel, beautiful patina with deep-brown color mixed with age spots. The leather grip wrap is excellent and original; the twisted wire is an undetectable restoration. The blade is overall smooth gray and light age patina with some deeper brown near the ricasso. Neatly stamped in tiny letters is, "C. Roby & Co." The scabbard is excellent with smooth brown surface, no dents, and a deeper-brown age patina with some heavy pitting on the drag and lower portion only. **1,150.00**

Enlisted artillery saber has 32" curved, fullered blade finished bright with only minor age spots, ricasso with faint, "Ames/Chicopee," maker stamp on obverse, and reverse with, "U.S./C.E.W./1864," proof, inspector, and date stamp. Single branch knuckle bow guard is stamped with several accountability numbers, "B.B.33", initials etched on either side of the cockscomb guard finial, Phrygian helmet pommel, and nice leather grip. Grip lacks wire cord wrap, but this is easily restored and the leather remains in fine condition. Sword is complete with scabbard retaining 60% old silvered finish with nice mellow age patina, complete with both original attachment rings....................... **675.00**

All brass-cast guard with simulated sharkskin grip. The blade has some moderate pitting, but is in pretty good polish and you can still see part of the "U.S." on the blade, as well as the inspector's initials, "L.D." The scabbard is also present, being moderately pitted over its length and showing a nice dark patina with no dents present. **425.00**

In original metal scabbard, the blade is clean and bright marked, "U.S. 1864 Ames." The grip and guard are original and in good shape, but do have remnants of old gold paint. The metal scabbard is in nice condition with dark, aged patina and no dents at all. Near the top of the scabbard are some old solder marks where a small plate was once affixed. **795.00**

Overall fine condition with beautiful brass guard and pommel with delicate patina. The leather grip covering and twisted wire wrap are near perfect, with just light wear on the leather. The blade is marked with the Ames Mfg Co marking, date of 1862, and, "Conn," to show purchase and issuance by the state. The blade is overall clean steel color with a couple spots of staining, but no pitting or bad edge nicks. The steel scabbard has a fine light-brown age patina and is dent free. There is a tiny crack in the scabbard's throat, rack number, "71," on the guard, very nice condition. **850.00**

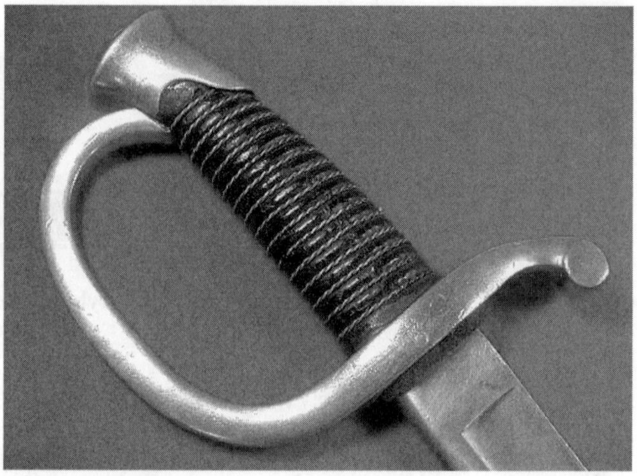

An import, this style of saber designated the "Model 1840 Light Artillery Saber" was used by troops, both North and South.

Middle Tennessee Relics

The blade is sparkling bright and clean, grip is perfect, 100% original wrap and wire. The scabbard is very nice as well, large number of import 1840 cavalry sabers, and artillery sabers were used by C.S. forces. **750.00**

Import, marked, "W. CLAUBERG-SOLINGEN," on the ricasso. The unusual thing about this artillery saber is that the entire brass D-guard is one solid cast piece, including the grip that has been painted black and has simulated wire cast in. The blade actually looks to be a cavalry-type blade in a brown patina. The brass guard has the recessed area for the scabbard to fit in, which is now lacking, crude brass casting. . . . **295.00**

Model 1840, Enlisted Man, Cavalry

"C. Hammond"-type with clear stamping on ricasso. Full wire, but no grip leather remains, totally untouched............................. **660.00**

Overall 42" with an iron gray 36" blade, unsharpened and in fine condition, would clean to brilliant. Right ricasso crisply marked, "US/ADK," left ricasso marked, "Ames Mfg. Co/Cabotville/1850." Deep mustard-colored patina on brass guard, pommel double inspected, "ADK," and, "JWK." Tine of knuckle bow has separated from the pommel, but could easily be pressed back in. Grips retain 100% original leather and double-twist wire wrap. Excellent heavy iron scabbard is a smooth almost blackish patina.................... **1,450.00**

Overall 42" with an iron gray 36" blade, unsharpened and in fine condition, would clean to brilliant if so desired. Right ricasso crisply marked, "US/ADK," left ricasso marked, "Ames Mfg. Co/Cabotville/1850." Deep mustard-colored patina on brass guard, pommel double inspected, "ADK," and, "JWK." Tine of knuckle bow has separated from the pommel, but could easily be pressed back in. Grips retain 100% original leather and double-twist wire wrap. Excellent heavy iron scabbard is a smooth, almost blackish patina. **1,450.00**

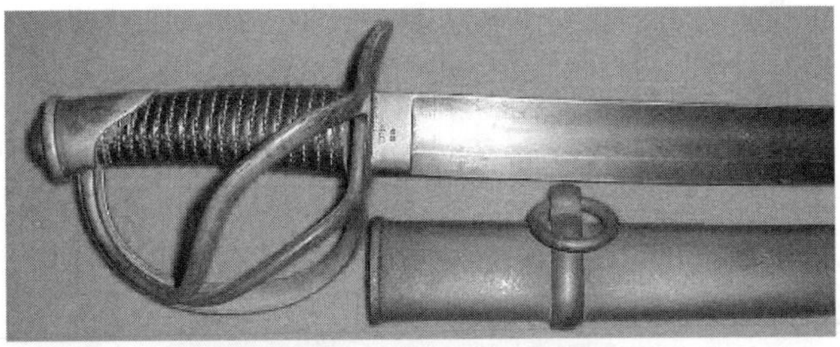

Hated by some because of the weight, and loved by others because of the devastating blows it could deliver, the Model 1840 Cavalry Saber was carried by troops on both sides. This example, bearing an 1847 date, could possibly have seen service in both the Mexican and Civil Wars.

Middle Tennessee Relics

Ames-manufactured heavy cavalry saber and scabbard, crisply marked, "N.P. Ames-Cabotville-1847." The grip is excellent with original wrap and wire, scabbard has a smooth-brown uncleaned age patina with no dents at all.. **1,250.00**

Blade marked, "US WD," and, "NP Ames Cabotville 1848," clean steel with one edge nick, leather handle wrap is very good. There are three strands of original twisted wire with the balance of the wire being a perfect replacement. Brass guard excellent with light age patina. Pommel marked, "JWR," and "WD." The scabbard is smooth, gray steel in fine condition, with one dent below the bottom ring mount. **975.00**

Classic import 1840-pattern cavalry saber. Retains the complete leather grip covering, all the wire wrap, it has a nice brass guard with good color, decent blade with "PDL" maker's mark, and complete with the scabbard, which is solid and free from dents, just having the expected age patina. **425.00**

"Old Wristbreaker" Model 1840 Saber dug on the Shiloh battlefield.

Middle Tennessee Relics

Complete Model 1840 "Old Wristbreaker" heavy cavalry saber. The blade is rusty, but very sound and complete. The brass guard is perfect with a brown-green patina. The wooden grip is decayed away, but remnants of the wire remain twisted around the tang. This is an early Shiloh find. **325.00**

Exceptionally scarce 1859-dated M1860 Ames Light Cavalry sword and scabbard (most do not realize that the sword was actually in production prior to the model designation with examples known as early as 1858). This example is an honest, brown sword with clear maker and inspector markings. The grip is shrunk and has flaking to the leather, and the wire wrap is complete. On the reverse in old painted script is "Appomattox C.H. 1865." **1,925.00**

This Model 1840 Saber is only one of 250 made by Smith, Crane & Co.

Sharpsburg Arsenal

Heavy cavalry saber by Smith Crane & Co., rarest of all contract swords. Total manufacture was only 250, delivered in 1861, dark patina on guard. Blade is in very good condition with very good, "S.C.& C." Grip has original twisted wire wrap on leather, which is about 70%. Missing leather ricasso washer, scabbard has nice patina with a few dents toward drag.. . . . . **1,795.00**

Model 1840, Enlisted Man, Cavalry, cont.

Made and marked by Sheble and Fisher of Philadelphia, markings were not struck cleanly and part is difficult to read, sword is untouched and unaltered. The handle wrap retains all the original leather and wire wrap (wire slightly loose). The blade is clean steel with absolutely no edge nicks or damage. The scabbard is free of dents or damage, having some expected surface rust and age patina **650.00**

Model 1840 Saber, sold with a scabbard that did not fit properly.

J.C. Devine Inc.

Made by "Sheble & Fisher/Phila<u>a</u>." The 35-1/2" long blade is gray, has some light pitting at the tip. The grip is missing, has a large crack, still has wire, iron scabbard does not fit. **300.00**

Made by P.S. Justice of Philadelphia, 36-1/4" long blade has a smooth, dark-gray patina and a couple of minor edge nicks. The brass guard has a couple of bent branches; the grip is missing all the leather and wire, no scabbard, good-plus condition. **200.00**

This P.S. Justice Model 1840 Saber did have its scabbard. Both sword and scabbard were in good condition.

Sharpsburg Arsenal

Manufactured in Philadelphia, Pennsylvania, very nice, complete cavalry saber with the hilt having a deep-mustard patina throughout, with the grip having original twisted wire and original leather. Blade is very nice with good, "PS Justice" markings, with four small nicks. Blade has not been sharpened or cleaned. Scabbard has dark-brown patina, having three very small dents on backside, very nice example. . . .**850.00**

Marked, "Horstman Phila," and, "N.J." Used extensively during the war, its weight and length made it a formidable weapon. Grip leather and wire intact, iron scabbard with even brown patina. **575.00**

Outstanding Model 1840, "Old Wristbreaker," cavalry-enlisted sword by William Glaze, Columbia, South Carolina, also known as the "Palmetto Armory." Absolutely brown overall. **5,250.00**

Signed on the ricasso with "C&J" (Clement & Jung of Solingen). It has a rich mirror-polish finish and all of the cross brushing at the ricasso. The brass guard is perfect with deep age patina mixed with traces of gilt. The leather handle covering is near perfect, as is the twisted wire wrap, though there is a horizontal split in the grip near the bottom edge. The scabbard is free from dents and covered with some light to moderate surface rust. **525.00**

This one is deeply marked on the blade, "1858 Ames Mfg Co Chicopee Mass," and, "US JH." The blade is steel gray, the handle wrap of leather and twisted wire is very nice. The scabbard is fine with light-brown age patina, some very minor pitting on the drag, and a very small dent on the scabbard. One ring on the scabbard is from a model 1833 dragoon saber, while the other is the standard 1840 ring. **975.00**

This piece is unmarked with full leather and wire, grip has a crack in it. The blade is mottled with no nicks and the scabbard is very good. **465.00**

This saber has the desirable date of 1845 stamped boldly on the ricasso. Blade is stamped, "US JH 1845 NP Ames Cabotville." The blade is a clean steel color, with some original polish. The brass guard is fine with a very appealing patina, the scabbard is likewise fine with deep-brown patina overall, and some pitting on the drag. The grip is void of leather and wire. **595.00**

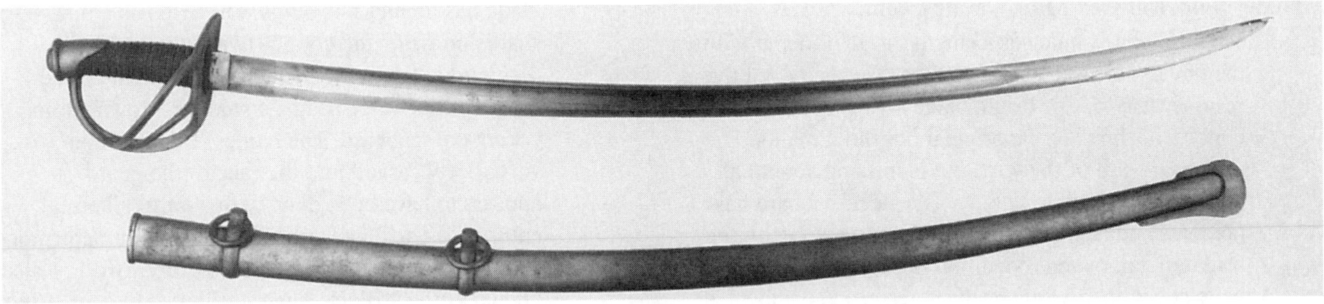

Bearing an 1848 date and the desirable "Ames/Cabotville" marking, this Model 1840 Saber was snatched up at auction.

J.C. Devine Inc.

Very appealing example of the Pennsylvania-made wrist breaker heavy cavalry saber. Leather and twisted wire nicely intact, with just honest wear. Blade is gray steel, no edge nicks, and deeply and boldly stamped on the ricasso, "P.S. Justice Philada." The brass guard has a delicate age patina. The scabbard is likewise very fine, with appealing attic patina and dirt and surface rust and no dents. **750.00**

The 35-3/4" blade is marked on the obverse ricasso, "US/WD," and on the reverse ricasso, "N.P. AMES/CABOTVILLE/1848." The blade is bright, showing much original luster and polishing marks with minor tarnish and tiny age spots. The brass guard has a stamped rack "692" and scratched "10." The brass has an ocher patina and the grip retains all the wire with only very light leather wear. The steel scabbard has no dents and is a light gray with minor rust spots. . . **800.00**

Model 1840 Saber with no scabbard and a couple of splits in the grip $125.00.

J.C. Devine Inc.

Import, 34-1/2" long blade is dark with scattered rust, the grip shows two splits and wear to leather wrapping, but has all the wire, the brass hilt with black patina has rack number, "65." No scabbard, good condition. . . . **125.00**

Untouched 41" overall import saber with tarnish freckled 36" bright blade. Marked "Walschied/Solingen" on the left ricasso. Walschied is a known exporter to both North and South during the Civil War. Brass guard is a beautiful untouched copper brown. Retains 95-98% leather wrap and a few coils of coppery wire wrap. Smooth, plum-brown, iron scabbard. **795.00**

Clemen & Jung (C & J) import cavalry saber and scabbard. This saber was imported to both sides during the Civil War. This piece is very nice, showing uncleaned brass hand guard and pommel cap. The grip has about 80% leather left and full wire. The front of the hand guard is turned down as Confederates liked to do and the scabbard is marked with an "X" and a "V." The blade is in nice condition with just a couple of nicks and the C & J marking is very nice and legible. The blade is unsharpened and full length, as it should be. The scabbard is in very nice condition as well, with only a minor ding here and there. Overall a very nice displayable piece! **495.00**

Marked "Germany" on the ricasso, this sword is patterned after the Model 1840 Saber. It is likely that it postdates the Civil War.

J.C. Devine Inc.

Model 1840, Enlisted Man, Cavalry, cont.

The 32-1/2" long blade has a knight's head trademark on the obverse ricasso and is marked "Germany" on the reverse ricasso. The bright blade is in excellent condition, showing the original polishing marks. The grip retains all of the wire, but is missing about half of the leather, due to flaking. The steel scabbard has no dents and has quite a lot of spider webbing on the bright metal, overall condition is very good." **225.00**

A fine blade with an eagle on the reverse, and on obverse is, "US." The blade is maker marked on the ricasso, "P D L." P.D. Luneschloss was a fine German maker who sold to a variety of U.S. contractors. The guard is highly decorated and has a soft brass patina. The blade has no nicks or dings. The grip has a fine sharkskin wrap and copper-twisted wire. The scabbard is fine with one dent, some wear on the drag. It shows nice usage, a smooth, brown patina covers the scabbard. The name, "F O Sherman," is very nicely carved into the face of the guard. It appears to have been done with a knife. Sherman enlisted in Sacketts Harbor, New York, on September 11, 1862, in the 10th New York Heavy Artillery, also known as the, "Black River Artillery." In April 1865, he became a member of the 6th New York Heavy Artillery and remained with that unit until August 24, 1865. This is a very nice sword that is associated with a unit that saw a good deal of action. **3,695.00**

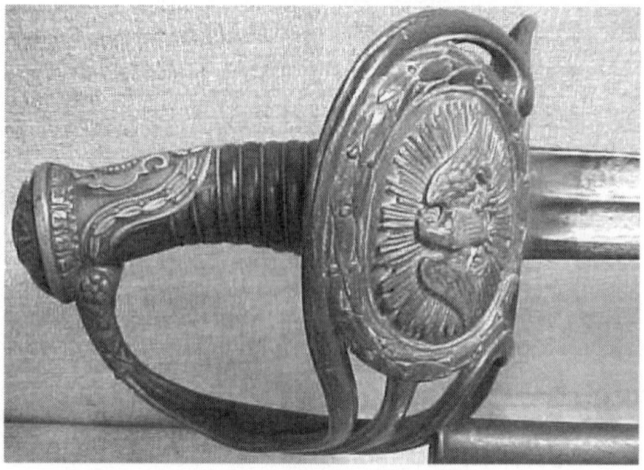

Officer's quality Model 1840 Saber made in France and bearing the arsenal date "1851."

Battleground Antiques, Inc.

Model 1840, Officer, Cavalry

Massive 37" long blade is straight with dual fullers and 1-1/4" wide at the ricasso. French-made with arsenal pattern date of 1855 etched on spine. Horn grip with original brass wire, monstrous pommel cap, three-branch and single branch guard, and oval sunburst disc on guard with spread-wing eagle device within. Even has the original scalloped buff leather throat washer, and original scabbard. **2,650.00**

Saber and scabbard, 39" overall length. Decorated three-branch guard is perfect with delicate light age patina with no dents or bends. The sharkskin grip covering is intact with some wear on the left side only. No wire wrap is present, blade is shiny steel and richly etched with "W.H. Horstmann & Sons Philadelphia," as well as having panoplies of arms and floral sprays. Blade has some traces of original factory luster, and is about the length of a staff blade, but curved for cavalry. The scabbard is all steel with a rich-brown patina and light surface pitting (fine and negligible). Of some interest is the fact that plainly visible on the outer branch of the guard are remnants of a wartime presentation inscription that was intentionally removed during this saber's period of use. ... **775.00**

Saber and brass, heavily engraved scabbard with traces of rich gilt, inscribed on reverse, "Presented to Capt. F.W. Coeler, by the Jaeger Comp., N. Orleans, Jan. 1st, 1855" (which became company I, 22nd. Louisiana Infantry, C.S.A.). Produced by Hyde and Goodrich, with 95% original leather grip and full wire wrap. Blade itself is a Solingen import type with gold-inlaid etched panels **22,500.00**

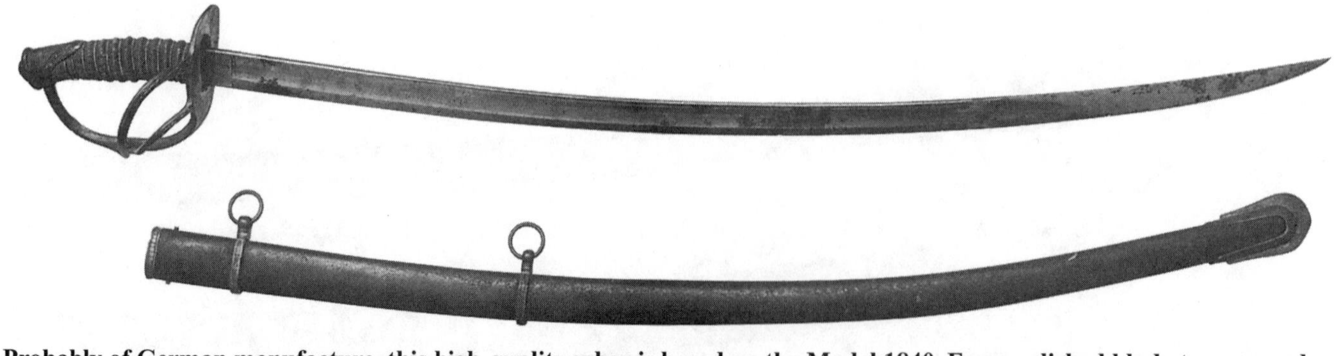

Probably of German manufacture, this high-quality saber is based on the Model 1840. From polished blade to engraved brass mounts on the scabbard, this entire sword belies a high investment upon the part of the original owner.

J.C. Devine Inc.

Import, 34-1/2" blade, etched on both sides with floral scrolls and martial panoplies, the obverse also has the American eagle with, "US," on the reverse. The bright blade has much of the original polish with quite a few patches of surface corrosion that should clean leaving little, if any, fine pitting. The blade does have several very small nicks in the edge with most of the etching bright. The brass pommel and guard are leaf engraved with the front of the guard having a raised relief eagle in flight. The guard has a break in one of the branches and retains 30% gilt. The grip retains all of the wire with only light wear on the fish skin wrapping. The iron scabbard has engraved gilt brass mounts and has a dark patina with light surface corrosion, no dents. This sword is probably of German manufacture and the condition is very good. **1,500.00**

Done on the British Pattern 1853 Cavalry Saber, 39-1/2" overall with a lightly curved 33" blade. Blade is a smooth, blackish tarnish that should clean to brilliant. Excellent, deep military etched decoration with fine eagle done on the right flat surrounded by stands of arms and, "E Pluribus Unum," in a riband. "W.H. Horstmann/& Sons/Philadelphia," in panel at right ricasso. Left has stands of arms and acanthus decorations, "US.". Iron three-tine guard, back strap and pommel. 100% gray skin grip wrap and fine double-twist copper wire, correct and fine iron scabbard is a smooth, slate-gray patina. . . . **1,700.00**

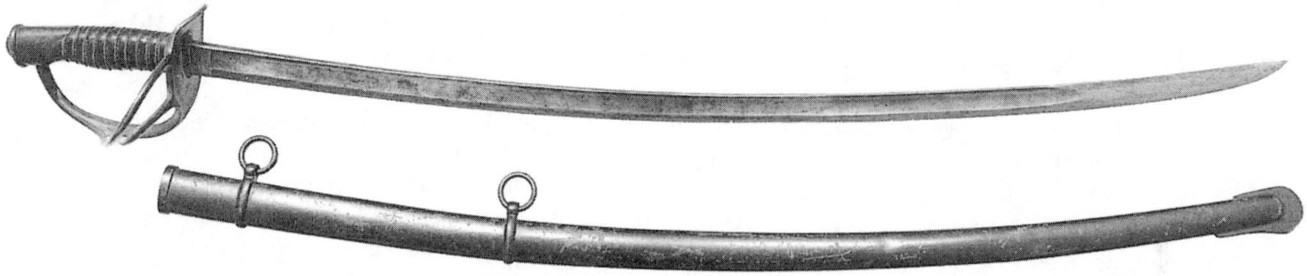

Model 1860 Cavalry Saber bearing the rather rare "1859" date.

J.C. Devine Inc.

Model 1860, Enlisted Man, Cavalry

1861 Ames Manufacturing saber and scabbard, full original grip and wire wrap, and crisp and clear markings on ricasso. Scabbard has been lightly cleaned. Blade only average, but no big nicks or rust, hilt looks like it has been painted black. **600.00**

Made by Ames, 34-1/2" blade is marked on the obverse ricasso, "US/JH/1859," and has very good manufacturer's markings on the reverse ricasso. The blade is gray with several small nicks in the edge, which has been sharpened. The brass guard has the initials, "HC," scratched into the top and bottom and has a dark patina. The grip retains all the wire with three small areas of wear to the leather wrapping. The iron scabbard has two shallow dents and shows scuffing to an old covering of black paint. **850.00**

1863-dated, Ames-marked saber with scabbard in good condition, original wrap and wire (very fine). Blade is in fine condition. **625.00**

1865-dated Ames specimen with nice blade and strong markings on the ricasso. This one lacks the throat on the scabbard and the leather on the grip, though the twisted wire is still present. Overall good solid condition, with perfect three-branch brass guard (no bends at all) even has the leather washer still present where the blade meets the guard. The scabbard has a couple minor dents, but is solid with a nice even light-brown age patina. **365.00**

Three-branch brass guard is dent free, and absolutely cruddy with patina, dirt, and grime encrusted over the brass. The leather grip covering is quite good. The wire is gone, the leather washer remains. Blade is outstanding with 80% mint factory luster. Blade is marked, "US JM 1864," and also, "Mansfield & Lamb Forestdale RI." The scabbard is dent free, though dirty, and appears to have a coat of hundred-year-old earth tone paint under the dirt. **595.00**

A really appealing example, blade stamped, "US/JF/186?," as well as bearing the Ames firm logo in a scroll design. Blade is gray steel with no edge nicks. Grip has very good leather and full wire. Brass is nicely aged with traces of gold G.A.R. post paint. Drag of scabbard deeply and legibly marked, "ADK." Scabbard has plum-brown patina mixed with age and dirt. **695.00**

A very good example that is 100% original and complete in every respect. This has a nice patina on the brass guard that is perfect and free from bends. The leather grip covering and twisted wire wrap are intact and original, with the leather showing normal handling wear. The blade is deeply stamped with the full Millard firm logo, as well as the 1862 date, U.S., and inspector's marks. There are several edge nicks in the blade, which is overall clean, gray steel. The leather washer is still present where the blade meets the guard. The scabbard has a nice light age patina mixed with age staining, and two small dents on each side about 7 north of the drag." **725.00**

Model 1860, Enlisted Man, Cavalry, cont.

A very presentable specimen with full original leather grip covering and twisted wire wrap. The guard is excellent and free from dents, and it bears a rack number of "616" as well as a unit mark of "E.C." in large characters. The blade is deeply stamped with the full Roby firm name as well as 1864 date and the "U.S.," and "AGM," inspector's mark. This is complete with the scabbard, which is free from dents. It has a nice, brown age patina covering the body of the scabbard with some scale and heavy rust at the drag. The only defect on this sword is that the blade tip has been rounded. **525.00**

An 1862-dated Ames specimen with nice blade and decent markings on the ricasso. This one lacks the throat on the scabbard and much of the leather on the grip is worn, though the twisted wire is still present. Overall good solid condition, with fine 3-branch brass guard with nice age patina. This even has the leather washer still present where the blade meets the guard. The scabbard has a couple dents but is solid with a nice even light brown age patina. ... **350.00**

An extremely desirable example with this scarce early date, and nice condition too. The ricasso is marked "US/J.H./1859" and also has a crisp deep maker's mark of "Ames Mfg. Co./Chicopee/Mass." The blade is a fine clean steel color with no rust or edge nicks. The 3-branch brass guard is excellent and free from bends or dents, it bears an issuance "rack" number of "B 52" on the underside. The leather grip covering is excellent, just showing expected light handling age, the twisted wire is a nearly undetectable restoration, which looks perfect. The leather washer is still present where the ricasso meets the guard. The scabbard is likewise fine. It has an inspector's initial "W" on the throat, a small rack number on the back near the throat, faint remnants of inspector's mark on the drag (illegible), and is overall clean steel color with some staining..................... **895.00**

Blade nicely marked "US/CEW/1863." Also signed with full "Emerson & Silver Trenton N.J." makers mark. Leather wrap is superb and the wire is still intact. Brass guard has a delicate patina and there is "JH" stamp on pommel and a tiny "167" rack marking. The blade is clean steel with one edge nick only, no leather washer present. The scabbard has a deep dark patina, no dents, one tiny push on the backside above the drag, and some pitting on the drag itself. A very appealing and solid specimen with really great leather grip. **795.00**

Brass guard richly and deeply aged. Leather grip covering and twisted wire are both truly excellent. The blade is gray steel deeply marked, "US 1865 AGM," and, "C Roby W. Chelmsford Mass." No edge nicks, scabbard has light and uniform age brown patina (smooth) with no dents, and only some superficial light pitting on the drag. **775.00**

Brass three-branch guard, excellent with no bends or dents, light age patina. A small, "A78," rack number is stamped into the outer branch, pommel marked, "CEW." Handle wrap is very good with leather, light handling age and twisted wire are original and intact. Leather washer at ricasso is perfect, blade is nearly mint with brilliant bright factory luster, much original cross brushing on the ricasso. It is signed, "US CEW 1865," and, "Mansfield & Lamb Forestdale RI." The scabbard has a fine, smooth brown patina (no rust no pitting), no dents or bends. Does have some light scrapes and scratches in the surface patina on the scabbard. **950.00**

Dated 1862, this piece has a nice hilt with turned down top guard and a very decent blade with good scabbard that has some old nickel plate on it. The grip is also nice, but needs wire, nice early piece. **695.00**

It is 100% complete in all respects, including the leather washer at the hilt. The blade is nicely marked with full Ames markings as well as 1865 date, inspector's marks, and "U.S." stamp. The blade is gray steel color and free from rust or pits, no edge nicks. The leather and twisted wire wrap are excellent with very little wear. The three-branch brass guard is free from bends and has a heavy brown patina mixed with dirt & soot. The scabbard has a deep brown patina with areas of moderate to heavy surface pitting on the lower half. There is one small "push" in the center of the scabbard, otherwise free from dents........ **625.00**

Made and marked by the Ames Manufacturing Company and dated 1863. These marks are on the blade near the hand guard. Very nice 35" blade with no nicks, bends, or rust, though there is just a little staining. Scabbard is nice with a few very small dings. Drag is marked, "CE," and the basket is marked, "53," painted leather. **416.00**

Marked horizontally, "Ames Mfg. Co." on the obverse ricasso. The 34-3/4" blade has a light gray patina with scattered pinprick pitting. The hilt has a three-branch brass guard slightly bent, the leather wrapping on the grip shows wear and is missing most of the wire. The iron scabbard is a dark gray with even light pitting. **125.00**

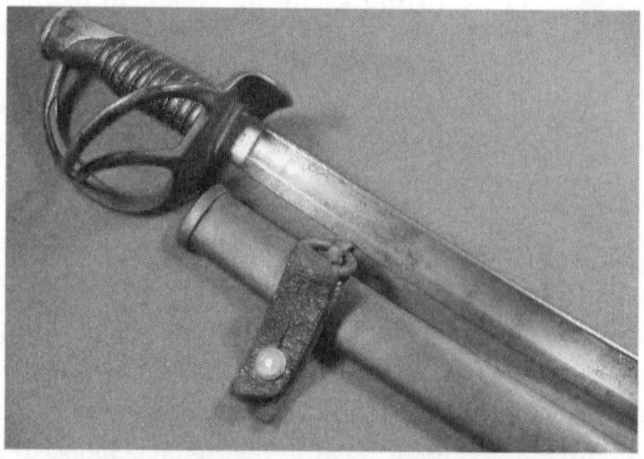

This Model 1860 Enlisted Man's Saber was dated 1860 and the scabbard, 1859.

Middle Tennessee Relics

Model 1860 Ames cavalry saber and scabbard dated 1859. The blade has a smooth gray patina with crisp, clear markings. The brass guard is excellent, with original wrap and wire on the grip. The scabbard has a thick brown patina with remnants of both leather sword straps. **1,250.00**

Model 1860 saber and scabbard by Ames, Chicopee, Massachusetts, dated and inspected in 1863. Original grip and wire wrap, 90%+ condition. Very honest and used wartime model, with numerous dings in the scabbard which look intentionally inflicted. . **550.00**

Ricasso stamped, "US JT 1860," on one side and, "Ames Mfg Co. Chicopee Mass," on the other. This has the full leather grip cover as well as the twisted wire wrap. The brass guard is perfect with no dents or bends. It has a deep rich patina on the brass and a rack number of "133." The pommel is stamped, "JH." Blade is gray steel with no rust, no pitting, and no edge nicks. The scabbard has no dents, overall smooth brown patina with light traces of silver paint or plate on the drag. **1,250.00**

The blade is stamped, "US JM 1863," other side marked, "Emerson & Silver Trenton NJ." The leather washer is still intact at the ricasso. The leather wrap on this sword is good. The twisted wire wrap is also still present. The guard is yellow brass with light patina and a slight bend in the outer branch of the guard. The blade is bright steel and has two tiny edge nicks. Pommel and drag are marked, "JM." The scabbard is plum-brown color. **895.00**

The brass guard is excellent with moderate age patina and shows honest use. The leather grip covering is excellent with just a couple light scuffs. The twisted wire wrap is firmly in place. The blade is clean steel color and nicely marked at the ricasso, "US 1865 AGM," as well as with the Roby firm marking all clear and legible. The original leather washer is present at the hilt. The scabbard is very nice with a couple minor dents. It was painted black sometime in the distant past. **625.00**

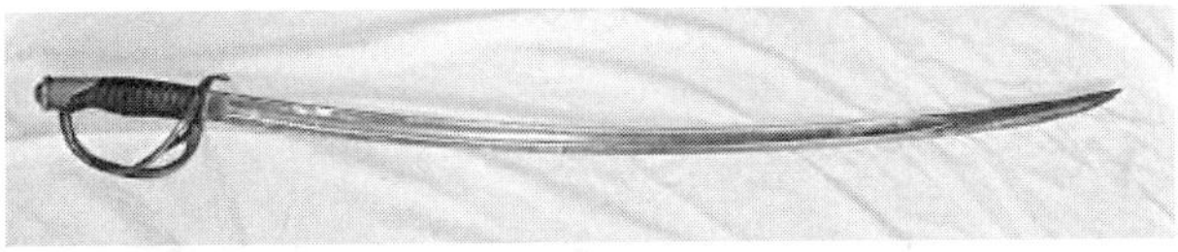

Ames-marked Model 1860 without a scabbard.

The U.S. mark is clearly visible on the ricasso. The first part of the date, "18-," is visible as is a letter "J" for the inspector's mark. The maker mark on the reverse side is no longer visible, which could indicate that it is from Ames Manufacturing Company, Chicopee, Massachusetts. The blade remains unsharpened, has a few very minor nicks and remnants of silver paint. The leather-wrapped grip and wire are complete. The knuckle bow and pommel cap are both marked "44." Hilt and blade are firmly attached. The knuckle bow rattles a little. Blade is approximately 34-3/4" long. Overall length approximately 41", no scabbard. **282.00**

These "Boker" marked light cavalry sabers are quite difficult to find. This is the regulation 1860 cavalry saber complete with the scabbard. The leather grip covering and twisted wire wrap are nicely intact with just a little chipping to areas of the leather on the backside of the grip (not visible when displayed). The brass guard is perfect, as is the gray steel scabbard. The blade is nice with gray steel color and it bears the crisp marking of "Henry Boker Solingen." Contracted for early in the Civil War exclusively for the Union Army. About "fine" condition. **595.00**

This saber possesses a very fine blade with a semi bright patina. There are no nicks or dings, ricasso is marked, "US/RPB/1862," and the reverse is marked, "PROV/TOOL/CO." The Providence Tool Company was the second smallest sword contractor to the U.S. Government, delivering only 10,434 swords, all of which were light cavalry swords. The leather grip is very fine and 100%, as is the twisted wire and the scabbard is perfect. **1,250.00**

Model 1860, Officer, Cavalry

38"overall with a curved 31-1/2" blade, black and steel patina with military etching on both sides of the flats. Right side features a spread-wing eagle surrounded by stands of arms. Left flat has a fine, "U.S.," encircled by an acanthus leaf decoration. German imported blade. Brass hilt has finely cast and chiseled acanthus leaf decorations on the guard, tines, and pommel. Grips retain 90-95% original rayskin wrap and 100% double-twist brass wire wrap. Smooth, plum iron scabbard with part of original sword sling, very good condition. **1,400.00**

It is a simple pattern, three-branch brass guard without casting or engraved decoration, rayskin grip covering with twisted-copper wire wrap (excellent with just light wear). The scabbard is very pretty with a plum-brown finish on the steel (no dents) and attractive brass throat, ring mounts, and drag. The drag looks like a standard drag as found on staff or foot swords. The blade is plain with an unmarked ricasso. Very nice with no rust or edge nicks, and also never having been etched, overall in excellent condition. **975.00**

Shows honest wear and is very nice, full grip wrap and twisted wire. The brass guard has the Ames eagle incorporated (embossed) into the quillon area on the guard, which is a signature feature on this Ames pattern. Gray steel blade with full etching that is characteristically very faint. The brass mounted steel scabbard is very good with a few dents in the brass drag, missing the brass throat. **1,695.00**

U.S. Swords

Made by Ames Manufacturing, ca. 1845, this sword was purportedly carried by Assistant Surgeon F.A. McVeigh of the 46th Virginia Infantry.

Battleground Antiques, Inc.

Militia, Officer

1840-1850 spread-wing eagle sword by Ames Manufacturing, Chicopee, Massachusetts, traces of heavy patina on all the gilt mounts. Nice, clear etching on blade with traces of original frosting as well—still has the original sword knot on it, as well as the chain guards. Family history states this item was carried by Assistant Surgeon F. A. McVeigh of the 46th Virginia Infantry who served from September of 1863. McVeigh was from Loudoun County, Virginia. The 46th saw action from Norfolk through Northern Virginia, North and South Carolina, Georgia and Florida. **4,500.00**

Circa 1840-1865 Ames militia officer's sword, nice carved ivory/bone grip with repair to minor hairline crack. Brass hilt retains 60% of original gilt finish and has chain from knight's head pommel to quillon. Blade is in good condition with good etching of eagle, stand of arms, and floral design, marked, "AMES MFG CHICOPPEE MASS." There is some age staining on blade, no pitting or scabbard. **535.00**

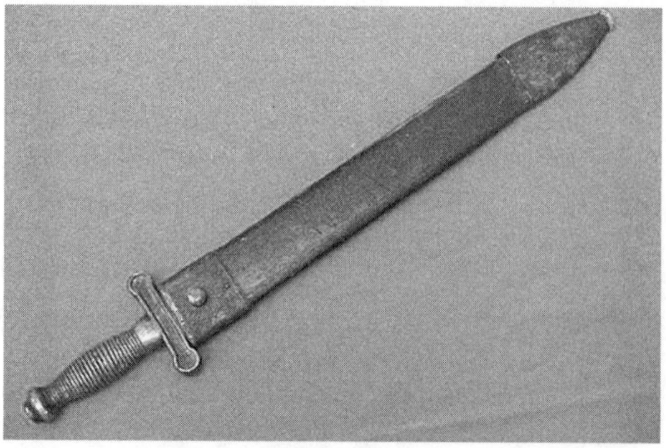

The Model 1832 Foot Artillery Short Sword was based on the gladiator sword of Roman era. Intended as the sole source of individual protection afforded to an artilleryman, they soon fell out of favor as heavy and useless.

Model 1832, Enlisted Man, Artillery, very nice Ames short with scabbard, part of the buff belt with frog and wreath, part of the two-piece belt buckle, 19" double-edged blade with three fullers in excellent shape and has great patina. The blade is marked with an eagle and, "Unite- Stat--, 1842, JCB inspector," as well as with traces of, "N.P. Ames Co. Springfield." Cast brass hilt in great shape with eagle on both sides of the pommel. Large "W.A.T." inspector's mark (Captain W.A. Thornton). The brass has beautiful patina. Excellent black leather scabbard with brass throat, drag, frog stud. The leather is in very nice shape and still supple. **961.00**

Import, Model 1832, Artillery

French-made artillery short sword complete with the perfect condition, matching scabbard. Blade marked with Paris maker's cartouche, excellent condition. **395.00**

Very-fine condition, marked "329" on brass guard, blade is marked "1832" and "L" which is worn, but readable. **350.00**

Model 1840, Musician

Blade is in very fine condition with no nicks or dings. The patina is gray to semi bright, with the usual age discoloring here and there, marked, "US/AHC/1862," and the ricasso is marked with a very light stamping, "AMES MFG./CHICOPEE/MASS." The brass guard has a nice aged brass patina, no scabbard. ...**295.00**

Sword without scabbard, brass is real nice as well as the Ames markings that include, "CABOTVILLE 1847," that makes this a Mexican War-dated piece. No scabbard is present and there is moderate pitting on the sword's tip.........................**325.00**

Excellent condition, bright blade, leather probably replaced on scabbard, crisp inspection markings and date. **550.00**

Import, very-fine condition, with full and solid scabbard. This is an import brought into the U.S. and sold in Philadelphia. **375.00**

Sword, U.S., Model 1840, NCO

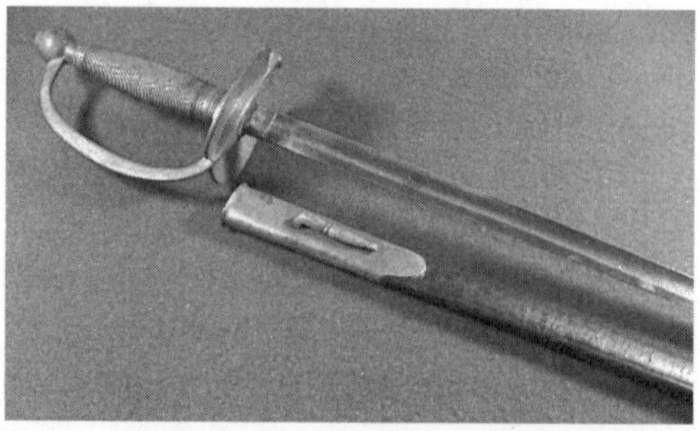

The N.C.O. sword remained a standard issue item until about 1910. This example, dated 1864 was in good condition, complete with scabbard.

Middle Tennessee Relics

The blade is sparkling bright, marked, "U.S. Ames 1864," cast brass guard is excellent with deep uncleaned patina. The leather scabbard is complete and in overall good sound condition. **595.00**

Blade does not have a maker mark, but has a faint inspection mark and date, "US," and, "1863." The guard is inspection marked, "AHC," and there is the number seven on the pommel, guard, and grip. Nice patina on the guard, blade is bright with no pitting or rust, all the black paint is gone from the scabbard, missing screws. **311.00**

29-1/2" long with a professionally cut down 23" blade, left flat has a handsome, "U.S.M.C.," panel flanked by acanthus leaf decoration. "Horstmann/Phila" etched in panel at left ricasso. Brass hilt is a very nice golden patina with the aforementioned turned down clamshell guard. Cut down black saddle leather scabbard with original brass guard and throat. **500.00**

33-1/2" overall with a bright 3" single-edged blade, "Horstmann/& Sons/Philadelphia," stamped on the right ricasso. Cast brass hilt is a deep reddish-bronze patina. Off side clamshell guard is turned down and this is sometimes considered to be the mark of a USMC-used NCO sword. Excellent condition, no scabbard. . . . **350.00**

Marked, "Emerson & Silver, Trenton, New Jersey," and, "US-DFM 1863." Blade is 32" long, original patina with brass-mounted iron scabbard having a couple of dents, overall length 38". **475.00**

Perfect brass grip and guard, "DFM" on guard, blade is near mint, boldly marked, "US DFM 1863," and, "Emerson & Silver Trenton NJ," Blade is excellent with 60% or more of the mint factory luster. The steel scabbard is likewise super, no body dents. One small dent in brass and drag. **595.00**

Perfect leather scabbard, bright minty blade, boldly signed with full Ames firm marking, U.S. inspector's marks, and date of 1864. . . . . **650.00**

The 31-3/4" straight blade is marked on the obverse ricasso, "U.S./DFM/1863," and the manufacturer's markings on the reverse ricasso are clearly stamped. The blade has a light-gray patina with some dried grease, should clean easily. The brass hilt is in fine shape with about 70% of the gilt remaining. The brass-mounted black leather scabbard is a reproduction in excellent condition. **250.00**

An 1865-dated sword with straight blade and all brass grip with double kidney-shaped handguards. Nice piece with the brass-mounted iron scabbard. . .**525.00**

Sword described by Peterson as being a non-regulation 1840 NCO sword. They were used from the 1840s through the years following the Civil War. Fine condition and complete with perfect leather scabbard. The pommel is a cast-brass knight's head, the grip is fluted bone, the cross guard is a T-shaped guard with floral scrolls and shield-shaped langet (much gilt finish present). The blade is bright and shiny with an elliptical cross section. The scabbard is tarred leather over a steel sheath, with brass drag and throat with button for attaching to a frog on the top mount. **135.00**

Very early manufacture date of 1848. The brass guard is perfect with light age patina, "JWR," and, "WD," inspectors' initials present. The blade is deep gray color, smooth with no rust pitting. It is stamped, "N.P. Ames Cabotville 1848," and, "US WD," on the ricasso, no scabbard, excellent overall condition. **325.00**

This sword has a mint blade with all the original factory luster, no nicks or dings, ricasso is marked, "U S/ G.W.C./1864," and the obverse is marked, "MADE BY/AMES MFG.CO./CHICOPEE / MASS." The brass guard has an uncleaned, soft brass patina, no scabbard. **375.00**

Sword is totally unmarked, except for a couple assembly numbers on the brass, no scabbard. **225.00**

Import, just the sword (no scabbard) with dark blade and rich patina on the brass, Solingen maker's mark on ricasso. **225.00**

Import, top-notch example with pretty brass grip, guard, and scabbard mounts. Blade is nice clean steel, the leather washer is still present at the ricasso, and the leather scabbard is full length, solid, very fine example. **395.00**

Model 1840, Officer, Medical

Complete with a fine brass scabbard. Langet has small separately applied letters, "MS" (Medical Staff). Blade is nice and shiny with great etching, "U.S.," eagle, and military motifs. Blade is excellent with just a few light spots of surface pitting, where some surface rust was removed. Scabbard is excellent and dent free. . .**2,100.00**

Probably dating to just before the Civil War, this Model 1840 Medical Staff Officer's Sword is quite typical of swords carried by military surgeons.

Model 1840, Officer, Medical, cont.

Nice example of a pre-Civil War medical staff officer's sword. The flat, double-edged blade measures 28" long and 7/8" wide at the ricasso. It is profusely etched on the obverse side with floral designs, "U.S." and an eagle with outstretched wings and more floral designs. The etching runs for over half of the blade length and shows much of its original luster and frosty contrast. The reverse side of the blade is etched, "Medical. Staff," in a large panel. Above the panel is a nicely etched American flag with a liberty cap hanging from atop the flagpole. There are only a couple of minor spots of dark staining. The heaviest staining is around the last "f" in the word "Staff." There are a couple of very minor spots of pin-size pits between the end of the etching and the blade tip. Unetched portion of the blade shows 98% original full luster. There are no maker's marks on the blade. Nicely cast hilt retains about 80% of its original gold gilt. Applied silver "MS" on the front langet. At the top of the hilt, on both sides is a nicely cast eagle with outstretched wings. The dent-free, brass scabbard only has a couple of minor scratches and pin-size nicks, mostly around the drag. The top mount lacks one of its ring mounts. The brass scabbard shows the gilt only in protected areas, and has a nice, soft patina look to it. **1,950.00**

Nice inscribed Model 1840 medical staff officer sword and scabbard, blade is in only fair condition (was Damascus and suffered from water damage). Back of scabbard ornately inscribed, "In Hoc Signo Vinces, Presented to Doctor J.G. Mackinsie by the Officers and Patients of St. Pauls Hospital Alexandria, Virginia, as a token of regard Sept. 17, 1862." **3,000.00**

Housed in an iron scabbard with rich brass fittings, this Model 1850 Foot Officer's Sword was manufactured by Horstmann and Son and possesses a finely etched blade.

Sharpsburg Arsenal

Model 1850, Foot Officer

Manufactured by Horstmann & Sons. Blade is finely etched with standard U.S. motif with some salt and peppering, but no rust. Guard and pommel are heavily engraved with handle being German silver with triple-twisted wire wrap. Scabbard is iron with a dark-brown patina. A brass throat with heavily engraved brass hangers and drag. **4,995.00**

Sword and scabbard by Horstmann, Philadelphia, circa 1862. Blade is about 90% mirror bright with crisp etching and frosting of U.S. military motifs. Hilt retains 35% original gilt. Full sharkskin grip covering and wire wrap. Scabbard has minor flaking, but no cracks or breaks. **1,350.00**

The blade is outstanding with 80% bright luster, superbly etched with military motifs, eagle, and "U.S." The guard has proper cast floral design with, "U.S.," incorporated into the casting. The scabbard is excellent. Steel finished with plum color, and adorned with attractive brass mounts. The brass has a delicate age patina with great appeal. The pommel and guard are likewise absolutely beautiful with undisturbed age patina. The rayskin grip covering is perfect and the triple wire wrap is intact with a small section repaired that is undetectable unless you look closely. The blade is signed on the ricasso, "PDL.".......... **1,950.00**

Superb color and patina, brass guard and scabbard mounts are truly beautiful, with a delicate undisturbed light age patina of uniform age and color. The leather grip coveting is near perfect with the fancy twisted wire wrap firmly in place. The wire is a double strand of twisted-brass wire flanked by single strands of brass wire. The blade is fine with bright steel color and etched with a widespread winged, federal eagle on one side and the letters, "U.S.," on the other. The spine is signed with a scarce Boston dealer's marking, "Palmers & Batchelders Boston." The leather scabbard is excellent with great life, strength, and finish. The finish is mostly smooth shiny leather, with just a few age crackles. The screw securing the drag is missing, and the previous owner put a spot of glue on it to hold the drag in place. **1,295.00**

Etched, "USMC," pattern is incorporated into the blade etching on this sword. The blade is signed, "W.H. Horstmann & Sons Philadelphia." It is also stamped with the Solingen blade maker's mark of a king's head with crown. The blade is gray steel with areas of dark age staining and wear. One side is etched with an eagle and panoply of arms. The other side is etched with military motifs and a faintly visible, "USMC." The grip wrap is leather and completely intact, as is the twisted wire wrap. **950.00**

32" blade is 1-1/16" wide at ricasso and etched with "U.S.," spread-winged eagle with shield, "E Pluribus Unum," and vine with scroll. Maker's mark reads, "F. Horster Solingen." Steel guard has eagle and shield sitting on a banner marked, "U.S.," and, "E Pluribus Unum." Sharkskin grip with wire wrap, correct metal scabbard with drag, throat piece, and dual suspension rings............................. **710.00**

37" overall with a brilliant 31" blade. "Ames Mfg. Co./ Chicopee/Mass," is etched in panel at right ricasso. Blade beautifully etched in a military motif featuring a stand of arms on the right below a Federal eagle. Left flat features a large block, "U.S.," under a stand of arms. Finely cast and chiseled guard with its acanthus leaf openwork tines retains 50-60% original bright gilt. Fine sharkskin gray grip wrap with gilt double-twist brass wire. Black saddle leather scabbard with brightly gilt brass furniture. Throat stamped with the Ames address again. Scabbard has been repainted to cover the crazing, but otherwise excellent. **2,450.00**

A very solid and appealing example of the standard combat infantry officer's sword (no scabbard). Perfect shagreen grip covering and twisted wire wrap. The cast floral brass guard is perfect with nice patina. The blade is nicely etched with military trophies, an eagle, "E Pluribus Unum," and "U.S.," It is also etched, "W.H. Horstmann & Son Philadelphia," just above the ricasso. The blade is dark gray with some age staining, very solid and representative.... **475.00**

A very solid and attractive example, steel guard manufactured with a spread-wing American eagle, letters, "U.S.," and, "E Pluribus Unum," nicely cut out of the steel guard. The blade is lightly etched with US military motifs and an eagle (nice steel color and no pitting). The grip is fully wrapped in the sharkskin (or rayskin) and the twisted wire is firmly in place. This is complete with the original dent-free steel scabbard, some expected age staining. There is a faint New York dealer's name etched on the ricasso. **795.00**

Crisp maker markings on both blade and upper brass mount, and a full-length leather scabbard with minor area of weakness near where drag connects. Nice strong etching on blade typical of the high quality. Still has one original sword hanger attached to upper ring. **2,000.00**

Etched and engraved black with a Chicopee, Massachusetts address, cast hilt with openwork, leather scabbard with brass bands and drag, engraved, "Lt. Geo. Trembley, 174th N.Y. S.I.," 30-1/4" blade, overall 36-1/4" long. **1,980.00**

Identified 3rd New York Cavalry sword, clearly dated and inspected 1865, full grip and wire shows age, but no major damage; a few combat-type nicks in the gray-silvery blade, untouched patina overall. Has great original tag on back of scabbard which reads, "S.C. Pierce 3rd NY Vet. Vol. Cav." Pierce mustered in at age 22 on August 20, 1861, from Rochester as a first lieutenant. He is listed as a POW at Reams Station, Virginia, 1864, and escaped from POW camp at Columbia, South Carolina, in November 1864, but was recaptured. The 3rd New York served in the Army of the Potomac under Banks and Stone, the Department of South Carolina, then in Virginia and later in the Army of the James. Comes with service records. **1,200.00**

Model 1850, Foot Officer, cont.

Inscribed from Massachusetts with a fine-condition blade. Ames Manufacturing marked sword, inscribed on upper mount, "Presented To Lt. B.F. Talbot by J.T. Bradlee Boston 1862." Full sharkskin grip and original wire wrap; clear Ames marking on upper scabbard brass mount as well. Blade etching is clear and good plus. Blade is bright with a few tiny edge nicks and some mottled pitting near the tip. One old, clean break about 5" above drag with small section missing. **2,750.00**

Marked, "Horstmann Sons, Philadelphia," not dated. Original leather and wire wrap grip still good. Even patina, good condition, no scabbard, blade length 30-1/2"; overall length 36-1/2." **425.00**

Presentation-grade infantry sword and scabbard, "Collins and Company, Hartford, Ct.," dated 1862. Etched blade includes a panel that reads, "Our Union Forever." Presentation plate on scabbard to, "Lt. W.H. Palmer from his Father, Feb. 1864." Palmer saw service in the 53rd Illinois Infantry at Corinth, Jackson, and Vicksburg. Also saw activity during the siege of Atlanta, Jonesboro, and the "March to the Sea." Above average blade, which shows honest light use and wear. **5,000.00**

Presentation-grade sword and scabbard with exceptional gilt and overall condition with Tiffany-style statue hilt and perched golden American eagle on the pommel. Presented to, "Col. Jacob DeForest, 81st New York Infantry (Second Oswego Regiment; Mohawk Rangers)" in March of 1864. DeForest enlisted in August 1861 and was elected lieutenant colonel. He was promoted to colonel in July 1862, and served until he was dismissed for disability in September 1864. The 81st served in the Army of the Potomac, Department of North Carolina and Virginia, and Army of the James. **20,000.00**

Presentation-grade sword, jeweled hilt, German silver scabbard with exceptional brass high-relief mounts, and a Tiffany-style standing Liberty statue hilt. Blade by Clauberg with exceptional etching and panels and traces of gilt overwash. Presented to, "Lt. Col. Henry B. Burgh, Company A, 9th Illinois Cavalry," Burgh served from September of 1861 until December of 1865. This unit fought both Nathan Bedford Forrest and John Bell Hood's troops and more for a full four years. **10,000.00**

Presentation sword and scabbard, uniquely engraved on both the scabbard mount and the sword hilt. Plain blade, full grip covering, but missing a strand of the treble-twisted brass, partial sword knot as well. Scabbard shows a minor repair near the drag. "Presented To Captain Henry Einwechter by the Elm Tree Council #26 O.U.A.M." This officer served in the 4th Reserve, 33rd Infantry in command of Company I. He was "damaged" in July 1862 at Seven Days Battle, and declared mentally unstable, forcing him to give up his commission. **1,850.00**

The acid-etched blade was bright on this Ames Model 1850 Foot Officer's Sword, and the leather scabbard was tight and sound.

Sharpsburg Arsenal

The acid-etched blade was bright on this Ames Model 1850 Foot Officer's Sword, and the leather scabbard was tight and sound.

Sharpsburg Arsenal

This is a 95% sword in excellent condition. Retaining a sharply acid-etched blade with all of the frosting and absolutely no rust or pitting. Cast-brass hilt with approx. 90% of original gold gilt remaining. Original leather ricasso washer, and sharkskin grip is tight. Leather scabbard is in excellent condition with the brass hangers and drag retaining 85% of original gold gilt. Top scabbard mount is stamped, "Ames Mfg. Co. Chicopee Mass." **4,295.00**

This is a fairly rare-type of foot officer's sword and, although not marked, is the typical Saurbier-type of blade with light etching. The pommel also has the typical Saurbier tang nut. The brass pommel cap and handguard are very dark patina and the leather is good, as is the wire. **550.00**

This sword is not marked, but is typical of Saurbier-made examples. The sword has full leather and wire with light etching on the blade, no scabbard. **525.00**

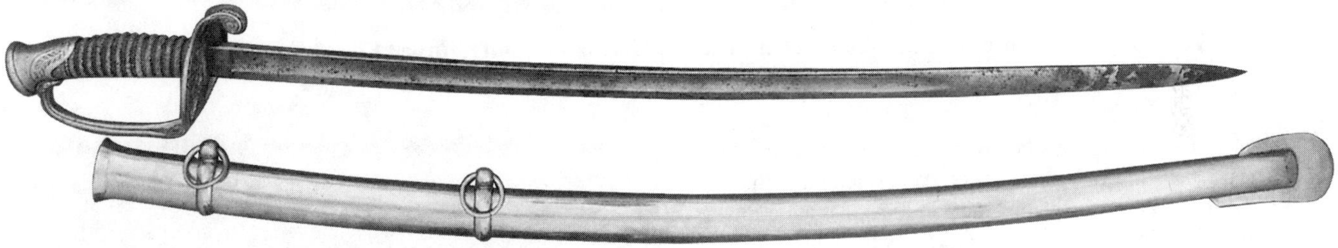

Virtually identical to a foot officer's sword made in the United States, this imported blade was lightly pitted. Matched to a reproduction scabbard for a Model 1860 Cavalry Saber.

J.C. Devine Inc.

The 30-1/4" long blade is not maker marked, etching is barely visible on the predominantly gray blade with deep pitting on the tip. The grip retains all the fish skin wrap, but is missing almost all the wire. The Civil War import is in very-good condition with a reproduction steel scabbard for a cavalry saber. **175.00**

Imported by Schuyler, Hartley, & Graham of New York, this sword was manufactured in Solingen by W. Slauberg. The sword is beautifully engraved on both sides of the blade and on the guard. The sharkskin grip is worn through in places, and the wire is partially missing and loose. The scabbard drag is worn down on the bottom, but the rest of the scabbard is very good. **730.00**

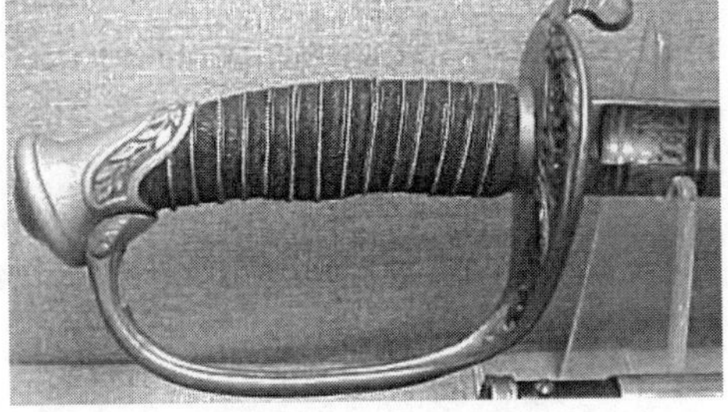

This German-made Model 1850 Foot Officer's Sword is identical to a United States-made version.

Battleground Antiques, Inc.

Import, museum-grade infantry officer sword, this Solingen-made Model 1850 infantry officer is original in all respects, with fine sharkskin grip, full wire, fancy brass mounted regulation steel scabbard (mounted type), and finely etched blade that retains close to 95% original frosting. **3,000.00**

Import, brass guard is perfect with beautiful age patina. Shagreen grip cover is very good and twisted-wire wrap is intact. The blade is clean steel with richly etched military motifs, federal eagle, and floral scrolls. The blade etching is identical to some Roby foot officer's swords, but interestingly is signed "Paris." The scabbard is missing the bottom 8" including the drag, but is otherwise superb with beautifully aged top and middle mount and really nice leather. **595.00**

Import, 38-1/2" overall with a slightly curved 33" blade. Blade is decorated in a military motif featuring an American eagle in the right-hand panel and a big decorative, "U.S.," in the left. Left ricasso has the knight logo surrounded by, "Clauberge/Solingen," maker's mark. Mellow brass hilt with fine openwork guard with, "U.S.," entwined in the tines. Grips retain 100% of the dark gray rayskin wrap and fine gilt double-twist wire wrap. Black saddle leather scabbard is good and sound with brass mounts and hangers. **1,850.00**

Model 1850, Foot Officer, cont.

Import, complete with the original scabbard. The brass grip, guard, pommel, and clamshell guard have beautiful patina with exactly the same color on the throat and drag of the scabbard. The blade is etched for two thirds of its length with floral scrolls, an urn, federal eagle, "E Pluribus Unum," and the large letters, "U.S." Very nicely etched with good detail and very little wear. The blade is overall steel gray in color with no rust, pits, or edge nicks. The scabbard is a plain leather scabbard with brass mount and drag. It is very solid with just one small crack where the drag meets the leather. The ricasso is signed with a knight's-head motif showing manufacture by one of the Solingen makers. **. 2,100.00**

Import, 30-1/2" blade is unmarked, gray patina with even fine pitting. The brass guard shows wear, grip retains all the wire with minor scuffs on the leather. The iron scabbard is a replacement from a cavalry saber, and has two small dents near the drag. **100.00**

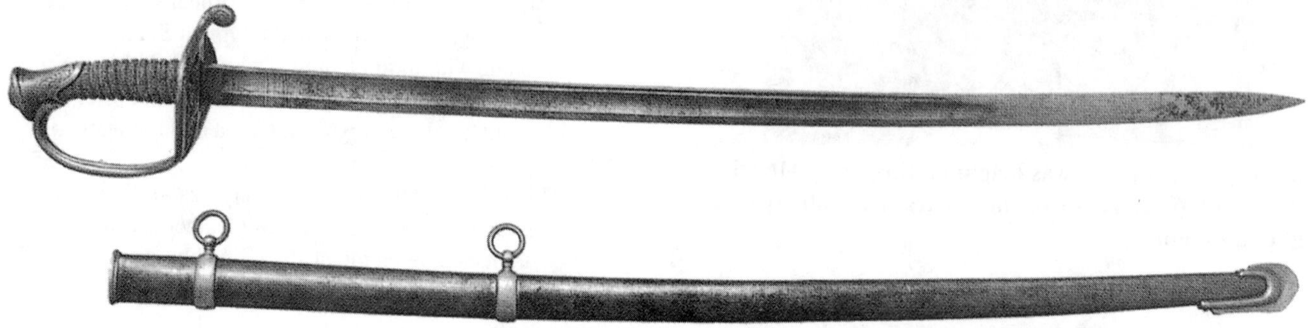

Model 1850 Foot Officer's Sword in metal scabbard marked to German manufacturer "Eisenhauer."

J.C. Devine Inc.

The 31" long blade is etched with the usual floral scrolls with large martial panoplies on each side and with, "U.S.," on the reverse and the American eagle on the obverse. The gray blade is marked by the German maker, Eisenhauer, and shows moderate etching wear. The brass guard and pommel are of standard form with pierced floral scroll, the grip is missing the wire and shows only two small areas of wear on the fish-skin wrapping. The brass-mounted iron scabbard has a dark gray patina on the iron and has only one small patch of corrosion, very-good condition...... **700.00**

The brass guard is excellent with an attractive aged patina. The grip is polished wood, very similar to those on Confederate E. J. Johnston swords. The blade is bright and clean with French markings on the top. The iron scabbard is in nice condition, and shows a lot of drag wear. **895.00**

Import, German-made blade, imported and marked by, "Horstmann/+Sons/Philadelphia." The 29" long blade is etched in standard patterns with, "U.S." Blade is dark, the edge nicked and pitted at the tip, wire wrap is missing, no scabbard.......... **175.00**

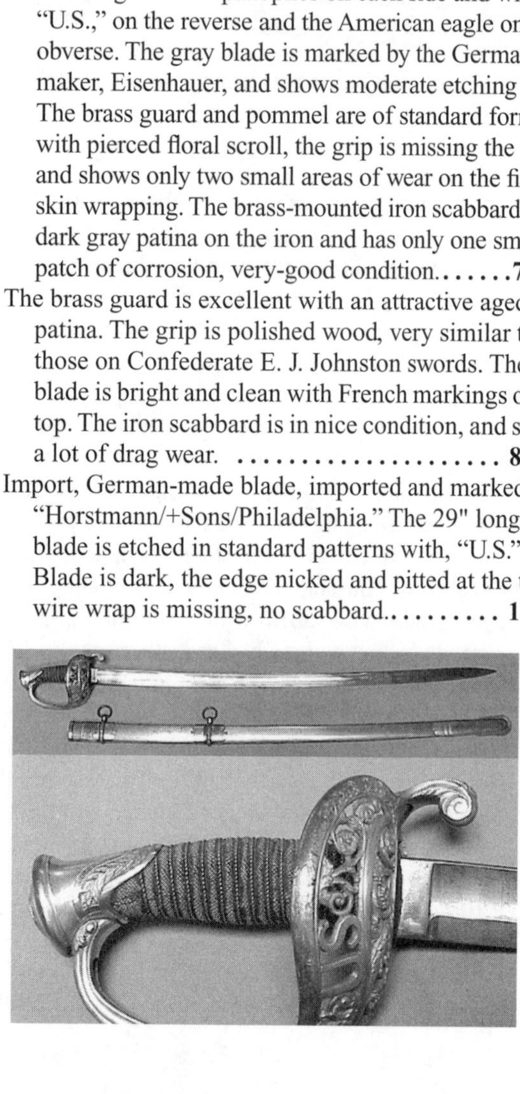

Lieutenant Colonel Edmund Shurly of the 26th New York Infantry carried this Model 1850 Field and Staff Sword. Shurly's records were included with this sword.

Sharpsburg Arsenal

Lieutenant Colonel Edmund Shurly of the 26th New York Infantry carried this Model 1850 Field and Staff Sword. Shurly's records were included with this sword.

Sharpsburg Arsenal

Presentation-grade field and staff sword presented to, "Lient. Col. Chas. H. Tay By the Enlisted Men of Co. E. 10th Reg. N.J.V. In the Field Maryland July 24, 1864." Records include copies of a letter from Tay's uncle asking for a, "Special Exchange of Prisoners," for his nephew with Confederate Col. George F. Maxwell and return letter to the uncle stating, "special exchanges are not approved except for such reasons of a public nature." **11,500.00**

Excellent sword, crisp etching on blade and fine wide brass mounts on metal field scabbard. Original rayskin grip is easily 95% plus; full original wire. Company name stamped on guard, "J. Hoey, NYC." John Hoey supplied 1,800 cavalry sabers in 1861 under Federal contract and was known to sell many types of arms up through 1862 in New York City. Rare example in fine condition. **2,500.00**

Civil War staff officer silver hilt sword. Exceptionally high, presentation-grade, silver-grip sword with eagle head quillon, "U.S.," in guard, German silver sheath with wide fancy brass mounts. Bright blade with crisp, "U.S.," and motifs. **4,000.00**

Ames engraved sword presented to, "H. C. Keith 1, Lient. Co. B 121, N.Y.V. Aug. 1, 1862." Brass-mounted, blued metal, presentation-grade scabbard. Blade and etching are 95% with approx. 80% of gold gilt retained on hilt. **6,500.00**

Presentation sword, blade by W. Clauberg with full etching of, "U.S.," eagles, and patriotic motifs. Silver hilt with original wire and a pommel cap inset with garnets and ruby in the filigree. The German silver scabbard has fancy high-relief cast mounts. **5,000.00**

Fine sword and scabbard, presentation-grade, lots of hand engraving. Grip is 95% intact with minor wear in rayskin and a tiny portion missing on the top; wire is two strands of single and one of double twist, and 100%; blade is marked "Iron Proof" on the spine and etched with military motifs. Blade is gray-silver and uncleaned, showing use, but no nicks or pitting. Mounts are wide and scalloped, and deeply hand engraved. **2,200.00**

Model 1850, Officer, Field and Staff

Ames field and staff sword presented to, "Edmund Richard Pitman Shurly, Lt. Col March 1865 By his friends in England." Shurly enlisted May 4, 1861 with 26th New York Infantry and was severely wounded at Fredericksburg. Later, he served with the 8th Veteran Reserve Corp. Shurly was the last Commanding Officer at Camp Douglas, Ohio. He later went on to serve during the Indian Wars where he was again severely wounded at the Battle of Goose Creek, Wyoming. Shurly retired from active duty on December 2, 1868, due to wounds received in the line of duty, records included. **10,000.00**

"I witnessed General Prentice surrender his sword to Colonel Moore (at the Battle of Shiloh) and saw the men lay down their arms and march to the rear under guard."

— Ralph J. Smith
2nd Texas Infantry

Model 1850, Officer, Field and Staff, cont.

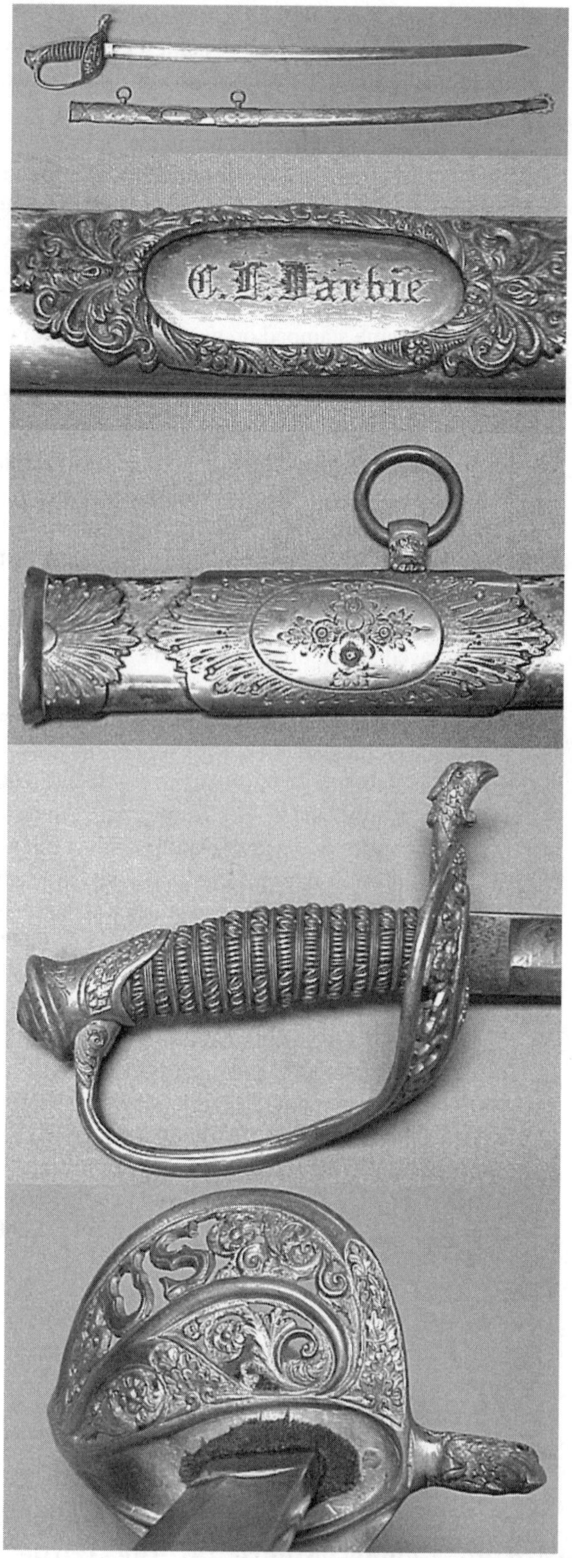

Though his regiment is unknown, the presentation plaque on this Model 1850 Field and Staff Sword signifies that it belonged to C.L. Darbie.

Sharpsburg Arsenal

Manufactured by G.W. Simms & Bros., Philadelphia, PA. Blade marked, "Collins & Co. Hartford, CT 1862." Blade is finely etched with a pattern seen on only high quality presentation-grade swords. Heavily engraved guard and handle retain 50% of original gold wash with eagle head retaining original ruby chip eyes. Scabbard is iron with German silver wash and heavily engraved brass throat, hangers, drag and presentation name panel. "C.L. Darbie" engraved in Old English letters on scabbard. **6,500.00**

Silver hilt presentation sword, fine example of the eagle quillon sword with ruby eyes and silver grip. Wonderful hand engraving on the M1850 Staff & Field pattern sword presented in 1862 to, "Capt. Francis S. Keese, Co. C, 128th New York State Volunteer Infantry." Keese has a brilliant war record beginning in 1861 with the 1st New Jersey Infantry, and ending up with a command post in the 128th New York. Bright blade by Clauberg with crisp center panel etching; much hand engraving and tooling on the wide brass mounts. **4,500.00**

Stunning presentation-grade inscribed sword made by Collins & Company, Hartford, Connecticut, and dated 1862 on the ricasso. Pressed leather scabbard is diamond shaped and a unique work of art, as are the gilt and strongly engraved patriotic mounts. Full original grip covering and wire, and superb inscription of "Presented to Capt. J.L. Yale by Co. K, 17th Vermont Volunteers, Sept. 23, 1864." Yale was originally mustered into the 13th Vermont in 1862, serving until 1863, then commissioned into the 17th Regiment seeing action at the Wilderness, Virginia, North Anna, Totopotomoy, Bethesda Church, Cold Harbor, Petersburg, Petersburg Mine, Weldon Railroad, Poplar Spring Church, and Hatchers Run. **12,500.00**

This import sword has a very nice blade with all its original factory luster. The etching on the blade has all the frosting and is factory crisp. On the reverse is an eagle sitting on a ribbon with, "E PLURIBUS UNUM," and floral designs. On the obverse is "U.S.," and floral designs. The ricasso is marked, "CLAUBERG/ SOLINGEN." The guard has all the gold gilt. There is 95% fish skin on the grip and the twisted wire is complete. The scabbard has brass hangers, drag, and throat, and retains 95% of its original, brown finish.. .... **2,895.00**

Very nice import staff officer sword and scabbard made by P.D. Lunenschloss, Solingen, Germany. Full etching of a U.S. eagle, banners, and military motifs very clear, full original rayskin grip and original wire wrap. Screws missing on reverse of mounts. **1,575.00**

Import, 37-1/2" overall with a nearly straight 33" blade. German blade handsomely etched with an eagle bearing an, "E Pluribus Unum," ribbon in panel on the right and broad, "U.S.," in panel on the left. Left ricasso stamped "Solingen," right ricasso has brass insert stamped, "proofed." Iron basket-style hilt with chiseled and engraved eagle, "U.S.," on guard. Iron pommel and back strap. Rayskin wrap is nearly perfect and sword retains 100% of the copper double-twisted wire. Bright iron scabbard in excellent condition. **1,575.00**

Import, 37" overall with a slightly curved 31-1/2" inch brilliant blade. Blade heavily etched in a military motif 2/3rds of its length. On the right a stand of flags, surmounted by a stand of war trophies and a fine American eagle below beribboned, "E Pluribus Unum." Left side of the blade has, "PDL," within an oval maker's mark. Lunenschloss of Solingen at the ricasso. This is surmounted by a large American flag scrolled in acanthus leaves leading to an open panel with a large, block, "U.S." This is surmounted by a stand of arms and flags. Bright blade in excellent condition. Superb openwork brass guard with, "U.S.," set into the tines along with cast and chiseled floral and acanthus-leaf decoration. Grips retain 98-100% of the gray rayskin wrap and 80-90% of the gilt triple-twist wire wrap. Fine red-lacquered iron scabbard with gilt brass mounts at throat, drag, and rings. **2,895.00**

Presentation-grade sword, French pattern, with exceptional brass scabbard with fine brass mounts; crisp and deep etching. Grip is rare white rayskin, 95% intact; full original wire as well. Hilt has fantastic eagle motif and form of an 18th Corps badge, exceptional example. **4,500.00**

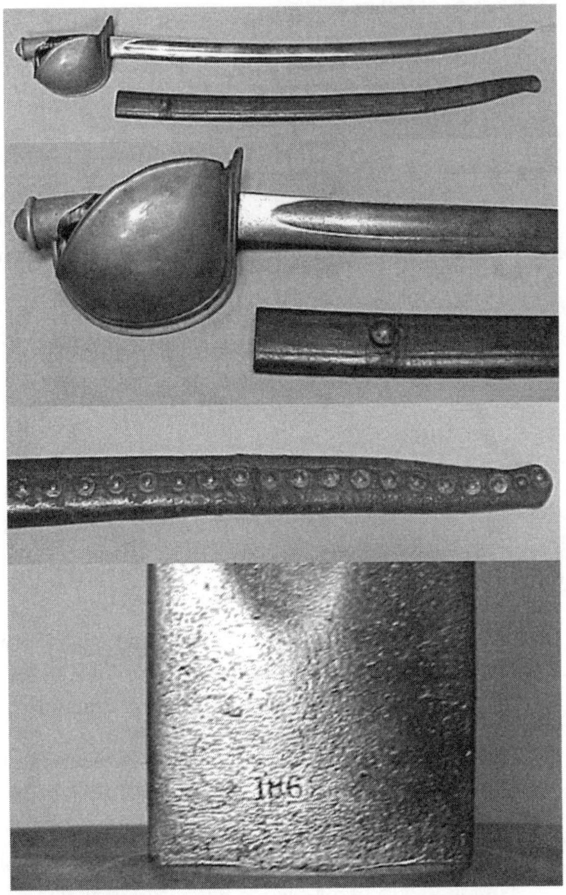

This example of the Model 1852 Naval Officer's Sword was in good, solid condition.

Sharpsburg Arsenal

Model 1852, Officer, Naval

Produced by Horstmann & Son's with a Clauberg blade. Naval anchor and, "USN," etching on blade still sharp, but blade has some discoloration. Blade has no nicks or rust. Hilt has approximately 75% original gilt. Sharkskin grip has wear on back top toward pommel cap. Leather wire wrap is all there, but has some repair. Brass mounted leather scabbard is strong with some finish flaking on leather and a few minor dents on drag.................... **1,895.00**

Inscribed Civil War navy officer sword with generous original gilt and crisp blade etching, full original wire wrap, grip, and scabbard. Inscribed in guard, "Edgar K. Sellen." Sellen enlisted in September of 1864 from Hartford, Connecticut, as Acting Assistant Paymaster aboard the *bark Gemsbok* where he served until honorably discharged October 3, 1865. .... **3,250.00**

Sword and scabbard clearly marked, "W.H. Horstmann," on ricasso. Fine scabbard with nice roped-brass mounts. Full original grip covering and wire wrap and beautiful etching. **1,500.00**

Made by W.G. Mintzer of Philadelphia, this Model 1852 Naval Officer's sword had several naval motif decorations, including a quillon shaped like a dolphin's head.

Sword has a single-edged blade measuring 29-1/4" long and 1-1/8" wide at the ricasso. There is a small fuller at the blade top that runs from the cross guard to within 10-1/2" of the tip. A type of blade seldom seen. The ricasso is stamped, "W.G.MINTZER, PHILA," in two lines. The reverse side of the blade is stamped with the logo of, "W. Clauberg." The blade is profusely etched with an elaborate eagle atop a cannon and stack of cannon balls. Above that is an anchor entwined in rope, a small "U.S.," and a ship's mast complete with a crow's nest and a U.S. flag atop of it. The obverse side is etched, "IRON PROOF U.S.N." in a banner, another anchor entwined in rope, and a most unusual trident amid oak leaves. Bright blade with lots of original luster and frosty contrast. There are no blade nicks and no pitting or serious stains. Only some very minimal staining in the small top fuller and a couple of gray spots. The hilt is very finely cast. One unusual feature is the serrated molded edge on the underside of the guard surrounding the blade. Extra fancy decorations on the knuckle bow, as it bends upwards to the pommel. The quillon is a well-detailed dolphin's head. The pommel cap is a finely detailed American eagle surrounded by 13 stars. The original sharkskin grips are completely intact with very little wear, and fancy twisted wire, along with two single strands of wire. The real plus is the presence of the original sword knot that is in excellent condition. The all-leather scabbard is in excellent condition with no bends, breaks, or repairs. The scabbard is very solid, has no open seams, but some surface flaking. The ridge running a 1/2" below the top of the drag. Only the drag has a few minor dings to it. **1,950.00**

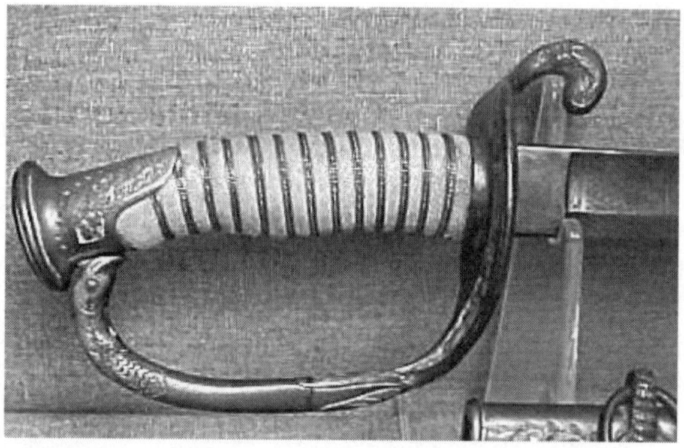

This sword belonged to John Van Bleecker, a sailor who had a career that spanned 1863 to 1897. Exceptional engraving on it includes the initials, "J.V.B.," and the slogan, "For the Old Flag."

Battleground Antiques, Inc.

Sword of Acting Ensign John Van Bleecker, ca. 1864, Acting Midshipman, October 10, 1863; Ensign, December 18, 1868; Master, March 21, 1870; Lieutenant, March 21, 1871; Lt. Commander, June 30, 1891; Commander, December 5, 1897. Exceptionally high-quality, presentation-grade sword by Clauberg, Solingen, with magnificent patriotic hand engraving on wide, rope border design mounts. Fine white sharkskin-covered grip with full wire wrap and full-length sharkskin-covered scabbard. Blade is etched with naval designs and motifs, and initials, "J.V.B.," in a panel beneath which is engraved, "For the Old Flag." The pommel cap has a superb eagle and stars motif; the face of the guard has, "U.S.N.," the drag is a curled dolphin. **2,500.00**

Model 1860, Field and Staff, straight blade staff sword carried by many officers and generals in the Civil War. Pattern stayed in use until the turn of the twentieth century. Sword has a very high-quality pommel, guard, and clamshell guard cast with great detail (eagle on pommel, leaves on "D" guard, eagle and flags on clam shell). The eagle and flags design on the clam-shell guard is highly detailed with a really crisp eagle's wings. The grip wrap is standard-style shagreen with double-twisted copper wire wrap. At the top and bottom of the grip are brass ferrules with intricate grooved designs. The blade has faint military etching and is signed, "W. Clauberg Solingen," with a standing knight motif marking associated with the 1860s and not the later period. The blade is quite wide with a subdued diamond cross section. The clamshell guard has one shell beautifully adorned with an eagle, and a smaller undecorated clamshell void of casting decorations. It is hinged identically to the 1840 Foot Officer's swords. The scabbard has high-quality, yet simple, ring mounts decorated with cast-raised floral designs, and the drag is totally symmetrical and is identical in design to those found on documented war-date inscribed specimens (the drag is made with open areas on the sides, so that there is a brass top and bottom which screws into the scabbard, but no brass on the side faces of the scabbard.) The scabbard is finished with a fine-smooth black paint that appears to be original to the date of manufacture. **1,250.00**

Sword Terminology

Saber: A cavalry sword with a curved blade.

Backstrap: A metal strap running down the back of the handle resting in the palm of the hand.

Ferrule: A metal washer between the guard and handle. It is there to make sure the handle doesn't move.

Fuller: A groove down the center of the blade, for strength and lightness. Usually misnamed the blood groove.

Knuckle bow: Single strap running from the quillon to the pommel. It guards the front of the hand.

Pommel: The part of the handle that keeps your pinky from sliding off. Also holds the whole sword together.

Quillon: The cross piece on a sword, also thought of as a guard.

Ricasso: The flattened portion of the blade that assists in the manipulation of the weapon. Often, one will find the maker's mark stamped here.

Scabbard drag: Tip of the scabbard that is reinforced. It is the part that literally drags on the ground.

See also: Bayonets, Knives, and Pikes, Groupings, and Accoutrements.

Chapter 18

Uniforms

Little transmits the depth of personal association quite the way an original Union soldier's four-button blouse or a Confederate officer's kepi does. Highly sought after by collectors since the end of the Civil War, uniform groupings, jackets, coats, and headgear are both rare and expensive today.

Though it is oversimplifying to say that Union troops wore blue uniforms and Southern troops gray, it is not difficult to recognize that not a lot of examples survived the war and the ensuing years. Collecting uniform pieces is an advanced form of the Civil War hobby, and it will become expensive in short order.

The upside of this, though, is that when pieces are found, they often have some sort of provenance. If you are looking for a representative piece such as a Union forage cap or a Confederate officer's frock coat, you will be able to find quality pieces available—provided you can afford the price tag!

Do exercise caution, though. As with any aspect of the hobby, fakes do exist. Also, bear in mind that people have been reenacting the Civil War in an organized fashion for more than forty years. Some early reenacting clothing, if worn hard on the campaign and put away dirty, will begin to have some convincing looking patina. Learn to recognize appropriate period construction techniques, fabrics, and styles before making your first purchase.

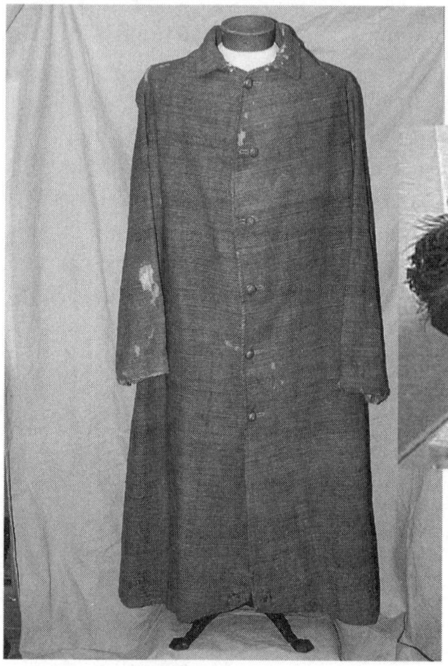

Battleground Antiques, Inc.

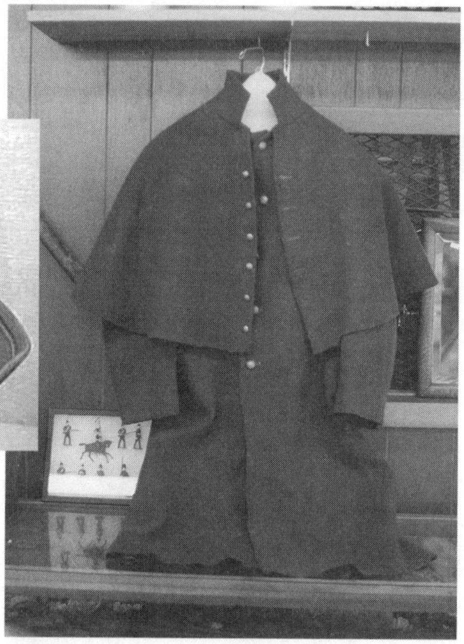

Collecting Hints

Pros:

- Uniforms and uniform pieces are extremely personal and probably impact with some of the strongest emotional force of any Civil War artifacts.
- It is difficult, but not impossible or unlikely, to create fakes. A person familiar with nineteenth-century fashion and Civil War uniforms can usually spot questionable pieces.
- If you have the money, quality pieces are available.

Availability ★
Price ★★★★★
Reproduction Alert ★★

Cons:

- Expensive! Uniforms, because of extreme delicate nature, have not survived in great numbers. When pieces become available, it is generally going to cost a lot to acquire them.
- Surviving examples of officer clothing far exceed the number of enlisted men's clothing. Therefore, it will be very difficult to assemble a representative Civil War soldier display complete with uniform.
- Uniforms are difficult to display. Special care has to be demonstrated in handling and storage. Proper storage materials can become costly.

Headgear, Confederate

Chapeau de Bras, Officer, Infantry, Confederate "Chapeau de Bras" worn by Surgeon Henry DeSassussure Fraser. Les Jensen, Curator of the Museum of the Confederacy, calls this hat the, "rarest piece of Confederate headgear known to exist," as it was made early in the war conforming to South Carolina style and regulation. This hat is made of black beaver with a large black cockade sewn directly to the front. In addition , it is accompanied by its original box marked, "C.S. Army." An incredible rarity, this hat was worn by Surgeon Fraser, as a doctor in Anderson's Division, when he was captured on July 5th, 1863, during the Gettysburg campaign. (Accompanied by Les Jensen Letter of Authenticity). **35,000.00**

Tennessee did not field 154 regiments of infantry, but this fabulous slouch hat was worn by a member of the "154th Tennessee Seniors"—a unit granted the right to serve the Confederacy with the special name.

Old South Military Antiques

Hat, Enlisted Man, Infantry, Confederate Soldier's irrepressible humor helped see him through the hardships of camp and field. This slouch hat illustrates that humor and displays the well-deserved pride he took in being a member of a distinguished, hard-fought regiment. Of course there were not 154 regiments enlisted in Tennessee, though this hat bears that designation. The 154th got its title in the following manner: Volunteers rushed to Tennessee's standard in April 1861, each vying to be designated the, "First Volunteer Regiment." On April 15th, the men that were to become the 154th Seniors embarked from the wharf at Memphis, rendezvousing under Colonel Preston Smith at Fort Randolph, Shelby County, Tennessee. The men who formed Preston Smith's and George Maney's units both claimed the honor of being designated the First Tennessee Infantry Regiment. When Maney's men were given the coveted title, Smith's good-natured boys insisted that if they couldn't be the lowest-numbered regiment, they would be the highest. They asked for, and received, permission to be numbered "154th" under the old militia system. The Regiment added the title "Seniors" to designate there early enlistment. No unit had a better fighting record than the gallant boys of the 154th. Having enlisted at the very outset, they fought at Belmont, losing thirteen men. At Shiloh, the 154th was devastated, losing thirty-one percent. They lost an even higher proportion at Murfreesboro, taking a staggering forty-one-percent casualties. After having fought through the Georgia campaign, the 154th became the first regiment to reenlist under J. E. Johnston at Dalton. Enlisting for "ninety-nine years or the war," the Seniors started a wave of patriotic enlistments among the dispirited Army of Tennessee. The Seniors fought through Hood's disastrous Tennessee campaign, the Carolina's campaign and had been virtually destroyed by the time of the Army of Tennessee's surrender, April 26, 1865. The hat's wearer took a well-earned pride in his regiment and his slouch hat. He fashioned a handmade pewter badge with his Regimental number and state cut into it, "154TH TENN," and decorated it with artistic scrollwork around the border. On the underside of the left brim, which was apparently worn pinned up, the bold designation "154 SENIOR" appears above, "TN Reg't". The designation is encapsulated by scrolls similar to the scrolls around the badge. This entire designation is done in ink and was probably red at the time it was executed. It still retains its original sweatband and decorative hatband. The hatband utilizes a braided, officer's sword knot complete with tassels. The hat's provenance is impeccable; donated to the Montgomery Museum of Fine Arts, circa 1930. The hat was stored in the museum's basement until the early 1980s, when it was rediscovered and preserved. In the 1990s, the museum began selling off artifacts that did not conform to the museum's primary goal of art promotion and preservation. During this restructuring, the museum sold the hat through the Flomation Auction House in Flomation, Alabama. Since that time, the hat has resided in one of the country's premier Confederate collections. **44,000.00**

Kepi

Enlisted Man, Artillery, Confederate Artillery Kepi worn by Private Robert Royall, Richmond Howitzers and signed by him inside the cap, "R Royall.00Rm'd Howitzers." He not only signed his name , but he also drew crossed cannons and, "Richmond Howitzers," inside the cap as well. A marvelous and historically important Confederate Artillery kepi gray wool cadet gray cap with a red band on top with confederate infantry "block" I pattern buttons both backmarked, "Extra Rich." Royall enlisted in the 1st Company of Richmond Howitzers in 1861 and served throughout the war. He fought briefly with the 23rd Virginia in 1864. He surrendered at Burkeville, Virginia, on April 24, 1865. Another identical kepi that belonged to Royall is now on display in the Museum of the Confederacy in Richmond. An extremely rare Confederate artillery man's cap made in Richmond, Capitol of the

Enlisted Man, Artillery, cont.
Confederacy, and worn by a member of one of the elite units of the Confederate Army of Northern Virginia. (Accompanied by Les Jensen letter of authenticity and research, with restoration by Jessica Hack.) . . **35,000.00**

Enlisted Man, Infantry, rare Confederate butternut kepi lined with red and white cotton checkered print. This kepi is in remarkably good condition, and is a classic early war-style Confederate headgear. Made with all Confederate materials, this kepi with oilcloth chinstrap and intricate side buttons is a true rarity. (Ex-Bill Turner Collection. Accompanied by Les Jensen Letter of Authenticity.) **25,000.00**

This pristine Confederate line officer's kepi is adorned with embroidered tape in a quatrefoil design indicating the rank of major or lieutenant colonel.

Battleground Antiques, Inc.

Officer, borderline pristine line officer kepi, early war pattern. Virtually no moth damage, full silk lining, tarred linen sweatband, and incredible rows of quatrefoil indicating the rank of major or lieutenant colonel. Buttons are typical early pattern-lined shield eagle staffs. **20,000.00**

Officer, Artillery, Confederate kepi worn by Captain Edward Owen of the famed Washington Artillery of New Orleans. This attractive kepi has a red body with a blue band around the base in accordance with Confederate uniform regulations. Captain Owen was the brother of Colonel William Miller Owen who wrote the acclaimed regimental history of the unit, *In Camp and Battle with the Washington Artillery of New Orleans.* Exceedingly rare as an identified Confederate artillery kepi worn by a member of the premier artillery regiment in the Civil War; the Washington Artillery of New Orleans. (Accompanied by Les Jensen Letter of Authenticity). **30,000.00**

General Officer, Confederate general's kepi that is a beautiful dark blue wool with four rows of gold braid signifying general's rank. The black leather visor is in good condition and there is a red, black, and gray lining in the inside of the crown, which could probably help identify the maker. (Accompanied by Les Jensen Letter of Authenticity.) **45,000.00**

Coats, Jackets; Confederate

Coat

Frock, Officer, Georgia, blue gray with red collar and cuffs and with Georgia State seal buttons, made in 1861 by Philadelphia tailor. **15,000.00**

Frock, Officer, Infantry
Single star on each side of collar denoting rank of major, two rows of seven buttons and blue pointed cuffs. **40,000.00**

Any form of Confederate cloth is rare and very desirable. When items do become available, they sell for strong dollars. This is an officer's frock coat.

Battleground Antiques, Inc.

Frock, Officer, Infantry, cont.

Deviating slightly from the Confederate regulations for an officer's frock coat, this major's coat has two rows of nine buttons. It most certainly was a state-issued or privately purchased item.

Battleground Antiques, Inc.

Regardless of fraying to the hem, a collector eagerly purchased this Confederate captain's frock coat.

Battleground Antiques, Inc.

Single star on each side of collar denoting rank of major, two rows of nine buttons. **40,000.00**

Three rows of gold tape on each side of collar denoting rank of captain, two rows of seven buttons. **40,000.00**

> **"I do not know what became of my bottle-green coat, with the bullet-holes through it, which would now be an object of interest to my children. It is remarkable that during the war no care was taken of any of these battle-marked articles."**
>
> ***— John B. Gordon***
> ***6th Alabama Infantry***

Officer, Navy, identified to a member of Whiteside's Naval Battalion of Columbus, Georgia, a period pencil note originally attached to the inside of the coat reads, "CONFEDERATE UNIFORM WORN BY LOUIS PHILLIPE HENOP." Research, all of which of course accompanies the coat, identifies Henop as an employee of the Columbus Naval Iron Works and as a member of this local naval militia battalion. The unit was activated and participated in the siege of Savannah. Subsequently, Henop was captured and paroled at Columbus, Georgia. The coat is of heavy cadet gray wool, double breasted with seven-button front. All buttons are Federal staff eagles with identical "Extra Quality" backmarks. All are original to the coat. Superb balloon sleeve cut. Body is lined with brown tabby-weave cotton, lightly padded in breast area. Tail pockets and breast pockets lined with unbleached osnaburg, as are the sleeves. Identical staff buttons also used on the tails, though the coat never had cuff buttons. The overall condition of the coat is truly remarkable, just some very minor nap mothing and a few very small seam openings. Shows no signs of ever having shoulder straps & doubtless saw very little use. The rolled collar coat was of course regulation for every Navy officer, but was also favored by many Army officers. Complete with the original belt and 1851 eagle belt plate with silver wreath, over the shoulder sling, but no provisions for sword hangers. Belt itself is unquestionably of C.S. manufacture. Coat is accompanied by a four-page letter from a leading authority on C.S. uniform/fabric/construction attesting to the authenticity of every detail of the coat. **22,500.00**

Vest, Confederate, Officer, single-breasted Confederate officer's vest is made of gray wool, lined with tan cotton twill. It originally had nine buttons, but the top button is missing. It has eight remaining Virginia state seal buttons including, "Mitchell & Tyler/Richmond," "Scovill," "Extra Quality," and, "Horstmann," backmarks. The reverse is made of black, glazed cotton twill. The pocket linings are completely intact and are made of the same cotton twill as the vest's reverse. The half belt adjuster on the reverse is broken. The tan cotton twill inner lining is in excellent condition, with the exception of the wear at the collar and hem resulting from much use. The style and cut is the standard three-pocket vest: an upper watch pocket in the left breast and two at the waist. The waist pockets have scalloped flaps with whipped interior eyelets, the pocket buttons are missing. The pocket linings are completely intact and are made of the same cotton twill as the vest's reverse. **9,900.00**

Vest bearing eight Virginia state seal buttons, with an unidentified original wearer.

Old South Military Antiques

> **"A movement had been started in Atlanta to uniform my mountaineers: but when the message was received from Governor Moore, inviting us to come to Montgomery, all thought of uniformity in dress was lost in the enthusiasm evoked by the knowledge that our services were accepted; and even after the hastily prepared uniforms were issued by the new Government my company clung tenaciously to "coonskin" head-dress, which made a striking contrast to the gray caps worn by the other companies."**
>
> ***— John B. Gordon***
> ***"Raccoon Roughs", 6th Alabama Infantry***

Headgear, Union

The Union Model 1858 forage cap is probably one of the most recognizable symbols of the Civil War.

Cap

Enlisted Man, Model 1858, Artillery, very solid example with fine silk lining and lots of padding, indicating high-grade custom tailoring with original, full gilt eagle, "A" side buttons. Exceptional gilt artillery officer false-embroidered insignia on the front of the cap as well. Cap has scattered moth or insect damage mainly on crown. **2,850.00**

Enlisted Man, Model 1858, Sharpshooter, excellent example of the Civil War Berdan-type forage cap as used by U.S. Sharpshooters. Early war, double-seam construction with tarred inner crown lining and original side buttons and chinstrap! Deep forest green, now faded slightly. This item was identified initially as a faded blue cap, but upon closer inspection in the protected seam areas, it is indeed green. Compared with another known and identified Berdan cap in a private collection, the crown construction and seam allowance is identical, indicating the same manufacturer! **7,500.00**

Enlisted Man, Model 1858

6.5" up the rear, 4.75" up the front, and 5.5" diameter crown. Generally excellent, clean, and tight. Made from typical "shoddy" wool which shows the under weave upon the least amount of wear to the nap. Hat body has two holes in the right rear, one 3/4", one 1/2", with some fraying around the edge. Crown has a couple worm holes (tracks) that go through the fabric. These holes need to be backed, to match the rest of the undamaged hat. Visor is flat, with edge binding, and dark green underside. Several wide heat cracks in tar finish. Sweatband is thin leather, finished with a thick brown tar-like substance. Interior lined with brown-black polished cotton, sweat stained, and frayed along the lower edge on one side and a little on top of the other side. Typical burlap stiffener inside the sweatband.. ...... **2,250.00**

Dark blue wool with a bound leather visor, leather chinstrap with eagle side buttons, and infantry horn insignia with "2" and "E"on the top. Has polished brown cotton lining with drawstring top. Complete with leather sweatband, few tiny nips. **785.00**

Federal forage cap with full original insignia! Unit and name faintly scratched in brim, "3rd N.J.V. S.G. Hendrickson." Records search finds only one guy, Private Samuel G. Hendrickson, Company H, 3rd New Jersey Infantry, mustered September 14, 1862, and discharged March 17, 1865, at Bristol, Pennsylvania, due to wounds received in action at Spotsylvania Court House, Virginia, May 10, 1864. The 3rd served in both the 1st and 6th Corps and saw action at Malvern Hill, Manassas, Chantilly, Cramptons Gap, Antietam, Fredericksburg, Salem Church, Gettysburg, Williamsport, Rappahannock Station, Mine Run, Wilderness, Spottsylvania, Richmond, North Anna River, Totopotomoy Creek and Cold Harbor. Cap is in overall good condition, but missing a portion of the lining, sweatband, chinstrap, and side buttons. Has scattered moth damage as well, mainly on the crown..... **2,950.00**

Forage cap, a.k.a., a "Bummer's Cap." Overall excellent condition with full lining, sweatband, and chinstrap. Excellent condition with just the smallest amount of moth repair. **2,950.00**

Standard-pattern blue wool "Bummer's" or "Forage" cap, having flat crown and black polished cotton lining with original label reading, "G & S/No. 3/N.Y." Leather sweatband and tarred leather brim intact. Leather chinstrap with infantry buttons present. Crossed sabers cap device on crown. Condition is very good. Shows a few scattered repairs and minor mothing. Lining shows moderate wear with minor seam separations. Cap device is probably a later addition. **1,725.00**

Kind of ratty, but still a great relic. Classic late-war forage cap with double-welted bands up the rear seam, brown polished cotton side linings open to expose a tarred or oilcloth circular stiffener in the crown. Wool is faded blue, chinstrap with eagle side buttons present as is sweatband. Body has a few moderate moth holes. Crown has a couple large holes, and visor has sewn bound edge. **795.00**

Officer, Model 1858, cap has a great look being 5" from the top to the brim. The color is a rich blue with a few very small moth nip holes including one small moth hole on the seam in the rear of the cap. Retains its original chinstrap and bound brim. Label inside reads, "DICKSON/STATE-STREET/ALBANY," and, "SEMPER FIDELIS." The silk lining is no longer present. **2,600.00**

Officer, "Smoking," blue velvet with yellow rick-rack trim, an embroidered green, black, and yellow sideband, and a long yellow tassel. Worn in camp when officer was off duty. A nice example in excellent condition..................... **125.00**

Union slouch hat with cavalry insignia without an identified wearer.

J.C. Devine Inc.

Hat

Officer, simply superb Union officer's slouch hat that is a fine specimen with full, original trim. Magnificent officer-embroidered infantry insignia and "Hardee" cockade device. Fully embossed maker mark, "Tomes, Melvain & Company," noted high quality New York outfitters. Silk lining is virtually flawless with only a minor area of deterioration. Full, super tall sweatband has some stitching coming loose, but mainly in place. Original heavy bullion acorn hat cord, too! An oral provenance states this hat was worn by Fred L. Atwood, First Lieutenant, Battery F, Pennsylvania Light Artillery, "Hamptons Battery." This battery was organized at Williamsport, Pennsylvania, December 7,1861, to serve three years. Atwood was wounded at Chancellorsville and was present at Gettysburg. Atwood died in 1871. . . . . **15,000.00**

Officer, Cavalry, black fur felt with 3-1/8" brim bound with silk braid, 4-1/2" crown dented front to rear, 3/8" silk hat band, 2-3/8" high black leather sweat band. The front of the crown has a gold bullion insignia on black velvet consisting of crossed cavalry sabers surmounted by a "1" in silver colored metal. The hat has three holes in the crown, the hatband is partially loose, but intact, the sweatband is partially loose with about 30% missing, the binding on the brim shows wear. Despite these shortcomings, a few minutes work with needle and thread will bind up the loose ends and give this hat a quite presentable appearance, would judge the overall condition as very good.. . . . **1,200.00**

A standard Model 1858 "Hardee" hat with yellow cord and possible postwar crossed sabers.

J.C. Devine Inc.

Enlisted Man, Model 1858, Cavalry, standard pattern "Hardee" hat of black felt. On the inside there is a brown label reading, "U.S. Army/Extra/Manufacture/3." Hat has an enlisted man's yellow wool cord and cavalry device. Condition is very good, though it does show a few insignificant small splits in brim edge and minor repairs. Sweatband is intact with minor seam separations. Hat device may be a later addition. **2,875.00**

The infantryman's Model 1858 hat was a standard issue to U.S. regulars and to many volunteer units. This nicely blocked example is trimmed with original cord and brass bugle insignia.

Battleground Antiques, Inc.

Enlisted Man, Model 1858, Infantry, "Hardee" with brass bugle and blue worsted hat cord. **4,500.00**

The embroidery on this enlisted sailor's hat provides a sense of the original owner.

Drumbeat Civil War Memorabilia

Enlisted Man, Sailor

Extremely rare Civil War enlisted man's hat as seen in all the photos of the period. This all-wool example is in pristine condition with fantastic embroidered star design on the top. The lining is cloth with a black and gold pattern. It has the original bow attached and part of the silk ribbon around the outside. There is no label. Accompanying the hat is an old handwritten note stating that, "these effects belonged to my father who fought in the Civil War," dated 1926. . . . . **4,995.00**

Naval uniform items are extremely rare, and yet, don't often command the highest prices. This enlisted man's cap is far rarer than a standard issue Model 1858 Hardee-style hat.

Drumbeat Civil War Memorabilia

Rare U.S. Navy enlisted man's "Donald Duck"-style hat, seen in all period photos of sailors. This all-black woolen hat has a full leather sweatband with a gold embossed Eagle emblem typical of the Civil War period. There is an embroidered star on the top. There is a grosgrain ribbon bow on the left. The condition is excellent with no mothing, and only a few light age stains. **4,200.00**

This all-wool example is in pristine condition with fantastic embroidered star design on the top. The lining is all cloth with a black and gold pattern. It has the original bow attached and part of the silk ribbon around the outside. There is no label. **5,595.00**

Kepi

Chasseur

Identified Civil War officer Chasseur-pattern kepivery nice example with positive identification to Captain John Foley, who served from 1861 until 1864, in the service of the United States. Cap is maker's marked as well, and missing the chinstrap. Comes in original box as found, with numerous calling cards of Captain Foley as a resident of New York. Research records included in portfolio format. **4,500.00**

Absolutely wonderful war-dated officer's blue wool cap with quilted silk lining which bears the maker's mark, "James Y. Davis / 356 Penn. Ave. / Washington, D.C." The body of the cap is beautiful midnight blue wool in excellent conditjust a couple tiny moth nips. The lining is 95% intact. The sweatband is all there with one break in it. The visor is a little loose and could use a stitch or two to tighten it up, as is the case with part of the black piping. The chinstrap is missing, but the small kepi staff buttons are still present on the cap's sides. The cap is piped with narrow black quatrefoil piping on the top of the crown. It is circled with the same piping around the band of the cap, and up the sides of the capion. **2,650.00**

Enlisted Man, Michigan, Kepi is of dark blue wool, side buttons are Michigan state seal with Scovill backmark. Very thin chinstrap with buckle. Crackling to surface with wear near side buttons. The thick visor (as usually seen on kepis) has surface crackling. Body of cap is nice with very tiny scattered moth nips. Recessed disk has crossed sabers with a number four above, 100% sweatband and lining, average wear. Altogether a nice enlisted kepi. **4,200.00**

Zouave-style kepi adorned with New York State buttons.

Battleground Antiques, Inc.

New York, Zouave, fine State of New York chasseur-style kepi, often associated with Zouave units or artillery officers. Beautiful deep blue wool body with scarlet trim, adorned with gilt New York state seal buttons. Lining is a bit tattered, but 95% intact. **1,850.00**

Officer, Artillery, blue wool with unbound leather visor, leather chinstrap and artillery officer's eagle, "A" buttons. Cardboard crown stiffener with black oil cloth covering, tan-polished lining , and deep leather sweatband. Has 1/4" hole in crown where insignia was attached.. . . . . 645.00

Officer, Cavalry, fine quality chasseur-pattern Cavalry Civil War officer's kepi with full chinstrap and virtually no moth or insect damage to the body. Sweatband is intact, but many stitches are rotten and it is a bit loose. Black silk quilted lining is heavily padded, typical of a custom-tailored kepi, and is a bit tattered and fragile. Traces of gilt-embossed maker name remains, but is illegible. Cavalry "C" buttons are in excellent form. Fine example with a rich, deep blue broadcloth wool construction. 2,450.00

Very rare, officer's embroidered insignia kepi.

Battleground Antiques, Inc.

Officer, Engineer, embroidered wreath and castle device affixed to the front. Chinstrap with buttons still present.. . . . . 5,500.00

Officer, Infantry, dark blue wool with bound leather visor, leather chinstrap and infantry officer's eagle "I" buttons. Cardboard crown stiffener, polished tan cotton lining, and remnants of a black silk lining, complete with sweatband. There is some staining to crown, otherwise, in excellent condition. 650.00

Officer, New York, Infantry, Civil War New York infantry M1859-pattern kepi with sky-blue trim, New York buttons, and rare New York front badge plate, all original and pre-1863, according to Les Jensen, former curator of the Museum of the Confederacy in Richmond, Virginia. New York regulations changed in 1863 to a buff trim for kepi hats. Very sound overall with a few minor moth nips and some cracking to leather sweatband. Upper crown is properly padded, and lining is fully intact. . . 2,100.00

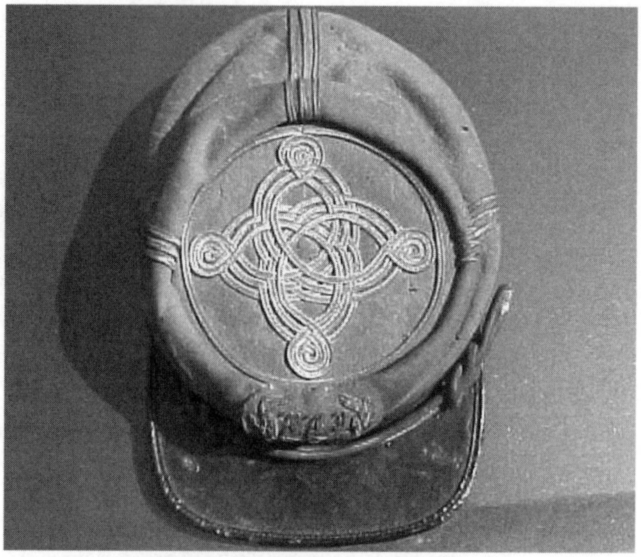

Elaborately embroidered kepi identified as belonging to an officer of the 1st Rhode Island Infantry.

Officer, Rhode Island, Infantry, rare Rhode Island First Light Infantry officer's kepi (rank of major). The kepi is fresh from a Rhode Island estate, and has not been offered before for sale. Some wear and missing one side button. 1,290.00

Shakos were worn by many militia units before the Civil War. There is a chance that several units even participated at the First Battle of Bull Run in 1861 wearing the tall, leather caps.

Shako, U.S., Enlisted Man, black pressed felt with black enameled leather crown and flat bound visor. Also has a leather chinstrap with crossed cannons on lined field buttons. M1858 7th Regiment, New York National Guard shako plate, a white wool pom-pom, and the label of "Baker & McKenny, N.Y." Owners name, "W.F. Ripley Co. B 7 Reg." written inside. 645.00

Coats, Overcoats, Jackets, Trousers; Union

Coat, Frock

Enlisted Man, one of the rarest Civil War uniforms is the nine-button enlisted man's frock coat. This particular example is clearly maker and inspector marked in the sleeves, and there is an identification written in the left sleeve. Definitely issued and worn during the Civil War, and not a surplus costume company coat. The overall condition is excellent, with only minor signs of wear in the lining and a very few tiny moth holes not detracting from the condition. The buttons all appear original and are Scovill marked, the light blue piping is all present and original. **12,500.00**

Officer, Infantry, uniform and effects of Captain VanDerzee, 44th and 25th New York Volunteers. Outstanding set of material owned by one officer. This group includes his regulation single-breasted line officer's frock coat with straps, two vests (one blue wool army example and one summer weight linen example), a fine 8"x10" oval albumen photo of him in uniform and armed, his bullion embroidered officer's eagle side plate hat insignia, his GAR membership medal, a loose portion of another medal, a wonderful 44th NYV GAR miniature flag made up to look like a 5th Corps Headquarters flag, and a Congressional record document. The coat is a regulation example in excellent condition (some wear on the collar top), with eagle infantry officer's buttons and double border bullion embroidered captain of infantry straps. The coat has classic long skirts, ballooned sleeve elbows, functional cuff, and rich quilted standard lining. It is as typical an example from the 1862-1863 period as can be found. The blue vest is outstanding, being the standard army pattern with small NY state buttons on the front and brown polished cotton back. The summer weight vest is a civilian example worn by him during warm weather. The embroidered Hardee hat eagle side plate is an outstanding example of the "tin back" variety covered with brown polished cotton on the reverse. It retains both attaching loops as well as the brass clips used to secure it to his hat. The albumen photo shows VanDerzee full standing wearing this frock coat, and also sporting a regulation sash and foot officer's sword. Excellent clarity, contrast, and condition housed in a period oval walnut frame. This material was owned by Captain John VanDerzee of the 25th New York, who served at the battles of Yorktown. Hanover Court House, Mechanicsville, Gaines Mill, Malvern Hill, 2nd Bull Run, Seven Days Battles, Antietam, Snickers Gap, Hartwood Church, Fredericksburg, Richards Ford, and Chancellorsville! VanDerzee had previous service as a private in the 44th NY Volunteers during 1861 and early 1862. A superb and historic lot of material. **9,500.00**

Officer, Cavalry, uniform and insignia of Captain Samuel N. Titus, 11th Pennsylvania Cavalry. The left sleeve bears a professionally printed (on cloth) label which reads, "T. McCormick / Merchant Tailor / Baltimore / 149 Baltimore Street." This label is inscribed in beautiful, ancient brown-ink script with the owner's name and location, "Lt. Titus / Portsmouth, Va." Included is the regulation Civil War line officer's frock coat of deep midnight blue wool in excellent condition, which has matching cavalry officer's eagle "C" buttons down the front (one missing), and small-size buttons on each cuff. It also has a pair of exquisite double-border, bullion-embroidered cavalry captain's shoulder straps on each shoulder with rich yellow velvet centers. The coat has a richly quilted and padded chest lining, wide elbows on each sleeve, and classic long skirts. In addition to the coat is included Titus' officer's embroidered crossed saber hat insignia on velvet in an oval with wire edge border and tin back covered with brown polished cotton, as well as his officer's eagle side plate (for the Hardee hat) also made of embroidered bullion on velvet with wire edge border and tin back covered with brown polished cotton. Includes a wealth of important historical and genealogical background which states that Titus enlisted as a private and rose through the ranks. He was wounded on October 7, 1864, in a fight on the Darbytown Road near Richmond by a gunshot wound through his right elbow, and he was taken prisoner at that time. He spent a short time in Libby Prison and then was exchanged. He nearly missed his appointment to major due to the fact that he had been wounded and captured, but his brigade commander saw to it that the promotion was indeed made. The regiment served in Virginia throughout the war, and one newspaper article states that Titus actually witnessed the battle between the Merrimac and Monitor. The 11th Cavalry was stationed at Portsmouth, Virginia, for much of 1862 and 1863 doing much raiding in southern Virginia and North Carolina, and fought at the Battles of Reams Station, Stony Creek, Petersburg, and others. **15,500.00**

Officer, Infantry

Double-breasted lieutenant colonel's frock coat and shoulder straps in overall very good condition with some light moth nips and repaired rips here and there. Top of collar shows real wartime wear. Body is double-breasted with two rows of seven Union staff buttons down each side. Three staff buttons on each cuff and four staff buttons on the tails. Shoulder straps are very worn, single border lieutenant colonel examples with sky-blue centers. Coat has repaired tear on left shoulder (well-done) and scattered small moth holes and a couple larger holes one on right cuff and one on the back. Lining is classic green quilted silk blend. **4,500.00**

Officer, Infantry, cont.

Excellent condition with beautiful midnight blue wool color and just a few scattered moth nips. Nine beautiful staff buttons on the front, three staff buttons on each functional cuff, and four more on the tails. Single border 1st lieutenant shoulder straps with dark blue velvet centers on the shoulders are excellent with the gilt bullion thread having grayed with oxidation. Lining is richly quilted classic green silk blend. **4,200.00**

The officer's frock coat is identified to a member of the 146th New York Infantry. There are also an enlisted man's cavalry shell jacket, and the fragment of a Union soldier's blanket.

Powder Horn Militaria LLC

Identified to Captain Joseph B. Cushman, Company C, 146th New York Infantry. Dark blue wool, full-length standard officer's coat with the full sleeves and lower thigh-length skirt. In near-perfect condition. The coat still retains all nine of its eagle "I" infantry officer's buttons with, "Schuyler H & G/New York," backmarks. Coattails retain four of the same buttons and both cuffs retain three each of small eagle "I" buttons also with the same backmark. Additionally, it has a beautiful pair of bullion-laced infantry captain's shoulder straps tacked on the shoulders. These are light blue velvet sewn onto a dark blue wool backing and heavily trimmed in thick gilt bullion thread. No moth nips or tears. The outside of the coat is near perfect. The inside of the coat is lined in a dark blue/green polished cotton with quilted padding at the chest. Couple of small tears in the middle of the back that are less than two inches long. Reinforced pockets at either breast that are lined in brown polished cotton or silk. The sleeves are lined in a natural color polished muslin. These have not worn well at the armpits. The barrel of the sleeve is fine, but the juncture with the inner lining is tattered. Right sleeve has written in old ink, "146 NY." Left sleeve initialed, "JBC." The 146th New York Volunteer Infantry left New York in October 1862 and served the Fifth Corps of The Army of The Potomac until the end of the War. Captain Cushman started as a lieutenant of Company K and was promoted to Captain October 28, 1863. He was then transferred to Company C of the Regiment. Captain Cushman served nobly with the regiment, but was often absent during the last six months of his career because of chronic diarrhea. He was in and out of the hospital and at home, until physically no longer able to perform his duties he resigned his commission in June 1864. Captain Cushman died in 1914, and this coat was auctioned along with much of his family's estate. Fine history, excellent condition. **7,500.00**

Outstanding condition, nine beautiful U.S. staff buttons on the front, three infantry eagle "I" buttons on each cuff, and four staff buttons on the tails. Classic quilted, greenish-brown lining. Condition is excellent with virtually no moth damage.. . . . . **3,950.00**

Regulation CW officer's nine-button frock coat of classic style and construction, with the original Smith's patent Captain's shoulder straps still on the shoulders, owned by George W Billow Co "F" 163rd Ohio Volunteer Infantry and having the original 100-year-old museum tag giving all the particulars. The coat is regulation and war date with fine, tightly quilted body lining, long skirts, balloon elbows on the sleeves, three-button cuffs, rich, brown polished cotton pocket linings, and eagle "I" buttons. Condition is very good with only a couple minor moth nips and some fading of the blue color from years of museum display. The shoulder straps have a couple bends in them. The museum tag states, "Coat worn by George W Billow Springfield, Ohio/Enlisted from Richland Co. O Company "F" 163rd Regiment. **4,350.00**

Standard grade U.S. Civil War infantry officer frock coat, excellent original condition with minor mothing and a slight stain on upper left arm. Has wonderful gilt eagle "I" buttons of a line officer and fine double embroidered second lieutenant of infantry straps. Lining is intact and well above average. . . . **4,720.00**

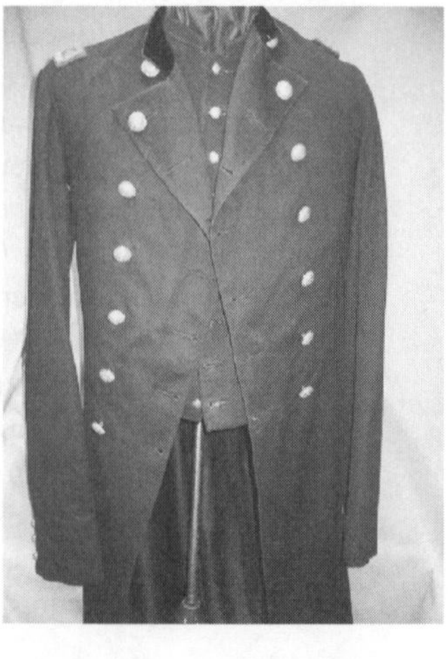

Double-breasted frock coat identified to a surgeon of the 6th Massachusetts Infantry.

Drumbeat Civil War Memorabilia

Officer, Surgeon, very high quality Civil War surgeon's frock coat belonging to Major Otis Humphrey, purchased originally from the family and passed through the collection of a well-known uniform collector. Comes with a letter from the seller and a letter from "The Horse Soldier of Gettysburg" and the original purchaser guaranteeing the authenticity and detailing the history of the coat. This is a dark-blue wool, double-breasted frock coat, unquestionably Civil War period. It has a plain dark green cotton lining, quilted breast area, plain white sleeve lining, and wide balloon sleeve, all the standard features of a Civil War frock. There is no moth damage and all the buttons are present, ("D. Evans" backmarks). The shoulder boards are for a major, and are not "MS" type. They have been added later. Dr. Humphrey enlisted at Lowell, Massachusetts and served as major with the 6th Massachusetts Infantry. He was surgeon in charge of the hospital at New Orleans, Louisiana and remained on duty until the end of the war. His records accompany the coats. **6,500.00**

Patterned after the Chasseur-style uniform, this jacket belonged to a member of the 22nd New York Infantry.

Hendershott Museum Consultants

Jacket, Enlisted Man

22nd New York Volunteer Infantry, rare and custom-made enlisted man's jacket of the 22nd New York Infantry-National Guard. It is single-breasted with New York state seal buttons made by, "Scovill Mf'g Co. Waterbury," with fancy blue trim, particularly on the jacket's back, where it is very ornate. The collar has blue stripes, as well as similar designs on each shoulder made to hold shoulder boards with a flat pocket at right along with a custom made belt loop and polished green linen lining inside. Organized at Troy, New York, the 22nd became part of the Army of the Potomac and fought throughout Virginia against Lee's Army of Northern Virginia, losing 102 men during the war. Their original uniforms were strawberry-trimmed gray, which looked too much like Confederate artillery uniforms. Therefore, they adopted this new style of uniform in the Chasseur pattern. With their new style uniforms they were also issued two-band Enfield rifles with saber bayonets, excellent condition.. . . . .**9,500.00**

Artillery

Civil War issue artillery shell jacket that is fully lined and bearing an inspector's mark in the sleeve with size marking. All original red piping is present. All buttons intact and appear with matching patina. No mothing nor stains. Some wear to piping on rear of neck area likely from actual use. **2,250.00**

Crisp and solid example of the regulation Union army artilleryman's coat with 12-button front, red piped collar, cuffs, and edge. Full body lining (slight fraying), full sleeve lining with inspector's stamp. 100% original and complete. . . . **1,950.00**

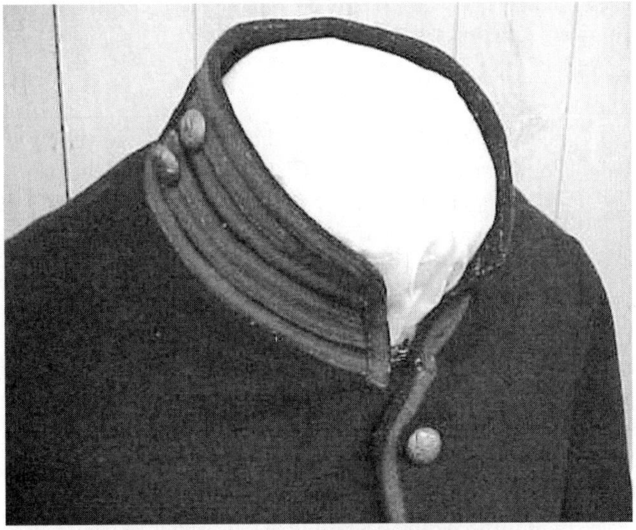

Circa 1862 enlisted man's artillery shell jacket in extremely good condition.

Battleground Antiques, Inc.

Regulation issue Union artillery shell jacket with bright crimson piping and trim; has scarcer blue wool interior lining circa 1862. Overall fine condition for one that actually saw use. Inspector stamps in sleeves. **2,450.00**

The standard pattern bolero-style shell jacket of navy-blue wool with red tape trim. Brass military buttons, small size. **1,150.00**

Beautiful Civil War artillery shell jacket, vivid crimson piping and full lining. Clear maker and inspector's marks in sleeve. **2,650.00**

Cavalry

Mint example of the regulation cavalry troopers short jackets piped in yellow with 12 buttons down the front, two on each side of the collar, and two on each cuff. Bright midnight blue wool body is perfect with great color and no moth damage. This is complete with the full body lining, and the white muslin sleeve linings with clear-size number and inspector's mark. Absolutely top notch in all respects. **2,950.00**

Cavalry, cont.

Striking enlisted man's cavalry jacket.

Battleground Antiques, Inc.

Beautiful Civil War cavalry shell jacket, vivid yellow piping and full lining. Clear maker and inspector marks in sleeve. **3,500.00**

Regulation cavalry troopers' short jackets piped in yellow with 12 buttons down the front, two on each side of the collar, and two on each cuff. Bright midnight blue wool body is fine with great color and no moth damage. This is complete with the full loosely woven blue woolen body lining, and the white muslin sleeve linings with clear size number "2" and inspector's mark, "FH. Shafer US Insp. CIN." Complete in all respects except for the two small pillows on the back of the coat, which were intentionally removed. **2,650.00**

Cavalry shell jacket bearing the maker's mark, "JOHN BOYLAN & CO./ NEWARK, N.Y."

Dale C. Anderson Co.

Regulation dark navy-blue wool coat body with dark yellow piping, 12 eagle buttons down front, two on each collar, and two at each cuff. Tall pillows are still in place on the rear. Light tan lining with some scattered thin spots intact. Marked in left shoulder lining with fairly legible ink stamp reading, "JOHN BOYLAN & CO./NEWARK, N.Y.," plus size mark "1." There is one 1/8" moth hole. **3,495.00**

Regulation, standard issue navy-blue wool body with yellow piping that was definitely issued and worn. Still very good condition, shows some use. Full body lining of coarse tan material and the right shoulder lining shows the size number "2" and a partial inspector's stamp. There is a pocket inside the left breast. Some restitching in the seam of lining has been done. Yellow piping still bright and very lightly faded, some lining is loose in cuffs. Cuffs are missing one cuff button. Jacket is complete with pillows on back. Piping is missing or never had been attached to the cuffs, no mothing. **2,595.00**

Dark blue wool roundabout jacket with complete yellow cavalry trim. Fine condition with all small brass eagle buttons and full muslin lining. Inside of right sleeve stamped with size number, "2." Still retains the belt pads in the back, no mothing or tears. **3,400.00**

Regulation issue Union cavalry shell jacket, vivid yellow worsted wool piping and trim, both pillows on reverse, standard eagle buttons. Fine specimen with virtually no moth damage, but shows a bit of use, unlike surplus ones on the market. Full lining with visible inspector marks in the sleeves. . . . **2,950.00**

U.S. cavalry jacket in need of repair, 100% real jacket that has had some pieces removed. The jacket itself is in very good condition. The collar was cut down, the liner was removed, some of the burlap is still there. The buttons were removed and replaced with half round ones. There is only yellow tape on the right sleeve. **323.00**

Enlisted Man, Zouave, original Civil War zouave jacket recently found in upstate New York. This pattern is standard issue to units such as the 5th New York, Duryea's Zouaves. Has inspector and quartermaster issue stamps in the sleeves! Unfortunately, the owner's name was removed from the inside by cutting out a section of fabric, scattered wear and insect damage. **22,000.00**

Overcoat, Enlisted Man, Infantry

1851 pattern infantry overcoat manufactured by E. Tracy, Philadelphia, Pennsylvania. Coat is complete with outer cape and six original eagle cape buttons and five original eagle coat buttons; and two collar closing hooks. Kersey blue color has turned somewhat green, due to age, but original color can be seen in protected areas. Coat has some staining on front, which is slightly noticeable and a small hole in left front cape panel. Two small holes are on the back under the cape. Hem has some fraying with four tears approx. 2" long with old sewn field repairs. Lining is in excellent condition with good maker marks. Owner's name is lightly on the inside lining, and appears to be, "A Pelky." Sleeve markings inside are "E. Tracy Phila. Oct 21st, 64." This contract was for 100,000 infantry greatcoats. This coat is in good to very-good condition overall. **6,595.00**

This fine enlisted man's infantry overcoat is identified to Private Franklin Denison of the 12th Vermont Infantry. It is made from satinette (the material used early in the war, only a few are known). The overall condition is excellent with a few minor moth holes, mostly under the cape and not visible. The coat has a red wool lining and is clearly marked with inspector's stamps and Denison's name on a sewn in label. Private Franklin Denison was born at Royalton, Vermont and enlisted at the age of 20 in Burlington on August 14, 1862. This regiment was present at the Battle of Gettysburg. Copies of the muster roll show his muster-out date of July 14, 1863. . . . . . . **8,900.00**

Overcoat, Enlisted Man, Mounted

Fine original specimen once the property of the great military artist George Woodbridge who used it as the basis for his illustrations. It comes with a letter from Peter Hlinka attesting to this, dated in 1964, when he sold it to the collector who just recently released it from his collection. Heavy sky-blue Kersey wool, double breasted, with long cape. Six buttons are in a double row down the front and the cape has 12 buttons, 3-1/2" cuffs. Belt across the back, threaded through single wide belt loop. Upper body lined in a brown fabric abrasive to the touch. Off-white arm lining. "Size 3" stamp in right shoulder with a faded contractor stamp. Something on each shoulder is inked-out. Left shoulder has partial, illegible inspector's stamp. Condition is clean, excellent. One worn edge (bit on edge of cape) and 2" of seam needs to be resewn where the collar joins coat at edge. Couple of subtly faded spots, no mothing or frayed lining **8,450.00**

Regulation enlisted man's mounted sky-blue greatcoat with Connecticut identification. Fine condition with full lining, all the buttons, and only a couple minor moth nips. Nicely marked in the sleeves with maker-inspector. This was worn by a soldier in the 2nd Connecticut Light Artillery. **6,850.00**

Cavalry or "mounted" trooper greatcoat complete with cape that belonged to Corporal Henry Berger, 1st Indiana Cavalry. The left cuff is missing, there are some moth holes, although this is a mostly intact original uniform. It is distinguished as a cavalry coat, because of the double-breasted design. There is a belt loop on the back, to adjust the slack in the coat. Coat has been de-acidified. Corporal Henry Berger, 1st Indiana Cavalry was drafted into Company M on November 14, 1862. His unit took part in the siege of Vicksburg, July 1863, and he was discharged shortly thereafter. Included with the jacket is a printout from the Civil War database, his service record from the National Archives, a page from a very old catalog where this jacket was offered for sale for $1,055! The jacket was originally sold at auction by Corporal Berger's grandson, who was moving to a retirement home, many years ago. **5,800.00**

Very rare, standard-issue enlisted cavalry greatcoat, or overcoat. Unlike the infantry ones, this is a double-breasted garment. Standard eagle buttons and wonderful sky-blue wool body. Full lining has some field repairs as well as some light restoration, but overall extremely nice example of a very difficult item to find. Inspector marking in sleeves make this one circa 1862. Full adjusting belt, outer cuffs, and cape. **5,600.00**

Trousers, Enlisted Man, Zouave, pants have "dished top" waistband and a slight reversed dish to the cuffs. Has a 1" woven gold bullion leg stripe. Red painted bone buttons (several of suspender buttons missing) A few scattered moth holes, but rates as excellent. **300.00**

Trousers, Officer, beautiful quality fabric, with extremely tight weave, thick, and with a rich, soft touch in one direction, and abrasive if rubbed the opposite way. Extraordinarily beautiful color between sky-blue and medium blue perhaps best called "Saxony Blue." Narrow waistband, bone suspender buttons inside, and tin-backed brass on the outside and down the fly. 1/8" golden cord welt down each outer seam. Side pockets along the side seam, and belt in back. Fully lined on top and at cuffs. Large size, clean, and in excellent condition showing light use. 1" tear at top of left pocket. **1,950.00**

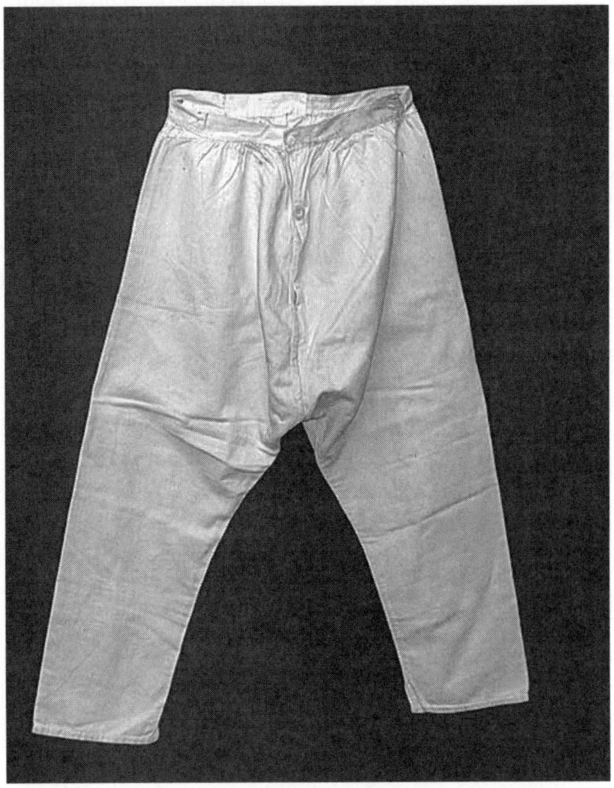

Seldom encountered, Civil War soldier underwear is a great find. Because many of these were home-supplied, finding issued drawers is even more difficult.

Drawers, Officer, cotton, identified, and seldom encountered, this pair of Civil War period drawers are made of a cotton flannel and muslin combination and are pieced together by both hand and machine. The front has a two-button closure and the back adjusts with a cotton tape tie. These drawers are very similar to the set pictured in *Echoes of Glory*. These were purchased in a lot of early clothing from upstate New York and are inscribed in the front of the waistband " Col. W or N (?) C. Raulston (?) N.Y. Vol." Drawers are in excellent condition with some minor yellowing and some minor stains but no tears or holes. Measure 37" from waist to cuff, waist measures about 30". **405.00**

Uniform, Officer

Infantry, exceptional, identified officer's frock coat and sky-blue pants. Coat is the standard nine-button with eagle "I" buttons, polished green lining and deep blue broadcloth construction. Captain of line (infantry) bars neatly sewn on, obviously a custom-tailored jacket—a lot of detailed and neat hand stitching throughout. Pants are typical, soft-brushed wool in sky-blue, with adjusting buckle on reverse with patent date of 1855. Button fly and slash front pockets. Bottom cuffs reinforced to reduce wear (worn with boots). Coat belonged to Captain Reynolds Laughlin, Company A, 103rd Pennsylvania Infantry. Laughlin mustered in service in September of 1861 and served until January of 1863. During that time, his unit saw action at Yorktown, Williamsburg, Fair Oaks, Seven Days Battles, Malvern Hill, Suffolk, and the 1862 Battle of Kinston, North Carolina, losing 53 officers and enlisted men killed in action during the term of service. Great condition overall, with positive ID inked in upper sleeve area. **7,500.00**

Uniform, Officer

Quartermaster, Civil War Quartermaster uniform grouping belonging to an officer of the 164th Ohio Infantry. Exceptional grouping from one officer that includes his beautiful frock coat with eagle "I" infantry buttons and super rare quartermaster bars; his vest; his trousers with blue officer welt down the leg; his sword; his fine belt rig with eagle buckle (name inscribed on reverse), and officer's silk sash. Azariah C. Baker enlisted on May 02, 1864, as a Quartermaster. On May 11, 1864, he was commissioned into the Field & Staff of the 164th Ohio Infantry. He was mustered out on August 27, 1864, at Cleveland, Ohio. This regiment was organized at Camp Cleveland, May 11, 1864, to serve for 100 days. It was composed of the 49th Regiment, Ohio National Guard, from Seneca county and the 54th Battalion, from Summit county. On May 14, it left Clevelandand proceeded (via Dunkirk, Elmira, Harrisburg, and Baltimore) to Washington, D.C. on the 17th. It took position in the defenses on the south side of the Potomac and during its 100 days' service garrisoned Forts Smith, Strong, Bennett, Haggarty, and other forts. At the expiration of its term of enlistment, it returned to Cleveland and was mustered out on Aug. 27, 1864. His widow, Harriet K. Baker, applied for a pension on February 01, 1888, from the state of Ohio. **22,000.00**

Uniform Terminology

Frock coat: A thigh-length outer garment fitted at the waist. Military examples will usually have a standing collar.

Blouse: Period term used to describe a waist-length outer garment. Blouses are not fitted at the waist.

Sack coat: Period term for a "blouse." Federally-issued Union sack coats had four-button fronts. Most, but not all, were lined.

Kepi: Drawn from the style of the French military, a low cap. Shaped with reed or wire to have a sharp rise on the rear, a standing front and a round crown.

Jacket: A fitted, waist-length outer garment.

Shako: Similar to a kepi, but generally taller, often standing 6" from visor to crown.

Zouave: A French soldier who wore a rather outstanding uniform consisting of short jackets, baggy pantaloons and a fez and/or turban. Both Union and Confederate regiments were raised, uniformed and drilled in the manner of the Zouave.

See also: Groupings.

Glossary of Terms

ADS: "Autograph Document Signed."

ALS: "Autographed Letter Signed."

Ambrotype: A positive effect achieved on glass coated with light-sensitive collodion, backed with black paint, fabric, or paper. Patented by James Ambrose Cutting of Boston, 1854. Encased in the then widely available daguerreotype cases, they are often confused with the early daguerrean photographs.

Armory brown: A term used today to describe a soft, even discoloring of a weapon's metal. Originally, bright metal was treated at the arsenals with a protective coating of brown lacquer.

Armory: The place where firearms are built.

Arsenal: A government location where weapons are stored. May also contain an armory where weapons are built.

Attributed: This term is used to associate an item to a particular soldier even though it is not marked as having belonged to him.

Backmark: Wet plate photographers often imprinted their name and address on the cards on which they mounted their photographs. These imprints served as an advertisement and today, can help identify the origin of a particular image. Abbreviated, "B/m."

Backstrap: (1) A metal strap running down the back of the handle resting in the palm of the hand. (2) That part of the revolver or pistol frame that is exposed at the rear of the grip.

Bannerman's: Francis Bannerman was an early surplus dealer, beginning his business in the late nineteenth century. He bought vast supplies of Civil War goods direct from the government and manufacturers for resale to early Civil War buffs. Bannerman was also the first individual to reproduce Civil War items on a large scale.

Barrel band: A metal band, either fixed or adjustable, around the forend of a gun that holds the barrel to the stock.

Battle honors: The names of battles or engagements in which the unit fought; honors are sewn or painted onto the flag or attached by streamers.

Belt plate: A belt plate is intended for wear on a leather belt, and generally has a decorative face.

Blank cartridge: A cartridge filled with powder, but having no projectile.

Blind shell: A projectile with a hollow cavity that was plugged and not intended for fitting with a fuse. This projectile weighed less than a solid shot of the same caliber, thereby increasing its velocity when it was fired.

Blouse: Period term used to describe a waist-length outer garment. Blouses are not fitted at the waist.

Bluing: The blue or black finish of the metal parts of a gun. Bluing minimizes light reflection, gives a "finish" to the bare metal, and protects somewhat against rust.

Bolt: An elongated, solid, rifled projectile that contains no explosive material that would fragment it. They were best used in counter-battery fire and against fortified positions. Because there are no explosives involved, they are also the safest artillery rounds to dig and collect.

Bormann fuse: This fuse is the invention of an officer of the Belgian service. The case is made of an alloy of tin and lead, cast in iron molds. Its shape is that of a thick circular disk. A screw thread is cut upon the edge, allowing it to be fastened into the fuse-hole of a projectile.

Breechloader: A long arm that is loaded from the area nearest the ignition system, rather than down the muzzle of the weapon. Most often involves a pre-made cartridge.

Broadside: Single-sheet notices or announcements printed on one or both sides, intended to be read unfolded.

Brogan: An early nineteenth century term meaning shoe. Somewhat erroneously, collectors and reenactors often refer to federally-issued Jefferson Pattern shoes as brogans. The error, though, is very slight as many soldiers also referred to their government-issued footwear as brogans.

Bundle: Period term to describe a sealed package of cartridges.

Bunting: The woolen fabric from which flags were traditionally made.

Caisson: A two-wheeled vehicle designed to carry artillery ammunition. It was pulled by a limber and team.

Canister: A metal cylinder made of tin, iron, or lead, with a removable thin iron top. A heavy iron plate is usually located between the canister balls and the wooden sabot at the bottom. The cylinder contains iron or lead balls that are arranged in rows with sawdust packed between them. The top edge of the vertical cylinder wall is bent over the iron top plate to help keep the canister contents in place and the bottom edge is nailed to the wooden sabot. Canister was designed to be used against infantry at close range.

Canton: Any quarter of the flag, but commonly refers to the upper-left corner. On the U.S. flag, it is the blue section.

Cap pouch: Small leather box carried on the waist belt for the storage and easy retrieval of percussion caps.

Cap: Short for percussion cap, the primer that when placed on the nipple and struck with the hammer, provides the fire to ignite the gunpowder charge.

Carbine: A breech or muzzle-loading shoulder arm having a smooth or rifled bore, using externally primed ammunition. Originally designed for horse-mounted troops.

Carte de viste: Also known as "cdv." A 2-1/2" x 4-1/2" photographic calling card, usually created as one of a number of images on a single photographic plate. Their introduction dates to 1854 by French photographer, Adolphe-Eugene Disderi, thought their popularity in America started in 1860. Their major competition was the lower-cost tintype.

Cartouche: A marking impressed on a firearm, usually denoting an inspector's initials.

Cartridge box plate: Similar to belt plates, cartridge box plates are decorative and generally have loops for fastening to a cartridge box flap. Though decorative, a cartridge box plate provided weight that kept the box flap closed.

Cartridge box sling plate: These are intended to be worn on the shoulder sling of the cartridge box strap. Its function was strictly decorative.

Cartridge box: Leather box carried on the waist belt or suspended from a shoulder strap for the storage and easy retrieval of cartridges.

Cartridge: A case usually made of paper for muzzle-loaders and of copper, brass, or combustible paper for breech-loaders that contains the powder charge, bullet, and sometimes, the primer.

Case shot: Also known as spherical case shot. Similar to the common shell except that the walls of the projectile were thinner. In both spherical and rifled projectiles, the bursting charge was usually located in a thin tin or iron container and placed in the center of the internal cavity. The case shot was placed around this container. The Confederates usually drilled into the case shot to form the bursting charge cavity. Due to the shortage of lead needed by the Confederates for small arms ammunition, iron case-shot balls were often substituted for lead.

Case: Due to the fragile nature of the photograph, and the familiar practice of housing a painted miniature in a jewel-like case, early photographers packaged daguerreotypes, ambrotypes, and many tintypes in a protective case. First, a thin brass mat was placed over the image, followed by a protective cover glass. After 1849, this sandwich was held together by a thin brass rim known as a preserver. A miniature case was then selected to house this package. The image was slipped into the right half opposite a pad, usually of velvet, on the left. (Some, however, were made to hold photographs on both sides.) The cheapest examples were made of embossed paper applied over a wooden shell. Leather was used as a covering as well. A molded thermoplastic (sometimes called "gutta-percha") "Union" case was the most expensive choice.

Centerfire: A design of ammunition in which the primer is centrally located in the base of the cartridge case.

Charge: An emblem or design added to the basic flag.

Chipped: Used to describe where small pieces are missing or where fraying has occurred on a dust jacket or the edge of a paperback.

Color: During the Civil War, this was the national, state, or regimental flag carried by dismounted units.

Combination fuse: Combination of the time fuse and percussion fuse system. The inertia of firing caused the plunger in the fuse to strike a chemical composition, thereby igniting the powder train. The fuse was designed to act as a percussion fuse if it struck an object before the preset time.

Concussion fuse: A chemical fuse designed to activate from the shock of striking an object. The chemicals were kept separate until impact when the action of the chemicals upon each other caused a flame.

Conversion: In terms of Civil War firearms, a conversion is where the ignition system of a weapon (usually a flintlock), is modified into a more modern system (usually percussion).

Corps badge: In 1863, the Union Army instituted a system of denoting corps affiliation by displaying specific symbols. These symbols, cut of wool felt, were initially issued to soldiers. Enthusiasm caught on for the idea and soldiers soon began buying commercial corps badges to decorate their hats, caps, coats, and jackets.

Cut-down: A collector term to describe a long arm that has had its original barrel length modified. In almost every case, a cut-down will not be worth as much as an original full-length weapon.

Cylinder scene: Many revolvers of the Civil War era had various pictures, or scenes engraved on the cylinders.

Daguerreotype: The first practical system of photography with a positive image produced on copper clad with a layer of burnished (mirror-like) silver, treated in the manner developed in France following successful efforts by Nicephore Niepce and J. L. M. Daguerre; announced to the world in 1839. Without a negative, the superior wet-plate system introduced about ten years later soon brought daguerrean era to an end.

D-Guard: This is the term applied to the over-the-fist guard on some Bowie knives. Most often associated with Confederate knives, there are many photographs of Union soldiers posing with D-Guard knives as well.

Double action: A revolver that may be fired by just pulling the trigger to cock the hammer and rotate the cylinder to the next chamber.

Drop: This is a collector term to describe a bullet that was dug and found to be in unfired condition. The idea is that the soldier who originally handled the round somehow dropped it and never recovered it.

DS: "Document Signed."

Dug: Any item that has been excavated, usually using a metal detector. Many collectors prefer dug items, because such pieces are more difficult to fake.

DuoDecimo: A book or document approximately 7" to 8" tall.

Edges: The outer surfaces of the leaves of a book.

Ensign: A flag flown on ships or boats.

Epaulette: Worn on the shoulder and fringed, epaulettes are part of a dress uniform. Rarely would they ever be worn in a combat situation.

Ephemera: Items that were intended to be used for a short period of time, then disposed.

Face: The front of a button on which the design is stamped or cast.

Ferrule: (1) A metal tip at the bottom of a staff used to plant the flag in the ground or rest the flag in a sling around the neck. (2) A metal washer between the guard and handle. It is there to make sure the handle doesn't move.

Field: The background color on a flag.

Finial: An ornamental device attached to the head of a flagstaff.

Fixed ammunition: A pre-assembled (or fixed) combination of a smoothbore projectile, sabot, and powder bag. This assembly allowed an increase in the rate of fire of the artillery crew by eliminating two steps in the process of loading and firing.

Flank markers: Small flags carried at each end of an infantry regiment's line of battle to mark the flanks

Flintlock: A firing mechanism used primarily on martial firearms prior about 1848. It uses a shower of sparks created when a piece of flint strikes a steel frizzen to ignite a priming charge, which in turn, ignites the main powder charge.

Flyleaf: A blank leaf, sometimes more than one, following the front free endpaper, or at the end of a book where there is not sufficient text to fill out the last few pages.

Fly: The part of the flag furthest from the staff.

Folio: Has several meanings: (1) a leaf numbered on the front; (2) the numeral itself; and (3) a folio-sized publication. When used as this third definition, it refers to the largest size of printed material. By the mid-1800s the normal folio size had increased to about 17" x 21", the size that is still standard to this day.

Foxing: Brown spotting of the paper caused by a chemical reaction, generally found in 19th century books, particularly in steel engravings of the period.

Frame buckle: This is simply a utilitarian buckle that was not intended to have any decorative value. Often associated with Confederate accoutrements, there are a wide variety of frame buckles.

Friction primer: A small brass or quill tube, known as the priming tube, filled with gunpowder and used to send a flame to the powder charge inside the bore. An artilleryman used a lanyard to pull the wire, thereby, igniting the fuse.

Frock coat: A thigh-length outer garment fitted at the waist. Military examples will usually have a standing collar.

Frog: Generally, a frog is a leather item that slips onto a belt and provides a means for carrying a bayonet scabbard or straight sword scabbard on the belt.

Fuller: A groove down the center of a blade, for strength and lightness. Usually misnamed the "blood groove."

Fuse: Devise used to detonate a shell or case shot. Fuses for projectiles are classified as time fuses, percussion-fuses, and combination-fuses. The time fuse serves to explode a projectile during flight, or at the end of a given period of time after its discharge from the gun. The percussion-fuse, rifled guns serve to explode a projectile either during flight or on impact. The combination fuse involves both of these elements.

Gemrig bone surgery set: A specialized surgical set issued to military surgeons for bone resection or removal. J. H. Gemrig was a supplier of military and civilian surgical sets before and during the war.

Gilt: The gold wash applied to the face of a button.

Grapeshot: Iron balls that, when bound together, formed a stand of grapeshot.

Grouping: The term used by collectors to identify items that are historically associated.

Guidon: A small flag or banner carried by military units to identify their origin or affiliation.

Hammer: The part of a gun's mechanism that, after being cocked, flies (usually) forward to strike the percussion cap or primer, thus firing the gun.

Haversack: A bag used primarily for an individual's eating tools and foodstuffs. Generally carried by means of a shoulder sling.

Hernstein military amputation set: Strictly for field amputation, marked instruments for U.S. Army Hospital Department. H. Hernstein was a supplier of military and civilian surgical sets before and during the War.

Hoist: The part of the flag nearest to the staff or flagpole.

Housewife: A small, usually rolled-up, portfolio for storing sewing supplies.

Identification disc: These are the precursors to the issued "dog tags." These items were not issued during the Civil War. Rather, soldiers purchased and made a variety of identification tags to wear while in service.

Identified: When a collector or dealer refers to an "identified" item, that means that the name of the soldier associated with the item is known.

Import: In Civil War terms, any weapon not produced in a Northern or Southern armory.

Imprint: A term that can refer either to the place of publication or to the publisher.

Jacket: A fitted, waist-length outer garment.

Keeper: Some belts were issued with a brass fitting that accepted the hook of the belt plate. This fitting was called the keeper.

Kepi: Drawn from the style of the French military, a low cap. Shaped with reed or wire to have a sharp rise on the rear, a standing front and a round crown.

Kern trepanning set: Civilian set for surgery of the skull. H. Kern was a supplier of military and civilian surgical sets before and during the War.

Kit: Term used to describe the entire trappings of accoutrements assigned to one soldier.

Knuckle bow: Single strap running from the quillon to the pommel. It guards the front of the hand.

Kolbe military set: Intended for major bone surgery, trepanning, amputation, a specialized set for bone resection or removal. Marked for U.S. Army Medical Department. Date of manufacture determined by label address of maker. D. Kolbe was a supplier of military and civilian surgical sets before and during the War.

Limber: A two-wheeled vehicle to which a gun or caisson is attached.

Lock: The firing mechanism of a muzzle-loading firearm.

LS: "Letter Signed."

Married: Items that were not historically together, but rather, put together some time after the Civil War.

Minié bullet: Perfected by Captain Claude Etienne Minié of the French Army in 1848. The U.S. Army adopted the design in 1855. The bullet was elongated, but was hollow at the base for about one-third of the length. When fired, gasses forced the lead into the rifling grooves in the barrel.

Musket: A muzzle-loading, smooth bore long arm that is equipped to support a bayonet.

Musketoon: A muzzle-loading shoulder arm having a smooth or rifled bore and a maximum barrel length of 26.5 inches.

Nipple: A small metal tube extending through the breech of a percussion firearm also called the cone.

Obverse: The right-hand page of a book, more commonly called the recto.

Octavo (8vo): A book or document of about 5" x 8" to about 6" x 9". Octavo is the most common size for current hardcover books. To make octavo books, each sheet of paper is folded to make eight leaves (sixteen pages).

Pamphlet: Published, non-serial volumes with no cover or with a paper cover, usually five or more pages and fewer than 49.

Paper boards: Stiff cardboard covered in paper.

Pennant: A flag made in the shape of an isosceles triangle, which has two equal sides.

Percussion cap: A slightly conical copper cap, shaped like a top hat, that contained fulminate of mercury. The cap was placed on the nipple of the fuse slider in the percussion fuse or simply the nipple of a musket. When struck, it sent a spark to the charge.

Pinfire: The pinfire system is one in which the firing pin is actually a part of the cartridge.

Plate sizes: Full (whole) plate 6-1/2 x 8-1/2 inches; half plate 4-1/4 x 6-1/2 inches; quarter plate 3-1/4 x 4-1/4 inches; one-sixth plate 2-3/4 x 3-1/4 inches; one-eighth plate 2-1/8 by 3-1/4 inches; one-ninth plate 1-1/2 x 1-3/4 inches; and one-sixteenth plate 1-5/8 by 2-1/8 inches.

Pommel: The part of the handle that keeps your pinky from sliding off. Also holds the whole sword together.

Primer: Device that when placed in the vent hole of a field piece and attached to a lanyard, is used to fire the gun. It replaced the process of priming the vent hole with fuse and powder and igniting with a slow match.

Provenance: The history of an item. Usually, provenance will identify the original owner and in some cases, subsequent owners of an item.

Puppy paw: Consisting of two studs, this is a style of attachment found on some U.S. belt plates.

Push: Slight dent, usually used to describe damage to a dug button.

Quarto (4to): A book or document between octavo and folio in size; approximately 11" to 13" tall. To make a quarto, a sheet of paper is folded twice, forming four leaves (eight pages).

Quillon: The cross piece on a sword, also thought of as a guard.

Ramrod: A wood or metal rod used to force a bullet down the barrel of a muzzle-loading firearm.

Receiver: The housing for a firearm's breech (portion of the barrel with chamber into which a cartridge or projectile is loaded) and firing mechanism.

Recto: The front side of a printed sheet or the front side of a leaf in a bound book; in other words, the right-hand page of an opened book. Also called the obverse.

Repeating firearm: A firearm that may be discharged repeatedly by recharging through means of deliberate, successive, mechanical actions of the user.

Ricasso: The flattened portion of the blade that assists in the manipulation of the weapon. Often, one will find the maker's mark stamped here.

Rifled musket: A muzzle-loading, rifled long arm that is equipped to support an angular bayonet.

Rifle: In terms of Civil War weaponry, a two-banded weapon (or of similar length to a two-banded weapon) equipped to support a saber bayonet.

Rimfire: A rimmed or flanged cartridge with the priming mixture located inside the rim of the case.

Ring: On the base of a conical bullet, rings will often be found. The idea is that, when fired, these rings expand and engage the rifling grooves in the barrel.

Rmdc: Used to describe hallmarks, usually on buttons. It means, "Raised mark depressed channel."

rm: Used to refer to hallmarks, usually on buttons. This refers to a "raised mark" maker's mark.

Saber bayonet: This is a wide-bladed (most often with a fuller) bayonet that has a handle that attaches to a lug on the side of a rifle barrel.

Saber belt: An enlisted man's grade leather belt fitted with straps for attaching a saber and often, also fitted with a shoulder strap.

Saber: A cavalry sword with a curved blade.

Sabot: The sabot served as the driving band for an artillery projectile. Generally, a sabot was made of wood, brass, copper, lead, or wrought iron. The sabot for a rifled projectile was attached directly onto the projectile. When the weapon was fired, the gases from the explosion caused the sabot to expand into the rifling grooves of the barrel.

Sack coat: Period term for a "blouse." Federally-issued, Union sack coats had four-button fronts. Most, but not all, were lined.

Sash: A sash was worn by officers and NCOs wrapped around their waist and under the sword belt.

Scabbard drag: Tip of the scabbard that is reinforced. It is the part that literally drags on the ground.

Sextodecimo (16mo): A small book or document, approximately 4" x 6". To make it, each sheet of paper is folded four times, forming sixteen leaves (32 pages).

Shako: Similar to a kepi, but generally taller, often standing 6" from visor to crown.

Shank: The loop on the back of a button for attaching to material.

Shell: A hollow projectile cast iron containing a bursting charge that was ignited by means of a fuse.

Shoulder scale: Not actually an insignia (though they were worn only by NCOs and lower ranks), shoulder scales were more of a form of body armor. The idea was that if a soldier wearing these was struck down by a swordsman, the blow would be diminished by the protecting scales.

Single action: The hammer has to be cocked manually on a single action revolver. Depressing the trigger will only fire a fully cocked revolver.

Solid shot: A solid projectile cast without a powder chamber or fuse hole. Also known as a "shot" or "cannon ball."

Standard: This was the national, state, or regimental flag carried by mounted units.

Sword belt: An officer's grade belt fitted with straps for carrying a sword. Often, there will be provisions for a shoulder strap.

Tang: A metal strip extending rearward from the breech plug that attaches to the stock of the weapon.

Tarred: Nineteenth century term used to refer to painted cloth.

Tax stamp: Images bearing a U.S. postage stamp on the back can be dated as having been produced before or during the period September 1, 1864, to August 1, 1866, when all such photographs transported in the U.S. mail were subject to this form of government tax in order to raise additional wartime revenue. Mainly found on cartes de visite, but also on some tintypes and ambrotypes as well.

Tintype: Also known as "Ferreotype" and "Melainotype" it is a direct-positive (that is, without a negative) photograph on a thin, tin-dipped iron sheet developed by a French process of 1853. Introduced to America beginning in 1856, its tonal range, durability, and low cost made it a popular process that continued in many places well into the early twentieth century.

Tongue: On a two-piece buckle, the "tongue" is the male half.

Trappings: Nineteenth century term used to described the sum of belt, cartridge box, cap pouch, bayonet scabbard, canteen, and haversack.

Trigger guard: A metal loop around the trigger designed to protect it.

Tube: Refers to the barrel of a gun, generally of bronze or cast iron.

Verso: The back of a printed sheet or the rear side of a leaf in a bound book; in other words, the left-hand page of an opened book.

War log: The term was first used in the early days of the Grand Army of the Republic and United Confederate Veterans to describe souvenir pieces of wood recovered from battlefields that showed the impact of bullets or artillery pieces. These early specimens served as reminders of the perils the veterans had faced. Today, war logs are reemerging on the market. No longer the branches or stumps stripped of bark, these are battlefield recovered specimens where the tree had actually "healed" around the projectile. Split open, these branches reveal the bullet, and often, the path it took to enter the wood. Definitely possessing a different feel than the earlier veteran-acquired specimens, they are, nonetheless, a true testament of the deadliness the soldiers had faced.

Water stained: Discoloration and perhaps actual shrinking. A greater degree of damp stained.

Wraps (a.k.a. Wrappers): The outer covers of a paperbound book or pamphlet. Not to be confused with the dust wrapper, which protects a hardcover book.

Zouave: A French soldier who wore a rather outstanding uniform consisting of short jackets, baggy pantaloons and a fez and/or turban. Both Union and Confederate regiments were raised, uniformed and drilled in the manner of the Zouave.

APPENDIX A

Civil War Memorabilia Sources

Advance Guard Militaria
270 State Hwy. HH
Burfordville, MO 63739
Phone:573-243-1833
E-mail: orders@advanceguardmilitaria.com
Web site: www.advanceguardmilitaria.com

Dale C. Anderson Co. Militaria and Americana
P.O. Box 3516
Gettysburg, PA 17325
Web site: www.andersonmilitaria.com

Antebellum Covers
Box 3494
Gaithersburg, MD 20885
Phone: 1-888-268-3235
E-mail: antebell@antebellumcovers.com
Web site: www.antebellumcovers.com

Barry'd Treasure—Civil War Relics
Barry L. Anderson
P.O. Box 16569
Louisville, KY 40256
Phone: 502-448-8772
E-mail: btreasure@iglou.com
Web site: www.iglou.com/btreasure

Battleground Antiques, Inc.
Will Gorges, Scott Ford
3910 US Hwy 70 East
New Bern, NC 28560
Phone: 252-636-3039
E-mail: rebel@civlwarantiques.com
Web site: www.civilwarshop.com

Blue Gray Relics
Mark Shuttleworth & Jocelyn Shuttleworth
3321 N. Reynolds
Mesa, AZ 85215
Phone: 480-641-8752
E-mail: mshutt3@aol.com
Web site: www.bluegrayrelics.com

Mike Brackin Civil War Americana
Mike Brackin
P.O. Box 23
Manchester, CT 06045
Phone: 860-647-8620
E-mail: info@mikebrackin.com
Web site: www.mikebrackin.com

Brian & Maria Green, Inc.
P.O. Box 1816
Kernersville, NC 27285-1816
Phone: 336-993-5100
E-mail: bmgcivilwar@triad.rr.com
Web site: wwwbmgcivilwar.com

Carolina Collectors
Rick Burton & Warren Vestal
P.O. Box 21864
Greensboro, NC 27420
Phone: 336-996-0787
E-mail: ccrelics@collectorsnet.com
Web site: www.ccrelics.com

The Carolina Rebel
Joe Haile
5426 Main Street
P.O. Box 1659
Spring Hill, TN 37174
Phone: 931-486-1561
E-mail: caroreb@aol.com
Web site: www.civilwarrelics.com

Civil War Artillery Man
Shane Cooper Neitzey
7595 Centreville Rd.
Manassas, VA 20111
Phone: 703-335-8185
E-mail: shanessigns@mindspring.com
Web site: www.cwartilleryman.com

Caldwell and Company Civil War Antiques
816 Pleasant St.,
Lebanon, IN 46052
Phone: 765-482-0292
E-mail: civilwr@in-motion.net
Web site: www.caldwellandcompany.net

The Civil War Connection
Dan and Teresa Patterson
128 Meadowdale Dr.
P.O. Box 2468
Madison, MS 39110
Phone: 601-856-0094
E-mail: cwtrader1863@E-mail.com
Web site: www.civilwarconnection.tripod.com

The Civil War Relicman
Harry Ridgeway
124 Selma Drive
Winchester, VA 22601
Phone: 540-662-6786
E-mail: relicman@shentel.net
Web site: www.relicman.com

CivilWarTokens.com
Steve Hayden
P.O. Box 571
Mauldin, SC 29662
Phone: 864-288-4375
E-mail: steve@civilwartokens.com
Web site: www.civilwartokens.com

CSA Military Collectables, Inc.
Robert S. Dodson, S. K. Dodson
P. O. Box 1111
Acworth, Georgia 30101
Phone: 678-354-2959
E-mail: info@csamilitary.com
Web site: www.csamilitary.com

Damon Mills Fine Antique Arms
Damon Mills, Antique Arms Dealer
Montgomery, AL
Phone: 334-281-0804
E-mail: damonmillsantiques@home.com
Web site: www.damonmills.com

Dave Taylor's Civil War Antiques
P.O. Box 87
Sylvania, OH 43560
Phone: 419-878-8355
E-mail: davetaylor.civilwar@Sylvania.sev.org
Web site: www.civilwarantique.com

Deep South Artifacts, Inc.
Keith B. Kenerly
11612 New Bond St.
Fredricksburg, VA 22408
Phone: 540-710-7841
E-mail: kbkdsa@aol.com
Web site: www.DeepSouthArtifacts.com

Drumbeat Civil War Memorabilia
Eric P. Kane
P.O. Box 119
Bayport, NY 11705
Phone: 631-472-3087
E-mail: info@DrumBeatMilitaria.com
Web site: www.erickaneantiques.com

N. Flayderman & Co., Inc.
P.O. Box 2446
Fort Lauderdale, FL 33303
Phone: 954-761-8855
E-mail: flayderman@aol.com
Web site: www.flayderman.com

Frohne's Historic Military
1963 Amy Jo Drive
Oshkosh, WI 54904
Phone:920-232-9839
E-mail: modoc1873@charter.net
Web site: www.modoc1873.com

Greybird's Relics
PO Box 126
Acworth, GA 30101
E-mail: greybirdrelics@mindspring.com
Web site: www.greybirdrelics.com

Gutterman Historical Weapons, Inc.
Neil & Julia Gutterman
P.O. Box 1022
Pearl River, NY 10965
Phone: 845-735-5174
E-mail: host@19thcenturyweapons.com
Web site: www.19thcenturyweapons.com

Heller's Antiques
Steve E. Heller
231 Juniata Park Way East
Newport, PA 17074-8725
Phone: 717-567-6805
E-mail: seheller@tricountyi.net
Web site: www.civilwarantiqueshop.com

Hendershott Museum Consultants
2200 N. Rodney Parham Rd., Suite 209
P.O. Box 22520
Little Rock, AR 72212
Phone: 501-224-7555
E-mail: hmc2000@swbell.net
Web site: www.garyhendershott.com

The Horse Soldier
Chet, Pat, Sam & Wes Small
777 Baltimore Street
Gettysburg, PA 17325
Mailing address:
P.O. Box 184
Cashtown, PA, 17310
Phone: 717-334-0347
E-mail: info@horsesoldier.com
Web site: www.horsesoldier.com

Steven L. Hoskin
P.O. Box 2148
Venice, FL 34284
Phone: 941-496-8427
E-mail: slhdoc@home.com
Web site: www.civilwarautographs.com

Jacques Noel Jacobsen, Jr.
Collector's Antiquities, Inc.
60 Manor Road
Staten Island, NY 10310
Phone: 718-981-0973
E-mail: Jjacobsen@SI.RR.com
Web site: www.home.fiam.net

J.C. Devine Inc.
P.O. Box 413, 20 South St.
Milford, NH 03055
Phone: 603-673-4967
E-mail: jcdevine@empire.net
Web site: www.jcdevine.com

JS Mosby's Antiques & Artifacts
Stephen W. Sylvia
125 East Main St.
Orange, VA 22960
Phone: 540-672-9944
E-mail: info@jsmosby.com
Web site: www.jsmosby.com

J & W Relics
Jack Masters
1049 Robertson Road
Gallatin, TN 37066
Phone: 615-748-3532
E-mail: jack@jackmasters.net
Web site: www.jackmasters.net

Keemakoo's Civil War Antiques James Dews
459 West Commodore Blvd.
Jackson, NJ 08527
Phone: 732-928-8973
E-mail: keemakoo@aol.com
Web site: www.hometown@aol.com/keemakoo/page3.html

Phillip B. Lamb, Ltd./Col. Lamb's Antiques
P.O. Box 206
Montreat, NC 28757
Phone: 504-236-6014
E-mail:lambcsa@aol.com
Web site: www.plamb.com

Lawrence Of Dalton
Lawrence Christopher
4773 Tammy Dr. N.E.
Dalton, GA 30721
Phone: 706-226-8894
E-mail: cw1861@vol.com
Web site: www.cw1861.com

McGowan Book Company
R. Douglas Sanders
P.O. Box 4226
Chapel Hill, NC 27515
Phone: 1-800-449-8406
E-mail: mcgowanbooks@mindspring.com
Web site: www.mcgowanbooks.com

Middle Tennessee Relics
Larry & Debbie Hicklen
3511 Old Nashville Hwy.
Murfreesboro, TN 37129
Phone: 615-893-3470
E-mail: DebHicklen@comcast.net
Web site: www.midtenrelics.com

Military Antiques & Museum
300 Petaluma Blvd North
Petaluma, CA 94952
Phone: 540-740-8065 (EST)
E-mail: WarGuys@sonic.net
Web site: www.militaryantiquesmuseum.com

Old South Books, Inc.
Larry and Vivian Wandling
Address: P.O. Box 757
Shalimar, FL 32579
Phone: 850-651-0709
E-mail: wandlinv@cybertron.com
Web site: http://home.cybertron.com/~wandlinv

Old South Military Antiques
Shannon and Lesia Pritchard
P.O. Box 175
Studley, VA 23126
Phone: 804-779-3076
E-mail: oldsouthantique@mindspring.com
Web site:www.oldsouthantiques.com

Barbara Pengelly, Autographs
13917 NO. Meadow Rd.
Hagerstown, MD 21742
Phone: 301-733-9070
E-mail: barbpengly@aol.com
Web site: www.autographdomain.com

The Powder Horn Gunshop, Inc.
Bob Daly, Owner
Cliff Sophia, Manager
Box 1001, 200 W. Washington St.
Middleburg, VA 20118
Phone: 540-687-6628
E-mail: info@phgsinc.com
Web site: www.phgsinc.com

Reb Acres
Sue Coleman
P.O. Box 215
Raphine, VA 24472
Phone: 540-377-2057
E-mail: scoleman@rebacres.com
Web site: www.rebacres.com

RelicAuction.com
Carson Jenkins & Steve Sylvia
Springfield, VA 22152
E-mail: auctioneer@relicauction.com
Web site: www.relicauction.com

Sharpsburg Arsenal
101 W. Main St. P.O. Box 568
Sharpsburg, MD 211782
Phone: 301-432-7700
E-mail: sarsenal@mip.net
Web site: www.sharpsberg-arsenal.com

Shiloh's Civil War Relics
Rafael & Lori Eledge
4730 Highway 22
Shiloh, TN 38376
Phone: 731-689-4114
E-mail: relics@shilohrelics.com
Web site: www.shilohrelics.com

Shotwell's Antiques & Civil War Memorabilia
Olin Shotwell
2935 Sycamore Lane
Bloomsburg, PA 17815
Phone: 570-387-1112
E-mail: OSCIVWAR@aol.com
Web site: www.shotwellsantiques.com

Jim Stanley & Associates
Jim Stanley
7613 Ensign Court
Fort Wayne, IN 46816
Phone: 219-447-7202
E-mail: cwartifax@home.com
Web site: www.cwartifax.com

Stone Mountain Relics, Inc.
John Sexton, Charles & Nan Nash, Lori Nash Cosgrove
968 Main Street
Stone Mountain, GA 30083
Phone: 770-469-1425
E-mail: SMRelics@aol.com
Web site: www.stonemountainrelics.com

Stones River Trading Company
Tom Hays
3500 Shacklett Rd.
Murfreesboro, TN. 37129
Phone: 615-895-7134
E-Mail: Whays@aol.com
Web site: www.stonesrivertrading.com

Sumter Military Antiques
Ray Davenport & Jay Teague
45 John Street
Charleston, SC 29403
Phone: 843-577-7766
E-mail: cwantiq@bellsouth.net
Web site: www.sumtermilitary.com

Sword and Saber
John Pannick, Betty Pannick
2159 Baltimore Pike
Gettysburg, PA 17325
Phone: 717-334-0205
E-mail: swordandsaber@blazenet.net
Web site: www.swordandsaber.com

Trader Ben's Civil War Relics
B. Thomas Martin
POB 7593
Garden City, GA 31418
Phone: 912 961-9868
E-mail: traderben@yahoo.com
Web site: www.trade4relics.com

www.civilwarbuttons.com
William Leigh
P.O.Box 145
Hamilton VA 20159
Phone: 540-338-7367
E-mail: wleigh@mindspring.com

Uniformbuttons.com
Ronald P. Pojunas
1605 Edwin Ct.
Bel Air, MD 21015
Phone: 410- 893-0923
E-mail: pojunas@uniformbuttons.com
Web site: www.uniformbuttons.com

Bibliography

Albaugh, William A., III, and Edward N. Simmons. *Confederate Arms.* Philadelphia: Riling and Lentz, 1963. The bible on the various manufacturers of small arms for the Confederacy. This was the first book written solely on the Confederate pistols and revolvers. It deals with only those arms made in the South or for the South during the Civil War.

Albaugh, William A., III, and Richard D. Steuart. *The Original Confederate Colt.* New York: Greenberg Publisher, 1953.

Albaugh, William A., III, Hugh Benet, Jr., and Edward N. Simmons. *Confederate Handguns.* Wilmington, NC: Broadfoot Publishing Company, 1993.

Albaugh, William A., III. *Confederate Brass-Framed Colts & Whitneys.* Wilmington, NC: Broadfoot Publishing Company, 1993. An illustrated history of two prominent Confederate revolver manufacturers, Gunniston and Spiller & Burr.

Albaugh, William A., III. *Confederate Edged Weapons.* New York: Harper & Brothers, 1960.

Albert, Alphaeus H. *Buttons of the Confederacy.* Boyerstown: Boyertown Publishing Co., 1963.

Allie, Stephen J. *All He Could Carry: US Army Infantry Equipment, 1839-1910.* Ft. Leavenworth: Frontier Army Museum, 1991.

Bartleson, John D. *Civil War Explosive Ordnance 1861-1865*, Washington: U.S. Government Printing Office, 1972.

Bazelon, Bruce S. and William F. McGuinn. *A Directory of American Military Goods Dealers & Makers 1785-1915.* Manassas, VA: REF Typesetting & Publishing, Inc., 1990. This is an important reference for tracking manufacturer marks. It will be vital to accurately establishing the background of an accoutrement collection.

Bengston, Bradley P., M.D.; and Julian E. Kuz, M.D. *Orthopaedic Injuries of the Civil War.* Medical Staff Press, 1996.

Bengston, Bradley P., M.D.; and Julian E. Kuz, M.D. *Photographic Atlas of Civil War Injuries.* Medical Staff Press, 1996.

Bennion, Elisabeth. *Antique Medical Instruments.* London, Sotheby Park Bernet, 1979.

Berg, Paul. *Nineteenth Century Photographic Cases and Wall Frames.* Huntington Beach: Huntington Valley Press, 1995.

Bezdek, Richard H. *American Swords and Sword Makers.* Boulder, CO: Paladin Press, 1994. A nice reference of data for U.S. and Confederate swords. Good compilation of data about who made swords, how many were made, or what the markings mean.

Bilby, Joseph G. *Civil War Firearms.* Conshockocken, PA: Combined Publishing, 1996.

Binder, Daniel J. *Civil War Collector's Guide to Albert's Button Book.* Orange, VA: Publisher's Press, 1993.

Brinckerhoff, Sidney B. *Boots and Shoes of the Frontier Soldier.* Tuscon, Arizona Historical Society, 1976.

Brinkerhoff, Sidney B. *Military Headgear in the Southwest, 1846-1890.* Tucson: Arizona Pioneer's Historical Society, 1963.

Campbell, J. Duncan and Edgar M. Howell. *American Military Insignia, 1800-1851.* Washington, DC: Smithsonian Institution, 1963. Although stopping short of the Civil War, this book does include good photographs of insignias that were introduced in 1851 and still in use during the Civil War.

Campbell, J. Duncan and Michael J. O'Donnell *American Military Belt Plates* Alexanderia, VA: O'Donnell Publications, 1996.

Cannon, Devereaux D., Jr. *The Flags of the Confederacy.* Memphis: St. Lukes Press, 1988. A very complete examination of the flags used in the South during 1861-1865. Discusses the more well-known flags, as well as state, battle, and nautical flags.

Catalogue of Uniforms: The Museum of the Confederacy. Richmond, VA: Museum of the Confederacy, 1987.

Coates, Earl J. and Dean Thomas. *An Introduction to Civil War Small Arms.* Gettysburg, PA: Thomas Publications, 1990. A very good basic overview. Best for the beginner.

Coates, Earl J. and John D. McAulay. *Civil War Sharps Carbines & Rifles.* Gettysburg, PA: Thomas Publications, 1990. Describes the various aspects of the Sharps firearms with a listing of regiments that were issued the weapons.

Coggins, Jack. *Arms and Equipment of the Civil War*. New York: Random House, Inc., 1962. Definitely dated in its research and presentation. It is, however, a good overview study. It will be a good starting point for someone contemplating entering the collecting arena.

Criswell, Grover C. and Herb Romerstien. *The Official Guide to Confederate Money & Civil War Tokens, Tradesmen & Patriotic*. New York: HC Publishers, 1971.

Criswell, Grover C. *Confederate and Southern States Currency.* Citra, FL: Criswell's Publications, 1992. Describes the real notes along with counterfeits and uncut sheets.

Crouch, Howard R. *Civil War Artifacts: A Guide for the Historian*. Fairfax, VA:SCS Publications, 1995. This book illustrates hundreds of hard to identify excavated Civil War artifacts.

Crouch, Howard. *Historic American Spurs, A Study of All Types: Western, US Military, Confederate, Civilian, Patents, Racing.* Fairfax, VA: SCS Publications, 1998. This is the book that collectors use as a standard when identifying spurs.

Crouch, Howard. *Historic American Swords.* Fairfax, VA: SCS Publications, 1999. A great new book on swords, military to fraternal. Great photos and descriptions.

Crouch, Howard. *Repro Buckles of the Civil War, Tell the Real from the Repro.* Fairfax, VA: SCS Publications, nd. This book illustrates and identifies hundreds of the many fake and reproduction buckles that are on the market today. If you plan on buying any expensive Civil War buckles, you should first invest in this book.

Crouch, Howard. *Virginia Militaria Of The Civil War Volume 1: Buckles, Buttons And Insignia.* Fairfax, VA: SCS Publications, 1991.

Crute, Joseph H., Jr., *Emblems of Southern Valor: The Battle Flags of the Confederacy.* Louisville, KY: Harmony House, 1990.

D'Otrange Mastai, Boleslaw and Marie-Louise D'Otrange Mastai. *The Stars and the Stripes.* New York: Alfred A. Knopf, 1973.

Dammann, Dr. Gordon. *Pictorial Encyclopedia of Civil War Medical Instruments and Equipment Volume I-III.* Missoula, Montana: Pictorial Histories Publishing Co., 1983, 1988.)

Dammann, Gordon Dammann. *Pictorial Encyclopedia of Civil War Medical Instruments and Equipment.* Vols. I and II. Missoula, MT: Pictorial Histories Publishing Company, 1983, 1988.

Datig, Fred A. *Cartridges for Collectors*. Beverly Hills, CA: Fadco Publishing Company, 1958.

Davis, Audrey B. and Appel, Toby. *Bloodletting Instruments in the National Museum of History and Technology.* Washington DC: Smithsonian Institution Press, 1979.

Davis, Audrey B. and Dreyfuss, Mark S. *The Finest Instruments Ever Made: A Bibliography of Medical, Dental, Optical and Pharmaceutical Trade Literature 1700-1939.* Arlington, MA: Medical History Publishing Associates, 1986.

Davis, Carl. *Arming the Union: Small Arms in the Civil War.* Port Washington, NY: Kennikat Press, 1973.

Davis, William C. *Memorabilia of the Civil War.* New York: Mallard Press. 1991.

Delano, Marfé Ferguson and Barbara C. Mallen. *Echoes of Glory: Arms and Equipment of the Union.* Alexandria, VA: Tim-Life Books, 1991.

Dickey, Thomas S. and George, Peter C. *Field Artillery Projectiles of the American Civil War, Revised and Supplemented 1993 Edition.* Mechanicsville, VA: Arsenal Publications II, 1993. This massive study encompasses all of the known field artillery shells of the American Civil War. The author documents many postwar and reproductions as an added service to the collector. The most comprehensive book on shells.

Dorsey, R. Stephen. *American Military and Naval Belts, 1812-1902.* Eugene, OR: Collectors Library, 2002. The result of 30 years of research, this huge book covers sword belts, waist belts, saber belts, shoulder belts, and cartridge belts.

Dorsey, R. Stephen. *American Military Belts and Related Equipments.* Union City, TN: Pioneer Press, 1984. A recent study, this book fills in many gaps about the variation and variety of belts.

Edmonson, James M. *American Surgical Instruments-An Illustrated History of their Manufacture and a Directory of Instrument Makers to 1900.* San Francisco, CA: Norman Publishing, 1997.

Edmonson, James M. *Nineteenth Century Surgical Instruments; A Catalogue of the Gustav Weber Collection at the Howard Dittrick Museum of Historical Medicine.* Cleveland: Cleveland Health Science Library, 1986.

Edwards, William B. *Civil War Guns.* Harrisburg, PA: The Stackpole Company, 1962. Dated, but interesting read.

Elting, John R. and Michael McAfee. *Military Uniforms in America Volume III: The Long Endure The Civil War Period 1852-1867.* Novato, CA: Presidio Press, 1982.

Emerson, William K. *Encyclopedia of United States Army Insignia and Uniforms.* Norman: University of Oklahoma Press, 1996. Although nearly lost in the volume of information regarding twentieth-century uniforms and insignia, Civil War items are well covered and photo illustrated.

Emilio, Luis Fenollosa. *Military Buttons, the Emilio Collection.* Salem, MA: Essex Institute, 1911.

Field, Ron. *Brassey's History of Uniforms: American Civil War Confederate Army.* London: Brassey's Ltd., 1996.

Flags of the American Civil War 1: Confederate by Philip Katcher & Rick Scollins; Osprey Publishing Ltd., London, 1992.

Flayderman, Norm and Stuart C. Mowbray. *American Swords from the Medicus Collection.* Lincoln, RI: Andrew Mowbray, 1998.

Flayderman, Norm. *Flayderman's Guide to Antique American Firearms...and Their Values,* 7th Ed., Iola, WI: Krause Publications, 1998. The basic starting point for any Civil War firearm enthusiast. Don't start shopping without first consulting this book! It provides a brilliant discussion of the hobby, grading systems, and assigns realistic values.

Fuller, Claud E. and Richard D. Steuart. *Firearms of the Confederacy.* Lawrence, MA: Quarterman Publications, 1944.

Fuller, Claud E. *Springfield Shoulder Arms, 1795-1865.* New York: Francis Bannerman & Son, 1930, reprinted by S & S Firearms, Glendale, NY, 1986. Classic reference and a standard for Springfield enthusiasts.

Fuller, Claud E. *The Breech Loader in Service 1816-1917: A History of All Standard and Experimental U.S. Breechloading and Magazine Shoulder Arms.* New Milfod, CT: N. Flayderman, 1965.

Gaede, Fred, *The Federal Civil War Shelter Half.* O'Donnell Publications, Alexandria, VA, 2001 Perhaps to esoteric for the general collector, this is, however, the definitive study on shelter tents. The text covers everything from government patents, records, and contract data to colorful soldier's descriptions.

Garavaglia, Louis A. and Charles G. Worman. *Firearms of the American West, 1803-1865.* Albuquerque: University of New Mexico Press, 1984.

Garofalo, Robert and Mark Elrod. *A Pictorial History of Civil War Era Musical Instruments and Military Bands.* Charleston, WV: Pictorial Histories Publishing, 1985. The first work dedicated to the study of musical instruments used during the War. It is a decent encyclopedia of period musical instruments fully illustrated with photos, and drawings.

Gavin, William G. *Accoutrement Plates North and South 1861-1865.* Philadelphia, PA: Riling and Lentz, 1963.

Gluckman, Arcadi. *United States Muskets, Rifles and Carbines.* Buffalo, New York: Otto Ulbrich Co., 1948. An old publication, it is still a good, standard reference.

Hamilton, Charles. *American Autographs: Signers of the Declaration of Independence, Revolutionary War Leaders, Presidents.* Norman, OK: University of Oklahoma Press, 1983.

Harris, Charles. *Civil War Relics of the Western Campaigns.* Mechanicsville, VA: Rapidan Press, 1987. This book focuses on excavated relics and gives decent attention to projectiles and bullets.

Hartzler, D.D., Yantz, L. and J. Whisker. *The U.S. Model 1861 Springfield Rifle-Musket as Manufactured by the United States Armory at Springfield, Massachusetts, and Various Private Contractors.* Bedford, PA: Bedford Village Press, 2000. Profusely illustrated history of the most-issued long arm in Civil War.

Haven, C.T., and F.A. Belden. *A History of the Colt Revolver.* New York: Bonanza Books, 1962.

Hazlett, James C., and Olmstead, Edwin, and Parks, M. Hume. *Field Artillery Weapons of the Civil War.* Newark: University of Delaware Press, 1983, 1988. This in-depth survey is for the person who wants to understand more about the variety of artillery used by both sides during the war.

Hicks, James E. *Nathan Starr.* Mt. Vernon, NY: James E. Hicks, 1940.

Hicks, James E. *Notes on United States Ordnance --Ordnance Correspondence.* Vol. 2. Mt. Vernon, NY: James E. Hicks, 1957.

Hicks, James E. *Notes on United States Ordnance --Small Arms, 1776-1956.* Vol. 1. Mt. Vernon, NY: James E. Hicks, 1957.

Hicks, James E., and Andrew Jandot *U. S. Military Firearms, 1776-1956.* Reprint Ed., La Canada, CA, 1962.

Hogg, Ian V., *Weapons of the Civil War.* Greenwich, Connecticut: Brompton Books, 1987. Edison, New Jersey: Book Sales, 1995.

Hopkins, Richard E. *Military Sharps Rifles and Carbines.* Campbell, CA: Published by the author, 1967.

Howell, Edgar M. and Donald E. Kloster. *United States Army Headgear to 1854.* Washington, DC: Smithsonian Institution Press, 1969.

Howell, *United States Army Headgear, 1855-1902.* Fredricksburg, VA: North South Press, 1986.

Jacobsen, Jacques Noel ed., *Regulations and Notes for the Uniform of the Army of the United States 1857.* Staten Island, NY: Manor Publishing, 1973.

Jensen, Les. *G.I. The Illustrated History of the American Soldier, His Uniform and His Equipment. Johnny Reb; The Uniform of the Confederate Army, 1861-1865.* Mechanicsburg, PA: Stackpole, 1996.

Johnson, David F. *Uniform Buttons, American Armed Forces, 1748-1848.* Watkins Glen, NY: Century House, 1948.

Johnson, Paul. *Civil War Cartridge Boxes of the Union Infantryman.* Lincoln, RI: Andrew Mowbray Publishers, 1998. Perhaps more in depth than the general collector needs, it is nonetheless, an outstanding reference.

Jones, Charles H. *Artillery Fuses of the Civil War.* Alexandria, VA: O'Donnell Publications, 2001. Fine, scholarly study of the vast array of artillery fuses employed by both sides, including those used by the sea coast, naval, and field artillery.

Katcher, Philip and Richard Scollins, *Flags of the American Civil War 1: Confederate*, Men-At-Arms Series, no. 252, London: Osprey Publishing, Ltd., 1992.

Katcher, Philip, Richard Scollins, and Gerry Embleton, *Flags of the American Civil War 3: State & Volunteer*, Men-At-Arms Series, no. 265, London: Osprey Publishing, Ltd., 1993.

Keim, Dr. Lon W. *Confederate General Service Accoutrement Plates.* Orange, Va.: Moss Publications, c1987. Outstanding reference on Confederate plates.

Kelbaugh, Ross J. *Directory of Civil War Photographers, vol. 1: Maryland, Delaware, Washington, D.C., Northern Virginia, West Virginia.* Baltimore: Historic Graphics, 1990.

Kelbaugh, Ross J. *Introduction to Civil War Photography.* Gettysburg, PA: Thomas Publications, 1991. A basic treatise, it describes early forms of photography, and its impact on the Civil War era. Examines various styles of photos and photographers, and includes a glossary and collector's guide.

Kerksis, Sydney C. *Plates and Buckles of the American Military, 1795-1874.* Stone Mountain, GA: Stone Mountain, Press, 1974. First published in 1974, this book stood as the pinnacle in belt plate study. Though some of the data is somewhat dated, it is an important work and every serious collector should have a copy.

Kerksis, Sydney C., and Dickey, Thomas S. *Field Artillery Projectiles of the Civil War, 1861-1865*, Atlanta: The Phoenix Press, 1968.

Kerksis, Sydney C., and Dickey, Thomas S. *Heavy Artillery Projectiles of the Civil War, 1861-1865*, Atlanta: The Phoenix Press, 1972. A solid reference on this specialized area of artillery projectile collecting. Covers data included in Dickey and George's exhaustive study.

Knopp, Ken R. *Confederate Saddles & Horse Equipment.* Orange, VA: Publisher's Press, Inc., 2001.

Krainik, Clifford & Michele, and Carl Walvoord. *Union Cases, A Collector's Guide to the Art of America's First Plastics.* Grantsburg: Centennial Photo Service, 1988.

Langellier, John P. *Army Blue: The Uniform of Uncle Sam's Regulars, 1848-1873.* Atglen, PA: Schiffer Military History, 1998. Fantastic book with lots of photos and diagrams of uniforms, insignia, and headwear, detailing U.S. government regulations from the time period specified.

Lanham, Howard G. *Straps: The Evolution of U.S. Army Shoulder Straps.* Westminster, MD: Freehold Publications, 1998. A thorough history of shoulder straps with adequate coverage to Civil War varieties.

Lewis, Berkeley R. *Notes on Ammunition of the American Civil War, 1861-1865.* Washington, DC: American Ordnance Association, 1960.

Lewis, Berkeley R. *Small Arms and Ammunition in the United States Service.* Washington, DC: Smithsonian Institution, 1960.

Lord, Francis A. and Arthur Wise. *Uniforms of the Civil War.* New York: A.S. Barnes and Co. Inc., 1962.

Lord, Francis A. *Civil War Collector's Encyclopedia.* New York: Castle Books, 1963. Long regarded as the paramount work on Civil War artifacts, this book has some misrepresentations of items. It does, however, illustrate many, many good items, so it should be studied carefully.

Mace, O. Henry. *Collector's Guide to Early Photographs,* 2nd Ed. Iola, WI: Krause Publications, 1999. From daguerreotypes to stereographs, this book contains a good background on the history, the processes, and the variety of factors that make 19th century photographs collectible.

Madaus, Howard Michael, and Robert D. Needham. *The Battle Flags of the Confederate Army of Tennessee.* Milwaukee: Milwaukee Public Museum, 1976.

Madaus, Howard Michael. *The Warner Collector's Guide to American Longarms.* New York: Main Street Press, 1981.

Marcot, Roy. *Spencer Repeating Firearms.* Irvine, CA: Northwood Heritage Press, 1983.

Mast, Greg. *State Troops and Volunteers; a Photographic Record of North Carolina's Civil War Soldiers, Vol. I.* Raleigh: State of NC, 1995.

McAfee Michael J. and John P. Langlier. *G.I. The Illustrated History of the American Soldier, His Uniform and His Equipment. Billy Yank; The Uniform of the Union Soldier, 1861-1865.* Mechanicsburg, PA: Stackpole, 1996.

McAfee, Michael J. *Zouaves: The First and the Bravest.* Gettysburg, PA: Thomas Publications, 1991.

McAulay, John D. *Carbines of the Civil War.* Union City, TN: Pioneer Press, 1981. Excellent survey covering all of the major types of carbines used during the War.

McAulay, John D. *Civil War Carbines, Volume II: The Early Years.* Lincoln, RI: Andrew Mowbray Inc., 1991.

McAulay, John D. *Civil War Pistols.* Lincoln, RI: Andrew Mowbray Inc., 1992. . Excellent overview of the subject.

McAulay, John D. *Civil War Small Arms of the US Navy and Marine Corps.* Lincoln, RI: Andrew Mowbray Publishers, 1999.

McGuinn, William F. and Bruces S. Bazelon. *American Military Button Makers and Dealers; Their Backmarks & Dates.* Chelsea, MI: BookCrafters, Inc., 1988.

McKee, W. Reid and Mason, M.E., Jr. *Civil War Projectiles II, Small Arms and Field Artillery, with Supplement,* Mechanicsville: Rapidan Press, 1980. Probably the single best work to own. This is the original authority on bullets and the "M&M" bullet numbering system is the standard still used today by most bullet collectors. This work will answer the vast majority questions of identifications, that you will encounter.

McPheeters, K.L. & R.S. Dorsey. *Bridle Bits of the American Military, 1776-1945.* Eugene, OR: Collectors Library, 2000.

McQueen, John C. *Spencer: The First Effective and Widely Used Repeating Rifle—And Its Use in the Western Theater of the Civil War.* Marietta, GA: Author, 1989.

Meadows, Edward Scott. *U.S. Military Holsters and Pistol Cartridge Boxes.* Dallas, TX: Taylor Publishing, 1987. A good study of these accoutrements. Important volume to add to a library.

Melton, Jack W., Jr., and Pawl, Lawrence E. *Introduction to Field Artillery Ordnance 1861-1865*, Kennesaw: Kennesaw Mountain Press, Inc., 1994. This work provides a decent background to the use of artillery pieces.

Melton, Jack W., Jr., and Pawl, Lawrence E. *Melton & Pawl's Guide To Civil War Artillery Projectiles*, Kennesaw: Kennesaw Mountain Press, Inc., 1996. A decent introduction to collecting projectiles.

Miller, David, ed. *The Illustrated Directory of Uniforms, Weapons, and Equipment of the Civil War.* London, UK: Salamander Books Limited, 2001.

Moller, George D. *American Military Shoulder Arms.* 2 Vols. Niwot, CO: University Press of Colorado, 1993. Great illustrations and a huge amount of new research published anywhere else.

Morrow, John Anderson. *The Confederate Whitworth Sharpshooters.* Atlanta, GA: Author, 1989.

Mullinax, Steve E. *Confederate Belt Buckles and Plates.* Alexandria, VA: O'Donnell Publications, 1998. This updated book on Confederate buckles is full of illustrations of Confederate buckles. It corrects the 1991 edition with new information and added at least forty buckles that were unknown in the first printing.

Murphy, John M. *Confederate Carbines and Musketoons.* Dallas: Taylor Publishing, 1986. Excellent resource on Southern short arms.

Murphy, John M., and Howard Michael Madaus. *Confederate Rifles & Muskets: Infantry Small Arms Manufactured in the Southern Confederacy, 1861-1865.* Newport Beach, CA: Graphic Publisher, 1996.

Noe, David, Larry W. Yantz, and James B. Whisker. *Firearms from Europe—Being a History and Description of Firearms Imported During the American Civil War by the United States of America and the Confederate States of America.* Rochester, NY: Rowe Publications, 1999.

O'Donnell, Michael J. and J. Duncan Campbell. *American Military Belt Plates.* Alexandria, VA: O'Donnell Publications, 1996. This massive study encompasses all of the known federal plates from the Revolutionary War through the Spanish American conflict, a sweeping, handsomely presented study that covers 1776 through 1910. This is the primary reference work for the buckle collector.

Olson, Kenneth E. *Music and Musket: Bands and Bandsmen of the American Civil War.* Westport, CT: Greenwood Press, 1981.

Paulding, J.N. *The Cannon and Projectiles Invented by Robert Parker Parrott*, New York, 1979.

Peterson, Harold L. *Round Shot and Rammers*, Harrisburg: Stackpole Books, 1969. Once the standard artillery reference, now somewhat outdated by fresher research. Still a worthwhile book for the beginner or veteran artillery enthusiast.

Peterson, Harold L. *The American Sword, 1775-1945.* Philadelphia: Ray Riling Arms Books Co., 1988. This reference was the first real reference available to U.S. sword collectors. Even though it was written in 1954, it is still a great book to have.

Phillips, Stanley S. *Civil War Corps Badges and Other Related Awards, Badges, Medals of the Period: Including a Section on Post Civil War and Spanish American War Corps Badges.* Lanham, MD: S.S. Phillips, 1982. This book has been long regarded the standard reference on corps badges. Though it is very thorough, new research shows that there are several identified and/or represented badges.

Phillips, Stanley. *Excavated Artifacts from Battlefield and Campsites of the Civil War 1861-1865.* Lanham, MD: privately printed, 1974.

Railsback, Thomas C. and John P. Langellier. *The Drums Would Roll: A Pictorial History of US Army Bands on the American Frontier, 1866-1900.* Poole, UK: Arms & Armour, 1987.

Rankin, Robert H. *Small Arms of the Sea Service.* New Milford, CT: N. Flayderman and Company, 1972.

Reedstrom, Ernest L. *Bugles, Banners and War Bonnets.* New York: Bonanza Books, 1986.

Reilly, Robert M. *United States Military Small Arms 1816-1865.* Baton Rouge, LA: Eagle Press, 1970.

Reinfeld, Fred. *The Story of Civil War Money.* New York: Sterling Pub. Co., 1959.

Rentschler, Thomas B. *Cosmopolitan and Gwyn & Campbell Carbines in the Civil War.* Lincoln, RI: Andrew Mowbray Publishers, 2000. This is a definitive study on these two carbines. Perhaps a bit too specific for the beginner, it is an important reference for the advanced.

Rickards, Maurice, ed. *The Encyclopedia of Ephemera: A Guide to the Fragmentary Documents of Everyday Life for the Collector, Curator, and Historian.* New York: Routledge, 2000. A rather scholarly work, it does force one to consider the context of collecting ephemera and what it means beyond the current generation.

Riling, Ray. *The Powder Flask Book.* Philadelphia: Robert Halter, 1953.

Ripley, Warren *Artillery and Ammunition of the Civil War.* 4th Ed., Charleston, SC: The Battery Press, 1984. Again, somewhat dated reference, but a standard book to add to your library, nonetheless.

Rollins, Richard (ed.) The Returned Battle Flags. Redondo Beach, CA: Rank and File Publications, 1995. In 1905, the U.S. government returned to the former confederate States over 500 flags captured during the Civil War. This reprint of an obscure southern railroad presented a 60-page souvenir that includes the government's inventory of all flags, containing all the information it could find on their background.

Rollins, Richard. *The Damned Red Flags of the Rebellion [sic]: The Confederate Battle Flag at Gettysburg.* Rank and File Publications, 1997. A special section includes 42 full-color photographs of flags captured during the Gettysburg campaign, most previously unpublished.

Russell, G. Michael. *The Collector's Guide to Civil War Period Bottles and Jars—With Prices.* Herndon, VA: Russell Publications, 1998. Strictly deals with makes and varieties of Civil War-era storage containers, also has a price guide. Good source for diggers.

Russell, G. Michael. *The Collector's Guide to Clay Tobacco Pipes.* Herndon, VA: Russell Publications, 1996. A great source for identifying clay pipes. Lots of hand-drawn illustrations.

Rywell, Martin. *Sharps Rifle: The Gun that Shaped American Destiny.* Union City, TN: Pioneer Press, 1984.

Sauers, Richard A. *Advance the Colors! Pennsylvania Civil War Battle Flags.* Harrisburg, PA: Pennsylvania Capitol Preservation Committee, 1987. Two-volumes that traces the history of the state's 215 regiments. It includes a background of Pennsylvania flags, and how they were procured.

Schuyler, Hartley and Graham. *Illustrated Catalog of Civil War Military Goods.* New York, NY: Dover Publications, 1985 [Reprint]. Originally printed in 1864, this valuable resource is available as a reprint.

Sellers, Frank M., and Samuel E. Smith. *American Percussion Revolvers.* Ottawa: Museum Restoration Service, 1973. The most important book published on Sharps weapons.

Slabaugh, Arlie R. *Confederate States Paper Money,* 10th Ed., Iola, WI: Krause Publications, 2000. Features a section on the Southern states, along with up-to-date pricing, a section on the financial history of paper money, and in-depth coverage of Confederate printing errors.

Smith, Robin. *Brassey's History of Uniforms: American Civil War Union Army.* London: Brassey's Ltd., 1996.

Smith, Robin. *Brassey's History of Uniforms: American Civil War Union Army.* London: Brassey's Ltd., 1996.

Smith, Samuel E., and Edwin W. Bitter. *Historic Pistols: The American Martial Flintlock, 1760-1845.* New York: Scalamandre Publications, 1985.

Smith, Winston O. *The Sharps Rifle.* New York: William Morrow Co., 1943.

Stahlberg, Rainer with Colin R. Bruce, II. *Standard Catalog of Stocks & Bonds. Iola, WI. Krause Publications, 2002.* The first comprehensive pictorial price guide of historic stocks and bonds.

Steffen, Randy. *United States Military Saddles, 1812-1943.* Norman, OK: University of Oklahoma Press, 1973.

Sumrall, Alan K., *Battle Flags of Texans in the Confederacy,* Austin: Eakin Press, 1995.

Sutherland, Robert Q., and R.L. Wilson. *The Book of Colt Firearms.* Kansas City, MO: Robert Q. Sutherland, 1971. Very good book that covers all the weapons produced by the Colt factory.

Sword, Wiley. *Firepower from Abroad: The Confederate Enfield and the Le Mat Revolver, 1861-1863.* Lincoln, RI: Andrew Mowbray, 1986.

Sylvia, Stephen W. and Michael J. O'Donnell. *Civil War Canteens.* Orange, VA: Moss Publications, 1990. No finer work has been published on this narrow slice of Civil War collecting.

Sylvia, Stephen and Mike O'Donnell. *Illustrated History of Civil War Relics.* Orange, VA: Moss Publications 1978. This book concentrates on identifying dug artifacts.

Thillmann, John H. *Civil War Cavalry & Artillery Sabres, A Study of United States Cavalry and Artillery Sabres,* 1833-1865. Lincoln, RI: Andrew Mowbray Publishers, 2001. Masterful history of the Civil War officers' and enlisted men's sabers. Contains an alphabetical listing of makers and contractors. New information on well-known suppliers and several new contractors identified.

Thomas, Dean S. *Cannons: An Introduction to Civil War Artillery*, Gettysburg: Thomas Publications, 1985. This is exactly what this inexpensive book is—an introduction. It is a good starting place for anyone interested in Civil War artillery.

Thomas, Dean S. *Ready...Aim...Fire! Small-Arms Ammunition in the Battle of Gettysburg.* Gettysburg, PA: Thomas Publications, 1981. Information and photos about more than 375 bullet and cartridge specimens used by the Northern and Southern armies.

Thomas, Dean S. *Round Ball To Rimfire. A History of Civil War Small Arms Ammunition, Part Two, Federal Breechloading Carbines & Rifles.* Gettysburg, PA: Thomas Publications, 2002. This extensive book explains in detail the evolution of ammunition and weapons from smoothbore weapons before the Civil War to the development of rifled musketry. Many variations of smoothbore balls, musket projectiles, and their specific association with the weapons of the period as well as the numerous manufacturers is explored.

Thomas, Dean S. *Round Ball to Rimfire; A History of Civil War Small Arms Ammunition.* Gettysburg, PA: Thomas Publications, 1997.

Thomas, James and Dean. *Handbook of Civil War Bullets and Cartridges.* Gettysburg, PA: Thomas Publications, 1996. Extensive information and illustrations of Civil War bullets, cartridges, and their manufacturers. It is a handy guide with illustrations and corrects many of the errors of earlier works.

Thompson, Charles J.S. *The History and Evolution of Surgical Instruments.* New York: Schuman, 1942.

Tice, Warren K. *Uniform Buttons of the United States 1776-1865.* Gettysburg, PA: Thomas Publications, 1997.

Time Life Books Eds. *Echoes of Glory: Arms and Equipment of the Confederacy.* Alexandria, VA: Time-Life Books, 1991. This has become the bible for researchers and reenactors, profusely illustrated.

Todd, Frederick P. *American Military Equipage, 1851-1872.* N.P.: Chatham Square Press, Inc., 1983. Though somewhat dated, this was the definitive work on accoutrements available in the 1970s. It is a crucial part of a complete reference library.

Waldsmith, John. *Stereo Views: An Illustrated History & Price Guide,* 2nd Ed., Iola, WI: Krause Publications, 2002.

Welling, William. *Photography in America: The Formative Years, 1839-1900.* New York: Crowell, 1978.

Whisker, J.B., D. Hartzler, and L.W. Yantz. *Arming the Glorious Cause--Weapons of the Second War for Independence—A Photographic Study of Confederate Weapons.* State College, PA: RR Books, 1998. A lot of information on makers, contracts, inspectors, and suppliers.

Wilbur, Keith. *Antique Medical Instruments. 4th ed.* Pennsylvania: Schiffer, 2000.

Winders, G.H. *Sam Colt and His Guns.* New York: John Day, 1959.

Winey, Michael J. *Union Army Uniforms at Gettysburg.* Gettysburg, PA: Thomas Publications, 1998.

Wise, Arthur and Francis A. Lord. *Bands and Drummer Boys of the Civil War.* New York: Thomas Yoseloff. 1966.

Witham, George F., comp. *Catalogue of Civil War Photographers: A Listing of Civil War Photographers' Imprints.* Portland, OR: G. F. Witham, 1988. By far, not comprehensive, but a very good place to start when researching the back marks on images.

Woshner, Mike, *India-Rubber and Gutta-Percha in the Civil War Era.* Alexandria, VA: O'Donnell Publications, 1999. Though not specifically about buttons, this source does present a good background on buttons bearing the "Goodyear" patent.

Wyckoff, Martin A. *United States Military Buttons of the Land Services, 1787-1902.* Bloomington, IL: The McLean County Historical Society, 1984.

Young, Anne Mortimer. *Antique Medicine Chests, or Glyster, Blister and Purge.* London: Vernier Press, 1994.

Index

"America has no north, no south, no east, no west. The sun rises over the hills and sets over the mountains...We are one and undivided."

— Private Sam Watkins
Company H, 1st Tennessee Infantry, CSA

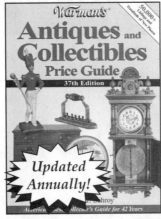

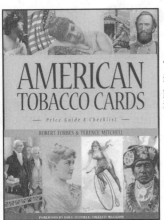

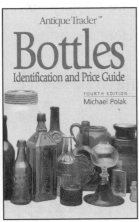

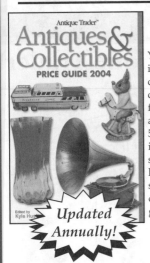

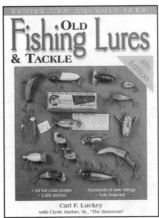

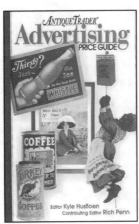